Intermediate Accounting

Lynn L Rees—Texas A&M University

David A. Rees—Southern Utah University

THOMSON

SOUTH-WESTERN

Australia · Canada · Mexico · Singapore · Spain · United Kingdom · United States

THOMSON

SOUTH-WESTERN

Intermediate Accounting, 1e

Lynn L Rees and David A. Rees

Editor-in-Chief:
Jack Calhoun

Publisher:
Melissa S. Acuña

Senior Acquisitions Editor:
Sharon Oblinger

Senior Developmental Editor:
Ken Martin

Marketing Manager:
Keith Paul Chassé

Senior Production Editor:
Marci Combs

Manufacturing Coordinator:
Doug Wilke

Production House:
Litten Editing and Production, Inc.

Compositor:
GGS Information Services, Inc.

Printer:
Quebecor World
Versailles, KY

Design Project Manager:
Rik Moore

Internal Designer:
Lou Ann Thesing

Cover Designer:
Rik Moore

Cover Photographer/Illustrator:
Anthony Weller, digital vision;
PhotoDisc, Inc.

Photography Manager:
John Hill

Photo Researcher:
Sam A. Marshall

Library of Congress
Control Number: 2002114161

ISBN: 0-324-06876-X

Dedication

To our wives

Barbara and LaRee

Enron. Worldcom. Imclone Systems. Waste Management. Sunbeam. Andersen. Global Crossing. The number of high-profile Fortune 500 companies involved in accounting irregularities within the last few years has brought the accounting profession under siege from regulators and the general public. We as accounting educators bear part of the blame. The accounting irregularities in these and other companies seem to validate the concerns of several groups and organizations who believe that poor training leads to inappropriate practices and to support their call for significant and meaningful change in accounting education. While many colleges and individual instructors have instituted revisions to meet the demands of their constituents, there is clearly room for more improvement.

Intermediate Accounting from a New Conceptual Approach

We see a growing commitment to teach students that good judgment is as necessary as a good grounding in accounting practices, particularly at the intermediate level. As students increase their knowledge of accounting principles, they must also understand that exercising judgment does not mean that any accounting solution that is not illegal is acceptable, nor does it give an accountant a license to do whatever is required to keep a client or to give management what it wants.

In *Intermediate Accounting* we teach analytical and decision-making skills along with accounting practices by taking an entirely new approach: we place a heavy emphasis on students learning accounting *concepts*. Of the book's 21 chapters, eight are devoted to the FASB's Conceptual Framework and accounting concepts. We believe this conceptual approach is consistent with the call for a focus on learning instead of memorizing.

What are the advantages of this conceptual approach to teaching intermediate accounting? First, such an approach effectively prepares students for the world of work, where accountants must identify alternative ways of accounting for new or unusual transactions, select an appropriate alternative, and defend its use. By focusing on the principles in the FASB's Conceptual Framework and allowing students to apply those principles, even to accounting problems not specifically covered in the chapter, students are trained to think analytically to solve unfamiliar problems.

Secondly, the conceptual approach actually allows the instructor to cover more material in greater depth within a shorter time period. In our discussions with accounting professors, many expressed frustration with the cumbersome presentation of material in most texts intended for a typical year-long course. While other intermediate accounting textbooks take up to eight chapters to cover the asset side of the balance sheet, the conceptual approach we use in *Intermediate Accounting* allows the instructor to cover thoroughly the same material in half the number of chapters.

Comprehensive Coverage of International GAAP

In addition to focusing on concepts, another innovative feature of *Intermediate Accounting* is its comprehensive coverage of international material. The remarkable

> I liked how your book went beyond the basic "how" to explaining "why" in today's accounting principles.

progress of the IASB and its predecessor, the IASC, has made familiarity with international GAAP a necessity within the accounting profession, and we expect the importance of international GAAP to only increase in the future. We believe that our textbook provides a valuable service to students by exposing them to international GAAP early in their careers, giving them a firm foundation to build on.

Besides making students more internationally aware, the presentation of international GAAP has another significant advantage. We have been frustrated with students viewing accounting as a science in which there is only one right way to account for and report transactions, and we are particularly concerned that students develop this viewpoint after they have taken the intermediate accounting courses. We want students to learn that accounting involves judgment, and we want them to begin learning to exercise judgment at the intermediate level. We want students to understand that there are correct alternative ways of accounting for and reporting certain transactions, and we think exposing them to international GAAP is a good way to do that. In *Intermediate Accounting* we strive to teach students that exercising judgment is an art, as well as a critical part of their education.

A Text Classroom-Tested for Proven Success

> I found the examples given in the chapters to be very helpful in grasping an understanding of the material.

Intermediate Accounting was thoroughly classroom-tested and revised before publication to ensure accuracy, completeness, clarity, and student comprehension. We conducted extensive testing in the classroom for two years, including summer school sessions. Student comments were obtained for each chapter, and based on those comments, chapters were rewritten as necessary to improve readability. We used the same evaluation method to ensure useful and insightful end-of-chapter materials. In addition to being classroom-tested, all the exercises and problems were verified by another experienced accounting instructor.

Some of the comments we received from student reviewers are included as marginal notes throughout this preface. We believe your students will have similar positive responses to the material and its presentation.

An Overview of the Text

A look at the structure of *Intermediate Accounting* demonstrates the differences between our text and other intermediate accounting texts currently in use and delineates the framework of our conceptual approach.

Part 1: Foundations

> Your book is far superior to any other technical textbook I have used.

The text begins with an in-depth look at the development of accounting and financial reporting—a unique introduction to an intermediate accounting book in that it introduces students to the evolution of both accounting and financial reporting and details the effect of cultural influences on financial reporting.

By starting with an international review of the history of accounting and demonstrating that accounting developed within a cultural context, we prepare students for a better understanding of the global issues that are critical factors in today's international business community. Chapter 1 covers the standard-setting function in the United States and positions it as a political process shaped by the inputs received from various affected groups. It reviews the movement to and the status of international GAAP and examines the keiretsu in Japan as an example of how culture impacts financial reporting. In addition to its strong content, this chapter also introduces the approach that defines the entire text. In user testing, students gave a high rating to this chapter, and some reviewers commented on how such an approach might encourage students to read the book.

Chapters 2, 3, and 4 continue to build a solid foundation for understanding intermediate accounting principles. These chapters cover the accounting cycle, preparation of basic financial statements, basic financial analysis, and the FASB's conceptual framework.

Part 2: Applying the Conceptual Framework

Chapters 5–16 comprise the core of the text, and it is here where our text differs most from other intermediate accounting textbooks. Using the conceptual approach, principles are presented and explained, and then applied. Both the manner of presentation and the relationships established between the principles are different from those found in more traditional texts.

These chapters present the historical cost principle, examine the matching principle and revenue recognition principle in depth, and detail methods of reporting assets, liabilities, legal capital and basic stockholders' equity transactions and accounts, and marketable securities and comprehensive income. The section ends with a detailed examination of the statement of cash flows.

Part 3: Special Reporting Issues

This section provides specific and detailed information on a variety of special reporting procedures. Chapters 17–19 look at accounting methods for leases, pensions, and income taxes. Chapters 20 and 21 cover foreign currency transactions and hedge accounting—topics not typically included in current intermediate textbooks but information we consider fundamental for accounting students in today's global business world.

Text Features: Tools for Teaching and Learning

Chapter Features Support Learning and Teaching

An array of well-designed features built into every chapter of *Intermediate Accounting* aids student comprehension of the concepts presented and gives instructors useful tools to expand learning beyond the text and classroom.

> Your textbook saved valuable study time with its concise and to-the-point style. Also, the examples and illustrations were easy to understand and very helpful.

- Each chapter begins with at least one real-world scenario that helps students relate the material they are learning to what actually occurs in the business world. Answers to the questions raised in the real-world scenarios are provided in the chapter.
- Throughout the text, relevant pronouncements of the FASB and its predecessors are paraphrased, set off as quotations, and discussed, with all references included.
- International accounting material, interlaced throughout each chapter, is denoted by a globe icon.
- A separate section of each chapter focuses on international accounting and financial reporting issues.
- Each chapter references one or more current Web sites where students can find extensive information about related topics that may be of interest to them and to the study of accounting. *Intermediate Accounting* also has its own Web site that provides additional support.

- Real-world examples of how information is reported in published financial reports are found in each chapter. These examples, including notes, have been taken from the published financial reports of various publicly traded corporations.

End-of-Chapter Materials Guide Discussion and Reinforce Concepts

We have provided a variety of end-of-chapter materials, each with its own pedagogical purpose and value.

> Instead of memorizing, your book helped me understand the reasoning behind the way problems are solved and why they are solved in that manner.

- The questions at the end of each chapter cover the essential concepts of the chapter and can be used in class to stimulate discussion and guide the students' thinking or as short written homework assignments.
- The exercises are designed to reinforce the basic concepts of the chapter.
- The problems are designed to stimulate the students' thinking and to give them the opportunity to apply what they have learned. Some problems also are designed to reinforce material covered in an earlier chapter, thus helping students to link their accounting knowledge.
- Research problems encourage students to examine the literature of the FASB, the AICPA, and international GAAP. The cases and research activities are designed to get the students out of the textbook and into other published materials with which accountants should be familiar.

Additional Features Enhance the Conceptual Approach

The unique conceptual approach of *Intermediate Accounting* is further supported with real-world examples plus questions that encourage the application of principles and stimulate class discussion.

> I liked your many examples, illustrations, and exhibits. They were very helpful.

- **This Is the Real World:** This boxed feature presents a real business situation that has been in the news and/or reported in a periodical and relates that situation to the topic being discussed in the chapter.
- **Extending the Concept:** This margin element poses a question related to the topic of the chapter and includes the answer if the chapter discussion does not explicitly provide one.
- **Conceptual Question:** This margin element is used occasionally to provide a question that prompts students to think broadly and analytically, beyond the chapter discussion.

Technology Tools for Connecting Intermediate Accounting with the Real World

Instructors can choose from our extensive **InfoAccess Menu** for informational resources that turbo-charge the learning experience and prepare students for the world beyond the classroom.

Guide to GAAP

Appearing on CD, this guide covers all FASB Statements, Interpretations, and Technical Bulletins; APB Opinions; ARBs; and relevant AICPA Statements of Position and FASB EITF issues, giving students practical experience researching accounting procedural guidelines. With its easy-to-use topical format, comprehensive disclosure checklists, and numerous practical considerations and examples, this resource is meant to be a timesaving tool.

Thomson Analytics—Business School Edition (BSE)

This premier web-based portal product provides integrated access to Thomson Financial content for the purpose of financial analysis. Thomson Analytics BSE offers the same features and functionality found in the full Thomson Analytics product, but for a subset of 500 companies. The 500 companies encompass global entities, spanning from large to small capitalization and consist of a minimum of:

- 150 Top Companies from the DJ Global Index
- 150 Middle Companies from the DJ Global Index
- 150 Bottom Companies from the DJ Global Index

Thomson Analytics—Business School Edition includes the following content sets:

I/B/E/S Consensus Estimates

The I/B/E/S Consensus Estimates includes averages, means, and medians; analyst-by-analyst earnings coverage; analysts' forecasts based on 15 industry standard measures; current and historic coverage for the selected 500 companies that are drawn from a database of 60 established and emerging markets. Current history is five years forward, and historic history is from 1976 for the United States and from 1987 for international. Current data is updated daily and historic is updated monthly.

Worldscope

Worldscope includes company profiles, financials and accounting results, and market per-share data for the selected 500 companies, drawn from a database of more than 55 established and emerging markets; and annual information and monthly prices going back to 1980, all updated daily.

Disclosure SEC Database

The SEC Disclosure Database includes company profiles, annual and quarterly company financials, pricing information and earnings estimates for U.S. and Canadian selected companies. The data is annual from 1987—quarterly data rolling 10 years—with monthly pricing, all updated weekly.

8-Hour Becker Conviser CPA Review

This CD contains eight free interactive hours of the Becker Conviser CPA review. Lectures on this easy-to-use, self-paced CD focus on both the content and skills needed to pass select CPA exam topics.

INSIDE LOOK: Analysis from All Angles

This feature brings accounting news into the classroom with this new Web site from Thomson/South-Western. The Access Card allows instructors and students to use information related to Enron, Andersen, and other accounting-related "names in the news." In addition to relevant articles, Inside Look includes related research links and questions to help students develop critical thinking skills. For a demo, go to **http://insidelook.swcollege.com**.

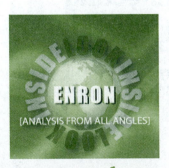

NewsEdge

This feature delivers news and information to fit individual classroom needs. The content is selected from the world's premier news and information sources and chosen for relevance by editorial experts.

InfoTrac® College Edition

This provides anytime, anywhere online access to a database of full-text articles from hundreds of popular and scholarly periodicals, such as *Newsweek, Fortune,* and *Journal of Accountancy*, among others. For more information, visit **http://www. swcollege.com/infotrac/infotrac.html**.

Other Support Materials

Available to Instructors

- Solutions Manual, prepared by David Rees and Lynn Rees. This manual contains independently verified answers to all end-of-chapter questions, exercises, problems, and cases.
- Instructor's Manual, prepared by Kathy Sevigny. This manual enhances class preparation with objectives, chapter outlines, teaching suggestions and strategies, transparency masters, and topical overviews of end-of-chapter materials. It also features assignment classifications with level of difficulty and estimated completion time.
- Test Bank and Examview, prepared by David Rees. The test bank is available in both printed and computerized version, Examview. Test items include multiple-choice questions and short examination problems for each chapter, along with solutions.
- PowerPoint Slides. Hundreds of slides in Microsoft® PowerPoint® format can be used in on-screen lecture presentations or printed out and used as traditional overheads. Additionally, they can be printed and distributed to students, allowing students to concentrate on the professor instead of hurrying to copy down information.
- Spreadsheet Templates, prepared by David Rees. Excel templates are provided on the Web site for solving selected end-of-chapter exercises and problems that are identified in the text with a spreadsheet icon.
- Instructor's Resource CD packages the Solutions Manual, Instructors Manual, Test Bank, Examview, PowerPoint slides, and Excel spreadsheet solutions on one convenient CD-ROM.

Available to Students

- Web Site (http://rees.swlearning.com). This content-rich Web site enhances the learning experience with PowerPoint slides, Excel spreadsheet templates, and online tutorials, and provides a real-world business connection through links to accounting-related sites.
- WebTutor Advantage on WebCT or Blackboard extends the classroom experience with an interactive educational learning tool. WebTutor provides real-time, self-correcting study outside the classroom that helps students grasp even the most complex topics. It includes:
  - Short *Topical Video* segments relating chapter content to a real business situation or events in the news.
  - *Tutorial* for reinforcing key chapter concepts.
  - *Annotated Spreadsheets*.
  - *Interactive Quiz* to test knowledge and provide immediate feedback on concept comprehension. Includes fill-in-the-blank, multiple-choice, and true/false questions.
  - *Crossword Puzzles,* a fun and engaging opportunity for testing understanding of each chapter's key terms.

- *Quiz Bowl,* providing the challenge of an online Jeopardy-style game to review chapter content.
- *Spanish Dictionary* of key financial accounting terms.
- Calculators for use in solving end-of-chapter materials.
- Links to relevant sites.

- **Xtra! for Intermediate Accounting CD-ROM** lets students test their understanding of text content through alternative study materials such as demonstration problems and quizzing. Available as an optional free package with each new text, students receive an access code so that they can receive Xtra! reinforcement in intermediate accounting.

- **Ethics in the Post-Enron Age.** With the Enron/Andersen debacle, ethics is becoming an increasingly important (and interesting) part of accounting education. This timely supplement contains ethics cases based on real situations in the business world. Examples include cases tied to Enron, Global Crossing, and Boston Chicken. Identifying ethical dilemmas and projecting their resolution allows students to develop essential skills for success in their future careers. In each section of the textbook, the problems will be labeled according to subject matter (i.e. bad debt expense, revenue recognition). This allows the instructor to select problems consistent with the needs of the course. Written by Iris Stuart, of California State University-Fullerton, and Bruce Stuart.

- **Accounting and Auditing Research: A Practical Guide, Fifth Edition.** This is the only step-by-step guide that provides methodology for conducting practical accounting research. In addition, the book offers up-to-date references to the primary sources of authoritative accounting literature, including electronic databases, and contains a special section on the Internet as a research tool. Written by Thomas Weirich, Central Michigan University, and Alan Reinstein, Wayne State University.

- **Practice Cases**
  - *Sharkey Incorporated*—In this case study, students assume the role of a financial consultant for Sharkey, Inc., for a two-year term. The goal of the case study is for students to maximize both earnings per share and return on assets.
  - *Foxcor Manufacturing Company*—This comprehensive practice case pulls together the concepts learned in the first half of the intermediate accounting course. The case also draws upon theory and concepts learned in foundation accounting courses. After completing this case, students will be able to read and interpret the financial statements and understand how individual journal entries support a set of financial statements and related note disclosures.

Acknowledgments

We gratefully acknowledge the following students who were instrumental in reviewing early drafts of the chapters and end-of-chapter material: Christy Anderson, Kevin Callister, Curtis Cox, Jan Jacobsen, Justin Lauderdale, Nattaly Manuel, Christine Schaller, and Doug Solstad.

We especially want to thank Jeff Barnes, who used the textbook in the Intermediate Accounting courses he taught. In addition, we are grateful for the constructive comments from the following reviewers of early drafts of the textbook:

Noel Addy
Mississippi State University

Joseph Anthony
Michigan State University

Craig Bain
Northern Arizona University

Otto Chang
California State University, San Bernardino

Stan Clark
University of Southern Mississippi

Tim Eaton
Marquette University

Susan Eldridge
University of Texas at Austin

Sheila Foster
Lynchburg College

Rich Houston
University of Alabama

Robert Koch
St. Peters College

Jerry Kreuze
Western Michigan University

Timothy Lindquist
University of Northern Iowa

Linda Nichols
Texas Tech University

Frederick Niswander
East Carolina University

Hong S. Pak
California State Polytechnic University, Pomona

Pamela Roush
University of Central Florida

Kathy Simons
Bryant College

Ross Stewart
Seattle Pacific University

Gary Taylor
University of Alabama

Peter Theuri
Northern Kentucky University

Judith Walo
Central Connecticut State University

David Wiest
University of Hartford

About the Authors

Lynn L and David A. Rees are brothers who have individually achieved success and earned great respect for their research and teaching in accounting. This text, their first collaborative effort, brings together a wealth of knowledge presented within a unique approach.

Lynn L Rees

Lynn L Rees is a Mays Faculty Fellow in the Mays Business School at Texas A&M University. He holds a bachelor's degree from Southern Utah University and a Ph.D. degree from Arizona State University. Prior to joining the faculty at Texas A&M, he was on staff at Washington State University, the University of Massachusetts—Amherst, and Arizona State University. Dr. Rees has taught various accounting classes at the undergraduate and masters level and has given seminars to Ph.D. students. His research papers have been presented in the United States, South America, Asia, and Europe. He has published papers in *The Accounting Review*, *Journal of Accounting Research*, and *Journal of Finance*, among others. He is an Associate Editor of Advances in Accounting and serves on the editorial boards of several other journals.

David A. Rees

David A. Rees is a Professor of Accounting at Southern Utah University. He holds a bachelor's degree from Brigham Young University, a Master's of Accountancy from Utah State University, and a Ph.D. degree from Texas Tech University. Dr. Rees joined the SUU faculty in 1985 to establish and oversee the Master's of Accountancy program there. Prior to this, he was at Wichita State University, Morehead State University, and Texas Tech University, where he taught extensively in both undergraduate and graduate programs in such diverse courses as financial accounting, not-for-profit accounting, and cost and managerial accounting, and conducted various graduate seminars. He has published papers and articles in several practitioner journals, and published and presented pedagogical materials in many venues. With his dissertation topic being in not-for-profit accounting, Dr. Rees is considered an expert in this area. He has worked for several years auditing not-for-profit entities and has served on the boards of directors of several not-for-profit organizations.

Brief Contents

Table of Contents

(2)

Applying the Conceptual Framework 175

③

Special Reporting Issues 799

Foundations

1

Development

OF

Accounting AND Financial Reporting

"First of all, let me be blunt: Bean counters need not apply. As we discussed, I need a strategic partner, a visionary, someone with global ties who can fill a much broader role than just supervising transactions and keeping tabs on employee expense reports. He or she should be a strategist, deft communicator, dealmaker, and financier—an expert in information technology and risk management."[a]

As a primary producer of information, the accountant is in a position to wield significant influence over the operations of a business. Accountants who can identify and produce information that clearly communicates the financial health of a company can be invaluable. Traditionally, chief financial officers (CFOs) of companies are well versed in accounting.

The authors believe that the material in this text will benefit students in acquiring some of the skills necessary for a twenty-first century accountant by tackling problems that have international implications and that require analytical thinking. The reward for a person with these types of skills is handsome. CFOs routinely earn compensation in excess of $1 million a year.

[a]SOURCE: M. Vickers, "Up from Bean Counter," *Business Week* (August 28, 2000), pp. 118–120.

Learning Objectives

- Summarize the long history of accounting and its significance to the development of civilization.
- Explain why the concept of financial reporting is relatively new.
- Explain why financial reporting is a reflection of culture and environment.
- Paraphrase the process of establishing generally accepted accounting principles in the United States.
- Summarize the U.S. "House of GAAP."
- Summarize the purpose and perceived necessity of the IASB.
- Extend the past history and present condition of accounting and financial reporting into the future.

A Brief History of Accounting

Accounting is ancient—at least as ancient as the beginning of civilization. When civilizations first began, the central authority needed a mechanism for measuring wealth, assessing and collecting taxes, and computing the cost of various projects, including the cost of waging war. As a result, every culture that advanced to the point of being considered a civilization developed a system of accounting and, in turn, the accounting system then contributed to the further development of the civilization. For example, it used to be presumed that the development of writing was a necessary prerequisite to the development of accounting. However, recent scholarship in the development of civilizations is showing that just the opposite is true—that the practice of accounting led to writing. One authority on ancient civilizations states, "A number of . . . elements characterize early civilizations. Of these, writing, or a system of notation, seems to be universal. The *need for an accounting system* to keep track of taxes, tribute, income, expenses, and all the additional data that go with the numbers *led to writing* in the Middle East and perhaps in Egypt."[1] This observation of accounting contributing to the development of writing in the Middle East also seems to be true of early civilizations in the Americas. The Incas are an excellent example of a civilization that developed an accounting system (by using knots tied in string) to record taxes, tribute, etc., but who never developed a system of writing.

Accounting is a reflection of its culture, and as civilizations grow and evolve, their accounting systems develop to meet the changing needs for information. The Bible, as an example of a record of an ancient civilization, contains many ac-

---

[1]Richard E. W. Adams, *Ancient Civilizations of the New World*, p. 22, emphasis added.

counting concepts that illustrate the antiquity and development of accounting. Some of the accounting concepts that are found in the Bible include the dual custody over funds,[2] seeking individuals with integrity as custodians of funds and verifying their integrity,[3] budgeting,[4] and surprise audits by owners.[5]

The advent of the mercantile era in Europe gave rise to modern-day accounting. In 1494, Luca Pacioli, an Italian mathematician and Franciscan monk, wrote a treatise that included a supplement describing the accounting system then used by Italian merchants. Although Pacioli only described accounting practices that had been common in Italy for many years, he is still regarded as the "Father of the Balance Sheet." Consistent with the approach taken by other authors of his day, Pacioli included homilies and observations about economics, business, and particularly religion (he was, after all, a Franciscan monk) throughout his book. In beginning his treatise, Pacioli observed: "The purpose of every merchant is to make a lawful and reasonable profit so as to keep up his business. Therefore, the merchants should begin their business with the name of God at the beginning of every book and have His holy name in their minds."[6] Obviously, and perhaps fortunately, accountants do not follow this practice today. But much of the basic accounting system Pacioli described is still used throughout the world. This includes:

- The use of a *journal* in which "the merchant shall put down all his transactions, small or big, as they take place."
- The use of a *ledger*, which is a summary by account (e.g., cash and receivables) of the transactions affecting the account total.
- The use of debits and credits to record transactions in both the journal and the ledger.
- The process (called *posting*) of transferring amounts from the journal to the ledger.
- The necessity of balancing the books yearly.

Although much of what Pacioli described has been retained, accounting has evolved in such a manner as to reflect its cultural environment. Thus, the Renaissance, being a time of rapid development in all aspects comprising Western civilization, was also a time for many innovations in accounting. And, just as in the biological world, where not all mutations give rise to viable species, so too in accounting not all innovations have been retained. Logismography was one of the more interesting experiments that did not prove viable. The accounting system described by Pacioli—and the same as that used today—was a **double-entry accounting system**. That is, every business transaction affects at least two ac-

[2]*New International Version*, 2 Corinthians 8: 16, 18, and 22.
[3]*New International Version*, 2 Corinthians 8: 18 and 23.
[4]*New International Version*, Luke 14: 28–29.
[5]*New International Version*, Matthew 24: 46–50.
[6]Luca Pacioli, as translated by John B. Geijsbeek, *Ancient Double-Entry Bookkeeping*, Houston, Texas: Scholars Book Co., 1974, pp. 33–34.

counts and is recorded in the books with at least one debit and at least one credit. Logismography was a quadruple accounting system designed for municipalities and other governments that used one double-entry in the real accounts and a second double-entry in the budgetary accounts for every transaction. Theoretically, it was a sound accounting system, but it was rather complex, was never widely adopted, and did not survive its creator. In the previous century, a triple-entry bookkeeping system was developed, although it was done more as an intellectual exercise rather than as a serious alternative to double-entry accounting.

During the Renaissance, companies in Germany, France, and the Lowlands adopted the Italian accounting system that Pacioli had described. Later, the Italian accounting system was adopted in Britain, which influenced the British Commonwealth, including North America, Australia, and India, to adopt it in the seventeenth and eighteenth centuries. Much the same thing occurred within the other European empires. Thus, the Dutch exported the Italian accounting model to Indonesia and South Africa; the French exported it to Polynesia and the French-dominated parts of Africa; and the Germans introduced it to the Swedes, Japanese, and Russians.

In this century, the United States (whose accounting system is based on Pacioli's Italian model) has had a significant impact on the global development of accounting because of its economic and political influence. But each country in the world has its own culture and, thus, has made minor adjustments to the Italian model to form its own unique accounting system. Each system is intended to provide the information individuals and organizations in that culture need to make informed decisions.

Today, accounting continues to be a primary information-gathering system for decision makers throughout the world. When providing reliable and relevant information, accounting contributes to the efficiency and effectiveness of business, the stability of securities markets, and the effectiveness of governments. But when accounting systems provide inaccurate data or data that is not timely or cannot be relied upon, then accounting may exacerbate the culture's problems. As an example, in the previous communist state of Russia, the performance of taxi cab drivers in Moscow at one time was measured according to how many miles they drove, with the result that taxi cabs were driven—empty—all over Moscow. When the measurement of performance was changed to the number of passengers carried, it was impossible to get a cab in Moscow without having to share it with several other individuals. In either situation, by reporting irrelevant information, accounting contributed to a social problem.

The Origin of Financial Reporting

As mentioned, accounting is as ancient as civilization. However, financial reporting is a relatively recent concept, having become an accepted practice only within the past century. In some areas of the world, financial reporting remains a novelty. The essence of **financial reporting** is the communicating to interested external parties the impact of economic events upon an enterprise, usually considered in the context of a business enterprise.

Until the advent of the Industrial Revolution, individuals outside a business had little need for economic information about a business. The business manager was the business owner, and he received whatever information he needed. When required, the manager/owner shared necessary information with his banker or the government—both of whom had the authority to ask for (or demand) the information that they needed. But everyone else had little need for information about a business; and when they had such a need, they usually did not have the authority to receive it.

Those interested in accounting history may want to access the Web site of the Academy of Accounting Historians at **http://weatherhead.cwru.edu/Accounting/**

The advent of the Industrial Revolution, with its massive undertakings requiring large accumulations of capital, resulted in the corporate form of business increasingly being used.[7] As a result, no longer was the business owner also the business manager. Rather, a corporation had hundreds or even thousands of absentee owners who were interested in information concerning their investment but who individually were powerless to demand and receive it. Thus, the notion of financial reporting was born. But having a need for financial reporting and having that need fulfilled was to take time and be the result of a series of interrelationships among many environmental influences and various bodies, the outcome of which is still evolving.

Initially, in the United States, financial reporting to stockholders and other interested external parties depended upon the whims or "good graces" of management, and it was a significant event whenever a corporation published any type of financial report to the public. Considerable time passed before corporate management recognized its accountability to provide information to present or prospective stockholders.[8]

The New York Stock Exchange was the first organization to request information that could be disseminated to stockholders. The response the stock exchange received in 1866 from the Delaware, Lackawanna & Western Railroad is indicative of the attitude of corporate management in that era towards supplying information to "outsiders." The railroad's reply was, "The Delaware, Lackawanna & Western R.R. Co. make no reports and publish no statements, and have not done anything of the kind for the last five years."[9] Neither did the railroad provide the stock exchange any information. However, by continuing to exert pressure, the New York Stock Exchange by 1905 was receiving financial information from applicants-for-listing that could be distributed to interested individuals.

© INDEXSTOCK INC.

At the beginning of the twentieth century, the president of United States Steel Corporation had a policy of not operating behind "locked doors and shut lips,"[10] and accordingly, United States Steel published the first true corporate annual report in 1902. But annual reports of the early twentieth century contained

[7]The corporate form of business organization was not adopted easily or without opposition. In 1840, the Governor of Massachusetts sent a message to the Great and General Court, expressing his views of corporations. He wrote, "[Corporations] are one of the vices of our time. They encourage speculation and fraud, mobilize landed property, overturn matrimonial arrangements, escape publicity in the transfer of real property, diminish the sense of individual responsibility, create property in mortmain, prevent all penal remedies, are lacking in moral sense, and constitute finally a grave social peril by concentrating too much power in the hands of certain of our citizens." William Z. Ripley, *Main Street and Wall Street*, Lawrence, Kansas: Scholars Book Co., 1972, p. 22.

[8]Illustrating the point of noncorporate disclosure of information to shareholders, a statement in a 1901 corporate report was as follows: "The settled plan of the directors has been to withhold all information from stockholders and others that is not called for by the stockholders in a body. So far no request for information has been made in the manner prescribed by the directors. Distribution of stock has not meant distribution of control." B. Bernard Greidinger, *Preparation and Certification of Financial Statements*, New York: The Ronald Press, 1950, p. 3.

[9]W. B. Flowers, *Some Criteria for Disclosure of Post-Statement Events*, unpublished dissertation, 1959, p. 13.

[10]Ibid., p. 15.

little information of worth. For example, in 1905 American Can Company presented a six-page condensed report, of which pages three and four of that report are included as Exhibit 1-1.[11]

EXHIBIT 1-1

Typical Balance Sheet in Early Twentieth Century American Can Company

Assets		
Plants, Real Estate, Patents, etc.		$74,854,298.82
New Construction and Improvements		3,376,042.76
Other Investment Items		649,298.64
Cash		3,311,519.53
Accounts and Bills Receivable		1,273,957.17
Merchandise Inventory		4,285,389.69
Total Assets		$87,750,506.61
Liabilities		
Capital Stock:		$82,466,600.00
Preferred	$41,233,300.00	
Common	41,233,300.00	
Accounts Payable		721,478.35
Dividends Payable, January 1, 1906		515,416.25
Surplus		4,047,012.01
Total Liabilities		$87,750,506.61

An examination of 20 financial statements published around 1905 revealed that "footnotes as they are used today were lacking; . . . disclosure of current assets was inadequate, but disclosure of fixed assets was practically nonexistent, [and] only one company among the twenty examined deducted depreciation from the asset account, and this deduction was questionable."[12] Regarding the six annual statements that were certified by public accountants as compared to those that were not, the examiner concluded that, "The statements certified by public accountants were by far the better statements for the period 1900–1905."[13] Likely, it is due to this higher quality of financial statements where a **certified public accountant (CPA)** was involved that later led to CPAs receiving a franchise from the **Securities and Exchange Commission (SEC)**[14] to audit financial statements of corporations whose stock was publicly traded.

Uniform Accounting

The development of financial reporting during the early years of the twentieth century and for some time thereafter was essentially laissez faire. Guidelines did not exist, and financial statement presentation was left to individual preference. As an obvious result, improvements in financial reporting evolved slowly and haphazardly. However, in 1917, a milestone in financial reporting was achieved

[11]Ibid., p. 17.
[12]Ibid., pp. 18–21.
[13]Ibid., p. 19.
[14]Many abbreviations are used from this point in the chapter, of which many and perhaps most will be new to the reader. To help in remembering the abbreviations and their meanings, a glossary is provided at the end of the textbook. All the items in bold in this chapter are in that glossary.

with the publication and wide distribution of the pamphlet "Uniform Accounting," which was a joint project of the Federal Trade Commission, the Federal Reserve Board, and the **American Institute of Accountants (AIA)**. The publication and distribution of the pamphlet was significant in that it was the first attempt to establish some minimum requirements for financial reporting. To show the age and origin of some current financial reporting principles, a few of these initial principles are included as Exhibit 1-2.[15]

EXHIBIT 1-2

Some Principles from Uniform Accounting Published in 1917

1. Notes receivable and accounts receivable from company officers and employees must be shown separately from customers' notes receivable. (Still in force today.)

2. Accounts receivable with credit balances should be shown separately from other accounts receivable and not [be] deducted from debit balances. (Apparently, accounts receivable with credit balances were shown as payables, which is the same procedure followed today.)

3. Only inventory owned and under the control of the owner was to be included in inventory. (Except for inventory owned by the company that is in transit, this is the same policy followed today.)

4. Disclosure needed to be made in the footnotes when the market price of inventory was higher than its cost. (This is not followed today, but perhaps it should be.)

5. No profit should be included in the price of finished products. (This is consistent with the present-day revenue realization principle, but today, an exception is permitted for certain goods where profit can be included in the cost of finished inventory.)

By the late 1920s, many individuals were recognizing that corporations had the responsibility to provide information to stockholders and that stockholders had the responsibility to demand accountability from corporate management. In 1926, *The Magazine of Wall Street* published an editorial expressing its opinion of the respective responsibilities of corporate management and shareholders regarding disclosure of corporate information. The editorial said: "[W]e believe that the general trend is already in the proper direction. The old business 'principle' of misleading the investor through incomplete reports is gradually losing favor among the better class of corporation heads. In the final analysis, it is the business of the shareholders to demand whatever information they deem necessary as to the position of their companies."[16]

Impact of the Securities and Exchange Commission

Both businesspeople and accountants were slow to respond fully to the need for full and fair disclosure, which was a contributing factor that led to the establishment of the SEC.[17] In retrospect, the establishment of the SEC probably did more than any other event in the twentieth century to professionalize accounting, to spur the development of standardized accounting principles, and to establish a set of ethical guidelines for the accounting profession to govern itself.

The SEC's Web site can be accessed at **http://www.sec.gov/**

---

[15]Flowers, op. cit., pp. 35–37.

[16]Editorial, *The Magazine of Wall Street*, Vol. XXVIII (September 11, 1926), p. 923, as quoted in Flowers, p. 48.

[17]Although there were a variety of abuses in the securities market during the 1920s, one of them was "outright deceit by issuing false and misleading statements." K. Fred Skousen, *An Introduction to the SEC, 3rd Edition*, South-Western Publishing Company, 1983, p. 4.

These characteristics distinguish accounting as a profession from accounting as a job.[18]

The Securities Act of 1933 requires disclosure of information at the time securities are issued, and the Securities Exchange Act of 1934—in addition to establishing the SEC—requires the continuing disclosure of information as long as a security is traded on the public market. The purpose of these two laws is to offer protection to the investing public through full and fair disclosure of information.

Although relatively unknown to most practicing accountants, the Securities Exchange Act of 1934 gave the SEC the power to determine accounting and financial reporting principles for all companies whose shares are sold in interstate commerce.[19] But early SEC Commissioners apparently did not perceive this to be a particularly important power, and instead of exercising it outright, *the SEC looked to the accounting profession to establish **generally accepted accounting principles (GAAP)***. That position was formalized in 1938 in **Accounting Series Release (ASR)** No. 4. However, in ASR No. 4, the SEC put itself in a position equivalent to a Supreme Court in that it stated its right to rule against a registrant even if the registrant followed GAAP as determined by the private sector, and further, the SEC affirmed its right to determine which accounting principles had substantive authoritative support.

The passage of these two securities acts requiring audited financial statements by all companies seeking registration gave accountants a franchise in regards to audits of corporations with publicly traded securities. Following the passage of these two acts, accountants quickly recognized that their profession had changed, that they had a new client—the shareholder—and that they had the responsibility of determining what constituted fair disclosure. In the 1934 annual meeting of the AIA, an address was given wherein was stated:

> One of the most radical changes brought about by the enactment of these two securities acts has been the complete abolition of the privity of contract between our profession and our immediate clients. . . . This can only mean that regardless of the source of our instructions or regardless of the person responsible for our fees, our ultimate client is now the investor, and it is to him that we are directly responsible for our part in the presentation of accounts.[20]

Structure for Establishing Generally Accepted Accounting Principles

One year after the SEC issued ASR No. 4, the AIA in response organized the **Committee on Accounting Procedure (CAP)** and gave it the authority to issue statements that would be GAAP. (Besides published pronouncements, GAAP also consists of the traditions that are generally accepted by all accountants.) Thus, the structure for establishing GAAP in the United States was put in place. This

---

[18]After passing the uniform national CPA exam and fulfilling all other requirements, the CPA candidate is required to swear an oath to abide by the professional rules of conduct before receiving a license to practice as a CPA. This code of conduct and the fact that CPAs generally have adhered to it has brought great prestige to the profession.

[19]This power given to the SEC to establish accounting principles and financial reporting practices was reiterated in the Public Utility Holding Company Act of 1935 and the Trust Indenture Act of 1939.

[20]Rodney F. Starkey, *Practice Under the Securities Act of 1933 and the Securities Exchange Act of 1934*, *Journal of Accountancy*, Vol. LVIII (December 1934), pp. 434 and 438.

structure is that the private sector has "primary" responsibility for determining GAAP, with the SEC maintaining an oversight responsibility. Today, the **Financial Accounting Standards Board (FASB)** is the private-sector body that is responsible for establishing authoritative standards that must be adhered to when issuing financial statements. Although the SEC considers the private sector as the primary source of authoritative guidance on accounting and financial reporting matters, it also issues guidance on such matters through Accounting Series Releases. These also deal with other matters, including sanctions taken against CPAs and their right to practice before the Commission.

The developments leading to the formation of the FASB and how the private sector and the SEC have related to each other in setting accounting and financial reporting standards is a fascinating topic. The highlights of these developments are shown in the timeline in Exhibit 1-3 and are covered in the next few pages.

EXHIBIT 1-3

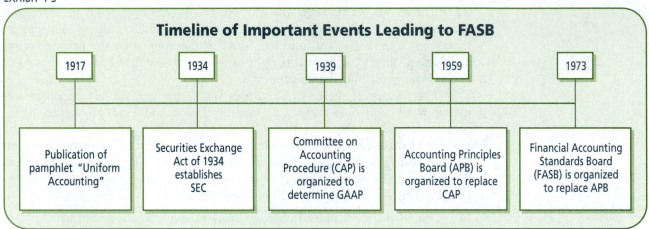

Timeline of Important Events Leading to FASB

1917	1934	1939	1959	1973
Publication of pamphlet "Uniform Accounting"	Securities Exchange Act of 1934 establishes SEC	Committee on Accounting Procedure (CAP) is organized to determine GAAP	Accounting Principles Board (APB) is organized to replace CAP	Financial Accounting Standards Board (FASB) is organized to replace APB

INTERNET

The FASB's Web site can be accessed at http://www.fasb.org/

Brief History of the Development of the FASB

The first organization designated to formulate accounting and financial reporting standards was the CAP, which was organized by the AIA in 1939. *The CAP's official pronouncements are labeled* **Accounting Research Bulletins (ARBs)***, and except where they are specifically superseded, they are still in force today.* Interestingly, practicing accountants of that time did not have to follow the ARBs, nor were they sanctioned when they failed to do so. The CAP's authority rested literally upon their pronouncements having "general acceptance."

The CAP was composed of practicing CPAs who devoted their efforts to the CAP on a part-time basis. Not having an established theoretical framework to guide them in setting standards, the CAP out of necessity used a "fire-fighting" approach to formulate their pronouncements. As the name suggests, a fire-fighting approach consists of developing solutions to problems independently of each other and only after they arise. Over time, this approach to standard setting led to inconsistencies among the ARBs and highlighted the need for an underlying conceptual framework for developing standards that would tie together all pronouncements under a theoretical model.

Beginning about 1950, the CAP attempted to develop such a conceptual framework but failed. Instead, in 1953, the CAP issued ARB No. 43, which is a restatement and revision of the previously issued 42 ARBs. ARB No. 43 eliminated many of the accounting and financial reporting inconsistencies, but as indicated in the title, it was not a set of concepts. As a result, the subsequent ARBs that the CAP issued were also developed using the fire-fighting approach. In its published standards, the CAP emphasized income measurement at the sacrifice of realistic balance sheet values.

The Accounting Principles Board

In 1959, the **American Institute of Certified Public Accountants (AICPA)**, which was the successor to the AIA, organized the **Accounting Principles Board (APB)** to replace the CAP, and gave it the authority to establish accounting and financial reporting standards, called Opinions, and also charged it to formulate a conceptual framework. *The **Accounting Principles Board's Opinions (APBO)**, like the CAP's Bulletins, remain in force, except where they have been specifically superseded.*

Regarding its charge to formulate a conceptual framework, shortly before establishing the APB, the AICPA commissioned Maurice Moonitz to prepare a set of accounting principles and postulates. Moonitz enlisted the help of Robert Sprouse and published two monographs, the essence of which was a call for current value accounting and reporting. Such a radical departure from historical cost resulted in the accounting profession voting to reject the monographs. In its next attempt to develop a conceptual framework, the APB commissioned Paul Grady to develop an inventory of currently accepted accounting principles, which was published in 1965. This inventory was also never accepted as an authoritative pronouncement. The APB's last attempt at developing a conceptual framework was publishing Statement No. 4 in 1970, which was a codification of supposed existing principles, rather than setting forth what accounting and financial reporting principles should be. Although widely quoted by accountants and subsequently referred to by the FASB, Statement No. 4 was never officially accepted as an authoritative standard of what accounting and financial reporting concepts should be, or even a description of concepts underlying accounting practice of the time. Because of the APB's failure to develop any sort of a conceptual framework, its Opinions were also developed utilizing a fire-fighting approach.

Other Attempts at Formulating a Conceptual Framework

From the 1920s through the 1960s, various accountants and accounting bodies published books and monographs attempting to establish an unofficial conceptual framework. (They would have been unofficial frameworks because they were not written at the request of any authoritative body.) Accounting educators—both as individuals and collectively through their association, the **American Accounting Association (AAA)**—were primary influences in these unofficial efforts. In 1936, the Executive Committee of the AAA issued the first in a series of publications addressing accounting theory. One of these publications, "A Statement of Basic Accounting Theory," which was published in 1966, made a significant contribution to establishing accounting principles and was widely quoted and substantially included in the FASB's subsequent conceptual framework.

Developments Leading to Establishing the FASB

During its existence, the APB was heavily criticized for (1) issuing several controversial opinions, (2) failing to act on a timely basis on emerging problems (which can be connected to its failure to develop a conceptual framework), and (3) lacking independence (i.e., too closely connected to the AICPA). As a result, in 1971

The AICPA's Web site contains information that is useful for planning a career in accounting. Access that Web site at **http://www.aicpa.org/index.htm** and check (a) the most recent issue of the Journal of Accountancy, (b) information on taking the CPA Exam, and (c) information on becoming a CPA.

the AICPA formed a study group to make recommendations for improving the organization and operations of the standard-setting body. The study group's recommendations were implemented in 1973, and the present day standard-setting structure was established (Exhibit 1-4), which consists of the Financial Accounting Foundation (FAF), the seven-member Financial Accounting Standards Board,[21] and the Financial Accounting Standards Advisory Committee (FASAC).

EXHIBIT 1-4

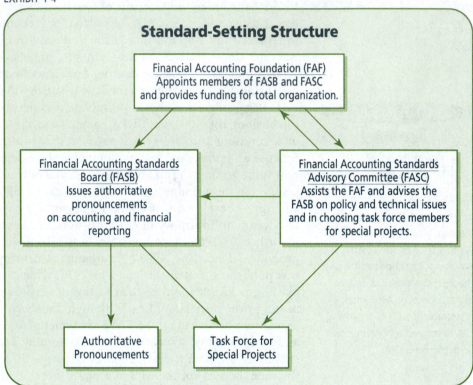

The FAF appoints the members of the FASB and the FASAC and provides funding for the total organization, whose financing is obtained primarily from contributions from CPA firms and industry and from sales of FASB literature.[22] The FASAC assists the FAF and advises the FASB on policy and technical issues and in choosing task-force members for special projects. The FASB issues authoritative pronouncements on accounting and financial reporting, which are called **Statements of Financial Accounting Standards (SFAS)**. The FASB has also issued authoritative **Interpretations**.

At about the same time that the FASB was organized, an important step was taken to ensure compliance to the official pronouncements of the FASB and also its predecessors. Where previously compliance had been based on the "general acceptance" of the pronouncements, now a rule was added to the AICPA's Code of Professional Conduct, allowing the AICPA to sanction members who issued financial statements that were not in compliance with official pronouncements.

---

[21]This seven-member board contrasts to the much larger CAP (22 members) and the APB (20 members). Besides the size of the board, another significant difference between the FASB and its predecessors is that the board members of the FASB are compensated for their full time, and they are expected to sever all ties with other organizations.

[22]In 1984, the Governmental Accounting Standards Board (GASB) also came under the auspices of the FAF. The GASB has final authority for establishing standards for state and local government entities and associated not-for-profit entities.

This provision is **Rule 203**, and *the documents that the CPA must adhere to when publicly issuing financial statements are called Rule 203 documents, which are:*

Rule 203 Documents

1. *Bulletins* issued by the CAP,
2. *Opinions* issued by the APB,
3. *Statements of Standards* issued by the FASB, and
4. *Interpretations* issued by the FASB.

Of course, the AICPA can only sanction its members, and that does not include being able to revoke a member's license to practice as a CPA, which is granted by a state. However, most state CPA societies have adopted the AICPA's ethical rulings, and their input to state agencies that grant licenses may result in the loss of the CPA license. Further, the SEC may also sanction CPAs and deny them the right to practice before it. Because of these linkages among the AICPA, state societies, state licensing agencies, and the SEC, violating Rule 203 or any other provision of the Code of Professional Conduct is a serious matter.

Dynamics of the Standard-Setting Process

For approximately 25 years from the time the CAP was established in 1939, the private sector establishing GAAP and the SEC maintaining an oversight responsibility worked reasonably well. Confrontations between the accounting profession and the SEC's staff regarding accounting and financial reporting issues were small. The first major confrontation between the SEC's staff and the private sector, with Congress also becoming involved, concerned the accounting for the investment tax credit that was passed in 1962. The Accounting Principles Board issued an opinion stating that the investment tax credit should be accounted for under the "deferral method." Noting the lack of support from businesspeople and accountants for the APB's decision, the staff of the SEC issued ASR No. 97, stating that the "flow-through" method was equally acceptable. As a consequence, the APB amended its decision and, although expressing a preference for its previous decision, stated that either the deferral method or the flow-through method was acceptable. Then, Congress destroyed the APB's position by passing legislation stating that taxpaying corporations could account for the investment tax credit any way they wanted.

Perhaps this controversy, particularly since it came shortly after the APB was established, was one reason why the SEC became much more active for the rest of the 1960s in issuing rules establishing GAAP (through ASRs). During the time that the APB issued its last six opinions, the SEC issued 14 ASRs. Continuing that tendency, during the first year of the FASB, the SEC issued 20 ASRs. This led the chairman of the FASB at the time to note that the SEC was pre-empting the private sector in establishing GAAP.[23]

Some years after its establishment, the FASB and SEC clashed. This time, the issue concerned the accounting for exploration costs in the oil and gas industry. At the beginning of the energy crisis in 1975, Congress was concerned with obtaining reliable energy data and authorized the SEC to prescribe adequate

---

[23]K. Fred Skousen, *An Introduction to the SEC, 3rd Edition*, South-Western Publishing Company, 1983, p. 136.

accounting practices in the matter. Congress also authorized the SEC to rely upon the FASB's decision, as long as the SEC felt that the FASB had received adequate input prior to issuing its decision and if the SEC felt that oil and gas producers would follow the FASB's pronouncement. Subsequently, the FASB issued a standard calling for "successful efforts" accounting, which many smaller oil and gas companies immediately opposed. The SEC, acting under its congressional mandate, held hearings and concluded that none of the existing methods of oil and gas accounting were adequate and stated it would develop a new method called "Reserve Recognition Accounting." In the interim, the SEC allowed oil and gas companies that filed reports with the SEC to continue using either the successful efforts or the "full-cost" methods of accounting. Again, the private sector's authority to establish GAAP had been undercut, and the FASB had to suspend the effective date of its published standard.

The nonsupport for the APB's accounting for the investment tax credit and the FASB's oil and gas accounting, along with the perceived interference of Congress,[24] has led many to believe that the accounting standard-setting function in the United States will be assumed eventually by the federal government. The recent accounting scandals have increased the cry for government oversight of the standard-setting function. Whether this will happen is not yet clear, but one thing that is evident is that accounting and financial reporting standards are not established in a vacuum. Accounting and financial reporting standards have economic impacts, and it is foolish to assume that those affected by them will not voice their opinions in an attempt to affect the outcome.

Another evident lesson from the past is that the FASB depends on the endorsement of the SEC for its existence. Aware of how crucial the SEC's support is to its existence, the FASB ensures that a representative of the SEC is present in all its deliberations. Such action undoubtedly has limited, but not eliminated, conflict between positions of the FASB and those of the SEC.

A recent example that demonstrates how dynamic the standard-setting process is concerns measuring compensation in certain stock options. The initial standard in accounting for stock options, APB Opinion No. 25, mandates that stock option compensation be measured usually at the date the stock options are granted and be computed as the difference between the option's exercise price and the stock price. Typically, this results in no compensation being recognized. Thinking that such an approach to measuring compensation denied economic reality, many critics lobbied the FASB to reconsider Opinion No. 25, and Congress also began considering legislation that would require companies to measure some compensation for all stock options. Subsequently, the FASB issued an exposure draft in which it proposed to measure compensation under a stock option-pricing model. As word circulated of the FASB's draft, opposition from business and accountants grew, and a politically reactive Congress reversed itself by introducing legislation that, if passed, would have prohibited the FASB from requiring financial statements to include compensation as measured under an option-pricing model. With support for its position having evaporated, the FASB had no choice but to allow two methods of accounting for compensation for certain stock options. However, following the accounting scandals at Enron, WorldCom, and other companies, pressure again mounted to measure stock option compensation only under an option-pricing model.

Each of these three examples of conflict in the standard-setting process were contentious and drawn-out affairs, but it should not be inferred that all adopted

---

[24]Several times during the 1970s, bills were introduced in Congress that would have brought the standard-setting function under the auspices of the government if they had passed.

standards cause such strong feelings. Nor should it be inferred that, when contention arises, the FASB (or its predecessors) always "lose the battle." Rather, the above situations were intended to illustrate that the standard-setting function is a political process and that the FASB must consider the views of all its constituents in order for its standard-setting process to be viable in establishing accounting and financial reporting standards. Exhibit 1-5 illustrates the way constituents can influence the FASB's decisions and thus influence the evolution of U.S. GAAP.

EXHIBIT 1-5

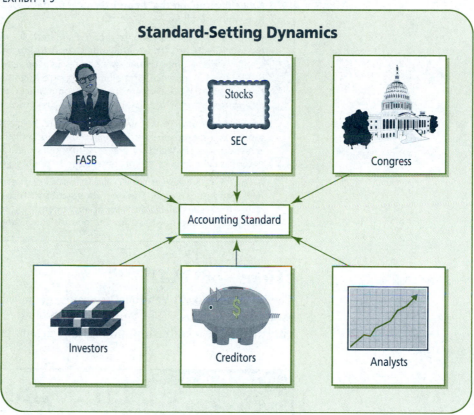

From Issue to Published Standard

When accounting and financial reporting standards impact so many different individuals and groups, it is inevitable that the standard-setting process is a political process. To respond to the needs of the various affected parties, the FASB consists—by requirement—of representatives drawn from a broad cross-section of the business community. Also, to provide all interested parties adequate input in its deliberations, the FASB follows a process that is open to public observation and participation. Each major project that the FASB undertakes may easily require two to four years before a standard is published.[25] For all standards that it issues, the FASB takes the steps as outlined in Exhibit 1-6, and throughout the process, extensive debate and lobbying occurs by all interested parties. As expected, corporations lobby against those standards that they perceive will have a negative impact on their financial statements.

---

[25]The FASB took 16 years in its deliberative process before issuing Statement No. 87, "Employers' Accounting for Pensions."

EXHIBIT 1-6

Steps in the FASB's Deliberative Process

1. The project is placed on the FASB's *agenda*.

2. A *task force* of outside experts is *appointed* to define the issues and alternatives related to the project.

3. The technical staff and the outside experts of the FASB *research* the project.

4. A *Discussion Memorandum* inviting comments from interested parties is released to the public. The Discussion Memorandum identifies the principal issues and includes a discussion of the various points of view, but it does not include specific conclusions.

5. *Public hearings* are held approximately 60 days following the release of the Discussion Memorandum.

6. The *public response is analyzed and evaluated*. During this phase of the deliberative process, the board (those individuals constituting the voting members of the FASB) meets as many times as necessary to discuss the issue. An agenda of these meetings is published in advance, and all meetings are open to the public. Throughout the entire process, the FASB maintains close communication with the SEC, including having a representative of the SEC present in discussions.

7. An *Exposure Draft* of the proposed standard is released to the public. The public response to the exposure draft is analyzed, evaluated, and if necessary, the exposure draft is revised. Also, if necessary, the board conducts field tests of the proposed standard to determine the impact the proposed standard would have on financial statements.

8. A *vote* by the board is taken, and if four of the seven members vote affirmatively, a new standard is issued. The new statement sets forth the new standard, the effective date of the standard, transition or implementation guidelines, pertinent background information, and the basis for the board's conclusions.

"House of GAAP"

The FASB's deliberative process negates the possibility of a timely standard, and as a result, various other authoritative bodies have arisen that provide timely guidance. The relationship among the various pronouncements from the sev-

This Is the Real World

As chairman of the U.S. Federal Reserve, Alan Greenspan makes decisions that have a substantial effect on the economy of the United States and, thus, of the world. Capital market participants eagerly await the announcement of decisions made in Federal Reserve meetings and hang on every word that Mr. Greenspan says during scheduled speeches to Congress. In fact, it is commonly believed that Mr. Greenspan has more power to influence the world economy than any other single individual. Mr. Greenspan has earned the respect shown to him by making weighty economic decisions (usually the right ones) that have kept the U.S. economy strong.

Given Mr. Greenspan's significant influence, it is no small matter that he has recently expressed his strong support for the current structure of the accounting standards process. During a time when the FASB was under attack from various constituents and

significant political pressure was being applied to Congress to assume responsibility for developing accounting standards, Mr. Greenspan wrote a letter to the chairman of the SEC, stating that he would oppose any type of legislation that would weaken the FASB. In the letter, Mr. Greenspan wrote, "The success of the U.S. accounting model has been due, in no small part, to the private sector's significant involvement in the process. An integral part of this process involves the Financial Accounting Standards Board working directly with its constituents to develop appropriate accounting standards that reflect the needs of the marketplace."

Mr. Greenspan concluded his letter saying, "While I have not always agreed with the FASB's ultimate conclusions, I have always felt that the openness of the process allows all affected parties sufficient opportunity to contribute to the debate."

eral authoritative bodies is known as the "House of GAAP." One such authoritative body is the **Emerging Issues Task Force (EITF)**, which was established in 1984 by the FASB. The EITF is a part-time body consisting of the senior technical partners of the major CPA firms and representatives from the major associations of financial statement preparers. If 11 of the 13 members of the EITF agree on the treatment of an issue, then that consensus defines the generally accepted accounting treatment on the issue until the time the FASB considers it. However, the FASB has the option of not considering the issue, and it may decide not to if it thinks the EITF's guidance is adequate. Abstracts of the EITF's decisions are published in the *Journal of Accountancy*, as are all other pronouncements of the FASB.

The AICPA, attempting to serve its members with timely guidance, has established several committees and charged them with providing guidance in auditing. Rather than being general pronouncements, these pronouncements relate to specific industries, such as construction, banking, and insurance. Concerned about the proliferation of accounting guidelines, the FASB has adopted all of these various guides as preferred accounting principles, subject to its review and possible subsequent issuance of a FASB statement.

With several bodies now providing accounting and financial reporting guidance, a pecking order has been developed that shows the relative authority of the several pronouncements comprising GAAP. That order is shown in Exhibit 1-7. In seeking guidance for accounting and financial accounting issues, Category A pronouncements are researched first. If guidance is not found from pronouncements in that category, then Category B pronouncements are researched, and so on, until guidance about the particular problem is found.

EXHIBIT 1-7

The "House of GAAP"

CATEGORY A
pronouncements are the most authoritative, and they consist of: Statements of the FASB, Interpretations of the FASB, Opinions of the APB, Bulletins of the CAP, and SEC releases.

CATEGORY B
pronouncements are the next most authoritative, and they consist of FASB Technical Bulletins and, if cleared by the FASB, AICPA Industry Audit and Accounting Guides and Statements of Position.

CATEGORY C
pronouncements consist of EITF pronouncements and AICPA Accounting Standards Executive Committee Practice Bulletins cleared by the FASB.

CATEGORY D
pronouncements consist of AICPA accounting interpretations and implementation guides published by the FASB staff, and practices that are widely recognized and prevalent generally or in a specific industry.

INTERNATIONAL

A Look at Financial Reporting in Japan

Some observations about Japanese business and business practices further illustrate how cultural factors affect accounting and financial reporting. For about a decade beginning in the mid-1980s, the average price-to-earnings ratio for Japanese companies has been two to five times higher than companies listed on the New York Stock Exchange, supposedly indicating that the stock of Japanese companies was more expensive than U.S. companies.[26] Also, the average return on assets for the S&P 500 companies has been consistently higher than for manufacturing companies headquartered in Japan, supposedly indicating that U.S. companies are more profitable than Japanese companies.[27] Using this data at face value, investors should conclude that the stocks of U.S. companies are a better investment compared to Japanese companies. However, this conclusion may not be appropriate because of the differences in Japanese accounting and financial reporting techniques as compared to U.S. GAAP.

The common explanation given for the differences in profitability performance measures mentioned above is that Japanese companies employ more conservative accounting procedures to measure net income. For example, Japanese companies typically use accelerated depreciation methods instead of the straight-line method that is often used in the United States. Also, Japanese companies use several income-decreasing discretionary reserves. The reason Japanese companies choose to employ these and other income-reducing procedures (as compared to U.S.-based companies that generally attempt to maximize the net income reported) is based in their respective cultures.

One study on cultural differences identified five major cultural dimensions that distinguish a culture's core values.[28] These dimensions are labeled: power-distance, uncertainty-avoidance, individualism, long-term orientation, and masculinity. Substantial differences were measured in every category between the Japanese culture and the U.S. culture, as shown in Exhibit 1-8, which defines each dimension and provides the respective U.S. and Japanese scores.

In addition to the previously mentioned differences in profitability ratios between U.S. and Japanese companies, Japanese companies also typically rely more on debt financing as compared to owner financing. Japanese companies commonly have debt levels two to three times greater than are found for comparable U.S. companies. Once again, a face value interpretation would suggest that the risk of default on debt is much higher for Japanese companies relative to U.S. companies. However, a closer look at the Japanese corporate structure indicates otherwise.

Many large Japanese companies are members of a **keiretsu**, which is a group of interrelated firms from various industries. Exhibit 1-9 illustrates the typical relationship among keiretsu companies. The intercompany holdings within the keiretsu are meant to facilitate cooperation. Company A provides raw materials to Company B, which in turn supplies inventory to Company C. Thus, the success of Company A depends, to a certain extent, on the success of Companies B and C. As a result, when Company A has financial difficulty, Companies B and C are expected to assist. Typically, a keiretsu is organized around a major bank, which provides financing on favorable terms to keiretsu members. This cheap

---

[26]M. E. Haskins, K.R. Ferris, and T.I. Selling, *International Financial Reporting and Analysis: A Contextual Emphasis*, Irwin Publishing Co., 1996, p. 571.
[27]Ibid., p. 572.
[28]G. Hofstede, *Culture's Consequences: International Differences in Work Related Values*, Sage, Beverly Hills, CA, 1980.

EXHIBIT 1-8

Hofstede's Cultural Characteristics

Large versus small power distance: Refers to a society's tolerance towards power inequality. A small power distance society would grant more power in establishing accounting and financial reporting standards to the private sector.

Uncertainty avoidance versus acceptance: Refers to a society's tolerance towards uncertainty. A high uncertainty avoidance society would prefer more rules and explicit standards, rather than flexibility in accounting and financial reporting standards.

Individualism versus collectivism: Refers to a society's aversion to integrate into strong, cohesive groups. Individualistic societies would tend to have more disclosure and be less conservative.

Long-term versus short-term orientation: Refers to a society's tendency to have long-term goals. Long-term oriented societies would focus less on short-term profits and more on long-term survival.

Masculinity versus femininity: Refers to a society's penchant for achievement and material success. A feminist society would be more concerned with relationships and the quality of life.

Hofstede's Characteristics	United States	Japan
Power Distance	40	54
Uncertainty Avoidance	46	92
Individualism	91	46
Long-Term Orientation	29	80
Masculinity	62	95

source of debt and reliance upon interrelated companies for help in times of financial difficulty are the reasons Japanese companies utilize more debt financing than comparable U.S. companies without necessarily incurring greater risk. The notion of keiretsu is consistent with a lower-risk-taking desire of the Japanese,

EXHIBIT 1-9

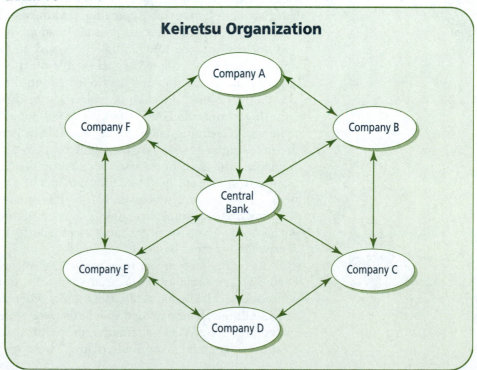

Keiretsu Organization

as evidenced by the lower cultural score on individualism shown previously in Exhibit 1-8.

These differences are only a few of the Japanese business practices that are the result of its different culture and which impact on accounting and especially financial reporting practices. Given the numerous political, legal, economic, and technological differences around the world, many different financial reporting systems should be expected. However, some accountants see the differences as becoming fewer. They believe that as economies become increasingly global, there will be an increasing need—and an increasing demand—for harmonized accounting and financial reporting procedures.

Short History of the International Accounting Standards Board

For some time, a call has been sounding for a set of harmonized financial reporting standards that multinational companies can use as guidance for providing financial information to investors in any country. Such harmonization is a Herculean task because all the cultural factors that have resulted in the different financial reporting systems in the world must be understood, considered, and transcended.

The **International Accounting Standards Board (IASB)** is leading the efforts to establish international accounting and financial reporting standards. The IASB is the successor of the **International Accounting Standards Committee (IASC)**, which was established in 1973 with representatives from eight countries (including the United States). The IASC issued its first standard one year later. Over the next 25 years, the IASC's influence over accounting issues increased substantially until in 2001 a major organizational restructuring occurred, and the IASB was formed, comprising 14 members from seven different countries (France, Germany, Japan, South Africa, Switzerland, the United Kingdom, and the United States).

A primary obstacle faced by the IASB (and its predecessor, the IASC) is its lack of enforcement authority. Currently, compliance to its pronouncements—**International Financial Reporting Standards (IFRS)**—is voluntary. To encourage as many companies as possible to adopt international GAAP and to avoid political conflict, the IASC initially followed an "anything goes" approach. Essentially, the IASC adopted as "acceptable practice" any financial reporting procedure that was used in any developed country. An advantage of this approach was that it lowered the costs of converting to its standards—**International Accounting Standards (IAS)**. However, it did not accomplish the objective of harmonizing accounting and financial reporting principles. Realizing that its success depended upon establishing a credible set of accounting and financial reporting principles, the IASC in the late 1980s began the "Improvements Project," whose main purposes were to (1) identify preferable accounting methods for transactions, (2) eliminate alternatives, (3) establish more disclosure requirements, and (4) provide more implementation guidance. In addition, the IASC aggressively encouraged various stock exchanges and security commissions to endorse IAS as acceptable for cross-border listings.

As a first step in the Improvements Project, the IASC released Exposure Draft 32, *Comparability of Financial Statements*, in January 1989. This document addressed several financial reporting topics where alternative treatments were allowed. Ultimately, ten revised standards were issued that eliminated many alternative practices. Where alternative procedures were retained, the "benchmark treatment" and an "allowed alternative" were identified. As expected, political pressures were exerted. For example, due to pressure primarily from the United States, the last-in, first-out (LIFO) method of inventory valuation was retained as an allowed alternative.

Given its lack of enforcement authority, the IASC made remarkable progress in achieving its objective of harmonizing worldwide accounting and financial reporting standards and promoting their acceptance. At the time of this writing, 41 International Accounting Standards[29] are in effect, and several hundred multinational companies specify that their financial statements conform to international GAAP. Also, several security exchanges (e.g., London, Frankfurt, and Paris) allow nondomestic companies to list by filing financial statements based on IAS, and some countries (e.g., France and Germany), while having their own set of national standards, allow even domestic companies to list using international GAAP.

A notable exception to this general acceptability is the SEC, which still requires all companies that list on a U.S. exchange to file either U.S. GAAP-based financial statements or to show in the footnotes a detailed reconciliation of reported earnings and stockholders' equity to what they would be if reported in accordance with U.S. GAAP. The SEC has been heavily criticized for its requirement, since many large non-U.S. multinational companies do not list on a U.S. exchange, and, thereby, U.S. investors may be deprived of favorable investment opportunities.[30] Despite these criticisms, the SEC has been rigid in its requirements based on the argument that its purpose is to protect the U.S. investor, and a way of doing this is to require comparable information.

In May 2000, the IASC gained a significant victory in its goal of obtaining worldwide acceptability of its standards when the **International Organization of Securities Commissions (IOSCO)** accepted them. IOSCO is an international body of representatives from securities regulating agencies (including the SEC) from more than 100 countries whose purpose is to improve the efficiency of securities markets on a domestic and international level. During the late 1990s, the IASC had campaigned heavily for the IOSCO's endorsement of its international accounting standards, which would significantly increase the credibility of these standards. Now, with the IOSCO's endorsement, that desired greater credibility has been achieved.

© GETTY IMAGES, INC./PHOTODISC

Although the SEC is a member of the IOSCO, the SEC's acceptance of international GAAP for cross-border listings does not automatically follow the IOSCO's endorsement. The SEC has made it abundantly clear that it will conduct a separate evaluation of IAS to determine whether the standards (1) form a comprehensive basis of financial reporting, (2) result in high-quality

---

[29]Unlike the FASB's method of assigning a new standard number to every adopted revision of a standard, the IASB retains the original number. At the time of this writing, the IASB has yet to issue an IFRS.

[30]Although U.S. investors could buy and sell securities on non-U.S. exchanges, it is generally much more expensive to do so.

information (i.e., comparable and providing full disclosure), and (3) will be rigorously interpreted and applied. Despite its supposed hard-line attitude, the SEC in April 1996 stated its support for the IASC's efforts as follows:

> The Commission supports the IASC's objective to develop, as expeditiously as possible, accounting standards that could be used for preparing financial statements used in cross-border offerings.

Furthermore, the SEC is susceptible to political pressure and is receiving such from the U.S. Congress. In October 1996, the Capital Markets Efficiency Act was passed, which essentially exhorts the SEC to do everything possible to support the establishing of international accounting and financial reporting standards and to report back to the Congress on its progress.

Many entities in the global economy are demanding a global financial language. They think accounting and financial reporting harmonization must be accomplished. Whether the IASB will be the body to establish global financial reporting standards is still unknown. Furthermore, whether it is possible to issue a set of international standards that will interface with the multitude of cultural factors and provide relevant information is also unknown. However, the IASB has gained a great amount of credibility, and it is the opinion of the authors that the pronouncements of the IASB will have an increasing influence on the worldwide development of accounting and financial reporting.

A Look to the Future

It has been 500 years since Pacioli wrote his book in which he described an accounting model that eventually became the foundation for accounting systems around the world. In that 500 years, the accounting system of capturing, recording, and summarizing economic events that impact an entity has changed very little. Pacioli would be quite comfortable using any of the accounting systems in the world—once he first learned how to use a computer. However, what amounts to a revolution in the concept of financial reporting has developed, with each country doing somewhat its "own thing." With the advent of the Information Age, financial reporting may be at its most dynamic point in history, with the possibility of more dramatic changes than were caused by the Industrial Revolution.

The following is a possible scenario of what may occur in the future. Rather than using journals and ledgers (which have been used since Pacioli), databases containing a plethora of financial data will be developed. Recording transactions will be done electronically and recorded directly into the database, rather than being done by the accountant leaving a paper trail. Recording transactions will still use the notions of debits and credits (i.e., double-entry accounting), but the debits and credits will be transparent (i.e., not seen or readily determinable). The Internet will make it possible for interested individuals to access a corporation's Web page and, from there, to access the corporation's financial database. There, individuals can request a particular report or even derive their own. Thus, information can be nearly instantaneous and customized, rather than being issued several months after year-end in a uniform package that might meet only limited needs for information. Some progressive companies are leading the charge to produce instantaneous information. Cisco Systems was the first company to generate hourly updates on revenues and other financial information. Upon its fiscal year-end, Cisco supposedly can close its books in one day, while it takes most companies up to two weeks. Also, users of financial information will not have to be content with just seeing numbers but will be able to use various graphical packages to enhance understanding of the numbers and to quickly analyze trends and relationships over time. Hypertext will be built into the databases, allowing users to probe into the background of the information that is appropriate to their analyses.

Existing technology makes all this available now. What is lacking is the desire of businesspeople and accountants to make it possible. Information is power, and to share information about a corporation threatens that power and could erode market position and ultimately profits.

Besides the impact of technology, there are other forces that are causing changes in accounting and financial reporting. Global communication and transportation systems are giving impetus to global business, with a resulting need for international accounting and financial reporting standards and the need for more relevant and timely information. The flow of capital among countries is expedited more quickly today than previously, and as evidenced by the Asian Crisis of 1998, the flow of capital across national boundaries has dramatic influence upon national economies, which then impacts the stability of the international economy. Capital flows are the result of the information available to decision makers, and the better the information available, the more stable are security markets and national economies.

Summary

Accounting is ancient. Information has always been needed, and that need will only increase. Hence, accounting will continue in some fashion to be a part of the world's cultures and civilization. In the United States, the professionalization of accounting was enhanced when CPAs received the franchise to audit the financial statements of publicly traded corporations. Undoubtedly, a significant factor in receiving that franchise was the higher quality of financial statements with which they were associated, as compared to those with which they were not associated. As long as accountants continue providing the highest quality information to interested users, their future is secure. However, the failure of financial reporting and accountants to evolve and meet the global need for information will cause them to go the way of the green-eye-shaded bookkeeper.

Markets, being the interaction of those demanding a product and those supplying it, are seemingly all-powerful. Information is a product, and the current demand for information is acute. Thus, there are unique opportunities for those capable of supplying the desired information. Because of their training and professional history, accountants have an edge in meeting the demands for information, but others also see opportunities and are positioning themselves to provide the desired relevant information in a timely manner. The current environmental changes are causing some accountants anxiety about their own future and that of their profession. Other accountants seem oblivious to the changes and the threats and opportunities available. For those young people with vision who seek opportunity in a respected and important profession, today is an exciting time to pursue a career in accounting. The opportunities for rewards and challenges seem limitless.

Questions

1. What are some reasons why students of accounting and financial reporting should know something about the history and development of accounting standards?

2. Some accountants argue that the development of accounting and financial reporting standards is linear. That is, as other countries achieve the degree of economic development that the United States has achieved, their accounting and financial reporting standards will mirror those of the United States. Therefore, these accountants argue that current accounting and financial reporting standards of other countries are inferior to those of the United States and that the SEC should resist any attempt to allow U.S.-based companies to issue their financial statements in conformity with the standards of the IASB (or other accounting standards bodies). Doing so, they conclude, would result in inferior financial reporting. Based on the information contained in this chapter, evaluate this assessment of the development of accounting and financial reporting standards.

3. List the principal influences of the last century or so that have resulted in broad acceptance of the financial reporting concept in the United States. Do these same influences exist in other cultures?

4. The basics of U.S. accounting were imported from Great Britain during the period of the founding of the original thirteen colonies through the late nineteenth century. Given that accounting was imported to the United States and that it happened relatively recently, is it to be expected that accounting, and particularly financial reporting, would be the same today in the two countries? Why or why not?

5. What was the first attempt to establish uniform financial reporting standards in the United States? Contrast this with the age of accounting.

6. What organization has statutory authority to issue accounting and financial reporting standards for all companies whose securities are traded on a U.S. exchange?

7. What is the fundamental purpose of the SEC?

8. Briefly explain what is meant by generally accepted accounting principles. Does this term apply only to those regulations that have been reduced to writing? Explain.

9. What was the first accounting group established under the auspices of the AICPA or its predecessor, the AIA, to promulgate accounting standards?

10. What accounting standard-setting organization preceded the FASB, and what were some of the reasons for its demise? Describe the primary differences between the FASB and its predecessors.

11. Describe the standard-setting process in the United States. Include in your answer the purpose of the "House of GAAP."

12. This chapter illustrates the dynamics of the standard-setting process in the United States, with many groups and individuals voicing their opinions of proposed standards. Is this voicing of opinions desirable? Is there a point where it becomes undesirable? How do you think the standard-setting process can be expedited but still allow interested individuals to give input?

13. Describe the process a proposed standard goes through before finally being issued as a FASB Statement of Financial Accounting Standard.

14. List the Rule 203 documents. What is the significance of Rule 203?

15. What are some of the key cultural differences between the United States and Japan that have resulted in different approaches to financial reporting between the two countries? In the future, will financial reporting in Japan and the United States become more similar, or will there continue to be differences? Why?

16. What factors have caused international accounting and financial reporting issues to become more complex in recent years?

17. According to the information in this chapter, why is accounting an outstanding career choice today? What other possible opportunities or cautions are ahead?

18. Define and briefly describe each of the following acronyms as they relate to accounting and financial reporting.
    a. SEC
    b. SFAS
    c. IASC
    d. IASB
    e. ARB
    f. FASB
    g. CAP
    h. FAF
    i. AAA
    j. IAS
    k. FASC
    l. IOSCO
    m. AICPA
    n. CPA

Discussion Questions

Note: The following questions do not have exact answers. They are meant to encourage awareness of international issues and factors affecting the future development of financial reporting.

1. The chapter emphasized that a country's financial reporting was a reflection of its culture. Social scientists broadly divide the world into seven or eight distinct cultures:
   a. Western, which principally comprises Western Europe, North America, and Australia
   b. Orthodox, comprising Russia as the core country and some Eastern European countries
   c. Sino, comprising China as the core country and Southeast Asia
   d. Japanese
   e. Hindu
   f. Moslem
   g. Latin, comprising Mexico and Central and South America
   h. African

   Select any two countries from the different cultures identified above, determine the key features of the cultures, and then predict what types of information would be provided in the published financial statements of businesses operating in those countries.

2. Recognizing that financial reporting is culturally influenced, discuss whether the attempt to establish a set of international accounting standards will be successful. Include in your answer the key cultural factors that you think will be a significant deterrent. Also, discuss whether such factors as increasing international business, communication, and the ability to easily transfer capital across national boundaries will overcome those cultural factors.

3. Do you consider it advisable for the SEC to allow companies that are registered on securities exchanges in the United States to issue financial statements that conform to the standards of the IASB but do not conform to the standards of the FASB and its predecessors? Why or why not?

4. What will be the success of a set of international accounting standards that most of the world perceives as being imposed upon them by a Western in-

fluenced standard-setting body? Is this an example of "Western cultural imperialism"?

5. Forecast what the result will be on securities markets and published financial statements if each country continues issuing its own financial reporting standards.

Research Activities

Activity 1–1: Using the World Wide Web (**http://www.iasc.org.uk/**), answer the following questions as they relate to the International Accounting Standards Board and its predecessor, the IASC.

a. What are the objectives of the IASB, as stated in its constitution?
b. Who were the founding countries of the IASC?
c. What are the country affiliations of the IASB members? Do you believe this representation will influence the content of the adopted standards? If so, do you believe this factor will affect the standards' acceptance in other countries?
d. What is the name of the body that provides authoritative guidance on the implementation and interpretation of IAS?
e. Provide a brief description of one project that is currently on the agenda of the IASB.
f. Based on the information provided on the IASB Web site, survey 10 countries and determine the extent of each country's acceptance of IAS. Summarize your findings in a table.

Activity 1–2: Another international accounting body that is striving to harmonize accounting and financial reporting is the International Federation of Accountants. Use the World Wide Web (**http://www.ifac.org/**) and write a two-page paper on the history and activities of the IFAC.

Activity 1–3: The U.S. economy has always been virtually inflation free, as compared to much of the rest of the world. This fact has had significant influence on the differences in the development of financial reporting around the world, particularly regarding the financial reporting of fixed assets. Identify a country where inflation has been a persistent problem in the past, and determine the country's policy for reporting fixed assets in financial statements.

Activity 1–4: Using the World Wide Web, access a foreign company's financial statements and determine the significant accounting policies of the foreign country, as identified in that company's financial statements.

2

Review

OF THE

Accounting Cycle AND
Financial Reporting

P arty City Corporation, an operator of retail party goods stores, experienced significant growth during 1998 and early 1999. Several new stores were opened, and sales grew at a double-digit rate. On April 18, 1999, the company announced a delay in its audit due to problems with its accounting system, which had not kept pace with the company's growth. Accordingly, the company could not take a physical inventory. On the day of the announcement, Party City's stock price dropped from $7.30 per share to $4.00 per share (a 45% loss in one day), which put Party City in default on some of its loan covenants. In addition, the inability to file an annual report with the SEC put the company in violation of its NASDAQ listing requirements, and trading in its stock was halted on May 6, 1999. The stock was delisted in July 1999.

Because of these inadequacies in the accounting system, shareholders filed suit against Party City. The poor quality of the accounting system also made it difficult for Party City to ob-

tain the necessary information to defend itself, and the company incurred significant losses. Ultimately, Party City was able to obtain alternative sources of financing and renegotiate the terms of some of its debt, but not without significant costs. Stores were closed, a member of the board of directors resigned, and substantial efforts were required to regain stockholder confidence.

Questions

1. A one-day 45% decline in equity value merely as a result of a delay in the company's audit appears excessive. What was the underlying reason for the market's decision to bid down the company's stock?

2. What financial statements were affected by Party City's inability to accurately determine the value of its inventory?

3. Could Party City Corporation have avoided its problems if it had had an effective accounting information system?

Learning Objectives

- Explain the necessity and purpose of an accounting information system.
- Explain the purpose of journals and ledgers and the posting process.
- Post journal entries and prepare a trial balance.
- Explain the purpose of and prepare necessary adjusting journal entries, as indicated from a trial balance.
- Construct the continuing operations section of an income statement, using either the single-step or the multiple-step format.
- Compute basic earnings per share.
- Construct a classified balance sheet.
- Describe some basic differences between U.S. financial reporting and other accepted international financial reporting alternatives.

In 1494, Pacioli wrote that accounting was "nothing else than the expressions in writing of the arrangement of [the business's] affairs, which the [business man] keeps in his mind." He also stated that "there are three things needed by anyone who wishes to carry on business carefully. The most important of these is cash or any equivalent. . . . The second thing necessary in business is to be a good bookkeeper and . . . the third and last thing is to arrange all the transactions in such a systematic way that one may understand each one of them at a glance."[1] The rules for a successful businessperson remain much the same today. In modern words, these rules are having cash, knowing enough about accounting to understand accounting reports, and having an accounting information system that captures and reports relevant and reliable information.

The Accounting Information System

Reporting relevant and reliable accounting information is the major objective of financial reporting in the United States. Providing such information is the purpose of a company's **accounting information system**, which comprises the set of procedures used to record, classify, and summarize accounting data, along with the necessary controls to prevent mistakes and guard against dishonesty. An accounting information system thus ensures that data are consistently captured and recorded, without either being lost or falsified, and that the resulting financial information is both relevant and reliable. Designing and using an effective accounting information system is not easy, and as was seen in the Party City Corporation example, the failure to do so can be quite devastating. When errors or irregularities are encountered in published financial reports, the source of them can frequently be traced to an inadequate accounting information system.

An accounting information system is a **transaction processing system**, meaning that data are entered into the system only when a transaction occurs. This concept is important to understanding what information an accounting information system can provide and what it cannot. For example, the current value of an

---

[1]John B. Geijsbeck, *Ancient Double-Entry Bookkeeping*, Houston, Texas: Scholars Book Club, 1974, p. 33.

entity's buildings, land, or equipment is not found in an accounting information system because no transaction occurred to capture that change in value. Rather, the accounting information system will provide historical cost data about the entity's land, buildings, etc., because that is the value that was determined when a transaction occurred. Many types of data are relevant to decision makers but are not included in an accounting information system because no transaction occurred in which the data could be captured.

Regardless of the nature, size, and needs of a business or whether the entity has a manual or an electronic accounting information system, the essential steps in processing transactions are always the same. First, data are entered into the system by being scanned in electronically, keyed in from a keyboard, or entered some other way, such as written manually. The system then classifies the data into accounts and summarizes the data in each account into a final total, which is called the account balance.

When an electronic system is used, the steps of classifying the data and determining an account balance happen simultaneously with the entering of the data into the system. However, when a manual accounting system is used, each of these steps is performed separately, with the source documents being sales receipts, invoices, time cards, etc. Two characteristics of manual systems are (1) the need for large amounts of personnel time and (2) time delays. Personnel time is required to enter data into the system, but this is not done until a sufficient quantity of data (i.e., a batch) has been accumulated, which causes a delay. Personnel time is also required to classify and summarize the data, but further time delays result because these functions are performed only at month-end. The need for large amounts of personnel time and the time delays inherent in manual systems increase the risk of errors entering the system, such as losing data or classifying them inappropriately.

Whether a manual or an electronic accounting information system is used, controls are established that ensure that all transactions are captured and that the data are accurately entered and classified. An important concept in implementing such controls is that *identical transactions are always handled in exactly the same way*. The presence of this control increases the reliability—and thus, the usefulness—of the resulting financial information. Also, auditors depend on this control being present, and one of their first audit objectives is to verify that identical transactions are recorded in exactly the same way. When their audit of the accounting information system verifies that this control is present and effective, then the presumption that the information generated is reliable is increased. When this control is not present, auditors must perform more testing of transactions to verify the reliability of the information generated, which increases both the time and cost of doing the audit. Obviously, electronic accounting systems, with their almost zero error rate, provide data that are much more reliable than the data provided by manual accounting systems. Finally, the concept that identical transactions should be recorded in the same way has implications for adjusting journal entries and explains why reversing entries are recommended.

Concepts in Recording Transactions

As mentioned earlier, only those events that are considered transactions are recorded in a company's accounting information system. A **transaction** is an external event that changes a business entity's assets, liabilities, owners' equity, or its revenues (and gains) and expenses (and losses). A transaction may be either reciprocal—where both parties receive something—or nonreciprocal—where only one party receives something. A sale is an example of a reciprocal transaction, as

OBSERVATION

Likely, the reason why audit problems were encountered on the audit of Party City Corporation's books is because the controls established to provide that identical transactions be recorded in the same way were not effective. Thus, the auditors had to spend more time auditing more transactions, and this caused the delay in completing the audit. It may be that all of Party City Corporation's problems began because an effective accounting control system had not been implemented or had been overridden by management.

the business obtains cash or a claim to cash and the buyer obtains goods or services. A dividend is an example of a nonreciprocal transaction, as the business distributes cash but receives nothing in return.[2]

Accounts, Ledgers, and Journals

When a transaction occurs, information is captured and classified into an **account**, such as Cash, Land, Building, and Sales, using an object code, such as 100 for Cash, 140 for Land, 400 for Sales, etc. The number of accounts and the names assigned to them are the foundation of the accounting information system. Just as the foundation of a building determines its size and shape, so too do the number of accounts and their names (referred to as the **chart of accounts**) determine the quality of the information generated. For example, having just one revenue account and one expense account is theoretically possible. However, the information generated would not be very useful. So a scheme of revenue and expense accounts is designed that hopefully classifies revenues and expenses into meaningful accounts, without having either too many (which would be cumbersome) or too few (which results in a loss of data). For example, failing to have an "advertising expense" account means that all advertising expenditures would be put in some other account (perhaps "Miscellaneous Expense"), and subsequently, the business would have difficulty determining the amount of expenditures incurred for advertising. This illustrates the importance of having an adequate number of appropriately titled accounts.

When it is important for a business to know information by department, program, activity or some other classification, the coding system (e.g., 100 for Cash) is expanded to facilitate such classification. Then, part of the code refers to the object (e.g., cash or advertising), part refers to the organizational component (e.g., department or location), and other parts of the code to other desired classifications, such as program or activity. This extensive classification is handled easily by an electronic information system, but it becomes very cumbersome under a manual accounting system.

When using a manual accounting system, information about a transaction is first recorded in a **journal**, which is also known as the "book of original entry." Each company usually uses a general journal and several special journals (which are time-saving devices), as appropriate for its needs. Seldom encountered transactions and end-of-period adjustments are recorded in the **general journal**. Frequent transactions (e.g., credit sales, the receipt of cash, and disbursing cash) are entered into **special journals** that are named for the respective repetitive transaction. Thus, the sales journal is used to record credit sales (but not cash sales), the cash receipts journal is used to record the receipt of cash from any source, the purchases journal is used to record the purchase of inventory on account, etc. Which particular specialized journals a company uses is determined by the nature of its transactions.

When an electronic accounting system is used, information about a transaction is recorded directly into the general ledger and (where appropriate) a subsidiary ledger. Under a manual accounting system, information contained in the various journals is transferred periodically to the general and subsidiary ledgers. The **general ledger** consists of all the company's accounts (e.g., Cash and Inventory), showing their respective balances and the transaction amounts that gave

---

[2]Other examples of nonreciprocal transactions are withdrawals of assets by owners and investments by owners.

rise to those balances. **Subsidiary ledgers** are used to show the detail for specific accounts in the general ledger. For example, knowing the amounts owed by individual customers is important and is provided in the accounts receivable subsidiary ledger. The total of the individual customer accounts in the accounts receivable subsidiary ledger equals the balance in the accounts receivable general ledger account, which is called the control account. Most companies also have subsidiary ledgers for such accounts as Accounts Payable, Inventory, Equipment, and Common Stock.

Thus, the chart of accounts is the foundation of the accounting information system, and the various journals and ledgers comprise the building blocks upon which the information system is built. The more care spent in designing these elements—and the corresponding controls that make sure all transactions are captured and consistently recorded—the more relevant and reliable the resulting accounting information is.

The Accounting Equation

When capturing data, whether manually or electronically, all accounting transactions are recorded using a **double-entry system**. That is, every accounting transaction affects and is classified into *at least two* accounts.[3] Also, account balances can only be increased or decreased, either by **debiting** the account (which refers to putting the amount on the left side of the account), or **crediting** the account (which refers to putting the amount on the right side of the account). Not only does every transaction affect at least two accounts, but the accounts are also affected in such a manner that *the debit entry amounts always equal the credit entry amounts*. The rules of debiting and crediting accounts are shown in Figure 2-1. The "books" are in balance when the total of all the debit entries in the general ledger equals the total of all the credit entries. This relationship is known as the **accounting equation** (Equation 2.1), and it is the relationship upon which the balance sheet is based.

$$\text{Assets} = \text{Liabilities} + \text{Owners' Equity} \qquad (2.1)$$

FIGURE 2-1

Rules for Debiting and Crediting Accounts

Assets, Owners' Withdrawls, Expenses and Losses		Liabilities, Owners' Contributions, Revenues and Gains	
Debit for increases	Credit for decreases	Debit for decreases	Credit for increases

Some criticize the learning of debiting and crediting accounts as being cumbersome and claim that automated accounting information systems make learning the rules unnecessary. True, accountants do not usually record transactions, but all accountants (and some nonaccountants) need to be adept at using debits

---

[3]In many electronic accounting information systems, this double-entry is not always obvious, but it is always present.

and credits as they are powerful analytical tools in both understanding and analyzing transactions and financial statements (as will be illustrated throughout the text). Essentially, the intricacies of debit and credit constitute an elegant way of thinking that is similar to understanding the language of the country where one lives. Accounting is the language of business and the more adept individuals are in using that language, the better they will understand the business information provided by the accounting information system.

T-Accounts and Normal Balances

T-accounts are representations or models of a general ledger account. T-accounts are excellent models to illustrate how general ledger accounts work, as debits can be put on the left side of the "T," credits on the right side, and the balance (or net amount) of the account at the bottom, on the left or right side as appropriate. For example, suppose that a business has a beginning cash balance of $1,000 and has activities during the month that increase Cash by $500 and $400 and decrease Cash by $800 and $200. Those data, and the ending balance in the cash account, are represented in a T-account as shown in Figure 2-2.

FIGURE 2-2

The Workings of a T-Account

Cash

Beginning Balance	1,000	
	500	800
	400	200
Ending Balance	900	

The **normal balance** of an account (i.e., whether it is expected that an account balance is a debit balance or a credit balance) is determined by the way that the account balance is increased. Thus, Figure 2-1 shows that a debit balance is the normal balance for asset accounts, expense (and loss) accounts, and owners' drawings accounts; and a credit balance is the normal balance for liability accounts, revenue (and gain) accounts, and owners' contributions accounts. An abnormal balance should always be investigated, as it might be an error. For example, a credit balance in the cash account is possible due to the business overdrawing its bank balance, or it may be due to an error. However, a credit balance in an equipment account is not possible and could arise only because an error occurred. To explain, when equipment is purchased, the equipment account is debited. When equipment is sold, the equipment account is credited *for its original cost*. Thus, having more credits than debits in the equipment account is impossible, and a credit balance indicates that an error was made.

The Accounting Cycle

Data must be recorded and processed in order to produce information. This is done in what is referred to as the **accounting cycle**, which consists of all the necessary procedures to process this year's transactions, prepare the financial statements, and get ready to process the next year's transactions. The steps in the accounting cycle, which are illustrated in Figure 2-3, consist of journalizing transactions (for manual systems only), posting to the ledger, preparing a trial balance, adjusting the trial balance, preparing the financial statements, closing entries (at year-end only), and—at the beginning of the next year—preparing reversing entries.[4]

FIGURE 2-3

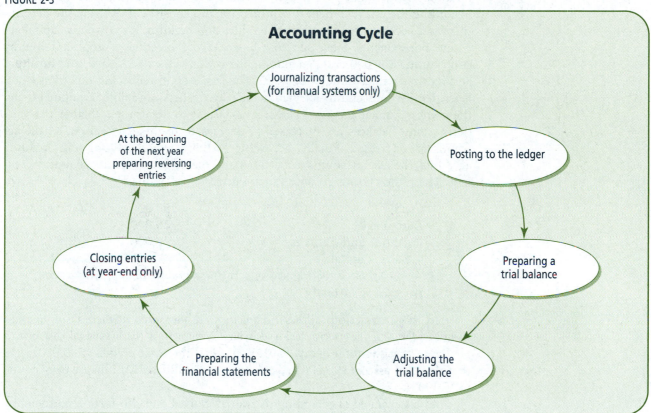

Accounting Cycle

Journalizing transactions (for manual systems only)

Posting to the ledger

Preparing a trial balance

Adjusting the trial balance

Preparing the financial statements

Closing entries (at year-end only)

At the beginning of the next year preparing reversing entries

Journalizing Transactions

Journalizing transactions is the beginning of the accounting cycle. The thought process in journalizing any transaction (or in designing an automated accounting system) consists of the steps as shown in Exhibit 2-1.

EXHIBIT 2-1

Procedures for Journalizing a Transaction

1. Identify the accounts affected by a transaction.

2. Determine whether the balances of those accounts are increased or decreased.

3. Determine whether those accounts are debited or credited, which is done by referring to the rules in Figure 2-1 for debiting and crediting accounts.

---

[4]Reversing entries is an optional step that is discussed in Appendix E at the end of this chapter.

The following paragraphs provide the general rules and some examples of preparing journal entries for establishing a business, acquiring assets, earning revenues and incurring expenses, and finally, making distributions to owners. These rules and examples will be expanded upon in subsequent chapters.

Establishing a Business

The form of the business organization (i.e., proprietorship, partnership, or corporation) only slightly affects the accounting when establishing a business. Recording the establishment of a proprietorship consists of debiting the descriptive asset accounts for their current values and crediting the owner's capital account. For example, Steve started a business, organized as a proprietorship, by contributing $50,000 cash, an automobile with a value of $20,000, and furniture and fixtures with a value of $25,000. The first step in recording this transaction is to identify the accounts affected, which are Cash, Automobile, Equipment, and the owners' capital account. The second step is to determine whether the various account balances are increased or decreased. In this transaction, all the accounts are increased. Finally, according to the rules of debiting and crediting accounts, the asset accounts are debited and the owners' capital account is credited. The transaction is recorded in a journal entry as follows:

Cash	50,000	
Automobile	20,000	
Furniture and Fixtures	25,000	
Steve, Capital		95,000

To record the establishment of a business proprietorship, with assets recorded at current value.

In this transaction, *all asset amounts were measured at their respective fair values at the time they were acquired, which is known as the historical cost principle.* Note that the total debits ($95,000) equal the total credits ($95,000), and that the total assets ($95,000) equal the total liabilities ($0) plus owners' equity ($95,000).

As an example of recording the initial journal entry to form a partnership, assume that Steve formed a partnership with Becky. Steve contributed the cash, as in the previous example, and Becky contributed the automobile and equipment. The only change in the previous journal entry is to *recognize the value of each partner's contribution in a separate capital account.* Thus, the journal entry is as follows:

Cash	50,000	
Automobile	20,000	
Furniture and Fixtures	25,000	
Steve, Capital		50,000
Becky, Capital		45,000

To record the establishment of a business partnership with assets recorded at current value.

Suppose instead that the state authorized Steve and Becky to form a corporation and authorized the corporation to issue one million shares of common stock with a par value of $5 per share. Steve and Becky decided that the assets they individually contributed entitled them to receive 7,500 and 7,000 shares of stock, respectively. The journal entry to record the establishing of the corporation is as follows:

Cash	50,000	
Automobile	20,000	
Furniture and Fixtures	25,000	
Common Stock		72,500[1]
Paid-In Capital in Excess of Par		22,500[2]

To record the establishment of a corporation with assets recorded at current value.

[1]14,500 shares of stock issued × $5 par value/share.

[2]The difference between the total value of the assets contributed and the par value amount of the stock.

The *stock account is credited only for the par value of the number of shares issued*, not for the total price received. When stock is assigned a par value, that value is established in the corporation charter and is printed on each stock certificate. Par value does not represent the fair value of anything. It is an arbitrary amount intended to be the corporation's **legal capital**,[5] which is the minimum amount of capital that the corporation must retain for the protection of creditors. Stockholders are not personally liable for the corporation's debts. To be able to identify a corporation's legal capital, the *par value is credited to the descriptive stock account, with any premium paid credited to the paid-in capital in excess of par account.* When stock has no par value, it may be given a stated value by the board of directors. The accounting for stated value stock is exactly the same as for par value stock. The stated value is the corporation's legal capital and is credited to the stock account, with any excess credited to paid-in capital in excess of stated value. When no-par stock is not assigned a stated value, the entire amount at which the stock is issued is recorded in the stock account and becomes the corporation's legal capital. In most states, it is illegal to issue stock at less than par value.[6]

The accounting for acquiring assets, recognizing revenue and expenses, and incurring liabilities is not affected by the way the business is organized. Whether the business is organized as a corporation, a partnership, or a proprietorship, the journal entries are the same.

EXTENDING THE CONCEPT

Herman Potter was the sole proprietor of a merchandise store that purchased and resold used sporting goods equipment. Sally Davis owned a store next door that purchased and sold outdoor clothing. Herman and Sally decide to join together and form a corporation.

At what values would the assets be recorded in the new general ledger when the two companies merged? Would the assets be recorded at the amounts on the general ledgers of the respective proprietorships, or would the assets be recorded at their current fair values?

Answer: All assets would be recorded at their current fair value amounts in accordance with the historical cost principle.

EXTENDING THE CONCEPT

Suppose that instead of paying cash and signing a mortgage note, Steve and Becky had acquired the land and building by issuing 6,000 shares of $5 par value common stock. For what amount is the common stock account credited?

Answer: The common stock account is credited for $30,000.

Acquiring Assets

Recording the acquisition of assets consists of debiting a descriptive asset account and crediting either the asset(s) given up, the liability incurred, or when stock is exchanged, a stock account and a paid-in capital in excess of par account. As an example, suppose that Steve and Becky purchased a building in which to conduct business. The building cost $200,000, of which $40,000 was deemed to be the fair value of the land on which the building was located. The transaction was financed by paying $25,000 cash

---

[5]State laws requiring legal capital are part of the "blue-sky" laws passed a century ago.

[6]Despite laws prohibiting issuing stock at a discount, it effectively happens when promoters and others receive stock in exchange for overvalued noncash assets or services.

and obtaining a mortgage for the remaining amount. Accordingly, the following journal entry is prepared:

Building	160,000	
Land	40,000	
Cash		25,000
Mortgage Payable		175,000

To acquire land by paying cash and signing a mortgage.

Recording Revenues and Expenses

For a retail or wholesale business, revenue is recorded in the accounts when sales are made. A sale has occurred either when the goods are delivered or when the goods are shipped by a common carrier with shipping terms of FOB[7] shipping point. FOB refers to who pays the freight charges and also indicates when title to the goods passes from the buyer to the seller. FOB shipping point means that the buyer pays the freight and obtains title when the common carrier receives the merchandise. FOB destination means that the seller pays the freight, and the goods remain his property until the buyer receives them. For a service entity, revenue is earned when the service is rendered. For either sales or services, revenue is recorded by crediting appropriately descriptive accounts.

© GETTY IMAGES, INC./PHOTODISC

Expenses that are clearly associated with the earning of revenues are measured when the revenues are earned and are recorded by debiting appropriately descriptive accounts. For example, assume that during the year, Steve and Becky purchased inventory on account in the amount of $60,000, which is recorded as follows:

| Inventory[8] | 60,000 | |
| Accounts Payable | | 60,000 |

To purchase inventory on account.

Sales during the year amounted to $95,000, of which $80,000 was on account and the rest cash. The cost of the merchandise that was sold was $42,000. The revenue and the associated cost of the inventory sold are recognized as follows:

Cash	15,000	
Accounts Receivable	80,000	
Sales		95,000

To recognize revenue from sale of inventory.

---

[7]FOB stands for "free on board."
[8]This is a typical journal entry in a perpetual inventory system, which is used in computerized accounting. When a periodic inventory system is used, a purchases account is debited instead of Inventory.

Cost of Goods Sold	42,000	
Inventory		42,000

To recognize the cost of inventory sold.

Recognizing the cost of goods sold as an expense when inventory is sold is an example of matching a product cost with the associated revenue. Other expenses—known as period costs—are not easily matched with revenue, and so they are recognized in the year they are incurred. Two examples of such expenses are rent expense and salary expense. Suppose that Steve and Becky incurred wages expense of $18,000 and other expenses of $7,000, all of which were paid in cash. The journal entry to record these expenses is as follows:

Wages Expense	18,000	
Other Expense	7,000	
Cash		25,000

To recognize the payment of various expenses.

Distributions to Owners

Accounting for distributions to owners depends on how the business is organized. When the business is organized as a proprietorship or a partnership, distributions to owners involves a "drawing" account. Using the example where Steve organized a business as a proprietorship, owners' withdrawals are recorded as follows:

Steve, Drawing	1,000	
Cash		1,000

To record withdrawal of cash by the owner in a business proprietorship.

Distributions to stockholders of a corporation are called **dividends** and are accounted in a slightly different manner. When cash dividends are distributed to stockholders, the following entry is prepared:

Dividends (or Retained Earnings)	1,000	
Cash		1,000

To record distribution of cash dividend to owners of a corporation.

Retained earnings is not cash, nor is it any other asset. The retained earnings account represents earnings accumulated by the corporation and reinvested into more assets rather than being distributed to the stockholders. Retaining earnings rather than distributing them as dividends is one way a corporation funds its growth. Thus, a company's retained earnings are seen in its assets. Like the drawing account(s) for a proprietorship or a partnership, the retained earnings account is a capital (or stockholders' equity) account.

EXTENDING THE CONCEPT

How would the distribution entry be recorded if Steve and Becky's business were organized as a partnership, and each of them withdrew $1,000 cash?

Answer:	Steve, Drawing	1,000	
	Becky, Drawing	1,000	
	Cash		2,000

Posting to the General Ledger

After transactions are journalized, the next step in the accounting cycle is to copy the dollar amounts of each transaction into the general ledger accounts. This process is referred to as **posting**. While posting, a reference or folio is attached in both the journal and the ledger, so that at a later time, amounts can be easily traced from the journal to the ledger or from the ledger to the journal. Also, these folios are used to verify account balances, to satisfy customers or clients as to the accuracy of their monthly bills, and for various internal management purposes.

Posting manually is a mundane, tedious task, but automated accounting systems have largely done away with the need to manually post amounts.

Preparing a Trial Balance

Preparing financial statements begins with a **trial balance**, which is a list of all the general ledger accounts and their respective balances at that time. Customarily, the asset accounts are listed first, followed by the liability, stockholders' equity, and revenue and expense accounts. The function of a trial balance is to verify that the total of debits in the general ledger equals the total of credits or that the "books balance." An example of a trial balance is presented in Exhibit 2-2, which is based upon the Steve and Becky data, assuming the corporate form of organization. (Not all entries to derive the trial balance are shown, but many of the amounts in the trial balance can be traced back to the previously recorded journal entries.)

Although the trial balance in Exhibit 2-2 does balance, it may not be free from error. Numerous errors could occur in the accounting system, and the books would still balance. Some of these errors include not journalizing a transaction, journalizing a transaction incorrectly or journalizing it twice, not posting a journal entry, posting a journal entry twice or posting an amount to the wrong account, and posting incorrect amounts. Thus, instituting controls in the accounting information system to guard against inadvertent errors is a necessity. The more effectively the accounting information system controls transactions, the better the resulting information will be. Fortunately, most errors are avoided when automated accounting systems are used, since transactions are recorded exactly the same way—every time.

EXHIBIT 2-2

Sample Unadjusted Trial Balance
Steve and Becky Corporation
Unadjusted Trial Balance
December 31, 2004

Cash	$ 22,000	
Accounts Receivable	20,000	
Inventory	18,000	
Prepaid Insurance	6,000	
Furniture and Fixtures	25,000	
Automobile	20,000	
Building	160,000	
Land	40,000	
Accounts Payable		$ 8,000
Mortgage Payable		175,000
Common Stock		72,500
Paid-In Capital in Excess of Par		22,500
Sales		95,000
Rent Revenue		6,000
Cost of Goods Sold	42,000	
Wage Expense	18,000	
Other Expense	7,000	
Dividends	1,000	
Totals	$379,000	$379,000

Adjusting the Trial Balance (Adjusting Entries)

Errors are not the typical cause of account balances being incorrect when the trial balance is prepared. Rather, the passage of time is a much more frequent cause of incorrect account balances. To explain, transactions typically occur at definite points in time and are recorded at that time, but some events that impact the financial statements occur continuously, such as the incurring of interest or the depreciating of an asset. Because continuously recording these events is impractical, the account balance is incorrect when the trial balance is prepared. The principal purpose of **adjusting journal entries** is to update—or adjust—account balances for unrecorded transactions.[9]

After preparing the trial balance, each account balance is reviewed to determine if its balance is correct and up-to-date or if an adjustment is necessary. When an account balance needs to be adjusted, the approach to preparing the adjusting journal entry is as shown in Exhibit 2-3.

EXHIBIT 2-3

Procedures for Preparing Adjusting Journal Entries

1. Determine what the current account balance *is*, which is the amount found on the trial balance or in the ledger.

2. Determine what the current account balance *should be*.

3. The adjusting journal entry amount is always the difference between the amount determined in Step 1 and the amount determined in Step 2.

Every adjusting entry affects a balance sheet account and an income statement account. Thus, every adjusting entry allocates an amount between the income statement and the balance sheet. The following discussion illustrates the basics of preparing adjusting entries, using the information in Exhibit 2-2.

Adjusting Entries for Prepayments

Prepayments is the term used to describe asset accounts where payments are made for goods or services that provide benefits for more than one month, and it is not appropriate to expense the entire amount in the period in which payment was made. Typical examples of prepayments include prepaid rent, prepaid insurance, office supplies, and prepayments for other goods and services. Since payments for these goods and services typically provide benefits for several months or even years, the amount paid is usually recorded in an asset account. Then, at year-end, all of these prepaid accounts—and the associated expense accounts—are analyzed to determine if the balances are correct. When they are not correct, an adjusting entry is made, which adjusts the balances of the asset and related expense accounts. Note that *all prepaid assets eventually become expenses.*

Prepayments made by an entity are asset accounts. But the company may also be the recipient of prepayments, in which case they are liabilities. Examples of typical prepayments received include amounts for rent (i.e., unearned rent revenue), insurance, magazine subscriptions, etc.; all such prepayments are

---

[9]Journal entries to correct errors are not adjusting entries; they are correcting entries.

recorded in an appropriately titled unearned revenue account. At year-end, these prepayment liability accounts are also analyzed—along with their associated revenue accounts—to determine if adjusting entries are needed. When adjusting entries are prepared, the entry affects the liability and related revenue accounts. Note that *all prepayments that are initially recorded as liabilities eventually become revenues, which occurs when the amounts are earned.*

On November 1, Steve and Becky issued a check in the amount of $6,000 for insurance. At a monthly amount of $2,000, the check pays the insurance for November through January. Remember that one control over recording transactions is that they are recorded the same way all the time. On November 1, the accountant chose (or the automated accounting system was programmed) to record the payment in an asset account, and the following journal entry was prepared:

Original entry:
| Prepaid Insurance | 6,000 | |
| Cash | | 6,000 |

To record the prepayment of three months of insurance.

By preparing the journal entry in this way, the prepaid insurance account has a balance of $6,000 on December 31, as can be seen in Exhibit 2-2. However, due to the passage of time, that account balance is not correct at December 31 because some of the insurance has expired, and that portion should be recorded as an expense. Using the steps outlined in Exhibit 2-3 for preparing an adjusting journal entry, the following is determined:

1. The current balance in Prepaid Insurance is $6,000, as per the trial balance.
2. The balance in Prepaid Insurance should be $2,000, which represents the insurance for January (1 month $\times$ $2,000 a month).
3. Therefore, the prepaid insurance account needs to be reduced by $4,000. This $4,000 also needs to be recorded as Insurance Expense, which represents the expired portion of the insurance for November and December. So the adjusting entry is as follows:

Adjusting entry:
| (a)[10] Insurance Expense | 4,000 | |
| Prepaid Insurance | | 4,000 |

The adjusting entry at December 31 to apportion the insurance payment amount between the asset and expense portions.

Posting both the original entry for the $6,000 payment and this adjusting entry results in the following balances:

Prepaid Insurance				Insurance Expense		
Nov. 1	6,000	4,000	Dec. 31	Dec. 31	4,000	
Balance	2,000			Balance	4,000	

The prepaid insurance account balance of $2,000 represents the future benefits of being covered by insurance for January, and the insurance expense account balance of $4,000 represents the previous coverage of insurance for November and December.

---

[10]This identification letter (and those to other adjusting entries) ties to the adjusting entries found in the worksheet in Appendix B at the end of this chapter.

To understand adjusting journal entries, realize that *how an adjusting journal entry is prepared depends upon how the original journal entry was prepared.* To illustrate, in the previous example the initial journal entry to record the insurance payment was debited to the prepaid insurance account. Suppose that, instead, the accountant chose (or the accounting system had been programmed) to record the payment by debiting Insurance Expense, which is also an acceptable way to record the payment. Then, the steps in preparing the adjusting journal entry would be as follows:

1. The current balance in the insurance expense account would be $6,000, and the balance in the prepaid insurance account would be zero.
2. The balance in Insurance Expense should be $4,000, and the balance in Prepaid Insurance should be $2,000.
3. Therefore, the adjusting journal entry reducing the insurance expense account by $2,000 and increasing the prepaid insurance account by $2,000 is as follows:

Adjusting entry:

Prepaid Insurance	2,000	
Insurance Expense		2,000

The adjusting entry at December 31 to apportion the insurance payment amount between the asset and expense portions.

EXTENDING THE CONCEPT

Suppose that on December 1, Steve and Becky rented a portion of the building to another company for four months and received a $4,000 payment in advance. Prepare the adjusting entry, assuming the payment received was recorded as (1) Rent Revenue, and (2) Unearned Rent Revenue.

Partial answers: The adjusting entries are:
(1) Debit Rent Revenue for $3,000.
(2) Credit Rent Revenue for $1,000.

Preparing the initial and adjusting entries in this manner results in ending account balances of $2,000 in the prepaid insurance account and $4,000 in the insurance expense account, which are exactly the same ending balances that were arrived at when the initial payment was recorded to Prepaid Insurance. Hence, it is not significant whether the initial payment was recorded as Prepaid Insurance or Insurance Expense, because no matter how the initial payment is recorded, the subsequent adjusting entry will make the ending balances correct as of the end of the year. The adjusting entry for insurance is an example of how all prepayments are adjusted at year-end so that the financial information communicated to readers is as accurate as possible.

Adjusting Entries for Long-Term Deferrals

In addition to adjusting prepayment accounts, companies also adjust the long-term deferral accounts at year-end. **Deferral** means to postpone recognizing the amount on the income statement.[11] Examples of long-term deferral accounts include Automobiles, Furniture and Fixtures, Buildings, and all long-term intangible assets, such as Patents and Copyrights. (Land is not a long-term deferral account because its usefulness never wears out, and so the cost of land is never reported on the income statement; it remains on the balance sheet.) Because these assets provide benefits for several years, the amounts to acquire them are initially recorded in asset accounts (i.e., deferred), and then each year a portion of the cost is recognized as an expense through an adjusting entry. This allocating of cost and reporting the amount on the income statement is called **depreciation**[12]

---

[11]All prepayments, whether received or paid, are deferrals because initially the amounts paid/received are recorded on the balance sheet and later reported on the income statement.

[12]In accounting, depreciation never refers to a decline in the value of an asset. It is always the allocating of cost. So, depreciation is applicable to assets that increase in value.

when referring to tangible assets or **amortization** when referring to intangible assets.

Earlier in the chapter, Steve and Becky contributed $25,000 of furniture and fixtures and a $20,000 automobile to a newly formed business. Suppose they expect the furniture and fixtures to have a useful life of 10 years and the automobile to have a useful life of five years. Then, the depreciation amount for the year on the furniture and fixtures is computed by dividing the $25,000 cost by its useful life of 10 years, which results in a depreciation amount of $2,500 per year. (This is called the straight-line method of depreciation, which is the most used method of depreciation.) The journal entry to record the depreciation is as follows:

(b) Depreciation Expense	2,500	
Accumulated Depreciation—Furniture and		
Fixtures		2,500

To record depreciation expense on furniture and fixtures and the related accumulated depreciation for the year.

EXTENDING THE CONCEPT

What is the depreciation expense amount for the year on the automobile?

Answer: $4,000 [also part of entry (b) in Appendix B].

Previously, Steve and Becky acquired a building at a cost of $160,000. Assuming that the building was acquired on April 1 and that it has a useful life of 40 years, the depreciation amount for the current year is $3,000. This amount is determined by first computing the amount of depreciation expense for an entire year, which is $4,000, and then multiplying that amount by the fraction of the year from the time the building was acquired to the end of the year, which is nine months, as follows:

Depreciation expense = (cost/life) × fraction of year
Depreciation expense = ($160,000 / 40 years) × 9/12 = $3,000[13]

The next year, the depreciation on the building will be $4,000, which represents depreciation for a full year.

Typically, the various accumulated depreciation accounts are separated by type of asset in the general ledger, but on the balance sheet they are combined and reported as one sum. Depreciation is credited to an accumulated depreciation account rather than to the asset account because the separate account gives the financial statement reader an idea as to the age and future usefulness of the assets and when cash may be needed to replace existing assets. The accumulated depreciation accounts, even though they have credit balances, are not liability or revenue accounts. Rather, accumulated depreciation is a **contra-asset account**, meaning that although the account has a credit balance, it is reported with the assets. The balance has no meaning by itself, only as it relates to the related asset account. Thus, the balance in an accumulated depreciation account provides no information unless the balance of the related asset account is also known. When reporting depreciation expense on the financial statements, there is usually little reason for the financial statement reader to know the amount of depreciation expense by type of asset, and so separate depreciation expense accounts by type of asset are not maintained. When it is important to know the amount of depreciation expense by asset type, then as many depreciation expense accounts as necessary can be used.

Allocating the cost of intangible assets is the same process as depreciation. Thus, the cost of the asset is allocated over the number of years of the

---

[13]Also part of entry (b) in Appendix B.

asset's useful life. The journal entry to record amortization debits Amortization Expense and credits the asset account, not an "accumulated amortization account."

Adjusting Entries for Accruals

Another category of adjusting journal entries is recording revenues earned or expenses incurred that are not yet entered in the accounting system. Such adjusting journal entries—called **accruals**—are typically needed to record interest revenue, interest expense, salaries expense, bad debt expense, etc.

When Steve and Becky acquired the building, they signed a mortgage note and borrowed $175,000. Immediately upon signing the note, interest begins accruing, but preparing entries daily to record the interest owed is not practical. So, at December 31, as seen in Exhibit 2-2, no interest expense or interest payable has been recorded. Yet, $7,875 of interest is owed (computed as $175,000 × 6% × 9/12 of a year) since the mortgage was signed on April 1. At December 31, the adjusting entry to record this interest is as follows:

Adjusting entry:
(c) Interest Expense   7,875
        Interest Payable   7,875
        To record the nine months of interest expense on a 6% note payable.

Steve and Becky pay their employees every Friday for the preceding five-day week, and a typical weekly payroll amount is $1,000. This year, December 31 is a Wednesday. Therefore, the wage expense and related liability for Monday through Wednesday (December 29 through December 31) must be recorded because the wage expense for those days is not on Steve and Becky's trial balance. The adjusting entry to record the wages for these three days is as follows:

Adjusting entry:
(d) Wages Expense   600
        Wages Payable   600
        To record wage expense for December 29 through December 31, which is computed as 3/5 × $1,000.

Recording bad debt expense is another example of a common accrual. When companies make sales where the customer promises to pay later, the companies know that some of the amounts owed eventually will be uncollectible. These are the companies' bad debt expenses. However, the concept in accounting for them is to record such expenses in the year that the sales are made and not when the company actually determines that a particular account will be uncollectible. Accounting for such expenses in this way—recording expenses in the same year in which the resulting revenue is also recorded—produces a better measure of net income, but accounting for these expenses in this way also requires the company to estimate its bad debt expenses.

To illustrate, Steve and Becky had recorded credit sales of $80,000 during the year. They have collected much of this amount by December 31, but they realize that some customers may not be able to pay, and at year-end—based upon industry experience—they estimate that 1% of the credit sales amount, or $800, will be uncollectible. The journal entry to record this bad debt expense is as follows:

Adjusting entry:
(e) Bad Debt Expense   800
        Allowance for Doubtful Accounts   800
        To record bad debt expense for the year.

Like accumulated depreciation, Allowance for Doubtful Accounts is a contra-account, meaning that although it has a credit balance, it is reported with the assets, and the only significance of the balance is how it relates to some asset account. The asset account to which Allowance for Doubtful Accounts relates is Accounts Receivable.

Assume that Steve and Becky also determine that a customer who owes them $150 will be unable to pay the amount owed, due to financial difficulty, and they decide to write off the amount. The journal entry to do so is as follows:

(f) Allowance for Doubtful Accounts   150
        Accounts Receivable   150
        To write off the account of Customer X who is unable to pay the amount owed.

Since a company's bad debt expense is an estimate, the estimate may be wrong. When the allowance account is growing slower than the receivable account, it indicates that the estimate may be too low. This is perhaps due to a downturn in the economy, a too lenient credit policy, or some other cause. When the allowance account is growing faster than the receivable balance, this indicates that the estimate is too high. In either case, *the solution is to modify the estimate of the bad debt expense for the current and future years* and not to redo prior years' estimates or financial statements. Changing the estimated rate of bad debts is an example of what is referred to as a "change in an accounting estimate," and all such changes are accounted by using the new estimate in the current and future years.

Adjusting Entries to Change to Accrual Accounting

Another common example of an accrual-type adjusting entry is switching a company's books from the cash basis of accounting to the accrual basis of accounting. Under cash accounting, transactions are not recorded until cash is paid or received. Under **accrual accounting**, transactions are recorded as they are incurred, regardless of their effect on cash. Issuing financial statements on the cash basis of accounting is not in accord with generally accepted accounting principles. However, many companies find it easier to keep their books during the year on the cash basis and then adjust them to the accrual basis at the end of the year. Primarily, this adjustment process consists of (1) putting receivables and payables on the books with their related revenues and expenses and (2) adjusting the inventory balance (when a periodic inventory system is used) to the correct end-of-year balance.

Deviating from the Steve and Becky example, suppose that during the year, Lodestone Co. records sales revenue when cash is received. At year-end, the necessary adjusting entry to update the receivable account and to correctly report sales for the year is prepared. Various customers owed Lodestone $8,000 at the beginning of the year, and an analysis of the individual customers' accounts shows that at the end of the year, the total amount owed is $9,500. Thus, the necessary adjusting entry to update accounts receivable and correctly report sales for the year is as follows:

Adjusting entry:
    Accounts Receivable   1,500
        Sales   1,500
    To adjust the books to the accrual basis at year-end.

When accounts payable (and all other current liabilities) are kept on a cash basis during the year, a similar adjustment is required at the end of the year. That is, the balance in accounts payable is actually the beginning-of-the-year balance, and so an adjusting entry is necessary to update the balance to what it should be at the end of the year. The offsetting accounts are to various expense accounts, depending upon the invoices or bills received.

Finally, depending on the inventory system used, retail companies (as compared to service entities) may need to prepare an additional adjusting entry. If a company utilizes a **perpetual inventory system**, purchases and sales are recorded directly in the inventory account, and thus *no adjusting journal entry is necessary* at the end of the year to correctly report the inventory account balance. However, when a **periodic inventory system** is used, the inventory account is not updated during the year for purchases and sales of inventory. Rather, the balance in the inventory account reflects the amount of inventory that was on hand at the beginning of the year. (Under a periodic inventory system, acquisitions of inventory are recorded in a purchases account, and sales of inventory are recorded only in the sales and accounts receivable accounts.) As a result, at the end of the year, the balance in the inventory account does not reflect the inventory that is actually on hand. Thus, at year-end, the inventory account balance needs to be adjusted to that amount.

Lodestone Co. uses a periodic inventory system, and at the end of the year, the inventory account has a balance of $5,000, which, remember, is the beginning-of-the-year balance. However, an inventory count shows that the actual amount of inventory on hand at the end of the year is $18,000. Purchases of inventory during the year were $45,000. Using these data, the following adjusting entry is prepared:

Adjusting entry:[14]

Inventory (ending)	18,000	
Cost of Goods Sold	32,000	
Purchases		45,000
Inventory (beginning)		5,000

To transfer the beginning inventory and purchase amounts to cost of goods sold and record the ending inventory.

Adjusted Trial Balance

Returning to the Steve and Becky example, when all the preceding adjusting entries for Steve and Becky are journalized and posted, an **adjusted trial balance** is prepared, as shown in Exhibit 2-4. Preparing and posting the necessary adjusting entries makes all account balances current and allows financial statements to be prepared.

Closing Entries

After the financial statements are prepared, the last phase of the accounting cycle, which occurs only at year-end, is to "close the books." Many companies prepare monthly or quarterly financial reports, which are known as interim reports,

---

EXTENDING THE CONCEPT

Suppose that a company records all its current payables (e.g., utilities, purchases of supplies, and inventory) in a single accounts payable account, and the beginning-of-the-year balance of this account was $5,000, which consisted of $1,100 for utilities, $3,800 for inventory, and $100 for purchases of supplies. At year-end, a review of outstanding bills and invoices received showed that amounts of $1,400, $4,500, and $250 were owing for utilities, inventory, and purchases of office supplies, respectively. Prepare the adjusting entry to switch from the cash basis of accounting to the accrual basis of accounting.

Answer:

Utility Expense	300	
Inventory (or Purchases)	700	
Supplies (or Supply Expense)	150	
Accounts Payable		1,150

---

[14]Some accountants prefer to adjust the inventory account when preparing closing entries, which is referred to as the closing entry approach. Those journal entries are included as Appendix A.

EXHIBIT 2-4

Adjusted Trial Balance

Steve and Becky Corporation
Adjusted Trial Balance
December 31, 2004

Cash	$ 22,000	
Accounts Receivable	19,850	
Allowance for Doubtful Accounts		$ 650
Inventory	18,000	
Prepaid Insurance	2,000	
Furniture and Fixtures	25,000	
Accumulated Depreciation—Furniture and Fixtures		2,500
Automobile	20,000	
Accumulated Depreciation—Automobile		4,000
Building	160,000	
Accumulated Depreciation—Building		3,000
Land	40,000	
Accounts Payable		8,000
Interest Payable		7,875
Wages Payable		600
Mortgage Payable		175,000
Common Stock		72,500
Paid-In Capital in Excess of Par		22,500
Sales		95,000
Rent Revenue		6,000
Cost of Goods Sold	42,000	
Wage Expense	18,600	
Insurance Expense	4,000	
Bad Debt Expense	800	
Other Expenses	7,000	
Interest Expense	7,875	
Depreciation Expense	9,500	
Dividends	1,000	
Totals	$397,625	$397,625

and this closing process is not done following the preparation of such interim reports. Closing the books prepares the revenue and expense accounts for the recording of next year's transactions.

Accounts are of two types: temporary (or nominal) and permanent (or real). Income statement accounts (i.e., revenues, expenses, gains, and losses) and the owners' drawing (or dividends) account are temporary accounts, in that new accounts are used each year. If new accounts are not used, then the income reported next year would be comingled with this year's income, making the determination of the current year's income difficult. Balance sheet accounts, however, continue from year to year and are permanent. For example, the cash balance at midnight December 31, 2004, is the same cash balance at 12:01 A.M. on January 1, 2005. A new cash balance does not occur, and so a new account is not necessary.

The objective of closing the books is to transfer the account balances in the temporary accounts to the permanent accounts. To do this, the revenue and gain accounts, which have credit balances, are debited. The expense and loss accounts, which have debit balances, are credited. The offsetting entry in both cases is to an income summary account. With the closing of the revenue/gain and expense/loss accounts, the balance in Income Summary is the net income/loss amount. Using the information on Exhibit 2-4, Steve and Becky prepared the following closing entries:

Closing entries:

Sales	95,000	
Rent Revenue	6,000	
Income Summary		101,000

To close the revenue accounts to Income Summary.

Income Summary	89,775	
Cost of Goods Sold		42,000
Wage Expense		18,600
Insurance Expense		4,000
Bad Debt Expense		800
Other Expense		7,000
Interest Expense		7,875
Depreciation Expense		9,500

To close the expense accounts to Income Summary.

The income summary account now has a credit balance of $11,225, which is Steve and Becky's income for the year before income taxes. This balance is transferred to the capital account for a proprietorship, or to the respective capital accounts for a partnership, or to Retained Earnings for a corporation. For a partnership, the amount in Income Summary is allocated to the various partners' capital accounts according to the partnership agreement or equally among all partners when the partnership agreement is silent as to how profits and losses are to be allocated.

The last step in the closing process is to close the withdrawals by owners (for a proprietorship or partnership) or the dividends paid to owners (for a corporation) to the appropriate capital account(s) or retained earnings account, respectively. Exhibit 2-5 demonstrates these closing entries. For the first entry, a net income of $11,225 was used as determined in the preceding example. For the partnership form, profits were divided 40% to Steve and 60% to Becky, which illustrates that profits are not necessarily divided among partners in relation to

EXHIBIT 2-5

Closing the Income Summary and the Distribution to Owners' Accounts

For Proprietorship		For Partnership			For Corporation		
Income Summary	11,225	Income Summary	11,225		Income Summary	11,225	
Steve, Capital	11,225	Steve, Capital		4,490	Retained Earnings		11,225
		Becky, Capital		6,735			
To close the income summary account.							
Steve, Capital	1,000	Steve, Capital	1,000		Retained Earnings	1,000	
Steve, Drawing	1,000	Becky, Capital	1,000		Dividends		1,000
		Steve, Drawing		1,000			
		Becky, Drawing		1,000			
To close the distribution to owners' accounts.							

their capital account balances or in relation to the amount of assets they have contributed to the partnership. For the second entry, the amounts used were those in the Distributions to Owners section of this chapter on page 37.

If Steve and Becky had a loss for the year of $11,225, then the journal entries for closing the income summary account would be exactly reversed—the debits would become credits and the credits would become debits.

Following the posting of the closing entries, a postclosing trial balance may be prepared. (This is the third time that a trial balance is taken in the accounting cycle.) Since the temporary accounts now have a zero balance, the postclosing trial balance consists of only the permanent accounts and their balances. The purpose of the postclosing trial balance is to make sure the "books balance" (i.e., the closing process was done correctly) before transactions for the next year are recorded. With the increasing use of automated information systems and a resulting nonexistent error rate for the posting type of activity, a postclosing trial balance is not usually needed. However, a postclosing trial balance should be prepared whenever a manual accounting information system is used.

All the above steps in the accounting cycle and the later step of preparing financial statements are expedited through a worksheet when a manual accounting system is used. An example of such a worksheet is included in Appendix B.

Preparing the Financial Statements

The objective of any accounting information system is to organize data so that financial statements can be generated that are useful for making decisions. *The financial statements that companies are required to provide are an income statement, a balance sheet, a statement of cash flows, a statement of changes in stockholders' equity, and a statement of comprehensive income.* The primary sections and classifications of the income statement and balance sheet are introduced in the following paragraphs. However, most of the rules and requirements regarding the preparation of all these financial statements and their uses are found in later chapters.

Income Statement

The primary function of the income statement is to measure the financial performance of a company during a specified time period. To assist the readers in extracting information useful to their purposes, companies are required to separate the components of income into those that are expected to persist in the future and those that are expected to be one-time events, including the nature of the one-time event. Accordingly, standard-setting bodies have been very active in defining the categories comprising the income statement and the criteria that determine in which category various revenues, gains, expenses, and losses are reported. Currently, GAAP requires that the income statement be classified into the categories as set out in Exhibit 2-6.

EXHIBIT 2-6

> ### Classifications on the Income Statement
> - Continuing operations, with separate reporting of items that are *either* unusual in nature *or* occur infrequently
> - Discontinued operations (which is covered in another chapter)
> - Extraordinary items, consisting of items that are *both* unusual *and* occur infrequently (covered here but also more extensively in a later chapter)
> - Changes in accounting principles (covered in another chapter)

INTERNET

An important resource for accounting is **http://raw.rutgers.edu**. This Web site offers numerous links to accounting information.

Income from Operations

Preparing the continuing operations section of the income statement requires that revenues be distinguished from gains and expenses be distinguished from losses. *Revenues and expenses result from the central or major activities of the company, while gains and losses result from incidental or peripheral activities.* Thus, the nature of the business defines what are revenues and gains and what are expenses and losses. For example, a retail store that sells surplus land will recognize a gain or a loss, but a real estate developer that sells land will recognize revenue. For most companies, revenues consist of the activities of selling inventory and rendering services, while gains and losses typically arise from selling investments and operating assets and writing off inventory or other assets due to obsolescence, casualties, or theft. The key to preparing the continuing operations of the income statement is to report gains and losses in such a way that they can be identified from the revenues and expenses that are part of the company's central purpose.

In addition to reporting expenses in such a way that they can be readily identified from losses, reporting expenses also involves separating product costs from period costs. **Product costs** are the costs of goods sold, and all other operating costs are **period costs**. Period costs are also usually classified in various categories. One common classification is to report period costs as either administrative expenses or selling expenses. Administrative expenses include such items as administrative salaries, legal, accounting, and personnel costs, depreciation on office furniture, office supplies, insurance, and property taxes. Selling expenses include such items as sales commissions, advertising, store displays, depreciation on store fixtures, and delivery expenses. Instead of reporting period expenses as either administrative expenses or selling expenses, they may be reported by a functional expense classification, such as administrative, occupancy, publicity, and selling expenses.

Income Statement Format

Exhibit 2-7 is an income statement for Steve and Becky in a multiple-step format, using the data in the adjusted trial balance of Exhibit 2-4. Exhibit 2-8, on page 51, is an income statement for Steve and Becky in a single-step format, using the same information. However, due to the small number of period expenses, the period costs are only listed and are not categorized into any classification. In each exhibit, important comments are made in an adjacent column.

In the multiple-step format at the top of the following page, there are several categories in which revenues, gains, expenses, and losses are reported, and thus there are several subtraction steps to obtain "Income from operations."[15] This is the reason for the name **multiple-step income statement**. The major advantage of a multiple-step income statement is the detail it provides. There is a gross profit amount that enables the reader to determine how much goods are marked up and thus how resilient the company is to possible pressures in the market to reduce selling

---

[15]This line goes by several other names, such as "Operating income."

EXHIBIT 2-7

Example of a Multiple-Step Income Statement

Steve and Becky Corporation
Income Statement
For the Year Ended December 31, 2004

Note that the heading begins with the name of the company, the title of the statement, and the date which is identified as "For the Year Ended" on the income statement.

Sales		$95,000
Cost of goods sold*		42,000
Gross profit		$53,000
Operating expenses:		
Wage expense	$18,600	
Insurance expense	4,000	
Bad debt expense	800	
Other expenses	7,000	
Depreciation expense	9,500	
Total operating expenses:		39,900
Income from operations		$13,100
Other revenue and expenses:		
Rent revenue	$ 6,000	
Interest expense	(7,875)	
		(1,875)
Income before taxes		$11,225
Income taxes		(3,143)
Net income		$ 8,082
Earnings per share		$0.56

Product costs are reported separately from period costs.

Gross profit is defined as sales less cost of goods sold, not sales less expenses.

This is an important line item. It indicates the viability of the company.

These are the items arising from peripheral or incidental activities. Interest expense is not considered part of the central operations of any business, except for financial-type businesses.

Technically, this is the only item on the income statement that should have the word "net" in its title.

This is computed as net income divided by the number of shares outstanding, which is 14,500. (See the journal entry where Steve and Becky contributed assets to the corporation.)

*Many companies report a detailed cost of goods sold, as follows:

Inventory, January 1, 2004	XXX
Purchases/cost of goods manufactured	+XXX
Cost of goods available	XXX
Inventory, December 31, 2004	−XXX
Cost of goods sold	XXX

prices. Also, the reader can easily distinguish the revenues from the gains and the expenses from the losses. However, the multiple-step's advantage in providing detail is also its disadvantage. As the number of accounts and the number of categories grow, the amount of detail provided may become overwhelming, so that communicating important information is actually hindered. (See Appendix C as an example of a complex multiple-step income statement published by the IVAX Corporation.) When this is the case, it may be better to prepare and issue

EXHIBIT 2-8

Example of a Single-Step Income Statement

Steve and Becky Corporation
Income Statement
For the Year Ended December 31, 2004

Note that the heading is the same as the one used for the multiple-step format, and no reference is usually made in the heading as to the format that is being used.

Sales		$ 95,000
Rent revenue		6,000
Total revenues		$101,000

Note that main revenues are reported first and then peripheral revenues. There is no gross profit line or income from operations line.

Expenses:		
Cost of goods sold	$42,000	
Wage expense	18,600	
Insurance expense	4,000	
Bad debt expense	800	
Other expenses	7,000	
Depreciation expense	9,500	
Interest expense	7,875	
Total operating expenses:		89,775
Income before taxes		$ 11,225
Income taxes		(3,143)
Net income		$ 8,082
Earnings per share		$0.56

Expenses are reported next to peripheral costs. Still, it is possible for the financial statement reader to extract the information.

Importantly, the net income is the same using either format.

a **single-step income statement**, where all elements of revenue and gains and expenses and losses are reported in the same section, as shown in Exhibit 2-8.

The difference between the single-step and multiple-step income statements is the number of categories in the statement and thus the number of subtraction steps to derive the income from operations line: one-step versus several. The primary advantage of the single-step income statement is its simplicity.

Note that dividends are not reported on the income statement. They are not expenses but instead are distributions to owners. Similarly, neither are drawings by a partner or a proprietor reported on the income statement. They, too, are not expenses but are also distributions to owners.

A final note of importance is that because a trend is always more significant than single numbers, the ARB encouraged corporations to issue **comparative income statements** for at least the prior year.[16] A comparative income statement is in columnar form, with one column used to report the current-year financial information and another column used to report the prior-year financial information. Additional years' data can be reported by adding additional columns. Appendix C contains an example of a comparative income statement where the information for two prior years is reported for comparative purposes.

Extraordinary Items

Transactions reported as extraordinary items are distinguished by their unusual nature and by the infrequency of their occurrence, taking into account the legal,

---

[16]ARB Bulletin #43, Chapter 2, Section A—Comparative Financial Statements, pars. 1–2.

geographical, and physical environment in which the entity operates. Having to consider the total environment in which a company operates means that what is an extraordinary item for one entity may not be an extraordinary item for another entity. Thus, judgment is required to identify those transactions that should be reported as extraordinary items.

Regarding the criteria for determining whether an event should be classified as an extraordinary item, *unusual in nature* means that the event or transaction possesses a high degree of abnormality and is clearly unrelated to, or only incidentally related to, the ordinary and typical activities of the entity. *Infrequency of occurrence* means that the event or transaction is not reasonably expected to recur in the foreseeable future. To illustrate that judgment is required in applying these two criteria, an event or transaction might not be considered to occur infrequently if it happens every five years. However, a transaction that occurs every 75 years might be considered to occur infrequently. Then what time is required for an event to be considered infrequent in occurrence? Is it ten years? Twenty-five years? Seventy-four years? The best that can be said regarding whether a transaction or event gives rise to an extraordinary item is that "judgment is required."

Regardless of the difficulty in applying the infrequent and unusual criteria, the APB has ruled that the write-down or write-off of receivables, inventory, and gains or losses that result from the sale or abandonment of property, plant, and equipment are not extraordinary items. Further, the FASB has ruled that *an extraordinary gain may arise when a company acquires another* (i.e., merger or acquisition) *and pays less than the current value for the net assets* (i.e., current value of the assets acquired minus the current value of the liabilities assumed). A more detailed explanation of an extraordinary item is beyond the scope of this chapter.

Events or transactions that are determined to be extraordinary items are reported separately on the income statement, net of tax, as shown in Exhibit 2-9 (emphasis added), which was extracted from a published financial statement of Dell Computers. This separate reporting is the same, regardless of whether the single-step or the multiple-step format is used. Thus, both formats of the income statement look exactly the same for the reporting of extraordinary items. Also, each extraordinary item is reported separately (unless related to the same event or transaction) and reported net of tax.

Intraperiod Tax Allocation

One important difference between the income statements in Exhibits 2-7 and 2-8 and in Exhibit 2-9 is that more than one income tax number is reported on the income statement in Exhibit 2-9. This reporting of the income tax within the various categories of the income statement (i.e., operations, extraordinary items, etc.) is called **intraperiod tax allocation**. As long as continuing operations is the only category on the income statement (as in Exhibits 2-7 and 2-8), there is only one income tax expense reported. However, if other categories of income are reported (e.g., extraordinary items), then *each item in those other categories is reported net of tax*. That is, if there are two extraordinary items, then each extraordinary item is reported net of taxes in addition to the tax expense reported for continuing operations. Also, if there is one extraordinary item and one item reported under change in accounting principle, then there is an income tax item for continuing operations, a second tax item for the extraordinary item, and a third tax item for the change in accounting principles. (See Appendix C for an extended example of intraperiod tax allocation on a published financial statement.) The

EXHIBIT 2-9

Reporting of Extraordinary Items

(in millions)	February 2, Year 2	January 28, Year 1
Net revenue	$7,759	$5,296
Cost of goods sold	6,093	4,229
Gross margin	$1,666	$1,067
Operating expenses:		
Selling, general and administrative	$ 826	$ 595
Research, development and engineering	126	95
Total operating expenses	$ 952	$ 690
Operating income	$ 714	$ 377
Financing and other income	33	6
Income before income taxes and extraordinary loss	$ 747	$ 383
Provision for income taxes	216	111
Income before extraordinary loss	$ 531	$ 272
Extraordinary items:		
Extraordinary loss, net of taxes of $xx	*(13)*	—
Net income	$ 518	$ 272

same principle applies for losses; each extraordinary loss, each change in accounting principle that reduces net income, etc., is reported net of its tax effect.[17]

Basic Earnings per Share (EPS)

As shown in Exhibits 2-7 and 2-8, earnings per share (meaning earnings per common share of stock) must be reported on the face of the income statement. The notion of computing EPS is to divide the income belonging to the common stockholders by the number of shares of common stock outstanding, as follows:

$$\text{Earnings per Share} = \frac{\text{Net Income to Common Stockholders}}{\text{Number of Shares of Common Stock Outstanding}} \quad (2.2)$$

The numerator in Equation 2.2, "Net Income to Common Stockholders," is computed by *subtracting preferred stock dividends declared from net income.* (Note that it is the year in which the dividends are *declared* that is important and not the date in which they were paid.) The only exception to this is if the preferred stock is cumulative. Usually, holders of preferred stock are entitled to dividends only when the dividends are declared by the board of directors and approved by the shareholders. Thus, if dividends are not declared in a particular year, holders of preferred stock lose their dividends for that year, and they have no claim to receive them in the future. However, when preferred stock is **cumulative**, the holders of preferred stock do not lose their rights to receive a dividend in a year when dividends are not declared. Instead, in future years when dividends are declared, the dividends that were not paid in prior years to the holders of the cumulative preferred stock are paid first. Then, the current-year preferred dividends are paid. Finally, any amounts left to be distributed are paid

---

[17]The intricacies of intraperiod tax allocation are covered in Chapter 19.

to the common stockholders. So, *dividends on cumulative preferred stock are deducted in the numerator, whether or not they are declared.*

The dividend on preferred stock is computed by multiplying the preferred dividend rate by the par value of the preferred stock. This computed amount is for one share of stock, so the total amount paid to the preferred stockholders is computed by multiplying the dividend amount for one share of stock by the number of shares of preferred stock *outstanding*. For example, Webster WordSmith, Inc., has outstanding 5,000 shares of 5%, $100 par preferred stock. The 5% is the dividend rate, which means that the preferred stock dividend amount is $5 per share (i.e., $100 par times 5%). The total preferred dividend is $25,000, which is computed by multiplying the $5 dividend per share by the 5,000 shares.

When the number of shares of common stock outstanding does not change during the year, the denominator used in computing EPS is the number of shares outstanding at year-end. When the number of shares of common stock outstanding changes because new shares are issued or the corporation acquires its own stock on the open market, EPS is computed using a weighted-average number of shares. For example, suppose that a company had 10,000 shares of stock outstanding at the beginning of the year and that it had several transactions in its own stock during the year, which are summarized as follows:

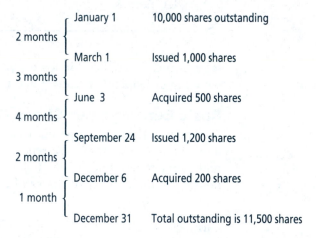

With this information, the weighted-average number of shares is determined as shown in Exhibit 2-10.

EXHIBIT 2-10

Calculation of Weighted-Average Number of Shares

Date	Number of Shares Outstanding	Fraction of Year Outstanding before Next Transaction	Weighted Number of Shares
January 1	10,000	2/12	1,666.667
March 1	11,000	3/12	2,750.000
June 3	10,500	4/12	3,500.000
September 24	11,700	2/12	1,950.000
December 6	11,500	1/12	958.333
Weighted-average number of shares			**10,825.000**

Reporting EPS is very similar to reporting intraperiod tax allocation. That is, when continuing operations is the only category of income, then there is only one earnings-per-share number reported, and that is for net income, as shown in Exhibits 2-7 and 2-8. However, when other categories of income are reported in addition to continuing operations, then an EPS number is reported for every item in those other categories. (See Appendix C for the reporting of earnings per share on a published financial statement.)

Comprehensive EPS Illustration

To illustrate the concepts of intraperiod tax allocation and the computing and presenting of earnings per share, assume the following information for the Roger Rabbit Corporation for the year ended December 31, 2004:

Description	Amount
Sales	$100,000
Cost of goods sold	$(40,000)
Operating expenses	$(28,000)
Gain on sale of land	$3,000
Extraordinary item	$(12,000)
Number of shares, January 1	18,000
Shares issued on May 31	2,400
Shares reacquired on September 30	900
Income tax rate	30%

To properly prepare the income statement for Roger Rabbit Corporation, it must be recognized that the income statement will consist of two major classifications: (1) continuing operations and (2) an extraordinary item. As a result, intraperiod tax allocation is necessary, and several EPS figures will be presented. Accordingly, the income statement will be prepared in four steps: (1) determining the basic format of the statement, whether to use a multiple-step or a single-step statement; (2) implementing intraperiod tax allocation; (3) computing the weighted-average number of shares; and (4) presenting the finished income statement.

Step 1: Basic single-step format

Roger Rabbit Corporation
Income Statement
For the Year Ended December 31, 2004

Revenues:	
Sales	$100,000
Gain on sale of land	3,000
Total revenues	$103,000
Expenses:	
Cost of goods sold	$ (40,000)
Operating expenses	(28,000)
Total expenses	$ (68,000)
Operating income before taxes	$ 35,000
Income taxes	
Income before extraordinary items:	
Extraordinary item	$12,000 loss less tax effect
Net income	

Step 2: Incorporating intraperiod tax allocation

Roger Rabbit Corporation
Income Statement
For the Year Ended December 31, 2004

Revenues:	
Sales	$100,000
Gain on sale of land	3,000
Total revenues	$103,000
Expenses:	
Cost of goods sold	$ (40,000)
Operating expenses	(28,000)
Total expenses	$ (68,000)
Operating income before taxes	$ 35,000
Income taxes	(10,500)
Income before extraordinary items	$ 24,500
Extraordinary item:	
Extraordinary item, less tax effect of $3,600	(8,400)
Net income	$ 16,100

Step 3: Computing weighted-average number of shares

Date	Number of Shares	Fraction of Year	Weighted-Average No. of Shares
January 1	18,000	5/12	7,500
May 31	20,400	4/12	6,800
September 30	19,500	3/12	4,875
Weighted-average number of shares			19,175

Step 4: Finished income statement

Roger Rabbit Corporation
Income Statement
For the Year Ended December 31, 2004

Revenues:	
Sales	$100,000
Gain on sale of land	3,000
Total revenues	$103,000
Expenses:	
Cost of goods sold	$ (40,000)
Operating expenses	(28,000)
Total expenses	$ (68,000)
Operating income before taxes	$ 35,000
Income taxes	(10,500)
Income before extraordinary items	$ 24,500
Extraordinary item:	
Extraordinary item, less tax effect of $3,600	(8,400)
Net income	$ 16,100
Earnings per Share	
Income before extraordinary item	$1.28
Extraordinary item	(0.44)
Net income	$0.84

If preferred dividends were declared during the year (or if the preferred stock is cumulative), then the preferred dividends would be deducted from income before extraordinary items and from net income, but they are not deducted from the extraordinary item. This same rule of deducting the preferred stock dividends from subtotals and from net income is applied regardless of the number of major classifications used (i.e., discontinued operations, accounting principles change, etc.). The reason for doing so is that dividends are paid from operating income and not from extraordinary gains/losses or other classifications of income.

The Balance Sheet

Like income statements, balance sheets are customarily classified into categories. In addition to providing other information, categorizing balance sheet elements tells the financial statement reader the intended use of assets, the maturity date of liabilities, and the source of funds received. Also, when a balance sheet is categorized, the relationships among the subtotals result in information for the financial statement user. Neither the FASB nor its predecessors have been as active in mandating definitive balance sheet classifications as they have been with the income statement. Thus, unlike the income statement, which is quite rigid in the classifications used and what is included in each classification, the balance sheet allows for some flexibility in content, form, and terminology. Accordingly, the classifications in Exhibit 2-11 are common classifications found in balance sheets today.

EXHIBIT 2-11

Typical Balance Sheet Classifications

Assets	Liabilities and Owners' Equity
Current assets	Current liabilities
Investments and funds	Long-term liabilities
Property, plant, and equipment	Owners' equity
Intangible assets	Contributed capital
Other assets	Retained earnings
	Accumulated other comprehensive income

A balance sheet can be presented in either the **account** or the **report format**. The account format presents the assets on the left side of the statement and the liabilities and owners' equity on the right side. Alternatively, the report form lists all accounts vertically, with assets first, followed by the liabilities and owners' equity accounts. As with the income statement, comparative reports are recommended. This facilitates detecting trends and changes from the prior year. Exhibit 2-12 presents an example of a balance sheet in report format with the data from the Steve and Becky example from Exhibit 2-4, adjusted for the income taxes. Explanations of the balance sheet and the elements that are reported in each category are shown both in the adjacent column in Exhibit 2-12 and also in more detail in the rest of the chapter.

Current Assets

Current assets are assets that are expected to be converted into cash, sold, or consumed within the business's operating cycle or one year, whichever is longer. The **operating cycle** is the length of time required to acquire inventory, process it (if necessary), sell it, and collect the resulting receivable. The time required to

EXHIBIT 2-12

Example of a Balance Sheet—Report Format

Steve and Becky Corporation
Balance Sheet
December 31, 2004

Note the familiar name of the company and name of the statement, but also note the different stating of the date.

Assets

Current assets:

Cash		$ 22,000
Accounts receivable (net of an allowance of $650)		19,200
Inventory		18,000
Prepaid insurance		2,000
Total current assets		$ 61,200

Disclosure of contra-asset amounts is often done by parenthetical notation.

Property, plant, and equipment:

Land	$ 40,000	
Furniture and fixtures	25,000	
Automobile	20,000	
Building	160,000	
Total	$245,000	
Less accumulated depreciation	(9,500)	
Total property, plant, and equipment		235,500
Total assets		$296,700

Note that each category is identified with a title and has a subtotal.

Accumulated depreciation is often reported in this fashion.

Liabilities and Owners' Equity

Current liabilities:

Accounts payable		$ 8,000
Wages payable		600
Taxes payable		3,143
Interest payable		7,875
Total current liabilities		$ 19,618
Mortgage payable		175,000
Total liabilities		$194,618

Amount comes from Exhibit 2-7 or 2-8.

Owners' equity:

Common stock		$ 72,500
Paid-in capital in excess of par		22,500
Retained earnings		7,082
Total owners' equity		$102,082
Total liabilities and owners' equity		$296,700

Retained earnings is computed as the amount of net income less dividends.

complete the operating cycle varies according to industry and even (to a lesser degree) among entities within the same industry. The most common current assets are cash and cash equivalents, prepaid items, inventory, receivables, and short-term investments. Current assets are listed in order of liquidity on the balance sheet, which means that cash is listed first, and then the other current assets are listed according to how close they are to cash or how quickly they could be turned into cash.

Cash is money or that which is used as a medium of exchange. Common examples of cash include currency, coins, and personal checks. Cash also includes certified checks, money orders, and cashiers' checks. Postdated checks are not cash but are classified as receivables. Cash with restrictions placed on it that prevent it from being used immediately is not classified as cash but is reported as restricted cash. It is classified as either current or long-term, depending upon when it will be available. Bank overdrafts are not cash but are reported with current liabilities. A bank overdraft at one bank may not be offset against a bank deposit in another bank. However, a bank overdraft *must be offset against a bank deposit in the same bank.*

Most companies use available funds to earn interest for even short time periods by investing in readily convertible, low-risk securities. Such investments are so near cash that they are called **cash equivalents**. To qualify as a cash equivalent, the asset must be highly liquid, meaning it can be converted into cash with no risk of loss. Cash equivalents have a short maturity date—90 days from the date of purchase is a typical rule of thumb. Because such securities are so near cash, they often are reported together with cash on the balance sheet under the caption Cash and Cash Equivalents.

Receivables are amounts expected to be collected from customers, officers, employees, and affiliates. Receivables are reported at their face value, less any estimated uncollectible amounts, which are based on past experience and are typically disclosed through a contra-asset account or by disclosure in the notes to the financial statements. Receivables from officers, employees, and affiliates should be reported separately from other receivables, which may be done in the notes to the financial statements.

Inventory for retail stores includes those goods that are primarily held for sale (or resale) in the ordinary course of business. Typically, manufacturing companies report inventory under one of three categories: raw materials, work-in-process, and finished goods, and this reporting may be done on the face of the balance sheet or in the accompanying notes.

Prepaids are expenditures made for the receipt of future benefits. In a sense, most of them are receivables, typically for services. Prepaid amounts usually include payments made for rent, insurance, advertising, and supplies.

Investments and Funds

The **investments and funds** classification is not always found in published financial statements. Sometimes, a company has no assets of this type, but other times, the company classifies such assets elsewhere. This classification includes all assets that are held for future use or for long-term price appreciation. Typical assets found in this category include:

1. Cash or securities that are physically separated and are to be used for a specific purpose, usually to retire long-term debt. This is the definition of a fund.
2. Idle land that will be either used in the future or sold.
3. Long-term receivables.
4. Investments in securities of other corporations.

Property, Plant, and Equipment

The **property, plant, and equipment** classification contains the operational assets of the company—those that accomplish the purpose for which the company is in business. The most common assets found in this category include furniture and fixtures, equipment, buildings, land, and natural resources, such as oil wells, timber stands, mines of all types, and gravel pits. Assets classified in this category must have all the following characteristics:

1. *Long-lived.* Such assets provide benefits for longer than one year or the current operating cycle. Being long-lived essentially distinguishes assets from expenses. Expenditures having future benefits of less than one year are expensed as period costs at the time of acquisition.
2. *Used in the company's operations.* Idle machinery and equipment (and their equivalents) are not classified as part of property, plant, and equipment. They would appropriately be classified elsewhere, depending upon management's intent regarding their ultimate disposition; e.g., idle machinery to be disposed of currently is recorded under current assets.
3. *Tangible.* Such assets can be seen, touched, etc.

These assets, except for land, are reported at historical cost less accumulated depreciation. The accumulated depreciation may be reported in a contra-asset account, in a parenthetical notation, or in the notes to the financial statements.

Intangible Assets

The **intangible assets** classification includes copyrights, patents, and trademarks. The lack of physical substance is the only characteristic that differentiates them from property, plant, and equipment. Thus, the primary qualities of the assets categorized as intangible assets are that they are long-lived and used in the operations of the company. The fluidity of classifying assets on the balance sheet is illustrated, in that intangibles are sometimes (perhaps inappropriately) recorded under property, plant, and equipment. Intangible assets are reported at historical cost less accumulated amortization, which is reported in the notes, if at all.

Assets that do not properly fit into any of these categories can be included as **other assets**. The types of assets located in this classification vary, depending upon the type of business and circumstances. Some examples of assets commonly found in this classification include deferred charges (i.e., items that are not properly classified as expenses but are not really assets), long-term receivables, and surplus land not held for future use.

Current Liabilities

Current liabilities are those obligations that will be liquidated within one year or the operating cycle, whichever is longer, by using a current asset or by incurring another current liability. Current liabilities include accounts payable, unearned revenue, accrued expenses, and current maturities on long-term debt. From this definition, current liabilities relate to current assets, in that a current liability is one that will be liquidated by using a current asset. Thus, when a maturing liability will not be liquidated by using a current asset, it is not a current liability. To illustrate, suppose that a company has a 20-year bond coming due in the next year, and it will be liquidated by using funds that have been accumulated in a bond sinking fund that is classified as a long-term asset. Because the bond will be liquidated by using a noncurrent asset—even though it will mature during the next operating cycle—the bond is classified as a long-term liability. Thus, whenever a liability is associated with an asset, the reporting should be consistent. Either both should be reported as current, or both should be reported as noncurrent. Current liabilities can be arranged according to (1) when they are due, (2) in descending order according to amount, or (3) according to preferences if the company is liquidated.

Long-Term Liabilities

Long-term liabilities are those that are not expected to be liquidated within one year or the current operating cycle by using a current asset. The long-term liabilities classification typically includes notes payable, mortgages, pension obligations, lease obligations, postretirement benefits (which are primarily medical benefits extended to individuals after they retire but may include other benefits as well), and bonds payable, which are a form of borrowing. Long-term debt is reported with any associated premiums and discounts related to it, which primarily applies to bonds payable. Two typical ways such a premium or discount is reported are (1) by parenthetical notation and (2) by a separate line. Both methods are shown in Exhibit 2-13 for bonds issued with a discount. For bonds issued with a premium, the premium amount is added to the bonds payable amount, rather than being subtracted.

EXHIBIT 2-13

Examples of Reporting Bond Discount with Long-Term Bonds

By parenthetical notation:

Bonds payable (less discount of $20,000)		$980,000

By a separate line:

Bonds payable	$1,000,000	
Less bond discount	(20,000)	$980,000

Owners'/Stockholders' Equity

Owners' or stockholders' equity can be described as the residual claim on assets or the claim on assets after creditors are paid in full. Another view is that owners' equity shows how much of the assets were financed either by contributions from owners or by a company retaining and reinvesting its profits in the business. The reporting of the owners' equity section depends on whether the business entity is a proprietorship, partnership, or corporation. For companies organized as a proprietorship, owners' equity consists of a capital account, which has a balance equal to the net assets of the company. For a partnership, owners' equity consists of a capital account for each partner.

For a corporation, the reporting of owners' equity, which is called stockholders' equity, is more lengthy due to the complexities of laws and restrictions placed on stock agreements. The basic classifications of stockholders' equity are contributed capital, retained earnings, and accumulated other comprehensive income.

The **contributed capital** classification represents the amount contributed by the stockholders. When shares of stock are authorized, a par or stated value may be assigned either by the state authorizing the corporate charter or by the board of directors of the corporation. This par or stated value has no relation to the market price of the stock and is often set at a low amount. The par or stated value is recorded in the stock account, and any excess received above that par or stated value is recorded in the paid-in capital in excess of par (or stated) value account. The rights and other characteristics of each type of stock are always fully described on the balance sheet.

Retained earnings represents the current and prior earnings of a business that have not been distributed to shareholders. The net income of a business increases the retained earnings account, while net losses and dividends reduce it. A **deficit** results when the accumulated losses and dividends exceed the accumulated profits and is labeled "Deficit," rather than Retained Earnings.

Accumulated other comprehensive income represents gains and losses that affect owners' equity but are not the result of an exchange transaction. Examples are the gains and losses that result from investments in certain debt or equity securities due to price changes and certain gains and losses associated with translating financial statements prepared in a foreign currency. (These topics are covered more extensively later in the text.)

Presentation of Financial Statements—An International Context

The differences among countries in terminology and formats used to present financial statements are significant. Familiarity with these differences facilitates more effective analysis of financial statements from countries other than the United States.

Appendix D contains the financial statements for BG Group PLC, which is a leading multinational energy company that follows UK GAAP when preparing its financial reports. Examination of the income statement reveals several differences in format and terminology used in the United Kingdom, compared to what is typically used in the United States. For example, "Turnover" is used in the United Kingdom in place of "Sales" in the United States. Results from discontinued operations are displayed throughout the income statement in the United Kingdom, instead of separately after continuing operations in the United States. "Exceptional items" is similar to "extraordinary items" in the United States. Finally, EPS numbers are presented for both "basic" earnings and "adjusted" earnings. The effects of items that are not expected to persist in the future, such as windfall taxes and gains/losses on disposals, are eliminated from basic earnings to derive adjusted earnings. Adjusted earnings are meant to provide a more accurate measure of the underlying performance of the company.

© GETTY IMAGES, INC./PHOTODISC

BG Group's balance sheet is also different in several ways from a typical balance sheet for a U.S. company. The ordering of the asset accounts in the balance sheet is inversely related to the asset's liquidity, which is exactly the opposite of what is presented in the United States. Presenting the share of assets and liabilities in joint ventures and associated undertakings (i.e., investments where ownership exceeds 20% of outstanding shares) separately is also different from U.S. practice, which is to net these amounts and lump them together with other investments. Instead of showing an amount for total assets, BG Group subtracts current liabilities from total assets to present a subtotal: "Total Assets less Current Liabilities."

Several terminology differences on the balance sheet can also be noticed. At first glance, "Stocks" might be thought of as part of stockholders' equity or perhaps an investment in stock. However, a closer examination indicates that "Stocks" is equivalent to inventory. "Debtors" refers to accounts receivable and "Debtors: amounts falling due after more than one year" is displayed in the current assets section. "Called up equity share capital" and "Share premium account" are used for common stock and paid-in capital in excess of par, respectively. Finally, the "Profit and loss account" is equivalent to retained earnings.[18]

The International Accounting Standards Committee addressed financial statement format in IAS No. 1. This statement indicates that presenting assets and liabilities in the balance sheet according to their liquidity is not required. Separating operating from nonoperating activities on the income statement is also not required.

Similar to U.S. GAAP, IAS No. 1 stipulates that the primary concern when presenting financial statements is that they should be presented fairly. In fact, IAS No. 1 allows companies to deviate from prescribed IAS when compliance would generate misleading information. This is referred to as the "true and fair view override" and has been very controversial with respect to the SEC's decision on whether to accept international GAAP for foreign listings on U.S. exchanges. The SEC argues that this override allows companies to follow any accounting principle they want and could ultimately weaken the standards through company abuse. To date, departure from international GAAP requirements via the override has not been tested. The IASC responded to the SEC's concern by indicating that use of the override can be justified only in very unusual circumstances. Nevertheless, the SEC has stated that one criterion for accepting international GAAP is that they be "rigorously interpreted."

Summary

One purpose of this chapter was to review the building blocks (i.e., accounts, ledgers, and journals) and the procedures of capturing information in an accounting information system, whether it is a manual or a computerized system. As demonstrated in the opening scenario of Party City Corporation, an inappropriately designed accounting information system, including one that cannot grow with the company's needs, can be very detrimental to the financial health of a corporation. Knowing these building blocks and procedures (1) is critical to designing and implementing any effective accounting information system, (2) facilitates an understanding of the effects that transactions have on a company's financial statements, (3) assists managers in determining what information can be obtained from the system, and (4) helps both managers and external financial statement readers better evaluate the relevance of information received.

Also, a review of income statement and balance sheet formats was provided, which focused on preparing such statements. For reporting income, the income statement is divided into various categories, including:

---

[18]Other equity accounts are associated with advanced topics that are discussed later in this textbook or in an advanced accounting course.

- Continuing operations
- Discontinued operations
- Extraordinary items
- Cumulative effect of accounting principles change

Reporting income by category is intended to aid the reader in differentiating between the nature of the various revenues/gains and expenses/losses and in determining which items will persist into the future. Within the continuing operations section, revenues are clearly differentiated from gains, and expenses are clearly differentiated from losses. The continuing operations section shows only one income tax number, but in the other sections, every item is shown net of its tax effect. In a like manner, only one EPS number is reported for continuing operations, but an EPS number is reported for every item in those other categories.

The balance sheet is also divided into classifications for the intent of providing meaningful information. Assets are reported under (1) current assets, (2) investments and funds, (3) property, plant, and equipment, (4) intangible assets, and sometimes (5) other assets. Current assets are defined in terms of the operating cycle and reported according to liquidity, with the most liquid asset (i.e., cash) reported first. Assets reported within investments and funds are held for future use or long-term price appreciation. Assets reported within the property, plant, and equipment category must be long-lived, tangible, and used in the operations of the company.

Liabilities are reported either as current liabilities or long-term liabilities. Current liabilities are defined in terms of the operating cycle and being liquidated by using a current asset. All other liabilities are reported as long-term liabilities. Because current liabilities are defined in terms of current assets, the related asset and liability should be consistently reported. That is, either both are reported as current or both are reported as long-term.

The reporting of owners' equity depends on how the business is organized. For a proprietorship, the owners' equity consists of one capital account. For a partnership, owners' equity consists of a capital account for each owner. For a corporation, owners' equity is reported under the categories (1) contributed capital, (2) retained earnings, and (3) other comprehensive income. Contributed capital is further divided between the par amounts and the amounts paid in that are in excess of par. This enables readers to determine the corporation's legal capital. Retained earnings is the income that has been kept by the company and reinvested into assets instead of being distributed as dividends. Other comprehensive income consists of other changes in owners' equity, such as price appreciation on certain long-term investments and adjustments that result from consolidating financial statements of a foreign subsidiary. Such gains/losses usually are not the result of a transaction.

Finally, financial reporting is a social development; it is not a science. Therefore, financial reporting is modified by its social, legal, and cultural environment. This chapter introduced some examples of how different financial reporting is between even culturally related countries, such as the United States and the United Kingdom. This single example should be enough to illustrate the impossibility of determining the "one right way" to account for a transaction or to report information. Rather, the accountant, business manager, and analyst must be able to use information in whatever form it is received. Also, the cultural significance of accounts must be understood by aspiring accountants so that they can better participate in directing the profession's future. Accounting will always be an important and rewarding career—when it provides useful information.

APPENDIX A: Closing Entry Scheme for Changing the Inventory Balance under a Periodic Inventory System

Throughout the chapter, Steve and Becky used a perpetual inventory system, and as a result, no adjusting entry was necessary to update the year-end inventory account balance. However, when a periodic inventory system is used, a year-end adjusting entry is necessary to update the inventory account balance. One such method of adjusting the inventory account balance was demonstrated for Lodestone Co. in the chapter.

Another way to adjust the inventory account balance is through the closing entry process, which credits the inventory account for the beginning inventory balance and debits the inventory account for the ending inventory balance. Using this approach and the data for Steve and Becky, the closing entries are as follows (note that no cost of goods sold account is used):

Closing entries:

Sales	95,000	
Rent Revenue	6,000	
Inventory (end-of-year balance)	18,000	
Income Summary		119,000

To close the revenue accounts to Income Summary and to establish the end-of-the year inventory account balance.

Income Summary	107,775	
Inventory (beginning-of-the-year)		0
Purchases		60,000
Wage Expense		18,600
Insurance Expense		4,000
Bad Debt Expense		800
Other Expense		7,000
Interest Expense		7,875
Depreciation Expense		9,500

To close the expense accounts and the beginning-of-the-year inventory account balance to Income Summary.

The closing entries to close Income Summary to the owners' equity account(s) and to close dividends or owners' drawings are the same as those illustrated in the chapter.

Under either the adjusting entry approach or the closing entry approach of adjusting the inventory account, the ending balances in all accounts will be exactly the same. Some accountants prefer the adjusting entry approach to changing the inventory account balance because they think it is a better representation of what actually happens to the accounts. Other accountants prefer the closing entry approach to changing the inventory account balance because of its perceived ease and convenience. Either approach accomplishes the same thing.

APPENDIX B: Worksheets

A worksheet is an optional tool that can be used to organize the steps in the accounting cycle from the trial balance to the point where financial statements are prepared. Worksheets are columnar in format and have at least five sets of columns, with each set having a debit column and a credit column. The worksheet begins with the trial balance in the first set of columns (see Exhibit 2-2). The adjusting entries obtained are recorded in the second set of columns. The identifying letters in the worksheet that follows identify the source of the particular adjusting entry in the chapter. The adjusted trial balance is in the third set of columns, obtained by adding or subtracting the adjusting entry amounts to/from the trial balance amounts (compare to Exhibit 2-4). Then, the adjusted trial balance numbers are placed either in the income statement columns or the balance sheet columns, as appropriate.

The Steve and Becky example is also used in the following worksheet example to illustrate the worksheet procedures. Carefully review the worksheet to see how each of these steps is done. Note that every number in the adjusted trial balance is extended to either the income statement columns or to the balance sheet columns, and that a debit/credit amount in the adjusted trial balance retains that balance in the other column. Net income is computed by totaling the numbers in the income statement columns and subtracting the total of the debit column from the total of the credit column. The net income is placed in the income statement columns so that the debit total equals the credit total, and it is also placed in the opposite column in the balance sheet set of columns. In this way, the debit column of the balance sheet also equals the credit column of the balance sheet.

The worksheet can be modified or expanded to include accounts other than those used here, so as to accommodate different businesses. Such modifications or expansions could include income taxes. Following the completion of the worksheet, the amounts in the income statement set of columns are then used to prepare the income statement, and the numbers in the balance sheet set of columns are used to prepare the balance sheet. The amounts in the income statement columns and the amount for dividends can then be used to prepare the closing entries.

Steve and Becky Corporation
Ten-Column Worksheet
For the Year Ended December 31, 2004

	Trial Balance Dr.	Trial Balance Cr.	Adjustments Dr.	Adjustments Cr.	Adj. Trial Bal. Dr.	Adj. Trial Bal. Cr.	Income State. Dr.	Income State. Cr.	Balance Sheet Dr.	Balance Sheet Cr.
Cash	22,000				22,000				22,000	
Accts. Receivable	20,000			150 (f)	19,850				19,850	
Allowance for Doubt. Accounts			150 (f)	800 (e)		650				650
Inventory	18,000				18,000				18,000	
Prepaid Insurance	6,000			4,000 (a)	2,000				2,000	
Furn. & Fixtures	25,000				25,000				25,000	
Accum. Depreciation				2,500 (b)		2,500				2,500
Automobile	20,000				20,000				20,000	
Accum. Depreciation				4,000 (b)		4,000				4,000
Building	160,000				160,000				160,000	
Accum. Depreciation				3,000 (b)		3,000				3,000
Land	40,000				40,000				40,000	
Accounts Payable		8,000				8,000				8,000
Interest Payable				7,875 (c)		7,875				7,875
Wages Payable				600 (d)		600				600
Mortgage Payable		175,000				175,000				175,000
Common Stock		72,500				72,500				72,500
Paid-In Capital in Excess of Par		22,500				22,500				22,500
Sales		95,000				95,000		95,000		
Rent Revenue		6,000				6,000		6,000		
Cost of Goods Sold	42,000				42,000		42,000			
Wage Expense	18,000		600 (d)		18,600		18,600			
Insurance Expense			4,000 (a)		4,000		4,000			
Bad Debt Expense			800 (e)		800		800			
Other Expenses	7,000				7,000		7,000			
Interest Expense			7,875 (c)		7,875		7,875			
Depre. Expense			9,500 (b)		9,500		9,500			
Dividends	1,000				1,000				1,000	
Subtotals	379,000	379,000	22,925	22,925	397,625	397,625	89,775	101,000	307,850	296,625
Net Income							11,225			11,225
Totals	379,000	379,000	22,925	22,925	397,625	397,625	101,000	101,000	307,850	307,850

APPENDIX C: Multiple-Step Format—Published Financial Statement

IVAX Corporation
Consolidated Statements of Operations
(in thousands except per share amounts)

	For the Years Ended December 31,		
	1998	1997	1996
Net revenues	$637,923	$ 594,286	$ 658,745
Cost of sales	396,752	479,982	496,776
Gross profit	$241,171	$ 114,304	$ 161,969
Operating expenses:			
Selling	$ 79,508	$ 100,220	$ 98,770
General and administrative	88,434	116,185	111,122
Research and development	48,615	53,409	51,729
Amortization of intangible assets	3,673	3,760	4,594
Restructuring costs and asset writedowns	12,222	38,088	69,073
Merger expenses	—	2,343	557
Total operating expenses	$232,452	$ 314,005	$ 335,845
Other income:			
Interest income	$ 11,972	$ 5,738	$ 1,126
Interest expense	(6,857)	(14,685)	(15,996)
Other income, net	20,427	53,366	6,623
Total other income	$ 25,542	$ 44,419	$ (8,247)
Income from continuing operations before income taxes and minority interest	$ 34,261	$(155,282)	$(182,123)
Provision (benefit) for income taxes	10,047	(60,166)	(52,488)
Minority interest	403	(4,086)	(5,354)
Income (loss) from continuing operations	$ 24,617	$ (99,202)	$(134,989)
Discontinued operations:			
Income (loss) from discontinued operations, net of tax	—	(21,324)	(23,690)
Gain on sale of discontinued operations, net of tax	48,904	12,623	—
Income before extraordinary item and cumulative effect of accounting change	$ 73,521	$(107,903)	$(158,679)
Extraordinary item:			
Gains (losses) on extinguishment of debt, net of a tax benefit of $1,382 in 1996	1,121	(2,137)	(2,073)
Cumulative effect of a change in accounting principle, net of a tax benefit of $1,295 in 1997	(3,048)	(2,882)	—
Net income (loss)	$ 71,594	$(112,922)	$(160,752)
Basic earnings (loss) per common share:			
Continuing operations	$ 0.21	$ (1.81)	$ (1.12)
Discontinued operations	0.41	(0.07)	(0.19)
Extraordinary item	0.01	(0.02)	(0.02)
Cumulative effect of accounting change	(0.03)	(0.02)	—
Net income	$ 0.60	$ (1.92)	$ (1.33)

APPENDIX D

Financial Statements from Another Country

BG Group PLC
Income Statement

for the year ended 31 December

	2001 Total £m	2001 Exceptional Items £m	2001 Business Performance £m	2000 Total £m	2000 Discontinued Operations £m	2000 Continuing Total £m	2000 Continuing Exceptional Items £m	2000 Continuing Business Performance £m
Turnover	2,672	34	2,638	4,769	2,427	2,342	—	2,342
Operating costs	(1,945)	—	(1,945)	(3,764)	(1,633)	(2,101)	(314)	(1,787)
Group operating profit	727	34	693	1,005	764	241	(314)	555
Share of operating profits in joint ventures and associated undertakings	140	—	140	132	(1)	133	—	133
Total operating profit	867	34	833	1,137	763	374	(314)	688
Profit (loss) on disposals	98	98	—	276	(4)	280	280	—
Profit on ordinary activities	965	132	833	1,413	759	654	(34)	688
Net interest	(63)	17	(80)	(459)	(379)	(80)	—	(80)
Profit before taxation	902	149	753	954	380	574	(34)	608
Tax	(287)	(28)	(259)	(281)	(167)	(114)	63	(177)
Profit after taxation	615	121	494	673	213	460	29	431
Minority interests	(29)	—	(29)	(19)	—	(19)	—	(19)
Profit for the financial year	586	121	465	654	213	441	29	412
Dividends	(105)	—	(105)	(223)	(122)	(101)	—	(101)
Transfer to reserves	481	121	360	431	91	340	29	311
Earnings per ordinary share:								
Basic	16.7p	3.4p	13.3p	18.8p	6.1p	12.7p	0.9p	11.8p
Diluted	16.7p	3.4p	13.3p	18.8p	6.1p	12.9p	0.9p	11.8p
Dividends per ordinary share:								
Interim	1.5p		4.95p					
Final	1.5p		1.45p					

BG Group PLC
Balance Sheet

as at 31 December	The Group		The Company	
	2001 £m	2000 £m	2001 £m	2000 £m
Fixed Assets				
Intangible assets	798	876	—	—
Tangible assets	3,707	3,863	—	—
Investments in subsidiary undertakings			2,269	2,269
Investments in joint ventures:			—	—
Share of gross assets	639	618		
Share of gross liabilities	(494)	(453)		
	145	165		
Loans	150	150		
Investments in associated undertakings:			—	—
Share of net assets	245	220		
Loans	109	14		
Other investments	14	13		
	5,168	5,301	2,269	2,269
Current assets				
Stocks	98	99	—	—
Debtors: amounts falling due within one year	616	522	31	14
Debtors: amounts falling due after more than one year	125	95	16	15
	741	617	47	29
Investments	326	129	—	—
Cash at bank and in hand	92	65	4	—
	1,257	910	51	29
Creditors: amounts falling due within one year				
Borrowings	(493)	(321)	—	—
Other creditors	(847)	(83)	(266)	(545)
	(1,340)	(1,152)	(266)	(545)
Net current liabilities	(83)	(242)	(215)	(516)
Total assets less current liabilities	5,085	5,059	2,054	1,753
Creditors: amounts falling due after more than one year				
Borrowings	(463)	(233)	—	—
Other creditors	(228)	(257)	—	—
	(691)	(490)	—	—
Provisions for liabilities and charges	(864)	(1,211)	(52)	(50)
	3,530	3,358	2,002	1,703
Capital and reserves				
Called up equity share capital	353	353	353	353
Share premium account	42	42	42	42
Other reserves	1,702	1,702	756	756
Profit and loss account	1,129	854	851	552
Joint ventures and associated undertakings	180	207		
BG shareholders' funds	3,406	3,158	2,002	1,703
Minority shareholders' interest	124	200		
	3,530	3,358	2,002	1,703

Appendix E

Reversing Entries

When reversing entries are used, they are prepared at the beginning of the year and are the first thing entered in the books for the year. Preparing them is optional, but because they expedite the accounting process for the coming year, they should be prepared. Accounting information systems are designed to record similar transactions in the same manner, and if these selected adjusting entries are not reversed, that consistency in recording does not occur. Reversing entries are prepared by taking selected adjusting entries and turning the debits of the adjusting entries into credits and turning the credits of the adjusting entries into debits. Thus, reversing entries reverse the effects of certain adjusting entries.

In the Steve and Becky example in the chapter, an adjusting entry was made at year-end to record wages expense and an associated payable for $600, as follows:

Wages Expense	600	
Wages Payable		600

Now, suppose that Steve and Becky's accounting information system is designed to record the payment of wages by debiting Wages Expense and crediting Cash. Then, if a reversing entry is not prepared, when wages are first paid in January, either the accountant would have to override the accounting system (which is not usually a good thing to do) or an error would occur. To illustrate, the T-accounts below show Wages Expense and Wages Payable as they would appear on January 1, after appropriate closing entries, and assuming that reversing entries were not prepared.

If the accounting information system was allowed to record the normal entry for

Wages Expense		Wages Payable	
Jan. 1 Balance 0		600	Jan. 1 Balance

recording the payment of wages, the following entry would be prepared:

Wages Expense	1,000	
Cash		1,000

But this entry results in two errors: (1) overstating wages expense for the year, which should be $400, not $1,000, and (2) still showing that $600 is payable when it is not.

One way to record the payment of wages so that these errors do not occur is to let the accountant override the accounting system and prepare the following entry:

Wages Expense	400	
Wages Payable	600	
Cash		1,000

To record the payroll entry for the first pay period of the new fiscal year. This entry requires reversing the amount previously accrued at the prior year-end, recognizing the appropriate amount of wage expense for the current fiscal year, and paying the entire amount.

Now, the wages expense for the new year are properly stated and the wages payable account correctly shows that nothing is owing. However, situations in which the accounting system is overridden should be kept to a minimum; there is no purpose for controls in the accounting system if they are allowed to be overridden.

A better way to avoid making the errors previously mentioned without overriding the accounting system is to prepare reversing entries. In the wages expense example, the reversing entry is as follows:

Reversing entry:
Wages Payable   600
    Wages Expense   600
To reverse the prior year's adjusting entry for wages expense.

After preparing this reversing entry and posting it, the wages expense and wages payable accounts appear as follows:

Wages Expense				Wages Payable			
Jan. 1 Bal.	0					600	Jan. 1 Bal.
		600	Reversing entry		600		
		600	New Jan. 1 Bal.			0	
Pay wages	1,000						
Bal.	400						

Subsequently, when wages are paid, the normal journal entry is recorded in which Wages Expense is debited for $1,000 and Cash is credited for $1,000. This entry results in the balance in Wages Expense being a $400 debit and in Wages Payable being zero. Thus, the accounting for the subsequent year has been expedited by preparing a reversing entry for wages expense.

Since only selected adjusting entries of the prior year are reversed, the question is: What adjusting journal entries should be reversed? Earlier, it was mentioned that adjusting entries are of three types: prepayments, deferrals, and accruals, and the following specific examples were illustrated in this chapter:

Prepayment Example	Deferral Example	Accrual Examples
Insurance	Depreciation	Interest expense (but also applicable to interest revenue)
		Wages expense
		Bad debt expense
		Cash-to-accrual:
		Accounts receivable
		Accounts payable
		Inventory (periodic inventory system)

An important key to learning which adjusting entries should be reversed is to remember that *reversing entries are intended to expedite the accounting process for the new year.* Therefore, *adjusting entries for deferrals are never reversed.* To explain, assets such as furniture and fixtures, automobiles, and buildings will provide benefits for many years, but eventually all those assets lose their usefulness. Therefore, the costs of all long-term assets eventually end up on the income statement. This is the purpose of depreciation—to move a portion of the cost each period from the balance sheet to the income statement. Reversing the depreciation entry would move the cost from the income statement back to the balance sheet, which would not expedite the accounting process. So, adjusting journal entries that record depreciation expense are never reversed.

The same logic can be applied to understanding which prepayments to reverse. As with the cost of long-lived assets, such as furniture and automobiles, the costs of all prepayments also eventually end up on the income statement. However, remember that the original prepayment entry can be recorded either in the asset account or in an expense account; either way is acceptable. Then, at year-end, the adjusting entry allocates the amount between the balance sheet and the income statement. Exhibit 2-1(A) summarizes these two ways of recording the original entries, the effect of the related adjusting entries, and which adjusting entries should be reversed.

EXHIBIT 2-1(A)

Reversing Entries for Prepayments

Original Entry Recorded	Effect of the Adjusting Entry	Reversing Entry
In an asset account as follows:	Moves an amount to the income statement:	Do not reverse this type of adjusting entry. To do so moves the amount back to the balance sheet.

Prepaid Insurance   XX
   Cash   XX
	Insurance Expense XX
	   Prepaid Insurance XX	

In an expense account as follows:	Moves an amount to the balance sheet:	Do reverse this type of adjusting entry because doing so moves the amount back to the income statement, which is eventually where it will end up.

Insurance Expense   XX
   Cash   XX
	Prepaid Insurance XX
	   Insurance Expense XX	

Regarding whether to reverse adjusting entries of the accrual type, *never reverse adjusting entries that convert the books to an accrual basis.* Accrual-based accounting is considered to be the best all-around accounting system, and after having converted the books to this better method, there is no need to reverse this effect. For the rest of the accrual-type adjusting entries, consider whether there will be future cash flows. Thus, there will be future cash flows for wages when the wages are paid. Also, there will be future cash flows for interest when the interest is paid. But there will not be future cash flows for the bad debt expense. As illustrated in the chapter, when those accounts that are uncollectible are identified, they are written off by debiting the allowance account and crediting the receivable account—no cash flow is involved. *Reverse all accrual-type adjusting entries where there will be future cash flows, and do not reverse those where there will not be future cash flows.*

Questions

1. What is the purpose of an accounting information system? What are the elements, or building blocks, that comprise an accounting information system?

2. Describe some advantages that an automated accounting information system has over a manual accounting information system.

3. Which of the following events is captured by an accounting information system?
   a. Selling inventory where the customer has 30 days to pay.
   b. Interviewing a prospective employee.
   c. Entering into an agreement to purchase goods from another company, ensuring a continuous supply of product.
   d. Declaring a dividend that is to be paid in cash.
   e. The company's vice president of finance retires.
   f. The U.S. Federal Reserve raises interest rates.

4. Describe the differences in the owners' equity accounts among a proprietorship, a partnership, and a corporation.

5. Design a chart of accounts that could be used by a plumbing business operated as a proprietorship. This chart of accounts should include all asset, liability, revenue, expense, and other accounts—appropriately grouped and numbered—that a plumbing business might need to record their ongoing and peripheral activities.

6. Design a chart of accounts that could be used by a not-for-profit nursing home organized as a partnership having three partners. This chart of accounts should include all asset, liability, revenue, expense, and other accounts—appropriately grouped and numbered—that a nursing home might need to record their on-going and peripheral activities.

7. Explain the difference between "real" and "nominal" accounts.

8. Which of the following accounts are permanent, and which are temporary?
   a. Salaries Expense
   b. Unearned Revenue
   c. Retained Earnings
   d. Accumulated Depreciation
   e. Sales Returns
   f. Cost of Goods Sold
   g. Dividends
   h. Cash

9. Explain the concept of an account's "normal" balance. What are the normal balances of (a) assets, (b) liabilities, (c) stockholders' equity, (d) revenues, (e) expenses, (f) gains, and (g) losses?

10. Review the basic steps in recording transactions.

11. Is the following statement true or false: "The preparation of a trial balance where debits equal credits ensures that clerical errors have not been made in recording transactions"? Explain your answer.

12. What is the meaning of an "accrual"? Provide an example. What is the meaning of a "deferral"? Provide an example.

13. Explain how the cost of goods sold is determined under the perpetual inventory system and under a periodic inventory system.

14. What is the journal entry to record a purchase of inventory for a company using the periodic inventory system?

15. a. Indicate which of the following items would likely need to be adjusted at the end of the reporting period, and indicate the name of the other account affected if an adjusting entry is necessary.
   (1) Prepaid Rent
   (2) Interest on Long-Term Debt
   (3) Cash
   (4) Unearned Revenue
   (5) Depreciation Expense
   (6) Accounts Payable
   (7) Land
   (8) Supplies on Hand
   (9) Salaries Expense

   b. From your answers to the items (1) through (9) above, what is the distinguishing factor between the items that need adjusting entries and the items that do not?

16. A company's insurance bill arrives on February 1, 2004. The amount owed, which is paid by the company, is $15,000 and covers the period from March 1 through August 31 of the current year. The company's fiscal year ends on December 31.
    a. Conceptually, what journal entry should be made to record the payment for the insurance?
    b. Practically, what journal entry would be more expedient for the company to make for the payment of the insurance?
    c. If the conceptual journal entry differs from the expedient journal entry, how would the year-end financial statements differ if appropriate adjusting entries are prepared under either alternative?

17. What is the purpose of closing entries?

18. a. Jumping Junipers, Inc., obtained debt financing from Lakeside Financing by signing a 10-year $1,000,000 note bearing interest at 9% on September 1, 2004. Semiannual interest payments are required every March 1 and September 1. When preparing the annual financial statements on December 31, 2004, what adjusting entry must be made to record the effects of this financing transaction?
    b. Appendix. If Jumping Junipers follows the practice of reversing adjusting entries, should this adjusting entry be reversed?

19. Which trial balance likely will have the most number of accounts on it: (a) preadjusted trial balance, (b) an adjusted trial balance, or (c) a postclosing trial balance? Which trial balance will likely have the least number of accounts on it?

20. Distinguish between a single-step income statement and a multiple-step income statement.

21. What are the primary categories of the income statement?

22. In which categories of the income statement are income taxes presented?

23. Fitzer Corp. had 100,000 shares of stock on January 1, 2004, (the beginning of its fiscal year) and issued 20,000 additional shares on July 1, 2004. The company's net income for the year was $200,000. Calculate Fitzer Corp.'s EPS for the 2004 fiscal year.

24. Provide a definition for current assets and current liabilities.

25. Which of the following items would be classified in a current category (i.e., either Current assets or Current liabilities) on a balance sheet?
    a. Accounts receivable
    b. Inventory
    c. Debt due in six months, where the company's operating cycle is three months
    d. A certificate-of-deposit that matures in three years
    e. An investment in stock of another company, where it is the company's intent to sell the securities within six months
    f. Equipment, used by the company, that has a 5-year life
    g. Land owned by a real estate company whose intent is to sell it
    h. Taxes payable

26. Identify and explain the three characteristics that assets must have to be classified as Property, Plant, and Equipment.

27. What is the primary difference between fixed assets and intangible assets?

28. The following is a list of accounts drawn from the financial statements exhibited in Appendix D that were prepared for a company headquartered in the United Kingdom. Indicate the U.S. terminology that corresponds with each account.

a. Provision for depreciation
b. Turnover
c. Share premium account
d. Creditors due within one year
e. Stocks
f. Debtors
g. Profit and loss account
h. Share capital

29. (Appendix) What is the purpose of reversing entries? Why are reversing entries optional? Discuss the advantages of preparing reversing entries.

30. (Appendix) If a company follows the practice of making reversing entries, which of the following accounts that were adjusted at the end of the period should be reversed?
a. Prepaid Rent
b. Interest Incurred on Long-Term Debt
c. Unearned Revenue
d. Depreciation Expense
e. Supplies on Hand
f. Salaries Expense

Exercises

Exercise 2-1: Analyzing Financial Statement Effects of Transactions. Complete the following table, showing how each of the transactions affect the balance sheet and income statement elements. Use I if the transaction increases the element, D if the transaction decreases the element, and NE if the transaction has no effect. Remember that transactions have a dual effect on the balance sheet equation, $A = L + OE$.

		Assets	Liabilities	Owners' Equity	Revenues & Gains	Expenses & Losses
a.	Issuing common stock for cash					
b.	Purchasing equipment on account					
c.	Depreciating equipment used in operations					
d.	Purchasing inventory with cash					
e.	Selling inventory on account, where the selling price is greater than the cost					
f.	Collecting cash on a previous credit sale					
g.	Paying salaries					
h.	Purchasing supplies for cash and debiting the amount to Supplies Expense					
i.	Selling equipment for cash in an amount greater than its book value					
j.	Declaring dividends					
k.	Paying utilities that previously had not been accrued					

Exercise 2-2: Information about Accounts. Indicate whether the following accounts are increased or decreased with a debit, normally have a debit or credit balance, and are real or nominal.

(1) Accounts Receivable	(11) Insurance Expense
(2) Purchases	(12) Investments
(3) Inventory	(13) Sales Returns and Allowances
(4) Land	(14) Service Revenue
(5) Retained Earnings	(15) Prepaid Rent
(6) Dividends	(16) Unearned Fees
(7) Loss on Sale of Fixed Assets	(17) Goodwill
(8) Amortization Expense	(18) Common Stock
(9) Sales	(19) Paid-In Capital in Excess of Par
(10) Cost of Goods Sold	

Exercise 2-3: Journal Entries and Trial Balance. Upon completing their graduate degrees from a prestigious Texas university, Tom and Frank established a consulting agency by forming a partnership called Business Solutions. The following events and transactions were some of those that occurred by July 31, which is their fiscal year-end.

June 15: Tom contributed $50,000 cash to the business, and Frank contributed $10,000 cash and furniture and equipment worth $10,000.

    20: Additional furniture and equipment costing $15,000 was purchased by paying $3,000 down and signing a lease that requires payments of $554 per month. The lease has an interest rate of 10% per year.

    30: Three computers were purchased for $1,200 each. A down payment of $500 was paid, and the balance is due in three months.

July   1: Rent for office space for the next six months in the amount of $3,000 was paid.

    8: A secretary was hired at $310 per week. She will be paid twice a month.

    12: A client was billed $2,500 for services rendered.

    16: Cash of $2,000 was received for services to be rendered next month.

    20: A lease payment on the furniture and equipment was paid.

    22: Paid the secretary's salary for the past two weeks.

    29: Received $1,500 in partial payment from the client billed on July 12.

1. Prepare the journal entries for the preceding transactions.
2. Prepare a trial balance.
3. Indicate which of the accounts in the trial balance, if any, may need to be adjusted prior to preparing the financial statements.

Exercise 2-4: Journal Entries and Trial Balance. Bob and Jerry formed a business, called Bob & Jerry's Inc., to sell office equipment. The company received state authorization to issue one million shares of $10 par value common stock. The following transactions occurred during the company's initial month of operations:

a. Issued 7,800 shares of common stock for $25 per share.

b. For services rendered in organizing the corporation, Bob and Jerry each received 1,000 shares of stock. (Debit Organization Expenses.)

c. Rented office and retail floor space, paying $3,500 for the first month.

d. Purchased $3,000 of equipment and $390 of office supplies, which will be used in operating the store, and paid cash.

e. Purchased office equipment that is to be resold for $15,600 on account.
f. Sold one-third of the merchandise on account for $7,540. Bob and Jerry use a perpetual inventory system.
g. Collections on accounts receivable totaled $4,250.
h. Paid salaries for the first month in the amount of $3,400. Of this amount, $800 was paid to a secretary/receptionist, and the rest was paid equally to Bob and Jerry.
i. Paid $8,000 to purchase merchandise that will be resold.

1. Prepare journal entries for the above transactions.
2. Prepare a trial balance.
3. Which of the accounts on the trial balance would need to be adjusted before financial statements are prepared?

Exercise 2-5: Adjusting a Trial Balance. The following trial balance does not balance.

Trial Balance
December 31, 2004

	Debit	Credit
Cash	$14,920	
Accounts Receivable	13,600	
Supplies	8,700	
Accounts Payable		$ 3,420
Unearned Service Revenue		4,280
Common Stock		15,000
Retained Earnings		3,000
Service Revenue		14,445
Wages Expense	4,500	
Rent Expense	500	
	$42,220	$40,145

Upon review, the following errors are found:

a. Transposition errors were made in the accounts payable account; the correct amount is $4,320.
b. A rent payment of $500 was debited to Rent Expense and debited to Cash.
c. Services were rendered in the amount of $750. Accounts Receivable was debited for $750, and Service Revenue was credited for $75.
d. A debit posting to Wages Expense for $500 was omitted.
e. $250 of the balance in Unearned Service Revenue was earned prior to December.

Prepare a corrected trial balance from the given information.

Exercise 2-6: Adjusting Entries. Prepare the necessary adjusting entries, using the following information. Assume that the company's year-end is December 31, 2005.

a. The prepaid rent account has a $3,300 balance, which occurred when a check was drawn on September 1 in payment for six-months' use of the building.

   b. A one-year insurance policy was acquired on November 1, 2005, for $2,000. The trial balance shows that the amount was debited to Insurance Expense.

   c. Interest from a bond investment is received each February 1. The $10,000 bond has an annual interest rate of 8%.

   d. The trial balance shows that the supplies account has a balance of $4,400, but a physical count shows only $2,230 on hand.

   e. Interest of $450 needs to be accrued on notes payable.

   f. Unearned Rent Revenue has a credit balance of $2,400, and at December 31, one-third of the amount has been earned.

   g. Equipment that was purchased on April 30, 1999, for $7,728 is being depreciated using an estimated life of seven years and no residual value. Depreciation through 2004 has been recorded.

Exercise 2-7: Cash and Accrual Basis. Assuming that 2003 is the first year for a business, the following information is provided:

	2003	2004
Total sales	$320,000	$395,000
Cash receipts from sales	243,000	347,000
Total expenses	280,000	341,000
Cash disbursements for expenses	205,000	353,000

Using only the given information, answer the following questions:

1. Using the accrual basis, what amounts would be reported on the financial statements at December 31, 2003, and December 31, 2004, for Revenues, Expenses, Accounts Receivable, Accounts Payable, and Cash?
2. Using the cash basis, what amounts would be reported on the financial statements at December 31, 2003, and December 31, 2004, for Revenues, Expenses, Accounts Receivable, Accounts Payable, and Cash?
3. What is net income for 2003 and 2004, using the accrual basis?
4. What is net income for 2003 and 2004, using the cash basis?
5. Assuming that the books were kept on the cash basis, prepare the adjusting entry(ies) necessary to switch from the cash basis to the accrual basis at January 1, 2004.
6. Assuming the books were kept on the cash basis through 2004, and independent of your answer to transaction #5, prepare the adjusting entry(ies) to switch from the cash basis to the accrual basis at December 31, 2004.

Exercise 2-8: Adjusting Entries. The trial balance for Mountain West, Inc., for December 31, 2003, included the following account balances, among others:

	Debit	Credit
Building	$210,000	
Accumulated Depreciation of Buildings		$ 29,250
Accounts Receivable	34,000	
Allowance for Doubtful Accounts		540
Bonds Payable		100,000
Service Revenue		148,000
Salaries Expense	64,230	
Interest Expense	4,000	

1. Prepare the adjusting entries based on the following information.
   a. The building has an estimated life of 18 years and a residual value of $48,000.
   b. Uncollectible accounts are estimated to be 2.5% of the accounts receivable balance.
   c. Bonds payable were issued on April 1, 2003. The annual interest rate is 8%, and interest payments are made on October 1 and April 1.
   d. Service amounting to $5,700 was still to be provided in January. The cash had been received, and the amount had been credited to Service Revenue.
   e. Accrued but unpaid salaries are $3,890.
2. What are the adjusted amounts in the accounts?
3. (Appendix) Indicate which, if any, of the adjusting entries should be reversed.

Exercise 2-9: Adjusting Entries. Based on the following information, prepare the necessary adjusting entries for the year ended December 31, 2004.

a. The supplies account balance is $3,200. A count reveals supplies on hand total $520.
b. December 31, 2004, was a Thursday. Employees are paid weekly for hours worked Monday through Friday. A typical weekly payroll amounts to $7,000.
c. Prepaid Rent has a balance of $36,200, which consists of the following payments for various stores:

Store	Date Paid	Coverage	Cost
1	April 1, 2004	5 months	$ 6,000
2	Nov. 30, 2004	6 months	11,000
3	July 31, 2004	12 months	19,200

Exercise 2-10: Closing Entries. Based on the following trial balance, prepare the four necessary closing entries.

	Debit	Credit
Cash	$ 46,000	
Accounts Receivable	82,000	
Allowance for Doubtful Accounts		$ 2,200
Prepaid Rent	6,000	
Plant and Equipment	118,000	
Accumulated Depreciation		31,000
Accounts Payable		24,500
Notes Payable		90,000
Common Stock		40,000
Retained Earnings		29,900
Dividends	30,000	
Earned Fees		190,000
Rent Expense	24,000	
Insurance Expense	14,500	
Wages Expense	72,000	
Bad Debt Expense	3,400	
Depreciation Expense	11,700	
	$407,600	$407,600

Exercise 2-11: Inventory Accounts. The following information was extracted, in summarized form, from the books of a local retailer:

Inventory	$ 17,900	Purchase Discounts	$ 2,300
Sales	579,540	Purchase Returns	7,430
Sales Returns	5,600	Administrative Expenses	34,660
Miscellaneous Revenue	43,820	Selling Expenses	29,540
Purchases	411,080	Retained Earnings	73,270

Also, a year-end count of the inventory showed an amount on hand of $15,300.

Assuming that the company uses the adjusting entry process to change the inventory account balance, prepare that adjusting entry and then prepare the necessary closing entries.

Exercise 2-12: Income Statement Relationships. The following information is provided for Lawson & Son, Inc. Determine the missing values.

	Year			
	2001	2002	2003	2004
Sales	(a)	$1,450	$1,731	(j)
Sales Returns	101	(d)	181	211
Net Sales	1,154	(e)	(g)	1,778
Beginning Inventory	115	187	(h)	210
Purchases	655	880	892	(k)
Purchase Discounts	41	(f)	58	62
Purchase Returns	98	81	67	102
Transportation In	11	15	18	20
Ending Inventory	(b)	258	210	295
Cost of Goods Sold	(c)	684	836	(l)
Gross Profit	699	707	(i)	1,017

Exercise 2-13: Financial Statement Effects of Errors. Indicate how each of the following errors would affect the selected financial statement items at the end of the reporting year. (O = the error causes an overstatement; U = the error causes an understatement; and NE = the error has no effect.)

Error	Net Income	Total Assets	Total Liabilities	Total Equity
1. Sales were not recorded.				
2. Interest payable was not accrued.				
3. Purchases on account are recorded as cash purchases.				
4. All purchases of supplies are debited to Supplies Expense, no adjusting entry was prepared, and the amount of unused supplies increased during the year.				
5. The adjusting entry for depreciation is not recorded.				
6. Shipping costs for inventory are expensed when incurred, and inventory increased during the period.				
7. No adjustment is made at the end of the period to accrue income taxes.				

Exercise 2-14: Weighted-Average Number of Shares. The Homestead Company began operations several years ago, financing most of its start-up capital and subsequent expansion through issuing common stock. At the beginning of the current year, there were 200,000 shares outstanding, and during the year, Homestead entered into the following transactions that affected the number of common shares outstanding:

April 1: Issued 40,000 shares of stock at $25 per share.

June 30: Issued 30,000 shares of stock at $28 per share.

December 2: Issued 36,000 shares of stock at $29 per share.

Determine the weighted-average number of shares that Homestead should use in computing earnings per share.

Exercise 2-15: Weighted-Average Number of Shares. Dynasty Restaurants operates a chain of Chinese restaurants along the west coast. They were organized in 1995 and immediately issued one million shares of $1 par value common stock. In 1997, another million shares were issued, and in 2000, another two million shares were issued. Now, in 2004, the following transactions have occurred:

February 1: Reacquired 400,000 shares of stock in a move to support the stock price, which had been experiencing a gradual downward trend in price.

April 29: Granted employees the opportunity to purchase shares of stock at specified dates, and immediately reacquired 250,000 shares that would be used to honor that agreement.

September 1: Issued 500,000 shares of stock to the owners of a competing restaurant chain as compensation for the net assets of that corporation.

November 1: The first date came when the employees could buy shares of stock, and employees purchased 50,000 shares.

Determine the weighted-average number of shares that Dynasty should use in computing earnings per share.

Exercise 2-16: Earnings per Share. The Kazan Company is completing its year-end financial reports and is seeking advice on properly presenting earnings per share. Selected information from the income statement, along with other pertinent data, are as follows:

Income before extraordinary items	$100,000
Extraordinary items	(25,000)
Net income	$ 75,000

In addition to 80,000 shares of common stock outstanding, Kazan also has 2,000 shares of $100 par value, 6% noncumulative preferred stock outstanding, which were issued two years previously. However, no dividends were declared or paid during the year to either the preferred or common stockholders.

1. Show how earnings per share should be presented for the current year.
2. Show how earnings per share should be presented for the current year, assuming that the preferred stock is cumulative.

Exercise 2-17: Income Statement. Use the following information to prepare a single-step income statement, including intraperiod tax allocation and earnings per share presentation.

Brinton Company
At December 31, 2004

Sales	$800,000
Cost of goods sold	$540,000
Operating expenses	$160,000
Gain on sale of securities	$20,000
Interest expense	$14,000
Loss due to hurricane damage (the damage was incurred in North Dakota)	$78,000
Extraordinary gain from foreign government expropriating assets	$9,000
Weighted-average number of shares	20,000
Tax rate	30%
Preferred dividends declared for the current year, but not paid	$10,000
Preferred dividends paid this year that were declared in the last fiscal year	$20,000

Exercise 2-18: Classifying Assets. A company maintains a stock of tuxedos, shoes, and related clothing items for the purpose of renting them to individuals. Every two years, the store buys new clothing items as replacements. At the end of each fiscal year, a complete inventory is taken of all items. What is the appropriate accounting classification of the clothing? Discuss when the cost of the clothing is recognized as an expense, and prepare the appropriate journal entry to do so.

Exercise 2-19: Income Statement. The Hard-Luck Company just completed its second year of operations, and again, the balance in Cash is negligible. Prospects are bleak, and an appointment has been made with officials at the bank to apply for another loan. In preparing for that meeting, the accountant prepared the following information from which he was going to prepare the income statement. However, the next day, he became ill and has not been to work since. Tomorrow is the meeting with the bank. You (an accounting intern) have been charged to prepare the income statement from the information the accountant had extracted previously.

1. Using the following information, prepare a multiple-step income statement.
2. From the multiple-step income statement, prepare a single-step income statement.

Accounts with credit balances:	
Sales	$120,000
Purchase Returns	5,000
Gain on Sale of Investments	12,000
Interest Income	2,000
Accounts with debit balances:	
Purchases	$ 60,000
Freight-In	3,000
Administrative Expenses	23,000
Selling Expenses	18,000
Tornado Loss (unusual and infrequent)	22,000
Sales Returns	4,000
Interest Expense	8,000

Other information:

Inventory, January 1, 2004	$ 10,000
Inventory, December 31, 2004	$ 13,000
Tax rate	30%
Number of shares of common stock outstanding	100,000

Exercise 2-20: Income Statement. Following the war, two brothers decided to use their savings and open a high-quality retail store of men's clothing. The following data were taken from the adjusted trial balance of Mr. R's Men's Wear for the year ended December 31, 2004:

Inventory, January 1, 2004	$ 69,000
Purchases	124,100
Sales Revenue	481,000
Purchase Returns	3,400
Common Stock ($10 par)	220,000
Depreciation Expense (60% administrative and 40% selling)	55,000
Rent Revenue	12,000
Interest Expense	16,000
Selling Expenses	108,000
General and Administrative Expenses	98,000
Loss on Sale of an Operating Asset	8,000
Gain on Sale of Investments	4,000
Extraordinary Gain	5,000
Merchandise Inventory, December 31, 2004	72,000
Reorganizing Charge	24,000
Income Tax Expense	?

For many years, the brothers had operated Mr. R's as a partnership; but because of changes in the legal environment, it was decided in August 2003 to reorganize as a corporation. Accordingly, lawyers and CPAs were hired to prepare the necessary legal documents, audit the books, and do all else necessary for the change. Following the reorganizing, each partner received 20,000 shares of common stock. The costs Mr. R's Men's Wear incurred were accumulated in the account called Reorganizing Charge.

1. Assuming an income tax rate on all items of 40%, prepare a multiple-step income statement.
2. From the multiple-step income statement, prepare a single-step income statement.

Exercise 2-21: Classified Balance Sheet. Use the code letters below to indicate for each balance sheet item the usual classification in which it is reported on the balance sheet.

A	Current assets	G	Long-term liabilities
B	Investments and funds	H	Capital stock
C	Property, plant, and equipment	I	Paid-in capital in excess of par
D	Intangible assets	J	Retained earnings
E	Other assets	K	Note reported on the balance sheet
F	Current liabilities		

Description	Code	Description	Code
Land held for speculation		Natural resource	
Accumulated depreciation		Paid-in capital in excess of par	
Accounts receivable on installment sales that will be collected over three years. The company does not normally sell on the installment basis.		Bonds due in six months that will be paid from an amount accumulated in a fund to pay it off. Thus, no current asset will be used.	
Cash to be used to retire bonds that mature in 10 years		Revenue earned but not collected	
		Bonds due in six months that will be paid from current assets	
Copyright			
Current maturity of long-term debt		Revenue collected in advance (concentrate on the noncash account)	
Damaged inventory that will not be sold in the normal course of business		Deficit	
		Goodwill	
Accrued salaries payable		Idle equipment—not being used currently, but not to be sold either	
Discount on bonds payable			
Franchise		Premium on bonds payable	

Exercise 2-22: Classified Balance Sheet. The following accounts and balances pertain to Duensen Corporation on December 31, 2004:

Accounts Payable	$ 50,000
Accounts Receivable	72,000
Accumulated Depletion	84,000
Accumulated Depreciation	130,000
Advances from Customers (Duensen will perform the services in 2005)	40,000
Advances to Suppliers (Duensen will receive the goods in 2005)	27,000
Allowance for Doubtful Accounts	12,000
Bonds Payable	500,000
Building	400,000
Cash	20,000
Cash Surrender Value of Life Insurance	15,000
Common Stock (no par, 500,000 shares authorized and 30,000 issued and outstanding)	150,000
Equipment	100,000
Furniture and Fixtures	75,000
Interest Payable	35,000
Investment in Common Stock of XYZ Corporation	80,000
Land	95,000
Merchandise Inventory	45,000
Note Payable (due April 2008)	40,000
Mineral Deposit	170,000
Patent	5,000
Prepaid Insurance	6,000
Salaries Payable	4,000
Retained Earnings (deficit)	?

1. Prepare a balance sheet in good form.
2. If all account balances were as shown, except that the balance in the accumulated depreciation account was $230,000, what would be the amount of the retained earnings, and how would it be presented on the balance sheet?

Exercise 2-23: Single-Step Income Statement and Classified Balance Sheet. From the following information for Cozzens Cabinets Co., prepare both a single-step income statement and a classified balance sheet for the year ended October 31, 2004. All accounts have normal balances.

Accumulated Depreciation	$ 24,000
Bonds Payable	100,000
Cash	20,000
Discount on Bonds Payable	5,000
Franchise	23,000
Building	150,000
Depreciation Expense	10,000
Land	40,000
Furniture and Fixtures	28,000
Investment Revenue	2,000
Extraordinary gain	2,500
Operating Expenses	20,000
Sales	50,000
Accounts Payable	23,000
Accounts Receivable	26,000
Long-Term Note Payable	40,000
Common Stock ($1 par value)	100,000
Deficit (as of November 1, 2003)	13,000
Income Tax Expense	6,500

Exercise 2-24: (Appendix) Reversing Entries. Prepare, where needed, the reversing entries for the following adjusting entries.

a.	Interest Expense	4,500	
	Interest Payable		4,500
b.	Depreciation Expense	11,000	
	Accumulated Depreciation		11,000
c.	Prepaid Rent	1,500	
	Rent Expense		1,500
d.	Revenue from Dues	76,000	
	Unearned Revenue from Dues		76,000
e.	Accounts Receivable	3,400	
	Revenue		3,400
f.	Interest Receivable	2,300	
	Interest Revenue		2,300

Problems

Problem 2-1: Journal Entries (Emphasis on Typical Operating Transactions). The January 1, 2004, balance sheet of Ed's Appliance Store was as follows:

Assets:			Liabilities and Stockholders' Equity:	
Cash		$ 5,000	Accounts payable	$ 3,500
Accounts receivable	$ 20,000		Salaries payable	800
Less allowance for doubtful			Interest payable	250
accounts	(2,400)	17,600	Notes payable	20,000
Interest receivable		150	Capital stock	8,000
Supplies		3,600	Paid-in capital in excess of par	32,000
Inventories		30,000	Retained earnings	31,800
Investment in bonds		5,000		
Buildings and equipment	$ 50,000			
Less accumulated depreciation	(15,000)	35,000		
Total assets		$96,350	Total liabilities and stockholders' equity	$96,350

The following summarized transactions occurred during 2004:

a. Sales on account were $200,000, and sales for cash were $80,000.
b. Collections on accounts were $189,500.
c. Paid the note payable amount plus interest of $1,000, which includes the interest payable at January 1, 2004.
d. Purchased merchandise on account at a cost of $104,000, assuming a periodic inventory system.
e. Rented a building under a five-year lease at an annual rental of $20,000 and paid the first year's rent. (Assume that the building was leased on January 1.)
f. Purchased office supplies for $1,200 cash.
g. Paid salaries totaling $40,000, which also includes the salaries accrued on December 31, 2003.
h. Purchased fixtures and equipment costing $30,000 and paid 20% down and signed a note that requires eight equal semiannual amounts of $3,000 plus interest at 8% on the unpaid balance.
i. Wrote off a customer's account of $500 as being uncollectible.
j. Paid accounts payable of $98,000.
k. A customer returned $250 of merchandise that had been sold on account.
l. Another customer returned $100 of merchandise that had been sold for cash and was granted a full refund.
m. Received $400 interest on the investment in bonds, which includes the interest receivable amount.
n. Paid the first payment on the fixtures and equipment purchased in transaction "h".
o. Declared a dividend of $10,000.
p. Paid the amount declared as a dividend.

Required:
1. For each of the transactions, prepare the appropriate journal entry.
2. Prepare a trial balance.

Problem 2-2: Journal Entries (Emphasis on Financing Transactions). The following transactions were incurred by the Slemboski Corporation during 2004.

    a. On January 2, Slemboski issued 50,000 shares of $1 par value common stock at an average price of $7.25.

    b. On January 2, Slemboski borrowed $100,000 from the Ninth Regional Bank, agreeing to pay 10% interest yearly and to begin in five years paying the principal amount of $20,000 per year.

    c. On January 3, the corporation purchased land for a building site for $120,000, paying 25% down and signing a 12%, 5-year note payable to the owner of the property for the remainder.

    d. Built a building on the site for $450,000, which was financed by paying 20% down and signing a 7% mortgage payable that requires annual payments of $34,000 on December 1 (which includes the interest amount), with the first payment due at the end of the year.

    e. Leased furniture and fixtures by signing a 3-year lease that requires annual payments of $25,000. The first payment was paid immediately. At the end of the three years, Slemboski has the option of renewing the lease for another three years, and if the option is not renewed, the furniture and fixtures return to the possession of the lessor.

    f. Acquired merchandise of $190,000 on account. (Assume a perpetual inventory system.)

    g. Sales on account amounted to $300,000. The company marks up merchandise 100%.

    h. Paid salaries of $60,000.

    i. Collected $290,000 of the accounts receivable.

    j. Paid the interest on the note to the Ninth Regional Bank. (See transaction "b.")

    k. Paid $24,967, which includes a full year's interest, to the holder of the note payable to acquire the land for a building site. (See transaction "c.")

    l. Paid the required mortgage payment. (See transaction "d.")

    m. Paid $120,000 of accounts payable.

    n. Paid operating expenses of $80,000.

    o. At year-end, the following bills had been received but not paid (credit Accrued Liabilities for each item):
        (1) Property taxes of $5,000.
        (2) Insurance bill of $2,400, covering the next two years.
        (3) Utilities of $650.

Required:
1. Journalize the transactions.
2. Prepare a trial balance.

Problem 2-3: Adjusting Entries. C, C, & T Company adjusts its books each December 31. The following information is available.

    a. Credit sales for the year were $350,000, and the estimated bad debt rate is 2½% of credit sales.

    b. Earned but unpaid wages amounted to $4,400.

    c. The company owns various fixed assets, the details of which are as follows:

Description	Cost	Life	Salvage	Purchased
Machine #1	$18,000	5 years	0	January 15, 2003
Machine #2	22,000	4 years	$1,000	September 1, 2004
Patent	34,000	17 years	0	January 1, 2002

(Note that the process of allocating the cost of an intangible asset is the same as allocating the cost of a tangible asset, except that the expense is called Amortization Expense and the asset account is credited rather than using an accumulated account.)

d. The company rented a warehouse on April 1, 2004, and paid the first year's rent of $6,000. The payment was recorded in a prepaid account.

e. A 2-year insurance policy was purchased on May 31, 2004, for $7,200. The amount was recorded in an expense account.

f. The company received its property tax statement on November 1 in the amount of $2,400. The county in which the company is located has a fiscal year ending on August 31 and levies taxes each October. When the company paid its bill in early November, the company accountant recorded the amount as an expense, but it is the company's policy to recognize the amount as an expense over the county's fiscal year.

g. On September 1, the company received a 6-month note from a customer in the amount of $5,000 that pays interest at 10%.

h. On October 15, the company borrowed $40,000 from a local finance company and signed a 16% note payable.

i. A year-end count of office supplies showed $400, but the general ledger account for office supplies shows $350.

j. The company records revenue during the year on the cash basis, and then at the end of the year, it converts to the accrual basis. The amount in Accounts Receivable on January 1 was $50,000 and a review of customer accounts shows that the amount owed at December 31 is $62,000.

Required:
Prepare the appropriate adjusting entries for 2004.

Problem 2-4: Adjusting Entries. The following information is available for Dallas, CPA (which is organized as a proprietorship):

a. Dallas holds a $120,000, 8% note receivable that is dated March 1, 2004.

b. Dallas purchased a three-year insurance policy on August 1, paying $30,600. When payment was made, Dallas debited a prepaid account.

c. Salaries during a typical 5-day workweek are $12,400. This year, December 31 is on a Wednesday, but employees are given New Year's Eve off with pay.

d. The office supplies account is as follows:

Office Supplies

Beginning balance	1,100
Purchase	450
Purchase	640
Purchase	330

A count of the office supplies at the end of the year showed that the value of the amount on hand was $450.

e. The depreciable assets have a cost of $260,000 and are being depreciated over five years, using the straight-line method of depreciation. Dallas uses a half-year convention, which is that all assets purchased any time during a year are considered to have been purchased on July 1 of that year. Of the total cost of assets, $40,000 was acquired during 2004.

f. Dallas rents office space in which to conduct business. On December 1, Dallas gave a check for $12,000 to the landlord, covering rent until March 1, 2005. Dallas debited Rent Expense for the payment.

g. During December 2004, Dallas received a check for $5,000 as a retainer for an audit that is to be done during February 2005. The payment was recorded as Unearned Revenue.

h. For part of the year, Dallas had his secretary/office manager do some of the bookkeeping for his CPA practice. (*Note: The secretary/office manager did not do the bookkeeping for any client.*) To avoid being interrupted, Dallas had informed the office manager to record any ambiguous transactions in a suspense account, and Dallas would correctly account for the transactions later. A review of the suspense account at December 31 disclosed the following:

Suspense Account

Two season tickets to the theater	1,200	
Cleaning of suits, shirts, etc.	400	
Sale of fully depreciated computer		175
Luncheons with clients and potential clients	1,000	
Balance at December 31, 2004	2,425	

Required:

Prepare the necessary adjusting entries, if appropriate, at December 31, 2004.

Problem 2-5: Accounting Cycle—S&G Inc. Account balances for S&G Inc. on November 1, 2004, using the periodic method of inventory, are as follows:

Cash	$ 60,000
Accounts Receivable	102,000
Allowance for Doubtful Accounts	3,430
Inventory on January 1, 2004	22,000
Prepaid Rent	8,400
Buildings and Equipment	232,000
Land	100,000
Accumulated Depreciation—Buildings	82,000
Accumulated Depreciation—Equipment	13,000
Accounts Payable	91,000
Note Payable	50,000
Common Stock, $5 par	200,000
Retained Earnings on January 1, 2004	78,000
Sales	342,770
Sales Returns and Allowances	32,000
Purchases	219,000
Purchase Discounts	7,200
Selling Expenses	22,000
Administrative Expenses	50,000
Insurance Expense	18,000
Interest Expense	2,000

Required:

1. Journalize the following transactions that took place in November and December.
   a. S&G bought additional equipment on December 1 for $8,000 cash. The equipment has a life of three years and is expected to have no residual value.
   b. Additional purchases of inventory were made on account in the amount of $10,000 (no discounts were taken).
   c. Additional sales of $60,320 were made on account, and $3,700 of sale returns were granted against amounts owed.
   d. Land was purchased in exchange for 800 shares of previously unissued stock. At the time of purchase, the shares had a market price of $32 per share.
   e. Additional selling expenses of $5,000 were incurred and paid in cash.
   f. A payment of $42,000 was made on accounts payable.
   g. Cash of $56,000 was collected on accounts receivable.
   h. Dividends in the amount of $20,800 were declared and paid.
2. Prepare a trial balance as of December 31, 2004.
3. Prepare a worksheet and enter the adjusting entries, based on the following information.
   a. $6,300 of the prepaid rent has expired.
   b. The allowance for doubtful accounts should be $5,400.
   c. Building depreciation expense is $23,000, and the depreciation expense for equipment owned at December 1 is $4,500. Additional depreciation expense needs to be computed for the equipment purchased on December 1. (See transaction "a" in part #1.)
   d. Twelve months' insurance was paid on April 1 and debited to an expense account.
   e. Wages were accrued in the amount of $2,500. Wages are normally accounted for as administrative expense.
   f. The note payable was issued in 1999 and bears interest of 8%. Annual payment of interest is required on July 1 of each year.
4. Complete the worksheet. Ending inventory on December 31, 2004, was $28,000. What is the net income?
5. Prepare the necessary closing entries.
6. (Appendix) Prepare the reversing entries that are appropriate.

Problem 2-6: Income Statement and Analysis. Bryce Valley Cabins was organized five years ago as a seasonal resort in southwestern Utah. The resort consists of 20 two-bedroom cabins that are rented either by the day or the week. A restaurant, laundry, and souvenir shop are located in the main building. In addition to renting the cabins, Bryce Valley also provides several tours of the surrounding sights, either from 4-wheel-drive vehicles or on horseback, which also includes either an outdoor BBQ or a Dutch Oven dinner.

Investors had anticipated losses for the first few years but expected profits to begin when total revenues exceeded $500,000. This past year, revenues did exceed that amount for the first time but profits were less than had been expected. The company generated a profit only because it sold an investment in a dot-com company at a gain.

In preparation for the upcoming meeting with the investors, the CPA was given the following information that had been extracted from the fiscal year-end (which is September 30) adjusted trial balance:

Room and related services revenues	$245,000
Cafeteria revenues	185,000
Retail stores revenues	95,000
Tour revenues	80,000

Gain on sale of investments	$ 60,000
Maid service expenses	80,000
Check-in, bell-hop, etc., expenses	25,000
Laundry expenses (65% used by rooms, 30% used by restaurants, and 5% used by tours)	50,000
Cost of food used in restaurant	70,000
Salaries of cook, waiters, dishwashers, etc.	60,000
Depreciation expense on cabins	80,000
Depreciation expense on equipment, etc., used in restaurant	25,000
Salaries of people working in souvenir shop	18,000
Administrative expenses	45,000
Stable expenses	10,000
Depreciation expense on main building	45,000
Depreciation expense on vehicles	14,000
Inventory of merchandise for sale, October 1, 2004	35,000
Inventory of merchandise for sale, September 30, 2005	30,000
Purchases of merchandise for resale	40,000
Cost of food and supplies connected with tours	21,000
Tour guide salaries	15,000
Repair and maintenance (40% on main building; the rest is on the cabins)	30,000
Winter loss	30,000
Tax expense	?

Winters in the high country of southwestern Utah are sometimes severe. However, this past winter was exceptionally cold, and although precautions had been taken during construction to protect the facilities, frost and other winter weather had caused more than usual damage. The old-timers couldn't remember such a winter since the one in '78.

The combined state, local, and federal tax rate was 38%.

Occupancy this past year was 60% for the 160 days that the resort is open.

Required:

1. Prepare an income statement in whatever format you think is best for the investors, showing the profitability of the various services offered by the resort (i.e., cabin rentals, restaurant, souvenir shop, and tours). Do not limit yourself to considering only the single-step and multiple-step formats.
2. Write a brief memo to management, recommending in which of the various services price increases may be necessary or where cost-cutting efforts should be focused.
3. Based upon your assessment as to whether the various costs are fixed or variable, determine the cost of renting a cabin for one day. What would that cost be if the occupancy rate could be increased to 80%? How do you explain the decrease in cost per day from 60% to 80%?
4. What recommendations might you make to the investors? (Don't limit yourself to the given financial data.)

Problem 2-7: Income Statement and Writing Assignment. The following list of items pertains to the 2004 calendar-year accounting period of Secard Pools & Spas:

Advertising expense	$ 18,000
Gain on sale of investments	12,200
Gain on early extinguishment of debt	14,400
Interest expense	20,000

Interest revenue	$ 8,000
Loss of inventory due to flood (considered unusual, but not infrequent)	40,000
Loss on write-off of plant assets due to obsolescence (considered infrequent, but not unusual)	24,000
Loss incurred when foreign government expropriated the company's assets (considered unusual and infrequent)	100,000
Merchandise inventory, December 31	22,000
Merchandise inventory, January 1	27,000
Miscellaneous expenses	4,000
Office salaries expense	21,000
Office supplies expense	2,900
Purchases	35,000
Sales	140,000
Sales returns	4,000
Sales salaries expense	35,000
Utilities expense	8,000
Income tax rate	40%

Required:
1. Prepare a multiple-step income statement.
2. If you were a potential investor, which income line would be most meaningful to you? Why?

Problem 2-8: Classified Balance Sheet and Writing Assignment. An accounting intern prepared the following balance sheet (which he now gives to you, his supervisor) for your critique. His professors in college had stressed the importance of summarizing data so as to not overwhelm the financial statement reader. So the intern had spent a considerable amount of time in developing this balance sheet, and you know that he is expecting to be complimented for the work he has done.

Haplea, Inc.
Balance Sheet
December 31, 2004

Assets	
Cash and cash equivalents	$ 100,000
Accounts receivable	180,000
Inventory	70,000
Other current assets	65,000
Land	1,200,000
Depreciable assets	800,000
Less accumulated depreciation	(250,000)
Total assets	$2,165,000
Liabilities and Owners' Equity	
Current liabilities	$ 210,000
Mortgage payable	540,000
Pension obligation	300,000
Total liabilities	$1,050,000
Common stock	1,000,000
Retained earnings	115,000
Total liabilities and owners' equity	$2,165,000

Along with this balance sheet, the accounting intern also provided you with the following notes:

a. Cash and cash equivalents consists of the following:

Petty cash	$ 500
Cash in the bank	73,250
U.S. government securities that will mature within 90 days or less from the time that they were purchased	20,000
IOUs from company employees that will be withheld from their next payroll check	1,250
U.S. government treasury bill that will mature in 180 days from date of purchase	5,000
Total	$100,000

b. Included in Accounts Receivable is the Allowance for Doubtful Accounts, which has a credit balance of $8,000. Also included is a note in the amount of $5,000 from the president of the corporation.

c. Inventory includes goods for resale in the amount of $65,000, office supplies of $700, and goods that have been ordered FOB destination but which have not arrived, $4,300.

d. Other current assets consist of $50,000 of securities that the company intends on selling during the next 60 days, prepaid insurance of $6,000, and cash surrender value of life insurance of $9,000.

e. Land includes the cost of the land on which the company's buildings are located, which is $200,000, but the remainder of the $1,200,000 consists of the cost of acquiring land on which there is a natural resource that the company is currently extracting.

f. Depreciable assets consist of the following:

Buildings	$400,000
Equipment	250,000
Furniture and fixtures	150,000

g. The current liabilities consist of the following:

Amounts payable to suppliers	$130,000
Salaries payable to employees at year-end	22,000
Income taxes payable to state and federal government	55,000
Interest payable	3,000
Total	$210,000

h. Of the $540,000 due on the mortgage, $40,000 will be paid during the next 12 months.

i. Presently, the company has no retirees and does not expect any employees to retire during the current year to whom pension benefits will be payable.

j. The company has 100,000 shares of stock issued and outstanding that were issued at an average price of $10 per share. The stock has a par value of $1. The company is authorized to issue one million shares of stock.

Required:
1. Prepare a corrected balance sheet.
2. Write a brief memo to the accounting intern, explaining why you made the

changes that you did and also suggesting that he needs to reread his intermediate accounting textbook—be gentle.

Problem 2-9: "Shoe-Box" Problem—Smart Solutions. Travis Burr and Jeremy Spencer started a partnership in 1997 and opened a business services and retail store in College Station, Texas, called Smart Solutions. The store catered to the needs of college students and business professionals in the area. Services offered were copying, binding, laminating, Internet access, and documents design. In addition, it offered business machines and supplies for sale at retail prices.

After realizing considerable success during its first four years, the partners opened a second store in Conroe, Texas, a small town about 50 miles south of College Station. Now, in 2004, the partners have decided to pursue significant expansion in the Houston and San Antonio areas. To finance the expansion, the partners have decided to incorporate and sell stock to private investors. In addition, they have decided to apply to First National Bank to obtain a significant loan.

As part of the loan application process, the bank requires the partnership to provide a current balance sheet, a projected income statement, and a projected balance sheet at the end of the first year of operations subsequent to receiving the loan. Upon completing the process of incorporation, issuing stock to each other and issuing additional shares of stock to some private investors, Burr and Spencer submitted the following balance sheet to First National Bank at the beginning of its 2005 fiscal year.

SMART SOLUTIONS, INC.
Balance Sheet
As of January 1, 2005

Assets		
Cash and cash equivalents		$ 25,569
Gross receivables	$ 79,253	
Less allowance for doubtful accounts	4,840	74,413
Inventories		76,010
Supplies		50,000
Prepaid expenses		8,807
Land		49,200
Buildings	$288,930	
Less accumulated depreciation	40,010	248,920
Equipment	$195,986	
Less accumulated depreciation	68,791	127,195
Total assets		$660,114
Liabilities		
Accounts payable		$ 23,814
Current maturities of long-term debt		70,000
Interest payable		10,500
Wages payable		4,110
Taxes payable		2,839
Long-term debt		140,000
Total liabilities		$251,263
Stockholders' Equity		
Common stock (par value $100; shares issued 3,000)		$300,000
Paid-in capital in excess of par		108,851
Total stockholders' equity		$408,851
Total liabilities and stockholders' equity		$660,114

Based on past experience and trends and the assumption that additional significant expansion would be realized, Burr and Spencer forecast the following transactions for the year 2005.

a. Revenues derived from the sale of business machines—$650,000. Revenues from services—$1,000,000. The company estimates that the balance in Accounts Receivable at December 31, 2005, will be 10% of the sales and service revenues for 2005. Also, it is estimated that at December 31, 2005, the balance in Allowance for Doubtful Accounts will equal 5% of the year-end outstanding accounts receivable.

b. The cost of goods sold equals 60% of the retail price. The company intends to purchase $500,000 of inventories, an equal portion each month of the year. All inventory purchases are made on account and left unpaid for approximately one month.

c. The cost of supplies purchased (all for cash) during the year is $550,000. Supplies used during the period are approximately 50% of service revenues.

d. Operating expenses incurred during the period (excluding bad debt and depreciation expense) are approximately $450,000, of which 6% will be wages left unpaid at the end of the year. In addition, the company intends to prepay additional operating expenses in the amount of $35,000, none of which will be used during the year. All current prepaid expenses will be used during the year.

e. All of the debt currently outstanding bears an interest rate of 10%. The current portion of this outstanding debt, plus interest of $21,000, will be paid on June 30, 2005. The next required principal payment of $70,000 is due on June 30, 2006. Burr and Spencer are applying to First National Bank for a loan of $400,000 to be received the first part of January 2005. The loan will bear an interest rate of 12%, and the company will be required to repay the loan by making five equal principal payments plus accrued interest. The first payment is due on December 31, 2005.

f. Capital expenditures to execute the expansion during the year, all of which will be paid with cash included in the requested loan, are planned as follows: land—$60,000; buildings—$150,000; equipment—$200,000. The useful lives of the new buildings and equipment are 30 and 5 years, respectively. The remaining useful lives of the old buildings and equipment are 26 and 3 years, respectively. Straight-line depreciation with no salvage value is used on all depreciable assets.

g. The company intends to issue 1,000 additional shares of stock for expected proceeds of $170,000.

h. The company's tax rate is 30%. At the end of the year, approximately 25% of the tax liability will be unpaid.

Burr and Spencer have indicated to private investors that a cash dividend of $5 per share will be declared at the end of 2005 if the company's financial position warrants such a declaration.

Required:
1. Construct the projected income statement for Smart Solutions, Inc., for the year ending 2005, assuming that First National Bank provides the company with the loan.
2. Construct the projected balance sheet for Smart Solutions, Inc., for the year ending 2005, assuming that First National Bank provides the company with the loan.

3. In your opinion, does the company's financial position warrant declaring the cash dividend? Explain.

Problem 2-10: Integrating Financial and Managerial Accounting. As a professor of soil science, Jean Wright conducted extensive research on developing instruments that measure moisture content in soils. After several years of research, Jean was able to develop a device that was particularly precise in its measurements. Upon recognizing its desirable properties, Jean patented the design and began to look for opportunities to use the instrument in other ways. It was quickly learned that many food companies were very interested in obtaining the instrument because, when packaging cookies, cakes, etc., that are to be baked upon opening, the precise amount of moisture is critical in obtaining quality products. Jean recognized a lucrative opportunity to sell the instrument and so took a leave of absence from her academic job to establish a corporation designed to manufacture and distribute the item.

On January 1, 2005, Jean established the company under the name HumiGon, Inc., by issuing 10,000 shares of stock to herself for services rendered and an additional 10,000 shares to various private investors for $40,000. Par value of the stock was $1 per share. Also, on January 1 additional financing was obtained through a small business loan in the amount of $25,000. The interest rate on the loan was 12%. HumiGon is required to repay the loan in 10 semiannual installments of $2,500 plus accrued interest for five years. The first payment is due on September 1, 2005. Subsequent payments are scheduled every March 1 and September 1. In addition, the bank offered a line of credit up to $10,000 for immediate cash needs. The bank charged an interest rate of 15% on any funds withdrawn from this line of credit. (For the shares of stock that Jean issued herself, debit Organization Expenses.)

Jean began work immediately on organizing space within a rented building to facilitate the production process. Personnel were hired to assist in purchasing, production, marketing, legal, and financial duties. Equipment was purchased and relationships with suppliers were established. Given the uniqueness of the product developed by HumiGon, marketing the product proved to be relatively simple, and the company immediately began to realize substantial sales. The following items summarize the transactions that took place during the company's first year in business.

a. Equipment to be used in the production process that has a useful life of 10 years was purchased with cash at the beginning of the year at a cost of $40,000. Straight-line depreciation is employed with no salvage value.

b. A 2-year insurance policy on the production facilities was purchased in January for $6,000.

c. Wages to production workers totaled $120,000 for the year. Salaries for accounting, marketing, and legal personnel were $85,000. The amount of unpaid wages and salaries at the end of the year was $25,000.

d. Purchases of raw materials amounted to $60,000. At year-end, $8,500 had not been paid. The value of raw materials on hand at the end of the year that had not been transferred to work in process is $1,500.

e. Work in process at the end of the year was $2,100.

f. Finished goods inventory at year-end was valued at $3,800.

g. Utilities costs and property taxes incurred and paid on the production facilities during the year were $6,600. (Overhead costs are debited directly to Work in Process.)

h. Rent expense incurred and paid on the building during the year was $15,000.

i. Invoiced sales for the year totaled $373,000. Sales returns were $16,000, cash collections from sales were $318,000. One customer that owes the company $3,100 has declared bankruptcy and notified HumiGon that payment will not be forthcoming. The company estimates that an additional $1,000 will not be collected.

   j. Other selling and administrative expenses paid during the year were $18,000.

   k. Legal fees of $28,000 were incurred and paid in December due to a lawsuit initiated against Jean by her academic employer. The issue was whether Jean had the right to patent and market the product since she was an employee of the university when she discovered the design. Jean was informed that the defense of the patent was successful.

   l. The company's income tax rate is 30%. Income taxes paid during the year were $1,000.

Required:
1. Analyze the effects of all transactions made by HumiGon during the 2005 fiscal year by constructing journal entries. A journal entry for income taxes will need to be made after determining net income before taxes.
2. Construct an income statement and balance sheet at December 31, 2005.

Research Activities

Activity 2-1: Start-Up Costs. Many one-time costs are incurred when a company first begins business, expands business into a new territory or with a new class of customers, etc., and it is not always clear whether such costs should be expensed or recorded as assets of the business. In recent years, a standard has been issued that provides guidance in the area. Find that publication and write a memo stating (1) what activities are defined as being start-up activities, and (2) which types of start-up costs of a business can be recorded as assets of the business, if any, and which have to be expensed.

Activity 2-2: Weighted-Average Number of Shares. The Warren Corporation had the following transactions in stock during 2004 and 2005:

January 1, 2004	1,000,000 shares outstanding
April 1	Issued 84,000 shares
August 4	Issued 120,000 shares
January 1, 2005	1,204,000 shares outstanding
June 1	Issued a 3-for-1 stock split

1. Research U.S. GAAP and write a brief description of how the weighted-average number of shares is computed when (a) shares are issued at other than the first day or the last day of the month, and when (b) there is a stock split or stock dividend. Also, note the citation.
2. Without regard to your answer in 1(a), compute the weighted-average number of shares to use to compute EPS in the 2005 income statement for both 2005 and 2004, which is reported for comparative purposes.

3

$\mathscr{I}$ntroduction TO Financial Statement Analysis

Zenith Electronics Corporation was founded in 1918 and quickly developed a national reputation for quality in the electronics industry. Initially, the company focused on the manufacturing of radio equipment and went on to produce monochrome and eventually color television sets and other video products. The company was a dominant leader in its industry until the 1980s, when superior technology gave foreign competitors (principally Japanese companies) the ability to produce a higher quality TV set for a lower price. In every year except one from 1985 to 1997, Zenith reported a net loss. During 1995, a Korean company executed a tender offer that effectively gave it control of Zenith, and subsequently, the prospects of the company improved considerably. In 1996, Zenith announced plans and agreements with partners to produce a new Web-cruising TV set that would allow the consumer to use the TV as a means to surf the Internet. The company's stock price shot up to $18 per share and settled in at a trading range of $10–$14 throughout most of the next year. However, significant sales of the Web-surfing TV sets never materialized, and when the company filed its 1997 Form 10-K with the SEC on March 31, 1998, the company's stock price was trading at around $7 per share. One month later, the company filed for Chapter 11 bankruptcy, and the per-share price plunged to $0.45. Today, the shares are not traded on a security exchange.

Questions

1. Was information available in the 1997 Form 10-K and the company's annual report signaling that the company was no longer solvent?

2. Did the stock market not fully realize the significance of the company continually reporting losses from the mid-1980s?

3. What types of information should a potential investor or creditor look for in order to avoid investing in insolvent companies?

Learning Objectives

- Identify the uses and limitations of financial statement analysis.
- Illustrate the procedures in preparing common-size financial statements.
- Use common-size financial statements and information provided in company footnotes and other sources to construct pro forma financial statements.
- Explain the procedures to conduct a horizontal analysis.
- Define and discuss basic financial statement ratios that provide information on a company's liquidity, long-term solvency, profitability, and asset management.
- Communicate the necessity of exercising judgment when conducting a financial statement analysis on any company.

A significant amount of cost and effort goes into preparing and publishing financial statements and their corresponding notes. But within those statements and notes, a large amount of information is available to financial statement users that should be beneficial in making economic decisions. *The purpose of **financial statement analysis** is to synthesize information in such a manner that additional insight into the operating performance and financial health of the company is provided.* The opening scenario suggests that proper financial statement analysis can identify warning signs when a company is on the brink of failure. Likewise, financial statement analysis can identify profitable investment opportunities.

This chapter introduces some basic tools of financial statement analysis. Learning these tools will enable you, as future readers of financial statements, to become familiar with the information that is contained in published financial reports and how to use it. It should be stressed, however, that the process of reading and understanding financial statement data is an *art*—not a *science*. This is clearly illustrated in the following excerpt from a magazine article in which professional analysts, using the same financial statement data, disagree on the future prospects of Amazon.com Inc:

"... On June 22, Lehman Brothers Inc. debt analyst Ravi Suria released a scathing report about Amazon's deteriorating credit situation. And the Holy War began in earnest.

"Suria painted the picture of a company hemorrhaging money. The only triple-digit growth that mattered, he argued, was in Amazon's cash flow losses. The report shook many remaining stalwarts, and the stock dropped 19% in one day. . . . [Suria argued] that excessive debt and poor inventory management will make Amazon's operating cash-flow situation worse the more it sells.

"[However, other] . . . analysts believe the Amazon of year 2000 is actually in a better position than ever. Operating losses fell from 26% of sales in the fourth quarter to 17% in the first quarter. . . . Says Merrill Lynch & Co. Internet analyst Henry Blodget: 'I'm not at all concerned about the cash side.'

"Where Bezos [Amazon's CEO] and his band of Wall Street believers think Lehman's report went astray was in focusing on the one year of Amazon's greatest expansion and projecting those costs forward into the *future. The costs came up front, but now, they argue, Amazon will exploit its ability to handle far higher volumes."*[1]

Besides the necessity of using judgment, financial statement analysis has several limitations that should be understood by all attempting to interpret financial statements. First, *virtually all financial decisions are based on future expectations; however, financial statements are an indication of past performance*. The FASB indicated in its conceptual framework that one of the objectives of financial reporting is to provide information about the amounts, timing, and uncertainty (i.e., riskiness) of *future* cash flows, and academic research has provided evidence that financial statements are meeting this objective. However, using historical data to extrapolate to the future is an inherent weakness of financial statement analysis.

Another limitation of financial statement analysis is that *financial statement data comprise only a small subset of all the information that is available about a company*. The analyst must interpret financial statement data within the context of all other available information, including the company's industry, growth prospects of the industry, company management, and macro-economic variables, such as the growth of the economy, inflation, and unemployment rates. All of these are key factors in determining a company's future performance.

Finally, *financial statements are affected, sometimes dramatically, by the accounting principles that the company uses*. In many cases, U.S. GAAP allows several different principles to be used to account for the same transaction (e.g., inventory valuation and depreciation methods). Hence, the analyst must consider not only the reported numbers but also the accounting principles that resulted in those numbers—especially when comparing data among several companies. This quality of information question is even more of a problem when the analyst reads the financial report of a foreign company that was prepared in conformity with its domestic GAAP. Even though foreign companies may provide a **convenience translation** (a financial statement prepared in the English language and sometimes even translated into U.S. dollars), such financial statements do not comply fully with U.S. GAAP. This is true even for companies that are registered with the U.S. Securities and Exchange Commission. Although the SEC requires all companies that list their securities on a U.S. exchange to comply with U.S. GAAP, such compliance is met when foreign companies present their financial statements based on their domestic GAAP, as long as they reconcile their earnings and stockholders' equity amounts to what they would have been had U.S. GAAP been followed. Hence, the analyst must always be concerned about the *quality* of the information provided in the financial statements.

Uses of Financial Statement Analysis

The potential uses of financial statement analysis are as varied as the users of financial statements. Lenders of capital are concerned with a company's ability to meet scheduled interest payments and the repayment of principal. So these readers of financial reports use financial statement analysis to obtain insight into a company's long-term solvency, focusing on the level of the company's debt and its ability to generate positive cash flows from internal operations.

Equity investors are concerned with a company's ability to enhance the value of its net assets. So the company's profitability is a primary concern to them. Some equity investors can wait years for their return and, as such, may

---

[1]Robert Hof, Debra Sparks, and Ellen Neuborne, "Can Amazon Make It?" *Business Week*, July 10, 2000, pp. 38–43.

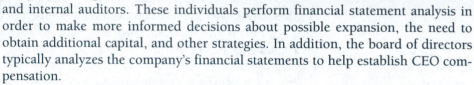

be attracted to a growth company that at present may have very little earnings or even be incurring a loss, but which has great potential for long-term profits. Other equity investors need a more immediate return and are attracted to a well-established company in which their investment seems more secure, where growth potential is not as promising, but dividends are larger and more immediate. In either case, information about the performance of a company over a period of time, including recent changes, is beneficial.

Financial statement analysis is also a vital tool for internal users, including company managers, boards of directors, and internal auditors. These individuals perform financial statement analysis in order to make more informed decisions about possible expansion, the need to obtain additional capital, and other strategies. In addition, the board of directors typically analyzes the company's financial statements to help establish CEO compensation.

Others who perform financial statement analysis include merger and acquisition specialists who analyze financial statements of a potential takeover target in order to assess the desirability of acquiring the company and to determine a reasonable acquisition price. Employees and short-term lenders, who are concerned about the short-term viability of a company, may use financial statement analysis as a way of determining whether a company can meet its short-term obligations.

In short, financial statement analysis can provide information concerning a wide array of questions to a wide array of readers. However, the primary questions that virtually all readers of financial statements ask can be summarized into the following categories:

Liquidity: What is the ability of the company to meet its short-term obligations?

Solvency: What is the probability that the company will have the ability to pay its long-term obligations?

Profitability: How much cash flow can the company generate from operations?

Asset management: How successful is the company in utilizing the resources provided to it?

Evaluating each of these areas can provide an assessment of a company's overall risk and return, and forms the basis for answering the question that guides all economic decisions: "Does the expected return from a cash investment justify the accompanying risk?"

Basic Types of Analysis

Just as a mechanic does not rely on one tool to accomplish his many tasks, so does an analyst have a variety of methods at his/her disposal to analyze financial statements. An extensive coverage of those available tools is beyond the scope of this book; however, the most basic financial statement analysis tools are introduced in this chapter.

This Is the Real World

Enron Corporation was formed in 1985 as a result of a merger of Houston Natural Gas and Internorth of Omaha, Nebraska. During the 1990s, this energy company became increasingly involved in the development of innovative commodity securities (i.e., derivatives) for the purposes of financial and risk management. The company was often used as a model of innovation and excellent management. By 2000, it was one of the largest companies in the world, with revenues of $101 billion and a market capitalization of $77 billion. The year 2001 began with the company's stock price at $84 per share, although it declined significantly during the first half of the year along with the general equity market. On July 31, 2001, Enron was added to the coveted Zack's #1 Ranked list of stocks because of its excellent valuation ($46 per share) and solid earnings performance. Just four months later, on December 2, 2001, Enron filed for Chapter 11 bankruptcy, and its stock price was trading at $0.68 per share.

How can a company lose 98% (and billions of dollars) of its market capitalization within a year without any warning? In Enron's case, fingers have been pointed at Enron's internal and external auditors. After the Enron meltdown, the chairman of the SEC, Harvey Pitt, noted the importance of internal auditors to signal how accounting principles affect financial statements:

"We are going to take steps to strengthen the role of audit committees [of

corporate boards]. We believe that it is appropriate for audit committees affirmatively to review with management, and also with outside auditors, the three, four, or five critical accounting principles that have the greatest impact on the company's financial posture."

Enron's case is particularly messy because Arthur Andersen acted as Enron's *internal and external* auditor, which begs the question of whether Arthur Andersen was independent in the performance of its duties. Internal audit committees ensure that a company's internal controls are adequate and working properly. However, if Arthur Andersen's internal auditors do not adequately perform their duties, will Arthur Andersen's external auditors perform the increased checks necessary to compensate for the internal weaknesses?

As expected, Arthur Andersen has claimed that Enron withheld important information during external audits of Enron's financial statements. However, given that Arthur Andersen's internal auditors were supposed to ensure that all relevant information was being captured in the information system, Andersen's argument might be difficult to defend, and Andersen will probably be subject to more litigation.

SOURCE: *"If You Violate the Law, You Will Pay for It,"* Business Week, December 24, 2001, p. 33.

Trend and Cross-Sectional Analyses

Regardless of the reason for conducting an analysis of financial statements, it is not typically meaningful to observe a set of data for one company at a point in time. Consider a company with earnings per share of $1.00, a price-to-earnings ratio of 10, and a gross margin of 40%. Are these numbers favorable? Do they represent a good investment opportunity? Is the company adequately using its resources? Without some reference point or benchmark, it is impossible to answer such questions. Thus, a proper analysis must include a "starting point," against which to compare current performance. Several good starting points are the performance of the same company in a previous year, the performance of other companies in the same industry, or the industry average.

Trend analysis refers to the performance of a company over an extended period of time. This tool attempts to identify trends in a company's performance, such as a company's earnings growth rate. Once a trend is found, the analyst then attempts to identify reasons to explain the trend to determine whether the trend will continue into the future. Projecting a trend into the future without identifying the reason(s) for a trend is little more than guessing. Thus, trend analysis uses the company's data in previous years as its starting point.

Cross-sectional analysis compares the performance of two or more companies on the same dimension at a point in time. When choosing companies on which to do a cross-sectional analysis, the analyst selects those companies that are a good match to each other. To illustrate, it is not very useful to compare an information providing Internet company that just recently went public with long established manufacturing companies like Ford or IBM. To obtain a meaningful comparison, the companies must be within the same industry. Other factors the analyst might want to consider when selecting comparable companies are company size, nationality, and product. Cross-sectional analysis uses other companies' operating performance or the industry average as its starting point.

Using trend and cross-sectional analyses simultaneously is a typical practice. That is, an analyst compares two or more companies over several time periods. This practice allows the analyst to obtain additional insights into the relative performance of not just the companies but also the industry.

Common-Size Financial Statements

Common-size financial statements display all amounts as a percentage of some base financial statement number. In the case of the income statement, the base number is net sales or, when it is available, total revenue. For the balance sheet, the base number is total assets. Common-size financial statements (which are also referred to as a **vertical analysis**) highlight the important components that comprise net income and total assets. Common-size financial statements are an efficient method to conduct both a trend analysis and a cross-sectional analysis.

Exhibits 3-1 and 3-2 (see p. 106) present common-size income statements and balance sheets, using information provided in the 2001 annual reports of Ford Motor Company and General Motors Corporation. The format of the common-size statements allows the analyst to quickly assess the relative profitability and efficiency of the two companies compared to each other and over time. Of course, a longer time period might be more beneficial and allow the analyst to more easily identify major trends.

The information in Exhibit 3-1 shows that both companies experienced a decline in their gross margins from selling cars from 2000 to 2001. Ford's decline

INTERNET

The financial statements of publicly-traded companies can be found at the SEC's EDGAR web site, **http://www.sec.gov/ edgar.shtm**.

EXHIBIT 3-1

Common-Size Income Statements

	Ford Motor Company (Automotive division)		General Motors Corporation (Automotive division)	
	2001	2000	2001	2000
Sales	100.0%	100.0%	100.0%	100.0%
Cost of sales	(98.2)	(89.3)	(89.5)	(86.1)
Gross margin	1.8%	10.7%	10.5%	13.9%
Other operating expenses	(7.6)	(7.0)	(10.6)	(10.1)
Operating income	(5.8%)	3.7%	(0.1%)	3.8%
Nonoperating income	(1.1)	0.0	(0.8)	(1.1)
Income from financing division	1.1	2.1	1.9	1.6
Tax provision (expense)	1.6	(1.9)	(0.5)	(1.5)
Income from continuing operations	(4.1%)*	3.9%	0.4%*	2.8%
Discontinued operations	—	(1.4)	—	—
Extraordinary items	—	—	—	—
Cumulative effect of acct. change	—	—	—	—
Net income	(4.1%)*	2.5%	0.4%*	2.8%

*Difference due to rounding.

was especially large—from 10.7% to 1.8%. That is, for every dollar of sales, the company realized a gross profit of 1.8 cents in 2001, which was inadequate to cover operating costs, and the company reported a loss for the year. The gross margin percentage is an important item that receives a lot of attention from professional analysts because it signals how well a company could tolerate an increase in its manufacturing costs. In addition, the gross margin provides information on how far a company could lower its retail prices during times of slowing sales before losses are incurred. General Motors' gross margin percentage is larger than Ford's in both years. Thus, it appears that General Motors earns a higher markup on its vehicles than does Ford. This is a significant reason why General Motors reported a profit in both 2000 and 2001.

The other operating expenses percentage provides information on the efficiency of the company. When a company executes a restructuring, the focus is often on reducing operating expenses by cutting sales forces and administrative personnel. General Motors' operating expense percentage is much higher than Ford's. Thus, it appears that Ford does not have to incur as many operating expenses relative to sales. However, given the difference in the gross margin percentages between the two companies, an alternative explanation is that the companies classify some costs differently. That is, Ford might capitalize as part of the cost of inventory some costs that GM expenses when incurred.

© GETTY IMAGES, INC./EYEWIRE

The operating income line considers how much of a sales dollar becomes profit after the company has paid all operating expenses during the period. Both companies experienced a significant decline in this percentage during 2001 (similar to the gross margin percentage), but General Motors appears to have the higher operating profitability. The same conclusion can be made when looking at the net income percentage. As a reflection of the poor operating performance during 2001, Ford's stock price declined significantly during the year. In addition, the company's CEO was forced to retire in October 2001 and was replaced by William Clay Ford Sr., the grandson of the company's founder, Henry Ford.

Overall, Exhibit 3-1 indicates that a common-size income statement can provide important information about a company's profitability relative to its sales and the company's ability to manage costs. Other percentages that are looked at closely are the income from continuing operations line and the net income line because they represent how much of a sales dollar the company actually retains as profits, which then can be distributed as dividends or retained by the company and reinvested into the business. Either or both numbers can be used, depending upon whether the analyst wants to exclude the items that are not expected to recur in the future. So important are these numbers that they are frequently computed independently of preparing a complete common-size income statement and are also frequently put on lists of accounting and financial ratios. When net income is used in this ratio, it is called the return on sales ratio:

$$\text{Return on Sales: } \frac{\text{Net Income}}{\text{Sales}} \tag{3.1}$$

Exhibit 3-2 presents common-size balance sheets for Ford and General Motors, using total assets as the base item. The exhibit reveals that the composition of the assets remained steady for both companies over the period examined. However, significant differences exist between the companies. The receivables percentage is much higher for Ford than for GM. This suggests that GM's collection policies result in less receivables being outstanding relative to total assets. Ford also has a higher percentage of its assets allocated to property, plant, and equipment, while GM has a higher percentage of its assets in "other assets," which are primarily prepaid pension assets and investments.

EXHIBIT 3-2

Common-Size Balance Sheets

	Ford Motor Company (Automotive division)		General Motors Corporation (Automotive division)	
	2001	2000	2001	2000
Assets:				
Cash and cash equivalents	6.6%	6.3%	6.0%	3.8%
Receivables	41.3	45.8	32.5	32.4
Inventory	2.2	2.7	3.1	3.6
Other current assets	3.5	3.2	7.1	7.8
Total current assets	53.6%	58.5%*	48.7%	48.5%*
Net PP&E	12.0	13.2	10.8	11.2
Other assets	34.4	28.7	40.6	41.2
Total assets	100.0%	100.0%*	100.0%*	100.0%
Liabilities:				
Trade payables	5.7%	5.3%	5.6%	6.0%
Accrued liabilities	8.7	8.2	10.5	11.0
Other current liabilities	2.9	3.5	3.7	3.8
Total current liabilities	17.2%*	17.1%*	19.8%	20.8%
Long-term debt	63.2	61.0	50.6	47.0
Other long-term liabilities	16.7	15.4	23.5	22.2
Total stockholders' equity	2.8	6.6	6.1	10.0
Total liabilities and stockholders' equity	100.0%	100.0%	100.0%	100.0%

*Difference due to rounding.

A third difference between the financial statements of the two automobile manufacturers is the percentage of long-term debt in relation to total assets. This relationship relates to financial leverage and risk, which are covered later in the chapter when solvency ratios are discussed.

Using Historical Information to Project Future Information

In addition to providing information to the analyst about the direction the company is going, common-size financial statements are very useful in constructing **pro forma** (i.e., as if) **financial statements**, which in this case are statements that project future operations. A pro forma income statement can be constructed in three steps:

1. Examine the relationship between sales and the various expenses/costs, separating the expenses into two categories, based on whether they vary directly with sales (variable costs) or whether they are relatively constant in relation to sales (fixed costs).
2. Project future sales, based on changes in expected demand.

3. Using the relationships determined from Step 1, compute the future expenses at the projected level of sales.

Step 1 requires some assumptions with respect to the behavior of costs, particularly whether the historical relationship of the expenses to sales will continue. As illustrated in the quotes about Amazon's future, not all analysts always agree as to whether past relationships of expenses to sales will continue into the future. Once that problem is solved to the analyst's satisfaction, then costs can be projected into the future by either of the following two methods:

1. Using judgment as to which costs vary with sales and which ones are essentially fixed in relation to sales. For example, the cost of goods sold basically varies directly with sales and so can be treated as a variable cost. Depreciation expense, on the other hand, basically remains the same from year to year and can be treated as a fixed cost.

2. Using various mathematical techniques to divide the expenses into their fixed and variable components. When the income statements of two years are all that is available, the high-low method can be used to separate the expenses/costs into their fixed and variable components. When data for more than two years are available, the more sophisticated linear regression procedures[2] can be used to separate expenses/costs into their fixed and variable components. In either case, both mathematical methods can be performed either upon individual expenses/costs or on the total expenses/costs, depending upon the amount of detail the analyst desires.

Step 2 is a more difficult procedure and usually requires that the analyst make judgments concerning the economic and industry growth potential and the company's share in these projected growth rates. As with most judgments that have to be made when performing financial statement analysis, projecting future sales is analyst specific. After future sales are projected, Step 3 is basically a mathematical procedure.

Exhibit 3-3 presents the 2001 income statement for Ford Motor Company and, after making some assumptions about the behavior of the various expenses, a pro forma income statement based on the premise that increased demand for

EXHIBIT 3-3

Projected Income Statement for Ford Motor Company

	2001 As Reported (in millions)	2002 Pro-forma (in millions)
Sales	$ 131,528	$ 138,104
Cost of sales (100% variable)	(129,159)	(129,473)
Gross margin	$ 2,369	$ 8,631
Other operating expenses (50% variable; 50% fixed)	(9,937)	(10,185)
Operating income	$ (7,568)	$ (1,554)
Nonoperating income (100% fixed)	(1,468)	(1,468)
Income from financing division (75% variable; 25% fixed)	1,452	1,506
Income before taxes	$ (7,584)	$ (1,516)
Tax expense (28% effective tax rate)	2,151	424
Income from continuing operations	$ (5,433)	$ (1,092)
Earnings-per-share (basic)	($3.02)	($0.61)

---

[2]Linear regression, including multiple regression, can be used very quickly and easily on Excel, Quatro Pro, and other electronic worksheets.

Ford's products will result in a 5% increase in sales. The amounts for the individual components were obtained as follows:

Cost of goods sold: This item is assumed to be 100% variable; thus, it varies directly with and is a fixed percentage of sales. Given the large change in the cost of goods sold percentage in 2001, the percentage applied to the pro forma statement is an average of the two years' percentages, or 93.75% [(98.2% + 89.3%)/2], which results in a cost of goods sold amount of $129,473 million.

Other operating expenses: This item is assumed to be equally distributed among variable and fixed costs. One-half of the amount that was recognized in 2001, or $9,937 million, will remain constant ($4,968.5) and the other half will increase with sales—5%, or $5,217 ($4,968 × 1.05). Thus, the total estimated operating expense amount is $10,185 million.

Nonoperating income: This item is assumed to be fixed at a $1,468 million loss.

Income from financing division: Financing revenue is directly related to sales, and so most of this component is assumed to be variable. The final amount is derived in the same way as was used for other operating expenses.

Tax expense: An effective tax rate is calculated for 2001 and applied to the pro forma statement. The rate is calculated by dividing tax expense by income before tax ($2,151/$7,584). This rate is equal to 28.4%, and the rate employed for the pro forma statement was rounded to 28%.

As indicated by the pro forma statement, a 5% increase in Ford's sales, combined with an improvement in the gross margin percentage, is projected to result in a 79.9% increase in net income [($5,433 − $1,092)/$5,433], or $2.41 per share.

EXTENDING THE CONCEPT

The assumption that Ford's cost of goods sold component is 100% variable is probably not a good one. The cost of goods sold is comprised of all the costs necessary to get the vehicles ready for sale. These costs include direct labor, direct materials, and manufacturing overhead. Ford's assembly line workers are typically paid an hourly wage, and therefore this component is a variable cost. Direct materials will also vary directly with the level of production, which will also be a function of sales. However, for a large, automated company such as Ford, manufacturing overhead will probably be comprised primarily of depreciation on large equipment and buildings and salaries paid to supervisors. These types of costs are fixed, and therefore Ford's cost of goods sold component must also have a fixed component.

Redo the pro forma income statement for Ford, assuming that the cost of goods sold is 40% fixed and 60% variable. With this new assumption, what was the percentage change in net income? As more costs become fixed, what is the effect on income?

A pro forma balance sheet can be developed from the information in the pro forma income statement and the common-size balance sheet. Absent any investments by or distributions to owners, the increase in total assets can be assumed to be equal to net income, where total assets serves as the base item upon which to construct all other balance sheet items, using the percentages as determined from the common-size balance sheet. Of course, if additional information is available concerning likely actions to be taken by management, this information should be taken into account. For example, management might obtain additional financing through issuing debt and/or equity securities, and if so, then long-term debt, common stock, paid-in capital amounts, and cash should all be adjusted, as should the accounts for which the cash raised will be used (e.g., expanding plant or acquiring land).

Pro forma financial statements, though based on several assumptions, provide insights into the future performance of a company. As already discussed, published financial statements are a picture of what has happened in the past, but financial statement users are concerned with future performance. As more information is obtained about the company and included in preparing the pro forma statements, the accuracy and usefulness of the statements are enhanced. In the Ford example, the pro forma financial statements were based primarily on a projection of sales and some assumptions of cost behavior. However, additional information could be gleaned about likely changes in other financial statement components in addition to their relationship to sales. Much valuable additional information is contained in the notes to the financial statements, such as information about scheduled interest payments, depreciation schedules, and the remaining lives on leases and fixed assets, along with national economic data and industry trends in refining the pro forma financial statements.

Horizontal Analysis

Horizontal analysis focuses on changes in magnitude and percentages in account balances over time. The beginning balance of each account represents the base on which a percentage is computed. Horizontal analysis is useful in evaluating trends. Exhibit 3-4 illustrates both vertical and horizontal analyses of the balance sheet of Eastman Chemical Company.

EXHIBIT 3-4

Vertical and Horizontal Analyses
EASTMAN CHEMICAL COMPANY AND SUBSIDIARIES
CONSOLIDATED STATEMENTS OF FINANCIAL POSITION
(dollars in millions)

December 31,	2001	Vertical Analysis %	2000	%	Horizontal Analysis % Change
Assets					
Current assets:					
Cash and cash equivalents	$ 66	1.08%	$ 101	1.54%	(34.65)%
Receivables	656	10.78	737	11.25	(10.99)%
Inventories	659	10.83	580	8.85	13.62%
Other current assets	77	1.27	105	1.60	(26.67)%
Total current assets	$1,458	23.96%	$1,523	23.25%*	(4.27)%
Properties:					
Properties and equipment at cost	$9,302	152.84%	$9,039	138.00%	2.91%
Less accumulated depreciation	5,675	93.25	5,114	78.08	10.97%
Net properties	$3,627	59.60%*	$3,925	59.92%	(7.59)%
Other noncurrent assets	1,001	16.45	1,102	16.82	(9.17)%
Total assets	$6,086	100.00%*	$6,550	100.00%	(7.08)%
Liabilities and shareowners' equity					
Current liabilities:					
Payables and other current liabilities	$ 958	15.74%	$1,258	19.21%	(23.85)%
Long-term borrowings	2,143	35.21	1,914	29.22	11.96%
Deferred income tax credits	452	7.43	607	9.27	(25.54)%
Postemployment obligations	1,043	17.14	829	12.66	25.81%
Other long-term liabilities	112	1.84	130	1.98	(13.85)%
Total liabilities	$4,708	77.36%	$4,738	72.34%	(0.63)%
Shareowners' equity:					
Common stock	$ 1	0.02%	$ 1	0.02%	0.00%
Paid-in capital	118	1.94	100	1.53	18.00%
Retained earnings	1,952	32.07	2,266	34.60	(13.86)%
Other comprehensive income (loss)	(251)	(4.12)	(117)	(1.79)	114.53%
	$1,820	29.90%*	$2,250	34.35%*	(19.11)%
Less treasury stock	442	7.26	438	6.69	0.91%
Total shareowners' equity	$1,378	22.64%	$1,812	27.66%	(23.95)%
Total liabilities and shareowners' equity	$6,086	100.00%	$6,550	100.00%	(7.08)%

*Difference due to rounding.

Ratio Analysis

A company's financial health can often be better measured in terms of the relationship among account balances than by the balance of a single account. Viewing the relationship among various account balances is referred to as ratio analysis. Actually, common-size financial statements are a sequence of ratios (i.e., the expression of one account to the base account) which are additive in nature. This section discusses other ratios where the denominator is not necessarily sales or total assets. Although the additive feature is forfeited in the following commonly used ratios, additional insights about company performance can be gained by examining the relationships of different financial statement components.

Liquidity

Liquidity refers to an entity's ability to pay its short-term liabilities as they mature, which is determined from the relationship between current assets and current liabilities. Since both current assets and current liabilities are accounts that relate to the operating cycle or one year, the readers of financial statements *by analyzing the relationship among the current accounts* can receive some insight as to whether an entity has enough short-term assets to meet all its short-term obligations. Common measures of financial liquidity are the following:

$$\text{Current Ratio: } \frac{\text{Current Assets}}{\text{Current Liabilities}} \qquad (3.2)$$

$$\text{Quick Ratio: } \frac{\text{Highly Liquid Assets (cash, marketable securities, receivables)}}{\text{Current Liabilities}} \qquad (3.3)$$

$$\text{Working Capital: Current Assets } - \text{ Current Liabilities} \qquad (3.4)$$

For a company to be liquid, *the current ratio must be greater than 1*; but other than that rule, there are no guidelines as to what the current ratio should be to indicate that the company has optimal liquidity. As a result, the current ratio, like all other financial statement ratios, must be interpreted with caution. For example, from the 2000 income statement and balance sheet for Intel Corporation (as shown in Exhibits 3-5 and 3-6), the current ratio is computed to be 2.68. Obviously, Intel is liquid. That is, Intel has enough current assets to meet its short-term obligations as they come due. But interpreting the ratio also requires a judgment about whether the current ratio is too high, which may indicate an inefficient allocation of resources among assets, resulting in less optimization of income. This is so because the expected return from holding short-term liquid assets is typically lower than from holding long-term operating assets. Thus, if a company is holding too many short-term assets rather than investing them in more

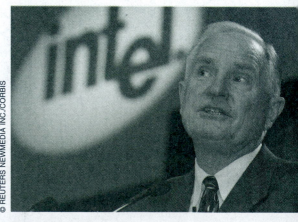

operating assets, it is probably not optimizing the company's income. The stockholders probably would prefer that such inefficiently managed assets be distributed to them in the form of dividends. However, having too little cash on hand might hinder the ability of the company to take advantage of profitable opportunities when they arise. Thus, interpreting what level of liquidity is optimal requires judgment.

EXHIBIT 3-5

Intel Corporation
Income Statement
(in millions, except per-share amounts)

	2001	2000	1999
Net revenues	**$26,539**	**$33,726**	**$29,389**
Cost of sales	13,487	12,650	11,836
Research and development	3,796	3,897	3,111
Marketing, general and administrative	4,464	5,089	3,872
Amortization of goodwill and other acquisition-related intangibles	2,338	1,586	411
Purchased in-process research and development	198	109	392
Operating income	$ 2,256	$ 10,395	$ 9,767
Gain (loss) on equity securities	(466)	3,759	883
Interest income and other, net	393	987	578
Income before taxes	**$ 2,183**	**$15,141**	**$11,288**
Provision for taxes	892	4,606	3,914
Net income	$ 1,291	$ 10,535	$ 7,314
Basic earnings per common share	$ 0.19	$ 1.57	$ 1.10
Diluted earnings per common share	$ 0.19	$ 1.51	$ 1.05

EXHIBIT 3-6

Intel Corporation
Balance Sheet
(in millions of dollars)

	2001	2000
Assets		
Current assets:		
Cash and cash equivalents	$ 7,970	$ 2,976
Short-term investments	2,356	10,497
Trading assets	1,224	350
Accounts receivable, net of allowance for doubtful accounts of $68 ($84 in 2000)	2,607	4,129
Inventories	2,253	2,241
Deferred tax assets	958	721
Other current assets	265	236
Total current assets	$17,633	$21,150
Property, plant, and equipment:		
Land and buildings	$10,709	$ 7,416
Machinery and equipment	21,605	15,994
Construction in progress	2,042	4,843
	$34,356	$28,253
Less accumulated depreciation	16,235	13,240
Property, plant, and equipment, net	$18,121	$15,013
Marketable strategic equity securities	155	1,915
Other long-term investments	1,319	1,797
Goodwill and other acquisition-related intangibles	5,127	5,941
Other assets	2,040	2,129
Total assets	$44,395	$47,945

Fortunately, as discussed in the previous section, some help in judging whether a ratio is appropriate can be obtained by comparing it to some "starting point" or benchmark. One such benchmark is the company's ratio from a prior year. Using Intel's current ratio for 2000 as the benchmark, its current ratio increased from 2.45 to 2.68, or by approximately 9%. This suggests that Intel's liquidity has improved during 2001, but the analyst still has to determine whether such an increase is favorable. So, a better benchmark is the comparison of the ratios of one company to those of other companies in the same industry or to an industry average. Using the ratios of another company in the same industry as the benchmark, the 2001 and 2000 current ratios for Micron Technology Incorporated are 4.57 and 3.26, respectively. Thus, it appears that Intel's ratios are similar to another company's ratios within the industry, and therefore, Intel probably does not have excess current assets. However, an analyst who is interested in assessing the liquidity of Micron Technology would want to investigate the reason for the dramatic increase in its current ratio during 2001.

Even though benchmarks are an aid to judging the appropriateness of ratios, eventually each analyst must determine his/her own answers as to what information a ratio conveys. Thus, judgment is required in properly interpreting a ratio—judgment that comes best through making decisions and learning from the results of those decisions.

The **quick ratio** (also called the acid-test ratio) measures how well a company can meet existing short-term obligations with assets that are easily converted into cash. The value of the quick ratio is that a measure is obtained of the company's ability to meet maturing obligations, regardless of future sales. That is, inventory is excluded from the ratio because the primary method of converting inventory to cash is through sales. Also, current assets such as the various prepaids and the deferred tax accounts are excluded because they cannot be turned into cash readily; rather, they represent reductions in future demands for cash. Thus, the quick ratio gives a more conservative measure of the company's ability to pay existing current liabilities, regardless of the amount of future sales. Intel has a quick ratio for 2001 of 2.15, which is a decrease from 2000's ratio of 2.8. The same ratio for Micron Technology in 2001 is 3.6, and for 2000, it was 2.68. Thus, the dramatic increase in Micron's current ratio is also revealed in the quick ratio, which is primarily the result of a significant increase in Micron's marketable securities. Perhaps the company is attempting to stockpile some cash for a future acquisition, for buying back securities, or for some other expenditure that would require a large amount of cash.

Working capital uses the same components as those used to calculate the current ratio. It measures the assets that are not required to meet existing obligations, that is, the amount of available assets that can be used to meet unexpected demands or take advantage of opportunities. Regardless of the similarity of the current ratio and working capital, some analysts prefer using working capital as a measure of liquidity because it is less susceptible to manipulation. For example, suppose that a company has $1,500 of current assets and $1,000 of current liabilities. The current ratio is 1.5, and working capital is $500. Now, suppose on December 31 that the company desires to improve the appearance of its liquidity prior to issuance of the financial statements, and to do this, it pays $500 of current liabilities. Now, current assets are $1,000 and current liabilities are $500. As a result of paying these liabilities, the current ratio has improved to 2.0, but working capital remains unchanged at $500. This simple example illustrates the notion that working capital cannot be manipulated as easily as the current ratio.

Solvency

In addition to assessing the liquidity of a company, financial statement analysts also assess **solvency**, which is a measure of the company's ability to generate cash to pay all its liabilities as they mature. Indirectly, then, it is also a measure of a company's ability to satisfy plant capacity needs and sustain growth. As with assessing liquidity, it is the relationship among accounts that is important when determining the solvency of a company. It is measured by comparing total assets or equity to long-term liabilities. An entity is insolvent when it has too few liquid assets and therefore cannot meet debt payments as they come due. It is also insolvent when its total obligations exceed its total assets, resulting in a negative net worth, which indicates it will at some time be unable to pay debts as they mature. Long-term solvency is measured in either of the following ways:

$$\text{Debt-to-Total Assets:} \ \frac{\text{Total Debt}}{\text{Total Assets}} \tag{3.5}$$

$$\text{Debt-to-Equity:} \ \frac{\text{Total Debt}}{\text{Stockholders' Equity}} \tag{3.6}$$

Both ratios measure the percentage of the company's assets that are financed by debt. As the amount of debt that a company carries increases, the probability that the company will not generate enough cash to meet scheduled interest and principal payments (i.e., insolvency) also increases. However, the flip side is that debt financing is usually a cheap form of financing. One reason is that interest payments paid on debt financing are tax deductible, and thus part of the cost of financing is borne by taxpayers, whereas dividend payments on equity financing are not deductible for tax purposes. A second reason why debt financing is usually a cheap form of financing is that the holders of the debt securities have the highest priority right to the company's assets in the event of bankruptcy, and so the holders of the debt securities do not demand as high a return compared to what equity investors may require.

Equation 3.6 is also commonly used to measure the **financial leverage** of a company.[3] As the name "leverage" implies, a company that is highly leveraged has disproportionately increased its ability to earn a profit, which occurs because the company has chosen to raise capital through debt financing—with its fixed interest rate charges—rather than through equity financing. For example, suppose that a company has an investment opportunity that will yield a 15% return. To take advantage of the opportunity, the company must raise $10 million, which it may do either by borrowing the money at 9% or by issuing stock. When the company decides to borrow the money at 9%—which it then invests at 15%—it has increased the net earnings to its stockholders through using financial leverage. But, financial leverage also has a downside that occurs during times of recession. With declining sales and profits, the company still must pay its interest commitments. Hence, financial leverage is also a measure of financial risk. As financial leverage increases, so does risk—the risk for increased profits and the risk for larger losses.

Whether financial leverage is favorable depends upon the viewpoint of the financial statement reader. Stockholders favor financial leverage; the higher the financial leverage, the better. Primarily, this is so because the stockholders are

EXTENDING THE CONCEPT

Return to Exhibit 3-2 (see p. 106) and determine which company has the greater financial leverage. During a period of national prosperity, which company's profits would increase at a more rapid rate? During a period of national recession, which company's profits would decrease at a more rapid rate?

---

[3]The phrase "trading on the equity" is synonymous with financial leverage.

shifting some downside risk from themselves to the creditors, while fully participating in the upside risk that comes from increased profits. Creditors, however,
become very anxious when financial leverage increases because they are assuming an undue risk in relation to the fixed return they are receiving. Hence, as a
company's financial leverage increases, so does the interest yield required by creditors. At some point, the company finds it unattractive to borrow more funds as
interest rates charged by creditors become prohibitive. Thus, companies strive to
find equilibrium between the benefits and costs of carrying debt.

One difficulty in computing solvency ratios (Equations 3.5 and 3.6) is deciding which accounts to include as total debt in the numerator. Two typical ways
that total debt is defined is as total liabilities and as total long-term liabilities.
However, some analysts exclude deferred taxes, or long-term contingencies, or
even other long-term liabilities from the numerator. Also, hybrid securities that
have both debt and equity characteristics present a significant problem to the analyst when deciding whether to count them as debt or equity and where to include them in the ratios. Some analysts spend a considerable amount of time
trying to decompose these securities into their equity and debt components. Furthermore, many analysts contend that off-balance-sheet financing, such as operating leases, should be included in the ratios. The decision as to which items to
include or exclude often depends upon the purpose the analyst has in computing the ratio. Whatever the decision as to which items to include, it is important
that the ratio be computed consistently from year to year and consistently for comparable companies.

As with interpreting other ratios, the analyst needs to compare the computed ratios with those of other companies in the same industry and to ratios in the same company in previous years. Traditionally, a debt-to-equity ratio of less than 50% has been considered advisable, with higher ratios indicating that a company may have potential problems meeting its debt obligations. However, the appropriate level of debt that a company should carry will be determined more by industry factors than anything else. So, judgment is required in interpreting these ratios to obtain the desired insights.

Including all reported liabilities in the numerator, the debt-to-equity ratio for Intel Corporation in 2001 was 23.9%, and in 2000, it was 28.5%. The same ratio for Micron Technology decreased dramatically—from 43.2% in 2000 to 17.1% in 2001. An analyst probably would desire to know the reason for Micron's decision to significantly reduce the level of debt during 2001.

Another form of leverage is **operating leverage**, which measures a company's ability to dispropor-tionately earn a profit as sales increase because of uti-lizing fixed costs as compared to variable costs. A company with higher fixed costs has greater operat-ing leverage. The concept is that with relatively high fixed costs and resulting lower variable costs, a com-pany's opportunity is greater for profits to increase rapidly when sales increase or for profits to decrease rapidly when sales decrease. This concept is illus-trated in Exhibit 3-7. Note that as sales increase or

EXTENDING THE CONCEPT

Micron Technology has a much higher financial leverage than Intel, as indicated by its higher levels of debt. This means that the com-pany's overall net income will be more sensitive to a change in op-erating income. To illustrate, assume the following facts for two companies: Company A and Company B.

	Company A	Company B
Operating income before interest and taxes	$2,000	$2,000
Debt outstanding (8% interest)	$1,000	$10,000
Interest expense	$80	$800
Tax expense (40% tax rate)	$768	$480
Net income	$1,152	$720
Shares outstanding (at $1 per share)	10,000	1,000
EPS	$0.1152	$0.72

Both companies received $11,000 of capital but in different forms. Company A received $10,000 of its capital through equity financing. Company B, on the other hand, received $10,000 of its financing through issuing debt.

For both companies, the profit before interest and taxes was the same. However, due to the tax deductibility of the interest, the stockholders of Company B earned a much higher return.

Now assume that the operating income before interest and taxes decreased by $1,000 for both companies. What is the new return to the shareholders of each company (i.e., EPS)? Why was the change in EPS so much larger for Company B than the change for Company A? Explain the advantages and disadvantages of financial leverage. Which company is the more risky company?

EXHIBIT 3-7

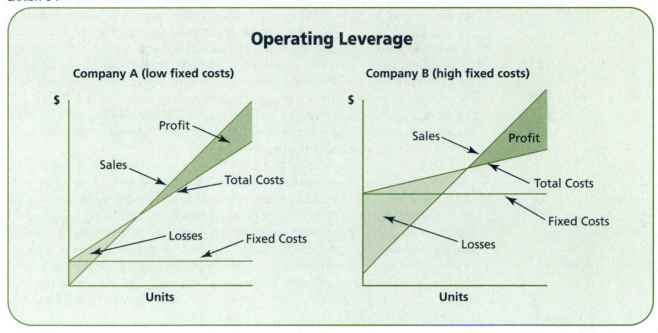

decrease, the change in net income is greater for the company with greater fixed costs. The degree of operating leverage—at a given level of sales—is measured by the following formula:

$$\text{Degree of Operating Leverage:} \quad \frac{\text{Contribution Margin}}{\text{Net Income}} \qquad (3.7)$$

Liquidity and solvency are closely related to the important concept of **financial flexibility**, which refers to an entity's ability to effectively respond to unexpected cash demands and to take advantage of new opportunities. For example, a company may become so loaded with debt—so financially inflexible—that cash is totally committed, leaving the company with no cash to accept opportunities. Also, an entity having financial flexibility can weather unexpected losses, recessions, or damage claims. Even the existence of large companies can be threatened because of the negative impact of such events, which may force them into the capital market to obtain needed funds. However, the availability of such funds becomes increasingly difficult to obtain for companies experiencing hard times. Hence, every company needs to have some financial flexibility.

EXTENDING THE CONCEPT

To make the debt-to-equity ratio more attractive, some financial consultants advise (1) retaining more earnings in the company by not paying a dividend until after the balance sheet date, or (2) paying off obligations before the balance sheet date and then borrowing again afterwards, or (3) deferring some expenses.

As an accountant, do you consider such actions ethical? Is accurate information being communicated to the financial statement reader? What advice would you give to improve the debt-to-equity ratio?

Profitability

The income statement is the best source of information about a company's profitability because it contains the most quoted and most referred to financial statistic of any business: earnings-per-share (EPS). Many analysts, accountants, businessmen, and others *consider EPS to be the single best overall indicator of the effectiveness and efficiency of the company and therefore an indication of the future profitability of the company.* Also, as mentioned when defining accrual accounting, net income is thought to be a long-run predictor of the amount and certainty of future cash flows.

While EPS on net income is important, it may be that EPS from continuing operations may be more indicative of future dividend payments and the ability to repay loans, as this is the income amount that can be depended upon to continue. By definition, nonoperating items of revenues, gains, expenses, and losses are infrequent and are not expected to persist. In addition, such nonoperating items often do not involve cash flows but consist of changing bookkeeping techniques, or they are the differences between book amounts and the cash received. Hence, giving users of financial statements an income statement that separates operating items from nonoperating items is important so that financial statement users can determine which income amount best fits their needs.

In spite of the popularity of using EPS as a summary measure of a company's performance, the same cautions about interpreting a single number without a cross-sectional or trend analysis apply here, too. As important as the current EPS may be, the trend of EPS figures over several years is a better gauge of the future profitability of any company, as it also indicates which direction net income is moving. For this reason, many companies include a five-year or a 10-year trend of significant financial numbers in their annual reports, which include earnings per share. The information contained in Exhibit 3-8 was extracted from an 11-year summary of an extensive list of what Dow Chemical considers to be significant data and illustrates this reporting of trend data.

EXHIBIT 3-8

The Dow Chemical Company
Supplemental Reporting of Trend Data
Eleven-Year Summary of Selected Financial Data
In millions, except as noted (unaudited)

	1998	1997	1996	1995	1994
Net sales	$18,441	$20,200	$16,742	$15,052	$15,493
Operating income	1,386	2,726	3,087	3,891	1,820
Net income (loss) available for common stockholders	1,304	1,802	1,900	2,071	931
Per share of common stock, net income: basic	5.86	7.81	7.71	7.72	3.37
Cash dividends declared	3.48	3.36	3.00	2.90	2.60
Total assets	23,830	24,040	24,673	23,582	26,545
Working capital	1,198	1,629	4,276	5,451	2,339
Net stockholders' equity	7,429	7,626	7,954	7,361	8,212

In addition to EPS, other important profitability ratios include:

$$\text{Return on Assets:} \frac{\text{Net Income}^4}{\text{Average Total Assets}} \tag{3.8}$$

$$\text{Return on Equity:} \frac{\text{Net Income}}{\text{Average Total Stockholders' Equity}} \tag{3.9}$$

---

[4]The prior discussion as to what net income should be for computing earnings per share applies also to computing the ratios in Equations 3.8 and 3.9.

The return on assets ratio, which is also frequently referred to as return on investment (ROI), is considered an overall measure of management's effectiveness and efficiency. The return on equity ratio is oriented towards the overall return to equity investors. In both ratios, the numerator is net income, and the denominator is a measure of resources available to management. The average amount is computed by taking the beginning and ending balances and dividing by two. Although the calculation of the ratios appears straightforward, various analysts choose to focus on different measures of income and even on different measures of total assets. Therefore, many different versions of these basic ratios are used. One common variation uses an operating income number (excluding taxes, interest, discontinued operations, etc.) in the numerator. A slightly different version includes taxes in determining the income number but does not include any other nonoperating items. Still other analysts focus on the return from only long-term assets and so exclude current assets from the denominator of ROI. Regardless of the variations, the most frequently used form of ROI is defining income as net income and assets as total assets. Although variations also exist for the return on equity components, the typical components are net income and total stockholders' equity.

When a company has negative stockholders' equity, computing the return on equity ratio gives nonsensical results. This is because, as net income increases, the overall ratio decreases. Thus, when an analyst is using a computer program to conduct an analysis on a large cross-section of companies, care must be taken to ensure that all comparisons are valid.

The profitability ratios for Intel Corporation for 2001 and 2000 are as follows (the 1999 balance sheet was obtained to compute the 2000 average total assets and stockholders' equity):

	2001	2000
Basic earnings per share	$0.19	$1.57
Return on assets	2.8%	22.4%
Return on equity	3.5%	28.6%

A useful decomposition of the return on assets ratio is frequently done in order to provide additional insights into the operating performance of a company. The decomposition is expressed mathematically as a combination of return on sales (see Equation 3.1) and the total asset turnover. The decomposition is as follows:

$$\text{Return on Assets: } \frac{\text{Net Income}}{\text{Net Sales}} \times \frac{\text{Net Sales}}{\text{Average Total Assets}} \qquad (3.8a)$$

$$\underbrace{\qquad\qquad}_{\text{(return on sales)}} \quad \underbrace{\qquad\qquad}_{\text{(total asset turnover)}}$$

This decomposition shows that a company's operating performance is a combination of its profitability (i.e., return on sales) and its efficiency (i.e., total asset turnover). Net income divided by net sales is often referred to as **profit margin** and indicates how much profit a company earns from each dollar of sales. This ratio indicates how efficiently the company turns sales into profits. The total asset turnover is an asset management ratio and indicates how efficiently the company uses its assets to produce sales.

Decomposing the return on asset ratio facilitates identifying the reason as to why ROI is less than expected or how to improve it. Suppose, for example, that a company's return on assets is 14.3% but that most of the other companies in the same industry are receiving a return on assets of 20%. Wanting to know where its efforts can best be focused to improve its company's return on assets, management decomposes the ratio as follows:

$$ROI = \frac{10}{150} \times \frac{150}{70}, \text{ which yields}$$

$$ROI = 6.67\% \times 2.14 \text{ times} = 14.3\%$$

Comparing the above computations to the results of other companies in the same industry, the company finds that the average return on sales is 10%, and the typical asset turnover is 2. Thus, the company knows that the best way of improving its overall return on assets is to focus on improving the return on sales. Improving the return on sales portion may require reducing expenses, focusing on core competencies, becoming more efficient, etc. Determining exactly how to improve the ROI will not be simple, but at least management now has a starting point.

Analysts benefit from decomposing the return on asset ratio and receive insights as to why particular companies are doing better (or worse) than their competitors. Thus, they can better determine in which companies they want to invest or loan funds, or they can make other decisions of interest.

Asset Management

Decision makers are frequently interested in how effective company management is in using the company's assets to produce revenues and ultimately profit. A commonly used tool that is used to assess management's effectiveness in utilizing its assets is the various turnover ratios. A turnover ratio is computed by using sales, generally, as the numerator of the ratio and some asset as the denominator. The one exception to this general equation is for computing the inventory turnover ratio, in which case the numerator is the cost of goods sold instead of sales. Turnover ratios can be calculated for any specific asset, classification of assets (such as property, plant, and equipment), or for total assets.

$$\text{Inventory Turnover}[5]: \frac{\text{Cost of Goods Sold}}{\text{Average Inventory}} \tag{3.10}$$

All Other Turnover Ratios:

$$\frac{\text{Sales}}{\text{Average of any Asset Account, Subtotal, or Total}} \tag{3.11}$$

Thus, when the total asset turnover ratio is less than optimal, management or analysts can decompose the ratio either into asset subtotals or even individual accounts so that the category or single asset that is being mismanaged can be identified. Once these assets or groups of assets have been identified, management can investigate the causes for the mismanagement and take steps to correct matters. Also, analysts are better able to make a judgment as to the possible success the company management will have in correcting the problems.

---

[5]Many times the inventory turnover is computed by using sales, rather than cost of goods sold, as the numerator.

As an example of computing and interpreting turnover ratios, assume that a company sells on account with credit terms of n/30. In this case, the dollar amount in Accounts Receivable could turn over optimally 12 times a year (i.e., 12 × 30 days equals 360 days or one year). Accordingly, the effectiveness of management in managing its accounts receivable (i.e., extending credit to worthy applicants and subsequently collecting amounts owed) is measured by computing an accounts receivable turnover and comparing the computed number to 12. Obviously, companies with different credit terms have different optimal turnover ratios, and each company should be evaluated against its own optimum. Further, higher turnover ratios do not necessarily indicate improved operating performance. For instance, in the previous example, an accounts receivable turnover ratio of 16 may indicate that the company's cash discount policies are too liberal. This is the same technique that is used to interpret other turnover ratios—comparing the actual turnover to some optimum, whether that optimum can be computed from company policy as was done with the previous accounts receivable turnover, or whether the optimum is some industry average.

In Equation 3.8a it was shown how the return on asset ratio can be decomposed into its two basic components, so that management, analysts, and others can focus their attention on how best to improve the company's performance. That same type of decomposition can be extended to include various other components, and to further narrow the problem areas in the company's operations, as follows:

$$\text{ROI:} \frac{\text{NI}}{\text{EBT}} \times \frac{\text{EBT}}{\text{EBIT}} \times \frac{\text{EBIT}}{\text{Sales}} \times \frac{\text{Sales}}{\text{Total Assets}} \qquad (3.12)$$

where,

NI is net income,
EBT is earnings before taxes, and
EBIT is earnings before interest and taxes.

The first component measures the percentage of operating income that the company is able to retain. The second component measures the impact of long-term debt on the company's profitability (i.e., the amount of income the company retains after paying interest and taxes). The third component measures the return on sales, and the fourth measures how effective management is in utilizing its assets.

Also, the return on equity ratio can be decomposed by just extending the decomposition of the ROI one step further, as follows:

$$\text{ROI:} \frac{\text{NI}}{\text{EBT}} \times \frac{\text{EBT}}{\text{EBIT}} \times \frac{\text{EBIT}}{\text{Sales}} \times \frac{\text{Sales}}{\text{Total Assets}} \times \frac{\text{Total Assets}}{\text{Common Equity}} \qquad (3.13)$$

Adding this last component measures the effect of financial leverage on return on equity.

EXTENDING THE CONCEPT

Is it possible to decompose the total asset turnover ratio (i.e., sales/total assets) into multiple components so that the sum of, for example, an inventory turn plus an accounts receivable turn plus other turnover ratios equals the total asset turnover?

Returning to Zenith Corporation

An obvious conclusion to this introduction to ratio analysis is that it is limited only by the imagination of the analyst. Referring back to the opening scenario of Zenith and using information provided in its annual report that was made public in March 1998, the following financial statement ratios are computed.

	1997	1996
Current ratio	0.67	1.05
Debt to equity	1.15	0.79
Return on assets	(46.3%)	(24.5%)
Return on equity	(820.3%)	(75.9%)
Inventory turnover	5.61	5.61
Total asset turnover	1.81	1.77

It can be seen that Zenith did not have the ability to pay its debts as they came due, that it carried too much debt, and that (because the return ratios are negative) it was not earning a profit. The asset management ratios (i.e., inventory and total asset turnover) remained relatively stable in spite of the significant decrease in the level of inventory and assets during 1997. Although hindsight is 20/20 and recommendations are easy to make after the fact, it does appear that information about the pending bankruptcy was available to the market in the company's annual report. Even the calculation of a few simple ratios would have provided ample warning of this fact.

Summary

Financial statement analysis is the means by which information about the financial health of a company is obtained in order to make economic decisions. Financial statement analysis is used by many readers of financial statements, including creditors to determine whether a loan should be granted, equity investors to assess the potential return of a company's stock, other businesses to assess the potential of a takeover and determine the appropriate market price, and boards of directors to evaluate company management.

No matter what decision is being considered, the decision maker will likely desire information about the company's liquidity, long-term solvency, profitability, and asset management. Several financial statement analysis tools are introduced in this chapter to assist the analyst in obtaining this type of information.

Preparation of common-size financial statements, which is also referred to as vertical analysis, requires that all amounts be displayed as a percentage of some base financial statement item—sales for the income statement and total assets for the balance sheet. Common-size financial statements highlight the important components that comprise net income and total assets and can facilitate comparisons with other companies (cross-sectional analysis) or with the same company over time (trend analysis).

Common-size financial statements, along with additional information from company footnotes and national economic indicators, are useful in constructing pro forma financial statements, which project the operating performance of a company given certain assumptions. Upon completion of the pro forma income statement, other financial statements also can be developed.

In this chapter, several financial statement ratios were introduced that are used to judge a company's liquidity, long-term solvency, profitability, and asset management. Care must be exercised in interpreting all ratios, since they are industry specific and may even justifiably vary within the same industry. Hence, the results of ratios for a specific company should be compared with industry averages before putting undue emphasis on them. In addition, ratios computed in the current year should be compared with those of the same company in previous years to identify trends. Many times, the primary result of ratio analysis is not to find answers but to raise questions that will require further analysis or research.

Questions

1. Discuss some of the limitations of financial statement analysis.

2. When conducting financial statement analysis, comparing company specific results to a benchmark is necessary. Identify some potentially useful benchmarks.

3. Define each of the following terms, and identify the financial statement readers who would likely be interested in this attribute:
   a. Liquidity
   b. Solvency
   c. Profitability
   d. Asset management

4. What is the difference between "trend analysis" and "cross-sectional analysis"? What type of analysis is horizontal analysis? Vertical analysis?

5. What information about a company's efficiency in managing assets and profitability can an analyst obtain from a common-size financial statement?

6. Review the three basic steps necessary to construct a pro forma income statement.

7. Assume that Company A, after analyzing the behavior of its operating expenses, estimates that 80% of its costs are fixed and 20% are variable. In contrast, Company B's costs are 30% fixed and 70% variable. Which company has the greater operating leverage? How does operating leverage affect earnings?

8. Identify specific ratios that can provide information about the following areas:
   a. Liquidity
   b. Solvency
   c. Profitability
   d. Asset management

9. When calculating solvency ratios, several different amounts could be used as a measure of debt. Identify some alternatives and discuss the rationale for using each one.

10. When calculating profitability ratios, several different income statement line items could be used as "net income" in the various ratios. Identify some alternatives and discuss the rationale for using each one.

11. Decompose the return on assets ratio into its profitability and asset management ratios.

12. Suppose that a company reports a profit of $700,000 on sales of $6,300,000, and the total asset turnover is 2. What is the return on assets for this company? What is the company's average total assets as reported on the balance sheet?

Exercises

Exercise 3-1: Financial Statement Ratios. Information related to the accounts of Twin City Galleries, Inc., for the year ended December 31, 2004, is as follows:

Sales	$2,000,000
Cost of goods sold	1,400,000
Net income	100,000
Merchandise inventory:	
Beginning	300,000
Ending	400,000
Total assets:	
Beginning	1,800,000
Ending	2,100,000

Calculate the following ratios for Twin City Galleries:

1. Return on assets
2. Profit margin
3. Total asset turnover
4. Inventory turnover
5. Gross profit percentage

Exercise 3-2: Asset Turnover Ratios. Financial statement data is presented below for Sherm's Merchandise, Inc.

Balance Sheet Data

	2004	2003
Cash	$ 12,000	$ 10,000
Accounts receivable (net)	32,000	25,000
Inventories	38,000	44,000
Property, plant, and equipment	120,000	104,000
Total assets	$202,000	$183,000

Income Statement Data

	2004	2003
Sales	$188,000	$167,000
Cost of goods sold	98,000	92,000
Gross profit	$ 90,000	$ 75,000
Selling, general, and administrative expenses	61,000	52,000
Net income	$ 29,000	$ 23,000

1. Calculate the 2004 turnover ratios for each individual asset presented and for total assets.
2. Compute the company's gross profit margin and total profit margin percentages for 2003 and 2004. What was the major reason for the increase in profit margin?
3. What is the company's return on assets for 2004?
4. If asset turnover increased to 1.2 times, but profit margin remained unchanged, what would the company's return on assets be for 2005?

Exercise 3-3: Inventory Turnover. Virent Technologies, Inc., had beginning inventory as of January 1, 2004, of $330,000. During the fiscal year, the company made purchases of $2,800,000. All purchases were made evenly throughout the year. Total sales for the year was $4,700,000, and ending inventory as of December 31, 2004, was $375,000. Calculate Virent's inventory turnover ratio for the 2004 fiscal year.

Exercise 3-4: Receivable Turnover. Thotley's Stores recorded sales for the year ended December 31, 2004, of $989,000. The gross profit realized on these sales was $450,000, and net income was $128,000. Accounts receivable on January 1, 2004, was $67,000, and on December 31, 2004, it was $83,000.

1. Calculate the receivable turnover ratio for Thotley's Stores for the year 2004.
2. Calculate the average time to collect a typical account receivable. If the company's policy is to extend credit for 30 days, comment on the effectiveness of the company's collection procedures.

Exercise 3-5: Current Ratio. The Sleigh Company had current assets in the amount of $125,000 and current liabilities of $82,000.

1. Calculate the company's current ratio and working capital.
2. Calculate the effect of the following independent transactions on the company's current ratio and working capital:
   a. The company purchased inventory of $25,000 on account.
   b. The company purchased equipment for $50,000 by issuing a long-term note that requires equal annual installments of $12,000 (including interest). The first installment is due within one year.
   c. The company refinanced a $15,000 short-term note. The new terms call for three annual installments of $7,000 (including interest). The first installment is due within one year.
   d. The company sold $10,000 of its accounts receivable for $9,000.
   e. The company accrued wage expenses of $8,000. The amount will be paid in one week.

Exercise 3-6: Financial Statement Ratios. Answer the following independent questions.

1. During the current year, Marcus Co. had beginning inventory of $78,000 and ending inventory of $92,000, and its inventory turnover was 4. Due to changes in demand for its product, the company expects sales to increase by 15 percent during the coming year. Historically, the gross profit percentage has been 40%, and during the coming year, unit costs are expected to remain unchanged. The company's goal is to have an inventory turnover of 5. What does ending inventory need to be at the end of the coming year to reach this goal?
2. Peterson, Inc., has current assets of $1,300,000, a current ratio of 2.0, and a quick ratio of 0.8. What is the total of the company's inventory and prepaid accounts?
3. Wondum, Inc., had a return on assets of 15% during the most recent fiscal year, based on average total assets of $1 million and sales of $1.8 million. What was the company's profit margin percentage?
4. Youngstown, Inc., reported total assets at the end of the most recent fiscal year of $2.5 million. The company's total debt-to-equity ratio was 1.5. Assuming that equity did not change during the year and net income was $200,000, what was the company's return on equity ratio?

Exercise 3-7: Asset Management. JCL, Inc., desires to cut costs related to holding inventories. The company hopes that by reducing the amount of inventories held, internally generated funds will be sufficient to pay for the needed purchases rather than having to borrow funds. The interest rate on short-term debt is 10%. The company's inventory turnover ratio for the most recent year was 5, based on cost of goods sold of $770,000. Assuming that cost of goods sold is expected to remain stable over the next year, calculate the amount of interest costs that would be saved if the company could increase the inventory turnover ratio from 5 to 7.

Problems

Problem 3-1: Interpreting Ratios. The following is a list of financial statement ratios for two separate companies.

	Company A	Company B
Profitability Ratios		
Net income	$1,800,000	$4,400,000
Earnings per share	$0.95	$1.80
Gross profit percentage	40%	45%
Return on assets	12%	9%
Return on equity	45%	23%
Asset Management Ratios		
Total asset turnover	0.97	1.50
Receivable turnover	3.73	6.72
Inventory turnover	6.02	7.33
Long-term assets turnover	1.75	2.48
Liquidity Ratios		
Current ratio	2.68	3.96
Working capital	$4,200,000	$14,500,000
Quick ratio	2.10	2.84
Solvency Ratios		
Long-term debt to equity ratio	2.13	1.31
Long-term debt to total asset ratio	57%	39%

Required:
Analyze the ratios and write a report to a client about the comparative investment prospects of both companies.

Problem 3-2: Analyzing Ratios. Refer to the ratios provided for each company in Problem 3-1.

Required:
Based on the information provided within the ratios, complete the following financial statements. Round all amounts to the nearest thousands.

Income Statements

	Company A	Company B
Sales		
Cost of goods sold		
Gross profit		
Operating expenses		
Net income		
Weighted-average number of common shares outstanding		

Balance Sheets

	Company A	Company B
Cash		
Accounts receivable		
Inventory		
Total current assets		
Property, plant, and equipment		
Total assets		
Current liabilities		
Long-term debt		
Stockholders' equity		
Total liabilities and stockholders' equity		

Problem 3-3: Analyzing Financial Statements that Use Different Accounting Principles. Provided are the income statement and balance sheet for JCPenney Co., Inc., for the year ended December 31, 1999. It uses the LIFO inventory valuation method for most of its inventory. *Note:* The LIFO reserve, as shown in the balance sheet, represents the reduction in inventory value as a result of using LIFO over FIFO.

INCOME STATEMENT

(in thousands of dollars)	1999	1998	1997
Revenue:			
Retail sales, net	$31,391	$29,439	$29,482
Direct marketing revenue	1,119	1,022	928
Total revenue	$32,510	$30,461	$30,410
Costs and expenses:			
Cost of goods sold	$23,374	$21,642	$21,294
Selling, general, and admin. expenses	7,164	6,623	6,566
Expenses of direct marketing	872	785	711
Real estate and other	(28)	(26)	(39)
Net interest expense	299	391	457
Acquisition amortization	129	113	117
Other charges and credits, net	169	(22)	379
Total costs and expenses	$31,979	$29,506	$29,485
Income before taxes	$ 531	$ 955	$ 925
Income taxes	195	361	359
Net income	$ 336	$ 594	$ 566

BALANCE SHEET

(in thousands of dollars)	1999	1998
Assets		
Current assets:		
Cash (including short-term investments of $1,233 and $95)	$ 1,233	$ 96
Retained interest in JCP Master Credit Card Trust	—	415
Receivables, net (bad debt reserve of $20 and $149)	1,138	4,268
Merchandise inventory (including LIFO reserves of $270 and $227)	5,947	6,060
Prepaid expenses	154	168
Total current assets	$ 8,472	$11,007
Property and equipment:		
Land and buildings	$ 3,089	$ 3,109
Furniture and fixtures	3,955	4,045
Leasehold improvements	1,151	1,179
Accumulated depreciation	(2,883)	(2,875)
Property and equipment, net	$ 5,312	$ 5,458
Investments, principally held by direct marketing	$ 1,827	$ 1,961
Deferred policy acquisition costs	929	847
Goodwill and other intangible assets, net (accumulated amortization of $340 and $227)	3,056	2,941
Other assets	1,292	1,294
Total assets	$20,888	$23,508
Liabilities and stockholders' equity		
Current liabilities:		
Accounts payable and accrued expenses	$ 3,351	$ 3,443
Short-term debt	330	1,924
Current maturities of long-term debt	625	438
Deferred taxes	159	107
Total current liabilities	$ 4,465	$ 5,912
Long-term debt	$ 5,844	$ 7,143
Deferred taxes	1,461	1,512
Insurance policy and claims reserves	1,017	946
Other liabilities	873	893
Total liabilities	$13,660	$16,406
Stockholders' Equity:		
Preferred stock authorized, 25 million shares; issued and outstanding, 0.7 million and 0.8 million shares Series B ESOP convertible preferred	$ 446	$ 475
Common stock, par value 50 cents: authorized, 1,250 million shares; issued and outstanding 261 million and 250 million shares	3,266	2,850
Reinvested earnings	3,590	3,791
Accumulated other comprehensive income/(loss)	(74)	(14)
Total stockholders' equity	$ 7,228	$ 7,102
Total liabilities and stockholders' equity	$20,888	$23,508

Required:

1. Assume that JCPenney's effective tax rate is 40%. If JCPenney had been using the FIFO inventory valuation method, determine the amount of net income that the company would have reported in 1999.
2. Calculate the following ratios for JCPenney for 1999 under both the LIFO and FIFO inventory valuation methods. (*Hint:* In addition to considering the change in inventory, be sure to also consider the change in income tax expense and income taxes payable due to any change in net income.)
   a. Current ratio
   b. Inventory turnover ratio
   c. Total debt to total assets ratio
   d. Total debt to equity ratio
3. Would you recommend the use of LIFO to JCPenney? Why do you suppose that JCPenney has chosen to use the LIFO method instead of the FIFO method?

Problem 3-4: Common-Size Financial Statements. Refer to the financial statements provided in Problem 3-3.

Required:

Construct common-size financial statements for the company for all years presented. Use total revenue as the base item for the income statement and total assets as the base item for the balance sheet. Given the information in the common-size financial statements, provide any insights you obtained from your analysis.

Problem 3-5: Horizontal Analysis. Refer to the financial statements provided in Problem 3-3.

Required:

Conduct a horizontal analysis for JCPenney Co., Inc. Prepare a brief statement that summarizes your results.

Problem 3-6: Pro Forma Financial Statements. Refer to the financial data for 1999 and 1998 in Problem 3-3 (and, if done, Problem 3-4) for JCPenney Co., Inc.

Required:

1. Using an electronic spreadsheet, determine the fixed and variable nature of each expense by using the high-low method.
2. Continuing to use the electronic spreadsheet, evaluate the sensitivity of JCPenney's net income to a change in economic conditions by constructing pro forma income statements, assuming that:
   a. Sales will increase by 15% during the next fiscal year. (Round amounts to the nearest dollar.)
   b. Sales will decrease by 15% during the next fiscal year. (Round amounts to the nearest dollar.)
3. Based upon your projected income statements, what expense must be brought under control for JCPenney Co. to earn an income next year?

Research Activities

Activity 3-1: JCPenney Co., Inc. Upon completing Problems 3-3, 3-4, and/or 3-5, augment your analysis of JCPenney Co., Inc., by evaluating the company's performance compared to a benchmark, as follows:

1. Determine the primary industry in which JCPenney conducts its operations. Using aggregated numbers provided by Moody's or Standard & Poor's services, obtain the industry average for some liquidity, profitability, solvency, and asset management ratios. Compare the industry averages with JCPenney's results, and prepare a statement that summarizes your analysis.

2. Choose a company within the same industry as JCPenney and calculate liquidity, profitability, solvency, and asset management ratios for the company and compare them with the same ratios for JCPenney for the same period. Prepare a statement that summarizes your findings.

3. Prepare common-size financial statements for both companies, using sales as the base item for the income statement and total assets as the base item for the balance sheet. Evaluate both companies' performance. Prepare a report that summarizes your findings.

Activity 3-2: Value-Line Analyst Reports. Obtain a recent Value-Line (**http://www.valueline.com**) report for three companies within the same industry. Summarize the reports in your own words by focusing on the following questions (other aspects of the report may be focused on as appropriate):

1. Do the analysts believe the outlook of the company is favorable?
2. What specific company characteristics did the analyst focus on?
3. Did the analyst refer to industry and/or national economic trends?
4. What accounting data were highlighted in the report?
5. Did the analyst focus on specific financial statement ratios?
6. What is the forecasted EPS for the company, and how does it compare to historical amounts?
7. How has the stock price changed for the company during the past year?

Activity 3-3: Other Ratios. The ratios introduced in this chapter are some of the basic ratios that are used. In the October 1998 *Journal of Accountancy* is an article by Mills and Yamamura that discusses cash flow ratios, and in the August 2001 *Journal of Accountancy* is an article by Wells that discusses ratios that may highlight financial difficulty. Read both of these articles and then write a short paper summarizing them.

Cases

Case 3-1. Amazon.com. Amazon.com, Inc., was incorporated in July 1994 and opened its virtual doors on the Web in July 1995. Amazon.com is an Internet retailer offering more than 18 million unique items in categories including books, music, DVD/video, toys, electronics, software, video games and home improvement products. Amazon.com offers a free electronic greeting card service and also provides a community of online shoppers with an easy and safe way to purchase and sell a large selection of products through Amazon.com Auctions and Shops.

In recent years, there has been a great deal of interest and attention paid to Amazon.com by analysts, investors, and others because of what is perceived to be its growth potential and because of its consistent large losses. Some investors have become millionaires because of investing in Amazon.com, but perhaps the time to profit from investing in Amazon.com is over. Or is it? Following are some recently published financial statements of Amazon.com for you to analyze and make that determination for yourself.

AMAZON.COM, INC.
CONSOLIDATED STATEMENTS OF OPERATIONS
(in thousands, except per share data)
Years Ended December 31,

	1999	1998	1997
Net sales	**$1,639,839**	**$ 609,819**	**$147,787**
Cost of sales	1,349,194	476,155	118,969
Gross profit	$ 290,645	$ 133,664	$ 28,818
Operating expenses:			
Marketing and sales	$ 413,150	$ 132,654	$ 40,077
Technology and content	159,722	46,424	13,384
General and administrative	70,144	15,618	6,741
Stock-based compensation	30,618	1,889	1,211
Amortization of goodwill and other intangibles	214,694	42,599	—
Merger, acquisition and investment-related	8,072	3,535	—
Total operating expenses	$ 896,400	$ 242,719	$ 61,413
Loss from operations	$ (605,755)	$(109,055)	$ (32,595)
Interest	45,451	14,053	1,901
Interest expense	(84,566)	(26,639)	(326)
Other income, net	1,671	—	—
Net interest income (expense) and other	(37,444)	(12,586)	1,575
Loss before equity in losses of equity-method investees	$ (643,199)	$(121,641)	$ (31,020)
Equity in losses of equity-method investees	(76,769)	(2,905)	—
Net loss	$ (719,968)	$(124,546)	$ (31,020)
Basic and diluted loss per share	$(2.20)	$(0.42)	$(0.12)
Shares used in computation of basic and diluted loss per share	326,753	296,344	260,682

AMAZON.COM, INC.
CONSOLIDATED BALANCE SHEETS
(in thousands, except per share data)
Years Ended December 31,

	1999	1998
Assets		
Current assets:		
Cash	$ 116,962	$ 25,561
Marketable securities	589,226	347,884
Inventories	220,646	29,501
Prepaid expenses and other current assets	85,344	21,308
Total current assets	$1,012,178	$ 424,254
Fixed assets, net	317,613	29,791
Goodwill, net	534,699	174,052
Other purchased intangibles, net	195,445	4,586
Investments in equity-method investees	226,727	7,740
Other investments	144,735	—
Deferred charges and other	40,154	8,037
Total assets	$2,471,551	$ 648,460

(continued)

	1999	1998
Liabilities and stockholders' equity		
Current liabilities:		
Accounts payable	$ 463,026	$ 113,273
Accrued expenses and other current liabilities	126,017	34,413
Accrued advertising	55,892	13,071
Deferred revenue	54,790	—
Interest payable	24,888	10
Current portion of long-term debt and other	14,322	808
Total current liabilities	$ 738,935	$ 161,575
Long-term debt and other commitments and contingencies	$1,466,338	$ 348,140
Stockholders' equity:		
Preferred stock, $0.01 par value: authorized shares—150,000; issued and outstanding shares—none	—	—
Common stock, $0.01 par value: authorized shares—1,500,000; issued and outstanding shares—345,155 and 318,534 shares at December 31, 1999 and 1998, respectively	$ 3,452	$ 3,186
Additional paid-in	1,195,540	298,537
Note receivable for common stock	(1,171)	(1,099)
Stock-based compensation	(47,806)	(1,625)
Accumulated other comprehensive income (loss)	(1,709)	1,806
Accumulated deficit	(882,028)	(162,060)
Total stockholders' equity	$ 266,278	$ 138,745
Total liabilities and stockholders' equity	$2,471,551	$ 648,460

Required:

1. Using an electronic spreadsheet, prepare a cross-sectional and trend analysis on the income statement and balance sheet. (That is, do a vertical and a horizontal analysis.) Then, make any observations of which a potential investor should be aware.

2. Compute the following ratios for 1999 an 1998, and make some general observations:
   a. Current ratio
   b. Long-term debt to equity ratio
   c. Return on assets
   d. Return on equity
   e. Inventory turnover (use ending inventory figures in lieu of average inventory)

Case 3-2. Southwest Airlines Co. Southwest Airlines is a national low-fare airline whose motto is focusing on customer satisfaction. Primarily, Southwest flies shorthaul city pairs, providing single class air transportation and targeting the business commuter and leisure travelers. The company commenced operations on June 18, 1971, with three Boeing 737 aircraft serving three Texas cities—Dallas, Houston, and San Antonio. At year-end 1997, Southwest operated 261 Boeing 737 aircraft and provided service to 52 airports in 51 cities throughout the United States. Southwest claims to have the lowest operating cost structure in the domestic airline industry and the lowest and simplest fares. It has one of the best overall customer service records in the airline industry. Financial statements are as follows.

SOUTHWEST AIRLINES CO.
CONSOLIDATED BALANCE SHEET
(in thousands, except share and per share amounts)
Years Ended December 31,

	1997	1996
Assets		
Current assets:		
Cash and cash equivalents	$ 623,343	$ 581,841
Accounts receivable	76,530	73,440
Inventories of parts and supplies, at cost	52,376	51,094
Deferred income taxes	18,843	11,560
Prepaid expenses and other current assets	35,324	33,055
Total current assets	$ 806,416	$ 750,990
Property and equipment, at cost:		
Flight equipment	$3,987,493	$3,435,304
Ground property and equipment	601,957	523,958
Deposits on flight equipment purchase contracts	221,874	198,366
	$4,811,324	$4,157,628
Less allowance for depreciation	1,375,631	1,188,405
	$3,435,693	$2,969,223
Other assets	4,051	3,266
Total assets	$4,246,160	$3,723,479
Liabilities and stockholders' equity		
Current liabilities:		
Accounts payable	$ 160,891	$ 214,232
Accrued liabilities	426,950	368,625
Air traffic liability	153,341	158,098
Current maturities of long-term debt	121,324	12,327
Other current liabilities	6,007	12,122
Total current liabilities	$ 868,513	$ 765,404
Long-term debt less current maturities	$ 628,106	$ 650,226
Deferred income taxes	$ 438,981	$ 349,987
Deferred gains from sale and leaseback of aircraft	$ 256,255	$ 274,891
Other deferred liabilities	$ 45,287	$ 34,659
Commitments and contingencies		
Stockholders' equity:		
Common stock, $1.00 par value: 680,000,000 shares authorized; 221,207,083 and 145,112,090 shares issued and outstanding in 1997 and 1996, respectively	$ 221,207	$ 145,112
Capital in excess of par value	155,696	181,650
Retained earnings	1,632,115	1,321,550
Total stockholders' equity	$2,009,018	$1,648,312
Total liabilities and stockholders' equity	$4,246,160	$3,723,479

SOUTHWEST AIRLINES CO.
CONSOLIDATED STATEMENT OF INCOME
(in thousands, except per share amounts)
Years Ended December 31,

	1997	1996	1995
Operating revenues:			
Passenger	$3,639,193	$3,269,238	$2,760,756
Freight	94,758	80,005	65,825
Other	82,870	56,927	46,170
Total operating revenues	$3,816,821	$3,406,170	$2,872,751
Operating expenses:			
Salaries, wages, and benefits	$1,136,542	$ 999,719	$ 867,984
Fuel and oil	494,952	484,673	365,670
Maintenance materials and repairs	256,501	253,521	217,259
Agency commissions	157,211	140,940	123,380
Aircraft rentals	201,954	190,663	169,461
Landing fees and other rentals	203,845	187,600	160,322
Depreciation	195,568	183,470	156,771
Other operating expenses	646,012	614,749	498,373
Total operating expenses	$3,292,585	$3,055,335	$2,559,220
Operating income	$ 524,236	$ 350,835	$ 313,531
Other expenses (income):			
Interest expense	$ 63,454	$ 59,269	$ 58,810
Capitalized interest	(19,779)	(22,267)	(31,371)
Interest income	(36,616)	(25,797)	(20,095)
Nonoperating (gains) losses, net	221	(1,732)	1,047
Total other expenses	$ 7,280	$ 9,473	$ 8,391
Income before income taxes	$ 516,956	$ 341,362	$ 305,140
Provision for income taxes	199,184	134,025	122,514
Net income	$ 317,772	$ 207,337	$ 182,626
Net income per share, basic	$1.45	$0.95	$0.85
Net income per share, diluted	$1.40	$0.92	$0.82

Required:
1. Using an electronic spreadsheet, prepare a cross-sectional and a trend analysis on the income statement. What are the significant trends identified on the income statement?
2. Using the high-low method, separate each operating expense on the 1997 income statement into its fixed and variable components. Then, prepare a prospective income statement for 1998, assuming that total revenues will increase by the average increase of the prior two years. (*Note:* You may want to obtain Southwest's published financial report for 1998 and see how close your pro forma statement was to the actual results.)

4

The Conceptual Framework OF Accounting

Accounting and financial reporting present many difficult challenges—particularly for intangible assets. Companies such as Coca-Cola and McDonald's have created worldwide brand recognition through highly effective advertising and marketing campaigns that undoubtedly will provide significant benefits to each company well into the future. However, the balance sheets of these companies do not recognize any increase in value to the company because of this brand recognition.

Another significant asset to many companies is human capital. Jack Welsh was the CEO for General Electric from 1981 until his retirement in 2001. During that time, the market value of GE's stock grew from $3 billion to well over $400 billion, and GE became one of the most highly valued companies in the world. Mr. Welsh established an outstanding reputation within the business world, and in 1999, *Fortune* magazine named him "Manager of the Century." Yet, during Welsh's tenure, GE's balance sheet never displayed an asset signifying the benefits from superior management.

Finally, accounting for goodwill continues to be the topic of much debate among accounting standard-setters and the business community. For almost thirty years, the Financial Accounting Standards Board required companies to record purchased goodwill as an asset and to amortize it over a period not to exceed forty years. But, as of 2002, the FASB requires companies to record purchased goodwill as an asset without amortization, but write it down when its value is determined to be impaired. Further, the FASB requires that internally developed goodwill be expensed as incurred. Thus, in the United States, there have been three different methods of accounting for goodwill. Alternatively, some people argue that goodwill should be written off directly to stockholders' equity and not affect reported earnings, which is a method of accounting for goodwill that is used in several countries.

Questions

1. What determines whether an item should be recognized on the balance sheet?

2. What information about goodwill should be reported that would be the most useful?

3. What measurement tools should be used to record assets and other financial statement elements, i.e., liabilities, revenues, and expenses?

4. How does the FASB justify keeping goodwill on the balance sheet without amortization? What was the justification for the old method of amortizing goodwill over a maximum of 40 years?

5. Ultimately, what are the main objectives of financial reporting in the United States? How do these objectives differ from those of some other countries?

Learning Objectives

1. Defend the need for a conceptual framework.
2. Identify the components of the FASB's user-oriented conceptual framework, including:
   - The assumption regarding the users of financial reporting,
   - The objectives of financial reporting,
   - The primary qualitative characteristics of financial reporting (i.e., those qualities that make accounting information useful),
   - The role of materiality and cost-benefit constraints in financial reporting,
   - The elements of financial reporting,
   - The measurement principles (e.g., historical cost and revenue recognition) and
   - The measurement tool.
3. Define the traditional assumptions of the accounting model and their implications in financial reporting.
4. Identify the similarities between the conceptual frameworks of the FASB and the IASB.
5. Describe the uniqueness of financial reporting in code-law countries, and recognize the impact that such uniqueness has upon implementing a conceptual framework in all countries.

The search for accounting and financial reporting principles parallels their respective lives. That is, the search for accounting principles, consisting of properly recording transactions, is as ancient as accounting. The search for financial reporting principles, however, which consist of reporting information to parties external to the business, is relatively new. After learning something about electronic data processing systems, Pacioli, who lived in the fifteenth century, would be quite comfortable with accounting systems of today. But identifying what information should be communicated to external parties has been, and continues to be, a source of controversy.

With (1) the impact that the Internet is having upon the dissemination of information, (2) the growth of international business, and (3) the accounting scandals of recent years, the debate about financial reporting is increasing—including the debate as to what role accountants will play in disseminating financial information about an enterprise. This chapter focuses upon the FASB's conceptual framework, which primarily is intended to give guidance to the FASB in developing financial reporting principles. The framework can also provide valuable guidance in both accounting and financial reporting issues facing all practicing accountants.

The FASB's Conceptual Framework

The FASB is constructing its conceptual framework through issuing **Statements of Financial Accounting Concepts (SFAC)**. In February 2000, the FASB issued its latest concept statement, SFAC No. 7, *Using Cash Flow Information and Present Value in Accounting Measurement*. This concept statement is the only one to be issued since 1985, when SFAC No. 3 was replaced by the issuance of SFAC No. 6. Since SFAC No. 4 deals with nonbusiness entities, the FASB's conceptual framework of accounting and financial reporting for businesses is comprised of SFAC Nos. 1, 2, 5, 6, and 7. The FASB's goal is to establish "a coherent system

INTERNET

Check the FASB's Web site at **http://www.fasb.org** and determine (a) what projects the FASB is currently working on and their status and (b) some interesting facts about the FASB, as provided on its Web site.

of interrelated objectives and fundamentals that is expected to lead to consistent standards and that prescribes the nature, function, and limits of financial accounting and reporting."[1]

The FASB adopted a financial statement user approach to developing its accounting and financial reporting conceptual framework. The essentials of this framework are covered in this chapter, but various components are elaborated on in future chapters. Essentially, the FASB's approach is to:

1. Identify potential readers of financial statements and their common needs for information (addressed in SFAC No. 1, which was issued in November 1978),
2. Determine the qualities that make information useful or more useful (addressed in SFAC No. 2, which was issued in May 1980),
3. Define the measuring tools to be used in determining the amounts reported on the financial statements (addressed in SFAC No. 6, which was issued in December 1985, and No. 7, which was issued in February 2000),
4. Identify those elements and attributes of those elements to be measured (addressed in SFAC Nos. 5, 6, and 7), and
5. Determine how best to present that information to the financial statement readers (addressed in SFAC No. 5).

The FASB's conceptual framework does not comprise "truth." Rather, it is the FASB's view as to what constitutes quality accounting and financial reporting, given the economic, legal, political, and social environment that gives rise to it.[2] So it is to be expected that as knowledge of the informational needs of the financial statement users increases and the need for information changes, and even as the medium through which financial information is communicated improves, so too will the FASB's conceptual framework evolve. Also, the FASB's conceptual framework pronouncements do not comprise accounting and financial reporting standards that must be complied with; that is, they are not Rule 203 documents. Rather, the conceptual framework pronouncements establish principles that will aid the FASB in formulating accounting and financial reporting standards and in assisting other accountants in understanding and implementing the published standards of the FASB.

EXTENDING THE CONCEPT

One significant reason the conceptual framework pronouncements are not Rule 203 documents is that knowing and following GAAP would be confusing in those areas where the conceptual framework pronouncements conflict with other previously issued Rule 203 documents. Rather, the FASB intends to implement the principles contained in the conceptual framework gradually, in a thought-out fashion, and in this way replace existing standards where appropriate.

The Financial Statement Reader and General-Purpose Financial Statements

Although many individuals and groups are interested in financial information about any particular business enterprise, the FASB noted that the objectives of financial reporting *are directed primarily towards the needs of those external users who lack the authority to receive the information desired.*[3] Further, the FASB identified the users of financial reporting as having "a reasonable understanding of business and economic activities and are willing to study the information with reasonable diligence."[4] Although the FASB's statements recognize the many and varied financial statement users, it gave a focus to the conceptual standards by phrasing its comments to investors and creditors. But those users are to be seen as representatives of all external users. Also, recognizing that the many individuals and groups external to a

---

[1] *Statement of Financial Accounting Concepts No. 6*, p. i.
[2] *Statement of Financial Accounting Concepts No. 1*, par. 9.
[3] Ibid., pars. 28 and 30.
[4] Ibid., par. 34.

business enterprise have a variety of different informational needs, the FASB stated its intent to focus only upon the common needs for information of the users.

These common needs for information are communicated through a set of **general-purpose financial statements**, which are the primary financial statements that a company issues to people who are external to the company. The information contained in the general-purpose financial statements comprises only a portion of a corporation's rather lengthy financial report. General-purpose financial statements are not "all-purpose" financial statements but have varied usefulness. Likely, all users will desire information not contained in the financial statements or the financial report. To take any other approach implies that the FASB is omniscient and also that providing information can be done without cost. Figure 4-1 presents the total information spectrum relative to investment and credit decisions and the role that financial reporting and financial statements have thereto.

FIGURE 4-1[5]

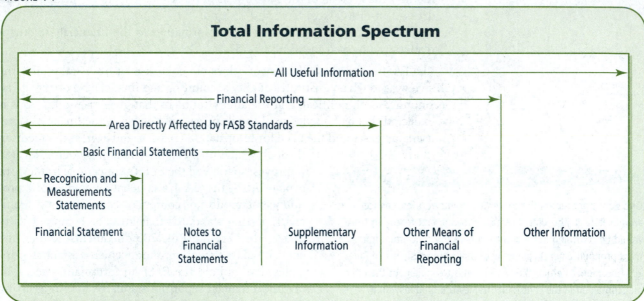

Total Information Spectrum

Objectives of Financial Reporting

Having defined who the users of financial information are and the role financial statements and financial reporting have in meeting the informational needs of those users, the FASB then set forth the objectives of financial reporting. These objectives are in the form of a hierarchy, each one elaborating on the previous one. The chief objective of financial reporting is to:

> "... *provide information that is useful* to present and potential investors and creditors and other users in making rational investment, credit, and similar decisions."[6]

Regarding this objective, the FASB noted that financial information is a tool, and like any tool, it is of no value to those who are unable to use it, including those who are unwilling to learn how to use it appropriately. Also, like any tool, the usefulness of financial reporting increases as efforts to learn its purpose and function are made. Thus, the financial statement user has the responsibility to learn how to use financial information. But the FASB also noted that it has the

---

[5]Adapted from *Statement of Financial Accounting Concepts No. 5.*
[6]Ibid., par. 34, emphasis added.

responsibility of continually assessing the usefulness of the financial information provided and, where indicated, to increase its understandability.

In the hierarchy of financial reporting objectives, the FASB's second objective of financial reporting is to define what constitutes useful information, which is:

> ". . . information to help . . . *[assess] the amounts, timing, and uncertainty of prospective cash [flows]. . . .*"[7]

Prospective cash receipts could be from interest, dividends, selling merchandise, redeeming securities, maturing loans, etc. The FASB considers information to be useful if it assists users in determining the amount of cash to be received, when the cash will be received, and the degree of uncertainty or risk that is attached to the cash flow prospects. All decisions to either loan or invest in a business enterprise are made with the expectation that cash flows received eventually will be greater than the cash loaned or invested, and as a result, total cash resources to the investor or creditor will increase. Ultimately, the test of any business decision is whether more cash is returned than was used. Investors and lenders are interested in both a return *of* their investment and a return *on* their investment, and it is usually from an enterprise's cash resources that a dividend is paid to the investor or interest and principal are paid to a creditor. Further, an enterprise's ability to generate cash is a determinant of the market price of its securities, which—by selling securities held—is another way an investor can receive a cash flow. So assessing future cash flow prospects is a vital function of both lending and investing decisions.

The third objective of financial reporting is to:

> ". . . provide information about *[a business enterprise's] resources, . . . the claims to those resources, . . . and [changes in those] resources and claims.*"[8]

Such information (elaborating upon the previous financial reporting objective of cash flows) aids the financial statement user in identifying the enterprise's cash flow prospects. With information about the enterprise's resources and obligations, the financial statement user can evaluate the cash flow potential of the resources and the cash flow requirements of the claims on those resources. Changes in resources and claims to those resources are a result of the enterprise's profitability; thus, information about an enterprise's profitability is also useful in assessing future cash flow prospects.

Accrual- and Cash-Based Financial Statements

Useful information about a business enterprise's ability to generate cash flow in the short run is found in cash-based financial statements, which focus on cash received and paid during the year. But such statements by themselves do not meet the needs of most investors and creditors whose decisions are typically long-run in nature. Information about a business enterprise's long-run ability to generate cash is better found in accrual-based financial statements. That is why the FASB stated that, "interest in an enterprise's future cash flows and its ability to generate favorable cash flows leads primarily [but not exclusively] to an interest in information about its earnings rather than information directly about its cash flows. . . . Information about enterprise earnings and its components measured by accrual accounting generally provides a better indication of enterprise performance than information about current cash receipts and payments."[9]

---

[7]Ibid., par. 37, emphasis added.
[8]Ibid., par. 40, emphasis added.
[9]Ibid., pars. 43–44.

Cash flows typically occur at the beginning and end of business transactions, and by focusing only on the two ends of a transaction and ignoring what happens in between, cash-based financial statements are short-term in nature. However, accrual accounting records the financial effects of transactions in the periods in which they occur, not just when cash is received or paid. Or stated differently, accrual accounting records the effects of an entire transaction or earnings process, not just the beginning or end of that transaction or earnings process. Accrual accounting recognizes that business activities, such as buying, producing, and selling, do not always coincide with cash flows, and so by relating effort to accomplishment, accrual-based financial statements are a better predictor of the company's long-run cash flow generating ability. Because cash-based statements focus on short-run cash flows and accrual-based statements focus on long-run cash flows, both types of statements are needed. Illustration 4-1 demonstrates the difference between the two bases of accounting.

ILLUSTRATION 4-1[10]

Comparing Accrual Accounting and Cash Accounting

Transaction #1. A retail company buys $5,000 of merchandise that it intends on reselling. It pays $1,500 now and promises to pay the difference in 30 days.

Accrual Accounting			Cash Accounting		
Inventory	5,000		Expense	1,500	
Cash		1,500	Cash		1,500
Accounts Payable		3,500			

Explanation: Accrual accounting recognizes the entire transaction, whereas only the cash portion is recognized under cash accounting, and then it is recognized as an expense.

Transaction #2: The company sells 20% of the merchandise for $3,200, collecting $1,200, with the customer promising to pay the difference later.

Accrual Accounting			Cash Accounting		
Cash	1,200		Cash	1,200	
Accounts Receivable	2,000		Sales		1,200
Sales		3,200			
Cost of Goods Sold	1,000				
Inventory		1,000			

Explanation: Again, accrual accounting recognizes the entire transaction of selling the merchandise, whereas under cash accounting, only the cash portion is recognized.

Transaction #3: Equipment that will be used in the company is purchased for $4,000. Financing is done with a short-term note payable.

Accrual Accounting			Cash Accounting		
Equipment	4,000		No Entry		
Note Payable		4,000			

Explanation: Since cash is not affected, there is no entry under cash accounting. However, under accrual accounting, the fact that an asset was acquired is recognized, and the means of financing it is also recognized.

---

[10]Also, see Chapter 2 for information on converting from cash accounting to accrual accounting.

Qualitative Characteristics of Information

Having determined the users of financial reporting and the objectives that financial reporting should meet, the FASB's next phase of the conceptual framework was to identify those qualities that make accounting information useful. In SFAC No. 1, the FASB stated that information about an enterprise's resources, claims to those resources, and changes in those resources is useful information.[11] The decision still had to be made as to what qualities of resources and claims to resources should be reported. For example, a building represents one resource of an enterprise, but what particular characteristic about that building should be reported? Its size? Its age? Or granting that the attribute reported should be financial in nature, what financial measurement should be used? The price paid to acquire the building? The price at which the building could be sold? The price at which the building could be replaced? Or some other financial measurement? By identifying those attributes that make financial information useful, the FASB and others are assisted in determining what should be reported to external parties to meet their common needs for information, and this was the FASB's next task in developing its conceptual framework.

So the objective of the FASB's second conceptual statement was to state those qualities that make information about a company's resources, claims to those resources, etc., useful. A recap of the FASB's conclusions is provided in Figure 4-2 and is presented here so that the reader can organize the material in the rest of this chapter into a coherent theory.

Primary Qualities

In SFAC No. 2, the FASB identified relevance and reliability as the two primary qualities that make accounting information useful for making business decisions. **Relevant** information is that which is capable of making a difference in a decision. If information has no effect on a decision, the information is not relevant. The FASB identified the following three components of relevance:

1. **Timeliness**—providing information to the decision maker while it has the capacity to affect a decision.
2. **Predictive value**—that quality of information that increases the likelihood the decision maker will correctly predict future events.
3. **Feedback value**—that quality of information that enables decision makers to confirm or correct prior expectations.

Relevance is decision-dependent, meaning that whatever information is relevant depends upon the question asked or the decision to be made. For example, a vehicle's selling price is relevant information when making a decision to sell it, but the vehicle's selling price is not relevant to the decision of whether to use a vehicle for business or pleasure. Further, the replacement cost of a vehicle is relevant when considering which new vehicle to buy but totally irrelevant to most other decisions.

Information is **reliable** when it contains the three following qualities:

1. It is reasonably free from error and bias (i.e., **neutrality**), meaning that the financial statements were not prepared to obtain a predetermined result or

---

[11]See objective of financial reporting #3. Resources seems to be another word for assets, and claims to resources seems to mean liabilities, but the FASB deliberately refrained from using those words in the earlier phases of its framework because it wanted to keep an open mind as to where the conceptual framework would eventually lead it.

FIGURE 4-2[12]

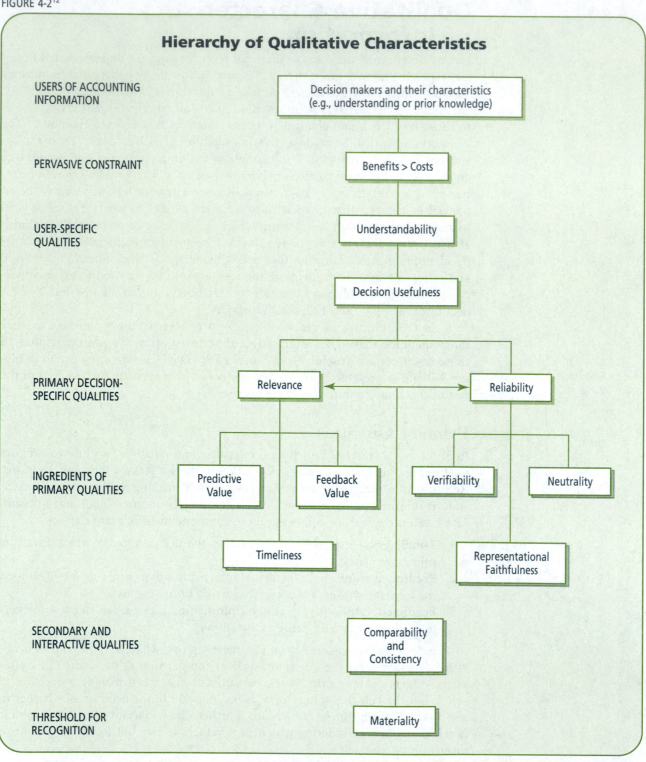

Hierarchy of Qualitative Characteristics

USERS OF ACCOUNTING INFORMATION — Decision makers and their characteristics (e.g., understanding or prior knowledge)

PERVASIVE CONSTRAINT — Benefits > Costs

USER-SPECIFIC QUALITIES — Understandability

Decision Usefulness

PRIMARY DECISION-SPECIFIC QUALITIES — Relevance ↔ Reliability

INGREDIENTS OF PRIMARY QUALITIES — Predictive Value | Feedback Value | Verifiability | Neutrality

Timeliness | Representational Faithfulness

SECONDARY AND INTERACTIVE QUALITIES — Comparability and Consistency

THRESHOLD FOR RECOGNITION — Materiality

to induce a particular mode of behavior or decision. Useful accounting information is neutral to any particular viewpoint, result, or party, and it is not consistently too high or too low.

---

[12]Adapted from *Statement of Financial Accounting Concepts No. 2.*

2. It faithfully represents what it professes to represent (i.e., **representational faithfulness** or validity), meaning there is a correspondence between the accounting measure and the phenomenon it represents. Useful accounting information reports in words and numbers the economic substance of reality, not its form or a misleading description.

3. It is **verifiable**, meaning that there is a consensus among measurers (e.g., accountants, analysts, etc.). However, verifiability does not require unanimity among measurers.

The most useful information is both completely relevant and totally reliable. But frequently a trade-off must be made between relevance and reliability; more of one can be obtained only by giving up some of the other. Sometimes, it seems that the most reliable information is the least relevant, and vice-versa. For example, the most reliable information is historical cost information, as it is relatively easy to verify, truly represents its original cost, and is neutral. Yet, all decisions are future-oriented, and historical data are often of little relevance to making future decisions. But as attempts are made to obtain more relevant data (for example, some current value), the information becomes less reliable. So both preparers and users of financial reporting must compromise as to the degree of reliability they will sacrifice in order to have more relevant information.

Secondary Qualities

The secondary qualities that make financial information useful are comparability and consistency. **Comparability** is that quality of information that enables users of financial reporting to identify similarities in and differences between sets of data of two or more different enterprises. In essence, information is more useful when it can be compared to some standard. For example, knowing that a business enterprise's net income is $1 million is not particularly useful. Knowing other business enterprises' net incomes makes the $1 million figure much more meaningful, particularly when the other business enterprises are in the same industry and are comparable in size.

Consistency is the application of the same accounting policies and procedures from period to period within the same business enterprise. Again, there is little usefulness of a $1 million net income figure if, during the same period, the business enterprise changed several accounting policies and procedures. In this case, the financial statement user cannot determine how much of the $1 million is due to business operations and how much is due to accounting changes. Hence, there is a presumption that an accounting policy or procedure, once adopted, should not be changed, unless the change is to a preferable accounting policy or procedure that will provide more relevant information. However, failure to permit a change to a preferable accounting procedure could adversely affect relevance, which is a more important quality of useful information than is consistency.

Cost-Benefit Constraint

Underlying the qualitative characteristics that make information useful are two constraints: the pervasive **cost-benefit constraint** and the **threshold materiality constraint**. The pervasive cost-benefit constraint means that the benefits of providing information should exceed the cost of providing it. Individuals often perceive information to be a "free" good; they think it is already available in the business enterprise's information system and only needs to be reported. But several times in the past, new requirements to provide additional information have resulted in increased costs to business. Examples include the requirement for segment information, reporting supplemental current cost information, and pension

This Is the Real World

Consistency and comparability are two important characteristics of accounting information according to the FASB's conceptual framework. The following excerpt from an article provided by *TheStreet.com* illustrates how confusing it can be for financial analysts to evaluate a company's performance when consistency is violated.

"Hashing out the reconstructed numbers provided by Hoechst for 1998 shows, according to German accounting methods, that earnings per share totaled 1.38 euros. But the shift to the new IAS standard means the company has reported no fewer than three separate EPS figures scattered about various official statements. These include two estimates that include goodwill charges—1.65 euros (according to an 'old' version of IAS) and 1.61 euros (according to a new, and current version of IAS)—as well as a number (2.40) that doesn't include a heap of previously unamortized goodwill.

"In Hoechst's case, as inscrutable as German accounting methods may or may not have been, the move to IAS standards has caused many an analyst headaches and sleepless nights. The new IAS standards

'most probably have improved transparency, but if you don't have a clearly defined and understandable basis, it does make life frustrating,' says Guy Phillips, an analyst for Societe Generale in London.

"Even with the data provided by the company, he and other analysts have adopted a wait-and-see attitude toward Hoechst's earnings this year. 'The ability to define exactly what constitutes the business at any one time, or have pro-forma comparisons, has been enormously difficult,' Phillips says.

"Unfortunately, investors figuring Hoechst's move to IAS standards will allow them to throw away their secret decoder rings next year may be in for a nasty surprise. Due to more favorable business conditions, the newly merged Hoechst-Rhone-Poulenc entity will be incorporated in France. In the merger prospectus the companies state the new firm, to be called Aventis, will adhere to French GAAP. . . ."

SOURCE: Marc Young, "Cracking the Books II: Despite Shift to International Accounting Standards, Transparency Still Evades Hoechst," TheStreet.com, October 21, 1999.

disclosures. However, increased cost to business is justified when the benefits of the information outweigh the costs of providing it. Applying the cost-benefit constraint seems easy at first glance, but the costs of providing the information and the benefits of the information are not easily quantifiable. In addition, the costs and benefits do not always occur in the same period.

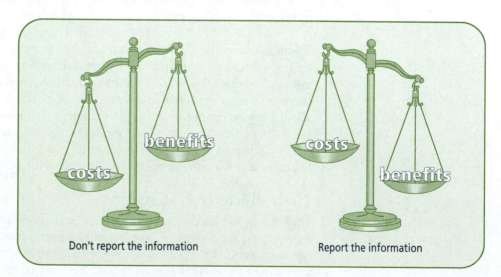

Don't report the information   Report the information

Materiality Constraint

Data are **material** when their omission or misstatement makes it probable that the judgments of a reasonable person will be changed or influenced. Materiality is frequently confused with relevance, but the two are different. Materiality allows for deviations from strict compliance with accounting procedures when the result is not material. Relevance has to do with that quality of information that makes a difference when making a decision.

Materiality has both a quantitative and a qualitative aspect. The quantitative aspect of materiality permits nonadherence to strict accounting procedures when the amount is not material. For example, according to the strict application of accounting principles, a $9.95 pencil sharpener should be depreciated over its useful life of several years. However, because of the immateriality of the results of strictly applying the accounting rule, the materiality constraint allows the $9.95 expenditure to be expensed in the year the pencil sharpener is acquired. This quantitative aspect of materiality considers not only the size of the expenditure (i.e., $9.95) but also the size of the expenditure in relation to the size of the business enterprise. Hence, a $10 million expenditure may be devastating to one business but not even justify separate disclosure for another much larger business enterprise. The qualitative aspect of materiality permits the nature of the transaction or event to be examined in determining materiality. So an expenditure may be material due to the nature of the transaction (e.g., embezzlement, bribing a public official, etc.), though the dollar amount is small enough to be considered immaterial.

© GETTY IMAGES, INC./PHOTODISC

Materiality requires judgment

Presently, there are few available guidelines to determine materiality. Hence, the financial statement preparers must use judgment in determining whether the failure to adhere strictly to accounting procedures would cause the judgment of a reasonable person to be changed or influenced.[13] There are difficulties in leaving

This Is the Real World

In determining materiality, many companies employ a "rule-of-thumb" of allowing a deviation from strict guidelines when the overall effect is less than a specified percent (typically 2% to 5%) of income. The U.S. Securities and Exchange Commission has criticized firms for exploiting the ambiguity of the materiality concept in this way. In a speech at New York University, the former SEC Chairman, Arthur Levitt, made the following remarks:

"[Some companies] intentionally record errors within a defined percentage ceiling. They then try to excuse that fib by arguing that the effect on the bottom line is too small to matter. If that's the case, why do they work so hard to create these errors?

Maybe because the effect can matter, especially if it picks up that last penny of the consensus estimate. When either management or the outside auditors are questioned about these clear violations of GAAP, they answer sheepishly, 'It doesn't matter. It's immaterial.'"

Recent anecdotal evidence and empirical research indicates that not meeting analysts' consensus forecasts results in serious stock price repercussions. Chairman Levitt believes that management is increasingly avoiding booking losses on the grounds of materiality, merely to report earnings that meet analysts' forecasts.

SOURCE: **http://www.sec.gov/news/speech/ speecharchive/1998/spch220.txt**

---

[13]Paragraph 165 of *Statement of Financial Accounting Concepts No. 2* provides some illustrations of what the courts have decided constitute materiality.

the determination of materiality to the judgment of a few, because what one individual considers immaterial, another may consider very material. But lacking any guidelines, the financial statement preparers are left with nothing but the following statement from the FASB's conceptual framework for guidance:

> The omission or misstatement of an item in a financial report is material if, in the light of surrounding circumstances, the magnitude of the item is such that it is probable that the judgment of a reasonable person relying upon the report would have been changed or influenced by the inclusion of the item.[14]

Traditional Assumptions of Accounting and Financial Reporting

There are several traditional assumptions of accounting and financial reporting that are not mentioned in the FASB's conceptual framework but that underlie it. The **separate entity assumption** means that the business enterprise is viewed as a separate economic unit from both its owners and from other business enterprises. That is, any user of financial information assumes that the accounting records and resulting financial statements comprise all the activities of a particular business entity and that the activities of any owner or any other business are not included. A violation of this assumption makes it impossible to assess the past performance or predict the future performance of a business entity, and hence, it would violate the relevance criterion.

The **going concern assumption**, in the absence of information to the contrary, assumes that the business enterprise will continue. This does not imply permanent continuance but rather a time period long enough for the entity to complete its contemplated operations, contracts, and commitments. This assumption adds focus as to which qualities (e.g., historical cost, selling prices, etc.) of information should be measured. For example, selling prices for long-lived assets are largely irrelevant when it is assumed that the enterprise will continue in business rather than be liquidated. Therefore, a financial measure other than selling price should be reported for long-lived assets. However, when a business enterprise's future is uncertain (i.e., the going concern assumption is violated), then selling prices of assets become very relevant and should be reported in the financial statements.

The **periodicity assumption** states that it is possible to divide the life of a business into arbitrary time periods and measure performance for that time period. The results of a business enterprise can be known with certainty only when it goes through final liquidation—a period of time that may encompass hundreds of years or more. However, users of financial information need more timely (i.e., relevant) information upon which to base their decisions. Hence, periodic reporting and the assumption that it is possible to divide the life of a business into segments are necessary, which result in also measuring transactions that are not yet complete. This assumption necessitates the recording of yearly accruals and deferrals.

Twelve months is currently recognized as the length of the basic financial reporting period, although quarterly interim reports also are frequently issued. Some enterprises' annual reporting periods coincide with the calendar year, while others select a 12-month period that coincides with the natural business cycle

---

[14]Ibid, par. 132.

(i.e., the low point of business activity in a year). Other variations on the 12-month reporting period are also found.

Financial Statement Elements

The objectives, qualitative characteristics, constraints, and traditional assumptions of accounting are the plans and the tools that are used to build useful financial statements. The material or building blocks (called elements) upon which

the usefulness of financial statements are based are assets, liabilities, revenues (and gains), expenses (and losses), and equities. Accountants and nonaccountants use these terms frequently but with different meanings. For example, company management often refers to its workforce as the company's greatest asset. However, the accountant never reports "company workforce" on the balance sheet as an asset. Similarly, the accountant is quite precise in his use of revenues and gains, while the businessperson may think of them as practically the same. An important part of understanding financial reporting, which then increases one's ability to analyze financial statements, is understanding the accountant's definitions of the various financial statement elements.

SFAC No. 6 provides definitions for the ten elements of financial statements, which are an important contribution of the FASB's conceptual framework and are presented in Exhibit 4-1. Although in most cases it is easy to classify items into their appropriate financial statement element (e.g., cash is obviously an asset), the FASB's deliberations on issues have been facilitated numerous times by referring to the definitions provided in the conceptual framework. Also, as another example, determining whether some costs should be accounted for as assets or expenses might prove to be difficult without explicit guidance from the framework.

The first three elements in Exhibit 4-1 (assets, liabilities, and owners' equity) are the building blocks of the balance sheet. The definition of an asset explains why "company workers" are not shown on the balance sheet as an asset. Although the workforce is controlled by the company and will provide future economic benefits, "company workers" were not acquired through a past exchange transaction.[15] Note that both assets and liabilities are expressed in terms of future economic benefits or transfer of benefits, and therefore, information about assets and liabilities should provide information about future cash flows. Equity is expressed merely as the mathematical equivalent of assets minus liabilities.

The next three elements in Exhibit 4-1 (investments by and distributions to owners and comprehensive income) provide information related to the third objective—which is to provide information about the company's resources, claims to those resources, and changes in those resources and claims (meaning comprehensive income, of which net income is a key component). Comprehensive income is a relatively new element and is discussed in greater detail later in the text.

---

[15]The qualitative characteristic of reliability would also explain why company management is not recognized as an asset. Measuring the value of the asset with precision would prove to be extremely difficult.

EXHIBIT 4-1

Definitions of Financial Statement Elements

Assets. (1) Probable future economic benefits (2) obtained or controlled by a particular entity (3) as a result of past transactions or events. Normally have a debit balance.

Liabilities. (1) Probable future sacrifices of economic benefits (2) arising from present obligations of a particular entity to transfer assets or provide services to other entities in the future (3) as a result of past transactions or events. Normally have a credit balance.

Equity. The residual interest in the assets of an entity that remains after deducting its liabilities. In a business enterprise, the equity is the ownership interest. Normally has a credit balance.

Investments by owners. They cause net assets (and owners' interests) to increase and are the result of the owners transferring something of value to the company. Normally have a credit balance.

Distributions to owners. They cause net assets (and owners' interest) to decrease as a result of transferring assets or rendering services to the owners or of incurring liabilities in behalf of the owners. The most common form of distributions to owners in a proprietorship and a partnership is owners' drawings, and the most common form of distributions to owners in a corporation is dividends. Normally have a debit balance.

Comprehensive income. All changes in owners' equity during a period, except those resulting from investments by owners and distributions to owners. Transactions captured by an accounting system are included in comprehensive income, but so are other events and circumstances that are not typically captured in an accounting information system. Could have either a debit or a credit balance.

Revenues. Inflows or other enhancements of assets of an entity or settlement of its liabilities (or a combination of both) during a period from delivering or producing goods, rendering services, or other activities *that constitute the entity's ongoing major or central operations.* Normally have a credit balance.

Expenses. Outflows or other using up of assets or the incurring of liabilities (or a combination of both) during a period from delivering services, producing goods, or carrying out other activities that constitute the entity's ongoing major or central operations. Normally have a debit balance.

Gains. Increases in equity from peripheral or incidental transactions of an entity and from all other transactions and other events and circumstances affecting the entity during a period, except those that result from revenues or investments by owners. Normally have a credit balance.

Losses. Decreases in equity from *peripheral or incidental transactions* of an entity and from all other transactions and other events and circumstances affecting the entity during a period except those that result from expenses or distributions to owners. Normally have a debit balance.

SOURCE: Statement of Financial Accounting Concepts No. 6, *"Elements of Financial Statements" (Stamford, CT: FASB, December 1985), pp. ix–x.*

The last four elements in Exhibit 4-1 (revenues, expenses, gains, and losses) are presented in the income statement and provide information about the past performance of the business enterprise. The sum (or net) of these revenues, gains, expenses, and losses constitute net income, which is expected to be a key indicator of future cash flows. The definitions of these elements clearly indicate that the key difference between revenues and gains (and also expenses and losses) is whether the transaction (or event) is related to the enterprise's ongoing operations. The definitions in Exhibit 4-1 are important, will be frequently referred to in the text, and, therefore, some time should be spent becoming familiar with the components of each definition.

To illustrate a model for determining which type of element (e.g., assets, liabilities, etc.) should be used and how these definitions are helpful in making that decision, consider the following examples:

- *Example 1:* A freight company acquires a vehicle to be used for short hauls around the city. Cash is credited, but determining which account to debit in this transaction begins with selecting the candidates from the ten elements previously listed. The candidates are those elements that normally have a debit balance: assets, expenses, losses, and distributions to owners. After the candidates are identified, one or several can be eliminated immediately as not fitting the description of the transaction. In this example, losses and distributions to owners are those that are immediately eliminated because they are not descriptive of what is occurring. Then, the definitions are consulted, and in this example, the following are noted: (1) expenditures that result in future economic benefits are assets, and (2) expenses result from selling products, rendering services, etc., none of which occurred when the vehicle was acquired. Thus, the conclusion is that the company should record the expenditure to acquire the truck as an asset.

- *Example 2:* The same delivery company sells some shares of stock in another company that it had acquired several years previously. Management of the company considered the stock price to have reached an optimum and, therefore, made the decision to sell. Cash is debited and one account that is credited is an investment account, but what other account should be credited for the excess received over the price paid for the investment? The candidates are those elements that normally have credit balances: liabilities, equities, investments by owners, revenues, and gains. Equities and investments by owners are eliminated immediately because they are not descriptive of what is happening. Liabilities are also eliminated because the company is not under any obligation, but should a gain or a revenue be credited? Referring to the above definitions, it is learned that the difference between a gain and revenue is whether the increase in net assets arose from the primary operations of the company or from a peripheral activity. Since the company's major or central operations consists of delivering freight, a gain is credited.

- *Example 3:* A new accountant is faced with recording a transaction in which the company is leasing an asset. The asset will remain the property of the leasing company, but the length of the lease is such that the company has substantially obtained the right to use the asset for its economic life. The questions the new accountant is considering are: Should the leased asset be recorded as an asset on the company's book? If an asset should be recorded, what account should be credited? (You may want to apply the preceding logic and then compare your answer to the following.) Reviewing the definition of an asset, it is noted that the essential elements are future economic benefits, obtained or controlled by an entity, a result of a past transaction. The description of the above lease seems to meet all three criteria, and thus, an asset should be recorded. Regarding the credit account, a liability is credited because there is a probable future sacrifice of making the payments that resulted from a past transaction and that also has given rise to a present obligation.

These examples emphasize the benefits that are obtained from knowing the definitions of the elements of financial statements. Accountants often solve relatively difficult accounting and financial reporting problems by considering the definitions of the various elements. There will be ample opportunities for you in this text to also resort to these definitions to solve accounting or financial reporting problems.

Measurement Tools and Attributes

The measurement tool used in financial reporting is money or **nominal dollars**. Of course, the ideal measurement tool is one that is stable over time, but unfortunately, unlike the typical yardstick that is always the same length, money or dollars change in real value constantly due to inflation. However, in the United States, both the preparers and the readers of financial reports have traditionally used financial statements prepared *assuming* a stable dollar. (In addition to the going concern and periodicity assumptions, this is another underlying assumption of accounting and financial reporting in the United States.) So the FASB noted that it "expects that nominal units of money will continue to be used to

This Is the Real World

The assumption that the value of the U.S. dollar is constant over time is an example of a country's economic environment having a significant influence on the financial reporting system. Historically, the United States has experienced relatively low rates of inflation, and, therefore, presenting assets at historical cost on the balance sheet has supposedly not presented serious problems. However, other countries have experienced hyper-inflationary rates, and in that type of environment, showing long-lived assets at historical cost amounts seriously understates the asset values in periods subsequent to acquisition.

As a result of persistent inflation, Brazil, Mexico, and other countries have implemented accounting systems that adjust year-end historical cost values of such assets as property, plant, and equipment for the effects of inflation, and a gain or loss is recognized in the income statement for the ef-

fect of holding cash and similar assets and liabilities in times of inflation. That is, holding cash during a period of inflation results in a loss, since the cash will not be able to purchase as much at the end of the year as it could at the beginning of the year.

During the late 1970s and early 1980s, the United States experienced higher than usual inflation rates in excess of 10%, which created considerable controversy concerning whether financial statements in the United States should be adjusted for inflation. In response, the FASB issued SFAS No. 33, *Financial Reporting and Changing Prices*, which required companies to include extensive footnote disclosures related to the impact of inflation and changing prices on the business's financial condition. However, inflation subsided in the mid-1980s, and the FASB eliminated the disclosure requirements of SFAS No. 33 (which is an example of applying the cost-benefit constraint).

Inflation Rates

Year	United States	Germany	Mexico	Brazil	Russia
1990	5.40%	2.70%	26.70%	2948.00%	5.60%
1991	4.20	3.50	22.70	477.00	92.70
1992	3.00	5.10	15.50	1022.00	1734.00
1993	3.00	4.50	9.80	1927.00	875.00
1994	2.60	2.70	7.00	2076.00	307.00
1995	2.80	1.70	35.00	66.00	197.00
1996	2.90	1.20	34.40	15.80	47.60
1997	2.30	1.50	20.60	6.90	14.70
1998	1.60	0.60	15.90	3.20	27.70
1999	2.20	0.70	16.60	4.90	85.90
2000	3.20	1.70	9.50	7.50	18.60
2001	2.60	1.50	8.20	5.00	13.20

SOURCE: *International Monetary Fund, The World Outlook Database, June 2002.*

measure items recognized in financial statements."[16] This assumption of a stable dollar means that, currently, there are no adjustments made in U.S. financial statements for the effects of inflation. This assumption of a stable dollar also presumes that the readers of financial reports can make whatever adjustments to reported information they consider necessary as a result of inflation.

Measurement Principles

With the financial statements being comprised of 10 elements, it is not surprising that different measurement principles are used. The historical cost principle is used to measure assets at acquisition, the revenue recognition principle specifies the time when revenue is measured, the matching principle determines when costs become expenses, and liabilities are measured using discounted cash flow procedures. Owners' equity is a residual interest, and once assets and liabilities

[16]*Statement of Financial Accounting Concepts No. 5*, par. 72.

are recognized, owners' equity is determined. Each of these measurement principles is defined in the following pages and covered in much more detail in subsequent chapters of the book.

Historical Cost Principle

When assets are acquired, they are recorded at their historical cost, which at the date of acquisition is the same as their fair value. Referring to what value is reported in the financial statements, the FASB in SFAC No. 5 stated that, "Property, plant, and equipment . . . are reported at their *historical cost, which is the amount of cash, or its equivalent, paid to acquire an asset.*"[17] Since fair value is also defined in terms of the amount that would be paid in a nonforced transaction, it is evident that at acquisition, historical cost and fair value are the same. Extending the preceding statement of the FASB, not only are property, plant, and equipment recorded at historical cost upon acquisition, but so are all other assets. Under the historical cost principle the necessary and reasonable costs incurred to acquire the asset and get it ready for its intended use become the historical cost of an asset. Examples of necessary and reasonable costs include sales taxes and shipping costs for purchased inventory or installation charges for purchased equipment. Also, the cost of manufacturing a product includes the cost of materials, labor, and overhead.

Measuring assets at their historical cost when they are acquired conforms with the primary qualitative characteristics of being relevant and reliable. The historical cost of an asset is relevant at the date of acquisition because it is also the asset's fair value at that date. Historical cost is also reliable, as the amount can be verified by referring to sales documents. This cost faithfully represents the market's perception of the asset's value, and such information is not biased when acquired in a nonforced transaction.

At times, the historical cost principle has been viewed as being such an important part of accounting in the United States that the entire accounting system has been, perhaps incorrectly, referred to as an historical cost accounting system. The reason for this reference is that, subsequent to acquiring assets, some of them continue to be carried on the accounting records and reported on the balance sheet at their historical cost, even though the asset's fair value has probably changed. However, when fair value information is available—as for most investments in securities and some inventories—then these assets are reported at their current fair value because that value is more reflective of the business enterprise's financial condition and thus is more relevant.

Why more assets are not reported at their fair value rather than at their historical cost continues to be a controversy. Those who want more assets reported at their fair value argue that the sacrifice of some reliability in getting more relevant information is in the best interest of those who rely upon financial statements. Those who want to continue reporting some assets at historical cost amounts argue that it is better to have information that can be relied upon, even if some relevance is sacrificed.

Regardless of the controversy, it is clear that when markets exist and are sufficiently developed so that current market values can be obtained at the financial statement date, then those market values are reported in the financial statements instead of historical cost amounts. However, when markets are not developed sufficiently to provide market values, then historical cost amounts are usually reported in the financial statements.

[17]*Statement of Financial Accounting Concepts No. 5*, par. 67.

Revenue Recognition Principle

Besides the historical cost–fair value controversy, another challenge accountants have is determining when to recognize revenue in the accounting records. The **revenue recognition** principle dictates that revenue must be (1) realized or realizable, and (2) earned before it is recorded in the financial records and reported on the income statement. **Realized** means that goods or services have been exchanged for cash or a claim to cash, such as a note receivable or an account receivable. **Realizable** means that goods or services have been exchanged for assets (e.g., stock) that are readily convertible into known amounts of cash or claims to cash. Readily convertible means that the asset received has a quoted price in an available, active market where the market price would not be affected by sale of the asset. Revenue is **earned** when the business entity has substantially completed what it must do to be entitled to the benefits represented by the revenues. Frequently, these two criteria are easy to apply, but at other times, identifying when revenue should be recorded is very difficult. The following examples relating to service revenue illustrate the basic aspects of the revenue recognition rule.

© GETTY IMAGES, INC./PHOTODISC

- *Example 1:* Service worth $1,000 is rendered with the customer paying cash.

    Transaction analysis: Revenue is recorded because the service has been rendered and is therefore earned. Also, cash is received and is therefore realized. This transaction is recorded by debiting Cash and crediting Revenue as follows:

Cash	1,000	
Service Revenue		1,000
To record cash received for services rendered.		

- *Example 2:* Service worth $1,000 is rendered with the customer promising to pay next month.

    Transaction analysis: Revenue is recorded because the service has been rendered (i.e., it is earned), and the rendering of the service has given rise to a claim to cash (i.e., it is realized), which is recorded as an accounts receivable. So the resulting journal entry is as follows:

Accounts Receivable	1,000	
Service Revenue		1,000
To record services rendered and customer's promise to pay.		

- *Example 3:* Payment of $1,000 is received for services to be rendered next month.

    Transaction analysis: Revenue is not recorded. Even though the realization criterion has been met (i.e., cash is received), the earned criterion has not (i.e., the company has not yet done what is required). Accordingly, the credit is to a liability account, inasmuch as there is a present obligation to render services in the future as a result of a past transaction.

Cash	1,000	
Unearned Revenue		1,000
To recognize the receipt of cash and that an obligation exists to provide agreed-upon services.		

- *Example 4*: An agreement is reached to provide a service next month for $1,000, and payment will be received after the service has been completed.

Transaction analysis: No journal entry is required, since there is no asset affected, no revenue earned, and no liability incurred.

The recording of sales revenue is analogous to these examples for recognizing service revenue. For sales of merchandise, the second requirement of the revenue recognition principle (i.e., earned) is generally met when ownership of the goods is transferred to the buyer. Ownership transfers when the goods are delivered or when they are shipped through a common carrier, with shipping terms of FOB shipping point.

Matching Principle

All businesses incur costs when trying to generate revenues. In its purest sense, a cost is an outlay, either in the form of cash paid, transferring other assets, or incurring a liability. When a cost is incurred, the first decision that must be made is whether to recognize the expenditure as an asset or as an expense. As discussed above, the cost is recorded as an asset when probable future benefits will result from the expenditure, which generally is interpreted to mean that the benefits will extend beyond one year. However, when benefits are immediate or there is doubt about future benefits, then the cost is not recorded as an asset. When these costs relate to the purpose for which the company exists, they are recognized as expenses. When these costs relate to a peripheral activity, they are recognized as a loss for the period. This immediate recognition of a cost as an expense/loss is one aspect of the **matching principle** and is referred to as **"immediate recognition."**

When the expenditure is recorded as an asset rather than immediately recognizing the amount as an expense/loss, a second decision must be made: When should the cost of that asset become an expense? This is another aspect of the matching principle. When an expenditure is recorded as an asset, all costs directly related to the selling of a specific product are expensed in the period in which the product is sold, in a cause-and-effect manner. These types of costs are referred to as **inventoriable costs**.[18] Until the product is sold, inventoriable costs are shown as inventories on the balance sheet, and then, when the product is sold, the cost of the product is moved from the balance sheet to the income statement. The following examples illustrate the accounting for inventoriable costs in acquiring and selling merchandise.

- *Example 1*: A retailer purchases merchandise on account for $8,000. Sales taxes on the order are $400. Payment for the inventory is to be made within thirty days after receipt of the invoice.

Transaction analysis: The expenditure of acquiring inventory results in acquiring an asset, as there is future benefit to the company from owning the inventory. Thus, at acquisition, the inventory account is debited and a liability account is credited because the company has an obligation that will result in the future transfer of an asset. Since an asset was acquired, the transaction is measured initially by using the historical cost principle. So the asset is recorded at the sum of the costs incurred to acquire it, which includes sales taxes because that is also a necessary cost in gaining ownership. The resulting journal entry to record the acquisition of the merchandise is as follows:

---

[18]Inventoriable costs are also referred to as product costs, as contrasted to period costs. Period costs have no relationship to a product and therefore are expensed according to the first aspect of the matching principle.

| Merchandise Inventory | 8,400 | |
| Accounts Payable | | 8,400 |

To record the acquisition of inventory using the perpetual inventory method.

Subsequently, the retailer sells one-fourth of the acquired merchandise for $4,000, of which cash of $2,500 is received, and the remainder is to be paid within 30 days. First, revenue is recorded because revenue has been both realized and earned, and the journal entry to record the sale is as follows:

Cash	2,500	
Accounts Receivable	1,500	
Sales		4,000

To record a sale with partial payment.

Second, those costs that were directly related to selling the merchandise are now recorded as expenses, according to the matching principle, and the journal entry to record the cost of the inventory sold as an expense is as follows:

| Cost of Goods Sold | 2,100 | |
| Merchandise Inventory | | 2,100 |

To record the cost of the merchandise sold in the above sale.

EXTENDING THE CONCEPT

How should the costs that an oil company incurs in extracting oil from the ground, transporting it to the refinery, storing the raw oil until it is refined, refining it, and storing the finished product be accounted for? As an asset or as an expense?

Assuming that the answer to the above question is that these costs should be recorded as an asset and be recorded in an inventory account, when should these costs be recognized as expenses?

Since one-fourth of the inventory was sold, then one-fourth of the cost of the inventory is recognized as an expense, which is called Cost of Goods Sold ($1/4 \times \$8,400 = \$2,100$).

The third aspect of the matching principle applies to the cost of long-lived assets and relates to when and how the costs of these long-lived assets become an expense. This aspect states that the costs of such long-lived assets (except for land and intangible assets with indeterminate lives, such as goodwill) are recorded as expenses, according to a **systematic and rational allocation procedure** over the time periods benefited. These systematic and rational allocation procedures are called depreciation for tangible assets, such as equipment or building, depletion for natural resources, and amortization for assets that do not have tangible substance, such as patents and copyrights.

To summarize the matching principle and the thinking process in applying it, the first decision the accountant faces when an expenditure is incurred is whether to record an asset or an expense/loss, which is made on whether future benefits will be obtained, as follows:

- When future benefits will not be obtained, an expense (or loss) is recorded immediately, according to the first aspect of the matching principle.
- When future benefits will be obtained and relate to inventory, then the costs of acquiring the inventory become an expense when the inventory is sold, according to the second aspect of the matching principle.
- When future benefits will be obtained because long-lived assets are acquired, then the costs of those long-lived assets (except land and intangible assets with indeterminate lives) are expensed, according to a systematic and rational allocation procedure according to the third aspect of the matching principle.

This relationship among costs, assets, and expenses is displayed graphically in Exhibit 4-2. One important point of Exhibit 4-2 is that all assets (except land and perhaps certain intangible assets) eventually become expenses.

EXHIBIT 4-2

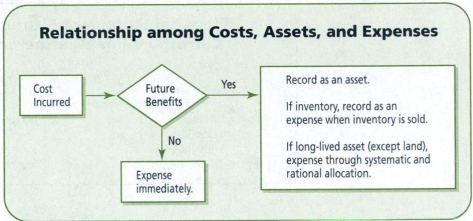

Relationship among Costs, Assets, and Expenses

Cost Incurred → Future Benefits

Yes → Record as an asset.

If inventory, record as an expense when inventory is sold.

If long-lived asset (except land), expense through systematic and rational allocation.

No → Expense immediately.

Present Value Principle

Theoretically, all liabilities are recorded at the amount that would be required to liquidate them at the date of the financial statements. This amount is not their maturity value (i.e., the amount that will be paid to satisfy the obligation when the liability comes due). Rather, the amount reported is that amount that is equivalent to the maturity value, given the difference in time. For example, $1 today is not equal to $1 in ten years or even one year from today. The reason is that, given the difference in time, the $1 today can grow to become more than a dollar because of interest. So it may be that $1 today is equal to $1.10 in one year, which is the case if the $1 could be invested and earn a 10% return. Saying the same thing in reverse, if the company owes a $1,000 debt that will be paid in one year, then the amount reported on today's balance sheet is not the $1,000 but rather the present value of the $1,000, which, at a 10% return, is equal to $909, and this is the amount that would be reported on this year's balance sheet. This present value concept is the basis of valuing liabilities.

As with the other measurement principles, the cost-benefit and materiality thresholds also apply to measuring liabilities. So liabilities that are due in a short period of time (i.e., less than one year) are reported at their maturity value because, due to the short period before they mature, the present value amount is essentially the same as the maturity value. This departure from the theoretically preferred measurement is justified because the difference is immaterial, and there is little benefit to reporting a present value. Thus, current liabilities are reported at their maturity value, and long-term liabilities are reported at their present value, which is an equivalent amount to the maturity value, given the difference in time.

In summary, the financial statement elements and the measurement principles that determine their reporting are shown in Exhibit 4-3.

Conservatism

Underlying all measurement and recognition principles is the **conservatism convention**, which means that when two equally viable alternatives are available, the accountant should choose the method that is least likely to overstate net income and/or total assets. The conservatism convention does *not* imply that accountants should purposely understate net income. Doing so would violate both primary qualitative characteristics of relevance and reliability. Intentionally distorted information is not relevant information. Nor is intentionally distorted information either neutral or representationally faithful. The conservatism convention when

EXHIBIT 4-3

Financial Statement Elements and Their Corresponding Measurement Principle

Element	Measurement Principle at Acquisiton
Assets	Historical cost
Liabilities	Present value concepts
Revenues/gains	Revenue recognition
Expenses/losses	Matching

used inappropriately results in bad accounting. Because of the continuing development of accounting theory, there now should be relatively few cases when the conservatism convention should be applied. Even when applied appropriately, some accountants criticize the conservatism convention because it has a preference for reporting bad news in preference to good news. Today, the most frequent application of the conservatism convention in U.S. GAAP is valuing inventory at the lower-of-cost-or-market.

International Perspectives on Financial Reporting

INTERNATIONAL

So far, this chapter has focused on the FASB's conceptual framework. However, as discussed in Chapter 1, not all countries have the same objectives for financial reporting due to legal, economic, cultural, and technological differences across countries.

The International Accounting Standards Board

The International Accounting Standards Board's (IASB) conceptual framework is very similar to the FASB's. According to the IASB, the main objective of financial reporting is to provide information, particularly information related to future cash flows, that is useful for making economic decisions. Similar to the FASB's focus, the IASB's objective is oriented to existing and potential stockholders and creditors who are *external* to the company. Under this model, financial reporting is critical in communicating unbiased information about the financial health of a company.

The IASB's conceptual framework establishes accrual accounting and going concern as the two basic underlying assumptions of accounting. And, as with the FASB's conceptual framework, the separate entity and periodicity assumptions are implicit in the IASC's conceptual framework. Also, the IASB's conceptual framework recognizes that the four qualities that make accounting information useful are understandability, relevance, reliability, and comparability. (Remember that the FASB does not recognize understandability as a quality, but rather as an objective, and that the FASB puts the qualities of relevance and reliability ahead of comparability.) Other components of the IASB's conceptual framework that are also stated in the FASB's framework include representational faithfulness, prudence (i.e., conservatism), substance over form, materiality, and neutrality. And finally, the definitions of the financial statement elements (e.g., assets, liabilities, etc.) closely mirror those of the FASB's conceptual framework.

From the similarities of their respective frameworks, the IASB obviously was influenced substantially by the FASB's previous work. A possible reason for this influence is that although the IASB is comprised of numerous countries, it was organized in the United Kingdom and, given the cultural, legal, and economic similarities between the United States and the United Kingdom, the similarity of the conceptual frameworks is not surprising. One question that has not been completely answered is how the IASB's conceptual framework will work in countries not having a cultural, legal, and economic environment similar to the United States and the United Kingdom.

Germany: A Code-Law Country

Both the United States and the United Kingdom are **common-law** countries, meaning that the respective federal governments generally allow private sector organizations to establish rules governing their profession. Other countries, such as Germany, Japan, and France, are described as **code-law** countries, meaning that a branch of the federal government typically establishes financial reporting rules. Thus, accounting systems in code-law countries are heavily influenced by the objectives of governmental organizations. These do not necessarily include the presentation of accurate financial information to investors and creditors, since governmental organizations have access to whatever information is desired through private communication with management. Instead, governmental organizations usually place a higher priority on macro-economic issues, such as tax revenue, unemployment, and foreign trade.

In addition to the government, the other major stakeholders of code-law countries are usually banks and employees. For instance, in contrast to the United States, where common stock is a primary source of capital, businesses in Germany rely heavily on banks for debt financing. Also, banks typically hold major blocks of common stock and have representatives on boards of directors. In addition, Germany has relatively strong labor unions that have been successful in having laws enacted that require employees (or their representatives) to hold 50% of the seats on company boards of directors. Because of these close relationships, banks and employees also have access to private communications with management and thus are not as concerned that financial statements reflect the true financial health of the company.

As with all financial reporting systems throughout the world, Germany's financial reporting system is organized to serve the primary stakeholders of a business: the government, banks, and employees. But due to the different cultural/economic environment, those needs are much different than they are in the United States. One difference is that the government makes the financial reporting rules and the tax rules, and so it is no coincidence that the two sets of rules are very similar. Also, the influence of the banks and employees has resulted in a very conservative financial reporting system (perhaps excessively conservative to a U.S. accountant) that allows German companies to "smooth" earnings. **Smoothing earnings** means that financial reporting techniques are used that dampen the income reported in good years and increase the income reported in not-so-good years. The essential characteristic—even goal—is to have less volatility in the reported earnings. One common technique used to smooth earnings is to use "reserve accounts." During years of high earnings, these reserve accounts are credited and are reported as liabilities, with the corresponding debit to an expense account, thus decreasing earnings. Then, during years of poor operating performance, companies can reverse these reserve accounts and thereby increase earnings. The overall result is to report a smooth flow of income.

All of the major stakeholders of German companies find this smoothing of earnings to be in their best interests. Banks benefit from smoothed earnings because excessive volatility increases the probability of penalties from government established regulations. Also, dividends received from companies are a primary source of bank income and thus smoothed earnings facilitate a smooth cash flow to the bank. In addition, remembering that bank loans are a primary source of business capital, companies are encouraged to report conservative balance sheets, which indicates a reduced ability to pay dividends in good years and, thus, also indicates an increased ability to meet debt payments. Smoothing earnings also protects the government's interests, in that smoothed earnings means a constant flow of tax revenues received. Finally, smoothing practices also serve the employees' interests by providing a continual flow of bonuses.

An interesting example of German companies' ability to smooth earnings is presented in Exhibit 4-4.

EXHIBIT 4-4

Daimler-Benz Lists on New York Stock Exchange

Prior to its merger with Chrysler Corp., Daimler-Benz announced in 1993 that it would list its equity securities on the New York Stock Exchange. A great amount of publicity surrounded this announcement because Daimler-Benz was the first German company to list its equity securities on a U.S. exchange. German companies had avoided listing their securities in the United States due to the SEC's requirement that all companies must reconcile their earnings and stockholders' equity to report what these amounts would be if reported in accordance with U.S. GAAP.

In conformance with the SEC's requirement, Daimler-Benz disclosed that its earnings for the first half of 1993 under U.S. GAAP was a loss of $548 million, as contrasted to a profit of $97 million under German GAAP for the same period. The difference was due to the reversal of reserve accounts that are allowed under German GAAP. This was believed to be the first time that Daimler-Benz had ever reported a loss.

Most observers believed that Daimler-Benz decided to comply with the SEC rules because it was in desperate need of capital and saw the listing of its stock on the New York Stock Exchange as the best solution to its capital needs. However, this reason does not explain entirely Daimler-Benz's action, as listing on the NYSE is accompanied by significant legal, listing, and accounting costs, and Daimler-Benz did not raise new capital. It merely listed its existing shares.

Another reason proposed for Daimler-Benz's choosing to list on the NYSE is that it wanted to overcome the entrenched incentives of its major stakeholders, which were to continually report positive earnings. By communicating through U.S. GAAP that the company was not performing well and that serious steps needed to be taken, management was later able to execute a corporate restructuring that included laying off 40,000 employees without incurring serious political repercussions from the labor unions.

Examining the financial reporting practices of a code-law country illustrates that the financial reporting objectives in the United States are fundamentally different from the financial reporting objectives of some other countries. Of importance is that the FASB's and the IASB's conceptual frameworks are oriented towards providing useful information to external financial statement users. On the other hand, in countries such as Germany, where major stakeholders have access to private communication with management, the accounting system is oriented towards the allocation of company resources among the major stakeholders. Although the European Community, of which Germany is a member, has adopted the common-law philosophy of presenting a "true and fair view" in financial statements, national influences have had a greater impact on the accounting system within Germany than have international financial reporting bodies. This is because the national financial reporting system better serves the needs of the major stakeholders.

Summary

The first step in formulating the FASB's conceptual framework was to identify those parties external to the company who were interested in obtaining information about the company but who did not have the authority to demand the desired information. These individuals and institutions were also assumed to have a reasonable understanding of business and economic activities and be willing to study the information provided with reasonable diligence. Although the conceptual statements are phrased in terms of creditors and investors, these groups are to be viewed as representatives of all the readers of financial reports.

Included in the first step of formulating the FASB's conceptual framework was to specify the objectives of financial reporting, which are in a hierarchal format, with each objective expanding upon the preceding objective. Thus, the first objective of financial reporting is to provide useful information. The second objective elaborates upon what useful information is, including the amounts, timing, and uncertainty of future cash flows. The third objective of financial reporting indicates that this information about future cash flows can be obtained from resources, claims to those resources, and changes in those resources and claims during the period.

The second step in formulating the FASB's conceptual framework was to specify those attributes of information that make it more useful than if these attributes were not present. The two primary qualities that make information useful are relevance and reliability. Information is relevant when it is (1) provided in a timely manner, (2) aids in predicting the future, and/or (3) enables readers of financial reports to confirm or correct prior expectations. Information is reliable when it (1) is reasonably free from error and bias, (2) represents what it professes to represent, and (3) is agreed to by a consensus of measurers. In addition to relevance and reliability, the secondary qualities that make information useful are consistency and comparability.

The elements that comprise the financial statements are: assets, liabilities, owners' equity, revenues, expenses, gains and losses, comprehensive income, and investment by and distributions to owners. Assets are measured using the historical cost principle. Liabilities are measured using present value concepts. Revenue and gains are measured using the revenue recognition principle. Expenses and losses are measured using the matching principle. Each of these measurement principles is the topic of a chapter later in the text.

The measurement tool is the dollar, which is assumed to be stable over time (i.e., inflation does not exist). This is acceptable because the readers of financial reports are accustomed to the dollar and presumably can make any necessary adjustments to the data because of inflation.

In addition to the assumption of a stable dollar, other assumptions of the financial reporting model are:

- The economic entity assumption, which assumes that the transactions of the business have been separately reported from the transactions of the owners and other business enterprises.
- The going concern assumption, which points to the type of information reported on financial statements. Thus, liquidation values, or the value at which assets could be sold, customarily are not reported because such values are only relevant should the business cease operations.

• The periodicity assumption, which indicates that it is possible to divide the life of a business into intervals and report performance for each interval. Because of this assumption, accruals and deferral are necessary.

These objectives, qualitative characteristics, elements, measurement tools, and underlying assumptions currently comprise the FASB's conceptual framework of financial reporting. When beginning the task of developing this framework, the FASB stated that these conceptual statements would guide them in developing sound accounting and financial reporting principles. Interestingly, since the issuance of SFAC No. 6, the FASB has taken a decided shift from emphasizing the measurement of income and now is focusing on properly measuring the elements of the balance sheet. Perhaps this shift in measurement is partly due to the insights the FASB gained in developing its conceptual framework.

This discussion of the FASB's conceptual framework is intended to provide a frame of reference for the study of subsequent chapters. Rather than providing a thorough coverage of all aspects of the conceptual framework, the authors choose to present the essentials here and will then build upon them throughout the text. Also, differences in financial reporting practices across countries will be discussed, which will assist the reader in understanding the diversity in financial reporting practices and allow the reader to assess the efforts being made to harmonize financial reporting practices.

Questions

1. What are the advantages derived from having a conceptual framework?

2. What is the difference between a Statement of Financial Accounting Standard and a Statement of Financial Accounting Concept?

3. According to the FASB, accounting information as derived under U.S. GAAP is oriented towards what type of user?

4. Should the FASB require all companies to disclose all the information that the readers of financial statements find useful? Defend your answer.

5. Distinguish between the cash basis and accrual basis of accounting.

6. According to the FASB's conceptual framework, what are the objectives of financial reporting?

7. According to the FASB's conceptual framework, what are the two primary qualitative characteristics of accounting information? Define each quality in terms of what determines whether an item has this quality.

8. What is conservatism and how might it conflict with the qualitative characteristics of relevance and reliability?

9. According to the FASB's conceptual framework, what are the secondary qualitative characteristics of accounting information, and how do they differ from each other?

10. What are the two constraints of accounting information?

11. What is the separate entity assumption, and why is it important for financial reporting purposes?

12. What is the going concern assumption, and what does it imply with respect to presenting liquidation values on the balance sheet?

13. What is the periodicity assumption, and why is this assumption necessary for financial reporting purposes?

14. What determines whether a cost that provides benefit to the company should be classified as an asset or an expense?

15. What is the difference between a revenue and a gain?

16. A company paid $15,000 to advertise its product. The advertising was meant to appeal to holiday shoppers and was to run from October 15 through December 15. If the company's year-end is October 31, how much of the $15,000 should be expensed at the end of the fiscal year?

17. What determines whether a cash outflow is classified as an expense or a loss?

18. a. Define the historical cost principle and defend its use in accounting.
    b. Now, defend why it would be more appropriate to use a current value model, rather than the historical cost model of accounting.

19. Define the revenue recognition principle as to when revenue is recognized.

20. Explain each of the three rules for recognizing costs as expenses under the matching principle and illustrate their use in specific examples.

21. Explain who the primary stakeholders are in common-law versus code-law countries. How does this difference affect the comparability of financial reporting between common-law and code-law countries?

22. Does the IASB's conceptual framework follow the financial reporting pattern of common-law or code-law countries? What aspects of its conceptual framework support your view?

Exercises

Exercise 4-1: Qualitative Characteristics. Answer the following questions as they relate to Statement of Financial Accounting Concept No. 2. (Use reliability and relevance only once.)

1. What quality of accounting information enables decision makers to confirm or correct prior expectations?
2. What term describes accounting information that is reasonably free from bias?
3. What are the two constraints of accounting information?
4. A company switches depreciation methods two times over a 3-year period. What qualitative characteristic of accounting has been violated?
5. The SEC requires that audited financial statements must be filed within 90 days after the fiscal year-end. This requirement is a result of trying to achieve information that contains what qualitative characteristic? (Do not use relevance.)
6. Fobley, Inc. uses the FIFO inventory valuation method, even though all other companies in its industry use the LIFO method. What qualitative characteristic of accounting is being compromised?
7. This qualitative characteristic of accounting implies that all information that is capable of making a difference should be reported.
8. Representational faithfulness is an ingredient of what qualitative characteristic of accounting?
9. This convention indicates that when two viable accounting alternatives exist, the alternative that is least likely to overstate assets and net income should be followed.

10. Not-Much-Good Inc. is liable for damages in a lawsuit; however, three different estimates of the liability have produced dramatically different results. This information lacks what qualitative characteristic of accounting?

Exercise 4-2: Qualitative Characteristics and Assumptions. Identify the qualitative characteristic of accounting information or accounting assumption that best relates to each of the following statements.

1. Historical cost, instead of current market values, is used to value property, plant, and equipment.
2. All expenditures under a certain amount are expensed.
3. Financial statements report the activities of a business independent of its owners.
4. Management must disclose and justify all changes in accounting principles.
5. Current market values, instead of historical cost, are used to value marketable securities.
6. Financial statements are presented in nominal dollars (i.e., unadjusted for inflation).
7. Assets are not reported at their liquidation values.
8. The SEC requires the issuance of quarterly and annual financial statements.
9. Companies within the same industry tend to follow the same accounting principles.

Exercise 4-3: Traditional Assumptions and Qualitative Characteristics. The following statements describe common accounting practices. Identify the accounting assumption that justifies each practice. The same answer can be used more than once.

1. Adjusting entries are made at the end of each fiscal year.
2. Historical cost, instead of liquidation value, is used to value property, plant, and equipment.
3. Inventory flow assumptions are frequently employed (e.g., FIFO and LIFO), instead of keeping track of the cost of specific items.
4. Companies must justify any change in accounting principle.
5. Current market values are reported for marketable securities that are traded on a national exchange.
6. Price level adjusted amounts are not reported for assets.
7. Inventories are valued at the lower of historical cost or market value.
8. Hand tools are expensed in the period they are purchased.
9. Accrual accounting is used.
10. Personal transactions of owners are not included on the books of the enterprise.
11. Significant events that occur after the reporting period but before the issuance of financial statements are disclosed in the financial statements.

Exercise 4-4: Assumptions, Qualitative Characteristics, and Measurement Principles. Below is a list of statements posing conceptual issues. For each statement, indicate whether it is correct or incorrect. For those statements that are correct, identify the assumptions, qualitative characteristics, measurement principles, etc., that are controlling. For those statements that are incorrect, state the correct principle.

1. The business entity is considered to be separate from the owners.
2. The dollar is stable over time and is a good measurement tool for measuring business transactions.
3. Inventories are reported on financial statements at the lower of their historical cost amount or their fair value.
4. The historical cost principle primarily relates to measuring income.

5. Revenue is recognized when cash is received.
6. Accruals and deferrals are necessary to appropriately measure income and assets.
7. Revenue should be recognized as late as possible and expenses as early as possible.
8. Relevance and reliability dominate the other qualitative characteristics of accounting.
9. The purchase of several small items of office equipment, such as staplers and pencil sharpeners, is expensed when acquired.
10. An accounting principle, once adopted, should not be changed unless another principle provides more relevant information.
11. Financial statements are more meaningful when similar transactions are accounted for in the same way by all companies in an industry.
12. Liabilities are reported only when it is known how much is owed and to whom it is owed.

Exercise 4-5: Materiality. Answer the questions for each of the following situations.

1. The purchase of a clerk/typist chair that costs $135 is expensed. What is the theoretical accounting treatment, and does the materiality concept permit this cost to be accounted for as the company has done?
2. Company policy requires that the capital acquisitions committee approve all purchases of assets of more than $1,000 in amount. A department in the company needing to buy 30 clerk/typist chairs has received a quote of $150 per chair. To avoid seeking approval of the capital acquisitions committee to purchase the chairs, the department submits 5 purchase requisitions for 6 chairs each (each purchase requisition is for $900) and expenses the $4,500. Assuming that the $4,500 in total is material to the company but that $900 is not, do you agree with the accounting treatment? Defend your answer.
3. A company conducts business in several foreign countries where business practices differ from those in the company's home country. In one such country, it is customary to pay bribes to low-level officials to receive permission to import the company's goods into that country. To avoid questions from the company's auditors, government officials in the company's home country, and others, the company records all such items in the freight account. The amounts involved are not quantitatively material to the company. Theoretically, how should these payments have been accounted for? Does the materiality concept permit this deviation from the theoretically correct accounting treatment?
4. To obtain a desired outcome in a foreign country, the company paid a high-level official an amount that is not considered material. Because the amount was not material, the company recorded the amount as a consulting fee. Do you agree with the company's treatment of this fee? Has the materiality concept been properly applied?

Exercise 4-6: Elements of Financial Statements. Identify the financial statement element that corresponds with the following definitions.

1. Increase in assets from sales of inventory.
2. Embodies a future economic benefit.
3. A decrease in equity due to a one-time event.
4. All changes in equity except from owner transactions.
5. Probable future sacrifices of economic benefits.
6. A decrease in net assets resulting from a transfer of assets to owners.
7. A peripheral transaction that results in an increase in net assets.
8. An inflow of cash due to the sale of the company's own stock.

9. Using up of assets or incurring liabilities from an entity's ongoing business activities.
10. Assets minus liabilities.

Exercise 4-7: Elements of Financial Statements. In the right column below are the elements of financial statements as defined in SFAC No. 6. In the left column below are some primary components of the definitions as listed in the same concepts statement. Match the primary components of the definitions with the elements. The primary components can be used more than once.

Primary Components of a Definition	Elements of Financial Statements
1. Decrease in ownership interest due to a single event	A. Assets
2. All changes in owners' equity, except for investments by and distributions to the owners	B. Liabilities
3. Consuming of an asset in the course of doing business	C. Owners' equity
4. Increases in net assets resulting from transfers from owners	D. Revenues
5. Inflows of assets from producing goods and services	E. Expenses
6. Probable future economic benefits	F. Gains
7. Increases in net assets from peripheral activities	
8. Probable future economic sacrifices	G. Losses
9. Outflows of assets from producing goods and services	H. Comprehensive income
10. Present obligation to transfer assets or provide services in the future	I. Investments by owners
11. Decreases in equity due to incidental transactions	J. Distributions to owners
12. Residual interest in the net assets	
13. Decreases in equity as a result of a transaction with owners	
14. The total change in owners' equity from (a) exchange transactions with nonowners, (b) the enterprise's productive efforts, and (c) price changes, casualties, etc.	

Exercise 4-8: Definition of an Asset. Determine whether each of the following is an asset as defined in SFAC No. 6 and should be included in Thompson's year-end balance sheet. Justify each of your answers.

1. Merchandise ordered from a supplier that will be shipped on January 4.
2. A patent on a new drug that currently is banned for sale by the Food and Drug Administration.
3. The excellent reputation Thompson has earned in the business community.
4. Cash that Thompson has received for some merchandise that Thompson will ship after the first of the next year.
5. Some equipment that Thompson is financing through a bank loan. The terms of the loan require monthly payments, and ownership of the equipment will become Thompson's in five years when the final payment is made.

6. Some equipment that Thompson is leasing and using. The terms of the lease require monthly payments, that ownership of the equipment will remain with the lessor, and possession of the leased asset will revert to the lessor in two years, which is the end of the lease term. The asset will have many more years of profitable use.
7. Same as (6), except that at the end of the lease term, the leased equipment will be worthless. Thus, Thompson has utilized all the economic benefits of the equipment during the time of the lease.
8. Some land that was given to Thompson by the city, upon which Thompson will build a new facility.
9. A note receivable from a customer who has just filed for bankruptcy protection.
10. The superior managerial talent Thompson has been able to hire and retain.
11. A park that Thompson has built on its land but that is often used by the city (with Thompson's permission) for various functions.
12. An advertising campaign over an extended period of time has been so successful that customers now consider the company's brand to be synonymous with the product.

Exercise 4-9: Definition of an Asset. From a theoretical point of view and without reference to what authoritative standards indicate should be done, state whether the following items should be recognized as an asset on a company's balance sheet. If asset recognition is not appropriate, indicate what the appropriate accounting should be and justify your answer.

1. Purchase of equipment with a useful life of 5 years.
2. Purchase of a patent with a useful life of 5 years.
3. Purchase of a wrench with a useful life of 20 years.
4. Legal fees incurred in the successful defense of a patent.
5. Research costs incurred to discover new knowledge.
6. Costs incurred to develop new products.
7. A building that is leased for 10 years.
8. Improvements to a building that is being leased for 5 years.
9. Costs incurred to register a trademark.
10. Land not being used.

Exercise 4-10: Definition of a Liability. Determine whether each of the following is a liability as defined in SFAC No. 6 and should be included in S&W's December 31, 2005, balance sheet. Explain your answers.

1. The cash outflow the company will need next month to purchase merchandise to resell. No purchase orders have been placed.
2. The cash outflow the company will need next month to honor warranties on products that were sold during the year.
3. The cash outflow the company will need on January 5 to pay salaries for the prior two weeks.
4. The obligation to ship merchandise in January to a customer who had prepaid with his order.
5. The obligation to ship merchandise in January to a customer who promises to pay within thirty days after receipt of the merchandise.
6. The obligation that may be incurred as a result of a lawsuit. The company is the defendant.
7. The obligation to pay a cash dividend that was declared on December 15 and is to be paid on February 1.

8. The obligation to pay a dividend in the company's stock that was declared on December 15 and is to be distributed on February 1.
9. The obligation to pay interest on a $10,000 note payable. The money was borrowed on December 1 and is to be repaid on March 1.

Exercise 4-11: Definition of Cost, Loss, and Expense.

1. Explain the meaning of the terms (a) cost, (b) loss, and (c) expense. In your definitions, identify the interrelationship among the terms.
2. Using your definitions, classify each of the following costs as to whether it is an expense, a loss, or should be recorded as something else. If you think the cost should be accounted for as something other than an expense or loss, identify the element and the account in which the cost should be recorded. Note, some costs may be classified in more than one account.
   a. The cost of goods sold.
   b. Purchasing inventory.
   c. The costs incurred in organizing a business, such as fees paid to lawyers and accountants, and fees paid to the state to receive a business charter and license.
   d. The estimation of the accounts receivable that will be uncollectible.
   e. Difference between the book value of some assets destroyed in a flood and the amount received from an insurance company.
   f. Advertising fees.
   g. Research and development expenditures.
   h. The difference between the amount paid to acquire a company and the fair value of the individual assets and liabilities of the company.

Exercise 4-12: Revenue Recognition. A publishing company is a unique model for determining when revenue should be recognized. For instance, should revenue be recognized when the subscription to the magazine is received, when the magazine is printed and shipped to homes and newsstands across the country, or should both events be considered?

1. What are the strengths and weaknesses of recognizing all the revenue when a subscription is received?
2. What are the strengths and weaknesses of recognizing the revenue according to the number of issues that are printed and shipped?
3. Using a combination of obtaining the subscription and shipping the magazine for recognizing revenue, develop an alternative model for recognizing revenue for a publishing company.

Exercise 4-13: Revenue Recognition, Definition of Assets, Matching, etc. A manufacturing company incurred the following transactions during the year:

a. Materials of $50,000 were acquired. These materials will be used in the production of the company's main product.
b. Direct material of $40,000 was put into production.
c. Labor of $15,000 was incurred, which was spent on building the company's main product.
d. Manufacturing overhead of $30,000 was applied to production. Manufacturing overhead consists of the heat, lights, power, property taxes, depreciation, etc., on the manufacturing portion of the business. (Credit Manufacturing Overhead.)
e. At the end of the period, all products were completed, and so the entire cost of $85,000 was moved to finished goods inventory.

f. The company reported the finished goods inventory at its current fair value of $120,000. (What account did you credit?)

g. All the inventory was sold for $120,000. (Make two entries, one for the sale of the product and another for the cost of the inventory. Consider your entry in (f) when preparing this entry.)

1. Prepare journal entries for each of the above events. Do not be overly concerned with the names of any accounts; the point to emphasize is when costs are assets or expenses, when revenue is recognized, etc. So when in doubt as to what account title to use, use "asset," "revenue," "expense," etc.

2. Determine the amount of profit (i.e., sales minus the cost of goods sold) that was recognized in journal entry (g) above.

3. Write a brief memo explaining (a) when costs related to inventories become expenses and (b) why it might be best to continue reporting inventories at historical cost until they are sold.

Exercise 4-14: Revenue Recognition. Determine whether revenue should be recognized in the current fiscal year for each of the following independent situations. Explain your answers, and if revenue is not recognized in the current fiscal year, identify the year (if any) in which revenue should be recognized.

1. A product is exchanged for cash.
2. A product is exchanged for a customer's promise to pay in 30 days.
3. A product is exchanged for shares of the customer company's stock, which is actively traded.
4. A company receives an order and ships the merchandise FOB shipping point on December 29. The customer is given 6 months before payment is expected.
5. A company receives an order and ships the merchandise FOB destination on December 29. The goods are expected to arrive in four business days, and the customer is given 30 days to pay.

Exercise 4-15: Measurement Principles. For each transaction below, identify the measurement principle, assumption, definition, etc., that was violated. The company's business is to warehouse and ship merchandise.

1. The company needed a small structure built and received a bid from a contractor to build it for $800,000. However, due to a temporary downturn in business, the company used surplus labor and built the structure itself at a cost of $750,000, which was paid in cash. The company prepared the following journal entry:

Building	800,000	
Cash		750,000
Gain on Constructing an Asset		50,000

2. Several vehicles were repaired during the year, including engine tune-ups, new tires and brakes, and alignments. The company prepared the following entry:

Trucks	3,500	
Cash		3,500

3. The company owned shares of stock in another corporation, which it sold during the year and made the following entry:

Cash	45,000	
Investment in Stock		32,000
Sales Revenue		13,000

4. The company acquired some equipment by exchanging 1,000 shares of its own unissued stock. The stock has a par value of $1 per share, and the fair value of the equipment was $20,000. The company prepared the following journal entry:

Equipment	1,000	
Common Stock		1,000

5. On December 30, the company collected $5,000 cash to ship some merchandise on January 3 of the next year. The following entry was prepared:

Cash	5,000	
Shipping Revenue		5,000

6. One of the company's warehouses is located near a river that overflows its banks every few years. During the current year, the river did overflow, and the company incurred a loss of $25,000 after reimbursement from the insurance company. The net journal entry prepared by the company was as follows:

Retained Earnings	25,000	
Cash	100,000	
Building		125,000

Exercise 4-16: Multiple-Choice Questions.

1. What was the intention of the FASB in issuing the Statements of Financial Accounting Concepts?
   a. To summarize in a concise manner all the pronouncements issued by its predecessors.
   b. To explain the reasons why the CAP and APB failed as accounting standard-setting bodies.
   c. To establish a conceptual framework that would serve as a foundation for the establishment of generally accepted accounting principles.
   d. To summarize current authoritative accounting principles.
2. According to the FASB's conceptual framework, which of the following choices is *not* an objective of financial reporting?
   a. To provide information that is useful for investment, credit, and similar decisions.
   b. To provide information that is useful in assessing the amounts, timing, and uncertainty of future cash flows.
   c. To form a basis for measuring taxable income to be reported to the IRS.
   d. To provide information about an enterprise's resources, claims to those resources, and changes in those resources and claims.
3. According to the FASB's conceptual framework, timeliness is an ingredient of:

	Relevance	Reliability
a.	Yes	No
b.	Yes	Yes
c.	No	Yes
d.	No	No

4. U.S. GAAP requires that probable future losses are to be recognized in financial statements. However, probable future gains are never recognized. According to SFAC No. 2, which characteristic describes this accounting practice?
   a. Prudence
   b. Conservatism
   c. Reliability
   d. Relevance

5. Which of the following items is *not* included in comprehensive income?
   a. Sale of an asset other than inventory.
   b. All increases or decreases in the fair value of assets during a year.
   c. A correction of an error that was made in a prior period.
   d. Dividends paid to shareholders.

Exercise 4-17: Violations of Conceptual Framework. The following items describe some transactions that D&H, Inc., incurred and also some decisions that were made during the most recent fiscal year. In regards to the conceptual framework, comment on the appropriateness of accounting for the transactions and of the accounting decisions made.

1. D&H, Inc., changed its method of accounting for inventory from LIFO to FIFO in order to increase earnings to meet analysts' forecasts.
2. The value of equipment that had been purchased five years ago was increased to its current market value according to an internal appraisal.
3. A new asset was recorded on the company's books to recognize the expected future benefit to be realized from the recent hiring of a chief executive.
4. In January of the following fiscal year, the company experienced a major employee strike that adversely affected production. Even though the financial statements had not been issued, the company decided not to report the incident in its financial statements since the strike began subsequent to the fiscal year.
5. For comparability purposes, the controller decided to adjust previous years' financial statements for the effects of general inflation.
6. It is reasonably certain that D&H, Inc., will be held liable for damages from a pending lawsuit. The controller believes that recognizing a liability in the financial statements is akin to an admission of guilt and accordingly decides not to recognize or disclose any information related to the lawsuit.
7. D&H, Inc., purchased land in exchange for stock that had a par value of $1 per share and a fair market value of $25 per share. The land was recorded on the books at the stock's par value.
8. Major improvements directly outside the company's primary place of business are being made by the city. Executives at D&H, Inc., believe that the improvements will boost sales by approximately 15% over the next several years. Accordingly, to recognize this future economic benefit, the controller decides that all city taxes paid during the next few years should be capitalized and amortized over the expected period of benefit.

Exercise 4-18: Conservatism. In a conversation with the management of Company B, you are told that the company has always taken a conservative view of measuring net income. According to management, this philosophy of measuring income has resulted in retaining cash in the company by not having to pay any more dividends than necessary. Also, management asserts that this philosophy, which has particularly resulted in undervaluing inventory and plant assets, has created a secret reserve that can be used during "hard times."

Comment on management's philosophy of measuring net income as it relates to the FASB's conceptual framework project.

Problems

Problem 4-1: Transaction Analysis. The following scenarios are independent:

1. A company has acquired some mountain property with the intent of constructing a ski resort. To that end, the timber, underbrush, and rocks are removed from the side of a hill. To what type of account (i.e., asset, expense, etc.) should the costs incurred be recorded? Why?
2. Three years after acquiring a patent, a company incurred $500,000 of legal fees in a successful defense of its patent. To what account should this cost be recorded? Why?
3. How would your answer change if in (2) the legal fees were incurred in an unsuccessful defense of a patent? Also, what should be done with the dollar amount in the patent account? Should it continue being recognized as an asset? If so, why? If not, then how should that cost be accounted for?
4. A publisher of a magazine receives 1,000 one-year subscriptions during a particular month. All subscriptions were accompanied with checks for the full subscription price. How or when should the revenue from these subscriptions be recognized? In this scenario, Cash is the account debited; but if you have decided that not all of the revenue should be recognized immediately, then what other account should be credited?
5. A company incurs substantial costs in rearranging the layout of its plant, which was done to expedite the flow of materials and decrease materials handling. How should these costs be accounted for?

Required:
Using the definitions and concepts in this chapter, answer each question.

Problem 4-2: Transaction Analysis. The following scenarios are independent:

1. After constructing an office building, a company hires professional landscapers to plant small trees, shrubs, and flowers. To what type of an account (i.e., asset, expense, etc.) should these costs be recorded?
2. A sports franchise signed an athlete to a guaranteed contract that requires payment for the next three years, regardless of whether the athlete makes the team or plays in any games. Should a liability be recorded? If so, what is the other account that should be recognized?
3. A corporation owns various assets, such as equipment, land, etc., all of which do not have active markets where prices of used assets can be determined readily. Should the corporation recognize increases or decreases in value on such assets? Why or why not?
4. College bookstores often return large amounts of unsold textbooks, which is in accordance with an agreed-upon policy with the publisher. So when should a publishing company recognize revenue on textbooks that it sells to college bookstores? Should revenue be recognized when the publisher receives the orders, when the textbooks are shipped, or after the books are returned?

5. A manufacturer of automobile tires warranties its premium tires for 80,000 miles. During the current year, the manufacturer sells 100,000 tires and appropriately recognizes the revenue. What accounting, if any, should be done for the warranties on these tires?

Required:
Using the definitions and concepts in this chapter, answer each question.

Problem 4-3: Transaction Analysis. The following scenarios are independent:

1. A land development company purchased several pieces of land with accompanying homes for $10 million. The company plans to demolish the homes in order to build a shopping mall. At the time the plots were acquired, competent appraisals indicated that the fair value of the homes was $4,000,000, and the fair value of the land plots was $6,000,000. How should the $4,000,000 be recorded? As an asset, expense, loss, etc.? If you select an asset account, what is the title of the asset? Buildings, land, etc.?
2. A company that builds furniture has 1,000 shares of stock in another major corporation whose stock is actively traded, which increased in value during the year. Should the company recognize this increase in the value of the stock? If so, what specific accounts are affected? If not, why should accountants not recognize this increase in value?
3. Many organizations sell season tickets, but when should the revenue be recognized? Defend your answer.
4. Many executives are paid a bonus based upon some measure or measures of performance, which are not known until the end of the year. In such cases, what should a corporation report in its monthly or quarterly financial statements in regards to bonuses?
5. Assets such as timber and animals increase in value due to their growth over time. Should accounting recognize the increase in value of such assets that grow? Why or why not?

Required:
Using the definitions and concepts in this chapter, answer each question.

Problem 4-4: Accrual Accounting. One of the objectives of accounting is to provide information that is useful to decision makers in assessing the amounts, timing, and uncertainty of future cash flows. This is consistent with finance theory, which suggests that the value of a firm is equal to the discounted value of all future cash flows. In fact, some finance textbooks teach that analysts should focus on a company's cash flows instead of earnings.

Required:
1. Explain why cash flow is the primary variable of interest to a potential investor or creditor.
2. If cash flow is what really determines firm value, why do accountants use accrual accounting to measure net income, rather than the cash basis of accounting?

Problem 4-5: Cash to Accrual (CPA adapted). Here is information pertaining to Ward Specialty Foods, a calendar-year sole proprietorship that maintains its books on the cash basis. At year-end, Mary, the accountant, adjusts the books to the accrual basis for sales, purchases, various expenses, and cost of sales, and records depreciation to more clearly reflect the business income.

Ward Specialty Foods
Trial Balance
December 31, 2005

	Dr.	Cr.
Cash	$ 18,500	
Accounts Receivable, December 31, 2004	4,500	
Inventory, December 31, 2004	20,000	
Equipment	35,000	
Accumulated Depreciation, December 31, 2004		$ 9,000
Accounts Payable, December 31, 2004		4,800
Accrued Expenses		900
Mary Ward, Drawings	24,000	
Mary Ward, Capital, December 31, 2004		33,600
Sales		187,000
Purchases	82,700	
Salaries Expense	29,500	
Payroll Taxes Expense	2,900	
Lease Expense	8,400	
Miscellaneous Expense	3,900	
Insurance Expense	2,400	
Utilities Expense	3,500	
Totals	$235,300	$235,300

At year-end, the following information was compiled:

a. Amounts due from customers totaled $7,900 at December 31, 2005.
b. A review of the receivables at December 31, 2005, disclosed that an allowance for doubtful accounts of $1,100 should be provided.
c. Unpaid vendors' invoices for food purchases totaled $8,800 at December 31, 2005.
d. The inventory amounted to $23,000 at December 31, 2005, based on a physical count of goods priced at cost. [Adjust the change in inventory and also the purchases account to Cost of Goods Sold. Also, see item (c).]
e. On signing the new lease on October 1, 2005, Ward paid $8,400, representing one year's rent in advance for the lease year ending October 1, 2006. The $7,500 annual rental under the old lease was paid on October 1, 2004, for the lease year ended October 1, 2005.
f. On April 1, 2005, Ward paid $2,400 to renew the comprehensive insurance coverage for one year. The premium was $2,160 on the old policy that expired on April 1, 2005.
g. Depreciation on equipment was computed at $5,800 for 2005.
h. Accrued expenses at December 31, 2004, and December 31, 2005, were as follows:

	December 31, 2004	December 31, 2005
Payroll taxes	$250	$400
Salaries	375	510
Utilities	275	450

Required:

Prepare a worksheet, with appropriate adjusting journal entries, to convert the trial balance of Ward Specialty Foods to the accrual basis for the year ended December 31, 2006. (*Hint:* When adjusting prior-year expense totals, debit or credit the Ward capital account.)

Problem 4-6: Nominal Dollars. Currently, the conceptual framework is based upon the assumption of no inflation, or stated differently, that the measurement tool is stable. When this is not the case, problems in interpreting financial data may result. The following requirements are intended to illustrate the nature of that difficulty.

Two hospitals serve the citizens of a particular community. One very large hospital was constructed forty years ago at a cost of $100 million dollars, and the other smaller hospital was constructed this year, also at a cost of $100 million dollars.

Assume that during the most recent year, the operating results of the two hospitals were as follows:

	40-Year-Old Hospital	New Hospital
Revenue	$ 200,000,000	$ 30,000,000
Expenses, other than depreciation	(160,000,000)	(24,000,000)
Depreciation (50-year life)	(2,000,000)	(2,000,000)
Net income	$ 38,000,000	$ 4,000,000

Required:

1. Compute the following ratios:
   a. Net Income/Revenue
   b. Net Income/Cost
2. From the results of the ratios, which hospital appears to be more profitable?
3. Recompute the ratios in (1), ignoring depreciation.
4. Why does the older hospital look to be much more profitable than the newer one when considering depreciation, but the two hospitals appear to be more equally profitable if depreciation is excluded? In addition to excluding depreciation from the ratios, what further adjustment is necessary to make the ratios more comparable?
5. As stated in the chapter, some countries allow financial statements to be restated or adjusted for the effects of inflation. Restate the historical cost of the 40-year-old hospital, assuming an annual inflation rate of (a) 2%, (b) 8%, and (c) 12%, and recompute the depreciation expense. Determine the net income for the year under each assumption.
6. What effect does adjusting the cost of the older hospital have upon the ratios in (1)?
7. Write a summary paragraph as to the difficulties of interpreting or comparing financial statements among companies that began business or acquired assets at different points in time, given the effects of inflation, even modest annual inflation rates.

Problem 4-7: Conservatism. An accountant has "sold" management that measuring income conservatively results in a lower net income and, therefore, less taxes and lessened expectations by shareholders for dividends. Thus, the company can more easily retain its cash to be used for internal expansion. Believing this argument, company management decides to adopt an accelerated method of depreciation for a recently acquired plant asset. The asset has an historical cost of $100,000, no salvage value, and a 5-year useful life. The following table shows the depreciation expense for each year under the accelerated depreciation method and the straight-line method.

Year	Accelerated Depreciation	Straight-Line Depreciation
1	$ 33,333	$ 20,000
2	26,667	20,000
3	20,000	20,000
4	13,333	20,000
5	6,667	20,000
Totals	$100,000	$100,000

Required:

1. Assuming that sales and expenses other than depreciation were stable for the five-year period at $250,000 and $150,000, respectively, compute net income for each of the years, using each depreciation method.
2. Does selecting a conservative accounting principle, such as an accelerated method of depreciation, always result in conservatively computed net income?
3. Do you think this observation is generally true of other supposed conservative methods of computing net income? There is one case when conservative measurement principles will consistently result in reporting conservative net income numbers for every year. What is that case?

Research Activities

Activity 4-1: Securities and Exchange Commission. Write a 2-page report on the United States Securities and Exchange Commission. In your report, you may address topics such as the SEC's objectives, organization, reason for its creation, duties of the office of the chief accountant, the rule-making process, or other topics of your choosing.

Activity 4-2: International Accounting Standards Board. Go to the International Accounting Standards Board's Web page (**http://www.iasb.org.uk**). The Web page contains a brief summary of the IASB's conceptual framework (click on "Standards" and then "Framework").

1. Summarize the benefits that a conceptual framework is expected to provide.
2. Identify some similarities and differences between the IASB and FASB frameworks.
3. Express your opinion on whether the differences between the frameworks are substantial or merely cosmetic. Would/could the differences result in significant differences in accounting requirements?

Activity 4-3: Financial Accounting Standards Board. Write a 2-page report on the Financial Accounting Standards Board. Your report might include information on the mission of the FASB, its organization, the process of adding topics to its agenda, the process of standard setting, etc.

Activity 4-4: International Comparison of Financial Statements. Monsanto Company, Bayer Group, and BASF Group are large multinational companies that operate in the chemicals and allied products industry. Monsanto is a U.S. company that issues financial statements in compliance with U.S. GAAP. Bayer Group is a German company that issues financial statements based on international GAAP. BASF Group is a German company that follows German GAAP. Look up the Web pages of each company (http://www.monsanto.com, http://www.bayer.com, and http://www.basf.com, respectively) and find their most recent annual reports.

1. Identify differences in financial reporting practices across the three companies. What valuation methods are used? How are the balance sheet accounts presented? Assess the level of disclosure across the three companies.
2. BASF Group has recently listed its shares on the New York Stock Exchange. As a result, the company is required to either present financial statements that comply with U.S. GAAP or reconcile any differences in net income and stockholders' equity in the footnotes. Find the reconciliations provided by BASF. What are the primary reconciling items for stockholders' equity? For net income? Is there a significant difference between these items under the different GAAPs?
3. Based on the evidence in the financial statements of Bayer and BASF, does it appear that the financial reporting of these companies is closely aligned with the tax laws of Germany?
4. Based on your analysis, do these German companies have the characteristics that are common of companies from code-law countries (i.e., relatively low levels of disclosure, smoothed income, conservative balance sheets, and high alignment of financial reporting and tax laws)? If not, why do you think these large companies are different from the typical German company?

Activity 4-5: Accrual Accounting. Net income can be divided into two components: operating cash flows and accruals. Find some published academic studies that investigate the value or relevance of these two components. Does the market appear to value accruals? What does this evidence suggest about the value or relevance of net income compared to cash flows?

Activity 4-6: International Properties of Accounting Earnings. Look up the following article and, without focusing on the research methodology, review its contents:

> R. Ball, S. P. Kothari, and A. Robin, 2000. "The Effect of International Institutional Factors on Properties of Accounting Earnings," *Journal of Accounting and Economics*, 29 pp. 1–51.

Prepare a 2-page report discussing the article's findings with respect to the properties of earnings in common-law and code-law countries.

$\mathscr{A}$pplying THE Conceptual Framework

PHOTODISC, INC

5

Historical Cost Principle: Acquiring Assets

New measurement and financial reporting problems arise as the world of business changes. For example, a certain company purchases airplanes to sell. While waiting to sell the airplanes and being located in a part of the country having several national parks, the company decides to charter the planes. At the end of the year, while preparing the financial statements, the company accountant wonders whether the airplanes should be classified as inventory (i.e., assets to be sold) or equipment (i.e., assets used in operations). Because the airplanes are for sale, they could be considered as inventory. Alternatively, because the airplanes are used as part of the business operations (i.e., chartered), they could be considered as equipment.

Questions

1. What are the financial statement ramifications for the classification of the airplanes?
2. What is the primary determinant on how the airplanes should be classified?

Pfizer Inc. is a research-based global pharmaceutical company that celebrated its 150th anniversary in 1999. During 1999, Pfizer reported net income of $3.2 billion on sales of $14.1 billion. Pfizer's longevity and profitability are due, in part, to an aggressive research and development program, as evidenced by just seven of its newest medicines generating 1999 revenues of over $1 billion. During 1999, Pfizer spent $2.8 billion on R&D activities, which represents 19.6% of sales, or 87.3% of net income.

Questions

1. Should these R&D expenditures be reported as an asset or an expense?
2. Alternatively, should only the R&D expenditures that result in a successful product be recorded as an asset? If so, how can it be determined during the R&D process which products will ultimately be successful?

Desperate for a center, the Utah Jazz drafted Luther Wright and signed him to a multi-year guaranteed contract. Although a talented basketball player, Luther's personal problems made it clear almost immediately that drafting him had been a bust. Nevertheless, despite the fact that he never played one year in the NBA, the Jazz still had to pay the amounts guaranteed by the contract.

Questions

1. How should the signing of Luther Wright have been recorded by the Jazz? How should the signing of Michael Jordan to a guaranteed contract have been recorded by the Chicago Bulls?
2. Is it appropriate to record people as assets? Because the guaranteed payments must be recorded as liabilities, what is the offsetting debit? How should the subsequent payments to Luther Wright be recorded? As expenses, losses, or neither?

INTERNET

The meanings of many financial terms can be found at **http://www.tiaa-cref.org/ libra/dictionary**. Information about investing or retiring can be found by backing up one level.

The Theory of Measuring Assets at Acquisition

For centuries, assets—at the time they were acquired—have been recorded at their fair value, which is subsequently known as the asset's historical cost. Today, every developed accounting system in the world continues to record assets at fair value at acquisition, which is known as the historical cost principle. The Financial Accounting Standards Board has stated that the historical cost of an asset " . . . is the amount of cash, or its equivalent, paid to acquire an asset."[1] In the United States, the historical cost of an item of inventory (which is an asset that will be resold) includes the price paid to acquire it and all necessary and reasonable costs in obtaining title (e.g., sales taxes), bringing it to the point where it will be sold (e.g., freight), and maintaining its value until it is sold. The historical cost of assets that will be used (rather than sold) includes the purchase price and all other costs incurred that are reasonably necessary to obtain title and bring the asset to where it will be used. *Appropriately applying the historical cost principle means that at acquisition, no asset is ever reported above its fair value as determined in an arm's-length transaction.*

The historical cost of an asset at acquisition can be determined in either of two ways. First, when assets are acquired by paying cash, the historical cost of an asset is the sum of the expenditures incurred to acquire it and prepare it for sale or use. Second, when assets are acquired in noncash transactions, the historical cost of an asset is the sum of the fair values of the assets given or received, whichever is more clearly evident. In all arm's-length transactions, the fair value of what is given is always equal to the fair value of what is received. Examples of transactions that are not considered to be arm's-length transactions are forced sales, liquidations, and transactions between related parties.

Undoubtedly, the reason for the historical cost principle's long and extensive use is because it provides relevant (at least at the time of acquisition) and reliable information. When assets are acquired, the most relevant financial in-

---

[1] FASB Statement of Concepts No. 5: *Recognition and Measurement in Financial Statements of Business Enterprises*, par. 67(a).

formation about them is their fair value, which is captured by the historical cost principle. And the historical cost of assets is reliable because such a price is what it purports to be, is neutral in that the current fair value of the asset does not give anyone undue preference, and is easily verifiable by referring to the sales documents.

However, as universal as the use of the historical cost principle is, various accounting systems in the world interpret and apply the principle somewhat differently. One difference arises from what is considered an asset. For example, in the earlier Pfizer R&D example, some accounting systems in the world define R&D expenditures as an asset, while other accounting systems do not. Another difference in applying the historical cost principle arises from what expenditures qualify to be recorded as part of the cost of the asset. For example, the purchase price of an automobile is an expenditure that is recorded as an asset, but what about sales tax on the automobile? Or title and license fees on the automobile? In this chapter, three examples—capitalization of interest, goodwill, and R&D costs—are presented to show how the historical cost principle is applied differently in various accounting systems in the world.

Asset Classification

Once it has been determined to capitalize[2] an expenditure as an asset, choosing the proper asset account in which to record the expenditure is done by referring to the primary purpose for acquiring the asset. The airplanes in the opening scenario were acquired with the primary intent of reselling them so they are classified as inventory and are not depreciated, even though they are used in charters. If the company's chartering activity becomes the main business activity and the primary reason for acquiring the airplanes is to use them in the operations of the company, then the airplanes are reclassified as equipment and are appropriately depreciated.

Journal Entry

The journal entry to record the acquisition of any asset consists of *debiting a descriptive asset account and crediting the source of the financing*. For example, if cash is used to acquire an item of equipment, then Equipment is debited and Cash is credited. Other possible credit accounts include Notes Payable (when financing is through borrowing), another asset account (when assets are exchanged), stock accounts (when a share in the ownership of the corporation is exchanged), or a combination of all of them. So the formula for preparing the journal entry when an asset is acquired is as follows:

Descriptive Asset	XXX	
Source of Financing		XXX

Expenditures that Comprise Historical Cost

As mentioned earlier, the historical cost of an asset includes all those expenditures that are incurred in obtaining title to the asset and in bringing it to the condition and location where it will be either sold or used. This section of the chapter

---

[2]*Capitalize* refers to recording an expenditure as an asset rather than expensing the amount. Thus, the expenditure is reported on the balance sheet instead of on the income statement.

sets forth some examples for identifying the expenditures that comprise an asset's historical cost.

Inventory

Inventories are assets that will be sold in the normal course of business or assets that will be used or consumed in producing goods for sale. The historical cost[3] of inventory includes all costs of acquiring it, of bringing it to the place where it will be sold, and of maintaining its value until sold. Examples of costs that are included in the cost of inventory include the acquisition price, sales taxes, freight-in (freight-out is a selling expense), and costs of receiving, storing, and insuring the inventory. For many companies, it is difficult to assign some of these expenditures (such as the costs of receiving and storage) to individual items of inventory. As a result, many of these expenditures are expensed as incurred. Such action may be justified in that (1) the costs of applying the theoretical principle outweigh the benefits of the resulting information, and (2) the amounts involved are too small to make a difference between expensing them or capitalizing them (i.e., materiality). The important point when deviating from the theoretical accounting treatment by expensing the amounts rather than capitalizing them is that such policy is consistently applied each year.

The historical cost principle requires that the cost of inventory be reduced for all **trade discounts**,[4] which are the discounts given to customers before considering payment or credit terms. Inventory also may be reduced for **cash discounts**, which are discounts received for timely payment. Under the **gross method**, purchases of inventory are recorded at the gross invoice amount. Subsequently, cash discounts received because of timely payment (including paying a portion of the total amount owed) are recorded in a purchase discounts account, which is included in determining the cost of goods sold. In other words, inventory is recorded at gross, whether or not the cash discount is taken, and the cost of goods sold is reduced by the amount of cash discounts taken.

Under the **net method**, purchases of inventory are recorded at the net invoice amount, which is the amount due less the cash discount, whether or not timely payment is actually made. Then, any cash discounts lost are recognized as an administrative expense. In other words, inventory is recorded at net, whether or not the cash discount is taken. Although either method is acceptable, the net method is conceptually preferable because it is more consistent with the historical cost principle, which is that the cost of inventory should include only the necessary and reasonable expenditures, i.e., net of the available cash discount. However, the gross method is used more frequently because many accountants consider it easier to apply. Illustration 5-1 shows the journal entries under both the gross and net methods of accounting for the acquisition of $1,000 of inventory under 2/10, n/30 terms.[5]

The historical cost of inventory that is produced includes the cost of direct materials, direct labor, an allocated portion of manufacturing overhead, and—in the United States—interest cost, which is discussed later in the chapter:

[3]This historical cost amount for inventories is also called product cost or inventoriable cost.
[4]When there is more than one trade discount, it is called a chain discount. Chain discounts are applied in steps, with each discount applied to the previously discounted price.
[5]The meaning of the phrase 2/10, n/30 is that a 2% discount is allowed when payment is made within 10 days; otherwise, the net (or total) amount is due in 30 days. Similarly, 3/20, n/60 reads that a 3% discount is allowed when payment is made within 20 days; otherwise, the net amount is due in 60 days.

ILLUSTRATION 5-1

Journal Entries for Recording Inventory Transactions

	Gross Method		Net Method	
Acquired $1,000 of merchandise for resale.				
Inventory[6]	1,000		980	
Accounts Payable		1,000		980
Payment is made within the time allotted to receive a discount for timely payment.				
Accounts Payable	1,000		980	
Cash		980		980
Purchase Discounts		20		—
Payment is not made within the time allotted to receive a discount for timely payment.				
Accounts Payable	1,000		980	
Purchase Discounts Lost[7]	—		20	
Cash		1,000		1,000

- Direct materials are those materials that become an integral part of the finished product and whose cost can be easily traced to specific finished products.
- Direct labor is the "hands-on" labor required to manufacture a finished product. Direct labor does not include the cost of the line supervisor or higher-level administrators, nor does direct labor include overtime.
- Manufacturing overhead cost includes all manufacturing costs except direct materials cost and direct labor cost. Unlike direct materials and direct labor costs that are assigned easily to individual inventory items, manufacturing overhead costs are allocated (the process is called "applied") to individual inventory items by using an overhead rate. The overhead rate is computed at the beginning of the year (and hence, the label "Predetermined Overhead Rate") by dividing the estimated yearly overhead costs by the estimated yearly activity base (such as direct labor hours), which is called the "cost driver." The amount of manufacturing overhead cost that is applied to any specific inventory item is then computed by multiplying this predetermined overhead rate by the actual amount of the cost driver incurred to produce that item of inventory.[8]

An example of financial reporting for inventories is shown in Exhibit 5-1, which was extracted from DuPont's 2001 annual report. The exhibit shows the inventory balance as reported on the balance sheet and the accompanying explanatory information found in the notes to the financial statements. Note particularly the portions italicized by the authors as they apply to the above

---

[6]This entry assumes the use of a perpetual inventory system. When a periodic inventory system is used, a purchases account is debited.

[7]Alternatively, an interest expense account could be debited, which indicates that a financing cost was incurred in acquiring the inventory.

[8]Costing of inventory that is produced is covered extensively in managerial and cost accounting classes and so is not discussed further in this text.

discussion on the historical cost of inventory. The exhibit also demonstrates the increasingly popular method of reporting abbreviated amounts on the balance sheet and then disclosing comprehensive information in the notes.

EXHIBIT 5-1

Example of Financial Reporting for Inventories
DuPont

Information found in the balance sheet:

	2001	2000
Inventories (in millions)	$4,215	$4,658

Information found in the notes in the financial statements (Notes 1 and 12):
Inventories

	2001	2000
Finished products	$2,652	$2,818
Semifinished products	1,185	1,504
Raw materials and supplies	844	907
Total	$4,681	$5,229
Less adjustment of inventories to a last-in, first-out (LIFO) basis	486	571
	$4,215	$4,658

Inventory values before LIFO adjustment are generally determined by the average cost method, which approximates current cost. Excluding Pioneer, inventories valued under the LIFO method comprised 79 percent and 81 percent of consolidated inventories before LIFO adjustment at December 31, 2001 and 2000, respectively. Pioneer inventories of $745 and $913 at December 31, 2001 and 2000, respectively, were valued under the LIFO method.

Investments

Assets classified in Investments (or Investments and Funds) are held by the company for future use or for long-term price appreciation. Typical assets found in this category include (1) cash or securities that are physically separated and are to be used for a specific purpose, usually to retire long-term debt, (2) land that either will be used in the future or sold, (3) long-term receivables, and (4) investments in bonds, stocks, or other securities of various corporations. The historical cost of all investments includes the acquisition price to acquire the asset and any other costs of obtaining title (e.g., broker's fees).

Property, Plant, and Equipment

To be classified as property, plant, or equipment, assets must be (1) long-lived, (2) used in the operations of the business, and (3) tangible, which means to have physical substance. The historical cost of such assets (e.g., equipment, buildings, land, and natural resources) consists of the acquisition cost and all other expenditures that are necessary to prepare the asset for its intended use, such as sales taxes and shipping costs. In determining the historical cost of these assets, the FASB's cost-benefit and materiality constraints are always effective, meaning that some expenditures frequently are treated differently from what the strict application of theory requires. Thus, companies expense some expenditures rather than capitalizing them because the amounts are immaterial or because the cost of capitalizing the amounts is greater than the benefits received. The following illustrates expenditures that are theoretically included in the cost of specific assets. When reading the list below, consider the various aspects of the definition of historical cost, such as "necessary" and "intended use."

Land

The historical cost of land includes expenditures for such items as:

- Purchase price,
- Title search fees, attorney's fees, closing costs, and other costs connected with obtaining title,
- Costs of surveying, grading, leveling, and clearing the land,
- Costs of removing an existing structure, net of any proceeds from the scrap that is sold,
- Obligations, such as back taxes, that are assumed by the purchaser, and
- Special assessments by local governments for improvements, such as lighting, curb, gutter, sidewalks and roads when such improvements will be maintained by the city.

To illustrate, on February 1, Callister Co. finalized negotiations to acquire land upon which it intends to construct a shopping center. Terms of the deal require a cash payment of $5 million and the assumption of back taxes of $500,000. Callister paid a lawyer $20,000 to help with the negotiations and consult in all legal matters connected with the acquisition. Immediately, Callister had the land surveyed to confirm property boundaries, which cost $5,000. Subsequently, Callister tore down an existing structure at a cost of $10,000 and was able to sell some scrap materials for $500. During March and April, preparations for laying the foundation of the building, including digging a hole, tamping the ground, etc., cost Callister $125,000.

The historical cost of the land includes the $5 million acquisition cost, the $500,000 for back taxes, the $20,000 lawyer's fees, the $5,000 surveying cost, and the $10,000 to remove the existing structure less the $500 received for scrap, for a total historical cost of $5,534,500. All of these costs were incurred with the intent of obtaining title to and preparing the land to build the shopping center. No cost is allocated to the structure that was torn down as it has no future benefits to the company. The costs of digging the hole, tamping the ground, etc., are part of the historical cost of the resulting building and are not included in the cost of the land. The journal entry to record each of the above expenditures is to debit Land and to credit Cash, and the journal entry for the scrap is to credit Land.

Land Improvements

A clear distinction is made between land costs and land improvement costs because, unlike land, land improvements have limited lives. Therefore, the land improvement costs are accumulated in a separate account from land and subsequently depreciated. Examples of land improvements include parking lots, private roads, company-maintained sidewalks, fences, and private lighting.

Equipment Acquired by Purchase

The historical cost of equipment that is purchased includes such expenditures as:

- Purchase price,
- Transportation costs to the location where the equipment will be used,

- Placement and installation costs,
- Costs of initially training employees to operate the equipment, and
- Costs associated with initial runs while calibrating the equipment to operate within specified parameters.

Buildings Acquired by Purchase

For buildings acquired by purchase or that are built under contract, historical cost includes such expenditures as:

- Contract price,
- Other initial charges, such as legal fees and closing costs, and
- Costs of reconditioning a recently acquired building to make it suitable for its intended purpose.

Self-Constructed Buildings and Equipment

As with inventory that is manufactured, the historical costs of buildings and equipment that are constructed include:

- Direct materials cost,
- Direct labor cost,
- The increase in *variable* overhead that was caused by the company undertaking the construction project, and
- Perhaps a portion of the fixed overhead.
  1. Some accountants argue that since fixed overhead does not increase because of the company undertaking a construction project, none of the fixed overhead should be included as part of the constructed asset's cost.
  2. Other accountants think that overhead attaches to all products made during the period—both those products sold and those used in the company's operations. Thus, they advocate assigning a portion of the fixed costs to the constructed asset. It should be noted that doing so reduces the cost of producing the routinely made inventory and thus increases income in the period in which the asset is constructed; income is increased by the amount of fixed overhead that is included in the cost of the manufactured asset.
  3. Still other accountants assign to the cost of the constructed asset the cost of the production that was lost (if any) because of building the operational asset rather than making inventory. Although conceptually appealing, this approach requires measuring the opportunity cost of the inventory that was not made, which is a difficult thing to do.
- Interest cost.
- Cost of insuring against property damage during construction.

Natural Resources

The historical cost of a natural resource includes:

- The acquisition price,
- Costs incurred in a title search and various other fees to obtain title,
- Costs of getting appropriate governmental permissions to extract the natural resource, and
- Costs of building roads, etc., that are necessary to extract the natural resource.

Exhibit 5-2, which was extracted from the annual report of Medtronic, Inc., illustrates the typical financial reporting for property, plant, and equipment in published financial reports. Again, note the tendency to report a summarized fig-

EXHIBIT 5-2

Example of Financial Reporting for Property, Plant, and Equipment

Medtronic, Inc.
(*in millions*)

	April 26, 2002	April 27, 2001
Information from the balance sheet:		
Property, equipment, and leasehold interests at cost, net	$1,451.8	$1,176.5

Information from the notes to the financial statements (Note 1)

	April 26, 2002	April 27, 2001	Lives
Land and land improvements	$ 64.0	$ 57.7	20 years
Buildings and leasehold improvements	650.8	510.1	up to 40 years
Equipment	1,547.5	1,215.4	3–7 years
Construction in progress	226.8	274.1	—
	$ 2,489.1	$2,057.3	
Less: Accumulated depreciation	(1,037.3)	(880.8)	
Property, plant and equipment, net	$ 1,451.8	$1,176.5	

ure in the balance sheet and to give supporting detail in the notes to the financial statements.

Capitalization of Interest

The assets that qualify for interest to be part of their historical cost are those *assets—whether for sale or for use—for which a period of time is required to construct them. Interest cost is not part of the historical cost of assets that are routinely manufactured in large quantities on a repetitive basis.*[9]

The FASB had two objectives in adopting this capitalization of interest requirement. The first objective was to more nearly align the accounting for purchasing an asset with the accounting for constructing an asset. For example, when a company purchases a manufactured asset, the manufacturer sets the purchase price at an amount high enough to cover cost—including the cost of financing the construction. Likewise, when the same company constructs an identical asset, the historical cost of the asset should include the financing costs. The FASB's second objective was to match future expenses (through depreciation) from using the asset with the revenues generated by the asset. Thus, the thought is that when the asset's historical cost is more accurate—which it theoretically is through including interest as part of its cost—then the subsequent allocation of the asset's cost through depreciation is also more accurate. Whether the resulting information obtained by capitalizing interest is more relevant is debatable, which is demonstrated by the fact that not many countries require interest to be capitalized as part of the cost of an asset.

EXTENDING *the Concept*

Even if the FASB is logical in its requirement of capitalizing interest on constructed assets, its position is an anomaly. Some countries, such as Japan, Germany, the United Kingdom, and Sweden, permit interest to be capitalized but do not require it, and other countries, such as Brazil, prohibit interest capitalization.

How does the capitalization of interest affect the comparability of U.S. GAAP financial statements with those from other countries?

[9]SFAS No. 34, "Capitalization of Interest Cost," pars. 6–9.

The amount of interest capitalized is the lesser of (1) the actual interest cost incurred for the year or (2) an amount called **avoidable interest**, which is the theoretical amount of interest that could have been avoided had the asset not been constructed. Avoidable interest is computed by multiplying the average accumulated expenditures by an interest rate.

For example, C. Schaller and Son began constructing a new office building on January 1, 2002, and moved into the new building on January 1, 2003. Costs of $3,000,000 were incurred uniformly during the period of construction. Schaller's typical rate to borrow money is 10%, and the actual interest incurred during the year was $135,000. The first step in computing avoidable interest is determining the average accumulated expenditures. Since the expenditures were incurred uniformly during the year, the weighted-average accumulated expenditures are one-half of the $3,000,000 incurred, or $1,500,000. The next step in computing avoidable interest is determining the appropriate interest rate, which in this situation is 10%. Avoidable interest is then computed as follows:

$$\text{Avoidable Interest} = \text{Average Accumulated Expenditures} \times \text{Interest Rate}$$
$$= \$1{,}500{,}000 \times 10\%$$
$$= \$150{,}000$$

As mentioned earlier, the amount capitalized is the lesser of the actual interest incurred of $135,000 and the avoidable interest of $150,000. So in this case, $135,000 of interest is capitalized as part of the cost of the building. (An extended example illustrating some complexities of interest capitalization is included as the appendix to this chapter.)

The *amount of interest to capitalize is not reduced by any interest revenue earned.* Thus, if Schaller and Son had borrowed the $3,000,000 on January 1 to finance the construction and had temporarily invested any unneeded portion, the amount of interest to capitalize is not reduced by the interest earned.

Capitalization of interest stops when the asset is substantially complete and ready for its intended use. In applying this rule, the FASB gave two examples. Suppose a complex of condominiums is being built in phases, where Phase I is completed before Phase II is begun. Then capitalization of interest stops on Phase I when it is substantially complete and ready for its intended use, but interest capitalization continues on Phase II. Also, suppose an oil pipeline and storage facilities are being constructed and that the pipeline is completed before the storage facility is ready to accept oil. Then, capitalization of interest on the pipeline continues because it cannot be used until the storage facility is also ready. Also, capitalization of interest stops when conditions internal to the company cause a disruption in construction (e.g., company approved vacations); but capitalizing interest continues when disruptions in construction occur because of conditions external to the company.

Exhibit 5-3, which is part of Boeing's 2001 annual report, illustrates the capitalizing of interest on constructed assets as reported in yearly financial reports. Note the amount of interest capitalized.

EXHIBIT 5-3

Example of Capitalizing Interest in Financial Reporting

Note 9: Property, Plant, and Equipment
Property, plant, and equipment at December 31 consisted of the following:

	2001	2000
Land	$ 489	$ 460
Buildings	8,598	9,241
Machinery and equipment	10,642	10,378
Construction in progress	1,099	891
	$20,828	$20,970
Less accumulated depreciation	(12,369)	(12,156)
	$ 8,459	$ 8,814

Depreciation expense was $1,140, $1,159, and $1,330 for 2001, 2000, and 1999, respectively.

Interest capitalized as construction-period property, plant and equipment costs amounted to $72, $70, and $69 in 2001, 2000, and 1999, respectively.

Intangibles

Like the assets categorized as property, plant, and equipment, intangible assets are long-lived and are used in the operations of the business. The only distinguishing difference between intangibles and property, plant, and equipment is that assets classified as intangibles lack physical substance. As with the accounting for acquiring any other asset, the accounting for acquiring an intangible asset is based on its fair value. However, *all costs incurred in internally developing an intangible asset are expensed as incurred.* Thus, intangible assets can be recorded only when purchased. The following are some illustrations of applying the historical cost principle to various intangible assets.

Patents, Copyrights, and Other Similar Intangible Assets

The historical cost of a patent, copyright, and other similar intangible assets includes the cost of acquiring them—but not the costs of internally developing them. All internal costs incurred to develop an intangible asset are expensed as incurred. Only purchased intangibles are recorded as assets.

Leasehold Improvements

Leasehold improvements are the improvements made to bring a *leased* property to the condition necessary where it can be used, or to improve its usefulness. Such costs are recorded as assets because the benefits received will benefit the company for several years. Improvements that are nondetachable from the build-

This Is the Real World

Priceline.com Inc. is an Internet company that allows consumers to name their own price over the Internet for airline tickets, hotel rooms, and other commodities. This unique business model was patented by the company. Perhaps because of the success of this business model, the market value of Priceline.com Inc. at June 30, 1999, was in excess of $15 billion. In contrast, the company's book value for the period ending June 30, 1999, was $171 million—approximately 10% of its market value. Also, reported EPS for the six months ending June 30, 1999, was a loss of 29 cents per share. The primary reasons for the large difference between book value and market value was attributed to the huge growth potential that the Internet offered and the protection against competitors that the patent provided.

On September 8, 1999, Microsoft Corporation announced plans to imitate the business model patented by Priceline.com. The threat that the software giant would become a competitor resulted in a one-day drop in Priceline.com's stock of 19% to $55 per share, which was the equivalent of a $2 billion loss in market value. Thus, if the patent holds up and Microsoft is not allowed to compete with Priceline.com, it can be assumed that the patent's market value is at least $2 billion. Currently, the patent is not even listed, at least as a separate line item, on Priceline.com's balance sheet because very little, if anything, was spent to patent the unique business model.

This example illustrates the inherent difficulty in valuing intangible assets and the inadequacy of reporting intangible assets at their historical cost amounts.

ing are amortized[10] over the shorter of the lease term or the life of the improvements.

Organization Costs

Organization costs are the start-up costs incurred in establishing a business or when a business opens a new facility, introduces a new product or service, or conducts business in a new territory or with a new customer. Typical organization costs include legal fees, accounting fees, advertising fees and other such costs. Until the issuance of SOP 98-5,[11] these costs were customarily recorded as assets and then amortized over a short, arbitrary period, such as five to ten years. However, the AICPA has concluded that all such costs must be *expensed as incurred.*

Development Stage Corporations[12]

Operating expenses and losses of **development stage corporations** are not deferred (not recorded as assets) but are expensed in the year incurred. A development stage corporation is one that is "devoting substantially all of its efforts to establishing [as contrasted to organizing] a new business and either of the following conditions exists:

---

[10]*Amortization* is a term that is comparable in meaning to *depreciation*. In a specific sense, assets such as buildings and equipment are depreciated; natural resources are depleted; and intangible assets are amortized. This is the meaning of the word as it is used here. However, amortization also has a general meaning, which encompasses depreciation and depletion. Hence, it is proper to talk of amortizing buildings, equipment, an oil well, or a patent. The amortization period is the length of time that benefits are expected to be received from a particular asset and the length of time over which the cost of the asset is expensed.

[11]SOPs (Statements of Position) are issued by the AICPA. The first number (98) refers to the year the statement was issued, and the second number (5) represents this statement as the 5th statement issued in 1998.

[12]See FAS No. 7 for the FASB standard on accounting for development stage corporations.

a. Planned principal operations have not commenced.

b. Planned principal operations have commenced, but there has been no significant revenue therefrom."[13]

Goodwill

From a business view, **goodwill** is the intangible asset that represents a company's ability to generate more than normal profits; or stated differently, goodwill is those intangibles that make a company more valuable than the sum of its individual identifiable components. Some examples of resources that may give rise to goodwill are brand names, superior management, or synergies between a parent and its subsidiary that result in improved operating efficiency. The resources comprising goodwill are inseparable from the company. (They cannot be bought or sold independently of the entire company.) For accounting purposes, goodwill is recorded only when an entire company is purchased and the amount paid exceeds the fair value of the **net assets** acquired. Expenditures to generate goodwill internally or to maintain existing goodwill are never recorded as assets but are expensed in the period incurred.

When an entire company is acquired, any goodwill that is present is measured through a subtraction process. First, the buyer and seller of a business, through a series of computations and negotiation, determine the value of the entire company. Then, fair values are assigned to the individual identifiable assets acquired and liabilities assumed. Finally, the historical cost of goodwill is measured as the difference between the sum of the fair value of the company's net assets[14] and the amount paid for the entire company. Mathematically, the formula for computing goodwill is as follows:

Price paid for the company		$ XXX
Fair value of individual assets:		
Accounts receivable	$ XXX	
Inventory	XXX	
Others	XXX	
Total fair value of assets		XXX
Less fair value of liabilities assumed:		
Accounts payable	$(XXX)	
Notes payable	(XXX)	
Others	(XXX)	
Total fair value of liabilities		XXX)
Subtract fair value of net assets		(XXX)
Goodwill		$ XXX

To illustrate determining and recording goodwill, consider the merger of Raytheon with Hughes Defense in 1997. According to information extracted from Raytheon's annual report, "The Hughes transaction was valued at $9.5 billion, . . . comprised of approximately $5.5 billion in common stock and $4.0 billion in debt, which was assumed by the merged company. . . . Assets acquired in conjunction with the merger with Hughes Defense [measured at fair value] include contracts in process of $1,820 million, inventories of $408 million, other current assets of $337 million, property, plant and equipment of $942 million, and other

[13]FAS No. 7, par. 8.
[14]Net assets means assets minus liabilities.

assets of $1,776 million (primarily pension related). Liabilities assumed include debt of $4,033 million, current liabilities of $2,659 million, and long-term liabilities of $961 million. Goodwill resulting from the preliminary estimates of fair value associated with this transaction was $7,950 million." Using the information provided, the following journal entry can be prepared:

Contracts in Process	1,820	
Inventories	408	
Other Current Assets	337	
Property, Plant, and Equipment	942	
Other Assets	1,776	
Goodwill	7,950	
Debt		4,033
Current Liabilities		2,659
Long-Term Liabilities		961
Common Stock		5,580

To record the net assets of an acquired company and recognize goodwill as the difference between the amount paid and the fair value of the identifiable net assets acquired.

Occasionally, the sum of the fair values of the net assets exceeds the cost paid for the entire company. In such a situation, the company is said to have "negative goodwill." (Actually, it is preferable to say that the company was acquired for a bargain price.) *When a company is acquired at a bargain price, the historical costs of the long-lived assets (except for long-term investments) are reduced proportionally according to their relative fair values.*[15]

In the summer of 2001, the FASB passed a new ruling requiring goodwill to be kept on the balance sheet as an asset without amortization. Previously, goodwill had to be amortized over a period not to exceed 40 years, a procedure that is used by many countries. Although declining in acceptability, other countries permit goodwill to be written off immediately to retained earnings. Writing off goodwill immediately, as compared to amortizing goodwill or recording goodwill as an asset without amortization, increases net income and reduces the amount of total assets and owners' equity on the balance sheet. The result is that the return-on-assets and return-on-equity ratios are improved, making the company look stronger and more profitable than companies that record goodwill as assets. In short, there are considerable differences in the treatment of goodwill among the accounting and financial reporting systems of the world that result in substantive and long-term differences among companies' published financial statements.

EXTENDING THE CONCEPT

In 1988, Philip Morris Companies acquired Kraft Inc. for $12.9 billion. This acquisition received much notoriety because the fair market value of Kraft's net assets was $1.3 billion. Thus, $11.6 billion—or 90% of the purchase price—was labeled as goodwill. Following U.S. GAAP at that time, Philip Morris amortized the purchased goodwill over 40 years, which resulted in an annual charge to income of $290 million. By comparison, Kraft's net income in the year prior to the merger was $489 million. U.S. GAAP has now been revised, so that companies may keep some goodwill on the balance sheet without amortization and write it down only when an assessment shows that its value has permanently declined. Philip Morris's profitability as shown on its financial statements would have been improved greatly if it had been allowed to write off the goodwill to retained earnings or to keep it as an asset on the balance sheet indefinitely.

The significance of the goodwill issue is further emphasized in the AOL/Time Warner merger, which resulted in $150 billion of goodwill and annual amortization expense of $7.5 billion per year for 20 years. Even Congress debated the merits of allowing companies to report a separate earnings-per-share amount that excluded goodwill amortization. This attention probably influenced the FASB to ultimately adopt the current standard. With the change in U.S. GAAP, Time Warner announced in January 2002 that it would be writing off $55 billion of goodwill for 2001. This change is seen as an attempt to improve the company's assets for future years, to which the company hopes the market will react favorably, and that it will not be penalized by taking a substantial loss in 2001.

1. What are the theoretical merits of (a) capitalizing goodwill with amortization, (b) writing off goodwill directly to retained earnings, or (c) keeping goodwill on the books without amortization?

2. How would each of these methods affect the comparability of financial statements?

3. Is Time Warner admitting that it overpaid for AOL?

---

[15]If it happens that the historical costs of all long-term assets (except long-term investments) are reduced to zero and an excess still remains, the difference is labeled as a "deferred credit" and included among the long-term liabilities on the balance sheet. Such a situation is extremely rare.

Research and Development (R&D)

The FASB mandates that "all research and development costs . . . shall be charged to expense when incurred."[16] However, the accounting for R&D is not as easy as this statement implies, because it is not easy to determine what the FASB meant by R&D costs. Identifying R&D costs is a two-step process. The first step is determining R&D *activities*, of which the following are some examples. Summarizing this list, generally once commercial production begins, R&D activities end.

- Laboratory research aimed at the discovery of new knowledge.
- Searching for applications of new research findings.
- Conceptual formulation and design of possible products or processes.
- Testing in search for, or an evaluation of, product or process alternatives.
- Modifying the formulation of a product or process.
- Design, construction, and testing of preproduction prototypes and models.
- Design of tools, jigs, molds, and dies involving new technology.

The second step is determining which costs of R&D activities are to be expensed, and when making this determination, the FASB implemented an "alternative future uses" test. *Any cost incurred in an R&D activity that has an alternative future use or use in another R&D project is not an R&D cost and therefore is not expensed.* For example, the cost of a building or a lab used for R&D activities is not expensed because the building or lab has alternative future uses. Similarly, laboratory equipment is not an R&D cost if it can be used in another R&D project or experiment.

The specific rules as applied to various types of costs are as follows:

1. Costs for materials, equipment, facilities, or intangible assets that have alternative future uses are not R&D costs. These costs are recorded as assets. When the material is subsequently used, then the cost of the material is an R&D expense. Likewise, when the equipment or facilities are used, the corresponding depreciation is an R&D expense.
2. Salaries, wages, fringe benefits, and other personnel costs of individuals doing R&D activities are expensed as incurred.
3. A reasonable allocation of general and administrative costs that are clearly related to R&D activities is expensed as R&D costs.
4. Costs of R&D activities performed for others are not expensed but are recorded as a receivable. R&D activities conducted by others for the benefit of the company are R&D costs and expensed when billed.

The FASB's rules eliminate the reporting of any R&D asset on a balance sheet. The FASB's requirement that all R&D costs are to be expensed directly conflicts with the accounting practices throughout most of the rest of the world,[17] which permit at least some development costs to be recorded as assets. Also, IAS No. 38 permits development costs (but not research costs) to be recorded as an intangible asset.

---

[16]See FAS No. 2, par. 12.
[17]Some of these major accounting systems include Australia, Brazil, Canada, France, Japan, Netherlands, Spain, Sweden, United Kingdom, and the IAS.

This Is the Real World

In most cases, management has a strong incentive to increase reported earnings. Not only are bonuses and other executive compensation related to the amount of reported earnings, but so are professional reputation and prestige. Hence, when it is questionable whether an expenditure has resulted in the acquisition of an asset or the incurring of an expense, management might be inclined to report the expenditure as an acquisition of an asset. Why? What effect do the two alternatives (i.e., expensing versus capitalizing) have on the current year's reported earnings? Is management's inclination in accord with the conceptual framework? Which rule, convention, principle, etc., is violated?

Manipulating earnings is not desirable, is often unethical, and in some cases may be illegal. However, due to the pressures to increase earnings, a few managers do succumb and use inappropriate accounting procedures to fraudulently inflate earnings. For example, during 1997 and 1998, five high-level managers at George Wimpey PLC, a leading builder of homes in England, inappropriately reported 4 million pounds of site development costs as assets rather than expenses and thus overstated net income during those two years. As another example, in the first four months of 1999, Sirena Apparel issued eight press releases in which it boasted of launching an online store, moving its corporate headquarters, introducing an intimate apparel division, reporting seven consecutive quarters of profits, and obtaining new financing. Then in June, Sirena filed for bankruptcy. The company stated the cause was due to "events arising from its discovery of financial irregularities..." These irregularities consisted of overstating inventory and "the write-off of certain deferred expenses." Again, management succumbed to the temptation to inappropriately defer costs rather than expense them.

Although the current year's earnings may be overstated by inappropriately deferring costs, what is the impact upon the income of future years by such action? Is this an example of a "slippery slope"? that is, once a course of action is begun, will maintaining control of one's actions become increasingly difficult and ultimately end in disaster?

As illustrated in the Pfizer opening scenario, the long-term success of many companies, particularly high-tech and pharmaceutical companies, is dependent upon the discovery and development of new products. R&D activities also have been the catalyst for technological change around the world, which, in turn, has been the primary driver of economic growth and the increased standard of living in many nations. Since the long-term benefits from R&D activities are unmistakable, the FASB's position seems unjustified. Because of these and other similar reasons, the FASB's approach to accounting for R&D costs has been criticized.

In defense of the FASB's position, the FASB recognized that "a high degree of uncertainty [exists] about the future benefits of *individual* [emphasis added] research and development projects;" and they also recognized the need for "a reasonable degree of comparability [of information] among enterprises." Since the future benefits of individual R&D projects cannot be determined objectively, and perceiving a need for comparable information, the FASB came to the entirely pragmatic conclusion of expensing all R&D costs.

General Observations on Measuring Intangible Assets

As illustrated with both the Raytheon and the Phillip Morris examples, often the most important assets of a business are its intangible assets. Yet, determining the historical cost of these intangible assets is often not possible. (This is the reason for measuring purchased goodwill through a subtraction process.) Complicating the accounting measurement problem is the number and nature of intangible assets that continue to grow and change in response to the business environment. For example, beginning in the mid-1980s, some Australian, UK, and other European companies began recording an intangible asset on their balance sheets for brand names, as illustrated in the following excerpt from the 1994 Annual Report for Guinness, PLC:

INTERNATIONAL

"The fair value of businesses acquired and of interests taken in associated undertakings includes brands, which are recognized where the brand has a value which is substantial and long-term. . . ."

An even more controversial accounting practice is to record as assets (without amortization) costs incurred internally for the purpose of developing a brand name. An example is the capitalization of advertising costs.[18]

Another example of a current accounting measurement problem occurs in bio-tech companies. The United States and parts of the rest of the world were involved with mapping the human genome, which (at least as a rough map) was completed in the summer of 2000. With a rough map of the human genome, bio-tech companies may be able to develop medications and treatments for genetic diseases. The efforts to date have taken several years and have cost a huge sum of money, and this is just the beginning of the costs to be incurred. Ahead is still a 5 to 10-year time frame to develop effective medications, and then another 5–10 years to obtain FDA approval to sell the medications—before any revenue can be recognized. Yet, the future potential profitability for some of these bio-tech companies is immense. So should the costs now being incurred be expensed, or should they be recorded as assets until revenue is generated? This is not an easy question, and the answer will affect dramatically the reported operating results of these bio-tech companies.

The problems of measuring and reporting relevant values at acquisition for intangible assets provide both challenges and opportunities for accountants. The problems in determining such values arise because:

1. Many intangibles are not acquired through an external transaction but instead are developed internally,
2. The costs of internally developing an intangible asset are often not reflective of the intangible asset's value (e.g., the cost of filing for a patent, the cost of developing a Web site, etc.), and
3. The marketplace cannot determine the value of many intangibles unless a transaction occurs.

Thus, not having recourse to a market value and with internally generated cost data not being reflective of fair value, how is the accountant to reliably determine a relevant value for many intangible assets? Just because measuring a relevant value for intangible assets is difficult and seemingly impossible, however, does not mean that accountants should give up trying to devise a way to measure relevant values for such assets. And this is where opportunities arise. Assuredly, a way will be derived to obtain such values in the future. The process will be slow, with many individuals making small contributions. But because the failure to appropriately measure intangible assets can lead to faulty decisions, measuring the value of intangible assets must be—and will be—an area of continuing interest to all accountants.

Measuring Historical Cost

Prior to this point, this chapter has defined the historical cost principle and given examples of the types of expenditures that constitute the historical cost of various assets. The final aspect of applying the historical cost principle is to measure the fair value of expenditures (1) where more than one asset is acquired in a sin-

---

[18]Many accounting regulators and practitioners believe the incentive behind the growth in the practice of capitalizing brands without amortization is to enhance reported stockholders' equity, which is understated due to goodwill being written off to retained earnings. In 1997, the United Kingdom adopted a standard that prohibits writing off goodwill to retained earnings and limits the capitalization of internally generated brand names.

gle transaction or (2) when expenditures are entered into and settled for non-cash consideration. These topics are covered in the following sections.

Lump-Sum Purchase of Assets

Occasionally, companies acquire a group of assets for a lump-sum amount. In such transactions, the historical cost of the individual assets is determined by *allocating the fair value of the consideration paid, using the relative fair values of the individual assets acquired as the basis for allocation.* This principle of allocating the cost paid for a group of assets applies whether the assets acquired are tangible assets (such as buildings and equipment) or intangible assets, other than goodwill (such as patents), or a combination of tangible and intangible assets.

Various indicators of fair value can be used, as long as such values are realistic indicators of the relative value (i.e., value in relation to each other) of the assets. Some indicators of relative fair value include tax assessed values, values used for insurance purposes, present value of future earnings, or appraisals. Whenever possible, indicators of fair value should be used that are market determined, as compared to those that are determined in appraisals or by individuals internal to the company (including members of boards of directors).

To illustrate, suppose that on June 20, 2004, Oat Company purchased for $870,000 a tract of land on which a warehouse and an office building were located. The data in Table 5-1 are the values of the respective properties.

TABLE 5-1

	Tax Assessed Values	Appraised Values	Seller's Original Cost
Land	$ 60,000	$ 90,000	$ 20,000
Warehouse	500,000	550,000	680,000
Office building	240,000	260,000	300,000
Totals	$800,000	$900,000	$1,000,000

In this illustration, either the tax assessed values or the appraised values may be used to allocate the cost of $870,000 to the three assets, even though the resulting answers may be different. The seller's original cost cannot be used as a basis of allocation because such values are not indicative of the *current relative values.* The tax assessed values can be used because, by law, governments are required to assess taxes on fair value and to update those values periodically.[19] Using the tax assessed values to allocate the fair value of the $870,000 consideration paid results in determining the historical cost amounts for the individual assets as shown in Table 5-2.

Once the respective historical cost amounts have been computed, the following journal entry is prepared:

Land	65,250	
Warehouse	543,750	
Office Building	261,000	
Cash		870,000

To record the assets acquired in a lump-sum purchase at historical cost.

---

[19]Many governments determine fair value and then, for various political reasons, reduce the fair values proportionately to determine actual taxes assessed. Even in this case, however, though tax assessed values may not reflect *actual* fair value, they do reflect *relative* fair value, which is what is required as a basis for allocation.

TABLE 5-2

	Tax Assessed Value	Percent of Total Value	Historical Cost
Land	$ 60,000	7.5%	$ 65,250*
Warehouse	500,000	62.5	543,750
Office building	240,000	30.0	261,000
Totals	$800,000		$870,000

*The $65,250 is obtained by multiplying the total consideration paid of $870,000 by 7.5%.

Since the appraised values are also reflective of relative value, they too can be used to allocate the $870,000 fair value to the various assets. Using those values to allocate the fair value of the consideration paid results in the historical costs of land, warehouse, and office building of $87,000, $530,700, and $252,300, respectively. The fact that using the appraised values results in different historical cost numbers does not indicate that either of the allocation methods is wrong. Rather, arriving at a set of different estimates of the historical cost amounts emphasizes that accountants are continually making estimates, and that judgments are an important part of accounting. Determining which of these two sets of historical cost numbers to use depends upon which set the accountant (in consultation with others) decides is most indicative to the company of the fair values of the acquired assets.

Assets Acquired through Noncash (i.e., Nonmonetary)[20] Transactions

Assets can be acquired in a variety of ways other than by paying cash. For example, assets may be acquired through exchanging assets other than cash, incurring a liability, or exchanging shares of the corporation's own stock. All such methods of acquiring assets are also measured using the historical cost principle. As previously defined, historical cost is the cash or cash equivalent price exchanged for goods (or services) at the date of acquisition. Therefore, *nonmonetary transactions are measured by referring to either the fair value of the asset received or the fair value of the consideration given, whichever is more clearly evident.* (The only exception to this rule is the exchange of similar assets.) Again, values obtained through markets are the best indicators of fair value.

Assets Acquired through Donation[21]

Assets acquired through donation are measured at the fair value of the property received, where fair value is often determined through competent appraisal, either by an external appraiser or by the board of directors. The credit in the journal entry is to a descriptive revenue account or gain account as determined by

---

[20]Monetary assets and liabilities are fixed as to dollar amount, regardless of price changes. Examples of monetary assets are cash and receivables. Most liabilities are fixed as to dollar amount and are, therefore, monetary. Nonmonetary liabilities are those that require payment in goods, such as warranties. The easiest way to determine if an asset or liability is fixed as to dollar amount is to ask if the amount would change during a period of severe inflation. For example, put some money in a sock, throw it under the mattress, and in five years take the sock out and count the cash. Since the number of dollars (not the value, as the value would have gone down) has not changed, it is monetary. This discussion then centers on accounting for acquiring assets where the consideration given is not fixed in terms of the number of dollars to be received.

the nature of the company's business. Thus, for not-for-profit companies that rely extensively on contributions, the appropriate credit may be to a revenue account, whereas for a business organized for profit the appropriate credit may be to a gain account.[22]

When assets are received subject to meeting some condition, the appropriate credit is to a descriptive liability account until the condition has been met. Then, at that time, the liability is debited and revenue or gain (as appropriate) is credited.

Assets Acquired through Exchanging the Company's Stock or Other Securities

A common practice among newly organized corporations is to compensate the organizers of the corporation or early providers of goods and services with company stock or other company securities. Because there is no established market for the securities (the company having been only recently organized), such transactions are best measured at the fair value of the services received or assets contributed.

When paying for goods or services with securities, the debit entry is to a descriptive account (either an asset or an expense), and the credit is to the security. When stock having a par value is the security used, then the credits are to Capital Stock for par, with the difference credited to Paid-In Capital in Excess of Par.

To illustrate, after several years of successful operations, Smith Glass Company decided to go public and subsequently issued its initial public offering of stock. To conserve cash, the company's common stock was used to compensate the CPA and the lawyer for their services. Six thousand shares of the corporation's newly issued $5 common stock were issued for services rendered. The CPA and the lawyer had billed Smith $18,000 and $22,000, respectively. The journal entry to record the above transaction is as follows:

Accounting Expenses	18,000	
Legal Expenses	22,000	
Common Stock		30,000
Paid-In Capital in Excess of Par		10,000

To record services at fair value in a noncash transaction.

When an established company exchanges securities for goods and services, the transaction is measured by the fair value of the securities given or the fair value of the assets received, whichever is more clearly evident. When the securities are broadly traded on a public exchange, the transaction is best measured by the fair value of the securities. But when the fair value of the securities is not easily determinable, perhaps because the securities are not traded broadly, the transaction is then measured at the fair value of the services received or assets contributed.

Assume, for example, that Staley Corporation exchanged 2,000 shares of its $10 par value common stock for a plot of land to be used for a future building site. The common stock is selling on an exchange at $45 per share. The asking price of the land is $100,000, and the board of directors was willing to pay as much as $94,000 cash for the land. In this illustration, there are many values from which to select in determining the historical cost of the land, and the process

EXTENDING the Concept

What are the effects on the financial statements if incorporators receive securities with a value in excess of the value of their services rendered?

---

[21]See FAS No. 116 for the standard on accounting for donated assets, particularly par. 8.

[22]Assets contributed to others are also measured at their fair value. The entry is to debit "Contribution Expense" (or some other descriptive expense account) for the fair value of the property, to credit the asset account for its carrying value, and to debit or credit a gain or loss, as appropriate, for the difference.

of deciding which value to use as being the best indicator of fair value may go something like this:

1. The general rule is to use the fair value of the asset received or the fair value of the consideration given, whichever is more clearly evident. In this example, the best indicator of fair value seems to be the value of the securities of $45 per share. As a result, the historical cost of the land is $90,000.

2. However, if Staley's stock was closely held and not actively traded on an exchange, the $45 per share value might not be indicative of the stock's current fair value. Furthermore, issuing 2,000 additional shares could have a significant negative impact on the stock's market value if considerably fewer shares are exchanged daily. If either of these two situations is present, some other measurement technique should be used. In such cases, the best determinant of historical cost of the asset acquired is the board of directors' appraisal.

3. The least preferable values to use as indicators of fair value (or historical cost) are "asking price" and par value of the stock. Asking price is viewed more as a starting point for negotiation and is seldom equivalent to fair value. The par value also is rejected as an indicator of fair value because it is an arbitrary number assigned to the stock at the time of incorporation.

To complete the preceding illustration, the journal entry to record the acquisition of the land by exchanging the company's stock is as follows:

Land (whichever value is determined from above)
    Common Stock   20,000
    Paid-In Capital in Excess of Par   (difference)
To record the acquisition of land by exchanging 2,000 shares of the company's stock.

Assets Acquired through Exchanging a Note Payable

When goods or services are acquired by exchanging a note payable or other liability, there is a presumption that the note's stated interest rate is fair and adequate compensation. Or, stated differently, the interest rate on the note is reflective of the interest rate the company would have to pay if it borrowed the money and used the money to acquire the asset. When the interest rate is reflective of the current borrowing rate for the company, the transaction to acquire the asset is *measured by the face value of the note.*

To illustrate, on January 2, 2005, Brown Company acquired an item of equipment with a list price of $180,000 and signed a 5-year, 9%, note payable. The 9% rate is indicative of what Brown would pay if it had borrowed the money from a local financial institution. Since the interest rate is fair and adequate consideration, the journal entry to record the acquisition of the equipment is as follows:

Equipment   180,000
    Note Payable   180,000
To record the acquisition of an asset through the exchange of an interest-bearing note where the interest rate is fair and adequate consideration.

The presumption as to the interest rate being fair and adequate consideration does not apply if:

1. The note does not have a stated interest rate.
2. The stated interest rate is clearly unreasonable (e.g., the proverbial 1%).
3. The note cannot be sold for its face amount or the asset cannot be purchased for a cash amount equal to the face amount of the note.

When any of these situations exist, the note and the historical cost of the asset are measured at the fair value of the note or of the asset, whichever is more

EXTENDING
the Concept

This is the key to the Utah Jazz/Luther Wright beginning scenario. An athlete's contract is considered an asset and is recorded at the fair value of any guaranteed contract. The offsetting account is a note.

clearly evident—in accordance with what was stated previously. Computing the fair value of the note involves the use of discounting cash-flow techniques, which is covered in Chapter 11.

Assets Acquired through Exchanging Dissimilar Assets

When an asset is acquired through exchanging another asset that is *dissimilar* in function from the asset being acquired, the transaction is measured at the fair value of either the asset received or the asset given up, whichever is more clearly evident. Also, a gain or loss, as appropriate, is recognized on the old asset. This gain or loss is the difference between the old asset's fair value and its carrying value.[23]

To illustrate, on September 1, Delivery Company acquired a truck from Developer Corporation in exchange for a 1/3-acre site suitable for building a residential home. Developer had purchased the truck several years ago for $45,000 and as of September 1, the truck had a carrying value of $30,000 and a fair value of $35,000. Delivery Company had originally purchased the building site for $32,000, and its current fair value was not readily determinable.

In every transaction, the fair value of the assets received is equal to the fair value of the assets given up. If this were not so, the two parties would never consummate the transaction. So the following relationship always exists in any transaction:

$$\text{Fair Value Consideration}_{\text{given}} = \text{Fair Value Consideration}_{\text{received}}$$

In the exchange of the delivery truck for the building site, the following is obtained:

$$\text{Fair Value of Truck} = \text{Fair Value of Land}$$

$$\$35,000_{(\text{known})} = \$35,000_{(\text{determined from this formula})}$$

So Delivery Company (1) records the truck at its fair value of $35,000, (2) writes off the land at its original cost, and (3) recognizes a gain or loss on the exchange for the difference between the land's fair value and its historical cost. The journal entry to record this is as follows:

Truck	35,000	
Land		32,000
Gain on Exchange		3,000

To record exchanging dissimilar assets.

Developer Corporation (1) records the land at its fair value of $35,000, (2) writes off the truck at its original cost along with its associated accumulated depreciation, and (3) recognizes a gain or loss for the difference between the truck's fair value of $35,000 and its carrying amount of $30,000 (i.e., the historical cost of $45,000 minus the accumulated depreciation of $15,000). The journal entry is as follows:

Land	35,000	
Accumulated Depreciation	15,000	
Truck		45,000
Gain on Exchange		5,000

To record the acquiring of an asset by exchanging a dissimilar asset.

---

[23]Carrying value is the amount at which the asset is shown on the balance sheet. So, for depreciable assets, carrying value is the asset's historical cost amount less any accumulated depreciation.

Note that in each entry, the gain is the difference between the asset's fair value and its carrying value. This illustration of the historical cost principle applies whether the assets are new or used (the truck was used in this example).

Acquiring Assets through Exchanging Similar Assets—No Boot (Cash) Involved

To this point, the historical cost principle has been consistently applied to measuring the acquisition of assets, regardless of whether cash was paid or some other means of financing was used to acquire the asset. That is, assets acquired were always recorded at their fair value, which is measured either by cash paid, the fair value of the asset received, or the fair value of the consideration given. However, an exception to the historical cost principle is when an asset is acquired in a transaction that "is not essentially the culmination of an **earnings process**."

Earnings Cycle

Record gains/loss

The earnings process is cyclical. It begins with cash, which is used to acquire inventory, which is then sold, and finally, cash is collected and the earnings cycle is completed. In 1973, the APB concluded that a company must complete each step of this earnings cycle before a gain or loss could be recognized.[24] Further, the APB concluded that exchanging assets that have a similar function, are of the same general type, or are employed in the same line of business does not complete this earnings process. As a result, current GAAP requires that *transactions involving the exchange of similar assets be measured at recorded amounts (i.e., book value) rather than at fair value*. The result of this opinion is that *gains are not recognized when similar assets are exchanged, but losses are*. If losses were not recognized, newly acquired assets would be inappropriately measured above their fair value. Transactions giving rise to an exchange of similar assets are those involving (1) an exchange of inventory for another item of inventory and (2) an exchange of one operational asset for another operational asset that serves the same function.

Suppose two baseball teams, Shirts and Skins, exchange the contracts of two players (i.e., operational assets). Shirts trades First Baseman, whose contract is recorded on the books at $3 million, and receives Shortstop, whose contract is recorded on Skins's books at $3.2 million. Each player's contract is currently valued at $4 million; since the values of the players' contracts are equal, no cash is paid by either company to complete the transaction. (Since these data are used in several subsequent examples, the details are summarized in Illustration 5-2.)

ILLUSTRATION 5-2

Data for Exchanges

Shirts:
Gives: First Baseman; contract on books at $3 million; contract worth $4 million
Skins:
Gives: Shortstop; contract on books at $3.2 million; contract worth $4 million

Assuming that the exchange of the two baseball players does not culminate the earnings process, Shirts records the following journal entry:

---

[24]This statement was issued long before the FASB's conceptual framework, wherein the FASB stated entirely different criteria for recognizing revenue. Perhaps, some day the two positions will be reconciled.

Contract—Shortstop	3,000,000	
Contract—First Baseman		3,000,000

To record the exchange of similar assets—at carrying value—where the earnings process is not complete.

The explanation of this entry is that since the earnings cycle was not completed, the entry is recorded at the book amount of "First Baseman" of $3 million. There is a gain on the contract, which is the difference between the fair value of $4 million and the book value of $3 million, but this gain is not recognized in accordance with the APB's guidelines.

Skins records the following journal entry, which is similar in nature and justification to the entry Shirts prepares:

Contract—First Baseman	3,200,000	
Contract—Shortstop		3,200,000

To record the exchange of similar assets—at carrying value—where the earnings process is not complete.

To illustrate how losses are recognized when similar assets are exchanged, assume that the book value of First Baseman's contract is $5 million but that the fair value of his contract is still $4 million. Then, Shirts records the following journal entry:

Loss on Exchange	1,000,000	
Contract—Shortstop	4,000,000	
Contract—First Baseman		5,000,000

To record the exchange of similar assets—at carrying value—where the earnings process is not complete, but a loss on the exchange is indicated and recognized.

Since the book value of First Baseman's contract is greater than its fair value, a loss is indicated and must be recognized. To not recognize the loss would result in Shortstop's contract being recorded at $5 million, which is above its fair value. Hence, a $1 million loss is recognized.

Acquiring Assets through Exchanging Similar Assets—Boot (Cash) Involved

When cash, or boot, is included in a transaction where similar assets are exchanged, measuring and journalizing the transaction is more detailed. *If the amount of cash is 25% or more of the total consideration in the transaction, the entire amounts of both losses and gains are recognized.*[25] However, when the amount of cash in the transaction is less than 25% of the total consideration, the *recipient of the cash* considers the exchange of assets as two transactions: a monetary transaction (represented by the amount of the cash received) and a nonmonetary transaction. In such transactions, the recipient of the cash *recognizes any indicated loss in full but recognizes only a portion of any indicated gain.* The steps to compute the amount of the gain to recognize are as follows:

1. Compute the total gain.
2. Allocate this gain among the monetary and nonmonetary transactions, based upon the relationship of the cash received to the fair value of the total consideration in the transaction.

---

[25]*EITF Issue No. 86-29*, "Nonmonetary Transactions: Magnitude of Boot and the Exception to the Use of Fair Value," *Emerging Issues Task Force Abstracts* (October 1, 1987).

To illustrate, assume the same exchange of baseball players' contracts example. Also, assume that First Baseman's contract is worth $4 million, but that Shortstop's contract is worth $4.5 million. As a result, Shirts pays Skins $500,000 as part of the transaction. From the viewpoint of Skins, who is the recipient of the cash and who must recognize some gain, the following is determined:

$$\text{Fair Value Consideration}_{\text{given}} = \text{Fair Value Consideration}_{\text{received}}$$

$$\$4,500,000_{\text{(shortstop)}} = \$4,000,000_{\text{(first baseman)}} + \$500,000_{\text{(cash)}}$$

Since the cash received is less than 25% of the total consideration, Skins considers the exchange of assets as two transactions. Skins first determines if a gain or loss is present by comparing the carrying value of Shortstop's contract of $3.2 million to its fair value of $4.5 million, indicating that there is a gain of $1.3 million on the exchange. Since Skins received some cash, a portion of that gain must be recognized. The amount recognized is determined from the ratio of the cash received to the total consideration received in the following manner:

TABLE 5-3

Type of Consideration	Fair Value of Consideration	Percent of Total Consideration	Allocated Gain
Cash	$ 500,000	11.11%	$ 144,444*
Noncash asset	4,000,000	88.89	1,155,556
Totals	$4,500,000	100.00%	$1,300,000

*($500,000/$4,500,000) × $1,300,000 gain

After these calculations are completed, Skins prepares the following journal entry:

Cash	500,000	(amount received)
First Baseman	2,844,444	("plug" figure)
Shortstop	3,200,000	(at cost)
Gain on Exchange	144,444	(per schedule)

To record the exchange of similar assets where the earnings process is not complete, cash is received, and a portion of the gain is recognized.

Since Shirts did not receive any cash, it cannot recognize a gain but must recognize any loss that is indicated. In this case, the fair value of First Baseman's contract was $4 million and was carried on Shirts' books at $3 million, indicating that there is a gain on the contract, which cannot be recognized. The journal entry to record the exchange on Shirts' books is as follows:

Shortstop	3,500,000	
Cash		500,000
First Baseman		3,000,000

To record the exchange of similar assets, cash paid, and gain indicated, which cannot be recognized.

When preparing the journal entry, it is usually easiest (and best) to journalize all accounts other than the cost of the asset acquired, leaving that amount until last, which is then determined as the amount needed to balance the journal entry. A flowchart that diagrams the steps to be taken in accounting for exchanges of nonmonetary assets is presented in Exhibit 5-4.

EXHIBIT 5-4

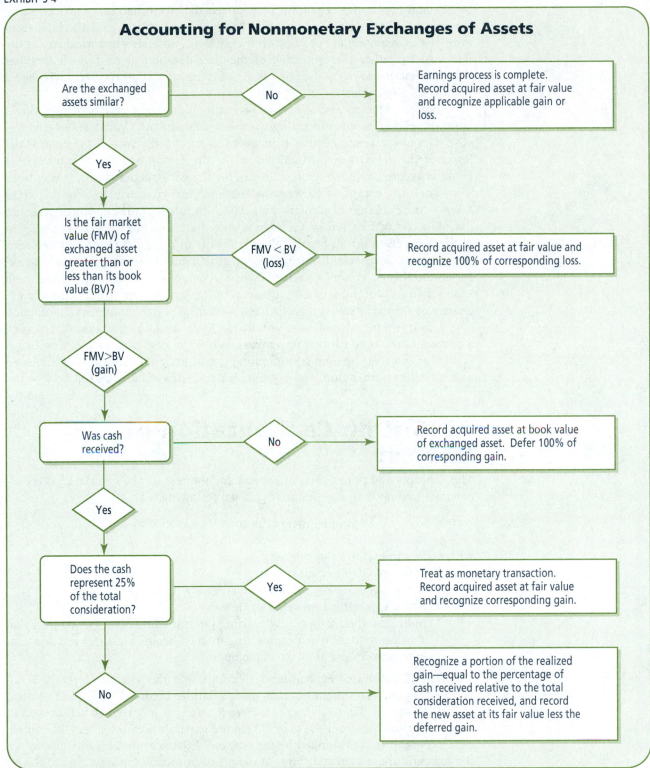

Accounting for Nonmonetary Exchanges of Assets

Are the exchanged assets similar? — No → Earnings process is complete. Record acquired asset at fair value and recognize applicable gain or loss.

Yes ↓

Is the fair market value (FMV) of exchanged asset greater than or less than its book value (BV)? — FMV < BV (loss) → Record acquired asset at fair value and recognize 100% of corresponding loss.

FMV>BV (gain) ↓

Was cash received? — No → Record acquired asset at book value of exchanged asset. Defer 100% of corresponding gain.

Yes ↓

Does the cash represent 25% of the total consideration? — Yes → Treat as monetary transaction. Record acquired asset at fair value and recognize corresponding gain.

No → Recognize a portion of the realized gain—equal to the percentage of cash received relative to the total consideration received, and record the new asset at its fair value less the deferred gain.

Summary

This chapter deals with using the historical cost principle to measure assets at acquisition. Historical cost is defined as the cash or cash equivalent price exchanged for assets at the date of acquisition, which is the same as the asset's fair value at that date. For cash transactions, an asset's historical cost is determined by (1) identifying the expenditures incurred that were necessary for acquiring the asset, (2) measuring the cash paid for each expenditure, and then (3) summing the cash amounts. For noncash transactions, an asset's historical cost is determined by either the fair value of the consideration given (which includes liabilities incurred) or by the fair value of the consideration received, whichever is more clearly evident.

For constructed assets, historical cost includes the direct materials, direct labor, a portion of manufacturing overhead, and, in the United States, interest cost. The interest amount that is included as part of the cost of the asset is the lesser of the actual interest incurred or the theoretical amount of interest that could have been avoided if expenditures for the construction had not occurred.

The only exception to applying the historical cost principle for acquiring assets is the exchange of similar assets. The APB ruled that the earnings cycle has not been completed, and so the asset acquired is valued at the carrying amount of the asset given up. Applying this rule results in recognizing losses when similar assets are exchanged but not recognizing gains. However, there is one exception to this exception, and that is when a company receives cash and the cash is less than 25% of the total consideration of the transaction. In this case, the exchange of similar assets is regarded as two transactions, a monetary transaction and a nonmonetary transaction, and the gain on the monetary transaction (i.e., a portion of the total gain) is recognized. When the cash portion of an exchange is 25% or more of the total consideration given, the entire transaction is treated as a monetary transaction, and both gains and losses are recognized.

APPENDIX: Capitalization of Interest

The concepts and procedures for capitalizing interest can be correlated to the elements in computing simple interest in the following way:

$$\text{Simple interest formula: } I = P \times R \times T$$

where, for capitalization of interest:

I is the avoidable interest cost,

P is the weighted-average accumulated expenditures,

R is the appropriate interest rate, and

T indicates when to begin capitalizing interest and when to stop. Note that T indicates only when capitalizing interest begins and ends but does not enter into calculating avoidable interest.

The definition of expenditures in computing the weighted-average accumulated expenditures includes: cash paid, liabilities incurred, or the fair value of assets transferred. That is, an expenditure is any cost incurred (whether paid in cash or not) to construct the asset. Once the expenditures have been identified, each expenditure is multiplied by the portion of the year that is remaining when the expenditure is incurred. Thus, an expenditure made on May 1 on a project that is not completed until December 31 is multiplied by 8/12 because there are eight months until year-end. However, the same expenditure made on May 1 on a project that is completed on September 30 is multiplied by 5/12 because there are five months from May 1 to September 30. After all of the expenditures have been averaged in this manner, they are totaled, which results in the desired average accumulated expenditures.

Regarding the interest rate to use, if the enterprise borrows money specifically for the construction, then the enterprise uses that interest rate, unless the average accumulated expenditures (as computed previously) exceed the amount borrowed. When that occurs, the interest rate on the newly borrowed money is used first and up to the amount borrowed, and the interest rate that is applied to the excess accumulated expenditures is the weighted-average of the interest rates of the other interest-bearing debt of the company. In computing this weighted-average rate, the objective is a "reasonable measure" of financing the acquisition of the asset. Accordingly, only those borrowings whose interest rates are reflective of the company's current ability to borrow money are used in calculating the weighted-average rate.[26]

The capitalization period begins when all the following conditions are present:

1. Expenditures have been made. Expenditures include the paying of cash, the transfer of other assets, or the incurring of an interest-bearing liability.
2. Necessary activities to get the asset ready for its intended use are in progress. Activities include more than actually constructing the asset. Activities also include the necessary preliminary functions, such as developing plans and obtaining needed permits from government authorities.
3. The company is incurring interest. It is not necessary that this interest be incurred on the debt related to constructing the asset, only that interest is being incurred on some debt.

The capitalization period ends when the asset is substantially complete and ready for its intended use. For assets in which part of the asset can be used when it is completed while work continues on other parts (e.g., constructing condominiums), interest capitalization stops on those components that are substantially complete and ready to be sold but continues on those components still under construction. For assets that cannot be used until a separate facility is completed (e.g., the Alaskan pipeline before the storage facilities are completed), interest is included in the cost of the asset (e.g., the pipeline) until the separate asset is completed.

Expenditures for activities necessary to get land ready for its intended use qualify for interest capitalization, but the amount of interest capitalized becomes part of the cost of the asset that results from those activities and is not part of the cost of the land. For example, if the resulting asset is a building, shopping center, etc., the interest incurred on the expenditures to acquire the land is part of the cost of the building, shopping center, etc. If the resulting asset is developed land that is to be sold (i.e., inventory), then the interest is capitalized as part of the cost of the developed land.

Lastly, once the avoidable interest amount is computed, the amount to include as part of the cost of the asset is the smaller of the actual interest or avoidable interest.

To illustrate, assume that K&S Corporation acquired a tract of land as a building site on January 1, 2005, for $60,000. A contractor is hired and subsequently paid quarterly payments of $25,000, with the first payment made on March 31, 2005. Also, on January 1, 2005, K&S borrows $100,000 on a 3-year, 12% note to finance the land purchase and building construction with interest

---

[26]Computing this weighted-average interest rate requires judgment. In some circumstances, it is appropriate to include all borrowings of both the parent company and its subsidiaries. "The objective is to obtain a reasonable measure of the cost of financing acquisition of the asset in terms of the interest cost incurred that otherwise could have been avoided." (SFAS No. 34, par. 14)

payable each December 31. K&S already has outstanding a $200,000, 10%, 5-year note, dated June 30, 2003, and a $50,000, 14%, 10-year note, dated January 1, 2002. K&S anticipates being able to internally generate any additional cash required to complete the project.

In this example, the procedures for computing the average accumulated expenditures for both 2005 and 2006 are covered first, and then determining the appropriate interest rate is demonstrated.

Average Accumulated Expenditures

The average accumulated expenditures of $97,500 for 2005 are computed as follows:

Weighted-Average Accumulated Expenditures
For 2005, First Year

| | Expenditures | | |
Date Incurred	Amount	Interest Period	Weighted-Avg. Accum. Expen.
January 1—Acquire land	$ 60,000	12/12	$60,000
March 31—1st Payment to contractor	25,000	9/12	18,750
June 30—2nd Payment to contractor	25,000	6/12	12,500
September 30—3rd Payment to contractor	25,000	3/12	6,250
December 31—4th Payment to contractor	25,000	0/12	0
Totals	$160,000		$97,500

Note that the expenditures for land are included in the calculation even though the amount of interest capitalized will be part of the cost of the building.

Now, assume that the building is not completed at the end of 2005 and that additional quarterly payments of $25,000 are made in March through September of 2006, with a final payment of $40,000 made on December 1 when the building is completed. The weighted-average accumulated expenditures of $177,917 for 2006 are computed as follows:

Weighted-Average Accumulated Expenditures
2006, Second Year

| | Expenditures | | |
Date Incurred	Amount	Interest Period	Weighted-Avg. Accum. Expen.
January 1—Amount from prior year	$160,000	11/12	$146,667
March 31—5th Payment to contractor	25,000	8/12	16,667
June 30—6th Payment to contractor	25,000	5/12	10,416
September 30—7th Payment to contractor	25,000	2/12	4,167
December 1—Final payment to contractor	40,000	0/12	0
Totals	$275,000		$177,917

Note that the accumulation of expenditures does not begin anew during 2006 but continues with the amount incurred at the end of the prior year. That is, $160,000 was the total expenditures at the end of 2005, and this entire amount is subject to interest during 2006, using the weighted-average accumulated expenditure calculations up to the time that the asset is complete and ready for its intended use. Interest capitalization stops on December 1 when the asset is complete and ready for use.

Interest Rate

The other component in the formula in computing avoidable interest is the interest rate. Continuing the K&S example, since the weighted-average accumulated expenditures of $97,500 for 2005 is less than the specifically borrowed amount of $100,000, the interest rate of 12% on the newly borrowed money is used for 2005.

For 2006, since the average accumulated expenditures of $177,917 exceeds the amount specifically borrowed ($100,000), a weighted-average interest rate based upon K&S's other appropriate borrowings is computed. This weighted-average interest rate is computed by dividing the total amount of interest incurred on those borrowings identified as being representative of what the company could borrow by the total principal. To illustrate the procedures in computing the weighted-average interest rate, assume that both of K&S's other interest-bearing debts do reflect interest rates at which K&S could borrow money currently. Calculating the weighted-average interest rate begins with computing the interest amount, as follows:

Principal		Rate		Interest
$200,000	×	10%	=	$20,000
+ 50,000	×	14%	=	7,000
$250,000				$27,000

Dividing the interest of $27,000 by the principal of $250,000 gives a weighted-average interest rate of 10.8%.

Avoidable Interest Amounts

The avoidable interest amount of $11,700 for 2005 is computed as follows:

Avoidable Interest = Average Accumulated Expenditures × Interest Rate

$$= \$97,500 \times 12\%$$

$$= \$11,700$$

The avoidable interest of $20,415 for 2006 is computed as follows:

Avg. Accum. Expenditures		Interest Rate		Avoid. Interest
$100,000	×	12.0%	=	$12,000
77,917	×	10.8%	=	8,415
$177,917				$20,415

Amount Recorded as an Asset

The avoidable interest amounts may not be the amounts included as part of the cost of the asset. That amount is the lesser of the actual interest incurred during the year or the avoidable interest. Since the same debts were outstanding during both 2005 and 2006, the actual interest incurred each year is $39,000, which is the sum of the interest on the new borrowings for the construction (i.e., $100,000 × .12%) and the interest on the other borrowings of $27,000 (as shown previously). In this example, since the avoidable interest amounts are less than the actual interest incurred for both 2005 and 2006, the avoidable interest amounts are capitalized as part of the cost of the asset for each year.

If more than one asset qualifies for interest capitalization, the amount of interest to be recorded as an asset is allocated among the various qualifying assets according to each asset's accumulated average expenditures.

Accounting Procedures

When a company has assets that qualify for interest capitalization, the interest capitalization requirement makes it impossible to know during the year whether incurred interest should be expensed or recorded as an asset. As a result, as interest is incurred during the year, it is debited to an interest suspense account. When the amount of interest to be recorded as an asset is later determined, a journal entry is prepared debiting the qualifying asset(s) for the appropriate interest amount(s), debiting Interest Expense for any remaining interest, and crediting Interest Suspense.

Questions

1. Explain what is meant by the historical cost of an asset.

2. Explain what is meant by "to capitalize." Explain what is meant by "to expense." What determines whether a cost is capitalized or expensed?

3. The materiality and cost-benefit thresholds have a role in the way that companies apply the historical cost principle. For example, most companies have a policy that requires all expenditures for acquiring fixed assets that are below a certain dollar amount to be expensed. Companies institute such policies because—in attempting to safeguard the assets of the company—they have established lengthy procedures to acquire expensive fixed assets, and such a policy permits the company to short-cut its policy when the amounts involved are not material. Although such a policy is desirous from a practical viewpoint, what are some of the possible impacts on the financial statements and on employee behavior from a company having such a policy?

4. Consumer, Inc., is a retail store that buys and sells various types of products. Indicate which of the following costs would be classified as a cost of inventory:
   a. The price to acquire inventory.
   b. Sales taxes paid on inventory purchased.
   c. Freight incurred to ship the purchased inventory to the retail store.
   d. Wages paid to sales employees.
   e. Utilities paid on the building.
   f. Freight paid to ship inventory sold to customers.

5. Acme Manufacturing, Inc., manufactures furniture that is sold to retail outlets throughout the country. Which of the following costs would be classified as the cost of the finished product?
   a. The cost of wood to be used in the manufacturing process.
   b. Wages for workers who manufacture the furniture.
   c. Wages for workers who distribute the furniture to retail outlets.
   d. Wages for janitorial services in the manufacturing plant.
   e. Administrative salaries.
   f. The cost of indirect materials, such as glue, nails, and knobs.
   g. Depreciation of administrative offices.
   h. Depreciation on manufacturing equipment.
   i. Utilities in the operating manufacturing plant.
   j. Utilities in the administrative offices.
   k. Legal and accounting services.

6. A company acquired several plots of land with houses on them and immediately tore down the houses so a shopping center could be constructed. The total cost of the purchases was $1,000,000, with approximately 70% of that amount considered the cost of the houses. Write a memo explaining the accounting treatment for the transactions, and show in summary form the appropriate journal entry for the $1,000,000 payment.

7. A company developed a tract of land into a ski resort, which included cutting the trees, clearing and grading the land and hills, and constructing ski lifts. To what account (e.g., Land, Land Improvements) should these various costs be recorded? Are these costs amortizable? How should the proceeds from the sale of the trees be accounted for?

8. A company is acquiring a one-of-a-kind piece of equipment, and as a result, the historical cost of the equipment cannot be determined by referring to the fair value of similar equipment. Describe how the historical cost should be determined for each of the following ways of financing the acquisition:
   a. Bonds having an established market price.
   b. Common stock not having an established market price.
   c. Donation.
   d. A long-term interest-bearing note, where the interest rate represents fair and adequate consideration.
   e. A long-term interest-bearing note, where the interest rate does not represent fair and adequate consideration.

9. Theoretically, what is the amount of interest that should be capitalized as part of the historical cost of assets that require an extended period of time to construct? Why does the FASB require the capitalization of interest on constructed assets? When does the capitalization of interest period begin and when does it end?

10. Under what conditions will the actual amount of interest be the amount of interest capitalized, rather than avoidable interest?

11. a. Determine the U.S. GAAP accounting treatment for each of the following items:

    (1) Laboratory research aimed at discovering new knowledge.
    (2) Searching for applications (e.g., products) of new research findings.
    (3) Modifying a design of a product as a result of research findings.
    (4) Engineering follow-through in an early phase of commercial production.

(5) Trouble-shooting in connection with breakdowns during commercial production.

(6) Quality control costs.

b. For which items would the accounting treatment for the above items be different under IAS?

c. What apparent influence did U.S. GAAP have upon the deliberations of the IASB for its eventual decision requiring research costs to be expensed in IAS No. 38?

12. Explain the accounting treatment for the exchange of similar assets. What is meant by similar assets? Give some examples of exchanges of similar assets. Do you agree with the APB's requirements for accounting for exchanges of similar assets? Is there a more appropriate procedure in accounting for exchanges of similar assets?

13. The Houston Rockets and Utah Jazz entered into an agreement to exchange basketball players. The Houston Rockets received a power forward and a point guard, and the Utah Jazz received a center and a small forward. Should gain/loss be recognized on this exchange? Explain your answer. Would your answer change if one of the teams also received $1 million? Why or why not?

14. Each year, sports franchises spend large amounts of money developing the talent of their players. What is the proper accounting for these expenditures? Should they be expensed or capitalized? Explain your answer.

Exercises

Exercise 5-1: Acquisition of Inventory. On July 1, 2004, R&R Company purchased inventory in the amounts of $50,000 and $70,000 under credit terms of 2/10, net 30. The payment due on the $50,000 was remitted on July 8, and the payment due on the $70,000 purchase was remitted on July 20.

1. Assuming a periodic inventory system (i.e., where purchases of inventory are debited to a purchases account), prepare the appropriate journal entries under (a) the gross method and (b) the net method.

2. What is the cost of the inventory under (a) the gross method and (b) the net method?

3. Assuming that R&R received trade discounts of 10% and 20% in addition to the cash discounts, what is the cost of the inventory purchased for $50,000 under the gross method?

Exercise 5-2: Historical Cost of Inventory. The following costs were among those incurred by Christensen Corporation for acquiring items of inventory during 2005:

Merchandise purchased for resale	$500,000
Freight charges for merchandise purchased	15,000
Insurance charges for merchandise during transit	800
Sales commissions	40,000
Interest on notes payable to vendors	5,000

1. Applying a strict application of the historical cost principle, what is the cost of inventory for the year?
2. Applying the modifying conventions of materiality and cost-benefit, what cost(s) would not be included in the cost of inventory for the year? What is your justification for excluding such costs?
3. If the net method had been used, with cash discounts averaging 3% and assuming (a) the theoretical approach and (b) the practical approach to determining historical cost, what would be the cost of inventory for the year?

Exercise 5-3: Classification of Expenditures. The following expenditures were among those incurred by Miller Company in 2000 in acquiring land and constructing a building on it. Using the following general ledger accounts, determine the appropriate one in which each of the expenditures should be recorded.

1. Land
2. Land Improvements
3. Building
4. Interest Expense
5. Miscellaneous Revenue
6. Landscaping Expense
7. Not Recorded

a.	Acquisition of land	$500,000
b.	Fees for title search	475
c.	Cost of surveying land	2,250
d.	Rental of temporary quarters for construction crew	13,000
e.	Cost of building permit	175
f.	Razing an old building located on the land	37,500
g.	Proceeds from sale of scrap from demolished building	(5,000)
h.	Excavation costs of digging the hole for the foundation	15,000
i.	Special assessment taxes levied by the city	3,250
j.	Actual interest cost	5,000
k.	Avoidable interest	7,500
l.	Cost of accident insurance during construction	2,000
m.	Costs of paving the parking lot	45,000
n.	Costs of landscaping, assuming the following:	10,000

(1) The landscaping consists mainly of annual flowers,
(2) The landscaping consists mainly of shrubs and bushes with an estimated life of 10 years before they will need to be replanted,
(3) The landscaping consists mainly of long-lived trees, and it is not anticipated that they will have to be replaced.

Exercise 5-4: Understanding the Historical Cost Principle. A company is considering relocating and has identified a building, ideally located, which may be purchased for $14 million, with $4 million considered to be the cost of the land. After a thorough inspection, some dry rot in the wood is discovered, and competent contractors estimate it will cost $2 million to repair the damage. Accordingly, the company makes an offer of $12 million to purchase the building and the offer is accepted.

1. Prepare the journal entries to record the $12 million expenditure to acquire the building and the subsequent expenditure of $2 million to make the building suitable for its intended use. Write a brief paragraph defending your treatment of the $2 million cost.

2. Now, assume the same scenario except that the dry rot in the wood is not discovered, and the company offers $14 million for the property. Then, while moving in, a heavy piece of equipment causes the floor to buckle and the dry rot is discovered. The company spends an additional $2 million to repair the dry rot. Prepare the journal entries to record the initial $14 million expenditure and the subsequent $2 million expenditure. Write a brief paragraph defending your treatment of the $2 million expenditure, assuming that the fair value of the land and building is still $14 million.
3. From your answers in parts (1) and (2), explain the connection between foreknowledge of a condition and whether a cost is an asset or a loss.
4. Assuming your answer to (2) is to not capitalize the $2 million dollars that was spent to fix the dry rot, then where on the income statement should that $2 million be reported? As an ordinary loss or as an extraordinary loss?

Exercise 5-5: Donated Assets. Pine City donated land to Skyview Corporation, upon which Skyview planned to build a plant. At the time of transfer, the land was valued at $100,000. The city had "bid in" (i.e., taken ownership of) the property five years previously when a taxpayer had failed to pay several years of taxes. When the property was bid in, it had a fair value of $65,000. Taxes owed had amounted to $20,000.

1. Prepare the journal entry (if any) on Skyview's books for the receipt of the land.
2. Would the entry in part (1) change if Pine City attached conditions to ownership of the land, such as Skyview having to hire a certain number of employees and to remain in business in Pine City for a minimum of five years? Then what entry would Skyview prepare at the time the land was received?
3. Refer to your answer in part (1). Until recently, the acceptable practice for donations was to credit a stockholders' equity account for the fair value of donated assets (which is not acceptable now). Assuming that immediately before the receipt of the land, Skyview's total assets were $1,000,000 and its total liabilities were $700,000, compare the effects on the financial statements of the journal entry you prepared in requirement (1) to previous practice on:
   a. Earnings per share,
   b. Debt-to-equity ratio [consider the formula (long-term liabilities/owners' equity)], and
   c. Return on assets.
4. Has the new ruling improved significant financial statement ratios, or has it made them present a less favorable picture?
5. Without regard to your answers in parts (1) through (4), suppose that instead Skyview purchased the land from Pine City for $45,000, which had previously bid in the property. Also, assume that Skyview was required to pay the existing back taxes of $20,000. Then what is the cost of the land to Skyview?

Exercise 5-6: Historical Cost of Land. Southern Utah Land Developers purchased a 10-acre tract of land for $900,000, which it intends to develop and subdivide into building lots. The following costs were incurred following acquisition:

Surveying	$10,000
Grading	15,000
Roads, curb, and gutter	40,000
Water and sewer lines	25,000
Administrative costs	20,000
Advertising costs	5,000
Legal fees	10,000

The legal fees were incurred in connection with obtaining title to the land. Approximately 20% of the land will be used for roads and green space. The remaining land will be subdivided into 24 lots that will sell for $50,000 each and five premium lots that will sell for $80,000 each.

1. Compute the historical cost amount of a typical lot and of a premium lot.
2. Prepare the journal entry(ies) to record the sale of a premium lot, assuming that Southern Utah Land Developers uses a perpetual inventory system.

Exercise 5-7: Lump-Sum Purchase. Rocket Corp. purchased land, building, and equipment from Comet, Inc., for a lump sum of $500,000, which was paid in cash. At the time of acquisition, the fair values of the land, building, and equipment were determined to be $150,000, $375,000, and $112,500, respectively.

1. Compute the costs of land, building, and equipment and prepare the appropriate journal entry. Round historical cost amounts to the nearest tens of dollars.
2. Prepare the journal entry to record the purchase of these assets, assuming that instead of paying cash, Rocket Corp. exchanged 12,500 shares of its $25 par value stock that currently was being broadly traded at $40 per share.

Exercise 5-8: Lump-Sum Purchase. Return to the Rocket Corp. problem in Exercise 5-7, but assume that the respective fair values of the assets as determined from the tax rolls of the county showed the land, building, and equipment were valued at $110,000, $264,000, and $66,000.

1. Compute the costs of land, building, and equipment and prepare the appropriate journal entry. Round historical cost amounts to the nearest tens of dollars.
2. Since the historical cost principle stipulates that the historical cost of assets at acquisition should not be greater than fair value, does your solution raise questions as to the appropriateness of the measurements and journal entry? Why or why not?

Exercise 5-9: Acquiring Assets through Exchanging Stock. On September 10, Wile-e Coyotee Company exchanged 2,000 shares of its $5 par value common stock for a new automobile. Wile-e's stock is traded on the NYSE, and approximately 100,000 shares trade each day. The previous day's closing price was $12. The automobile dealership was asking $28,000 for the automobile but commonly discounted the asking price by 5%. Prepare the journal entry to record Wile-e's acquisition of the automobile and justify your answer.

Exercise 5-10: Acquiring Assets through Exchanging Stock. On December 1, Tiffany Corporation exchanged 2,000 shares of its $50 par value common stock for a plot of land to be used for a future plant site. The shares had been acquired on the open market two years ago at a cost of $74 per share. Tiffany's common stock is actively trading on a securities exchange, and the closing quote on November 30 was $89 per share. Management conservatively estimates that the land could have been purchased for $170,000, as other parcels of land of the same size in that area have recently sold for that amount. At what amount should the land be recorded? Justify your answer.

Exercise 5-11: Exchange of Assets—Dissimilar. Riverton Company traded in a used delivery vehicle that had a book value of $12,000 for some used computer equipment for which the owner was asking $34,000, and Riverton also paid a cash difference of $20,000.

1. Assuming that Riverton thinks the fair value of the old vehicle is $12,000, what is the cost of the computer equipment, and how much gain or loss should be recognized?
2. Assuming that Riverton thinks the fair value of the old vehicle is $8,000, what is the cost of the computer equipment, and how much gain or loss should be recognized?
3. Assuming that Riverton thinks the fair value of the old vehicle is $14,000, what is the cost of the computer equipment, and how much gain or loss should be recognized?
4. What is the relationship among the cost of an asset, the amount of gain/loss recognized, and management's estimation of what the old asset's fair value is?

Exercise 5-12: Exchange of Assets—Similar. Tinker Auto Parts traded in a used delivery vehicle having a book value of $12,000 for a new delivery vehicle with a list price of $34,000, and paid a cash difference of $20,000. Tinker also paid $1,800 in sales tax, $185 in vehicle registration fees, and $150 in documentation fees.

1. Assuming that Tinker thought the fair value of the old vehicle was $12,000, what is the cost of the new vehicle, and how much gain or loss should be recognized?
2. Assuming that Tinker thought the fair value of the old vehicle was $8,000, what is the cost of the new vehicle, and how much gain or loss should be recognized?
3. Assuming that Tinker thought the fair value of the old vehicle was $14,000, what is the cost of the new vehicle, and how much gain or loss should be recognized?

Exercise 5-13: Exchange of Assets. Microstrategy Inc. is a worldwide provider of e-business software and services that enable companies to conduct business transactions through the Internet, wireless, and voice communication channels. The company made the following statement to describe one of several restatements made to its 1999 and 1998 financial statements:

> In addition, we reduced fixed assets by approximately $8.8 million, net of the decrease in depreciation, in order to record software received for resale and software acquired for internal use in barter transactions at the book value of our assets surrendered in the exchange. Approximately $5.0 million of the reduction in fixed assets is a reduction in revenue, as restated. Of this amount, no revenue will be recorded unless this software is resold.

1. Describe how Microstrategy apparently originally accounted for the exchange of assets. Include a journal entry, and rather than use numbers, indicate whether the amount is fair value, book value, etc.
2. The note explains that Microstrategy later restated (i.e., revised its method of accounting for an event), and it appears that the exchange of assets was accounted for in another way. Describe how Microstrategy then accounted for the exchange, including journal entries.

Exercise 5-14: Interest Capitalization. On the first day of February 2004, Desert Image signed a contract with D&L Contractors to construct an office building on some land that had been acquired previously for $9.5 million. Following the signing of the contract, work commenced immediately, and cash expenditures paid by Desert Image to D&L during the year consisted of the following payments:

Date Payment Made	Amount
February 21	$ 100,000
May 5	400,000
July 18	1,000,000
October 29	1,200,000
Total	$2,700,000

Compute the amount of the average accumulated expenditures for 2004.

Exercise 5-15: Interest Capitalization (Appendix). Return to the Desert Image problem in Exercise 5-14, but assume that work on the office building continued un-interrupted during 2005, and during the year, the following interim payments were made by Desert Image:

Date Payment Made	Amount
January 5	$1,500,000
April 20	2,000,000
June 30	1,800,000
October 2	1,000,000
Total	$6,300,000

Assuming that the building is not yet completed, compute the amount of the average accumulated expenditures for Desert Image for 2005.

Exercise 5-16: Interest Capitalization. On April 23, Tone's Interiors signed a con-tract to have a new warehouse built, which qualifies for capitalization of interest. Dur-ing the current year, total expenditures amounted to $2,300,000, and the average accumulated expenditures were $1,100,000. To finance the construction, Tone's bor-rowed $1,500,000 at 10% on May 1 from Second National Bank, which is payable in five payments of $300,000 each, plus accrued interest. The first payment is due one year from May 1. Tone's will finance the rest of the construction from internally gen-erated cash. Interest incurred during the year on borrowings other than the note with Second National amounted to $83,000.

1. How much is avoidable interest?
2. What amount of interest should Tone's capitalize for the year?

Exercise 5-17: Interest Capitalization. Using the same information in Exercise 5-16, but assuming that Tone's borrowed only $1,000,000 to finance the construction, com-pute (1) avoidable interest and (2) the amount of interest to capitalize for the year. Also assume that Tone's has the following liabilities on its books:

Accounts payable, with terms of 2/10, n/30	$ 40,000
180-day, 6% note payable	20,000
3-year, 10% note payable	50,000
10-year, 12% note payable	650,000

Exercise 5-18: Interest Capitalization. On March 1, 2003, Vasquez Corporation signed a fixed-price contract to have Houston Builders construct a manufacturing

plant at a cost of $20 million. The project was estimated to take 3 years to complete. To help finance the construction, Vasquez also borrowed $4 million that is payable in 5 annual installments of $800,000 plus interest at 14%. This is the only interest-bearing liability that Vasquez has. During 2003, Vasquez paid Houston Builders $6 million (the average accumulated expenditures being $2 million). Because all of the $4 million was not needed immediately, $3 million was invested in short-term securities, and income of $300,000 was earned. What amount of interest should Vasquez capitalize for 2003?

Exercise 5-19: Research & Development. Wolfe Corporation records revealed the following information for 2003:

Salaries and other personnel costs of individuals involved in R&D activities	$100,000
Consulting fees paid to outside consultants	20,000
Equipment purchased for R&D activities, which has an estimated useful life of three years.	24,000
Depreciation on the building where R&D activities are conducted	8,000
Indirect costs reasonably allocated to R&D projects	12,000
Materials purchased ($1,000 is in inventory and the rest of the materials have no other possible uses)	40,000

Most of the R&D activities conducted by Wolfe were done to discover new products, but Wolfe did contract to do R&D work for one outside company on which Wolfe spent 10% of its time and resources. What is the total amount of R&D costs that should be expensed for 2003?

Exercise 5-20: Goodwill. On February 1, 2004, Nikel Company purchased the net assets of Foote Company for $12.5 million. To record the individual assets and liabilities on its general ledger, the following values were obtained for the various assets and liabilities:

	Carrying Value On Foote's Books	Fair Value
Accounts Receivable	$ 2,000,000	$ 2,000,000
Inventory	3,000,000	3,500,000
Equipment	1,000,000	1,500,000
Land	500,000	2,000,000
Building	2,500,000	3,000,000
Patent	500,000	1,000,000
Accounts Payable	(1,000,000)	(1,000,000)
Notes Payable	(2,000,000)	(2,000,000)
Net assets	$ 6,500,000	$10,000,000

1. Prepare the journal entry to record the individual assets and liabilities on the books of Nikel Company.
2. Prepare the journal entry to record the individual assets and liabilities on the books of Nikel Company, assuming that Nikel purchased the net assets for $9,000,000.

Problems

Problem 5-1: Historical Cost of Property, Plant, and Equipment. On February 1, Speculators' Corporation purchased a parcel of land as a factory site for $225,000. An old building on the property, with an appraised value of $70,000 was demolished immediately and construction began on a new building that was completed on November 1. Costs incurred during this period were:

Demolition of old building	$ 20,000
Architect's fee (incurred prior to February 1)	300,000
Legal fees for title investigation, etc.	40,000
Construction costs:	
Direct materials	1,200,000
Direct labor	1,000,000
Predetermined variable overhead rate, 65% of direct labor	
Salvaged materials resulting from demolition	7,000

Information relating to capitalization of interest:
- Expenditures for materials, labor, and overhead were incurred uniformly from February through October and were paid on the first day of the following month. The other expenditures occurred at the first of February.
- Speculators' did not allocate any fixed overhead to the project.
- Speculators' did not borrow any new funds to acquire the land or construct the building.
- The weighted-average interest rate being incurred on borrowings that represent interest rates at which money has been borrowed is 10%.
- Actual interest incurred by Speculators' for the year was $120,000.

Required:
1. Determine the costs of the land and the building.
2. Write a brief memo to the controller defending your answer.

Problem 5-2: Historical Cost of Equipment and Related Party Transactions. Associates Country Club made a lump-sum purchase of three pieces of used machinery for $105,000 from Bloomington Country Club, which is an unaffiliated company. The following information is available.

	Cost if Acquired New	Appraisal Value	Value on Seller's Books
Machine A	$20,000	$15,000	$12,000
Machine B	40,000	30,000	24,000
Machine C	90,000	45,000	64,000

Required:
1. Determine the cost of each machine.
2. What difficulties would arise in determining cost if the transaction occurred between related parties? What changes or additional reporting requirements must be done when a transaction occurs between related parties?

Problem 5-3: Exchange of Assets. Sundance Company exchanged 1,000 shares of Robbers Roost Company stock for a building in a remote location in southern Utah that it plans to use as a place for its chief executives to "get away from it all." The Robbers Roost Company stock had been purchased for $33.50 per share but was currently broadly trading on a national exchange for $57.50 per share. Butch Cassidy Company had acquired the building several years ago for $40,000 but thought it was worth twice that much. To date, Butch Cassidy had recorded depreciation of $8,000 on the building. Because of a long-standing friendship with Sundance, Butch Cassidy Company agreed to the exchange if Sundance also paid an additional $5,000. Sundance thought the deal was equivalent to "highway robbery," but it eventually paid the money. There have been no other sales of similar buildings in the area to assist in obtaining an approximate fair value.

Required:

1. Prepare the appropriate journal entries for Sundance and Butch Cassidy.
2. Would the journal entries change if instead of exchanging the stock for the building, the two entities exchanged a building in Southern Utah for a condominium in Houston? If the journal entries would change, prepare the journal entries for this new exchange.
3. What determines whether assets are similar or dissimilar?

Problem 5-4: Acquisition of Assets—Various. At December 2004, Applegate Corp. had the following accounts and balances classified as property, plant, and equipment:

Land	$ 450,000
Buildings	1,300,000
Leasehold improvements	240,000
Machinery and equipment	1,500,000

During 2005, the following transactions occurred:

a. A tract of land on which a new factory will be built was purchased for $1 million cash. In addition, Applegate paid an $80,000 commission to a real estate agent. Following acquisition, costs of $20,000 were incurred to clear the land of timber and prepare it for its intended use. The timber was sold for $8,000.

b. A second tract of land with a building was acquired for $1,500,000 cash, of which $500,000 was assigned as the cost of the building. Shortly after acquisition, the building was demolished at a cost of $30,000, and a new building was constructed for $2 million.

c. A third tract of land was acquired for $800,000 and was put back on the market for resale.

d. Extensive work was done to a building under lease, which expires on December 31, 2009. The work consisted of the following expenditures:

Description	Cost	Estimated Useful Life
Painting of walls and ceiling	$12,000	3 years
Electrical work	60,000	20
Building of walls and partitions	40,000	40
New floor coverings	38,000	5

The lessor reimbursed Applegate for one-half of the expenditures except for the painting.

e. New machines were purchased under a royalty agreement that provides for payment of royalties[27] based on units of production from the machines. The invoice price of the machines was $135,000, freight costs were $2,000, unloading costs were $3,000, and royalty payments for 2005 were $24,000.

Required:
1. Prepare journal entries to record the acquisition of each of the assets.
2. Ignoring depreciation, prepare a worksheet to update the account balances for the property, plant, and equipment accounts.
3. For all acquired assets that were not included in the property, plant, and equipment category, indicate where they would be reported on Applegate's balance sheet.

Problem 5-5: Exchange of Assets. Mustang Corporation has a 4-year-old tractor that was purchased for $28,000 and has accumulated depreciation of $10,000. Having recently purchased a much larger tractor, Mustang is exploring its options for disposing of the tractor.

Required:
Prepare the journal entry in accordance with current GAAP for each of the following options that Mustang is considering. When preparing the journal entries, consider all *previous* offers. That is, when preparing the entry for Requirement (2), consider the offer in Requirement (1), etc.

1. Accept a cash offer of $12,000 for the tractor.
2. A used farm implements dealer has offered Mustang $15,000 as a trade-in on a new $40,000 tractor, with the difference to be paid in cash. Using the dealer's trade-in allowance as an indication of fair value, prepare the appropriate journal entry. Comment on the appropriateness of not recognizing a loss as was done in Requirement (1), particularly if the dealer has marked up the merchandise in anticipation of giving a liberal trade-in allowance.
3. Mustang has an offer to exchange the tractor for some land for which the owner is asking $50,000 but would accept the used tractor and $25,000 cash. In addition to preparing the journal entry, and considering both this offer and also the previous two offers, write a brief paragraph explaining why recording the land at $50,000 seems inappropriate. (*Note:* Does it appear that the fair value of the land is really $50,000?)
4. Mustang can exchange the tractor for a neighbor's older tractor that it would use as a yard tractor. Mustang would also receive $12,000. The neighbor had offered previously to sell Mustang the tractor for $2,000, but Mustang had refused because it thought the price was too high. Prepare the journal entry, assuming that the offer is accepted, and write a brief paragraph commenting on your answer.

Problem 5-6: Exchange of Assets. Trader Sue has a policy of trading all long-term assets after one year's use. The following information is available:

January 1, 2004: Acquired Asset A for $35,000 cash.
January 1, 2005: Exchanged Asset A for Asset B, which had a market value of $30,000, and paid $13,000 in cash.
January 1, 2006: Exchanged Asset B for Asset C, which had a market value of $32,000, and paid $5,000 in cash.

---
[27]A royalty is a cost of continuing to use an asset.

January 1, 2007: Exchanged Asset C for Asset D, which had a market
                  value of $24,000, and received $6,000 in cash.
January 1, 2008: Exchanged Asset D for Asset E, which had a market
                  value of $11,700, and received $4,100 cash.

Assume that all assets have a 5-year life, no salvage value, and that the straight-line depreciation method is used.

Required:
1. Assuming that the assets are all dissimilar, prepare the journal entries for each exchange.
2. Assuming that the assets are all similar, prepare the journal entries for each exchange.

Problem 5-7: Capitalization of Interest (Appendix). On January 1, 2003, Brown Company signed a fixed-price contract to have D&L Builders construct a major plant facility at a cost of $14 million. It was estimated it would take two years to build the facility. Also, on March 1, 2003, Brown borrowed $10 million at 9% to finance the construction, with installment payments to be paid to the financing company each March 1 for the next five years. Brown expects to raise the remaining $4 million to construct the facility from cash generated from operations. The first progress payment of $1.2 million was made to D&L on April 30, 2003; the second progress payment of $2.8 million was made on October 1, 2003; and a third payment of $2 million was made on December 31, 2003. In addition to the $10 million, Brown had other outstanding debt as follows:

$15 million bonds, 14%, due on December 31, 2020.
$12 million unsecured bonds, $16\frac{1}{3}$%, due on December 31, 2015.

Work on the plant facility continued in 2004, and additional progress payments in the amount of $2 million each were made on March 1, July 1, November 1, and December 31. Also, the required debt payment of $2 million plus interest was paid on the scheduled date. The plant facility was finished and ready to be occupied on December 31, 2004. If necessary, assume that both of the outstanding bonds are to be used to compute the weighted-average interest rate.

Required:
Determine the amount of interest to be capitalized on this plant facility for 2003 and 2004.

Problem 5-8: Research and Development (International). Currently, the IASB permits R&D costs to be capitalized if a company can prove that a market does (or will) exist for its proposed product. The 1996 financial statements of Goodyear Tire & Rubber Co. (which followed U.S. GAAP) reveal that R&D expenses totaled $1,032 million, $1,067 million, and $1,047 million in 1996, 1995, and 1994, respectively. Net income amounts totaled $3,636 million, $3,293 million, and $2,727 million for 1996, 1995, and 1994, respectively.

Required:
Assuming that Goodyear could apply the IASB's standard and is able to demonstrate that a market will exist for its proposed products, calculate the after-tax dollar effect on Goodyear's 1995 and 1996 earnings. The aggregate income tax rate from all taxing entities is 50%, and amortization period is five years.

Problem 5-9: Goodwill. Large Company is considering acquiring Tiny Company by acquiring its net assets, except cash, for cash. The following data have been collected regarding Tiny Company:

Description	Book Value	Estimated Market Value
Identifiable assets, other than cash	$400,000	$440,000
Total liabilities	250,000	280,000
Owners' equity	150,000	Not Applicable

Required:

1. Assuming that Large Company paid $200,000 for the net assets of Tiny, compute the amount of goodwill.
2. Assuming that Large Company paid $140,000 for the net assets of Tiny, compute the amount of goodwill, or state how any difference between the fair value of the net assets and the acquisition price is accounted for.

Problem 5-10: Comparability of Financial Statements (International). Mr. Hathaway was performing an analysis on two companies within the same industry. One company was domiciled in the United States and followed U.S. GAAP. The other company was based in Sweden and followed accounting principles that were in conformity with European Union Directives. Mr. Hathaway noticed the following differences in accounting principles followed by the two companies:

a. The Swedish company capitalized, without amortization, the costs incurred that promoted brand names (i.e., primarily advertising costs).
b. The Swedish company wrote off immediately to retained earnings any goodwill resulting from acquisitions.

Using the following table, indicate how each accounting practice followed by the Swedish company will affect the following financial statement items and ratios (i.e., increase or decrease) compared to U.S. GAAP.

	Net Income	Return on Equity	L-T Debt/SE	Net Sales/ Total Assets	Market Price/Book Value per Share
a.					
b.					

Problem 5-11: Fixed Asset Worksheet. Previously, the Nile.com Company had owned very few fixed assets; but due to increasing business, it had found it necessary to expand its facilities, equipment, and other fixed assets. Thus, it undertook an aggressive campaign of buying assets during 2004. At the beginning of the year, its fixed asset records disclosed the following accounts and balances:

Detail of Land, Building, and Equipment

Description	Cost
Land	$ 450,000
Buildings	4,000,000
Automobiles	150,000
Building improvements	200,000
Equipment	2,500,000

During 2004, Nile.com completed the following transactions:

a. On January 26, a building to be used as a warehouse was acquired in exchange for 300,000 shares of Nile.com Company's $1 par value common stock. At the time, the common stock was being actively traded on an exchange at $18 per share, and on average, approximately 7,000,000 shares are traded each day. The county's tax rolls showed that the land was appraised at $450,000 and the building at $4,500,000.

b. On March 15, improvements to the recently acquired land were completed, which included repaving the parking lot, installing lighting for the parking lot, and putting in new landscaping (consisting primarily of bushes and small trees). The cost of the expenditures was $120,000, which was paid in cash.

c. After acquiring the building, various improvements were completed, including installing lighting and a security system and carpeting an area of the newly acquired building that will be used as offices. The lives of the lighting and security system are as long as the building, but the life of the carpet is thought to be eight years. The costs of the respective improvements are $40,000, $50,000, and $15,000.

d. Several forklifts were purchased to move large items; the total cost was $60,000.

e. Unrelated to acquiring the building and improving it, Nile.com also purchased two new automobiles by trading in two used vehicles. The total cost of the old vehicles was $65,000, and the accumulated depreciation was $50,000. The combined suggested manufacturer's retail price on the two new automobiles was $80,000. Nile.com was required to pay $60,000 to acquire the automobiles in addition to trading the old vehicles.

f. Toward the end of the year, after seeing many advantages of its new warehouse location, Nile.com purchased an adjacent plot of land that it intends to hold as an investment, expecting that the price will increase and a tidy profit will be recognized. The land was purchased by paying cash of $50,000 and signing an 8% note payable for $400,000, which is fair and adequate consideration.

Required:

1. Prepare an electronic spreadsheet and enter the beginning balances. Then, enter the amounts from the various transactions in the appropriate accounts/columns on the spreadsheet and determine the ending balance of each account.

2. What was the gain or loss recognized on the exchange of the automobiles? Show all computations.

3. Where on the balance sheet is the investment in land reported?

4. Assuming that total accumulated depreciation is $1,000,000, prepare the Land, Building, and Equipment section of Nile.com Company's balance sheet for the year ending December 31, 2004, rounding amounts to the nearest thousand.

5. In addition, inventory acquisitions during the year totaled $15,000,000. Freight on those purchases was $80,000; insurance during shipping was $25,000; and costs of preparing the inventory to be shipped to customers were $100,000. Nile.com uses the net method of costing its inventory and all purchases are acquired on terms of 2/10, n/30. At year-end, 8% of the inventory remained on hand. What is the total cost of the inventory at December 31, 2004? (Do not consider materiality on any of these items.)

Problem 5-12: "Shoe-Box" Problem—TJ's Men's Store. On March 1, 2003, two men's clothing stores merged. The move was prompted because of increasing competition in men's clothing, a national upsurge in catalog sales, and the construction of a new shopping mall in the area. The owners hoped the merger would help them be more competitive. The assets and liabilities of the two companies just prior to the merger were as follows:

	Mr. T's Men's Store		Mr. J's Men's Store	
	Book Value	Fair Value	Book Value	Fair Value
Cash	$ 10,000	$10,000	$ 8,000	$ 8,000
Accounts Receivable	6,000	5,500	16,000	7,500
Inventory	50,000	55,000	60,000	58,000
Fixtures	45,000	12,000	50,000	16,000
Accumulated Depreciation	(30,000)		(40,000)	
Accounts Payable	(5,000)	(5,000)	(6,000)	(6,000)

The owners decided on the partnership form of business and organized accordingly, with the name of TJ's Men's Store. Each received a capital contribution equal to the net fair value of their investments and all profits and losses from operations will be shared equally. The total legal cost of drawing up the partnership papers was $1,500, which was paid. (*Hint:* When recording the accounts receivable, use two accounts. Debit Accounts Receivable for the gross amount and then record the difference between the fair value and the book value in Allowance for Doubtful Accounts.)

The following transactions, in summarized form, occurred from the time of forming the partnership to December 31, 2003.

a. On March 1, TJ's signed a 5-year lease contract for space in a more centrally located building. The lease requires a monthly rental of $3,000 a month, payable at the first of each month. The first payment was made immediately, and all payments during the year were made on time. (*Note:* No asset is recorded for this type of lease. Instead, an expense is recognized each month.)

b. On April 1 and prior to opening, all the old fixtures were sold to a local scrap dealer for cash of $26,000, and new fixtures were acquired by signing a 3-year, 12% note payable for $60,000. The note is payable in yearly installments, with the first payment due on April 1, 2004. Labor costs to install the fixtures was $2,000. The fixtures have a 10-year expected life and will have no significant salvage value at the end of that time. If the lease is not renewed, the fixtures will be moved out of the building. Depreciation is computed to the nearest month.

c. Also on April 1, TJ's borrowed $10,000 from the local bank at 14% to install new carpeting that will not have to be replaced for five years. The note is due in two years.

d. On March 24, existing inventory was transferred to the new store. During the move, merchandise with a retail price of $600 was soiled. The merchandise could not be sold during normal business, and accordingly the merchandise was donated to a local charity. The charity gave TJ's a letter thanking them for their donation and, for tax purposes, stating that it thought the merchandise had a fair value of $50. Both previous proprietors maintained a relationship between cost and retail of 250%. (That is, inventory that cost $100 was priced to sell for $250.)

e. Sales of merchandise during the nine months that TJ's was open during 2003 totaled $160,000, all on account. Subsequently, 80% was collected. Of the accounts receivable that were transferred when the business began, collections totaled $14,000, and the balance was written off as being uncollectible. TJ's uses a perpetual inventory system, and accordingly records cost of goods sold at the time of sale. TJ's does not grant cash discounts to its customers.

f. Merchandise of $60,000 (gross) was acquired on terms of 2/10, n/30. TJ's uses the net method of recording inventory. At the end of the year, the total accounts payable that TJ's still owes is $10,000 (gross). Timely payments were made during the year to receive discounts of all but $360.

g. During the year, TJ's exchanged with another retailer, who specialized in outdoor clothing, $2,000 (retail price) of its slower moving merchandise.

h. Operating expenses amounted to $40,000, of which $38,000 was paid by the end of the year.

i. During the year, each owner withdrew $24,000 cash from the business.

j. Other information available was as follows (for making any adjusting journal entries necessary):

   (1) TJ's estimates that of the outstanding accounts receivable, $2,600 will be uncollectible. (*Hint:* When preparing this entry, be sure to consider the current balance.)

   (2) TJ's tax rate is 30%. No taxes were paid during the year.

Required:

1. Prepare the journal entries for these transactions.

2. Prepare a multiple-step income statement and classified balance sheet for the year ending December 31, 2003. For financial statement reporting purposes, combine accounts as you consider appropriate.

Research Activities

Activity 5-1: Write-Up of an Asset. In 1954, a corporation acquired 1,000 acres of land for $100 per acre. The purpose for acquiring the land never came to fruition, and the company has never been able to sell the land to anyone else. Recently, a valuable mineral deposit was discovered on the land, and it is now worth many times more than the $100 per acre that was paid for it.

1. Under what conditions is it permissible to write up land to its fair value under U.S. GAAP?

2. Assuming that the accounting requirements of a particular country require the land to be written up to fair value, what is the journal entry to record the write-up?

3. If consolidated statements are issued, what are the appropriate procedures for consolidating a foreign subsidiary in which assets have been written up to fair value?

Activity 5-2: Development Stage Enterprises. A development stage corporation cannot defer the expenses incurred but must follow GAAP for recognizing revenues and expenses. However, development stage corporations have additional reporting requirements that must be followed. What are these other reporting requirements?

Activity 5-3: Fair Value Determination of Acquired Subsidiary's Assets. When a company acquires another company, the individual assets and liabilities are recorded at their respective fair values. Research U.S. GAAP and determine the principles/techniques that should be used to ascertain the fair values of the individual assets and liabilities.

Activity 5-4: Goodwill (International). In the past, UK companies have been accused of making excessive allowances for goodwill when acquiring other companies. Mergers and acquisition specialists on Wall Street have claimed that the method of accounting for goodwill in the United Kingdom, which allowed corporations to immediately write off any purchased goodwill to retained earnings, puts U.S. firms at a competitive disadvantage in the market for acquiring other corporations. In 1998, the UK practice was changed, and now goodwill is capitalized and amortized over a period, usually of 20 years.

1. Given the differences in accounting for goodwill between UK and U.S. GAAP prior to 1998, why would UK companies have a competitive advantage in mergers and acquisitions over U.S. companies?
2. What are the disadvantages on the financial statements of writing off goodwill immediately to retained earnings?
3. Compare the UK and U.S. accounting rules for goodwill that exist currently. In your opinion, which country's accounting rules are more advantageous?

Matching Principle: Recognizing Costs OF Inventory AS Expenses

Where Has All the Inventory Gone?

During the year, a retailer of computers bought several desktop computers, all of which were the same make. Those purchased in January cost $1,000, those purchased in April cost $850, and those purchased in May cost $800. In May, the retailer sold one of these computers for $1,200. The customer never saw the actual computer he or she was buying but purchased it from inventory after looking at a floor display model.

Questions

1. What is the cost to the retailer of the computer that was sold and how much profit did the retailer earn?

2. Since the amount of profit that the retailer earns is dependent on the cost of the item, should the retailer be allowed to choose which cost is assigned to the item sold?

Several years ago, a manufacturing facility hired a cost accounting manager to replace its fired controller after each of the preceding four quarters had shown an inventory shortage. The manager's first responsibility was to supervise the counting of inventory. Following each quarterly count, the company had taken steps to curb further losses. First, tighter controls over requisitioning materials from the warehouse were instituted. Next, a high fence was built, then a night guard with guard dogs was hired, and finally, all vehicles leaving the premises were inspected. However, each quarter when the inventory was counted, another shortage was indicated. Interestingly, the company did not keep—and had never kept—any record of how much inventory should have been on hand.

Questions

1. How did the company know there really was an inventory shortage?

2. What inventory control system was the company using, and what inventory control system should it have been using to ensure a more accurate record-keeping system and more control over inventory?

Companies whose financial statements are audited must count the inventory on hand at least once a year. Everyone who has ever counted inventory is aware of the many errors that can occur in the count, particularly in a manufacturing company that has a large amount of work-in-process inventory.

Questions

1. What effect does an error in counting inventory have on the published financial statements? For instance, what is the effect of overstating or understating inventory on net income, total assets, or stockholders' equity?

2. What is the effect on published financial statements of subsequent years of misstating inventory in the current year?

1. Explain the matching principle as it relates to recognizing costs of inventory.

2. Explain the necessity of a cost-flow assumption to recognizing the costs of inventory.

3. Distinguish between a periodic inventory control system and a perpetual inventory control system, and describe when each is appropriate.

4. Apply the various cost-flow assumptions (i.e., FIFO, LIFO, average cost, and specific identification) to determining the cost of goods sold.

5. Compare the advantages and disadvantages of FIFO and LIFO cost-flow assumptions in computing net income and the inventory value reported on the balance sheet.

6. Use dollar-value LIFO procedures to restate a FIFO inventory value to a LIFO inventory value.

7. List the reasons why estimating an inventory value is sometimes necessary, and apply both the gross profit percentage method and the various applications of the retail method to estimating inventory.

8. Explain the effects on various financial statement numbers because of errors in counting inventory in the current and subsequent years.

9. Make appropriate journal entries to the LIFO reserve account.

The Theory of Expensing the Cost of Inventory

The previous chapter discussed the historical cost principle as it applies to acquiring inventory, showing that the cost of inventory consists of those necessary costs to acquire it, bring it to the place where it is to be sold, and to maintain its value. A primary purpose of this chapter is to cover the essential principle and conventions of *recognizing the historical cost of inventory as an expense on the income statement for the purposes of determining net income*. A related purpose is to determine the historical cost of the inventory that remains on hand and will be reported on the balance sheet. Stated differently, this chapter covers the matching principle and how it, in conjunction with a cost-flow assumption, determines when and how much cost of inventory is recognized as an expense and how much remains as an asset on the balance sheet.

Matching Principle

The **matching principle** requires that the *cost of inventory be recorded as an expense in the period that the revenue is recognized from selling the inventory*. This principle is shown in Figure 6-1, which continues the development of the accounting and financial reporting model.

Applying the matching principle requires that revenues from selling the inventory be recognized first, and then the cost of inventory is matched against that revenue (i.e., expensed in that period). For example, a retailer of men's clothing initially reports the cost of acquiring inventory as an asset. Then, when a sale is made, revenue is recognized, and the cost of the inventory that is sold is moved from the balance sheet to the income statement and becomes the cost of goods sold amount. In general, this is how the matching principle is applied in expensing the cost of inventory.

FIGURE 6-1

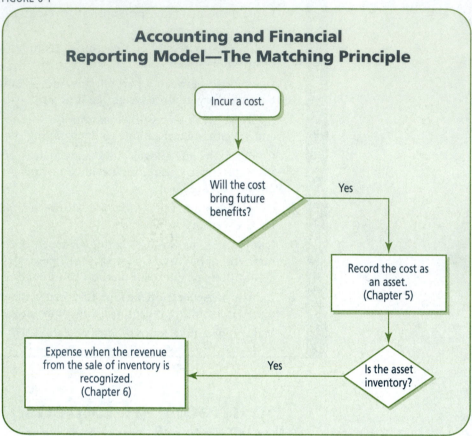

Cost-Flow Assumption

Although the matching principle determines when the cost of inventory is expensed, it is the **cost-flow assumption** that *determines how much of the inventory cost becomes an expense*. The case of the computer retailer in the opening scenarios, where a cost has to be matched with the $1,200 revenue, is an example of applying a cost-flow assumption. Since the computers were purchased for different amounts, it is possible to assign one of several different costs to each computer that was sold. Some alternatives are assigning the oldest cost, assigning the newest cost, or assigning some average cost. In almost all cases, it is impractical and provides no relevant information to identify the specific cost of the sold item and expense that amount. For example, labeling the hundreds of bolts in a hardware store is time consuming and costly and does not provide any useful information. That same rationale applies to almost all items of inventory in any store. Hence, it is customary to separate the physical flow of the inventory from the cost flow of the inventory. That is, business entities typically arrange their inventory so that the oldest items are sold first, but selling the oldest item first has no implication as to what cost is assigned to the item sold. Business entities may assign the oldest cost to the item sold, the most recent cost, or

EXTENDING THE CONCEPT

The costs of many other products are accounted for in the same way. For example, the labor, materials and other direct costs of extracting oil from the ground, and shipping, storing, and refining the crude oil are first accounted for as the cost of inventory and reported on the balance sheet. Then, when the inventory is sold, those costs are moved from the balance sheet and are reported as cost of goods sold on the income statement. This is the same procedure used in accounting for the costs of extracting many natural resources, the costs of manufacturing items, as well as the cost of inventory that is purchased for the purpose of reselling it to others.

some other cost. Determining which cost to assign to the inventory sold—and to the inventory still on hand—is a function of the cost-flow assumption.

Regarding the qualitative characteristics of relevance and reliability, the information provided from the various cost-flow assumptions is equally reliable because the same cost data are used and the same documentation is available to verify the results of any of them. Thus, the choice of which cost-flow assumption to use depends upon which cost provides the most relevant information.

Financial Reporting

On the income statement, the cost of the inventory sold is reported separately from other costs of doing business. *The cost of the sold inventory is reported as cost of goods sold*, and the other operating costs of the business are reported as operating expenses.

Since the cost-flow assumption has a significant impact on determining the income reported, *the business entity's cost-flow assumption must be disclosed in the Summary of Significant Accounting Policies, which either precedes the notes to the financial statements or is the first note.* Furthermore, once a cost-flow assumption has been selected, it should not be changed unless a business entity can show that another cost-flow assumption is preferable, which is demonstrated by the new cost-flow assumption providing more relevant information.[1] Allowing frequent or repeated changes to the cost-flow assumption violates the qualitative characteristic of consistency.

To illustrate the typical disclosure of the inventory cost-flow assumption, the following excerpts from the annual reports of Dell Computers and Honeywell Corporation, respectively, (with emphases added) are shown here.

EXTENDING THE CONCEPT

One of the secondary-level concepts of the FASB's Conceptual Framework is comparability; but how comparable are the net income numbers of two different companies if their inventory cost-flow assumptions are different? Can an analyst or other user of the financial statements draw meaningful comparisons from them? Should the FASB mandate only one cost-flow assumption so that comparability is achieved?

Inventories—Inventories are stated at the lower of cost or market. *Cost is determined on a first-in, first-out basis.*

Inventories—Inventories are valued at the lower of cost or market using the *last-in, first-out (LIFO) method* for certain qualifying domestic inventories and the *first-in, first-out (FIFO) or the average cost method* for all other inventories.

The preceding disclosure statements show that companies may use different cost-flow assumptions[2] and that the same company may use different cost-flow assumptions for various inventories.

Goods Included in Inventory

The first step in determining the cost of inventory (and the associated cost of goods sold) is to determine those goods that should be included in inventory. The idea is that once the quantity of goods that the company owns has been determined, then a cost can be attached to each item and the sum of these individual costs will yield the total cost of inventory. When counting inventory,

---

[1] *Opinions of the Accounting Principles Board No. 20*, "Accounting Changes" (New York: AICPA, July 1971), pars. 15–16. Preferability should not be based upon income tax implications but should be judged upon the relevance of the accounting information provided.
[2] Even within the same industry, companies sometimes use different accounting principles.

the theoretical rule is to include in inventory all items that the company owns. Although theoretically appealing, this rule is difficult to apply because it requires that a document verifying the company's ownership be presented for each item of inventory, which would be a long and tedious process. Rather, when taking a physical count of the inventory, the operational rule is to include all items that the company has in its possession, subject to the following exceptions:

- Ownership of goods in transit and not in the possession of either the buyer or seller is determined from the shipping terms. *The company paying the freight includes the goods in its inventory.* Thus, for goods being shipped FOB shipping point, title passes when the goods are loaded on the common carrier (e.g., truck or train) and the goods are included in the inventory of the buyer. For goods shipped FOB destination, title does not pass to the buyer until they are delivered to the buyer's place of business.
- *Goods on consignment are included in the inventory of the consignor, not of the consignee.*[3]
- In some cases, even though legal title has apparently passed, it is best to continue reporting the goods in the inventory of the seller. A **sale with a buy-back agreement** is one example in which the seller continues including the goods in its inventory. The nature of such transactions means that a company transfers inventory to another company and agrees to buy back the inventory at specified prices over an agreed-upon period of time. Thus, the essence of the transaction is that the seller has temporarily "parked" the inventory among the buyer's assets. Such transactions raise the question as to whether an actual sale has occurred; for this reason, the inventory continues being reported by the seller. Sales with a high risk of return are another example where the goods may continue being included in the inventory of the seller until the time expires in which the buyer has the right to return the goods or until payment is received.[4]

© GETTY IMAGES, INC./PHOTODISC

- Goods shipped subject to the buyer's approval are included on the seller's inventory until payment is received or a statement is received indicating that the goods meet the buyer's specifications.

Inventory Control Procedures

Although determining net income and the value of inventory are the primary purposes of accounting for inventories, another important accounting function is safeguarding the inventory against theft or other forms of loss. Depending upon

---

[3]A consignment transaction is one where the potential seller (the consignor) delivers merchandise to an agent (the consignee) for the agent to sell. Title to the merchandise does not pass to the consignee but remains with the consignor.

[4]This topic is covered more extensively in Chapter 8.

whether a few safeguards are needed because the items are relatively inexpensive or whether more controls are needed, companies use either a periodic inventory control system or a perpetual inventory control system.

Under a **periodic inventory control system**, the accounting records do not show either the quantity or the cost of the inventory on hand. The quantity can be known only by physically counting the items, and the cost of the inventory can be known only by determining the cost of each item counted. So at any time during the year, both the *quantity of inventory and its cost as reported in the general ledger are the amounts as of the date of the last inventory count*. Under the periodic inventory system, the journal entry to record the acquisition of inventory is to debit a purchases account and credit either Cash or Accounts Payable, and the only entry to record the sale of inventory is to debit Accounts Receivable (or Cash) and to credit Sales. Thus, under a periodic inventory system, the basic entry is as follows:

Purchases	XXX	
Accounts Payable (or Cash)		XXX

To record the acquisition of inventory under the periodic inventory system.

Under a periodic inventory system, the cost of goods sold amount is computed mathematically by adding the cost of the beginning inventory to the cost of the net purchases for the period and subtracting from this sum the cost of the ending inventory amount as determined from the physical count, as shown in Illustration 6-1. Net purchases means the cost of purchases plus freight to ship them to the company's location, less both purchase returns and purchase discounts.

ILLUSTRATION 6-1

Cost of Goods Sold Calculation—Periodic Inventory System

Inventory, January 1, 2004	$ 1,000
+ Purchases (net)	8,000
= Cost of goods available for sale	$ 9,000
− Inventory, December 31, 2004	(1,500)
= Cost of goods sold	$ 7,500

The advantages of the periodic inventory system are its simplicity and low cost. The disadvantage is the lack of information provided concerning the amount of inventory that should be on hand and the resulting lack of control over inventory. That is, since the cost of goods sold number is determined by mathematical calculation, the inventory system provides no information about possible inventory theft, breakage, waste, or other causes of inventory shrinkage. Losses due to all these reasons are simply counted as part of the cost of goods sold. Thus, since there is no information about possible inventory losses, no signals are sent that further inventory control procedures are needed, and no information is provided as to the effectiveness of controls in reducing losses. Because of its simplicity and low cost, the periodic inventory system may be of use in a manual accounting system for low-cost inventory items, but a perpetual inventory system probably should be used in all other situations.

A **perpetual inventory control system** shows—at any point in time—both the quantity of inventory on hand and its cost. The inventory is still counted at least once a year (usually as close to year-end as feasible, although continuous counting on a rotational basis is frequently used), but such counting is done more to confirm what is shown on the accounting records than to determine the amount of inventory on hand. After counting the inventory, the inventory records are adjusted so that they agree to the physical count, with any difference recognized as a loss (or gain).

Under a perpetual inventory control system, journal entries are prepared that change the inventory account balance each time inventory is purchased or sold. Purchases of merchandise are recorded by debiting the inventory account rather than a purchases account, as was done under the periodic inventory system. When a sale is made, in addition to debiting Accounts Receivable (or Cash) and crediting Sales, a journal entry is prepared debiting Cost of Goods Sold and crediting Inventory for the cost of the items sold. The dollar amount of the cost of goods sold entry is determined by the business entity's cost-flow assumption. Thus, under the perpetual inventory system, the basic journal entries are as follows:

Inventory	XXX	
Accounts Payable (or Cash)		XXX

To record the acquisition of inventory under a perpetual inventory system.

Cost of Goods Sold	XXX	
Inventory		XXX

To record the cost of inventory sold (i.e., move the amount to the income statement) under a perpetual inventory system.

The chief advantage of using a perpetual inventory system is that it is possible to determine the effectiveness of current physical procedures to protect the inventory against theft, spoilage, or other forms of loss by comparing the inventory on hand as determined by counting it to the amount of inventory reported in the general ledger. When an inventory loss is evident because the inventory count is less than what the general ledger indicates should be on hand, various physical controls can be implemented to safeguard the inventory (as in the opening scenario). The primary disadvantage of the perpetual inventory control system is the additional record-keeping expense.

Some companies use a combination of the periodic and perpetual inventory systems, which is called a **modified perpetual inventory control system**. Like a perpetual system, changes in quantities are recorded as they occur (i.e., both for purchases and sales of inventory) but not in the general ledger. But like the periodic system, journal entries are not prepared that affect the inventory account for either purchases or sales of inventory. The advantage of such a system is that information is provided as to the amount of inventory the company should have, without incurring the entire expense of maintaining a perpetual inventory system.

CONCEPTUAL *Question*

In the opening scenario, which inventory control system was the second company using? Since the company was using a periodic inventory control system, how did it know that there was an inventory shortage each time an inventory count was conducted? (*Note:* This question is answered later in the chapter.)

Cost-Flow Assumptions

The information in Table 6-1 about a particular item of inventory will be used to illustrate the procedures of various cost-flow assumptions. As previously mentioned, the purpose of a cost-flow assumption is to *determine the cost of the units*

TABLE 6-1

Inventory Data

	Units Purchased	Units Sold	Unit Cost	Total Cost
Inventory, January 1	400		$10.00	$4,000.00
	100		10.50	1,050.00
January 5		200		
January 11	300		11.00	3,300.00
January 14		300		
January 19		200		
January 27	100		11.50	1,150.00
Total to account for	900			$9,500.00
Quantity sold during January	(700)	700		
Inventory, January 31	200			

that were sold and of the cost of the units that remain on hand. Table 6-1 shows that, at the end of January, there are 200 units in inventory and 700 units have been sold. In the illustrations that follow, the cost-flow assumption will first be applied using a periodic inventory system and then using a perpetual inventory system.

First-In, First-Out (FIFO)

Under the FIFO cost-flow assumption, the oldest cost is assigned to the cost of goods sold, and the newer costs are assigned as the value of the inventory on the balance sheet. In other words, FIFO means that the first cost incurred becomes the first cost moved to the income statement to become the cost of goods sold.

This Is the Real World

An important question every manager with responsibility over inventory faces is, "How much inventory should be available for sale?" Holding inventory includes the cost of space, hiring employees to record and monitor the inventory, and the opportunity cost of the return that could have been earned if the funds spent on inventory had been spent on some other asset. However, inventory is the life-blood of retail and manufacturing companies, and therefore, having sufficient inventory on hand is crucial to a company's survival. A balance must be found where the cost of holding inventory is minimized while meeting customers' demands.

The importance of finding the appropriate amount of inventory was highlighted by Amazon.com, Inc.'s experience during the 1999 and 2000 holiday seasons, which were critical times for Internet retailing businesses. During 1999, to ensure that it could satisfy customer demands, Amazon.com heavily stocked its shelves with inventory, and as a result, Amazon was successful in shipping 99% of its orders before the holidays. But afterwards, during the first quarter of 2000, the company wrote down $39 million of unsold inventory, which represented over 20% of the largest quarterly loss in its history. Much the same thing, but to a lesser extent, occurred during the 2000 holiday season.

Was the company correct in its decision to overstock inventory? Amazon.com may have received future benefits in the form of repeat buyers as a result of having met customer demands, but the costs to do so were significant.

Periodic System

Illustration 6-2 demonstrates a FIFO cost-flow assumption under a periodic inventory system. The most important column is the one titled "Determination," where the cost is assigned to cost of goods sold or to inventory. Remember that regardless of which physical items were sold, under a FIFO cost flow, the costs of the 700 units sold are assumed to be the first costs that the company incurred. Thus, the first cost to be moved from the balance sheet to the income statement is the cost of the beginning inventory, which is $10.00 per unit. Then, the next cost to be moved to the income statement is the $10.50 per unit. This process continues until the costs of the 700 units sold have been identified and the costs of the 200 units in inventory have been identified. Once these costs have been identified, computing the cost of inventory and the cost of goods sold is a mathematical summation procedure. Illustration 6-2 shows that the cost of the 700 units goods sold (Table 6-1) under a FIFO cost-flow assumption and a periodic inventory system is $7,250 and the cost of the inventory is $2,250.

ILLUSTRATION 6-2

FIFO Cost-Flow and Periodic Inventory System

Totals to account for: 900 units; $9,500 (see Table 6-1).

	Units	Determination	Unit Cost	Cost of Goods Sold	Cost of Inventory
Inventory, January 1	400	Sold	$10.00	$4,000	
	100	Sold	10.50	1,050	
Purchase, January 11	300	200 Sold	11.00	2,200	
		100 Inventory	11.00		$1,100
Purchase, January 27	100	Inventory	11.50		1,150
Totals				$7,250	$2,250

Summary: 700 sold and 200 in inventory for a total of 900 units.
$7,250 in cost of goods sold and $2,250 in cost of inventory for a total of $9,500.

Illustration 6-2 shows that—according to a FIFO flow—the first units purchased were the first ones sold. The accuracy of these calculations can be checked by verifying that the total quantities and total costs in Illustration 6-2 agree with those in Table 6-1. Thus, in Illustration 6-2, the 700 units sold and the 200 units in inventory agree with the 900 total units in Table 6-1, and the sum of the $7,250 cost of goods sold and the $2,250 cost of inventory agree with the total cost of $9,500 in Table 6-1. The journal entry to change the inventory account to its correct end-of-the-year balance is prepared by using either the adjusting-entry approach or the closing-entry approach, as demonstrated in Chapter 2.

Perpetual System

Illustration 6-3 demonstrates the use of the FIFO cost flow with a perpetual inventory system. Note that each time a sale is made, the oldest cost is assigned to the cost of goods sold, and the inventory is valued at the newer costs. Illustration 6-3 should be carefully followed so that the cost flows become readily apparent. (The arrows indicate the order of liquidation; that is, the units that are moved first to the cost of goods sold.)

ILLUSTRATION 6-3

FIFO Cost-Flow and Perpetual Inventory System

	Purchases		Sales		Inventory	
	Quantity	Unit Cost	Quantity	Unit Cost	Quantity	Cost
Inventory, January 1	400	$10.00			400 @ $10.00	$4,000
	100	10.50			100 @ 10.50	1,050
						$5,050
January 5			200	$10.00	200 @ $10.00	$2,000
					100 @ 10.50	1,050
						$3,050
January 11	300	11.00			200 @ $10.00	$2,000
					100 @ 10.50	1,050
					300 @ 11.00	3,300
						$6,350
January 14			200	10.00		
			100	10.50	300 @ $11.00	$3,300
January 19			200	11.00	100 @ $11.00	$1,100
January 27	100	11.50			100 @ $11.00	$1,100
					100 @ 11.50	1,150
Totals	900		700	$7,250		$2,250

FIFO Method

Perpetual = Periodic

An interesting point about the FIFO cost-flow assumption is that regardless of whether a periodic or a perpetual system is used, the values of ending inventory and the cost of goods sold are always identical. In the example given, the value of the ending inventory is $2,250 under either inventory system, and the cost of goods sold is $7,250 under either system. This uniformity of results does not occur with any other cost-flow assumption.

Last-In, First-Out (LIFO)

With a LIFO cost-flow assumption, the most recently incurred costs are assigned as the cost of the inventory sold, and the older costs are assigned as the value of the inventory. That is, LIFO means that the last (or most recent) cost is the first cost that is transferred to the cost of goods sold.

Periodic System

Using the same data in Table 6-1, Illustration 6-4 demonstrates a LIFO cost-flow assumption with a periodic inventory system. Again, the most important column is the one titled "Determination." As before, the information in the Determina-

ILLUSTRATION 6-4

LIFO Cost-Flow and Periodic Inventory System

Totals to account for: 900 units; $9,500 (see Table 6-1).

	Units	Determination	Unit Cost	Cost of Goods Sold	Cost of Inventory
Inventory, January 1	400	200 Inventory	$10.00		$2,000
		200 Sold		$2,000	
	100	Sold	10.50	1,050	
Purchase, January 11	300	Sold	11.00	3,300	
Purchase, January 27	100	Sold	11.50	1,150	
Totals				$7,500	$2,000

Summary: 700 sold and 200 in inventory for a total of 900 units.
$7,500 in cost of goods sold and $2,000 in cost of inventory for a total of $9,500.

CONCEPTUAL
Question

Which cost-flow assumption, FIFO or LIFO, would result in a higher cost of goods sold number and a lower inventory value during a period of falling prices?

Answer: FIFO cost flow

tion column is obtained by knowing that there are 200 units in inventory and 700 units have been sold. Then, a LIFO cost-flow assumption is applied, where the costs of the 700 most recently acquired items are moved to the income statement and the older costs are the cost of the inventory on hand.

Note that—just opposite to the FIFO cost flow—the inventory on hand comes from the earliest layer, and the goods sold come from the more recent layers. Note also that in relation to the FIFO cost-flow assumption, a LIFO cost flow results in a higher cost of goods sold number *during a period of rising prices* and a lower inventory value. The explanation as to why this is so is illustrated in Figure 6-2, which shows that in a period of rising prices, a LIFO cost flow matches newer—and higher-priced—goods with sales, and thus results in a lower net income as compared to a FIFO cost flow.

FIGURE 6-2

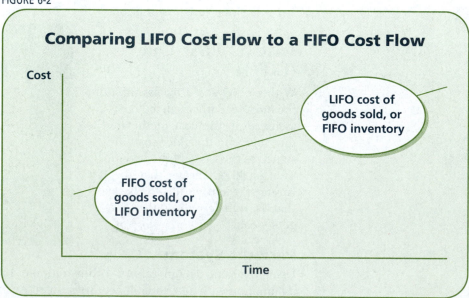

Comparing LIFO Cost Flow to a FIFO Cost Flow

Cost

LIFO cost of goods sold, or FIFO inventory

FIFO cost of goods sold, or LIFO inventory

Time

Perpetual System

Illustration 6-5 shows a LIFO cost-flow assumption applied to a perpetual inventory system. Note that in contrast to a FIFO cost flow, each time a sale is made, the cost of the inventory that is moved to the income statement is the newest cost. Otherwise, the procedures are exactly the same as in Illustration 6-3. (Again, the arrows indicate the order in which the units in inventory are moved to the cost of goods sold.)

ILLUSTRATION 6-5

LIFO Cost-Flow and Perpetual Inventory System

	Purchases		Sales		Inventory	
	Quantity	Unit Cost	Quantity	Unit Cost	Quantity	Cost
Inventory, January 1	400	$10.00			400 @ $10.00	$4,000
	100	10.50			100 @ 10.50	1,050
						$5,050
January 5			100	$10.50	300 @ $10.00	$3,000
			100	10.00		
January 11	300	11.00			300 @ $10.00	$3,000
					300 @ 11.00	3,300
						$6,300
January 14			300	11.00	300 @ $10.00	$3,000
January 19			200	$10.00	100 @ $10.00	$1,000
January 27	100	$11.50			100 @ $10.00	$1,000
					100 @ 11.50	1,150
						$2,150
Totals	900	$9,500				
Inventory, January 31					200	$2,150
Sold during January			700	$7,500		

Unlike the FIFO cost-flow assumption, different inventory and cost of goods sold figures result from using a LIFO cost flow and applying it to a periodic inventory system versus a perpetual inventory system. To clarify why this is so, consider the purchase made on January 27. Under a perpetual system, this last purchase is still in inventory, since no sale occurred after it; but under a periodic system, this last purchase is the first layer liquidated (see Illustration 6-5), even though the sale occurred before the purchase.

The journal entries to record the above transactions using a LIFO cost-flow assumption are the same as illustrated with a FIFO cost-flow assumption. Only the amounts change.

Choosing between FIFO and LIFO

Some contend that a FIFO cost-flow assumption is flawed in that it matches an "old cost" on the income statement with a "current revenue." That is, a July 1 sale would result in reporting a July 1 revenue value, against which is matched

CONCEPTUAL *Question*

Given the comparative advantages of FIFO and LIFO, why do you think many companies in the 1970s and 1980s chose to report lower net income numbers and switched to the LIFO cost-flow assumption?

Answer: The use of LIFO in the United States undoubtedly is based on increased cash flows through tax savings. For example, LIFO is an allowed alternative for accounting purposes, but not for tax purposes, in the United Kingdom and Hong Kong. As a result, LIFO is rarely used for financial reporting purposes there.

an older cost value, perhaps even many months older. Thus, the net income number is not as relevant as it could be. But, conversely, an obvious advantage of a FIFO cost flow is that the inventory on the balance sheet is valued at a current value. Another advantage of a FIFO cost-flow assumption is that it approximates the physical flow of goods.

Generally, the advantages and disadvantages of a LIFO cost flow are just the opposite of those mentioned for a FIFO cost flow. So an advantage of a LIFO cost flow is that it matches a current cost with a current revenue, but the inventory value is not reflective of its current cost. Over time, this old inventory cost becomes less and less reflective of current costs and thus less relevant to the financial statement users. In essence, choosing between FIFO and LIFO often depends upon which financial statement figure—net income or inventory—is considered more relevant. When a more relevant net income is desired, a LIFO cost-flow assumption is generally preferred;[5] when a more relevant balance sheet inventory number is desired, a FIFO cost-flow assumption is generally preferred.

Besides the advantage of matching a current cost with a current revenue, a further advantage of using a LIFO cost-flow assumption is the increased cash flow because of decreased taxes. (This discussion presumes rising prices over time.) That is, *when prices are rising*, LIFO results in a higher cost of goods sold and, correspondingly, a lower taxable income and fewer taxes paid. Hence, more cash is available.

However, a disadvantage of LIFO is that, in a manual accounting system, it is cumbersome and costly for businesses whose inventory is either large or growing because, over time, there is a tendency for many small layers of inventory to be created but never liquidated. Another and more significant disadvantage of using LIFO is when technological obsolescence occurs, which causes old units of inventory to be liquidated, and thus old costs are matched against current revenues—exacerbating the very problem that LIFO was meant to avoid. A further disadvantage of LIFO is that by planning the timing of purchases, management can, to some degree, manipulate the amount of net income reported. That is, by postponing the acquisition of inventory, management can liquidate older layers of inventory with a lower per unit cost and thereby report a higher income for the period. Also, by acquiring large amounts of inventory just before the financial statement date—when a periodic inventory control system is used—a lower net income is reported. This ability to manipulate income is not desirable. Under a FIFO cost-flow assumption, it is not possible to manipulate income by choosing when purchases of inventory will be made.

The FASB determines the rules that govern financial reporting, and the IRS, Treasury Department, Congress, courts, etc., determine the rules that determine taxable income. Most times, a company may choose to apply one accounting rule for financial reporting and a different accounting rule to determine its taxable income. But when Congress permitted the use of LIFO to determine taxable income, it attached a provision to the law—known as the **LIFO conformity rule**—that permits LIFO for determining taxable income only when the company also uses LIFO for financial reporting.

---

[5]Presumably, if a LIFO cost-flow assumption better matches current costs with current revenues, then an even better cost-flow assumption is next-in, first-out (NIFO). Such a cost-flow assumption matches current revenue with the cost that will be incurred to replace the inventory sold. However, NIFO is not an accepted procedure under generally accepted accounting principles because it is not based on actual cost but on an expected cost.

Average Cost

Besides the FIFO and LIFO cost-flow assumptions, a third option is to use an average cost-flow assumption. Although it may seem that an average cost-flow assumption would overcome the failings of both FIFO and LIFO, another way to view average cost is that it has the problems of both FIFO and LIFO, just not to the same magnitude. That is, the cost reported on the income statement is not as relevant as that reported under LIFO, and the inventory value on the balance sheet is not as relevant as that reported under FIFO. Perhaps because it has the deficiencies of both FIFO and LIFO, the average cost-flow assumption is not applied very widely in financial reporting.

Periodic System

Using the data in Table 6-1, the computations to determine the cost of goods sold and the value of inventory to report on the balance sheet are shown in Illustration 6-6 for an average cost-flow assumption and a periodic inventory control system. These procedures are called a **weighted-average cost flow**.

ILLUSTRATION 6-6

Weighted-Average Cost Flow

	Units Purchased	Unit Cost	Total Cost
Inventory, January 1	400	$10.00	$4,000
	100	10.50	1,050
January 5			
January 11	300	11.00	3,300
January 14			
January 19			
January 27	100	11.50	1,150
Total to account for	900		$9,500
Inventory, January 31	200		
Quantity sold during January	700		

Average cost = $9,500/900 units = $10.56/unit (rounded)

Inventory value = 200 units × $10.56/unit = $2,112

Cost of goods sold = $9,500 − $2,112 = $7,388

Two points need to be stressed. First, the unit cost figure usually will have to be rounded, with the number of digits to the right of the decimal being arbitrary. Second, either the inventory value or the cost of goods sold number, but not both, is computed by multiplication and the other is computed by subtraction. Computing both inventory and cost of goods sold by multiplication will result in rounding errors.

Perpetual System

Illustration 6-7 presents the use of an average cost-flow assumption and a perpetual inventory system applied to the data in Table 6-1, which is referred to as a **moving-average cost flow**. The *major point is that a new unit cost is computed after each purchase*, and, if desired, a new unit cost may also be computed after each sale. When sales are made, the cost of goods sold is computed by multiplying the newest unit cost by the number of units sold.

ILLUSTRATION 6-7

Moving-Average Cost Flow

	Purchases	Sales	Total
Inventory, January 1	400 × $10.00 = $4,000 100 × $10.50 = $1,050		500 @ $10.10 = $5,050
January 5		200 × $10.10 = $2,020	300 @ $10.10 = $3,030
January 11	300 × $11.00 = $3,300		600 @ $10.55 = $6,330
January 14		300 × $10.55 = $3,165	300 @ $10.55 = $3,165
January 19		200 × $10.55 = $2,110	100 @ $10.55 = $1,055
January 27	100 × $11.50 = $1,150		200 @ $11.03 = $2,205
Totals	900 units and $9,500		
Inventory, January 31			200 @ $11.03 = $2,205
Quantity sold during January		700 units and $7,295	

The procedures in computing this unit cost are found in the "Total" column in Illustration 6-7 and consist of the following sequential calculations:

1. Computing the total number of units,
2. Computing the total cost, and
3. Computing the unit cost by dividing the total cost by the total units.

Specific Identification

When the quantity of inventory is relatively small, but individually the items are unique and costly, it may be relevant to match the inventory cost flow with the quantity flow. Examples in retailing where associating cost flow and physical flow may be relevant include automobiles, jewelry, and furs. To use a specific identification cost flow, each inventory item must have a unique identifying number, symbol, or characteristic. The inventory value and the cost of goods sold figures are computed by identifying each unit that is sold and each unit that is still on hand. Then, from invoices, the cost of each unit is determined. An automobile dealership, for example, takes an inventory by referring to the VIN number of each vehicle on hand and then finding the cost of each car from invoices.

Although the specific identification system appears ideal, it has two undesirable results. One is the large and detailed amount of record keeping required if it is applied to most inventory items. A second undesirable result is the possible manipulation of income. Assume there are three identical "Big Screen TVs" in a retailer's inventory, each of which was acquired at a different time, and therefore at a different cost. A customer buys one from inventory by looking at a floor model. If the specific identification method of determining cost is used, the retailer can control the amount of net income to be reported by selecting which of the three units is shipped to the customer. Because of these defects (i.e., costly to use and ability to manipulate income), the specific identification cost flow should only be used when each item of inventory has unique characteristics that appeal differently to customers, and thus the customer selects which item is sold.

Dollar-Value LIFO

As mentioned previously, the two disadvantages of LIFO are: (1) the many layers that result cause it to be a costly and cumbersome system for businesses whose inventory is either large or growing, particularly when the inventory records are kept manually, and (2) technological changes cause inventory to be

CONCEPTUAL
Question

Returning to the first of the three opening scenarios, how does the cost-flow assumption make it possible to have several different correct net income amounts? In your opinion, is this desirable, or should the FASB mandate only one correct cost-flow assumption? Why or why not?

liquidated, which results in very old costs being matched with current revenues. A solution to the problem of many layers is to apply LIFO to pools of inventory rather than to individual units; the solution to liquidating old layers is to compute the cost of inventory by referring to price changes (i.e., a price index) rather than using the cost of individual items. By using pools, LIFO procedures are greatly simplified, as the number of inventory layers is replaced by a greatly reduced number of pools. By costing the inventory by using price indexes, a very old cost is rarely matched with a current revenue, even when technological changes occur.

Combining the use of pools of inventory with price indexes has given rise to the most popular method of applying LIFO cost-flow procedures, called dollar-value LIFO. It is easiest to apply dollar-value LIFO procedures when the inventory records are kept during the year on a FIFO cost-flow assumption, although an average cost-flow assumption can also be used.[6]

The Concept and Procedures

Graphically, the dollar-value LIFO theory and procedures can be explained as shown in Figure 6-3.

FIGURE 6-3

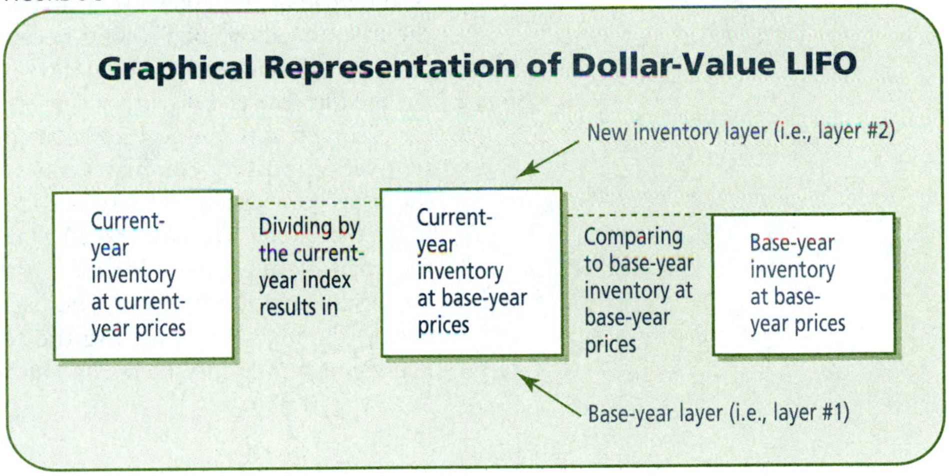

Graphical Representation of Dollar-Value LIFO

New inventory layer (i.e., layer #2)

| Current-year inventory at current-year prices | Dividing by the current-year index results in | Current-year inventory at base-year prices | Comparing to base-year inventory at base-year prices | Base-year inventory at base-year prices |

Base-year layer (i.e., layer #1)

At year-end, the dollar-value LIFO procedures are applied to the ending inventory cost to convert from a FIFO cost to a LIFO cost. The procedures to make this conversion are as follows:

Step 1: *Determine the current-year price index,* which can be an appropriate published index, or it can be computed by dividing the current end-of-year prices by the base-year prices. (This assumes that all price-level indexes for prior years have been computed already.)

Step 2: *Deflate the year-end inventory cost,* computed by using a FIFO cost-flow assumption (which is the value in the general ledger), divided by this index. *Explanation:* Inventory value is a function of quantity and cost. Deflating the cost of the ending inventory eliminates price as a reason for a change in inventory value. Thus, any increase in the cost of inventory as compared to the prior

---

[6]The dollar-value procedures that may be used by companies that switch fom FIFO to LIFO are discussed in Appendix A at the end of this chapter.

year's cost of inventory is due to an increase in the quantity of inventory.

Step 3: *Identify the inventory layers* and the years in which inventory quantities changed, remembering that any inventory liquidations occur in a LIFO order.

Step 4: *Reinflate each inventory layer by multiplying it by the corresponding price index.* This results in each layer of inventory being valued at the end-of-the-year prices in effect for the year in which the inventory was acquired.

Step 5: *Sum the results* in Step 4. This is the LIFO cost as computed by applying dollar-value procedures.

To illustrate the dollar-value LIFO procedures, assume that Davis Corporation's FIFO cost of inventory for one of its inventory pools at the end of 2004 was $11,200 and that the cost of inventory at December 31, 2003 (the base year), was $10,000. The end-of-year price indexes for 2003 and 2004 were 100 and 105, respectively. Using this information, the steps in converting the FIFO inventory cost of $11,200 to a LIFO cost are as follows:

Step 1: *Compute the current-year price index.* This is given as 105,[7] meaning that prices increased 5% relative to the base year. From this, it is known that the 2004 FIFO inventory of $11,200 is higher than the base inventory of $10,000 because of an increase in price and possibly an increase in the quantity on hand.

Step 2: *Deflate the year-end inventory cost of $11,200 by dividing by the current-year price index*, $11,200/1.05 = $10,667. Deflating the current-year inventory eliminates any increase in inventory cost over the base-year amount of $10,000 due to price increases. The difference between $10,667 and $10,000 is due only to an increase in the quantity of goods on hand.

Step 3: *Identify the inventory layers.* The base inventory is $10,000, so the cost of the inventory added in the current year is $667.

Step 4: *Reinflate the inventory layers by multiplying by the price index in effect for that year.*

	Layer		Price Index		Inventory Cost
Base year:	$10,000	×	1.00	=	$10,000
Current year:	667	×	1.05	=	700

Step 5: *Sum the results.* The LIFO cost of the ending inventory using dollar-value procedures is $10,700.

Illustration 6-8 continues the example of Davis Company for the years 2005 through 2007, reinforcing the dollar-value LIFO procedures and also illustrating how liquidations and subsequent additions to inventory are handled. Price indexes for all years are given, as are the ending inventory values using a FIFO cost-flow assumption. Review carefully the procedures for a year before proceeding to the next year. Note in particular how the liquidation was treated in Year 2006 and how a new inventory layer was subsequently valued in 2007. Note also that in 2007, the index for 2006 (i.e., 110) is not used. The reason is that no inventory was added in 2006.

---

[7]Price indexes are percentages, and therefore they are decimal values. Although they are typically stated without decimals, when doing the calculations, always use the decimal form.

ILLUSTRATION 6-8

Dollar-Value LIFO

	2005	2006	2007
FIFO Ending Inventory	$12,150 (given)	$11,825 (given)	$12,600 (given)
Step 1: Index	108 (given)	110 (given)	112 (given)
Step 2: Deflate year-end inventory	$12,150/1.08 = $11,250 (Because this amount is greater than it was for this step in the prior year, a new layer of inventory has been added.)	$11,825/1.10 = $10,750 (Because this amount is less than the amount in Step 2 for the year 2005, inventory has been liquidated. The amount of liquidation is $500.)	$12,600/1.12 = $11,250 (Comparing this number to the amount in Step 2 for 2006 shows that inventory has been added.)
Step 3: Identify inventory layers	Base year = $10,000 2004 = 667 2005 = 583 Total = $11,250 (This step identifies the amount of that new layer.)	Base year = $10,000 2004 = 667 2005 = 83 Total = $10,750 (Note the LIFO order of liquidation.)	Base year = $10,000 2004 = 667 2005 = 83 2007 = 500 Total = $11,250 (This step identifies the amount of the new layer.)
Step 4: Reinflate inventory layers	$10,000 × 1.00 = $10,000 667 × 1.05 = 700 583 × 1.08 = 630	$10,000 × 1.00 = $10,000 667 × 1.05 = 700 83 × 1.08 = 90	$10,000 × 1.00 = $10,000 667 × 1.05 = 700 83 × 1.08 = 90 500 × 1.12 = 560
Step 5: Summation	$11,330	$10,790	$11,350

External and Internal Indexes

In practice, the most popular price-level index is the Consumers Price Index for All Urban Consumers (CPI-U). Other price-level indexes published by the federal government or various trade associations may be used if they are more representative of the price changes for specific inventory. When a relevant price index is not available, a business may compute its own internal price index. *An internal price index is computed by dividing the ending inventory under a FIFO cost-flow assumption by the value of the current inventory quantity at base-year prices.*[8] The result is the price index for the current year, and once this index is computed, the dollar-value LIFO procedures as previously illustrated are applied.

To illustrate the computing of an internal price index, suppose that Davis Company has two items in a particular inventory pool, Items A and B. Further, on January 1 of the base year, inventory consisted of 500 items of A at a cost of $20 each and 2,000 items of B at a cost of $5 each. Thus, the total cost of the base-year inventory is $20,000, which is computed as follows:

---

[8]This method of computing a price index is referred to as the double-extension method.

Base-Year Inventory at Base-Year Prices

Item	Quantity	Unit Cost	Total Cost
A	500	$20	$10,000
B	2,000	5	10,000
Total			$20,000

At the end of the next year, the inventory records show that there are 650 units of Item A on hand and 2,200 units of Item B on hand at the following costs:

Current-Year Inventory at Current-Year Prices

Item	Quantity	Unit Cost	Total Cost
A	550	$22.00	$12,100
	100	24.00	2,400
B	2,200	6.50	14,300
Total			$28,800

Note that the quantities in the preceding schedule are the quantities for the current year. Also, note that the time of purchasing the merchandise (i.e., the layers) is retained. The next step in determining an internal index is to multiply these same quantities by the base-year prices, which is shown in the next schedule.

Current-Year Inventory at Base-Year Prices

Item	Quantity	Unit Cost	Total Cost
A	550	$20.00	$11,000
	100	20.00	2,000
B	2,200	5.00	11,000
Total			$24,000

Having computed the current-year inventory at both the current-year and base-year prices, the final step in computing an internal price index is to divide the inventory at current prices by the inventory at base-year prices. This results in an internal price index of 1.20 (i.e., computed by dividing the $28,800 by the $24,000).

International Accounting for Inventory Valuation

INTERNATIONAL

The International Accounting Standard that provides accounting guidance on inventories is IAS No. 2. This standard specifies that the benchmark treatment for inventory valuation is FIFO or an average-cost system. LIFO is an allowed alternative, but if it is used, companies must disclose the lower of the inventories' net realizable value or cost based on the FIFO or the weighted-average method.

Including LIFO as an acceptable cost-flow assumption under International GAAP is an example of the political environment within which the IASC operated and the IASB must continue to operate. During the late 1980s, in an effort to enhance the credibility of IAS, the IASC began what was referred to as the Comparability Project. The primary goal of this project was to reduce the number of options allowed by international GAAP. By the end of 1993, the IASC had issued 10 revised standards that eliminated 16 accounting choices.

As part of the Comparability Project, the LIFO cost-flow assumption was one of the methods that the IASC originally had proposed eliminating. The basis for this proposal was that the LIFO assumption of selling the most recently purchased inventory was not realistic and it distorted the balance sheet. In addition, LIFO was not an allowed method in several countries that were members of the IASC (e.g., Australia, Sweden, and at the time the issue was being debated, Germany).

Of course, LIFO is a very popular inventory valuation method in the United States, primarily because of the tax benefits that it provides. When the IASC proposed eliminating LIFO, it was readily apparent that support for this proposal from the United States would not be forthcoming. The IASC recognized that without this support, accomplishing its objective of a worldwide set of accounting principles was very unlikely. Thus, the final standard provided the use of LIFO as an allowed alternative.

Estimating Inventory

It might be necessary to estimate the dollar amount of inventory for several reasons. One reason is to verify the accuracy of an inventory count, particularly when a periodic system of inventory control is used and it is not possible to determine the quantity of inventory that should be on hand by referring to the inventory records. A second reason is to file an insurance claim in the event of loss, where the amount of lost inventory cannot be counted, and either a periodic inventory system is kept or the perpetual inventory records are destroyed or lost. A third reason, when using a periodic inventory system, is to be able to compute an ending inventory cost so interim financial statements[9] can be prepared without taking the time or incurring the cost of counting the inventory and computing its cost. The two accepted methods of estimating an inventory dollar amount are the gross profit percentage method and the retail method.

Gross Profit Percentage Method

As the name implies, the gross profit percentage estimation technique assumes *relative stability in the relationship between gross profit and sales* over time. In a competitive market and considering only the short run, this seems a logical assumption, as the only two ways the gross profit percentage (i.e., gross profit/sales) can be changed are either (1) to charge more for the product being sold or (2) to buy the product at a lower price. Given competitive markets, it is not logical that a business can raise prices very much without suffering loss of customers, with a possible decrease in total revenues earned. Also, given competitive markets, it is not logical that the business can purchase inventory at a considerably cheaper price without also having a loss of quality in the inventory, which again would likely result in a loss of customers and less total revenues earned. Rather, assuming competent management, it is more reasonable to suppose that the optimum price is being charged for the product sold and that the lowest price, given the quality of the inventory, is currently being paid. Thus, although small fluctuations in the gross profit percentage are expected, large changes are unusual. Given this stability, the most recent gross profit percentage or a simple average

---

[9]Interim financial statements are statements issued at any time other than the fiscal year-end.

of the gross profit percentages for several years can be used to estimate the cost of the inventory on hand.

To illustrate, suppose that Price Company needs to estimate its ending inventory amount so as to prepare its quarterly financial statements. It has compiled the information in Illustration 6-9.

ILLUSTRATION 6-9

Price Company
Income Statement
For the Quarter Ended September 2004

Net sales		$1,000,000	per the general ledger
Inventory, January 1	$160,000		per the general ledger
Purchases	510,000		per the general ledger
Cost of goods available	$670,000		
Inventory	?		number unavailable
Cost of goods sold		?	number unavailable
Gross profit		?	

At this point, the income statement cannot be completed because of the missing ending inventory number; but the cost of the ending inventory can be estimated by assuming that the gross profit percentage for this period is the same as that in the prior year. If the gross profit percentage for the prior year was 45%, the gross profit amount for the current period can be estimated by multiplying the net sales of $1,000,000 by 45%, giving $450,000. Once the gross profit is computed, the cost of goods sold is computed as the difference between net sales and gross profit, which is $550,000. Then, ending inventory of $120,000 is computed as the difference between the cost of goods available and the cost of goods sold. Finally, the rest of the income statement is completed.

Because the gross profit percentage method provides an estimate of inventory based on the cost-to-retail relationship that existed in prior periods, *it is not acceptable for year-end financial reporting purposes*. Also, when using the gross profit percentage method to estimate inventory, a separate gross profit percentage should be applied to separate classes of inventory when each class has significantly different markup rates. Finally, because the gross profit percentage is based upon historical numbers, the cost-flow assumption that was used in computing the gross profit percentage is retained in the estimation of the current inventory. That is, if the gross profit percentage is based upon last year's income statement, when a FIFO cost-flow assumption was used, then a FIFO cost-flow will be implemented in this period's estimate of inventory.

EXTENDING THE CONCEPT

Referring back to the second of the opening scenarios, the company was able to determine that its cost of inventory was too low by using the gross profit percentage method. Thus, the cost of the physical count of inventory was verified by estimating how much inventory should have been on hand. Each time, the procedure indicated that there was less inventory than there should have been. So confident was management in the estimation technique and its bookkeeping procedures that it concluded there was an inventory shortage. However, much to the chagrin of management, the bookkeeping procedures were eventually determined to be in error. This experience does not discredit the gross profit percentage method; the method is valid. However, just like any other tool, it produces valid results only when the inputs are valid—the better the inputs, the better the results. In the experience related, because the inputs were flawed, so too were the outputs and the conclusions of management.

Retail Method

The retail method of estimating inventory receives its name because it is commonly used by retail businesses, especially department stores, to determine the cost of inventory. The retail method provides a more accurate estimate of the inventory on hand than the gross profit percentage method does because it is based on the current relationship between cost and retail prices, rather than on a prior year's relationship. As a result, the method *is accepted for both year-end financial reporting and determining taxable income.* Further, the retail method is more flexible than the gross profit percentage method, in that it allows estimates of inventory to be based upon any cost-flow assumption (i.e., LIFO, FIFO, etc.), and it also allows inventory to be estimated either at cost or at the more conservative lower-of-cost-or-market. Finally, it expedites the taking of a physical inventory because the inventory can be taken at retail prices—which are readily available on each item as the inventory is counted—and then that count at retail prices can be converted to a cost number without the necessity of referring to purchase documents.

The essence of the retail method is the computing of a cost-to-retail percentage, which is the relationship between the total cost of inventory available for sale and the total retail value of the inventory available for sale. Because the retail method is based upon the relationship of current costs to current retail prices, records must be kept outside the general ledger of retail prices or the markup on cost for both the beginning inventory and the purchases of inventory for the year. In its simplest form, the sales figure is subtracted from the goods available for sale at retail, giving an ending inventory at retail figure, which then is multiplied by the cost-to-retail percentage to determine the inventory at cost.

© GETTY IMAGES, INC./PHOTODISC

The computations in Illustration 6-10 show the application of the retail method of estimating the cost of inventory on hand. Since the beginning inventory and purchases are added together to determine the cost-to-retail percentage, the preceding procedures result in an inventory cost number based upon an average cost-flow assumption.

ILLUSTRATION 6-10

Basics of Retail Method Computations

	Cost	Retail
Inventory, January 1	$36,000	$ 54,000
Purchases during period*	60,000	96,000
Goods available for sale	$96,000	$150,000
Cost-to-retail percentage, computed as ($96,000/$150,000)	64%	
Sales for the period		114,000
Ending inventory at retail		$ 36,000
Ending inventory at cost ($36,000 × 64%)	$23,040	

*Purchases includes freight and all other charges that are appropriately part of the cost of the inventory in accordance with the historical cost principle (see Chapter 5).

Conventional Retail

The preceding calculations assumed that the retailer made no changes in the retail price after the initial markup. Frequently, however, such is not the case. There are markdowns due to periodic sales, which are followed by markdown cancellations after the sale ends. Also, superior quality merchandise occasionally receives an additional markup, which may then be followed by a markup cancellation. In addition, many retailers give discounts to their employees for merchandise they buy, and the retailer also may incur spoilage, shrinkage, or other forms of inventory loss. All of these can be built into the retail method. Illustration 6-11 shows how these additional items are handled under the most commonly used method, called conventional retail.

ILLUSTRATION 6-11

Conventional Retail Method

	Cost	Retail	
Inventory, January 1	$36,000	$ 54,000	This is the initial markup to retail.
Purchases	60,000	96,000	
Additional markups		3,000	This is the additional markup on
Additional markup cancellations		(1,000)	superior quality merchandise.
Goods available for sale	$96,000	$152,000	
Cost percentage			
($96,000/$152,000)	63.2%		
Deduct sales		$ (90,000)	
Markdowns		(2,000)	This is the markdown for sales
Markdown cancellations		800	and the subsequent cancellations.
Employee discounts, spoilage, etc.		(500)	
		$ (91,700)	
Ending inventory, at retail		$ 60,300	
Ending inventory, at cost	$38,110		

Under the conventional retail method, it is important to note where in relation to the cost-to-retail percentage the various items are. So the markups and markup cancellations are placed before the cost-to-retail percentage (and thus are included in the cost-to-retail percentage calculation); whereas the markdowns, subsequent markdown cancellations, employee discounts, and inventory shrinkage are all placed after the cost percentage. Including items in this way results in valuing the ending inventory at the lower-of-cost-or-market, using an average cost-flow.[10]

Dollar-Value LIFO Retail

A LIFO cost-flow assumption can also be applied in the retail method and most commonly is done by combining the dollar-value LIFO procedures discussed earlier with the retail method procedures just illustrated. Assuming the same data and a price-level index of 105, Illustration 6-12 demonstrates the dollar-value LIFO procedures applied to the retail method.

The first thing to note in Illustration 6-12 is that two cost-to-retail percentages are computed, one for each layer of inventory. The two layers are (1) the inventory that was purchased prior to this year and (2) the inventory that was

[10]The reasons why inventory is valued on the year-end balance sheet at the lower-of-cost-or-market and the procedures for how this is done are covered in Chapter 10.

ILLUSTRATION 6-12

Retail Dollar-Value LIFO Method

	Cost	Retail	
Inventory, January 1	$36,000	$ 54,000	Prior-year cost-to-retail percentage: $36,000/$54,000 = 66.7%
Purchases	60,000	96,000 ⎫	
Additional markups		3,000 ⎪	
Markup cancellations		(1,000) ⎬	Current-year cost-to-retail percentage:
Markdowns		(2,000) ⎪	$60,000/$96,800 = 62%
Markdown cancellations		800 ⎭	
Goods available for sale	$96,000	$150,800	
Deduct sales		(90,000)	
Employee discounts, spoilage, etc.		(500)	
Ending inventory, at retail		$ 60,300	

purchased this year. Having two layers makes it possible to have various cost-flow assumptions, including being able to liquidate layers, either in a LIFO order or a FIFO order.[11] Hence, two cost-to-retail percentages are needed, one for each year.

The next thing to notice is that, unlike the conventional retail method, the markdowns and markdown cancellations are included in computing the cost-to-retail percentage for the second layer of inventory. The reason that markdowns are treated differently is that, under the conventional retail method, markdowns are not considered to reflect the normal relationship between cost and retail but rather indicate that the utility of the goods has decreased and the inventory should be written down below cost to reflect this decrease in value. However, LIFO does not consider this lower-of-cost-or-market value.

Lastly, note that the ending inventories at retail in Illustrations 6-11 and 6-12 are exactly the same. The amount of inventory on hand is not affected by the bookkeeping method used.

Having determined the cost-to-retail percentages and the ending inventory amount at retail, the dollar-value LIFO procedures are now applied as follows:

Step 1: *Determine the price-level index.* A price-level index of 105 was given.

Step 2: *Deflate ending inventory at retail.* $60,300/1.05 = $57,429.

Step 3: *Identify the layers.* Since the ending inventory at retail of $57,429 is greater than the beginning inventory at retail of $54,000, additional inventory of $3,429 was acquired during the year. Therefore, the layers are:

$54,000 which is the inventory at the beginning of the year, and
$3,429 which is the amount of inventory acquired during the current year at base-year prices.

Step 4: *Reinflate the layers.* This is done by multiplying the respective layers by the price indexes for each year, which are 1.00 and 1.05, respectively, as follows:

$54,000 × 1.00 = $54,000
$3,429 × 1.05 = $3,600

---

[11]An introduction of other cost-flow assumptions using the retail method is included in Appendix B at the end of this chapter.

Step 5: *Multiply each inventory layer by the respective cost-to-retail percentages.* This is a new step in the typical dollar-value LIFO procedures, and it is necessary to convert *ending inventory at retail* to an *ending inventory at cost* number.

$$\$54,000 \times 0.667 \text{ (from the data in Illustration 6-12)} = \$36,000$$
$$\$3,600 \times 0.620 \text{ (from the data in Illustration 6-12)} = \$2,232$$

Step 6: *Sum the various layers.* This is the ending inventory at cost, using dollar-value LIFO procedures, which is $38,232.

Liquidations of inventory and increases in inventory following a liquidation are handled in exactly the same way as shown previously in the chapter for the general dollar-value LIFO procedures. Continuing with this same company, Illustration 6-13 shows the procedures when an inventory liquidation occurs. As with previous illustrations, study each step carefully.

Evaluation of the Retail Method

Although the retail method is very accurate, an inventory count is still necessary at least once a year, and following the count, the inventory records should be ad-

ILLUSTRATION 6-13

Dollar-Value LIFO—Retail Method

	Initial Year (See previous calculations.)	1st Subsequent Year	2nd Subsequent Year
Ending inventory at retail	$60,300 (given)	$61,600 (given)	$68,000 (given)
Step 1: Index	1.05 (given)	1.1 (given)	1.12 (given)
Step 2: Deflate year-ending inventory at retail	$60,300/1.05 = $57,429	$61,600/1.10 = $56,000 Since this amount is less than the previous year, there has been an inventory liquidation.	$68,000/1.12 = $60,714
Step 3: Identify inventory layers (still at retail prices)	Base year* = $54,000 Next layer* = 3,429	Base year* = $54,000 Next layer = 2,000 (Note the LIFO order of liquidation.)	Base year* = $54,000 Next layer = 2,000 Current year = 4,714
Step 4: Reinflate inventory layers	$54,000 × 1.00 = $54,000 3,429 × 1.05 = 3,600	$54,000 × 1.00 = $54,000 2,000 × 1.05 = 2,100	$54,000 × 1.00 = $54,000 2,000 × 1.05 = 2,100 4,714 × 1.12 = 5,280
Step 5: Multiply by the respective cost-to-retail percentages to obtain ending inventory at cost	$54,000 × 0.667* = $36,000 3,600 × 0.620 = 2,232	$54,000 × 0.667* = $36,000 2,100 × 0.620* = 1,302	$54,000 × 0.667* = $36,000 2,100 × 0.620* = 1,302 5,280 × 0.650** = 3,432
Step 5: Summation	$38,232	$37,302	$40,734

*See Illustration 6-12
**Given

justed to agree with the count. As with the gross profit percentage method of estimating inventory, when there are different markups in various departments, the retail method should be applied separately to the different departments.

By including spoilage, shrinkage, and other inventory losses after the calculation of the cost-to-retail percentage in the previous examples, they are treated as normal costs of doing business. However, if the spoilage, etc., is abnormal (i.e., not anticipated), then the inventory losses should be included in calculating the cost-to-retail percentage.

Effects of Errors in Inventory on Financial Statements

A key to determining the effects of inventory errors on financial statements is remembering that the ending inventory amount is reported both on the income statement—as part of the cost of goods sold—and on the balance sheet—under current assets. Thus, an error in counting inventory affects both the income statement and the balance sheet. A second key is knowing that the error in counting inventory will affect the income statement and balance sheet accounts in such a way that the basic balance sheet equation of assets equaling liabilities plus owners' equity will still balance.

To illustrate, suppose that a company miscounted its inventory and overstated it by $1,000. Illustration 6-14 shows both what the income statement and balance sheet figures should have been and what they were because of the error.

From this illustration, it can be seen that, when ending inventory is overstated, cost of goods sold is understated and that all of the following are over-

ILLUSTRATION 6-14

Effects of Misstating Ending Inventory

	Should Have Been	Difference	As Reported
Income Statement:			
Sales	$100,000		$100,000
Inventory, January 1	$ 20,000		$ 20,000
Purchases	70,000		70,000
Cost of goods available	$ 90,000		$ 90,000
Inventory, December 31	24,000	$ 1,000	25,000
Cost of goods sold	$ 66,000	(1,000)	$ 65,000
Gross profit	$ 34,000	1,000	$ 35,000
Operating expenses	24,000		24,000
Net income	$ 10,000	1,000	$ 11,000
Balance Sheet:			
Inventory	$ 24,000	1,000	$ 25,000
Other current assets	46,000		46,000
Total current assets	$ 70,000	1,000	$ 71,000
Property, plant, and equipment	230,000		230,000
Total assets	$300,000	1,000	$301,000
Current liabilities	$ 35,000		$ 35,000
Long-term liabilities	105,000		105,000
Stock	120,000		120,000
Retained earnings	40,000	1,000	41,000
Total liabilities and stockholders' equity	$300,000	1,000	$301,000

250

stated: gross profit, net income, current assets, total assets, retained earnings, and total liabilities and stockholders' equity. Retained earnings is overstated because an overstated net income is closed to Retained Earnings. Also, note that overstating ending inventory causes working capital and the current ratio to be overstated.

This error in counting inventory at year-end also affects the following year's income statement because this year's ending inventory becomes next year's beginning inventory. However, *overstating the beginning inventory causes the net income to be understated. There are no errors on the balance sheet for the subsequent year.* This is because last year's error in counting inventory has no effect on this year's count of ending inventory, and therefore all asset account balances are correct. And, when this year's understated net income is closed to last year's overstated retained earnings, the resulting retained earnings balance is correct.

To summarize, an overstatement of an inventory count will cause net income, current assets, total assets, and retained earnings to be overstated for the current year. Also, the overstatement of inventory then causes net income for the subsequent year to be understated; but there is no other effect on any subsequent year account balance, subtotal, or total. All balance sheet numbers for the subsequent year (because of an error in counting the inventory last year) are correct. This canceling out of effects on the balance sheet in the subsequent year is what is meant by a **counterbalancing error**.

EXTENDING THE CONCEPT

Several articles have appeared on inventory fraud where companies have intentionally overstated inventory with the purpose of artificially inflating income. Assuming inventory fraud in one year but a correct inventory count the following year, how is the balance sheet affected at the end of the second year as a result of the fraud?

If unscrupulous management desires to use inventory fraud to show an increasing trend of net income, they must increasingly overstate the ending inventory. Otherwise, the inventory errors begin to counterbalance. Inventory fraud is an example of a slippery slope where, once the fraud is begun, it becomes increasingly difficult to maintain, and eventually, detection is almost inevitable. In the famous Salad Oil Swindle, Tino DeAngelis increasingly overstated ending inventory until, at one point, his reported inventory of vegetable oil supposedly was greater than the amount of vegetable oil in the entire United States.

Inventory errors can occur in ways other than miscounting the amount of inventory. All such other errors should be analyzed very closely to determine the impact on the financial statements. For example, failure to include in inventory goods that are in transit causes both inventory and accounts payable to be understated. However, net income as reported is correct. The reason that net income is correct is that the goods in transit have not been included in purchases, and so the cost of goods available number is understated by the same amount that the ending inventory count is understated. Thus, subtracting a misstated number from another equally misstated number that is opposite in direction results in a correct cost of goods sold number.

Because of the various ways in which inventory can be misstated, it is generally not a good idea to memorize the effects that a particular inventory error will have on the various account balances, subtotals, and totals on the financial statements. Rather, it is preferable to analyze each inventory error and the cause of the error to determine the impact upon the financial statement numbers.

Summary

This chapter deals with recognizing the cost of inventory as expenses, which is done according to the matching principle. In applying the matching principle, revenue is first realized, and then the cost of inventory sold is matched against it. The amount of cost recognized during a period is dependent primarily upon the cost-flow assumption but is also influenced (except for FIFO) by the inventory system used (i.e., perpetual or periodic).

The two major record-keeping systems over inventory are the periodic and the perpetual inventory control systems. Under a periodic inventory system, the amount of inventory on hand can be known only by counting it, because no entries are recorded in the inventory account, either when the goods are purchased or when they are sold. A periodic inventory system should be used only in manual accounting systems for goods that are relatively inexpensive. When a perpetual inventory control system is used, entries to the inventory account are recorded both when the goods are purchased and when they are sold. Using a perpetual inventory system makes possible the determining of inventory shrinkage caused through loss, spoilage, or other means. This is done by comparing the amount of goods on hand, as determined by counting, to the amount of inventory as reported in the general ledger. Thus, a perpetual inventory system makes it possible to determine the effectiveness of present controls to safeguard the inventory.

Different cost-flow assumptions (e.g., FIFO, LIFO, etc.) are made possible because of inventory layers, meaning that inventory items are purchased at different times and costs. The LIFO cost-flow assumption results in matching current costs against current revenues and thus reports a more relevant net income but a less relevant inventory value on the balance sheet. The results of using a FIFO cost-flow assumption are just the opposite. An average cost-flow assumption is also possible, as is a specific identification cost flow that is used when the customer determines which inventory items are sold. The cost-flow assumption selected should be the one that provides the most relevant information to the financial statement user.

Because of several difficulties in implementing a LIFO cost-flow assumption, companies that elect LIFO most commonly apply it by using dollar-value LIFO procedures. These are based on pools of inventory rather than individual units and the use of price indexes rather than unit prices.

Reasons for estimating inventory include (1) to confirm an inventory count, (2) to file an insurance claim when the inventory has been lost, stolen, or destroyed, and (3) to prepare interim financial reports. The two accepted methods of estimating inventory are the gross profit percentage method that relies on the past relationship between cost and retail prices and the retail method that relies on the current relationship between cost and retail prices. Because the retail method maintains two inventory layers, it is possible to use different cost-flow assumptions, the two most popular methods being conventional retail and dollar-value LIFO retail.

Errors in inventory can arise in various ways. All errors in inventory should be analyzed closely to determine their effects on the financial statements. Inventory errors result in the balance sheet equation of Assets = Liabilities + Owners' Equity being maintained. Thus, inventory errors affect at least two account balances. Inventory errors counterbalance, meaning that after two years, there is no longer any effect on the balance sheet account balances, subtotals, or totals.

APPENDIX A: LIFO Reserve

Companies that base their inventory records on a FIFO cost-flow assumption during the year and then switch to LIFO for financial reporting at year-end by applying the dollar-value procedures may prepare a journal entry as shown, assuming a period of rising prices:

Cost of Goods Sold	XXX	
LIFO Reserve		XXX

Illustration 6-15(A) continues the Davis Corporation example of Illustration 6-8 and the two prior years and shows how journal entries are prepared at each year-end to report a LIFO number on the financial statements.

ILLUSTRATION 6-15(A)

Summary of Inventory Values for the Dollar-Value LIFO Example

Line		Base Year	2004	2005	2006	2007
1	FIFO inventory (see line 1 on Illustration 6-8 and prior material)	$10,000	$11,200	$12,150	$11,825	$12,600
2	LIFO inventory (see Step 5 on Illustration 6-8 and prior material)		10,700	11,330	10,790	11,350
3	Balance needed in the LIFO reserve account (line 1 minus line 2)		$ 500	$ 820	$ 1,035	$ 1,250
4	Balance already in the LIFO reserve account		0	500	820	1,035
5	Adjusting journal entry amounts		$ 500	$ 320	$ 215	$ 215

Using this information, the adjusting journal entries to change Davis Corporation's books from a FIFO cost flow to a LIFO cost flow are as follows:

	2004	2005	2006	2007
Cost of Goods Sold	500	320	215	215
LIFO Reserve	500	320	215	215

To adjust the company's books so that inventory is valued at a LIFO cost in preparation to issuing the financial statements at year-end.

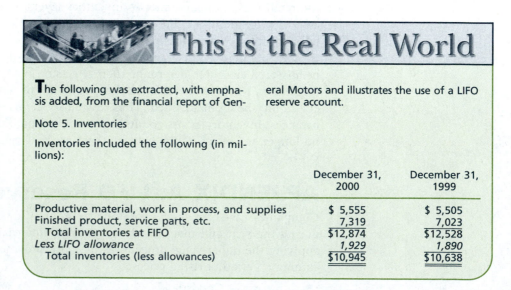

This Is the Real World

The following was extracted, with emphasis added, from the financial report of General Motors and illustrates the use of a LIFO reserve account.

Note 5. Inventories

Inventories included the following (in millions):

	December 31, 2000	December 31, 1999
Productive material, work in process, and supplies	$ 5,555	$ 5,505
Finished product, service parts, etc.	7,319	7,023
Total inventories at FIFO	$12,874	$12,528
Less LIFO allowance	1,929	1,890
Total inventories (less allowances)	$10,945	$10,638

APPENDIX B: Various Cost-Flow Assumptions under the Retail Method

As noted in the chapter, the possibility of different cost-flow assumptions (e.g., FIFO, LIFO, etc.) is based on inventory being purchased at different times for different amounts. In short, different cost-flow assumptions are possible because there is more than one inventory layer. The retail method has two inventory layers (prior-year and current-year), and so it is possible to apply different cost-flow assumptions in the retail method, as shown in Illustration 6-16(A). In reviewing Illustration 6-16(A), note that the average, lower-of-cost-or-market (LCM) method is the same as the conventional retail method shown in the chapter.

ILLUSTRATION 6-16(A)

Various Cost-Flow Assumptions

	Average Cost		Average, Lower-of-Cost-or-Market		FIFO Cost		FIFO, Lower-of-Cost-or-Market	
	Cost	Retail	Cost	Retail	Cost	Retail	Cost	Retail
Inventory, January 1	$36,000	$ 54,000	$36,000	$ 54,000	$36,000	$ 54,000	$36,000	$ 54,000
Purchases	60,000	96,000	60,000	96,000	60,000	96,000	60,000	96,000
Additional markups		3,000		3,000		3,000		3,000
Markup cancellations		(1,000)		(1,000)		(1,000)		(1,000)
Markdowns		(2,000)		NA		(2,000)		NA
Markdown cancellations		800		NA		800		NA
Goods available for sale	$96,000	$150,800	$96,000	$152,000	$96,000	$150,800	$96,000	$152,000
Cost percentage		63.7%		63.2%		62.0%		61.2%
Deduct sales		$ 90,000		$ 90,000		$ 90,000		$ 90,000
Markdowns		NA		(2,000)		NA		(2,000)
Markdown cancellations		NA		800		NA		800
Employee discounts, spoilage, etc.		(500)		(500)		(500)		(500)
Ending inventory, at retail		$ 60,300		$ 60,300		$ 60,300		$ 60,300
Ending inventory, at cost	$38,411		$38,110		$36,000		$36,000	
					3,906		3,856	
					$39,906		$39,856	

Note that using a FIFO cost-flow assumption requires that a cost-to-retail percentage be computed for each layer of inventory, as was done with dollar-value LIFO: one cost-to-retail percentage for the January 1 inventory layer and another cost-to-retail percentage for the current-year purchases, which comprises all other numbers. So for FIFO cost, the cost-to-retail percentage is computed as $60,000/($150,800 − $54,000) and the FIFO lower-of-cost-or-market cost-to-retail percentage is computed as $60,000/($152,000 − $54,000). Then, the ending inventory at retail is divided into layers and each layer multiplied by its appropriate percentage. Actually, the oldest retail layer does not need to be multiplied by a cost-to-retail percentage because the cost of that layer is already given as the cost of the beginning inventory. Thus, once the retail inventory is divided into the two layers, only the newest layer needs to be restated to cost, and that amount is added to the cost of the beginning inventory.

Note also that the only difference between the two cost methods and the two lower-of-cost-or-market methods is where markdowns and markdown cancellations are included. The LCM methods include the markdowns below the cost-to-retail percentage, whereas the cost methods do not. Finally, note that in all cases the ending inventory at retail numbers are identical, regardless of the cost-flow assumption or whether LCM procedures were applied.

Questions

1. Describe the application of the matching principle to recognizing the cost of inventory as an expense.

2. Contrast a perpetual inventory system with a periodic inventory system. Which method requires the least amount of bookkeeping? What circumstances would justify using a system that requires more record keeping (and thus a higher cost)?

3. Is it always the case that the inventory shown on the books of a perpetual inventory system equals the amount of inventory on hand? What circumstances could cause these amounts to differ?

4. Describe what is meant by a modified perpetual inventory system.

5. Indicate for each of the following questions whether they are True (T) or False (F).
   ____ Companies should choose an inventory cost-flow method that approximates the physical flow of goods.
   ____ Selecting an inventory cost-flow assumption is not a significant choice for companies, since any of them will result in similar financial statement results.
   ____ A company's inventory cost-flow assumption must be disclosed in the notes to the financial statements.
   ____ The FIFO cost-flow assumption assigns the oldest inventory costs to the income statement as cost of goods sold and the most recent inventory costs to the balance sheet.
   ____ Under the FIFO cost-flow assumption, the perpetual and periodic inventory systems give identical results for the value of inventory and for the cost of goods sold.
   ____ Under the LIFO cost-flow assumption, the perpetual and periodic inventory systems give identical results for the value of inventory and for the cost of goods sold.

6. Discuss the reasons why cost-flow assumptions, such as FIFO, are used instead of using the specific identification method. When is the specific identification method justified?

7. What is the LIFO conformity rule?

8. Describe the advantages the dollar-value LIFO procedures have over the conventional LIFO procedures.

9. What inventory cost-flow assumptions are benchmark cost-flow assumptions under IAS No. 2? How did the LIFO cost-flow assumption become an allowed alternative?

10. Assume that Thomas Corporation has beginning and ending inventory levels of $20,000 and $25,000, respectively, using FIFO. Also, assume that the beginning and ending price levels are 110 and 120, respectively. Calculate the LIFO in-

ventory layer that was created during the year and the LIFO cost of the ending inventory, using dollar-value LIFO procedures.

11. Identify some possible sources to obtain the price-level index used in the dollar-value LIFO method.

12. Anderson Co. uses dollar-value LIFO to value inventory on its balance sheet and reports inventory of $7,500. The notes to the financial statements disclose that a LIFO reserve having a $1,000 debit balance exists. What would the inventory cost have been on the balance sheet if Anderson had used FIFO to value its inventory? In general, are inventory costs for Anderson increasing or decreasing?

13. List some situations when it is necessary or may be desirable to estimate the cost of inventory. Can the ending inventory value as determined by the gross profit percentage method be used in the annual financial statements issued to the public?

14. Discuss the various ways that net markups and net markdowns are treated when using the retail method of estimating inventory.

15. When employing the conventional retail method to estimate ending inventory, indicate how the following items are used in the cost-to-retail calculation:
    a. Markups
    b. Markup cancellations
    c. Markdowns
    d. Markdown cancellations
    e. Normal spoilage and theft
    f. Abnormal spoilage and theft
    g. Discounts offered to employees

    How would your answers differ if the dollar-value retail LIFO method was used?

16. Suppose that Rieser Co. had beginning inventory of $10,000, purchases during the period of $7,500, and net sales of $25,000. Also, assume that the company's average gross profit percentage for prior years is 50%. Estimate the company's ending inventory, using the gross profit percentage method.

17. Using the information provided in question 16 and assuming that the estimated retail prices of the beginning inventory and purchases are $18,000 and $16,000, respectively, estimate the company's ending inventory, using the retail method.

18. Suppose that Howard Corporation overstated its 2004 ending inventory. How does this error affect the following items:
    a. Cost of goods sold in 2004?
    b. Net income in 2004?
    c. Cost of goods sold in 2005?
    d. Net income in 2005?
    e. Retained earnings in 2004?
    f. Retained earnings in 2005?

19. Suppose that ABC Company and XYZ Corporation operate within the same industry. The inventory turnover ratios of these two companies are 5.6 and 6.1, respectively. According to this ratio, which company manages its inventory levels more efficiently? Can the same answer be given as to which company is managing its inventory more effectively? Would your answer be different if the companies used different cost-flow assumptions (e.g., ABC used the FIFO method and XYZ used the LIFO method)?

20. Why do you suppose that the FASB allows several different inventory cost-flow assumptions? What qualitative characteristic is violated when two companies use different inventory cost-flow assumptions? What qualitative characteristic is violated when the same company changes its cost-flow assumptions?

Exercises

Exercise 6-1: LIFO versus FIFO. Over an extended period of time, the LIFO and FIFO cost-flow assumptions can result in substantially different financial statement results.

1. List the theoretical and practical advantages and disadvantages of using each cost-flow assumption relative to the other one.
2. In an inflationary economy, explain how the different cost-flow assumptions affect the income statement and balance sheet.
3. Conduct a small survey of the following companies to determine which cost-flow assumption they employ:

   U.S. Companies:
   a. International Business Machines
   b. Johnson & Johnson
   c. Bristol-Myers Squibb Co.
   d. Alcoa Inc.
   e. International Paper Co.

   Non-U.S. Companies:
   a. Sony Corporation
   b. Total Fina Elf S.A.
   c. Bayer A.G.
   d. Nokia

Exercise 6-2: Journalizing Transactions. Hardaway Corporation incurred the following transactions during 2004:

Sept. 2 Ordered $15,000 of inventory, FOB shipping point, with terms of 2/10, net 30.
  5 Hardaway received the merchandise ordered on September 2 and paid $1,000 for shipping.
  11 Ordered $12,000 of inventory, FOB destination, with terms of 1/10, net 60.
  12 Paid the invoice for the September 2 order of inventory, less the stipulated discount.
  15 Hardaway received the merchandise ordered on September 11.
  30 Paid the invoice for the September 11 order of inventory.

1. Journalize the above transactions, assuming that Hardaway Corporation uses a periodic inventory system and records all purchases at the (a) gross amount and (b) net amount.
2. Assume that Hardaway's fiscal year ends on September 30, the company's beginning and ending inventories are $37,000 and $41,000, respectively, and the balance in the purchases and the freight-in accounts are $300,000 and $9,000, respectively. Considering only these accounts, prepare the necessary adjusting entry that must be made with respect to the preceding transactions.
3. When using the net method, where is the balance in the purchase discounts lost account reported?

Exercise 6-3: Percentage Markups.

1. CPI, Inc., purchased inventory for $22,000 and sold the inventory at an 80% markup on cost. Calculate the selling price of the inventory, the gross profit, and the gross profit percentage.
2. Goods-in-the-Attic, Inc., purchased inventory for $325 and sold it for $540. What is the inventory markup expressed as a percentage of cost? What is the inventory markup expressed as a percentage of selling price? What is the gross profit percentage?
3. ABC Corporation's gross profit percentage last year was 23%. Determine ABC Corporation's inventory markup as a percentage of cost.

Exercise 6-4: Inventory Valuation.
The following purchases and sales transactions occurred during the month of November for L&L Industries:

Purchases	Sales
Nov. 1 300 units @ $4.00 (opening balance)	Nov. 4 100 units @ $8.00
Nov. 7 500 units @ $4.25	Nov. 6 100 units @ $9.00
Nov. 16 400 units @ $4.30	Nov. 9 200 units @ $8.50
Nov. 21 300 units @ $4.40	Nov. 11 100 units @ $9.00
Nov. 28 400 units @ $4.50	Nov. 17 300 units @ $8.50
	Nov. 20 100 units @ $9.00
	Nov. 22 150 units @ $9.50
	Nov. 25 250 units @ $9.25

1. Assume that L&L Industries uses a periodic inventory system. Compute the ending inventory and the cost of goods sold under each of the following inventory cost-flow assumptions:
   a. FIFO
   b. LIFO
   c. Average cost
2. Repeat part (1), assuming that L&L Industries uses a perpetual inventory system.

Exercise 6-5: Inventory Valuation—Six Cost-Flow Assumptions.
Sporty Dog Co. is a seller of pets and pet supplies. The beginning inventory of dog collars in the month of February was 20 units at a cost of $3.00 per unit. The following sales and purchase transactions were made by Sporty Dog Co. for the month of February.

Date	Transaction	No. of Units	Unit Cost	Selling Price
Feb. 2	Purchase	100	$3.10	
3	Sale	10		$7.00
5	Sale	20		7.00
8	Sale	50		7.00
10	Purchase	50	3.20	
12	Sale	40		7.25
15	Sale	20		7.25
20	Purchase	70	3.50	
21	Sale	25		7.30
23	Sale	35		7.50
25	Purchase	20	3.40	
27	Sale	30		7.50
28	Purchase	20	3.45	

1. Using the given information, compute the cost of goods sold and the cost of inventory for Sporty Dog under each of the following scenarios:
    a. FIFO method using a periodic inventory system
    b. FIFO method using a perpetual inventory system
    c. LIFO method using a periodic inventory system
    d. LIFO method using a perpetual inventory system
    e. Weighted-average method using a periodic inventory system
    f. Moving-average method using a perpetual inventory system
2. Which of these methods results in the highest net income? Which method results in the lowest inventory on the balance sheet? Which method requires the most record keeping?

Exercise 6-6: Inventory Valuation—Net Method, Periodic System. Franklin Co. uses a periodic inventory system. The beginning inventory of Item No. 725 was 1,400 units at a net cost of $7.00 per unit. The following information was obtained from the purchasing department of Franklin Co. for the 2004 annual period:

Date	Units Purchased	Cost per Unit	Payment Terms
Jan. 10	1,500	$7.50	2/10, net 30
Apr. 17	2,000	7.25	1/10, net 60
July 7	1,000	7.60	2/15, net 30
Sept. 20	1,200	7.75	net 60
Oct. 5	2,500	8.10	3/10, net 45

All purchases are recorded at the net amounts, and all discounts were taken, except for the October 5 purchase. Total sales for the period were 8,400 units.

Compute the ending inventory that would be presented on the balance sheet and the cost of goods sold on the income statement, using the following cost-flow assumptions:

1. FIFO
2. LIFO
3. Weighted-average

Exercise 6-7: Inventory Valuation—Net Method, Perpetual System. Repeat the requirements of Exercise 6-6, assuming that Franklin uses a perpetual inventory system. Also assume that all sales for the month were shipped FOB shipping point at the end of the month and total sales for each month were 700 units.

Exercise 6-8: Dollar-Value LIFO. Lewis adopted the dollar-value LIFO inventory method on December 31, 2004. Lewis's entire inventory consisted of one pool, and the inventory value on December 31, 2004, was $200,000, and the price index was 100. At the end of 2005, the value of the ending inventory at base-year prices was $210,000, and the price index was 105. At the end of 2006, the value of the ending inventory at current-year prices was $247,250, and the price index was 115.

Using dollar-value LIFO procedures, compute the value of Lewis's inventory at December 31, 2006.

Exercise 6-9: Dollar-Value LIFO. On January 1, 2004, Barnes Company adopted the dollar-value LIFO inventory method. The inventory, which consists of a single pool, was valued on that date at $140,000. Inventory data for the years ended December 31, 2004 through 2006, are as follows:

Year Ended	Inventory at End-of-Year Prices	Price Index
December 31, 2004	$146,000	104
December 31, 2005	156,400	110.5
December 31, 2006	165,300	112.5

Compute the value of the ending inventory, using dollar-value LIFO procedures, for the years 2004 through 2006.

Exercise 6-10: Dollar-Value LIFO—Internal Price Index. Jacob's Toybox is a retail outlet for baby toys. Dollar-value LIFO was adopted at the beginning of 2004 for inventory valuation, and the following information was gathered for a pool of inventory:

	Base-Year Cost	Current-Year Cost
January 1, 2004	$100,000	$100,000
December 31, 2004	120,000	140,000
December 31, 2005	125,000	180,000
December 31, 2006	115,000	200,000

1. Calculate an internal price index for each of the years ended 2004, 2005, and 2006. (Round the index to three decimals.)
2. Determine the value of inventory that should be shown on the balance sheets for each year, using the dollar-value LIFO method.

Exercise 6-11: Dollar-Value LIFO—External Price Index. Memory Lane, Inc., sells gifts and scrapbook and stationery supplies. The company uses FIFO for financial reporting purposes and then converts to LIFO by applying dollar-value LIFO procedures at year-end, using one cost pool. The following information is related to the company's inventory.

		Current Value of:	
	Gifts	Scrapbooks and Stationery	Price Index
January 1, 2004	$ 82,000	$ 56,000	100
December 31, 2004	95,000	52,000	120
December 31, 2005	101,000	87,000	140
December 31, 2006	126,000	99,000	145
December 31, 2007	110,000	115,000	155
December 31, 2008	118,000	120,000	170

1. Determine the ending inventory for Memory Lane, Inc., using dollar-value LIFO procedures for the years 2004–2008.
2. **(Appendix)** Prepare a table similar to the one in Appendix I that shows the adjusting entry amounts for each year 2004–2008 to adjust the general ledger of Memory Lane, Inc., and report LIFO numbers on the financial statements.

Exercise 6-12: Gross Profit Percentage Method of Estimating Inventory. Jensen & Sons accounting records indicate the following:

Inventory, January 1, 2004	$ 500,000
Net purchases during 2004	2,000,000
Sales during 2004	3,200,000

A physical inventory taken on December 31, 2004, showed that the value of inventory on hand was $550,000. Jensen's gross profit on sales consistently has been 40%. Compute the amount of inventory that apparently was lost or stolen during the year.

Exercise 6-13: Gross Profit Percentage Method of Estimating Inventory. Alleycat Enterprises sells various inventory items to retail stores in the southwest. On April 1, 2004, a tornado caused the roof of a warehouse to collapse, resulting in a total loss of stored inventory items. For insurance purposes, the company gathered the following information to estimate the amount of the loss:

	For the Year		
	2001	2002	2003
Sales	$1,078,000	$1,305,000	$1,698,000
Cost of sales	501,000	689,000	848,000
Gross profit	$ 577,000	$ 616,000	$ 850,000

Beginning inventory as of January 1, 2004	$169,000
Purchases for the year	312,000
Sales for the first quarter of 2004	479,000

1. Provide an estimate for the inventory losses incurred by Alleycat as a result of the tornado.
2. Instead of assuming a total loss, assume that sales for the first quarter were $500,000, and that $20,000 of the goods reported as inventory were located elsewhere. Determine the amount of the loss.

Exercise 6-14: Retail Method of Estimating Inventory. Callister Clothing Company uses the retail method to estimate its inventory when preparing interim financial statements. Data relating to computing the value of the ending inventory at cost for September 30, 2004, are as follows:

	Cost	Retail
Inventory, January 1, 2004	$220,000	$ 500,000
Purchases	900,000	2,350,000
Freight-in	20,000	
Sales		2,140,000
Markdowns		20,000

Compute the cost of the ending inventory, using the lower-of-cost-or-market retail method (i.e., conventional retail).

Exercise 6-15: Retail Method of Estimating Inventory. Shorty Shirttails Co. sells men's clothing and prepares interim financial statements based on the retail method of accounting for inventory. The following information was gathered from the accounting records for the first quarter of 2004:

	Cost	Retail
Beginning inventory	$63,000	$104,000
Purchases for the year	89,000	146,000
Sales for the year		154,000

1. What is the company's cost-to-retail ratio for the year 2004?
2. Compute the company's cost of ending inventory to be shown on the quarterly balance sheet.
3. Compute the company's cost-of-goods-sold for the first quarter of 2004.

Exercise 6-16: Retail Method of Estimating Inventory. The following information relates to the operations of Shelley's Attic Co., a retailer of women's clothing.

	Cost	Retail
Inventory, January 1, 2004	$124,000	$189,000
Purchases	252,000	378,000
Purchase returns	(25,000)	
Net markups		17,000
Net markdowns		39,000
Employee discounts		16,000
Sales		435,000

1. Estimate the ending inventory, using the conventional retail method.
2. Estimate the ending inventory, using the retail LIFO method and assuming that the beginning inventory consists of the base-year layer when the price index was 100 and the end-of-the-year price index is 105.
3. Redo parts (1) and (2), assuming that sales are $300,000 rather than $435,000.

Exercise 6-17: Inventory Errors. Andy Inc. uses a periodic inventory system and takes a physical count of inventory only at the end of each year. When counting the inventory for 2003, the following events occurred.

a. Merchandise in transit (FOB destination) from Andy's warehouse to the retail store was excluded from the physical count.
b. Merchandise in transit (FOB shipping point) from a supplier was excluded from the physical count but correctly recorded as a purchase.
c. Merchandise received (FOB destination) was included in the physical count but not recorded as a purchase since the invoice had not yet arrived.
d. Merchandise returned by a customer was received on December 30 but was not included in the physical count and was not recorded in the books as a sales return.

Indicate how each of the above errors affects the ending inventory, income before taxes, total assets, and retained earnings for the years 2003 and 2004.

Exercise 6-18: Inventory Errors. Jackson, Inc., uses a periodic inventory system. At the end of each annual period, Jackson takes a physical count of inventory to determine the cost of goods sold for the period. Net income for the years 2003–2005 follows.

Year	Net Income
2003	$222,000
2004	238,000
2005	237,000

The ending inventory for each year was taken without knowledge of the following events:

a. Merchandise with a cost of $15,000 was shipped FOB shipping point and was in transit as of December 31, 2003. The purchase was recorded in 2003, but the merchandise was not included in the physical count.

b. The inventory count for 2004 included inventory that was held on consignment on behalf of Roberts Corporation. The inventory was valued at $5,000.

c. The 2005 count of inventory was understated by $7,000.

d. Merchandise with a cost of $22,000 was shipped to a customer on December 28, 2005, and was still in transit at December 31, 2005. This merchandise was not included in the ending inventory physical count. The shipping terms were FOB shipping point.

1. Compute the correct amount of net income for each year.
2. Make the necessary adjusting entry at the end of 2005, based on the given information and assume that the books for 2005 have been closed.

Exercise 6-19: Inventory Errors. During the first years of operations, the employees of Pawn Company made several errors in taking and computing the ending inventory value. In addition, purchases of inventory that were in transit at the end of each year were not always accounted for correctly. From the following net income figures that were reported and the inventory and purchase errors that were discovered, compute the revised net income figures.

Description	2004	2005	2006
Net income, as reported	$ 5,000	$10,000	$14,000
Overstate (understate) ending inventory	(3,000)	1,000	10,000
Purchases FOB destination that were not journalized or included in inventory	2,000	4,000	8,000
Purchases FOB shipping point that were not journalized or included in inventory	5,000	2,000	1,000

Exercise 6-20: Inventory Errors. Christensen Corp. uses a periodic inventory system, and at the end of 2004, the general ledger showed the following balances:

Inventory	$120,000
Accounts receivable	90,000
Accounts payable	45,000
Sales	450,000
Net purchases	180,000

During an audit of the company's accounting records, the following data were found:

a. The count of ending inventory showed a value of $75,000 on hand.

b. Merchandise that cost $1,000 shipped FOB shipping point on December 28, 2004, and received on January 3, 2005, was not included in the December 31, 2004 inventory. However, the purchase was recorded in the general ledger for 2004.

c. Merchandise that cost $1,500 and was segregated in the warehouse awaiting shipment was not included in the December 31, 2004 inventory because there was a "tentative order by phone." A sale of $3,000 was recorded for 2004.

d. Merchandise costing $6,000 that was received on consignment was excluded from the count of ending inventory.

e. Merchandise that cost $2,500 and received on January 5, 2005, was excluded from the 2004 ending inventory, and the purchase was not recorded in the general ledger for 2004. The shipping documents indicate the merchandise had been shipped prior to the end of 2004, with terms FOB shipping point.

f. Merchandise that cost $2,000 was sold on December 31, 2004, but was not shipped until January 2, 2005. A sale was recorded in 2004, and the merchandise inventory was also included in the December 31, 2004 count of inventory.

g. Merchandise that cost $3,000 was included in the count of the ending inventory on December 31, 2004, although an inspection had shown that it did not meet the company's specifications and was going to be returned. Approval had been received from the supplier to return the merchandise for a full refund. The purchase had not been recorded.

1. Prepare a worksheet with one column for each of the five general ledger accounts. Recompute the correct balance for each of the accounts.
2. Prepare a journal entry to correct the accounts, assuming that the general ledger has not been closed for 2004.

Problems

Problem 6-1: Inventory Issues.

Required:
Answer each of the following questions.

1. Ishmael Corporation made various purchases of inventory on December 30, 2003. Inventory Item A was shipped FOB destination, and inventory Item B was shipped FOB shipping point. Neither shipment had arrived at Ishmael's warehouse by the end of the year. When should Ishmael record the purchase of each inventory item and include the inventory items in its end-of-year balance sheet?
2. Fujimoto Co. received inventory on December 29, 2003, via train. The shipping terms were FOB destination. The common carrier required Fujimoto to sign a receiving document, but since Fujimoto did not want to include the inventory in its end-of-year balance sheet, the goods were not unloaded from the train car until after the end of the year. When should Fujimoto record the purchase of the inventory? Would your answer change if the reason Fujimoto did not unload the train car was because it didn't have room in the warehouse? Would your answer change if Fujimoto had stipulated that it did not want the inventory delivered until after the end of the year?
3. Haywood Industries purchased inventory with an invoice cost of $2,000. Payment terms were 2/10, net 30. Discuss the theoretical arguments for recording the inventory at the gross invoice cost or net of the early payment discount. Assume that Haywood intended to forgo the early payment discount.
4. Harriston Corporation received goods and signed the appropriate receiving document on December 23, 2003. However, the goods were not exactly what had been ordered, and Harriston intends on returning the goods in exchange for other items. Due to the holiday rush and end-of-year procedures, Harriston did not return the items until January 5, 2004. Should the items be included in Harriston's ending inventory for 2003?

Problem 6-2: Inventory Cost-Flow Assumptions. Computer Universe, Inc., sells customized computer systems to companies and individuals. The company was organized and began operations during 2003. The following information relates to purchases and sales of inventory Item No. 4112 for the years 2003 and 2004:

	Purchases	Sales
2003— 1st quarter	5 units @ $300	2 units
2nd quarter	18 units @ $320	15 units
3rd quarter	25 units @ $300	20 units
4th quarter	23 units @ $290	30 units
2004— 1st quarter	35 units @ $275	26 units
2nd quarter	22 units @ $250	30 units
3rd quarter	10 units @ $220	12 units
4th quarter	2 units @ $150	3 units

Required:

1. Assume that Computer Universe uses a periodic inventory system. Compute the number of units and the cost of the ending inventory for 2003 and 2004, using the following inventory cost-flow assumptions:
   a. FIFO
   b. LIFO
   c. Average cost
2. Redo Requirement (1), assuming that Computer Universe uses a perpetual inventory system, and all purchases are made the first day of each quarter.
3. Compare the results from Requirements (1) and (2). Which method results in the highest net income at the end of the two years? Explain these results.

Problem 6-3: Alternative LIFO Methods. Harry Cooper runs a small business that sells various items on a retail basis to customers. Harry has heard about the income tax benefits associated with LIFO inventory and has decided to adopt some convention of LIFO. Harry's beginning inventory for the first quarter of 2004 was 6,400 units at a cost of $32,000. The following transactions occurred during the first quarter:

Date	Purchases	Sales
Jan. 3	500 units @ $5.00	
Jan. 4–Feb. 10		2,200 units @ $9.50
Feb. 10	2,200 units @ $5.07	
Feb. 10–22		2,500 units @ $9.55
Feb. 23	800 units @ $5.10	
Feb. 24–Mar. 9		1,500 units @ $9.70
Mar. 10	1,500 units @ $5.25	
Mar. 11–Mar. 15		500 units @ $9.70
Mar. 16	2,000 units @ $5.50	
Mar. 17–Mar. 31		2,200 units @ $9.95

The sales price of the item at January 1 was $9.50, and the cost to replace the item on March 31 was $5.50.

Required:

1. Calculate ending inventory, using the following LIFO conventions:
   a. Conventional LIFO, using a periodic inventory system.
   b. Conventional LIFO, using a perpetual inventory system.
   c. Dollar-value LIFO method, where the price index at the beginning of the quarter is 1.00, and an internal price index for the quarter is calculated by comparing the end-of-quarter unit price of inventory with the beginning-of-quarter price.

 d. Dollar-value retail LIFO method. Use the same price index as computed in (c). (*Hint:* To compute the retail value of the purchases, use the sales price that was realized immediately subsequent to each purchase.)
 2. Explain the advantages of using one of the dollar-value LIFO methods.

Problem 6-4: Dollar-Value LIFO—Inventory Liquidations. Jones Retail Outlet Store has used the dollar-value LIFO method to value its inventory for several years. The following information relates to the company's operations:

	2004	2005	2006	2007
Ending inventory, using FIFO	$27,000	$41,000	$38,000	$50,000
Price index	1.80	1.90	1.95	2.10

The ending inventory in 2003, using dollar-value LIFO, consisted of the following layers:

	Base-Year Prices	Index	Dollar-Value LIFO
Base-year layer	$ 9,000	1.00	$ 9,000
Layer created in 2002	3,000	1.40	4,200
Layer created in 2003	1,175	1.60	1,880
Total	$13,175		$15,080

Required:
 1. Determine the ending inventory as of December 31, 2003, if Jones had used FIFO to value its inventory.
 2. Calculate the company's ending inventory, using dollar-value LIFO, for the years 2004–2007.

Problem 6-5: Dollar-Value LIFO—Multiple Products. The following information is related to inventory for Jordan's Jewelers, a manufacturer of fine jewelry. The company adopted dollar-value LIFO as of January 1, 2004, when inventory was $200,000 for diamond rings, $70,000 for ruby rings, and $35,000 for emerald rings.

Inventory Item	Ending Inventory in Units	Base-Year Cost Cost/Unit	Base-Year Cost Total	Current Cost Cost/Unit	Current Cost Total
As of December 31, 2004:					
Diamond rings	350	$600	$210,000	$650	$227,500
Ruby rings	225	300	67,500	310	69,750
Emerald rings	125	250	31,250	230	28,750
As of December 31, 2005:					
Diamond rings	375	$600	$225,000	$690	$258,750
Ruby rings	235	300	70,500	365	85,775
Emerald rings	110	250	27,500	275	30,250
As of December 31, 2006:					
Diamond rings	325	$600	$195,000	$720	$234,000
Ruby rings	230	300	69,000	360	82,800
Emerald rings	120	250	30,000	300	36,000

Required:

Assume that the company uses a single inventory pool and calculates an internal price index based on the double-extension method. Compute the ending inventory that should be shown on the balance sheet for Jordan's Jewelers for the years 2004–2006.

Problem 6-6: Gross Profit Percentage Method. Rose Gardens, Inc., is preparing quarterly financial statements for the first quarter of 2004. Inventory is estimated by using the gross profit percentage method. The following information was obtained:

Gross sales during first quarter	$545,000
Sales returns during first quarter	19,000
Inventory December 31, 2003	63,000
Purchases	453,000
Purchase returns	21,000

Required:

Calculate the estimated cost of goods sold and ending inventory for the period, assuming that the historical gross profit percentage rate is:

1. 20%
2. 25%
3. 40%

Problem 6-7: Conventional and Dollar-Value Retail LIFO Method. McMillan Corporation adopted the dollar-value retail LIFO method for inventory valuation in the year 2004. The price index used by McMillan was based on the change in CPI for the year. Other information related to McMillan's operations is as follows.

	Cost	Retail
Beginning inventory	$22,000	$ 40,000
Purchases	89,000	168,000
Net markups		10,000
Net markdowns		38,000
Sales		160,000
CPI as of January 1, 2004	310	
CPI as of December 31, 2004	341	

Required:

1. Compute McMillan's ending inventory at cost, using the conventional retail method.
2. Compute McMillan's ending inventory at cost, using the dollar-value LIFO retail method.
3. Compute the ending inventory at cost again under the conventional retail and dollar-value LIFO retail methods assuming that sales for the period were $120,000.

Problem 6-8: Conventional Retail and Dollar-Value Retail LIFO Method (Continuation of Problem 6-7). Information related to McMillan Corporation's 2005 transactions is as follows.

	Cost	Retail
Purchases	$95,000	$180,000
Net markups		5,000
Net markdowns		18,000
Sales		155,000
CPI as of December 31, 2005	392	

Required:
Using the information from Problem 6-7, when sales were $160,000 for 2004, compute McMillan's ending inventory at cost for the year ended December 31, 2005, using both the conventional retail and the dollar-value LIFO retail methods.

Problem 6-9: Dollar-Value Retail LIFO Method. Outdoor Fitters, Inc., is a retail store that sells various types of hunting and camping apparel. The company uses the dollar-value retail method for financial reporting purposes, and its inventory as of January 1, 2006 (which is the same as December 31, 2005), *stated in end-of-year 2005 prices*, consists of three LIFO layers, as follows:

	Cost	Retail
Layer #1—acquired in base year 2003	$56,000	$106,000
Layer #2—acquired in year 2004	15,000	27,000
Layer #3—acquired in year 2005	21,000	34,000
Total	$92,000	$167,000

The price indexes as of December 31 for each year are as follows:

Year	Price Index
2003	125
2004	135
2005	150
2006	155

Transaction data for 2006 are as follows:

	Cost	Retail
Purchases	$232,000	$441,000
Purchase discounts	2,500	
Purchase returns	8,200	13,000
Markups		22,000
Markup cancellations		7,000
Markdowns		35,000
Markdown cancellations		9,000
Normal spoilage and theft		13,000
Employee discounts		10,000
Sales		420,000

Required:
1. With the retail price of the beginning inventory at end-of-year 2005 prices being $167,000, compute the retail price of the beginning inventory at base-year prices.

268

Chapter 6

2. Using the values computed in Requirement (1), compute the dollar-value LIFO retail amounts for each year by reinflating the values by the appropriate indexes.
3. Using the values computed in Requirement (2), compute the dollar-value LIFO retail amounts at cost for each year by multiplying by the cost-to-retail percentages.
4. Using the information for the current year and your answers to Requirements (2) and (3), calculate the December 31, 2006 inventory, at cost, for Outdoor Fitters.

Problem 6-10: Retail Method Using Various Cost-Flow Assumptions (Appendix).
Bryan's Fishing Things, Inc., is investigating the effects of using different retail methods for valuing inventory. The following information pertains to the operations of the company for the first half of 2004:

	Cost	Retail
Beginning inventory	$23,000	$ 45,000
Purchases	92,000	170,000
Net markups		7,000
Net markdowns		18,000
Employee discounts		2,000
Normal theft and damage		11,000
Sales		150,000

The CPI for the year was 1.05.

Required:
For Bryan's Fishing Things, calculate the ending inventory at retail and at cost, using the following cost-flow assumptions:

a. average cost,
b. average, lower-of-cost-or-market,
c. FIFO, and
d. FIFO, lower-of-cost-or-market.

Research Activities

Activity 6-1: Purchase Commitments. To guarantee future prices, companies frequently enter into contractual arrangements to purchase specified quantities of merchandise at guaranteed prices. Between the time of entering into such contracts and the date of delivery of the merchandise, it is possible that the price of the merchandise has declined. In other words, the company would have gotten a better price if it had not entered into such a contractual arrangement. But having done so, delivery must be accepted and payment made. When such occurs, has the company incurred a loss? Research generally accepted accounting principles and summarize the appropriate accounting for such purchase commitments. Consider in your answer the case when the market price increases above the contracted purchase price.

Activity 6-2: Comparing Accounting Practices for Inventory. The inventory flow assumptions used by companies can have a significant effect on the amount of inventory that is reported on the balance sheet and the net income that is reported on the income statement. Generally accepted accounting principles (GAAP) can vary across countries with respect to what inventory valuation alternatives companies are allowed to employ.

Research the inventory flow assumption alternatives allowed by the following list of countries and summarize your findings in a table. Possible sources of information are the Internet and PricewaterhouseCoopers' *Doing Business In . . .* books.

a. United Kingdom
b. Japan
c. Germany
d. France
e. Brazil
f. Australia

Cases

Case 6-1: Boise Cascade Corporation. Boise Cascade Corporation is a major distributor of office products and building materials and an integrated manufacturer and distributor of paper and wood products. The company owns and manages over two million acres of timberland in the United States and is headquartered in Boise, Idaho, with domestic and international operations.

The following excerpt is from Boise Cascade's 1998 annual report:

INVENTORY VALUATION. The company uses the last-in, first-out (LIFO) method of inventory valuation for raw materials and finished goods inventories at substantially all of our domestic wood products and paper manufacturing facilities. In 1998, our building products segment reduced certain inventory quantities that were valued at lower LIFO costs prevailing in prior years. The effect of this reduction was to increase operating income by approximately $6,100,000. All other inventories are valued at the lower-of-cost-or-market method, with cost based on the average or first-in, first-out (FIFO) valuation method.

Manufactured inventories include costs for materials, labor, and factory overhead. Inventories include the following:

	December 31,	
	1998	**1997**
	(expressed in thousands)	
Finished goods and work in process	$456,577	$453,268
Logs	87,688	107,625
Other raw materials and supplies	145,319	149,870
LIFO reserve	(64,366)	(77,473)
	$625,218	$633,290

The company reported the following results in its income statement:

| | December 31, | |
	1998	1997
	(expressed in millions)	
Sales	$6,162	$5,494
Total operating costs	6,021	5,386
Equity in net income (loss) of affiliates	(4)	(5)
Operating profit	137	102
Net income	(37)	(30)

Required:

1. Explain what the term "LIFO reserve" means, and the typical journal entry to record it.
2. Restate operating profit for 1998, assuming that Boise Cascade used the FIFO cost-flow assumption instead of LIFO since inception.
3. Assuming that Boise Cascade's marginal tax rate was 40%, compute the tax effect of using LIFO instead of FIFO for 1998.
4. During 1998, was the cost of inventory for Boise Cascade increasing or decreasing?

Case 6-2: Harley-Davidson Inc. The current asset and current liabilities section of Harley-Davidson Inc., as obtained from the company's 1999 annual report, follows along with the financial statement note that discusses inventories. Harley-Davidson's sales for the years ended 1999 and 1998 were $2,453 million and $2,064 million, respectively.

HARLEY-DAVIDSON, INC.
CONSOLIDATED BALANCE SHEETS
(In thousands, except share amounts)

| | December 31, | |
	1999	1998
ASSETS		
Current assets:		
Cash and cash equivalents	$183,415	$165,170
Accounts receivable, net	101,708	113,417
Current portion of finance receivables, net	440,951	360,341
Inventories	168,616	155,616
Deferred income taxes	29,434	29,076
Prepaid expenses	24,870	21,343
Total current assets	$948,994	$844,963
LIABILITIES AND SHAREHOLDERS' EQUITY		
Current liabilities:		
Accounts payable	$137,660	$122,722
Accrued and other liabilities	199,331	199,051
Current portion of finance debt	181,163	146,742
Total current liabilities	$518,154	$468,515

NOTE 1. SUMMARY OF SIGNIFICANT ACCOUNTING POLICIES (continued)
INVENTORIES—Inventories are valued at lower-of-cost-or-market. Substantially all inventories located in the United States are valued using the last-in, first-out

(LIFO) method. Other inventories, totaling $40.9 million in 1999 and $43.7 million in 1998, are valued at lower-of-cost-or-market, using the first-in, first-out (FIFO) method.

NOTE 2. ADDITIONAL BALANCE SHEET AND CASH FLOW INFORMATION (continued)

	December 31,	
	1999	**1998**
	(In thousands)	
Inventories:		
Components at the lower of FIFO cost or market:		
Raw materials and work in process	$ 61,893	$ 55,336
Motorcycle finished goods	29,977	27,295
Parts and accessories and general merchandise	97,422	93,710
	$189,292	$176,341
Excess of FIFO over LIFO cost	20,676	20,725
	$168,616	$155,616

Required:

1. Calculate the working capital, current ratio, and quick ratio for Harley-Davidson for the years 1999 and 1998. Comment on the usefulness of these ratios.
2. What percentage of Harley's inventories is valued using LIFO, and what percentage is valued using FIFO? Why do you suppose that Harley uses the LIFO method for U.S. inventories but not for non-U.S. inventories?
3. How would the ratios computed in Requirement (1) change if Harley valued all of its inventories using FIFO?
4. Discuss the effects that LIFO has had on Harley's balance sheet and income statement over the life of the company.

Case 6-3: Ingersoll-Rand Company. Ingersoll-Rand Company is a diversified multi-national company that produces a wide array of products, including air compressors, electric- and gas-powered golf carts, power-operated doors, precision-bearing products, and many more. Information from the company's 1997 annual report is provided. Ingersoll-Rand uses the LIFO valuation method for some of its inventories.

Financial Highlights
(*At and for the years ended December 31*)

	1997	1996
Net sales	$7,103.3	$6,702.9
Earnings before income taxes	$613.7	$568.3
Provision for income taxes	$233.2	$210.3
Net earnings	$380.5	$358.0
Basic earnings per common share	$2.33	$2.22
Dividends per common share	$0.57	$0.52
Average number of common shares outstanding	163.2	161.2
Expenditures for property, plant, and equipment	$186.0	$195.0
Depreciation and amortization	$212.3	$202.6
Number of shareholders	12,109	12,884
Number of employees	46,567	41,874

(*All dollar and share amounts in millions except per share data*)

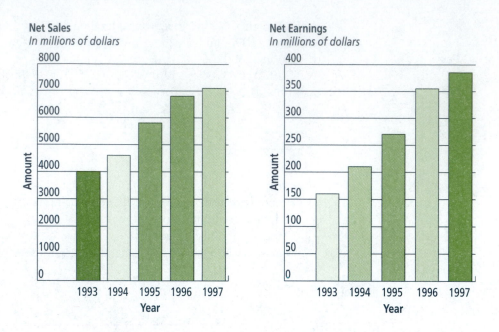

Net Sales
In millions of dollars

Net Earnings
In millions of dollars

NOTE 4. Inventories.
At December 31, inventories were as follows:

In millions	1997	1996
Raw materials and supplies	$ 174.1	$156.2
Work-in-process	218.6	238.7
Finished goods	613.8	538.1
	1,006.5	933.0
Less-LIFO reserve	151.7	157.9
Total	$ 854.8	$775.1

Work-in-process inventories are stated after deducting customer progress payments of $17.8 million in 1997 and $24.9 million in 1996. At December 31, 1997 and 1996, LIFO inventories comprised approximately 40% and 43%, respectively, of consolidated inventories.

During the periods presented, certain inventory quantities were reduced, resulting in partial liquidations of LIFO layers. This decreased cost of goods sold by $4.1 million in 1997, $4.8 million in 1996, and $3.4 million in 1995. These liquidations increased net earnings in 1997, 1996, and 1995 by approximately $2.5 million, $2.9 million, and $2.1 million, respectively.

Required:
1. Evaluate the company's financial performance based on what was reported in the financial statements, with particular focus on the EPS growth percentage.
2. In compliance with FASB requirements, the inventory note refers to LIFO liquidations that occurred in 1995–1997. How did these liquidations affect earnings and gross profit for the years reported in both absolute and percentage terms? Based on this information, what was Ingersoll-Rand's marginal tax rate?

3. Discuss the cumulative effect of the three years' LIFO liquidations on cash flows.
4. In your opinion, were the LIFO liquidations realized by Ingersoll-Rand material? Why do you suppose that the FASB requires companies to disclose the effects of LIFO liquidations on earnings?

7

*M*atching Principle: Immediate Recognition AND Systematic AND Rational Allocation

On September 28, 1999, Amazon.com announced that on the following morning it would make a statement that would significantly affect the e-commerce world. Based on that announcement, the stock market during that day's trading boosted Amazon.com's value by $1.5 billion. At nine the next morning, in a room crammed with reporters and analysts, Jeff Bezos, the CEO of Amazon.com, stepped to the riser and declared that the future Amazon.com would be the "place where you can buy anything." Bezos's vision for Amazon.com is that it will be the center of the e-commerce universe. To that goal, Amazon.com subsequently acquired 46% of Drugstore.com, 35% of HomeGrocer.com, 54% of Pets.com, and 49% of Grear.com, and it launched other on-line auctions. Because of its expansion efforts, operating expenses grew by 252% to $869 million. Amazingly, Amazon.com had never made a profit for any year of its existence. Yet, opinions about Amazon.com could be categorized into two groups of people. One group thought, "Oh no, its not profitable!"

And the second group believed in Amazon.com's strategy of building market share and did not worry about its continuing losses.

Questions

1. Is Amazon.com growing a business in which assets should be recorded for some of the $869 million that was being expensed? Or was Amazon.com incurring large losses that were being camouflaged by Wall Street hype?

2. Is it always possible to tell whether an expenditure should be recorded as an asset or an expense?

3. Is determining whether an expenditure should be recorded as an asset or as an expense contingent upon the expectations of management? That is, if management thinks the expenditure will result in future benefits, should it be recorded as an asset? If so, is a principal function of accounting the reporting of management's expectations?

Learning Objectives

- Explain how the conservatism convention and the "immediate recognition" aspect of the matching principle relate to recognizing some expenditures as period costs.
- Apply the immediate recognition aspect of matching to the accounting for expenditures incurred subsequent to when an asset is acquired and placed into service.
- Explain how costs are recognized as expenses through the "systematic and rational allocation" aspect of the matching principle.
- Apply the systematic and rational notion in allocating the cost of various long-lived assets under the commonly accepted cost-allocation techniques for both a full year and a partial year.
- Compare the advantages and disadvantages of the various commonly used cost-allocation methods.
- Demonstrate the accounting for a change in an accounting estimate.
- Apply some principles for accounting for errors.

INTERNET

A recent history of the price of Amazon.com's stock can be found at the Amazon.com Web site **http://www.amazon.com**.

Click on About Amazon.com, click on Investor Relations, and then click on Stock Quote and Chart.

The Theory of Expensing Costs, Including the Costs of Long-Lived Assets

This chapter and the previous two chapters are closely linked together. They have to do with recognizing and appropriately reporting costs on the financial statements. Chapter 5 covered the recording of expenditures as assets, which occurs when it is expected that the expenditures will result in benefits for more than one year. The expensing of those costs that initially are reported as inventory was covered in Chapter 6. Chapter 7 covers two other aspects of the matching principle: (1) the immediate expensing of some expenditures and (2) the expensing of the costs of some long-lived assets through a systematic and rational allocation technique. The relationship among these three chapters is illustrated in Exhibit 7-1.

Immediate Recognition

The difference between an expenditure that results in acquiring an asset and one that results in the incurring of an expense is whether or not it is expected that probable future economic benefits will be obtained. Including the word "probable" in that phrase emphasizes that there is always a degree of uncertainty whether those future economic benefits will be received. Thus, whether an expenditure is accounted for as the acquisition of an asset or as the incurring of an expense depends to some extent upon management's expectations regarding the future. When management thinks an expenditure probably will result in future economic benefits, the expenditure is recognized as an asset in accordance with the historical cost principle. Otherwise, the expenditure is *immediately recognized as an expense of the period.*

EXHIBIT 7-1

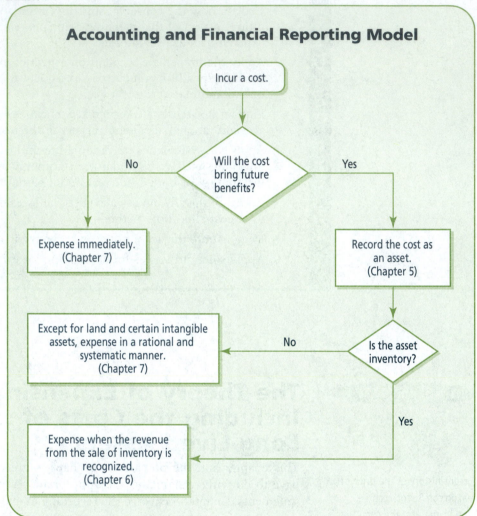

Accounting and Financial Reporting Model

There are many situations where it is difficult to know whether an expenditure has resulted in the acquisition of an asset or in the incurring of an expense. One example that illustrates this difficulty and also illustrates the correct application of the "immediate recognition" aspect of the matching principle is the accounting for **start-up costs**, which are the initial costs of establishing a business, a new division, or a new facility, and which are incurred before principal operations have commenced and significant revenues are earned.[1] In the past, many companies deferred such costs on the basis that these costs gave rise to a business that presumably would result in future benefits. Also, in the early stages of a business there are no revenues against which such costs can be matched. However, the AICPA decided that start-up costs (i.e., principally lawyer and accounting fees) should not be given special treatment. Since at other times, legal and accounting fees are expensed in the period incurred, start-up costs also are expensed as incurred.[2]

---

[1]Such new business entities are called development stage corporations. Once principal operations have commenced, then the company is no longer a development stage corporation.
[2]SOP 98-5, *Reporting on the Costs of Start-Up Activities*.

This Is the Real World

As an example of how accounting reflects management's expectations, consider the following statement that was taken from Cendant's 1998 financial report:

"On October 5, 1998, the Company announced the termination of an agreement to acquire, for $219 million in cash, Providian Auto and Home Insurance Company ("Providian"). Certain representations and covenants in such agreement had not been fulfilled and the conditions to closing had not been met. The Company did not pursue an extension of the termination date of the agreement because Providian no longer met the Company's

acquisition criteria. *In connection with the termination of the Company's proposed acquisition of Providian, the Company wrote off $1.2 million of costs.*" (emphasis added)

This statement illustrates that accounting does to some extent report on management's expectations. Prior to October 5, 1998, Cendant management thought that the $1.2 million of expenditures would result in future benefits and so had capitalized the costs. Subsequently, management changed its view, and as a result, the expenditures were then written off and recorded as a loss.

Other examples of transactions where it is difficult to know whether to record an expenditure as an asset or as an expense include advertising costs that may result in future benefits to the company and employee training and education costs from which the company will benefit for several years.

In considering these and similar issues, the conservatism convention[3] helps. According to this convention, *when in doubt whether an expenditure should be capitalized or expensed, the accounting alternative is chosen that has the most immediate and least favorable impact on net income and total assets.* Thus, the conservatism convention requires that when there is doubt about whether an expenditure will result in future benefits, the expenditure should be recorded as an expense.

EXTENDING THE CONCEPT

Return to the Amazon.com scenario and again consider whether it is properly accounting for expenditures by expensing them as they are incurred.

Systematic and Rational Allocation

The final aspect of the matching principle is the allocation of costs of long-lived assets (except land and certain intangible assets) in some systematic and rational manner to the time periods in which benefits from using those assets are received. This is the justification behind the concepts of depreciation, depletion, and amortization. For accounting purposes and in published financial statements, depreciation, depletion, and amortization are cost allocation techniques and have nothing to do with asset valuation. These concepts are applied in accounting in order to more appropriately measure net income. They are not attempts to arrive at current balance sheet values.[4]

---

[3]Some accountants inappropriately apply the conservatism convention to many areas of accounting and, as a result, have erroneously concluded that the conservatism convention is a pervasive concept in accounting. However, the only appropriate time to apply the conservatism convention is when *the accounting for a transaction cannot be determined between two or more equally acceptable alternatives.*

[4]Failure to report fair value information (i.e., more relevant information) for long-lived assets on the balance sheet is a major criticism of current depreciation theory and procedures.

For accounting purposes:

- **Depreciation** is the process of allocating the cost of long-lived tangible assets (such as plant and equipment) to the time period benefited.
- **Depletion** is the process of allocating the cost of natural resources to time periods.
- **Amortization** is the process of allocating the cost of long-lived intangible assets (such as patents and copyrights) to time periods. Amortization is also frequently used to refer to all of these allocation techniques.

The concept of depreciation and amortization is that the service potential of long-lived assets declines over time due to physical wear and tear and/or technological obsolescence. The concept of depletion is similar in that the potential usefulness of the natural resource also declines over time.[5] The yearly expense amounts computed are not measures of the actual decrease in the service potential that occurred during the period (which usually is impossible to measure), but rather, the yearly expense amount is a reasonable allowance for the physical wear and tear and obsolescence that occurred during the period.

Despite depreciation being a cost-allocation technique and the service potential of assets declining over time, not-for-profit entities under the auspices of the FASB[6] do not need to depreciate assets whose economic value diminishes slowly over a long period of time (e.g., historical works of art and historical treasures). To qualify, the entity must be technologically and financially capable of preserving, essentially undiminished, the service potential of the asset and must be taking steps to do so.[7]

Essentially, any technique to allocate the cost of long-lived assets to expense can be used as long as the technique is both systematic and rational. **Systematic** means that clear, unambiguous guidance is provided *in advance* as to the amount of the cost of the long-lived asset to allocate to expense for any particular time period. **Rational** means that the allocation method is defensible in associating cost with the time period.

Because depreciation, depletion, and amortization calculations are estimates, amounts are usually rounded to the nearest hundreds or even thousands of dollars. Carrying depreciation calculations to pennies is never appropriate because it implies a precision in the calculations that does not exist.

Because management's plans or expectations for an asset may change, periodic reviews of an asset's remaining service potential and its salvage value should be conducted. In 1995, the FASB mandated periodic reviews of tangible assets,[8] and in 2001 the FASB extended such periodic reviews to intangible assets.[9] When indicated, changes in the allocation formula being used should be made. Changes in the allocation formula are changes in accounting estimates, which is covered later in this chapter.

---

[5]Depletion is discussed in more detail in Appendix B at the end of the chapter.

[6]Not-for-profit entities (such as cities, states, and entities associated with them) are not under the auspices of the FASB but follow the pronouncements of the Governmental Accounting Standards Board. Those not-for-profit entities (such as hospitals and universities) that are not connected with a government follow the pronouncements of the FASB.

[7]*Statement of Financial Accounting Standard No. 93*, "Recognition of Depreciation for Not-for-Profit Organization" (Stamford: Financial Accounting Standards Board, August 1987), pars. 6 and 36.

[8]*Statement of Financial Accounting Standard No. 121*, "Accounting for the Impairment of Long-Lived Assets and for Long-Lived Assets to Be Disposed Of" (Stamford: Financial Accounting Standards Board, 1995).

[9]*Statement of Financial Accounting Standard No. 142*, "Goodwill and Other Intangible Assets" (Stamford: Financial Accounting Standards Board, June 2001), pars. 15 and 17.

Applying the "Immediate Recognition" Aspect

Under the immediate recognition aspect of the matching principle, all of the following types of expenditures are expensed in the period incurred[10] because benefits are received from such expenditures for only the current period or because benefits are uncertain:

- Expenditures incurred that are a function of time (e.g., rent, interest, property taxes).
- Expenditures incurred for services that are part of the normal ongoing operations of the company and that are not part of the cost of producing inventories (e.g., utilities and salaries that are part of the administrative and selling functions).
- Expenditures incurred for past services that will not result in probable future benefits that extend beyond one year.
- Expenditures incurred to maintain the value of long-lived assets.
- All research and development costs (see Chapter 5).

There are no unique accounting problems for expenditures that (1) are a function of time, (2) are incurred as part of normal operations, or (2) are for past services. Also, the accounting for these topics is amply covered in elementary accounting textbooks and has been reviewed in prior chapters of this text and so will not be covered in this chapter. The unique accounting questions for research and development costs were covered in Chapter 5. Thus, the only immediate recognition topic that will be covered further in this chapter is the accounting for expenditures that are incurred to maintain assets.

Expenditures to Maintain or Increase the Value of Long-Lived Tangible Assets[11]

Subsequent to placing long-lived assets into operation, business entities frequently incur additional expenditures to maintain, repair, or improve these operating assets. These subsequent expenditures are routinely divided into two classifications: revenue expenditures and capital expenditures. **Revenue expenditures** are incurred for the purpose of maintaining the assets in normal operating condition and are incurred routinely as part of the ongoing operations of the company. Typically, the business entity derives benefits for only the current time period from revenue expenditures, and such expenditures will be incurred again in other periods. A final characteristic of revenue expenditures is that, at the time the asset was acquired, it is anticipated that these expenditures will be incurred. All of these characteristics do not need to be present for a cost to be a revenue expenditure. Because of their nature, revenue expenditures are expensed in the period incurred. Revenue expenditures for an automobile, for example, maintain the normal operating condition of the automobile and include oil changes, cleaning, and periodic engine checkups.

---

[10]The period incurred does not mean the period in which the cash was paid. From Chapter 2, "incurred" means the period in which the services or products were used. The period in which the cash was paid may be different.

[11]Recall from Chapter 5 that all expenditures incurred *before the asset is placed in service* with the intent of getting the asset ready for its intended use are always debited to the asset account. This discussion deals with expenditures incurred *after the asset is placed in service*.

Capital expenditures are incurred for the purpose of improving the nature of the asset (e.g., adding air conditioning in an automobile), substantially improving the productive life of the asset (e.g., putting a new engine in an automobile), or improving the productivity of the asset (e.g., an improvement that will result in the automobile being driven more miles). These types of expenditures are not expensed in the period incurred but instead are capitalized either to the asset account or to the accumulated depreciation account associated with the asset. The choice of whether to debit the asset account or the accumulated depreciation account depends upon the purpose of the expenditure and the following guidelines.

Additions are capital expenditures that are incurred for the purpose of increasing the productive capacity of the asset. A typical example is constructing a new wing of a hospital. Such expenditures are intended to generate additional future revenues, and accordingly, they are debited to an asset account. Subsequently, such expenditures are recognized as expenses according to some systematic and rational allocation plan.

Replacements are expenditures that are incurred to replace a worn-out component of an asset with the *same quality* component, whereas **betterments** are expenditures that result from substituting a worn-out component with a *higher quality* component or adding something to an asset that improves the quality of the asset. Examples of betterments, as contrasted to replacements, include replacing an old roof on a building with a higher quality roof and installing air conditioning in a building. Both replacements and betterments improve the existing quality of an asset, but they may not improve the overall life or productivity of the asset. For example, replacing a leaking roof with a newer roof may increase the overall quality of the existing building, but likely it will not affect the overall life of the building as that life is affected more by such things as the condition of the foundation and electrical systems.

The preferred accounting procedures in accounting for replacements and betterments are to:

1. Remove the cost and associated accumulated depreciation of the old asset or component (if they are known),
2. Recognize the indicated loss, and
3. *Debit the asset account* for the cost of the replacement or betterment.

To illustrate, Confidential Security has had trouble with its roof leaking in inclement weather and accordingly has decided to replace it with a higher-quality roof. The accounting records show that the cost of the old roof was $225,000, and the accumulated depreciation is $150,000. Subsequently, the old roof is torn off and has no salvage value, and a new roof is installed for $350,000. The following journal entries are prepared to account for these transactions:

Accumulated Depreciation	150,000	
Loss on Replacing Roof	75,000	
Building		225,000

To remove the cost and accumulated depreciation of a component of an old asset and recognize the associated loss.

| Building | 350,000 | |
| Cash | | 350,000 |

To record the cost of installing a new component of an asset.

When the cost and associated accumulated depreciation of the old asset (or component) are not known, then:

1. The accumulated depreciation account is debited when the useful life of the asset is extended; otherwise,
2. The asset account is debited.

Practically, whether the asset account or the accumulated depreciation account is debited does not make any difference in the current or future years. Neither the amount of depreciation nor net income is affected by the choice, and neither is any other financial subtotal, total, or ratio.

Rearrangements and reinstallations and other such remodeling enhance the effectiveness and productivity of current and future operations. Thus, accounting for these costs according to the same rules for replacements/betterments is appropriate. So, if the cost of the old installation is known, it is removed from the general ledger along with the associated accumulated depreciation, and a loss is recognized. Then, the cost of the rearrangement or reinstallation is debited to an asset account. When the cost and associated accumulated depreciation of the old asset are not known, the cost of the rearrangement/reinstallation is debited to an asset account.

Extraordinary repairs are those that were not anticipated when the asset was acquired but are necessary for the company to continue deriving benefits from using the asset. For example—and to further clarify the differences in the previous definitions—consider the following expenditures connected to an automobile.

Which costs of repairing/maintaining a car are expensed, and which are capitalized?

- When buying an automobile, the owner expects to change the oil and have periodic checkups. So, when expenditures for these items are incurred, they are expensed because they are anticipated, they are part of maintaining the automobile in its normal operating condition, and they will be incurred again in the future.
- If air conditioning is added to a vehicle when it is acquired, the expenditure becomes part of the cost of acquiring the vehicle and getting it ready for its intended use. So, according to the historical cost principle, the cost of installing the air conditioning is capitalized. If air conditioning is added some time after the vehicle has been in operation, it is a betterment, and the expenditure is still debited to the asset account.
- Replacing the engine in an automobile is handled according to the replacement rules.
- But what is the proper procedure for an engine overhaul? Such repairs are called extraordinary repairs. Extraordinary repairs were not anticipated when the asset was acquired, they likely do not extend the life of the asset

© GETTY IMAGES, INC./PHOTODISC

A company acquired a new vehicle and at the same time decided to have the name of the company and other information about the company printed on the sides. How should the company account for the cost of painting the signs? Why?

Answer: The cost of painting should be capitalized as part of the cost of the vehicle because it is a necessary expenditure in getting the vehicle ready for its intended use.

What is the appropriate accounting when the information about the company is repainted two years later because of severe fading? Explain your answer.

Answer: This seems to be an extraordinary repair. Likely, it was not anticipated that the information would have to be repainted in two years, the expenditure does not improve the nature of the vehicle from what management originally intended, and the expenditure will not increase the life of the vehicle. But the expenditure is being incurred to derive future benefits. Hence, the preferable accounting treatment is to write off the cost and accumulated depreciation (if known) of the original paint job and to capitalize, by debiting the vehicle account, the cost of the new paint job.

beyond what management expected when the asset was purchased, and they do not improve the asset over management's expectations when it was purchased. However, because the expenditure is incurred for the purpose of deriving future benefits, the expenditure is capitalized according to the rules for replacements/betterments.

Exhibit 7-2 summarizes the accounting treatment of expenditures incurred subsequent to the purchase of long-lived tangible assets.

Expenditures to Protect Intangible Assets

Since one of the defining characteristics of intangible assets is that they lack physical substance and thus are not subject to physical wear and tear, the previous discussion of additions and repairs does not apply to them. Rather, the typical reason a company incurs subsequent expenditures on intangible assets is to protect the exclusive right to use them. For example, a company may incur legal costs to protect its patent, trademark, or copyright. Regardless of when

EXHIBIT 7-2

Summary of Accounting Treatment for Subsequent Expenditures

Type of Expenditure	Purpose	Accounting Treatment
Revenue Ordinary repair	To maintain asset in normal working condition. Such expenditures are anticipated when the asset is purchased and are incurred on a regular basis. Benefits are received only for the current period.	Debit an expense account in the period incurred.
Additions	To increase the productive capacity.	Debit an asset account.
Replacements and betterments	To replace a worn-out component with the same quality (replacement) or a higher quality (betterment) component.	(1) Carrying value known: remove cost and accumulated depreciation of the old component and recognize any loss. Debit the asset account for the cost of the new component. (2) Carrying value not known: a. If the asset's life is increased, debit Accumulated Depreciation. b. Otherwise, debit the asset account.
Rearrangements and reinstallments	Remodeling to enhance the effectiveness and productivity of current and future operations.	Account for the cost according to the rules for replacements and betterments.
Extraordinary repair	To make repairs that were not anticipated when the asset was purchased.	Account for the cost according to the rules for replacements and betterments.

the cost to protect an intangible asset is incurred, if the litigation is successful, all such costs incurred are capitalized to the appropriate intangible asset account and then amortized over its remaining life. When the litigation is unsuccessful, the cost of litigation is recognized as an expense of the period, and any unamortized cost of the asset is written off as a loss. The costs of maintaining or restoring intangible assets (including goodwill) that are not specifically identifiable, or that have indeterminate lives, or are related to the business entity as a whole are expensed in the period incurred.

International Accounting Standards

INTERNATIONAL

International GAAP requirements are very similar to U.S. GAAP in accounting for subsequent expenditures on tangible assets. All costs that extend the useful life of the asset, improve the quality of its output, and/or increase its capacity are capitalized. Ordinary repairs and maintenance costs are expensed as incurred. When capitalizing a cost, international GAAP do not stipulate whether to debit the asset account or the accumulated depreciation account. Presumably, either method is acceptable.

Subsequent expenditures to protect intangible assets is a topic where some of the most significant differences exist between U.S. and international GAAP. IAS No. 38 stipulates that costs incurred to protect intangible assets must be expensed, unless it is probable that those costs will enable the asset to generate future economic benefits in excess of what was originally estimated. Thus, even though a company might be successful in defending a patent, the legal costs in doing so are expensed, unless the company can demonstrate that the patent is now more valuable than it was before the litigation occurred. On the other hand, if a company is not successful in defending its intangibles, then similar to U.S. GAAP, IAS No. 38 requires not only the expensing of the litigation costs but also recognizing as a loss the impairment of the intangible asset.

Applying the "Systematic and Rational" Aspect—Depreciation

The amount of depreciation expense reported in any given year depends upon (1) the cost of the asset, (2) its anticipated useful life, (3) the estimated salvage value at the end of its anticipated useful life, and (4) the depreciation method chosen. The cost of the asset is determined at acquisition according to the historical cost principle, as covered in Chapter 5, and as modified by subsequent expenditures as discussed previously in this chapter.

The **anticipated useful life** (also referred to as the service life) of an asset is the length of time the business entity estimates it will use the asset as determined at the time the asset is acquired or as modified thereafter. The asset's anticipated useful life is determined by such physical factors as wear and tear, deterioration, decay and destruction, and by technological factors such as inadequacy, supersession, and obsolescence. **Inadequacy** results when an asset ceases to be useful because it is not capable of meeting the demands placed on it. **Supersession** is the replacing of one asset by another that is more efficient or economical. **Obsolescence** is the catch-all phrase used to indicate all other possible technological reasons for replacing an asset. In today's economy, the anticipated useful life of an asset is determined more by technological factors than by physical factors, and hence, the length of time the company will use the asset is frequently less than the actual life of the asset.

Salvage value is the expected amount to be realized through sale or trade-in that will be received at the end of the asset's useful life. Again, this estimate is made when the asset is acquired or as modified thereafter. The estimate of salvage value is reduced by the costs of dismantling and disposing of the asset. In practice, salvage values are frequently ignored in depreciation calculations, which is acceptable when salvage value is immaterial or when more relevant information is not obtained by including salvage value. When salvage value is used in depreciation calculations, including when salvage is presumed to be zero, assets must be depreciated to salvage by the end of their anticipated useful lives. No additional depreciation is taken when an asset is used longer than its useful life because the cost of the asset has been fully allocated.[12]

Methods of Depreciation

Theoretically, a company could select a different method of depreciation for each asset or asset type, but practically a company selects a depreciation method and then applies it to all assets.[13] All of the following commonly used methods of depreciation are accepted as being systematic and rational allocation methods:

Time-factor methods of depreciation:

1. Straight-line depreciation,
2. Sum-of-the-years'-digits depreciation, and
3. Declining-balance depreciation.

Activity methods of depreciation:

1. Service-hours depreciation, and
2. Productive-output depreciation.

Regardless of the depreciation method used, the form of the journal entry to recognize depreciation expense for the year is exactly the same and is shown as follows:

Depreciation Expense	XXX	
Accumulated Depreciation		XXX

To record depreciation expense for a year.

The following discussion focuses on the more commonly used depreciation methods, but other methods of depreciation are possible—including those that a company may develop. GAAP does not prescribe the depreciation methods that are allowed. All that is required is that whatever method the company uses, it must meet the criteria of being systematic and rational.

Straight-Line Depreciation Method

The **straight-line depreciation method** is based on the assumption that time is the most significant factor in the declining service potential of an asset and that decline is relatively constant. The result of these assumptions is that equal amounts of depreciation expense are recorded for equal periods of time. The method gets its name because straight lines are obtained for depreciation expense, accumulated depreciation, and book value when they are graphed against time, as shown in Exhibit 7-3.

INTERNET

Over 14,000 calculators can be found at **http://www. sciencegems.com**. At this site, click on "Calculators On-Line Center." Several depreciation calculators can be found under Management and Business. In addition, one particularly useful calculator for determining the true cost of using credit cards can be found under Finance—Personal—Credit Cards—Cardcalc Wizard.

---

[12]This is the essence of cost allocation; the cost of the asset less salvage is fully allocated to the periods benefited.

[13]Depreciation calculations may also be applied to groups of assets, as explained in Appendix A at the end of the chapter.

EXHIBIT 7-3

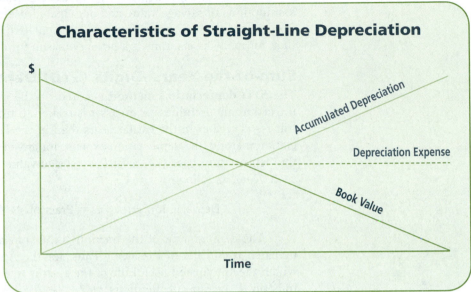

Characteristics of Straight-Line Depreciation

The formula for computing depreciation expense under the straight-line method is as follows:

$$\text{Depreciation Expense} = \frac{\text{Cost} - \text{Salvage}}{\text{Life (in years)}}$$

To illustrate, Anderson Company purchased a new machine on January 1, 2001, for $45,000. Anderson estimates that the machine will be used for five years, at which time it expects to be able to sell the machine for $4,500. Using the straight-line depreciation method to allocate the cost of the machine, the depreciation expense for each year is $8,100. Illustration 7-1 summarizes the cost allocation process for the life of the asset, using the straight-line method of depreciation. Note that (1) the depreciation amount is the same each year and (2) the asset is depreciated to the estimated salvage value of $4,500 by the end of its anticipated useful life.

© CORBIS, INC.

ILLUSTRATION 7-1

Straight-Line Depreciation

End of Year	Depreciation Formula	Depreciation Expense	Accumulated Depreciation	Book Value
2001	($45,000 − $4,500)/5	$8,100	$ 8,100	$36,900
2002	($45,000 − $4,500)/5	8,100	16,200	28,800
2003	($45,000 − $4,500)/5	8,100	24,300	20,700
2004	($45,000 − $4,500)/5	8,100	32,400	12,600
2005	($45,000 − $4,500)/5	8,100	40,500	4,500

The straight-line depreciation method is systematic because as soon as the assumptions of salvage value and anticipated useful life are made, the depreciation expense for any given year can be calculated. The method is also rational in that, for many assets, time is a primary reason for declining economic usefulness.

Sum-of-the-Years'-Digits (SYD) Depreciation

The **SYD depreciation method** is based on the assumption that the decline in the economic usefulness of an asset is related to time but that the decline in usefulness is greater in the earlier years than in the later years. For the SYD depreciation method, the depreciation expense for any year is computed by multiplying the depreciation base (i.e., cost less salvage value) by a fraction (that decreases each year), as follows:

$$\text{Depreciation Expense} = \text{Fraction} \times (\text{Cost} - \text{Salvage})$$

The denominator of the fraction is the sum of the digits from 1 to the anticipated useful life of the asset. Thus, for the Anderson Company example in which the anticipated useful life of the asset is five years, the denominator of the fraction is the sum of the digits $1+2+3+4+5$, or 15. As another example, the denominator in the fraction for an asset with an anticipated useful life of eight years is $1+2+3+ \ldots +8 = 36$.[14] The numerators of the fractions are the years in reverse order. So, for an asset with a five-year anticipated useful life, the fraction for the first year's depreciation expense is 5/15; for the second year, the fraction is 4/15; for the third year, it is 3/15, etc.

Illustration 7-2 summarizes the cost allocation process for the asset used in the Anderson Company example, using the SYD method of depreciation.

ILLUSTRATION 7-2

Sum-of-the-Years'-Digits (SYD) Depreciation

End of Year	Depreciation Formula	Depreciation Expense	Accumulated Depreciation	Book Value
2001	5/15 × ($45,000 − $4,500)	$13,500	$13,500	$31,500
2002	4/15 × ($45,000 − $4,500)	10,800	24,300	20,700
2003	3/15 × ($45,000 − $4,500)	8,100	32,400	12,600
2004	2/15 × ($45,000 − $4,500)	5,400	37,800	7,200
2005	1/15 × ($45,000 − $4,500)	2,700	40,500	4,500

EXTENDING THE CONCEPT

If the anticipated useful life of an asset is five years and the depreciation expense amount for the first year is $8,000, verify that the depreciation expense amounts for the second, third, and fourth years are $6,400, $4,800, and $3,200, respectively, using the sum-of-the-years'-digits method. Also, verify that the cost of the asset is $24,000, assuming that the salvage value is zero.

Note that as with the straight-line method, the asset is depreciated to its estimated salvage value at the end of its useful life. Also, note that in this case, the depreciation expense declined by $2,700 each year, which is 1/5, or 20%, of the depreciation expense amount of the first year (i.e., $13,500). So another and perhaps quicker way of computing depreciation expense for a year is to divide the depreciation expense of the first year by the life of the

---

[14]The sum of the years for any life can be quickly computed by the following formula: $n(n+1)/2$, where n is the life of the asset. For an asset with a life of five years, the formula is $5(5+1)/2$, which is equal to $(5 \times 6)/2$, or 15.

asset (e.g., $13,500/5 = $2,700$) and then subtract this amount from the depreciation expense of the previous year. For an asset with an anticipated useful life of eight years, the depreciation expense each year will decline by 1/8 of the first year's deprecation amount.

Declining-Balance Depreciation Methods

Declining-balance depreciation methods have the same assumption as the SYD method; that is, there is a greater decline in the economic usefulness of an asset in the earlier years, with the result that depreciation expense amounts decrease over time. To accomplish this decreasing depreciation amount per year, depreciation expense is computed by multiplying the asset's cost less accumulated depreciation by a constant percentage as expressed in the following formula:

$$\text{Depreciation Expense} = \text{Percent} \times (\text{Cost} - \text{Accumulated Depreciation})$$

The most popular percentages in the above equation are (150%/life) and (200%/life), where "life" is expressed in terms of years. When the (200%/life) percentage is used, the method is called the **double-declining-balance (DDB) depreciation method**. The name "double" comes from the fact that the rate is twice the rate used in the straight-line method.

Illustration 7-3 summarizes the cost allocation process for the Anderson Company example, using the double-declining-balance depreciation method. Note that since the life of the asset is five years, the straight-line rate is 1/5. Therefore, twice the straight-line rate is 2/5.

ILLUSTRATION 7-3

Double-Declining-Balance (DDB) Depreciation

End of Year	Depreciation Formula	Depreciation Amount	Accumulated Depreciation	Book Value
2001	(2/5) × ($45,000 − $0)	$18,000	$18,000	$27,000
2002	(2/5) × ($45,000 − $18,000)	10,800	28,800	16,200
2003	(2/5) × ($45,000 − $28,800)	6,480	35,280	9,720
2004		2,610	37,890	7,110
2005		2,610	40,500	4,500

Because the declining-balance depreciation methods do not incorporate salvage value into the formula, it is unlikely that the asset will be depreciated to salvage value by the end of the asset's anticipated useful life. To overcome this calculation problem, most companies *at some point in the asset's useful life switch to the straight-line method of depreciation.* In the above illustration, Anderson Company switched to the straight-line depreciation method at the beginning of 2004.[15] At that time, with a book value of $9,720 and an expected salvage value of $4,500, there is only $5,220 left to depreciate. Since there are two years remaining over which to depreciate the asset, the depreciation expense is $2,610 each year.

The SYD and declining-balance methods of depreciation also meet the systematic and rational criteria. They are systematic methods because, once the assumptions of salvage value and life are made, the calculations of depreciation

---

[15]See Illustration 7-4 for an example where a switch to the straight-line method was not made.

expense can be determined in advance for any year. They are rational methods because the economic usefulness of many assets does decline in relation to time. Accelerated methods of depreciation may be appropriate for those assets whose economic usefulness is a factor of technology, where it may be that the decline in usefulness is greater in the earlier years of the asset's life than in the later years. Accelerated methods of depreciation may also be appropriate for those assets where maintenance charges are expected to increase during the later years, thus causing the sum of the maintenance and depreciation costs to be fairly constant each year over the life of the asset, as shown in Exhibit 7-4.[16]

EXHIBIT 7-4

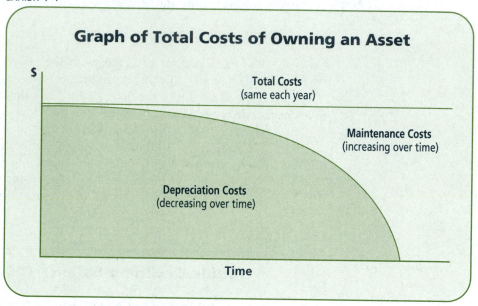

Graph of Total Costs of Owning an Asset

Activity Methods of Depreciation

The previously discussed depreciation methods are based upon the assumption that time is the most important factor leading to a decline in the economic usefulness of an asset. However, for some assets, this assumption is not valid. Rather, the decline in economic usefulness is more a function of use. The activity methods of depreciation (i.e., service-hours and productive-output) are based on this assumption.

The formula for computing depreciation expense under either activity method is as follows:

$$\text{Depreciation Expense} = \frac{(\text{Cost} - \text{Salvage})}{\text{Total Estimated Units}} \times \text{Units for the Year}$$

For the Anderson Company to use an activity method, the company has to estimate the total amount of activity (i.e., hours or units) that the machine will produce and then count the number of hours the machine was used or the number of units that were produced for the year. Suppose that Anderson estimated—at the time the machine was purchased—that the machine would produce 90,000

---

[16]*Accounting Research Bulletin No. 44 (Revised)*, "Declining-Balance Depreciation" (Stamford: Financial Accounting Standards Board, October 1954), par. 2.

units and that 16,000 units were actually produced during the year. Then, depreciation expense for the year using the activity method of depreciation is $7,200, which is computed as follows:

$$\text{Depreciation Expense} = \frac{(\$45,000 - \$4,500)}{90,000} \times 16,000$$

$$= \$0.45 \times 16,000$$

$$= \$7,200$$

In subsequent years, depreciation expense is more quickly computed by multiplying the depreciation cost of $0.45 per unit by the number of units produced. As with the depreciation methods that are based upon time, the asset cannot be depreciated below its salvage value, even if more than 90,000 units are produced. This is true because once 90,000 units have been produced, the cost of the asset has been fully allocated to expense.

Activity methods of depreciation also meet the criteria of being systematic and rational. They are systematic because the unit depreciation charge can be determined at the time the asset is acquired, and as a result, the depreciation expense can be computed in advance for any level of activity. They are rational because the economic usefulness of many assets is directly related to their use.

Evaluating Depreciation Methods

The reliability of the information provided by various depreciation techniques is the same, since all the methods essentially use the same inputs. Thus, a company should select the depreciation method that provides the most relevant information. Also, since the purpose of depreciation is to measure income, companies should use the method that most appropriately matches expenses of the period to the revenues recognized. In this regard, it may be that the activity methods best measure income, as there is a more clear association between the revenues generated and the costs incurred than exists with revenues and time-based depreciation methods. However, activity-based depreciation methods are not used extensively because they are infeasible for many assets (such as a building, whose service hours or productive output is not measurable), and they are more costly to apply than just counting the passage of time.

The selection of a depreciation method is usually based on practicality rather than on a conceptual basis. Given the ease of calculations of the straight-line method and that it meets the criteria of being systematic and rational, it is not surprising that the straight-line method is by far the most commonly used depreciation method for financial reporting purposes.

Regardless of the method chosen for financial reporting purposes, *a company does not have to use the same depreciation method for tax purposes in the United States*. There is no similar rule for depreciation, like the LIFO conformity rule for inventory. Thus, many companies use the straight-line method of depreciation for financial reporting and some accelerated method of depreciation for tax purposes and thereby achieve what appears to be the best of all worlds—lower taxes paid (in the earlier years of an asset's anticipated useful life) and a higher reported net income on the financial statements.

Finally, when considering which depreciation method to use, realizing its impact upon the important return-on-assets ratio is important. Frequently, management evaluations and incentives (such as bonuses) are at least partially based on this (or a similar) ratio. Exhibit 7-5 compares the effects of the straight-line

INTERNATIONAL

Recall in Chapter 1 the discussion of the effects of culture on financial reporting across countries. The United States is a country where the standard-setting function for financial reporting is done in the private sector, whereas tax regulations are a government function. In Sweden, Germany, and Japan, for example, both roles of prescribing financial accounting and tax regulations are governmental functions, with the result that companies tend to use the same accelerated depreciation method for financial reporting that they use to compute taxes.

and double-declining-balance methods on this ratio over the 5-year anticipated useful life of the machine acquired by Anderson Company.

As shown in Exhibit 7-5, an assessment of management's ability and stewardship can be initially enhanced when the straight-line method is used, but with older assets, the accelerated depreciation methods give a better assessment of management's ability. Exhibit 7-5 also shows that trends in income and apparent profitability are significantly affected by the choice of a depreciation method. The exhibit also highlights the difficulty of comparing financial statements between two or more companies when different depreciation methods are used.

EXHIBIT 7-5

Effects on ROA of Various Depreciation Methods

Straight-Line

Line	Year 1	Year 2	Year 3	Year 4	Year 5
1. Cost of assets	$1,000,000	$1,000,000	$1,000,000	$1,000,000	$1,000,000
2. Less accumulated depreciation	8,100	16,200	24,300	32,400	40,500
3. Total assets	$ 991,900	$ 983,800	$ 975,700	$ 967,600	$ 959,500
4. Income before depreciation	$100,000	$100,000	$100,000	$100,000	$100,000
5. Depreciation expense	8,100	8,100	8,100	8,100	8,100
6. Net income	$ 91,900	$ 91,900	$ 91,900	$ 91,900	$ 91,900
7. Return on assets (Line 6/Line 3)	9.3%	9.3%	9.4%	9.5%	9.6%

Double-Declining-Balance

Line	Year 1	Year 2	Year 3	Year 4	Year 5
1. Cost of assets	$1,000,000	$1,000,000	$1,000,000	$1,000,000	$1,000,000
2. Less accumulated depreciation	18,000	28,800	35,280	37,890	40,500
3. Total assets	$ 982,000	$ 971,200	$ 964,720	$ 962,110	$ 959,500
4. Income before depreciation	$100,000	$100,000	$100,000	$100,000	$100,000
5. Depreciation expense	18,000	10,800	6,480	2,610	2,610
6. Net income	$ 82,000	$ 89,200	$ 93,520	$ 97,390	$ 97,390
7. Return on assets (Line 6/Line 3)	8.4%	9.2%	9.7%	10.1%	10.2%

EXTENDING THE CONCEPT

In Exhibit 7-5, the ROA for the straight-line method is initially higher than it is for the DDB method of depreciation, but these magnitudes are reversed in subsequent years. However, because most companies are growing in size and their total assets are increasing, the ROA of companies that use accelerated methods of depreciation will typically be lower than the ROA of companies that use the straight-line method of depreciation.

Depreciation for Partial Years

Of course, acquiring assets on the first day of the year, as was assumed with the Anderson Company example, is unusual. When assets are purchased at times other than January 1, depreciation must be calculated for partial years. The following are all accepted methods of computing depreciation for a partial year:

1. Recognize depreciation to the nearest month. Assets acquired by the fifteenth day of the month are considered to have been purchased on the first day of the current month, and assets acquired after the fifteenth day are considered to have been purchased on the first day of the following month.

2. Recognize depreciation to the nearest whole year. Assets acquired by June 30 are considered to have been purchased on January 1 of the current year; otherwise, the asset is considered to have been purchased on January 1 of the subsequent year.
3. Recognize depreciation for one-half of a year for all assets that are either acquired or sold during the year.
4. Recognize depreciation for an entire year on all acquisitions and no depreciation in the year of disposal.
5. Recognize depreciation for an entire year on all disposals of assets, but no depreciation in the year that assets are acquired.

These variations for computing depreciation for a partial year are acceptable because depreciation is only an estimate. Thus, to compute depreciation to the nearest day is to include an illusion of accuracy. Alternative 1 seems to be the most frequently used technique, and its use is reflected in the subsequent discussion (but not all of the problems at the end of the chapter).

For the straight-line and declining-balance methods of depreciation, computing depreciation for a partial year requires minimal additional calculations in the year of acquisition and disposal, and no additional calculations are required in any other year. For the activity methods, no additional calculations are required in any year, as the number of hours worked or units produced are already stated in terms of a partial year. Continuing with the facts of the Anderson Company example, assuming that the asset was acquired on March 10 and that depreciation expense is computed to the nearest month, ten months of depreciation is taken in 2001 and two months of depreciation is taken in 2006. Illustration 7-4 shows the depreciation amounts under both the straight-line and DDB methods for acquiring the asset on March 10.

ILLUSTRATION 7-4

Partial-Year Depreciation Calculations

End of Year	Straight-Line Depreciation Formula	If Purchased March 10	Double-Declining Depreciation Formula	If Purchased March 10
2001	($45,000 − $4,500)/5 × 10/12	$ 6,750	($45,000 − $0)[1] × (2/5) × (10/12)	$15,000
2002	($45,000 − $4,500)/5	8,100	($45,000 − $15,000) × (2/5)	12,000
2003	($45,000 − $4,500)/5	8,100	($45,000 − $27,000) × (2/5)	7,200
2004	($45,000 − $4,500)/5	8,100	($45,000 − $34,200) × (2/5)	4,320
2005	($45,000 − $4,500)/5	8,100		1,980[2]
2006	($45,000 − $4,500)/5 × 2/12	1,350		
Totals		$40,500		$40,500

[1]The formula for computing depreciation expense under a declining-balance method is to subtract accumulated depreciation from cost.
[2]For this example, the switch to the straight-line method was not done. Instead, the depreciation expense amount for the year 2005 is computed as the amount needed to depreciate the asset to salvage value, which is less than the amount would be if the formula had been used.

Although computing depreciation for a partial year is straightforward for the straight-line and declining-balance methods, computing depreciation for partial years using the SYD method requires additional calculations for every year. This is because depreciation is first computed for each whole fraction (e.g., 5/15 and 4/15), which is then allocated to the various years. Finally, the depreciation amounts are summed by year. Illustration 7-5 shows the calculations necessary to compute depreciation expense for the years 2001–2006 under the SYD method, assuming that Anderson Company acquired the asset on March 10.

ILLUSTRATION 7-5

Partial-Year Depreciation Calculations, SYD

Col. 1 Fraction	Col. 2 Depreciation Calculation (See Illus. 7-2.)	Col. 3 Depreciation Amount Allocated to the Various Years	Col. 4 Year	Col. 5 Depreciation Amount
5/15	$13,500	2001: 10/12 × $13,500 = $11,250 2002: 2/12 × $13,500 = $2,250	2001	$11,250
4/15	10,800	2002: 10/12 × $10,800 = $9,000 2003: 2/12 × $10,800 = $1,800	2002	$2,250 + $9,000 = 11,250
3/15	8,100	2003: 10/12 × $8,100 = $6,750 2004: 2/12 × $8,100 = $1,350	2003	$1,800 + $6,750 = 8,550
2/15	5,400	2004: 10/12 × $5,400 = $4,500 2005: 2/12 × $5,400 = $900	2004	$1,350 + $4,500 = 5,850
1/15	2,700	2005: 10/12 × $2,700 = $2,250 2006: 2/12 × $2,700 = $450	2005	$ 900 + $2,250 = 3,150
			2006	450
Totals	$40,500			$40,500

The steps in computing the amounts in the table are as follows:

- The fractions in Column 1 were computed previously in the Anderson Company example.
- The depreciation calculations in Column 2 are as computed in Illustration 7-2. These amounts represent the depreciation expense amounts for the twelve-month period from March of one year to March of the next year.
- The formulas in Column 3 are used to allocate the year's depreciation amount in Column 2 between the 10 months of one year and the two months of the following year.
- The amounts in Column 5 are the depreciation amounts for the respective years.

International Accounting Standards

INTERNATIONAL

IAS No. 16 provides guidance on depreciation of fixed assets, and its requirements are essentially identical to U.S. GAAP. The depreciation methods mentioned in IAS No. 16 as being acceptable are straight-line, sum-of-the-years'-digits, declining-balance, and units of production. The standard does permit other methods to be used if the company can demonstrate that another method would provide a more accurate matching of costs with revenues. The standard also mentions the importance of considering salvage value and periodically reviewing the estimated useful life of the assets. Also, similar to U.S. GAAP, the purpose of depreciation under international GAAP is to allocate historical costs in a systematic and rational basis over the periods benefited and is *not* a basis for valuation.

IAS No. 16 does not address partial-year depreciation. However, approaches similar to those followed under U.S. GAAP presumably would be acceptable.

Applying the "Systematic and Rational" Criteria—Amortization[17]

As with depreciation, the purpose of amortizing intangible assets is to match the cost of using them with the revenue generated from that use. Thus, all the comments made about depreciation being an estimate, that the cost of the asset must be depreciated to salvage but not below salvage, etc., apply as well to amortizing intangible assets. Hence, the following comments regarding amortization of intangible assets focus only on how it differs from depreciation accounting.

An intangible asset with a finite useful life is amortized. An intangible asset with an indefinite useful life (which is not the same as infinite useful life) is not amortized. The useful life of an intangible asset is the length of time over which the asset is expected to contribute, either directly or indirectly, to generating cash flows. The useful life is based upon all pertinent factors, including:

- The expected useful life to the entity.
- Any legal, regulatory, or contractual provision that may limit the useful life.
- The effects of obsolescence, demand, competition, and other economic factors.
- The level of required maintenance expenditures to obtain the expected future cash flows from the asset.

If there are no legal, regulatory, contractual, competitive, economic, or other factors that could limit the useful life of the intangible asset to the entity, the useful life is considered to be indefinite and the intangible asset is not amortized.

The amortization method used should reflect the pattern in which the economic benefits from the intangible asset are consumed. If the pattern of those benefits cannot be determined, then the straight-line method must be used. *Salvage value of intangible assets is assumed to be zero.* An exception is allowed if, at the end of the useful life to the entity, the intangible asset will have economic value to some other entity. Amortization is usually credited to the applicable asset account, rather than credited to an "accumulated amortization" account.

To illustrate, assume that Mountain West Eye Institute purchased a patent for $96,000 early in 2004. The patent has a 12-year legal life, but the registration on the patent was granted in early 2003. Regardless of the legal life, Mountain West believes that, because of rapidly changing technology, the patent will have a life of only six years, at which time it will have no value to any entity. During December 2006, Mountain West won a patent infringement lawsuit against a competitor. The cost of the legal defense was $24,000.

© GETTY IMAGES, INC./PHOTODISC

Like depreciation calculations, computing the amortization expense involves identifying the (1) cost of the asset, (2) useful life, (3) salvage value, and (4) the amortization method. For this example, the cost of the asset is $96,000. There is no salvage value, and the useful life is six years because that is the period of time that Mountain West is planning on receiving cash flows from the use of the patent. Also, since no definite correlation can be established between the use of the patent and the

---

[17]*Statement of Financial Accounting Standard No. 142*, "Goodwill and Other Intangible Assets," (Stamford: Financial Accounting Standards Board, June 2001).

revenues generated, the straight-line method of amortization is used. Accordingly, the amortization expense for 2004–2006 is computed as follows:

$$\text{Amortization Expense} = \$96{,}000/6 \text{ years} = \$16{,}000$$

Because the patent was successfully defended, the cost of the defense is then added to the cost of the patent, with the result that amortization expense for 2007 through 2009 is computed by determining the amount of the unallocated cost and spreading that amount over the three years of the remaining useful life, as follows:

Cost of the patent		$ 96,000
Amortization per year	$16,000	
Number of years amortized	× 3	
Total amortization taken on the patent . . .		(48,000)
Unallocated amount of original cost		$ 48,000
Cost of successful defense		24,000
Total unallocated cost		$ 72,000
Remaining useful life		÷ 3 years
Amortization amount per year		$ 24,000

Goodwill

As discussed in Chapter 5, when a company purchases another company at a cost that exceeds the market value of the net identifiable assets, the remaining balance (i.e., the "unidentified" asset) is referred to as goodwill. In many cases, goodwill may represent a significant portion of a company's overall value. Consider, for example, the value of the brand name Coca-Cola or the name familiarity of McDonald's. Other factors that can contribute to the overall market value of a company exceeding the value of its identifiable net assets is superior management, intellectual capital, and a history of realizing abnormal profits. Whatever the cause, when a company acquires another entity and pays more than the sum of the fair values of the net assets, the difference is defined as goodwill.

Determining how to account for goodwill (i.e., record an asset, immediately expense the amount, or charge the amount immediately to retained earnings) has been a controversial issue in accounting for many years, and each of the positions has been taken by at least one accounting standard-setting body in the world at some time, with standard-setting bodies in the United States having adopted different positions at different times. Also, when the decision has been reached to record goodwill as an asset subject to amortization, another difficult issue has been deciding over what period of time to amortize it. Years ago, the APB established a 40-year maximum period over which goodwill was to be amortized. When establishing this maximum period, the APB did not intend it to become *the* period over which goodwill should be amortized—although it did. Then, in recent years, many companies began questioning the use of such an arbitrary and long amortization period. For a time, the FASB proposed changing the maximum amortization period for goodwill to something less than 40 years; but after much discussion with various constituents, the FASB concluded that goodwill should not be amortized. Instead, companies are now required to conduct an annual assessment of the recorded goodwill, and if it is determined that the value of the goodwill has been impaired, companies must write it down to its market value and record a loss on the income statement. This is a significant change from traditional accounting methods and also departs from the international norm.[18]

International Accounting Standards

In IAS No. 38, the IASC presumed that the useful life of all intangible assets would not be greater than 20 years. This means that if a company desires to amortize its intangible assets beyond 20 years, it must provide persuasive evidence that the useful life is greater than 20 years and disclose this evidence in its financial statements. Looking 20 years into the future seems like a very difficult task to accomplish.

Financial Reporting

Depreciation on tangible assets that are used in manufacturing inventory is included in the cost of finished goods inventory. Once the inventory is sold, the cost of the inventory, including the related portion of depreciation, is moved from the balance sheet and reported in the cost of goods sold section of the income statement. The depreciation on selling and administrative assets is reported as operating expenses of the period.

Amortization and depletion follow the same principles. Amortization of intangible assets used in the manufacturing of a finished product (or depleting a natural resource) is reported as part of the cost of inventory until the inventory is sold, at which time the cost is reported as cost of goods sold. Amortization on intangible assets that are used in the administrative or selling function is reported in operating expenses for the period.

Change in Accounting Estimate

Depreciation and amortization calculations require estimating both the anticipated useful life and salvage value, and as was discussed in Chapter 5, even the cost of the asset is subject to the application of judgment. One result of these estimates is that the reported depreciation expense and net income are also only estimates. Also, because of these estimates, a problem that arises is what to do when better estimates become available.

Since future events are always uncertain, it is likely that some estimates of residual value or anticipated useful life will change. In fact, changing an estimate is a normal and recurring part of many aspects of accounting. When a **change in an accounting estimate** occurs, no adjustment is made to the financial statements of prior periods, neither is a catch-up adjustment made to adjust balances to what they would have been if the revised estimates had been used initially. Rather, the *procedure for any change in an accounting estimate*—and not just those related to depreciation calculations—*is to use the new estimates in the current and future periods*. To determine depreciation expense following a change in an estimate, the cost of the asset that remains to be amortized is computed (considering any salvage value), and that amount is amortized over the revised anticipated useful life.

---

[18]This topic of recognizing an impairment of value is covered in Chapter 10.

To illustrate, assume that Anderson Company acquired a machine at a cost of $45,000 and estimated a salvage value of $4,500 and a useful life of five years for the machine. Suppose that after depreciating the machine for two years, Anderson in 2003 determined that its initial estimates were wrong and that the machine will be used five more years, for a total of seven years. At that time, the machine will have a salvage value of $800. Using the straight-line method, computing the depreciation expense for 2003 requires that the amount of cost remaining to be allocated first be determined, as follows:

Cost of the machine		$45,000
Depreciation expense/year (straight-line method)	$8,100	
Number of years the asset has been depreciated	× 2	
Accumulated depreciation		16,200
Unallocated cost		$28,800
New estimate of salvage value		800
Remaining cost to be depreciated		$28,000

Once the "remaining cost to be depreciated" of $28,000 is determined, the depreciation expense for 2003 is computed by dividing the $28,000 by the 5-year remaining life, which results in a depreciation expense amount of $5,600. This amount is also the depreciation expense for each of the next four years of the anticipated useful life of the asset, unless another estimate is changed.

All changes in accounting estimates—when care is employed—are treated prospectively, as illustrated earlier. When the estimate was erroneous because of inadequate judgment or incorrect information, the resulting change is treated as a correction of an error, which is covered in Chapter 14 of this book. Finally, changes made in the depreciation method (e.g., from straight-line to double-declining-balance) are a change in an accounting principle, which is covered in Chapter 9 of this book.

Disposal of Long-Lived Assets

Long-lived assets (whether plant, equipment, or intangible assets) that are traded are accounted for according to the guidelines involving exchanges of assets, as discussed in Chapter 5. Accounting for the disposal of long-lived assets through sale, abandonment, or loss requires applying the following procedures:

1. Compute and record depreciation expense from the time that depreciation was last recorded to the date of disposal,
2. Remove the cost of the asset and any associated accumulated depreciation from the books,
3. Record any consideration received, and
4. Recognize the difference as a gain or loss, as needed.

Disposal by Sale

Returning to the Anderson Company example, assume that Anderson had used the machine for two years after revising the estimates of its anticipated useful life and salvage value. Now, presume that Anderson sold the machine for $16,000 on March 23, 2005—making a total of four years and three months that Anderson had used the machine. Also, assume that Anderson depreciates assets to the nearest whole month. The journal entries to reflect the listed procedures of selling this machine are as follows:

To record depreciation for the current year from January 1 to March 23, which is the date the asset was disposed of:

Depreciation Expense	1,400	
Accumulated Depreciation		1,400

*To depreciate the machine from
January 1, 2005, through March 23,
according to Step 1 above.*

Supporting calculations: the depreciation expense amount of $1,400 was computed as follows:

Depreciation expense per year, following the revised estimates	$5,600
The machine was sold on March 23, making 3/12 of a year	× 3/12
Depreciation expense from January 1 through March 23	$1,400

The journal entry to record the disposal of the asset by selling it is as follows:

Cash	16,000	
Accumulated Depreciation	28,800	
Loss on Sale of Machine	200	
Machine		45,000

To record the sale of an asset.

Supporting computations for the accumulated depreciation amount are as shown:

Depreciation for years 2001 and 2002 at $8,100/year	$16,200
Depreciation for years 2003 and 2004 at $5,600/year	11,200
Depreciation for year 2005, see previous entry	1,400
Total accumulated depreciation	$28,800

The "Loss on Sale of Machine" is merely a balancing figure. It does not represent cash or anything else of economic value. If Anderson had sold the machine for $17,000 instead of $16,000, the company would have had a gain of $800. So the gain or loss can be viewed as a correction of the net income for previous years in which the asset was being used and the net income amounts were misstated because of incorrect depreciation charges. In other words, if more correct depreciation charges could have been determined during the years that the asset was being depreciated, there would have been no gain or loss at the date of sale.

Disposal by Other than Sale

The only change to the previously illustrated journal entry if Anderson Company were to **scrap or abandon the machine** is that no cash proceeds would be received. Thus, the loss would be equal to the machine's book value on the date it was scrapped or abandoned.

The accounting procedures for the disposal of assets that arise through **involuntary conversions** (i.e., acts that are not under the control of the entity), such as fire, flood, theft, or government condemnation through the right of eminent domain, are exactly as illustrated for sales. However, when the gains or losses meet the extraordinary item criteria, they are reported as such on the income statement.

This Is the Real World

Lockheed Martin Space Systems, a unit of the nation's largest defense contractor, Lockheed Martin, has several billion dollars worth of government contracts with the Pentagon and NASA. Government contracts are frequently devised to compensate the service provider (in this case, Lockheed Martin) for all costs incurred, as reported by the accounting system, plus a predetermined profit percentage.

In a letter to the Defense Department, Democratic Senator Tom Harkin from Iowa accused Lockheed Martin of using accounting procedures to cheat the government and hence, the American taxpayers, out of nearly $100 million. The accusations from Senator Harkin were based on the fact that during 2001, Lockheed Martin Space Systems sold some defense facilities for several million dollars. Although the book value of the buildings was $95 million, the company determined that, at the time of sale, the facilities had no value and the entire proceeds were allocated to the sale of the land. Since the government paid for repairs, maintenance, and $22 million worth of improvements on the facilities (as late as 1999), it could have participated in any realized gain from the sale of the facilities. However, regulations prohibit the government from participating in any gains from the sale of land. Senator Harkin claimed that the company intended to lease back some of the "worthless" buildings and pointed out that the county tax records had an appraised value for the buildings of several million dollars.

The company defended its accounting policy, stating that various buyers wanted only the land and have torn down the buildings or plan to do so in order to build new office facilities.

Questions:
1. Suppose the proceeds received from the sale of the facilities were $150 million and the book value of the land was $20 million. Prepare the journal entry to record the sale, assuming (a) the market value of the buildings was equal to their book value and (b) their market value is equal to $0. What are the implications to the taxpayers under both scenarios?
2. How should the market value of the buildings be determined? Should the following items be considered?
   • Lockheed Martin leased back the buildings after their sale.
   • The buyers of the buildings demolished them to build new ones.
   • The appraised value of the buildings is recorded on county tax records.

Source: *Edward T. Pound, "Senator: Lockheed Trying $100M Scam," USA Today, April 5, 2001, p. A1.*

A gain or loss must be recognized on all involuntary conversions in the period the loss is incurred, even if the company reinvests the proceeds or plans to reinvest the proceeds in similar assets. For example, companies having property condemned by government edict have proposed that they must invest the proceeds in other similar assets, and therefore, they are in the same economic position as they were before the condemnation. Thus, they argue that no gain or loss should be recognized. However, the FASB has ruled that *gains/losses shall be recognized on "involuntary conversions . . . even though an enterprise reinvests or is obligated to reinvest the [proceeds] in replacement . . . assets."*[19]

Effects of Errors[20]

Just as inventory errors affect various accounts and the determination of net income, so do errors in other accounts (both revenue and expense) have an effect on various aspects of the financial statements. But, since errors in other accounts do not always counterbalance and because the effect of an error is dependent

---

[19]*FASB Interpretation No. 30*, "Accounting for Involuntary Conversions of Nonmonetary Assets to Monetary Assets," (Stamford: Financial Accounting Standards Board, November 1979), par. 2, emphasis added.

[20]The financial reporting requirements in correcting errors will be covered in Chapter 14.

upon how it was caused, the accountant must be able to identify errors and then analyze (as compared to memorize) the effects that such an error has. Despite there being many different ways in which errors can be made and though the effects of each type of error may be different, here are some guidelines that help in understanding the effects that errors have and in being able to correct them.

Errors that are noticed in the same year in which they were made are analyzed and corrected in the same way that adjusting entries are prepared. That is, the process of analyzing the effects of the errors and correcting them are to:

1. Determine what the account balances currently are with the error,
2. Determine what the account balances should be, had the error not been made, and
3. Prepare the correcting entry.

To illustrate, assume that Brown Company acquired an asset on January 1, 2005, for $40,000. It was anticipated that the asset would have a useful life of four years and a salvage value of $4,000. Using this information, the amount of depreciation expense for each year of the asset's useful life is $9,000; but on December 31, Brown Company forgot about the anticipated salvage value and prepared the following journal entry:

Depreciation Expense	10,000	
Accumulated Depreciation		10,000

To correct this error, the accountant compares what should have been done with what was done and prepares a journal entry to properly state depreciation expense. In this case, the correcting entry is as follows:

Accumulated Depreciation	1,000	
Depreciation Expense		1,000
To correct entry when the error was made in the same year.		

When an error is discovered in a year subsequent to when the error was made, the same procedures as previously outlined are used to analyze the effects of the error—except that when preparing the adjusting entry, instead of adjusting expense and revenue accounts, the adjusting entry is made to the retained earnings account (or to a prior-period adjustment account). The reason for adjusting Retained Earnings is that at year-end, the balances in all revenue and expense accounts are transferred (through the closing process) to the retained earnings account. So there is no balance in any prior-year revenue or expense account to correct. Rather, the account (i.e., Retained Earnings) into which the revenue or expense account balance was closed must be corrected.

Suppose that the above error in recording depreciation in 2005 was not discovered until 2007. Then, since the depreciation expense account cannot be corrected—because it has been closed to Retained Earnings—the correcting entry is as follows:

Retained Earnings	1,000	
Accumulated Depreciation		1,000
To correct a prior-year error.		

Just like errors in counting inventory counterbalance, so do some other errors counterbalance. Errors made by omitting an accrual-type adjusting entry (e.g., accruing wages or interest) counterbalance over a 2-year period. Failing to record accrued wages at the end of the year will result in wages expense and wages payable being understated, and when they are paid in the following year, wages expense will be overstated for that year. Thus, failing to make an accrual-type adjusting entry results in the following effects:

	Current Year	Subsequent Year[21]
Wages expense	Understated	Overstated
Wages payable	Understated	No effect
Net income	Overstated	Understated
Retained earnings	Overstated	No effect

Other types of errors may also counterbalance, but the time period may be longer than two years. For example, an error of expensing the acquisition cost of a machine when it should have been capitalized and then depreciated will counterbalance over the life of the machine.

For errors that counterbalance and are caught subsequent to the counterbalancing, there is no need to prepare a correcting entry. Otherwise, a correcting entry is prepared.

Errors in classification (e.g., classifying a sales expense as a general and administrative expense) do not affect the determination of net income, nor do they affect any balance sheet account. Further, such errors affect only the current year and subsequent years in which the amounts are reported for comparative purposes. These types of errors are corrected by correctly classifying the amount on the financial statement, and no journal entry is required to correct the general ledger.

When many errors are discovered, it is usually best to prepare a worksheet in order to analyze the effects of the various errors and to make sure that correcting entries have been appropriately prepared. In addition, using a worksheet makes it possible to prepare only one correcting entry for all errors discovered, and the worksheet becomes support for how and why the correcting entry was made. The following example both illustrates the use of a worksheet to correct several errors and reviews the preceding rules regarding the effects of errors.

XYZ Company began operations early in 2004 with a small but dedicated group of individuals and an innovative product. Not wanting to be bothered with the details of running an office, an individual who had some experience as a bookkeeper was hired, given the title of office manager, and among other duties, was given the responsibility of keeping the books. By March 2007, the owners had become dissatisfied with the quality of information they were receiving. Because the office manager's workload in other areas had substantially increased, an accountant was hired and given the title of controller. One of the controller's initial responsibilities was to review the records for previous years to become acquainted with the company's financial position and to ascertain the status of the books. From this review, the following errors were discovered.

1. Adjusting entries for accrued wages were not made in any year. The controller estimates that the amounts that should have been accrued are $5,000, $8,000, and $9,500 for 2004, 2005, and 2006, respectively.
2. The office manager had expensed the entire amount of insurance premiums when they were paid. The controller has determined that the amounts representing prepaid insurance for the three years are $2,000, $2,500, and $3,600, respectively.

---

[21]This assumes that the adjusting entry for the subsequent year was correctly prepared.

3. Depreciation expense was incorrectly computed. The amounts and direction of the errors were that depreciation expense was understated by $1,500 for 2004, understated by $4,000 for 2005, and overstated by $3,000 for 2006.

4. In 2005, $2,500 of expenses that should have been classified as general and administrative expenses were classified as selling expenses. The same error occurred in 2006 in the amount of $4,000 except that the amount should have been reported as selling expenses but was classified instead as general and administrative expenses.

5. In January of the current year, some used machinery was sold for $1,000 that originally had cost $5,000 and on which $3,500 of depreciation had been taken. The office manager had correctly written off the cost of the machinery and had recognized the receipt of the $1,000 but had not recorded the $500 loss.

Having discovered these errors, the controller prepared the worksheet shown in Illustration 7-6 to assist in preparing the correcting entry.

ILLUSTRATION 7-6

Worksheet for Error Corrections

Description	Effect on Income				Accounts Needing Adjusting	
	2004	2005	2006	2007	Dr.	Cr.
Income reported	$(5,000)	$10,000	$ 8,500	NA		
1. Accrued wages—2004	(5,000)	5,000			Error has counterbalanced.	
Accrued wages—2005		(8,000)	8,000		Error has counterbalanced.	
Accrued wages—2006			(9,500)	$ 9,500	Retained Earnings, $9,500	Wage Expense, $9,500
2. Prepaid insurance—2004	2,000	(2,000)			Error has counterbalanced.	
Prepaid insurance—2005		2,500	(2,500)		Error has counterbalanced.	
Prepaid insurance—2006			3,600	(3,600)	Prepaid Insurance, $3,600	Retained Earnings, $3,600
3. Depreciation	(1,500)	(4,000)	3,000		Accumulated Depr., $2,500	Retained Earnings, $2,500
4. Classification					No correcting entry necessary for error of this type.	
5. Loss on machinery				(500)	Loss on Sale, $500	Accumulated Depr., $500
Income as adjusted	$(9,500)	$ 3,500	$11,100			

*Bracketed amounts indicate that the effect is to reduce reported net income.

Note the following from Illustration 7-6:

• Errors in accruals (i.e., the failure to accrue wages) and the failure to adjust the prepaid accounts (i.e., expensing the insurance premiums in the year they were paid) reverse over two years. So the only correcting entry required is for the error in the previous year, 2006.

- Errors in the long-term deferrals (i.e., depreciation) have not reversed; regardless of how many years it has been since the error was made, a correcting entry is necessary.
- Errors in classification have no effect on the general ledger, and correcting entries are not necessary.
- Errors to revenue and expense accounts in prior years are adjusted to the retained earnings account.
- The failure to record a loss on disposal of machinery is adjusted to the loss account, and since it is assumed that the journal entry to record the sale balanced and both the cash and machinery accounts are correct, the error must have been in the accumulated depreciation account.

Using the information in Illustration 7-6, the following correcting entry is prepared:

Prepaid Insurance	3,600	
Accumulated Depreciation	2,000	
Loss on Sale	500	
Retained Earnings	3,400	
Wage Expense		9,500

To correct the accounting records for various mistakes that were made from 2004 through 2007, in accordance with the attached worksheet.

Summary

This chapter covered two aspects of the matching principle: (1) the immediate recognition aspect and (2) the systematic and rational allocation aspect. Examples of costs that are recognized according to the immediate recognition aspect of the matching principle include:

- Expenditures incurred that are a function of time (e.g., rent, interest, and property taxes).
- Expenditures incurred for services that are part of the normal ongoing operations of the company and that are not part of the cost of producing inventories (e.g., utilities and salaries that are part of the administrative and selling functions).
- Expenditures incurred for past services that do not result in probable future benefits that extend beyond one year.
- Expenditures incurred for the normal maintaining of assets or for the restoration of assets that have broken down during the current period.

Expenditures incurred subsequent to placing long-lived assets in service that are additions to those assets are debited to the asset account. For replacements, betterments, rearrangements, and extraordinary repairs, the preferred accounting procedure is to remove the cost and accumulated depreciation of the component of the old asset that is worn out and then to debit the asset for the cost incurred. When the cost and accumulated depreciation of the component are not known, the accumulated depreciation account is debited for replacements and betterments when the asset's life is increased. In all other situations, the asset account is debited.

Depreciation is an estimate of the decrease in the economic usefulness of an asset because of physical wear and tear or technological factors. The purpose of depreciation is to report a more relevant net income number and is not an attempt to report the asset at its current value. Thus, the criteria for selecting a depreciation method should be based on which method best measures income. Any method of allocating the cost of long-lived assets to the periods benefited is acceptable as long as the allocation method is both (1) systematic—gives clear guidance in advance—and (2) rational—is defensible. Commonly used methods of depreciation are the time-based straight-line, sum-of-the-years'-digits, and declining-balance methods, and the activity-based productive-output and service-hours methods. Assets are depreciated to salvage value, but not below, by the end of their anticipated useful life.

Just as depreciation allocates the cost of tangible assets, so too does amortization allocate the cost of intangible assets. The straight-line method of amortization is typically used, although the method selected should be the one that most appropriately matches expenses with revenues earned from the use of the intangible asset.

All changes in accounting estimates are handled in the current and future years; the financial statements of prior periods are never restated. For changes in an estimate involving depreciation calculations, the procedure to compute the revised depreciation expense amounts is to compute the cost that remains to be allocated and to allocate it over the remaining anticipated useful life.

Since depreciation expense is computed and recorded infrequently during the year, disposing of long-lived assets requires updating the depreciation calculations to the date of disposal of the asset. Then, the cost and accumulated depreciation amounts are removed from the general ledger, any cash or other consideration received is recorded, and the difference is recognized as a gain or loss. This procedure is the same whether the asset is sold, abandoned, exchanged, or disposed of through some involuntary conversion.

Just as errors can occur in accounting for inventory, they can also occur when accounting for other expenses. Errors can have a variety of effects on the financial statements. Some guidelines are available to assist in determining the effects of errors, but the accountant needs to be able to recognize when an error has occurred, determine its effects on account balances, and prepare the necessary correcting entry(ies)—regardless of the nature of the error.

APPENDIX A: Group/Composite Depreciation Method

In the chapter, it was assumed that depreciation calculations are applied to individual assets. Obviously, to literally do this would entail an extremely large number of calculations and would also entail a very cumbersome and costly record-keeping system. To reduce the cost and the burden of applying depreciation calculations to single assets, either the group or composite depreciation methods may be used, which apply depreciation calculations to pools of assets. The group and composite depreciation methods use the same procedures, and the names refer only to the types of assets comprising the pools. In the **group depreciation method**, the assets comprising the pool are physically similar or homogenous, and this method could be used to depreciate, for example, all the vehicles of a company. In the **composite depreciation method**, the assets comprising the pool are not physically similar, but are heterogeneous in nature, and this method could be used to depreciate, for example, all the office furniture of a company. When using either group or composite depreciation methods, depreciation expense is computed by multiplying the total cost of the pool by an average depreciation rate.

To illustrate, suppose that Christensen Company uses the composite depreciation method and has compiled the information about cost, salvage value, and anticipated useful life for various assets shown in Illustration 7-7A for each pool. In this example, $65,150 of depreciation would be expensed each year for the next 5.55 years.

ILLUSTRATION 7-7A

Composite Depreciation

Asset	Cost	Salvage	Depr. Cost	Anticipated Life	Depr. per Yr.
Computers	$160,000	$16,000	$144,000	4	$36,000
Desks	70,000	3,500	66,500	10	6,650
Filing cabinets	40,000	0	40,000	10	4,000
Other office furniture	120,000	9,000	111,000	6	18,500
Totals	$390,000		$361,500		$65,150

$$\text{Group Depreciation Rate} = \frac{\$65,150}{\$390,000} = 16.71\%$$

$$\text{Group Life} = \frac{\$361,500}{\$65,150} = 5.55 \text{ years}$$

As long as the essential nature of the assets in the pool remains the same, assets can be either added to the pool or disposed of without having to compute a new depreciation rate.[22] Thus, to compute the new depreciation expense amount when an asset is added to or dropped from a pool, all that needs to be done is to multiply the new cost of the pool by the depreciation rate of 16.71%. This ease of computation is a tremendous advantage to using the group and composite methods of depreciation.

When assets in the pool are disposed of, no gain/loss on disposal is recognized, since the amount in accumulated depreciation relates to the pool and not to individual assets. Rather, the cost of the asset is removed from the general ledger, any cash or other consideration received is recorded, and the difference is recorded in Accumulated Depreciation.

In the preceding example, suppose that a computer that had cost $8,000 was sold for $2,500 at the beginning of the third year. The entry to record this sale would be as follows:

Cash	2,500	
Accumulated Depreciation	5,500	
Computer		8,000

To record the disposal of an asset under
either the group or composite method.

The above calculations assumed that the straight-line method was used. However, declining-balance procedures can be applied as well.

---

[22]Some accountants agree with this statement, while others are of the opinion that when new assets are added to a pool, it is necessary to compute a new group or composite depreciation rate.

This Is the Real World

From the Financial Statements of AT&T (emphasis added)

We state property, plant and equipment at cost and determine depreciation based upon the assets' estimated useful lives *using either the group or unit method.* The useful lives of communications and network equipment range from three to 15 years. The useful lives of other equipment range from three to seven years. The useful lives of buildings and improvements range from 10 to 40 years. *The group method is used* *for most depreciable assets,* including the majority of the telecommunications and network equipment. *When we sell or retire assets depreciated using the group method, the cost is deducted from property, plant and equipment and charged to accumulated depreciation, without recognition of a gain or loss.* The unit method is used primarily for large computer systems and support assets. When we sell assets that were depreciated using the unit method, we include the related gains or losses in Other Income (net).

APPENDIX B: Depletion of Natural Resources

The most important difference in depletion accounting from depreciation accounting is that *the productive-output method is the only acceptable method.* Hence, an estimate of the total number of extractable units (e.g., barrels of oil, yards of gravel, or tons of ore) contained in the property must be made at the time of acquisition, which is often difficult to do. Once this estimate is made, a depletion charge per unit is computed in the same way as was illustrated in the chapter for computing depreciation calculations, which is as follows:

$$\text{Per-Unit Depletion Charge} = \frac{(\text{Cost} - \text{Salvage})}{\text{Total Estimated Extractable Units}}$$

The term "Cost" in this equation is the historical cost of the natural resource, which was covered in Chapter 5,[23] plus the estimated costs of restoring the land to government prescribed conditions after the natural resource has been extracted. The total depletion included in determining net income for a year is computed by multiplying the per-unit charge by the number of units extracted during the year.

Since the extracted natural resource becomes inventory, the amount of depletion as computed according to the above formula is reported as part of the cost of inventory until the time the inventory is sold. So the amount of depletion reported on the income statement (and included in the cost of goods sold) is computed by multiplying the per-unit charge by the number of units sold.

Special depreciation problems may arise for tangible assets, such as buildings or equipment that is used to extract natural resources, when the expected life of the tangible assets is longer than the expected time to extract the natural resource and the tangible assets will be abandoned. In such situations, the tangible assets are depreciated using the productive-output method, with the number of extractable units of the natural resource as the base. Special depreciation

---

[23]The historical cost includes all costs in getting title to the natural resource and all other costs that are necessary to begin extracting the natural resource. Some of these other costs include the cost of constructing roads and tunnels, drilling costs, and the costs of wells and shafts.

problems do not exist (1) when the tangible assets have a life that is shorter than the time expected to extract the natural resource or (2) when the tangible assets will not be abandoned when the natural resource is exhausted but will be moved to another site and will continue being used. In those situations, the tangible assets are depreciated over their anticipated useful lives, using the company's normal depreciation method and policies.

When recording depletion, it is more common to credit the particular asset account, rather than crediting Accumulated Depletion. However, some companies do credit such an account.

Questions

1. What is the determining factor as to whether a cost is classified as an asset or an expense? What does this suggest about the importance of management's intentions and expectations? How is it possible for managers to communicate their superior information about firm value through accounting procedures?

2. Which of the following costs would not be reported as inventoriable costs?
   a. Depreciation on equipment used for the sales function.
   b. Advertising costs.
   c. Freight for shipping merchandise to the company's warehouse.
   d. Wages paid to workers involved in the manufacturing process.
   e. Depreciation on a manufacturing plant.
   f. Research and development costs.
   g. Freight to ship sold inventory to a customer.

3. Describe where the costs that are not typically part of the cost of inventory are reported in the income statement and where the costs that are inventoriable are typically reported.

4. James Burgess is an accountant for VIC Inc., which recently paid several thousand dollars in a successful defense of its patent. Although James realizes that the costs of the legal defense can be capitalized as part of the cost of the patent, based on the conservatism convention, he decides to expense the amount immediately. Comment on the appropriateness of James's decision. Explain the conservatism convention, and indicate under what circumstances it should be applied.

5. What is the reason for expensing costs on a systematic and rational allocation basis?

6. T F A company may adopt any depreciation method it chooses, even one that was invented by the company, as long as the method is systematic and rational.

   T F A fixed asset should never be depreciated below its salvage value.

   T F A purpose of depreciation is to report long-lived assets at market value.

   T F When a company changes the estimated useful life of a machine that had been depreciated for three years, previously issued financial statements are never restated to reflect this change.

   T F Similar to the LIFO conformity rule, if a company uses an accelerated depreciation method for tax purposes, the same method also must be used for financial reporting purposes.

7. Distinguish between ordinary repairs, extraordinary repairs, additions, and replacements. Explain the accounting for each type of expenditure.

8. George Lucas purchased a new car and simultaneously purchased a car stereo and had it installed in the new car.
   a. How should George account for the cost of the car stereo?
   b. Would your answer change if George Lucas had waited a year before buying and installing the stereo?
   c. Assume that George purchased another car stereo five years after acquiring the car as a replacement for the original stereo. How should George account for the new stereo purchased?

9. George Lucas II purchased a new car, at which time he estimated the useful life of the car to be seven years. Four years later, George had the engine completely overhauled, which resulted in the car running more efficiently but did not extend its useful life. How should George account for the cost of the engine overhaul? Would your answer change if the engine overhaul extended the useful life of the car?

10. Identify a depreciation method that is based on the passage of time. Identify a depreciation method that is based on activity. Which method is theoretically superior? Why? Which method is easier to implement?

11. How does salvage value affect the calculation of depreciation under the double-declining-balance method? How does this fact affect the idea of not depreciating an asset below its salvage value?

12. An asset was purchased at a cost of $70,000, had no salvage value, and its useful life was 45 years. Using the sum-of-the-years'-digits method and a calculator, determine the depreciation expense for this asset in the thirty-seventh year.

13. Henry Washburn purchased a machine for $50,000. Henry estimates that the machine will produce 200,000 units of inventory over its useful life, at which time Henry believes the machine can be sold for $2,000. If Henry produces 30,000 units in the first year, how much depreciation should be recorded on this machine, using the units-of-production method?

14. Using the same information provided in Question 13, answer the following question. After the third year, the machine had produced 100,000 units and had been depreciated using the original assumptions. During the fourth year of operations, Henry realizes that the machine is becoming obsolete and will need to be replaced after the fifth year of use, at which time Henry believes the total number of units produced by the machine will be 175,000 and its salvage value will be $0. Calculate the depreciation expense for the machine in the fourth year if 35,000 units were produced in that year.

15. Malcolm Harris sold a machine for $5,000. The machine had an original cost of $25,000 and accumulated depreciation of $18,000. What is the journal entry to record the sale?

16. (Appendix) Distinguish between group and composite depreciation methods. Under what circumstances would these methods likely be used?

Exercises

Exercise 7-1: Reporting Costs. Determine where on the income statement each of the following expenditures should be recorded. If the cost is not reported on the income statement but should be capitalized, identify the asset account to be debited.

a. Rewired a section of the factory to accommodate the electrical needs of a new machine. The rewiring will be of benefit long after the machine has worn out.
b. Incurred repair costs during the first year of a machine's operation. The machine is used in the manufacturing of the company's products.
c. State sales taxes incurred when equipment was purchased.
d. The cost of materials to test a newly acquired machine.
e. The direct materials on a self-constructed asset.
f. The variable factory overhead on a self-constructed asset.
g. A portion of the fixed factory overhead on a self-constructed asset.
h. Assessment of $2,300 by the city to repave roads that access company headquarters.
i. Legal fees incurred to close the purchase of a building.
j. Costs incurred to demolish a building on a recently purchased property.
k. Manufacturing supervisor's salary.
l. Salary of administrative personnel.
m. Charges paid for shipping of purchased equipment.
n. Charges paid for shipping of sold inventory.
o. Landscaping charges (trees, shrubs, etc.).

Exercise 7-2: Costs Incurred Subsequent to Acquisition. Kelley Publishing incurred the following expenditures during the 2004 calendar year. The company depreciates all buildings over 20 years, using the straight-line depreciation method and no salvage value. Equipment is depreciated over its useful life, using the double-declining-balance method and no salvage value. The company follows a policy of taking a half-year's depreciation in both the year of acquisition and disposal.

Jan.   15 A building was repainted at a cost of $4,500.
Mar.   31 A bed on a hauling truck was replaced at a cost of $10,000. The old bed was installed in 1999 at a cost of $6,500 and at that time, the truck had an estimated useful life of eight years. The remaining useful life of the truck is four years.
June   1 A building that was purchased in 1992 at a cost of $185,000 was sold in 2004 at a price of $140,000.
Aug.   15 A special device was attached to the building's heating unit to make it run more efficiently. The cost of the device was $2,300.
Nov.   30 An ordinary repair was made on a machine. The cost of the repair was $500.

Prepare a journal entry to record each of the above transactions.

Exercise 7-3: Costs Incurred Subsequent to Acquisition. Determine the proper accounting for each of the following costs by preparing appropriate journal entries.

a. Legal costs of $5,500 were incurred related to a successful defense of a patent.
b. Costs of $800 were incurred to paint the office buildings.

c. The cost of normal maintenance on a company owned vehicle was $250.
d. The air conditioning system was replaced in a company warehouse at a cost of $26,500. The old air conditioning unit was installed six years ago at a cost of $13,200 and was being depreciated on a straight-line basis over eight years, with no salvage value.
e. The company added a new wing to the office building at a cost of $100,000.
f. A major overhaul of a machine was incurred at a cost of $7,000, which should extend the useful life of the asset an additional two years.

Exercise 7-4: Depreciation Methods Based on Time. Johnson Company purchased a $40,000 machine with an estimated useful life of five years and estimates the salvage value of the machine will be approximately $3,000. Calculate the depreciation expense for each year (assuming the machine was purchased at the beginning of Year 1), using the following depreciation methods:

a. Straight-line
b. Sum-of-the-years'-digits
c. Double-declining-balance, assuming a change to the straight-line method at the beginning of Year 4

Exercise 7-5: Depreciation Methods. At January 1, King Manufacturing Company purchased a machine to be used in the manufacturing process. At the beginning of its service life, King Manufacturing made the following estimates with respect to the productive output of the machine:

Production capacity over life of machine	160,000 units
Total estimated service hours over life of machine	18,000 hours
Estimated service life	4 years

The historical cost of the machine was $35,000. Residual value was estimated to be $5,000 at the end of the fourth year of service. During Years 1 and 2, the machine produced 36,000 and 44,000 units, respectively, and was used 4,200 and 4,800 hours, respectively.

Assuming that the machine was purchased at the beginning of Year 1, calculate the amount of depreciation to be recognized on the machine for Years 1 and 2, using the following depreciation methods:

a. Straight-line
b. Activity method based on units produced
c. Activity method based on hours used
d. Sum-of-the-years'-digits
e. Double-declining-balance

Exercise 7-6: Depreciation Methods. Villesse, Inc., purchased an asset on January 2, 2003, at a cost of $40,000. The expected useful life of the machine is eight years, and the expected total productive output is 100,000 units. Actual units produced during 2003 and 2004 were 12,000 and 15,000, respectively. Based on this information, Villesse determines that the following depreciation amounts would be recognized for the years 2003 and 2004, using various depreciation methods:

Year	Method A	Method B	Method C	Method D
2003	$8,888	$5,000	$10,000	$4,800
2004	7,777	5,000	7,500	6,000

1. Without computations and based only upon your knowledge of the cost behavior of the various depreciation methods, identify each of the depreciation methods.
2. Verify your answer to Requirement 1 by computing depreciation amounts for 2005 where possible.

Exercise 7-7: Depreciation Methods; Partial Years. Toby, Inc., purchased equipment with a cost of $72,000 on March 1, 2004. Toby expects the useful life of the equipment to be seven years, with a residual value of $9,000.

Calculate the amount of depreciation to be recognized on the equipment for the years 2004 and 2005, using:

a. Straight-line,
b. Sum-of-the-years'-digits, and
c. Double-declining-balance methods.

When calculating the depreciation for 2004, make two separate independent assumptions. First, assume that Toby uses a half-year convention, where a half-year's depreciation is recognized on all depreciable assets in the years of acquisition and disposal. Next, assume that Toby calculates depreciation to the nearest month.

Exercise 7-8: Partial-Year Depreciation. McGowan, Inc., purchased a building on September 10, 2004, at a cost of $125,000. The useful life of the building is expected to be 20 years, after which the building will have no residual value. Straight-line depreciation is to be employed. Determine the five possible amounts of depreciation that McGowan could recognize for the building in the year 2004. Explain the depreciation convention that is employed for each amount.

Exercise 7-9: Disposal of Assets. Layton Corporation has an asset with a historical cost of $23,000 and accumulated depreciation of $20,000. Provide a journal entry to record the following means of disposing of the asset:

a. Layton Corporation sold the asset for $5,000 cash.
b. Layton Corporation exchanged the asset for 1,000 shares of ABC Co. common stock. The stock had a par value of $1 and a market value of $5.
c. Layton Corporation donated the asset to a charity. An appraisal of the asset indicated its market value was $5,000.
d. Layton Corporation abandoned the asset for no compensation.
e. The asset was completely destroyed by fire, and Layton received an insurance settlement in the amount of $5,000.

Exercise 7-10: Disposal of PP&E. In December 2002, National Sciences Corporation moved into a new building and began the process of trying to sell its existing building. National purchased the old building in January of 1992 for $1,100,000, of which $100,000 was allocated to land, and it was being depreciated on a straight-line basis over 40 years. The building was sold in April 2005 for $750,000, and again $100,000 was allocated to the land.

1. Record the journal entry to dispose of the building.
2. Where should the building be classified on the balance sheet while National Sciences Corporation is trying to find a buyer?
3. Explain where on the income statement any gain or loss on disposing of the building is reported.

Exercise 7-11: Disposals of Assets. Bryce Incorporated owned a building that at the end of December 31, 2004, had a cost of $1 million, a book value of $160,000, and a remaining useful life of five years. The building is being depreciated over a 40-year life, using the straight-line method and a salvage value of $40,000. Bryce's policy is to depreciate assets to the nearest month. Prepare the entries to (1) record depreciation up to date and (2) dispose of the building under the following independent situations:

a. The building is sold for $200,000 on October 1, 2005.
b. The building is exchanged for a similar building having a fair value of $180,000 on April 1, 2005.
c. The building is exchanged for some equipment having a fair value of $160,000 on March 1, 2005.
d. On June 1, 2005, the building is exchanged for a similar building having a fair value of $150,000, and $30,000 cash is received.
e. On November 1, 2005, the building is exchanged for a similar building having a fair value of $135,000, and $45,000 cash is received.

Exercise 7-12: Change in Estimate. Hogle Industries purchased a machine on January 3, 2001, at a cost of $36,000. The straight-line method was used to depreciate the machine over its anticipated useful life of seven years, and the estimated salvage value was set at $3,000. In the late summer of 2004 and before any depreciation expense had been recorded for the year, Hogle determined that the machine will be replaced at the end of 2005 and that it is likely it can be sold for $8,000. Calculate the depreciation expense that should be recognized for 2004 and 2005.

Exercise 7-13: Change in Estimate. Bees-Wax Incorporated purchased a machine on January 1, 2000, for $164,000. At the time, it was thought that the machine would have a useful life of 10 years, after which it could be sold for $24,000. Bees-Wax uses the straight-line method for all long-lived tangible assets. On January 1, 2008, it was decided the machine had a remaining life of five years, after which it could be sold for scrap for $2,000.

1. Determine the amount of deprecation for the years 2000–2007.
2. Determine the amount of depreciation for the years 2008–2012.
3. Compute the gain or loss if the asset is sold for $12,000 cash on May 1, 2011.

Exercise 7-14: Amortization of Intangibles. Tingey's Sporting Goods incurred the following costs during 2004. Indicate whether the expenditures should be capitalized as an intangible asset or expensed as incurred. Assuming that the company amortizes all intangibles with determinate lives over the shorter of their legal life or 10 years and a full year's amortization is recognized in the year an intangible asset is acquired, calculate the amount of amortization expense to be recognized for each of the following intangible assets in 2004.

a. Research and development expenditures of $12,000 were incurred. Tingey fully expects to receive future benefits for the next 10 years as a result of the R&D.
b. Tingey registered a brand-name that was developed for one of its products. Total research and marketing costs to develop the brand-name were $500,000. The cost to register the brand-name with the proper authorities was $1,000.
c. Tingey purchased the rights to an established trademarked product from a competitor for $750,000. It is thought that the trademark has an indeterminate life.
d. A patent with a remaining legal life of five years and a book value of $20,000 was successfully defended in a lawsuit at a cost of $5,000.

(*continued*)

e. Goodwill in the community was established as a result of a special service campaign. The actual cost of the campaign was $50,000. In addition, the company estimated that employees donated a total of 800 service hours to various community projects. The average employee wage is $12 per hour.

f. Tingey acquired the net assets of Lytle Corporation at a cost of $450,000. The estimated market value of the identifiable net assets was $380,000.

Exercise 7-15: Intangibles. Whitney Corporation had the following transactions dealing with intangible assets during 2004:

Jan. 2 Paid $60,000 attorney's fees and other related costs in securing the corporate charter, drafting bylaws, and advising on operating in various states.

 31 Paid $100,000 for television commercials advertising the grand opening. During the grand opening, the company gave away samples of its products that cost $15,000.

Mar. 1 Paid $200,000 to a franchisor for the right to include his products in the business operations. The franchise runs for 20 years and is renewable upon payment of a second amount that will be determined then and will be based on past sales.

May 1 Purchased a patent for $80,000. The patent had been registered on January 1, 2000 and has a legal life of 20 years. Due to technological innovations in the area, Whitney does not expect the patent to generate any cash flows after five years from the date of purchase.

July 1 Paid consultants for providing feedback on a new trademark.

Sept. 1 Acquired the net assets of another business by paying cash of $50,000 and issuing 33,000 shares of $0.01 common stock that was broadly selling for $15 per share. The book value of the net assets was $400,000, but the fair value was $500,000.

Prepare a schedule that shows (1) the treatment of each expenditure (i.e., whether it should be expensed or capitalized, and if capitalized, what account is debited), (2) the amount of amortization expense for the year, and (3) any unamortized cost at December 31, 2004. Assume that amortization expense is computed to the nearest month.

Exercise 7-16: Correction of Errors. Lezzin, Corp. discovered the following errors after the 2007 financial statements were issued:

a. Inventory of $20,000 being held on consignment during 2006 was included in ending inventory.

b. An insurance premium of $18,000 paid on November 1, 2006, was debited to Insurance Expense. The premium was for 24 months, and no adjusting journal entry was made at the end of 2006 or 2007.

c. Equipment was purchased on January 3, 2007, for $40,000. Inadvertently, Repair Expense was debited. The equipment has a life of four years, and salvage value is considered to be 10% of the historical cost of the asset.

1. Prepare journal entries to correct the errors.

2. Explain the effects of these errors on the 2008 financial statements, assuming that the errors have not been discovered and corrected.

3. What would the correcting entries be, assuming that the errors were discovered prior to the closing of the books for 2007?

Exercise 7-17 (Appendix): Group/Composite Depreciation Methods. TLJ Inc. purchased four assets that it intends to pool together for depreciation purposes. Details related to each asset are as follows:

Asset	Historical Cost	Salvage	Estimated Life
Asset A	$18,000	$ 0	6 years
Asset B	63,000	3,000	4 years
Asset C	25,000	1,000	4 years
Asset D	10,000	1,000	9 years

1. Distinguish between the group and composite methods of depreciation.
2. Determine the amount of annual depreciation to be recorded for the pool of assets and the number of years this amount will be recognized.
3. Assume that Asset C was disposed of at the end of its third year for $10,000. Provide a journal entry to record the transaction. Would this sale of Asset C affect the amount of depreciation to be recorded in subsequent years?

Problems

Problem 7-1: Historical Cost and Depreciation Methods; Partial Year. Tucker Company ordered a machine that is expected to improve operating efficiency. The machine was shipped to Tucker on August 25, 2004, FOB shipping point. Details of the transaction are as follows.

Retail price of the machine	$24,000
Sales tax rate	6.5%
Shipping costs paid by Tucker	$350
Installation costs	$570
Financing terms	2/10, net 60

The machine has an expected useful life of seven years, after which it is expected to have a salvage value of $1,500. Tucker Company paid for the machine upon delivery on September 2, 2004. Financial statements are prepared on a calendar-year basis.

Required:
1. Assuming that Tucker calculates depreciation to the nearest whole month in the years of acquisition and disposal, compute the depreciation expense on the machine for the years 2004, 2005, and 2006, using the following methods:
   a. Straight-line
   b. Sum-of-the-years'-digits
   c. Double-declining-balance
2. If Tucker Company believes that stockholder wealth is maximized when earnings are at their highest levels, which depreciation method should the company adopt so as to maximize stockholder wealth in the earlier years of the asset's life?
3. Suppose that the CEO of Tucker Company believes the company will benefit from implementing a depreciation method that expenses more costs in the early years, because, according to the CEO, this policy will allow the company to generate replacement funds at a faster rate, which in turn will allow the company to quickly replace old equipment. Ignoring income taxes, comment on this philosophy.

Problem 7-2: Depreciation Methods. Oswald Widget Co. purchased new equipment on January 3, 2003. The cost of the new equipment was $19,000. The company made the following estimates related to the machine's operations:

Estimates

Life in years	6 years
Production capacity over life of machine	84,000 units
Service hours over life of machine	12,000 hours
Residual value at the end of six years	$500

Oswald recognizes depreciation to the nearest whole month.

Required:
1. Assume that during the first year of operations, the equipment produced 17,000 units and was in service for 2,500 hours. Calculate the amount of depreciation that would be recognized, based on each of the following methods:
   a. Straight-line
   b. 150% declining-balance
   c. Units-of-production
   d. Service-hours
   e. Sum-of-the-years'-digits
2. On June 1, 2007, Oswald sold the old equipment for $3,200. Data related to actual usage of the old equipment for the year 2007 and for its entire life are as follows.

	Year 2007	Entire Useful Life
Units produced	4,000 units	67,000 units
Service hours	2,500 hours	11,500 hours

Calculate the depreciation expense for 2007 on the old equipment, using each of the depreciation methods in Requirement 1.
3. Prepare journal entries for the disposal of the old equipment for each of the depreciation methods in Requirement 1.
4. Which depreciation method results in the largest loss on disposal?
5. Which depreciation method resulted in the highest net income *over the life of the equipment*?

Problem 7-3: Accounting for Equipment, Depreciation, Postacquisition Costs, and Disposal. The equipment and corresponding accumulated depreciation accounts for John Taylor, Inc., as of January 1, 2003, are as follows.

Equipment (January 1, 2003)		Accumulated Depreciation	
$110,550			$61,800

Because much of the equipment was relatively old, John Taylor entered into the following transactions during 2003:

Feb.   2 Equipment with a fair market value of $9,000 was donated to the company by a retired employee.

Mar. 11 Old equipment that was originally purchased in 1996 with a historical cost of $40,000 was sold for $2,500.

Apr.   5 The company purchased new equipment at a price of $55,000.

May 31 A major part on a piece of equipment was replaced at a cost of $15,000; the cost of the old part was not known and the life of the asset is not extended.

Sept.   3 An old air conditioning unit, which had originally cost $5,000 and had been in service since 1992, was replaced at a cost of $17,000.

Dec. 15 The total maintenance cost on all equipment for the year was $4,300.

The following information is also provided.

a. All of the equipment is depreciated using the straight-line method at a 10% annual rate, with no estimated salvage value.

b. As part of the $110,550 opening balance in Equipment, $23,000 was equipment that was fully depreciated. All other equipment has at least one year left on its anticipated useful life.

c. The company's policy is to take a half-year's depreciation in the year of purchase and a half-year's depreciation in the year of disposal.

Required:

1. Prepare journal entries for the equipment-related transactions that took place in 2003.
2. Prepare the year-end adjusting entry to record depreciation.

Problem 7-4: Costs Incurred Subsequent to Acquisition, Partial-Year Depreciation, and Change in an Accounting Estimate. Darrin's Home Products purchased a machine in 2002 at a historical cost of $42,000. At the time of purchase, the estimated useful life of the machine was four years, and the estimated salvage value was $2,000. The company uses straight-line depreciation and takes a half-year's depreciation in the year of acquisition and disposal. During 2004, the following expenditures on the machine were incurred:

Jan.   20 Normal maintenance costs of $700 were incurred.

Apr.   5 A new and improved part installed in the equipment improved the efficiency of the machine. The cost of the part was $4,700. The company financed this expenditure and incurred finance charges of $350.

Sept.   3 A consultant was hired to train the workers how to better use the machine, which is expected to extend the machine's useful life by two years. The consultant's fees were $2,000.

Dec.   8 The machine was adapted to perform additional tasks. The cost of the up-grade was $2,500 and does not improve the machine's efficiency but adds to the usefulness of the machine. In addition, the expenditure increases the estimated salvage value of the machine to $5,000.

Required:

1. Journalize each transaction.
2. Calculate the amount of depreciation to be recognized on the machine in 2004.

Problem 7-5: Depreciation Changes. Ozark Computer Company has two pieces of machinery that are used in business operations. Details related to each piece of machinery as of January 1, 2003, are as follows:

	Machine No. 1	Machine No. 2
Year of purchase	1999	2001
Historical cost	$50,000	$75,000
Estimated useful life	8 years	5 years
Depreciation method	straight-line	double-declining-balance
Estimated salvage value	$5,200	$12,000

The company follows the policy of recognizing a half-year's depreciation in both the year of purchase and the year of disposal. During 2003, the company made two decisions related to the machinery. First, the company decided that technological advances will require Machine No. 1 to be replaced at the end of 2004, and that the machine will have to be scrapped at that time. Second, the company decided that Machine No. 2 will be used until the end of 2007, and that its anticipated salvage value will be $2,000. When using the DDB method, the company also follows the policy of converting to the straight-line method halfway through the useful life.

Required:
Compute the amount of depreciation expense for both machines for 2003.

Problem 7-6: Disposal of Assets. Griffey Company incurred the following transactions related to the disposition of assets in 2004.

a. A building was sold for $550,000 on April 1. The historical cost of the building was $300,000 and was being depreciated over a 30-year life, using the straight-line method. At the beginning of 2004, the accumulated depreciation on the building was $120,000. The land upon which the building was set had a historical cost of $75,000. Prior to the sale of the building, the appraised market value of the building and land were $450,000 and $150,000, respectively.

b. On June 1, Griffey sold used machinery to Reds, Inc., for $1,000 cash and 100 shares of stock in Reds, Inc. The stock had a market value of $50 per share and a par value of $1 per share. The machinery was originally purchased by Griffey on October 2, 2001, at a historical cost of $10,000 and was being depreciated using the double-declining-balance method over five years, with no salvage value.

c. A copyright with a book value of $4,000 at the beginning of 2004 and an estimated remaining life of four years was donated to a local charity on October 30.

Griffey Company records depreciation and amortization on all assets to the nearest month.

Required:
Prepare journal entries to record the disposition of each of these assets.

Problem 7-7: Intangible Assets. Brian Harris Corporation incurred the following expenditures during the 2004 calendar year:

Jan. 12 Expenditures related to organizing a research division within the business cost $12,000.

28 Legal fees of $23,800 were incurred in the successful defense of a patent. The patent has a carrying value of $120,000 and a useful life of 10 years.

May 15 A machine to be used in a research and development project was purchased for $37,000. The R&D project is expected to last for three years, after which the machine will be scrapped.

June   5 The company, trying to improve its brand-name, launched an advertising campaign at a cost of $50,000. The company expects to receive benefits from the campaign for approximately two years.

Aug. 11 A subsidiary was purchased. As part of the purchase price, goodwill was computed to be $22,000. Assume that the goodwill has an indeterminate life.

Dec. 20 Employee wages related to R&D activities were $172,000.

Required:

1. Prepare the journal entries for the transactions.
2. Prepare the necessary year-end adjusting entries, assuming that the company calculates amortization to the nearest month.

Problem 7-8: Errors. Torry Corporation acquired land and a building in Townsend City on January 2, 2004. Operations did not begin until July 1, 2004, because of the need to construct a suitable building. At the beginning of 2005, but before the books were closed for 2004, an analysis of the building account was undertaken, which showed the following:

Date	Activity	Amount
Jan. 1	Purchase of land and building	$ 200,000
Feb. 15	Paid the cost of removing the old building	230,000
Mar. 1	Legal fees paid	86,000
10	Payment to contractor	2,000,000
Apr. 20	Special tax assessment	20,000
May 1	General expenses	64,000
Jun. 30	Final payment to contractor	5,000,000
30	Asset write-up	200,000
Dec. 31	Depreciation expense	(195,000)
31	Account balance	$7,605,000

The following information was gathered in support of these expenditures:

Jan.   1 The company paid $50,000 cash and issued 30,000 shares of its $5 par common stock as payment for the land and building. At the time, the tax rolls of the county showed a fair value of $500,000 for the land and $1,000,000 for the building. Torry's stock was widely traded, and its price at January 1, 2004, was $45 per share

Feb. 15 The contractor who removed the building kept all salvage materials as part of his compensation.

Mar.   1 The bill received from legal counsel for services rendered showed the following detail:

Fees for obtaining necessary permits and licenses to open for business in the city, county, and state	$50,000
Fees for examining title to land	20,000
Fees for preparing contract with building contractor	16,000

Apr. 20 The special assessment was for installing new sewer lines, curbs, and gutters. The improvements will be maintained by the city.

May 1 The general expenses consisted of the following:

Travel expenses of corporate executives to select the site	$24,000
Travel expenses of corporate personnel to review progress on and quality of construction of the building	40,000

June 30 Due to the increase in construction costs in the area, which also resulted in market prices of all buildings in the area increasing in price, the board of directors felt that the fair value of the building was $200,000 more than what had been paid. Accordingly, this write-up was made with an offsetting credit to Gain, Price Appreciation.

It is the corporation's policy to depreciate buildings over 40 years, using the straight-line method, with a salvage value of 10%, using the one-half year convention.

Required:
Prepare the necessary journal entries to correctly state the balance of the building account and all other accounts affected, including Depreciation Expense.

Problem 7-9: Errors with Worksheet. Due to employee turnover during the prior two years, the recently hired controller of Midwest Manufacturing decided to review all account balances to determine their correctness. As a result of that review, the following errors were discovered but too late to correct the 2004 financial report:

a. Revenue received in advance in 2004 of $50,000 was credited to a revenue account when received. Of the amount, only $5,000 had been earned by December 31, 2005.
b. Accrued salaries and wages payable were not recorded at the end of either 2003 or 2004. The amounts were $40,000 and $33,000, respectively.
c. The entire amount of $60,000 was expensed for a 3-year insurance policy that was purchased on March 1, 2004.
d. Depreciation expense was overstated for 2003 in the amount of $22,000 and was also overstated for 2004 by $20,000.
e. Some equipment was acquired on May 1, 2004, for $80,000. The equipment has a 5-year life, after which it is anticipated that its salvage value will be $10,000. Instead of capitalizing the equipment, the entire cost was miscoded as a repair expense. As a result, no depreciation was recorded for 2004. Depreciation is computed to the nearest month.
f. Inventory on consignment to a retailer was not included in the year-end count, and as a result, the ending inventory at December 31, 2003, was understated by $50,000.
g. Merchandise shipped on December 29, 2004, from a supplier with shipping terms FOB shipping point was not included in the ending inventory count nor was the purchase recorded in the general ledger at December 31, 2004. The purchase price of the inventory was $36,000.

Midwest Manufacturing had reported net income of $400,000 for 2003 and $440,000 for 2004.

Required:
1. Prepare a worksheet in which the corrected net incomes for 2003 and 2004 are computed.

2. Prepare the necessary correcting entry(ies) to bring all accounts to their proper balances as of December 31, 2004. (*Hint:* Since the general ledger for 2004 has been closed, correct Retained Earnings when it is necessary to correct an account that has been closed.)

Problem 7-10: Cumulative and Comprehensive Review (Chapters 2, 3, 5–7).
On January 1, 2004, Martin formed a new corporation (The Best Corporation) by issuing to himself 200,000 shares of $1 par value common stock in exchange for $10,000,000. Immediately, The Best acquired the net assets of an existing corporation by paying cash of $8,000,000. At that date, information about the net assets acquired was as follows:

Description	Fair Value	Useful Life
Accounts receivable	$2,000,000	
Inventory, 900 units	4,500,000	
Land	1,000,000	
Equipment	1,500,000	5 years
Building	3,000,000	20 years
Accounts payable	4,500,000	
Long-term debt	1,000,000	

Any goodwill resulting from this acquisition is deemed to have an indeterminate life.

The debt pays interest yearly on December 31 at an interest rate of 12%.

During 2004, The Best had the following transactions, which are in summarized form and classified by type of transaction for ease of analysis.

Acquisition of Assets:
 a. On March 1, The Best exchanged $96,000 of inventory (20 units) that was located in a warehouse in another state for similar inventory (15 units) that was located nearby and that had a fair value of $72,000. The Best also received $25,000 cash.
 b. On June 30, The Best acquired several assets from a competitor for $150,000. The assets and their respective fair values on that date were as follows:

Equipment	$ 60,000	useful life of 4 years
Patent	120,000	useful life of 10 years

 c. On October 2, The Best acquired some land in exchange for 10,000 shares of its $1 par value common stock. Before acquisition, The Best had had the land appraised, and the appraisal valued the land at $450,000. The Best's stock was selling for $43 a share on October 2.

Inventory Data:
The following purchases (not including the initial acquisition when the other company was acquired) and sales of units occurred during the year:

Purchases	Sales
100 @ $4,800 each	
15 units	20 units
(see previous acquisition of assets)	
	250
50 @ $5,200 each	
	400
100 @ $5,400 each	
	350
200 @ $5,500 each	
	500
100 @ $5,600 each	
400 @ $5,400 each	

Subsequent Expenditures:

a. On April 1, The Best paid a contractor for improvements made to the building acquired on January 1. The cost of the improvements was $790,000. The improvements do not extend the useful life of the building but will make it more suitable to The Best's needs.

b. On July 1, The Best paid $50,000 for an advertising campaign that is intended to enhance its goodwill in the community. The campaign did not mention The Best's products but rather the charitable programs and other community development programs in which The Best was involved.

c. On September 1, The Best served legal papers in which it notified a competitor that it was suing for infringing the patent purchased on June 30. The suit was settled out of court on November 1 for $20,000. The Best's legal fees were $34,500.

Other Data:

a. Sales for the year were $11 million, 90% of which was collected, as was the beginning balance of accounts receivable.

b. Besides the cost of the inventory sold, depreciation expense, and the items listed under subsequent expenditures, $2.5 million of other expenses were paid.

c. All purchases of merchandise inventory were made on account, 80% of which were paid, along with the beginning balance of accounts payable.

d. The income tax rate is 40%. If a net loss should result, compute the taxes as usual and record the amount as an income tax receivable and an income tax benefit.

e. The Best's depreciation/amortization policy is to depreciate/amortize to the nearest month.

f. Income tax amounts on any net loss is to be reported as a receivable.

Required:

1. Prepare a single-step income statement (including EPS) and a balance sheet under the assumptions that The Best uses straight-line depreciation and a FIFO cost flow.

2. Prepare a single-step income statement (including EPS) and a balance sheet under the assumptions that The Best uses double-declining-balance depreciation and a LIFO cost flow.

3. Compute the return-on-assets for Requirements 1 and 2.

4. What are the effects of the two quite different financial statements? For example, is it likely that the stock price of the company would differ, depending upon which set of financial statements was issued? Do the financial statements tell different stories about the future prospects of the company? Explain.

Problem 7-11: Depletion and Depreciation (Appendix). Montana Mining acquired a new mine site for $15 million that it estimated will yield 2 million tons of ore. At the time of acquiring the land, management anticipated having to spend $5 million to restore the land to government-approved standards, but then the land could be sold to developers for $2,000,000. Management thinks it will take 10 years to extract the ore.

To work the mine, roads and structures had to be built. The cost of the roads was $1 million, and they are permanent in nature. The cost of building the structures was $2 million, and such structures have a life of 40 years. Finally, the mine shaft was dug at a cost of $1,000,000 and the necessary machinery installed, which had a cost of $4,000,000. The machinery has a life of 10 years. Following the removal of the ore, the company does not anticipate removing the structures, and the cost of removing the equipment will be equal to its anticipated salvage value. Montana normally depreciates all assets by using the straight-line method and the half-year convention.

At December 31, 2004, Montana Mining had extracted 150,000 tons of ore, of which 120,000 tons were sold for $6,000,000. Besides depreciation and depletion, other costs of extracting the ore were $2 million, and general and administrative expenses for the year were $1 million. The income tax rate is 40%.

Required:
1. Compute the cost of depletion for the year, and state to what account it should be charged.
2. Compute the cost of depreciation for the year, and state to what account it should be charged.
3. What was the total cost of extracting the 150,000 tons of ore?
4. What was Montana's net income/loss for the year?

Research Activities

Activity 7-1: MACRS. What is the modified accelerated cost recovery system (MACRS)? What was the reason for Congress initially adopting an accelerated depreciation method for tax purposes?

Activity 7-2: Impact of Depreciation Policy. Managers of capital-intensive companies can significantly affect their financial statements by the depreciation methods they choose to employ. Consider the following questions.

1. Listed next are some financial statement ratios that are often used by financial analysts. Indicate how each ratio would be affected if a company that is continually replacing its old fixed assets with newer ones chose to use straight-line depreciation instead of double-declining-balance. Assume that the same depreciation method that is used for financial reporting purposes is also used for tax purposes.
   a. Return on assets (Net income/Total assets)
   b. Return on equity (Net income/Stockholders' equity)
   c. Fixed asset turnover (Sales/Total fixed assets)
   d. Debt-to-equity (Total liabilities/Stockholders' equity)
   e. Earnings per share (Net income/Shares outstanding)
   f. Cash flow per share (Cash flows from operations/Shares outstanding)

(continued)

2. From a theoretical standpoint, when should a company use straight-line depreciation and when should double-declining-balance be used? In the United States, a large majority of fixed assets are depreciated using straight-line depreciation. Why do you suppose this is the case? Do you suppose other companies that are domiciled in countries where financial reporting is affected by tax law would typically choose to use straight-line depreciation? Why?

3. The automotive industry is one where fixed assets comprise a large portion of a company's total assets. The following automotive companies are from various countries. Look up their most recent financial statements and determine what depreciation policies are followed by each company, including the depreciation method(s) employed, average useful lives of assets, and estimated salvage values (if available).

United States
Ford Motor Company
General Motors Corporation

Germany
BMW
DaimlerChrysler Corporation
Volkswagon

Japan
Toyota Motor Corporation
Honda Motor Company

4. Calculate the ratios listed in Question 1 for each company listed in Question 3. Make a table that compares the ratios across countries. Summarize your analysis.

Activity 7-3: International Financial Reporting. Research generally accepted accounting principles for depreciation of fixed assets and amortization of intangible assets for the following countries. Include the prescribed methods allowed, limitations in estimated useful lives, and to what extent tax laws influence financial reporting. Include a table to summarize your findings.

a. United Kingdom
b. Japan
c. Sweden
d. Germany
e. France

Cases

Case 7-1: America Online, Inc. For the fiscal year ending June 30, 1996, America Online (AOL) reported net income of $29,816,000, which was equal to $0.28 per share. The results were a significant improvement over the prior year's loss of $0.51 per share and were particularly noteworthy, given that other Internet companies were not even close to making a profit. However, soon after the reporting of earnings for the period, some financial analysts began to question an accounting policy followed by the company. The following note was extracted from the company's 1996 annual report.

Deferred Subscriber Acquisition Costs The Company expenses the costs of advertising as incurred, except direct response advertising, which is classified as deferred subscriber acquisition costs. Direct response advertising consists solely of the costs of marketing programs, which result in subscriber registrations without further effort required by the Company. These costs, which relate directly to subscriber solicitations, principally include the printing, production, and shipping of starter kits and the costs of obtaining qualified prospects by various targeted direct marketing programs and from third parties. To date, all deferred subscriber acquisition costs have been incurred for the solicitation of specifically identifiable prospects. No indirect costs are included in deferred subscriber acquisition costs.

The deferred costs are amortized, beginning the month after such costs are incurred, over a period determined by calculating the ratio of current revenues related to direct response advertising versus the total expected revenues related to this advertising, or twenty-four months, whichever is shorter. All other costs related to the acquisition of subscribers, as well as general marketing costs, are expensed as incurred.

On a quarterly basis, management reviews the estimated future operating results of the Company's subscriber base in order to evaluate the recoverability of deferred subscriber acquisition costs and the related amortization period. It is possible that management's future assessments of the recoverability and amortization period of deferred subscriber acquisition costs may change based upon actual results and other factors.

Required:
1. Explain in your own words the accounting treatment followed by AOL for "deferred subscriber acquisition costs." What was AOL's theoretical justification for following this accounting policy?
2. The balance of the deferred subscriber acquisition costs account as of June 30, 1996, was $314,181,000. Where would this account show up on the financial statements? What other alternative could AOL follow to account for these costs? Calculate what net income and earnings per share would have been in 1996 if AOL had followed the alternative accounting treatment. Assume a 40% effective tax rate.
3. Which alternative (the one that AOL follows or your identified alternative) is most consistent with U.S. GAAP? Justify your answer.

Case 7-2: Delta Air Lines, Inc., and American Airlines, Inc. The 1999 annual report for Delta Air Lines, Inc. (DAL), describes a change in estimate that the company made in that fiscal year. Go to the Securities and Exchange Commission's Web site at **http://www.sec.gov** and use the Edgar Database to answer the following questions.

Required:
1. Look up DAL's 1999 Form 10-K. Describe the change in accounting estimate that was made by Delta in the 1999 fiscal year.
2. How did this change in estimate affect reported earnings for the 1999 fiscal year? Did the company restate previous years' earnings to account for the change in estimate? (*Hint:* You might want to look at Delta's 1998 Form 10-K to answer this question.)

(continued)

3. To compare the depreciation policies of DAL with another company within the same industry, look up the Form 10-K for American Airlines, Inc., for the fiscal year ending March 27, 2000. Make a table that compares the two companies on the depreciation methods used, the estimated useful lives employed for various types of assets, and the salvage value assumed. How did the change in estimate made by DAL affect the comparability between the two companies?

Case 7-3: Vishay Intertechnologies, Inc. Vishay Intertechnologies, Inc., is a leading international manufacturer and supplier of electronic components, particularly resistors, capacitors, inductors, diodes and transistors. Components manufactured by the company are used in many types of high-tech electronic products. Given the ever changing environment of this industry, research and development is critical to the company in order to maintain its market position.

The following income statement was extracted from Vishay's 1999 annual report. In addition, the note that discusses research and development expenditures is provided.

Vishay Intertechnology, Inc.
Statement of Operations
(in thousands of U.S. dollars)

For the year ending December 31,	1999	1998	1997
Net sales	$1,760,091	$1,572,745	$1,125,219
Costs of products sold	1,299,705	1,189,107	858,020
Gross profit	$ 460,386	$ 383,638	$ 267,199
Selling, general, and administrative expenses	254,282	234,840	136,876
Amortization of goodwill	12,360	12,272	7,218
Unusual items	—	29,301	14,503
Purchased research and development	—	13,300	—
	$ 193,744	$ 93,925	$ 108,602
Other income (expense):			
Interest expense	(53,296)	(49,038)	(18,819)
Other	(5,737)	(2,241)	(222)
	$ (59,033)	$ (51,279)	$ (19,041)
Earnings before income taxes and minority interest	134,711	42,646	89,561
Income taxes	36,940	30,624	34,167
Minority interest	14,534	3,810	2,092
Net earnings	$ 83,237	$ 8,212	$ 53,302
Basic earnings per share	$ 0.99	$ 0.10	$ 0.63
Diluted earnings per share	$ 0.97	$ 0.10	$ 0.63

(Extracted from company notes)

Research and development expenses

The amount charged to expense for research and development (exclusive of purchased in-process research and development) aggregated $35,038,000, $28,857,000, and $7,023,000 for the years ended December 31, 1999, 1998, and 1997, respectively. The Company spends additional amounts for the development of machinery and equipment for new processes and for cost reduction measures.

Assume that beginning in 1997, the company began to follow international accounting standards with respect to research and development costs. Also, assume that one-half of the R&D costs incurred in each year are related to research and the other half are development costs. The company decides that future benefits from R&D expenditures will be approximately 10 years and a half-year convention is followed in the year the expenditures are made. Also, assume an effective tax rate of 30%.

Required:
1. Determine what net income and earnings per share would be for each year, given this change in accounting.
2. Calculate the amount of deferred R&D costs that would be shown on the balance sheet for each year.

Case 7-4: Cendant Corporation. Cendant Corporation was formed in December 1997 from the merger of HFS Inc. and CUC International Inc. Headquartered in Parsippany, New Jersey, the company has more than 40,000 employees and operates in over 100 countries. The company operates in three principal segments: Travel services, Real estate services, and Alliance marketing. In Travel services, Cendant is the leading franchisor of hotels (Ramada) and rental car agencies worldwide (Avis) and the largest provider of vacation exchange services. In Real estate services, Cendant is the world's largest franchisor of residential real estate brokerage offices (Coldwell Banker). In Alliance marketing, Cendant provides access to insurance, travel, shopping, auto, and other services.

One of the membership clubs offered by Cendant is called *TravelAdvantage*. Members of this club are provided with discounts on travel. As a marketing strategy, Cendant offers prospective customers free membership for three months, after which, if the customer decides to retain the membership, an annual fee is charged. However, at any time during the membership period, customers are offered a full money-back guarantee if they decide to revoke their membership for any reason.

Cendant incurs significant amounts of solicitation costs as part of its selling process. The company is able to demonstrate that future economic benefits are derived from these solicitation costs in the form of increased membership fees.

Required:
How should Cendant account for the solicitation costs?

8

Revenue Recognition Principle

Professional sports organizations depend heavily on season ticket sales for their revenue, with most of the tickets being sold during the current playoff season and extending through the next "off-season." Another significant source of revenue is the annual television and radio broadcasting contracts, which are signed in advance of any games played.[1]

Questions

1. Is it appropriate to recognize revenue when the season tickets are sold and when the broadcasting contracts are signed?

2. Besides selling a season ticket or signing a broadcasting contract, what else, if anything, needs to occur before the professional sports organization may recognize revenue? That is, when should revenue be recognized?

Because of the costs involved, manufacturers of large commercial aircraft do not start production until a contract has been signed. Contracts are usually fixed-price contracts, and production extends over a considerable period of time.

Questions

1. Should revenue be recognized when the contract is signed? Why or why not?

2. When do you think revenue should be recognized?

The number of on-line auction companies has grown significantly in recent years. One such on-line company auctions airline tickets, hotel rooms, and several other products and services. For selling the airline tickets and hotel rooms, companies are paid a commission. However, according to the published financial statements of this on-line auction company, revenue is recognized in "the amount received from the customer, net of taxes." Partly due to this manner of recognizing revenue, this on-line auction company's revenues grew from $35 thousand in 1998 to $482 thousand in 1999.

Question

What is your assessment of this company's policy of recognizing revenue?

---

[1]The signing of broadcasting contracts is a function of the NBA, NFL, etc., and not of individual teams. However, for illustrative purposes this distinction is ignored.

- Define the revenue recognition principle.
- State why companies might overstate revenues and the ways in which it might be done.
- Prepare the necessary journal entries when revenue is recognized at the point of sale.
- Describe when revenue can be recognized after production is completed, and compute the amount of revenue to be recognized.
- Explain when it is appropriate to recognize revenue (i.e., gross profit) during the production process, and apply the percentage-of-completion method to compute the revenue to be recognized.
- Explain when it is appropriate to postpone recognizing revenue until cash is received, and apply the installment-sales and cost recovery methods to recognizing revenue.
- Explain when investment revenue (i.e., interest and dividends) is recognized, and prepare appropriate entries.

The previous chapters have focused upon the accounting for costs. This chapter deals with recognizing revenue, and Chapter 9 will cover the reporting of costs and revenues on an income statement. Adding to the theoretical framework that is being constructed, the accounting for revenues is graphically illustrated in Exhibit 8-1.

The Theory of When Revenue Should Be Recognized

Transactions that result in net asset inflows and are connected with earning revenue are among the most significant transactions of any company. Earning revenue—and ultimately profits—is the reason businesses are formed. So, deciding when to recognize revenue and how much revenue to recognize are significant issues in accounting. This chapter primarily deals with determining *when* it is appropriate to recognize revenue.[2]

The **revenue recognition principle** determines when revenue is recorded in the general ledger of the company and reported on its financial statements. The revenue recognition principle specifies that the earliest point in time that revenue may be recorded in the company's ledgers and reported in its financial statements is when the revenue is both (1) realized or realizable and (2) earned.[3] Once this date is determined, the amount of revenue to be recognized is measured by the amount of cash received or by the fair value of the assets or rights received.

---

[2]Recognition and realization are frequently used interchangeably in the accounting literature. However, they are not the same, and in its conceptual framework, the FASB drew a clear distinction. Recognition is the "process of formally recording or incorporating an item in the accounts and financial statements of an entity." *SFAC No. 5*, par. 6, and *SFAC No. 6*, par. 143. Realization is the "process of converting noncash resources and rights into money." *SFAC No. 6*, par. 143. Also, see *SFAC No. 5*, par. 83–84.

[3]*Statement of Financial Accounting Concepts No. 5*, "Recognition and Measurement in Financial Statements of Business Enterprises," Stamford: Financial Accounting Standards Board, December 1984, par. 83.

EXHIBIT 8-1

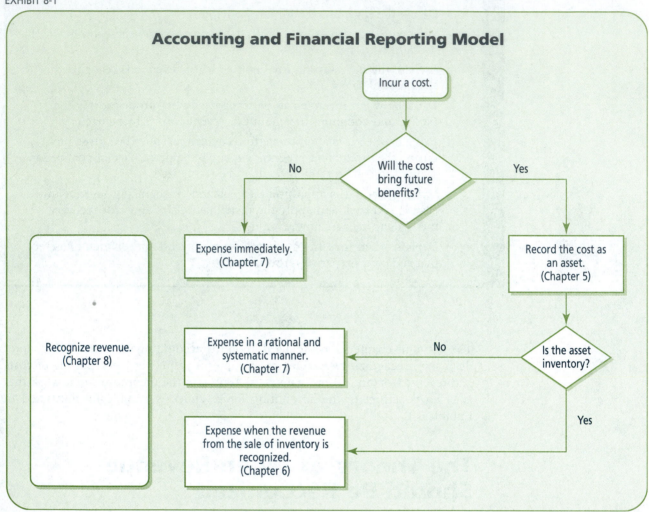

Accounting and Financial Reporting Model

Incur a cost.

Will the cost bring future benefits?

No → Expense immediately. (Chapter 7)

Yes → Record the cost as an asset. (Chapter 5)

Is the asset inventory?

No → Expense in a rational and systematic manner. (Chapter 7)

Yes → Expense when the revenue from the sale of inventory is recognized. (Chapter 6)

Recognize revenue. (Chapter 8)

INTERNET
WWW

The Boston Celtics is a public company and therefore must provide to the general public financial statements that comply with Generally Accepted Accounting Principles. You can learn about the company by going to a financial tool website that provides general information about listed companies (e.g., **http://cbs.marketwatch.com**; **http://www.hoovers.com**) and look up the ticker symbol BOS.

Revenue is **earned** when the company has substantially accomplished what it must do to receive the benefits represented by the revenues. Revenue is **realized** when goods or services are exchanged for cash or claims to cash, such as a receivable. Revenue is **realizable** when goods or services are exchanged for an asset that is readily convertible to cash or a claim to cash. Readily convertible assets have the characteristics of unit interchangeability (i.e., not being able to differentiate one unit from another) and have a quoted price in an active market. An investment in a share of stock is an example of a typical "readily convertible asset" because one share of stock cannot be differentiated from another share of stock of the same company, and there is a quoted price in an active market for the stock. Thus, the stock can be sold readily and converted into cash.

© GETTY IMAGES, INC./PHOTODISC

To illustrate the application of the revenue recognition principle, return to the opening scenario of the sale of season tickets by a professional sports organization and the signing of broadcasting contracts. The professional sports organization must answer "yes" to two questions prior to recognizing revenue when the season tickets are sold and the broadcast contracts are signed: (1) Is the revenue realized or realizable and (2) is the revenue earned? Regarding the first question, the answer is "Yes, the revenue is realized or realizable when the season tickets are sold and the broadcast contracts are signed." That is, the sports organization has received either cash or a promise to pay from the season ticket holders and the broadcasting company. Regarding the second question, the answer is "No, the organization has not substantially accomplished what it must do." It now is obligated to play the sports games, and revenue cannot be recognized until the organization has done that.[4]

EXTENDING THE CONCEPT

So when should the professional sports organization recognize revenue on the sale of season tickets and the signing of broadcast contracts? Should it wait until the end of the season to recognize any revenue? What financial reporting difficulties would that cause?

Also, if revenue should not be recognized when a season ticket is sold, what type of account should be credited (i.e., revenue, liability, etc.) when season tickets are sold and cash is received?

Answer: A liability account should be credited. Typically, this liability account is labeled Unearned Revenue.

Once revenue can be recognized, it is recorded in a company's books by debiting a descriptive asset account, such as Cash or Accounts Receivable, and crediting a descriptive revenue account, such as Rent Revenue, Sales, or Accounting Fees Revenue.

Generally, the point of sale is considered to be when revenue is both realized or realizable and earned. However, there are exceptions to this rule, some of which are are summarized in Table 8-1. Other lesser used revenue recognition methods are covered in an appendix to the chapter. This chapter is organized to discuss (1) some difficulties of recognizing revenue at the point of sale, including some techniques used by unethical managers to manipulate the recognizing of revenue, and (2) some exceptions to recognizing revenue at the point of sale.

General Rule—Point of Sale (or Time of Service)

Realistically, most types of revenue are the joint result of many activities of an enterprise. Purchasing, receiving, manufacturing, etc., all add value to the final product. Therefore, revenue can be considered as being earned continuously. However, because of the inherent difficulties in measuring revenue continuously, standard-setting bodies have focused on a single point in time when revenue should be recognized. For most transactions, the point in time *when revenue is considered realized or realizable and earned is when a sale is made or a service is rendered.* This is the general rule for determining when revenue is recognized.[5]

The typical retail store or wholesale outlet recognizes revenue when the sale of inventory occurs, regardless of whether payment is made with cash, with a charge card, or arrangements have been made for the customer to pay later. Also, a CPA, lawyer, or other provider of services recognizes revenue when the service is rendered, regardless of the nature or timing of the payment.

Applying the general rule of recognizing revenue at the point of sale is not without its difficulties. One difficulty concerns **goods in transit** at year-end. Has

---

[4]See Appendix A for a description of the deposit method, which is a method of recognizing revenue when the cash is received first and the services are rendered later.

[5]This reasoning also applies to goods on consignment, which are discussed in Appendix B at the end of the chapter.

TABLE 8-1

Methods for Recognizing Revenue

Time	Revenue Recognition Method	When Used
• During production	Percentage-of-completion method	For long-term construction contracts.
• When production is complete	Production method	The following three criteria must be met: 1. No significant remaining costs, 2. Immediate marketability at quoted prices, and 3. One item cannot be distinguished from another.
	Accretion method (Appendix A)	Currently not permitted under U.S. GAAP.
	Discovery method (Appendix A)	Currently not permitted under U.S. GAAP.
• Point of sale	Point-of-sale method	The predominant revenue recognition method.
• After point of sale	Installment sales method	When uncertainty with respect to the collectibility of sales receivables is higher than normal.
	Cost recovery method	When the probability of collecting cash from sales receivables is remote.
	Deposit method (Appendix A)	When cash has been received, but the seller has a further obligation to the buyer.

a sale been made if neither the seller nor the buyer has possession of the goods at year-end, but the goods are in the possession of the common carrier? The answer as to whether a sale has occurred depends upon the shipping terms. A sale has been made for goods in the possession of the common carrier that are shipped FOB shipping point, but no sale has been made for goods shipped FOB destination.

Another difficulty in recognizing revenue under the point-of-sale method is in the way in which it is applied, as illustrated in Exhibit 8-2 by comparing the revenue recognition policies of AT&T and Caterpillar. Both companies recognize revenue at the point of sale, but note the difference in how the method is applied.

EXHIBIT 8-2

Revenue Recognition Policies of Two Companies

"We recognize products and other services revenues when the products are delivered and accepted by customers and when services are provided in accordance with contract terms." (AT&T 1998 Annual Report)

"Sales of machines and engines are generally unconditional sales that are recorded when product is shipped and invoiced to independently owned and operated dealers or customers." (Caterpillar 1998 Annual Report)

As illustrated by the revenue recognition policies of AT&T and Caterpillar, even when companies utilize the same method of recognizing revenue, it is still possible to recognize revenue differently. So it is with other companies and many other accounting policies. There are variations as to how an accounting policy is actually implemented, thus making it possible for a wide variation of financial reporting results, even when the same accounting policies are used.

Managing Earnings through Overstating Revenue

When reporting to owners, creditors, and others through published financial statements, managers desire to present the best picture possible of the future of the company and their ability to manage for that future. To this end, some unscrupulous managers try to also manage earnings by inappropriately applying accounting principles and procedures so as to obtain a desired result. It should be noted that all attempts to increase the current year's income always result in decreasing some other year's income; that is, managing earnings results in shifting income from one year to another.

In recent years, manipulating the recognition of revenue seems to be a particularly popular method of managing earnings. For example, during early 2000, it was reported that SCB Computer Technology had overstated its net income by $4.2 billion during the previous three fiscal years. A major portion of the overstatement was related to the timing of recognizing revenue. Chapter 2 mentioned that controls are instituted in all accounting information systems—whether manual or automated—to ensure that similar transactions (e.g., revenue recognition) are accounted for in the same way. So the question may be asked as to how the recognition of revenue can be manipulated, as was done at SCB. Unfortunately, the answer too many times is that management overrides the accounting system controls. Such apparently is what happened at SCB. In its 1997 annual report, SCB stated that its policy is to "... [recognize] revenue as professional services are performed." But illustrating how revenue was actually recognized—and how the company's revenue recognition policy was overridden—SCB later disclosed that during its 2000 fiscal year $50 million of revenue had been recognized inappropriately. Note that in all four cases below, SCB recognized revenue contrary to its stated policy and before either the "earned" criteria or the "realized or realizable" criteria had been met.

1. Revenue of $10 million was recognized on a contract that was subsequently canceled, evidently before any services had been performed, which is in obvious conflict with SCB's stated policy.
2. Another $10 million of revenue was recognized on a contract where specific purchase orders were to be issued over a 3-year period. In its financials, SCB stated that it thought the purchase orders would generate $10 million over that 3-year period, and so it had recognized the entire $10 million immediately.
3. Revenue of $3.2 million was immediately recognized on another contract that encompassed a 3-year period, where the $3.2 million was the maximum amount that could be paid in total to SCB and several other service providers.
4. Finally, revenue of $26.3 million was recognized on a contract—which was shared with five other contractors—where the maximum amount that could be paid to all five contractors—in total—was $26.3 million.

A second way that revenue can be overstated is through an inappropriate revenue recognition policy. For example, the revenue recognition policy of one company that sells memberships in time-share condos, generally for 1-year periods, is to initially record a liability and then to recognize revenue ratably over the membership term. At first glance, this revenue recognition policy seems reasonable; but because the company permitted cancelation anytime within one year with a full refund, it is doubtful that the revenue has been earned until a refund cannot be obtained.

EXTENDING THE CONCEPT

The third scenario at the beginning of this chapter told of a company that recognizes as revenue the amount received from the customer, net of taxes, and records as the cost of earning that revenue the amount that the company pays the respective airline or hotel. After having read of various ways in which creative business practices have been implemented with the objective of hyping sales and considering the requirements that revenue must be realized or realizable and earned before being recognized, what is your suggestion for recognizing revenue for this company? When should it be recognized, and how much?

A third way in which revenue can be overstated is through creative management practices. For example, Sunbeam reported substantially increased revenues for 1997, but an investigation found that a major part of Sunbeam's increase in revenue resulted because of two programs: (1) an "early buy" program and (2) a "bill and hold" program. The early buy program was implemented in the fourth quarter of 1997 and allowed retailers to buy merchandise in November and December of 1997 but to not pay for it until as late as June 1998. Sunbeam counted all shipments of merchandise made in November and December as revenue in 1997. With the retailers' aisles filled with merchandise, Sunbeam then instituted its bill and hold program, which permitted Sunbeam's customers to store merchandise in its warehouse, apparently without paying any rent. Thus, Sunbeam had custody of the merchandise and also counted the sale. Sales under both programs were nothing more than next year's sales recognized in the current year. Such policies are known as "channel stuffing" or "trade loading."

EXTENDING THE CONCEPT

What is the effect on a subsequent year's income as a result of such policies to manage earnings?

Answer: Income is reduced from what it otherwise would have been.

In summary, revenue can be recognized inappropriately either through overriding the accounting controls, inappropriate revenue recognition policies, or creative management practices. Illustrating the extent to which revenue can be overstated, KnowledgeWare Inc. was charged with overstating its 1994 fiscal-year income by more than triple the actual amount. For all business practices that are designed to falsely increase sales, it is important to *record the substance of the transaction and not its form.*

This Is the Real World

The number of ways in which revenue can be overstated are seemingly limitless. For example, two telecommunications companies (Global Crossing and Qwest Communications International) bought and sold network capacity from each other. Each transaction was accompanied with cash, which gave them the appearance of being independent transactions, but they were so close in time that the thought that they were connected should be considered. If the transactions were essentially a swap of ca-

pacity, then neither company should recognize revenue. Instead, the transactions should be treated as exchanges of similar assets, and revenue/gain should not be recognized, as discussed in Chapter 5. However, each company treated the sale of network capacity as a revenue-generating transaction and the purchase of network capacity as a capital expenditure that was amortized over a period of time. The result was an immediate increase in reported net income for the period.

Sales with Buy-Back Agreements[6]

Another example of a business practice designed to hype sales is the practice of selling goods with an agreement to buy them back if certain conditions occur or fail to occur. For this type of sales transaction, the FASB has stated that if the buy-back agreement includes a set price and that price covers the cost of inventory and the buyer's associated holding costs, a sale has not occurred. Rather, the seller of the goods should record the transaction as a liability and not recognize a sale until after the buy-back period has elapsed.

Sales with the Right of Return[7]

All companies expect to incur some level of sales returns. When the sales returns are small, they may be recorded as incurred, as has been assumed in the text. Thus, the company records the sales at gross amounts when they occur, and when merchandise is returned, the company debits Sales Returns and credits Accounts Receivable when credit is given or credits Cash when a cash refund is given.

When an enterprise sells goods and gives the buyer the right to return the goods, the enterprise recognizes revenue either (1) after all return privileges have expired or (2) at the point of sale, reducing the amount of revenue recognized by a reasonable estimate of the amount of returns and the costs incurred with the returns. This second option may be used only if all of the following conditions are met:

1. The selling price is substantially fixed or determinable at the date of sale.
2. The buyer's payment or obligation to pay is not contingent upon the resale of the product.
3. The buyer's payment or obligation to pay is not contingent upon theft or physical damage to the product.
4. The buyer exists on more than paper.[8]
5. The seller does not have significant obligations to assist the buyer in selling the product.
6. The amount of future returns can be reasonably estimated.

The intent of these criteria is that a sale cannot be recognized until the rights and risks of ownership have been transferred (see criteria 2 and 3) to a buyer that is a real entity (see criterion 4) with real and determinable obligations (see criteria 1 and 2). When all the preceding conditions are met, *revenue—as reduced by an estimate of the amount of returns and costs that may be incurred in connection with the merchandise returned—can be recognized at the point of sale.* When these conditions are not met, revenue is not recognized until the return privilege expires.

When the six criteria are met, revenue can be recognized at the point of sale, and the following journal entry is recorded:

Accounts Receivable	XXX	
Sales		XXX
Allowance for Sales Returns		XXX
To record sales with right of return because		
the appropriate criteria have been met.		

---

[6]*Statement of Financial Accounting Standard No. 49*, "Accounting for Product Financing Agreements," Stamford: Financial Accounting Standards Board, June 1981, par. 8.

[7]*Statement of Financial Accounting Standard No. 48*, "Revenue Recognition when Right of Return Exists," Stamford: Financial Accounting Standards Board, June 1981, par. 6.

[8]This is meant to exclude buyers who were created by the seller and, as a result, have little or no physical facilities or employees.

The allowance for sales returns account is a balance sheet account that is reported with accounts receivable, thus reporting accounts receivable at the amount expected to be collected. Likewise, sales are recorded at the net amount expected to be realized. Later, when any goods are returned, the allowance and sales accounts are adjusted.

To illustrate, Gigantic Publishing Co. sends books to colleges and universities on credit but requires any unsold books to be returned no later than six weeks after the start of the semester. In August, Gigantic sent books to Small College Bookstore in the amount of $500,000. Returns were estimated to be 20%. In September, Gigantic received payment of $380,000 for the sold books, which was accompanied with the return of all other books. The journal entries Gigantic would record to recognize revenue for these transactions are shown in Illustration 8-1:

ILLUSTRATION 8-1

Journal Entries for Sales with Right of Return

August	Accounts Receivable	500,000	
	Sales		400,000
	Allowance for Sales Returns		100,000
	To record sales when there is the right of return.		
September	Cash	380,000	
	Allowance for Sales Returns (reversal of above)	100,000	
	Sales (adjustment)	20,000	
	Accounts Receivable (reversal of above)		500,000
	To record receipt of payment and returned books and to adjust sales for actual books sold.		

CONCEPTUAL
Question

In the journal entries shown, why is Accounts Receivable debited for the gross amount of the books shipped, even though it is known that not all books will be sold?

Recognizing Revenue Before Sale— When Production Is Complete[9]

Having covered some of the difficulties that can arise regarding recognizing revenue at the point of sale and also some ways in which unethical managers manipulate the revenue recognition criteria, attention is now turned to recognizing revenue before the point of sale. In its conceptual framework project, the FASB identifies these times and some of them are shown in Table 8-1 on p. 330.

One result of recognizing revenue at the point of sale is that inventories are never recorded at an amount greater than cost. The reason why inventory cannot be stated above cost is that—because of the double-entry nature of accounting—to do so would require revenue to be recognized before the inventory is sold. That is, the journal entry to write up inventory requires debiting the inventory account, but what account is credited? The possible candidates (i.e., those accounts that normally have credit balances) are (1) a liability account, (2) some stockholders' equity account, or (3) a revenue or gain account. Options (1) and (2) are eliminated because writing up inventory does not result in any obligation

---

[9]*Accounting Research Bulletin No. 43*, Chapter 4, "Inventory Pricing," Stamford: Financial Accounting Standards Board, June 1953, Statement 9.

to an external party, nor is it a transaction with owners. Hence, if inventory is written up, a revenue or gain would have to be recognized—and that violates the revenue recognition general rule.[10]

Years ago, however, the Committee on Accounting Procedure (CAP) stated (and its statement has been accepted by subsequent standard-setting bodies) that, in exceptional cases, inventories can be stated above cost—meaning that *in exceptional cases, revenue can be recognized before the point of sale.* The CAP's statement requires that all exceptions to reporting inventories above cost be justified by the following criteria:

1. No significant costs to dispose of the inventory,
2. An immediate marketability of the inventory at quoted prices, and
3. An inability to distinguish one item of inventory from another.

Concerning these criteria, the CAP gave the example of "an effective government-controlled market at a fixed monetary value" when revenue can be recognized before sale. But there are other instances when inventories can be recorded above cost. For example, agricultural operations frequently meet these three criteria. In that industry, there are many farmers, each of whom can sell all their inventory at the quoted price and not adversely affect quoted market prices. The costs of selling the harvested crop are negligible, and one bushel of wheat, for example, is much like any other bushel of wheat.[11]

© GETTY IMAGES, INC./PHOTODISC

To illustrate how revenue is recognized when production is complete, consider a Kansas wheat farmer who harvests 2,200 tons of wheat in 2004. The market quotation for wheat at harvest time is $48 per ton. The farmer stores 1,200 tons but sells the remaining 1,000 tons at the market price of $48 per ton. The farmer's cost of producing the wheat is $79,200. Under the concept of recognizing revenue when production is complete, the farmer may recognize revenue for 2004 on the entire 2,200 tons at $48 per ton, or $105,600, for a profit of $26,400. However, the farmer may still choose to follow the general rule of recognizing revenue at the point of sale, and in that case the revenue recognized for 2004 would be $48,000, which is computed as 1,000 tons at $48 per ton.

Using the information about the wheat farmer, the journal entries to write up the inventory and recognize revenue at the point where production is complete are shown in Illustration 8-2. Companies that recognize revenue upon completion of production must (1) disclose that policy and (2) reduce the amount of revenue by any costs of disposing of the inventory. That is, such *inventory is reported at its net realizable value.*

---

[10]With the FASB's recent use of comprehensive income, an alternative method of writing up inventory to fair value (and possibly other assets as well) is now available without recognizing revenue.

[11]Sufficiently broad and reliable markets also exist for other commodities, such as metals and chemicals, where inventory can be disposed of at known prices and where no one producer, by selling all inventory, can negatively affect the quoted market price. When such markets exist, revenue may be appropriately recognized at the completion of production.

ILLUSTRATION 8-2

Journal Entries for Recognizing Revenue When Production Is Complete

1. To record the costs of production during 2004:

Inventory (assumed amount)	79,200	
Cash, Accounts Payable, etc.		79,200

2. At completion of production, to write up the inventory to market in 2004:

Inventory	26,400	
Profit		26,400

Supporting computations:

Market price of wheat	$105,600
Costs of production (see entry 1)	79,200
Difference	$ 26,400

When the CAP issued the standard allowing revenue to be recognized when production is complete, it was using a "fire-fighting approach" to standard-setting, which is to address problems as they arise and without any overall coordination with other standards. This particular standard was issued to address an inventory valuation problem; but due to the double-entry nature of accounting, the standard also affects revenue recognition. The standard is in obvious conflict with the FASB's conceptual framework in that (although wheat is a realizable asset that can be readily converted to cash) an exchange transaction is implicit in the definition of realized or realizable. Hence, the farmer mentioned earlier has not met the realized or realizable criterion as intended by the FASB. As yet, no attempt has been made to address the discrepancy between the FASB's conceptual framework and the official standard.

Recognizing Revenue Before Sale— Percentage-of-Completion

A second exception to recognizing revenue at the point of sale is required when *it is more meaningful to report revenue while inventory is being produced*, rather than to wait for the point of sale. The most typical example is for companies that enter into long-term construction contracts (i.e., those contracts that require more than a year to complete). If a construction company waits until a project is complete before recognizing any revenue, the income statement— loaded with expenses and without any revenue—may not report a meaningful result of the construction company's current year's achievement. However, an implication of recognizing revenue during production is that an estimate of revenue/profit will have to be used, rather than reporting actual revenues/ profit, as would be done if the point-of-sale method had been used. But, in accordance with the FASB's conceptual framework, a measure of reliability is sacrificed to achieve a much more relevant measure of the construction company's performance.

When all the following conditions exist, revenue *must be* recognized during production, using the percentage-of-completion method.[12] Otherwise, the completed-contract method (which is a point-of-sale-method of recognizing revenue) is used. Note that these two methods of recognizing revenue for long-term construction contracts are not alternatives. The percentage-of-completion method must be used unless the following criteria are not met, and then the completed-contract method must be used.

1. Dependable estimates can be made of contract revenues, costs, and the progress towards completion;
2. The contract clearly specifies the enforceable rights to be provided and received by the parties, the consideration to be exchanged (e.g., a fixed-price contract), and the manner and terms of settlement; and
3. Both buyer and contractor are expected to satisfy their contractual obligations.[13]

Procedures for Computing Income or Loss

To illustrate the accounting for long-term construction contracts under the percentage-of-completion method, assume that Western Construction, Inc., started construction on a $5,000,000 fixed-price construction contract and reported data for the next three years, as shown in Illustration 8-3(a); all amounts are in the thousands.

ILLUSTRATION 8-3(a)

Summarized Data for Western Construction, Inc.

Entry		First Year	Second Year	Third Year	Totals
1	Cost incurred for the year	$1,050	$2,100	$1,200	$4,350
	Estimated costs to complete	3,450	1,050	0	NA
2	Billings on contract	900	2,000	2,100	$5,000
3	Collections during the year	750	1,800	1,800	4,350
			Total profit to recognize		$ 650

The entries to record the above transactions are shown in Illustration 8-3(b) with all amounts in thousands. The numbers in the first column of each table indicate where the amounts are coming from for the respective entries.

---

[12]*Statement of Financial Accounting Standard No. 56*, "Designation of AICPA Guide and Statement of Position 81-1 on Contractor Accounting and SOP 81-2 concerning Hospital-Related Organizations as Preferable for Purposes of Applying *APB Opinion 20*," Stamford: Financial Accounting Standards Board, February 1982, par. 3. The primary reason the profession prefers the percentage-of-completion method is that yearly costs incurred are better matched with revenue.

[13]*Statement of Position 81-1*, New York: American Institute of Certified Public Accountants.

ILLUSTRATION 8-3(b)

Journal Entries for the Percentage-of-Completion Method

Entry		First Year		Second Year		Third Year	
1	Construction in Progress	1,050		2,100		1,200	
	Cash, Accounts Payable, etc.		1,050		2,100		1,200
	To record costs incurred.						
2	Accounts Receivable	900		2,000		2,100	
	Billings on Contract		900		2,000		2,100
	To record billings.						
3	Cash	750		1,800		1,800	
	Accounts Receivable		750		1,800		1,800
	To record cash collections.						

Under the percentage-of-completion method, gross profit (as contrasted to revenue) is recognized each year in proportion to how complete the project is. Gross profit is measured based upon the relationship between effort-to-date as compared to estimated total effort required for the contract, with effort usually expressed in terms of cost.[14] Procedurally, the profit recognized for a year is computed through the following steps:

1. Compute the total costs to date. This includes not only the current year's costs, but also the costs expended on the contract in prior years.
2. Estimate the costs that remain to complete the contract.
3. Determine the total expected costs required for the contract, which is the sum of the amounts in Steps 1 and 2.
4. Determine the total expected profit on the contract, which is the contract price less the amount computed as the total costs in Step 3.
5. Determine the cumulative profit earned on the contract to date, which is computed by taking the costs to date (Step 1) divided by the total expected costs (Step 3) and multiplying the result by the expected profit (Step 4).
6. Finally, determine the year's profit by subtracting the profit earned in prior years from the cumulative profit on the contract to date (Step 5).

The profit amounts for Western Construction Inc. for each year under the percentage-of-completion method are computed as shown in Illustration 8-3(c).

Following the computing of the gross profit, the journal entries to record that gross profit for each year are as follows:

	2001		2002		2003	
Construction in Progress	117		483		50	
Profit from Long-Term Construction Contracts		117		483		50
To recognize profit.						

Loss Is Indicated for the Year

These procedures for computing the gross profit are also used when a loss is indicated in any particular year, but a gross profit is still indicated on the contract.

---

[14]Effort can also be expressed in terms of inputs, such as labor hours or machine hours, or in terms of outputs, such as contract goals or objectives.

ILLUSTRATION 8-3(c)

Computing Profit under Percentage-of-Completion Method

Row	Descriptions	2001	2002	2003
1	Contract price	$5,000	$5,000	$5,000
2	Step 1: Compute costs incurred to date [See Illustration 8-3(a)]	$1,050	$1,050 + 2,100 = $3,150	$3,150 + 1,200 = $4,350
3	Step 2: Estimated costs remaining to complete the contract [See Illus. 8-3(a)]	$3,450	$1,050	$0
4	Step 3: Total expected costs (Row 2 plus Row 3)	$4,500	$4,200	$4,350
5	Step 4: Total expected gross profit (Row 1 minus Row 4)	$500	$800	$650
6	Step 5: Cumulative gross profit earned to date (Row 2/Row 4) × Row 5	($1,050/$4,500) × $500 = $117	($3,150/$4,200) × $800 = $600	($4,350/$4,350) × $650 = $650
7	Step 6: Profit for the year	$117	$600 − $117 = $483	$650 − $600 = $50

For example, assume that in 2002 in the preceding example the total expected costs on the contract (both those incurred and those anticipated) are $4,900 instead of $4,200. A gross profit of $100 is still anticipated on the contract, but since a gross profit of $117 was recognized in the prior year, a loss must be recognized in the current year. Otherwise, the gross profit of $117 recognized to date would exceed the $100 total estimated gross profit to be earned. However, the amount of the loss to recognize is not $17. Rather, the amount of the loss to recognize in 2002 is measured by using the same procedures, as follows:

Step 4: Total expected gross profit on the contract = $5,000 − $4,900
$$= \$100$$

Step 5: Cumulative gross profit earned to date
$$= (\$3,150/\$4,900) \times (\$5,000 - \$4,900)$$
$$= \$64$$

Step 6: Year's loss = $64 − $117 = $(53)

The entry to recognize this loss is just the opposite of the entry to recognize a gross profit for the year. Loss on Long-Term Construction Contract is debited and Construction in Progress is credited.

Loss Is Indicated on the Contract (as Compared to a Loss for the Year)

When a loss is indicated on the *entire contract*, the *entire loss* is recognized in the earliest year that it is anticipated. To illustrate, suppose in the given example that in 2002 the total expected costs on the contract (both those incurred and those anticipated) are $5,100. Therefore, since the contract price is $5,000, a loss of $100 is indicated on the contract. In this case, *the loss recognized in 2002 must be an amount large enough so that the sum of any previously recognized profits plus the recognized loss in the current year equals the total indicated loss.* Since a $117 gross profit was recognized in the previous year, a loss of $217 must be recognized in 2002. This is substantiated as follows:

Profit earned in previous years	$ 117
Loss recognized in the current year	(217)
Total anticipated loss on the contract	$(100)

The journal entry to record this loss is:

Loss on Long-Term Construction Contract	217	
Construction in Progress		217

To recognize the loss for a particular year when a loss is indicated on the contract.

There is a difference between a loss for a year and a loss on the contract, and this difference can be determined by comparing the total estimated costs to complete the contract to the contract price. When the total estimated costs exceed the contract price, a loss is indicated on the contract. Then, the entire loss is recognized including the reversal of all previously recognized profits. On the other hand, it may be necessary to recognize a loss for the year, even when a gross profit on the contract is expected (i.e., the contract price still exceeds the total estimated costs). Such a situation arises when (because of changing estimates) too much gross profit was recognized in prior years. Hence, a loss is recorded in the year. The amount of this loss is computed in the usual manner.

EXTENDING THE CONCEPT

Referring back to the opening scenario with the airplane manufacturer, do you think that the company should use the percentage-of-completion method or the completed-contract method to recognize revenue? Why?

Financial Reporting

In the journal entries for accounting for long-term construction contracts, Construction in Progress is an inventory account, and Billings on Contract is a contra-account to Construction in Progress. When the balance in the construction in progress account is greater than the balance in the billings on contract account, the excess represents the construction costs incurred and gross profit earned that have not been billed, and this excess amount is reported as a current asset, labeled Costs in Excess of Billings. When the balance in the billings on contract account exceeds the balance in the construction in progress account, the excess (labeled Billings in Excess of Costs) is reported as a current liability. When a construction company has several long-term contracts, the projects in which the construction in progress amounts exceed the billings on contract amounts are reported as a net current asset, and the other projects are also netted and reported as a net current liability.

Reporting these accounts in this fashion raises the opportunity to highlight the nature of assets and liabilities. Initially, assets are often thought of as being "good" and liabilities as being "bad," which may not be so. For long-term construction contracts, when a company is incurring costs faster than they are being billed—and thus reporting a current asset—the company's cash flows are negatively affected. So having a current asset might be a negative signal concerning the company's cash management policies. The opposite is true when costs are billed faster than they are being incurred. The net balance is reported as a liability, but in fact, the improved cash flow to the company is good.

Whether Costs in Excess of Billings and Billings in Excess of Costs are reported as current or noncurrent depends upon a particular company's operating cycle. Because the operating cycle of a company involved in long-term construction projects is longer than a year, these amounts typically are classified as either a current asset or a current liability.

The Point-of-Sale Method for Long-Term Contracts—Completed-Contract Method

The completed-contract method is used to recognize gross profit when dependable estimates of progress towards completion cannot be made or other conditions of using the percentage-of-completion method are not met. It is also used when the contractor has primarily short-term contracts (i.e., time to complete is less than a year) or there are uncertainties beyond normal business risk. Under this method, gross profit is recognized when the project is completed and transferred to the buyer, except when it is anticipated that there will be a loss on the contract. Then the entire loss is recognized immediately.

The same example that was used to illustrate the percentage-of-completion method will be used to illustrate recognizing gross profit under the completed-contract method. Procedurally, all costs connected with the construction contract are accumulated in Construction in Progress, as was done under the percentage-of-completion method. Also, accounting for billings on contract and collection of amounts owed is done in the same manner as demonstrated for the percentage-of-completion method.[15] (See Illustration 8-3b.) When the project is complete, gross profit is recognized on the contract, and the following entry is recorded. Note that this entry reverses the amounts in both Billings on Contract and Construction in Progress and reports the difference as the gross profit on the contract.

Billings on Contract	5,000,000	
Construction in Progress		4,350,000
Income on Contract		650,000[16]

To recognize gross profit under the completed-contract method when the project is complete.

As mentioned previously, when a loss is anticipated on the contract, the entire anticipated loss is recognized immediately. However, since no gross profit was recognized in any previous years, there is no necessity to back out any previously recognized gross profit. In comparison, in the percentage-of-completion example, when a loss of $100 was indicated on the entire contract, a loss of $217 was recognized in the current year, consisting of the $100 anticipated loss and the backing out of the $117 previously recognized. However, when the completed-contract method is used and a loss for the year of $100 is anticipated on the entire

---

[15]The reason the entries are the same for the completed-contract method is that the costs incurred do not change. Also, the amounts billed the customer do not change because billings are a function of the contract, which specifies amounts that can be billed and when.

[16]An alternative entry is:

Billings on Contract	5.00 m		per ledger
Revenue on Contract		5.00 m	balancing amount
Construction Costs	4.35 m		per ledger
Construction in Progress		4.35 m	balancing amount

INTERNATIONAL

The percentage-of-completion method of accounting for long-term construction contracts is required under U.S. GAAP when the company has sufficient information to implement the procedure. As a result, the completed-contract method is rarely used by companies registered with the U.S. Securities and Exchange Commission. This accounting practice is a significant departure from German GAAP. Germany's conservative accounting system tries to protect the creditor, which is the primary source of capital in Germany (see Chapter 4). Thus, the completed-contract method is the predominant method of accounting for long-term construction contracts in Germany.

The financial statement effects of this difference are that German companies report lower income than do U.S. companies during the years of production, which also affects stockholders' equity and total assets. Then, when production is complete, German companies report higher income. In addition, the completed-contract method tends to introduce greater volatility in earnings. However, the German practice of recognizing secret reserves allows managers to offset this undesirable effect.

contract, then the amount recognized as a loss is just the $100. Finally, under the completed-contract method, no attention is given to losses in a particular year when a gross profit is expected on the entire contract.

Recognizing Revenue After the Point of Sale—Installment-Sales Method[17]

Having covered the general rule of recognizing revenue at the point of sale and two exceptions for when revenue is recognized before the point of sale, attention is now turned to two methods of deferring the recognition of revenue until sometime after the point of sale. The first of these two methods is the installment-sales method.

All businesses occasionally fail to collect all amounts owed. Bad debts are a natural part of doing business. But when there is a more than normal uncertainty surrounding future collectibility of the amounts owed, revenue *"may be* recognized on the basis of cash received."[18] The most common example of postponing recognizing revenue until cash is collected is for companies selling merchandise and collecting installment payments. But *just because a company has installment sales does not mean it can use the installment-sales method of recognizing revenue from those sales.* Rather, revenue from installment sales ordinarily should be recognized according to the point-of-sale method. Similarly, the installment-sales method of recognizing revenue can be used for any sale regardless of whether the terms of sale call for periodic payments over an extended period of time or a single payment at some future point. The rationale for the installment-sales method of recognizing revenue is that although the company has recorded an account receivable in conjunction with a sale, the uncertainty of collection is so large that the realization criterion has not been met.

© CORBIS, INC.

General Procedures for Recognizing Income/Loss

When using the installment-sales method, revenue is recognized proportionately to the cash collected.[19] The essential characteristics of the installment-sales method are:

1. Gross profit (not sales or cost of goods sold) is deferred and then recognized as cash is collected.
2. Because gross profit rates may vary from year to year, a gross profit rate is computed for each year.

---

[17]Installment sales of real estate is not covered in this section. The reader can consult *Statement of Financial Accounting Standard No. 66*, "Accounting for Sales of Real Estate," October 1982, for guidance on this topic.

[18]*Statement of Financial Accounting Concepts No. 5*, "Recognition and Measurement in Financial Statements of Business Enterprises," Stamford: Financial Accounting Standards Board, December 1984, par. 84g (emphasis added). The discussion and illustrations focus upon sales, but the methods of revenue recognition discussed here apply to other revenue transactions as well.

[19]The amount of cash collected may include interest, which affects the amount of sales revenue recognized. This topic is discussed in Appendix D at the end of the chapter.

3. Cash collected must be identified with the sales of a particular year in order to compute how much gross profit is recognized for the reporting period.

4. The amount of gross profit to recognize is computed as follows:

Gross Profit Rate × (Amount of Cash Received from that Year's Sales).

Assume that Harter Corporation uses the installment-sales method for recognizing revenue on sales when future collectibility of amounts owed is lower than normal. The information in Illustration 8-4(a) has been compiled regarding such sales.

ILLUSTRATION 8-4(a)

Data to Illustrate Installment-Sales Method of Recognizing Revenue

Entry		2004	2005
1	Sales for the year	$1,000,000	$1,200,000
2	Cost of goods sold	600,000	735,000
	Gross profit on these sales	$ 400,000	$ 465,000
	Gross profit percentage (i.e., gross profit divided by sales)	40%	38.75%
3	Cash collections:		
	Connected to 2004 sales	$ 450,000	$ 300,000
	Connected to 2005 sales		400,000

The journal entries under the installment-sales method of recognizing revenue are shown in Illustration 8-4(b).

The journal entries under the installment-sales method are the same as the familiar entries under the point-of-sale method, except for the two additional entries that are required at year-end. The first such entry closes Sales and Cost of Goods Sold and establishes a deferred gross profit amount. The second entry then recognizes the appropriate amount of gross profit for the year.

Financial Reporting

Regarding the balance sheet, classifying installment accounts receivable depends upon the length of the company's operating cycle. When there is a higher than normal risk of the receivables being uncollectible due to a longer than normal collection period, installment accounts receivable may be classified as long-term. Otherwise, the resulting accounts receivable are classified as current assets. In either situation, installment accounts receivable should be *reported separately from other accounts receivable*, as shown in Exhibit 8-3.

According to the FASB's conceptual framework project, Deferred Gross Profit is most appropriately reported on the balance sheet as an asset valuation account to the related Installment Accounts Receivable (similar in nature to how Accumulated Depreciation is reported in relation to Property, Plant, and Equipment).[20] However, because accountants do not need to adhere to the conceptual statements, Deferred Gross Profit is often reported under Current Liabilities.

Regarding the income statement, normally there is no need to separately report the amount of revenue recognized under the installment-sales method from

---

[20]*Statement of Financial Accounting Concepts No. 3*, "Elements of Financial Statements of Business Enterprises," Stamford: Financial Accounting Standards Board, December 1980, par. 157.

ILLUSTRATION 8-4(b)

Journal Entries for the Installment-Sales Method of Recognizing Revenue

Entry		2004			2005	
1	Install. Accounts Receivable	1,000,000		Install. Accounts Receivable	1,200,000	
	Install. Sales		1,000,000	Install. Sales		1,200,000
2	Install. Cost of Goods Sold	600,000		Install. Cost of Goods Sold	735,000	
	Inventory		600,000	Inventory		735,000
3	Cash	450,000		Cash	700,000	
	Install. Accounts Receivable		450,000	Install. Accounts Receivable		700,000

These journal entries are the same as those that would have been recorded under the point-of-sale method. However, it is necessary to separate sales where revenue is recognized under the installment-sales method from other sales because of the different methods of recognizing revenue. This is why, in the preceding journal entries, the word "Install." was added.

Install. Sales	1,000,000		Install. Sales	1,200,000	
Install. Cost of Goods Sold		600,000	Install. Cost of Goods Sold		735,000
Defer. Gross Profit—2004		400,000	Defer. Gross Profit—2005		465,000

This entry is made at year-end before preparing the financial statements. The entry closes the sales and cost of goods sold accounts and establishes the deferred gross profit account.

Defer. Gross Profit—2004	180,000		Defer. Gross Profit—2004	120,000	
Realized Gross Profit		180,000	Defer. Gross Profit—2005	155,000	
			Realized Gross Profit		275,000

This entry is prepared at year-end, and it computes the amount of deferred gross profit to recognize for the year. These amounts were computed as follows:

	2004			2004	2005
Cash collected	$450,000		Cash collected	$300,000	$400,000
Gross profit percentage	× 0.40		Gross profit percentage	× 0.40	× 0.3875
Realized gross profit	$180,000		Realized gross profit	$120,000	$155,000

EXHIBIT 8-3

Balance Sheet Reporting for Receivables under the Point-of-Sale and the Installment-Sales Methods

Current Assets	2003	2002
Accounts and notes receivable (includes receivables from significant affiliates of $694 million in 2003 and $234 million in 2002), less allowance for doubtful accounts of $28 million in 2003 and $22 million in 2002	$3,955	$4,120
Installment receivables collectible (net of deferred gross profit of $782 and $653, respectively)	2,567	2,095

other sales revenue. However, if such is deemed necessary, it may best be done in the notes to the financial statements rather than on the face of the income statement. This position is in accord with current trends of reporting totals and subtotals on the face of the financial statements and disclosing the details of these amounts in the related notes. If revenue recognized under the installment-sales method is reported separately on the face of the income statement, it may be reported as shown in either Exhibit 8-4 or Exhibit 8-5, depending upon how much detail the company desires to report.

EXHIBIT 8-4

Income Statement for Revenue Recognized under the Installment-Sales Method

Harter Corporation
Income Statement
For the Year 2005

	Install. Sales	Other Sales	Total
Sales	$1,200,000	$ 870,000	$ 2,070,000
Cost of goods sold	(735,000)	(580,000)	(1,315,000)
Gross profit on sales	$ 465,000	$ 290,000	$ 755,000
Gross profit deferred to future years	(310,000)		(310,000)
Gross profit recognized	$ 155,000		$ 445,000
Gross profit recognized on prior years' sales	120,000		120,000
Total gross profit recognized this year	$ 275,000	$ 290,000	$ 565,000

EXHIBIT 8-5

Income Statement for Revenue Recognized under the Installment-Sales Method

Harter Corporation
Income Statement
For the Year 2005

Sales	$ 870,000
Cost of goods sold	(580,000)
Gross profit on sales	$ 290,000
Gross profit recognized from installment sales	275,000
Gross profit recognized	$ 565,000

The acceptability of the installment-sales method has fluctuated over time. For instance, in 1966, the APB stated that ". . . the installment method of recognizing revenue is not acceptable."[21] The justification was that the installment-sales method was not in accordance with accrual accounting. Then, the franchise and land development booms occurred during the late 1960s and 1970s where companies recognized revenue according to the point-of-sale method.[22] Subsequently,

[21]*Opinions of the Accounting Principles Board No. 10*, "Omnibus Opinion—1966," New York: AICPA, December 1966, par. 12.
[22]Recognizing franchise fees as revenue is discussed in Appendix C at the end of the chapter.

The gross profit percentage can also be computed by the relationship between the balances in Accounts Receivable and Deferred Gross Profit. For example, suppose that it is necessary to compute the amount of gross profit to recognize for a year, but the gross profit percentage has been lost. However, the general ledger shows beginning-of-the-year balances of $100,000 and $40,000 in Installment Accounts Receivable and Deferred Gross Profit, respectively. Also, the end-of-the-year balance in Installment Accounts Receivable is $60,000. How much realized gross profit should be recognized during the year?

Answer: Gross profit of $16,000 should be recognized for the year. This answer is determined by first computing the gross profit percent, which is based upon the relationship of the *beginning-of-the-year balances of Accounts Receivable and Deferred Gross Profit*. So the gross profit percent is 40%. The amount of cash collected during the year can be determined from the change in the installment accounts receivable account, which is $40,000. The $16,000 of gross profit to recognize is then computed by multiplying the 40% by the $40,000 of cash collected.

a substantial number of such ventures failed, and it was learned that the point-of-sale method had resulted in "front-end loading," meaning that revenue had been recognized prematurely. As a result, the FASB now accepts the installment-sales method but restricts its use to where there is a larger-than-normal uncertainty regarding collectibility of the amounts owed.

Today, the general rule is that revenue should be recognized when a sale is made, subject to a reasonable estimation of uncollectible amounts. The fact that collection expenses, bad debts, and repossession of merchandise all increase as the collection period increases does not justify using the installment-sales method for recognizing revenue. Rather, the justification for using this method rests on the risk of the future collectibility of amounts owed being so great that the realization criteria has not been met. When this uncertainty becomes sufficiently large, the installment-sales method of recognizing revenue may be used.

Repossessions

In the event that merchandise sold is subsequently repossessed—whether the sale is being accounted for under the installment-sales method or according to the point-of-sale method—it is necessary to remove the account receivable amount. For sales accounted for under the installment-sales method, the associated deferred gross profit amounts must also be removed from the general ledger. The repossessed inventory is reported at its net realizable value, which is its selling price less any costs of disposal, and any difference is recognized as a gain or loss on repossession.

To illustrate, assume that H. Althouse owes $2,000 to Harter Corporation for a sale made in 2004, for which Harter Corporation is recognizing revenue under the installment-sales method. In 2005, H. Althouse notifies Harter that it is unable to pay the amount owed and Harter repossesses the merchandise. Given the condition of the merchandise, Harter thinks it can sell the merchandise for $800, less sales commissions of $160. The journal entry to record the repossession of the merchandise, the removal of the amount owed with its associated deferred gross profit, and the resulting gain or loss is as follows:

Inventory[23]	640	
Deferred Gross Profit[24]	800	
Allowance for Doubtful Accounts	560	
Accounts Receivable		2,000

To record the repossession of inventory and recognize the resultant loss.

---

[23]This is the net realizable value of the repossessed inventory, computed as the sales price of $800 less the estimated costs of disposal (i.e., sales commissions) of $160. Repossessed inventory, if material, is separately classified from normal inventory, as it may not be sold in the normal course of business.

[24]Computed as the amount owed of $2,000 multiplied by the gross profit percentage for Year 1 of 40%, which was the year the sale to H. Althouse was made.

Allowance for Doubtful Accounts is debited because businesses establish an allowance for uncollectible accounts at the end of each year (with an offsetting expense), and when a specific account is deemed to be uncollectible or when a repossession occurs, the resulting loss is written off to the previously established allowance account. If the repossession had resulted in a gain, a gain account could be credited.

EXTENDING THE CONCEPT

A customer finances a car loan through her local bank. After missing six payments, the bank repossesses the car. The bank thinks it can sell the car to a local dealer for $7,000. The balance owed on the car is $10,000, and the gross profit percentage is 20%. What gain or loss did the bank incur on the repossession?

Answer: The bank incurred a $1,000 loss.

If the repossessed inventory can be sold under normal terms in the ordinary course of business, it is included under Current Assets in the balance sheet. Otherwise, the repossessed inventory is reported under some other balance sheet classification, depending upon when it will be sold. The only change to this journal entry when the point-of-sale method is used to recognize revenue is that there is no need to write off the deferred gross profit. As a result, Harter Corporation would recognize a loss on repossession of $1,360.

Recognizing Revenue After the Point of Sale—Cost Recovery Method

Another technique besides the installment-sales method for recognizing revenue after the point of sale is the cost recovery method. Choosing between the installment sales and cost recovery methods depends upon the degree of uncertainty concerning the future collectibility of amounts owed. As mentioned previously, the installment-sales method of recognizing revenue is used when there is more than normal uncertainty surrounding the future collectibility of the amounts owed. However, when the probability of collection is remote and thus the probability is large that the realization criterion has not been met, the cost recovery method is used in preference to the installment-sales method. As with the installment-sales method, gross profit is initially deferred; but under the cost recovery method, *no gross profit is recognized until cash receipts exceed the cost of the product*. After the cost of the product has been recovered, any additional cash collected is reported as realized gross profit.

Assuming the same data as were used for the installment-sales method illustration, the journal entries shown in Illustration 8-5 recognize gross profit under the cost recovery method in comparison to the installment-sales method.

Gross profit of $150,000 is recognized on 2004 sales because the total amount collected from 2004 sales of $750,000 (i.e., $450,000 in 2004 and $300,000 in 2005) exceeds the cost of goods sold of $600,000 in 2004. However, no gross profit is recognized on 2005 sales because, as yet, the amount collected of $450,000 does not exceed the cost of goods sold for 2005.[25]

Investment Revenue

The general rule for investment revenue is that it is recognized when the interest is earned or when the dividends are declared. Unlike revenue that is earned

---

[25]Besides installment sales, another example of how the cost recovery method may be used is when bonds are purchased whose interest payments are in default for several years. In that case, it seems appropriate for future cash amounts to be treated as a return of capital, and once the amount paid for the bonds has been recovered, to recognize any future cash payments as revenue.

ILLUSTRATION 8-5

Journal Entries under the Installment-Sales and the Cost Recovery Methods

2004 Entries

	Installment-Sales Method		Cost Recovery Method
Installment Accounts Receivable	1,000,000		Same entry
Installment Sales		1,000,000	
Installment Cost of Goods Sold	600,000		Same entry
Inventory		600,000	
Cash	450,000		Same entry
Installment Accounts Receivable		450,000	
Installment Sales	1,000,000		Same entry
Installment Cost of Goods Sold		600,000	
Deferred Gross Profit—2004		400,000	
Deferred Gross Profit—2004	180,000		**No entry**
Realized Gross Profit		180,000	

No entry is recorded to recognize gross profit because the amount collected of $400,000 is less than the cost of goods sold of $600,000.

2005 Entries

	Installment-Sales Method		Cost Recovery Method
Installment Accounts Receivable	1,200,000		Same entry
Installment Sales		1,200,000	
Installment Cost of Goods Sold	735,000		Same entry
Inventory		735,000	
Cash	700,000		Same entry
Installment Accounts Receivable		700,000	
Installment Sales	1,200,000		Same entry
Installment Cost of Goods Sold		735,000	
Deferred Gross Profit—2005		465,000	
Deferred Gross Profit—2004	120,000		**150,000**
Deferred Gross Profit—2005	155,000		**0**
Realized Gross Profit		275,000	**150,000**

from sales or from providing services, which occurs at definite points in time, interest revenue is earned continuously from the moment the debt security is purchased, the credit is extended, or the money is loaned. Since there is not a definite point that interest is earned, most accountants usually recognize interest revenue when the payment of interest is received. The only exception is that interest is accrued at year-end for amounts that have been earned but not received.[26]

---

[26]Interest is computed as $I = P \times R \times T$, where P is the amount borrowed, R is the interest rate, and T is the amount of time that has passed since the amount was borrowed.

The major difference between interest and dividends that impacts accounting is that dividends do not continuously accrue as interest does. Thus, an owner does not recognize revenue until a dividend has been declared and approved by the stockholders. Hence, in general, dividends are recognized as revenue when they are declared, and at year-end, dividends that have not been declared are not accrued.

When dividends are declared, the journal entry to record the resulting revenue is as follows:

Dividends Receivable	XXX	
Dividend Revenue[27]		XXX
To record dividend revenue when dividends are declared.		

This method of accounting for dividends is appropriate for all investments in preferred stock and for "small" investments in common stock of a corporation, which is usually interpreted to mean investments of 20% or less of the corporation's outstanding common stock. For investments in common stock that are larger than 20% of the outstanding shares, the equity method is used, which is covered in Chapter 15.

Summary

The revenue recognition principle determines *when* revenue is recorded in the general ledger and reported on financial statements. Revenue is recognized when it is both (1) earned and (2) realized or realizable. Realized means goods or services are exchanged for cash or claims to cash and realizable means goods or services are exchanged for an asset that is readily convertible to cash or a claim to cash. Earned means that the company has substantially accomplished what it must do to receive the benefits represented by the revenues.

Generally, the earliest time that revenue is both earned and realized or realizable is when a sale is made or a service is rendered. This is the general rule for recognizing revenue and is referred to as the point-of-sale method. The completed-contract method is a point-of-sale method for recognizing revenue.

When certain conditions are met, revenue can be recognized before the point of sale. One exception allows revenue to be recognized when production is complete. This method may be used (it is not required) when (1) there are no remaining significant costs connected with the inventory, including marketing costs, (2) the inventory can be sold immediately at quoted prices, and (3) one unit of inventory cannot be distinguished from other units of inventory.

Another exception to recognizing revenue at the point of sale is for long-term construction contracts. Then, revenue must be recognized during the construction process when (1) dependable estimates can be made of contract revenues, costs, and the progress towards completion; (2) the contract clearly specifies the enforceable rights to be provided and received by the parties, the consideration to be exchanged (e.g., a fixed-price contract), and the manner and terms of settlement; and (3) both buyer and contractor are expected to satisfy their contractual obligations. The percentage-of-completion method recognizes profit in proportion to the amount of effort expended in relation to

[27]Investment Revenue is another appropriate account title that can be used.

the total expected effort to be expended, where effort is usually measured by the costs incurred. When a loss is expected on the contract, the entire loss is recognized, meaning that all previously recognized profits must also be reversed.

Just as there are exceptions allowing revenue to be recognized before the point of sale, there are also exceptions that allow the recognizing of revenue to be postponed past the point of sale. When collectibility of amounts owed is greater than usual, revenue may be recognized when the cash is collected. The most commonly used revenue recognition method for doing this is the installment-sales method. Under that method, revenue is recognized by multiplying the gross profit percentage by the amount of cash collected. When the uncertainty of collection increases, the cost recovery method may be used, which does not recognize any revenue until the cost of the product has been recovered. Then, all subsequent cash collected is recognized as revenue.

Regarding investment revenue, interest revenue is earned continuously but usually is recorded when it is received. The only exception is at year-end, and then an adjusting entry is prepared in which the interest earned but not received is recorded. Dividend revenue is not recognized until the dividends are declared. No adjusting entry is made at year-end to accrue dividend revenue.

APPENDIX A: Other Times To Recognize Revenue

Recognizing Revenue Before Sale— Accretion Method

Accretion is the increase in value of an asset over time because of natural growth. Examples of assets that accrete are timber and livestock. Currently, revenue is not recognized due to accretion. The reasons why are because the asset often is not realized or realizable, nor has the company substantially accomplished what it must do to consider the revenue earned. This policy of not recognizing the steady increase in value of some assets is a frequent cause of misleading financial statements. For instance, the Boston Celtics basketball organization reports the value of its NBA franchise at approximately $4 million,[28] whereas current NBA franchises sell for around $200 million, assuming a franchise can even be purchased. Hence, the balance sheet of the Boston Celtics greatly understates the value of the organization's assets.

Recognizing Revenue Before Sale— Discovery Method

The difference between accretion and discovery is that accretion is the steady increase in the value of an asset, whereas discovery is the sudden detection that an asset is more valuable than was previously thought. An example is the discovery of a precious natural resource on land that previously was considered to be of little value. Present GAAP states that "property, plant, and equipment should not be written up . . . to reflect appraisal, market, or current values which are above

---

[28]This $4 million is the price originally paid for the NBA franchise, less amortization taken since acquisition.

cost."[29] Again, the reason for not recognizing this increase in value is that to do so violates the revenue recognition principle.[30]

Recognizing Revenue After Point of Sale—Deposit Method[31]

In some cases, the realization criterion is met at the point of sale, but the seller has not performed sufficiently to consider the revenue to have been earned. The seller still has the obligation to accomplish what it must do to earn the benefits represented by the cash received. In addition to the season ticket sales scenario mentioned at the beginning of the chapter, other common examples of postponing revenue to some time after the point of sale are magazine subscriptions and rent payments. In these cases, revenue is not recognized until the seller or service provider has substantially performed what it must do to consider the revenue to be earned. This method of recognizing revenue receives its name of "deposit method" because the initial payment is treated as a deposit that is subject to refund (and is thus a liability) if the promised product/service is not provided. The initial payment is recorded as "Unearned Revenue" or "Deferred Revenue." Subsequently, *revenue is recognized as the promised product/service is delivered and in proportion to the total product/services to be provided.* Hence, for a professional basketball organization that plays 41 home games, 1/41 of the total cash received is recognized as revenue each time the team plays a home game, with a corresponding decrease in the related liability account.

EXTENDING THE CONCEPT

Suppose that a professional basketball organization, in order to increase ticket sales, offers a free ticket to a subsequent game for each two tickets purchased for an upcoming game. How much revenue should be recognized for ticket sales made for the upcoming game? 100%? Two-thirds of the amount? Or some other amount?

APPENDIX B: Consignment Sales

A consignment transaction is one where the potential seller (the consignor) delivers merchandise to an agent (the consignee) to sell. Title to the merchandise remains with the consignor, and the merchandise is included on the consignor's balance sheet. The consignor does not recognize any revenue until the consignee sells the inventory. The consignor also includes all expenses incurred (e.g., freight charges) as part of the cost of the consigned inventory in accordance with the historical cost principle.

The consignee does not make a formal entry to record receipt of the merchandise, nor is the inventory included on its balance sheet. The consignee records as a receivable all expenses incurred that will be reimbursed by the consignor. When the consignee sells some merchandise, the consignee recognizes its commission as revenue, reimburses itself for expenses incurred in behalf of the consignor, and sends the difference to the consignor.

Illustration 8A-1 illustrates the journal entries for accounting for consignment sales for both the consignor and the consignee.

---

[29]*Opinions of the Accounting Principles Board No. 6*, "Status of Accounting Research Bulletins," New York: AICPA, 1965, par. 17.

[30]Recently, the FASB has allowed certain marketable securities to be reported at current market values when such market values are readily determinable. Perhaps this is just the beginning to other assets being reported at market values.

[31]The deposit method is also called the proportional performance method of recognizing revenue. The method receives its name because revenue is recognized proportionally as the service is provided. Thus, for advance sales of magazine subscriptions, a proportion of the total cash received is recognized as revenue each month as the promised magazine is delivered.

ILLUSTRATION 8A-1

Journal Entries for Consignment Sales

Entries on Consignor's Books			Entries on Consignee's Books		
Inventory on Consignment	100		Memorandum entry only		
Inventory		100			
Shipment of consigned merchandise.					
Inventory on Consignment	5		No entry		
Cash		5			
Payment of freight charges.					
No entry			Accounts Receivable	15	
			Cash		15
			Payment of expenditures to be reimbursed by consignor.		
No entry			Cash	150	
			Payable to Consignor		150
			Sales of ¾ of the merchandise at the retail price.		
Cash	105		Payable to Consignor	150	
Commission Expense	30		Accounts Receivable		15
Inventory on Consignment*	15		Commission Revenue		30
Consignment Revenue		150	Cash		105
Notification of sale and receipt of cash.			*Notification of sale and payment of cash. (Commission revenue is computed as the commission rate multiplied by the amount of sales.)*		
(*This is the expense paid by the consignee in behalf of the consignor.)					
Cost of Goods Sold	90				
Inventory on Consignment		90			
Cost of sold inventory.					
(The total cost of the consigned inventory is $120, and ¾ of the inventory was sold.)					

APPENDIX C: Franchise Fees

Franchise fees are of two types: initial fees and ongoing fees. The initial fees pay for the right to use the franchise name, purchasing equipment from the franchisor, preopening services such as finding a suitable location, employee training, and other such costs. The ongoing fees are for ongoing services such as advertising. The ongoing fees, which are typically computed as a percentage of the franchisee's sales, *are recognized by the franchisor as revenue in the same period that the sales are made by the franchisee.* But determining when to recognize the initial fees as revenue has been a difficult issue. Current authoritative guidance specifies that *initial franchise fees should be deferred* and then be recognized as revenue when "all material services or conditions relating to the sale have been *substantially performed* or satisfied."[32]

---

[32]*Statement of Financial Accounting Standard No. 45*, "Accounting for Franchise Fee Revenue," Stamford: Financial Accounting Standards Board, March 1981, par. 5 (emphasis added).

"Substantially perform" means that (1) the franchisor has no obligation or intent to refund any of the cash received, (2) substantially all of the initial services have been performed, and (3) the franchisor has no remaining conditions or obligations to meet. The earliest point at which these three conditions can be met is the commencement of operations. Once the franchisor has substantially performed what it must, then the initial fees are recognized using the most appropriate revenue recognition method (e.g., point-of-sale, installment-sales, etc.). Regardless of the revenue recognition method used, the amount of revenue recognized is reduced by an appropriate provision for estimated uncollectibles.

To illustrate, suppose that a franchisor signs an agreement with a new franchisee that calls for an initial cash payment of $10,000, and a note is also signed that calls for four yearly cash payments of $10,000 each, plus interest at 10% on the unpaid balance. In addition, the agreement requires the franchisee to pay 2% of sales for ongoing services. In return, the franchisor will help the franchisee find a suitable location, assist in arranging financing for a building, provide needed equipment and initial supplies, and will train the employees of the franchisee. The franchisor's journal entries to account for these events are as follows:

Entry 1		
Cash	10,000	
Note Receivable	40,000	
Deferred Revenue		50,000

To record signing of the franchise agreement and receipt of initial cash.

Accounting When Collection on Note Is Reasonably Assured

When the franchisor has substantially performed the initial services, revenue may be recognized using the most appropriate method, which could be the point-of-sale method when it is reasonably assured that the note receivable will be collected. If so, then the $50,000 is recognized as revenue—reduced by any allowance for uncollectibles and future costs, as shown in the following journal entry:

Deferred Revenue	50,000	
Franchise Fees—Initial Revenue		45,000
Allowance for Estimated Uncollectibles		5,000

To recognize revenue due to having substantially performed as specified in the franchise contract.

At the beginning of the following year, the franchisor receives a report from the franchisee showing sales of $150,000, and included with the report is a check for $17,000 in payment of the ongoing fees, the first installment on the note, and interest. Then, the franchisor prepares the following journal entry:

Cash	17,000	
Note Receivable		10,000
Interest Revenue		4,000
Franchise Fee—Ongoing Revenue		3,000

To record receipt of cash, including interest computed at 10% on the unpaid balance of $40,000 for one year and 2% of the year's sales of $150,000.

Accounting When Collection on Note Is Not Reasonably Assured

When the franchisor decides that there is a higher than normal uncertainty that the note receivable will be collected, the installment-sales method (or the cost recovery method) of recognizing revenue may be used. In this scenario, after installing the equipment, providing the initial supplies, and training the employees, the franchisor prepares the following journal entry in addition to Entry 1, which recognizes revenue to the extent that cash has been received:

Deferred Revenue	10,000	
Franchise Fees—Initial Revenue		10,000

To recognize revenue based upon having substantially performed according to the contract but only to the amount of cash received that will not be refunded.

Later, when the $17,000 payment is received, the franchisor prepares the following journal entries:

Cash	17,000	
Note Receivable		10,000
Interest Revenue		4,000
Franchise Fee—Ongoing Revenue		3,000

To record receipt of cash, including interest computed at 10% on the unpaid balance of $40,000 for one year and 2% of the year's sales of $150,000.

Deferred Revenue	10,000	
Franchise Revenue—Initial Revenue		10,000

To recognize revenue based upon having substantially performed according to the contract.

APPENDIX D: Interest on Installment Sales

Because of the extended time period required to collect the amounts owed on installment sales, the buyer of the merchandise is always charged interest. Thus, each payment consists of an amount for interest and an amount that is applied to reducing the principal. Although the payment amounts are equal, the portion that is interest declines over time, while the portion representing the return of the amount borrowed increases over time. This procedure results in a *constant rate of interest* for each period. For example, suppose that Harter Corporation sells merchandise costing $2,700 for $3,600 on January 1, 2001. The customer makes a down payment of $600 and is required to make monthly payments of $99.64 at the beginning of each succeeding month. That amount includes both interest and an amount applied to reducing the principal. The interest rate is 1% per month. At the date of sale, Harter Corporation establishes a schedule separating the $99.64 between interest and principal, showing how much gross profit to recognize in each period, and the balance still owing, as shown in Illustration 8A-2.

ILLUSTRATION 8A-2

Installment Receivable Schedule

Date	Cash	Interest	Receivable	Balance	Gross Profit
				$3,000.00	
Jan-01	$ 99.64	$ 30.00ᵃ	$ 69.64ᵇ	2,930.36ᶜ	$ 17.41ᵈ
Feb-01	99.64	29.30	70.34	2,860.02	17.59
Mar-01	99.64	28.60	71.04	2,788.98	17.76
⋮					
Oct-03	99.64	2.93	96.71	196.45	24.18
Nov-03	99.64	1.96	97.68	98.78	24.42
Dec-03	99.64	0.86	98.78	0.00	24.70
Totals	$3,587.04	$587.04	$3,000.00		$900.00

ᵃComputed by multiplying the interest rate of 1% by the unpaid balance.
ᵇComputed as the difference between the cash paid and the interest amount.
ᶜComputed as the previous unpaid balance reduced by the amount applied to the receivable.
ᵈComputed by multiplying the gross profit percentage (25%) by the amount applied to reducing the receivable.

Note that the major change in using the installment-sales method when interest is introduced into the discussion is that the *amount of gross profit recognized* for the period is computed by multiplying the *gross profit percentage by the amount of cash applied to reducing the principal* rather than to total cash received.

Questions

1. As relating to revenue, define (a) realized, (b) realizable, and (c) earned.

2. Explain the difference between *realized* and *recognized*.

3. When is a company justified in recognizing revenue at the point production is complete? Provide a specific example.

4. When recognizing revenue for a long-term construction contract, indicate when the percentage-of-completion method should be used, and when the completed-contract method should be used instead.

5. One of the conditions for revenue to be recognized at the point of sale when the buyer has the right to return the goods is that the amount of future returns can be reasonably estimated. With respect to this condition, indicate whether a company can recognize revenue at the point of sale under each of the following circumstances:
   a. The rate of sales returns is 1%–2% per annum,
   b. The rate of sales returns is 10%–50% per annum.
   c. The time period in which the product can be returned is relatively long.
   d. The company has no experience with sales of this or similar products.

6. List the costs that are accumulated in the construction-in-progress account and in the billings-on-contract account. Then, describe the appropriate balance sheet classification for the accounts Costs in Excess of Billings and Billings in Excess of Costs.

7. When possible, U.S. GAAP requires the use of the percentage-of-completion method instead of the completed-contract method. Explain why the percentage-of-completion method might be superior to the completed-contract method.

8. Would U.S. GAAP or German GAAP be more likely to recognize revenue faster for a long-term construction contract? Why do you suppose the respective GAAP's differ on this principle?

9. When should revenue be recognized under the installment-sales method rather than at the point of sale?

10. Explain the fundamental difference between the installment-sales method and the cost recovery method of recognizing revenue. Under what circumstances would each of these methods be appropriate for recognizing revenue?

11. Assume that Hanson Co. has the following account balances at the end of its 2004 fiscal year:

Accounts Receivable	$95,000
Allowance for Uncollectible Accounts	1,780

During 2005, a customer notified Hanson that it has declared bankruptcy and will be unable to pay the $500 owed to Hanson on a sale that was made in 2004. Accordingly, Hanson appropriately writes off the customer's account as uncollectible by debiting the allowance account and crediting Accounts Receivable. Should revenues recognized in 2004 be adjusted for the $500 that will not be collected? Explain.

12. (Appendix) During December 2003, Image Publishing Co. received $12,000 for 500 new annual subscriptions for magazines to be issued in 2004. Image Publishing recognized the payment as income for tax purposes. How should Image Publishing recognize cash receipts for financial reporting purposes?

13. (Appendix) Briefly explain the deposit method of recognizing revenue. Provide an example of when this method would be used, and explain the basic accounting entries.

14. (Appendix) When should initial franchise fees be recognized when the franchisor is obligated to provide assistance to the franchisee in locating a suitable business site and training employees?

15. (Appendix) ABC Co. (the consignor) placed on consignment $2,000 worth of inventory with XYZ Co. (the consignee). XYZ Co. charged an up-front 15% fee for holding the goods. If the inventory does not sell within 90 days, it can be returned to ABC Co., along with two-thirds of the consignment fee. When should ABC Co. and XYZ Co. recognize revenue with respect to the inventory?

Exercises

Exercise 8-1: Recognizing Revenue from Royalties. Drill Co. receives royalty payments of 20% on all oil sales from its ownership share in an oil well. Payments are made to Drill Co. on June 30 for oil sold during the previous December through May, and on December 31 for oil sold during the previous June through November. Drill is provided with actual oil sold information as follows:

	Oil Sold
December 1, 2003–May 31, 2004	$600,000
June 1, 2004–November 30, 2004	750,000
December 1, 2004–May 31, 2005	680,000

Sales are made evenly throughout the year.

How much revenue should Drill Co. recognize for the year ending December 31, 2004?

Exercise 8-2: Recognition of Revenue. Luvridge Co. ordered 2,000 tons of wheat from Morton Feed Co. on October 21, 2004, to be delivered as needed. The purchase price was $78 per ton. Morton delivered 1,500 tons of wheat on December 20, 2004, and the remaining 500 tons were delivered on February 16, 2005. Luvridge Co. paid for the wheat in three equal monthly payments of $52,000, beginning on December 28, 2005.

If revenue is recognized at the point of sale, how much revenue should Morton Feed Co. recognize in 2004?

Exercise 8-3: Recognition of Revenue. Quincy Co. sells merchandise to various retail outlets and allows its customers to purchase on credit and return any items within 30 days. Historically, Quincy's returns have averaged about 1% of gross sales. Customers are responsible for all shipping costs. Gross sales (before any adjustments for the following information) for the year ending December 31, 2004, were $575,000. Additional information regarding possible adjustments to gross sales is as follows:

- Goods with an invoice amount of $25,000 were shipped to a customer on December 28, 2004. The sale was recorded on January 4, 2005.
- On January 3, 2005, goods shipped in December 2004, with an invoice amount of $1,500, were returned for a full refund.
- Goods with an invoice amount of $10,000 that were shipped to a customer on consignment in December 2004 were not recorded as a sale.

What net revenue should Quincy report for 2004?

Exercise 8-4: Recognizing Revenue on Interchangeable Products with a Ready Market Value. Morton Feed Co. entered into an agreement with Olden Acres Corp. to purchase all the wheat Olden Acres could produce at the quoted market price at the time of harvest, with delivery to be made as needed by Morton. By the end of October 2004, Olden had harvested 900,000 pounds of wheat, the market price of which was $0.70 per pound. Costs to deliver the wheat are immaterial. Between October and December, Olden Acres delivered 600,000 pounds of wheat to Morton, and the remaining 300,000 pounds were delivered in January 2005, when the market price had increased to $0.73 per pound.

1. What are the two methods that Olden may use to recognize revenue for 2004?
2. Under each method, how much revenue should Olden Acres Corp. recognize in 2004?

Exercise 8-5: Revenue Recognition—Point of Sale. Consider each of the following independent situations:

1. Vanity Faire, a department store, in addition to selling merchandise sells gift certificates, which expire one year after issuance. At December 31, 2004, the following information is available regarding the sale of gift certificates:

Unredeemed certificates at December 31, 2003	$ 20,000
2004 sales of gift certificates	300,000
Redemptions of certificates sold in 2003	8,000
Redemptions of certificates sold in 2004	220,000

Approximately 10% of the certificates sold are never redeemed. How much revenue should Vanity Faire recognize in connection with its gift certificates for 2004?

2. At the beginning of 2004, Super Heroes Comics sold a comic book to Fantastic Stories Comics for 20% of all future sales. At December 31, 2004, Super Heroes reported a receivable from Fantastic of $30,000. During 2005, Super Heroes received payments totaling $80,000 from Fantastic, who reported sales from the comic book of $500,000. At December 31, 2005, Super Heroes reported a receivable of $50,000. How much royalty revenue should Super Heroes report from the comic strip for 2005?

3. Susan is an author who receives cash from her publisher for royalties on sales of books and advances on books currently being written. Each December, Susan receives a sales report from her publisher from which she records revenue, which typically precedes the actual payment by 90 days. During 2006, Susan received cash totaling $400,000. The following information is also available for 2006 and 2007:

	2006	2007
Revenue receivable	$50,000	$38,000
Advances received	25,000	75,000

Based upon this information, how much revenue should Susan report for 2007?

Exercise 8-6: Revenue Recognition. Answer each of the following independent situations.

1. Seagull sells subscriptions of a specialized directory that is published quarterly on March 1, June 1, September 1, and December 1. Subscribers who pay more than 60 days prior to a publication date receive the next publication; otherwise, the publication is not sent until the following quarter. Cash is received evenly during the year. From 2003 through 2005, cash was received of $4,800,000, $5,400,000, and $5,700,000, respectively. How much revenue should Seagull report for 2004?

2. As part of its business, Vanity Publishing publishes novels of new authors. Sometimes the books are immensely successful, and sometimes they are not. Vanity allows bookstores to return all unsold books for a full refund ninety days after receiving a shipment. During the fourth quarter of 2004, Vanity published two books by new authors, with shipments to bookstores totaling $2,000,000. Historically, about 30% of the books are returned. At December 31, cash of $1,100,000 had been received from sales to bookstores. How much revenue may Vanity report for the fourth quarter of 2004 from these two books, assuming that all conditions are met to recognize revenue at the point of sale?

3. To finance the construction of a ski resort in Colorado, WWT sold partnerships that allow the partners the right to stay free at the resort for up to one week at a time. The partners can visit the resort an unlimited number of times during the year, and the partnership is a lifetime partnership but cannot be bequeathed to anyone at death. Under the plan, $100 million was collected. Without giving a

dollar figure, discuss when the $100 million should be recognized as revenue. Be specific.

Exercise 8-7: Revenue Recognition. Answer each of the following independent situations.

1. A manufacturer of home playground equipment for children has an innovative product that is in great demand. Currently, it will take the company a minimum of three months to fill orders received, and there does not seem to be any decrease in the amount of orders that will be received. Any order must be accompanied by a 20% down payment, which is fully refundable should the customer cancel before the product is delivered. The president of the company desires to present an accurate picture of the financial health of the company to obtain needed financing to expand production capacity. Accordingly, the president has approached you with the notion that, since demand for the product is strong, revenue should be recognized when the order for the product is received. Respond and defend your answer.
2. The Workout Place is a new health club that sells membership by the month but also sells lifetime memberships. Discuss how revenue should be recognized for sales of the lifetime memberships. Include in your answer the accounting for any cash received at the time of the signing of a contract, subsequent collections, and the recognition of revenue.
3. Catfish Charlie's began business in New Orleans with a tasty menu and an unusual ambience. Due to its success, Catfish began selling franchises. For a fee of $200,000, Catfish will allow the franchisee the rights to the menu, help the franchisee find a suitable location, and train the franchisee in all areas of restaurant management. The franchisee also pays a yearly royalty of 2% of gross sales. Discuss when Catfish should recognize as revenue the initial fee and the yearly royalties.

Exercise 8-8: Percentage-of-Completion Method. Riser Corp. uses the percentage-of-completion method to account for long-term construction contracts. On June 1, 2004, Riser began working on a $4 million construction contract that is expected to be completed on March 31, 2006. On June 1, 2004, the estimated costs of the project were $2,750,000. Updated data at December 31, 2004, are as follows:

Total costs incurred to date	$ 900,000
Estimated remaining costs to complete	2,100,000
Billings to customer	750,000

1. How much gross profit should Riser Corp. recognize on the project for the year ending December 31, 2004? (Round answer to the nearest thousand.)
2. Upon recognizing the gross profit computed in 2004, assume that on December 31, 2005, total costs incurred were $2,500,000, and estimated costs to complete the project were an additional $1,000,000. How much gross profit should Riser recognize in 2005? (Round the percentage of completion to the nearest tenth of a percent.)
3. How would your answer in part (2) change if the total costs incurred on December 31, 2005, were $2,500,000, and the estimated costs to complete the contract were $1,800,000?

Exercise 8-9: Percentage-of-Completion Method. Peterson Co. uses the percentage-of-completion method to account for all its long-term construction contracts. During

2004, Peterson worked exclusively on one large project that had a contract price of $6 million. Cost information related to the project is as follows:

Costs incurred during the year	$1,750,000
Estimated remaining costs to complete	2,250,000
Billings on contract	2,000,000
Cash collections from customers	1,500,000

1. Calculate the gross profit to be recognized on this project in 2004.
2. What is the balance in the construction-in-progress account related to this project?
3. How would the billings-on-contract and construction-in-progress accounts be reported on Peterson's financial statements?

Exercise 8-10: Percentage-of-Completion Method. Lee's Construction Co. began working on a large construction project in 2004 and continued work on the project throughout 2005. The company recognizes revenues based on the percentage-of-completion method. The following information provides appropriate balances for some of the company's accounts:

	2004	2005
Accounts receivable	$ 80,000	$120,000
Contract-to-date construction expenses	215,000	525,000
Construction in progress	250,000	680,000
Billings on contract	90,000	350,000

1. How much gross profit did Lee's Construction recognize in 2004 and 2005?
2. How much did Lee's Construction bill its customer during 2004 and 2005?
3. How much cash did Lee's Construction collect from the customer in 2004 and 2005?
4. Given that the total contract price will remain constant, does it appear that the estimated costs to complete the project increased or decreased during 2005?

Exercise 8-11: Completed-Contract Method. Norsick AG is a German construction company that uses the completed-contract method to account for long-term construction projects. The following information relates to two projects that were started in 2004:

	2004		2005	
	Project 1	**Project 2**	**Project 1**	**Project 2**
Contract price	$550,000	$250,000	$550,000	$250,000
Costs incurred during year	150,000	30,000	300,000	200,000
Estimated costs to complete	250,000	100,000	0	40,000
Billings on contract	300,000	0	550,000	200,000
Cash proceeds from customers	220,000	0	180,000	75,000

How much gross profit should Norsick AG recognize for the years 2004 and 2005?

Exercise 8-12: Completed-Contract Method. Using the following cost information, determine how much gross profit (loss) should be recognized by year on a $100 million contract, using the completed-contract method:

	2001	2002	2003	2004
Cost incurred for the year	$20,000,000	$40,000,000	$35,000,000	$7,000,000
Estimated remaining costs	60,000,000	45,000,000	8,000,000	0

Exercise 8-13: Installment-Sales and Cost Recovery Methods. Anderson Inc. began operations in October 2003. The company sells expensive network computing systems to corporations and requires payment for the systems over a 24-month period. Customers of Anderson are typically start-up companies that carry a high level of risk. Accordingly, Anderson decided to recognize revenue as cash is collected. The following schedule provides information on sales and cash receipts over a 3-year period:

	2003	2004	2005
Sales	$150,000	$800,000	$950,000
Cash collected from:			
2003 sales	10,000	70,000	60,000
2004 sales	—	300,000	325,000
2005 sales	—	—	375,000
Gross profit percentage	45%	50%	60%

1. Determine the amount of recognized gross profit and deferred gross profit that would be shown for each year on the financial statements of Anderson Inc., using (a) the installment-sales method and (b) the cost recovery method.
2. Assuming that Anderson Inc. continues to experience the same success in collecting receivables as was experienced during 2003–2005, estimate the amount of *net* installment accounts receivable that would be shown on the balance sheet at the end of 2005, after writing off the remaining uncollected accounts from 2003 sales as being uncollectible. Show how that amount would be reported on the year-end balance sheet.

Exercise 8-14: Installment-Sales and Cost Recovery Methods. The following information relates to the sales activity of Andrew Systems, Inc.:

	2004	2005
Installment sales	$100,000	$120,000
Collections:		
On 2004 sales	50,000	40,000
On 2005 sales		50,000
Cost of goods sold	60,000	75,000

Compute the amount that Andrew Systems should present on its financial statements for 2004 and 2005 as realized gross profit and deferred gross profit, using (1) the installment-sales method and (2) the cost recovery method.

Exercise 8-15: Installment-Sales Method. Stumble and Sly sell merchandise and use the installment-sales method for recognizing revenue. At December 31, 2005, while preparing the financial statements, it was discovered that the sheet of paper which listed the gross profit percentages for the past few years had been lost. Fortunately, the following information was available from the general ledger:

From Sales Made During	Accounts Receivable, January 1, 2005	Accounts Receivable, December 31, 2005	Deferred Gross Profit, January 1, 2005
2002	$ 140,000	$ 20,000	$ 42,000
2003	300,000	140,000	100,000
2004	650,000	445,000	227,500
Totals	$1,090,000	$605,000	$369,500

In addition, sales for 2005 were $1,000,000, the cost of the merchandise sold was $625,000, and amounts still owing were $875,000.

Determine the following amounts:

1. Total realized gross profit for the year.
2. Total deferred gross profit for the year.

Exercise 8-16: Consigned Inventory (Appendix). Harris Corp. offers some merchandise to retailers to sell on a consignment arrangement. As of the end of 2004, Harris had transferred 100 units of inventory to various retailers and received notice that 90 units had been sold for $500 per unit. The cost to Harris to purchase the units (including freight-in) was $300 per unit. Harris also incurred $2,000 to ship the inventory to the consignees. Harris pays the consignees a commission of 20% of the selling price.

1. What is the balance in the consignment inventory account at the end of 2004?
2. Prepare a pro-forma income statement for the information related to consigned goods.

Exercise 8-17: Accounting for Revenues from Franchises (Appendix). The Malt Shop sells franchises and charges a nonrefundable franchise fee of $75,000. One-third of the fee is required at the initiation of the contract, and the remaining $50,000 is paid equally over 12 months. In addition to the franchise fee, the franchisor requires 5% of gross sales to be remitted at the end of each month to pay for ongoing services. Prior to opening the franchise, The Malt Shop is required to perform significant services related to site location, employee screening and training, and accounting services. All services are expected to be substantially complete after six months from the contract signing and before officially opening for business. Local advertising and annual training meetings are held on an annual basis subsequent to opening.

1. Indicate through journal entries how The Malt Shop should account for:
   a. The receipt of the initial franchise fee of $25,000, assuming that collectibility is reasonably assured.
   b. Employee screening, training, etc., has occurred after a suitable site has been found.
   c. Collecting the monthly payments on the note of $4,167.
   d. Collecting a royalty payment of $2,000, which is 5% of the first month's gross sales.
2. Would any of your answers to part (1) change under the following independent assumptions?
   a. Collectibility of the franchise fee is not assured.
   b. The entire franchise fee is collected on the date of contract signing.
   c. The franchisor promises to refund the entire franchise fee for whatever reason within 60 days of signing the contract.

Problems

Problem 8-1: Revenue Recognition with High Return Rates. Alpine Publishing Co. distributes textbooks to college bookstores. As a service to the bookstores, Alpine ships a generous supply of all textbooks to ensure that the textbooks do not sell out and also allows any unsold books to be returned for full credit. Payment for textbooks is made soon after the return period expires. In October 2004, Alpine shipped 500 textbooks to ABC Books at a price of $50 each. Historically, ABC Books typically returns about 20% of the total textbooks shipped and pays for the other textbooks within 30 days after returning the unsold units.

Required:
1. Alpine Publishing conceivably could recognize revenue:
    a. When the books are shipped and provide an estimate of future returns,
    b. When the books are shipped and account for the returns when they occur,
    c. When the return period expires, and
    d. When cash is collected.

    Provide journal entries for shipping the books under each alternative.

2. Which alternative identified in part (1) is most consistent with U.S. GAAP?
3. Assume that ABC Books returned 150 books in the first part of January 2005, and that cash was received for the sold books. Provide the appropriate journal entry for the returns and the receipt of the cash under each identified alternative in part (1). (*Note:* Ignore the entries to account for the inventory and cost of goods sold.)

Problem 8-2: Alternative Revenue Recognition Methods. Norris Corporation began operations on January 1, 2004, by issuing 5,000 shares of its no-par common stock to its founders in exchange for land valued at $30,000, a building with a 20-year useful life valued at $20,000, and equipment with a 10-year useful life valued at $40,000. (Straight-line depreciation is employed, and depreciation is considered a cost of manufacturing.) A 10% loan in the amount of $50,000 was received from a local bank for working capital, and interest during the year (which was not paid) amounted to $5,000. During 2004, Norris produced 2,000 chairs at a cost of $40,000 (excluding depreciation, which is considered part of the cost of producing the chairs). Each chair sells for $60. By the end of the year, a total of 1,800 chairs were sold, and cash was collected in the amount of $86,000. Operating expenses (excluding interest) for the period were $50,000.

Required:
Prepare an income statement, including earnings per share, and a balance sheet for Norris Corporation, assuming that revenue is recognized:

1. When chairs are sold,
2. When the chairs are produced, and
3. When cash is collected using the installment-sales method.

(*Hint:* After preparing the income statement and balance sheet for Alternative (1), the only changes in the statements for the other alternatives are for sales, retained earnings, and inventory.)

Problem 8-3: Long-Term Construction Project. Acme Construction Co. received a contract from a city in California to construct a new freeway around the city for $75 million. Construction on the project began in 2004, and Acme expects to complete the project by the end of 2007. The following cost information relating to the project was gathered at the end of each year:

	2004	2005
Labor directly related to the project	$ 2,500,000	$ 3,800,000
Materials directly related to the project	3,000,000	4,000,000
Equipment purchased	10,000,000	0
Overhead costs incurred	1,500,000	1,200,000
Estimated costs to complete the project (excluding depreciation)	27,000,000	20,000,000

The equipment purchased in 2004 has an estimated 4-year useful life, no salvage value, is to be used exclusively on the freeway construction, and will be used evenly throughout the construction process.

Required:

Compute the amount of gross profit that Acme should recognize on this project for 2004 and 2005, using the:

1. Percentage-of-completion method, and the
2. Completed-contract method. (Round amounts to the nearest thousand.)

Problem 8-4: Long-Term Construction Project (Percentage-of-Completion Method). LB Construction Co. received a contract to construct a building. The contract is for $4 million, and it is anticipated that it will take three years to complete the building. Cost information related to the contract is as follows:

	2004	2005	2006
Total construction costs to date	$1,200,000	$3,400,000	$4,200,000
Estimated costs to complete	2,000,000	1,000,000	0
Billings on contract	1,300,000	3,700,000	4,000,000
Accounts receivable	800,000	1,200,000	500,000

Required:
1. Compute the profit to be recognized on the project for each year, using the percentage-of-completion method.
2. Provide the necessary journal entries for the three years.

Problem 8-5: Long-Term Construction Project (Completed-Contract Method).

Required:
Using the cost data provided in Problem 8-4, (1) compute the gross profit to be recognized on the project for each year, using the completed-contract method, and (2) prepare the necessary journal entries.

Problem 8-6: Long-Term Construction Project (Percentage-of-Completion Method). Concrete & Steel Co. began construction on a bridge during 2004 that the company estimates will cost $100 million over the life of the contract. The expected completion date is February 2007, and the proceeds from the contract are fixed at $170 million. During the third year of construction, several unforeseen events (e.g., a trucker strike that cut off materials from suppliers, a labor shortage, etc.) resulted in the company incurring significantly more costs than expected. To offset these unfavorable events, the company placed substantial effort in increasing efficiency and cutting costs and eventually realized a small profit on the project.

Cost information by year for the project is as follows:

	2004	2005	2006	2007
Construction costs incurred	$45 million	$45 million	$ 60 million	$ 15 million
Estimated costs to complete	70 million	35 million	25 million	0
Billings on contract	45 million	90 million	140 million	170 million
Accounts receivable	5 million	10 million	12 million	2 million

Required:

1. Compute the gross profit to be recognized on the project for each year, using the percentage-of-completion method. (Round amounts to the nearest thousand.)
2. Provide the necessary journal entries, using the percentage-of-completion method.

Problem 8-7: Long-Term Construction Project (Completed-Contract Method).

Required:

Using the cost data provided in Problem 8-6, (1) compute the revenue and gross profit to be recognized on the project for each year and (2) provide the necessary journal entries.

Problem 8-8: Installment-Sales Method. Sam's Electronics and Appliances sells inventory to customers on a cash or an installment basis. Installment sales where the risk of collection is more than normal are accounted for using the installment-sales method. The following information relates to operations for Sam's for the years 2004–2006:

	2004	2005	2006
Cash sales	$70,000	$65,000	$40,000
Installment sales	$125,000	$139,000	$150,000
Gross profit percentage:			
On cash sales	55%	52%	50%
On installment sales	48%	45%	45%
Cash collections:			
From 2004 installment sales	$35,000	$80,000	$10,000
From 2005 installment sales		$29,000	$90,000
From 2006 installment sales			$65,000
Operating expenses	$50,000	$62,000	$67,000
Interest expense	$1,000	$3,000	$4,000

Sam's income tax rate is 30%.

Required:

1. Compute the realized gross profit for Sam's on all sales for each year.
2. Prepare an income statement for Sam's for each year. (Assume that there is no income tax expense/effect on net losses.)

Problem 8-9: Installment-Sales Method. Haskins' Car Dealership sells used cars on a long-term installment basis and appropriately recognizes revenues using the installment-sales method. Haskins estimates that bad debt expense will be approximately 1% of installment sales. Information related to sales during the period 2004–2006 is as follows:

	2004	2005	2006
Installment sales	$4,000,000	$4,700,000	$5,500,000
Cost of sales	2,800,000	3,243,000	3,685,000
Cash collections:			
From 2004 sales	1,000,000	2,000,000	880,000
From 2005 sales		2,400,000	1,900,000
From 2006 sales			2,400,000

The following information relates to repossessions that occurred during the same period:

	2004	2005	2006
Repossessions of 2004 sales:			
Retail sales price	$40,000	$ 30,000	$ 50,000
Less cash collected on sales	(5,000)	(15,000)	(40,000)
Amounts owed	$35,000	$ 15,000	$ 10,000
Repossessions of 2005 sales:			
Retail sales price		$ 50,000	$ 70,000
Less cash collected on sales		(10,000)	(25,000)
Amounts owed		$ 40,000	$ 45,000
Repossessions of 2006 sales:			
Retail sales price			$ 65,000
Less cash collected on sales			(10,000)
Amounts owed			$ 55,000

The retail sales price is the price at which Haskins originally sold the car. Cars that are repossessed in the first, second, and third year of sale are, on average, revalued to 60%, 40%, and 25% of the original sales price, respectively. Commissions to salesmen are normally 20% of the price at which the cars can be sold.

Required:
1. Determine the gross profit percentage for each year.
2. Record the journal entries that would be made in 2006 for (a) sales, (b) cost of goods sold, (c) cash collections, (d) bad debt expense,[33] (e) deferring gross profit for 2006, (f) recognizing gross profit for 2006, and (g) repossessions.
3. Assuming that operating expenses other than bad debts were $1,400,000, prepare an income statement for 2006.

---

[33]If necessary, review Chapter 2 as to how to prepare this entry. Also, information about how and why this entry is prepared can be found in Chapter 10.

Problem 8-10: Cost Recovery Method.

Required:
Rework Problem 8-8, using the cost recovery method.

Problem 8-11: Cost Recovery Method.

Required:
Using the information in Problem 8-9, (1) compute the realized gross profit on all sales for each year, and (2) prepare an income statement for each year, ignoring income tax effects.

Problem 8-12: Deposit Method (Appendix).

Bloomer's TVs is a retail company that sells television sets on a cash or credit basis. As a customer service, Bloomer's also offers an extended service warranty to each customer at an additional cost of $20 on TV sets with 19-inch or smaller screens and $30 on TV sets with greater than 19-inch screens. Estimated (and actual) warranty costs over the 2-year service period are presented in the following table:

	Estimated Actual Service Costs	
	First Year Following Sale	Second Year Following Sale
TVs with screen ≤19 inches	$4	$12
TVs with screen >19 inches	8	19

Sales data for 2006 are as follows:

	Units Sold	Average Price per Unit	Extended Warranties Sold
TVs with screen ≤19 inches	375	$280	40
TVs with screen >19 inches	450	825	110

Required:
1. Compute the amount of revenue that Bloomer's should recognize in 2006, assuming that Bloomer's uses the deposit method of recognizing revenue for warranties. Separately indicate the amount of revenue that should be recognized from the sales of TVs from the amount to recognize from sales of the extended warranties.
2. Prepare appropriate journal entries for 2006.

Problem 8-13: Reconciliation from German GAAP to U.S. GAAP.

Berger, Inc., is a construction company domiciled in Germany that works on long-term construction contracts. Berger prepares financial statements in conformity with German GAAP and accordingly uses the completed-contract method. Information related to the only two projects that Berger worked on during 2004 follows.

	Project A		Project B	
	2003	2004	2003	2004
Contract price	$9,500,000	$9,500,000	$6,300,000	$6,300,000
Total construction costs as of December 31	4,500,000	5,200,000	400,000	1,700,000
Estimated costs to complete	1,000,000	0	4,000,000	2,600,000

German tax rules require that taxes be paid according to the method used for German financial reporting purposes. Berger's effective tax rate is 50%. Berger's 2004 income statement is as follows:

Berger, Inc.
Income Statement
For the Year Ended December 31, 2004

Revenues from long-term construction contracts	$ 9,500,000
Expenses from long-term construction contracts	5,200,000
Gross profit on long-term construction contracts	$ 4,300,000
Other operating expenses	(800,000)
Interest expense	(500,000)
Income before taxes	$ 3,000,000
Income tax expense	(1,500,000)
Net income	$ 1,500,000

Required:
1. Beginning with the caption "Net income under German GAAP," reconcile German GAAP net income using the completed-contract method to U.S. GAAP net income using the percentage-of-completion method.
2. Since the gross profit recognized under U.S. GAAP differs from the gross profit under German GAAP, the income taxes payable to the German government ($1,500,000) will differ from the income tax expense under U.S. GAAP (50% of income before taxes). How should this difference be shown on the financial statements?

Research Activities

Activity 8-1: Accounting and Market Performance Measures. During the Gulf War, the *Patriot* missile proved very successful in defending Saudi and Israeli populations from Iraq's scud missiles. The first successful firing of the *Patriot* missile occurred in January 1991.

1. Research the quarterly stock price performance of Raytheon Company, which is the manufacturer of the *Patriot* missile, from December 1990 to December 1992. How did the stock perform, particularly during the first quarter of 1991? Did the successful firing of the *Patriot* missile have an impact on the stock price?
2. How would Raytheon's financial statements be impacted by the success of the *Patriot* missile? How quickly would the financial statements be affected?
3. Compare total quarterly revenues and EPS for Raytheon for the 1990 through 1992 quarters. Compare these accounting performance measures with the stock price performance. Did the income statement reflect the success of the *Patriot* missile in a timely fashion?

Cases

Case 8-1: Revenue Recognition—Cendant Corporation. Cendant Corporation was formed in December 1997 from the merger of HFS Inc. and CUC International, Inc. Headquartered in Parsippany, New Jersey, the company has more than 40,000 employees and operates in over 100 countries. The company's business is separated into three principal segments: Travel Services, Real Estate Services and Alliance Marketing. In Travel Services, Cendant is the leading franchisor of hotels (Ramada) and rental car agencies worldwide (Avis) and the largest provider of vacation exchange services. In Real Estate Services, Cendant is the world's largest franchisor of residential real estate brokerage offices (Coldwell Banker). In Alliance Marketing, Cendant provides access to insurance, travel, shopping, auto, and other services.

One of the membership clubs offered by Cendant is called *TravelAdvantage*. Members of this club are provided with discounts on travel. As a marketing strategy, Cendant offers prospective customers free membership for three months, after which, if the customer decides to retain the membership, an annual fee is charged. However, at any time during the membership period, customers are offered a full money-back guarantee if they decide to revoke their membership for any reason.

Identify alternatives for recognizing revenue from selling *TravelAdvantage* memberships. Recommend a specific alternative for Cendant to follow.

Case 8-2: Ethics—Cendant Corporation. In December 1997, Walter A. Forbes, CEO of CUC International, Inc., and Henry R. Silverman, CEO of HFS Inc., agreed to merge and form a new company called Cendant Corporation. In April 1998, a Cendant audit committee discovered some improprieties by management of the former CUC International. Management of CUC had inflated accounting earnings by $500 million over three years, and additional errors made by the company inflated earnings further by $200 million. In what would be termed the accounting scandal of the decade, Cendant's stock dropped from $35 per share to $19 per share on the day the improprieties were made public (nearly $13 billion of market capitalization). Only days prior to this, the market price of Cendant was trading at an all-time high of $41 per share.

Both Forbes and Silverman claimed they knew nothing about the accounting practices. In July 1998, Forbes resigned as chairman of the company and took a severance package of $35 million and options valued at $12.5 million. In September 1998, Silverman accepted a recommendation by the board of directors to reprice his 17.2 million outstanding options, which put the market value of the options close to $85 million. Prior to the repricing, the options were virtually worthless. The New York State comptroller expressed this action as "egregious."

1. Evaluate the claim made by Forbes that he knew nothing about the accounting improprieties of CUC. Should a CEO of a company know the accounting practices followed by the company?
2. Evaluate the claim made by Silverman that he knew nothing about the accounting improprieties of CUC. Did Silverman have a "due diligence" responsibility to shareholders of HFS before agreeing to the merger? Could any amount of due diligence reasonably be expected to reveal the improprieties prior to a merger?

(continued)

3. Did Forbes earn the compensation provided to him in the severance package? Should he have accepted such a lucrative package?

4. Evaluate the board of directors' decision to reprice Silverman's options. What was the board's motivation behind its decision? Were Silverman's ethics compromised when he accepted the board's recommendation?

5. The total earnings effect of the accounting improprieties totaled approximately $700 million over three years. Correction of the errors reduced the book value of stockholders' equity by the same amount. However, upon public release, Cendant's market value of equity declined almost $13 billion. In your opinion, what is the reason for such a large discrepancy between the changes in book value and market value of equity?

Case 8-3: Revenue Recognition—Priceline.com Inc. Priceline.com Inc. has pioneered a unique business concept that uses the Internet as a means to connect buyers and sellers of various goods and services. Priceline.com allows customers to set a price at which they would be willing to purchase something (e.g., an airline ticket). These data are used to assess consumer demand, which is communicated to participating sellers. This system offers customers goods and services at a discounted price, while simultaneously offering sellers the opportunity to earn incremental revenues by selling an excess supply of goods and services.

Priceline.com's income statements for 1999 and 1998, as obtained from its 1999 annual report, follow.

Priceline.com Incorporated
Statements of Operations
(in thousands, except per share data)

	Year Ended December 31,	
	1999	1998
Revenues	$ 482,410	$ 35,237
Cost of revenues:		
Product costs	$ 423,456	$ 33,496
Supplier warrant costs	1,523	3,029
Total cost of revenues	$ 424,579	$ 36,525
Gross profit	$ 57,831	$ (1,288)
Operating expenses:		
Warrant costs, net	$ 998,823	$ 57,979
Sales and marketing	79,577	24,388
General and administrative	27,609	18,004
Systems and business development	14,023	11,132
Total operating expenses	$ 1,120,041	$ 111,503
Operating loss	$(1,062,210)	$(112,791)
Total other income (expense)	7,120	548
Net loss	$(1,055,090)	$(112,243)
Accretion on preferred stock	(8,354)	(2,183)
Net loss applicable to common stockholders	$(1,063,444)	$(114,426)
Net loss per share	$(7.90)	$(1.41)
Weighted average number of shares	134,622	81,231

E-commerce companies, such as Priceline.com, typically realize large operating losses during their first few years in business but are considered to have extremely high growth potential. Since these companies don't have earnings, investors rely heavily on total revenues. Instead of stating price as a ratio of earnings (i.e., the P/E ratio), analysts often assess firm value based on revenue as a percentage of price revenues/earnings and revenue growth. Thus, revenue recognition policies become very significant for these companies. The following is an excerpt from the notes of Priceline.com's 1999 annual report:

> Revenues and Cost of Revenues—The Company recognizes and records revenues in a variety of ways, depending on the product or service sold. With respect to airline ticket, hotel room, and rental car services, the Company recognizes as revenue the amount received from the customer, net of taxes, and records as the cost of revenues the amount that the Company pays the respective airline or hotel.

Given this information, answer the following questions:

1. Calculate Priceline.com's revenue growth for 1999 in both absolute and percentage terms. Priceline.com's stock price at the end of 1999 was approximately $50. Calculate Priceline.com's price-to-revenues ratio for 1999.
2. Evaluate Priceline.com's revenue recognition policies related to airline tickets and hotel rooms. That is, do you agree with the company's policy to recognize the entire amount received from customers as revenue and the cost of the item as cost of goods sold? What other alternatives could Priceline.com follow?
3. Assume that all of Priceline.com's recognized revenues in 1999 and 1998 were from the sale of airline tickets and hotel rooms. Calculate Priceline.com's revenue growth for 1999 in absolute and percentage terms, assuming that the company recognized only the commission received from the product as revenue. What is the price-to-revenues ratio?

Case 8-4: Ethics. Review the case of SCB in the chapter (page 331). Applying a company's revenue recognition criteria is considered the responsibility of the accountants. So in the SCB scenario, why did they fail to "hold the line" when requested to inappropriately recognize revenue in the various situations described? What would you have done if a senior official in the company where you worked had asked you to recognize revenue when you knew that the "earned" and "realized or realizable" criteria had not been met? For how long would you maintain an ethical stance? Until it was evident your chances for a raise were jeopardized? Until you were threatened with being fired?

9

$\mathcal{R}$eporting Income: Classifications AND EPS

I n April, following an investigation, The Company announced the discovery of accounting fraud. The market's reaction was swift and harsh, and The Company's stock price plunged and then fell further as the full extent of the problem was disclosed. The cost to conduct the investigation, including the hiring of various external professionals, was $33.4 million.

Company management reacted swiftly to restore the lost equity value—and its credibility—by changing its strategic direction from buying companies to selling noncore assets. Accordingly, The Company sold (1) its publishing activities on which it expected a gain of approximately $380.0 million and (2) its computer software activities, recognizing a gain of $206.9 million. The Company also ended plans to acquire other companies. The costs incurred in acquiring these other companies, which were now written off, totaled $433.5 million. The Company also incurred $52.5 million in terminating certain executives, including the chairman of the board of directors.

Because of the accounting fraud, more than 70 lawsuits were filed in various courts against The Company. Further, the Securities and Exchange Commission and the U.S. attorney general began investigations relating to these matters.

Because of the accounting irregularities, The Company did not have audited financial statements and therefore was temporarily prohibited from accessing public debt markets. As a result, The Company paid $27.9 million in fees associated with waivers and various financing arrangements that it otherwise would not have incurred. Additionally, The Company exercised its option to redeem its 4¾% convertible senior notes and incurred a $7.2 million loss on extinguishing the debt before maturity.

In August, the SEC requested that The Company change its accounting policies with respect to recognizing revenues for its membership businesses.

Ex. 9-1 summarizes the various items The Company incurred or expected to incur during the year as a result of the accounting fraud.

Questions

1. Should these costs in Exhibit 9-1 be reported separately on the income statement?

2. If they should be reported separately, should any be reported in the operating section? As an extraordinary item?

3. Are there some items which do not fit comfortably in either the operating section or as an extraordinary item? Which ones?

EXHIBIT 9-1

Items the Company Incurred during the Year

Event or Cause	Amount
1. Hiring professionals	$33.4 million
2. Sale of noncore businesses	$206.9 million gain and an expected expected $380.0 million gain
3. Costs written off when plans to proceed with acquisitions were terminated	$433.5 million
4. Severance costs	$52.5 million
5. Lawsuits filed	Unspecified amount
6. Financing costs, including the loss on the early extinguishing of debt	$27.9 million and a $7.2 million loss on extinguishment
7. Change in the way that revenue is recognized	Unspecified amount

Learning Objectives

- Distinguish between the economic approach and the transactions approach to measuring income.
- Explain the difference between the current operating and the all-inclusive concepts of measuring income.
- Paraphrase the criteria and the test for determining whether a component of a business qualifies to be reported under discontinued operations.
- Measure the amounts reported as income from discontinued operations.
- Paraphrase the criteria for determining whether an event qualifies to be reported as an extraordinary item.
- Compute the amount reported under the cumulative effect of an accounting principles change.
- Compute diluted EPS.

Chapter 2 presented an overview of the concepts of preparing the income statement, with emphasis on the operating section and computing basic earnings per share (EPS). Chapters 6 and 7 dealt with measuring expenses, and Chapter 8 covered recognizing revenue. Having covered these topics, it is now possible to cover in more depth the concepts of reporting income, with emphasis on reporting (1) the operations of a company that have been or are being discontinued, (2) extraordinary items, (3) the general case for a change in an accounting principle, and (4) diluted EPS. Adding this topic of reporting income, the accounting and financing reporting model being developed is shown in Exhibit 9-2.

EXHIBIT 9-2

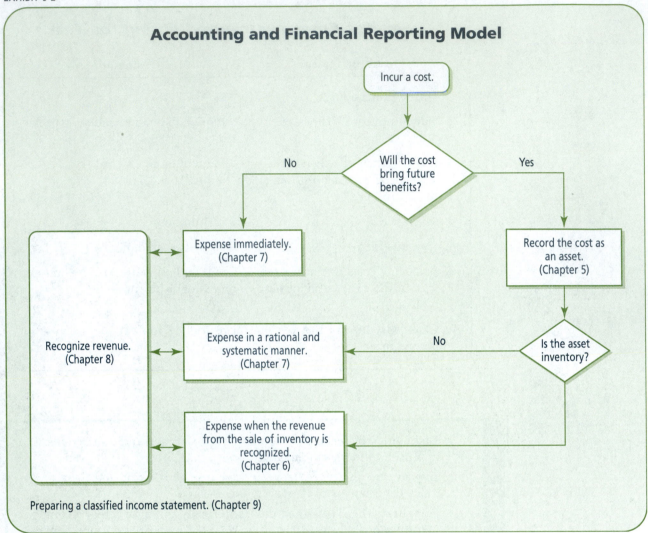

Accounting and Financial Reporting Model

Incur a cost.

Will the cost bring future benefits?

No → Expense immediately. (Chapter 7)

Yes → Record the cost as an asset. (Chapter 5)

Is the asset inventory?

No → Expense in a rational and systematic manner. (Chapter 7)

Expense when the revenue from the sale of inventory is recognized. (Chapter 6)

Recognize revenue. (Chapter 8)

Preparing a classified income statement. (Chapter 9)

The Theory of Measuring and Reporting Income

According to the FASB's conceptual framework, a major objective of financial reporting is to aid the readers of financial statements in making projections of future cash flows. In making these projections, all available data should be used, including the information contained in financial statements. But it is important to recognize that some of the amounts on the income statement are for one-time events. Since these events will not persist, the amounts should not be considered in making a cash flow projection. Deciding which amounts on the income statement to exclude is a decision for the readers of the financial statements. But the management of the company and the independent auditors—because of their knowledge of the company—certainly should help the readers to make such assessments. That is the reason why various revenues, gains, expenses, and losses are classified on the income statement into categories. To illustrate the difficulty of deciding what amounts represent one-time events, return to Exhibit 9-1 (p. 373) and decide which of the amounts should be excluded when making forecasts of future cash flows because they are one-time events.

The following discussion focuses on the difficulties of measuring and reporting income. Then the FASB's requirements for classifying the income statement will be better appreciated.

Economic Approach to Defining and Measuring Income

Income (as contrasted to revenue) is not easy to measure. Economists define income as the maximum amount an entity can consume during a period and still be as well off at the end of the period as it was at the beginning. This is a nice theoretical definition, but it is difficult to apply to a real-world business. One reason is because the term "well off" must be defined, which involves measuring psychic income in addition to changes in physical wealth. For example, a college student who works during the summer and part-time during the school months and earns a total of $8,000, but who spends more than that on tuition, fees, books, and room and board, may seem to have incurred a net loss for the year. But under the economic definition of well off, the value of the college education received would also have to be considered, as would the vacation spent on the beaches of Florida during spring break. Such psychic rewards—especially in a business setting—are impractical, and perhaps impossible, to measure.

Income can also be measured by valuing an entity at its current value at the beginning of the period and then again at the end of the period, with the difference between the two current values being economic income. Thus, another problem with the economic approach to measuring income is that current values for a business are seldom readily available.

Further, this method does not provide any detailed data on which to make decisions. Under the economic approach, the only number provided is the one labeled income. The economic approach gives no information about how income was generated or the factors that caused income to be less than it might have been. So if this method is used, management and financial statement readers have limited information on which to manage or base their decisions.

Transactions Approach to Defining and Measuring Income

Because of the disadvantages of using the economic approach to measuring income, businesses today use a **transactions approach**, where each transaction is measured in terms of the revenue realized, the expenses incurred, the assets acquired, etc. The primary advantage of the transactions approach is that detailed information is provided for managers in overseeing the business and for creditors and investors in making decisions.

But there are concerns about the transactions approach, too. One concern pertains to which revenues/gains and expenses/losses should be included on the income statement and which should be excluded. For example, should the income statement focus on income as measured by *all* the revenues and gains minus *all* the expenses and losses, or should it focus only on current operating income? Those who argue for an income statement that focuses on operating income justifiably state that the readers of financial statements are not too interested in nonoperating items because such items cannot be relied upon to portray a picture of future earnings or cash flows. They state further that a company's capacity to pay dividends and repay loans is contingent upon its cash flows from operations and not from cash flows from nonoperating transactions. However, those who argue for measuring income by subtracting all expenses and losses from all revenues and gains justifiably claim that focusing on anything less gives management the discretion as to which items of income and expense to include or exclude from income. The likely result would be that all questionable transactions that increase income would be included and all questionable transactions that decrease income would be excluded. Therefore, they say that all transactions that affect owners' wealth, regardless of whether the transactions are connected to operations or not, should be included in measuring income. These different viewpoints to measuring income are known as the **current operating** and the **all-inclusive** concepts, respectively. These concepts are summarized in the following table.

Current Operating	All-Inclusive
Revenues − Expenses	Revenues and Gains − Expenses and Losses
= Operating Income	= Operating Income

Today, U.S. GAAP supports the all-inclusive view—subject to specific exceptions mandated by the FASB—with the additional requirement that, because of its importance to the readers of financial statements, *income from operations should be disclosed prominently on the income statement. So all items of revenue and expense—except those defined as prior-period adjustments or reported as a component of other comprehensive income[1]—are included in determining net income.* In addition, U.S. GAAP requires that information be communicated regarding the nature of the revenues and expenses reported on the income statement (i.e., issue a classified income statement), which assists the financial statement readers in assessing the amounts, timing, and uncertainty of future earnings and cash flows. For example, income from operations is more likely to persist than is an extraordinary gain, and by separately classifying these items on the income statement, financial statement readers can analyze the income by classification and make their own determinations regarding expectations of the amount, timing, and uncertainty of future cash flows. It should be noted that one result of classifying an income statement is that, in effect, both the current operating concept and the all-inclusive concept are accommodated.

Although the accounting profession has essentially solved the issue as to what items of revenue and expense should be included on the income statement, a more troubling concern is that the transactions approach to measuring income results in several acceptable income numbers. This is so because of the acceptable alternative measurement principles that are available to measure transactions. For example, an asset can be depreciated using the straight-line method, an accelerated method, or some method based upon the number of units produced or hours operated. Each alternative method of depreciation is acceptable, but each results in a different measurement of income. In reality, there are a plethora of possible acceptable measurement alternatives, compounded by a variety of ways of applying them, thus giving rise to a possible multitude of acceptable income numbers that a company can appropriately report.

---

[1]Recall from Chapter 2 that "other comprehensive income" represents gains and losses that affect owners' equity but are not the result of an exchange transaction.

Currently, there does not seem to be an easy way to decrease the number of acceptable alternative accounting principles. Rather, the readers of financial statements must realize, as stated in the FASB's conceptual framework, the importance of becoming knowledgeable about the financial reporting process, including its strengths and concerns.

Because a company can report various "correct" income numbers, the readers of financial statements must assess the **quality of a company's earnings**, or the likelihood that the amount of reported income will persist, before they put much reliance on reported financial data. Allowing readers of financial statements the ability to assess a company's quality of earnings is a major reason why earnings are categorized and separately reported on the income statement and why a summary of a company's significant accounting policies are attached, either before the notes to the financial statements or as the first note.

Besides the quality of earnings, another concept that has arisen from having acceptable alternative accounting principles to measure transactions is **income smoothing**. Under this concept, it is considered appropriate to select those measurement principles that decrease income in very successful years and boost income in unsuccessful years. Today, it is widely accepted (at least in the United States) that smoothing out the highs and lows of income is artificial and does not reflect economic reality. Efforts are being made to encourage companies (and accountants) to report more realistic income numbers and not to use income-smoothing techniques.

U.S. GAAP Requirements for Reporting Income

Presently, U.S. GAAP requires that income be classified into several major categories (or sources of income) and reported in the following specified order:

- Continuing operations, with separate reporting of items that are *either* unusual in nature *or* that occur infrequently;
- Discontinued operations;
- Extraordinary items, which are items that are *both* unusual in nature *and* that occur infrequently; and
- Changes in accounting principles.

U.S. GAAP also requires that the tax effects of the various classifications of income be reported within each respective classification. This is called intraperiod tax allocation, or allocating the taxes of the year within the income statement.

U.S. GAAP requires that two earnings per share figures—basic and diluted—be reported on the face of the income statement. The reporting of these EPS numbers must be consistent with the income statement presentation, meaning that if the company has discontinued operations, an extraordinary item, or a change in an accounting principle, it must also report EPS data for discontinued operations, an extraordinary item, or a change in an accounting principle. (EPS is covered later in this chapter.)

Finally, because trends in financial data are more useful than single numbers, the income statement for at least the prior year should be presented for comparative purposes, including the reporting of associated EPS data. If the

EXTENDING THE CONCEPT

Return to Exhibit 9-1, p. 373, and determine in which category or classification each item would best be reported: as ordinary income, as an extraordinary item, etc.

prior-year data are not comparable due to reclassifications or other reasons, then the financial statements of the prior period(s) are restated so that they are comparable.[2]

Exhibit 9-3 (with simplified language and format for ease of reading and understanding) is the published financial statement of the Company that was introduced in the opening scenario. As you examine this income statement, note the following items:

1. The statement is a comparative statement with two prior periods being presented.
2. The following classifications are used: continuing operations, followed by discontinued operations, extraordinary items, and changes in accounting principles, respectively.
3. The single-step format is used because, within the continuing operations classification, the revenues and gains are grouped together, as are the expenses and losses.
4. Intraperiod tax allocation is used, in that a tax number is reported within each major classification of the income statement.

Continuing Operations

The first major classification of any income statement is the continuing operations classification, which consists of revenues and expenses and all gains and losses except for those specifically mandated by the FASB and its predecessors to be reported in another classification. In Exhibit 9-3, this classification consists of all items from Revenues to the subtotal "Income from continuing operations." In Exhibit 9-3, income from continuing operations is $159.9 for 2002. When a multiple-step format is used, the continuing operations classification is subdivided into various sections, such as revenues, cost of goods sold, other gains/losses, etc., as discussed in Chapter 2. When a single-step format is used, the only major sections are revenues and expenses.

From the single-step format, any difference between "Income from operations" and "Income from continuing operations" is not evident. But when the multiple-step format is used, the difference between the two amounts is evident because income from operations (or operating income) is reported separately and consists of revenues less expenses, where *revenues and expenses are the result of the central or major ongoing activities of the company.* Even though income from operations is not distinctly identified in Exhibit 9-3, it can be determined by reviewing the statement and identifying the ongoing revenues and expenses, as shown here.

Estimate of Income from Operations

Membership and service fees, net	$5,080.7
Expenses:	
Operating	1,869.1
Marketing and reservation	1,158.5
General and administrative	666.3
Depreciation and amortization	322.7
Income from operations	$1,064.1

[2]AICPA, ARB *Bulletin No. 43*, Chapter 2, "Form of Statements," New York, June 1953, pars. 1–3.

EXHIBIT 9-3

A Published Income Statement (Single-Step Format)
Consolidated Statements of Operations
(in millions)

For the Year Ended December 31	2002	2001	2000	
Revenues:				
Membership and service fees, net	$5,080.7	$4,083.4	$3,147.0	
Fleet leasing	88.7	59.5	56.7	
Other	114.4	97.1	34.0	These are the
Net revenues	$5,283.8	$4,240.0	$3,237.7	revenues and
				expenses connected
				to the reason the
				company is in
Expenses:				business.
Operating	$1,869.1	$1,322.3	$1,183.2	
Marketing and reservation	1,158.5	1,031.8	910.8	
General and administrative	666.3	636.2	341.0	
Depreciation and amortization	322.7	237.7	145.5	
Other charges				These are the
Litigation settlement	351.0	—	—	gains/losses
Termination of proposed acquisitions	433.5	—	—	connected with
Executive terminations	52.5	—	—	peripheral activities.
Investigation-related costs	33.4	—	—	These various
Merger-related costs and other unusual charges (credits)	(67.2)	704.1	109.4	gains/losses are unusual or
Financing costs	35.1	—	—	infrequent, but not
Interest, net	113.9	50.6	14.3	both.
Total expenses	$4,968.8	$3,982.7	$2,704.2	
Income from continuing operations before income taxes	$ 315.0	$ 257.3	$ 533.5	
Provision for income taxes	(104.5)	(191.0)	(220.2)	
Minority interest, net of tax	(50.6)	—	—	
Income from continuing operations	$ 159.9	$ 66.3	$ 313.3	
Discontinued operations:[3]				
Income (loss) from discontinued operations, net of tax	(25.0)	(26.8)	16.7	Intraperiod tax
				allocation, with a tax
Gain on sale of discontinued operations, net of tax	404.7	—	—	amount reported for income from
Income before extraordinary gain and cumulative effect of accounting change	$ 539.6	$ 39.5	$ 330.0	operations and every item thereafter being
Extraordinary items:				reported net of tax.
Extraordinary gain, net of tax	—	26.4	—	
Cumulative effect of accounting change, net of tax	—	(283.1)	—	
Net income (loss)	$ 539.6	$ (217.2)	$ 330.0	

[3]This format was acceptable for presenting discontinued operations prior to the issuance of *SFAS No. 144*, which was issued in 2001 and became effective for financial statements whose fiscal year began after December 15, 2001.

This Is the Real World

The fall of Enron Corporation in 2001 from one of the largest companies in the world as measured by market capitalization to declaring bankruptcy in less than a year reinforced to investors the importance of analyzing financial statements to better assess a company's actual operating performance. Companies are required to assist investors in assessing the quality of their earnings by formatting their income statements in such a manner that income from core operations can be easily distinguished from transitory and/or peripheral transactions. The following excerpt from a *Business Week* article illustrates what can happen when investors suspect that company management might be trying to stretch accounting rules to artificially inflate reported income from operations.

"There's no doubt the market is already penalizing those who ignore this demand for openness. On February 15, when The New York Times *reported that Big Blue had used the gain on the sale of one of its businesses to lower reported expenses, its shares got slammed, dropping 5%, to $103. On February 19 and 20, they dropped 3% more, to $99, falling below $100 for the first time since last October.*

Some accounting pros say the move was within the bounds of financial-reporting rules. And IBM says the transaction was properly disclosed and approved by its auditors. Big Blue notes that it has offset such sales against expenses on its income statement since the mid-1990s. But investors weren't buying it. Many argued that the accounting makes IBM's operations look more robust than they actually are—not a good thing at a time when quality of earnings is all the rage. 'Most investors are going to feel that gains on the sale of property are not core operations, no matter how frequent it is,' says Robert Willens, a tax-and-accounting analyst at Lehman Brothers Inc."

Source: A. Barrett, S.E. Ante, W.C. Symonds, and M. McNamee, "Slammed," Business Week, March 4, 2002, pp. 34–35.

Only one tax expense number is reported in the income from operations section. Further, only two EPS numbers (one basic and the other diluted, shown later in the chapter in Exhibit 9-7) are reported for this classification. No amounts within the classification have an EPS number reported for them.

At the end of the continuing operations classification, the subtotal is labeled "Income from continuing operations." Occasionally, this subtotal is modified to reflect the types of classifications that follow it. For example, when a company has amounts in the discontinued operations section, the subtotal may be labeled "Income from continuing operations before discontinued operations." If the company has extraordinary items but no discontinued operation amount, then the subtotal may be labeled "Income from continuing operations before extraordinary items." Any caption, as long as it is descriptive, is acceptable. So a caption such as "Income from continuing operations before discontinued operations and extraordinary items" is acceptable—although lengthy.

Discontinued Operations[4]

The discontinued operations section follows immediately after the income from continuing operations subtotal and is used when both of the following criteria are met:

- A component of an entity has been disposed of or is being held for sale, and
- The cash flows from the component are clearly distinguished, both operationally and for financial reporting purposes, from the rest of the entity.

Failure to meet either criterion means that the results of operations of the component are reported under continuing operations.

---

[4]See *SFAS No. 144*, "Accounting for the Impairment or Disposal of Long-Lived Assets."

As used here, a component of a business entity may take the organizational form of an operating segment,[5] a reporting unit,[6] a subsidiary, or a group of assets. Obviously, the size of the organizational unit is not relevant in determining whether the results of operations of the component should be reported under discontinued operations.

To be considered as being held for sale, all of the following criteria must be met as of the fiscal year-end of the business entity:

- Management has committed itself to a plan to sell a component of the business entity,
- An active program to locate a buyer has been initiated,
- The sale of the component of the business entity is probable and will occur within one year,
- The asking price is reasonable, and
- It is unlikely that significant changes to the plan will be made.

If all of the above criteria are not met at the end of the fiscal year but are met before the financial statements are issued, all amounts related to the business component being sold (e.g., operating income and gains/losses) still must be reported under continuing operations.

When the component meets both criteria, the amount reported under discontinued operations consists of all of the following:

- The results of operations of the component from the beginning of the fiscal year to the date the component is sold or to the end of the fiscal year, whichever occurs first.
- Any estimated loss[7] on the date that the decision is made to sell the component. This estimated loss is the difference, on that decision date, between the carrying value of the net assets (i.e., assets being sold minus the liabilities that also are being sold) of the component and the fair value of the net assets less any costs of disposing of the net assets (i.e., net realizable value).
- Any gain or loss when the component is sold.
- Or, if the component is not sold as of the end of the fiscal year, any gain or additional loss between the carrying value of the net assets of the component and the net realizable value of the net assets. While a gain can be recognized, the amount of the gain is limited to no more than the amount of the previously recognized loss on the decision date.

EXTENDING THE CONCEPT

In recent years, several lines and models of automobiles have been discontinued (e.g., Oldsmobile and Mercury). Obtain recent financial statements and determine whether these operations were reported under discontinued operations.

Measuring the Amounts to Be Reported under Discontinued Operations

Examples of measuring the amount to report under discontinued operations are shown in Illustration 9-1. Situation 1 illustrates measurement scenarios in which the component is sold before the fiscal year-end. The measurement of the amount to report under discontinued operations is slightly more complicated when the component has not been sold by fiscal year-end, illustrated in Situation 2.

---

[5]According to *SFAS No. 131*, "Disclosures about Segments of an Enterprise and Related Information," an operating segment of a business is a component (1) that engages in business activities from which it earns (or is expected to earn) revenues and incurs expenses, (2) whose operating performance is reviewed regularly by the chief operating decision maker, and (3) for which discrete financial information is available.

[6]According to *SFAS No. 142*, "Goodwill and Other Intangible Assets," a reporting unit is an operating segment (see footnote 5) or one operating level below an operating segment.

[7]Gains are not recognized because the realization criterion (i.e., a claim to cash) is not met.

ILLUSTRATION 9-1

Determining the Amount to Report as Discontinued Operations

Situation 1: Component is sold before the fiscal year-end.

Scenario	Operating Income/Loss for the Year	Gain/Loss on Decision Date	Additional Realized Gain/Loss on Disposal	Total to Report under Discontinued Operations
1	$(50,000)	$(65,000)	$ 5,000	$(110,000)
2	50,000	(65,000)	(5,000)	(20,000)
3	35,000	10,000	(5,000)	40,000
4	(40,000)	20,000	13,000	(7,000)

Situation 2: Component is not sold before the fiscal year-end.

Scenario	Operating Income/Loss for the Year	Estimated Gain/Loss on Decision Date	Additional Estimated Gain/Loss from Decision Date to Fiscal Year-End	Total to Report under Discontinued Operations
1	$(50,000)	$(65,000)	$5,000	$(110,000)

Explanation: The estimated loss on the decision date is recognized, and because the subsequent gain or loss recovery is less than the loss on the decision date, it too is recognized.

2	$50,000	$(65,000)	$(5,000)	$(20,000)

Explanation: All losses are recognized as is operating income.

3	$35,000	$10,000	$(5,000)	$35,000

Explanation: The $10,000 estimated gain on the decision date is not recognized, and since the net realizable value of the net assets at fiscal year-end is still greater than their carrying value (as indicated by the gain on the decision date being greater than the subsequent loss), that loss is not recognized either.

4	$(40,000)	$10,000	$(13,000)	$(43,000)

Explanation: The $10,000 estimated gain on the decision date is not recognized; however, since the net realizable value of the net assets at fiscal year-end is less than their carrying value (as indicated by the gain on the decision date being less than the subsequent loss), the net loss is recognized.

5	$(40,000)	$(20,000)	$33,000	$(40,000)

Explanation: The $20,000 estimated loss is recognized, and $20,000 of the subsequent gain is also recognized.

Financial Reporting Requirements

The discontinued operations section is prepared as shown in Exhibit 9-4,[8] which reports the results for the year in which the decision was made, the year prior, and the year subsequent. The amount reported under the "Year of the Decision to Sell" was computed as illustrated previously. The amount reported for the prior year includes all items of revenues, expenses, losses, and gains that are connected with the discontinued component for that year, which are reclassified from the categories where they were reported previously (e.g., sales, cost of goods sold), so that the income statements for all years are comparable. The amount reported in the subsequent year consists of (1) the operating income/loss for that year and (2) any gain on sale or adjustment to the estimated loss that was recognized in

---

[8]Because of the issuance of *SFAS No. 144*, the financial reporting of discontinued operations as shown in Exhibit 9-3, p. 379, is no longer acceptable.

EXHIBIT 9-4

Bear Hugs by LaRee
Financial Reporting for Discontinued Operations

	Year of Disposal	Year of the Decision to Sell	Year Prior to the Year of Decision
Income from continuing operations	$124,000	$118,500	$112,000
Discontinued operations:			
Income from operations of discontinued Division Y (less income taxes)	(34,200)	11,850	18,600
Income before extraordinary items*	$ 89,800	$130,350	$130,600

*If the company has no extraordinary items or a change in an accounting principle, then this title is "Net income."

the previous year (i.e., the year in which the decision to sell was made). *All amounts reported under discontinued operations are reported net of tax expense or benefit.*

In addition to reporting these amounts, the business entity must disclose the following information:

- A description of the facts and circumstances leading to the expected disposal, the expected manner and timing of that disposal, and the carrying amounts of the major classes of assets and liabilities included in the component;
- The gain or loss recognized on the date the decision was made to dispose of the component;
- The gain or loss recognized on the sale;
- If applicable, the amounts of revenue and pretax profit or loss reported in discontinued operations; and
- If applicable, the identification of the segment in which the component is located.

It may happen that after making the decision to sell a component, either (1) the criteria for being considered held for sale are no longer met or (2) the decision is made to not sell the component. Under either situation, the net assets of the business component are revalued at the lower of their (a) carrying amount at the time the *decision to sell was made, adjusted for any depreciation since the decision to sell,* or (b) fair value at the time the decision to sell is rescinded (or the criteria for being considered held for sale are not met). Any gain or loss recorded in order to revalue the net assets is reported in the continuing operations section of the income statement. Examples of this concept are shown in Illustration 9-2.

In either scenario, a $5 million loss is recognized when the decision is made to sell the component. This loss is measured by comparing the carrying value of the net assets of $20 million to the net realizable value of the net assets of $15 million. One year subsequent, the decision to sell the component is rescinded, with the possibilities that the fair value of the net assets may have increased (Scenario 1), or the fair value of the net assets may have decreased (Scenario 2). In either situation, when the decision to sell is rescinded, the carrying value of the net assets on that date is $15 million.[9]

---

[9]As will be discussed in more detail in Chapter 10, once the decision is made to sell a component, the long-lived assets are no longer depreciated or amortized.

ILLUSTRATION 9-2

Measuring Loss When Decision to Sell a Component Is Rescinded

	Scenario 1	Scenario 2
Information available when the decision is made to sell the component:		
Carrying value of the net assets	$20 million	$20 million
Fair value of the net assets	16 million	16 million
Costs to dispose of the net assets	1 million	1 million
Information available when the decision is rescinded:		
Carrying value of the net assets (see above)	$15 million	$15 million
Fair value of the net assets	$18 million	$13 million
Economic life of the net assets	5 years	5 years
Time elapsed before decision is rescinded	1 year	1 year

Once the decision to sell is rescinded, the business entity must now determine whether a gain or loss should be recognized. A loss is recognized when the new carrying value of the net assets (i.e., net realizable value as of the decision to sell date) is greater than *either* (a) the new fair value of the net assets or (b) the original carrying value of the net assets adjusted for depreciation. A gain should be recognized when the new carrying value of the net assets is less than *both* (a) and (b). The calculations for each scenario are as follows:

	Scenario 1	Scenario 2
Computing the adjusted carrying value of the net assets to the time that the decision to sell the component is rescinded:		
1. Carrying value of the net assets when the decision is made to sell the component (see Illustration 9-2)	$20 million	$20 million
2. Economic life of the net assets (see Illustration 9-2)	5 years	5 years
3. Time elapsed before the decision is rescinded (see same)	1 year	1 year
4. Depreciation/amortization for one year (Row 1 ÷ Row 2)	$4 million	$4 million
5. Adjusted carrying value of the net assets (Row 1 − Row 4)	$16 million	$16 million
Computing the amount that should be reported on the books as the carrying value of the net assets at the time the decision to sell the component is rescinded (i.e., lesser of adjusted carrying amount or fair value):		
6. Fair value of the net assets (see Illustration 9-2)	$18 million	$13 million
7. Amount that now should be reported as the carrying value of the net assets of the component (lower of Row 5 or Row 6)	$16 million	$13 million
Computing the gain/loss when the decision to sell is rescinded:		
8. Carrying value of the net assets at the time the decision to sell the component is rescinded (see Illustration 9-2)	$15 million	$15 million
9. Gain (or loss) to recognize (compare Row 7 and Row 8)	$1 million	$(2 million)

To repeat what was stated earlier, this gain/loss from rescinding the decision to dispose of the component is reported as part of continuing operations. Further, if a business reports a caption such as "Income from operations," the loss must be reported as part of that subtotal.

When a company decides to sell a group of assets that do not qualify as a component, a loss is still computed as of the date of the decision to sell and is calculated as the difference between the carrying value and the net realizable value of the net assets. As before, gains are not recognized. Further, if the asset group is not sold by the end of the fiscal year, an additional loss is recognized if the group of assets' net realizable value has declined further. Or a gain may be recognized to the extent of any previously recognized loss when the assets' net realizable value has recovered. In fact, the accounting for the disposal of an asset group is the same in all respects as illustrated for a component, except that any gain/loss is reported as part of continuing operations. And as stated previously, if a business reports a caption such as "Income from operations," the gain/loss on disposing of an asset group is reported as part of that subtotal.

Extraordinary Items

The criteria for determining an extraordinary item are that the event or transaction must be unusual in nature *and* infrequent in occurrence, taking into account the environment in which the entity operates. The amount should also be material. **Unusual in nature** means that the event or transaction possesses a high degree of abnormality and is clearly unrelated to, or only incidentally related to, the ordinary and typical activities of the entity. Infrequency of occurrence means that the event or transaction would not reasonably be expected to recur in the foreseeable future.

In the first sentence of APB *Opinion 29*, concerning identifying whether an event or transaction is extraordinary, the APB wrote, "Judgment is required. . . ." This phrase clearly indicates that recognizing an extraordinary item is not an easy task, regardless of the comfort that is received from doing textbook problems. To illustrate the difficulty in recognizing extraordinary items, refer back to Exhibit 9-1 and the opening scenario, pp. 371–372, and decide which of items 1 and 3–6 should be reported as an extraordinary item, and then compare your decisions to how the Company actually reported them, as shown in Exhibit 9-5.

EXHIBIT 9-5

How the Company Reported Atypical Events and Transactions

Event or Cause (the numbering refers to the order in Exhibit 9-1, p. 372)	Determination	Where Reported on the Company's Income Statement
1. Hiring professionals	Not extraordinary	"Investigation-related costs"
3. Costs written off when plans to proceed with acquisitions were terminated	Not extraordinary	"Termination of proposed acquisition"
4. Severance costs	Not extraordinary	"Executive terminations"
5. Lawsuits filed	Not extraordinary	Unknown
6. Financing costs, including the loss on the early extinguishing of debt	Not extraordinary	"Financing costs"

Since judgment is required in determining what constitutes an extraordinary item, do you disagree with the way in which some items were reported? What is your rationale for reporting these items differently from The Company?

Likely, your decisions/recommendations were not always consistent with how the Company actually reported the amounts; accountants often disagree as to what constitutes an extraordinary item.

Specifically, the APB gave the following as examples of transactions or events that do not qualify as extraordinary items:

a. Write-down or write-off of receivables, inventories, equipment leased to others, and various intangible assets and deferred charges;
b. Gains/losses from foreign currency exchange rate fluctuations;
c. Gains/losses on the disposal of a component of a business;
d. Gains/losses on the sale or abandonment of property, plant, or equipment;
e. Effects of a strike, including those against a competitor or a supplier; and
f. Adjustments of accruals on long-term contracts.

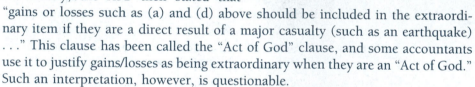

Interestingly, immediately following this listing of events that are not extraordinary, the APB then stated that "gains or losses such as (a) and (d) above should be included in the extraordinary item if they are a direct result of a major casualty (such as an earthquake) . . ." This clause has been called the "Act of God" clause, and some accountants use it to justify gains/losses as being extraordinary when they are an "Act of God." Such an interpretation, however, is questionable.

To date, *there is only one transaction that is always classified as an extraordinary item, and that results from purchasing a company for less than the book value of its net assets*, which is discussed in advanced accounting texts.[10] These gains/losses are extraordinary items because the FASB declared them to be so.

For financial reporting purposes, extraordinary items are grouped by type (e.g., all gains and losses resulting from several hurricanes after insurance settlements, etc.), and *each type of extraordinary item is presented separately and reported net of its tax or tax effect*, as shown in Exhibit 9-6.

The subtotal following the reporting of extraordinary items should be descriptive. Thus, when a company has a change in an accounting principle, the subtotal can be labeled "Income before the cumulative effect of a change in an accounting principle," or some other descriptive title. When a company does not report the effects of a change in an accounting principle, the amount is labeled "Net income."

International Practices

Soon after its organization, the International Accounting Standards Board (IASB) began a project to review and increase the quality and consistency of its standards, referred to as the IASB's Improvement Project. In May 2002, the IASB released an exposure draft that proposes to revise 12 of its 34 active standards. One of the proposed changes is to no longer permit companies to use the label of ex-

---

[10]FASB, *Statement No. 141*, "Business Combinations," Stamford, CT: July 2001, par. 45.

EXHIBIT 9-6

Bear Hugs by LaRee
Financial Reporting for Extraordinary Items

Income before extraordinary items and change in accounting principle	$130,350
Gain from acquiring company for less than book value (net of taxes of $12,600)	47,400
Losses from earthquake (net of tax effect of $4,200)	(15,800)
Income before the cumulative effect of a change in an accounting principle	$161,950

traordinary items on the income statement. The IASB believes that the extraordinary items label is used too inconsistently across accounting regimes to be useful for cross-country comparisons.

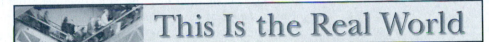

This Is the Real World

On September 11, 2001, a tragedy of epic proportions occurred on U.S. soil. Four commercial airlines were hijacked. Two of the hijacked planes crashed into the World Trade Towers in New York City, resulting in their collapse. Another plane crashed into the Pentagon Building in Washington D.C., and a fourth plane crashed in an open field in Pennsylvania. Although paling in comparison to the devastating loss of human life, the tragedy also had a very significant effect on business—including accounting. Obviously, many companies in New York City lost substantial physical assets. However, numerous other companies were indirectly affected due to transportation problems, cancelled orders, and the significant shock to the economy.

In the wake of the disaster, the FASB's Emerging Issues Task Force (EITF) attempted to develop some additional guidelines for companies to determine whether their realized losses could be attributed to the September 11 attacks and thus classified as extraordinary. After two weeks of deliberations, the EITF declared that it was impossible to develop a set of criteria, given the widespread effects of the disaster. Essentially, the EITF recognized that only management can decide whether something is extraordinary or not.

Several analysts expressed concern that management might abuse this power by claiming that some ordinary expenses and losses would not have occurred had the September 11 tragedy not happened. Stated one analyst, "There is going to be a tendency to overestimate the economic impact of the attack because it allows managements to shift responsibility for their own mistakes to Osama bin Laden." Nobody can say for certain whether this has occurred or not. One must rely on management credibility or form an opinion, based on critical analysis of the financial statements.

SOURCE: D. Henry, "Putting on a Grim New Face," Business Week, October 15, 2001, pp. 46–47.

Change in Accounting Principle[11]

This text has stated in various places that the income a company reports is determined by its choice of accounting principles and that the trend of income is more informative than a single number, which is why companies issue comparative financial statements. But when a company changes its accounting princi-

---

[11]APB *Opinion No. 20,* "Accounting Changes," New York, July 1971.

ples, the trend of income is distorted. So it is evident that the consistent use of accounting principles enhances the relevance of financial statements. Thus, there is a presumption that once an accounting principle has been selected, it should not be changed. However, that presumption should not prohibit a company from changing to an accounting principle that is preferable, such as conforming to a new accounting standard or when economic conditions change and current accounting principles no longer represent economic conditions. This is so because relevance is a more important qualitative characteristic than is consistency.

A change in an accounting principle is the result of changing from one generally accepted accounting principle to another generally accepted accounting principle. Examples of changes in an accounting principle are changing the inventory cost-flow assumption (e.g., from LIFO to FIFO) and changing from the straight-line method of depreciation to an accelerated method of depreciation.[12] A change from an accounting principle that is not generally accepted to a principle that is generally accepted is the correction of an error and is reported as a prior-period adjustment. The adopting of an accounting principle to account for events or transactions that have not occurred previously is not a change in an accounting principle. Finally, when a change in an accounting principle occurs simultaneously with a change in an accounting estimate *and the effects of the two changes cannot be separated*, the APB concluded that the *entire change is accounted for as a change in an accounting estimate*.

When specifying the financial reporting for a change in an accounting principle, the APB was torn between two competing views. One view was that the prior-year's financial statements must be restated in the current years' financial report, as failure to do so would result in the data between the two years not being comparable. The other view was that the prior-year's financial statements must not be restated because to do so would erode the confidence of the financial statement readers in the accounting profession, as they would perceive that such restatement meant that the prior-years' financial statements were in error.

General Case: Reporting a Cumulative Effect

For most changes in an accounting principle, the course the APB chose was to require that the financial statements of prior periods that are presented for comparative purposes *not be restated*. But to compensate for the resulting income statements not being comparable, *pro forma data are reported for all periods presented (i.e., the current year and all prior periods) "as if" the newly adopted accounting principle had been used for all periods*. These pro forma data (including the related per-share amounts) are reported only for net income and, if necessary, income before extraordinary items. Finally, a cumulative effect is reported as a component of the current year's net income, which is computed as *the difference between (a) the balance of retained earnings as of the beginning of the year of change and (b) what the balance of retained earnings at the beginning of the year would have been if the newly adopted accounting principle had always been used*. These procedures are summarized as follows:

1. Do not restate prior-year financial statements,
2. Present pro forma amounts, and
3. Compute a cumulative effect.

---

[12]A planned change to the straight-line method of depreciation from an accelerated method of depreciation at a specific point in the service life of an asset is not a change in an accounting principle; that is the accounting principle.

To illustrate how the cumulative effect is computed, assume that in December 2006 L&B Company, which had been using an accelerated depreciation method, switched to the straight-line method. Using fixed asset records, depreciation amounts were recomputed for all assets for all prior periods and summarized by year, shown in Illustration 9-3. The income tax rate for both years was 30%.

ILLUSTRATION 9-3

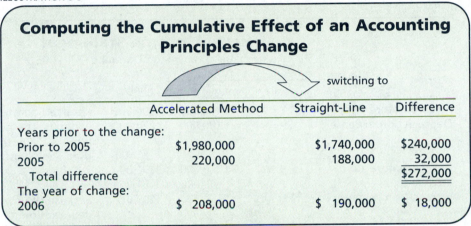

Computing the Cumulative Effect of an Accounting Principles Change

switching to

	Accelerated Method	Straight-Line	Difference
Years prior to the change:			
Prior to 2005	$1,980,000	$1,740,000	$240,000
2005	220,000	188,000	32,000
Total difference			$272,000
The year of change:			
2006	$ 208,000	$ 190,000	$ 18,000

Taking this information to its CPA, L&B is told that the amount of depreciation expense to deduct for 2006 is $190,000, which is computed by using the newly adopted accounting principle, and that a cumulative effect of $272,000 must also be reported. This amount is the difference prior to the year of change between using the old depreciation principle as compared to the new depreciation principle.

The journal entry to record the cumulative effect is prepared by analyzing the effect on accumulated depreciation. Since more depreciation was recorded under the accelerated method than needs to be recorded under the straight-line method, the accumulated depreciation account needs to be reduced. So, Accumulated Depreciation is debited, and the cumulative effect account is credited, as shown.

Accumulated Depreciation	272,000	
Cumulative Effect of an Accounting		
Principle Change		190,400
Tax Effect ($272,000 × 30%)		81,600

To record an accounting principle change—changing from an accelerated depreciation method to the straight-line method.

The entry to record depreciation expense for 2006 is as follows, which is based upon the new depreciation principle:

Depreciation Expense	190,000	
Accumulated Depreciation		190,000

To record the depreciation expense for 2006, using the straight-line method.

Concluding his advice, the CPA tells L&B that the prior year's income statement that is included in the current years' financial report for comparative purposes is presented just as previously reported. Since the income statement data between the two years are not comparable, pro forma data must be reported. The income statement for 2006 with the comparative income statement for 2005, along with pro forma data and supporting calculations, is shown in Illustration 9-4.

Note from the calculations in Illustration 9-4 that the pro forma amounts are computed by using the newly adopted accounting principle for both years. Also, note that the cumulative effect is not included in computing the pro forma amounts.

ILLUSTRATION 9-4

Partial Income Statement
For the Year Ended December 31, 2006

	2006	2005	
Income before depreciation[13]	$410,000	$390,000	Assumed amount
Depreciation expense	190,000	220,000	For 2005, the accelerated method is used and for 2006, the straight-line method is used. (See Illustration 9-3)
Income before taxes	$220,000	$170,000	
Income taxes	66,000	51,000	
Income before extraordinary items	$154,000	$119,000	Because of using two different depreciation methods, these numbers are not comparable.
Extraordinary item (net of taxes of $10,000 and $30,000, respectively)	20,000	(60,000)	Assumed amount for illustration purposes only.
Accounting principle change (net of taxes of $81,600)	190,400	0	See journal entry to recognize the cumulative effect of the accounting change.
Net income	$364,400	$ 59,000	These numbers are not comparable.
Earnings per Share			
Income before extraordinary items	$ 1.54	$ 1.19	Author constructed.
Net income	$ 3.64	$ 0.59	Author constructed.
Pro Forma			
Income before extraordinary items	$154,000	$141,400	These numbers are comparable.
Net income	$174,000	$ 81,400	These numbers are comparable.
Pro Forma Earnings per Share			
Income before extraordinary items	$ 1.54	$ 1.41	
Net income	$ 1.74	$ 0.81	

Pro Forma Calculations

	2006	2005	
Income before depreciation	$410,000	$390,000	See first part.
Depreciation expense	190,000	188,000	Both amounts were computed using the straight-line method, which is the newly adopted accounting principle.
Income before taxes	$220,000	$202,000	
Income taxes	66,000	60,600	
Income before extraordinary items	$154,000	$141,400	Reported on the income statement.
Extraordinary item (net of taxes of $10,000 and $30,000, respectively)	20,000	(60,000)	See first section.
Net income	$174,000	$ 81,400	Reported on the income statement.

[13]There is no such line on the income statement. It is used here for teaching purposes only.

As another illustration of applying the general principle of accounting for a change in an accounting principle, presume that in early 2004, J&M Company changed from using a FIFO inventory cost-flow assumption to an average system. The ending inventory amounts under the two cost-flow assumptions are as shown.

Year	FIFO Cost-Flow Assumption	Average Cost-Flow Assumption
2002	$43,000	$38,000
2003	52,000	45,000
2004	64,000	51,000

In this illustration, the journal entry to recognize the cumulative effect and to change the inventory records to an average cost-flow assumption, assuming an income tax rate of 30%, is as follows:

Cumulative Effect of Change in Accounting Principle	4,900	
Tax Effect	2,100	
Inventory		7,000

Inventory is credited because the dollar amount of inventory is being reduced, and the cumulative effect is debited for the same amount, less taxes. It is not necessary to compute a cumulative effect by adding the differences in each year, as was done with depreciation, because the ending inventory amounts computed under the two cost-flow assumptions represent the total difference between the values of inventory under the two methods. So the amount in the preceding journal entry is the difference in the ending inventory as of the end of the 2003 fiscal year. The additional difference that resulted in 2004 will be reflected in the company's operating earnings for 2004.

Exception 1 to the General Case: Reporting a Prior-Period Adjustment

The APB decided that, for certain changes in an accounting principle, restating prior-year financial statements is necessary. In those cases, *the prior-year financial statements that are presented for comparative purposes are restated, using the newly adopted accounting principle.* This retroactive restatement is required for the following changes:

1. A change from the LIFO cost-flow assumption to another cost-flow assumption.
2. A change in the method of accounting for long-term construction contracts.
3. A change either to or from the "full cost" method in the extractive industries.[14]

---

[14]The question arises in the oil industry when no oil is found as to whether the exploratory costs should be expensed or capitalized as an asset. One notion is that these costs should be expensed as a cost of the period in accordance with the "immediate recognition" part of the matching principle because no benefits resulted from the expenditures. This is known as the "successful efforts" approach, meaning that only the costs incurred when oil is successfully discovered are capitalized. Another notion is to view the asset in a larger sense—as an oil field rather than individual oil wells. Under this view, all costs incurred in finding the oil, even if individual wells are unproductive, are capitalized. This is the "full cost" approach. Changing either to or from the full cost approach is a change in an accounting principle that requires the prior-period's financial statements that are presented in the current year for comparative purposes to be restated.

4. A closely held corporation issuing public financial statements for the first time to obtain equity financing, to effect a business combination, or to register securities.[15]
5. A change in a reporting entity.[16]
6. When a newly issued financial standard requires retroactive restatement for companies that must change their accounting principles to comply with the new standard.

In addition to restating the financial statement data for all prior periods that are issued for comparative purposes in the current year's financial report, a prior-period adjustment is computed.[17] The prior-period adjustment is computed in exactly the same way as the cumulative effect in the general case of a change in an accounting principle. The only difference is where it is reported. Reporting prior-period adjustments will be covered in Chapter 15.

Exception 2 to the General Case: Change to LIFO

A second exception to the general case for reporting a change in an accounting principle is for a change *to LIFO*. For that change, the APB concluded that computing the cumulative effect was impossible or impractical and, therefore, mandated that the beginning inventory in the year that the change to LIFO is made becomes the beginning LIFO inventory, and that LIFO procedures be applied from that time. Hence, when a change to LIFO occurs, the only accounting or reporting requirement is to *disclose the effect on income* in the year of change.

Computing Diluted Earnings per Share

Some corporations are required to report two EPS numbers: a basic and a diluted EPS. Diluted EPS numbers are reported for the same line items on the income statement as those for which basic EPS numbers are reported. The difference between the two EPS figures is that basic EPS is computed only upon the weighted-average number of shares of common stock outstanding, whereas diluted EPS is computed upon both the weighted-average number of shares *and* all other securities that may in the future be exchanged for shares of common stock. Thus, diluted EPS gives information (primarily to the common stockholders) as to the potential dilution to their share of income if the holders of all those securities that could be exchanged for common stock actually did exchange them. *Basic and diluted EPS must be reported with equal prominence on the face of the income statement.*

Those corporations that must present this **dual presentation** (i.e., basic and diluted EPS) are those that have a **complex capital structure**. A corporation has a complex capital structure when it has bonds, preferred stock, stock options, warrants, rights, or other securities outstanding that may be converted into common stock and which, upon conversion, would reduce basic EPS.

[15]Financial reporting for closely held corporations does not have to comply with GAAP, as long as the financial statements are not publicly issued. Hence, when a closely held corporation uses accounting principles that are not in accord with GAAP and is now issuing financial statements to the public, those financial statements—including amounts for prior years that are reported for comparative purposes—must be restated. Normally, changing from an accounting principle that is not accepted to one that is accepted is an accounting error, but the APB permitted this exception.
[16]A change in a reporting entity usually occurs when the subsidiaries that are being consolidated are different from those consolidated in prior years.
[17]An exception for reporting a prior-period adjustment is allowed for companies that are publicly issuing financial statements for the first time.

Review of Basic EPS Procedures

To review, the following fundamental procedures apply in calculating and presenting basic EPS as well as diluted EPS:

- The reporting of EPS data must be consistent with the income statement presentation. Specifically, basic and diluted EPS data must be shown for income from continuing operations, net income, and—when necessary—for discontinued operations, extraordinary items, and a change in an accounting principle.
- Basic EPS, which is the starting point for calculating diluted EPS, is computed as:

$$\frac{\text{Net Income to the Common Stockholders}}{\text{Weighted-Average Number of Shares of Common Stock}}$$

where "Net Income to the Common Stockholders" is computed as either:
  a. Net income minus preferred stock dividends that are declared, or
  b. When the preferred stock is cumulative, net income minus the yearly preferred dividend requirement, whether or not the preferred dividend is declared.

- The weighted-average number of shares is computed by weighting the number of shares of common stock outstanding by the portion of the year that they were outstanding.

Regarding computing the weighted-average number of shares, one issue that was not covered in Chapter 2 was the effect of stock dividends and stock splits on the weighted-average number of shares. A **stock dividend** is a dividend paid to the stockholders of the company in shares of the company's stock. Usually, stock dividends increase the number of shares by relatively small amounts (e.g., 10% or 15%) Similarly, a **stock split**[18] also is the issuing to stockholders of the company additional shares of the company's stock, but usually in much greater amounts. Thus, in a 2-for-1 stock split, two new shares of the company's stock are given in exchange for each old share of stock surrendered. A 3-for-1 stock split triples the number of shares outstanding.

Both stock dividends and stock splits have an impact on computing basic and diluted EPS. When stock dividends or stock splits occur, it is assumed that they occurred at January 1 of the earliest year reported—regardless of the actual date they were declared and issued. To demonstrate, the data in Illustration 9-5(a) will be used.

The weighted-average number of shares for 2003 in the 2003 financial statements is computed as shown in Illustration 9-5(b). The procedures are the same as those illustrated in Chapter 2.

---

[18]More information will be given in Chapter 14 about what stock dividends and stock splits are and how they are accounted for.

ILLUSTRATION 9-5(a)

Data for Illustrating How Stock Splits/Dividends Affect the Computing of the Weighted-Average Number of Shares

January 1, 2003	Number of shares of stock outstanding	120,000
June 1	Shares of stock issued	24,000
November 29	Shares of stock reacquired	(12,000)
January 1, 2004	Number of shares of stock outstanding	132,000
April 1	Shares of stock reacquired	(24,000)
August 12	2-for-1 stock split	108,000
December 1	Shares of stock reacquired	(18,000)
December 31	Number of shares outstanding	198,000

ILLUSTRATION 9-5(b)

Basic Computations for Weighted-Average Number of Shares

Date	Fraction of a Year	Number of Shares	Weighted-Average Number of Shares
January–June	5/12	120,000	50,000
June–November	6/12	144,000	72,000
December	1/12	132,000	11,000
Total weighted-average number of shares in computing basic EPS			133,000

When issuing the 2003 financial statements, the weighted-average number of shares to use in computing EPS figures is 133,000. However—and this is the important point—when issuing the 2004 financial statements, the weighted-average number of shares for computing the 2003 comparative EPS figures is 266,000, because even though the stock split occurred in August 2004, *it is assumed that the stock split occurred in January 2003*. The computations to obtain this 266,000 weighted-average number of shares for 2003 in the 2004 financial report are shown in Illustration 9-5(c).

ILLUSTRATION 9-5(c)

Computations for Computing Weighted-Average Number of Shares When a Stock Split/Dividend Occurs

Date	Fraction of a Year	Number of Shares	Effect of the Stock Split/Dividend	Weighted-Average Number of Shares
January–June	5/12	120,000	2	100,000
June–November	6/12	144,000	2	144,000
December	1/12	132,000	2	22,000
			Total	266,000

This same type of adjustment to the weighted-average number of shares is done for stock dividends. So, if a 10% stock dividend had been declared in 2004, the adjustment to the 2003 weighted-average number of shares would be to multiply the amounts by 110%, rather than 2, as is done in Illustration 9-5(c).

The computations for deriving the weighted-average number of shares to compute the 2004 EPS figures are shown in Illustartion 9-5(d).

ILLUSTRATION 9-5(d)

Computations for Computing Weighted-Average Number of Shares When a Stock Split/Dividend Occurs

Date	Fraction of a Year	Number of Shares	Effect of the Stock Split/Dividend	Weighted-Average Number of Shares
January–April	3/12	132,000	2	66,000
April–August	4/12	108,000	2	72,000
August–November	4/12	216,000	NA	72,000
December	1/12	198,000	NA	16,500
			Total	226,500

Illustration 9-5(d) shows that it is not necessary to adjust the transactions that occurred after the stock split, only those that occurred before. Handling stock dividends and stock splits in this manner makes the computed EPS numbers comparable. If the dividends and splits had not been retroactively treated to 2003, the EPS computations for 2004 would have been based on a much larger number of shares—and resulted in correspondingly much smaller EPS numbers—as compared to 2003, thus giving the impression of diminished profitability.

Computing Diluted EPS

As stated earlier, the difference between basic and diluted EPS is how securities that can be converted into common stock are handled. Once basic EPS numbers have been computed, diluted EPS numbers are calculated by making the necessary adjustments in the basic EPS formula, assuming that each of these convertible securities is exercised or converted. This assumption of exercise or conversion is made under several parameters, two of which are as follows:

Parameter 1: It is presumed that the *conversion of each potentially dilutive security occurs at the later of (a) the beginning of the earliest year presented or (b) when the potentially dilutive security is issued.*

Parameter 2: It is assumed that *only those securities whose effects would be to reduce the basic EPS are converted.*[19] It is not assumed that securities whose effects are to increase EPS numbers are converted. (This is called antidilution.)

---

[19]Some convertible securities have graduated rates of conversion, so that, depending upon the length of time that the security is held, conversion rates are more preferable to the holder. For example, in the first few years, the holders of convertible securities may be permitted to exchange each security for four shares of common stock, but this rate of conversion increases the longer the convertible securities are held. For purposes of computing diluted EPS when securities have such graduated rates of conversion, it is assumed that the securities are converted into the maximum number of shares issuable.

Diluted EPS Example 1—Convertible Debt Securities

The application of the preceding parameters is called the **as-if converted method**. To illustrate the as-if converted method, the following information was extracted from the financial statements of the Company in the opening scenario, p. 372, whose income statement is shown in Exhibit 9-3, p. 379, and whose EPS data is shown later in the chapter in Exhibit 9–7. From information available in the financial report, it was determined that basic EPS on income from continuing operations is computed by dividing the income to common stockholders of $159.9 million by the weighted-average number of shares of 848.4 million, as follows:

$$\text{Basic EPS} = \frac{\$159.9 \text{ Million}}{848.4 \text{ Million Shares}} = \$0.19 \text{ per share}$$

Other information in the financial statements shows that the Company has $550.0 million of 3% *convertible* notes outstanding that were issued two years previously and that each $1,000 note can be exchanged for 32.6531 shares of the Company's common stock. Assuming an effective tax rate of 33%, the adjustments to the basic EPS formula are as follows:

1. *Income adjustment*, assuming the 3% notes are converted:

   Assuming that the notes had been converted at the earliest possible date (which is the beginning of the year), the Company would not have paid any interest during the year. The interest amount on these notes is $16.5 million, which is computed as $550.0 million × 3%, and net income would have increased correspondingly. However, this increase in net income would have meant that the Company would have to pay $5,445 more in taxes, which is computed as $16.5 million × 33%.

   So the net increase in income, assuming that the 3% notes had been converted, is $11.055 million, which is the $16.5 million savings in interest less the $5.445 million additional taxes.

2. *Share adjustment*, assuming the 3% notes are converted:

   Assuming that the notes had been converted, the number of shares of common stock outstanding would increase. The number of outstanding new shares is determined by (1) computing the number of notes that are outstanding and then (2) multiplying the number of notes by the conversion ratio of 32.6531 shares of stock for each note. The financial statements show that each note has a face amount of $1,000, so there are 0.55 million notes outstanding, which is computed as $550.0 million of notes divided by $1,000 per note. So the number of new shares of common stock that would be issued is 17.96 million shares (0.55 million × 32.6531 shares per note).

   Based upon these assumptions and computations, the adjustments to the basic EPS formula to compute diluted EPS are as follows:

$$\text{Diluted EPS} = \frac{\$159.9 \text{ Million} + \$11.055 \text{ Million}}{848.4 \text{ Million} + 17.96 \text{ Million}} = \$0.197$$

In the preceding computations, note how Parameter 1 was applied: income and the number of shares are adjusted, assuming that the 3% notes are converted at the first of the year. Thus, a full year of interest is included in the adjustment of income, and the number of additional shares issued is not weighted for a fractional year. *If the 3% notes had been issued during the year, then it would have been assumed that the notes were converted to common stock as soon as they were issued, and fractional-year adjustments to both the interest and the number of shares would have been made.*

Before reporting the $0.197 as the diluted EPS amount, it is first necessary to compare it against the second parameter, which is the assumption of converting the notes to shares of common stock only if basic EPS decreases. Because the newly computed EPS of $0.197 is greater than the basic EPS of $0.19 (the 3% notes are antidilutive), it is assumed that the 3% notes are not converted.

The previous example illustrates how the adjustments to income and the number of shares are made for all debt-type securities, such as bonds and notes. *For convertible preferred stock, the income adjustment is the preferred dividends that are declared for the year, unless the preferred stock is cumulative, and then the income adjustment is the preferred dividend requirement for the year.* (This dividend amount is the same amount that is subtracted from net income when computing basic EPS.) So when it is assumed that the preferred stock is converted, the dividend amounts that were initially deducted are then added back. A difference in computing the income adjustment for debt-type securities versus equity-type securities, such as preferred stock, is that there is no tax effect on the preferred dividends because dividends are not tax deductible. Regarding the share adjustment for convertible preferred stock, it is computed in the same way that the share adjustment is computed for debt-type securities, as illustrated earlier.

Having covered the basic procedures in computing diluted EPS, the procedures are now expanded by introducing three other parameters for assuming the conversion of potentially convertible securities.

Parameter 3: When there is more than one potentially dilutive security, it is assumed that the potentially dilutive securities are *converted one at a time, beginning with the most potentially dilutive security and proceeding to the least dilutive security.* A security's dilutive effect is computed by dividing the security's income adjustment by its share adjustment. The smaller the resulting number, the more dilutive the security is.

Parameter 4: Diluted EPS is computed after including each potentially dilutive security, one at a time, until all potentially dilutive securities are included or until a point of antidilution is reached.

Parameter 5: Because the assumed conversion of a security could result in a dilutive effect on one income statement item (e.g., income before extraordinary items) and an antidilutive effect on another income statement item (e.g., net income), the *effect on income from continuing operations is used to determine whether a potentially dilutive security is dilutive or antidilutive.* Once the point of antidilution has been determined on income from continuing operations, then the EPS numbers for the other items on the income statement are computed using the same income and share adjustments.

Diluted EPS Example 2—Stock Options, Rights, Warrants, etc.

To illustrate these parameters, information (modified somewhat for illustration purposes) again is extracted from the Company's financial statements that are referred to in the opening scenario. In addition to the 3% convertible notes, the Company has two other potentially dilutive securities: 4¾% convertible notes and some stock options. There are $240.0 million of 4¾% notes outstanding, with a $1,000 face amount for each note, and each note can be converted into 36.030

shares. There are also 177.8 million stock options outstanding that can be exercised at an average price of $14.64. The average market price of the Company's common stock was $16.56 per share during the year.

In accordance with Parameter 4, the first step in computing diluted EPS is to determine the order in which the three potentially dilutive securities are assumed to be converted. This order is based upon the dilutive effect of the respective securities (as defined in Parameter 3), which is computed by dividing the income adjustment by the share adjustment, assuming that the security is converted to common stock.

The dilutive effect of the 3% notes is $0.6155, which was computed in the previous illustration as follows:

1. Income adjustment (computed previously): $11.055 million
2. Share adjustment (computed previously): 17.96 million
3. Dilutive effect: $11.055 million/17.96 million = $0.6155 per share

The dilutive effect of the 4¾% notes is $0.8833, computed as follows:

1. Income adjustment, assuming the 4¾% notes are converted:

    Total interest saved if the notes are converted: $240.0 million × 4¾% = $11.4 million

    Additional taxes that will have to be paid because of not having $11.4 million of tax deductible interest expense: $11.4 million × 33% = $3.762 million

    Net increase to income from continuing operations, assuming that the 4¾% notes are converted is: $11.4 million − $3.762 million, or $7.638 million.

2. Share adjustment, assuming the notes are converted:

    Number of notes that are outstanding: $240.0 million/$1,000 per note = 0.24 million

    Number of new shares of common stock that would be issued, assuming the 4¾% notes are converted: 0.24 million × 36.030 = 8.647 million shares.

3. Dilutive effect:

    Income adjustment/Share adjustment = $7.638/8.647 = $0.8833.

The as-if converted method is not used to compute the dilutive effect of the stock options. Rather, the **treasury stock method** is used to compute the dilutive effect of stock options and other securities, such as warrants and rights. Under the treasury stock method, it is assumed that the holder of the stock options exercises the options (or warrants, rights, etc.) by paying the exercise price. The exercise occurs on the earlier of the first day of the earlier year presented or the day the options are issued. Thus, the number of shares increases, and the corporation receives an influx of money. Then, it is assumed that the money is used to repurchase the corporation's common stock (treasury stock) at the average price for the year, and the number of shares decreases.

Applying the treasury stock method means that the share adjustment is computed in two steps. There is no income adjustment under the treasury stock method. Hence, stock options, warrants, and rights, having only a share adjustment, are always the most dilutive securities. Under Parameter 3, they are the first securities assumed to be converted into shares of common stock when computing diluted EPS.

In the example of the Company, the dilutive effect of the stock options is $0.00. There is no income adjustment, and the share adjustment for the options is computed as follows:

Because there are 177.8 million stock options outstanding, the number of new shares of common stock that would be issued, assuming that all stock options are exercised, is 177.8 million. Then, the number of shares of common stock that would be repurchased with the money received is:

Cash received: 177.8 options × $14.64 option price = $2,602.99 million

Number of shares that could be repurchased: $2,602.99 million/$16.56 (average stock price) is 157.2 million shares.

Thus, the net number of new shares of common stock that would be issued, assuming that all stock options are exercised, is 177.8 million − 157.2 million = 20.6 million.

Having computed the dilutive effects of the Company's three potentially dilutive securities, it is now possible to specify the order in which it is assumed that these securities are converted, which is as follows:

1. Stock options with a dilutive effect of $0.00, then the
2. 3% notes with a dilutive effect of $0.6155, and finally the
3. 4¾% notes with a dilutive effect of $0.8833.

As mentioned in Parameter 5, the income from continuing operations is the number that is used to test for antidilution. Thus, diluted EPS is computed in the following steps:

1. Basic EPS:

$$\frac{\text{Income from Continuing Operations}}{\text{Weighted-Average Number of Shares}} = \frac{\$159.9 \text{ million}}{848.4 \text{ million}} = \$0.19$$

2. Including the stock options in computing diluted EPS and making the necessary income and share adjustments, tentative diluted EPS is computed as follows:

$$\frac{\$159.9 \text{ million} + \$0}{848.4 \text{ million} + 20.6 \text{ million}} = \$0.18$$

Since the $0.18 is less than basic EPS, the stock options are dilutive. (They always will be unless the exercise price is greater than the average market price for the year.) So the iterative process—Parameter 4—continues and the next potentially dilutive security, which is the 3% notes, is included to compute diluted EPS.

3. Including the 3% notes in computing diluted EPS and making the necessary income and share adjustments, tentative diluted EPS is now:

$$\frac{\$159.9 \text{ million} + \$0 + \$11.055 \text{ million}}{848.4 \text{ million} + 20.6 \text{ million} + 17.96 \text{ million}} = \frac{\$170.955 \text{ million}}{886.96 \text{ million}} = \$0.19$$

Because the new calculation of diluted EPS is greater than the previous calculation, the 3% notes are antidilutive, and the diluted EPS number for income from continuing operations is $0.18. Since the 3% notes are antidilutive, so will be all other securities (i.e., the 4¾% notes) that had a greater dilutive impact than the 3% notes.

Once diluted EPS for income from continuing operations has been computed, diluted EPS numbers are then computed for the other income statement items, as shown in Illustration 9-6.

ILLUSTRATION 9-6

Computing Diluted EPS Numbers for Other Income Statement Items

Description	Income for 2002 (See Exhibit 9-3)	Number of Shares (see previous computation)	Diluted EPS
Income from discontinued operations[20]	$ (25.0) million	886.96 million	$(0.03)
Gain on sale of discontinued operations	404.7 million	886.96 million	0.46
Extraordinary gain	0	886.96 million	0
Cumulative effect of accounting change	0	886.96 million	0
Net income	539.6 million	886.96 million	0.61

Exhibit 9-7 shows the EPS numbers the Company actually reported in its annual income statement. As you review it, note the following:

- The format of the EPS presentation agrees with the income statement format. (Compare Exhibit 9-7 with Exhibit 9-3, p. 379.) That is, EPS numbers are reported for each major classification of the income statement, and

EXHIBIT 9-7

EPS Data as Reported in The Company's Income Statement

Income (loss) Per Share	2002	2001	2000
Basic			
Income from continuing operations before extraordinary gain and cumulative effect of accounting change	$ 0.19	$ 0.08	$0.41
Income (loss) from discontinued operations	(0.03)	(0.03)	0.03
Gain on sale of discontinued operations	0.48	—	—
Extraordinary gain	—	0.03	—
Cumulative effect of accounting change	—	(0.35)	—
Net income (loss)	**$ 0.64**	$(0.27)	$0.44
Diluted			
Income from continuing operations before extraordinary gain and cumulative effect of accounting change	$ 0.18	$ 0.08	$0.39
Income (loss) from discontinued operations	(0.03)	(0.03)	0.02
Gain on sale of discontinued operations	0.46	—	—
Extraordinary gain	—	0.03	—
Cumulative effect of accounting change	—	(0.35)	—
Net income (loss)	**$ 0.61**	$(0.27)	$0.41

---

[20]Remember that this format for discontinued operations (i.e., two lines) is no longer appropriate. It is used here to illustrate the EPS calculations only.

after the "Income from continuing operations" line, EPS is reported for every item on the income statement.
- Because the Company has a complex capital structure, a dual presentation of EPS is given, consisting of basic EPS and diluted EPS.
- Finally, the diluted EPS numbers computed previously agree with the diluted EPS numbers the Company reported for 2002.

Diluted EPS Example 3—Comprehensive Example

Throughout the chapter, information has been given about the company Bear Hugs by LaRee. That information, along with the following, is used as a further review of the process in computing diluted EPS. The student is encouraged to do all specified calculations and then to compare results with the solution in the appendix to this chapter. Supporting computations are also given in the appendix.

- The weighted-average number of shares before conversion or exercise of any potentially dilutive securities is 119,000.
- Stock options to purchase 20,000 shares of common stock were issued the prior year, and each option has an exercise price of $20. No options were exercised during the year. The average stock price during the year was $25 per share.
- One hundred, 7%, $1,000 convertible bonds were outstanding during the entire year. The bonds pay interest annually, and each bond can be converted into 63 shares of common stock. The bonds were issued at par.
- Also, on July 1 of the current year, two hundred, 8%, $1,000 convertible bonds were issued at par. These bonds pay interest semiannually, and each bond can be converted into 60 shares of common stock.
- Finally, 3,000 shares of 6% cumulative, convertible preferred stock with a par value of $50 were outstanding for the entire year. Each preferred share can be converted into 4 shares of common stock. Dividends were declared of $2 per share on preferred stock during the year.
- The effective tax rate for Bear Hugs by LaRee is 30%.
- Bear Hugs by LaRee reported the following income statement items, all of which are net of tax (as shown in exhibits throughout the chapter):

Income from continuing operations	$118,500
Income from discontinued operations	11,850
Income before extraordinary items	$130,350
Extraordinary gain	47,400
Extraordinary loss	(15,800)
Accounting principles change	(18,960)
Net income	$142,990

© GETTY IMAGES, INC./PHOTODISC

Required:

1. Compute basic EPS for income from continuing operations.

   Answer: $0.920

2. Compute the dilutive effects of the convertible securities.

   Answer: The dilutive effect of the 7% convertible bonds is $0.777; the 8% convertible bonds, $0.933; and the convertible preferred stock, $0.75.

3. Determine the order in which it is assumed the securities will be converted when computing diluted EPS, and explain when the iterative process of bringing the potentially dilutive securities ends.

   Answer: The securities are brought into calculating diluted EPS in the following order: (1) stock options, (2) convertible preferred stock, (3) 7% convertible bonds, and then (4) the 8% convertible bonds. This iterative process will continue until either all securities have been included in computing diluted EPS or until a point of antidilution is reached.

4. Compute diluted EPS on income from continuing operations after including just the stock options, and then determine if the iterative process should continue.

   Answer: $0.890, and since this amount is less than basic EPS, the iterative process continues.

5. Continue the iterative process until diluted EPS for income from continuing operations is computed.

   Answer: Diluted EPS is $0.873.

6. Show how the basic and diluted EPS would be reported for Bear Hugs by LaRee.

   See the appendix for the answer.

Summary

This chapter covered some of the more difficult measurement problems and reporting techniques of reporting the results of operations. It began with a real-world scenario in which the Company had many atypical transactions/events that were used to illustrate the importance of issuing an income statement that classifies the various items of revenue, gains, expenses, and losses. Also, the economic and transaction approaches to measuring income were discussed in order to highlight some problems with both approaches Thus, readers of financial statements must become educated as to the financial reporting process in order to judge the quality of a corporation's earnings when making decisions based wholly or partly upon published financial reports.

When reporting discontinued operations, the group of assets sold or being held for sale must meet the criteria of (1) being a component of an entity and (2) being held for sale. In determining whether the group of assets is a component of an entity, organizational size is not important, but being able to distinguish the cash flows of the component from the rest of the business entity is. There are various criteria for determining whether a group of assets is being held for sale—all of which must be met—and which are listed on page 381. The amount reported under discontinued operations consists of (1) operating income/loss for the year, (2) the estimated loss on the decision date, and (3) any gain/loss on disposal (when disposal occurs before the end of the year) or any adjustment to the estimated loss at the end of the fiscal year. The estimated loss is the amount by which the carrying amount of the net assets exceeds their net realizable value. When the decision to sell a component is rescinded or the criteria for being held for sale are no longer met, an additional gain or loss is recognized. This is computed as the difference between (1) the fair value of the net assets at the time the decision to sell is rescinded (or the criteria are not met) and (2) the carrying amount of the net assets at the time the decision to sell was made, adjusted for any depreciation or amortization since the decision to sell. This gain/loss, however, is reported as part of continuing operations. Estimated losses on the planned sale of assets or groups of assets that do not meet the criteria of a component are reported also in continuing operations.

The general rule for measuring and reporting the change in an accounting principle is to not restate prior-years' financial statements. Rather, a cumulative effect is computed and reported on the income statement. This amount is computed as the change in retained earnings as of the beginning of the year of change under the prior accounting principle and the newly adopted accounting principle. Pro forma amounts are also reported, which are computed using the new accounting principle.

For some changes in accounting principles, this cumulative amount is not reported on the income statement, but instead is reported as a prior-period adjustment. For those types of changes in an accounting principle, all prior-period financial statements that are reported in the current year for comparative purposes are restated. Finally, when changing to LIFO, neither of these approaches is used. Instead, LIFO inventory costing techniques are applied in the current year.

Calculations to determine diluted EPS numbers for corporations with complex capital structures require making the assumption that all potentially dilutive securities are either exercised or converted. For stock options, warrants, and rights, this assumption is applied according to the treasury stock method, which assumes that the money received when the options, warrants, or rights are exercised is used to acquire treasury stock. This results in an adjustment to the number of shares in the basic EPS formula but not to income. For other potentially dilutive securities, the assumed conversion to common stock is applied according to the as-if converted method. This method requires adjustments to both the number of shares and the income, including, where appropriate, the result of additional taxes that would result from not having the interest deduction. It is assumed that all potentially dilutive securities are converted one at a time, beginning with the most dilutive security. This iterative process continues until either all the potentially dilutive securities are included in computing dilutive EPS or until a point of antidilution is reached. For corporations with complex capital structures, both the basic EPS numbers and the diluted EPS numbers are reported on the face of the income statement with equal prominence.

In conclusion, the income statement in Illustration 9-7—in single-step format—for Bear Hugs by LaRee is presented as an example of a completed income statement with all necessary EPS figures. After having read and studied this chapter, all headings, subtotals, and calculations should be familiar. Also, the reasons for the various classifications and the significance of reported numbers, including EPS numbers, should be understandable.

ILLUSTRATION 9-7

Bear Hugs by LaRee
Income Statement
For the Year Ended December 31, 20XX

Revenues:	
Sales	$1,058,000
Gain on sale of securities	42,000
Total revenues	$1,100,000
Expenses:	
Cost of goods sold	$ 570,000
Operating expenses	352,700
Loss on disposal of equipment	27,300
Total expenses	$ 950,000
Income before taxes	$ 150,000
Income tax expense	(31,500)
Income from continuing operations	$ 118,500
Discontinued operations:	
Income from discontinued operations (net of taxes of $8,400)	11,850
Income before extraordinary items	$ 130,350
Extraordinary items:	
Gain from acquiring company for less than book value (net of taxes of $12,600)	47,400
Loss from earthquake (net of tax effect of $4,200)	(15,800)
Accounting principles change (net of tax effect of $5,040)	(18,960)
Net income	$ 142,990

EPS		
	Basic	Diluted
Income from continuing operations	$ 0.920	$ 0.873
Income from discontinued operations	0.100	0.084
Income before extraordinary items	1.020	0.957
Extraordinary gain	0.398	0.335
Extraordinary loss	(0.133)	(0.112)
Accounting principles change	(0.159)	(0.134)
Net income	$ 1.126	$ 1.046

APPENDIX: Solution to Diluted EPS Example

1: Compute basic EPS for income from continuing operations.

Income from continuing operations is used as the base income figure. The preferred stock dividend is $9,000,[21] and since the preferred stock is cumulative, the dividend requirement is used rather than the actual dividends paid. So basic EPS is computed as:

$$\frac{\$118,500 - \$9,000}{119,000} = \$0.920$$

---

[21]The preferred stock dividend was computed as the dividend rate of 6% multiplied by the preferred stock par value of $50 multiplied by the number of preferred stocks outstanding of 3,000.

2: Compute the dilutive effects of the convertible securities.

The purpose of this step is to determine the order in which the securities are assumed to be converted. This assumed order of conversion is determined by computing the income and share adjustments for each of the potentially convertible securities.

Stock Options

Stock options are converted into shares of common stock according to the procedures known as the treasury stock method. This method assumes that the money the corporation receives when the stock options are exercised is used to purchase shares of treasury stock at the average share price for the year. So the share adjustment under the treasury stock method is:

Assuming exercise of the options:
    20,000 new shares are issued.

Amount of money the corporation receives:
    20,000 options × $20 option price, or $400,000.

Number of shares of common stock that are repurchased at the average market price is:
    $400,000/$25 = 16,000 shares

Net number of new shares issued is:
    20,000 issued − 16,000 repurchased = 4,000 shares

There is no income adjustment for the stock options.

The dilutive effect of the stock options is $0, determined by dividing the income adjustment by the share adjustment.

All other securities are assumed converted into common stock, using the as-if converted method.

7% Convertible Bonds
    Share adjustment: 100 bonds × 63 shares/bond = 6,300 shares
    Income adjustment: $100,000 bonds × 7% × (1 − 0.30) = $4,900

Explanation: The income adjustment calculation is the after-tax effect of the interest savings. Since the bonds were outstanding during the entire year, it is assumed that they are converted at the beginning of the year, thus saving the interest expense of $100,000 × 7%, or $7,000. But not having the interest expense as a tax deduction results in more taxes being paid, which reduces the overall savings. Multiplying the interest expense of $7,000 by one minus the tax rate results in the net-of-tax savings from the assumed conversion of the bonds to common stock.
    EPS dilutive effect: $4,900/6,300 = $0.777

8% Convertible Bonds
    Share adjustment: 200 bonds × 60 shares/bond × ½ year = 6,000 shares
    Income adjustment: $200,000 bonds × 8% × (1 − 0.30) × ½ year = $5,600

Explanation: These calculations are the same as above, except for the ½ year factor, which is necessary because the bonds were not issued until July of the current year, and so July is the earliest they could have been converted.
    EPS dilutive effect: $5,600/6,000 shares = $0.933

Convertible Preferred Stock

Share adjustment: 3,000 preferred shares × 4 shares each = 12,000 shares

Income adjustment: 3,000 shares × $50 par × 6% = $9,000

Explanation: The dividend amount of $9,000 is not multiplied by one minus the tax rate because dividends are not tax deductible.

EPS dilutive effect: $9,000/12,000 = $0.750

3: Determine the order in which it is assumed that the securities will be converted when computing diluted EPS, and explain when the iterative process of bringing the potentially dilutive securities ends.

The securities will be brought into the calculation of diluted EPS in the following order: (1) stock options, (2) convertible preferred stock, (3) 7% convertible bonds, and then (4) the 8% convertible bonds. This iterative process continues until either all securities have been included in computing diluted EPS or until a point of antidilution is reached.

4: Compute diluted EPS on income from continuing operations after including just the stock options.

Adding this share adjustment to the preceding basic EPS calculation results in a tentative diluted EPS number of:

$$\frac{\$118,500 - \$9,000}{119,000 + 4,000} = \frac{\$109,500}{123,000} = \$0.890$$

Since the $0.890 is less than basic EPS, the iterative process continues.

5: Determine diluted EPS for income from continuing operations.

After the stock options, the next potentially dilutive security that is included in computing diluted EPS is the preferred stock. Since the income and share adjustments are already computed, the new tentative diluted EPS is computed as follows:

$$\frac{\$109,500 + \$9,000}{123,000 + 12,000} = \frac{\$118,500}{135,000} = \$0.877$$

Since the $0.877 is less than the previously computed $0.890, the preferred stock is dilutive, and the next potentially dilutive security, which is the 7% convertible bonds, is included in the calculation. Doing this, the new tentative diluted EPS number is computed as:

$$\frac{\$118,500 + \$4,900}{135,000 + 6,300} = \frac{\$123,400}{141,300} = \$0.873$$

Again, the $0.873 is less than the previously computed diluted EPS, so the iterative process continues, and the next potentially dilutive security is included, which is the 8% convertible bonds:

$$\frac{\$123,400 + \$5,600}{141,300 + 6,000} = \frac{\$129,000}{147,300} = \$0.876$$

In this case, the EPS number of $0.876 is larger that the previously computed number of $0.873, and so the 8% convertible bonds are antidilutive, and the diluted EPS for income from continuing operations is $0.873.

6: Show how the basic and diluted EPS would be reported for Bear Hugs by LaRee. The reporting of the two EPS numbers for Bear Hugs by LaRee is as follows:

	Basic	Diluted
Income from continuing operations	$ 0.920	$ 0.873
Income from discontinued operations	0.100	0.084
Income before extraordinary items	$ 1.020	$ 0.957
Gain on insurance settlement from loss due to earthquake	0.398	0.335
Extraordinary loss	(0.133)	(0.112)
Accounting principles change	(0.159)	(0.134)
Net income	$ 1.126	$ 1.046

For basic EPS, the EPS numbers for all subtotals were computed by dividing the income or loss amount less the preferred dividends by the weighted-average number of shares of 119,000. For example, the EPS for net income was computed as: ($142,990 − $9,000)/119,000. The other basic EPS numbers were computed by dividing the income number by 119,000 shares of stock. For example, the EPS for the accounting principles change was computed as: $18,960/119,000.

For diluted EPS, the EPS numbers for all subtotals were computed by dividing the income or loss amounts per the basic EPS computations and *adding back the preferred stock dividend and interest saved on bonds assumed converted* by 141,300 shares of stock. For example, the EPS for net income was computed as: ($142,990 − $9,000 + $9,000 + 4,900)/141,300. The other diluted EPS numbers were computed by dividing the income number by 141,300 shares of stock.

Questions

1. From an economic point of view, define net income. Why is this concept to measuring net income virtually impossible to use? As a result, what approach is used to measure net income in financial statements?

2. Due to the inability to measure a company's "true net income" under the transactions approach, what other items of information should an analyst consider when evaluating a company's performance during a period?

3. Distinguish between the current operating and the all-inclusive approaches to measuring accounting income. What are the advantages and disadvantages of each method? Which method is prescribed by the FASB, and how has the FASB attempted to overcome the primary disadvantage of this approach?

4. Why would managers prefer to report a smooth earnings stream as opposed to more volatile earnings, even when the average earnings are the same?

5. Identify, in order, the classifications in which the income statement is divided.

6. In a multiple-step income statement, what is the difference between income from operations (or operating income) and income from continuing operations?

7. Indicate whether the following items would be included as part of income from operations and as part of income from continuing operations:
   a. Depreciation on office furniture.
   b. Cost of inventory sold.
   c. The loss from operating a discontinued component of a business.

(continued)

    d. Gain on selling land by a manufacturing company.
    e. Gain on selling land by a real estate company.
    f. Loss due to a foreign currency being devalued.
    g. Gross profit.
    h. Correcting an error made in a prior period.
    i. Costs of keeping accounting records and constructing financial statements.
    j. Interest revenue.

8. Explain the meaning of intraperiod tax allocation.

9. Discuss the criteria that must be met in order for a company to classify operations as discontinued on its income statement.

10. In July 2004, ABC Corp. sold a component of the business that qualified to be reported as a discontinued operation. The 2004 realized loss from operations prior to the decision to sell was $12,000. Subsequent to the decision date, ABC Corp. realized additional operating losses during 2004 of $18,000 and estimated continued operating losses in 2005 of $10,000. On the date of the decision to sell, the component's net assets had a carrying value of $150,000 and a fair value of $130,000. The company estimated that it would incur direct selling costs of $5,000. Prepare the discontinued operations section of the income statement for ABC Corp. for the year ending December 31, 2004, assuming a 30% income tax rate. Should the company restate prior-years' financial statements if comparative financial statements are prepared?

11. Referring to the details of Question 10, assume that as of the 2004 fiscal year-end, the net assets had a fair value of $160,000, and the estimated disposal costs were unchanged at $5,000. Prepare the discontinued operations section of the income statement for ABC Corp. for 2004.

12. Using the following classification, indicate how each of the items from (a) to (i) should be classified:

    1. Operating income

    2. Income from continuing operations, but not operating income

    3. Discontinued operations

    4. Extraordinary item

    5. Cumulative effect—Accounting principle change

    6. None of the above

    a. An increase in the accumulated depreciation account because of changing from the straight-line to the double-declining-balance depreciation method.
    b. An increase in depreciation because of changing the estimated useful life of some equipment.
    c. Due to the untimely death of an important executive, a gain was recognized as the difference between the insurance proceeds and the cash surrender value of the life insurance policy.
    d. A Utah company incurred significant losses due to a tornado where less than six have been verified in the last 100 years.
    e. A manufacturing company incurred a significant gain as a result of selling marketable securities, which it does frequently.
    f. A company has a substantial decrease in its bad debt expense due to successfully implementing a new collection policy.
    g. A media company recognizes a gain from disposing of all its radio stations.
    h. A company incurred a loss from extinguishing its outstanding debt before the regularly scheduled maturity date.

i. Establishing an allowance for bad debts because of changing from recognizing bad debts expense as specific accounts are identified to recognizing bad debt expense as a percentage of sales.

13. Which of the following should be reported as a change in accounting principle: (1) changing from the straight-line method of depreciation to an accelerated method, or (2) changing the estimated useful life of an asset from 10 years to 6 years? Explain the differences in accounting for the above two changes.

14. Restate the basic arguments for and against restating the prior-year financial statements when a company changes its accounting principles and provides comparative financial statements. In general, what does U.S. GAAP require? List those changes in an accounting principle when accounting procedures under the general rule are not followed, but instead the financial statements are restated.

15. For purposes of computing basic earnings per share, explain how cash dividends are treated for each of the following types of stock: (a) common stock, (b) non-cumulative preferred stock, and (c) cumulative preferred stock.

16. How does diluted EPS differ from basic EPS? What characteristics must a company have to report diluted EPS? Under what circumstances, if any, is the diluted EPS figure greater than the basic EPS figure?

17. Kojak Company had 10,000 shares of stock outstanding at January 1, 2004. On May 1, 2004, Kojak issued 4,800 shares; on June 15, the company issued a 2-for-1 stock split; and on September 1, Kojak reacquired 3,600 shares. Net income for the year was $55,440. Calculate Kojak's basic EPS for 2004.

18. Describe how the income and share adjustments are computed for the following securities when calculating diluted EPS:
    a. Convertible bonds
    b. Convertible preferred stock
    c. Stock options

19. Under what conditions are stock options antidilutive?

20. When computing the dilutive effect of convertible bonds, XYZ Corp. determined that the effect of assuming the bonds to be converted on income from continuing operations was dilutive, but the effect on net income was antidilutive. Should XYZ Corp. include the effects of converting the bonds into stock when calculating diluted EPS?

21. Ken Griffey Company wanted to report higher earnings per share, so management has inquired about the possibility of doing so by purchasing and retiring the company's shares of common stock immediately before the fiscal year-end. Comment on the effectiveness of this strategy.

Exercises

Exercise 9-1: Preparing the Income Statement. The following pretax information relates to the operations of Dixon's Electronics, Inc., for the year ending December 31, 2004.

• The company changed its method of depreciation from the straight-line to the sum-of-the-years'-digits method and appropriately increased the accumulated depreciation account by $96,000.

- The company disposed of a component of a business that qualifies as a discontinued operation. Income of $12,000 was recognized prior to the date of the decision to sell, and an operating loss of $25,000 was recognized after the decision date to the disposal date. As of the decision date, the net assets of the component had a carrying value of $430,000 and a net realizable value of $530,000. The component was disposed of by the end of the fiscal year, resulting in net proceeds of $550,000.
- The company had an extraordinary gain of $66,000.
- Last year, the company neglected to record an expenditure for maintaining equipment in the amount of $2,500. The error was corrected in the current period.
- Income from continuing operations before taxes for 2004 was $140,000.
- Dividends of $20,000 were declared and paid during 2004.
- Dixon's effective tax rate was 40%.
- The balance of Retained Earnings at January 1, 2004, was $69,000, and the number of shares of common stock outstanding for the entire year was 100,000.

Prepare an income statement including EPS data in proper form, beginning with income from continuing operations before taxes for Dixon's Electronics for the 2004 fiscal year.

Exercise 9-2: Preparing the Income Statement. Allways, Inc., is preparing its income statement for the year ending December 31, 2005, and has computed that its net income, before taxes, is $220,000. However, questions have arisen as to the proper reporting for the following items, all of which are included in the $220,000:

Loss from hurricane, considered both unusual and infrequent	$(300,000)
Loss from worker strike	(160,000)
Loss from discontinued operations prior to decision to sell	(65,000)
Gain from discontinued operations from decision date to December 31	120,000
Extraordinary gain	40,000
Cumulative effect of accounting change on prior-periods' earnings	20,000

Dividends in the amount of $25,000 were declared, but not paid, on preferred stock. Further, Allways estimates the net realizable value of the component's net assets is $60,000 greater than their carrying value. There are 20,000 shares of common stock outstanding at the end of the year, and the company was not involved in any transactions in its common stock during the year. The company's effective tax rate is 40%.

Prepare the income statement, including EPS data, in proper form, beginning with income from continuing operations before taxes for Allways, Inc., for the 2005 fiscal year.

Exercise 9-3: Reporting Income. Indicate the financial reporting classification and treatment for each of the following items.

a. Changing from the completed-contract method to the percentage-of-completion method.
b. A company that produces and distributes many different varieties of foods discontinues producing broccoli and mushrooms.
c. Changing the estimated useful life of equipment from seven years to five years.
d. Changing from the FIFO inventory cost-flow assumption to LIFO.
e. Changing from the LIFO inventory cost-flow assumption to FIFO.
f. Writing down a significant amount of inventory due to obsolescence.
g. A company incurs a significant loss as a result of a workforce strike.
h. Changing from capitalizing and amortizing advertising costs to expensing them.

i. Adopting the installment-sales method of recognizing revenue for certain transactions involving higher than normal risk of collection. This is the first year the company has had such transactions.

Exercise 9-4: Discontinued Operations Including Subsequent Year. The board of directors for Couch Potato Company decided on September 9, 2004, to sell all assets associated with a division that qualified to be reported under discontinued operations. The following information about this component was obtained from the company records:

Operating loss for the division from January 1, 2004, to September 9, 2004	$ (55,000)
Operating loss for the division from September 9, 2004, to December 31, 2004	(20,000)
Estimated profit from operations from January 1, 2005, to the disposal date	10,000
Carrying value of assets as of September 9, 2004 and December 31, 2004	510,000
Net realizable value of assets as of September 9, 2004	470,000
Net realizable value of assets as of December 31, 2004	440,000

The company's effective tax rate is 30%.

1. Prepare the company's discontinued operations section for the year ended December 31, 2004.
2. Repeat (1), assuming that the net realizable value of net assets as of December 31, 2004, is $580,000.
3. Assuming the original data from part (1), suppose that actual results during 2005 for Couch Potato Company are operating profit of $20,000 and net cash proceeds from the sale of assets of $550,000. Present the discontinued operations section of comparative income statements for Couch Potato Company for 2004 and 2005.

Exercise 9-5: Discontinued Operations—Changes to a Plan of Sale. On December 31, 2004, the board of directors for Vaughn Company approved a plan to dispose of a group of assets (with a remaining useful life of five years) that qualifies to be reported under discontinued operations. The business component incurred an operating loss of $110,000 during the year. The carrying value of the assets is $600,000, and Vaughn Company has found a buyer for the component for $550,000 less disposal costs of $20,000. On June 30, 2005, the date the sale was scheduled to culminate, the buyer was unable to obtain sufficient funding and backed out of the purchase agreement. Continued operating losses for the component during 2005 were $30,000, and the net realizable value of the assets as of June 30, 2005, was $580,000. The company's income tax rate is 30%.

1. Prepare the company's discontinued operations section as of December 31, 2004.
2. Explain how the company should report the results from the business component in 2005. Include an explanation on whether depreciation is recorded and how the net assets are valued.
3. Explain how your answer to part (2) would differ if the assets' net realizable value as of June 30, 2005, is $380,000.

Exercise 9-6: Discontinued Operations—Restatement Including Prior Year. Mann Company issued the following income statement for the year ending December 31, 2005:

	2005	2004
Operating income	$500,000	$450,000
Gain on sale of division	50,000	0
	$550,000	$450,000
Income tax expense (30% effective rate)	165,000	135,000
Net income	$385,000	$315,000

On April 22, 2005, the company had agreed to dispose of a business component for $900,000. The book value of the component's net assets was $850,000, and the sale was completed on November 30, 2005. The division's operating losses for the period were $95,000. All of these amounts are included in the financial data for 2005 in the preceding table.

For 2004 in relation to this component, Mann incurred an operating loss of $45,000 and had gains of $15,000 from disposing of assets.

Beginning with income from operations before taxes, revise the income statement for Mann Company to properly report the discontinued component. Assume that all amounts are included in the income statement numbers but need to be properly reported.

Exercise 9-7: Discontinued Operations—Measuring the Gain/Loss on Disposal.
For each of the following cases, determine the amount that should be reported as the gain/loss from discontinued operations. Assume that actual disposals did not take place until after the fiscal year.

Case	Operating Income/(Loss)	Gains/(Losses) on Decision Date	Additional Gains/(Losses) From Decision Date to Fiscal Year-End
A	$ 10,000	$ 5,000	$ 3,000
B	(6,000)	(3,000)	(4,000)
C	10,000	5,000	(4,000)
D	(6,000)	(3,000)	3,000
E	6,000	(3,000)	(3,000)
F	10,000	(5,000)	4,000
G	(10,000)	5,000	(4,000)

Exercise 9-8: Extraordinary Items. Kevin Callister, a new staff accountant for CMS Chemicals, Inc., has been assigned to summarize the nonrecurring items incurred by the company during the year. He has come to you to discuss whether certain items should be classified on the income statement as extraordinary items or included in the continuing operations section of the income statement.

1. Review the criteria that must be met for an item to be classified as extraordinary.
2. Determine/discuss whether each of the following items/events would typically meet the extraordinary item criteria:
   a. A gain from selling equipment.
   b. Explosion within a plant that caused extensive damage.
   c. An earthquake that caused significant damage at the company's San Francisco plant.
   d. Significant increases in sales revenues as a result of a major competitor being unable to fulfill orders due to a workforce strike.
   e. A tornado in Boise, Idaho, that caused damage to the company's plant located there.

    f. Writing off an account receivable due to the bankruptcy of a customer. The write-off was significantly more than what had been provided in the company's allowance for bad debts account.

    g. Gain from an early extinguishment of debt.

    h. Significant costs associated with environmental cleanup.

Exercise 9-9: Extraordinary Items. Determine whether the following items should be reported as extraordinary items:

    a. A gain on a note receivable from a customer in Mexico that was to be paid in pesos. The gain occurred because of a change in the exchange rate. The company rarely sells to customers in Mexico.

    b. Loss of the citrus crop on a farm in Florida.

    c. A loss of $10 million due to disposing of one of three factories. Otherwise, the company's net income for the year was $3 million.

    d. A nationwide shutdown in a foreign country due to civil unrest that resulted in disrupting the supply of a raw material to a company in the United States, causing that company to incur material losses.

    e. A foreign country nationalized a company's assets, paying them more than the carrying value but less than the fair value of the assets.

    f. A company acquired a parcel of land upon which it built a factory and then sold the unused land at a gain. The company had never done this before, but due to rising real estate prices in the area, it had decided that this would provide such an opportunity now. The company does not foresee doing this again in the near future.

    g. Before some bonds matured, several bondholders, at their option, converted their bonds into shares of common stock, and as a result, the issuing company recognized a gain. The bonds do not mature for another 10 years.

Exercise 9-10: Extraordinary Items. Determine whether the following items should be reported as extraordinary items:

    a. Earthquake damage to a plant located near the San Andreas fault in southern California.

    b. Earthquake damage to a plant located along the Wasatch Mountains in Utah where geological surveys have shown a major fault exists. Over several thousand years, it has been the cause of only minor earth movements. For the past 25 years, scientists have been predicting that it was very likely that such a major earth movement could occur soon. Today, the fault caused extensive damage.

    c. A gain of 5% of net income that resulted from insurance proceeds being more than the property damage caused by a fire that has been determined to have been deliberately set.

    d. Actual damages paid due to a lawsuit.

    e. Punitive damages paid due to a lawsuit.

    f. A ransom paid to Colombian kidnappers to ransom the company's operating head in that country.

    g. A loss of $25,000 to the company's property located in the downtown area, caused by citizens celebrating their team winning the NBA championship.

    h. The loss in (g) was 10 times that amount. 100 times.

Exercise 9-11: Accounting Principle Change. During 2004, Gray Company decided to change its method of depreciating fixed assets from the straight-line method to the double-declining-balance method. The company follows the policy of recognizing a full year's depreciation in the year of acquisition, and its effective tax rate is 30%.

1. Compute the amount of depreciation expense for 2004 that Gray should report on a machine that cost $81,000, was purchased in 2002, has an estimated useful life of six years, and no salvage value.
2. Determine the amount that Gray Company should report on its 2004 financial statements as the cumulative effect of an accounting change.
3. What qualitative characteristic(s) does a company violate when it changes accounting principles?
4. What would justify a company changing an accounting principle?
5. When switching to a new accounting principle, how should Gray Company show comparative data? That is, should Gray restate its 2003 income statement data that are reported in its 2004 financial statements? If not, how are comparative data presented?

Exercise 9-12: Accounting Principle Change to LIFO. Kenny's Bike Shop began operations in 2002 and has been using the FIFO method to account for its inventory. Now, in 2004, the company's accountant has advised Kenny to change to the LIFO inventory method in order to take advantage of tax savings. The accountant provided the following data:

Inventory based on FIFO (Jan. 1, 2004)	$43,000
Inventory based on LIFO (Dec. 31, 2004)	46,000
Inventory based on FIFO (Dec. 31, 2004)	62,000

The company has an effective tax rate of 35%.

1. Determine the *effect* on Kenny's net income for the year ending December 31, 2004, as a result of changing to the LIFO inventory valuation method.
2. How much did Kenny save in taxes as a result of changing inventory methods?
3. Prepare the journal entry to switch to the LIFO inventory valuation method.
4. Prepare the journal entry to switch to the LIFO inventory valuation method for financial reporting purposes, assuming that Kenny continues using a FIFO valuation method for bookkeeping purposes. (*Hint:* It may be necessary to review Chapter 6.)

Exercise 9-13: Weighted-Average Number of Shares with Stock Splits/Dividends. At January 1, 2004, Buttercup had 100,000 shares of common stock outstanding. During the next two years, Buttercup had the following transactions in its own stock:

Date	Transaction
Mar. 1, 2004	Issued 20,000 shares
July 30	Acquired 6,000 shares
Sept. 30	Issued 11,000 shares
Feb. 1, 2005	Issued 25,000 shares
May 31	Acquired 6,000 shares
Aug. 1	Acquired 9,000 shares
Nov. 30	Issued 25,000 shares

If an income statement is issued in 2005, with the 2004 data presented for comparative purposes, compute the weighted-average number of shares to use to compute EPS for 2004 and 2005, assuming that:

1. A 10% stock dividend is declared on August 1, 2004.
2. A 2-for-1 stock split is declared on July 1, 2005.
3. A 15% stock dividend is declared on May 1, 2004, and a 3-for-1 stock split is declared on November 1, 2005.

Exercise 9-14: Earnings per Share with Preferred Stock. Curt Cox Company has the following stockholders' equity accounts for the year ending December 31, 2004:

8% cumulative preferred stock, $100 par value,	
50,000 shares authorized and outstanding	$ 5,000,000
Common stock, no par value, one million shares authorized,	
700,000 shares issued, 680,000 shares outstanding	14,000,000
Paid-in capital in excess of par	800,000
Treasury stock, 20,000 shares	(400,000)
Retained earnings	2,100,000
Total stockholders' equity	$21,500,000

Net income for the year was $2,500,000. No dividends were declared or paid during the year.

On March 31, 2004, Curt Cox purchased 100,000 shares of its own stock for $2,000,000 and later, on December 1, 2004, reissued 80,000 of these shares at a price of $30 per share.

1. Calculate Curt Cox Company's basic EPS for the year ending December 31, 2004.
2. Assuming that each share of preferred stock is convertible into five shares of common stock, compute diluted EPS.

Exercise 9-15: Earnings per Share, Several Line Items. Kramer Foods, Inc., had the following stock outstanding as of December 31, 2004:

8% preferred stock, $50 par value, 10,000 shares	
authorized and outstanding	$ 500,000
Common stock, $10 par, 400,000 shares authorized	
and outstanding	4,000,000

On April 1, 2004, the company issued 50,000 shares of common stock along with the 10,000 shares of preferred stock. Preferred stock dividends declared, but not paid, for the period were $40,000.

The following net-of-tax information was extracted from Kramer's income statement:

Income from continuing operations	$ 2,255,000
Income (loss) from discontinued operations	(1,075,000)
Extraordinary gain	750,000
Net income	$ 1,930,000

1. Prepare a partial income statement with appropriate EPS data for the year ending December 31, 2004.
2. Prepare a partial income statement with appropriate EPS data for the year ending December 31, 2004, assuming that each share of preferred stock is convertible into 3.6 shares of common stock.

Exercise 9-16: Earnings per Share with Potentially Dilutive Debt Security. Greer Company issued 200 8% convertible bonds with a ten-year life on January 1, 2001. Each $1,000 bond is convertible, at the holder's option, into 100 shares of Greer Company's common stock. Greer Company reported net income of $380,000 during 2004 and had 500,000 shares of common stock outstanding for the year. No transactions in the company's common stock occurred during 2004.

Calculate Greer Company's basic and diluted EPS for the 2004 fiscal year, assuming a tax rate of 30%.

Exercise 9-17: Earnings per Share, Several Potential Dilutive Securities. The following information was extracted from the balance sheet of Leon's Financial Services, Inc.:

	2003	2004
7% convertible bonds	$500,000	$500,000
Common stock, $1 par	50,000	50,000
Additional paid-in capital in excess of par	325,000	325,000
10% convertible preferred stock; $100 par	500,000	500,000
Retained earnings	400,000	550,000

During 2004, the company paid dividends of $1 per share on common stock and $10 per share on the preferred stock. Each share of preferred stock is convertible into three shares of common, and the convertible bonds are convertible, in total, into 12,000 shares of common. The company's tax rate is 30%.

Compute the basic and diluted EPS for the company for 2004.

Exercise 9-18: Earnings per Share with Options. At December 31, 2007, Built-Just-Rite had several different types of stock options outstanding, the details of which are as follows:

Identification	Date Issued	No. of Options	Option Price
A	June 20, 2005	20,000	$13
B	Jan. 2, 2006	50,000	14
C	Sept. 30, 2007	70,000	16

Compute the share adjustment necessary for each option under each of the following assumptions and watch for antidilution:

a. The average price of Built-Just-Rite's common stock was $12 per share.
b. The average price was $14 per share.
c. The average price was $18 per share.

Exercise 9-19: Testing for Dilution. Putnam has several potentially dilutive securities outstanding at year-end. Because you are an accounting intern who also is currently enrolled in an intermediate accounting course and studying EPS, you have been asked to assist in determining whether any of these securities should be included in computing diluted EPS. For the year, Putnam reported net income of $278 million and had 60 million shares of common stock outstanding. The details of each potentially dilutive security follow:

- Convertible bonds—$100 million par value, 7%, with each $1,000 bond convertible into 11 shares of common stock.
- Preferred stock—10 million shares of 8%, $100 cumulative preferred stock with each share convertible into 2.5 shares of common stock.

Putnam's effective tax rate is 40%.

Compute diluted EPS.

Exercise 9-20: Multiple-Choice Questions.

1. Which of the following items should probably be reported as an extraordinary item on the income statement?
   a. An insurance company receives a significant number of claims from customers who sustained losses from a hurricane.
   b. A company has assets expropriated, without compensation, by a foreign government.
   c. A company sustains significant losses due to a workforce strike.
   d. A company's CEO dies and the company realizes a significant gain from holding a life insurance policy on the CEO.
2. With respect to the income statement, which of the following statements is *true*?
   a. The income statement reveals the total of economic changes in the enterprise for the period.
   b. The income statement separates the items derived from normal operations and those that are not, which provides information that is more useful in predicting future earnings.
   c. The current operating approach is adopted in reporting income.
   d. Many items are reported on the income statement before they are actually realized.
3. On January 1, 2004, Russell, Inc., changed its inventory valuation method from LIFO to FIFO, and as a result, the inventory value on January 1 increased by $200,000. The effective tax rate for Russell, Inc., is 30%. Considering the tax effect, how should this change in accounting principle be reported in the company's financial statements?
   a. As a separate line item in the income statement that increases income by $200,000.
   b. As a separate line item in the income statement that increases income by $140,000.
   c. As a prior-period adjustment in the retained earnings statement that increases beginning retained earnings by $200,000.
   d. As a prior-period adjustment in the retained earnings statement that increases beginning retained earnings by $140,000.

Exercise 9-21: Miscellaneous Questions. Answer each of the following independent questions.

1. On October 1, 2002, Burns Corp. approved a formal plan to sell Hall Division, which qualifies as the disposal of a business component. The sale was scheduled to take place on March 31, 2003. Hall had operating income of $100,000 for the quarter ended December 31, 2002, and expected to incur an operating loss of $50,000 for the first quarter of 2003. Burns estimated that it would incur a $375,000 loss on the sale of Hall's assets. Burns' income tax rate for 2002 was 30%. In its 2002 income statement, how much should Burns report as the loss on disposal of Hall Division?

(continued)

2. Burl Company incurred the following gains and losses during 2004:

- A loss of $50,000 as the result of an unanticipated strike by its employees.
- A gain of $25,000 as the result of early extinguishments of bonds payable.
- A loss of $125,000 from the abandonment of equipment used in the business.

Burl's income tax rate for 2004 was 30%. How much should Burl's 2004 income statement report as extraordinary items?

3. On January 1, 2004, Dart, Inc., entered into an agreement to sell the assets and product line of its Jay Division, considered a component of the business. The sale was consummated on December 31, 2004, and resulted in a gain on disposition of $400,000. The division's operations resulted in losses before income tax of $225,000 in 2004 and $125,000 in 2003. Dart's income tax rate is 30% for both years. Prepare the discontinued operations section in the comparative income statement for Dart, Inc., for the years 2003 and 2004.

4. On December 31, 2004, Kerr, Inc., appropriately changed its inventory valuation method to FIFO cost from weighted-average cost for financial statement and income tax purposes. The change will result in a $700,000 increase in the beginning inventory at January 1, 2004. Assume a 30% income tax rate. What is the cumulative effect of this accounting change that should be reported for the year ended December 31, 2004?

Exercise 9-22: Miscellaneous Questions. Answer each of the following independent questions.

1. On January 1, 2003, Aker Corp. acquired a machine at a cost of $200,000. It was to be depreciated using the straight-line method over a 5-year period, with no residual value. Because of a bookkeeping error, no depreciation was recognized in Aker's 2003 financial statements. The oversight was discovered during the preparation of Aker's 2004 financial statements. What is the amount of depreciation expense that should be recognized in Aker's 2004 income statement?

2. Jones Corp.'s capital structure is as follows:

	December 31	
	2004	2003
Outstanding shares of common stock	110,000	110,000
Outstanding shares of convertible preferred, $100 par	10,000	10,000
8% convertible bonds	$1,000,000	$1,000,000

During 2004, Jones paid dividends of $3.00 per share on its preferred stock. The preferred shares are convertible into 20,000 shares of common stock. The 8% bonds are convertible into 30,000 shares of common stock. Net income for 2004 is $850,000. Assume that the income tax rate is 30%. What is the diluted EPS for 2004?

3. Tack, Inc., reported a retained earnings balance of $150,000 at December 31, 2000. In June 2001, Tack discovered that merchandise costing $40,000 had not been included in inventory in its 2000 financial statements. Tack has a 30% tax rate. By what amount should Tack adjust its beginning retained earnings in its statement of retained earnings at December 31, 2001, and should retained earnings be increased or decreased?

4. On January 2, 2005, to better reflect the variable use of its only machine, Holly, Inc., elected to change its method of depreciation from straight-line to the units-of-production method. The machine was purchased on January 2, 2003, for $50,000, and at that time it was estimated that its useful life was 10 years, or 50,000 machine hours. The machine was used 8,500 and 3,500 hours during 2004 and 2003, respectively. Holly's income tax rate is 30%. Compute the cumulative effect of the accounting principles change and determine whether it should be treated as a gain or loss.

Problems

Problem 9-1: Earnings Announcement. The following earnings announcement was made by Advanced Digital Information Corporation.

> Advanced Digital Information Corporation (ADIC) today announced earnings of more than $14.2 million, or 27 cents per diluted share, for the third quarter ending July 31, 2000. ADIC earnings include a pretax gain of $14.3 million on the sale of shares of Crossroads Systems, Inc., owned by the Company. Excluding the effect of this asset sale, earnings were $4.9 million with diluted earnings of 9 cents per share versus 11 cents per share the same period a year ago. The consensus analyst estimate for the period was 14 cents per share. Revenues were $66.0 million, an increase of 15% from the same period last year.

Required:
1. Identify the different EPS amounts that were announced and explain why they differ from each other.
2. Why did the company feel it necessary to announce an EPS amount other than for net income? Which earnings amount is the best indicator of future earnings? Why?
3. Is the information provided in the announcement a positive or negative indicator of future trends? Why?
4. Suppose that, during 2004, the company adopts a formal plan to dispose of a business component that qualifies to be reported under discontinued operations. The actual disposal date will not occur until 2006 or later. The operations of the component to be discontinued were profitable and, as a result, the company announced EPS that exceeded analysts' forecasts. Explain the incentives and propriety of including the operating performance of this business component in an announcement of EPS. As part of this requirement, consider the following questions:

   - Is it likely that the classification of the business component profit would affect the interpretation of the operating performance by analysts?
   - If the company reported the component profit in continuing operations and did not disclose to the auditors its intention to dispose of the component, is it likely that the auditor would identify the misclassification?

Note: On the day of the announcement, ADIC's share price declined 15%.

Problem 9-2: Earnings Announcement. The following article provides a report of an annual earnings announcement made by Clorox Company:

Clorox quarterly profits beat expectations

THURSDAY, AUGUST 3, 2000, 7:37:00 AM EST

OAKLAND, Calif., Aug. 3 (Reuters)—Consumer products company Clorox Co. on Thursday said earnings rose 20% in its fiscal fourth quarter, beating analysts' estimates by a penny a share, as the firm benefitted from strong sales of new products and cost-saving initiatives.

The maker of Clorox bleach, Armour All car care products, and Formula 409 cleaner said net income for the quarter ended June 30 before merger-related and other one-time charges was $138 million, or 58 cents a diluted share, up from $115 million, or 48 cents a diluted share, a year ago.

The consensus financial analysts estimate called for profit of 57 cents a share, according to market research firm First Call/Thomson Financial. Revenue rose 5% to $1.15 billion. Analysts had expected revenue growth of about 7%.

Including restructuring and merger-related charges, net earnings were 52 cents a share compared with 21 cents a share in the year-ago period.

Required:

1. Identify the different EPS amounts that were announced, and explain why they differ from each other.
2. Why did the company feel it necessary to announce an EPS amount other than for net income? Which earnings amount is the best indicator of future earnings? Why?
3. Is the information provided in the announcement a positive or negative indicator of future trends? Why?

Note: Although the company met earnings expectations, the stock price dropped about 5% for the day. Analysts explained this was due to the market's disappointment in the company's revenue growth.

Problem 9-3: Discontinued Operations. Shantell, Inc., is a diversified corporation that has operations in restaurants, clothing retail stores, hardware stores, and food distributors. Due to stiff competition and persistent losses, on May 15, 2004, the company adopted a plan to dispose of all business assets associated with food distribution.

According to company records, the clothing retail stores division had incurred a loss of $135,000 for the 2003 fiscal year, and the operating loss from January 1, 2004, to May 15, 2004, was $175,000. The carrying value of the component's net assets was $2.5 million, and the company estimated the net assets' net realizable value at $2.2 million. During the remainder of the 2004 fiscal year, the company began selling the assets of the division and operated on a reduced scale. Additional operating losses incurred after May 15 were $105,000 from operations, and the actual loss from the sale of assets was $80,000. In addition, the company incurred severance payments to employees in the amount of $50,000.

As of December 31, 2004, the company had completely closed two plants and was still operating two other plants on a reduced scale. The company estimated that further operating losses of $120,000 would be incurred prior to the plants being sold. Estimated additional losses on disposing of the remaining assets were estimated to be $215,000. Further severance payments of $25,000 were also estimated to be incurred. The company's effective tax rate for all years is 40%.

Required:

1. Prepare the discontinued operations section of the income statement for Shantell, Inc., as of December 31, 2004. Include comparative amounts for the year 2003.

2. Assume that, during 2005, actual results were as follows:

Loss from operations	$ 95,000
Additional loss from disposing of assets	205,000
Severance payments to employees	65,000

Prepare the discontinued operations section of the income statement for Shantell, Inc., as of December 31, 2005. Include comparative amounts for the year 2004.

Problem 9-4: Accounting Changes (CPA Adapted). There are various types of accounting changes (e.g., estimate, principle requiring restatement, principle not requiring restatement, etc.), each of which is required to be reported differently.

Required:
1. Identify the type of accounting change each of the following is and also specify the way in which it should be reported:
   a. A change from the sum-of-the-years'-digits method of depreciation to the straight-line method for previously acquired assets.
   b. A change from the LIFO inventory method to FIFO inventory method.
   c. A change in the expected service life of an asset arising because of more experience with the asset.
2. With respect to a change in accounting principle, how should a company calculate the (a) cumulative effect and (b) pro forma amounts?
3. Why are accounting principles, once adopted, normally continued?
4. What is the justification for changing from one accounting principle to another?

Problem 9-5: Effects of Accounting Changes. During 2004, the management of Whetton Corp. decided to change the way it depreciated certain equipment from an accelerated method (double-declining-balance) to the straight-line method. All the equipment had been purchased on January 1, 2000, had cost $2 million, and had an estimated useful life of six years, with no salvage value. The company has a 30% tax rate.

Required:
1. How should Whetton Corp. report the change in accounting principle under U.S. GAAP?
2. Calculate (a) depreciation expense for 2004 and (b) the cumulative effect to be reported in the current year's financial statements.
3. Besides the method required by U.S. GAAP, another method of reporting a change in an accounting principle is to restate the financial data of the prior year(s) that is presented for comparative purposes. Why did the APB decide upon the requirements that it did?
4. Suppose that instead of changing an accounting principle, Whetton Corp revised the useful life of the equipment from six years to 10 years. How should the effects of this change be reported in the income statement? Calculate depreciation expense for 2004.
5. What reason(s) justify an accounting principle change? Do you suppose that company management might be motivated to change accounting principles for other reasons?

Problem 9-6: Change in Accounting Principle—Inventory. Below is the income from continuing operations, before taxes, of Tiffany and Associates since it was incorporated in 2002, as computed under three different inventory assumptions and using a periodic inventory system.

Year	FIFO	Weighted-Average	LIFO
2002	$20,000	$15,000	$10,000
2003	30,000	20,000	12,000
2004	35,000	28,000	16,000
2005	40,000	31,000	18,000

Other information is as follows:

- Tiffany's effective tax rate is 30%.
- Tiffany had an extraordinary gain of $10,000, net of tax, in 2005.
- There are 10,000 shares of common stock outstanding at December 31, 2005, and there were no transactions in the company's stock during the year.

Required:

Beginning with income from continuing operations before taxes, prepare the income statement in proper format (e.g., EPS, intraperiod tax allocation, pro forma—if necessary—etc.)

1. Assuming that Tiffany changes from the FIFO method to the weighted-average method on December 1, 2005.
2. Assuming that Tiffany changes from the LIFO method to the FIFO method on December 1, 2005.
3. Assuming that Tiffany changes from weighted-average to LIFO on December 1, 2005. (*Hint:* Focus on the change in inventory during the year under the LIFO and weighted-average methods.)

Problem 9-7: Change in Accounting Principle—Depreciation. On March 1, 2007, the Keep'm Guessin Company changed its method of depreciating fixed assets from the straight-line method to the sum-of-the-years'-digits method. Relevant information about this change is as follows:

Year	Straight-Line Method	Sum-of-the-Years'-Digits Method
	Depreciation Expense Computed under the	
Incorporation	$6,667	$12,500
2003	6,667	11,667
2004	6,667	10,833
2005	6,667	10,000
2006	6,667	9,167
2007	6,667	8,333

The effective tax rate for all years is 35%. In 2006, Keep'm Guessin reported a net income of $100,000, with an extraordinary gain (after taxes) of $13,000. In 2007, the income from operations before depreciation expense and taxes was $130,000, and there are no extraordinary items.

At December 31, 2007, Keep'm has 200,000 shares of common stock outstanding, and its only stock transaction during the year was declaring and issuing a stock dividend on July 1.

Required:
Prepare a partial income statement, beginning with income from operations before depreciation and taxes for Keep'm for December 31, 2007. Round all amounts to the nearest dollar.

Problem 9-8: Change in Accounting Principle. Larsen's Greenhouse, Inc., has been in business for several years as a landscaping company and has used the LIFO inventory valuation method and periodic inventory system for both financial reporting and tax purposes for all inventory items in order to minimize taxes. Recently, the industry has been experiencing a decrease in the cost of a particular inventory item (Item X), and accordingly, LIFO inventory valuation has lost its tax advantage for this item. Thus, effective January 1, 2005, the company switched to using the FIFO valuation method for Item X. Cost information for Item X as of December 31, 2005, is as follows:

LIFO Layers for Item X at January 1, 2005

Date Purchased	No. of Items	Unit Cost	Total Inventory Cost
Jan. 23, 2000	170	$5.40	$ 918
May 18, 2001	110	7.20	792
Nov. 13, 2002	150	9.80	1,470
Oct. 2, 2004	80	6.30	504
Total	510		$3,684

Purchases Made During 2005

Date Purchased	No. of Items	Unit Cost	Total Inventory Cost
Feb. 8	700	$6.40	$ 4,480
May 11	1,000	6.20	6,200
July 30	500	5.80	2,900
Sept. 22	1,000	5.15	5,150
Dec. 10	600	5.10	3,060
Total	3,800		$21,790

During 2005, Larsen sold 3,700 units at $12.00 per unit. The company's tax rate is 30%.

Required:
1. Compute the amount of gross profit that Larsen would report for 2005 using the LIFO inventory method.
2. Compute the amount of gross profit that Larsen would report for 2005 using the FIFO inventory method.
3. How much did Larsen save in income taxes by switching to FIFO? Round to the nearest dollar.
4. Explain how this change would be reported in the 2005 financial statements.

Problem 9-9: Potentially Dilutive Securities. K&K Associates reported net income of $698,000 for the year ending December 31, 2004. The company had outstanding 200,000 shares of common stock for the entire year. In addition, the company had the following potentially dilutive securities outstanding at year-end:

- 9% convertible preferred stock: $100 par, 3,000 shares outstanding. Each share of preferred stock is convertible into $2\frac{1}{2}$ shares of common stock.
- 12% convertible preferred stock: $50 par, 10,000 shares outstanding. Each share of preferred stock is convertible into 3 shares of common stock.
- 4.5% convertible bonds: $500,000 face value. Each $1,000 bond can be converted into 25 shares of common stock.
- 8.5% convertible bonds: $250,000 face value. Each $1,000 bond can be converted into 15 shares of common stock.
- Stock options: 100,000 options outstanding; each option can be used to acquire one share of stock at an exercise price of $15. The average market price for the year was $18.

All appropriate dividends to the preferred stockholders were declared and paid during the year.

Required:
Assuming an income tax rate of 30%,

1. Determine the dilutive effect of each of the above securities.
2. Indicate the assumed order of conversion.
3. Calculate basic and diluted EPS for K&K Associates.

Problem 9-10: Earnings per Share—Complex Capital Structure. Kutler, Inc., is a department store that sells a wide variety of household goods. During 2004, the company had net income of $223,000, including a loss before taxes of $85,000 from disposing of a component of the business that qualified to be reported under discontinued operations and an extraordinary loss before taxes of $38,000. The company's effective tax rate is 40%.

Information about the company's outstanding capital as of December 31, 2004, is as follows:

6% cumulative preferred stock, $100 par value, 10,000 shares issued and outstanding. Each share is convertible into 14 shares of common stock.	$1,000,000
Common stock, $10 par value	5,000,000
Additional paid-in capital, common stock	7,500,000

On April 1, 2004, the company issued 50,000 shares of common stock at $35 per share. The common stock price at the beginning of the year was $29; the average price during the year was $33; and the closing price on December 31, 2004, was $36.

In addition to the above equity capital, the company has outstanding $5\frac{1}{2}$% convertible bonds with a maturity value of $3,000,000. Each $1,000 bond can be converted into 30 shares of common stock.

Finally, 20,000 common stock options, which were issued to employees in 2003, were still outstanding at the end of 2004. Each option allows the holder to purchase one share of stock at a price of $30.

Required:
1. Calculate the weighted-average number of shares.
2. Beginning with income from continuing operations, prepare the income statement.
3. Prepare the basic EPS presentation for 2004.
4. Prepare the diluted EPS presentation for 2004.

Problem 9-11: Earnings per Share—Complex Capital Structure. Wolfe, Inc., reported net income of $450,000 for the year ending December 31, 2007. Included in this net income was an extraordinary loss, net of tax, of $75,000. In addition, the company recorded a loss of $45,000, net of tax, as a result of an accounting change.

The number of common shares outstanding at the end of 2006 was 225,000, and the transactions affecting the company's shares during the year were as follows.

February 1, 2007	Issued 25,000 shares
April 1, 2007	Issued a 10% stock dividend
October 1, 2007	Acquired 5,000 shares of the company's common stock

The company had outstanding for the entire year 10,000 shares of $100 par value convertible preferred shares. Each share of preferred stock is convertible into 4.5 shares of common stock at the option of the holder. The dividend rate on the preferred stock is 8%, and the stock is noncumulative. Dividends on the preferred stock were paid in full during 2007, and cash dividends of $0.50 per share were paid on all outstanding shares of common stock.

The company also had outstanding for the entire year 50,000 stock options. For each option, one share of common stock can be purchased. The exercise price for 60% of the options is $10 per share, and the exercise price for the remaining options is $25 per share.

During the year, the average market price of Wolfe's common stock was $24 per share, and the closing price on December 31 was $28 per share.

The company's tax rate is 30%.

Required:

1. Determine the weighted-average number of shares to use in calculating Wolfe's basic EPS for 2007.
2. Prepare a partial income statement, beginning with income from continuing operations.
3. Compute basic EPS for all required income statement amounts.
4. Calculate all necessary diluted EPS amounts for Wolfe, Inc., for the year ending December 31, 2007.

Research Activities

Activity 9-1: Researching Current Annual Reports with Writing Assignment. Research annual reports and find a company that has executed one of the following accounting changes:

    Voluntary accounting principle change
    Mandatory accounting principle change
    Change in accounting estimate
    Correction of an error

Provide a brief report that consists of the following:

a. The company name
b. A summary of the accounting change
c. The effect of the change on the current period's earnings

(continued)

d. The effect of the change on the prior-periods' earnings
e. The justification for the change as stated by management and your opinion on whether management had other incentives to execute the change.

Cases

Case 9-1: Thomaston Mills, Inc. Thomaston Mills, Inc., manufactures cotton, synthetic, and blended textile products and markets these products to the home furnishings, apparel fabrics, and industrial products industries. At the beginning of the company's 1995 fiscal year, the company changed accounting methods with respect to inventory valuation. Information related to the company's financial performance and the accounting change follows.

EXHIBIT 1

Partial Balance Sheet

Thomaston Mills Inc.
As of July 1, 1995

Cash and cash equivalents	$ 1,543,579	$ 1,109,975
Trade accounts receivable less allowance of		
$415,000 in 1995 and 1994	50,924,234	56,157,445
Inventories—Note 2	39,665,948	36,502,342
Deferred income taxes—Note 5	790,345	384,676
Prepaid expenses and other current assets	400,896	528,369
Total current assets	$93,325,002	$94,682,807

EXHIBIT 2

Income Statement

Thomaston Mills Inc.
Statement of Income

For the Year Ended	July 1, 1995	July 2, 1994	July 3, 1993
Net sales	$276,490,994	$279,479,091	$277,875,811
Cost of sales	249,690,536	242,245,990	232,783,675
Gross profit	$ 26,800,458	$ 37,233,101	$ 45,092,136
Selling, administrative and			
general expenses	18,847,382	18,338,717	17,734,879
Operating income	$ 7,953,076	$ 18,894,384	$ 27,357,257
Interest expense	3,044,358	1,885,870	2,182,432
Other income, net	424,320	428,209	493,161
Income before income taxes	$ 5,333,038	$ 17,436,723	$ 25,667,986
Income taxes—Note 5	1,959,542	6,727,133	10,093,000
Net income	$ 3,373,496	$ 10,709,590	$ 15,574,986
Net income per common share	$ 0.52	$ 1.63	$ 2.37

EXHIBIT 3

Selected Notes

NOTE 2—INVENTORIES

Inventories consisted of the following.

	July 1, 1995	July 2, 1994
Raw materials and supplies	$ 10,087,236	$ 9,579,814
Work in process	21,008,342	21,945,409
Finished goods	21,198,049	15,300,583
LIFO reserve	(12,627,679)	(10,323,464)
Total	$ 39,665,948	$ 36,502,342

Through July 2, 1994, the Company accounted for the cotton, polyester, labor, and overhead components of raw materials, work in process, and finished goods at the lower of cost, determined under the LIFO method of accounting, or market. Purchased cloth and yarn and certain supplies inventories were accounted for at the lower of cost, determined under the FIFO method of accounting, or market. Effective July 3, 1994, the Company changed to the LIFO method of accounting for purchased cloth and yarn. This change will result in better matching of revenues and expenses and will conform substantially all manufacturing inventories to the LIFO method. The cumulative effect of this change is not determinable. The effect of this change was to decrease net income for 1995 by approximately $550,000 ($0.08 per share). In connection with this change, the Company conformed the manner of applying the LIFO method for its cotton and polyester inventories to the dollar value method. Management believes the effect of this change was not significant.

A number of the Company's competitors use the FIFO method of inventory valuation. Had the Company reported its LIFO inventories at values approximating current cost, as would have resulted from using the FIFO method; and had applicable tax rates in 1995, 1994, and 1993 been applied to changes in operations resulting therefrom; and had no other assumptions been made as to changes in operations, net income would have been approximately $4,834,000 ($0.74 per share) in 1995; $10,864,000 ($1.65 per share) in 1994; and $15,509,000 ($2.36 per share) in 1993.

Required:
1. Describe the change in accounting for inventories that Thomaston Mills made during the fiscal year 1995.
2. What effect did this change in accounting have on 1995 reported net income? Give the answer in both absolute and percentage amounts. What was the stated reason made by the company for the accounting change? What other potential benefits could the company realize from using LIFO?
3. The company stated that the cumulative effect of the accounting change is not determinable, which indicates that the previous years' inventory amounts have not been adjusted to reflect this change. Why is it almost impossible to determine the cumulative effect of this type of accounting change?
4. By what amount and in what direction did inventory change from 1994 to 1995? Calculate the inventory turnover ratio for 1994 and 1995. Calculate the inventory turnover ratio for 1995, assuming that Thomaston Mills did not change its inventory accounting. (Assume an effective tax rate of 40%.) Provide an analysis of the calculated ratios.

Case 9-2: Johnson & Johnson. Johnson & Johnson is a large, multinational corporation that is involved in the manufacture and sale of a broad range of health-care products. The company was organized in 1887 and today employs close to 100,000 people worldwide. The company has experienced remarkable sales growth. In 1999, total sales recorded for the company were $27.5 billion, which was an increase from 1998 sales of 14.5% and represented the sixty-seventh consecutive year of positive sales growth. Earnings growth has also been significant. In the company's Management Discussion and Analysis section of its 1999 annual report, management made the following disclosure concerning its earnings growth:

> "Worldwide net earnings for 1999 were $4.2 billion, reflecting a 38.8% increase over 1998. Worldwide net earnings per share for 1999 equaled $2.94 per share, an increase of 38.7% from the $2.12 net earnings per share in 1998. Excluding the impact of special charges, both worldwide net earnings and net earnings per share increased 13.8% over 1998. The special charges included costs associated with the Centocor merger in 1999 and the reconfiguration of the worldwide manufacturing network and in-process research and development (IPR&D) charges in 1998."

In addition, the following graph was presented to highlight the consistent growth in earnings that the company has realized.

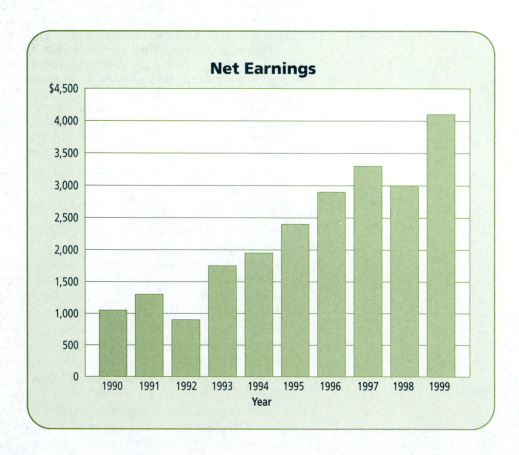

Johnson & Johnson reported both basic and diluted EPS amounts for 1999 and 1998 in its annual report. The following note was extracted from the company's 1999 annual report that provides details about the company's capital structure.

EARNINGS PER SHARE

The following is a reconciliation of basic net earnings per share to diluted net earnings per share for the years ended January 2, 2000, January 3, 1999, and December 28, 1997:

Basic earnings per share	$ 3.00	$ 2.16	$ 2.40
Average shares outstanding—basic	1,390.1	1,389.8	1,380.6
Potential shares exercisable under stock option plans	68.7	68.8	70.5
Less shares repurchased under treasury stock method	(40.6)	(41.4)	(35.7)
Adjusted average shares outstanding—diluted	1,418.2	1,417.2	1,415.4
Diluted earnings per share	$ 2.94	$ 2.12	$ 2.34

The diluted earnings per share calculation does not include approximately six million shares related to convertible debt and 11 million shares of options.

1. What types of potentially dilutive securities did Johnson & Johnson have outstanding in 1999? Which of these securities were dilutive, and which were antidilutive?
2. Refer to management's discussion of earnings growth. On what types of EPS did management focus? Why do you think management decided to focus on these earnings numbers?
3. Johnson & Johnson executed several company mergers during the decade of the 1990s. Refer to the graph that was provided by management to highlight the realized earnings growth of the company. What effect would mergers likely have on reported net income? Do you suppose that reported EPS would have the same trend?

10

Financial Reporting FOR Assets

Consider the following scenarios and the effects that changing prices have upon the relevance of reporting historical cost amounts.

Change in Price Due to Discovery During the first half of the 20th century, the desert land in eastern Utah was considered almost worthless. Then, in the 1950s, uranium was discovered around Moab. Almost overnight, the value of that desert ground appreciated considerably.

Questions

1. For financial statements prepared shortly after discovery of the precious metal, at what value should that land be reported on the balance sheet—the price originally paid or some current "asking price" for land in the area?
2. Is asking price relevant?
3. Is it reliable?
4. Now that uranium is not in demand, the value of the land has gone down. At what value should the land be reported now?

Change in Price Over an Extended Period In the 1970s, Nelson A. Rockefeller was nominated as vice president of the United States. As part of the confirmation hearings, he submitted his financial statements to Congress, and these statements revealed that his family owned substantial amounts of real estate in New York City that had been purchased more than 60 years previously. Congress was concerned that the financial statements—prepared under the auspices of reputable CPAs—continued to report this real estate at the price paid 60 years previously and not at the land's current value. Mr. Rockefeller stressed that there was no intent to mislead the congressional committees and that it was routine to value such long-lived assets at their historical cost amounts.

Questions

1. If Mr. Rockefeller did not intend on selling the land, is selling price relevant?
2. How would a selling price be obtained?
3. Is this land unique, so that the quotations available in real estate listings are not reflective of its current value?

Change in Price Due to Inflation During the 1970s and early 1980s, the highest inflation rates (a rise in all prices as compared to a change in a specific price) ever encountered in the United States caused many businessmen and even the FASB to question the relevance of historical-cost-based financial statements. The FASB issued an exposure draft, which, if it had resulted in a formal statement, would have required companies to adjust their financial statements for the effects of inflation and also to report certain current value information. That exposure draft led to a 5-year experiment in which certain companies provided supplementary price-level-adjusted and current value information, and during which time the FASB issued eight standards addressing price-level-adjusted information.[1] Finally, the FASB issued *SFAS No. 89*, which superceded all eight of the previous standards and provided guidance to companies who *desired* to issue supplementary information on the effects of changing prices. Undoubtedly, one reason the FASB never mandated that such information be reported is that the inflation rate decreased during the latter part of the 1980s. However, the impact of inflation upon financial statements has not gone away; it is just not as noticeable when inflation rates are low. High rates of inflation continue to be a problem throughout much of the world, and, as business be-

comes more global, questions will be raised—again—as to whether financial statements should reflect the impact of changing prices.

[1]The standards are *SFAS Nos. 33, 39, 40, 41, 46, 54, 70, & 82.*

Learning Objectives

- Describe what constitutes cash for proper reporting on the balance sheet.
- Compute and report the net realizable value of receivables.
- Prepare the necessary journal entry to recognize bad debts and adjust the corresponding allowance for doubtful accounts, using both the income statement approach and the balance sheet approach.
- Explain the difference between pledging receivables and transferring receivables with and without recourse, and describe the financial reporting of each.
- Apply the lower-of-cost-or-market procedures to valuing and reporting inventory on the balance sheet.
- Explain the FASB's criteria for determining when long-lived assets are impaired, and measure the amount of the impairment.
- Recognize how a typical current cost system functions for revaluing long-lived assets, and describe the effects of a current cost system on financial statements.
- Compute the cash proceeds when discounting notes, and prepare the appropriate journal entries.

Theory of Reporting Assets

As discussed in Chapter 5, all assets at acquisition are reported at the fair value of the consideration paid to acquire them and to bring them to the location where they can be used or sold. This fair value amount is called the historical cost of the asset. At acquisition, this historical cost amount (which by definition is also the fair value of the asset) is the most relevant and reliable information that can be reported concerning the asset. But as pointed out in the opening scenarios, the historical cost of an asset may lose its relevance over time. So the questions arise: When preparing a balance sheet at year-end, at what value should assets continue being reported—at their historical cost amount, or at some other more relevant value? If some other value is more relevant, can that value be obtained? Finally, even though some other value is more relevant, does reporting that value result in the loss of reliability to the extent that it is not advisable to report the more relevant value?

Exhibit 10-1 illustrates the relationship of reporting assets with the previously developed model for recognizing and accounting for costs, recognizing revenue, and reporting income. Note that the revenues and expenses represent "flows," or the movement of costs and revenues through the accounts and eventually to the income statement as a result of operating activities during the year, whereas the reporting of assets (and later liabilities and stockholders'/owners' equities) represents stocks or the balances on hand at the end of the year.

Remember that a fundamental objective of financial reporting is to provide useful information, which the FASB defined as information about the amount,

EXHIBIT 10-1

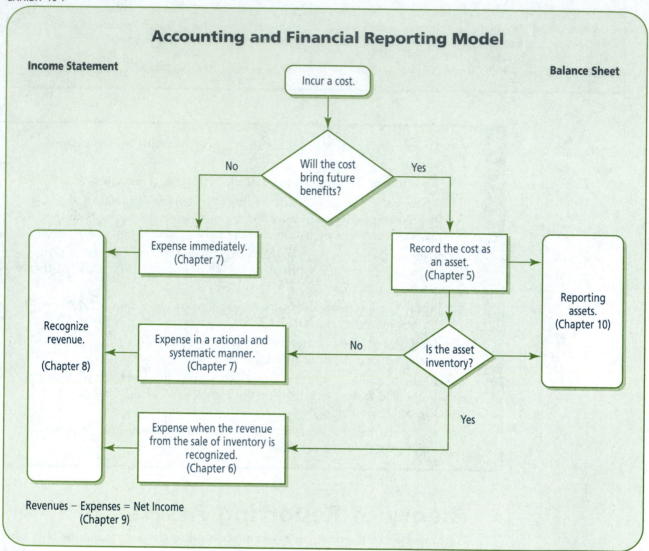

Accounting and Financial Reporting Model

Income Statement

Balance Sheet

Incur a cost.

Will the cost bring future benefits?

No → Expense immediately. (Chapter 7)

Yes → Record the cost as an asset. (Chapter 5)

Reporting assets. (Chapter 10)

Recognize revenue. (Chapter 8)

Is the asset inventory?

No → Expense in a rational and systematic manner. (Chapter 7)

Yes → Expense when the revenue from the sale of inventory is recognized. (Chapter 6)

Revenues − Expenses = Net Income (Chapter 9)

timing, and uncertainty of future cash flows. Given the FASB's objective of providing information about future cash flows, it is to be expected that the values reported for assets on the balance sheet should be connected in some way with expected future cash flows.

Future cash flows, or the amount at which to report an asset, can be measured in one of two ways. One way is to obtain a market price or quotation, which is the market's assessment as to what the potential cash flows of the asset will be. Thus, the historical cost of an asset was the market's assessment at the time the asset was acquired as to what the future cash flows of the asset would be. The second way of determining the amount at which to report an asset is to discount the estimated future cash flows the asset will generate, using some appropriate interest rate.

Theoretically, either approach is acceptable, but both methods have their drawbacks. For example, for many assets (particularly those assets that are unique or fill a specialized function), no market quotation is available. Also, market quotations are not particularly relevant when there is no intent to sell the asset. Regarding the second method of discounting an asset's potential future cash flows, a synergistic effect among assets often makes it impracticable or impossible to identify the future cash flows of specific assets.

Regardless of the difficulties of measuring the cash flows of assets, the FASB has concluded that measurements other than historical cost should be used to report the value of assets. These other measurements include the following:

- Selling price or current market value, which is the price that would be received if the asset were sold. The major advantages of this measurement are that it is determined by a market and is therefore objective, and since the measure is market-determined, frequent updates are obtainable.
- Net realizable value, which is the selling price of an asset less the costs of completing the asset and selling it. Since this measure begins with selling price (from which various costs are deducted), its advantages are the same as mentioned for using a selling price to measure the value of assets.
- Replacement cost or current cost, which is the price that would be paid to obtain a similar asset. This measure differs from the selling price because replacement cost is the price the company would pay to obtain an asset, whereas the selling price is the price the company would receive when selling the asset. Thus, the two measures differ by the amount of the company's gross profit. Since replacement costs are determined by the market, the advantages of using this measurement are much the same as those listed for the selling price.

Some reliability is sacrificed, regardless of which measurement from the previous list is reported in place of historical cost. The reason lies in the fact that historical cost is based upon a past transaction and is, therefore, verifiable, neutral, and representative of the fair value of the asset when it was acquired. In contrast, a market quotation (such as selling price or replacement cost) is a supposed transaction, therefore, it is subject to some variability due to negotiations, the condition or location of the asset, etc.

When deciding to report a market quotation or some value based upon a market price, the issue arises as to how much reliability should be sacrificed to achieve a more relevant measurement. Different cultures take different approaches to this matter. Generally, those cultures where price changes are frequent and volatile are more willing to move away from reporting historical cost values. Also, as market-based measurements have become more reliable and available, all financial reporting systems have more willingly reported such measures. Financial reporting in the United States illustrates the interplay between these two factors. Here, where markets have been very stable, the financial reporting system has reported historical cost numbers for a longer period of time than other cultures have;[2] but even in the United States, as reliable market measures are being developed, the financial reporting system is moving to report those numbers.

The objective of a country's financial reporting system is another factor that influences a country's willingness to give up some reliability to achieve a more relevant number. For example, as discussed in Chapter 4, Germany is a code-law country, where establishing accounting rules is done by governmental organizations. There, a primary objective is not to report the information desired by financial statement users but rather to report information to determine a company's tax liability. In addition, the primary providers of capital in Germany are banks and private shareholders who obtain their desired information by communicating directly with management. Thus, reporting relevant financial statement information to other interested parties is not a priority in Germany, and accordingly, the country tends to report historical cost numbers.

---

[2]At times, the financial reporting system in the United States has been called the last bastion of historical-cost-based financial statements.

Given this background into the difficulty of measuring an individual asset's potential future cash flows, which measurement best reports those future cash flows, and the issue of how much reliability should be sacrificed to obtain more relevant information, the measuring and reporting of assets can be addressed and more fully appreciated. *In general, the notion is that when markets are sufficiently developed so that the market quotation provides relevant information that can be used without sacrificing too much reliability, either that market quotation or some value based upon it is substituted for historical cost and reported on financial statements.*

Cash and Cash Equivalents

Measuring cash is not difficult. It is measured by simply counting it. The two accounting issues related to cash are (1) providing adequate internal controls to ensure that cash is safeguarded and (2) deciding what is included in cash on the balance sheet. The controls-over-cash question is beyond the scope of this text. You may learn about it in either an information systems class or in an auditing course.

Concerning the second issue as to what is included in cash on the balance sheet, cash is money—that which is used as a medium of exchange. Cash includes currency, coins, savings accounts, and demand deposits.[3] Cash also includes certified checks, money orders, and cashiers' checks that are not yet deposited at the end of the year. *To be reported as cash on the balance sheet, such items must be readily available and have no restrictions on their use, either to pay debts, acquire assets, or finance operations.* Any items that are considered as cash but that have restrictions—either self-imposed, legally imposed, or imposed by others—limiting their use to pay debts, to acquire assets, or finance operations are separately classified, either among the current assets or among the investments and funds, depending upon when the cash will be available. Such restrictions are a concern because, if such amounts are reported with cash, the readers of financial statements may assume that the entire amount is immediately available to meet current obligations or to expand operations, when such is not the case. Examples of restricted cash that are typically reported in the investments and funds classification include cash set aside for plant expansion, cash set aside to pay for losses when the company is self-insured, and cash in the bank of a foreign country where limitations have been imposed on transferring the cash out of the country.

Per *SFAS No. 95*, those items that are determined to be equivalent to cash are also reported under cash on the balance sheet, and then the caption is more appropriately labeled as "Cash and cash equivalents." **Cash equivalents** are readily convertible, low-risk securities. To be a cash equivalent, the security must be readily convertible into cash and have a short maturity date from the time it was acquired, so there is little risk of a change in value because of a change in interest rates. A typical rule of thumb is that highly liquid securities that will mature within *90 days from when they were acquired* qualify as cash equivalents.

Time deposits are funds deposited in a bank where prior notification is legally required before the amounts can be withdrawn without incurring a penalty. Examples of time deposits include certificates of deposit (i.e., CDs), money market funds and savings certificates, and similar types of short-term investments. Because of the requirement that prior notification must be given before withdrawal, time deposits are reported under "restricted cash" and classified as either

---

[3]A demand deposit is a checking account.

current assets or investments and funds, depending upon the maturity date of the deposits. An exception to reporting short-term paper separately from cash is money market funds that provide checking account privileges; these are reported with cash.

Another type of restriction on cash is a **compensating balance**, which is the amount a lender requires to be retained in a demand deposit to support an existing loan arrangement. The SEC recommends that compensating balances resulting from legal restrictions be reported separately from cash and cash equivalents. When the legal restriction will be satisfied within the year or operating cycle, the cash should be reported in the current assets section but separately from cash and cash equivalents. Otherwise, the compensating balance should be reported with investments and funds. Compensating balances that are not legally restricted can be included with cash and cash equivalents.

Bank overdrafts are caused when a company writes checks for more than the cash that is available in the account. Bank overdrafts are not included in cash, but are reported under current liabilities. An exception is when a company has other accounts at the same bank, and then the overdraft may be offset against positive balances in the other accounts, with the net amount reported as either a current asset or a current liability, as appropriate.

Exhibit 10-2, which is an excerpt from Boeing's published financial report, along with accompanying note information, illustrates the typical reporting of cash and cash equivalents today.

EXHIBIT 10-2

Reporting of Cash and Cash Equivalents

(in millions except per share amounts) December 31,	2001	2000
Assets		
Cash and cash equivalents	633	1,010

Note 1
Summary of Significant Accounting Policies

Cash and cash equivalents
Cash and cash equivalents consist of highly liquid instruments, such as certificates of deposit, time deposits, treasury notes and other money market instruments, which generally have maturities of less than three months.

Receivables

EXTENDING
the Concept

Which of the attributes listed earlier in the chapter is used to measure receivables?

Receivables consist of future payments from customers, employees, financial institutions, etc., and they are classified on the balance sheet as either current or long-term, depending upon their anticipated receipt. Receivables classified as current are those expected to be collected within the year or the current operating cycle, whichever is longer. All other receivables are classified as long-term. Furthermore, receivables are typically reported on the balance sheet as "trade receivables" and as "all other" or "nontrade receivables." All receivables are reported at **net realizable value**, which is the gross amount to be received minus an estimate of the dollar amount that will not be collected.

Financial Reporting

Exhibit 10-3 was taken from the financial statements of Ace Hardware Corporation and illustrates the typical reporting for receivables. Note that (1) the receivables are classified into two groups: Trade and Other, (2) the total amount that is expected to be uncollectible for 2001 is $2,419, (3) Allowance for Doubtful Accounts is reported as a contra-account to Accounts Receivable, and (4) the net realizable value of Ace's receivables at December 29, 2001, is $369,035.

One convenient place to obtain company financial reports is the following Web site: **http://www.reportgallery.com/**. Over 2,200 annual reports are offered in addition to links to company Web pages and many other financial Web sites.

EXHIBIT 10-3

Ace Hardware Corporation

ASSETS	December 29, 2001	December 30, 2000
Current assets:	(000's omitted)	
Cash and cash equivalents	$ 25,213	$ 24,644
Short term investments	17,158	12,772
Receivables:		
Trade	308,390	316,339
Other	63,064	59,090
	371,454	375,429
Less allowance for doubtful accounts	(2,419)	(2,458)
Net receivables	369,035	372,971
Inventories	412,568	395,565
Prepaid expenses and other current assets	16,295	15,105
Total current assets	$840,269	$821,057

Determining Net Realizable Value

In determining the net realizable value of receivables, either the income statement approach or the balance sheet approach may be used. These methods are commonly referred to as the percent-of-sales approach and the percent-of-receivables approach, respectively. Both methods employ a year-end adjusting entry, where Bad Debts Expense is debited and Allowance for Doubtful Accounts is credited. (Because both of these methods use an allowance account, both are also referred to as an "allowance method.") The income statement approach focuses on measuring the Bad Debts Expense amount in the journal entry, which is an income statement account, while the balance sheet approach focuses on measuring the Allowance for Doubtful Accounts, which is a balance sheet account.

The Income Statement Approach—Percent of Sales

The income statement approach to computing the net realizable value of a company's receivables is based on a company's bad debts expense being related to its credit sales. That is, as a company's credit sales increase, so too does its bad debts expense. Based on past experience and making allowance for changing economic conditions, bad debts expense is estimated as a percentage of credit sales, as follows:

$$\text{Bad Debts Expense} = \text{Percent} \times \text{Credit Sales}$$

When the amount of credit sales is not available, other sales number can be used. The only change is to adjust the estimate of the percentage of those sales that will be uncollectible. Thus, if bad debts are estimated as a percent of total sales rather than as a percent of credit sales, the percentage that is expected to be uncollectible is reduced, since there are no bad debts on cash sales.

Assume that Ace Hardware had credit sales of $500 million for 2004. Based on past experience, it estimates that 2% of these sales will be uncollectible. From this information, Ace determines that the bad debts expense for the year is $10 million (which is computed as 2% of $500 million). *This $10 million is both the ending balance of Bad Debts Expense and the adjusting entry amount.* The reason why it is the adjusting entry amount is that Bad Debts Expense for 2003 was closed to Income Summary, and so at the beginning of 2004, Bad Debts Expense had a zero balance. Since there are no entries during the year that affect Bad Debts Expense, the balance at the end of the year—before the adjusting entry is prepared—is still zero. This concept of the computed amount being both the ending balance of Bad Debts Expense and the adjusting entry amount is shown in Illustration 10-1.

ILLUSTRATION 10-1

Bad Debts Expense (amounts in thousands)		
Dec. 31, 2003 balance (assumed) Closing of the account at December 31, 2003	$ 8,000	$8,000
January 1, 2004 balance Never any transactions to this account during the year[4]	0	
Balance in the account before year-end adjusting entry Year-end adjusting entry amount	10,000	0
Year-end balance	10,000	The adjusting entry and year-end balance are the same.

Having computed that $10 million is the amount needed in Bad Debts Expense, Ace prepares the following year-end adjusting entry:

Bad Debts Expense	10,000 (computed)	
Allowance for Doubtful Accounts		10,000 (plugged in)

To recognize the amount of bad debts expense for the year.

---

[4]Like all other expense accounts, Bad Debts Expense begins the year with a balance of zero. During the year, the only event to affect this balance is the recognizing of bad debts expense.

Besides recognizing bad debts expense for the period, this entry also adjusts the allowance for doubtful accounts, and as a result, reports the company's receivables at their net realizable value.

Balance Sheet Approach—Aging of Accounts Receivable

The balance sheet approach to determining the net realizable value of receivables is based upon analyzing the receivables outstanding at the end of the year. The most common technique of doing this is an aging schedule that separates the receivables into categories based on the number of days that amounts have been owed. The uncollectible receivables are computed by multiplying an estimated percentage by the dollar amount in each age category. When estimating the percentages to use, it is assumed that the likelihood of not collecting the amounts owed increases as the time that the receivables have been outstanding increases. Illustration 10-2 shows a typical aging schedule.

ILLUSTRATION 10-2

Accounts Receivable Aging Schedule

Number of Days Outstanding	Accounts Receivables (in thousands)	Likelihood of Default	Doubtful Accounts (in thousands)
Less than 30	$24,000	3.5%	$ 840
Greater than 30 but less than 60	18,000	6	1,080
Greater than 60 but less than 90	12,000	20	2,400
Greater than 90 but less than 180	5,000	60	3,000
Greater than 180	2,000	100	2,000
Ending balance needed in doubtful accounts			$9,320

Since the balance sheet approach of estimating the receivables that will be uncollectible is a different estimation technique than the income statement approach illustrated earlier, it should not be expected that the estimates will be the same. Unlike the income statement approach, *the amount computed as the ending balance of the allowance account (i.e., $9,320,000) is not the amount of the adjusting journal entry.* The reason is because Allowance for Doubtful Accounts is not closed to Income Summary at the end of each year, and so it does not begin each year with a zero balance. The adjusting entry amount is determined by comparing the current balance in the allowance account to the balance that is needed as computed from the aging schedule (i.e., $9,320,000), with the adjusting entry amount being the difference.

Using the data in Illustration 10-2 and assuming that (1) the beginning balance in Ace's Allowance for Doubtful Accounts was $8,000,000 and (2) Ace wrote off $8,400,000 of receivables during 2004, the adjusting entry amount of $9,720,000 is computed as shown in Illustration 10-3. Thus, the adjusting entry is the amount needed to obtain the desired ending balance of $9,320,000, given the present debit balance of $400,000.

Based on this analysis, Ace's adjusting entry at year-end is as follows (with amounts expressed in thousands):

Bad Debts Expense   9,720 (plugged in)
    Allowance for Doubtful Accounts   9,720 (computed)
To recognize the amount of receivables
that will not be collected.

ILLUSTRATION 10-3

Allowance for Doubtful Accounts
(amounts in thousands)

Accounts written off	$8,400	$8,000	Balance, January 1, 2004
Balance at December 31 before adjustment	400		
		$9,720	**Bad Debts Expense for 2004**
		$9,320	Balance, December 31, 2004. (See Illustration 10-2.)

The journal entry under the balance sheet approach has the same debits and credits as the adjusting entry under the income statement approach. However, the computed and plugged in numbers are not the same accounts. The reason is that, under the income statement approach, the balance in another income statement account (i.e., Bad Debts Expense) is computed, whereas under the balance sheet approach the balance in another balance sheet account (i.e., Allowance for Doubtful Accounts) is computed.

To further illustrate the balance sheet approach of determining the adjusting entry amount, assume that in the given example the allowance account had a credit balance of $1,500 before the year-end adjusting entry. Then, the adjusting entry is as follows:

Bad Debts Expense	7,820 (plugged in)	
Allowance for Doubtful Accounts		7,820 (computed)

To adjust the allowance for doubtful accounts to its current estimated amount.

Supporting calculations:	
Needed balance in the allowance account	$9,320 Cr.
Balance before adjustment in the allowance account	1,500 Cr.
Required adjusting entry amount	$7,820 Cr.

Until recently, accounting standard-setting bodies in the United States emphasized computing net income in preference to reporting more relevant balance sheet figures, and as a result, the income statement approach was considered the preferred technique for estimating bad debts expense and the related allowance for doubtful accounts. However, in recent years, the FASB has shown a preference for measuring balance sheet figures, and now it may be that the balance sheet approach is the preferred technique.

Direct Write-Off Method

The direct write-off method of accounting for bad debts expense does not use an allowance account, nor is bad debts expense estimated at the end of the year. Rather, bad debts expense is recognized when a specific account is deemed to be uncollectible, and the entry to write off the account consists of debiting Bad Debts Expense and crediting Accounts Receivable. The direct write-off method is not a generally accepted technique, but it is commonly used by small companies that are not subject to SEC regulations or FASB pronouncements. Also, it is the *only* method that is accepted for income tax reporting to the IRS. When this method is used, no year-end entry is made to recognize bad debts expense and adjust the allowance for doubtful accounts, as is done for either of the allowance methods.

The direct write-off method is not in accordance with GAAP for two reasons: (1) on the balance sheet, receivables are reported at their gross amount, rather than being adjusted to net realizable value and (2) bad debts expense is not reported in the same year in which the related sales are recognized, and thus, the matching principle is violated. In short, the direct write-off method does not provide information as relevant as those methods that use an allowance account.

Of interest is the notion that estimating an allowance for doubtful accounts and recognizing bad debts expense in the same year that the related sales are recognized is used in every developed accounting system in the world.

INTERNATIONAL

Writing Off an Uncollectible Account Receivable—Allowance Method

Under either of the allowance methods, as specific accounts are identified that will not be collected, they are written off the books *by reducing both Accounts Receivable and Allowance for Doubtful Accounts.* Suppose that on January 22, 2005, Ace Hardware receives notification from Harris Corporation, who owes Ace $15,000, that it has filed for bankruptcy and does not have the means to pay Ace the amount owed. To write off this receivable, Ace prepares the following entry:

Allowance for Doubtful Accounts	15,000	
Accounts Receivable		15,000
To write off an uncollectible receivable.		

It should not be expected that the total amount of the accounts receivable written off during the year will equal the amount that was estimated and recorded as the company's bad debts expense. Instead, if the balance in the allowance account gradually grows to an unreasonable level (either a large debit balance or a large credit balance), then in future years the estimate of the percentage of credit sales (or accounts receivable) that is expected to be uncollectible is increased or decreased as needed. As a result, either more or less expense will be recognized in future years. This is another example of a change in an accounting estimate, and, as discussed in Chapter 7, the accounting for such is done in the current and future years, rather than retroactively restating the financial statements.

Interestingly, the act of writing off an uncollectible receivable does not affect the net realizable value of the receivables. Illustration 10-4 demonstrates why this is so.

ILLUSTRATION 10-4

Effect of Writing Off a Receivable

	Amounts before the Write-Off	Amounts Written Off	Amounts after the Write-Off
Receivables, gross amount	$400,000	$15,000	$385,000
Allowance for doubtful accounts	40,000	15,000	25,000
Net realizable value—did not change	$360,000		$360,000

The writing off of an uncollectible account having no effect on the net realizable value of the receivables is illustrated graphically in Figure 10-1. The larger circle represents the total amount of receivables, and the smaller circle represents the subset of the receivables that are presumed to be uncollectible. The portion of the larger circle that is outside the smaller circle represents the net realizable value of the receivables. When it is determined that a specific account is uncollectible and is written off, the smaller circle decreases in size, which also causes the larger circle to decrease in size but does not affect the area in the larger circle that is outside the smaller circle (i.e., the net realizable value of the receivables remains unchanged).

FIGURE 10-1

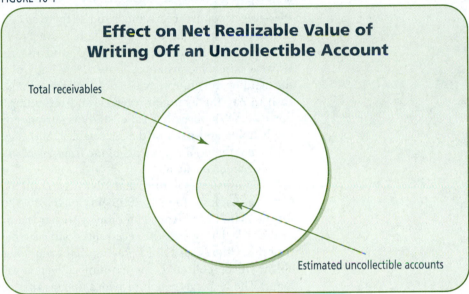

Effect on Net Realizable Value of Writing Off an Uncollectible Account

Total receivables

Estimated uncollectible accounts

Collecting Accounts Receivable that Previously Were Written Off

Occasionally, a receivable that was written off as uncollectible is subsequently collected. When this happens, two entries are prepared. The first entry reverses the previous write-off of the account receivable, correcting the misconception that the amount was uncollectible, and the second entry records the collection of the cash. Suppose that through the bankruptcy process, Ace is eventually able to collect $1,000 of the amount that was owed by Harris Corporation. The following journal entries would then be prepared:

Accounts Receivable	1,000	
Allowance for Doubtful Accounts		1,000
To put back on the books an account *receivable that previously had been* *written off as uncollectible.*		
Cash	1,000	
Accounts Receivable		1,000
To collect an amount owed.		

Using Accounts Receivable as a Means of Financing

Because of their relatively low risk and high liquidity, accounts receivable are frequently used as a means of meeting a company's immediate need for cash. They can be used as a source of cash, either through (1) pledging them as collateral on a loan, (2) transferring the receivable without recourse (i.e., selling them), or (3) transferring them with recourse (i.e., borrowing against them). Not only are companies able to meet their immediate cash needs through such financing arrangements, but such arrangements also allow the company to avoid the opportunity cost of holding the receivables and the cost of collection.[5]

Pledging (or Assigning) Accounts Receivable

Pledging accounts receivable is to use them as collateral on a loan. The more traditional way of doing this is for the borrower to keep physical custody of the receivables, collect the amounts owed, and use the collections to pay the loan. However, in some instances, physical custody of the receivables is transferred to the lending institution, with the lender making collections, keeping sufficient cash to pay the loan and interest, and refunding any remaining amounts to the borrower. Whether physical custody is surrendered or not, the transferor retains the benefits and risks of the receivables, and they *continue being reported on the books and financial statements of the transferor/borrower*. In addition, *a liability is recognized for the loan*.

To illustrate, assume that DNR Corporation borrowed $100,000 from First National Bank on June 1, 2005, and pledged $120,000 of receivables as security for the loan. (The pledged amount is greater than the amount of the loan because of the risk that not all the receivables will be collected. Thus, the financial institution has the security of knowing that even when less than 100% of the receivables will be collected, the amount collected still will be sufficient to pay the loan.) The loan agreement provides that, as the receivables are collected, the proceeds will be forwarded to First National Bank to pay the loan. The annual interest rate on the loan is 10%. At the time the cash is borrowed, DNR Corporation makes the following entries:

Cash	100,000	
Note Payable		100,000
To record the cash received on a note payable.		
Accounts Receivable Pledged	120,000	
Accounts Receivable		120,000
To reclassify accounts receivable to reflect pledging them for a loan.		

The second entry has no effect on total assets; it merely reclassifies the accounts receivable to disclose that these receivables have been pledged to secure a loan and are not available for other purposes.

To illustrate the settling with the bank, assume that by August 1, 2005, $112,000 of receivables have been collected, $5,000 of receivables were uncollectible, and $3,000 of receivables were reduced because of sales returns granted.

---

[5]Notes receivable can also be used as a source of cash by discounting them. Discounting notes receivable is discussed in the appendix at the end of this chapter.

Then, DNR Corporation would prepare the following entries to adjust the receivables and pay the note payable:

Cash	112,000	
Allowance for Doubtful Accounts[6]	5,000	
Sales Returns and Allowances	3,000	
Accounts Receivable Pledged		120,000

To record settlement of the accounts receivable.

Note Payable	100,000	
Interest Expense[7]	1,666	
Cash		101,666

To record settlement of loan from First National Bank.

Factoring Receivables without Recourse

Transferring receivables without recourse is referred to as factoring or selling them. Since the transfer is without recourse, the factor cannot go to the transferor/borrower for satisfaction in case of nonpayment. So the transferor has clearly surrendered control over the receivables and has transferred all economic benefits and risks to the factor. As a result, the receivables are written off the transferor's books, and either a loss or a financing expense, as appropriate, is recognized.

From the factor's point of view, accepting the receivables exposes him to the risks of (1) uncollectibility and (2) sales returns, discounts, and allowances. To compensate for the risk of uncollectibility—and to earn a profit—the factor charges a fee, which varies according to the factor's assessment of the quality of the receivables. Regarding the sales returns, discounts, and allowances, the factor holds back some cash, with the understanding that when the receivables are collected and all sales returns, etc., have been granted, the factor will settle with the borrower. This holdback feature is used because sales returns, allowances, and discounts are arrangements between the buyer and seller of the merchandise and do not involve the factor.

To illustrate, using the facts in the previous example, assume that instead of pledging the $120,000 receivables to First National Bank that DNR Corporation factored them without recourse. National Bank charged an 8% or $9,600 nonrecourse factoring fee to cover any uncollectible accounts and to provide a profit. In addition, First National retained an additional $10,000 to protect against sales returns, discounts, etc., which are beyond the bank's control and so are borne by DNR Corporation. After the fee and holdback, the bank issued a check to DNR for $100,400, which is verified as follows:

Total accounts receivable	$120,000
Less factoring fee	(9,600)
Amount potentially payable to DNR	$110,400
Holdback for returns, discounts, etc.	(10,000)
Cash advanced	$100,400

---

[6]Remember that this account normally has a credit balance. By debiting the account, the company is writing off its uncollectible accounts.

[7]This interest amount is computed as $100,000 \times 0.10 \times 2/12$.

444

Chapter 10

Given these assumptions, DNR prepares the following entry when the receivables are transferred or sold to First National:

Cash	100,400	
Due from First National	10,000	
Financing Expense[8]	9,600	
Accounts Receivable		120,000

To record a factoring of accounts receivable without recourse.

Following the collection of receivables, First National Bank settles with DNR. If sales returns and discounts are less than the anticipated $10,000, then First National pays DNR the difference. If sales returns and discounts are greater than the anticipated $10,000, then DNR pays First National the difference. That is, First National keeps only the cash equal to the actual sales returns and discounts, and DNR may potentially receive as much as $110,400 for the receivables.

Assuming the same collection history as recorded previously under the pledge example—that $112,000 is collected, $3,000 is granted for sales returns, and $5,000 is written off as uncollectible—DNR prepares the following journal entry to settle with the bank:

Cash	7,000	
Sales Returns and Allowances	3,000	
Due from First National		10,000

To record final settlement with factor.

Note two items in the foregoing journal entries. First, DNR does not adjust the allowance for doubtful accounts for the uncollectible accounts because the nonrecourse provision results in First National having to absorb any nonpayment. Second, the net result to First National Bank is a profit of $4,600, which is the difference between the amount paid to DNR of $107,400 and the amount collected of $112,000. This profit figure can be verified also as the difference between the fee of $9,600 and the amount of uncollectible accounts of $5,000.

Factoring Receivables with Recourse[9]

The major difference between the transfer of receivables with recourse and the transfer of them without recourse is that *the borrower/transferor retains the responsibility of ensuring payment on the receivables and absorbing the loss of any uncollectibles.* Determining whether a sale has actually occurred or whether the transfer is merely collateral for a loan may not be readily apparent. Because of the difficulty of determining the actual nature of the transaction and to ensure some comparability among published financial reports, the FASB has stated that all of the following conditions must be met before a transferor has effectively surrendered control over the receivables and may account for the transfer as a sale:

1. The transferor and its creditors do not have legal access to the receivables,
2. The transferee(s) obtains the right to pledge or exchange the receivables, and

[8]Instead of recognizing an expense, the account may be labeled "Loss from Sale of Accounts Receivable."

[9]Factoring with recourse arose because some companies had such a poor history of receivable collectibility that factors were willing to purchase the receivables only if a substantial fee was charged. When a company thought its receivables were of a higher quality than was being granted by the factor, the substantial fee was avoided by allowing the factor recourse against the company in the event of uncollectibility.

3. An agreement has not been entered into that entitles nor obligates the transferor to repurchase or redeem the receivables before their maturity.[10]

If all the stated criteria for transferring control over the receivables are met, the accounting is the same as was done for a transfer without recourse. However, if any of these conditions are not met, the transfer of receivables is accounted for as a secured borrowing, and the transferor continues to report the receivables and, in addition, reports a liability for the estimated amount of the recourse provision, which is to cover the amount of uncollectible accounts. Determining the amount of the recourse provision requires judgment, but one possible estimation technique is to analyze the transferred receivables in an aging schedule or to use some other way to determine the amount that is expected to be uncollectible. Another method that may be more objective is to compare the factor fees charged for transfers with and without recourse.

To illustrate the accounting for a transfer with recourse, return to the DNR example and further assume that:

1. All the FASB's criteria to record the transfer of receivables as a sale are not met,
2. First National Bank charges a factoring fee of 3%, which is much less than the fee charged when the transfer was without recourse because now the bank does not absorb the loss of the uncollectibles,
3. First National Bank retains $10,000 to cover sales returns, discounts, etc., which will be settled later, and
4. Since DNR Corporation must compensate First National Bank for any uncollectible accounts, it has a liability to the bank for the estimated amount of the uncollectibles, which is $4,800.

Given these assumptions, the journal entry to record the transfer of the accounts receivable with recourse is as follows:

Cash (see the following supporting computations)	106,400	
Due from First National (given)	10,000	
Allowance for Doubtful Accounts	4,800	
Financing Expense	3,600	
Obligation to Factor (given)		120,000
Estimated Liability for Recourse Provision (given)		4,800

To record the transfer of accounts receivable with recourse.

As in the prior example, the cash amount advanced can be verified as follows:

Total accounts receivable	$120,000
Less factoring fee	(3,600)
Amount potentially payable to DNR	$116,400
Holdback for returns, etc.	(10,000)
Cash advanced	$106,400

The primary differences between the preceding journal entry and the entry of receivables without recourse are:

1. The amount of estimated uncollectible accounts is written off against the allowance account and is recognized as a liability.

---

[10]*Statement of Financial Accounting Standards No. 125*, "Accounting for Transfers and Servicing of Financial Assets and Extinguishments of Liabilities," June 1996, par. 9.

2. Instead of crediting the accounts receivable, an obligation to the factor is recognized. This difference is due to the nature of the transaction—instead of transferring all interest in the receivables, the borrower of the money continues to have an interest in them.

3. By factoring with recourse, DNR received an additional $6,000 as compared to factoring without recourse. This $6,000 is the difference between the factoring fee without recourse of 8% and the factoring fee with recourse of 3% multiplied by the accounts receivable factored of $120,000.

$$\$120,000 \times (8\% - 3\%) = \$6,000$$

Assuming the same collection pattern as previously, DNR prepares the following journal entry to settle with the factor:

Cash (see the following supporting computations)	2,000	
Estimated Liability for Recourse Provision		
(reversal of prior entry)	4,800	
Sales Returns and Allowances (given)	3,000	
Allowance for Doubtful Accounts (see the following		
supporting calculations)	200	
Due from First National (reversal of prior entry)		10,000

To record final settlement with factor for receivables transferred with recourse.

Obligation to Factor	120,000	
Accounts Receivable		120,000

To write off the receivables that have been collected and to show the settling with the factor.

The amount of cash received or paid is (1) the difference between the estimated and actual sales returns, allowances, etc., and (2) the amount of bad debts incurred. Since the uncollectible accounts totaled $5,000 but only $4,800 had been provided in the previous entry, an additional $200 is recognized in this entry. If the amount of defaulted receivables had been less than the estimated amount of $4,800, DNR would have credited the allowance for doubtful accounts at the time of settlement. From the preceding journal entries, it can be seen that the total cash DNR received was $108,400, which can be verified as follows:

Total accounts receivable factored		$120,000
Less: Sales returns	$ 3,000	
Bad debts	5,000	
Factoring fee (3%)	3,600	(11,600)
Total cash to be received		$108,400
Consisting of:		
Amount advanced	$106,400	
Amount received at settlement	2,000*	

*The difference between the estimated and actual sales returns, etc. ($10,000 − $3,000), minus the uncollectible accounts of $5,000.

Illustration 10-5 summarizes the journal entries when the factoring is considered a sale and a borrowing because one or more of the FASB's criteria were not met. Note that the key difference in the entries is due to who absorbs the losses due to uncollectible accounts. This is why the allowance for doubtful ac-

ILLUSTRATION 10-5

Journal Entries for Factoring: With and Without Recourse

Name of Accounts if Considered a Sale	Debit Amounts	Credit Amounts	Borrowing	Debit Amounts	Credit Amounts
1. Journal entry when receivables are factored:					
Cash	100,400		Cash	106,400	
Due from Factor	10,000		Due from Factor	10,000	
Financing Expense	9,600		Financing Expense	3,600	
			Allowance for Doubtful Accounts	4,800	
Accounts Receivable		120,000	Obligation to Factor		120,000
			Estimated Liability		4,800
2. Journal entry at time of settling with factor:					
Cash	7,000		Cash	2,000	
			Estimated Liability	4,800	
Sales Returns	3,000		Sales Returns	3,000	
			Allowance for Doubtful Accounts	200	
Due from Factor		10,000	Due from Factor		10,000
In addition to the above entry, the following journal entry is also prepared:					
			Obligation to Factor	120,000	
			Accounts Receivable		120,000

counts is affected, an estimated liability to the factor is recognized, and an obligation to the factor is recognized rather than writing off accounts receivable.

Inventories

One accounting issue connected with reporting inventories is determining which inventories to include on the balance sheet, which was discussed in Chapter 6. Recall that the theoretical rule is to include all items that the company owns, and the operational rule is to include all items in the possession of the company, subject to a few exceptions.

Another accounting issue is determining at what value to report the inventory on the year-end balance sheet. Inventories that will be sold in the normal course of doing business are reported at the lower-of-cost-or-market (LCM). All other inventories (e.g., obsolete, damaged, etc.) are reported at **net realizable value**, which for inventories means selling price less costs of disposal. Except in rare situations, inventory is never reported above its historical cost.[11] Although the LCM rule seems capricious in requiring inventory to be reported at market when such is below cost but not allowing inventory to be reported at market when such is above cost, valuing inventory at fair value when it is above

EXTENDING *the Concept*

Which of the attributes listed earlier in the chapter could be used to measure inventories?

[11]An exception to not reporting inventory above its historical cost amount was covered in Chapter 8, which is that inventory is reported at its net realizable value when (1) the inventory can be marketed immediately at quoted prices, (2) inventory could be sold without incurring significant marketing costs, and (3) one unit of inventory cannot be distinguished from any other unit. As covered in Chapter 8, the revenue recognition criteria are seriously violated when inventory is recorded at an amount greater than its historical cost.

cost seriously violates the revenue recognition criteria and distorts the financial statements.[12]

Elaborating on why inventory is not reported above its historical cost and using extremes to illustrate the point clearly, suppose that a company acquires inventory throughout the year with the intent of selling it but never sells any of it so at the end of the year its showroom and warehouses are overflowing with inventory. In reality, the business is poorly managed, and the income statement should reflect that. But if the market price of the inventory increased during the year and the company is allowed to report the higher price for its inventory, then the company by writing up its inventory would recognize a large net income for the year. Although this example uses extremes that should never occur, it illustrates the point that recognizing gains on inventory before it is sold violates the revenue recognition principle and distorts the measuring of net income.

Lower-of-Cost-or-Market Procedures

When applying the lower-of-cost-or-market procedures, market means current replacement cost when it is between a ceiling and a floor. When replacement cost exceeds the ceiling, then ceiling is the market value; when replacement cost is less than the floor, the floor is the market value, as shown in Figure 10-2.

FIGURE 10-2

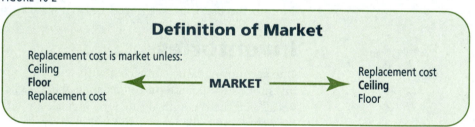

Definition of Market

Replacement cost is market unless:
Ceiling
Floor
Replacement cost
⟵ **MARKET** ⟶
Replacement cost
Ceiling
Floor

The ceiling and floor values are defined as follows:

Ceiling: Net realizable value, or the selling price of the inventory less the costs of completing and selling it.

Floor: Net realizable value (i.e., the ceiling) minus a normal profit, which is defined as gross profit.

The LCM value is determined in two steps.

1. *Determine the market in accordance with the listed ceiling/floor notions.*
2. *Determine the LCM value by comparing the market number, as determined in Step 1, to the historical cost of the inventory, with the lower of the two numbers reported on the year-end balance sheet.*

---

[12]The revenue recognition principle is also violated when gains are recognized on assets other than inventory, but the result is not as serious because (1) selling inventory is the primary operating activity of many businesses, (2) there are many more inventory transactions during a year in comparison to buying and selling other assets, and (3) the amount of inventory on the balance sheet is significantly larger than for most other assets.

TABLE 10-1

LCM Data

(Col. 1) Inventory Item	(Col. 2) Historical Costs	(Col. 3) Costs to Complete	(Col. 4) Selling Costs	(Col. 5) Replacement Costs	(Col. 6) Selling Price	(Col. 7) Normal Profit Margin
A	$10	$0	$1	$15	$25	$10
B	8	0	3	6	12	2
C	12	2	2	13	15	6

To demonstrate this 2-step procedure, the data in Table 10-1 are used.

Step 1: Determining the Market

For each inventory item, the ceiling is computed as the selling price (Col. 6) minus the sum of the costs to complete (Col. 3) and the selling costs (Col. 4). The ceiling values for each of the items are as shown in Table 10-2.

TABLE 10-2

Ceiling Computations

Item	Selling Price	Costs to Complete	Selling Costs	Ceiling
A	$25	$0	$1	$24
B	12	0	3	9
C	15	2	2	11

The floor is computed by subtracting the normal profit margin (Col. 7) from the previously computed ceiling amounts. So, the floor values for Items A, B, and C are computed as shown in Table 10-3.

TABLE 10-3

Floor Computations

Item	Ceiling (See Table 10-2)	Normal Profit Margin	Floor
A	$24	$10	$14
B	9	2	7
C	11	6	5

Having computed the ceiling and floor values and having the replacement cost available, it is now possible to determine the value that is to be used for *market, which is the midvalue of the floor, replacement cost, and ceiling.* Thus, the market values are determined as shown in Table 10-4, with the market values in bold.

TABLE 10-4

Determining the Market

Item	Ceiling (See Table 10-2)	Replacement Cost (See Table 10-1)	Floor (See Table 10-3)
A	$24	$15	$14
B	9	6	7
C	11	13	5

Step 2: Determining the Lower-of-Cost-or-Market Value

Having determined the market values, the second step in the LCM procedures is to compare the market value with the historical cost amounts and select the lower of the two values, as shown in Table 10-5.

TABLE 10-5

Determining the LCM Amount

Inventory	Cost Amount (See Table 10-1)	Market Amount (See Table 10-4)	LCM Amount
A	$10	$15	$10
B	8	7	7
C	12	11	11

Finally, assuming that there are 1,000 units of inventory Item A and 2,000 units each of inventory Items B and C, the inventory value to be reported on the balance sheet is computed as shown in Table 10-6.

TABLE 10-6

Determining Total Inventory Value

Inventory	Quantity	LCM Value	Inventory Value
A	1,000	$10	$10,000
B	2,000	7	14,000
C	2,000	11	22,000
		Total inventory value	$46,000

Recording the Adjusting Entry

Since the historical cost of the inventory is $50,000 [(1,000 × $10) + (2,000 × $8) + (2,000 × $12)],[13] a journal entry is required to write down the inventory to its LCM value. The simplest procedure, when a periodic inventory system is used, is to use the typical adjusting entry (as illustrated in Chapter 2), where be-

---

[13]See Table 10-1.

ginning inventory is closed and the ending inventory is recorded. It is now recorded at the LCM number, as follows:

Cost of Goods Sold (assumed amount)	180,000	
Inventory (ending)	46,000	
Purchase Returns	XXX	
Inventory (beginning)		49,000
Purchases		XXX

To close beginning inventory, record the ending inventory applying the LCM rule, and establish the cost of goods sold.

Note that the ending inventory is recorded at the LCM value. This way of recording the LCM adjustment is known as the **direct method**. If the decline in the value of the inventory is material and it is considered desirable to track this decline in value, a more appropriate entry may be as follows (with emphasis added):

Cost of Goods Sold (assumed amount)	176,000	
Inventory (ending)	46,000	
Inventory Holding Loss[14]	*4,000*	
Purchase Returns	XXX	
Inventory (beginning)		49,000
Purchases		XXX

To close beginning inventory, record the ending inventory applying the LCM rule, and establish the cost of goods sold.

In the illustrative journal entries, numbers are shown for Cost of Goods Sold to illustrate the impact on that number. Since there is no impact on any of the other numbers, they are not presented. Another method of recognizing the holding loss is called the allowance method. Using this method, the entry to record the inventory loss is as follows:

Cost of Goods Sold (assumed amount)	180,000	
Inventory (ending)	50,000	
Purchase Returns	XXX	
Inventory (beginning)		49,000
Allowance to Reduce Inventory to LCM		4,000
Purchases		XXX

To close beginning inventory, record the ending inventory applying the LCM rule, and establish the cost of goods sold.

As with the direct method, when the inventory loss is significant, the debit may be to an inventory holding loss account.

Applying LCM Procedures

LCM procedures can be applied to individual inventory items, as was done in the previous example, to groups or classifications of inventory items or to the inventory as a whole. When applying LCM procedures to either groups of inventory or to the inventory as a whole, unit costs (as were used in the preceding example) cannot be used. Rather, total amounts must be determined for all items: ceiling, replacement cost, floor, and historical cost. These total amounts are then used in the same 2-step process to determine (1) market and then (2) LCM. Regarding

---

[14]A gain/loss from holding an asset and having the value change is—for brevity—referred to as a holding gain/loss.

the effect of applying LCM procedures to individual items, categories, or to the total inventory, the lowest net income generally is reported when LCM procedures are applied to individual items, and the highest net income generally is reported when they are applied to total inventory.

Reasons for Using a Ceiling and Floor

The United States is one of the few nations in the world that employs a ceiling and a floor when determining the LCM value. The importance of the ceiling and floor concepts is illustrated in the following examples, using the data in Table 10-1 (see p. 449). Regarding the reason for using a ceiling, consider what would happen if the ceiling is ignored for Item C and replacement cost is used as market value. Then, since historical cost is less than replacement cost, there would be no write-down of the inventory. Subsequently, the sale of the inventory would result in recognizing revenue of $15 and expenses of $16 (which is the sum of the $12 cost of inventory plus the $2 cost to complete the inventory and the $2 cost to dispose of the inventory). Hence, the sale would result in a

© GETTY IMAGES, INC./PHOTODISC

$1 loss, and the more that is sold the greater the loss becomes. Such a result might actually create a disincentive to sell the inventory. To eliminate this situation, *the inventory is carried at an amount that is not greater than the net cash inflows from selling the inventory (which is the ceiling)*, and hence when the inventory is subsequently sold, there is no loss on the sale. In the world of business, the ceiling becomes the market value when there has been a substantial decrease in the demand for a product and to sell the product the company has to reduce its selling price.

Although other countries besides the United States require inventory to be valued at LCM, significant differences exist as to how market is defined. Most countries define market as meaning net realizable value, and others define market as meaning replacement cost. Another difference from U.S. GAAP is the types of inventory to which LCM procedures are applied. Germany, for example, applies LCM procedures only to raw material inventory.

Regarding the reason for using a floor, assume that the replacement cost of Item A is $8 but that all other data remain the same. Then, if the floor is ignored, the inventory is written down because the cost of $10 is greater than the replacement cost of $8. Thus, a loss of $2 per unit is recognized. Subsequently, when the inventory is sold, a higher-than-normal profit of $16 is recognized (which is the $25 selling price minus the $1 selling cost and the $8 cost of inventory). This floor prohibits companies from recognizing an inventory loss in one period that will be offset in the next period when the inventory is sold. In the world of business, the floor value typically becomes the market value when there has been a drop in the replacement cost that is not accompanied by a corresponding drop in the selling price. This could occur when the production costs of a product decrease, but the demand for the product remains high.

Criticisms of the LCM Rule

One criticism of the LCM rule is that it is a conservative accounting method in that losses are recognized but gains are not. The appropriate response to this criticism is that, as mentioned previously, the revenue recognition principle is seriously violated when holding gains are recognized on inventory, which leads to reporting results of operations that are contrary to economic reality and makes possible the manipulating of net income.

A second criticism of LCM is that writing down inventory in the current year results in reporting higher earnings in a future year than would have been recognized if the inventory had not been written down. This does occur and the reason is that by writing down inventory today, future costs of goods sold are decreased and net income is increased when those marked-down goods are sold. Thus, management can use LCM procedures to report, to some degree, the desired net income. Academic research has shown that managers occasionally do select accounting policies and procedures to report a desired income. For example, managers generally want to report a smooth flow of earnings, but when they perceive that the operating performance for the current period will be poor, they tend to select as many income decreasing rules and procedures as possible and thereby reduce net income further in order to enhance future earnings.[15] Such a strategy is referred to as taking a "big bath." Ways to minimize the possible manipulating of net income through LCM procedures are to (1) apply LCM procedures to either categories of inventory or to the entire inventory and perhaps (2) have a standard-setting body require that LCM procedures always be applied to some specific inventory level (i.e., items, category, or total).

Finally, critics question the relevance of the financial statement numbers that LCM procedures produce because the resulting inventory value is neither a historical cost value nor a market value. A response to this criticism is that questions can always be raised as to the relevance of numbers that are substituted for historical cost numbers, but to make no effort to improve the relevance of re-

This Is the Real World

The following excerpts from an article in **USA Today** illustrate the financial statement effects of inventory write-downs.

Huge inventory write-offs taken this year by technology companies could instantly turn into dramatic profit when the industry finally recovers.

A nuance of accounting will give firms . . . an artificial boost to their profit—and possibly their stocks—if they sell the massive amounts of inventory they've written down. For goods that firms have completely written off, any sales mean[s] a 100% profit.

Nortel could get a sizable bump to profit if it sells even a fraction of the $650 million of inventory and other manufacturing items it has just written off. That write-off equals 14% of expected second-quarter revenue.

Micron Technology last month wrote down the value of its inventory of memory products by $260 million, or 32% of revenue for the quarter ended May 31. If Micron sells that inventory at or above market prices, its earnings will be higher than they would have been before the write-down.

SOURCE: USA Today, *Monday, July 16, 2001.*

---

[15]For example, within a certain range of earnings, executive compensation plans frequently provide managers with a bonus that is an increasing function of earnings. As long as earnings are within the bonus range, managers should be motivated to increase earnings in order to increase their bonus. However, if it is clear that earnings will fall outside the range (either below the lower bound or above the upper bound), then any additional earnings will not be accompanied by an increased bonus. Under these circumstances, managers might be motivated to make choices that will decrease earnings. Any reduction in earnings today, due to recognizing an inventory holding loss, for example, will result in higher earnings in the future. Managers might desire to manipulate earnings for other reasons; the LCM rule is just one tool that could be used to achieve that purpose.

ported numbers dooms the financial reporting system to its present status and denies it the opportunity to evolve and improve.

Long-Lived Assets

Because operating assets are held for long periods of time in relation to current assets, the impact of changing prices on operating assets is more dramatic, as was illustrated in the opening scenarios. However, of all the assets on a balance sheet, it is most difficult to obtain relevant information concerning current assessments of the cash flow potential of such assets. Three reasons for this difficulty were discussed earlier in the chapter: (1) Market quotations are not as readily available for long-lived assets in comparison to other assets; (2) even when market quotations are available, because such quotations are based on the presumption that the assets will be sold, the quotation often is not relevant because the company plans to continue using the assets; and (3) determining a fair value based upon cash flows cannot be used because of the synergy that exists among operational assets, which causes difficulty in separating the cash flows due to one asset from the cash flows of all other assets.

Because of these problems in determining relevant numbers for long-lived assets concerning their cash flow potential, U.S. GAAP has persisted in reporting historical-cost-based numbers for long-lived assets. But even U.S. GAAP in recent years has begun reporting nonhistorical-cost-based numbers for all long-lived assets (except land) through the use of impairment tests.

Currently, U.S. GAAP has the following requirements concerning the financial reporting of long-lived assets.

- Long-lived tangible and intangible assets (either individually or as groups) that are being held for sale are reported at the lower of their carrying amount or their net realizable value (i.e., selling price less costs of disposal). These assets are not depreciated or amortized while waiting to be sold and are reported separately from other assets.
- Long-lived tangible and intangible assets that are being used in the operations of the business are reported at the lower of their carrying amount or fair value. These assets are depreciated or amortized while continuing to be used.
- Goodwill (and similar intangible assets with indeterminate useful lives) is reported on the balance sheet at the lower of its historical cost or implied fair value. It is not amortized but is subject to an impairment test.

Long-Lived Assets to Be Sold

EXTENDING
the Concept

Of the attributes listed earlier in the chapter, which ones are used to measure long-lived assets?

A long-lived tangible or intangible asset (or asset group)[16] that is to be sold is reported at year-end at the lower of its (1) carrying amount or (2) fair value less costs of disposal (i.e., net realizable value), with a corresponding loss recognized in accordance with the requirements covered in Chapter 9. Since markets for used, long-lived, specialized assets (or groups of assets) often are not readily available, determining net realizable value is usually difficult. Nevertheless, the com-

---

[16]The term "asset group" refers to all assets and liabilities to be jointly disposed. For purposes of balance sheet reporting, it is not necessary to identify whether the asset group qualifies as a component of an entity. The balance sheet reporting is the same, whether or not the asset group qualifies as a component of an entity.

pany must use due diligence to obtain a selling price for the asset and thus have a reasonable estimate of the asset's net realizable value.

As given in Chapter 9 and repeated here, all of the following criteria must be met at the balance sheet date for the asset (or asset group) to be considered as held for sale. Failure to meet these criteria at the balance sheet date means that the assets (or asset group) must be reported as held for use.

- Management has committed itself to a plan to sell a component of the business entity,
- The asset is available for immediate sale in its present condition,
- An active program to locate a buyer has been initiated,
- The sale of the asset (or asset group) is probable, and will occur within one year,
- The asking price is reasonable, and
- It is unlikely that significant changes to the plan will be made.

Any long-lived asset (or asset group) that is being held for sale is presented separately in the balance sheet. Also, the assets and liabilities of any asset group are not netted (or offset). *SFAS No. 144* does not give any guidance as to the balance sheet classification in which these assets, including liabilities of an asset group, should be reported. However, if the assets are taken out of service while waiting to be sold, it seems that they (including all liabilities of the asset group) should be reported in their respective current classification because of the one-year requirement that has to be met for them to qualify as being held for sale. But if the assets continue to be used while waiting to be sold, it seems then that they should be reported in their normal balance sheet classification (i.e., property, plant, and equipment), making sure that they are separately reported from other assets.

While long-lived assets are waiting to be sold, no further depreciation or amortization is recorded. Further, *additional losses may be recognized* as the fair value of the asset (or asset group) continues to fall. Or *a gain is recognized* if the fair value of the asset (or asset group) recovers, but a gain cannot be recognized for an amount in excess of the cumulative losses previously recognized. According to *SFAS No. 144*, the adjustment for such gains/losses is to be done to the "carrying amount," meaning that the accumulated depreciation account is adjusted for any impairment loss on tangible assets rather than changing the asset's historical cost.

To illustrate the accounting for asset impairments, assume that Travis Oil Inc., as part of its exploration activities, uses special seismic equipment that provides information about the possibility of oil reserves in an area. The equipment currently in use was purchased on January 1, 2004, at a price of $500,000, and is being depreciated on a straight-line basis over 10 years, with no salvage value. During 2006, more technologically advanced equipment became available. Management at Travis Oil realizes that not using it would place the company at a competitive disadvantage. Accordingly, during the fourth quarter of 2006, Travis Oil made arrangements to lease the new equipment and began looking for a buyer for the old equipment. For illustration purposes, assume that the old equipment's approximate net realizable value is $50,000 and that the book value of the old equipment, prior to any write-down, is $350,000, which is the asset's historical cost of $500,000 less three years of depreciation. So, the impairment loss is $300,000, which is the difference between the old equipment's book value of $350,000 and its net realizable value of $50,000. The journal entry to record the write-down is as follows:

Impairment Loss on Equipment   300,000
        Accumulated Depreciation   300,000
    To record an impairment loss on a long-
    lived asset or asset group.

Should plans change for selling the asset or should the criteria to qualify as being held for sale no longer be met, the asset (or asset group) is reclassified as held for use. In doing so, the asset (or asset group) is recorded at the lower of (1) the fair value of the asset (or asset group) on the date of reclassifying as held for use and (2) the carrying value of the asset (or asset group) on the date of the decision to sell, adjusted for any depreciation or amortization since the date of the decision to sell.[17]

Long-Lived Assets Being Held for Use

For long-lived assets (including an asset group) that are continuing to be used, an assessment as to whether an asset (or asset group) is impaired is made whenever events or changes in circumstances indicate that the carrying amount of an asset (or asset group) may not be recoverable. The FASB gave the following examples of events or changes in circumstances that might indicate an asset (or asset group) is impaired:

1. A significant decrease in the market price of the asset (or asset group).
2. A significant adverse change in the extent or manner in which the asset (or asset group) is used or a significant physical change in the asset (or asset group).
3. A significant adverse change in legal factors or in the business climate that could affect the value of the asset (or asset group), including an adverse action or assessment by a regulator.
4. An accumulation of costs significantly in excess of the amount originally expected to acquire or construct an asset (or asset group).
5. A current-period operating or cash flow loss combined with a history of operating or cash flow losses or a projection or forecast that demonstrates continuing losses associated with the long-lived asset (or asset group).
6. A current expectation that, more likely than not, a long-lived asset (or asset group) will be sold or otherwise disposed of significantly before the end of its previously estimated useful life.

When such an event or circumstance occurs, a **recoverability** (or **impairment**) **test** is conducted. A long-lived asset (or asset group) in use is impaired *when the sum of the* undiscounted *future cash flows over its useful life[18] (including cash from disposal) is expected to be less than the asset's book value.* In other words, the asset is impaired when the sum of future cash flows is less than the book value. This is only a test to determine impairment. It is not the amount of the impairment loss.

By not discounting the cash flows, the recoverability test is biased against concluding that an asset is impaired. Popular opinion among financial analysts and accounting regulators was (and still is) that companies use asset impairments as a way to report desired earnings. Similar to inventory write-downs, asset impairments cause current earnings to be less in the current year but then result in higher future earnings because of lower depreciation (or amortization) charges. If a com-

---

[17]See Chapter 9, under discontinued operations, for examples of how this gain/loss is computed.
[18]The useful life of an asset group is based on the remaining useful life of the primary asset of the group, which is the principal long-lived identifiable asset that is the most significant asset in generating cash flows.

pany is reporting low earnings anyway, there might be motivation to take a big bath in the current year by recording an asset impairment so as to enhance future earnings. Not discounting the cash flows results in fewer asset write-downs and gives some protection that only those asset impairments that actually occurred will be recorded. Also, not discounting the cash flows has the additional advantage of avoiding small write-downs in the current year that may reverse in the near future.

When the recoverability test indicates that a long-lived asset (or asset group) is impaired, the asset (or asset group) is *written down to its fair value (not the net realizable value as is done for assets that are to be sold), and an impairment loss is recognized*. The reason for not valuing the assets at their net realizable value is that disposal costs are not relevant when the assets are to be used in operations. Regarding determining fair value, the FASB indicated that the best source of fair value is quoted market prices. However, since such quotations are often not available, particularly for specialized assets, the FASB indicated that other valuation techniques can be used, including discounted cash flow information.

Following the recognition of an impairment loss, *the fair value of the asset (or asset group) is depreciated over its remaining useful life, and the asset (or asset group) is never written up in later years to reflect a reversal of an impairment loss*. This rule eliminates the possibility of recognizing a huge impairment loss in one period and then reversing the write-off in another period. For example, in 1992, Federal Express Corp. recognized an impairment loss of $254 million during the third quarter—a period of already significant losses—and then reversed approximately $25 million of the write-down in the next quarter and an additional $15 million in the first quarter of the following fiscal year.

The impairment rules are summarized in Exhibit 10-4.

EXHIBIT 10-4

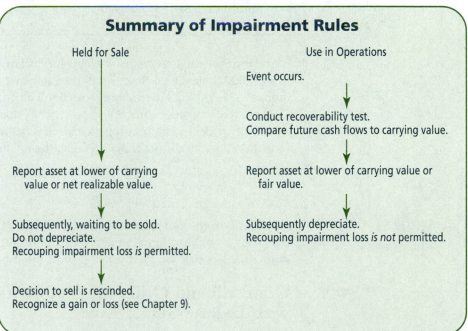

To illustrate the application of the impairment rules, assume that on May 1, 2004, Stillwell Corp. conducts a recoverability test and determines that the undiscounted cash flows of the asset group will be less than the carrying value. Accordingly, an impairment loss must be determined. On May 1, 2004, Stillwell gathers the following data about the various assets comprising the asset group.

Asset	Carrying Value
Inventory	$ 150,000
Long-Lived Asset 1	200,000
Long-Lived Asset 2	400,000
Long-Lived Asset 3	800,000
Total carrying value	$1,550,000

Stillwell also determines that the fair value of the asset group is $1,359,000, with the fair value of the inventory being $120,000. *The amount of the impairment loss is the difference between the carrying value and the fair value*, which, in this case, is a loss of $191,000. The first step in accounting for that loss is to write down all current assets and liabilities and all long-term assets that are not covered under *SFAS No. 144* to their fair value.[19] Thus, inventory is written down to $120,000. The remaining amount of the impairment loss (i.e., $161,000) is allocated among the long-lived assets in relation to their respective carrying amounts, as shown in Illustration 10-6.

ILLUSTRATION 10-6

Allocation of Impairment Loss

Asset	Carrying Value	Allocation Percentage	Allocation of Impairment Loss	Adjusted Carrying Value
Long-Lived Asset 1	$ 200,000	1/7	$ 23,000	$ 177,000
Long-Lived Asset 2	400,000	2/7	46,000	354,000
Long-Lived Asset 3	800,000	4/7	92,000	708,000
Allocation base	$1,400,000		$161,000	$1,239,000

However, *no asset can be written down below its fair value*. So if its fair value is $375,000, Long-Lived Asset 2 will have to be written up to $375,000, and an additional $21,000 will have to be allocated to Long-Lived Assets 1 and 3, based upon their relative carrying values. Of importance is that this allocation is done primarily for future depreciation purposes and does not affect the actual journal entry to record the loss impairment. Accordingly, the following journal entry is prepared:

Impairment Loss on Asset Group	191,000	
Inventory		30,000
Accumulated Depreciation[20]		161,000

Long-lived assets that are to be disposed of through means other than by sale, such as by abandonment or by distribution to owners, are accounted for the same as assets that are held for use, until the time that they are disposed.

Goodwill and Other Intangible Assets with Indeterminate Lives

Recall from Chapter 5 that goodwill is computed in a residual manner. That is, when a company pays more than the underlying book value for the net assets of

---

[19]Examples of long-lived assets not covered by *SFAS No. 144* include goodwill and any other intangible asset not being amortized, financial instruments, and deferred tax assets.

[20]Assuming that the company uses only one accumulated depreciation account and none of the impaired assets are intangible assets.

another company, that excess is first allocated to the identifiable assets whose fair values are greater than their carrying amount, and any remaining excess is assigned as the cost of goodwill. When assessing whether goodwill is impaired for financial reporting purposes, a similar measurement process is used. Thus, the amount by which goodwill is impaired is measured in the following steps:

1. Compute the fair value of a reporting unit.
2. Compute the fair value of the individual assets and liabilities of the reporting unit.
3. The current value of goodwill is the difference between the amount in Step 1 and the amount in Step 2.
4. Goodwill is impaired when the amount in Step 3 is less than the carrying value of goodwill, and this is also the amount of the impairment loss.

Once an impairment loss is recognized, subsequent reversal is prohibited.

Any intangible asset that is not being amortized because its useful life is indefinite is evaluated at least once each reporting period to determine if events and circumstances continue to support the fact that the asset has an indefinite life. When it is determined that an intangible asset no longer has an indefinite life, an impairment loss is recognized for the amount by which the asset's carrying amount exceeds its fair value. The asset's fair value is subsequently amortized over the useful life of the intangible asset.

Financial Reporting

Impairment losses are reported as part of income from continuing operations, in the other income/loss section. It is unlikely that any such impairment losses could ever be considered an extraordinary item, since to do so requires that the event be both infrequent in occurrence and unusual in nature, given the environment

This Is the Real World

The notion that financial analysts and accounting regulators would accuse managers of trying to minimize assets on the balance sheet appears confusing. After all, a strong balance sheet should signal investors and creditors that the company's financial position is strong. Although managers certainly are aware of the picture sent by the balance sheet, the following excerpt from a *Wall Street Journal* article suggests that the SEC believes managers use asset write-downs in order to enhance future earnings.

"The Securities and Exchange Commission's year-long campaign against corporate accounting abuses seems to be having an impact. The total amount of corporate write-offs in some major areas dropped 24% in 1999's first half to $25.8 billion from $33.9 billion a year earlier. The decline in these corporate write-offs is an important indicator of how chief executive and chief financial officers lately have been handling their bookkeeping. In recent years, companies have been reporting increasingly large hits to earnings, which the SEC considers fruitful ground for accounting abuses. By

taking large hits to earnings early in the game—and including inappropriate items in these write-offs—companies can make their future earnings glow, impressing Wall Street."

To explain, assets can be viewed in two different ways: 1) as a measure of future earnings to a company, or 2) as a measure of future expenses. Depending on the asset and the circumstances of the company, both views are appropriate. So one sure way to enhance future earnings is to accelerate the recognition of expenses by writing off assets. Even though one purpose of SFAS #121 by the FASB was to mitigate the manipulation of earnings through asset write-downs, the SEC's continuing battle on write-downs indicates that the standard did not eliminate the subjective nature of determining whether an asset impairment has occurred, and, if so, by how much the asset should be written down.

SOURCE: *"Amount of Certain Corporate Write-Offs Falls 24% after SEC Battle on Abuses,"* The Wall Street Journal *(September 13, 1999): A4.*

in which the company operates. If material in amount, an impairment loss is reported separately; otherwise, an impairment loss is included with some other amount.

Non-U.S. GAAP Financial Reporting Practices

INTERNATIONAL

Many countries, including the United Kingdom, The Netherlands, and Hong Kong, allow long-lived assets to be revalued to a current cost amount for financial reporting purposes, and many financial statement readers think that such information is more relevant than the historical-cost-based numbers.

Some questions must be addressed when a current-cost-based financial reporting system is used. For instance, should the revaluation take place for all long-lived assets, only tangible assets, or only for those assets that are not specialized in nature and have a quoted market value? How often should revaluations occur? What account should be credited when assets are written up: a stockholders' equity account or an income statement account? If a stockholders' equity account is credited, how should this amount be reported in subsequent periods (e.g., as part of retained earnings, as contributed capital by the owners, etc.)? And what happens to this revaluation amount when the revalued asset is sold? Also, should depreciation be based on the historical cost amount or on the current cost amount? Then, too, what is meant by current cost? Does it mean the amount at which a replacement asset can be acquired, or is it the amount at which the current asset can be disposed? Given the many alternatives, it should not be surprising that there are several different variations of current cost systems throughout the world.

In Hong Kong, companies have the option of recording long-lived assets at either historical cost less accumulated depreciation or at current cost.[21] If current cost is chosen, companies must revalue assets at regular intervals to ensure that the carrying value of the assets at the balance sheet date approximates their current cost. In addition, if one asset is revalued, then all other assets within the same class (e.g., land)[22] must be revalued at the same time.

To illustrate Hong Kong's revaluation procedures, assume that Asian Parkview, a real estate investment company, decided to record all of its holdings in buildings and land at current cost. Prior to the revaluation, the carrying values of all the assets were as follows (in HK$):

Buildings	HK$45,000,000
Less accumulated depreciation	(20,000,000)
Land	15,000,000
Total	HK$40,000,000

---

[21]*Statement of Standard Accounting Practice* 2.117, "Property, Plant, and Equipment," issued July 1995 and reviewed May 1999.

[22]Hong Kong GAAP stipulates nine different kinds of asset classes: (1) land, (2) land and buildings, (3) construction in progress, (4) machinery, (5) ships, (6) aircraft, (7) motor vehicles, (8) furniture and fixtures, and (9) office furniture.

Recording the Revaluation

To effect the revaluation, professional appraisers were hired who determined that the market value of the buildings was HK$30 million (as compared to the carrying amount of HK$25 million) and the market value of the land was HK$25 million. Accordingly, Asian Parkview prepared the following journal entry:

Land	10,000,000	
Accumulated Depreciation	5,000,000	
Revaluation Reserve (Buildings)		5,000,000
Revaluation Reserve (Land)		10,000,000
To record an upward revaluation for		
land and buildings.		

To the extent possible, the adjustment for the buildings is made through the accumulated depreciation account. If it is necessary to adjust the buildings by an amount greater than the HK$20 million in the accumulated depreciation account, two accounts are debited. First, the accumulated depreciation account is completely eliminated, and then the building account is debited for the remaining revaluation amount. The **revaluation reserve** accounts are reported in stockholders' equity and do not affect current or accumulated earnings.

Recording Subsequent Depreciation Charges

Continuing with the example, assume that the remaining useful life of the buildings is 10 years with no residual value. After the revaluation, the depreciation base for the buildings is the current cost amount of HK$30 million, and using straight-line depreciation, the annual depreciation expense is HK$3 million. In addition, the revaluation reserve that is related to the buildings (HK$5 million) is amortized to retained earnings over the life of the buildings. Thus, the following entries are made annually:

Depreciation Expense	3,000,000	
Accumulated Depreciation		3,000,000
Revaluation Reserve (Buildings)	500,000	
Retained Earnings		500,000

From these entries, it can be seen that under Hong Kong GAAP, an upward revaluation results in more expense being recognized over the life of the assets. This result is due to the revaluation reserve being amortized directly to retained earnings, instead of using it as an offset to depreciation expense.

Recording Subsequent Disposals of Assets

Now assume that the land that had been revalued to HK$25 million is sold for HK$30 million. Then, the following journal entry is made to record the sale:

Cash	30,000,000	
Land		25,000,000
Gain on Sale of Land		5,000,000
Revaluation Reserve (Land)	10,000,000	
Retained Earnings		10,000,000

The total gain on the sale of land is equal to the difference between the sales price of HK$30 million and the asset's new carrying value of HK$25, which is $10 million less than it would have been had the asset been recorded at historical cost. The revaluation reserve is closed to retained earnings, without affecting operating income.

Downward Revaluation

The accounting for a downward revaluation is considerably different from an upward revaluation. If the appraised value of the buildings is $15 million rather than the carrying amount of $20 million, then the accumulated depreciation account is increased by $5 million, but the corresponding debit is to a *loss account*. Subsequently, if an upward revaluation is made on the same assets, a gain is recognized (instead of crediting the revaluation reserve) to the extent that a previous revaluation loss had been recognized.

Such current cost procedures required by Hong Kong GAAP appear to be becoming the norm for countries that implement a current-cost accounting system, and they are also consistent with international GAAP. The effects of an upward revaluation on financial statements in any particular year are to increase assets and stockholders' equity and to decrease subsequent earnings because of increased depreciation charges. Thus, profitability ratios, such as return-on-assets and return-on-equity, will be decreased relative to what they would have been if based on historical cost numbers. However, debt-to-equity ratios are favorably impacted.

Summary

Regarding the financial reporting of assets, the goal is to report information that is relevant for financial statement readers to project the amount, timing, and uncertainty of future cash flows. To do this requires that, for many assets, various measures are substituted for historical cost numbers when the balance sheet is prepared. Substituting these measures raises the issues of (1) how to measure an individual asset's potential future cash flows, (2) which measure best reports those future cash flows, and (3) the trade-off between relevance and reliability when some measure other than historical cost is reported. Different cultures give different answers to these questions and issues.

On the balance sheet, cash is valued by counting it. The primary problem in reporting cash is determining what is meant by cash. Cash is money—that which is accepted as a medium of exchange. Cash includes coins, currency, checking account balances, savings accounts, certified checks, money orders, and cashiers' checks. Any of these items that have restrictions placed on them that prevent their immediate use as a medium of exchange, such as amounts in foreign banks or compensating balances, are not included in cash. Cash equivalents are those securities that are so near cash that there is little risk of loss. To qualify as a cash equivalent, the security must be highly liquid and have a maturity date that is 90 days or less (as a rule of thumb) from the date it was acquired. When cash equivalents are reported with cash, the balance sheet caption is labeled "Cash and cash equivalents."

Receivables are reported at net realizable value, which can be determined using either an income statement approach or a balance sheet approach. The income statement approach computes the bad debts expense amount for the year; the amount so computed is also the year-end adjusting entry amount. The balance sheet approach computes the balance of the allowance for doubtful accounts, and the year-end adjusting entry is then determined by comparing that ending balance amount to the current balance of the allowance account. Under either method, uncollectible receivables are written off against the allowance account.

Because of their relatively low risk and high liquidity, accounts receivable are used to finance a company's short-term need for cash. The financing can take the form of pledging, transferring with recourse, or transferring without recourse. When accounts receivable are pledged, the receivables are reclassified from the typical accounts receivable account to an "accounts receivable pledged" account. The major accounting differences between the two types of transfers are (1) the recording of a liability, as opposed to writing off the accounts receivable and (2) the matter of who incurs losses due to uncollectible accounts. When a transfer of receivables meets all the criteria as specified by the FASB to qualify as a sale of the receivables, the accounts receivable are written off the transferor's books; otherwise, a liability is recorded when the transfer does not meet all the criteria. For a transfer without recourse, the factor incurs losses due to receivables being uncollectible; otherwise, the transferor incurs those losses. For both types of transfers, a financing fee, or loss, is recognized.

Inventories are reported at the lower-of-cost-or-market, where market is defined as the middle of three values: (1) net realizable value (i.e., ceiling), (2) replacement cost, and (3) net realizable value less a normal profit (i.e., floor). LCM procedures are applied in two steps. The first step is determining which of these three values is the market value. The second step is selecting the lower of that market value or the historical cost amount. The lower of these two amounts is reported as the value of inventory. LCM procedures can be applied to individual items, classifications of inventory, or the total inventory. The results are more conservative—result in lower values for assets and net income—when they are applied to the individual items of inventory. Although LCM procedures are criticized, the method is still well accepted throughout the world.

Long-lived assets (or asset groups) that are to be sold are reported at the lower of their carrying value or net realizable value, and impairment losses are recognized. Such assets are not depreciated while they are waiting to be disposed. In subsequent years, further losses may be recognized, or previous impairment losses may be reversed. Long-lived assets (or asset groups) that are still in use are periodically submitted to an impairment test, which is done by comparing the asset's carrying amount to its expected undiscounted cash flows. When the carrying amount is greater, the asset is determined to be impaired and an impairment loss is recognized for the difference between the asset's carrying amount and its fair value. Subsequently, reversals of an impairment loss are prohibited. Goodwill and other such intangible assets with indeterminate lives are also subject to an impairment test. Goodwill is determined to be impaired when a newly computed value for goodwill is less than its book value. In that case, goodwill is written down to the newly computed value, and an impairment loss is recognized.

APPENDIX: Discounting Notes Receivable

Just as a company can use its accounts receivable as a source of cash by pledging or factoring them as shown in the chapter, so, too, can it use its notes receivable as a source of cash by **discounting** them. The accounting problems connected with discounting notes receivable are (1) determining whether a sale has occurred so that the appropriate accounting and reporting are done (similar to the accounting problem in accounting for transferring accounts receivable) and (2) computing the amount to be received.

Regarding the first issue, determining whether a note is sold or is a source of borrowing is done according to the criteria on pages 444–445. Those discounting of notes transactions that meet all three criteria are recorded as a sale and those that do not are recorded as a borrowing. *When notes are sold, they are removed from the books and a gain/loss is recognized.*

Regarding the second issue, the amount of cash that will be received when a note is discounted is computed through the following steps.

1. *Determine the maturity value of the note*, which is the principal plus any interest, where interest is computed according to the formula for simple interest:

$$\text{Interest} = \text{Principal} \times \text{Interest Rate} \times \text{Time}$$

Then, the maturity value is determined as:

$$\text{Maturity Value} = \text{Principal} + \text{Interest}$$

2. *Compute the amount of interest the bank will earn*, which is referred to as the discount amount. This discount amount is computed by multiplying the maturity value of the note by the discount interest rate and the fraction of the year remaining until the note matures. Expressed as a formula, the discount amount is determined in the following way:

$$\text{Discount Amount} = \text{Maturity Value} \times \text{Discount Rate} \times \text{Time}$$

3. The final step is to compute the amount of cash to be received, which is computed by subtracting the amount in Step 2 from the amount in Step 1.

$$\text{Proceeds} = \text{Maturity Value} - \text{Discount Amount}$$

Discounting a Customer's Note

To illustrate, on June 1, Richardson's Boat Store sold a boat to a customer and as part of the payment accepted a 180-day, 8% note in the amount of $20,000. On September 10, Richardson's discounted the note at its local bank, incurring a 12% discount rate. The amount of cash Richardson's will receive is computed as follows:

1. Computing the maturity value:

$$\text{Interest} = \$20,000 \times 0.08 \times 180/360 \text{ days} = \$800$$
$$\text{Maturity Value} = \$20,000 + \$800 = \$20,800$$

2. Computing the discount amount:

$$\text{Discount Amount} = \$20,800 \times 0.12 \times 80/360 \text{ days} = \$554.67$$

In this calculation, it is important to note that the discount rate of 12% is used and not the interest rate that is specified on the note receivable. Also, the number of days (i.e., 80) the bank or finance company will hold the note is used in the formula. (For simplicity, it is assumed that each month has 30 days and that there are 360 days in a year.)

3. Computing the cash proceeds:

$$\text{Cash} = \$20,800 - \$554.67 = \$20,245.33$$

Depending upon whether the discounting is considered a sale or a borrowing, the appropriate journal entries follow, with all amounts rounded to the nearest dollar.

Transaction Is Considered a Sale (i.e., without recourse)			Transaction Is Considered a Borrowing (i.e., with recourse)		
Cash	20,245		Cash	20,245	
Note Receivable		20,000	Note Payable to Factor		20,000
Gain on Sale of Note Receivable		245	Interest Revenue		245

These journal entries are similar to those prepared for assigning accounts receivable. Subsequent entries depend upon whether the discounting transaction was considered a sale or a borrowing and whether the customer pays the amount when due. Thus, there are four scenarios.

1. The discounting transaction was considered a sale, and the customer paid the amount owed when it was due.
2. The discounting transaction was considered a sale, and the customer did not pay the amount owed when it was due.
3. The discounting transaction was considered a borrowing, and the customer paid the amount owed when it was due.
4. The discounting transaction was considered a borrowing, and the customer did not pay the amount owed when it was due.

Regarding the accounting for when the discounting transaction is a sale (Scenarios 1 and 2), no subsequent journal entries are necessary because the company acquiring the note has assumed all risks and benefits of collection, and the company discounting the note receivable has written off the note and has not recorded any liability to the factor.

Regarding the accounting for when the discounting transaction is considered a borrowing and the customer pays the amount owed, the subsequent entry is to write off both the customer's note receivable and the obligation to the factor. When the customer does not pay the amount owed, then—since the discounting was done with recourse—the company discounting the note pays to the financial institution the maturity amount of the note plus any protest fee charged.

To illustrate the accounting for a note discounted with recourse that is not collected at maturity, suppose in the prior example that on the note's maturity date, Richardson's was notified by the bank that the customer had not paid the amount owed. Therefore, Richardson's paid the bank the maturity value of $20,800 plus a $50 protest fee. Then, Richardson's would prepare the following journal entry:

Note Payable to Factor	20,000	
Note Receivable	850	
Cash		20,850

To pay the bank the maturity amount of the note plus protest fee and to establish the amount owed by the customer.

This entry reflects the "with recourse" nature of the discounting transaction. And, since the balance in the note receivable account is now $20,850, it also shows that the customer is still expected to pay the maturity amount—and the protest fee. Usually, interest continues to accrue on the note from the maturity date until it is paid.

Discounting a Company's Own Note

Another situation in which discounting procedures are used is when a company borrows money by discounting its own notes. For example, Purple Crayon Bookstore borrowed money from a local financial institution and issued in return a 90-day, $20,000 note payable that the bank discounted at 12% and remitted the difference to Purple Crayon. Borrowing money on a discounted basis means that the total amount to be repaid when the note matures will be $20,000. Thus, when the note is signed, some amount less than $20,000 will be received. Determining the amount Purple Crayon will receive when borrowing on a discounted basis is done using the same three steps as outlined previously for discounting a customer's note receivable.

1. Determine the maturity value of the note.
2. Compute the discount amount.
3. Compute the amount of the cash proceeds.

For the Purple Crayon example,

1. The maturity value of the note is the amount Purple Crayon Bookstore will pay the bank in 90 days, which is $20,000.
2. The discount amount is computed according to the following formula:

$$\text{Discount Amount} = \$20,000 \times 0.12 \times 90/360 = \$600$$

3. The cash that Purple Crayon actually receives is $19,400, which is the difference between the maturity value of $20,000 (Step 1) and the discount amount of $600 (Step 2).

Purple Crayon prepares the following journal entry to record the borrowing:

Cash	19,400	
Discount on Note Payable	600	
Note Payable to Factor		20,000
To borrow money by discounting a note.		

Finally, the $600 is recognized in a straight-line manner as interest expense over the 90-day period. If the fiscal year-end occurs within that 90-day period, the portion of the $600 to recognize as interest expense is computed in proportion to the number of days elapsed before year-end in relation to the total number of days of the note.

Questions

1. Identify some environmental or cultural factors that influence whether a country might embrace fair values or historical costs for financial reporting purposes. From your answer, write a brief statement as to why a worldwide shift to reporting fair values on a balance sheet may occur more quickly in some countries and, perhaps, take much longer in others.

2. Indicate whether each of the following would be classified under "Cash and cash equivalents" on a balance sheet. If the item should not be classified as Cash and cash equivalents, indicate its appropriate classification.

   • Money order
   • Certified check

- Postdated check
- Money held in a fund for the specific purpose of paying a bond at maturity
- Certificate of deposit that matures six months after the date that it was purchased

3. Identify the two criteria an asset must meet to be classified as a cash equivalent.

4. Discuss how a bank overdraft is reported on a classified balance sheet when (a) the company has other bank accounts at the same bank that have money in them and (b) the company does not have other bank accounts at the same bank.

5. To maintain a line of credit, a company is required by the bank to keep a compensating balance of $25,000. What is a compensating balance, and how is it reported on a classified balance sheet?

6. Explain the difference between the direct write-off method and the allowance method for recognizing bad debts expense. Why is the allowance method accepted under U.S. GAAP, but the direct write-off method is not?

7. Explain the income statement approach and the balance sheet approach for estimating uncollectible accounts.

8. What is the effect on net accounts receivable and working capital from writing off a receivable as uncollectible?

9. Distinguish between (a) pledging, (b) factoring with recourse, and (c) factoring without recourse.

10. Describe in your words the conditions that must be met for a transfer of receivables (either accounts receivable or notes receivable) to be considered a sale.

11. Why are inventory holding losses recognized, but inventory holding gains are not?

12. Define "market" as it applies to the lower-of-cost-or-market rule for valuing inventory. How are the ceiling and floor calculated? How does the meaning of market value differ according to international GAAP?

13. What is the purpose of having a ceiling and a floor when determining the market value of inventory? In a business setting, what are the circumstances that cause the ceiling and floor to become the market value of inventory? (*Note:* Do not give as your answer the procedures for determining when the ceiling and floor become the market values.)

14. What are some criticisms—and responses to those criticisms—of the lower-of-cost-or-market rule as applied to inventories?

15. A company stopped manufacturing a line of products and discontinued using the machinery and equipment used in manufacturing that line. Should the idle machinery and equipment continue to be depreciated? How should the idle machinery and equipment be classified on the balance sheet?

16. Describe when a recoverability test as it relates to long-lived assets that will continue to be used is conducted and what the recoverability test is. When the recoverability test indicates an asset is impaired, how is the amount of the impairment loss computed?

17. When a long-lived asset (or group of assets) is retired from service and waiting to be disposed, at what amount should it be reported on a year-end balance sheet? In what category should it be classified? Could retiring an asset from service in the current year have any impact on net income of a future year?

18. Where in the income statement (e.g., extraordinary items, discontinued operations, etc.) is an impairment loss reported for (a) assets that are continuing to be used and (b) a group of assets that are to be sold?

19. What is the effect on total assets, net book value, and net income of an upward revaluation of a depreciable fixed asset according to international GAAP as implemented in Hong Kong? How are the net income amounts for subsequent years affected? How would your answer differ if the depreciable fixed asset was written down?

20. (Multiple-choice) According to Hong Kong GAAP and international GAAP, the correct accounting for the amount credited to the revaluation reserve includes which of the following procedures?
    a. Amortize the amount over the life of the asset through income as an adjustment to depreciation expense.
    b. Amortize the amount over the life of the asset directly to retained earnings.
    c. Do not amortize the account so that it will be informative of the total revaluations made by the company.
    d. All of the above are acceptable alternatives.

21. (Appendix) What does "discounting a note receivable" mean? Describe the three steps in discounting a note to determine the amount of cash proceeds.

22. (Appendix) Staley Company discounts the following three notes at Big State Bank and is charged a discount rate of 12%. Compute the amount of cash that will be received from each note. Round all amounts to the nearest dollar and assume that each month has 30 days.
    a. A 90-day, 8% note receivable for $10,000 that Staley has held for 60 days.
    b. A 90-day, 14% note receivable for $10,000 that Staley has held for 30 days.
    c. Staley's own 90-day, $10,000 note.

Exercises

Exercise 10-1: Defining Amounts to Be Reported as Cash. Determine whether the following items should be classified as cash, cash equivalents, or something else. If something else, specify within what account on the balance sheet the item belongs.

1. A bank certificate of deposit that matures 90 days from date of purchase
2. A Treasury Bill that matures six months from date of purchase
3. Currency that is contractually restricted for use in retiring long-term debt
4. A check that is postdated one week after the balance sheet date
5. A cashiers' check
6. A share of stock in Microsoft
7. Stock in a mutual fund where the brokerage house allows a limited number of checks to be written on the fund
8. Checking account balance
9. Money order
10. Travel advances to employees not yet cleared by travel documents
11. Savings account balance
12. Petty cash

Exercise 10-2: Cash and Cash Equivalents. As a junior accountant, you were given the following information and charged to determine the amount to report as "Cash and cash equivalents" on Cornell Company's current year's balance sheet.

1. Cornell Company had several checking accounts at First Union Bank. One checking account was used to pay payroll, and a balance of $5,000 was maintained in it. Another checking account was used for international exchanges, and its balance was overdrawn by $2,000 at the end of the year. The third checking account was used to pay purchases and operating expenses, and its reconciled balance at the end of the year was $20,100.

2. The petty cash balance in the general ledger was $500, but a review showed cash of $350 and receipts of $150.

3. Undeposited customer checks on the last day of business amounted to $1,200.

4. Cornell Company had a savings account of $150,000 at Third National Bank. The account is being used to accumulate an amount to pay some bonds that will mature in eight years.

5. Cornell buys and sells U.S. Treasury securities as a means of investing excess funds. It purchased $50,000 of such securities on September 20 that mature on February 20 and an additional $70,000 of such securities on November 30 that mature on May 30.

Exercise 10-3: Cash and Cash Equivalents. The following information was extracted from the records of T&R Company as of December 31, 2004, relating to its dealings with First Union Bank.

Checking account	$ 90,000
Money market account	25,000
90-day certificate of deposit, due March 15, 2005	70,000
180-day certificate of deposit, due February 28, 2005	30,000
Line of credit	170,000

How much should T&R report in its balance sheet as cash and cash equivalents?

Exercise 10-4: Journal Entries for Receivables. On December 31, 2005, Heidi's Pets, Inc., estimated that its bad debts expense for the period had been $5,000. Prior to any adjusting entry, the allowance for doubtful accounts had a debit balance of $500. During the first quarter of 2006, total receivables of $2,000 were written off, and subsequently receivables of $150 that had been written off were collected.
   Prepare the journal entries for these events.

Exercise 10-5: Estimating Bad Debts Expense. Ketchy Can Co. uses the allowance method to account for bad debts expense. Information relating to the company's accounts receivable as of December 31, 2004, prior to any adjusting entry to record bad debts expense for the year, is as follows:

Accounts receivable	$ 400,000
Allowance for doubtful accounts (credit balance)	10,000
Credit sales during 2004	1,125,000

Determine the amount of bad debts expense to be reported for the period, assuming that Ketchy Can estimates bad debts expense as (1) 1.5% of credit sales and (2) 6% of outstanding accounts receivable.

Exercise 10-6: Bad Debts Expense. Baker Industries estimates its bad debts expense (and the related net realizable value of the receivables) by analyzing its receivables. Based on such analysis, the company estimates its uncollectible accounts to be $10,000. Show the journal entry necessary in each of the following independent cases to record bad debts expense for the year.

1. Allowance for Uncollectible Accounts has a credit balance of $3,500.
2. Allowance for Uncollectible Accounts has a zero balance.
3. Allowance for Uncollectible Accounts has a debit balance of $4,200.

Exercise 10-7: Estimating Bad Debts Expense. The following account balances were obtained from the records of Anderson, Inc., as of December 31, 2004.

	Debit	Credit
Accounts receivable	$667,000	
Allowance for doubtful accounts		$ 2,000
Total sales		8,900,000
Credit sales		3,700,000

1. Assume that the company estimates bad debts expense based on credit sales, and that past experience has shown that approximately 2.5% of total credit sales will become uncollectible.
   a. Prepare the adjusting entry as of December 31, 2004, to record bad debts expense.
   b. What is the ending balance in the allowance for doubtful accounts?
   c. How would your answers change if prior to preparing any adjusting entry the allowance for doubtful accounts had a $1,500 debit balance?
2. Assume that the company estimates bad debts expense based on accounts receivable and that from past experience approximately 5% of the amounts owed will become uncollectible.
   a. Prepare the necessary adjusting entry as of December 31, 2004, to record bad debts expense.
   b. What is the ending balance in Allowance for Doubtful Accounts?
   c. How would your answers change if prior to preparing any adjusting entry, Allowance for Doubtful Accounts had a $1,500 debit balance?

Exercise 10-8: Uncollectible Accounts and Effects on Financial Statements. At the end of 2005, Smith & Company estimates that its bad debts for the current year will be 1% of sales, which totaled $300,000. The ending balance in Accounts Receivable is $40,000, and there is a $200 credit balance in Allowance for Doubtful Accounts before any adjusting entry for bad debts expense is prepared.

1. Compute the net realizable value of the accounts receivable before the adjusting entry to recognize bad debts expense for the year is recorded.
2. Prepare the journal entry to record bad debts expense for 2005.
3. Compute the net realizable value of the accounts receivable after preparing the journal entry to record bad debts expense, then write a conclusion as to what effect recognizing bad debts expense has upon the net realizable value of the receivables.
4. Based upon your previous answers, prepare a journal entry as of January 3, 2006, to write off as uncollectible a $400 amount owed by Jones & Sons.
5. Compute the net realizable value of the accounts receivable after writing off the Jones & Sons account, then write a conclusion as to what effect writing off an uncollectible account has upon the net realizable value of the receivables.

Exercise 10-9: Pledging/Factoring Accounts Receivable. On September 1, 2005, Red Rock Cycle Shop transferred $80,000 of accounts receivable to First State Bank, which advanced 80% of the amount to Red Rock. First State required Red Rock to sign a note payable in the amount of the advance, which bears interest at 1½% per month. Red Rock retains possession of the receivables, and any amounts received will be used to pay the note. The note was paid on October 1.

1. What is the nature of this transaction—is it a pledging of accounts receivable, or a factoring of accounts receivable? Defend your answer.
2. Prepare all necessary journal entries on September 1 and October 1.

Exercise 10-10: Factoring Accounts Receivable. Fast-n-Loose sells small, portable vacuum cleaners door to door. The typical contract requires the purchaser to make a small down payment and to make monthly payments for two years. At the end of each month, Fast-n-Loose factors its accounts receivable to a local finance company. On June 30, Fast-n-Loose factored $50,000 of accounts receivable to a factor and was charged a fee of 3%. Also, to cover sales returns, discounts, etc., the factor withheld 5% of the accounts receivable.

1. Prepare the necessary journal entries for transferring the receivables, assuming that (a) the transfer was done without recourse and (b) the transfer was done with recourse, assuming the obligation to the factor was $5,000.
2. Prepare the necessary journal entries for both scenarios in part (1) to settle with the factor, assuming that collections totaled $43,500, uncollectible accounts were $3,000, and sales returns, allowances, etc., totaled $3,500.

Exercise 10-11: Factoring Accounts Receivable. Castro & Son sells fine and custom-made jewelry. Sales on account are net/60, and customers are expected to arrange other financing during this time. To finance the acquisition of additional raw materials and finished goods inventory, Castro factors its receivables at Up-Town Bank and is charged a 5% factoring fee. During the current month, Castro transferred $100,000 of accounts receivable, and because of the historical high quality of its receivables, Castro was advanced $85,000.

1. Prepare the necessary journal entries for factoring the receivables, assuming that (a) the factoring qualifies as a sale and (b) the factoring does not qualify as a sale and there is a liability of $6,000 connected with the recourse provision.
2. Prepare the necessary journal entries for both scenarios in part (1) to settle with the factor, assuming that collections totaled $84,000, uncollectible accounts were $10,000, and sales returns, allowances, etc., totaled $6,000.

Exercise 10-12: Computing the Ceiling and Floor on Inventory. Kitty Express has partially completed scratching posts with a total sales value of $58,000 and projects that it will cost $20,000 to complete the units. The company's standard gross profit margin is 30% of sales. Determine the ceiling and floor prior to applying lower-of-cost-or-market procedures.

Exercise 10-13: Computing Lower-of-Cost-or-Market and Preparing Journal Entries. At the beginning of 2006, Pineapple Computers paid $1,000,000 for some computers that it intended to resell for $1,250,000. However, shortly after the purchase, technological changes made it impossible to sell the computers through regular sales channels, and now the replacement cost of the inventory is no more than $750,000. Recently, Pineapple found an overseas buyer who is willing to pay $960,000 for the computers, but Pineapple will have to pay freight, tariffs, and other charges totaling $100,000 to complete the sale.

1. Using the lower-of-cost-or-market procedures, determine the value at which the inventory should be reported in the financial statements.

2. Assuming that the appropriate lower-of-cost-or-market value for the inventory is $890,000 and that any holding loss is considered immaterial, prepare the necessary journal entry to write down Pineapple's inventory under (a) the direct method and (b) the allowance method, assuming Pineapple uses a perpetual inventory system.

Exercise 10-14: Lower-of-Cost-or-Market. Nelson Company uses the FIFO cost flow to value inventory items. Information pertaining to the company's inventory is as follows.

FIFO historical cost	$580,000
Replacement cost	$560,000
Estimated selling price	$720,000
Estimated costs to sell	$80,000
Normal profit margin	60% on sales

1. Determine the market value of the inventory.
2. Determine the lower-of-cost-or-market value of the inventory.
3. Assuming that Nelson uses a perpetual inventory system, prepare the necessary journal entry to record the inventory at lower-of-cost-or-market using the (a) direct method and the (b) allowance method.
4. Prepare the necessary journal entries to recognize the cost of goods sold under both the direct and the indirect methods, assuming that the inventory was sold in the next year.

Exercise 10-15: Lower-of-Cost-or-Market on Individual Items and on Total Inventory. The following information pertains to five different inventory items held by Sherm's Auto Parts, Inc. For each inventory item, assume that the company has 100 units on hand.

Inventory Item	Historical Cost per Unit	Replacement Cost	Selling Price	Estimated Selling Cost	Normal Profit Margin
Item A	$ 9.25	$ 8.00	$14.30	$0.50	50% of replacement cost
Item B	2.60	2.55	4.20	0.20	40% of selling price
Item C	7.50	7.75	8.00	1.00	30% of selling price
Item D	14.85	10.50	21.50	1.50	50% of replacement cost
Item E	1.15	1.10	2.55	0.05	40% of selling price

1. Assuming that the company applies LCM procedures to individual items, determine the LCM amount to report on the company's balance sheet.
2. Assuming the company applies LCM procedures to the inventory as a whole, determine the LCM amount to report on the company's balance sheet.

Exercise 10-16: Impairment of Assets. Regal Brewing Co. bought a distilling device in 2000 for $1,000,000. By December 31, 2004, $400,000 of the machine's cost had been depreciated. Regal estimates that the distiller will produce cash flows of $300,000 next year and $200,000 the year after that, at which time Regal estimates the asset can be sold for $50,000. At December 31, 2004, the asset's fair market value is approximately $450,000.

1. Determine if the distilling device is impaired. If so, prepare the necessary journal entry to recognize the impairment loss.

2. At December 31, 2005, an offer is received to sell the distilling device for $600,000. Assume that Regal recorded $200,000 of depreciation for the machine during 2005 (in addition to the impairment in 2004). Prepare any necessary journal entry to write up the asset because of its apparent increase in value at December 31, 2005.

Exercise 10-17: Impairment of Assets. The following information is related to equipment owned by Beebo Company as of December 31, 2004.

Historical cost	$400,000
Accumulated depreciation	$160,000
Expected future cash flows	$200,000
Remaining estimated useful life	5 years
Current selling price	$170,000
Costs of disposing of the asset	$10,000
Salvage value in five years	$0

The company intends to continue using the equipment in the business operations.

1. Perform a recoverability test to determine whether Beebo should recognize a loss from an asset impairment. If you determine that an impairment loss should be recognized, prepare the necessary journal entry.
2. Assuming that the equipment is depreciated using the straight-line method, calculate depreciation expense for the year ended December 31, 2005.
3. Suppose that the selling price of the equipment as of December 31, 2005, has recovered to $225,000. Prepare the necessary journal entry to record this event under U.S. GAAP.
4. How would parts 1–3 differ, assuming the same facts, except that on December 31, 2004, management decided to dispose of the equipment and the sale had not taken place as of December 31, 2005?

Exercise 10-18: Asset Impairment. On December 31, 2004, the management of Benoit Company is evaluating whether an item of equipment is impaired and should be written down on the books. The historical cost of the equipment was $150,000. It was purchased on January 1, 2003, and at the time of purchase, the expected useful life of the equipment was 10 years. As part of its analysis, management determines that the expected future cash flows from using the equipment is $100,000 and its current fair value is $75,000. Benoit Company uses the straight-line method to depreciate the equipment. The equipment is continuing to be used.

1. Prepare the journal entry (if any) to record the impairment as of December 31, 2004.
2. Where should impairment losses be reported on the income statement?
3. If the equipment continues to be used in operations and has a recovery of fair value, how should Benoit recognize this recovery? Why?
4. Suppose that all the facts remain the same, except that management determines the future cash flows from using the machine are $125,000. Prepare the journal entry (if any) to record the impairment as of December 31, 2004.

Exercise 10-19: Asset Revaluations. British Manufacturing Co. is domiciled in the United Kingdom and follows UK GAAP when preparing its financial statements. Accordingly, the company has the option of revaluing assets to their fair market values. Explain the effect(s) of an upward asset revaluation on the following ratios:

1. Current ratio
2. Debt-to-equity ratio
3. Return on assets
4. Return on equity
5. Total asset turnover ratio

Exercise 10-20: Discounting a Note Receivable (Appendix). On April 1, Charlie's Cycle Shop received a $1,000, 60-day, 9% note receivable from a customer that it immediately discounted at the local finance company. The finance company discounted the note without recourse at a discount rate of 12%. Assuming that each month has 30 days, compute the amount of the proceeds from the note and prepare the entry when discounting the note to recognize both the interest expense and the interest income. (*Note:* Keep all amounts accurate to the nearest cent.)

Exercise 10-21: Journal Entries for Notes Receivable (Appendix). On June 3, Adriane's Tuxedo Supply Store sold 10 tuxedos to Mr. T's Men's Store on terms of 2/10, n/30. On August 3, Mr. T's was unable to pay the amount due of $2,000, but as a sign of good faith paid $500 and gave Adriane's a $1,500, 12%, 60-day note receivable. Thirty days after receiving the note, Adriane's discounted the note with recourse at 18%. (*Note:* Keep all amounts accurate to the nearest cent.)

Prepare the following journal entries for Adriane's.

1. Record the receipt of the cash and note receivable on August 3.
2. Discount the note 30 days later, assuming that each month has 30 days.
3. Assume that Mr. T's paid the note when it was due.
4. Assume that Mr. T's did not pay the note when it was due, and Adriane's was charged a protest fee of $25.

Exercise 10-22: Journal Entries and Discounting a Note Receivable (Appendix). On December 1, 2004, The Party Shoppe received a 10%, 90-day note receivable from a customer who owed it $2,000. The Party Shoppe discounted the note with recourse on February 1, 2005, at a 12% discount rate. Assume that all months have 30 days. (*Note:* Keep all amounts accurate to the nearest cent.)

Prepare all necessary journal entries for this transaction, assuming that December 31 is the fiscal year-end and that the note is paid when it is due.

Exercise 10-23: Discounting a Company's Own Note Receivable (Appendix). Victoria's Gardens discounted its own 90-day, $4,000 note at the bank at 14%. Compute the amount Victoria's will receive and prepare the necessary journal entry. Also, prepare the journal entry when the note matures and is paid. Assume that each month has 30 days. (*Note:* Keep all amounts accurate to the nearest cent.)

Exercise 10-24: Discounting a Company's Own Note with Interest Accrual (Appendix). On April 1, to finance the purchase of some seasonal inventory, Cameo Florist and Landscaping borrowed $10,000 from the First Union Bank on a discount basis. The note is for 90 days and has a discount rate of 12%. Assume that each month has 30 days. (*Note:* Keep all amounts accurate to the nearest cent.)

Prepare the following journal entries.

1. Record the borrowing of the money.
2. Record the accrual of interest on April 30 and May 31.
3. Record the payment of the note on June 30.

Problems

Problem 10-1: Aging Method of Estimating Bad Debts Expense (CPA Adapted).
Sigma Company began operations on January 1, 2005. On December 31, 2005, Sigma estimated its uncollectible accounts to be 1% of credit sales. During 2006, Sigma changed its method of estimating uncollectible accounts by applying the following percentages to its accounts receivable.

Days Past Invoice Date	Percent Deemed to Be Uncollectible
0–30	1%
31–90	5
91–180	20
Over 180	60

The following additional information relates to the years ended December 31, 2006, and 2005.

	2006	2005
Credit sales	$3,000,000	$2,800,000
Collections	2,915,000	2,400,000
Accounts written off	27,000	None
Recovery of accounts previously written off	7,000	None
Days past invoice date at December 31		
0–30	$ 300,000	$ 250,000
31–90	80,000	90,000
91–180	60,000	45,000
Over 180	25,000	15,000

Required:
1. Compute the December 31, 2006 balance in Allowance for Uncollectible Accounts before any adjusting journal entry.
2. Compute what the December 31, 2006 balance in Allowance for Uncollectible Accounts should be, and prepare the appropriate adjusting journal entry at December 31, 2006.

Problem 10-2: Review of Receivables. Toy Time had the following balances in its receivables and associated accounts at January 1, 2004.

Accounts receivable	$15,000
Receivables from officers and employees	1,500
Allowance for uncollectible accounts	(750)
Allowance for sales returns	(500)

Toy Time had the following transactions relating to its receivables for 2004 and 2005.
For 2004:
a. Sales on account were $130,000.

b. Sales returns during the year were $3,000. Toy Time uses the allowance method of accounting for sales returns.

c. Collections from customers were $98,000.

d. Toy Time accepted a 12%, 90-day note receivable from a customer who was unable to pay his account when due. The amount owed was $2,000.

e. Toy Time collected $1,200 of the amounts owed to it by its officers and employees, but a disgruntled employee who owed the company $300 quit and refused to pay the amount owed. Toy Time decided not to pursue legal action.

f. Amounts written off as uncollectible totaled $2,800.

g. During the year, Toy Time continued the policy of advancing amounts to its officers and employees, and at year-end Toy Time was owed $2,100.

h. At the end of the year, Toy Time estimated that its sales returns would total 3% of credit sales and that its bad debts would total 4% of credit sales.

For 2005:

a. Credit sales totaled $170,000.

b. Sales returns were $4,500.

c. Collections from customers were $150,000.

d. Collected the note receivable with interest.

e. Collected the amounts owed from the employees and officers of the company, except for $200 that was owed by an employee whose spouse had passed away during the year. The company wrote off the $200. Due to problems with collectibility, the company discontinued the policy of loaning to employees and officers.

f. Wrote off $1,800 of uncollectible accounts.

g. Collected $300 on accounts that had been written off in 2004.

h. Revised its estimate of uncollectible accounts to 2.5% of credit sales and also recorded the estimate of sales returns.

Required:

1. Prepare the journal entries to record these transactions for 2004 and 2005.

2. Show how information about the receivables would be shown on the balance sheets for 2004 and 2005.

Problem 10-3: Analysis Problem. Agassi Sports manufactures three styles of high performance tennis rackets, which are sold exclusively to players on the ATP Tour for tournament play. The company has been in business for four years and has used absorption costing to complement its FIFO perpetual inventory system since its inception. With the exception of overhead, the costs of production are accumulated using actual costs. Predetermined overhead rates are used to apply overhead to production. The balances of the inventory accounts at fiscal year-end at cost, before any year-end adjustments, are as follows.

Finished goods	$1,230,000
Work in process	413,000
Raw materials	604,000
Factory supplies	145,000
Total cost	$2,392,000

Additional information:

a. The details of the finished goods inventory are as follows.

	Cost	Market
Sweet Spot:		
Extra large head	$ 140,000	$ 138,000
Large head	122,000	121,000
Standard head	106,000	104,000
Total Sweet Spot	$ 368,000	$ 363,000
Power Stroke:		
Extra large head	$ 230,000	$ 234,000
Large head	195,000	202,000
Total Power Stroke	$ 425,000	$ 436,000
Finesse:		
Large head	$ 232,000	$ 233,000
Standard head	205,000	212,400
Total Finesse	$ 437,000	$ 445,400
Total finished goods	$1,230,000	$1,244,400

b. One-third of the Power Stroke finished goods inventory is held by elite tennis pro shops on consignment.

c. One-half of the Sweet Spot finished goods inventory is used as collateral for a short-term bank loan.

d. The total market value of the work in process inventory is $402,500.

e. Included in the cost of factory supplies are obsolete items with a historical cost of $12,000. The market value of the remaining factory supplies is $135,600.

f. One-half of the materials inventory is titanium that is used for framing and was purchased at a price 30% above the current market price. The market value of the remaining materials is $314,000.

g. Agassi applies the lower-of-cost-or-market method independently to each of the three models of tennis rackets in finished good inventory. For work-in-process inventory, Agassi applies the lower-of-cost-or-market method to the total inventory.

h. Assume that all amounts are material.

Required:

1. Prepare the inventory section of Agassi Sports' balance sheet at year-end, including the necessary note disclosures.

2. Assume that Agassi has a firm purchase commitment for titanium and the contracted price is 22% greater than the current market price. The titanium will be delivered to Agassi next year. Explain the impact, if any, that this purchase commitment has on Agassi's financial statements for the current year.

Problem 10-4: Lower-of-Cost-or-Market (CPA Adapted). York Company sells one product, which it purchases from various suppliers. York's trial balance at December 31, 2005, includes the following accounts.

Sales (33,000 units @ $16)	$528,000
Sales discounts	7,500
Purchases	368,900
Purchase discounts	18,000
Freight-in	5,000
Freight-out	11,000

York Company's inventory purchases during 2005 were as follows.

	Units	Cost per Unit	Total Cost
Beginning inventory, January 1	8,000	$8.20	$ 65,600
Purchases, quarter ended March 31	12,000	8.25	99,000
Purchases, quarter ended June 30	15,000	7.90	118,500
Purchases, quarter ended September 30	13,000	7.50	97,500
Purchases, quarter ended December 31	7,000	7.70	53,900
	55,000		$434,500

Additional information:
York's accounting policy is to report inventory in its financial statements at the lower-of-cost-or-market as applied to total inventory. Cost is determined under the last-in, first-out method, using a periodic inventory system.

York has determined that, at December 31, 2005, the replacement cost of its inventory was $8 per unit, and the net realizable value was $8.80 per unit. York's normal profit margin is $1.05 per unit.

Required:
1. Prepare York's schedule of cost of goods sold, with supporting details. York uses the direct method of reporting losses from market decline of inventory.
2. Explain the rule of lower-of-cost-or-market and its application in this situation.

Problem 10-5: Lower-of-Cost-or-Market. The following information is available at year-end for AmSouth Construction Company.

Inventory Item and Quantity	Unit Cost	Current Replacement Cost	Current Selling Price	Cost to Complete and Dispose	Normal Profit Margin
A, 100	$ 4.00	$ 3.60	$ 3.90	$0.20	$0.20
B, 50	8.00	8.20	8.60	0	0.30
C, 20	12.00	12.50	12.90	0.50	0.50
D, 120	5.00	5.10	5.20	0.15	0.10
E, 40	9.00	8.75	9.20	0.35	0.40

Required:
Using the lower-of-cost-or-market procedures, calculate the dollar amount of inventory on the following bases.

1. An individual item basis.
2. A total inventory basis.

Problem 10-6: Recovery of Asset Impairment—U.S. GAAP vs. International GAAP. Stockton, Inc., possesses a machine with a historical cost of 100 units of currency. The company depreciates the machine over a 5-year useful life using the straight-line method, with no salvage value. At the end of Year 2 and after recording depreciation expense, Stockton gathers the following information.

Estimated total future cash flows from holding machine	55 units
Present value of cash flows	42 units
Net future cash flows at the time the machine will be sold	0 units

Stockton concludes that the remaining useful life of the machine has not changed.

Required:
1. Determine whether this machine is impaired. If it is, prepare the necessary journal entry.
2. Record the journal entry to recognize depreciation expense for Year 3.
3. Assume that at the end of Year 3, Stockton concludes the machine has fully recovered its previous impairment loss and actually has a fair market value of 120 units. How is this event recognized?
4. Redo Requirements 1–3, assuming that Stockton has decided to sell the asset at the end of Year 2. Also, assume that the selling price information is as follows.

Estimated selling price of machine	65 units
Estimated costs to dispose after sale	7 units

5. Explain for Requirements 1–3 how the accounting would be different under international GAAP as illustrated under Hong Kong GAAP and assuming that the asset will continue in use. Prepare appropriate journal entries.

Problem 10-7: Asset Impairment. On January 1, 2005, Maglebys purchased several pieces of specialized mining equipment and opened operations in Delta, Utah, which meets the test of being a component of a business. The total purchase price of all items of equipment was $3,555,000, all of which are being depreciated using the straight-line method. At the end of 2007 and after recording depreciation for the year, it was determined that the operation was a failure, and management devised a plan to sell the operation. The plan meets all the requirements for the results of operation to be reported under discontinued operations. In preparing to dispose of the operation, the following information about the various assets was obtained.

Asset	Original Cost	Carrying Value	Fair Value
Asset 1	$ 355,500	$ 142,200	$ 125,000
Asset 2	782,100	547,470	365,000
Asset 3	1,244,250	995,400	670,000
Asset 4	1,173,150	938,520	600,000
Totals	$3,555,000	$2,623,590	$1,760,000

Maglebys fully expects to be able to sell the operation for $2,000,000 and considers this to be the operation's fair value. The costs of selling the operation are estimated to be $200,000.

Required:
1. Determine the amount of impairment loss, if any, that should be recognized by Maglebys at the end of 2007, and prepare the appropriate journal entry.
2. Determine the adjusted carrying value for each asset. (Round amounts to the nearest ten dollars.)

Problem 10-8: Revaluation of Assets. Long Shorts, Inc., is a company domiciled in Hong Kong that follows Hong Kong GAAP. Due to significant increases in real estate values, management has decided to revalue its real estate assets in order to better reflect the true financial position of the company. As part of the revaluation process, the following appraisals were obtained for its land and buildings at December 31, 2004.

Asset	Historical Cost	Date Acquired	Estimated Useful Life	Fair Value
Land	$ 90,000	March 10, 1987	Indefinite	$330,000
Building 1	225,000	September 1, 1988	30 years	180,000
Building 2	550,000	May 28, 1999	30 years	540,000

The company uses the straight-line depreciation method for all depreciable assets, and a full year's depreciation is taken in the year of acquisition. Expected salvage value for the buildings at the end of their useful lives is zero.

Required:

1. Assuming that the revaluation is effective as of December 31, 2004, after depreciation is recognized for the year, prepare the journal entry to revalue the assets to their fair market values.
2. Prepare the necessary journal entry to record depreciation on the buildings and the related adjustments to the revaluation accounts for the year ended December 31, 2005.
3. In January 2006, Long Shorts accepts an offer to sell Building 1 for $150,000. Prepare the journal entry to record the disposal of the building (assuming that no depreciation is recognized in the year of disposal).
4. Assume all the preceding facts, except that the fair market value of Building 1 as of December 31, 2004, is $52,000. Redo Requirements 1–3 under this new assumption.

Problem 10-9: Review of Concepts. Answer each of the following independent questions.

Required:

1. Burr Company had the following account balances at December 31, 2004.

Cash in banks	$2,250,000
Cash on hand	125,000
Cash legally restricted for additions to plant (expected to be disbursed in 2005)	1,600,000

Cash in banks includes $600,000 of compensating balances against short-term borrowing arrangements that are not legally restricted as to withdrawal by Burr. In the current assets section of Burr's December 31, 2004 balance sheet, what should be the reported amount for total cash?

2. Roxy Company had the following information relating to its accounts receivable.

Accounts receivable at December 31, 2003	$1,300,000
Credit sales for 2004	5,400,000
Collections from customers for 2004	4,750,000
Accounts written off September 30, 2004	125,000
Collection of accounts written off in prior years (customer's credit was not reestablished)	25,000
Estimated uncollectible receivables per aging of receivables at December 31, 2004	165,000

At December 31, 2004, what is Roxy's accounts receivable before deducting the allowance for uncollectible accounts?

3. Orr Co. prepared an aging of its accounts receivable at December 31, 2004, and determined that the net realizable value of the receivables was $250,000. Additional information is as follows.

Allowance for uncollectible accounts at January 1, 2004—Credit balance	$ 28,000
Accounts written off as uncollectible during 2004	23,000
Accounts receivable at December 31, 2004	270,000
Uncollectible accounts recovery during 2004	5,000

For the year ended December 31, 2004, what is Orr's uncollectible accounts expense?

4. Mill Co.'s allowance for uncollectible accounts was $100,000 at the end of 2004 and $90,000 at the end of 2003. For the year ended December 31, 2004, Mill reported bad debts expense of $16,000 in its income statement. What amount did Mill write off during 2004?

5. The following information pertains to an inventory item.

Cost	$12.00
Estimated selling price	13.60
Estimated disposal cost	0.20
Normal gross margin	2.20
Replacement cost	10.90

What is the inventory value for this item under the lower-of-cost-or-market rule?

6. (Multiple-choice) A method of estimating uncollectible accounts that emphasizes asset valuation rather than income measurement is the allowance method based on:
   a. Aging the receivables.
   b. Direct write-off.
   c. Gross sales.
   d. Credit sales less returns and allowances.

7. The original cost of an inventory item is above the replacement cost but below the net realizable value less the normal profit margin. As a result, at what amount should the inventory item be reported under the lower-of-cost-or-market method?

8. The original cost of an inventory item is above the replacement cost and above the net realizable value. The replacement cost is below the net realizable value less the normal profit margin. At what amount should the inventory item be reported under the lower-of-cost-or-market method?

9. The original cost of an inventory item is above the replacement cost, and the replacement cost is above the net realizable value. At what amount should the inventory item be reported under the lower-of-cost-or-market method?

10. The replacement cost of an inventory item is below the net realizable value and above the net realizable value less the normal profit margin. The original cost of the inventory item is above the replacement cost and below the net realizable value. As a result, at what amount should the inventory item be reported under the lower-of-cost-or-market method?

11. During 2005, the management of West Inc. decided to dispose of some of its older equipment and machinery. By year-end, these assets had not been sold, although the company was negotiating their sale to another company. At what amount should the equipment and machinery be reported on the December 31, 2005, balance sheet of West Inc.?

12. Taft Inc. recognized a loss in 2004 related to long-lived assets that it intended to sell. These assets were not sold during 2005, and the company estimated at December 31, 2005, that the loss recognized in 2004 had been more than recouped. At what amount should these long-lived assets be reported on Taft's December 31, 2005 balance sheet?

Cases

Case 10-1. Fruit of the Loom (Comprehensive). Fruit of the Loom is one of the largest marketing oriented and vertically integrated apparel companies in the world, emphasizing branded products for consumers ranging from children to senior citizens. It is one of the largest producers of men's and boys' underwear, activewear for the imprinted market, casual wear, jeanswear, women's and girls' underwear, and children's wear, selling products primarily under the Fruit of the Loom, BVD, Screen Stars, Best TM, Munsingwear, Wilson, Gitano, and Cumberland Bay TM brand names. Under the Pro Player and Fans Gear brands, Fruit of the Loom designs, manufactures, and markets licensed sports apparel bearing the names, trade names, and logos of the National Football League, the National Basketball Association, Major League Baseball, Major League Soccer, the National Hockey League, professional sports teams, and many colleges and universities, as well as the likenesses of certain popular professional athletes.

Fruit of the Loom is a low-cost producer in the markets it serves. Fruit of the Loom states that its primary strengths are its excellent brand recognition, cost-effective production, and strong relationships with mass merchandisers, discount chains, and the wholesale distribution network. Fruit of the Loom sells its products primarily in the United States, Europe, Canada, Japan, and Mexico to over 10,000 accounts worldwide, including all major mass merchandisers, discount stores, wholesale clubs, and screenprinters. Fruit of the Loom's basic apparel products are designed, manufactured, sold, and distributed by more than 33,500 employees at 70 facilities around the world.

Despite its name recognition, wide marketing, being a low-cost producer, and other strengths, Fruit of the Loom's financial statements, which follow, contain some disturbing information.

Fruit of the Loom, Inc., and Subsidiaries
Consolidated Balance Sheet

(In thousands of dollars)	January 2, 1999	December 31, 1997
ASSETS		
CURRENT ASSETS:		
Cash and cash equivalents (including restricted cash)	$ 1,400	$ 16,100
Notes and accounts receivable (less allowance for possible losses of $12,000,000 and $11,900,000, respectively)	109,700	98,100
Inventories		
Finished goods	500,700	570,400
Work in process	183,100	212,300
Materials and supplies	$ 58,200	$ 64,800
Total inventories	$ 742,000	$ 847,500
Other	41,100	53,900
Total current assets	$ 894,200	$1,015,600

(In thousands of dollars)	January 2, 1999	December 31, 1997
PROPERTY, PLANT, AND EQUIPMENT:		
Land	$ 14,400	$ 14,700
Buildings, structures and improvements	303,300	330,500
Machinery and equipment	862,500	882,800
Construction in progress	11,900	4,200
Total	1,192,100	1,232,200
Less accumulated depreciation	758,200	717,800
Net property, plant and equipment	$ 433,900	$ 514,400
OTHER ASSETS:		
Goodwill (less accumulated amortization of $336,200,000 and $309,600,000, respectively)	$ 686,300	$ 712,900
Net deferred income taxes	36,700	30,300
Other	238,700	209,900
Total other assets	$ 961,700	$ 953,100
TOTAL ASSETS	$2,289,800	$2,483,100
LIABILITIES AND STOCKHOLDERS' EQUITY		
CURRENT LIABILITIES:		
Current maturities of long-term debt	$ 270,500	$ 28,200
Trade accounts payable	119,700	234,100
Acme Boot guarantee	—	67,000
Other accounts payable and accrued expenses	226,700	195,900
Total current liabilities	$ 616,900	$ 525,200
NONCURRENT LIABILITIES:		
Long-term debt	$ 856,600	$1,192,800
Other	267,400	343,000
Total noncurrent liabilities	$1,124,000	$1,535,800
COMMON STOCKHOLDERS' EQUITY:		
Common stock and capital in excess of par value, $0.01 par value; authorized, Class A, 200,000,000 shares, Class B, 30,000,000 shares; issued and outstanding:		
Class A Common Stock, 66,465,255 and 66,216,720 shares	$ 323,000	$ 315,300
Class B Common Stock, 5,684,276 shares	3,700	3,700
Retained earnings	276,600	140,700
Accumulated other comprehensive income	(54,400)	(37,600)
Total common stockholders' equity	$ 548,900	$ 422,100
TOTAL LIABILITIES AND STOCKHOLDERS' EQUITY	$2,289,800	$2,483,100

Consolidated Statement of Operations

	Year Ended		
(In thousands, except per-share data)	January 2, 1999	December 31, 1997	December 31, 1996
Net sales	$2,170,300	$2,139,900	$2,447,400
Cost of sales	1,564,800	1,644,400	1,724,500
Gross earnings	$ 605,500	$ 495,500	$ 722,900
Selling, general and administrative expenses	344,000	751,800	378,000
Goodwill amortization	26,600	26,800	26,700
Impairment write-down of goodwill	0	4,600	0
Operating earnings (loss)	$ 234,900	$ (287,700)	$ 318,200
Interest expense	(97,300)	(84,700)	(103,600)
Other income (expense)—net	5,400	(79,300)	(36,400)
Earnings (loss) from continuing operations before income tax provision	$ 143,000	$ (451,700)	$ 178,200
Income tax provision	7,100	(66,300)	31,600
Earnings (loss) from continuing operations	$ 135,900	$ (385,400)	$ 146,600
Discontinued operations—LMP litigation	0	(102,200)	0
Net earnings (loss)	$ 135,900	$ (487,600)	$ 146,600
Earnings (loss) per common share:			
Continuing operations	$ 1.89	$ (5.18)	$ 1.92
Discontinued operations—LMP litigation	0	(1.37)	0
Net earnings (loss)	$ 1.89	$ (6.55)	$ 1.92
Earnings (loss) per common share—assuming dilution:			
Continuing operations	$ 1.88	$ (5.18)	$ 1.90
Discontinued operations—LMP litigation	0	(1.37)	0
Net earnings (loss)	$ 1.88	$ (6.55)	$ 1.90

1. Prepare a cross-sectional and a trend analysis on the income statement and balance sheet. (That is, do a vertical and a horizontal analysis.) What are the major expenses during 1998, and what significant trends, if any, are identified on the income statement?

2. Determine Fruit of the Loom's liquidity by computing current ratio, quick ratio, and working capital. What is your assessment of Fruit of the Loom's liquidity?

3. Compute the accounts receivable turnover and the average number of days it takes Fruit of the Loom to collect a receivable. (This is computed by dividing 365 days by the accounts receivable turnover.) What is your general observation regarding Fruit of the Loom's management of its accounts receivable?

4. Compute the inventory turnover for each of its three components. Where is Fruit of the Loom particularly having difficulty managing its inventory? Also, compute the number of days of inventory, by category, that Fruit of the Loom is carrying. (This number is computed by dividing 365 days by the inventory turnover.) What comments do you have regarding Fruit of the Loom's management of its inventory?

5. The length of the operating cycle can be computed by adding the number of days of inventory on hand [see part (4)] to the number of days it takes to collect its receivables [see part (3)]. What is the length of Fruit of the

Loom's operating cycle? How long should the operating cycle be for this type of company?

6. Compute the degree of Fruit of the Loom's leverage, or its "riskiness." Do you think Fruit of the Loom is carrying too much debt?

7. Compute the return on assets and return on equity. Using these amounts and the EPS numbers reported on the income statement, comment regarding the overall effectiveness and efficiency of Fruit of the Loom.

8. Overall, what is your assessment of Fruit of the Loom's future?

Case 10-2: Sunbeam Corporation. For several years, Sunbeam Corporation has been an international leader in designing, manufacturing, and marketing durable household consumer products. However, in 1995, the company was coming under increased scrutiny from Wall Street. Annual EPS was reported at $0.61 per share, which was a decline from the previous year by more than 50%. Moreover, Sunbeam had missed analysts' expectations in EPS for five consecutive quarters as earnings steadily declined from $0.36 per share in the first quarter of 1995, to $0.14, $0.11, and $0.00 in the second through fourth quarters, respectively. Virtually every analyst had taken Sunbeam off its "buy" list, and the stock price languished at around $12 per share.

In an attempt to solve the problems inherent in Sunbeam, the company hired a new CEO, Albert J. Dunlap, in July 1996. Mr. Dunlap was famous for turning struggling companies into profitable ones within a very short time. He had previously worked his magic with American Can Co., Lily Tulip, Crown Zellerback, and Scott Paper. The hiring of Mr. Dunlap was cheered by Wall Street, and the day after the announced hiring, Sunbeam's shares soared 60%, to $18.63.

After only three days on the job, Mr. Dunlap informed analysts that he would turn the company around within a year. To properly motivate his top managers (many of whom were brought in with Mr. Dunlap), Mr. Dunlap rewarded them with stock options that would reward them handsomely if the stock price increased. The vesting requirements of the options were three years.

The consultation services of Coopers and Lybrand were retained to assist in the restructuring of the company. The restructuring plan called for the layoff of over 50% of the employees, including many high-ranking managers, and the discontinuance of 87% of the company's products. The restructuring note, as disclosed in Sunbeam's 1996 financial statements, follows.

Note 2: Restructuring

On November 12, 1996, the Company announced the details of its restructuring and growth plan for the future. The cost reduction phase of the plan includes the consolidation of administrative functions within the Company, the rationalization of manufacturing and warehouse facilities, the centralization of the Company's procurement function, and reduction of the Company's product offerings and stock keeping units ("SKU's"). The Company also announced plans to divest several lines of business which it determined are not core for Sunbeam (see Note 3).

Since the restructuring plan was announced, the Company has consolidated six divisional and regional headquarters functions into a single worldwide corporate headquarters in Delray Beach, Florida and outsourced certain back office activities resulting in a 50% reduction in total back-office/administrative headcount. Overall, the restructuring plan calls for a reduction in the number of production facilities from

26 to 8 and warehouses from 61 to 18. The restructuring plan will result in the elimination of over 6,000 positions from the Company's workforce, including 3,300 from the disposition of non-core business operations and the elimination of approximately 2,800 other positions. The Company completed the major phases of the restructuring plan by January 1997.

In conjunction with the implementation of the restructuring and growth plan, the Company recorded a pre-tax special charge to earnings of approximately $337.6 million in the fourth quarter of 1996. This amount is allocated as follows in the accompanying Consolidated Statement of Operations: $154.9 million to Restructuring, Impairment and Other Costs as further described below; $92.3 million to Cost of Goods Sold related principally to inventory write-downs from the reduction in SKU's and costs of inventory liquidation programs; $42.5 million to Selling, General and Administrative expenses principally for increases in environmental and litigation reserves (see Notes 12 and 13) and other reserve categories; and the estimated pre-tax loss on the divestiture of the Company's furniture business of approximately $47.9 million.

Amounts included in Restructuring, Impairment and Other Costs in the accompanying Consolidated Statement of Operations include cash items such as severance and other employee costs of $43.0 million, lease obligations and other exit costs associated with facility closures of $12.6 million, $7.5 million of start-up costs on back office outsourcing initiatives and other costs related to the implementation of the restructuring and growth plan. Expenditures for the cash restructuring items will be substantially completed in 1997. Non-cash Restructuring, Impairment and Other Costs include $91.8 million related to asset write-downs to net realizable value for disposals of excess facilities and equipment and non-core product lines, write offs of redundant computer systems from the administrative back-office consolidations and outsourcing initiatives and intangible, packaging and other asset write-downs related to exited product lines and SKU reductions.

Although Sunbeam was operating at a small profit during the first two quarters of 1996, the restructuring resulted in a fiscal-year loss of $2.75 per share. Nevertheless, analysts were optimistic that the company had turned the corner, and even some of the more skeptical were advising investors to buy some Sunbeam shares.

During 1997, Sunbeam did not disappoint. EPS for the first three quarters of 1997 were $0.24, $0.30, and $0.39, respectively, meeting or exceeding analysts' forecasts in each case. In much of October 1997, Sunbeam's stock price was flying high at over $50.

Mr. Dunlap promised analysts and investors that the company's profitability would continue to rise. Indeed, in January 1998, Sunbeam reported profits for the fourth quarter in the amount of $0.47. However, the stock price on the earnings announcement date dropped over 10%, even though the earnings was only one penny below analysts' expectations. The price drop was due largely to some reports that the earnings increase was primarily the result of taking the restructuring accrual through earnings. In spite of the disappointing earnings announcement in January, the stock price regained the losses realized on the announcement date and again appreciated to the $50-per-share level.

On April 3, 1998, a PaineWebber analyst downgraded Sunbeam's stock, which caused a stir among other analysts and investors. In response to several phone calls to Sunbeam, Mr. Dunlap provided a press release disclosing that Sunbeam expected to report an operating loss for the first quarter of 1998. By the end of the day, in spite of a conference call where Mr. Dunlap attempted to convince analysts that the market was overreacting, Sunbeam's stock price had lost nearly 25% of its value and closed at $34.375. During the second quarter of 1998, the stock price continued its downward spiral. On June 13, 1998, Mr. Dunlap was unexpectedly fired as Sunbeam's CEO. Subsequently, the stock price declined to $6 per share. Shareholder lawsuits and a formal investigation by the SEC ensued.

What happened to Sunbeam?

Mr. Dunlap was very demanding and required managers to meet earnings targets, using any means possible. If goals were not met, managers were ridiculed, humiliated, and threatened with their jobs. Mr. Dunlap developed a nasty reputation and was widely known throughout the company as Chainsaw Al. Given the large gains in stock price during 1997, managers had huge incentives to stay with the company to profit from the employee stock options, which had a 3-year vesting period.

The pressure to hit earnings targets resulted in accounting games being played. One of the games was the reversal of the large restructuring accrual that was recognized in 1996. Another was the acceleration of revenues through heavy product discounts and extended credit terms. In November 1997, in an effort to show increasing profits for the fourth quarter, Sunbeam allowed retailers to order barbecue grills but did not require payment for six months. Since the grills were not needed by the retailers until the following spring, Sunbeam agreed to hold the inventory until needed by the retailers; nevertheless, the orders were recorded as sales. Mr. Dunlap was recorded as saying, "There is absolutely nothing improper about this practice."[23] Although warned by a Sunbeam internal auditor, the questionable accounting practices were not discontinued.

The following financial statement data were provided in Sunbeam's 9-Q and 9-K reports filed with the Securities and Exchange Commission.

Sunbeam Consolidated Quarterly Income Statement

	Three Months Ended			Fiscal Year Ended
	March 31, 1997	June 30, 1997	September 30, 1997	December 31, 1997
Net sales	$ 253,450	$ 287,609	$ 289,033	$1,168,182
Cost of goods sold	(185,669)	(213,080)	(200,242)	(837,683)
Selling, G&A expenses	(33,008)	(31,559)	(33,863)	(131,056)
Operating earnings	$ 34,773	$ 42,970	$ 54,928	$ 199,443
EPS from continuing operations	$ 0.24	$ 0.30	$ 0.39	$ 1.41
Net EPS	$ 0.08	$ 0.30	$ 0.39	$ 1.25

[23]John A. Byrne, "Chainsaw: The Notorious Career of Al Dunlap in the Era of Profit-at-Any-Price," *HarperBusiness*, 1999.

Sunbeam Quarterly Consolidated Balance Sheet
(dollars in thousands)

	Three Months Ended			Fiscal Year Ended
	March 31, 1997	June 30, 1997	September 30, 1997	December 31, 1997
ASSETS:				
Cash and cash equivalents	$ 30,415	$ 57,970	$ 22,811	$ 52,378
Receivables, net	296,716	252,045	309,095	295,550
Inventories	148,011	208,374	290,876	256,180
Net assets of discontinued operations	20,655	5,549	2,900	
Deferred income taxes	75,132	58,582	56,854	36,706
Prepaid and other current assets	38,725	52,328	10,016	17,191
Total current assets	$ 609,654	$ 634,848	$ 692,552	$ 658,005
PP&E, net	217,453	229,339	229,152	240,897
Trademarks and trade names, net	199,028	197,651	195,851	194,372
Other assets	27,020	27,507	27,516	27,010
Total assets	$1,053,155	$1,089,345	$1,145,071	$1,120,284
LIABILITIES AND SHAREHOLDERS' EQUITY:				
Short-term debt	$ 848	$ 749	$ 668	$ 668
Accounts payable	100,648	136,489	132,686	105,580
Restructuring accrual	45,309	31,223	20,068	10,938
Other current liabilities	113,349	89,688	92,575	80,913
Total current liabilities	$ 260,154	$ 258,149	$ 245,997	$ 198,099
Long-term debt	175,235	174,855	199,855	194,580
Other long-term liabilities	151,074	144,738	145,509	141,109
Deferred income taxes	53,532	55,894	55,894	54,559
Shareholders' equity:				
Common stock	892	896	899	900
Other shareholders' equity	475,656	518,057	560,048	594,082
Treasury stock (at cost)	(63,388)	(63,244)	(63,131)	(63,045)
Total liabilities and shareholders' equity	$1,053,155	$1,089,345	$1,145,071	$1,120,284

Sunbeam Quarterly Consolidated Statement of Cash Flows

	Three Months Ended March 31, 1997	Six Months Ended June 30, 1997	Nine Months Ended September 30, 1997	Fiscal Year Ended December 31, 1997
Net earnings	$ 6,848	$ 33,082	$ 67,654	$ 109,415
Adjustments to reconcile net earnings to net cash used in operating activities:				
Depreciation and amortization	10,587	19,790	29,770	38,577
Loss on discontinued operations	13,713	13,713	13,713	13,713
Deferred income taxes	13,128	32,029	33,746	57,783
Change in working capital	(66,969)	(102,792)	(205,655)	(227,737)
Cash flows from operations	$(22,693	$ (4,178)	$ (60,772)	$ (8,249)

1. What were the primary objectives of the Sunbeam restructuring? What benefits did the company hope to obtain? What are the potential problems that accompany a restructuring?

2. What was the total restructuring charge to pretax earnings in the fourth quarter of 1996? Itemize the restructuring charge into its different components. Were all of the itemized costs incurred in 1996? In 1997? How will the charge affect future earnings? Given the effect of the restructuring on future earnings, what incentives do incoming managers face when joining a struggling company?

3. One of the restructuring components is called "environmental, litigation, and other reserve categories." Construct a journal entry that establishes this account. Where would the account be shown on the financial statements? How would this be accounted for in the future; i.e., when would the account be eliminated? Construct a journal entry to eliminate the account.

4. Review some alternative revenue recognition practices with respect to Sunbeam's barbecue grill sales in the fourth quarter of 1997. Do you agree with Mr. Dunlap's claim: "There is absolutely nothing improper about this practice"?

5. Review the Sunbeam financial statements provided in the case. Find some warning signals from the financial statements that might have been the cause for Sunbeam's stock downgrade by some analysts on April 3, 1998.

6. Determine how Sunbeam has performed since the case was written. In conducting your analysis, obtain accounting and stock market information. Determine what steps have been taken by the company to improve performance. Have the strategies implemented by the company worked? How does the future look for Sunbeam?

11

Present Value: Measuring Long-Term Liabilities

Occasionally, stories appear in the newspaper of individuals who have won a large jackpot at some casino or of individuals who have won a state lottery. Usually, their winnings are paid out at a certain sum per year over a considerable number of years. Suppose an individual wins a $1 million jackpot at a casino and that the winnings are to be paid at the rate of $50,000 per year for the next 20 years.

Questions

1. What amount of liability has the casino incurred?

2. Does the casino have a liability for $1 million?

A similar measurement problem arises in professional sports. It is common for professional athletes to earn, say, $2 million a year. However, that $2 million is typically paid out over several years. When an athlete signs a new contract but is already being paid in the current year under a previous contract, he often elects to defer being paid until payments expire under the older contract. Thus, athletes who have signed more than one previous contract and whose payments are each being spread over multiple years may not be paid anything for several years on the new contract.

Questions

1. So, when an athlete signs a new contract for $2 million and has played the games required, how much expense should the professional organization record?

2. How is the amount of its long-term liability determined?

- Explain why all liabilities are theoretically measured by using the concept of the time value of money.

- Apply time value of money techniques to measuring the long-term liability amount at the time of issuing bonds and long-term notes.

- Prepare amortization tables, using both the effective-interest and straight-line methods for bonds and long-term notes.

- Using amortization tables, prepare journal entries for the subsequent accounting for bonds and long-term notes, including recognizing interest and retiring bonds before maturity, and prepare financial statements.

Previous chapters have described the accounting and financial reporting model that involves (1) the accounting for costs and (2) the recognizing of revenue. Exhibit 11-1 summarizes this model. The accounting for costs and the principles for determining when those costs become expenses were covered in Chapters 5 through 7. The revenue recognition principle was presented in Chapter 8, while the reporting of net income (with its various categories) and assets on the balance sheet was discussed in Chapters 9 and 10, respectively. In this chapter, the final measurement principle, the concept of discounted cash flow—which is how long-term liabilities are measured—will be explained. Chapter 12 will cover the basic financial reporting concepts for reporting both current and long-term liabilities. The financial reporting for the liabilities associated with leases, pensions, and deferred taxes is reserved for later chapters.

The Theory of Discounting Cash Flows

© GETTY IMAGES, INC./PHOTODISC

Theoretically, all liabilities, whether they are classified as current or long-term, are reported on the year-end balance sheet at the hypothetical amount that would be required on that date to liquidate them. This hypothetical amount is called the liability's **present value**. But when the time between the balance sheet date and the maturity date of the liability is very short, the liability's face amount and its present value amount are only slightly different. Therefore, *current liabilities are reported on the year-end balance sheet at their face amount.* This deviation from the theoretically preferred reporting treatment is justified on the grounds of both materiality and cost benefit. However, when the time between the balance sheet date and the maturity date of the lia-

EXHIBIT 11-1

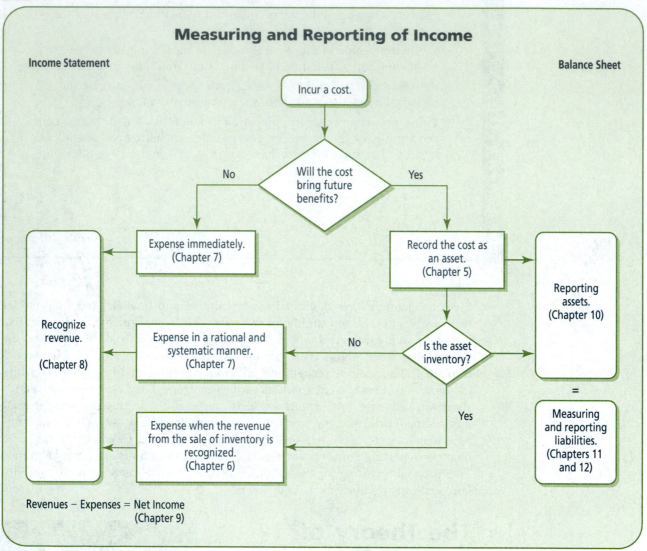

bility is long, a considerable difference between the liability's face amount and its present value amount exists. For this reason, *long-term liabilities are generally reported at their present value amount.*[1]

Since most long-term debt is incurred to finance the acquisition of long-lived assets, transactions in which a company acquires a long-lived asset that is financed by incurring a long-term liability may be measured by using either the historical cost principle to value the asset or by determining the present value of the long-term debt, whichever is more clearly evident. For example, a transaction in which a building is acquired by signing a mortgage can be measured either at the historical cost of the building (with the value of the *liability* being determined in a "plug" manner) or at the present value of the mortgage (with the value of the *building* being determined in a plug manner). Either approach is appropriate.

---

[1]Some long-term liabilities are not reported at their discounted cash flow amounts. The primary example of this exception is deferred taxes, which are tax amounts that will be paid in the future and result from differences between the tax treatment and the financial reporting treatment of certain assets and liabilities. Accounting for deferred taxes is covered in Chapter 19.

Review of Time Value of Money Concepts that Apply to Long-Term Liabilities

The notion of the time value of money is that having $1 today is preferable to having $1 in the future. Aesop, in 600 B.C., may have been the first to express this notion when he said, "A bird in the hand is worth more than two in the bush." The reason that $1 today is worth more than $1 in the future is that the dollar today can be invested, and so it will be worth more than $1 in the future.

But how much more is $1 today worth than $1 that is to be received, say, one year from today? The answer depends upon the interest rate (which is referred to as the **discount rate**) used in the calculations. If a 10% discount rate is assumed, then $1 today is equivalent to $1.10 one year from today, since the $1 today can be invested, and, at a 10% interest rate, it will become $1.10 one year later. Thus, a person investing at an interest rate of 10% is ambivalent between having $1 today or $1.10 one year from today. Individuals using a discount rate higher than 10% will prefer receiving $1 today, as at a higher rate than 10%, that $1 will be worth more than the $1.10 that is to be received in one year. But individuals using a discount rate lower than 10% will prefer receiving $1.10 in one year. *This equating of money over time is the purpose of all present value and future amount computations.* As the number of future payments becomes more than $1 or if the payments extend over more than one year, the calculations become more complex, but the central idea remains the same: equating amounts of money over a period of time. For these more complex calculations, time value of money tables are provided at the end of this chapter, or alternatively, financial calculators can be used.

Review of Basic Terminology

Regardless of the form in which a long-term liability is packaged (whether as a bond, lease, note, etc.), the essential nature of a long-term liability consists of borrowing money now in return for repaying that amount—with interest—sometime in the future. This interest component is always present, even on those long-term liabilities that are labeled as non-interest-bearing.[2]

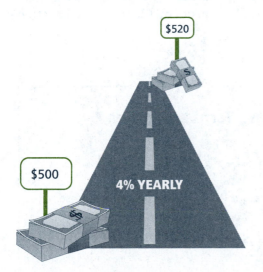

The time value of money concepts that are the most relevant to accounting for long-term liabilities are (1) the present value of a single sum and (2) the present value of an annuity or of an annuity due. An **annuity** is the paying of an equal amount of cash over equal periods of time. Both of these elements—equal amounts and equal periods—must be present in order to use the annuity time value of money tables or the annuity function on a calculator. For cash payment amounts or patterns that are not equal in amount or time intervals, calculations are done on single sums. Under an **annuity due** contract, the first payment is made immediately, whereas under an **ordinary annuity** contract, the first payment is due one time period in the future.

---

[2]As mentioned previously, all liabilities are reported at their present value. The APB specifically noted that the face amount of non-interest-bearing notes does not represent the present value of the note (*APB Opinion 21*, par. 1), and therefore non-interest-bearing notes must have an element of interest.

The essence of measuring a long-term liability using the time value of money concepts entails the following steps, which should be used in solving end-of-chapter problems:

1. *Determine the amount(s) of the cash flow(s).*
2. *Determine the timing of the cash flows.* This pertains to determining whether the amounts can be treated as an annuity, including what type of annuity, or whether the amounts will have to be treated as single sums.
3. *Determine the discount interest rate.* The discount rate is the interest rate demanded by the market.

Review of Basic Procedures

To illustrate applying time value of money concepts to the accounting for long-term liabilities, assume that on December 30, 2004, Newel, Inc., purchased some new equipment from the local farm implements dealership in exchange for a $60,000 non-interest-bearing note that requires three annual payments of $20,000 each, with the first payment due immediately and the other payments due the following two years on December 30. At December 30, 2004, the interest rate at which Newel could have borrowed the money from a bank is 11%. What is the historical cost of the tractor, and what is the amount of the liability that Newel should report on its December 31, 2004 balance sheet? These questions and answers are summarized as follows:

Questions	Answers
1. What are the amounts of the cash payments?	$20,000 each
2. When will these cash payments be paid?	Yearly, beginning immediately
3. What is the discount interest rate?	11%

Measuring Newel's long-term liability by discounting the future cash flow is graphically illustrated in Figure 11-1. This illustration shows that the present value of long-term liabilities is measured by determining how much the future cash payments are worth now. For Newel, Inc., the long-term liability is measured by discounting the two future cash payments of $20,000 to today at an 11% interest rate.

FIGURE 11-1

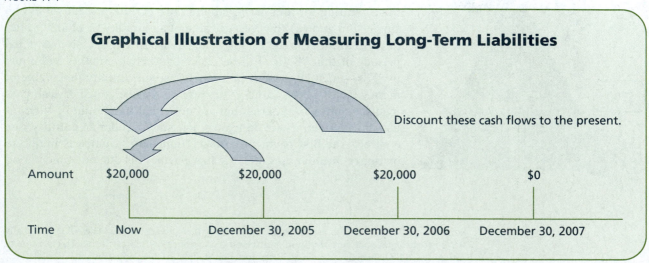

Graphical Illustration of Measuring Long-Term Liabilities

Discount these cash flows to the present.

Amount	$20,000	$20,000	$20,000	$0
Time	Now	December 30, 2005	December 30, 2006	December 30, 2007

Since the payment amounts are equal—with the first payment to be made immediately—and since the time periods between the payments are equal, a factor from the Present Value of an Annuity Due Table is used.[3] The correct present value factor is found by looking down the 11% column to three payments (or periods), which is 2.71252 (from Table 5 in Appendix A). So the cost of the equipment, or the amount of Newel's liability, is computed as follows:

$$\$20,000 \times 2.71252 = \$54,250$$

The journal entry to record the purchase of the equipment is as follows:

Equipment	54,250	
Note Payable		54,250

To record the acquisition of equipment in exchange for a $60,000 non-interest-bearing note.

If desired, the note payable can be reported at its gross amount of $60,000 by preparing the following journal entry:

Equipment	54,250	
Discount on Note	5,750	
Note Payable		60,000

To record the acquisition of equipment in exchange for a $60,000 noninterest bearing note.

The $5,750 (the amount in Discount on Note) is computed as the difference between the note payable of $60,000 and the present value of the note of $54,250 and represents the amount that will be recognized as interest expense over the next two years. Verifying that the $54,250 actually is the present value of the note and computing the interest expense amounts for 2005 and 2006 can be done as follows:

Note Payable (net)

Balance, Dec. 30, 2004		54,250	
Payment, Dec. 30, 2004	20,000		
Balance, Jan. 1, 2005		34,250	
Recognize interest for 2005		3,768	computed as 11% × $34,250
Payment, Dec. 30, 2005	20,000		
Balance, Jan. 1, 2006		18,018	
Recognize interest for 2006		1,982	computed as 11% × $18,018
Payment, Dec. 30, 2006	20,000		
Balance, Dec. 31, 2006		0	

The journal entries to recognize interest expense are shown in Illustration 11-1. When the note payable is recorded at net, the journal entry for either 2005 or 2006 is a debit to Interest Expense and credit to Note Payable. As illustrated in the T-account, if this option is chosen, the balance in the note payable account will be zero after the final payment is made. When the discount on the note payable account is used to record the initial entry, Interest Expense is debited and Discount on Note Payable is credited. If this is the option chosen, Discount on Note Payable also will be zero at December 2005.

---

[3]Present Value and Future Value tables are located in Appendix A at the end of this chapter.

ILLUSTRATION 11-1

Entries for Interest

When Note Is Recorded at Net	When Note Is Recorded at Gross

Interest Expense 3,768
   Note Payable   3,768
	Interest Expense 3,768
	   Discount on Note Payable 3,768

Present value analysis can also be used to calculate payment amounts. For example, a leasing company is asked to arrange the financing of a $24,000 automobile. Terms of the lease specify seven annual payments, with the first payment due immediately and an interest rate of 12%. Computing the annual lease payments requires algebraic manipulation of the basic discounted cash flow problem as follows:

$$\text{Basic formula: Present Value} = \text{Future Cash Flow Amount(s)} \times \text{Present Value Factor}$$

$$\text{So: Future Cash Flow Amount(s)} = \frac{\text{Present Value}}{\text{Present Value Factor}}$$

Since the first payment is made immediately, the present value factor is found by locating the factor for seven periods and 12% in a Present Value of an Annuity Due Table, which is 5.11141. Thus, the annual payment amount is determined as follows:

$$\text{Annual Payment Amount} = \frac{\$24,000}{5.11141} = \$4,695.38$$

EXTENDING THE CONCEPT

Since all long-term liabilities are measured initially by discounting the future cash flows, does the casino in the opening scenario have a liability for $1 million? Or, is it a lower amount?

Describe how the liability for the casino should be measured.

Since the amount of the casino's liability depends upon the discount rate used, what factors should the casino consider in selecting a discount rate?

Partial answer: The casino's liability is less than $1 million. It is computed by discounting the future payments, using an appropriate discount rate.

Having reviewed the basic time value of money concepts as they relate—in general—to accounting for long-term liabilities, these time value of money concepts are now applied to specific long-term liabilities.

Bonds Payable

Companies often issue bonds (i.e., borrow money from the public on a long-term basis) when the amount needed is too large for a single lender to provide. The typical **bond** contains a promise to pay (1) a sum of money (i.e., the principal) at the maturity date and (2) periodic interest at a certain interest rate at specified dates. The terms of the contract between the company borrowing the money—also known as the seller or issuer of the bonds—and the lenders of the money or the buyers of the bonds are referred to as the **bond indenture**. When issuing bonds, a business may either elect to sell the bonds directly to the lenders, or use the services of an investment banker. In turn, the investment banker may either elect to buy the entire bond issue and take the risk of selling it at a higher price to institutional investors or on a bond exchange,[4] or it may sell the bonds on commission.

---

[4]Buy and sell quotations for bonds are available in the same way that stock quotations are available.

Bonds usually sell in increments of $1,000. Unless otherwise stated, this text will assume such increments are being used. Statements that a bond is selling for 97, 100, or 104 mean that the bond is selling at 97%, 100%, or 104%, respectively, of the dollar amount printed on the bond. For example, a $1,000 bond selling at 97 is selling for $970.

The price at which a bond will sell depends upon many factors, one of which is the relationship between the coupon rate of interest on the bond and the market rate of interest. In theory, the market determines the price of a bond by discounting the cash flows (both principal and interest), using a market interest rate that is indicative of the bond risk.

The **coupon interest rate** (which is also called the **nominal rate** or **stated rate**) is the interest rate stipulated in the bond indenture and is the interest rate used to determine the periodic cash payments. The **yield rate of interest** (which is also called the **market**, **real**, or **effective-interest rate**) is the rate demanded by the market, given the risk associated with the bond.

When the coupon rate offered by the company is *higher* than the yield rate demanded by the market, the bond sells for more than its face amount, and the excess amount is called a **bond premium**. Conceptually, people who desire to own bonds that are paying an interest rate above the market rate bid up the price of the bonds to an amount where the actual return they receive is equal to the market rate of interest. At that price, they have no greater desire to own those bonds in relation to other bonds and the bidding up of the price stops. Conversely, when the coupon interest rate is less than the market interest rate, people are not willing to pay the face amount of the bond, which results in the bond selling at a **discount**. Theoretically, this bidding process to acquire a bond always results in the investor receiving a return on his investment equal to the market rate of interest, given the risk of the bond.[5] Finally, this relation between bond prices and market interest rates continues to exist after the bonds are issued. Thus, as interest rates rise (but the coupon rate remains constant), prices at which bonds are exchanged fall.

When bonds sell at a premium or discount, the premium or discount is kept in a separate account and is amortized as interest expense over the life of the bond. This amortization process will be illustrated throughout the chapter.

Interests Rates　　　Bond Prices

Issuing Bonds

To illustrate the time value of money concepts in measuring the price at which bonds are issued, assume that on December 31, Year 1, Ellsworth Company issues $1,000,000 of 10%, 20-year bonds with interest payable annually on De-

---

[5]As discussed previously, the price at which any bond will sell depends also on the relative risk. Hence, two bonds having the same coupon rate do not sell for the same price. In this chapter, the impact of risk on determining the market price of a bond is ignored, which allows the focus of the chapter to be upon the *accounting* for bonds rather than on the market dynamics of determining the bond price.

cember 31. At the time of issuance, the market interest rate for bonds of comparable risk is 12%.

As mentioned in the first part of this chapter, the steps in applying the time value of money concepts are to determine (1) the cash flow amounts, (2) the timing of the cash flows, and (3) the market interest rate, as follows:

1. The cash flows are: $1,000,000 principal and the $100,000 yearly interest amounts. (The $100,000 interest amounts are computed by multiplying the principal of $1,000,000 by the *coupon* interest rate of 10%.)
2. The timing of the cash flows are: the $1,000,000 will be paid in 20 *years*, and the $100,000 interest payments will be paid *each December 31*.
3. The discount rate is 12%.

Having identified these three items, it is now possible to refer to the appropriate time value of money tables (or to use a financial calculator) and determine the discounted cash flow amounts. Since interest is paid every year, discounting the $100,000 is done by referring to the Present Value of an Ordinary Annuity of $1 and finding the factor where the market rate of interest (i.e., 12%) intersects with 20 periods, which is the number of times that interest will be paid. Since the principal amount is paid only once, discounting the $1,000,000 is done by referring to the Present Value of a Single Sum Table and finding the factor where the market rate of interest intersects with the same number of periods as was used to discount the interest amount.[6] The following computations show how the price at which the bonds will be issued or sold is determined:

Present value of the principal: $1,000,000 × 0.10367[7] = $103,670
Present value of the interest: $100,000 × 7.46944[8] = $\underline{746,944}$
     Price of the bond $\underline{\underline{\$850,614}}$

Theoretically, the bonds will sell for $850,614.

The way the information will be quoted on the bond market is that the bond is selling at 85, meaning that, to buy one $1,000 bond, an investor will have to pay 85% of the face amount of $1,000. The fact that Ellsworth's bonds are selling at a discount is expected, because the coupon interest rate of 10% is less than the market rate of 12%. But at the price of 85, investors will earn a return that is equal to the market rate of 12%.

The journal entry Ellsworth would prepare to record the borrowing of the money and the issuing of the bonds is as follows:

Cash	850,614	
Discount on Bonds	149,386	
Bonds Payable		1,000,000

To record the issuance of 10%, 20-year bonds with interest paid annually.

The process of computing the price at issuance of a bond that has a coupon rate higher than the market rate or that pays interest more frequently than annu-

---

[6]The number of periods is not necessarily equivalent to the number of years. They are the same only when interest is paid annually. When interest is paid semiannually, then the number of periods is twice the number of years; when interest is paid quarterly, the number of periods is four times the number of years, etc.

[7]This is the factor from the Present Value of a Single Sum Table at 12% and 20 periods.

[8]This is the factor from the Present Value of an Ordinary Annuity of $1 Table at 12% and 20 periods.

ally is similar in all respects to the preceding example. Suppose that on December 31, Year 1, Brown Company issues $1,000,000 of 14%, 20-year bonds when the market rate of interest for bonds of similar risk is 12%. The bonds pay interest semiannually. (Since the coupon interest rate is greater than the market interest rate, the bonds are anticipated to sell for a premium.) In this case, the cash flows of the $1,000,000 principal and the $70,000 semiannual interest[9] are discounted for 40 periods. The reason for using 40 periods is that interest will be paid 40 times. Doubling the number of periods from 20 to 40 results in halving the effective interest rate, and so the amounts will be discounted at 6%, which is one-half the yearly market rate of interest. The mathematics of discounting the cash flows of the bond at the effective interest rate of 6% for 40 periods are as follows:

© GETTY IMAGES, INC./PHOTODISC

Present value of the principal: $1,000,000 × 0.09722[10] =	$	97,220
Present value of the interest: $70,000 × 15.04630[11] =		1,053,241
Price of the bond		$1,150,461

As expected, the bonds sold at a premium because the coupon rate of interest was greater than the market rate on bonds of similar risk. In this example, the bonds are said to sell at 115. The journal entry that Brown Company would record on issuing the bonds is as follows:

Cash	1,150,461	
Bonds Payable		1,000,000
Premium on Bonds		150,461

To record the issuance of 14%, 20-year bonds with interest paid semiannually.

Buyers and sellers of bonds do not actually pay a price based only upon the relationship between the coupon and market interest rates, such as was illustrated. Rather, the market determines a price for a bond based upon many factors, including the company's previous earnings, expectations of future earnings, the stability of the economy and the industry in which the company operates, other investment opportunities available, and the coupon interest rate. But the market's process of computing the price at which a bond will be issued based upon these and other factors is comparable to the discounting procedures illustrated earlier. In other words, the previous calculations are a simplistic model of how the market works to determine bond prices at issuance. Further, the relationship between the coupon rate and the market rate of interest is so critical in determining the price of a bond that there is justification for using the model.

---

[9] The $70,000 interest was computed in the same manner as in the preceding example by multiplying the principal amount of $1,000,000 by the coupon rate of 7% per period. This is in accordance with the simple interest formula of computing interest: Interest Amount = Principal × Interest Rate × Time.

[10] This is the factor from the Present Value of a Single Sum Table at 6% and 40 periods.

[11] This is the factor from the Present Value of an Ordinary Annuity of $1 Table at 6% and 40 periods.

Issuing Deep Discount or Zero-Interest Bonds

Issuing deep discount bonds, which was fashionable during the 1980s, will be used to further illustrate that regardless of the packaging, the accounting for a long-term liability at time of issuance is the same. A **deep discount bond** is one that does *not* pay periodic interest. Rather, the total payout is paid or received when the bond matures. Suppose that on January 3, 2004, Cain Corporation issues $10,000,000 of deep discount bonds that will mature on January 3, 2014. At the time, the market is demanding a return of 15% on bonds of similar risk. Issuing such bonds means that the total payout will be $10,000,000, which includes both the principal and the interest. It must now be determined how much Cain will receive at issuance by determining (1) the cash flow amounts, (2) the time when the cash flows will occur, and (3) the market rate of interest.

1. The cash flow is just the $10,000,000; there are no periodic cash flows for interest.
2. The timing of the cash flow is that the $10,000,000 will be paid in 10 years.
3. The discount rate is 15%.

The calculations are as follows:

$$\$10,000,000 \times 0.24718 = \$2,471,800$$

Thus, the amount Cain will receive on issuing the zero coupon bonds is $2,471,800, and the journal entry to record the issuing of the bonds is as follows:

Cash	2,471,800	
Discount on Bonds	7,528,200	
Bonds Payable		10,000,000
To issue deep discount bonds with the resulting discount.		

Accounting by the Investor

For all practical purposes, the accounting for an investment in bonds is the mirror image of the accounting for the issuing of bonds. The issuing of bonds by Brown Company is used to illustrate this mirror image of accounting, which (for ease of illustration) assumes that one investor buys all of the bonds.

Issuing Bonds			Investing in Bonds		
Cash	1,150,461		Investment in Bonds	1,150,461	
Bonds Payable		1,000,000	Cash		1,150,461
Premium on Bonds		150,461			

Note that the main difference in the journal entries is that only one account (as contrasted to two accounts) is used to account for the investment. This using of one account is in accordance with the historical cost principle, where assets are recorded at the sum of the necessary expenditures incurred to acquire them.

Determining Interest Amounts and Accounting for the Premium/Discount

Amortization tables are prepared when bonds are issued; they are a vital tool in the subsequent accounting for bonds because they aid in preparing journal entries for interest, correctly classifying amounts as current or long-term on the balance sheet, and preparing journal entries to retire bonds before their scheduled maturity date. An amortization table has columns for the cash to be paid each period, for the interest expense to be recognized each period, and for the **carrying amount of the bonds** (which is the face amount of the bonds plus any premium or less any discount). Also, at the preparer's option, an amortization table may have other columns, such as a column to show the unamortized premium or discount.

The two accepted methods of preparing an amortization table—and the resulting accounting for interest—are the effective-interest and straight-line methods. The effective-interest method results in a constant rate of interest for each period of time, and it is the amortization method that must be used unless the results obtained under the straight-line method are not materially different. The straight-line method of amortization results in a constant amount of interest (as compared to a constant rate of interest) for each period of time.

Effective-Interest Amortization

Using the information provided in the Brown Company example, where the bonds were issued at a premium with an effective-interest rate of 12%, Table 11-1 demonstrates the preparation of an amortization table using the **effective-interest method**.

TABLE 11-1[12]

Bond Amortization Table—Brown Company
Effective-Interest Method, at 12%

Period	Cash[13]	Interest Expense	Amortization of Premium (Difference between Cash and Interest)	Carrying Amount of Bonds
				$1,150,461
1	$ 70,000	$ 69,028	$ (972)	1,149,491
2	70,000	68,969	(1,031)	1,148,460
3	70,000	68,908	(1,092)	1,147,368
4	70,000	68,842	(1,158)	1,146,210
37	70,000	62,079	(7,921)	1,026,730
38	70,000	61,604	(8,396)	1,018,334
39	70,000	61,100	(8,900)	1,009,434
40	70,000	60,566	(9,434)	1,000,000*
Totals	$2,800,000	$2,649,537		

*Rounding errors often occur. Such amounts are usually just adjusted through the interest expense and amortization amounts in the last period or throughout the life of the bond. For this example, the adjustments were made throughout the table.

The amounts in the preceding amortization table were computed in the following manner:

- **Cash** is computed from the formula for simple interest, which is $I = P \times R \times T$. For this example, the $70,000 was computed by multiplying the face

[12]Appendix B at the end of the chapter contains the Excel commands to construct a worksheet to compute the present value of a bond and prepare the amortization table under the effective-interest method of amortization.
[13]This column actually may have several different titles, including: "Cash Paid," "Cash Interest," "Interest Paid," or as shown here, just "Cash."

amount of the bonds of $1,000,000 by the bond *coupon rate* of 14%, which—because interest is paid twice a year and the interest rate of 14% is a yearly rate—is then multiplied by $\frac{1}{2}$. The cash amount is the same for all years.

- **Interest expense** is computed by multiplying the *effective-interest rate* by the bond carrying amount at the end of the previous period.[14] So, the interest expense for Period 1 is computed by multiplying the bond carrying amount of $1,150,461 by the effective-interest rate of 12% and then by $\frac{1}{2}$ to change the yearly interest rate to a semiannual interest rate. Note that when bonds are issued at a premium, interest expense decreases over time.
- **Amortization** is the difference between the amount in the Cash column and the amount in the Interest Expense column.
- **Carrying amount of the bonds** is computed by deducting the amount in the Amortization of Premium column from the carrying amount of the bonds in the previous period. If the bonds had been issued at a discount, then this amount would be computed by adding the amount in the Amortization of Premium column to the carrying amount of the bonds in the previous period. Whether bonds are issued at a premium or a discount, the ending amount in this column will be equal to the face amount of the bonds at maturity.

EXTENDING THE CONCEPT

What amount would be amortized for the thirty-eighth period?

Answer: $8,396

To illustrate how an amortization table is used to prepare the periodic entries for interest, the following journal entry is prepared to record the interest expense, cash paid, and the amortization of the discount for the first period, based on Table 11-1.

Interest Expense	69,028	
Premium on Bonds	972	
Cash		70,000

To record the payment of cash, the interest incurred, and the amortizing of the premium for the first period.

The bond investor also prepares an amortization table to aid in his subsequent accounting for the bond purchased. That amortization table is prepared by using the same columnar headings and techniques as illustrated for the corporation issuing the bonds. The only difference is that the amounts will differ because it is unlikely that the investor will have acquired all the bonds that were issued. However, assume that in the Brown Company example the bond investor did buy the entire bond issue and, therefore, can use exactly the same amortization table that the issuer of the bonds prepared. Then, the investor in bonds prepares the following entry for the receipt of cash and the recognition of interest income for the first payment period:

Cash	70,000	
Bond Investment		972
Interest Revenue		69,028

To record the receipt of cash and the recognition of interest income for the first period.

Note again the mirror image of accounting. The issuer has interest expense, whereas the investor has interest revenue, but both for the same amount. Note

---

[14]This end-of-the-previous-period amount is, of course, the same as the beginning-of-the-current-period amount, which is an important observation because many times the equation for interest is stated in those terms.

also that the amortization of the liability by the issuer and the amortization of the asset by the investor are the same amount.

Amortization tables are also used to prepare the necessary adjusting entries at financial statement dates. To illustrate, suppose that the Brown Company bonds pay interest every September 1 and that the financial statement date is December 31. Then, the following journal entry is prepared for December 31 of Period 4:

Interest Expense	22,947[a]	
Premium on Bonds	386[b]	
Interest Payable		23,333[c]

To record the accrual of interest at December 31 of Period 4.

[a]Computed as $68,842 (which is the interest expense for Period 4) $\times$ 4/12 (the fraction of the year from September 1 to December 31).
[b]The difference between the interest expense and the interest payable.
[c]Computed as $70,000 $\times$ 4/12.

The investor of the bonds prepares a similar—but mirror-image reverse—of the preceding entry to record the accrual of interest revenue at December 31 of Period 4.

Straight-Line Amortization

As stated earlier, the **straight-line method** of preparing an amortization table may be used when the results obtained are not materially different from the effective-interest method. *APB Opinion No. 21* is silent regarding how "materially different" is to be interpreted, so judgment is required to decide when the straight-line method of amortization is acceptable. Table 11-2 was prepared using the straight-line method and the Ellsworth Company example.

TABLE 11-2[15]

Bond Amortization Table—Ellsworth Company
Straight-Line Method

Period	Cash	Interest Expense (Cash plus Amortization)	Amortization	Carrying Amount of Bonds
				$ 850,614
1	$ 100,000	$ 107,469	$7,469	858,083
2	100,000	107,469	7,469	865,552
3	100,000	107,469	7,469	873,021
4	100,000	107,469	7,469	880,490
17	100,000	107,469	7,469	977,593
18	100,000	107,469	7,469	985,062
19	100,000	107,469	7,469	992,531
20	100,000	107,469	7,469	$1,000,000*
Totals	$2,000,000	$2,149,386		

*Rounding errors usually occur and are adjusted through the expense and amortization amounts, either in the last period or throughout the table. In this example, these adjustments were made throughout the table.

---

[15]Refer to Table 11-1, p. 501, to recall how the initial carrying amount was determined.

- **Cash** is computed in exactly the same way as under the effective-interest method.
- **Amortization** is equal for each period—hence its name: straight-line. The amount is computed before the interest expense amount is computed. It is computed by dividing the total discount by the number of periods. For this example, the discount of $149,386[16] was divided by 20 periods, which results in a yearly amortization amount of $7,469.
- **Interest expense** is computed by *adding* the amortization amount to the cash amount. If the bonds had been issued at a premium, the interest expense amount would be computed by *deducting* the amortization amount from the cash amount.
- **Carrying amount of the bonds** is computed in the same way as under the effective-interest method, which is that the amount in the Amortization column is added to the carrying amount of the bonds in the previous period. Again, if the bonds had been issued at a premium, then these amounts would have been computed by subtracting the amount in the Amortization column from the carrying amount of the bonds in the previous period. As with the effective-interest method, the ending amount in this column should be equal to the face amount of the bonds at maturity.

The amortization table can now be used to prepare the journal entries to record the periodic interest expense and the payment of cash. That journal entry takes the same format as under the effective-interest method and is as follows for any payment period:

Interest Expense	107,469	
Discount on Bond		7,469
Cash		100,000

To record the payment of cash and the incurring of interest expense.

When amortization tables are prepared using the straight-line method, year-end adjusting entries, when necessary, are prepared as illustrated for the effective-interest method example. Also, when the purchaser of bonds uses the straight-line method of amortization, the accounting for the receipt of cash, the recognition of interest revenue, and year-end accruals are again the mirror image of the entries used by the issuer of the bonds who uses the straight-line method.

The final illustration of an amortization table is for a deep discount bond, which is shown in Table 11-3 and was prepared using the earlier data in the section on deep discount bonds. Note that (as defined) no cash is paid during the interim periods, but the issuer of the bonds recognizes interest expense each period, and the purchaser of the bonds recognizes interest revenue each period.

The journal entry to recognize interest expense for the first period is as follows:

Interest Expense	370,777	
Discount on Bonds		370,777

To recognize interest expense for Period 1.

Comparing the Effective-Interest and Straight-Line Methods of Amortization

Amortization tables are prepared quite differently under the effective-interest and straight-line methods. Under the effective-interest method, interest expense is

---

[16]This discount is computed as the maturity amount of the bonds of $1,000,000 minus the present value of the bonds of $850,614.

TABLE 11-3

Amortization Table, Deep Discount Bonds
Effective-Interest Method

Period	Cash	Interest	Discount/ Premium	Carrying Amount
				$ 2,471,847
1	$0	$ 370,777	$ 370,777	2,842,624
2	0	426,394	426,394	3,269,018
3	0	490,353	490,353	3,759,370
4	0	563,906	563,906	4,323,276
5	0	648,491	648,491	4,971,767
6	0	745,765	745,765	5,717,532
7	0	857,630	857,630	6,575,162
8	0	986,274	986,274	7,561,437
9	0	1,134,216	1,134,216	8,695,652
10	0	1,304,348	1,304,348	10,000,000

computed directly, and the amortization amount is the difference between the cash paid and the interest expense. But under the straight-line method, the amortization amount is computed directly, and the interest expense amount is the difference between the cash paid and the amortization amount. The cash amount and the procedures to compute the carrying amount of the bonds are the same under either method.

An insight into the effect these two amortization methods have on the financial statements can be grasped by realizing that *regardless of which amortization method is used, the total interest expense over the life of the bonds is exactly the same.* As a result, the difference between the two amortization methods lies in how the total interest expense is allocated over the life of the bonds. Figure 11-2 shows that when bonds are issued at a premium, the effective-interest

FIGURE 11-2

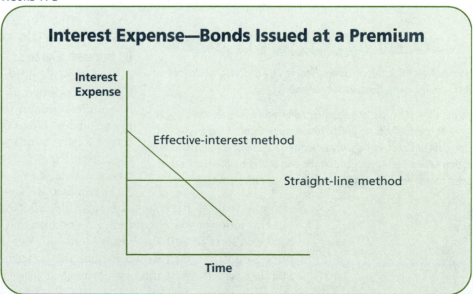

Interest Expense—Bonds Issued at a Premium

Interest Expense

Effective-interest method

Straight-line method

Time

EXTENDING THE CONCEPT

What would the graph look like, and how would it be interpreted, if the bonds had been issued at a discount?

method results in a greater initial interest expense as compared to the straight-line method. This seems logical because interest expense under the effective-interest method is computed by multiplying a decreasing carrying value by a constant percentage.

These concepts can be further verified by referring to Figure 11-3, which illustrates the relationship between the carrying amount of the bonds under the effective-interest method versus the straight-line method when the bonds are issued at a premium. Note that under either amortization method, the carrying amount of the bonds begins and ends at the same points but that at all points in between the carrying amount of the bonds under the two methods is different. Again, the amount of amortization for each individual period is different, even though the total amortization under the two methods is the same. Thus, the straight-line method initially is a quicker amortization technique when the bonds are issued at a discount.

FIGURE 11-3

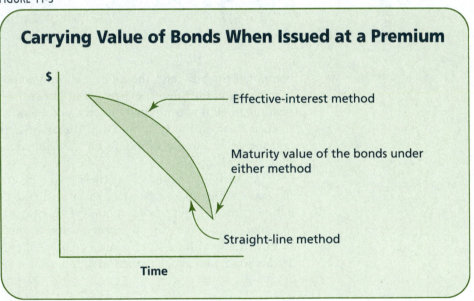

Carrying Value of Bonds When Issued at a Premium

EXTENDING THE CONCEPT

How do you think the graphs in Figures 11-2 and 11-3 would look if the bonds were issued at a discount?

Prepare amortization tables under the effective-interest and straight-line methods to justify your answer. (*Hint:* Using an electronic spreadsheet will greatly expedite your preparation of amortization tables. See Appendix B at the end of this chapter for a set of Excel commands to prepare an electronic amortization table.)

Issuing Bonds between Interest Dates

In the preceding illustrations, it was assumed that the bonds were issued on an interest payment date, but it is more common for bonds to be issued between interest dates. When that occurs, the price paid or received for the bonds will also include an amount for the interest that has accrued since the last interest payment date.

To illustrate, in the preceding Brown Company example (page 449), it was computed that the bonds would sell for $1,150,461. But this amount was computed by assuming that the bonds were issued on December 31, Year 1. If the bonds were sold two months later on March 1, the price paid or received would include the accrued interest from December 31 to March 1. On the first interest payment at June 30, investors in the bonds will receive interest for the full six months, even though they held the bonds for only four months, and, therefore, at the date of purchase, investors must "pay" for this benefit.

Similar to the preceding illustrations, the accrued interest is determined by multiplying the carrying amount of the bonds (i.e., $1,150,461) by the market rate of interest (i.e., 12%) and then by 2/12 of a year (i.e., the time from December 31 to March 1):

$$\text{Accrued interest} = \text{Carrying Amount} \times \text{Market Rate} \times \text{Time Elapsed}$$

$$\text{Accrued interest} = \$1,150,461 \times 12\% \times 2/12$$

$$= \$23,009$$

Consistent with previous examples, this $23,009 is comprised of two components: (1) interest payable that will be paid in cash to investors at June 30 (along with the additional four months of interest that will have accrued on that date) and (2) amortization of the premium from December 31 to March 1. The interest payable component is determined by multiplying the face amount of the bonds ($1,000,000) by the stated coupon rate (14%) and adjusting for time (2 months), as follows:

$$\text{Interest payable} = \$1,000,000 \times 14\% \times 2/12$$

$$= \$23,333$$

The amortization of the premium from December 31 to March 1 is the difference between the accrued interest ($23,009) and the interest payable ($23,333), which is $324.

Thus, in this case, the bonds will sell for a total of $1,173,470, which is the sum of the initial price and accrued interest since December 31 less the premium amortization of $324. The appropriate entry to record the issuing of the bonds on March 1 is as follows:

Cash	1,173,470	
Bonds Payable		1,000,000
Interest Payable		23,333
Premium on Bonds		150,137

To record the issuance of bonds on
March 1 and the accrual of interest since
December 31.

Another approach to preparing the journal entry is *to credit Interest Expense* rather than crediting Interest Payable. This is usually a better entry, as it expedites the later entry when payment is made for the accrued interest, as shown in Illustration 11-2.

Under either approach the total interest expense for the six-month period is $46,667. Therefore, the decision as to which journal entry scheme to use can be based upon ease, which for most accountants will be to initially credit the Interest Expense account.

Bond Issue Costs

Issuing bonds is a lengthy and costly endeavor. During such a process, the legal, accounting, underwriting, and other direct costs that are incurred are accu-

ILLUSTRATION 11-2

Journal Entries for Issuing Bonds, Crediting Interest Payable vs. Interest Expense

Crediting Interest Payable			Crediting Interest Expense		
Transaction A: Issuing the Bonds					
Cash	1,173,470		Cash	1,173,470	
Bonds Payable		1,000,000	Bonds Payable		1,000,000
Interest Payable		*23,333*	*Interest Expense*		*23,333*
Premium on Bonds		150,137	Premium on Bonds		150,137
Transaction B: Subsequent Paying of Interest on June 30					
Interest Payable	23,333		Interest Expense	70,000	
Interest Expense	46,667*		Cash		70,000
Cash		70,000			

*1,000,000 × 14% × 4/12 (i.e., March 1–June 30)

mulated in a separate account called **Bond Issue Costs**. The bond issue costs account has a debit balance and is reported as an asset in accordance with *APB Opinion No. 21*, even though it does not meet the definition of an asset according to the FASB's conceptual framework.[17] Usually, the bond issue costs account is reported with the intangible assets or as a deferred charge. In a **deferred charge**, there is a delay (i.e., deferral) in expensing the amount (i.e., charging the amount to the income statement). The bond issue costs amount is amortized over the life of the bonds in a straight-line manner. That is, the yearly amortization amount is determined by dividing the bond issue costs by the number of interest periods. When amortizing bond issue costs, the corresponding debit is to Interest Expense.

Retiring Bonds

Bonds are always issued with a specified maturity date, and accounting for retiring bonds on the maturity date is done by debiting Bonds Payable and crediting Cash for the face amount (i.e., principal) of the bonds. (The accounting by bond investors is, again, the mirror image of the bond issuer's accounting. In other words, the bond investor records a debit to Cash and a credit to Bond Investment.) Neither the issuer of the bonds nor the investor in the bonds records an entry to the premium/discount account or to the bond issue costs account because both accounts are fully amortized at the time the bonds mature.

Illustrating further the usefulness of an amortization table in preparing necessary journal entries, consider the retiring of bonds before their maturity date.

---

[17]*Opinions of the Accounting Principles Board No. 21*, "Interest on Receivables and Payables," New York: American Institute of Certified Public Accountants, August 1971, par. 16. When *APB No. 21* was issued, the APB was emphasizing the measurement of income, and as a result, the balance sheet became a place to "dump" costs that did not appropriately belong on the income statement. However, the FASB, in *SFAC No. 3* and *SFAC No. 6*, expressed a preference for including bond issue costs with any bond premium or discount and to then amortize the net amount over the life of the bonds. However, the FASB's conceptual statements do not establish generally accepted accounting principles.

Bonds may be retired before maturity if the issuer (1) purchases them on the market, (2) exercises a call privilege, or (3) refunds the bonds. When bonds are retired before their maturity by any of these methods, the basic accounting procedures are:

1. *To recognize any interest on and amortize any premium/discount on the bonds being retired since the last interest payment date.*
2. *To write off the face amount of the bonds that are being retired.*
3. *To write off any remaining associated premium/discount and bond issue costs that relate to the bonds being retired.*
4. *To account for the cash or other assets that are used to retire the bonds.*
5. *To recognize a gain/loss as the difference between the debits and credits— which is also equal to the difference between the carrying value of the bonds (including bond issue costs) and the fair value of the consideration given to retire them.*

To be classified as an extraordinary item, the gain/loss on the early extinguishment of debt must meet the unusual and infrequent criteria, the same as all other items that are reported as extraordinary items.

Acquiring Bonds on the Market

The issuing corporation may buy its own bonds on the market in the same manner that investors purchase bonds on the market. This is usually done when the corporation has excess cash and interest rates have risen, with a resulting decline in bond prices to such an extent that it is advisable to buy the bonds and retire them.

Returning to the Ellsworth Company example of issuing bonds at a discount and the amortization table prepared under the straight-line method (see Table 11-2 on page 503), assume that four months after the end of Period 3 Ellsworth Company purchased 10% of the outstanding bonds at 90, not including an amount for interest, and then retired them. Following the steps given previously, the first journal entry to amortize the discount since the last interest payment date is as follows:

Interest Expense (4/6 × $107,469 × 10%)	7,165	
Discount on Bonds (4/6 × $7,469 × 10%)		498
Interest Payable (4/6 × $100,000 × 10%)		6,667

To amortize the discount and record interest expense accrued prior to retiring 10% of the bonds that were acquired on the open market.

All these amounts were computed by multiplying the time elapsed since the last payment date (i.e., 4/6) by the amount in the amortization table (see Table 11-2 on page 503) and the percentage of bonds being retired. Then, the entry to record the acquisition and retirement of the bonds is as follows:

Bonds Payable (10% × $1,000,000)	100,000	
Interest Payable (see preceding entry)	6,667	
Loss on Retiring Bonds (difference)	2,200	
Cash [$90,000 + $6,667 (see prior entry)]		96,667
Discount on Bonds (see following computation)		12,200

To record the acquisition and retirement of 10% of the bonds.

EXTENDING the Concept

Would this journal entry for Ellsworth Company change if the bonds were acquired for 110 rather than 90? Why or why not?

Answer: No, the entry would not change. The amortizing of the discount and the recognizing of accrued interest does not depend on the amount paid to acquire the bonds. These amounts depend on the coupon interest rate and the price at which the bonds sold.

The amounts in the prior journal entry were computed in the following manner.

- The bonds payable amount is 10% of the face amount of the bonds of $1,000,000.
- The discount on bonds amount is computed as follows:

Maturity value of the bonds	$1,000,000
Carrying amount of the bonds at the end of Period 3	873,021
Total discount at the end of Period 3	$ 126,979
Percentage of the bonds being retired	× 10%
Discount related to the bonds being retired	$ 12,698
Amount of this discount amortized in previous entry	498
Discount written off in the prior entry	$ 12,200

EXTENDING THE CONCEPT

Would this entry change if the bonds were acquired for 98 rather than 90? If so, which parts of the entry would change?

Answer: Yes, the entry would change. The amount of cash and the loss would both change. The amount of bond discount and bonds payable would remain the same.

EXTENDING THE CONCEPT

Refer back to Figures 11-2 and 11-3 (on pages 505 and 506, respectively) and predict whether the loss would have been higher or lower if the effective-interest method of amortization had been used instead of the straight-line method.

Answer: The loss would have been higher because the carrying amount would have been lower.

- The interest payable amount was computed in the previous entry.
- The cash amount is the price paid for the bonds, plus the amount paid for interest, which was computed in the previous entry.
- The gain/loss amount is computed as either (1) the amount needed to balance the journal entry or (2) the difference between the fair value of the consideration given (i.e., $90,000) and the carrying amount of the bonds (i.e., $100,000 − $12,200). Amounts paid for interest do not affect the amount of gain or loss.

Before continuing on, review this exercise and note how many times the amortization table was referred to in preparing the necessary computations.

Exercising a Call Provision

A call is typically exercised to avoid further interest payments. The terms of the call provision are determined before the bonds are issued and are communicated to the investor in the bond indenture. Typical call provisions require that the call be exercised on an interest payment date and that a premium above the face amount be paid. Because of this second provision, one effect of a call is to set a ceiling on the price at which the bond will sell because investors would not pay more for a bond than the amount that they could reasonably expect to receive. Thus, no investor would pay an amount greater than that at which the bond issuer can call the bonds.

Using the Brown Company illustration and the amortization table prepared using the effective-interest method (Table 11-1, p. 501), suppose that at the end of Period 3 (when the carrying amount of the bonds is $1,147,368), Brown called 20% of the bonds at the call price of 102. Also, to introduce another aspect to retiring bonds, assume that *total unamortized* bond issue costs were $84,000. Since a call provision is exercised on an interest payment date, no entry is necessary to amortize the discount since the last interest payment date. So, Step 1 of the preceding outlined procedures is not necessary. Then, the journal entry to record the call transaction is as follows:

Bonds Payable (20% × $1,000,000)	200,000	
Bond Premium (computation follows)	29,474	
Gain on Retiring Bonds (the difference)		8,674
Bond Issue Costs (20% × $84,000)		16,800
Cash (102 × $200,000)		204,000

To record the call and retirement of 20% of the bonds outstanding at 102 and to write off the associated bond premium and bond issue costs.

The bond premium amount is computed as follows:

Maturity value of the bonds	$1,000,000
Carrying amount of the bonds at the end of Period 3	1,147,368
Total premium at the end of Period 3	$ 147,368
Percentage of the bonds being retired	× 20%
Discount related to the bonds being retired	$ 29,474

As before, the gain/loss amount can be computed either as (1) the amount needed to balance the journal entry or as (2) the difference between the fair value of the consideration given (i.e., $204,000) and the carrying amount of the bonds being retired minus the bond issue costs (i.e., $200,000 + $29,474 − $16,800).

Refunding Bonds

A third way of retiring bonds early and perhaps taking advantage of falling interest rates is to issue new bonds and use the proceeds to retire all or part of the existing bonds. Retiring bonds in this way does not involve any new issues. When the refunding bonds are issued, they are accounted for in the same way as when any other bonds are issued. When the proceeds of the bonds are used to retire the already outstanding bonds, two entries are recorded, as illustrated previously. The first entry accrues interest and amortizes any premium/discount, and the second entry writes off the bonds that are being retired, along with any associated premium/discount and bond issue costs, and also accounts for the cash paid and any resulting gain or loss.

Treasury Bonds

Thus far, it has been assumed that the bonds being acquired were retired. However, it may be that the bonds are not retired but rather are held by the corporation for possible future reissuance.[18] Such bonds are called **treasury bonds** and they are *reported on the balance sheet as a deduction from Bonds Payable*, with the net figure reported as Bonds Payable. At acquisition, treasury bonds are accounted for "as if" they had been retired. So, the only change required in the prior journal entries for retiring bonds is that Treasury Bonds is debited instead of Bonds Payable. Subsequently, when treasury bonds are reissued, they are accounted for "as if" they were newly issued bonds, which may give rise to a new premium/discount that is then amortized over the remaining life of the bonds.

Long-Term Notes

The measuring and subsequent accounting for long-term notes uses the same time value of money measurement techniques as used for bonds, and amortization tables are prepared to assist in the subsequent accounting for interest, as was

---

[18]The primary advantage to doing this is that the corporation can more quickly issue these treasury bonds than going through the process and incurring the cost of issuing new bonds.

done for bonds. In the following paragraphs, we discuss the accounting for notes that are exchanged (1) for cash only, (2) for cash and other rights and consideration, and (3) for property, goods, or services.

Notes Issued Solely for Cash[19]

When a note is issued solely for cash, the *present value of the note is equal to the amount of cash received.* There are no exceptions, even if the interest rate is clearly unreasonable (i.e., 3%) or if there is no interest rate. For example, On October 1, 2004, Agreka Video and Music signed a 2-year, 3% note with First National Bank and received $30,000 cash, and the note is due on October 1, 2006, with interest paid yearly on October 1. Since the note was exchanged solely for cash, the present value of the note is equal to the cash proceeds so the transaction is measured at $30,000. The entries to record the borrowing of the money, the year-end accrual of interest, and the first payment of interest are as follows:

Cash	30,000	
Note Payable		30,000
To record money borrowed from First National Bank.		
Interest Expense	225	
Interest Payable		225
To record accrual of interest at December 31, 2004. The amount is computed as $30,000 \times 3\% \times 3/12$.		
Interest Payable	225	
Interest Expense	675	
Cash		900
To record payment of interest on October 1, 2005. The cash amount is computed as $30,000 \times 3\% \times 1$.		

When a note is issued solely for cash and the cash proceeds are less than the face amount of the note, the present value of the note is still equal to the cash proceeds. (This example is similar to issuing deep discount bonds.) The resulting discount is amortized over the life of the note, using the effective-interest method, unless the results obtained from the straight-line method are substantially the same.

Again, assume that on October 1, 2004, Agreka Video and Music signed a non-interest-bearing, 2-year, $30,000 note with First National Bank and received $25,250 in cash. At maturity, the entire $30,000 is to be repaid to the bank. In this case, the present value of the note is still equal to the cash proceeds of $25,250, which could have been computed by using time value of money concepts if a market interest rate had been given. However, it is not necessary to know the market interest rate to record the borrowing because the amount of cash received is known. So, the appropriate journal entry to record the borrowing is as follows:

Cash	25,250	
Discount on Note	4,750	
Note Payable		30,000
To record money borrowed on a non-interest-bearing note.		

---

[19]*APB Opinion No. 21,* "Interest on Receivables and Payables," New York: American Institute of Certified Public Accountants, August 1971, par. 11.

To properly account for the yearly interest expense, it is necessary to know the market rate of interest that the bank used. The interest rate the bank used can be determined by algebraically manipulating the time value of money formula as shown:

$$\text{Present Value} = \text{Cash Flow} \times \text{PV Factor}$$

$$\text{PV Factor} = \frac{\text{Present Value}}{\text{Cash Flow}}$$

$$= \frac{\$25,250}{\$30,000}, \text{ or } 0.84167$$

Then, referring to the Present Value of a Single Sum table for two periods and reading across that row, it can be seen that the bank discounted the note at 9%.

Based upon this 9%, the amortization table in Table 11-4 is prepared by using the effective-interest method. The Cash column is excluded because there are no cash payments until the maturity of the note.

TABLE 11-4

Amortization Table
Non-Interest-Bearing Note

Period	Interest	Carrying Amount
		$25,250
Oct. 1, 2005	$2,273	27,523
Oct. 1, 2006	2,477	30,000

The journal entries to accrue interest at December 31, 2004, and at October 31, 2005, are as follows:

Dec. 31, 2004
    Interest Expense   568
      Discount on Note Payable   568
    To record accrual of interest at December 31, 2004. The amount is computed as 3/12 × $2,273.

Oct. 1, 2005
    Interest Expense   1,705
      Discount on Note Payable   1,705
    To recognize interest on October 1, 2005. The amount is computed as 9/12 × $2,273, or as $2,273 − $568.

Finally, when the note matures, the following journal entry is prepared:

Oct. 1, 2006
    Note Payable   30,000
      Cash   30,000
    To record payment of maturing note.

Notes Issued for Cash and Other Consideration

When notes are exchanged for cash and other rights and privileges are also included, recognition must be given to those rights and privileges. The fair value of such rights and privileges can be measured (1) directly—by referring to a market value or (2) indirectly—as the difference between the discounted cash flows and the face amount of the note, which is usually the more practical approach. Either approach results in the note being measured at its present value.

To illustrate, on January 1, Colorland Company borrowed $100,000 from a major customer and signed a 3-year non-interest-bearing note. Colorland also agreed to supply the customer's inventory needs for the next three years at lower than market prices. The prevailing rate of interest on such notes is 10%.

Directly measuring the value of purchasing inventory at less than market value for the next three years is very impractical, so the second method of indirectly measuring the rights to acquire inventory at reduced prices is used. Measuring these purchase rights is done through the same discounting procedures as has been illustrated throughout the chapter. Thus, it must be determined (1) what the cash flows will be, (2) when those cash flows will occur, and (3) what market rate of interest should be used to discount the cash flows. Thus, the calculations in this example are as follows:

Discount the $100,000, using the present value of a single sum for three years at 10% as shown:

$$\$100,000 \times 0.75131 = \$75,131$$

The present value of the note is $75,131, and the right to acquire merchandise at lower than market prices is thus measured at $24,869, which is the difference between the discounted cash flows of $75,131 and the face amount of the note of $100,000. The entry to record the transaction is as follows:

Cash	100,000	
Discount on Note Payable	24,869	
Note Payable		100,000
Obligation to Provide Purchase Rights		24,869

To record the borrowing of $100,000 and
the incurring of an obligation to provide
purchase rights to a major customer.

The discount on note payable amount is amortized by using the effective-interest method. The obligation to provide purchase rights is a liability. The part of the liability that relates to the purchase rights that will be exercised next year is classified as a current liability, and the rest of the obligation is classified as a long-term liability. The obligation is amortized using the straight-line method, unless some other pattern of amortization is more consistent with the benefits received. For example, if it is known that the major customer's needs for merchandise will be increasing each year, it is appropriate to amortize less in Year 1 than in Year 2 and less in Year 2 than in Year 3. The actual amounts to be amortized will depend upon the best estimate of what the customer's purchases will be. When amortizing the amount, the appropriate credit is to some descriptive revenue account. Table 11-5 illustrates the amortization for the discount on the note, using the effective-interest method, and for the obligation to provide purchase rights, using the straight-line method.

TABLE 11-5

Amortization Table
Non-Interest-Bearing Note with
Other Rights and Privileges

| | Interest Expense Component | | Revenue Component | |
| | Interest | | | Obligation to Provide |
Period	Expense	Note Payable	Revenue	Purchase Rights
		$ 75,131		$24,869
Year 1	$7,513	82,644	$8,290	16,579
Year 2	8,264	90,908	8,290	8,289
Year 3	9,092	100,000	8,289	0

The journal entries to record interest expense under the effective-interest method for each of the three years are as follows:

	Year 1		Year 2		Year 3	
	Debit	Credit	Debit	Credit	Debit	Credit
Interest Expense	7,513		8,264		9,092	
Discount on Note		7,513		8,264		9,092

The journal entries to amortize the obligation to provide purchase rights are as follows:

	Year 1		Year 2		Year 3	
	Debit	Credit	Debit	Credit	Debit	Credit
Obligation to Provide Purchase Rights	8,290		8,290		8,289	
Sales		8,290		8,290		8,289

Whether the major customer subsequently buys more or less merchandise than was estimated at the time the $100,000 was borrowed does not affect the above entries. However, the amounts for these entries are affected if it is later determined that the major customer will not make purchases in equal amounts each year. Then, in accordance with the principle of accounting for a change in an accounting estimate, the unamortized amount of the obligation to provide purchase rights is amortized over the remaining years in which the rights can be exercised and according to the revised estimate of how much will be purchased in each year.

Notes Exchanged for Property, Goods, or Services

When a long-term note is exchanged for property, goods, or services, it is presumed that the stated interest rate is reasonable. When that presumption is correct, the present value of the note is equal to the face amount of the note, and the note, property, goods, or services are all valued at the note's face amount. Then, interest expense is equal to the cash paid each period for interest. Hence, the accounting for such notes is the same as demonstrated earlier under "Notes Issued Solely for Cash."

However, the presumption that the stated interest rate is reasonable does not apply if:

1. There is no interest rate,
2. The interest rate is clearly unreasonable, or
3. The fair value of the property, goods, or services is clearly not equal to the face amount of the note.

Then, the note payable and the property, goods, or services are measured at either the fair value of the property, goods, or services or the fair value of the note, whichever is more clearly determinable. The fair value of the property may be determined by referring to available exchange prices, appraisals, etc., as discussed in Chapter 5. The fair value of the note is determined by discounting all future cash flows, using the market rate of interest as demonstrated in this chapter. Any resulting premium or discount is amortized over the life of the note, using the effective-interest method, unless the straight-line method yields substantially the same results.

© GETTY IMAGES, INC./PHOTODISC

Assume that on January 1, Colorland Company issued a $100,000 face value note payable in exchange for services received. The note is due in three years and has an interest rate of 4%, with interest payable annually. At the time of issuance, the market rate of interest on similar notes is 10%. Because the 4% coupon rate is clearly unreasonable as compared to the market rate, this note and the services received cannot be valued at the face amount of the note. Assuming no value can be readily placed on the services received, the transaction is measured by discounting the future cash flows as follows:

Principal: $100,000 \times 0.75131$ (the present value of a single sum for three years, 10%)

Interest payments: $4,000 \times 2.48685$ (the present value of an annuity for three years, 10%)

These computations yield a present value of $85,078, and the entry to record the exchange of the note for services received is as follows:

Service Expense[20]	85,078	
Discount on Note Payable	14,922	
Note Payable		100,000
To record the exchange of a long-term		
note for services received.		

The resulting amortization table, using the effective-interest method, is illustrated in Table 11-6.

---

[20]Some more descriptive account is actually used and is determined by what services were provided.

TABLE 11-6

Amortization Table
Note Exchanged for Property, Goods, or Services

Period	Cash	Interest Expense	Amortization Amount	Carrying Amount of Note
				$ 85,078
Year 1	$4,000	$8,508	$4,508	89,586
Year 2	4,000	8,959	4,959	94,545
Year 3	4,000	9,455	5,455	100,000

When deciding which market interest rate is appropriate for use in the discounting procedures, consideration should be given to such factors as the credit standing of the issuer, the value of any collateral, and any restrictive covenants. The prevailing rates of interest for similar instruments are often helpful. The interest rate should be at least equal to the rate the issuer would have to incur if money were borrowed from another source.

Creditor's Accounting for Long-Term Notes

As with bonds, the accounting for the creditor in long-term note transactions is the mirror image of the accounting for the debtor (or issuer of the note). In place of a note payable, the creditor has a note receivable, which initially is measured and recorded at its present value. Subsequently, the creditor accounts for the receipt of cash and the recording of interest revenue, using an amortization table.

International Accounting Standards

INTERNATIONAL

Recording long-term liabilities at the present value of future cash flows is a well accepted practice throughout the world. This practice makes economic sense, and the resulting interest expense entries capture the cost of using funds. Similar to U.S. GAAP, international GAAP requires most long-term liabilities to be shown at net present value amounts. However, in some countries, such as Sweden, Japan, and Italy, reporting long-term debt at present value amounts is acceptable but is not required. As a result, the prevalent practice in these countries is to show all debt, both long-term and short-term, at face value. This represents a significant difference between U.S. GAAP and these other countries' GAAP.

The financial statement effects of this accounting difference depend on whether the debt bears an interest rate that is less than or greater than the market rate of interest. When the stated interest rate is greater than the market rate and the debt is issued at a premium, the amount of debt reported on the balance sheet is higher, which negatively impacts debt-to-equity ratios. The opposite happens when debt is issued at a discount. In addition to affecting the balance sheet, interest expense is also affected when debt is issued at a premium or discount because in such cases the amount of interest is not equal to the amount of cash paid. When interest amounts differ, net income is also affected, which in turn affects various other financial statement ratios. Thus, there are significant differences in the financial statements when companies, in those countries where it is permitted, do not measure long-term liabilities at present value amounts.

Summary

This chapter discussed the basic issues of accounting for long-term liabilities, with emphasis placed on bonds and notes payable. At the time of issuance, long-term liabilities are recorded at their present value, which is computed by discounting all future cash flows at the market rate of interest. Following a review of the time value of money, examples of this discounting process were given for bonds (issued at a discount and a premium) and long-term notes payable (exchanged for cash; cash with other rights and privileges; and for property, goods, or services).

Examples of amortization tables were constructed, using both the effective-interest and straight-line methods. These tables expedite the subsequent accounting for interest. The effective-interest method must be used, unless the results obtained under the straight-line method are not materially different. Amortization tables were also used to aid in preparing entries for the retirement of bonds before their maturity, whether that early retirement was done by (1) acquiring them on the market, (2) exercising a call privilege, or (3) refunding the bonds. The procedures in retiring bonds early consist of:

1. Recognizing any interest and amortizing any premium/discount on the bonds being retired since the last interest payment date,
2. Writing off the face amount of the bonds that are being retired,
3. Writing off any remaining associated premium/discount and bond issue costs that relate to the bonds being retired,
4. Accounting for the cash or other assets that are used to retire the bonds, and
5. Recognizing a gain/loss, which is the difference between the carrying value of the bonds (including bond issue costs) and the fair value of the consideration given to retire them.

Gains/losses on retiring debt before its scheduled maturity date must meet the criteria of being infrequent in occurrence and unusual in nature to be reported as an extraordinary item. Otherwise, they are reported as part of normal operations.

Although the chapter focused primarily on accounting for the debtor, brief mention was made of accounting for the creditor. The fact that accounting for the creditor is the mirror image of accounting for the debtor was stressed several times.

APPENDIX A: Future Amount/Present Value Tables

TABLE 1

Future Amount of a Single Sum
FVF = (1 + i)ⁿ

(n) periods	2%	3%	4%	5%	6%	7%
1	1.02000	1.03000	1.04000	1.05000	1.06000	1.07000
2	1.04040	1.06090	1.08160	1.10250	1.12360	1.14490
3	1.06121	1.09273	1.12486	1.15763	1.19102	1.22504
4	1.08243	1.12551	1.16986	1.21551	1.26248	1.31080
5	1.10408	1.15927	1.21665	1.27628	1.33823	1.40255
6	1.12616	1.19405	1.26532	1.34010	1.41852	1.50073
7	1.14869	1.22987	1.31593	1.40710	1.50363	1.60578
8	1.17166	1.26677	1.36857	1.47746	1.59385	1.71819
9	1.19509	1.30477	1.42331	1.55133	1.68948	1.83846
10	1.21899	1.34392	1.48024	1.62889	1.79085	1.96715
11	1.24337	1.38423	1.53945	1.71034	1.89830	2.10485
12	1.26824	1.42576	1.60103	1.79586	2.01220	2.25219
13	1.29361	1.46853	1.66507	1.88565	2.13293	2.40985
14	1.31948	1.51259	1.73168	1.97993	2.26090	2.57853
15	1.34587	1.55797	1.80094	2.07893	2.39656	2.75903
16	1.37279	1.60471	1.87298	2.18287	2.54035	2.95216
17	1.40024	1.65285	1.94790	2.29202	2.69277	3.15882
18	1.42825	1.70243	2.02582	2.40662	2.85434	3.37993
19	1.45681	1.75351	2.10685	2.52695	3.02560	3.61653
20	1.48595	1.80611	2.19112	2.65330	3.20714	3.86968
21	1.51567	1.86029	2.27877	2.78596	3.39956	4.14056
22	1.54598	1.91610	2.36992	2.92526	3.60354	4.43040
23	1.57690	1.97359	2.46472	3.07152	3.81975	4.74053
24	1.60844	2.03279	2.56330	3.22510	4.04893	5.07237
25	1.64061	2.09378	2.66584	3.38635	4.29187	5.42743
26	1.67342	2.15659	2.77247	3.55567	4.54938	5.80735
27	1.70689	2.22129	2.88337	3.73346	4.82235	6.21387
28	1.74102	2.28793	2.99870	3.92013	5.11169	6.64884
29	1.77584	2.35657	3.11865	4.11614	5.41839	7.11426
30	1.81136	2.42726	3.24340	4.32194	5.74349	7.61226
35	1.99989	2.81386	3.94609	5.51602	7.68609	10.67658
40	2.20804	3.26204	4.80102	7.03999	10.28572	14.97446

(continued)

TABLE 1 (CONTINUED)

Future Amount of a Single Sum
$FVF = (1 + i)^n$

(n) periods	8%	9%	10%	11%	12%	15%
1	1.08000	1.09000	1.10000	1.11000	1.12000	1.15000
2	1.16640	1.18810	1.21000	1.23210	1.25440	1.32250
3	1.25971	1.29503	1.33100	1.36763	1.40493	1.52088
4	1.36049	1.41158	1.46410	1.51807	1.57352	1.74901
5	1.46933	1.53862	1.61051	1.68506	1.76234	2.01136
6	1.58687	1.67710	1.77156	1.87041	1.97382	2.31306
7	1.71382	1.82804	1.94872	2.07616	2.21068	2.66002
8	1.85093	1.99256	2.14359	2.30454	2.47596	3.05902
9	1.99900	2.17189	2.35795	2.55804	2.77308	3.51788
10	2.15892	2.36736	2.59374	2.83942	3.10585	4.04556
11	2.33164	2.58043	2.85312	3.15176	3.47855	4.65239
12	2.51817	2.81266	3.13843	3.49845	3.89598	5.35025
13	2.71962	3.06580	3.45227	3.88328	4.36349	6.15279
14	2.93719	3.34173	3.79750	4.31044	4.88711	7.07571
15	3.17217	3.64248	4.17725	4.78459	5.47357	8.13706
16	3.42594	3.97031	4.59497	5.31089	6.13039	9.35762
17	3.70002	4.32763	5.05447	5.89509	6.86604	10.76126
18	3.99602	4.71712	5.55992	6.54355	7.68997	12.37545
19	4.31570	5.14166	6.11591	7.26334	8.61276	14.23177
20	4.66096	5.60441	6.72750	8.06231	9.64629	16.36654
21	5.03383	6.10881	7.40025	8.94917	10.80385	18.82152
22	5.43654	6.65860	8.14027	9.93357	12.10031	21.64475
23	5.87146	7.25787	8.95430	11.02627	13.55235	24.89146
24	6.34118	7.91108	9.84973	12.23916	15.17863	28.62518
25	6.84848	8.62308	10.83471	13.58546	17.00006	32.91895
26	7.39635	9.39916	11.91818	15.07986	19.04007	37.85680
27	7.98806	10.24508	13.10999	16.73865	21.32488	43.53531
28	8.62711	11.16714	14.42099	18.57990	23.88387	50.06561
29	9.31727	12.17218	15.86309	20.62369	26.74993	57.57545
30	10.06266	13.26768	17.44940	22.89230	29.95992	66.21177
35	14.78534	20.41397	28.10244	38.57485	52.79962	133.17552
40	21.72452	31.40942	45.25926	65.00087	93.05097	267.86355

TABLE 2

Present Value of a Single Sum
$$PFVF = 1/(1 + i)^n$$

(n)	1%	2%	3%	4%	5%	6%	7%	8%
1	0.99010	0.98039	0.97087	0.96154	0.95238	0.94340	0.93458	0.92593
2	0.98030	0.96117	0.94260	0.92456	0.90703	0.89000	0.87344	0.85734
3	0.97059	0.94232	0.91514	0.88900	0.86384	0.83962	0.81630	0.79383
4	0.96098	0.92385	0.88849	0.85480	0.82270	0.79209	0.76290	0.73503
5	0.95147	0.90573	0.86261	0.82193	0.78353	0.74726	0.71299	0.68058
6	0.94205	0.88797	0.83748	0.79031	0.74622	0.70496	0.66634	0.63017
7	0.93272	0.87056	0.81309	0.75992	0.71068	0.66506	0.62275	0.58349
8	0.92348	0.85349	0.78941	0.73069	0.67684	0.62741	0.58201	0.54027
9	0.91434	0.83676	0.76642	0.70259	0.64461	0.59190	0.54393	0.50025
10	0.90529	0.82035	0.74409	0.67556	0.61391	0.55839	0.50835	0.46319
11	0.89632	0.80426	0.72242	0.64958	0.58468	0.52679	0.47509	0.42888
12	0.88745	0.78849	0.70138	0.62460	0.55684	0.49697	0.44401	0.39711
13	0.87866	0.77303	0.68095	0.60057	0.53032	0.46884	0.41496	0.36770
14	0.86996	0.75788	0.66112	0.57748	0.50507	0.44230	0.38782	0.34046
15	0.86135	0.74301	0.64186	0.55526	0.48102	0.41727	0.36245	0.31524
16	0.85282	0.72845	0.62317	0.53391	0.45811	0.39365	0.33873	0.29189
17	0.84438	0.71416	0.60502	0.51337	0.43630	0.37136	0.31657	0.27027
18	0.83602	0.70016	0.58739	0.49363	0.41552	0.35034	0.29586	0.25025
19	0.82774	0.68643	0.57029	0.47464	0.39573	0.33051	0.27651	0.23171
20	0.81954	0.67297	0.55368	0.45639	0.37689	0.31180	0.25842	0.21455
21	0.81143	0.65978	0.53755	0.43883	0.35894	0.29416	0.24151	0.19866
22	0.80340	0.64684	0.52189	0.42196	0.34185	0.27751	0.22571	0.18394
23	0.79544	0.63416	0.50669	0.40573	0.32557	0.26180	0.21095	0.17032
24	0.78757	0.62172	0.49193	0.39012	0.31007	0.24698	0.19715	0.15770
25	0.77977	0.60953	0.47761	0.37512	0.29530	0.23300	0.18425	0.14602
26	0.77205	0.59758	0.46369	0.36069	0.28124	0.21981	0.17220	0.13520
27	0.76440	0.58586	0.45019	0.34682	0.26785	0.20737	0.16093	0.12519
28	0.75684	0.57437	0.43708	0.33348	0.25509	0.19563	0.15040	0.11591
29	0.74934	0.56311	0.42435	0.32065	0.24295	0.18456	0.14056	0.10733
30	0.74192	0.55207	0.41199	0.30832	0.23138	0.17411	0.13137	0.09938
35	0.70591	0.50003	0.35538	0.25342	0.18129	0.13011	0.09366	0.06763
40	0.67165	0.45289	0.30656	0.20829	0.14205	0.09722	0.06678	0.04603

(continued)

TABLE 2 (CONTINUED)

Present Value of a Single Sum
$PFVF = 1/(1 + i)^n$

(n)	9%	10%	11%	12%	14%	15%	16%
1	0.91743	0.90909	0.90090	0.89286	0.87719	0.86957	0.86207
2	0.84168	0.82645	0.81162	0.79719	0.76947	0.75614	0.74316
3	0.77218	0.75131	0.73119	0.71178	0.67497	0.65752	0.64066
4	0.70843	0.68301	0.65873	0.63552	0.59208	0.57175	0.55229
5	0.64993	0.62092	0.59345	0.56743	0.51937	0.49718	0.47611
6	0.59627	0.56447	0.53464	0.50663	0.45559	0.43233	0.41044
7	0.54703	0.51316	0.48166	0.45235	0.39964	0.37594	0.35383
8	0.50187	0.46651	0.43393	0.40388	0.35056	0.32690	0.30503
9	0.46043	0.42410	0.39092	0.36061	0.30751	0.28426	0.26295
10	0.42241	0.38554	0.35218	0.32197	0.26974	0.24718	0.22668
11	0.38753	0.35049	0.31728	0.28748	0.23662	0.21494	0.19542
12	0.35553	0.31863	0.28584	0.25668	0.20756	0.18691	0.16846
13	0.32618	0.28966	0.25751	0.22917	0.18207	0.16253	0.14523
14	0.29925	0.26333	0.23199	0.20462	0.15971	0.14133	0.12520
15	0.27454	0.23939	0.20900	0.18270	0.14010	0.12289	0.10793
16	0.25187	0.21763	0.18829	0.16312	0.12289	0.10686	0.09304
17	0.23107	0.19784	0.16963	0.14564	0.10780	0.09293	0.08021
18	0.21199	0.17986	0.15282	0.13004	0.09456	0.08081	0.06914
19	0.19449	0.16351	0.13768	0.11611	0.08295	0.07027	0.05961
20	0.17843	0.14864	0.12403	0.10367	0.07276	0.06110	0.05139
21	0.16370	0.13513	0.11174	0.09256	0.06383	0.05313	0.04430
22	0.15018	0.12285	0.10067	0.08264	0.05599	0.04620	0.03819
23	0.13778	0.11168	0.09069	0.07379	0.04911	0.04017	0.03292
24	0.12640	0.10153	0.08170	0.06588	0.04308	0.03493	0.02838
25	0.11597	0.09230	0.07361	0.05882	0.03779	0.03038	0.02447
26	0.10639	0.08391	0.06631	0.05252	0.03315	0.02642	0.02109
27	0.09761	0.07628	0.05974	0.04689	0.02908	0.02297	0.01818
28	0.08955	0.06934	0.05382	0.04187	0.02551	0.01997	0.01567
29	0.08215	0.06304	0.04849	0.03738	0.02237	0.01737	0.01351
30	0.07537	0.05731	0.04368	0.03338	0.01963	0.01510	0.01165
35	0.04899	0.03558	0.02592	0.01894	0.01019	0.00751	0.00555
40	0.03184	0.02209	0.01538	0.01075	0.00529	0.00373	0.00264

TABLE 3

Future Amount of an Ordinary Annuity
$FVF - OA = [(1 + i)^n - 1]/i$

(n)	2%	3%	4%	5%	6%	7%	8%
1	1.00000	1.00000	1.00000	1.00000	1.00000	1.00000	1.00000
2	2.02000	2.03000	2.04000	2.05000	2.06000	2.07000	2.08000
3	3.06040	3.09090	3.12160	3.15250	3.18360	3.21490	3.24640
4	4.12161	4.18363	4.24646	4.31013	4.37462	4.43994	4.50611
5	5.20404	5.30914	5.41632	5.52563	5.63709	5.75074	5.86660
6	6.30812	6.46841	6.63298	6.80191	6.97532	7.15329	7.33593
7	7.43428	7.66246	7.89829	8.14201	8.39384	8.65402	8.92280
8	8.58297	8.89234	9.21423	9.54911	9.89747	10.25980	10.63663
9	9.75463	10.15911	10.58280	11.02656	11.49132	11.97799	12.48756
10	10.94972	11.46388	12.00611	12.57789	13.18079	13.81645	14.48656
11	12.16872	12.80780	13.48635	14.20679	14.97164	15.78360	16.64549
12	13.41209	14.19203	15.02581	15.91713	16.86994	17.88845	18.97713
13	14.68033	15.61779	16.62684	17.71298	18.88214	20.14064	21.49530
14	15.97394	17.08632	18.29191	19.59863	21.01507	22.55049	24.21492
15	17.29342	18.59891	20.02359	21.57856	23.27597	25.12902	27.15211
16	18.63929	20.15688	21.82453	23.65749	25.67253	27.88805	30.32428
17	20.01207	21.76159	23.69751	25.84037	28.21288	30.84022	33.75023
18	21.41231	23.41444	25.64541	28.13238	30.90565	33.99903	37.45024
19	22.84056	25.11687	27.67123	30.53900	33.75999	37.37896	41.44626
20	24.29737	26.87037	29.77808	33.06595	36.78559	40.99549	45.76196
21	25.78332	28.67649	31.96920	35.71925	39.99273	44.86518	50.42292
22	27.29898	30.53678	34.24797	38.50521	43.39229	49.00574	55.45676
23	28.84496	32.45288	36.61789	41.43048	46.99583	53.43614	60.89330
24	30.42186	34.42647	39.08260	44.50200	50.81558	58.17667	66.76476
25	32.03030	36.45926	41.64591	47.72710	54.86451	63.24904	73.10594
26	33.67091	38.55304	44.31174	51.11345	59.15638	68.67647	79.95442
27	35.34432	40.70963	47.08421	54.66913	63.70577	74.48382	87.35077
28	37.05121	42.93092	49.96758	58.40258	68.52811	80.69769	95.33883
29	38.79223	45.21885	52.96629	62.32271	73.63980	87.34653	103.96594
30	40.56808	47.57542	56.08494	66.43885	79.05819	94.46079	113.28321
35	49.99448	60.46208	73.65222	90.32031	111.43478	138.23688	172.31680
40	60.40198	75.40126	95.02552	120.79977	154.76197	199.63511	259.05652

(continued)

TABLE 3 (CONTINUED)

Future Amount of an Ordinary Annuity
$FVF - OA = [(1 + i)^n - 1]/i$

(n)	9%	10%	11%	12%	15%	16%
1	1.00000	1.00000	1.00000	1.00000	1.00000	1.00000
2	2.09000	2.10000	2.11000	2.12000	2.15000	2.16000
3	3.27810	3.31000	3.34210	3.37440	3.47250	3.50560
4	4.57313	4.64100	4.70973	4.77933	4.99338	5.06650
5	5.98471	6.10510	6.22780	6.35285	6.74238	6.87714
6	7.52333	7.71561	7.91286	8.11519	8.75374	8.97748
7	9.20043	9.48717	9.78327	10.08901	11.06680	11.41387
8	11.02847	11.43589	11.85943	12.29969	13.72682	14.24009
9	13.02104	13.57948	14.16397	14.77566	16.78584	17.51851
10	15.19293	15.93742	16.72201	17.54874	20.30372	21.32147
11	17.56029	18.53117	19.56143	20.65458	24.34928	25.73290
12	20.14072	21.38428	22.71319	24.13313	29.00167	30.85017
13	22.95338	24.52271	26.21164	28.02911	34.35192	36.78620
14	26.01919	27.97498	30.09492	32.39260	40.50471	43.67199
15	29.36092	31.77248	34.40536	37.27971	47.58041	51.65951
16	33.00340	35.94973	39.18995	42.75328	55.71747	60.92503
17	36.97370	40.54470	44.50084	48.88367	65.07509	71.67303
18	41.30134	45.59917	50.39594	55.74971	75.83636	84.14072
19	46.01846	51.15909	56.93949	63.43968	88.21181	98.60323
20	51.16012	57.27500	64.20283	72.05244	102.44358	115.37975
21	56.76453	64.00250	72.26514	81.69874	118.81012	134.84051
22	62.87334	71.40275	81.21431	92.50258	137.63164	157.41499
23	69.53194	79.54302	91.14788	104.60289	159.27638	183.60138
24	76.78981	88.49733	102.17415	118.15524	184.16784	213.97761
25	84.70090	98.34706	114.41331	133.33387	212.79302	249.21402
26	93.32398	109.18177	127.99877	150.33393	245.71197	290.08827
27	102.72313	121.09994	143.07864	169.37401	283.56877	337.50239
28	112.96822	134.20994	159.81729	190.69889	327.10408	392.50277
29	124.13536	148.63093	178.39719	214.58275	377.16969	456.30322
30	136.30754	164.49402	199.02088	241.33268	434.74515	530.31173
35	215.71075	271.02437	341.58955	431.66350	881.17016	1120.71295
40	337.88245	442.59256	581.82607	767.09142	1779.09031	2360.75724

TABLE 4

Present Value of an Ordinary Annuity

$$PVF-OA = \frac{1 - \dfrac{1}{(1+i)^n}}{i}$$

(n)	1%	2%	3%	4%	5%	6%	7%	8%
1	0.99010	0.98039	0.97087	0.96154	0.95238	0.94340	0.93458	0.92593
2	1.97040	1.94156	1.91347	1.88609	1.85941	1.83339	1.80802	1.78326
3	2.94099	2.88388	2.82861	2.77509	2.72325	2.67301	2.62432	2.57710
4	3.90197	3.80773	3.71710	3.62990	3.54595	3.46511	3.38721	3.31213
5	4.85343	4.71346	4.57971	4.45182	4.32948	4.21236	4.10020	3.99271
6	5.79548	5.60143	5.41719	5.24214	5.07569	4.91732	4.76654	4.62288
7	6.72819	6.47199	6.23028	6.00205	5.78637	5.58238	5.38929	5.20637
8	7.65168	7.32548	7.01969	6.73274	6.46321	6.20979	5.97130	5.74664
9	8.56602	8.16224	7.78611	7.43533	7.10782	6.80169	6.51523	6.24689
10	9.47130	8.98259	8.53020	8.11090	7.72173	7.36009	7.02358	6.71008
11	10.36763	9.78685	9.25262	8.76048	8.30641	7.88687	7.49867	7.13896
12	11.25508	10.57534	9.95400	9.38507	8.86325	8.38384	7.94269	7.53608
13	12.13374	11.34837	10.63496	9.98565	9.39357	8.85268	8.35765	7.90378
14	13.00370	12.10625	11.29607	10.56312	9.89864	9.29498	8.74547	8.24424
15	13.86505	12.84926	11.93794	11.11839	10.37966	9.71225	9.10791	8.55948
16	14.71787	13.57771	12.56110	11.65230	10.83777	10.10590	9.44665	8.85137
17	15.56225	14.29187	13.16612	12.16567	11.27407	10.47726	9.76322	9.12164
18	16.39827	14.99203	13.75351	12.65930	11.68959	10.82760	10.05909	9.37189
19	17.22601	15.67846	14.32380	13.13394	12.08532	11.15812	10.33560	9.60360
20	18.04555	16.35143	14.87747	13.59033	12.46221	11.46992	10.59401	9.81815
21	18.85698	17.01121	15.41502	14.02916	12.82115	11.76408	10.83553	10.01680
22	19.66038	17.65805	15.93692	14.45112	13.16300	12.04158	11.06124	10.20074
23	20.45582	18.29220	16.44361	14.85684	13.48857	12.30338	11.27219	10.37106
24	21.24339	18.91393	16.93554	15.24696	13.79864	12.55036	11.46933	10.52876
25	22.02316	19.52346	17.41315	15.62208	14.09394	12.78336	11.65358	10.67478
26	22.79520	20.12104	17.87684	15.98277	14.37519	13.00317	11.82578	10.80998
27	23.55961	20.70690	18.32703	16.32959	14.64303	13.21053	11.98671	10.93516
28	24.31644	21.28127	18.76411	16.66306	14.89813	13.40616	12.13711	11.05108
29	25.06579	21.84438	19.18845	16.98371	15.14107	13.59072	12.27767	11.15841
30	25.80771	22.39646	19.60044	17.29203	15.37245	13.76483	12.40904	11.25778
35	29.40858	24.99862	21.48722	18.66461	16.37419	14.49825	12.94767	11.65457
40	32.83469	27.35548	23.11477	19.79277	17.15909	15.04630	13.33171	11.92461

(continued)

TABLE 4 (CONTINUED)

Present Value of an Ordinary Annuity

$$PVF-OA = \frac{1 - \dfrac{1}{(1+i)^n}}{i}$$

(n)	9%	10%	11%	12%	14%	15%	16%
1	0.91743	0.90909	0.90090	0.89286	0.87719	0.86957	0.86207
2	1.75911	1.73554	1.71252	1.69005	1.64666	1.62571	1.60523
3	2.53129	2.48685	2.44371	2.40183	2.32163	2.28323	2.24589
4	3.23972	3.16987	3.10245	3.03735	2.91371	2.85498	2.79818
5	3.88965	3.79079	3.69590	3.60478	3.43308	3.35216	3.27429
6	4.48592	4.35526	4.23054	4.11141	3.88867	3.78448	3.68474
7	5.03295	4.86842	4.71220	4.56376	4.28830	4.16042	4.03857
8	5.53482	5.33493	5.14612	4.96764	4.63886	4.48732	4.34359
9	5.99525	5.75902	5.53705	5.32825	4.94637	4.77158	4.60654
10	6.41766	6.14457	5.88923	5.65022	5.21612	5.01877	4.83323
11	6.80519	6.49506	6.20652	5.93770	5.45273	5.23371	5.02864
12	7.16073	6.81369	6.49236	6.19437	5.66029	5.42062	5.19711
13	7.48690	7.10336	6.74987	6.42355	5.84236	5.58315	5.34233
14	7.78615	7.36669	6.98187	6.62817	6.00207	5.72448	5.46753
15	8.06069	7.60608	7.19087	6.81086	6.14217	5.84737	5.57546
16	8.31256	7.82371	7.37916	6.97399	6.26506	5.95423	5.66850
17	8.54363	8.02155	7.54879	7.11963	6.37286	6.04716	5.74870
18	8.75563	8.20141	7.70162	7.24967	6.46742	6.12797	5.81785
19	8.95011	8.36492	7.83929	7.36578	6.55037	6.19823	5.87746
20	9.12855	8.51356	7.96333	7.46944	6.62313	6.25933	5.92884
21	9.29224	8.64869	8.07507	7.56200	6.68696	6.31246	5.97314
22	9.44243	8.77154	8.17574	7.64465	6.74294	6.35866	6.01133
23	9.58021	8.88322	8.26643	7.71843	6.79206	6.39884	6.04425
24	9.70661	8.98474	8.34814	7.78432	6.83514	6.43377	6.07263
25	9.82258	9.07704	8.42174	7.84314	6.87293	6.46415	6.09709
26	9.92897	9.16095	8.48806	7.89566	6.90608	6.49056	6.11818
27	10.02658	9.23722	8.54780	7.94255	6.93515	6.51353	6.13636
28	10.11613	9.30657	8.60162	7.98442	6.96066	6.53351	6.15204
29	10.19828	9.36961	8.65011	8.02181	6.98304	6.55088	6.16555
30	10.27365	9.42691	8.69379	8.05518	7.00266	6.56598	6.17720
35	10.56682	9.64416	8.85524	8.17550	7.07005	6.61661	6.21534
40	10.75736	9.77905	8.95105	8.24378	7.10504	6.64178	6.23350

TABLE 5

Present Value of an Annuity Due

$$PVF - AD = 1 + \frac{1 - \dfrac{1}{(1 + i)^n}}{i}$$

(n)	2%	3%	4%	5%	6%	7%	8%
1	1.00000	1.00000	1.00000	1.00000	1.00000	1.00000	1.00000
2	1.98039	1.97087	1.96154	1.95238	1.94340	1.93458	1.92593
3	2.94156	2.91347	2.88609	2.85941	2.83339	2.80802	2.78326
4	3.88388	3.82861	3.77509	3.72325	3.67301	3.62432	3.57710
5	4.80773	4.71710	4.62990	4.54595	4.46511	4.38721	4.31213
6	5.71346	5.57971	5.45182	5.32948	5.21236	5.10020	4.99271
7	6.60143	6.41719	6.24214	6.07569	5.91732	5.76654	5.62288
8	7.47199	7.23028	7.00205	6.78637	6.58238	6.38929	6.20637
9	8.32548	8.01969	7.73274	7.46321	7.20979	6.97130	6.74664
10	9.16224	8.78611	8.43533	8.10782	7.80169	7.51523	7.24689
11	9.98259	9.53020	9.11090	8.72173	8.36009	8.02358	7.71008
12	10.78685	10.25262	9.76048	9.30641	8.88687	8.49867	8.13896
13	11.57534	10.95400	10.38507	9.86325	9.38384	8.94269	8.53608
14	12.34837	11.63496	10.98565	10.39357	9.85268	9.35765	8.90378
15	13.10625	12.29607	11.56312	10.89864	10.29498	9.74547	9.24424
16	13.84926	12.93794	12.11839	11.37966	10.71225	10.10791	9.55948
17	14.57771	13.56110	12.65230	11.83777	11.10590	10.44665	9.85137
18	15.29187	14.16612	13.16567	12.27407	11.47726	10.76322	10.12164
19	15.99203	14.75351	13.65930	12.68959	11.82760	11.05909	10.37189
20	16.67846	15.32380	14.13394	13.08532	12.15812	11.33560	10.60360
21	17.35143	15.87747	14.59033	13.46221	12.46992	11.59401	10.81815
22	18.01121	16.41502	15.02916	13.82115	12.76408	11.83553	11.01680
23	18.65805	16.93692	15.45112	14.16300	13.04158	12.06124	11.20074
24	19.29220	17.44361	15.85684	14.48857	13.30338	12.27219	11.37106
25	19.91393	17.93554	16.24696	14.79864	13.55036	12.46933	11.52876
26	20.52346	18.41315	16.62208	15.09394	13.78336	12.65358	11.67478
27	21.12104	18.87684	16.98277	15.37519	14.00317	12.82578	11.80998
28	21.70690	19.32703	17.32959	15.64303	14.21053	12.98671	11.93516
29	22.28127	19.76411	17.66306	15.89813	14.40616	13.13711	12.05108
30	22.84438	20.18845	17.98371	16.14107	14.59072	13.27767	12.15841
35	25.49859	22.13184	19.41120	17.19290	15.36814	13.85401	12.58693
40	27.90259	23.80822	20.58448	18.01704	15.94907	14.26493	12.87858

(continued)

TABLE 5 (CONTINUED)

Present Value of an Annuity Due

$$\text{PVF} - \text{AD} = 1 + \dfrac{1 - \dfrac{1}{(1 + i)^n}}{i}$$

(n)	9%	10%	11%	12%	14%	15%	16%
1	1.00000	1.00000	1.00000	1.00000	1.00000	1.00000	1.00000
2	1.91743	1.90909	1.90090	1.89286	1.87719	1.86957	1.86207
3	2.75911	2.73554	2.71252	2.69005	2.64666	2.62571	2.60523
4	3.53129	3.48685	3.44371	3.40183	3.32163	3.28323	3.24589
5	4.23972	4.16987	4.10245	4.03735	3.91371	3.85498	3.79818
6	4.88965	4.79079	4.69590	4.60478	4.43308	4.35216	4.27429
7	5.48592	5.35526	5.23054	5.11141	4.88867	4.78448	4.68474
8	6.03295	5.86842	5.71220	5.56376	5.28830	5.16042	5.03857
9	6.53482	6.33493	6.14612	5.96764	5.63886	5.48732	5.34359
10	6.99525	6.75902	6.53705	6.32825	5.94637	5.77158	5.60654
11	7.41766	7.14457	6.88923	6.65022	6.21612	6.01877	5.83323
12	7.80519	7.49506	7.20652	6.93770	6.45273	6.23371	6.02864
13	8.16073	7.81369	7.49236	7.19437	6.66029	6.42062	6.19711
14	8.48690	8.10336	7.74987	7.42355	6.84236	6.58315	6.34233
15	8.78615	8.36669	7.98187	7.62817	7.00207	6.72448	6.46753
16	9.06069	8.60608	8.19087	7.81086	7.14217	6.84737	6.57546
17	9.31256	8.82371	8.37916	7.97399	7.26506	6.95423	6.66850
18	9.54363	9.02155	8.54879	8.11963	7.37286	7.04716	6.74870
19	9.75563	9.20141	8.70162	8.24967	7.46742	7.12797	6.81785
20	9.95011	9.36492	8.83929	8.36578	7.55037	7.19823	6.87746
21	10.12855	9.51356	8.96333	8.46944	7.62313	7.25933	6.92884
22	10.29224	9.64869	9.07507	8.56200	7.68696	7.31246	6.97314
23	10.44243	9.77154	9.17574	8.64465	7.74294	7.35866	7.01133
24	10.58021	9.88322	9.26643	8.71843	7.79206	7.39884	7.04425
25	10.70661	9.98474	9.34814	8.78432	7.83514	7.43377	7.07263
26	10.82258	10.07704	9.42174	8.84314	7.87293	7.46415	7.09709
27	10.92897	10.16095	9.48806	8.89566	7.90608	7.49056	7.11818
28	11.02658	10.23722	9.54780	8.94255	7.93515	7.51353	7.13636
29	11.11613	10.30657	9.60162	8.98442	7.96066	7.53351	7.15204
30	11.19828	10.36961	9.65011	9.02181	7.98304	7.55088	7.16555
35	11.51784	10.60857	9.82932	9.15656	8.05985	7.60910	7.20979
40	11.72552	10.75696	9.93567	9.23303	8.09975	7.63805	7.23086

APPENDIX B: Preparing an Electronic Spreadsheet Amortization Table Using Excel

Electronic spreadsheets are a tremendous labor-saving tool for accountants—particularly for amortization tables, where just a few key commands can result in a completed amortization table. The following commands are just one example of how an amortization table can be constructed on an electronic spreadsheet, using Excel. With only minimal knowledge, other commands can be used to either expedite the process or to "dress up" this rather bland worksheet.

The easiest way to execute the copy command is to use the mouse: highlight the cells from B16 through E16 by holding the left mouse button down while scanning across the cells and then releasing the mouse; then move the mouse to the lower right-hand corner where the shape of the cursor changes to a plus sign; then, left click on the mouse and drag it down to the end of the table.

	A	B	C	D	E	F
4	FACE AMOUNT OF THE BONDS				$400,000	
5	COUPON RATE OF INTEREST				4	
6	MARKET RATE OF INTEREST				5	Inputs
7	NO. OF INTEREST PERIODS				20	
8						
9	COMPUTING PV OF THE NOTE					
10	PV OF THE PRINCIPAL				=((1/(1+E6/100)^E7)*E4)	
11	PV OF THE INTEREST				=((1-(1/(1+E6/100)^E7))/E6*100)*(E4*E5/100)	
12	TOTAL PV				=SUM(E10:E11)	
13						
14	PERIOD	CASH	INTEREST	DISCOUNT /PREMIUM	CARRYING AMOUNT	
15					=E12	
16	1	=1$E$4*$E$5/100	=$E$6*E15/100	=C16−B16	=E15+D16	
17	2		(Then use the "Copy" command to complete the table)			
35						
37	20					

Questions

1. Theoretically, how should all liabilities be valued, even those classified as current liabilities? What is the justification for not using the theoretically preferred measurement for current liabilities?

2. Each of these three present value factors corresponds with a 10% interest rate and 10 periods. Without referring to present value/future amount tables, identify the table from which each factor was obtained, and explain what the factor represents:

   a. 0.38554
   b. 6.14457
   c. 6.75902

3. Explain the difference between an ordinary annuity and an annuity due.

4. Suppose that a 5% annual return was guaranteed (the return would be no more and no less). Considering only financial factors, would a logical person prefer to receive $100 today or $105 one year from today? Why?

5. What three data items must be identified in order to determine the present value of a liability?

6. Suppose that Woodruff Corp. has two long-term notes payable, which both require payments of $12,000 each year for 10 years. The only difference in the notes is that Note 1 requires monthly payments of $1,000 per month, whereas Note 2 requires a payment at the end of the year for $12,000. Will the carrying value of the notes be equal? If not, and without doing the math, which note will have the higher carrying value? Explain your answer.

7. What is the relationship between premiums/discounts and the coupon interest rate on a bond versus the market interest rate?

8. Suppose a company issues a $1,000 bond at 94. Is the bond selling at a premium or discount? Was the stated interest rate on the bond lower or higher than the market rate of interest? If the company sells 1,000 of such bonds, what will the proceeds received be? How is the discount or premium reported on the balance sheet?

9. Indicate how a bond's face value will compare to its present value (or maturity value) under each of the following circumstances.
   a. The stated interest rate is greater than the market rate for debt of similar risk.
   b. The stated interest rate is less than the market rate for debt of similar risk.
   c. The stated interest rate is equal to the market rate for debt of similar risk.
   d. The stated interest rate is equal to the market rate for debt of greater risk.

10. Suppose that Hewlett-Packard (a Fortune 500 company) and Be Free Inc. (a company that helps its customers manage Internet business and made its initial public stock offering in late 1999) issued bonds on the same day. Both issuances carry the same interest rates and require cash payments to be made on the same future dates. Which company would probably receive the most proceeds from its respective issuance? Why?

11. Would an investor receive the same rate of return on two bonds that are of equal risk if one bond had a coupon rate of 8% and the other had a coupon rate of 12%?

12. Why is accrued interest recognized when bonds are sold between interest dates? For the issuer of the bonds, what alternative accounts are available for recording the accrued interest?

13. How is interest expense determined under the effective-interest method? How is interest expense determined under the straight-line method? Over the life of the bonds, will the interest expense as computed under the effective-interest method be greater than, equal to, or less than the interest expense as computed under the straight-line method?

14. Using the effective-interest method and assuming that a bond was issued at a discount, will the amount of the amortization of the discount increase, remain the same, or decrease over time? Answer the same question, except assume that the bond was issued at a premium. (*Hint:* Prove your answers by constructing amortization tables.)

15. For the issuer of bonds, under what circumstances will the effective-interest method result in a higher net income than the straight-line method? Will this be true over the life of the bonds?

16. How is the gain or loss on early extinguishment of debt determined? How is the gain or loss on early extinguishment of debt reported on the income statement?

17. What are bond issue costs? What is the recommended accounting and financial reporting treatment for bond issue costs under GAAP?

18. Stuppor Co. receives used equipment from another company in exchange for a non-interest-bearing $50,000 note. The terms of the note require Stuppor to pay annual payments of $10,000 for the next five years, with the first payment due upon delivery of the equipment. The market rate of interest for notes having a similar risk is 12%. Due to the specialized nature of the used equipment, a readily determinable value is not available. Explain how the historical cost of the equipment is determined, and then determine that amount.

19. Suppose a note is exchanged for property, goods, or services.
    a. How is the transaction measured if the note has a reasonable interest rate? Explain.
    b. How is the transaction measured if the note does not have an interest rate or the interest rate is unreasonable? Explain.

20. Distinguish between (a) secured and unsecured bonds, (b) term and serial bonds, and (c) callable and convertible bonds.

Exercises

Exercise 11-1: Financial Statement Classification. Jorgenson, Inc., had the following accounts in its records. Define where and how each should be presented in the financial statements.

a. Treasury bonds
b. Premium on bonds payable
c. Bond issue costs
d. Discount on bonds payable
e. Accrued interest payable on bonds issued between interest payments
f. A 5-year note payable
g. That portion of long-term debt that is due within one year

Exercise 11-2: Market Value of Bonds. Hickson Corporation desires to raise new capital for working capital purposes by issuing 20-year bonds that will pay interest semiannually. The face value of the bonds will be $1,000,000, but management is still trying to determine the stated interest rate. The market rate of interest for bonds of this type is 10%.

Determine the amount of proceeds that would be raised from the bond issue, assuming that the stated annual interest rate on the bonds is:

1. 8%
2. 10%
3. 12%
4. Non-interest-bearing

Exercise 11-3: Computing Issuing Price and Preparing Amortization Tables. For each of the following issuances of 100 bonds with a face amount of $1,000 per bond and a market rate of interest of 10%, compute the price at which each of the bonds will be issued, and then prepare amortization tables for each bond issuance for the first three years using (1) the effective-interest method and (2) the straight-line method.

Bond issuances:

a. A 10-year, 8% bond paying interest annually
b. A 20-year, 12% bond paying interest semiannually
c. A 10-year, non-interest-bearing bond (frequently referred to as zero-interest bonds or deep discount bonds). Discount assuming an annual rate of interest.

Exercise 11-4: Computing the Issuing Price of Bonds and Preparing Effective-Interest Amortization Table, Using an Electronic Spreadsheet. On December 31, 2003, SS Minnow, Inc., issued 20-year bonds with a face value of $50 million to the public to purchase a new ship. The bonds carry an interest rate of 12%, and interest payments are to be made each December 31. The market interest rate on securities of similar risk is 10%.

1. Prepare the journal entry for SS Minnow to issue the bonds.
2. Prepare an amortization table, using an electronic spreadsheet and the effective-interest method.
3. From the amortization table, prepare the journal entry to recognize interest and amortize any bond premium/discount as of December 31, 2004.

Exercise 11-5: Electronic Spreadsheets and Amortization Tables, Using the Effective-Interest Method. On December 31, 2004, Stepley, Inc., issued $100,000 of 10-year bonds with an interest rate of 6%. The market rate of interest for bonds of similar risk is 9%. The bonds pay interest semiannually at December 31 of each year.

1. Prepare the journal entry to record the issuing of the bonds.
2. Using an electronic spreadsheet, prepare an amortization table that tracks the carrying value of the bonds, using the effective-interest method.
3. From the amortization table, prepare the journal entries to recognize interest for the first two interest periods.

Exercise 11-6: Accounting for Discounts/Premiums on Bonds. Suppose that Hemli Corp. issued 5-year, 8% bonds with a face value of $100,000. The bonds pay interest annually and were sold on the market for $96,000.

1. Assuming that the market price of bonds is determined only by the relationship between the coupon rate of interest and the market rate, what is that relationship?
2. For this same bond, will the total interest expense over the life of the bonds as computed under the effective-interest method be greater than, equal to, or less than the interest expense as computed under the straight-line method?
3. For the earlier years of the bonds, will interest expense using the effective-interest method be greater than, equal to, or less than the interest expense as computed under the straight-line method?
4. Using the effective-interest method, will the amount of amortization of the discount increase, remain the same, or decrease over time?
5. Prove your reasoning is correct by determining the effective yield on the bonds and constructing an amortization table, using the effective-interest method.

6. Answer Parts 3–5, except assume that the bond was issued at $104,000 instead of $96,000.

Exercise 11-7: Issuing Bonds between Interest Payment Dates. Sherlock Co. desires to build a new office building. The company explored various financing alternatives and ultimately decided the best option was to issue bonds to the public. Accordingly, a total of 5,000 bonds with a face value of $1,000 each were issued on March 1, 2004. The bonds were dated as of January 1, 2004, and pay interest semiannually on June 30 and December 31 of each year and expire on December 31, 2013. The stated interest rate on the bonds is 9% compounded semiannually, and the bonds were issued at 94.

1. Prepare the required journal entry for issuing the bonds.
2. Using an electronic spreadsheet, prepare an amortization table, using the straight-line method.
3. From the amortization table, prepare the required journal entry for each of the interest payments in 2004.

Exercise 11-8: Issuing Bonds between Interest Payment Dates and Bond Issue Costs. On April 1, 2004, Ash Company sold 2,000 of its 8%, $1,000 bonds at 99 plus accrued interest. The bonds are dated January 1, 2004, and mature in 10 years. Interest is paid semiannually on June 30 and December 31. The cost of issuing the bonds was $130,000. Prepare the following journal entries, assuming the straight-line method is used to amortize the bond discount and bond issue costs.

1. Issuing the bonds, including the cost of issuing the bonds
2. First interest payment, assuming that bond issue costs are amortized only at year-end
3. Year-end interest payment, including amortizing the bond issue costs

Exercise 11-9: Issuing and Retiring Bonds. On January 2, 2004, Watson, Inc., issued $4 million of 9% bonds that mature in 10 years and pay interest annually. At the time, the market rate of interest on bonds of similar risk was 8.5%. On January 2, 2010, interest rates were at 9.5%, and so Watson, Inc., repurchased $1 million of the bonds at their current market values of $984,000.

1. Calculate the price at which the bonds were issued at January 2, 2004.
2. Prepare an amortization table, using the effective-interest method.
3. Prepare the required journal entries to record the repurchase of the bonds, assuming that
   a. The bonds are retired.
   b. The bonds are held in the treasury.
4. How should the gain/loss on early extinguishment of debt be reported on the income statement?

Exercise 11-10: Issuing and Retiring Bonds. Desert Image Company issued $500,000 of 10%, 10-year bonds at 103 on January 1, 2002. The bonds pay interest annually on December 31, and Desert Image amortizes the premium using the straight-line method. Also, the bonds are callable at 105 at the option of Desert Image any time after December 31, 2005. On December 31, 2006, Desert Image called $100,000 of the bonds and retired them.

1. Prepare the journal entries for issuing the bonds, the first interest payment, and the call of the bonds.

(continued)

2. Prepare the journal entries for an investor who purchased 20% of the bonds for acquiring the bonds, the first interest payment, and the call of the bonds, assuming that all the bonds retired were owned by this investor.
3. State how the gain/loss for Desert Image is reported on the December 31, 2006 income statement?

Exercise 11-11: Computing Interest Expense on Long-Term Debt. On January 2, 2004, Kobe Bryant Associates (KBA) issued three separate issues of debt as follows:

a. $25 million, 20-year bonds that bear interest at 11% and require semiannual payments on June 30 and December 31 of each year. The market rate of interest for similar bonds is 8%.
b. A $500,000 note payable that requires end of the month payments for three years. The interest rate on the note is 10%, which is similar to the market rate of interest for similar notes.
c. $1 million, zero-interest bonds were issued that expire in 10 years. The bonds were issued to yield a 9% return.

Calculate the amount of interest expense that KBA should report on its 2004 income statement, assuming that it uses the effective-interest method of amortization.

Exercise 11-12: Non-Interest-Bearing Note. On August 1, 2003, Entrada Company sold some used equipment that originally cost $80,000 and had accumulated depreciation of $60,000. The equipment was rather unique and did not have any ready second-hand market. As a result, Entrada was pleased that it had been able to find a buyer. In exchange, Entrada received a non-interest-bearing note of $25,000 that is due in two years. Entrada's management thinks that a reasonable rate of interest on the note is 14%.

Assuming that Entrada's fiscal year-end is December 31, prepare the necessary journal entries for the note for the 2-year period.

Exercise 11-13: Issuing Long-Term Notes. On January 1, 2004, Johnson Company issued a $1,000, 3-year note to pay for special equipment. The note stipulates an annual interest rate of 4%, which is considerably below the market rate for similar notes. Prepare journal entries for the purchase of the equipment and the cash flows related to the note over the three years, including paying the note at maturity, under each of the following assumptions.

1. The same type of equipment is sold for cash of $925. Interest is paid yearly, and the principal is paid at maturity. The straight-line method of amortization is used.
2. The fair value of the equipment is not readily determinable, and the note requires annual interest payments and a lump-sum principal payment at the expiration of the note. The market rate for similar notes is 8%. Use the effective-interest method of amortization.
3. The fair value of the equipment is not readily determinable, the market rate of interest is 8%, and the note is to be paid in three equal annual installments, with the first payment due one year from the signing of the note. Use the effective-interest method of amortization. (*Hint:* You must first compute the annual payment amount.)

Exercise 11-14: Acquiring Assets with Long-Term Notes. Howard Corporation purchased three different machines during 2004. In each case, due to the nature of the machines, a readily available market value was not available. Determine the amounts at which Howard should record each machine if Howard's cost of borrowing money is 10%.

1. Machine No. 1 was purchased by exchanging a $10,000 note with a stated interest rate of 4%. The note requires annual interest payments, and the principal is paid at the end of five years.
2. Machine No. 2 was purchased by exchanging a non-interest-bearing note that requires three annual payments of $4,000 with the first payment made in one year.
3. Machine No. 3 was purchased by exchanging a $9,000 note that bears interest at 8%. Four equal annual installments of $3,492 are required.

Exercise 11-15: Building Acquisition. On January 2, 2004, Progressive Insurance acquired a building by exchanging a $700,000 5-year non-interest-bearing note. The building does not have an established exchange price, but competent appraisal put the value of the building at $420,000. If Progressive had borrowed the money from the bank, it would have paid an interest rate of 12%.

Prepare the journal entries for the first three years of the note by (1) assuming that it is valued at the appraisal price of the building and by (2) discounting the cash flows of the note at the market rate.

Exercise 11-16: Long-Term Notes Payable. Hazel Manufacturing, Inc., purchased new equipment from Longley Corporation that will be used in its manufacturing process. The equipment was custom-made for Hazel and therefore does not have a readily available market value. Hazel financed the purchase by signing a 5-year note in the amount of $40,000. Explain how Hazel should account for this transaction under each of the following scenarios, including amounts.

1. The interest rate stated on the note is 9%, which approximates a fair value compensation for notes of this type.
2. Hazel Manufacturing is a preferred customer of Longley, and Longley regularly provides favorable financing terms to such customers. Accordingly, Longley charges Hazel 4% interest on the note, and the interest is due at the end of each year, with the principal due in five years. The market rate on the note is 9%.

Exercise 11-17: Note with Other Rights and Privileges. Dixie Medical Supply borrowed $50,000 from a major customer, signing a non-interest-bearing note for the amount that is due in three years. In return, Dixie promised to supply the customer's needs for inventory at less than market prices for the 3-year period. Prior to borrowing the money from the major customer, Dixie had tried to borrow the needed funds from a bank, but the best interest rate it had been able to obtain was 14%. Dixie presumes that the major customer's needs will be approximately equal each year.

Prepare the journal entries necessary to account for the life of the note, including the appropriate recognition of revenue.

Exercise 11-18: Issuing Notes for Cash and Other Privileges. Howard Company borrowed $1,050 from Miller Corporation. In exchange, Howard signed a $1,000 note bearing interest at a compound rate of 6% that is payable in two years. The current market rate of interest for notes of similar risk is 9%. In addition, Howard agreed to sell merchandise to Miller at preferential prices.

1. Determine the present value of the note payable. Contrast this amount with the cash proceeds received by Howard Company. (Round amounts to the nearest cent.)

(continued)

2. Prepare the journal entry that should be made by both Howard Company and Miller Corporation to record the above transaction.

Exercise 11-19: Implicit Interest Rate. Morgan Corporation purchased $24,000 of merchandise from Stanley, Inc., and was given two options to finance the purchase. Morgan could pay cash upon delivery and receive a $2,400 discount, or Morgan could finance the purchase by paying 24 equal monthly payments of $1,150, with the first payment due one month after delivery.

1. Determine the monthly interest rate that is implicit in the transaction.
2. Record the transaction, assuming that Morgan chose to purchase the merchandise by paying cash upon delivery.
3. Record the transaction, assuming that Morgan decided to finance the purchase by making 24 monthly payments of $1,000, and also record the first month's payment.

Exercise 11-20: Note Amortization Tables. On January 1, 2004, Jones Company signed a 5-year note payable with a face value of $10,000 to purchase a new vehicle. The stated annual interest rate on the note is 6%, and the market rate of interest for similar notes is 12%. The note requires equal monthly installments to pay off the accrued interest and part of the principal amount.

1. Compute the amount of the monthly payments.
2. Using the effective-interest method, prepare an amortization table that shows the monthly payment, interest expense, and the remaining principal amount on the note for the 60 periods.
3. Prepare the journal entries for the first two monthly payments.

Exercise 11-21: Types of Bonds. Define and distinguish between the following types of bonds:

  a. Deep discount bonds
  b. Registered bonds
  c. Callable bonds
  d. Treasury bonds
  e. Unsecured bonds
  f. Zero-coupon bonds
  g. Serial bonds
  h. Term bonds
  i. Convertible bonds

Problems

Problem 11-1: Various Bond Issues.

Required:
Answer the following questions:

1. Explain the effective-interest method of amortizing a bond premium/discount. How does this method differ from the straight-line method? Which is the more appropriate method to use?

2. Consider a 10-year bond that was issued at a premium. Which method of amortization—effective-interest or the straight-line method—will result in the higher interest expense in the first year of issuance? Graphically present how the bond premium is amortized under each method.

3. Explain how appropriate journal entries are prepared when a bond is issued between interest payment dates.

4. Assume that a company repurchases its bonds on the open market at a time when interest rates have increased subsequent to the bond issuance. Will the company recognize a gain or loss when extinguishing early this debt? Where is this gain or loss reported?

Problem 11-2: Payment Options. Donald Enterprises, Inc., purchased office furniture at a local furniture store on July 1, 2003, for $5,200, which Donald will use in its office. The furniture store offered two options for paying.

a. As part of a marketing campaign, the furniture store allowed customers to take possession of the furniture without making any payments until January 2, 2004, at which time customers could pay the entire amount or pay equal monthly payments for two years at a monthly interest rate of 1%. If this option is chosen, the first monthly payment is due on January 2, 2004.

b. Customers could pay the entire amount on the date of purchase and receive a 5% discount.

Required:

1. Assume that Donald Enterprises chooses the financing option.
   a. Calculate the monthly payment Donald will pay.
   b. Calculate the total interest Donald will pay.
   c. Calculate the implicit interest rate that Donald Enterprises is paying for the privilege of not paying cash from July 1, 2003, to January 2, 2004, and verify this amount by constructing an amortization table.
   d. Prepare the journal entry that Donald should make on:
      (1) July 1, 2003, for the purchase of the furniture.
      (2) December 31, 2003, for the adjusting entry to record depreciation and to recognize interest expense for the period July 1–December 31, 2003. Assume that the equipment has a 10-year life and no salvage.
      (3) January 2, 2004, to record the initial monthly payment.
      (4) February 1, 2004, to record the payment of the second monthly payment.
2. Assume that Donald Enterprises chooses to pay cash at the date of purchase. Prepare the journal entry that should be made to acquire the furniture.

Problem 11-3: Notes Payable to Purchase Equipment.

Required:
Answer the following questions related to Dickenson Electronics:

1. Dickenson purchased a new computer system with a fair market value of $52,500 and financed the purchase by paying $10,000 down and agreeing to pay semiannual payments of $5,000 for six years. Determine the effective interest rate on the note, and prepare the journal entries to purchase the computer system and to pay the first semiannual payment.
2. Dickenson sells $22,000 worth of merchandise to a preferred customer. Due to the customer's status, Dickenson allows the customer to pay nothing for six months and then to pay $1,000 per month for two years. Dickenson's cost of bor-

rowing money is 12%. Determine the amount of revenue that Dickenson should recognize on the sale of merchandise, and prepare the appropriate journal entry.

3. Dickenson has outstanding bonds with a face value of $1,000,000 that will expire in five years. Dickenson invests $650,000 for the purpose of retiring the bonds. What interest rate is necessary in order for the investment to accumulate to $1,000,000?

4. Dickenson exchanged a non-interest-bearing note for land. The face value of the note is $120,000 and has a 5-year life. Determine the cost of the land that should be recorded on Dickenson's financial statements. Dickenson uses a discount rate of 10%.

Problem 11-4: Understanding an Amortization Schedule. Johnson Products issued long-term bonds on January 1, 2002, dated as of January 1, 2002, and immediately prepared the following amortization schedule:

Amortization Schedule

Date	Cash Payment	Interest Expense	Unamortized Discount	Carrying Value
1/1/02			$13,421	$ 86,579
12/31/03	$6,000	$6,926	12,495	87,505
12/31/04	6,000	7,000	11,495	88,505
12/31/05	6,000	7,080	10,415	89,585
12/31/06	6,000	7,167	9,248	90,752
12/31/07	6,000	7,260	7,988	92,012
12/31/08	6,000	7,361	6,627	93,373
12/31/09	6,000	7,470	5,157	94,843
12/31/10	6,000	7,588	3,569	96,431
12/31/11	6,000	7,715	1,854	98,146
12/31/12	6,000	7,854	0	100,000

Required:

1. What amount of cash was received from the bonds?
2. Were the bonds issued at a discount or a premium? What was the amount of the discount or premium?
3. Is the bond discount/premium being amortized using the straight-line or the effective-interest method? How can you tell?
4. Determine the stated interest rate and the effective yield on the bonds.
5. Prepare the journal entry that the company would have recorded to issue the bonds on January 1, 2002.
6. Prepare the journal entries to record interest on December 31, 2006, and January 1, 2007.

SPREADSHEET

Problem 11-5: Accounting for Bonds. Aikman Industries issued 10-year bonds with a face value of $250,000 on January 1, 2003. The bonds have a stated interest rate of 6%, and annual interest payments are paid on December 31 of each year. The market rate of interest for similar bonds on that date was 8%.

Required:

1. Compute the amount received for the bonds.
2. Using a spreadsheet, construct an amortization table for the bonds, using the effective-interest method. Prepare all necessary journal entries for the bonds through December 31, 2005.

3. Assume the same facts, except that the stated interest rate on the bonds is 10%. Prepare all necessary journal entries for the bonds through December 31, 2005, using the straight-line method.
4. Assume the original facts, except that the bonds were issued on March 31, 2003. Prepare the journal entries related to the bonds for the years 2003 and 2004 using the effective-interest method of amortization.

Problem 11-6: Retiring Bonds. Sherry's Electronics issued 20-year callable bonds at 96 on January 1, 1999. The bonds have a face value of $2 million, make annual interest payments on December 31, and have a stated interest rate of 8%. The callable feature allows the company to repurchase the bonds in the future at 102½. On January 1, 2004, the company decided to exercise the call feature for the entire bond issue and to finance the bond retirement by issuing 10-year bonds, also with a face value of $2 million. The bonds were issued at 102. The stated rate of interest on those bonds was 7%.

Required:
1. Determine the market rate of interest on January 1, 1999, and January 1, 2004.
2. Prepare the journal entries that Sherry's Electronics would make on January 1, 2004, to retire the old bonds and issue the new bonds. Explain the income statement treatment for the gain/loss on retiring the debt.
3. Given the imputed interest rate calculated in Part (1) and the amount of cash paid to retire the old bonds, determine how much money Sherry's Electronics saved as a result of exercising the call feature on the old bonds instead of having to purchase them at their market value.

Problem 11-7: Cash-Flow Analysis of Retiring Bonds. On December 31, 2004, Cowbell, Inc., issued 20-year bonds at their face value of $1,000,000. The bonds bear annual interest at a rate of 10%, payable at the end of each year, and are callable any time at 104. On December 31, 2009, market conditions have changed, and Cowbell is considering whether to issue new bonds with an 8% interest rate (the market rate is also 8%) and use the proceeds to retire the old bonds.

Required:
Considering all options, use a cash-flow analysis to determine whether Cowbell should issue the new bonds and retire the old bonds.

Problem 11-8: Cash-Flow Analysis of Retiring Bonds. On December 31, 2004, Campbell, Inc., issued 20-year callable bonds at their face value of $1,000,000. The bonds have an interest rate of 10% and pay interest at the end of each year. The callable feature stipulates that Campbell must pay 108 for all bonds repurchased. On December 31, 2010, the market rate of interest has fallen to 8%, and Campbell is considering whether the old bonds should be called and new identical bonds (i.e., having the same expiration date, schedule of payments, etc.) issued that would have an interest rate of 8%.

Required:
1. Compute how much cash Campbell would pay as a penalty to repurchase the old bonds. (*Note:* This is the difference between the call provision and the face amount of the bonds.)
2. Compute how much cash Campbell would save in interest each year if the old bonds were retired and new bonds were issued, assuming that Campbell issues new bonds for the entire amount needed to call the old bonds.
3. Compute the present value of the annual cash savings.

(continued)

4. Would you advise Campbell to repurchase the old bonds and issue new bonds?
5. Would your answer change if the market rate of interest was 9%? How about 6%?

Problem 11-9: Multiple Retirements of Bonds. The following amortization table was prepared for some bonds payable issued by Sebaggio Inc.:

Period	Cash	Interest	Discount/ Premium	Carrying Amount
				$ 893,580
1	$87,500	$89,358	$ 1,858	895,438
2	87,500	89,544	2,044	897,482
3	87,500	89,748	2,248	899,730
4	87,500	89,973	2,473	902,203
5	87,500	90,220	2,720	904,923
6	87,500	90,492	2,992	907,915
7	87,500	90,792	3,292	911,207
8	87,500	91,121	3,621	914,828
9	87,500	91,483	3,983	918,811
10	87,500	91,881	4,381	923,192
11	87,500	92,319	4,819	928,011
12	87,500	92,801	5,301	933,312
13	87,500	93,331	5,831	939,143
14	87,500	93,914	6,414	945,557
15	87,500	94,556	7,056	952,613
16	87,500	95,262	7,762	960,375
17	87,500	96,038	8,538	968,913
18	87,500	96,891	9,391	978,304
19	87,500	97,831	10,331	988,635
20	87,500	98,865	11,365	1,000,000

Required:

1. At the fourth interest payment date, Sebaggio called $200,000 of the bonds at 101 and retired them. Prepare the appropriate journal entry.
2. At the twelfth interest payment date, Sebaggio purchased on the open market $100,000 of the bonds for $97,500 and held them in the treasury. Without preparing a new amortization table, prepare the appropriate journal entry to show the acquisition of the treasury bonds.
3. At the fifteenth interest period, $100,000 of the bonds were converted into 5,000 shares of Sebaggio's common stock that had a par value of $10 per share. Without preparing a new amortization table, prepare the appropriate journal entry to show the conversion of these bonds into stock.

Problem 11-10: Issuing and Retiring Serial Bonds. On January 3, 2002, Scholzen Company sold directly to underwriters $3 million of 8% serial bonds at an effective annual interest rate of 10%. The serial feature is that 25% of these bonds mature on January 1, 2007; 35% mature on January 1, 2010; and the remaining 40% mature on January 1, 2012. Interest is payable annually, with the first interest payment due on January 1, 2003. Scholzen uses the effective-interest method to amortize any premium/discount.

Required:

1. Calculate the proceeds from issuing the bonds.

2. Construct an amortization table for the 10-year period that the bonds will be outstanding.
3. Referring to the amortization table, prepare the journal entry to recognize the interest expense on December 31, 2003.
4. Show how the bonds would be reported on the December 31, 2006 balance sheet.
5. Referring to the amortization table, prepare the journal entry on January 1, 2007, to make the interest payment and retire the bonds maturing on that date.

Problem 11-11: Issuing and Retiring Bonds. To take advantage of a recent health craze and the increasing popularity of bicycling, Ladies-Nite-Out Bicycle Rental Shoppe issued on July 2, 2003, $4 million of bonds to finance expansion into various states. The bonds have a coupon rate of 8%, pay interest semiannually on June 30 and December 31, and mature in 10 years. Ladies-Nite-Out uses the effective-interest method to amortize any premium or discount. At the time the bonds were issued, the market rate of interest was 10%.

Required:
1. Compute the amount at which the bonds will be issued.
2. Prepare an amortization table for the 20 periods.
3. Assume that on July 1, 2004, Ladies-Nite-Out purchased $1 million of the bonds on the open market at 98 and retired them. Prepare the necessary journal entry to record the retirement of the bonds.
4. In addition, assume that on January 1, 2006, Ladies-Nite-Out purchased another $1 million of bonds on the open market at 101 and held them in the treasury. Prepare the necessary journal entry to record the purchase of the bonds.

Problem 11-12: Issuing and Retiring Bonds with Financial Reporting. Sherlock Co. wants to build a new office building. The company explored various financing alternatives and ultimately decided that the best option was to issue bonds to the public. Accordingly, a total of 500 bonds, dated December 31, 2003, with a face value of $1,000 each, were issued on March 1, 2004, at 77.26%. The bonds pay interest semiannually on June 30 and December 31 and mature on December 31, 2013. The stated interest rate on the bonds is 8% compounded semiannually, and bonds of similar type bear a market interest rate of 12%.

Required:
1. Determine the amount of proceeds to be received from the bonds, including interest.
2. Prepare the journal entries for each of the interest payments in the year 2004, using the effective-interest method. (Present an amortization table for the 20 periods as support for your answer.)
3. Show how the bonds and any interest should be shown on Sherlock's balance sheet at December 31, 2005.
4. Assume that Sherlock acquires 10% of the bonds at June 30, 2007, for $40,000. Prepare the journal entry to retire the bonds, and explain where the gain/loss would be reported on the income statement.

Problem 11-13: Accounting for Interest-Bearing Note with Unreasonable Interest Rate. On January 1, 2001, Rasper Corporation purchased some equipment for $20,000, which it financed by signing a 6-year note that bears interest at a rate of 5%. Equal annual payments are required at the beginning of each year, with the first payment due on the date of purchase. Similar notes have a market interest rate of 10%.

Required:

1. Compute the amount of the annual payments and the present value of the payments. (For this and all subsequent answers, round answers to the nearest dollar.)
2. Prepare the journal entry to record the purchase of the equipment, including the first payment.
3. Prepare an amortization schedule for the life of the note, using the effective-interest method.
4. Prepare the journal entry to record the annual installment one year after the purchase.
5. What is the total cost of borrowing to purchase the equipment?

Problem 11-14: Purchase of Equipment—Profit Analysis. Andersen Manufacturing purchased and placed into production a machine on January 1, 2001, with an output capacity of 400,000 units per year. On March 30, 2003, due to an engineering breakthrough, the manufacturers of the machine introduced a newer model with a 10% increase in annual output and lower operating costs. Andersen Manufacturing paid $64,000 for the original machine and is depreciating it on a straight-line basis over 10 years, with no scrap value. Andersen is considering purchasing the newer model and has an interested buyer who will pay $30,000 for the original machine. The new machine will cost $150,000, has a useful life of eight years, and a scrap value of $3,000. Production engineers do not foresee any start-up problems with the new machine, stating that production could commence immediately. The production costs for one unit of each machine are as follows.

	Old Machine	New Machine
Labor	$0.12	$0.10
Materials	0.48	0.46
Overhead	0.24	0.20

The product produced by this machine has a selling price of $0.95. To sell the additional output from the new machine, Andersen estimates advertising costs will increase by $5,500 per year. All other production and selling and general administrative costs are expected to stay the same. The company requires a return on this particular investment of 10%.

Required:
Answer the following questions, assuming that Andersen Manufacturing purchases the equipment.

1. What journal entries would be made to dispose of the old machine and purchase the new one?
2. Using a discounted cash-flow analysis, should Andersen purchase the machine?

Research Activities

Activity 11-1. Retiring Debt. Jones & Co. has $5 million of debt outstanding that it would like to not report on its balance sheet. It has been informed that if it placed assets into a trust that was sufficient to pay the interest and the principal

on the debt when it comes due, it would not have to include the debt on its balance sheet. Jones comes to you, its CPA, for official guidance. Research GAAP sufficiently to respond fully to Jones' query.

Cases

Case 11-1: Circus-Circus, Inc. The following information was extracted from the
1998 Circus-Circus financial report.

Note 4 : Long-Term Debt

Long-term debt consists of the following:

(in thousands)	January 31, 1998	January 31, 1997
Amounts due under corporate debt program at floating interest rates, weighted average of 5.8% and 5.6%	$ 981,310	$ 501,191
6.45% senior notes due 2006 (net of unamortized discount of $352 and $396)	199,648	199,604
7⅝% senior subordinated debentures due 2013	150,000	150,000
6¾% senior subordinated notes due 2003 (net of unamortized discount of $87 and $103)	149,913	149,897
7.0% debentures due 2036 (net of unamortized discount of $146 and $160)	149,854	149,840
6.70% debentures due 2036 (net of unamortized discount of $279 and $327)	149,721	149,673
10⅝% senior subordinated notes due 1997 (net of unamortized discount of $7)	—	99,993
Other notes	11,443	6,078
	$1,791,889	$1,406,276
Less current portion	(3,071)	(379)
	$1,788,818	$1,405,897

1. Why do the interest rates differ among the various debt issues?
2. If the current market interest rate is 7½%, which of the securities would sell
   above par, and which would sell below par?
3. Using the time value of money concepts and assuming that interest is paid
   semiannually, if the managers of Circus-Circus have excess cash that is to be
   used to retire debt and the current market interest rate is 7½%, which of
   the securities would it choose to acquire on the market and retire if its objective is to increase reported net income in the current year?
4. The following information was extracted from the financial report of Circus-
   Circus regarding the issuing of several long-term obligations in 1996:

   "In November 1996, the company issued $150 million principal
   amount of 7.0% debentures due November 2036 (the "7.0% debentures"). The 7.0% debentures may be redeemed at the option of the
   holder in November 2008. Also, in November 1996, the company

issued $150 million principal amount of 6.70% debentures due November 2036 (the "6.70% debentures"). The 6.70% debentures may be redeemed at the option of the holder in November 2003. Both the 7.0% debentures, which were discounted to $149.8 million, and the 6.70% debentures, which were discounted to $149.7 million, have interest payable each May and November, are not redeemable by the company prior to maturity, and are not subject to any sinking fund requirements."

Based upon this information, prepare an amortization table for the 6.7% bonds through 2006, and then prepare the journal entry in November 2003, assuming that all holders of the bonds exercise their option and that the bonds are redeemed at their maturity value.

Case 11-2: Resorts International. In 1988, Donald Trump and Merv Griffin engaged in a bidding war for Resorts International, an Atlantic City-based casino operation. Eventually, Griffin purchased all the stock in the company by issuing $325 million in "secured" junk bonds. This debt was in addition to an already existing "unsecured" debt of $600 million issued by Resorts prior to the takeover. For 1989, Resorts' projected cash flow was estimated at $55 million, compared to its debt service costs of $133 million. Griffin had hoped to sell some of Resorts' assets and use the cash to reduce the debt load, but those transactions never materialized. So less than a year after issuing the $325 million in new debt, Resorts filed bankruptcy.

1. In this case, what claims to specific assets did the secured junk bonds have when they were issued?
2. Why would investors purchase the new bond issue when Resorts already had $600 million of outstanding debt, especially given the inherent cash flow problems?
3. Who are the big losers when Resorts International went bankrupt? Was it the stockholders, or the holders of the secured junk bonds?
4. Have the rights of the stockholders and bondholders been reversed in this (and similar) situations?

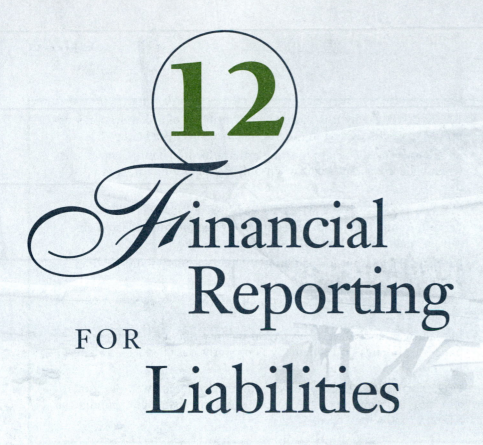

12

Financial Reporting FOR Liabilities

Does a Liability Exist?

Suppose that a few days before the end of the fiscal year, an explosion occurs in one of a company's plants, causing extensive property damage to the buildings and vehicles in the surrounding area. By the end of the year, no claims have been filed against the company, although management is certain that such claims will be forthcoming. Several months later, when the financial statements are being finalized and prior to their being issued, claims totaling $1,000,000 have been filed, and management estimates that an additional $500,000 of claims will soon be filed, although the identities of those suing are not known.

Questions

1. Since no claims were filed by year-end, does the company have a liability?
2. If so, what amount of liability should be reported on the company's fiscal year-end financial statements? Why?

The manager of the accounting department of a major corporation began working for the corporation shortly after the Korean War. The manager had never taken a day off because of illness. The corporation had a policy that sick days could be accumulated without limit, and as a result, it was certain that the corporation had a liability for accumulated but unpaid sick days.

Question

1. How is a liability for unpaid sick days, warranties on products, product premiums, or many other such items measured?

In Chapter 2, a current liability was defined as an obligation that will be liquidated within one year or during the operating cycle, whichever is longer, by using a current asset or incurring another current liability. A company whose fiscal year-end falls on December 31 has a liability due in May of the next year. According to the previous definition, this liability would normally be classified as a current liability. But suppose the company issues stock during January and uses the proceeds to liquidate the debt.

Questions

1. Since a current asset was not used to liquidate the debt, should the debt be classified as a current liability?
2. Suppose further that, instead of actually issuing stock, the company only intends to issue stock and use the proceeds to liquidate the debt. Should the liability be classified as a current liability now?

As illustrated in these scenarios, the financial reporting problems dealing with liabilities are (1) identifying the liabilities that exist, (2) determining the amounts to be reported, and (3) ascertaining the proper classification.

PHOTODISC, INC.

- Briefly describe why it is difficult to identify all of a corporation's liabilities, particularly relating to "off-balance-sheet financing."
- Summarize the financial reporting criteria for loss contingencies (i.e., when such are accrued and when only disclosure in a note is required).
- Summarize the financial reporting treatment for gain contingencies.
- Paraphrase the criteria for accruing liabilities for compensated absences, and estimate the liability amount.
- Estimate the amount for liabilities such as warranties and product premiums.
- Using the operating cycle concept, classify liabilities as either current or long term.
- Explain why and when a short-term liability that a company refinances or intends on refinancing is properly classified as a long-term liability.
- Use amortization tables for classifying the amounts owed on bonds and long-term notes payable as to the amount that is current and the amount that is long term.

Theory—Existence of Liabilities

The FASB's conceptual framework stipulates that a **liability** is a (1) probable *future* sacrifice of economic benefits that (2) arises from a *present* obligation to transfer assets or provide services to other entities (3) as a result of *past* transactions or events. All components of this definition must be met before an entity reports a liability on its balance sheet. The definition does not require that the amount of the liability be known with certainty, nor is it necessary that the company know the identity of the specific entity or entities to which it is obligated or even to know the date when payment will be made. Also, the definition does not require that cash will be used to liquidate the liability.

© CORBIS INC.

How and when is the damage to surrounding property accounted?

However, because this definition requires that a past transaction or event occur before a liability is recorded, all *contracts that are wholly executory are not reported as a liability.* A wholly **executory contract** is an exchange of promises where neither party has fulfilled any part of its promise. When the promises are partially executed, the contracts are partially executory; when the promises are fulfilled, the contracts are no longer executory but are wholly executed contracts. Thus, as long as the contracts represent mere promises—as many labor contracts are on the date they are signed—no liability is recorded.

Also, from the earlier definition of a liability, it only needs to be *probable* that an obligation has been incurred for the company to report a liability. The company should not wait until it is known with certainty that a liability has been incurred before recording it. Rather, the company should recognize a liability when it is probable that a future event will occur and confirm that a liability has been incurred. This criterion is particularly applicable to lawsuits where a future event must occur (e.g., the jury returning a verdict) before it is known whether a liability exists. Thus, according to the definition of a liability, to recognize lawsuits and similar obligations as liabilities, it is only necessary that the future event (e.g., the jury returning with an adverse verdict) is probable and will confirm the existence of a liability.

Most liabilities are incurred at definite points in time through identifiable transactions, and as a result, the existence of the liability is not in question. For example, accounts payable are incurred as merchandise is purchased and the existence of a liability is known. Also, the existence of many other liabilities, such as sales taxes, notes payable, interest payable, leases, mortgages, and bonds payable, are known. For all of these liabilities and many others, there is no question about the existence of the liability; it is known that the company has one.

Off-Balance-Sheet Financing

One of the more difficult issues dealing with reporting liabilities is being sure that all the liabilities are reported on the balance sheet. One satirist who commented on this difficulty quipped that only three things in life are certain: death, taxes, and the propensity for businessmen to keep liabilities off the balance sheet—which is referred to as **off-balance-sheet financing**. Leases (which are covered in detail in a later chapter) are classic examples of this propensity. Both the FASB and APB have grappled unsuccessfully with establishing—without loopholes—financial reporting standards for leases. The reason why businesses try to structure agreements in such a way as to exclude the liability from the balance sheet is that supposedly by not reporting the debt on its balance sheet, the financial strength of the company appears better than it actually is.

Product financing arrangements are another popular form of off-balance-sheet financing, where, due to the reciprocal nature of a transaction, all liabilities are excluded from the balance sheet. The purpose of product financing arrangements is for one party to receive financing to construct a facility or to complete a project where the party loaning the money has an interest in seeing the facility or project completed, usually to ensure a continuing supply of the product or a continuance of the service. An example of a product financing arrangement is a **take-or-pay contract** (see Exhibit 12-1), where the purchaser of goods promises to make specified payments to the seller, even if no goods are shipped. The guaranteed payments enable the seller to make payments on any

This Is the Real World

Enron appears to have excluded some $500 billion of liabilities from its balance sheet by shifting them to special-purpose entities. The reporting of this off-balance-sheet financing had repercussions on other companies involved in similar financing activities. One such company who suffered from the Enron fallout was Krispy Kreme donuts, whose stock on February 5, 2002, plunged more than 10% when details of a synthetic lease were reported. In essence, the synthetic lease allowed Krispy Kreme to benefit from all the practical effects of an asset without reporting the related liability. From this and other examples, it appears that the market is currently punishing companies who are involved in off-balance-sheet financing—at least when it was not previously known that companies were involved in such activities.

loan obtained to finance a project of mutual benefit to buyer and seller. Such agreements are entered into when two companies are highly dependent upon the other for their existence. For example, one company depends upon the other to supply its material, and the other company is dependent upon such purchases for its existence.

EXHIBIT 12-1

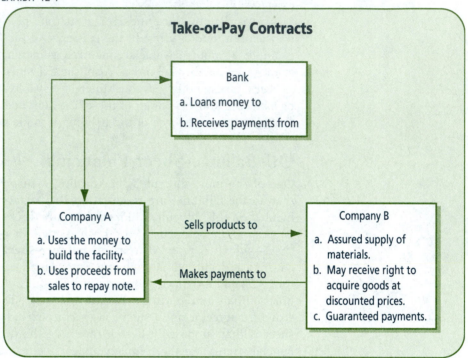

A **through-put contract** is the same type of arrangement, except that the agreement is for a service rather than a product. An example of a through-put contract is an agreement between an oil refinery and a pipeline company, where the refinery makes payments to the pipeline company for the delivery of oil or gas, even though no shipments may actually be made.

The FASB realizes the futility of combating this attitude that leaving debt off the balance sheet is good and knows that it cannot specify rules for every possibility. To this end, it has taken the approach of requiring that when it *is unclear whether a liability has been incurred, the essence of the agreement must be disclosed in the notes to the financial statements.* This approach assumes that neither the market nor knowledgeable investors are fooled about the correct financial position of a company that enters into off-balance-sheet financing activities. So the following information must be disclosed in the notes to the financial statements for each off-balance-sheet financing agreement:

- The nature and terms of the agreement;
- The amount of the fixed and determinable portion of the obligation in the aggregate and, if determinable, for each of the next five fiscal years;
- The amount of any variable component of the obligation; and
- For years in which an income statement is issued, the amounts actually purchased under the obligation (for example, under a take-or-pay contract).[1]

---

[1]*FASB Statement No. 47*, "Disclosure of Long-Term Liabilities," March 1981, par. 7.

The information contained in Exhibit 12-2 was extracted from a recently issued financial report of Eastman Chemical Company and Subsidiaries and is typical of the disclosures regarding off-balance-sheet financing activities found in notes accompanying published financial statements.

EXHIBIT 12-2

Off-Balance-Sheet Financing Activities

4. Equity Investments and Other Noncurrent Assets and Liabilities [portion only]

Eastman has entered into an agreement with a supplier that guarantees the Company's right to buy a specified quantity of a certain raw material annually through 2007 at prices determined by the pricing formula specified in the agreement. In return, the Company will pay a total of $239 million to the supplier through 1999 ($218 million and $196 million of which have been paid through December 31, 1998 and 1997, respectively). The Company defers and amortizes those costs over the 15-year period during which the product is received. The Company began amortizing those costs in 1993 and has recorded accumulated amortization of $96 million and $79 million at December 31, 1998 and 1997, respectively.

12. Commitments

Lease Commitments

Eastman leases facilities, principally property, machinery, and equipment, under cancelable, noncancelable, and month-to-month operating leases. Future lease payments, reduced by sublease income, follow:

(Dollars in millions)
Year ending December 31,

1999	$ 53
2000	45
2001	42
2002	29
2003	18
2004 and beyond	55
Total minimum payments required	$242

Loss Contingencies[2]

Loss contingencies are another area where liabilities may arise and must be reported on a balance sheet where the liabilities have not been recorded in the general ledger. A **contingency** is an existing condition or situation that has given rise to an uncertain gain or loss. This uncertainty will be resolved when a future event occurs or fails to occur. From this definition, the essence of a loss contingency is that there is uncertainty regarding possible loss, and the uncertainty will be resolved sometime in the future. However, not all uncertainties result in contingencies. For example, estimates are an ongoing part of accounting, but the necessity of using an estimate (due to uncertainty) does not result in a contingency. So, too, general business risks are an inherent part of doing business, and they, too, do not result in a loss contingency. To clarify further, typical examples of **loss contingencies** are lawsuits, product warranties and guarantees, self-insurance, and premiums and coupons. To synthesize, business risks are not transactions, and so

---

[2]Loss contingencies can result in either an asset being impaired or a liability being incurred. Loss contingencies on assets being impaired were covered in Chapter 10. The discussion here applies mainly to loss contingencies that may give rise to liabilities being incurred.

there is no contingency for them. Also, the use of estimates means that it is known a transaction has occurred, and so there is no uncertainty there either. But when a product is sold with an attached warranty, it is uncertain whether a claim will be submitted or whether a lawsuit will result. Further, when a lawsuit is filed, it is uncertain as to what the eventual outcome will be. For these situations, there is uncertainty as to whether the business has incurred a gain or a loss.

Accrual of a Loss Contingency

When uncertainty concerning a loss contingency exists, the probability of the future event occurring that will confirm that a loss has resulted and a liability has been incurred is either probable, reasonably possible, or remote. Three alternatives are available to the accountant as to what to do with a loss contingency: accrue the loss, disclose the loss, or do nothing. Figure 12-1 illustrates these options.

FIGURE 12-1

Accounting for Loss Contingencies

Probable	Reasonably possible	Remote
Accrue	Disclose in note	Do nothing

A loss contingency is accrued when the two following criteria are met:

1. Information available at the balance sheet date indicates (a) it is *probable* that an asset has been impaired or a liability has been incurred and (b) it is *probable* that a future event will confirm this fact, and
2. The amount of the loss can be *reasonably estimated*.

Product Warranties or Guarantees

Based on information available at the balance sheet date, if it is probable that customers will make claims under warranties relating to the company's goods or services, such loss contingencies are accrued.

Note that according to the definition of a liability, it is not necessary to know the identities of those who will file warranty claims prior to accruing a loss and recording a liability. Failure to accrue such loss contingencies on sales for the year because there is a significant uncertainty regarding future claims raises questions about the acceptability of recording a sale prior to the expiration of the warranty period. These same guidelines also apply to accounting for coupons (or proofs-of-purchase), premiums, etc.

To illustrate, suppose that a company wishes to promote a new product and accordingly offers customers an attractive product (called a premium) for turning in five proofs-of-purchase and $2.00 to cover handling and shipping costs. The premiums cost the company

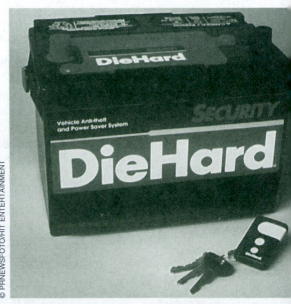

© PRNEWSFOTO/HIT ENTERTAINMENT

When do companies account for warranties or product recalls?

$5.00 each, and actual shipping costs are $1.20. During the year, the company sells 250,000 units of the new product of which they expect 60% of the proofs-of-purchase to be redeemed eventually. At December 31, a total of 90,000 proofs-of-purchase have been redeemed. The company's liability for premiums at December 31 is computed by focusing on what the balance in the liability account should be, as follows:

1. Total number of proofs-of-purchase that probably will be redeemed:

$$60\% \times 250{,}000 \text{ proofs-of-purchase issued} = 150{,}000 \text{ proofs-of-purchase}$$

2. Total number of proofs-of-purchase that the company still must honor:

$$150{,}000 \text{ proofs-of-purchase} - 90{,}000 \text{ proofs already honored} = 60{,}000 \text{ proofs}$$

3. Total liability for the number of premiums that are still outstanding:

$$60{,}000 \text{ proofs}/5 \text{ proofs for each premium} = 12{,}000 \text{ premiums}$$

4. The amount of the liability that the company should accrue is the cost (including handling and shipping) of honoring the 12,000 premiums less the amount the customers send in. Thus, the net cost to the company is computed as follows:

$$12{,}000 \times (\$5.00 + \$1.20 - \$2.00) = \$50{,}400$$

The journal entry to record this liability at year-end is as follows:

Premium Expense[3]	50,400	
Liability for Premiums		50,400

To record the year-end liability for unredeemed proofs-of-purchase.

To further illustrate the accounting for a contingency and introduce the concept of a change in an accounting estimate relating to it, the same company during the second year sells 290,000 units. During the year, a total of 100,000 more proofs-of-purchase were received by the company, and 20,000 premiums were shipped. At the end of this second year, company management now thinks that it is more reasonable that only 50% of the total proofs-of-purchase issued will be redeemed. Computing the amount of the company's liability and the associated adjusting entry at the end of the second year is done as follows:

1. Total number of proofs-of-purchase that probably will be redeemed:

$$50\% \times (250{,}000 + 290{,}000 \text{ proofs-of-purchase}) = 270{,}000 \text{ proofs-of-purchase}$$

2. Total number of proofs-of-purchase that the company still must honor:

$$270{,}000 \text{ proofs-of-purchase} - 190{,}000 \text{ proofs already honored} = 80{,}000 \text{ proofs}$$

3. Total liability for the number of premiums that are still outstanding:

$$80{,}000 \text{ proofs}/5 \text{ proofs for each premium} = 16{,}000 \text{ premiums}$$

---

[3]As always, any descriptive account could have been used. So it is acceptable to also debit Advertising Expense or some other account.

4. The amount of the liability that the company should report is the cost of honoring the 16,000 premiums less the amount the customers send in. Thus, the company's liability is:

$$16,000 \times (\$5.00 + \$1.20 - \$2.00) = \$67,200$$

This $67,200 is the amount needed as the ending balance in the liability account, but it is not the amount of the adjusting entry, which is obtained by first considering the balance that already exists in the liability account. Assuming that the typical entry that the company prepares when proofs-of-purchase are submitted and premiums sent is to debit a premium expense account and credit the premium account, then the balance in the liability account prior to the adjusting entry is still the $50,400 from last year's adjusting entry. The adjusting journal entry for this year is as follows:

Premium Expense	16,800	
Liability for Premiums		16,800

To record the year-end liability for unredeemed proofs-of-purchase.

In addition to seeing how the amount of the adjusting entry was obtained, note how the change in the accounting estimate was handled. Prior-year amounts were not changed. Instead, the new estimate was implemented for the current and, if necessary, future years.

Risk of Damage to Company Property

Many companies self insure against possible loss due to fire or casualty, meaning that such companies consider it less expensive in the long run to pay for property losses arising from fire and casualty than to pay yearly insurance premiums. Such companies have loss contingencies from future fires or casualties, and it is probable that at some time the company will incur the costs of such property losses. But having such loss contingencies usually does not cause the company's assets to be any less functional, nor does lack of insurance give rise to a liability. Therefore, since no asset has been impaired and no liability has been incurred, no loss accrual is necessary.

Threat of Expropriation

If information is available at the balance sheet date indicating that it is *probable* that expropriation[4] is imminent and the amount of compensation to be received will be less than the carrying amount of the assets to be expropriated, then *the loss is accrued.* However, when the amount to be received is greater than the carrying amount of the property, no gain is accrued.

Litigation

The accrual of a loss is not necessary when a lawsuit is filed. Rather, the nature of the litigation, the progress of the case, the opinions of legal counsel, the company's experience in similar cases, and management's decision as to how to respond to the lawsuit are all considered in deciding whether it is *probable* that future events will confirm that a liability has been incurred. The fact that legal counsel is not able to express an opinion that the outcome will be favorable to the company also does not indicate that the conditions for accrual have been met.

Do companies actually accrue losses on lawsuits before such suits have been settled? Not usually, although Exhibit 12-3, which was extracted from a finan-

[4]*Expropriation* means to take away by force the possession of or the right to use property.

cial report of Eastman Chemical Company and Subsidiaries (with emphasis added), illustrates that occasionally such does happen. (It causes a person to wonder whether the prosecuting attorneys read financial reports. Also, if Eastman discloses that they are willing to pay $8 million, how much more would they actually pay?)

EXHIBIT 12-3

Disclosure of Litigation Information

In addition, the Company, along with other companies, has been named as a defendant in seven antitrust lawsuits brought subsequent to the Company's plea agreement as putative class actions on behalf of certain purchasers of sorbates. The Company recognized a charge to earnings in the fourth quarter of 1998 of $8 million for the estimated costs, including legal fees, related to the *pending sorbates litigation*.

In regards to lawsuits, it may be necessary on occasion (at least theoretically) to accrue losses for lawsuits that have not been filed, which are called **unasserted claims**. Losses on such potential lawsuits are accrued when it is probable that a lawsuit will be filed, and it is also probable that the resulting outcome will be unfavorable to the company. Also, it must be possible to reasonably estimate the amount of the loss before accruing such.

EXTENDING THE CONCEPT

Returning to the first of the opening scenarios, where an explosion occurs, and based upon the preceding theoretical discussion, what is your opinion regarding whether a liability should be reported at the end of the fiscal year? If a liability should be reported, at what amount should it be reported?

Answer: A liability should be recognized for $1,500,000.

Estimating the Amount of Loss Contingencies

Regarding the criterion that it must be possible to reasonably estimate the loss before recording an accrual, it is not necessary to wait until a single number is determined as the amount of the loss. Rather, a loss is accrued, even if the loss is estimated to be within a range of possible losses. When an amount within the range is more likely than any other amount (see Exhibit 12-4), then that is the amount accrued.

EXHIBIT 12-4

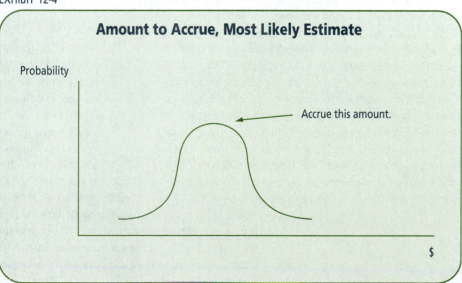

Amount to Accrue, Most Likely Estimate

Probability

Accrue this amount.

$

When no amount in the range is a more likely estimate of the loss than any other amount, then the low end-point of the range is accrued, with the difference between the low end-point of the range and the high end-point of the range being disclosed in the notes as a possible additional loss (see Exhibit 12-5). For example, when it is deemed that the amount of the loss could be between $2 million and $5 million, the $2 million is accrued, and a note discloses that there is an additional possible loss of $3 million.

EXHIBIT 12-5

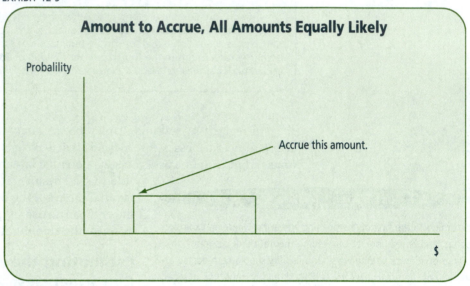

Amount to Accrue, All Amounts Equally Likely

Probalility

Accrue this amount.

$

EXTENDING THE CONCEPT

During the past several years, Philip Morris Companies Inc. has vigorously defended itself against literally thousands of tobacco-related lawsuits. In its 2001 annual report, a note that fills nearly eight pages discusses the status of various lawsuits that have been brought against the company. As of December 31, 2001, over 1,500 suits had been filed against the company in the United States, with lawsuits filed in at least 10 other countries. The federal government also has filed suit against Philip Morris. However, the company did not accrue a liability and did not recognize any expense in 2001 related to the lawsuits, claiming that "Management is unable to make a meaningful estimate of the amount or range of loss that could result from an unfavorable outcome of pending tobacco-related litigation, and the Company has not provided any amounts in the consolidated financial statements for unfavorable outcomes, if any." In your opinion, should Philip Morris have recognized a liability for tobacco-related lawsuits in its financial statements? Look up a more recent annual report for Philip Morris and determine whether contingencies have now been accrued.

The year-end adjusting entry to record the accrual for a loss contingency is to debit an appropriately described expense or loss account and credit an appropriately described liability account, as was illustrated for the previous examples regarding premiums.

Disclosure of Loss Contingencies

Disclosure in a note regarding loss contingencies is necessary when:

1. No loss is accrued because it is only *reasonably possible that a loss contingency has occurred*;
2. It is probable that a loss contingency has occurred, but *the loss cannot be reasonably estimated*;
3. It is probable that a loss contingency has occurred, but it *occurred after the balance sheet date but before the financial statements are issued*; and
4. Certain loss contingencies are disclosed, even though the possibility of loss is remote. The common characteristic of this type of loss contingency involves *a guarantee with the right to proceed against a third party* (i.e., the reporting entity), *should the guarantor be required to satisfy the guarantee.* Examples include a guarantee of the indebtedness of another, standby letters of credit, and a guarantee to repurchase receivables that have been sold.

EXTENDING THE CONCEPT

This information on page 554 focuses on loss contingencies that give rise to possible liabilities. However, as can be seen from the definition of a contingency, a loss contingency can also arise when it is probable that an asset has been impaired. When such a contingency arises, the journal entry to recognize the contingent loss changes slightly. Rather than crediting an estimated liability account, the asset account is credited, as covered in Chapter 10 under the discussion of impairment of assets.

Included in the disclosures of contingencies should be the nature of the contingency and an estimate of the loss or range of loss.

Gain Contingencies

The prior discussion regarding the accrual and/or disclosure in a note applied only to uncertainties regarding loss contingencies, but it also is possible that a company may be exposed to uncertainties regarding gain contingencies. The financial reporting for gain contingencies can best be illustrated by referring to Figure 12-1 (page 550) for loss contingencies and then sliding the accounting treatment part of the scale one category to the left as shown in Figure 12-2.

FIGURE 12-2

Accounting for Gain Contingencies

Probable	Reasonably possible	Remote
Disclose in a note	Do nothing	Do nothing

So gain contingencies are not accrued until the realization criterion has been met; that is, the company has a claim to cash. Even when a gain contingency is probable and the amount can be reasonably estimated, the appropriate accounting treatment is to—perhaps—disclose such gain contingency in the notes to the financial statements. But even then, "care shall be exercised to avoid misleading implications as to the likelihood of realization."[5]

Environmental Remediation

The estimated costs of cleaning up the environment due to the current or past actions of some businesses are huge and most likely will continue to grow as new legislation is passed. Currently, most companies acknowledge the existence of such potential liabilities but do not accrue charges related to them because they claim that the amount is not estimable or that it is immaterial in regards to the operations (e.g., net income) of the company. Whether a company accrues charges related to environmental remediation or discloses the existence of such in the notes, the Securities and Exchange Commission requires that any estimated amount that may be recovered through insurance be reported separately. In essence, then, estimated recoverable amounts through insurance are deemed to be gain contingencies, and in accordance with the rules of accounting for such, they are not reported on the balance sheet.

The information contained in Exhibit 12-6 was extracted from a recent financial report of The Goodyear Tire & Rubber Company (with emphasis added) and is indicative of the typical financial reporting disclosures for contingencies relating to environmental remediation.

---

[5]*FASB Statement No. 5*, "Accounting for Contingencies," par. 17, March 1975.

EXHIBIT 12-6

Disclosure of Environmental Remediation

[In Note 1] Goodyear expenses environmental expenditures related to existing conditions resulting from past or current operations and from which no current or future benefit is discernible. Expenditures that extend the life of the related property or mitigate or prevent future environmental contamination are capitalized. *Goodyear determines its liability on a site by site basis and records a liability at the time when it is probable and can be reasonably estimated.* Goodyear's estimated liability is reduced to reflect the anticipated participation of other potentially responsible parties in those instances where it is probable that such parties are legally responsible and financially capable of paying their respective shares of the relevant costs. *The estimated liability of Goodyear is not discounted or reduced for possible recoveries from insurance carriers.* Refer to Note 22.

[And in Note 22] *At December 31, 1999, Goodyear had recorded liabilities aggregating $66.5 million for anticipated costs related to various environmental matters, primarily the remediation of numerous waste disposal sites and certain properties sold by Goodyear.* These costs include legal and consulting fees, site studies, the design and implementation of remediation plans, postremediation monitoring and related activities and will be paid over several years. The amount of Goodyear's ultimate liability in respect of these matters may be affected by several uncertainties, primarily the ultimate cost of required remediation and the extent to which other responsible parties contribute. Refer to Environmental Cleanup Matters at Note 1.

Theory—Valuation of Liabilities

Theoretically, all liabilities (both current and long-term) are reported on the year-end balance sheet at their discounted cash flow amount. However, because the discount period for current liabilities is very short and the resulting premium or discount is immaterial, current liabilities are reported on the balance sheet at face amount, meaning the amount that will be paid to liquidate them. Long-term liabilities, however, are generally reported at their discounted cash flow amount, using the effective interest rate when the liability was incurred.[6]

Regarding valuation, few difficulties arise when determining the amounts for liabilities that are incurred at definite points in time through identifiable transactions. At year-end, companies usually have to estimate amounts for accrued salaries, interest, or other liabilities. Estimating these amounts is usually done on the basis of the time passed in relation to the total time, and several acceptable estimation techniques can often be used, although the different techniques will give slightly different answers.

Accruing property taxes at year-end is one example of a liability that can be accrued under several different estimation techniques and where any of several answers is appropriate. To illustrate, suppose that a company acquires a piece of property on March 1 in an area where property tax assessments are mailed in September. But wanting to have monthly or quarterly financial statements, the company decides to accrue property taxes on a monthly basis. One acceptable approach to estimating the amount of the monthly accrual is to obtain information about last year's property tax assessment and to accrue 1/12 of that amount each month. Then, when the actual property tax assessment is received in September, a catch-up adjustment is made (because it is a change in an accounting estimate) to correct the

---

[6]Some long-term liabilities are not reported at their discounted cash flow amounts. The primary example of this exception is deferred taxes, which are tax amounts that will be paid in the future that result because of differences between the tax treatment and financial reporting treatment of certain assets and liabilities. Accounting for deferred taxes is covered in a later chapter.

current balance in the payable account to what it should be, based upon the actual property tax statement. Another acceptable approach to estimating the amount of the monthly property tax accrual is to adjust last year's property tax assessment for the expected change in this year's property tax assessment and then to accrue 1/12 of that amount. Again, when the actual property tax assessment is received, a catch-up adjustment is made. Undoubtedly, other acceptable estimation techniques exist besides these two.

Compensated Absences

Several acceptable techniques are also available for determining the liability for **compensated absences**, which is the liability companies incur for allowing their employees time off—with pay—for vacation and sick days. Because the matching principle specifies that an *expense must be recognized in the time period when the benefit is earned*, the liability for compensated absences and its associated expense must be accrued, rather than being recognized as an expense in the year that the time off is taken. This liability for compensated absences is accrued when *all* of the following conditions exist:

© CORBIS INC.

How and when does the business account for this vacation?

- The employer's obligation to compensate employees *arises from services already performed*,
- The obligation *vests*[7] or *accumulates*,[8]
- Payment is *probable*, and
- The amount of the payment can be *reasonably estimated.*[9]

Acceptable alternatives for estimating the amount of the liability for compensated absences exist because the FASB did not state whether the liability should be accrued at the wage rate in effect when the compensated time off was earned or the wage rate that will be in effect when the compensated time off will be taken. Thus, the liability can be accrued using either wage rate.

Another reason that acceptable estimation alternatives exist is because the FASB allows, but does not require, an accrual for nonvesting sick pay benefits when the right to receive those benefits is contingent upon an illness. That is, accrual is not required (but still may be done) for those companies where employees must be sick to receive benefit for the sick days earned. Accrual is not required because the FASB thought (1) the amount would be immaterial and (2) the costs of estimating the accrual exceeded the benefits of doing so. However, sick leave benefits must be accrued if employees do not have to be sick to receive compensation or if they are paid for their accumulated, unused sick days should employment be terminated. So the various alternatives to accounting for compensated absences are as follows:

[7]Vested rights are those for which the employer has an obligation to the employee, even if the employee is terminated or resigns. Vested rights are not dependent upon future services.

[8]Rights that accumulate are those that, if unused, can be carried forward to succeeding years, even if there is a limit to the amount that can be carried forward.

[9]*FASB Statement No. 43*, "Accounting for Compensated Absences," par. 6, November 1980.

1. Accrue both sick and vacation leave at existing wage rates,
2. Accrue only vacation leave at existing wage rates,
3. Accrue both sick and vacation leave at estimated future wage rates, and
4. Accrue only vacation leave at estimated future wage rates.

All alternatives are equally acceptable, depending upon the company's policy for sick leave.

As demonstrated earlier in the chapter in the premium example, the easiest approach to determining the year-end adjusting entry for liabilities that must be estimated in amount is to *focus on the liability account*, rather than on the corresponding expense account. Using this approach, the procedure in preparing the year-end adjusting entry is the same as was illustrated in Chapter 2 for preparing any other adjusting entry, which is as follows:

1. Determine what the balance in the liability account is,
2. Determine what the balance in the liability account should be, and
3. The adjusting entry amount is always the difference between what the current balance is and what the balance should be.

To illustrate, Quad-City Motors employs 10 individuals who customarily work a 5-day week, 8 hours per day. As part of the benefit package, Quad-City grants each employee 10 days of paid annual vacation and eight days of paid annual sick leave. Employees cannot take the vacation days until they have worked one year, but each employee earns two sick days each quarter, and compensated time off may be taken as the sick days are earned, including for reasons other than sickness. Both vacation days and sick days accumulate. At December 31, 2004, a total of 120 vacation days and 140 sick days were owed to all employees. The average rate of pay during 2004 was $10.50, and Quad-City uses that rate to determine its liability for compensated absences. The balance in Estimated Liability for Compensated Absences at the beginning of 2004 is $18,240. During the year, the company accountant recorded the compensated time off that was taken by debiting Wage Expense and crediting Cash.[10]

Since the company accountant did not make any entry to the liability account during the year, the end-of-year balance (before adjusting entry) in Estimated Liability for Compensated Absences is the same as its beginning balance of $18,240. Since Quad-City accrues at existing wage rates, the ending balance in the account is computed as follows:

Ending Balance = Number of Days Owed × 8 Hrs./Day × Existing Rate of Pay

$21,840 = (120 vacation days + 140 sick days) × 8 hrs./day × $10.50/hr.

The adjusting entry at December 31, 2004, is for $3,600, which is the difference between what the ending balance should be ($21,840) and what the balance currently is ($18,240) and is recorded as follows:

Wage Expense	3,600	
Estimated Liability for Compensated Absences		3,600
To accrue the expense and related liability for compensated absences.		

This technique of focusing on the liability account and determining what the balance is and what it should be gives the proper year-end adjusting entry for any liability whose amount must be estimated, even when it may be necessary to re-

---

[10]This journal entry is the usual entry that is made when employees are paid. No attempt is typically made to distinguish the pay of those individuals who worked and those individuals who received compensated time off. All individuals are paid by check, and the same journal entry is made for all checks issued.

duce the liability account. For example, suppose that the employees for Quad-City took more compensated time off during the year than what they had earned. (This is possible by taking compensated time off in the current year for days earned in several previous years.) As a result, at the end of the year, Quad-City owes only 200 total days for compensated absences (rather than 260). Under this assumption, the ending balance in Estimated Liability for Compensated Absences should be:

$$\$16,800 = 200 \text{ days} \times 8 \text{ hrs./day} \times \$10.50/\text{hr.}$$

Since the balance in the liability account needs to be reduced by $1,440, the required adjusting entry is:

Estimated Liability for Compensated Absences	1,440	
Wage Expense		1,440

To accrue the expense and related liability for compensated absences.

In this case, it is necessary to reduce Wage Expense because of the way in which the company accountant recorded the entry when compensated time off was taken—which was to debit Wage Expense. This action resulted in Wage Expense being recorded twice, once when the right to take compensated time off was earned and then again when the compensated time was taken. As long as employees take less compensated time off than they earn in the current year, the balance in both the liability and expense accounts will need to be increased at year-end. But, when employees take more compensated time off than they have earned, this double counting of the wage expense and not decreasing the liability account results in having to decrease both the liability and the wage expense accounts at year-end.

Warranties

Many retail and wholesale companies warranty the products that they sell against defect for a specified period of time. Determining the amount of expense related to warranties and the amount of the year-end liability balance is another example of the need of estimation in accounting.

To illustrate, assume that Allied Electronics warranties its products for two years against defect or failure. From past experience, Allied has learned that the cost of warranties approximates 7% of total sales, and sales during the current year amounted to $2,200,000. At the beginning of the current year, the balance in Estimated Liability for Warranties was $138,000, and total expenditures during the year related to warranties were $130,000, which were recorded by crediting the liability account. Two questions are relevant at the end of the year.

- What is the amount of warranty expense for the year?
- What should be the ending balance in the liability account?

Illustrating a different estimation technique than shown previously by measuring the expense amount rather than the liability amount, the computations in determining the answers to these two questions and reasons for them are described as follows.

The total estimated cost for warranties associated with the sales during the current year are computed by multiplying the 7% estimated defect rate by the total sales of $2,200,000, which is $154,000. According to the matching principle, where expenses are recognized in the same time period in which the associated revenues are earned, this $154,000 is the amount of warranty expense for the year. Then, the balance in the liability account can be determined through a T-account analysis, as follows:

Estimated Liability for Warranties

		$138,000	Beginning balance
Warranty expenditures	$130,000	154,000	Warranty expenses for the year
		$162,000	Ending balance

The year-end balance must be estimated for many other liabilities. In most of these situations, the year-end adjusting entries are best determined by focusing on the liability account—determining what the balances are and what they should be, with the adjusting entry amount always being the difference between them. The offsetting account is to an appropriately described expense account.

Theory—Classification of Liabilities

Liabilities are classified on the balance sheet as either current or long term; that determination is made when the financial statements are prepared. At that date and looking ahead, liabilities that will be liquidated within the upcoming current operating cycle or one year (whichever is longer), by using a current asset or the incurring of another current liability, are classified as current liabilities. Liabilities that are due in yearly installments are partly current and partly long term, with the current liability portion being that amount of the principal that will be liquidated in the current operating cycle or one year by using a current asset. For these types of liabilities, amortization tables are very useful in separating the total amount owed into the current and long-term components. All other liabilities are classified as long term.

Liabilities Expected to Be Refinanced[11]

Liabilities due within one year that are expected to be refinanced on a long-term basis are excluded from the current liability classification because a current asset (as of the balance sheet date) will not be used to liquidate them, nor will another current liability be incurred to settle them. Instead, such liabilities are classified as long-term liabilities. However, all short-term liabilities "arising from transactions in the normal course of business that are due in customary terms"[12] (such as accounts payable, taxes payable, accrued expenses, collections received in advance of the delivery of the goods, and payments received for services that will be rendered within the year or operating cycle) can never be reclassified as long term.

To classify a short-term liability as long term, *the company must demonstrate both the* intent *and the* ability *to refinance the debt on a long-term basis.* Demonstrating intent requires only that management express the intent to refinance the debt. Demonstrating the ability to refinance can be done in either of two ways:

1. After the balance sheet date but before the financial statements are issued, long-term debt or equity securities are issued, and the proceeds are used (or will be used) to retire the short-term obligation(s).

---

[11]Liabilities may be settled by restructuring, rather than refinancing. Accounting for such restructurings is covered in the appendix at the end of this chapter.
[12]*FASB Statement No. 6*, "Classification of Short-Term Obligations Expected to Be Refinanced," par. 8, May 1975.

EXTENDING
the Concept

What is the effect on liquidity ratios (such as the current ratio, working capital, etc.) of reclassifying currently maturing long-term liabilities in the long-term liability classification? Does this give some insight into the possible reasons why companies may desire to reclassify some currently maturing liabilities as long-term liabilities?

Partial answer: Reclassifying liabilities from short-term to long-term will increase liquidity ratios and working capital.

2. After the balance sheet date but before the financial statements are issued, a refinancing agreement is entered into that contains all of the following:
   a. The refinancing agreement does not expire, is not callable, and is not cancelable for one year from the balance sheet date, except for a violation of the agreement. (That is, the refinancing must be done on a long-term basis.)
   b. There is no violation of the refinancing agreement when the financial statements are issued, or if a violation has occurred, a waiver has been obtained. (If a violation exists, then the lender has no obligation to refinance the short-term loan, and so the company has not demonstrated the ability to refinance on a long-term basis.)
   c. The lender is capable of fulfilling the agreement.

Refinancing a short-term liability with another short-term liability or a series of other short-term obligations does not demonstrate the ability to refinance on a long-term basis, and so the short-term obligation is classified as a current liability. A short-term liability that is paid after the balance sheet date from existing funds (i.e., before the long-term financing is obtained) is also classified as a current liability because a current asset was used to liquidate the debt, even though the current asset is subsequently replenished.

When the short-term liability has actually been refinanced because long-term debt or equity securities have been issued, *the amount of the short-term obligation that is excluded from the current liability classification is the lesser of the net proceeds of the securities issued or the amount of the short-term liability.*

When a refinancing agreement is entered into, the amount of the short-term obligation that can be excluded from the current liability classification is the lesser of the amount available under the refinancing agreement or the amount of the short-term liability. However, the amount available under the refinancing agreement is reduced by any funds that will not be available to pay the debt, such as amounts that must be maintained in checking accounts that are larger than what the company usually carries. Also, if the amount available under the refinancing agreement may fluctuate (e.g., the amount available is a percentage of some collateral), then the amount to exclude from the current liability classification is limited to a reasonable estimate of the minimum amount expected during the fiscal year. And if no minimum amount can be reasonably estimated, then the short-term liability is classified as current.

To illustrate these concepts, suppose that on December 31, which is the end of its fiscal year, Insolvency Corp. has the following short-term liabilities coming due within the next year:

12% note payable maturing March 30	$150,000
14% note payable maturing November 1	250,000

Insolvency does not want to classify these liabilities as current because the resulting current ratio would violate the covenants on a long-term borrowing, which would cause the long-term debt to be due and payable immediately. So on January 15, Insolvency issues preferred stock for $135,000, net of all commissions and fees, and uses the proceeds and some cash on hand to liquidate the 12% note payable. Also, on March 1, just before the financial statements are finalized and issued, Insolvency enters into a debt refinancing agreement that allows it to borrow a maximum of $250,000 on a long-term basis, subject to the further restriction that the amount borrowed cannot exceed 80% of the value of the collateral, which at March 1 was $300,000. Assuming that the creditor is capable of honoring the agreement and that there is no violation of the refinancing agreement, what are the amounts that are classified as current on Insolvency's balance sheet at December 31?

The answer is that $25,000 must be reported as a current liability, and the rest, or $375,000, is classified as a long-term liability. The reasons are as follows:

- Regarding the 12% note, since only $135,000 was raised through equity financing, the rest of the $150,000 liability (or $15,000) was liquidated through using existing cash, and this $15,000 must be classified as a current liability.
- Regarding the 14% note, the maximum amount that can be borrowed at the balance sheet date is $240,000 (80% × $300,000). So the remaining $10,000 of the liability must be classified as a current liability.

Finally, the preferred stock that was issued to pay the 12% note is not shown on the year-end balance sheet because, as of December 31 (the date of the financial statements), no preferred stock had been issued. But a note to the financial statements should explain how the refinancing was effected, and that will alert the financial statement readers that preferred stock had been issued subsequent to the balance sheet date.

EXTENDING THE CONCEPT

Return to the third of the opening scenarios and answer the questions posed there.

Answers: In the first case, the short-term liability can be excluded from the current liability category and instead reported under long-term liabilities. In the second case, if the refinancing agreement met all the conditions specified previously, the short-term liability also could be excluded from the current liability category; otherwise, it would have to be reported as a long-term liability.

Using Amortization Tables to Classify Debt

For long-term liabilities that were issued with a premium/discount or that are due in installments, the amount to report on the balance sheet or the amounts to report as current or as long term on the balance sheet are found from associated amortization tables. The bond amortization table in Illustration 12-1 is used to demonstrate how the amount to report on the balance sheet is determined when the debt is issued with a premium/discount and is paid in full at maturity, as contrasted to a debt that is paid in installments.

ILLUSTRATION 12-1

Using Bond Amortization Tables to Classify Debt Amounts Due in a Lump Sum

Period	Cash	Interest Expense	Amortization	Carrying Amount of Bonds
				$ 850,614
2004	$ 100,000	$ 102,073	$ 2,073	852,687
2005	100,000	102,322	2,322	855,009
2006	100,000	102,601	2,601	857,610
2007	100,000	102,913	2,913	860,523
2020	100,000	112,710	12,710	951,964
2021	100,000	114,235	14,235	966,199
2022	100,000	115,944	15,944	982,143
2023	100,000	117,857	17,857	1,000,000
Totals	$2,000,000	$2,149,389		

Using Illustration 12-1, it can be seen that for the years ending December 31, 2005 and 2006, the total carrying amounts of the bonds are $855,009 and $857,610, respectively, and these carrying amounts are reported on the respective year-end balance sheets, as shown in Exhibit 12-7.

EXHIBIT 12-7

Findley Company
Partial Balance Sheet
For the Years Ended December 31,

	2006	2005
Long-term liabilities:		
Bonds payable	$1,000,000	$1,000,000
Less bond discount	(142,390)*	(144,991)
Net bonds payable	$ 857,610	$ 855,009

*Reporting the discount/premium in a parenthetical note is also acceptable.

As shown, premiums and discounts on long-term debt are not separately classified but are reported with their associated long-term liability. (This financial reporting procedure is similar in nature to reporting depreciable assets net of their associated accumulated depreciation.) Presenting long-term liabilities with their associated premium/discount in this way results in reporting them at the theoretical amounts that would be required at the balance sheet date to liquidate them.

Regarding debt that is paid in installments, the amortization table in Illustration 12-2 is used to separate the total liability amount into its current and long-term components.

ILLUSTRATION 12-2

Using Amortization Tables to Classify Debt
Amounts Due in Installment Payments*

Period	Payment	Interest	Obligation
			$170,000
Dec. 31, 2004	$25,152	$ 0	144,847
Dec. 31, 2005	25,152	14,485	134,180
Dec. 31, 2006	25,152	13,418	122,446
Dec. 31, 2007	25,152	12,245	109,538
Dec. 31, 2008	25,152	10,954	95,340
Dec. 31, 2009	25,152	9,534	79,722
Dec. 31, 2010	25,152	7,972	62,542
Dec. 31, 2011	25,152	6,254	43,645
Dec. 31, 2012	25,152	4,364	22,857
Dec. 31, 2013	25,152	2,295	0

*Small rounding errors throughout the table due to not carrying amounts to cents.

EXTENDING
the Concept

For a financial report prepared for 2008, how much of the obligation is current and how much is long-term?

Answer: The amount of $15,618 is classified as current, and $79,722 is classified as long-term.

As with the bond amortization table in the previous example, it can be seen that at December 31, 2004, the total amount owing is $144,847. It can also be seen that at December 31, 2005, the total amount owing is $134,180. Hence, during 2005, the total amount owing decreased by $10,667, and this decrease in the principal amount is the amount that is reported as a current liability on the December 31, 2004 balance sheet. The rest of the $144,847, or $134,180, is reported as a long-term liability because that amount will not be liquidated during the coming year through using a current asset. Exhibit 12-8, which is a partial comparative balance sheet for the year ended December 31, 2005, is prepared from this amortization table.

EXHIBIT 12-8

Name of the Company
Partial Balance Sheet
For the Years Ended December 31,

	2005	2004
Current liabilities:		
Currently maturing portion of long-term liability	$ 11,734	$ 10,667
Long-term liabilities:		
Debt	122,446	134,180

For installment debt that pays interest other than on December 31, the rule for determining the current liability is that it is the change in the carrying value as illustrated above, plus any accrued interest. The long-term liability is read from its amortization table for the next period, the same as illustrated above.

General Comments Regarding Financial Reporting

In recent years, all companies have tended to prepare highly condensed balance sheets and then to provide details in the notes. Hence, the number of pages of notes to the financial statements is growing, and it could be said that the importance of the financial statements is decreasing. See Exhibit 12-9 for an example of this, which is the liabilities section of E.I. du Pont de Nemours and Company's balance sheet. Note particularly the number of references to notes where additional information about that particular liability total can be found. Note 19 is also attached for illustration purposes.

International Accounting Standards

INTERNATIONAL

Because of the differences that exist across countries in recognizing and measuring liabilities, comparability of the resulting financial statements is somewhat difficult. With respect to liabilities, some countries' GAAP allow companies to recognize liabilities for *future* contingencies (as contrasted to contingencies in this chapter where a contingency was an *existing* condition or situation that would be resolved in the future). That is, provisions are sometimes taken today for events that may occur in the future. Germany, for example, allows this practice.

EXHIBIT 12-9

Typical Reporting of Liabilities in Published Financial Reports

Dollars in millions	2001	2000
Current liabilities		
Accounts payable (Note 19)	$ 2,219	$ 2,731
Short-term borrowings and capital lease obligations (Note 20)	1,464	3,247
Income taxes (Note 9)	1,295	250
Other accrued liabilities (Note 21)	3,089	3,027
Total current liabilities	$ 8,067	$ 9,255
Long-term borrowings and capital lease obligations (Note 22)	5,350	6,658
Other liabilities (Note 23)	7,336	7,729
Deferred income taxes (Note 9)	2,690	2,105
Total liabilities	$23,443	$25,747

Note 19. Accounts Payable

December 31	2001	2000
Trade	$ 1,565	$ 1,900
Payables to banks	169	237
Compensation awards	111	191
Miscellaneous	374	403
	$ 2,219	$ 2,731

Accounting for Contingencies under German GAAP

As mentioned in Chapter 4, Germany is a code-law country, where the financial reporting rules are established by the government. In addition to the government, the other major stakeholders of financial reporting in Germany are banks and employees. Presenting a fair view of the financial health of the company is not as high a financial reporting priority as it is in the United States and other common-law countries. The major stakeholders in Germany have access to private communication with management and thus do not depend as much on external reports to obtain the desired information.

All of the major stakeholders in Germany desire a pattern of earnings that is evened out over time, which results in a smooth flow of tax revenue to the government and less risk to employees. The banks benefit in two ways by a smooth flow of earnings. First, banks are the major stockholders in Germany, and an even flow of company earnings will result in a steady flow of dividend revenue to banks, which is a primary source of their earnings. Second, the accounting rules that facilitate the smoothing of earnings also result in earnings that are relatively more conservative, which protects creditors from large dividend distributions that could harm the companies' ability to service debt to the bank. In fact, the principle of **prudence** (which is similar to the conservatism convention in the United States) dominates German financial reporting.

So how do German companies effectively smooth reported earnings and simultaneously follow the prudence principle? They practice what has been commonly referred to as **reserve accounting**. That is, German GAAP allows companies to establish liabilities that U.S. GAAP would not allow. The recognition and measurement of these liabilities (i.e., reserves) is up to the discretion of management. Sufficient disclosure is often not provided in the financial statements for the reader to determine how much of the reserves were recognized and for what reasons, which explains why Germany is notorious for hidden reserves.[13]

Some examples of reserves that a German company might recognize are reserves for *future* expenditures related to R&D projects, repairs and maintenance, environmental cleanup, advertising, and lawsuits. In all these cases, it is important to realize that the actual expenditure has not taken place, and in fact, it might not be probable that the expenditure will ever occur. Further, to recognize a contingent liability under German GAAP, the probability that an event will occur that will result in a liability to the company needs only to be *reasonably possible*, which is significantly less stringent than the *probable* criterion under U.S. GAAP. Also, it should be noted that whether to recognize a liability and expense—even when the reasonably possible criterion is met—is up to the discretion of management.

Exhibit 12-10 presents some information extracted from the financial statements of BASF Aktiengesellschaft, a Fortune-500 German company. BASF has established provisions (i.e., reserves) for pensions, taxes, and other. Note 24 to the financial statements indicates that the other provisions consist of several types of contingencies. Most notably, the contingency for future maintenance and repair costs would not be allowed under U.S. GAAP, which requires repairs and maintenance costs to be expensed as incurred. However, even the other contingencies might not be allowed under U.S. GAAP if the likelihood of them actually occurring is less than probable.

This practice of providing reserves for future costs is conservative in that net assets are understated, which protects creditors' interests. In addition, it is an effective method to smooth earnings. During years with high earnings, managers can recognize additional reserves, which would increase expenses and cause earnings to be decreased. Then, in years with poor operating performance, the reserves represent a "pool of earnings" that managers can dip into by reversing the entry that was made in prior years, or at the very least, the manager would not need to recognize additional expenses for items where reserves have been established already.

The power of reserve accounting was clearly illustrated in 1993 when Daimler-Benz became the first German company to list on the New York Stock Exchange. In order to register with the SEC, Daimler-Benz was required to reconcile its earnings and stockholders' equity from German GAAP to U.S. GAAP. In so doing, its earnings for the first half of 1993 went from a healthy profit of $97 million under German GAAP to a loss of $548 million under U.S. GAAP. The primary difference was Daimler-Benz's reversal of previously established

INTERNET

The German Accounting Standards Board (GASB) is actively revising German GAAP to more closely harmonize with other stockholder-oriented accounting regimes, including international GAAP as promulgated by the IASB. To find up-to-date information on the activities of the GASB, go to its Web site at **http://www.drsc.de/eng/ index.html**.

[13]Hidden reserves means that, in reference to the accounting equation A = L + OE, owners' equity is understated, which could occur either because assets are understated or because liabilities are overstated, which is more the case with German companies. U.S. companies that have hidden reserves generally have understated assets. (The discussion in this chapter about the desire of businessmen to leave debt off the balance sheet will result in understating owners' equity, and that is called watered stock.)

EXHIBIT 12-10

Selected Information from Financial Statements of BASF Aktiengesellschaft

Millions €

Stockholders' equity and liabilities	Note	1999	1998
Subscribed capital	(21)	1,589.7	1,594.7
Capital surplus	(21)	2,675.2	2,590.1
Retained earnings	(21)	9,001.7	8,695.1
Currency translation adjustment		549.3	39.5
Minority interests	(22)	329.3	330.7
Shareholders' equity		**14,145.2**	**13,250.1**
Provisions for pensions and similar obligations	(23)	4,170.0	4,062.5
Provisions for taxes		662.6	487.3
Other provisions	(24)	3,805.1	3,196.1
Provisions		**8,637.7**	**7,745.9**
Bonds and other liabilities to capital market		516.7	590.5
Liabilities to credit institutions		777.7	725.3
Accounts payable, trade		2,316.0	1,871.2
Liabilities to affiliated companies		208.0	202.8
Miscellaneous liabilities		3,217.4	2,115.1
Liabilities	(25)	**7,035.8**	**5,504.9**
Deferred income		**190.3**	**200.8**
Stockholders' equity and liabilities		**30,009.0**	**26,701.7**

NOTE 24—Other Provisions

	1999	Thereof likely use within one year	1998	Thereof likely use within one year
Oil and gas production	350.2	—	326.3	3.1
Environmental protection and remediation costs	255.1	125.8	293.4	120.6
Personnel costs	1,129.2	709.8	983.5	599.9
Sales and purchase risks	533.7	526.8	419.9	401.1
Shutdown and restructuring costs	222.7	164.6	207.3	160.9
Legal, damage claims, and related commitments	726.7	265.8	448.3	95.3
Maintenance and repair costs	125.5	61.1	172.6	107.8
Other	462.0	431.1	344.8	304.4
Total	**3,805.1**	**2,285.0**	**3,196.1**	**1,793.1**

reserves that were not allowed under U.S. GAAP. In addition, in 1996, Deutsche Bank admitted to having accumulated over $12 billion marks in hidden reserves.[14]

The effect of recognizing hidden reserves has been mitigated significantly in the last few years as a result of many German companies adopting international

---

[14]S. Ascarelli, "Deutsche Bank Says Net Jumped 24% in 1995, Discloses Big Hidden Reserves," *The Wall Street Journal*, March 29, 1996, p. A8.

The IASC's conceptual framework defines a liability as follows:

> A present obligation of the enterprise arising from past events, the settlement of which is expected to result in an outflow from the enterprise of resources embodying economic benefits.

This definition of a liability contains the same basic elements as provided in the FASB's conceptual framework. As a result, financial reporting under international GAAP with respect to liabilities is very similar to U.S. GAAP. Also, in the authors' opinion, significant differences do not arise between international GAAP and U.S. GAAP when reporting liabilities for warranties, compensated absences, proofs-of-purchase, premiums, bonuses, and long-term notes and bonds.

GAAP, which, similar to U.S. GAAP, explicitly prohibits recognizing liabilities for expected future operating costs and requires the probable criterion to be met before recognizing a contingent liability. According to the IASC Web site, at the time of this writing, 161 German companies have adopted international GAAP, including Fortune-500 companies, such as Henkel, MAN, Lufthansa, Deutsche Bank, and Volkswagen.

Summary

Three primary issues arise when reporting liabilities at year-end: existence, valuation, and classification. Determining the existence of liabilities is often the most difficult issue to deal with of the three. This is so because of the many commitments that constitute off-balance-sheet financing and because of various loss contingencies. For agreements that result in off-balance-sheet financing, the FASB requires complete disclosure of such in the notes to the financial statements. Another issue concerning the existence of liabilities is loss contingencies, which are accrued where (1) it is probable that a future event will occur, confirming that it is probable that presently an asset is impaired or a liability has been incurred, and (2) when the amount can be reasonably estimated. Gain contingencies are not accrued until the realization criterion is met. Also, care should be taken in disclosing information about gain contingencies in the notes.

Regarding valuation, theoretically, all liabilities are reported at their present value amount. However, those liabilities that have a short discount period are reported at face amount. This is the usual situation for liabilities classified as current. Most liabilities occur at definite points in time from recognizable transactions, and so the amount of the liability is known. However, other liabilities must be estimated. Usually, the best approach to estimating the amounts of the liabilities is to focus on estimating the liability. The resulting adjusting entry is the difference between what the end-of-year balance is and what it should be.

Liabilities are classified as either current liabilities or long-term liabilities. Those liabilities that will be liquidated in the current operating cycle or one year, whichever is longer, and that will require the use of an existing current asset or the incurring of another current liability to liquidate them are classified as current liabilities. Short-term liabilities are reclassified as long-term when management has the intent and can demonstrate the ability to refinance on a long-term basis. Ability is proven either by actually refinancing after the end of the fiscal year and before the financial statements are issued or by entering into a refinancing agreement. Those liabilities that are incurred in the normal course of doing business and that are due in customary terms (e.g., accounts payable and salaries payable) can never be reclassified as long term. Amortization tables are useful for classifying and reporting long-term liabilities. The amount shown in the Carrying Amount column of the amortization table is the total amount due. For long-term liabilities that mature at a point in time, the amount in the Carrying Amount column is reported as a long-term liability. For long-term liabilities that are paid in installments, the carrying amount for the next year is the long-term portion, and the amount by which the carrying amount decreases during the current period is the current portion plus accrued interest. Premiums and discounts are reported with their associated debts.

APPENDIX: Troubled Debt Restructuring

The late 1970s and early 1980s were times of general business recession in the United States, and many businesses experienced more than usual financial difficulty. During that time, many creditors, in order to make the best of a difficult situation, settled various debts by restructuring them. Because of the typical economic and/or legal pressures that the creditor was under to restructure these troubled debts as compared to typical debt restructurings,[15] many accountants had concerns as to whether the accounting for troubled debt restructurings, as they have come to be called, also ought to be different.

Accordingly, the FASB followed its due process procedures and issued *SFAS No. 15,* "Accounting for Debtors and Creditors for Troubled Debt Restructurings." Since issuing *SFAS No. 15,* the board has issued two other standards that amend the manner in which the creditor accounts for troubled debt restructurings and another standard that changes the manner in which the debtor reports any gain. Standards No. 114 and No. 118 contain the accounting changes for the creditor, and Standard No. 145 addresses the change in reporting for the debtor. These three standards constitute GAAP for troubled debt restructurings.

Since the accounting and financial reporting for *troubled* debt restructurings are different from the accounting and financial reporting of other debt restructurings, the first step in accounting for them is distinguishing between them. A **troubled debt restructuring** occurs when the creditor grants a concession that he ordinarily would not,[16] which is done with the objective of recovering as much money as possible. This concession may be imposed by a court or be the result of an agreement between the debtor and creditor. Even though a debtor is in financial difficulty, a troubled debt restructuring does not occur when:

- The creditor settles a debt at a current interest rate, even though that rate is less than the rate on the debt;
- The creditor accepts assets that have a fair value at least equal to the carrying amount of the debt;
- The creditor accepts less than the fair value of the note because of his own cash flow problems;
- The creditor fails to collect a trade account receivable, even if he has taken legal action, unless there has been a restructuring agreement on the trade account between the debtor and creditor; and
- Lease agreements change.

Also, if the debtor can obtain funds from sources other than the existing creditor at a current market interest rate, given the terms and conditions of the debt, the debt restructuring is not troubled.

---

[15]Examples of more typical debt restructurings are (1) the early extinguishing of debt, (2) refunding the debt by issuing new debt securities for those presently outstanding, and (3) calling the debt. The accounting for these typical restructurings was covered in Chapter 11 of this text.

[16]A troubled debt restructuring could occur in a bankruptcy proceeding, unless the restructuring was part of a general restructuring of the debtor's liabilities.

A troubled debt restructuring may include, but is not limited to, one or any combination of the following:

1. Accepting assets whose fair value is less than the amount owed,
2. Accepting an equity interest in the debtor corporation, or
3. Modifying the terms of the debt, such as one of the following or a combination of the following:
   a. Reducing the interest rate for the remaining life of the debt,
   b. Extending the maturity date,
   c. Reducing the amount of the debt, and/or
   d. Reducing the accrued interest owed.

The accounting and financial reporting requirements for both the creditor and the debtor are explained in the following sections for each of the stated methods of restructuring a troubled debt.

Accepting Assets Whose Fair Value Is Less Than the Amount Owed

In the debtor's accounting for this type of troubled debt restructuring, the resulting gain should be separated into two components. A gain on restructuring is recognized for the difference between the fair value of the assets transferred and the carrying amount of the debt, and a gain or loss on transferring assets is recognized for the difference between the fair value of the assets transferred and their book value. Exhibit 12-1(A) illustrates how these two gains are computed for the debtor.

EXHIBIT 12-1(A)

**Separating the Extraordinary Gain
from the Ordinary Gain/Loss when Assets Are Tranferred
in Full Settlement of the Amount Owed**

(Debtor accounting only)

Carrying amount of the debt

This is the gain on restructuring.

Fair value of the assets transferred

This is the gain/loss on transferring assets. If the book value is greater than the fair value, the difference is an ordinary loss.

Book value of the assets transferred

The fair values of the assets transferred are determined by considering the amount that the debtor could have reasonably expected to receive in a sale with a willing buyer. However, if the fair value of the receivable is more clearly determinable, then that value is used to measure the transaction. When assets are transferred in *partial* settlement of a debt, the fair value of the asset must be used to measure the transaction; the fair value of the receivable cannot be used. (Application of this concept is covered later in this appendix where the troubled debt restructuring is done by accepting assets in partial settlement of the amount owed, and then the terms of the debt are restructured.)

For the creditor, the allowance for uncollectible accounts is first reduced to the extent that the loss had been previously provided, and any excess loss is recognized as an ordinary loss of the period. For both the debtor and creditor, the loss is not an extraordinary loss because it is the nature of business to incur losses on monies borrowed or loans made, and thus the unusual in nature and infrequent in occurrence criteria to be considered an extraordinary item are not met.

To illustrate, The Blindman is a custom window covering company that is indebted to the First Bank of Southern Texas for a $300,000, 12%, 4-year note that pays interest each December 31 and is due December 31, 2006. During 2004, The Blindman incurred severe financial difficulties, and at December 31, 2004, it is likely that The Blindman will default on the note and on the accrued interest of $36,000. In an effort to make the best of a difficult situation, First Bank agreed to settle the note and interest for a tract of land having a current market value of $220,000, which The Blindman had acquired in 1999 for $180,000. First Bank had previously established a $20,000 allowance for bad debts on this loan. The accounting for the debtor and creditor for this troubled debt restructuring is shown in Illustration 12-1(A).

ILLUSTRATION 12-1(A)

Troubled Debt Restructuring—Transfer of Assets

Accounting by the Debtor

Note Payable	300,000	
Interest Payable	36,000	
Land		180,000
Gain on Transfer of Land[a]		40,000
Gain on Restructuring Debt[b]		116,000

[a]This is the difference between the fair value and the carrying value of the land.
[b]This is the difference between the fair value of the land and the total amount owed.

Accounting by the Creditor

Land[c]	220,000	
Allowance for Uncollectible Accounts[d]	20,000	
Loss on Restructuring Debt[e]	96,000	
Note Receivable		300,000
Interest Receivable		36,000

[c]Recorded at fair value.
[d]The amount of the loss previously provided by First Bank is removed from the books.
[e]The excess of the total loss over that previously accounted for is recognized as a loss of the period.

Accepting an Equity Interest in the Debtor Corporation

When the debtor grants an equity interest in his corporation to settle a debt, both the debtor and creditor account for the equity interest at its fair value. The debtor recognizes a gain for the difference between the fair value of the equity interest and the carrying amount of the debt. The creditor first reduces its allowance account for the amount of the loss previously provided for and then recognizes any excess as a loss of the period.

Assume that instead of transferring assets, The Blindman offers to issue to First Bank 10,000 shares of its $5 par common stock that is selling currently at $22 per share, an offer that First Bank accepts. As before, First Bank had previously established a $20,000 allowance for bad debts on this loan. The accounting for the debtor and creditor for this troubled debt restructuring is demonstrated in Illustration 12-2(A).

ILLUSTRATION 12-2(A)

Troubled Debt Restructuring—Granting an Equity Interest

Accounting by the Debtor		
Note Payable	300,000	
Interest Payable	36,000	
Common Stock		50,000
Paid-In Capital in Excess of Par		170,000
Gain on Restructuring Debt		116,000

Accounting by the Creditor		
Investment in The Blindman	220,000	
Allowance for Uncollectible Accounts	20,000	
Loss on Restructuring Debt	96,000	
Note Receivable		300,000
Interest Receivable		36,000

To measure this transaction, the fair value of the equity interest should be used, unless the fair value of the receivable is more readily determinable. However, when the equity interest is given in partial settlement of the amount owed, then the fair value of the equity interest must be used to measure the transaction.

Modifying the Terms of the Debt

To this point, the accounting for the debtor and the creditor for a troubled debt restructuring has been symmetrical (i.e., whatever one party did, the other party did the same). However, when the terms of the debt are modified, the accounting for the debtor and the creditor is not symmetrical. For this reason, accounting for creditors and debtors is discussed separately, with the debtor's accounting being covered first.

Accounting for the Debtor Essentially, the debtor accounts for a troubled debt restructuring involving a modification of terms prospectively. The debtor does not reduce the principal or the accrued interest, nor is any gain recognized, unless the total future cash flows—under the new terms—will be less than the carrying amount of the debt, including the accrued interest. Hence, the first step in the debtor's accounting is to compute the total future cash flows (principal and accrued interest) and then to compare that total to the carrying value of the principal and interest and apply the following rules:

- When the total future cash flows will be less than the carrying amount of the principal and accrued interest, the debtor reduces the carrying amount of the debt to equal the future cash flows and recognizes a gain. Subsequent collections are recognized totally as a payment of the principal, and no interest expense is recognized.

- When the total future cash flows will exceed the carrying amount of the principal and accrued interest, the debtor does not change the carrying amount of the debt, and no gain on restructuring is recognized. Rather, a discount rate is computed that equates the current carrying amount to the future cash flows, and the debtor uses that discount rate in subsequent years to recognize interest expense.

To illustrate these two situations, assume that The Blindman, on December 31, 2004, agreed with First Bank to restructure the $300,000, 12%, 4-year note under the following terms:

- The accrued interest of $36,000 is forgiven;
- The principal amount is reduced to $250,000;
- The interest rate is reduced to 8%; and
- The term is extended to December 31, 2007, which is one year beyond the original maturity date.

The future cash flows are computed as follows:

Future principal amount	$250,000
Future interest amounts:	
for 2005 ($250,000 × 8%)	20,000
for 2006	20,000
for 2007	20,000
Total future cash flows	$310,000

Once the total future cash flows are computed, they are compared to the total carrying amount of the debt, which is $336,000 ($300,000 principal plus the $36,000 accrued interest). Because the future cash flows are less than the current carrying amount, the debtor reduces the carrying amount to the future cash flows of $310,000 and recognizes an extraordinary gain, as follows:

Accrued Interest Payable	36,000	
Note Payable		10,000
Gain on Restructuring		26,000

To recognize a gain from restructuring a troubled debt and reduce the carrying amount of the debt to the future cash flow amount.

The debtor records subsequent cash payments by the usual credit to Cash and debits Note Payable for the amount paid. No interest expense is recognized in any year.

To illustrate the second scenario where the future cash payments exceed the current carrying amount of the debt, suppose that First Bank restructures the note as before, except that the principal amount of the note will not be reduced but will remain at $300,000. The future cash flows are now computed as follows:

Future principal amount	$300,000
Future interest amounts:	
for 2005 ($300,000 × 8%)	24,000
for 2006	24,000
for 2007	24,000
Total future cash flows	$372,000

Since the future cash flows exceed the current carrying amount of $336,000, The Blindman does not recognize any gain on the restructuring nor adjust the carrying values of any of its accounts. It is suggested that the only journal entry to prepare is to debit Accrued Interest Payable and credit Note Payable. Doing this expedites the accounting process when subsequent interest payments are made. In preparing its amortization table, the debtor computes a discount rate that equates the future cash flow amount of $372,000 to $300,000. This rate is used to recognize interest expense over the next three years. For The Blindman, this discount rate is 3.70%,[17] and it is used to prepare the amortization table in Illustration 12-3(A).

ILLUSTRATION 12-3(A)

Amortization Table—Modification of Terms Where the Future Cash Flows Exceed the Current Carrying Amount
(Debtor only)

Year	Cash	Interest	Carrying Value
			$336,000
2005	$24,000	$12,434	324,434
2006	24,000	12,006	312,440
2007	24,000	11,560	300,000

The journal entry to account for the first interest payment is as follows:

Interest Expense	12,434	
Note Payable	11,566	
Cash		24,000

To record the interest payment for 2005.

Also, the journal entries for paying interest and principal in 2007 are as follows:

Interest Expense	11,560	
Note Payable	12,440	
Cash		24,000

To record the interest payment for 2007.

| Note Payable | 300,000 | |
| Cash | | 300,000 |

To record the payment of principal at the maturity date.

Accounting for the Creditor The accounting for the creditor for a troubled debt restructuring that involves a modification of terms is established in *SFAS No. 114*, "Accounting by Creditors for Impairment of a Loan," as amended by *SFAS*

---

[17]This interest rate can be estimated by dividing the carrying amount of the note ($336,000) by the total of the future cash flows ($372,000) and then referring to the Present Value of a Single Sum Table. The interest rate is found by referring to the number of periods and reading across the line until the computed value is found. Interpolation can also be used to refine the percentage. This procedure gives an approximate interest rate. A more precise amount can then be determined in a trial-and-error fashion. Another way to find the appropriate interest rate is to use the "Solver" function in Excel.

No. 118, "Accounting by Creditors for Impairment of a Loan—Income Recognition and Disclosure." *SFAS No. 114* applies to all loans—not just troubled debt restructurings—except for:

- Large groups of smaller-balance loans that are evaluated as a group for collectibility,
- Loans that are measured at fair value or at the lower-of-cost-or-market,
- Leases, and
- Investments in debt securities.

According to *SFAS No. 114, a loan is impaired when it is probable that the creditor will be unable to collect all amounts due according to the terms of the contract.* The amount of loss on impairment is based upon *discounting the future cash flows at the loan's original contracted rate to the new maturity date,* and then comparing that amount to the carrying amount of the receivable (i.e., the principal plus the interest). Returning to the most recent example of First Bank and The Blindman, the following calculations are made to determine the amount of impairment that First Bank has incurred.

Carrying amount of the receivable (principal and interest)		$336,000
Present value of the restructured loan:		
Principal ($300,000 × 0.71178)[18]	$213,534	
Interest ($24,000 × 2.40183)	57,644	
Total		271,178
Loss on restructuring		$ 64,822

Assuming that First Bank had previously provided for $20,000 of this loss, then the journal entry to record the impairment of the loan is as follows:

Allowance for Uncollectibles	20,000	
Loss on Impairment	44,822	
Accrued Interest Receivable		36,000
Note Receivable		28,822

To record the impairment of a note receivable.

The preceding entry assumes that adequate provision for the loss had not been made previously in the allowance account. If adequate provision had been made, then the entire impairment of $64,822 would be debited to Allowance for Uncollectible Accounts.

Note that an important part of the previous calculation is that the carrying amount of the note receivable is reduced from $300,000 to $271,178. This is important because the creditor's subsequent amortization table is based upon the $271,178, as shown in Illustration 12-4(A).

Interest income is computed using the originally contracted 12% interest rate, thus assuring that the creditor will continue to recognize interest revenue based upon the originally contracted interest rate. This is made possible by recognizing a larger loss immediately than would have been recognized if the loss had been computed on an undiscounted future cash flow basis. Thus, the entry to recognize interest income for 2005 is as follows:

---

[18]This is the time value of money factor for the present value of a single sum at 12% (the original contracted rate) for three years, which is the time remaining to the new maturity date. These same discounting concepts also apply to determining the present value for purposes of discounting the interest.

Cash	24,000	
Note Receivable	8,542	
Interest Revenue		32,542

To recognize interest for 2005 and to reduce the note payable appropriately based upon the originally contracted 12% interest rate.

ILLUSTRATION 12-4(A)

Amortization Table—Modification of Terms Where the Discounted Future Cash Flows Are Less than the Current Carrying Amount
(Creditor only)

Year	Cash	Interest	Carrying Value
			$271,178
2005	$24,000	$32,542*	279,720
2006	24,000	33,566	289,286
2007	24,000	34,714	300,000

*Computed as 12% (the originally contracted rate) times the carrying value.

As a result of this scheme of journal entries, the balance in the note receivable account at the end of 2007 will be $300,000, which is the amount that will be received when the note matures.

Combination of Types

When a troubled debt restructuring involves both a transfer of an asset or the granting of equity interest and a modification of terms, both the debtor and creditor first account for the assets transferred or the equity interest granted according to the rules specified earlier, and then account for the modification of terms. In both steps, the same procedures as set forth previously are followed. The only exception to the rules is that when assets are transferred, no gain on restructuring is recognized by the debtor. The debtor recognizes only the gain or loss from transferring assets, which is the difference between the fair value and the carrying value of the asset(s) transferred.

Final Comments on Troubled Debt Restructuring

At the time the issues of troubled debt restructuring were first being discussed by the FASB, which was prior to 1977, many financial institutions lobbied strongly for recognizing losses on loans on an undiscounted cash flow basis when the debt was restructured under a modification of terms. Eventually, that is the position the FASB took, and it is the position still used for accounting by the debtor. The FASB justified its position based upon the notion that modifying the terms of a debt was not a new event that required changing the values of assets and liabilities or recognizing gains or losses. Rather, the FASB reasoned that "troubled debt restructurings typically resulted from the debtor's financial difficulties that existed before restructuring, ... [that] the creditor should have considered the debtor's financial difficulties in estimating an allowance for uncollectible amounts ... [and, therefore,] the restructuring event in itself [had] no accounting significance except to sometimes provide more definitive evidence of the effect on the debtor's financial difficulties."[19]

As a result of requiring creditors to recognize losses on an undiscounted cash-flow basis during the savings and loan crisis of the 1980s, financial institutions were "saved" from having to recognize the larger losses that would have otherwise resulted—as is now required. So to some extent, the magnitude of the savings and loan crisis was camouflaged by the accounting principles used. Thus, accounting for troubled debt restructurings is another example of the influence that accounting techniques have had on economic events.

Questions

1. What criteria must be met before a liability can be recognized? Given these criteria, prior to recognizing a liability, is it necessary to:
   a. Know the identity of the person to whom the obligation is owed?
   b. Know the amount of the obligation?
   c. Know the date the liability will be satisfied?
   d. Know that the obligation will be paid in cash?
   e. Know that the obligation is certain?

2. At what amount, theoretically, should liabilities be valued on a balance sheet? Practically, how are short-term liabilities valued? Why?

3. How should a long-term bond be classified that is due within one year and will be liquidated using proceeds from a bond sinking fund that is classified under investments in funds? Why?

4. Discuss the meaning of off-balance-sheet financing, and indicate some arrangements by which businesses accomplish this. What disclosures are required for companies that enter into off-balance-sheet financing arrangements?

5. With respect to loss contingencies, what is the appropriate accounting procedures when the probability of a loss occurring is (a) probable, (b) reasonably possible, or (c) remote? How does your answer differ for gain contingencies?

6. Randall Corporation is a defendant in a lawsuit. Management believes it is probable that the outcome of the case will be unfavorable and that estimated damages will be within a range of $800,000 to $1,500,000. What, if anything, should Randall accrue for this loss contingency, and what disclosures should Randall make in the notes?

7. Thomas Hills Co. uses different types of chemicals in its manufacturing process. Recently, the company has been ordered by the courts to clean up the environment as a result of disposing of these chemicals. Although the total cost for the cleanup is unknown, the company expects to incur total costs of approximately $20 million. The company has insurance that will reimburse Thomas Hills in the amount of $5 million. How should Thomas Hills account for the liability and the insurance proceeds?

8. Identify the conditions that must be met before a liability for compensated absences can be accrued.

---

[19]*FASB No. 115*, "Accounting for Certain Investments in Debt and Equity Securities," pars. 65–66 and 76.

9. In all cases where an estimated liability must be recognized (e.g., warranties, coupons, compensated absences, and bonuses), describe the procedures that an accountant should take to properly recognize the year-end liability and the expense for the reporting period.

10. Discuss the rationale for excluding from current liabilities obligations due within one year that are expected to be refinanced on a long-term basis. What criteria must be met before a company can exclude short-term liabilities from the current liabilities category? What short-term liabilities can never be excluded from current liabilities?

11. Digger Co. has long-term debt outstanding that will expire on March 15, 2005. In February 2005, the company enters into a noncancelable arrangement that allows it to borrow sufficient cash to pay that maturing debt. How should Digger classify the long-term debt that is maturing on February 15 on its December 31, 2004 financial statements? Why? Where should the debt that will be incurred in April be reported on the December 31, 2004 financial statements? Why?

Exercises

Exercise 12-1: Known Liability, Definite Amount. On February 1, 2004, Ranchers Company borrowed $200,000 from a lending institution at a stated interest rate of 12%, which is equal to the market rate. Terms of the note stipulate that Ranchers is to pay annual interest payments, and the entire principal is due in three years. Indicate the amounts that should be reported as a liability for this note and how the amounts should be classified on Ranchers' balance sheet as of December 31, 2004.

Exercise 12-2: Known Liability, Definite Amount. Ryan's Stores, Inc., operates several stores in a state that charges a 7.5% sales tax. The company collects the tax from customers and makes estimated monthly payments to the state government. Then, at the end of each quarter, Ryan's Stores completes a quarterly sales tax return, at which time any underpayment of sales taxes is paid.

During the first quarter of 2004, Ryan's Stores recorded sales revenues of $670,000, $750,000, and $824,600, for the months of January, February, and March, respectively. These amounts include the sales tax collected. During February, the company submitted a sales tax payment of $50,000 for taxes collected in January, and the same amount was paid in March for taxes collected in February.

Determine the amount of the sales tax liability that Ryan's Stores has as of March 31, 2004.

Exercise 12-3: Known Liability, Known Amount. Achiever has an incentive compensation plan under which the store manager receives a bonus equal to 10% of some predetermined amount. During the current year, income before the bonus and taxes equaled $160,000, and the effective tax rate is 40%. Any bonus is deductible for determining income before taxes.

1. How much is Achiever's liability for bonus if the predetermined amount is defined to be income before taxes and bonus?

2. How much is Achiever's liability for bonus if the predetermined amount is defined to be income after taxes and bonus?

Exercise 12-4: Known Liability, Several Correct Amounts. On March 1, 2005, Zecco acquired some property in an area in which property tax assessments are made each August. Wanting to prepare monthly financial statements (and therefore having to make monthly accruals for property taxes), Zecco learned that the property taxes assessed on the property in the previous year had been $15,000. The average increase in property taxes over the past 10 years had been 3%, although in some years there had been no increase in property taxes and in one year the property tax assessment had decreased. (*Note:* The property taxes for the months prior to March would be paid into escrow by the previous owner, and that amount should not be considered part of Zecco's liability.)

Determine at least two amounts that Zecco could properly report as the liability for property taxes on its March 31, 2005 balance sheet.

Exercise 12-5: Known Liability, Known Amount. Grand Vista, Inc., has seven employees, all of whom work eight hours a day, five days a week. The wage rate and other information for each employee as of the last pay period are as follows:

Employee(s)	Wage/Hr.	No. of Weeks Worked during the Current Year for Each Employee
1	$19.60	48
2–4	9.70	50
5	8.00	45
6–7	6.00	38

The company pays a total of 3.5% of eligible gross wages to the federal and state governments for unemployment benefits. Eligible gross wages are defined as the first $20,000 earned by each employee during the year. Grand Vista, Inc., has made periodic payments to the government totaling $3,500 during the year. As of December 31, 2004, all seven employees have three days of accrued wages.

Determine the liability that Grand Vista should report on its balance sheet for unemployment benefits and wages and prepare any necessary journal entry.

Exercise 12-6: Contingencies. During 2004, Goodrick Company filed a $1 million lawsuit against McDaniel, Inc., for patent infringement. The lawyers of both companies believe it is probable that the outcome of the lawsuit will be favorable for Goodrick. McDaniel lawyers are refusing to pay the $1 million and believe that the actual damages will be between $400,000 and $750,000, with their best estimate being $600,000. However, Goodrick's lawyers believe that the actual award will be about $500,000.

1. Prepare necessary journal entries as of December 31, 2004, for both Goodrick and McDaniel.
2. Considering that the annual reports of both companies are publicly available, can you identify a potential ethical dilemma that might be faced by either company?

Exercise 12-7: Contingencies. A lawsuit was filed against McGraw, Inc., during 2003, and as of December 31, 2003, company lawyers believed it was probable McGraw will have to pay damages within the range of $150,000 to $325,000, with no amount within the range being more likely than any other.

1. Explain how this contingency should be accounted for, and if necessary, prepare the appropriate journal entry.
2. Late in 2004, McGraw was pleasantly surprised when a favorable judgment was returned in which the court decided on McGraw's behalf, and in addition, the plaintiff was required to pay McGraw's legal fees of $40,000. At December 31, 2004, the plaintiff is appealing the ruling, but management believes that the likelihood of the plaintiff winning an appeal is very remote. McGraw has not received any of the $40,000. Prepare any necessary journal entry.

Exercise 12-8: Contingencies. Crunch-em Rent-a-Car has always carried its automobile insurance through All Nation, but due to rising insurance rates, upper management has decided to "just pay the repair bills, or sue the other party." Last year, auto premiums for its fleet of cars were $200,000. The company issues quarterly reports, and for the first quarter of 2004, Crunch-em had no accidents involving its auto fleet. The controller knows this is a highly abnormal situation, and it is probable there will be several accidents later in the year. Also, he is concerned because having no insurance costs and no repair costs, the reported net income is much greater than it usually is. He wants your opinion as to what should be done before the financial statements are issued.

Can an accrual be made for repair costs? For insurance costs? Should a note explaining the abnormality be included in the financial report? Should anything else be included?

Exercise 12-9: Contingencies. Good Citizen, Inc., guaranteed a long-term loan for Little Brother Company. During 2004, Good Citizen was informed by the creditor that Little Brother had defaulted on the loan, and Good Citizen would be required to pay the remaining balance of the loan, plus interest, if Little Brother did not pay the loan by April 10, 2005. As of December 31, 2004, Little Brother had not yet paid the loan and is about to file for bankruptcy. Legal counsel for Good Citizen has indicated that it is probable Good Citizen will be held liable for the loan and interest, which total $250,000.

Little Brother had been an important customer of Good Citizen, and as a result of Little Brother's bankruptcy, Good Citizen is planning a restructuring that will require closing a plant and laying off employees. If the restructuring proceeds, Good Citizen estimates that the costs of closing the plant, disposing of the plant assets, and providing severance pay to workers will be approximately $1 million. The restructuring has not yet been approved by the board of directors, although such a plan has been submitted to them.

1. Determine the amount of the contingent liability that Good Citizen, Inc., should record on its books as of December 31, 2005, and prepare the necessary journal entry.
2. Comment on how the balance sheet should be presented because of the loss accrual.

Exercise 12-10: Estimated Liability for Warranties. In 2004, Montgomery, Inc., began selling washing machines on which it offers a warranty for one year at a price of $45 per machine. During 2004, 150 warranties were sold, of which 70 required service during the year. Total costs (including labor and parts) to service these warranties were $2,000. Based upon industry experience, Montgomery estimates that the total cost of servicing warranties is approximately 70% of the revenues received from selling the warranties.

How much warranty expense should Montgomery recognize for 2004, and what is the amount of Montgomery's liability for warranties at December 31, 2004?

Exercise 12-11: Estimated Liability for Coupons. In an effort to sell more products, Super Crunch Cereal began a promotional campaign in the latter part of 2004 in which it will provide a toy to customers that submit three proofs-of-purchase plus $1.50 for shipping and handling. The company estimates that proofs-of-purchase will be submitted for approximately 20% of the cereal boxes sold within the promotional period. The cost to Super Crunch Cereal for each toy is $2.25, and the cost of shipping is $0.75. As of December 31, 2004, 300,000 boxes of cereal had been sold, and 12,000 box tops had been received or redeemed.

1. Estimate the liability for the promotional campaign that Super Crunch Cereal should report on its December 31, 2004 balance sheet.
2. During 2005, an additional 400,000 boxes of cereal were sold, but at the end of 2005, only 72,000 (including the 12,000 that had been redeemed the prior year) of the proofs-of-purchase had been redeemed, and the company now believes that only 15% of the total proofs-of-purchase sold will be redeemed. Assuming that during the year the company accounts for redeemed proofs-of-purchase by crediting the liability account, prepare the necessary adjusting entry to report the liability for the promotional campaign as of December 31, 2005.

Exercise 12-12: Estimated Liability for Compensated Absences. Oh Buoy, Inc., has 10 employees who participate in a vacation and sick leave plan. Each employee earns approximately $100 per day and is provided with 10 paid days of annual sick leave and an additional 10 paid days of annual vacation leave. If not used within the year, both vacation and sick leave days can be carried over indefinitely. As of January 1, 2004, there were 65 vacation days and 54 sick days that were being carried over by employees. During 2004, employees were paid for 108 vacation days taken and 85 sick leave days taken. The accountant's normal practice when paying for compensated time off is to debit Wage Expense and credit Cash.

1. Determine the amount that should be recorded as a liability for compensated vacation and sick leave as of December 31, 2004. Prepare the necessary adjusting entry on December 31.
2. Determine the amount that should be recorded as a liability for compensated vacation and sick leave as of December 31, 2004, assuming that employees must be sick before they are paid for sick leave taken, and prepare the necessary journal entry on December 31.

Exercise 12-13: Estimated Liability for Compensated Absences. Redo Part (1) of Exercise 12-12, assuming that instead of accruing amounts at current wage rates, Oh Buoy computes the liability at estimated future wage rates, and it is anticipated that the employees will receive a 6% raise during the coming year.

Exercise 12-14: Estimated Liability for Compensated Absences. Thomson Company has 35 employees who work 8-hour days and are paid by the hour. On January 1, 2004, the company began granting its employees 10 days' paid vacation each year. Vacation days earned in 2004 may first be taken on January 1, 2005, etc. Information relative to these employees is as follows:

Year	Hourly Wage	Vacation Days Earned by Each Employee	Vacation Days Used by Each Employee
2004	$8.60	10	0
2005	9.00	10	8
2006	9.50	10	10

Thomson has chosen to measure the liability for compensated absences at the rates of pay in effect for the current year.

1. What amount of expense relative to compensated absences should be reported on Thomson's income statements for 2004–2006?
2. What is the amount of the accrued liability for compensated absences that should be reported at December 31, 2006?

Exercise 12-15: Estimated Liability for Warranties. In 2004, Ididit Corporation began selling a new line of products that carry a 2-year warranty against defects. Based upon past experience with other products, the estimated warranty cost as a percentage of dollar sales is as follows:

First year of warranty	1%
Second year of warranty	4%

Sales and actual warranty expenditures for 2004 and 2005 are as follows:

	2004	2005
Sales	$350,000	$500,000
Actual warranty expenditures	4,000	16,000

What is the estimated warranty liability at the end of 2005?

Exercise 12-16: Estimated Liability for Gift Certificates. Zach's Inc. operates a retail store and frequently sells gift certificates that must be redeemed for merchandise within one year. Past experience indicates that approximately 10% of the certificates sold will never be redeemed. Zach's credits Unearned Revenue at the time the certificates are sold. The following information was obtained from the company's records:

Gift certificates not redeemed as of January 1, 2004	$31,000
Gift certificates sold during 2004	77,000
Redeemed gift certificates that were sold in 2003	25,000
Redeemed gift certificates that were sold in 2004	60,000

How much should Zach's report as unearned revenue as of December 31, 2004?

Exercise 12-17: Classification, Refinancing Short-Term Debt. On January 21, 2005, Hagler Company issued common and preferred stock for $500,000, and on February 3 used the proceeds, along with an additional $100,000, to retire maturing bonds in the amount of $600,000. The annual report for 2004 was issued on March 13, 2005.

Show how the maturing bonds will be presented on Hagler's 2004 balance sheet.

Exercise 12-18: Classification, Refinancing Short-Term Debt. On December 31, 2004, Goof Company had $500,000 of debt outstanding that will mature on May 15, 2005, but management intends to refinance the note. Accordingly, in January 2005, Goof Company entered into a noncancelable agreement with First Union Bank to borrow $500,000 on May 1, 2005, to refinance the debt. Subsequently, in February 2005, Goof used excess cash to prepay $100,000 of the outstanding debt but still intends to receive the entire $500,000 from First Union on May 1 and use the extra $100,000 to replenish working capital.

Determine how much, if any, of the debt outstanding on December 31, 2004, should be classified as long-term debt.

SPREADSHEET

Exercise 12-19: Classification, Reporting Bonds Payable. On January 1, 2001, Wil-e Coyote Company issued $5 million of 10% bonds that will mature in 10 years and pay interest annually every December 31. The market rate of interest for similar bonds, when the bonds were issued, was 8%. Wil-e Coyote also incurred $150,000 of bond issue costs.

Show how these bonds and related bond issue costs will be reported on Wil-e's balance sheet at December 31, 2006, assuming that Wil-e uses the effective-interest method to amortize the bond premium/discount and the straight-line method to amortize the bond issue costs.

Exercise 12-20: Multiple-Choice Questions.

1. Which of the following is the best criterion for determining whether a liability should be classified as a current liability?
   a. It is expected to be settled in the normal course of the entity's operating cycle or 12 months from the balance sheet date, whichever is longer, by using a current asset.
   b. It is expected to be settled in the normal course of the entity's operating cycle or 12 months from the balance sheet date, whichever is shorter, by using a current asset.
   c. It is expected to be settled in the normal course of the entity's operating cycle.
   d. It is expected to be settled within 12 months from the balance sheet date.
2. Which of the following is *not* normally considered a current liability?
   a. Trade accounts payable arising from the entity's normal business activities.
   b. Currently scheduled payments on long-term obligations.
   c. Dividends declared and payable in eight months.
   d. Cash received for services that will be rendered in 15 months.
3. Which principle or concept justifies showing accounts payable at face value instead of discounted present value?
   a. Consistency; all other liabilities are generally stated at face value.
   b. Relevance; face value is more relevant than discounted present value.
   c. Conservatism; presenting liabilities at face value typically results in lower net assets.
   d. Materiality; the short holding period results in an immaterial difference between the two valuation methods.
4. Which of the following is a criterion that must be met in order for a company to classify a short-term obligation as a long-term liability?
   a. The company must have completed the refinancing prior to issuing the financial statements.
   b. The company must intend to refinance the debt on a long-term basis.
   c. The company must show an ability to refinance the debt on a long-term basis.
   d. Both b and c.
5. When should a contingent gain be recognized?
   a. When the chances are remote that the inflow of economic benefits will arise.
   b. When the chances are reasonably possible that the inflow of economic benefits will arise.
   c. When the chances are probable that the inflow of economic benefits will arise.
   d. Contingent assets should never be recognized until the economic benefits have been realized.

Exercise 12-21: Troubled Debt Restructuring—Transfering Assets and Granting an Equity Interest (Appendix). Spendit is experiencing financial adversity, and as a result, Big Bank is considering granting some allowance to Spendit that it normally would not consider. To settle the $250,000 note plus accrued interest of $35,000, Big Bank is considering two alternatives offered by Spendit, as follows:

> Alternative 1: Accept land owned by Spendit that is valued at $225,000. Spendit's historical cost is $140,000.

> Alternative 2: Accept an equity interest in Spendit, consisting of 24,000 shares of $1 par common stock. Currently, the stock is trading for $8.50 a share.

Big Bank has established an allowance for this account in the amount of $40,000.

Prepare the journal entries for Spendit and Big Bank for both alternatives, and explain where Spendit should report any gains/losses as a result of the restructuring.

Exercise 12-22: Troubled Debt Restructuring—Modification of Terms (Appendix). Due to a downturn in the economy and poor management, Deep-Trouble has negotiated a restructuring of its $85,000 note payable that is payable to Tight-Wad Bank, which has agreed to the restructuring in order to make the best of a difficult situation. Tight-Wad has agreed to reduce the face value of the note to $60,000, reduce the interest rate from 14% to 10%, and extend the due date of the note two years from the date of restructuring. However, Deep-Trouble is expected to pay the current interest owing of $11,900 and to pay the interest amount owing in one year.

1. Prepare the journal entries for Deep-Trouble and Tight-Wad for the restructuring, assuming that Tight-Wad has established a $25,000 allowance for this account. Show all supporting computations.
2. Prepare the journal entries for Deep-Trouble for the interest payment in the first year after restructuring and when the note matures.
3. Prepare the journal entries for Deep-Trouble and Tight-Wad for the restructuring, assuming that instead of extending the due date of the note by two years, it is extended for five years.

Exercise 12-23: Troubled Debt Restructuring—Transfer of Assets (Appendix). On December 31, 2005, Pride Inc., which was experiencing cash flow difficulties, transferred real estate to the Last National Bank of Prussia in full settlement of a debt for $700,000. The real estate was carried on Pride's books at $500,000 but had a fair value of $800,000, based upon sales of similar real estate in the past year. Last National had established an allowance of $100,000 related to this debt.

Discuss the proper accounting treatment of settling this debt, and record the appropriate journal entries for Pride and Last National Bank.

Exercise 12-24: Troubled Debt Restructuring—Modification of Terms (Appendix). To make the best of a difficult situation, the Only Bank of Antwerp agreed to restructure a debt that was due on this date from Irresponsible, as follows:

- Reduce the principal from $100,000 to $90,000.
- Forgive $6,969 of accrued but unpaid interest.
- Extend the maturity date of the loan five years.
- Reduce the interest rate from 10% to 6%.
- Interest is payable at the end of each year.

Only Bank had established an allowance related to this account of $15,000.

1. Prepare the journal entries for Irresponsible and Only Bank at the time of re-structuring.
2. Prepare the journal entries for the first interest payment for Irresponsible and Only Bank.

Exercise 12-25: Troubled Debt Restructuring—Transfer Asset and Modify Terms (Appendix). On December 31, 2005, due to financial difficulties and in an attempt to maximize the amount of cash received, Lone Star Bank agreed to restructure a $1,000,000 loan with Soggy Bottom Ltd. The terms of the restructuring require Soggy to transfer land to Lone Star that has a fair value of $200,000 and is carried on Soggy's books at $230,000. Further, Lone Star will:

- Reduce the remaining amount owing (after considering the transfer of the land) from $800,000 to $750,000;
- Reduce the interest rate from 12% to 8%;
- Extend the maturity date from the present to December 31, 2009; and
- Forgive one-half of the accrued interest of $120,000, or $60,000, with the other $60,000 payable immediately, with interest to be paid each December 31.

1. Prepare the journal entries for Lone Star and Soggy Bottom for the debt restructuring, assuming that Lone Star had established an allowance for bad debts of $150,000 related to this loan.
2. How much interest expense and interest income should Soggy Bottom and Lone Star recognize, respectively, for 2006 as a result of the restructuring?

Problems

Problem 12-1: Known Liabilities, Known Amounts. Jack's Donuts has five full-time employees. The following chart shows the year-to-date compensation paid to each employee, along with the compensation paid for the month of October. Relevant tax information also follows.

Federal income tax rate: 15%
State income tax rate: 5%
Federal unemployment tax rate: 0.75% up to $7,000 paid to each employee
State unemployment tax rate: 1% up to $7,000 paid to each employee
FICA tax: 7.65% up to $65,000 for each employee and 1.45% on all compensation greater than $65,000. Jack is required to match all FICA contributions.

Employee	Year-to-Date Wages	October Wages
Rivers, D.	$82,400	$8,240
Brown, L.	68,000	6,800
Sloan, J.	56,900	5,690
Riley, P.	3,220	3,220
Jackson, P.	8,100	3,100

The company is required to withhold federal and state income taxes, along with FICA, from each employee's paycheck and submit the amount to the respective governments two weeks after the end of the month. Federal and state unemployment taxes are paid by the employer.

Required:

1. Calculate the amount of taxes that should be withheld from each employee's October paycheck.
2. Prepare the journal entry to record and pay the October payroll.
3. Calculate Jack's liability for FICA and unemployment taxes for October, and prepare the appropriate adjusting entry.

Problem 12-2: Contingencies. The following contingencies relate to Stevenson, Inc.:

1. During 2004, a former employee sued Stevenson, and at December 31, 2004, Stevenson's lawyers believe that an unfavorable outcome is probable, estimating that damages will be awarded in the amount of $300,000–$450,000, with no single amount within the range being more likely to occur than any another amount.
2. During 2004, the government informed Stevenson that it was responsible to clean up the environment as a result of using a toxic chemical. As of December 31, 2004, management believes that the liability for the cleanup will be within the range of $750,000–$1.5 million, with the most likely amount being $900,000.
3. How would Stevenson's situation change if, in February 2005 and prior to issuing its financial statements, it signed a contract with an environmental cleanup company that will clean up the area for $800,000?
4. While working for the company, an employee of Stevenson's was involved in a traffic accident late in 2004. Although property damage was not significant, several individuals were involved in the accident and management expects medical claims to be asserted against the company. Management believes that it is probable that the company will be held liable for damages approximating $750,000. The company has a liability insurance policy that will pay $500,000 but has a $50,000 deductible.

Required:

For each contingency, indicate the proper accounting treatment. If a journal entry is necessary, prepare the proper entry.

Problem 12-3: Contingencies (CPA Adapted). The following items present various contingencies of Townsend Inc. at December 31, 2004:

1. On December 1, 2004, Townsend was awarded damages of $75,000 in a patent infringement suit that it brought against a competitor. Although management thinks that the competitor will appeal, as of December 31, 2004, the defendant had not done so.
2. What would change if Townsend received payment from the defendant on January 19, 2005, and before the financial statements were issued?
3. A former employee of Townsend has brought a wrongful dismissal suit against Townsend. Townsend's lawyers believe the suit to be without merit.
4. In December, Townsend became aware of a design flaw in its product that poses a potential safety hazard. A recall of the product appears unavoidable, and such action will most likely cost the company $150,000, although the possible loss may range anywhere from $100,000 to $250,000.

5. A government contract completed during 2004 is subject to renegotiation. Although Townsend estimates that it is reasonably possible that a refund of approximately $200,000–$300,000 may be required by the government, it does not wish to publicize this possibility.

6. Townsend has been notified by a government agency that it will be held responsible for the cleanup of toxic materials at a site where it formerly conducted operations. Townsend estimates that its share of remedial action may be as high as $500,000.

Required:

For each item, indicate the reporting requirements for Townsend Inc.

Problem 12-4: Estimated Liabilities for Warranties. Near-Zero-Defects Company has developed a new way to produce a product that greatly enhances the product's reliability. As a result, Near-Zero-Defects undertook a comprehensive marketing campaign, a part of which is a 6-year warranty against defects of any kind. Near-Zero-Defects expects an 0.8% (8/10 of 1%) return for which the sales price will be refunded. The typical return pattern for the 6-year warranty period is expected to be as follows:

Year	Percent of Total Returns Expected During the Year
Year of sale	10%
Second year	10
Third year	10
Fourth year	20
Fifth year	20
Sixth year	30
Total	100%

For example, for sales made in 2004, 10% of the returns from those sales are expected to be presented in 2004, 10% in 2005, etc.

Gross sales and actual returns of this new product for 2004 through 2006 are as follows:

Year	Sales	Returns
2004	$100,000	$200
2005	150,000	150
2006	225,000	250

Required:

1. Compute Near-Zero's warranty expense for the years 2004–2006.
2. Compute Near-Zero's estimated liability for warranties at the end of 2006, based upon its present policy of accruing 0.8%.
3. In your opinion, is Near-Zero's policy of accruing 0.8% adequate? Why or why not?

Problem 12-5: Estimated Liabilities for Warranties and Coupons. Westside Sporting Goods has been in business for several years, selling a wide variety of sporting equipment, and has frequently offered promotions to boost sales. Two of the most used promotions relate to warranties of certain equipment and the use of coupons, the details of which are as follows:

- One-year warranties are provided on selected equipment, wherein if the equipment becomes defective within one year, Westside will repair or replace the item free of charge. Past experience indicates that warranty costs average approximately 3% of total sales. During the current year, total warranty expenditures were $31,400, of which $14,700 related to sales of the prior year.
- Westside has found it profitable to offer coupons to customers to purchase selected items within the store. For every $20 spent in the store, the company gives a coupon to the customer. Coupon items change after a period of time to help maintain interest in the program and to assist in moving inventory items that are becoming stale. Recently, the company offered a basketball in exchange for 10 coupons. Next month, the company intends to change the promotion to a sleeve of golf balls for every two coupons redeemed. In general, the company attempts to offer promotions that give a $2 value for each coupon. Past experience indicates that approximately 80% of the coupons will be redeemed.

During 2004, sales for Westside were $1,056,000, and a total of 49,000 coupons were issued. During the year, a total of 47,500 coupons were redeemed.

The following information provides the balances in the warranty and coupon liability accounts as of the beginning of the year:

Estimated warranty liability	$15,100
Estimated coupon liability	76,400

Westside records entries to liability accounts only at year-end.

Required:

Compute the ending balances related to liabilities for warranties and coupons for 2004, and prepare the necessary journal entries.

Problem 12-6: Estimated Liabilities. The following three situations are independent.

Required:

Answer the questions related to each situation.

1. Needleman, Inc., inserts coupons in boxes of its products providing discounts on future purchases. When the coupons are redeemed, Needleman reimburses retailers for the face amount of the coupon plus a 10% premium for handling costs. The coupons expire two years after being distributed. As of January 1, 2005, the balance in the liability account related to coupons was $50,000. During 2005, coupons with a face value of $225,000 were distributed to retailers, and $120,000 of coupons were redeemed. Needleman estimates that approximately 60% of the coupons will ultimately be redeemed. Determine the amount of the estimated liability for coupons that should be presented on Needleman's financial statements for the year 2005.
2. Bradshaw Company offers gift certificates that have a 1-year expiration date to its customers. At the time of sale, Bradshaw credits Unearned Revenue. The company estimates that approximately 10% of the gift certificates will never be redeemed. The balance in Unearned Revenue at January 1, 2004, was $23,000. During 2004, gift certificates totaling $55,000 were sold, and gift certificates totaling $60,000 were redeemed. How much should Bradshaw report in its financial statements as unearned revenue?

3. Miller was awarded $80,000 in a lawsuit, $50,000 of which is punitive damages. The defendant is appealing only the $50,000 punitive damage award. Legal counsel for Miller believes it is probable that the appeal will not be successful. What amount should Miller report on its year-end financial statements in regards to this lawsuit, and how should it be reported?

Problem 12-7: Refinancing Short-Term Debt (CPA Adapted). At December 31, 2004, Manuel Escobar Corporation has a $12 million debt coming due within 12 months of the balance sheet date. Management intends to refinance the debt on a long-term basis, so that no portion of the $12 million will be paid from current assets during the coming year.

Required:
1. Is management's intent sufficient to classify the maturing debt as a long-term liability?
2. Assume that in 2005 and before the financial statements are issued, Escobar issues $10,000,000 of long-term bonds at 98. The amount received, supplemented as needed with cash from a sinking fund established for the purpose of retiring the maturing debt, was used to pay the debt. How, then, should the maturing $12 million debt be classified on the 2004 balance sheet?
3. Independent of Requirement 2, assume that in 2005 and before the financial statements for 2004 were issued, Escobar issues common stock whose proceeds amount to $12,100,000 and that this amount is used to retire the maturing debt. Under this scenario, how should the maturing $12 million debt be classified on the 2004 balance sheet? How (if at all) should the newly issued common stock be classified on the 2004 balance sheet?
4. Independent of Requirements 2 and 3, assume that in 2005 and prior to issuing the 2004 financial statements, Escobar entered into a financing agreement with a large national bank that permits Escobar to borrow, at any time through 2006, up to $15,000,000. Any amounts borrowed under this arrangement are to be paid in installments, with the first installment due January 1, 2006. The only way the agreement can be canceled by the bank is for a violation of a loan covenant, none of which exists at December 31, 2004. It is presumed that the bank will be financially capable of honoring the agreement. Using these facts, how should the $12 million maturing debt be reported in the financial statements for 2004?

Problem 12-8: Measuring and Classifying Liabilities. The following situations relate to Robinson's Pet Shop. The appropriate annual discount rate on all present value calculations is 12%.

1. During 2004, the company initiated a retirement plan for all employees who have worked at least 10 years for the company. The plan promises to make a lump-sum payment of $100,000 at retirement to each vested retiree. The company currently has 22 employees, 10 of whom are expected to accumulate enough service to participate in the retirement plan. The average time to retirement for these 10 employees is 15 years. The company plans to administer the plan, but it did not fund any amount during the current year.
2. On January 1, 2004, the company initiated a marketing campaign, where any customer that purchases at least $100 can sign up for a drawing that will take place at the end of the year, the winner of which will receive $500 (based on

retail prices) of pet supplies every year for 10 years, starting at the beginning of 2005. The company's average markup on pet supplies is 100%. (For convenience, assume that all purchases by the customer are made at the beginning of each year.)

3. On December 31, 2004, the company signed a non-interest-bearing note payable with a face amount of $75,000. Three payments of $25,000 each must be paid on the note at the end of the next three years.

Required:

Determine the amount of each liability that will be shown on the company's balance sheet on December 31 of the current year, and determine whether it (or how much of it) will be classified as current and as long-term on the December 31, 2004 balance sheet.

Problem 12-9: Various Liabilities. The following information relates to some liabilities of Wall Flowers for its fiscal year-end, December 31, 2004:

Trade payables. Accounts payable for supplies on open accounts amounts to $440,000, all of which are payable by February 1, 2005.

Payroll-related items. Outstanding items related to payroll as of December 31, 2004, are:

Accrued salaries and wages	$80,000
FICA taxes	9,000
Sate and federal taxes withheld from employees	22,000
Other payroll deductions	5,000

Bonds payable. The company issued $10,000,000 of 8% bonds on July 1, 2000. The price received for the bonds resulted in an effective yield of 7.9%. The bonds will mature on June 30, 2020, and pay interest annually, and Wall Flowers amortizes the premium by using the effective-interest method.

Notes payable. Wall Flowers has several notes payable outstanding, the maturities of which follow. The total accrued interest on these notes at December 31, 2004, is $120,000.

April 1, 2005	$1,000,000
June 30, 2005	140,000
October 30, 2005	2,000,000
December 31, 2005	1,200,000
After December 31, 2005	2,000,000

Concerning the note due on April 1, on February 1, 2005, Wall Flowers borrowed $1,000,000 from another financial institution and paid the amount. The amount so borrowed is due on February 1, 2006.

Concerning the note due on October 30, on February 10, 2005, Wall Flowers signed a series of 60-day refinancing agreements that allow them to borrow $2,000,000 on a recurring basis. During February, Wall Flowers borrowed an amount sufficient to pay the trade payables and to increase the amount of working capital available. Wall Flowers also plans to use the agreement and borrow money on October 30 to pay the maturing note.

Lease obligation. Wall Flowers is leasing some equipment that requires annual payments each December 31. Wall Flowers has paid the amount for 2004. The following amortization table is available for the remaining lease term.

Period	Cash	Interest	Carrying Amount
Dec. 31, 2004	$29,630	$9,464	$98,137
Dec. 31, 2005	29,630	7,851	76,358
Dec. 31, 2006	29,630	6,109	52,837
Dec. 31, 2007	29,630	4,227	27,435
Dec. 31, 2008	29,630	2,195	0

Taxes. The following taxes have been incurred but are not due until some time in 2005:

State and federal income taxes	$110,000
Property taxes	33,000
Sales and use taxes	54,000

Miscellaneous accruals. Other accruals not separately classified on the general ledger amount to $50,000 as of December 31, 2004.

Contingencies. Wall Flowers was involved in two lawsuits, both of which are expected to be settled within the next year, the details of which are as follows:

1. A previous employee is suing Wall Flowers for sexual harassment, claiming that she was fired because she refused the advances of her male supervisor. In public, Wall Flowers states that the claim is without merit and is vigorously defending the case. However, in the board of directors' minutes, it is disclosed that an offer to settle has been made in the amount of $100,000. At December 31, 2004, no word had been received from the plaintiff's lawyer as to whether the offer will be accepted.
2. A customer is suing Wall Flowers, claiming product failure caused physical and emotional distress. The attorneys for Wall Flowers are in the discovery phase, and no consideration is being given to settling out of court.

Required:
Prepare the current liability section of the balance sheet for Wall Flowers as of December 31, 2004, as it *theoretically* should appear in the annual report to stockholders that will be issued on March 10, 2005.

SPREADSHEET

Problem 12-10: Reporting Bonds Payable (Comprehensive Review). On January 1, 2004, Road Runner Company issued $10 million of 7% bonds that mature in 20 years (the bonds are dated January 1, 2004) and pay interest semiannually on June 30 and December 31. The market rate of interest for similar bonds at the time they were issued was 8%.

Required:
1. Compute the amount Road Runner will receive on January 1, 2004, and prepare the necessary journal entry.

(continued)

2. Prepare an amortization table, using the effective-interest method, for 20 years.

3. Prepare the journal entry to pay interest on June 30, 2004.

4. Show how the bonds would be reported on Road Runner's balance sheet at December 31, 2005.

5. Compute the gain/loss on extinguishing $1 million of bonds on December 31, 2007, assuming that Road Runner buys them on the open market when the market rate of interest is 8½%. (*Hint:* First use discounted cash flow concepts to compute the price that would be paid to acquire the bonds.)

6. Show how the bonds (after the acquisition of the $1 million in Requirement 5) should be reported in the balance sheet, and beginning with Income from Operations, show how all amounts related to the bonds, including the gain/loss, are reported on the income statement at December 31, 2007. Assume that the effective income tax rate is 30%, net income is $450,000.

Problem 12-11: Various Problems.

Required:

Solve each of the following independent problems.

1. Included in Witt Corp.'s liability account balances at December 31, 2004, are the following:

14% note payable issued October 1, 2004, maturing September 30, 2005	$500,000
16% note payable issued April 1, 2004, payable in six equal annual installments of $200,000, beginning on April 1, 2005	$800,000

Witt's December 31, 2004 financial statements were issued on March 31, 2005. On January 15, 2005, the entire $800,000 amount of the 16% note was refinanced by issuing a long-term obligation payable in a lump sum. In addition, on March 10, 2005, Witt consummated a noncancelable agreement with the lender to refinance the 14%, $500,000 note on a long-term basis, on readily determinable terms that have not yet been implemented. Both parties are financially capable of honoring the agreement, and there have been no violations of the agreement's provisions. On the December 31, 2004 balance sheet, what amount of these notes should Witt classify as current liabilities? (Ignore interest.)

2. Games, Inc., has $500,000 of notes payable due June 15, 2005. Games signed an agreement on December 1, 2004, to borrow up to $500,000 to refinance the notes payable on a long-term basis with no payments due until 2006. The financing agreement stipulated that borrowings may not exceed 80% of the value of the collateral Games was providing. At the date of issuing the December 31, 2004 financial statements, the value of the collateral was $600,000 and is not expected to fall below this amount during 2005. In Games' December 31, 2004 balance sheet, how much of the obligation for these notes payable should be classified as short term, and how much as long term?

3. On November 1, 2004, Beni Corp. was awarded a judgment of $1,500,000 in connection with a lawsuit. The decision is being appealed by the defendant, and it is expected that the appeal process will be completed by the end of 2005. Beni's attorney feels it is highly probable that an award will be upheld on appeal but that the judgment may be reduced by an estimated 40%. What amount should be reported as a receivable on Beni's balance sheet at December 31, 2004?

4. During 2004, Tedd Company became involved in a tax dispute with the IRS. At December 31, 2004, Tedd's tax advisor believed that an unfavorable outcome was probable. A reasonable estimate of additional taxes was $400,000 but could be as much as $600,000. After the 2004 financial statements were issued, Tedd received and accepted an IRS settlement offer of $450,000. What amount of accrued liability should Tedd report in its December 31, 2004 balance sheet?

5. In May 2001, Croft Company filed suit against Walton, Inc., seeking $950,000 damages for patent infringement. A court verdict in November 2004 awarded Croft $750,000 in damages, but Walton's appeal is not expected to be decided before 2006. Croft's counsel believes it is probable that Croft will be successful against Walton for an estimated amount between $400,000 and $550,000, with $500,000 considered the most likely amount. What amount should Croft record as a gain from the lawsuit in the year ended December 31, 2004?

6. Gavin Company grants all employees two weeks of paid vacation for each full year of employment. Unused vacation time can be accumulated and carried forward to succeeding years and will be paid at the salaries in effect when vacations are taken or when employment is terminated. No employee turnover occurred in 2004. Additional information relating to the year ended December 31, 2004, is as follows:

Liability for accumulated vacations at December 31, 2003	$35,000
Pre-2004 accrued vacations taken from January 12, 2004 to September 30, 2004 (the authorized period for vacations)	20,000
Vacations earned for work in 2004 (adjusted to current rates)	30,000

Gavin granted a 10% salary increase to all employees on October 1, 2004, its annual salary increase date. For the year ended December 31, 2004, how much vacation pay expense should Gavin report?

7. In packages of its products, Curran Co. includes coupons that may be presented at retail stores to obtain discounts on other Curran products. Retailers are reimbursed for the face amount of coupons redeemed plus 10% of that amount for handling costs. Curran honors requests for coupon redemption by retailers up to three months after the consumer expiration date. Curran estimates that 70% of all coupons issued will ultimately be redeemed. Information relating to coupons issued by Curran during 2004 is as follows:

Consumer expiration date	December 31, 2004
Total face amount of coupons issued	$600,000
Total payments to retailers as of December 31, 2004	$220,000

What amount should Curran report as a liability for unredeemed coupons at December 31, 2004?

Research Activities

Activity 12-1: Disclosure of Long-Term Liabilities in Notes to the Financial Statements (CPA Adapted). At December 31, 2006, Brown Corporation had long-term borrowings with annual sinking fund requirements and maturities as follows:

Year	Sinking Fund Requirements	Maturities
2006	$ 1,000,000	$ 0
2007	1,500,000	2,000,000
2008	1,500,000	2,000,000
2009	2,000,000	2,500,000
2010	2,000,000	2,500,000
2011	2,400,000	2,500,000
	$10,400,000	$11,500,000

In the notes to its December 31, 2006 balance sheet, how should Brown report the above data?

Activity 12-2: German GAAP. WestLB Group is a Fortune 500 German bank. Unlike many other German companies that have adopted international GAAP in recent years, WestLB still follows German GAAP. WestLB's income statement as provided in its 1999 annual report follows.

Group Statement of Income for the Year Ended December 31, 1999

	€	€	31. 12. 1999 €	1. 1–31. 12. 1998 € thousands
Interest from				
a) lending and money market transactions	15,384,526,518.37			(13,919,869)
b) interest-bearing securities and book-entry securities	5,047,125,146.13			(4,334,014)
		20,431,651,664.50		
Interest paid		18,352,430,191.10		(16,593,744)
			2,079,221,473.40	1,660,139
Current income from				
a) shares and other non-interest-bearing securities		82,831,191.46		(219,362)
b) equity investments in non-affiliated companies		194,480,910.88		(162,738)
c) equity investments in affiliated companies		10,281,836.32		(99,345)
			287,593,938.66	481,445
Income from equity investments in associated companies			79,543,512.18	20,095
Income from profit pooling, profit transfer and partial profit transfer agreements			15,375,173.10	26,124
Commission income		1,140,563,858.44		(843,727)
Commission paid		419,992,487.22		(291,683)
			720,571,371.22	552,044
Net result from trading operations			103,312,780.36	295,461
Other operating income			515,876,840.79	447,143
Income from reversal of special item with partial reserve character			107,946.50	2,788

(continued)

	€	€	31. 12. 1999 €	1. 1–31. 12. 1998 € thousands
General administrative expenses				
a) personnel expenses				
aa) wages and salaries	1,139,833,880.75			(940,925)
ab) compulsory social security contributions and expenses for pensions and other employee benefits	343,293,825.85			(313,912)
including:		1,483,127,706.60		
for pensions 216,846,109.08				
b) other administrative expenses		991,712,531.97		(900,754)
			2,474,840,238.57	2,155,591
Depreciation and value adjustments on intangible and tangible fixed assets			202,055,618.21	169,165
Other operating expenses			211,521,857.19	195,592
Write-downs and value adjustments on loans and certain securities as well as allocations to loan loss provisions			550,880,319.69	1,033,634
including:				
allocation to fund for general bank risks 105,338,555.92				
			362,305,002.55	68,743
Income from revaluation of equity investments in non-affiliated companies, equity investments in affiliated companies and securities treated as fixed assets			543,780,047.90	617,594
Expenses from the assumption of losses			2,068,551.01	1,717
Allocations to special item with partial reserve character			88,846,173.53	1,641
Profit or loss on ordinary activities			815,170,325.91	545,493
Extraordinary income		—		(253,273)
Extraordinary expenses		373,097.97		(333)
Extraordinary result			−373,097.97	252,940
Taxes on income and revenues		361,503,044.29		(379,800)
Other taxes not shown under other operating expenses		17,186,046.28		(4,906)
			378,689,090.57	384,706
Net income for the year			436,108,137.37	413,727
Withdrawals of net income from reserves on retained earnings				
a) legal reserves		—		(—)
b) reserves required by WestLB's statutes		—		(—)
c) other reserves		—		(—)
d) Group reserves		5,391,175.06		(16,482)
			5,391,175.06	16,482
Allocation to capital of Wohnungsbauförderungsanstalt Wfa/Investitionsbank of Landesbank Schleswig-Holstein			86,070,529.57	72,053
				(continued)

	31. 12. 1999	1. 1–31. 12. 1998
€	€	€ thousands

Allocations of net income to reserves from retained earnings

a) legal reserves	—		(—)
b) reserves required by WestLB's statutes	22,224,388.11		(20,452)
c) other reserves	87,940,158.40		(81,807)
d) Group reserves	131,037,430.78		(86,665)
		241,201,977.29	188,924

Profit attributable to shareholders outside the Group

	19,126,805.57		(74,285)

Loss apportionable to shareholders outside the Group

	—		(—)
		19,126,805.57	74,285
Group profit		95,100,000.00	94,947

1. What is meant by the following accounts?
   a. Income from reversal of special item with partial reserve character
   b. Allocations to special item with partial reserve character
   c. Withdrawals of net income from reserves on retained earnings
   d. Allocations of net income to reserves from retained earnings
   Indicate for each account whether it is subtracted or added in the income statement.
2. What is the difference between "net income for the year" and "group profit"?
3. Explain the differences between U.S. and German GAAP on accounting for future contingencies.
4. Comment on any other differences, including format and terms used, between WestLB's income statement and a typical U.S. company income statement.

Activity 12-3: Debt Due on Demand. Allegheny Co. has an obligation to a financial institution that is due in five years. As part of the debt agreement, Allegheny is required to maintain a certain level of debt-to-equity, and at the end of the current year the company's debt-to-equity ratio is less than it should be. Being in violation of the debt covenant, the financial institution can call the debt and make the entire amount due and payable. However, Allegheny has a 90-day grace period in which to remedy the violation. This period begins after the financial statements are issued. Research GAAP and determine whether this debt should be reported as current or long term.

Activity 12-4: Definition of "Probable." How does U.S. GAAP define the term "probable"? Contrast this definition to the guidance provided in international GAAP. Explain how different meanings attached to the term probable could result in financial statement differences.

Cases

Case 12-1: Circus-Circus Inc. The liability and stockholders' equity sections of Circus-Circus's 1998 balance sheets, along with a note describing the company's outstanding long-term debt, follow.

	January 31, 1998	January 31, 1997
Long-term debt	$1,788,818	$1,405,897
Other liabilities:		
Deferred income tax	175,934	152,635
Other long-term liabilities	8,089	6,439
Total other liabilities	184,023	159,074
Total liabilities	$2,139,799	$1,694,739
Redeemable preferred stock		$ 17,631
Temporary equity		44,950
Stockholders' equity:		
Common stock $0.01 2/3 par value		
Authorized—450,000,000 shares		
Issued—113,609,008 and 112,808,337 shares	$ 1,893	1,880
Preferred stock $0.01 par value		
Authorized—75,000,000 shares		
Additional paid-in capital	558,658	498,893
Retained earnings	1,074,271	984,363
Treasury stock (18,496,125 and 18,749,209 shares), at cost	(511,073)	(513,345)
Total stockholders' equity	$1,123,749	$ 971,791
Total liabilities and stockholders' equity	$3,263,548	$2,729,111

Note 4 : Long-Term Debt

Long-term debt consists of the following:

(in thousands)	January 31, 1998	January 31, 1997
Amounts due under corporate debt program at floating interest rates, weighted average of 5.8% and 5.6%	$ 981,310	$ 501,191
6.45% senior notes due 2006 (net of unamortized discount of $352 and $396)	199,648	199,604
7⅝% senior subordinated debentures due 2013	150,000	150,000
6¾% senior subordinated notes due 2003 (net of unamortized discount of $87 and $103)	149,913	149,897
7.0% debentures due 2036 (net of unamortized discount of $146 and $160)	149,854	149,840
6.70% debentures due 2096 (net of unamortized discount of $279 and $327)	149,721	149,673
10⅝% senior subordinated notes due 1997 (net of unamortized discount of $7)	—	99,993
Other notes	11,443	6,078
	$1,791,889	$1,406,276
Less—current portion	(3,071)	(379)
	$1,788,818	$1,405,897

Required annual principal payments as of January 31, 1998, are as follows:

Year Ending January 31,	(in thousands)
1999	$ 3,071
2000	3,481
2001	488
2002	262
2003	981,584
Thereafter	803,003
	$1,791,889

"The Company has established a corporate debt program, whereby it can issue commercial paper or similar forms of short-term debt. Although the debt instruments issued under this program are short term in tenor, they are classified as long-term debt because (i) they are backed by long-term debt facilities (see below), and (ii) it is management's intention to continue to replace such borrowings on a rolling basis as various instruments come due and to have such borrowings outstanding for longer than one year. To the extent that the Company incurs debt under this program, it maintains an equivalent amount of credit available under its bank credit facility, discussed more fully below."

Based on this information, answer the following questions:

1. Identify the dollar amount of "commercial paper or similar forms of short-term debt" that is classified as long-term debt. Why do you suppose that the company chose to classify it as long term? Do you think it should have been classified as current or long term on the financial report? Give your justification.
2. Determine the long-term debt-to-equity ratio and the long-term debt-to-total-assets ratio. Identify alternative amounts that could be used as "debt" in the ratios. Justify why you chose the amount you did in your calculation.
3. If you were one of the lending institutions that had extended long-term credit to Circus-Circus, what actions would you now propose to improve the probability that you would be repaid? Write a memo to the president explaining your proposed course of action.

*L*egal Capital AND Basic Stockholders' Equity Transactions

Aero West and Kids Korner

During a typical year, a corporation does not enter into as many transactions involving its stockholders' equity accounts as those transactions that affect its asset, liability, revenue, and expense accounts. Yet, when it enters into transactions with owners, the accounting issues are usually interesting. For example, consider the following rather typical transactions that involve stockholders' equity accounts.

How Are Typical Stockholders' Equity Transactions Measured? On January 2, 2004, Aero West Corporation was incorporated with the authorization to issue 5,000,000 shares of $5 par value common stock. The various incorporators of Aero West consist of several individuals and two businesses that previously had been organized as proprietorships. Each of these entities transferred various assets to the new corporation in exchange for shares of common stock. At what value should these assets and the common stock that was issued in exchange be recorded on Aero West Corporation's books: at their current fair values, at the par value of the stock, or at the values at which they had been recorded on the books of the individuals and proprietorships donating them to the new corporation?

Can a Corporation Have Gains or Losses on Its Stock? A corporation may buy and sell shares of its stock on the market. Suppose that Kids Korner Corporation acquired 1,000 shares of its own common stock at $14 per share and subsequently sold them for $20 per share.

Questions

1. Should Kids Korner recognize a gain of $6 per share?

2. Since Kids Korner has access to insider information (i.e., information that is not generally available to others), does Kids Korner's ability to trade in shares of its own stock potentially harm present and potential investors because it may know more about when it is appropriate to buy or sell?

- Define *legal capital*, and explain why it is the foundation of the accounting for transactions involving stock.
- Apply the legal capital notion to transactions where stock is issued for cash, for other assets, or on a promise to pay in the future.
- Account for a corporation acquiring shares of its own stock under the cost method.
- Explain the various dates for dividends, and prepare the journal entries for cash dividends.
- Explain the nature of retained earnings and why a corporation may appropriate retained earnings.

After adding the accounting for transactions that affect owners' equity accounts, the accounting and reporting model in Exhibit 13-1 now shows an almost completed theoretical framework. All that is lacking is the reporting of investments in securities.

History and Theory

Corporations are a relatively new way of organizing a business. At the time that the U.S. Constitution was being framed, only two profit-oriented corporations existed in the country.[1] Then and for decades later, the corporate form of doing business was generally viewed with public disapproval. One of the first publications on American business stated in 1820 that corporations were "injurious to the national wealth, and ought to be looked upon by those who have no money with jealousy and suspicion."[2] Twenty years later, the governor of Massachusetts echoed that opinion, stating that corporations were:

> ". . . one of the vices of our time . . . [because] they encourage speculation and fraud, . . . overturn matrimonial arrangements, escape publicity in the transfer of real property, diminish the sense of individual responsibility, . . . prevent all penal remedies, are lacking in moral sense, and constitute finally a grave social peril by concentrating too much power in the hands of certain of our citizens."[3]

During the Industrial Revolution, businesses increasingly needed large amounts of capital which in turn caused them to turn to the corporate form of doing business. As more businesses organized as corporations, concerns grew about the potential that such organizations provided to the unscrupulous to de-

[1]William Z. Ripley, *Main Street and Wall Street*, Scholars Book Co., Lawrence, Kansas, 1972, p. 20.
[2]Ibid., p. 22.
[3]Ibid.

EXHIBIT 13-1

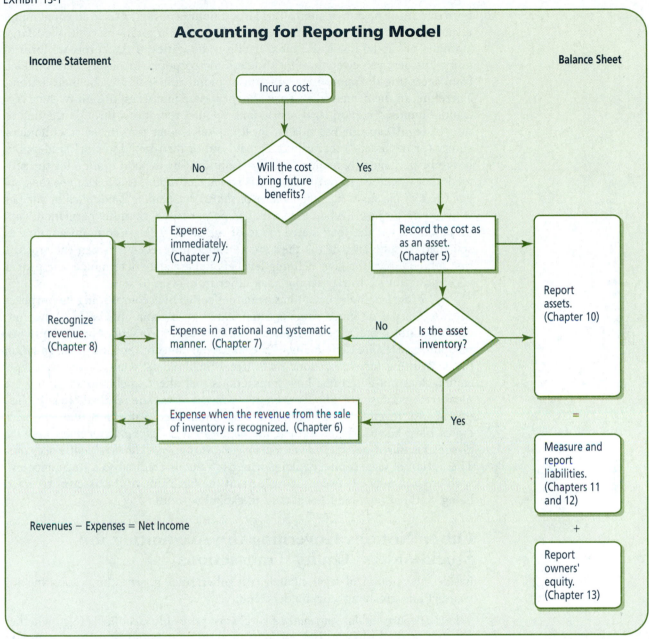

fraud the unwary. Around the turn of the twentieth century all states passed laws, known as "blue sky" laws, which were designed to protect creditors and potential investors from corporations that were selling stock in business ventures that consisted of nothing more than "blue sky."

Legal Capital

From a review of literature, it is apparent that critics of corporations were particularly concerned with the limited liability[4] (i.e., the so-called "corporate shield") of corporations. The prevailing notion of western civilization has always

---

[4]Limited liability means that shareholders' losses are limited to the amount they have invested—that neither creditors of the corporation nor others who sue the corporation may seek the personal assets of the shareholders for satisfaction of their claims. This limited liability arises because the law views the corporation as a legal (though fictional) entity that is separate from its owners.

been that those having or controlling large amounts of capital have an equal moral responsibility for the use of that capital. Because corporations controlled large amounts of capital but had limited liability, the critics of the corporate form of doing business perceived that stockholders and corporate managers were shielded from accepting the appropriate amount of moral responsibility for their actions. Therefore, in the perceived absence of appropriate moral responsibility, state legislators imposed certain legal restrictions upon corporations through the definition of **legal capital**. Essentially, legal capital is that portion of stockholders' equity (or net assets[5]) that cannot be paid out or distributed to stockholders but has to be permanently retained (until dissolution) by the corporation for the protection of creditors. In most states, *this permanent capital is defined to be the total par value of the stock (i.e., the number of shares outstanding[6] multiplied by the par value for each share)*. When the stock has no par value, then the permanent capital is either (1) the total stated value of the stock, (2) a minimum amount as specified in state law, or (3) the total consideration received when the stock is first issued. Since the laws defining legal capital are state determined, the proper accounting for such transactions may differ from state to state.

The legal capital concept has been ineffective in accomplishing its purposes because (1) par or stated value is often stated at low amounts and (2) the concept does not protect the creditors from poor business practices or the truly unscrupulous. Despite these faults, the legal capital concept remains the foundation for accounting for transactions that affect stockholders' equity. Note that legal capital does not determine how transactions that affect stockholders' equity are measured, because stockholders' equity is measured as the residual after the historical cost, revenue recognition, matching, and present value measurement principles have been applied. Rather, *the notion of legal capital determines how the already measured amount is divided among the various stockholders' equity accounts*. The notion of legal capital explains why par value is credited to a stock account, with any difference between par value and the fair value of the asset(s) received being credited to an additional paid-in capital account.

Other Notions Governing the Accounting for Stockholders' Equity Transactions

Besides the notion of legal capital, two other rules govern the accounting for transactions involving stockholders' equity:

1. *The* source *of the contributed capital must be readily identifiable* (e.g., whether the capital was contributed from preferred stockholders or from common stockholders), and
2. *Neither gains nor losses are incurred in transactions with owners in their role as owners.*[7] That is, a corporation does not recognize either a gain or a loss when the corporation issues stock, reacquires stock previously issued, has a stock split or stock dividend, or becomes involved in any other transaction with stockholders in their role as owners of the corporation.

These three rules—(1) legal capital, (2) identifying the source of the capital, and (3) not recognizing either gains or losses in transactions with the owners—are the basis for the accounting for stockholders' equity transactions.

---

[5]Net assets means the difference between the corporation's assets and its liabilities, which is stockholders' equity.

[6]In a minority of states, total legal capital is based upon the number of shares *issued* rather than the number of shares outstanding.

[7]Transactions with owners in their role as owners are referred to as capital transactions. See *SFAC No. 5*, "Recognition and Measurement in Financial Statements of Business Enterprises," note 36.

Additional Paid-In Capital

So as to easily identify legal capital, *only the legal capital amount is recorded in the capital stock accounts*. However, since most transactions in the company's stock are not for amounts equal to par/stated value, paid-in capital accounts are used to capture such differences. For example, when stock is issued at an amount greater than its par/stated value, the journal entry to record the transaction is as follows:

Cash	Amount received
Capital Stock	Par/Stated value
Paid-In Capital in Excess of Par/Stated Value	Difference

This notion of capturing the legal capital amount in the capital stock accounts and any difference in a paid-in capital account applies to all transactions in a company's capital stock.

In keeping with the notion of identifying the source of the capital, each paid-in capital account is labeled as to the reason for (or source of) the additional capital. Thus, corporations usually have many paid-in capital accounts in their general ledger, with each one identifying the type of stock transaction that gave rise to it. So there is a paid-in capital in excess of par account that is used when stock is issued at an amount greater than the par value, a paid-in capital from treasury stock account that is used when the corporation buys and sells its own shares of stock, and other paid-in capital accounts are used to identify the source of other capital amounts. As with the labels attached to any other account, there are no rules to naming the various paid-in capital accounts, except that the name should be descriptive.

Regardless of the number of paid-in capital accounts a corporation may have in its general ledger, the balances of all the accounts usually are summarized into one paid-in capital account for financial reporting purposes (see Exhibit 13-2). A variation on this is that the common stock paid-in capital accounts are summarized and reported as one total, and the preferred stock paid-in capital accounts are summarized and reported as another total.

EXHIBIT 13-2

Stockholders' Equity Section[8]

Circus-Circus
(in thousands)

	1998	1997
Stockholders' equity		
Common stock $0.01 2/3 par value		
Authorized—450,000,000 shares		
Issued—113,609,008 and 112,808,337 shares	$ 1,893	$ 1,880
Preferred stock $0.01 par value		
Authorized—75,000,000 shares	—	—
Additional paid-in capital	558,658	498,893
Retained earnings	1,074,271	984,363
Treasury stock (18,496,125 and 18,749,209 shares),		
at cost	(511,073)	(513,345)
Total stockholders' equity	$1,123,749	$ 971,791

[8]This example is included because it is a little unusual. Normally, preferred stock is listed first, but Circus-Circus lists its common stock first. This illustrates that some flexibility is permitted in acceptable financial reporting.

Rights and Characteristics of Capital Stock

Since transactions involving capital stock have to be recorded so as to distinguish the amount of capital contributed by class of stock, the topic of what stock is and the characteristics that attach to the various classes of stock are discussed first. Originally, corporations had only one class of stock, with all shareholders having the same rights and risks of ownership. Traditionally, these rights are to:

1. Share equally in profits and losses.
2. Participate equally in management.
3. Share equally in the assets, or the proceeds from the sale of assets, upon liquidation and after the creditors' claims are satisfied.
4. Have the first opportunity to acquire shares of newly offered stock so as to preserve the ownership percentage in the corporation. This right is called the **preemptive right**.

Over time, some of these rights have been eroded or negotiated away. For example, the right to participate in management now usually means the right to vote either "Yes" or "No" for those persons who are nominated to the board of directors, which is done either for individuals or for a slate of candidates. Also, many corporations have eliminated the preemptive right because its existence makes it difficult to issue new shares of stock as a means of acquiring other corporations. Still, other shareholders have traded their right to participate in management for a preference in receiving dividends or a preference in receiving assets when the corporation is liquidated—and thus the traditional preferred stock was created. Since stockholders' rights have been variously modified, most corporations now customarily have more than one class of capital stock.

See Exhibit 13-3 for definitions of some common terms relating to preferred stock.

EXHIBIT 13-3

Terms Relating to Preferred Stock

Callable: Allows the corporation to acquire the security at its option, usually at specified prices and times. The call price typically is higher than the original issuing price, thus giving the holder some incentive to buy the stock and some reward for having held it should the corporation exercise the call option.

Convertible: Allows the holder of the preferred stock at his option to exchange his stock for shares of the corporation's common stock at specified times, rates of exchange, and perhaps subject to other conditions as well. This gives the holder the opportunity to participate in the greater rewards that accrue to the common stockholders should the corporation become very profitable but also the security of a set return if such does not occur.

Cumulative: The right to dividends is not lost in those years in which a dividend is not declared, but the right to those dividends accumulates and must be satisfied before dividends are paid to the common stockholders in any later year.

Participating: Allows preferred stockholders to receive an additional dividend above the regular preferred dividend, usually after certain conditions are met.

Redeemable: Has a fixed or determinable redemption date, or is redeemable at the option of the holder, or has conditions regarding redemption that are not totally within the control of the issuer. Such stock cannot be reported under the stockholders' equity caption.

Because of the various ways in which stockholder rights can be combined, not only is there a distinction between preferred stock and common stock, but there are also various categories of both preferred and common stock. For example, preferred stock may be participating, callable, convertible, redeemable, or have some other preferential right, or a combination of several of these rights. Common stock, too, has a variety of preferences in regards to each other. As a result, it is sometimes difficult to distinguish common stock from preferred stock.

Financial Instruments with Debt and Equity Characteristics

Not only has there been a blurring between common and preferred stock, but due to the creation of innovative financial instruments having both debt and equity characteristics, it is sometimes difficult to identify whether a financial instrument should be reported among the long-term liabilities or as part of stockholders' equity. For example, a characteristic of a debt instrument is that a set amount of interest is paid at a known point in time, and a characteristic of an equity instrument is that both the amount and timing of a dividend is uncertain. However, preferred stock has characteristics of both debt and equity instruments in that, like debt, a known amount is paid, but, like equity, the time the amount will be received is not certain. Traditionally, preferred stock has been reported in the equity section of the balance sheet, but accountants struggle with how to report other financial instruments that take on more characteristics of debt. In classifying innovative financial instruments, too much regard should not be attached to their label, but rather *financial instruments that are more like debt instruments should be classified among the long-term liabilities on the balance sheet.* Redeemable preferred stock is an example of a financial instrument that has the label "stock" attached to it but which—by SEC mandate—must not be reported under the caption of "stockholders' equity."[9] **Redeemable preferred stock**, like a debt instrument, has a fixed or determinable redemption date or is redeemable at the option of the holder or has conditions regarding redemption that are not totally within the control of the issuer.

Currently, the FASB is grappling with developing better guidance for determining when financial instruments should be reported as debt securities and when they should be reported as equity securities. Some (although inadequate) guidance in differentiating between debt and equity securities is found in the conceptual framework. There, the FASB stated that the "essential characteristics of equity center on the conditions for transferring enterprise assets to owners. . . . Generally, an enterprise is not obligated to transfer assets to owners except in the event of the enterprise's liquidation unless the enterprise formally acts to distribute assets to owners."[10] But if this guidance is followed precisely, then common stock and noncumulative preferred stock would be the only securities to be reported under stockholders' equity, with all other financial instruments being reported among the long-term liabilities. Exhibit 13-4 illustrates (in the italicized portion) how one company reports securities that have some debt and some equity characteristics. Looking at the stockholders' equity section, it can be seen that the company also has two types of common stock.

---

[9]SEC *Release No. 33-6097.*
[10]*SFAC No. 6,* "Elements of Financial Statements," par. 61.

EXHIBIT 13-4

Reporting Securities with Debt and Equity Characteristics

Time Warner
(in millions)

	1997	1996
Long-term debt	$11,833	$12,713
Borrowings against future stock option proceeds	533	488
Deferred income taxes	3,960	4,082
Unearned portion of paid subscriptions	672	679
Other liabilities	1,006	967
Company-obligated mandatorily redeemable preferred securities of subsidiaries holding solely subordinated notes and debentures of subsidiaries of the Company	575	949
Series M exchangeable preferred stock, $0.10 par value, 1.9 and 1.7 million shares outstanding and $1.903 and $1.720 billion liquidation preference	1,857	1,672
Shareholders' equity:		
Preferred stock, $0.10 par value, 35.4 and 35.6 million shares outstanding, $3.539 and $3.559 billion liquidation preference	4	4
Series LMCN-V Common Stock, $0.01 par value, 57.1 and 50.7 million shares outstanding	1	1
Common stock, $0.01 par value, 519.0 and 508.4 million shares outstanding	5	5
Paid-in capital	12,680	12,250
Accumulated deficit*	(3,299)	(4,296)
Total shareholders' equity	9,713	8,852

*Author's note: This is the caption used (instead of retained earnings) when a company's accumulated operating losses and dividends exceed their operating profits.

Wall Street will certainly continue creating new and innovative financial instruments due to the demand for such securities both by businessmen and investors. As a result, accountants will be increasingly challenged in determining where to report such financial instruments so as to communicate financial information in a clear and understandable manner. More on this topic of accounting for securities that have both debt and equity characteristics will be given in Chapter 14.

Issuing Stock

Individuals desiring to conduct business as a corporation must adhere to the accounting rules established by the state in which they desire to incorporate. No *federal* laws of incorporation exist. Given the diversity among the 50 states, the following is only typical of the incorporation process:

1. *The articles of incorporation are prepared.* These articles give such information as the nature of the business, its place of doing business, names of the organizers, classes of and numbers of shares of capital stock to be authorized with their par value (if given) and the amount and nature of the consideration to be paid by the organizers for their respective shares.

INTERNET

www

The laws governing the organizing of a corporation usually can be found on the internet by referring to a search engine and typing in the words "organizing a corporation," followed by the name of a state. Try this for your state.

2. *The articles of incorporation are filed* with a state official, usually the secretary of state.
3. *The corporate charter is issued*, making the articles of incorporation operative and giving the corporation authorization to issue a maximum number of shares of stock. This number of authorized shares is usually—but not always—disclosed on the face of the balance sheet. (Compare Exhibits 13-2 and 13-4.)
4. *The corporation collects the amounts specified from the organizers* per the articles of incorporation.
5. *A board of directors is elected*, which approves the bylaws that are supplemental to the articles of incorporation and appoints the corporate officers.

Issuing Stock at Incorporation

Three brothers, Vince, Dee and Kent Brown, have thought of a novel way to provide exercise activities in a club setting and have chosen to organize their new business as a corporation, called Ponce de Leon's Fountain. The brothers have agreed to donate tangible and intangible assets, and they have also agreed upon the valuations of the assets, as shown in Illustration 13-1:

ILLUSTRATION 13-1

Contributed Assets with Corresponding Valuations

	Vince	Dee	Kent
Cash			$200,000
Land		$ 30,000	
Building		175,000	
Equipment		50,000	
Expertise	$150,000		

In the articles of incorporation, the brothers request authorization to issue 100,000 shares of $10 par common stock and agree to give themselves 10,000 shares of stock each, regardless of these asset valuations.

Upon approval of the corporate charter, the journal entries are prepared, which are shown individually for ease of presentation and understanding. So the journal entry to record Kent's cash contribution is as follows:

Cash	200,000	
Common Stock, $10 par value		100,000
Paid-In Capital in Excess of Par—Common		100,000

To record the receipt of cash from Kent and the issuance of 10,000 shares of $10 par value stock in exchange.

Note that this journal entry identifies the amount of legal capital by crediting Common Stock only for par value. Also, the difference between the cash received and the par value of the stock given is credited to Paid-In Capital in Excess of Par in accordance with not recognizing gains in transactions with owners. Finally, the source of the capital is identified in both credit entries. Thus, the rules of (1) identifying legal capital, (2) showing the source of the capital (i.e., common stock), and (3) not recognizing either a gain or a loss in a transaction with an owner are met.

This journal entry, and the ones to follow, emphasize that *par value has no relation to fair value of the corporation's assets or the fair value of its stock.* The only significance of par value is that it is an arbitrary amount set forth in the articles of incorporation, and it becomes the corporation's permanent capital—that portion of the corporation's assets that cannot be distributed to owners but must be maintained for the protection of the creditors.

The following journal entry to record Dee's contribution of tangible assets is based on the historical cost principle—where assets are recorded at fair value—and the rules described in this chapter for accounting for stockholders' equity transactions:

Land	30,000	
Building[11]	175,000	
Equipment	50,000	
Common Stock, $10 par value		100,000
Paid-In Capital in Excess of Par—Common		155,000

To record various tangible assets received from Dee at their respective fair values and the issuance of 10,000 shares of $10 par value stock in exchange.

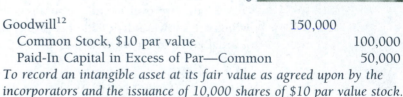

As discussed in Chapter 5, the assets are recorded at their respective fair value, which can be determined by referring to markets where such assets are bought and sold or by appraisal by either a competent outside appraiser or the board of directors. Again, the amount credited to Common Stock is the par value amount, and the amount credited to Paid-In Capital in Excess of Par is the difference between the fair value of the assets received and the par value (i.e., legal capital) of the common stock given in exchange. All three rules that govern the accounting for transactions involving stockholders' equity accounts are met.

Finally, the journal entry to record the stock given to Vince in exchange for his expertise (i.e., an intangible asset) in running a business is as follows:

Goodwill[12]	150,000	
Common Stock, $10 par value		100,000
Paid-In Capital in Excess of Par—Common		50,000

To record an intangible asset at its fair value as agreed upon by the incorporators and the issuance of 10,000 shares of $10 par value stock.

---

[11]A condition known as "watered stock" results when assets are contributed to the corporation in exchange for stock and the assets are recorded at more than their fair value. That is, overvalued assets result in a condition called "watered stock." Also, undervalued assets result in a condition known as a "secret reserve."

[12]In Chapter 5, it was mentioned that goodwill is only recognized when an entire company is acquired and the amount paid exceeds the fair value of the net assets received. That is the general rule; this example is an exception. Here, goodwill can be recorded as long as the corporation's stock is not traded on a public exchange that is subject to SEC oversight and rules. Many proprietorships, partnerships, and small closely held corporations do not follow all the rules of the SEC or the FASB, nor need they do so. And such entities may record an intangible asset at incorporation, as illustrated in this journal entry.

EXTENDING
the Concept

Return to the opening scenario of the incorporation of Aero West (p. 599) and describe at what value the various contributed assets should be recorded on Aero West's books.

Answer: The contributed assets should be recorded at their current fair value.

As with the tangible assets in the previous journal entries, *intangible assets are recorded at their fair value*, which usually is determined by the incorporators or the board of directors.

Issuing Stock Subsequent to Incorporation

In all three prior journal entries, regardless of the type of assets received, the corporation identified the nature of the stock issued, recorded that stock at its par value, and then recorded the difference between the fair value of the asset(s) received and the par value of the stock issued in a paid-in capital in excess of par account. This is the pattern for recording the issuance of all stock, regardless of whether the stock is issued to the incorporators, as was shown, or whether the stock is sold on an exchange sometime after incorporation.

The following journal entries illustrate the issuing or selling of various types of stock on an exchange. In all cases, the important differences between the following examples and how the journal entries were recorded previously are italicized.

Issuing preferred stock that has a par value:

Cash	200,000	
Preferred Stock, $10 par value		100,000
Paid-In Capital in Excess of Par—*Preferred*		100,000

Note that the type of stock is identified, the legal capital is recorded in the stock account, and the difference between the amount received and the legal capital amount is recorded in Paid-In Capital in Excess of Par, which in this example is identified as being associated with the preferred stock.

Issuing common stock that has a stated value:

Cash	200,000	
Common Stock, $10 *stated* value		100,000
Paid-In Capital in Excess of *Stated*		
Value—Common		100,000

From this journal entry, it should be clear that, from an accounting viewpoint, there is no difference between par value stock and stated value stock. Stated value stock is no-par stock that has been given a value by the board of directors. Note that again the type of stock is identified, legal capital is separately recorded, and an appropriately descriptive paid-in capital account is used to record any amount received in excess of the legal capital amount.

Issuing no-par common stock:

Cash	200,000	
Common Stock, *no par value*		200,000

For no-par stock, the entire amount received becomes the corporation's legal capital. Hence, there is no need for a paid-in capital in excess of par account.

Issuing Stock at Less than Par Value

In most states, it is illegal to issue stock at less than its par or stated value. In those few states where stock can legally be issued at a discount, the same principles apply as set forth previously. That is, the stock account is credited for the par or stated value, and the difference between the fair value of the consideration received and the par or stated value of the stock issued is *debited* to Discount on Capital Stock.

Issuing stock at a discount results in the corporation receiving less than the required permanent capital, and, therefore, those who acquire such stock have a contingent liability to the creditors of the corporation. The liability is a contingent liability because the purchasers of the stock may never be asked to contribute the additional amount. However, if subsequent losses are sufficiently large so that the net assets of the corporation are less than the permanent capital, the creditors can force these stockholders to pay the discount amount to the corporation, which then can pay it to the creditors. This contingent liability pertains only to the individuals who initially acquire the stock at a discount, and it is not passed to others when the stock is subsequently sold—unless such is specifically contracted.

Costs of Issuing Stock

It is costly to issue shares of stock on the market. For example, a corporation incurs legal fees, accounting fees, SEC registration fees, and the cost of printing stock certificates. Then, an underwriter is customarily hired who either buys the issue of stock or sells it for a fee, which also becomes a cost of issuing stock. All of these fees and costs are debited to Paid-In Capital in Excess of Par/Stated Value, or in the case of no-par stock, these amounts reduce the amount credited to the capital stock account.[13]

Subscribed Stock

Although used very infrequently today, a corporation may choose to offer shares of its stock to prospective stockholders on contract in an agreement called a **stock subscription**. Such agreements usually require that a portion of the total contracted price be paid immediately, with installments paid at future specified times. So because a legal contract exists, including the exchange of consideration, accounting recognition must be given to the transaction. When preparing the journal entry at the subscription date, the rules of separating the legal capital and showing the source of the capital are followed. But the contracted shares are not issued until the agreed-upon price is completely collected. To show that stock has been subscribed but not issued, a common stock subscribed account is used to capture the legal capital amount. When the amounts owed are collected and the shares are issued, the legal capital amount is transferred from Common Stock Subscribed to Common Stock.

To illustrate, suppose that Caleb and Tiffany each subscribe to 5,000 shares of common stock in Ponce de Leon's Fountain. The subscription price is $18 per share, 20% of which is paid immediately. The journal entry to record this subscription is as follows:

Cash (10,000 shares × $18/share × 20%)	36,000	
Subscriptions Receivable		
(10,000 shares × $18/share × 80%)	144,000	
Common Stock Subscribed, $10 par value		100,000
Paid-In Capital in Excess of Par Value—Common		80,000
To record the subscription to 10,000 shares of common stock.		

As the amounts owed are subsequently received, the cash account is debited and Subscriptions Receivable is credited. For financial reporting, the SEC requires that *subscriptions receivable be reported as a deduction from stockholders' equity* (as shown in Exhibit 13-5) *and not be reported among the current assets.*

[13]An alternative, but lesser used, accounting treatment is to debit these costs to an intangible asset account—called Organization Costs. Previously, these costs were amortized over a period not to exceed 40 years. Current guidelines require organization costs to be expensed in the period incurred, as discussed in Chapter 7.

EXHIBIT 13-5

Proper Reporting of Subscriptions Receivable

Stockholders' Equity

Contributed capital:

Common stock of $1.00 par value. Authorized shares: 900,000; issued and outstanding shares: 407,450	$ 407,450
Common stock subscribed	100,000
Paid-in capital in excess of par	1,655,550
Total contributed capital	$2,163,000
Retained earnings	6,123,000
Total contributed capital and retained earnings	$8,286,000
Less subscriptions receivable	(144,000)
Total stockholders' equity	$8,142,000

The SEC's reasoning is that most states do not allow corporations to proceed against individuals who fail to pay the amounts contracted. The only time that subscriptions receivable may be reported among the current assets is when the amounts owed are collected before the financial statements are issued.

Most state laws give individuals who have entered into subscription contracts the same rights as all other stockholders of the same class of stock, including the right to vote and the right to participate in dividends. State laws also prescribe what corporations must do in the event a subscriber defaults. Some possible actions the corporation may be required to take include:

1. *Return the consideration received* to the subscriber, which essentially *returns the parties to their original position* before the stock was subscribed. The journal entry for such an action is to reverse the initial subscription entry.

2. *Issue the number of shares of stock for which the subscriber paid.* Using the Caleb and Tiffany example, the journal entry for this option is as follows:

Common Stock Subscribed (Reverse entire amount, as there is no stock currently subscribed.)	100,000	
Paid-In Capital in Excess of Par (Adjust the balance to the excess amount on the 20% of the shares that are issued.)	64,000	
Subscriptions Receivable (Reverse entire amount, as there is no amount still due.)		144,000
Common Stock (par value of common shares issued)		20,000
To issue the 20% of the stock that was paid for.		

3. *Sell the subscribed stock to other parties and then return to the subscriber of the stock any payments less the costs of selling the stock and any losses incurred.* Losses arise when the stock is sold for a lesser amount than that for which the stock had been subscribed.

To illustrate, suppose Tiffany, who had subscribed to 5,000 shares in Ponce de Leon's Fountain at $18 per share, eventually paid $54,000, but was then unable to pay the additional amount owed. Subsequently, Ponce de Leon's Fountain sold those 5,000 shares for $16. Hence, Ponce de Leon incurred a loss of $2 per share, or a total of $10,000, because Tiffany defaulted on her subscription payments. So of the total $54,000 that Tiffany paid, Ponce de Leon must refund to her only $44,000, and the journal entry to settle matters with Tiffany is as follows:

Common Stock Subscribed (see subscription entry)	50,000		
Paid-In Capital in Excess of Par	30,000		
Cash		44,000	
Subscriptions Receivable (amount still owing)		36,000	

*To refund Tiffany's money after adjusting for the loss
of $10,000 on reselling the stock.*

Selling Several Securities as a Unit

Occasionally, a corporation issues two or more securities for a single sum. Since it is necessary to account for the source of the capital, the cash received must be separated among the various types of securities issued. The two allocation methods to separate the single sum are the same two methods discussed in Chapter 5 for determining the cost of individual assets that were acquired as a group: (1) the proportional method and (2) the incremental method.

Whenever possible, the proportional method should be used to allocate the cash received among the various securities issued. Under the proportional method, the transaction is first measured (usually by considering the fair value of the assets received), and then the consideration received is divided—proportionally—among the various securities based upon their *relative* fair values. For instance, suppose a corporation issued the securities shown in Illustration 13-2 for a lump sum of $197,100.

ILLUSTRATION 13-2

Proportional Method of Allocating Proceeds Among Securities

Description of Security	Number of Units Issued of Each	Par Value of Each	Fair Value of Each
Common stock	5,000	$ 10	$ 15
Preferred stock	1,000	25	50
Bonds	100	1,000	940

The first step in applying the proportional method is to measure the transaction at the fair value of the assets (i.e., cash) received of $197,100. The second step is to then determine the total fair values of each class of security, which are $75,000, $50,000, and $94,000, respectively, with the total fair value of all securities being $219,000. Finally, the $197,100 received is allocated among the three securities, based on their relative fair values, as shown in Illustration 13-3.

ILLUSTRATION 13-3

The Proportional Method of Allocating the Cost

Type of Security	Fair Value of Security/Total Fair Value	Total Cost	Cost of Security
Common stock	($75,000/$219,000)	× $197,100 =	$67,500
Preferred stock	($50,000/$219,000)	× $197,100 =	$45,000
Bonds	($94,000/$219,000)	× $197,100 =	$84,600

The journal entry to record selling the three securities for the single sum—remembering to separate the legal capital from the other capital and to separate the bond discount from the face amount of the bond—is as follows:

Cash	197,100	
Discount on Bonds	15,400	
Bonds Payable		100,000
Common Stock, $10 par		50,000
Paid-In Capital in Excess of Par—Common		17,500
Preferred Stock, $25 par		25,000
Paid-In Capital in Excess of Par—Preferred		20,000

Explanation: The cost of the bonds was computed to be $84,600. The maturity value or face amount of $100,000 is recorded in the bonds payable account, with the difference of $15,400 being recorded in Discount on Bonds. The cost of the common stock was computed to be $67,500. The par value is captured in the stock account, and the excess is recorded in the paid-in capital account. The accounting for preferred stock follows the same pattern.

The incremental method of allocating the amount received among the various securities is used when the fair value of one security is not known. When using this method, again the transaction is first measured (usually by the fair value of the assets received), and then the amount received is assigned first to those securities where the fair values are known, and the remaining amount is assigned to the remaining security. Utilizing the same information as used for illustrating the proportional method, except that the fair value of the preferred stock is not known, then the procedures outlined in Illustration 13-4 are used to allocate the $197,100 among the three securities.

ILLUSTRATION 13-4

The Incremental Method of Allocating the Cost

	Number	Fair Value	Total
Amount assigned to bonds	100 bonds	× $940/bond	= $94,000
Amount assigned to common stock	5,000 shares	× $15/share	= $75,000
Amount assigned to preferred stock	$197,100 − $94,000 − $75,000 = $28,100		

The journal entry to record issuing these securities is as follows:

Cash	197,100	
Discount on Bonds	6,000	
Bonds Payable		100,000
Common Stock, $10 par		50,000
Paid-In Capital in Excess of Par—Common		25,000
Preferred Stock, $25 par		25,000
Paid-In Capital in Excess of Par—Preferred		3,100

The same rationale for capturing the amounts in Discount on Bonds and the various paid-in capital accounts is followed here, as was used in the proportional method.

In situations where neither the proportional nor the incremental method can be used because the fair value of more than one security is not known, a temporary arbitrary allocation can be used until the time that either the proportional or the incremental method is appropriate.

Treasury Stock Transactions—Cost Method

Shares of a corporation's own stock that have been reacquired but have not been retired are called **treasury stock**. Treasury stock has the same status as authorized but unissued stock. Acquiring treasury stock reduces the number of shares outstanding but does not change the number of shares issued. A corporation may acquire shares of its stock for several reasons, including:

1. The stock appears to be underpriced. So the corporation attempts to improve its net assets by buying the shares when the price is low and selling them again when the price is higher.
2. To meet employee stock compensation contracts or other future needs for stock (e.g., to issue a stock dividend).
3. To thwart takeover attempts by reducing the number of shares available to be purchased and in this way prohibiting "outsiders" from acquiring enough shares to gain control or significant influence.
4. To buy out disgruntled stockholders.[14]
5. To support the market price of the stock. By buying its own stock, the corporation creates a demand for the stock that may stabilize the stock price.

Because a corporation has access to insider information, its actions of trading in its own stock may be detrimental to existing and potential stockholders, and Rules 10b-5 and 10b-6 of the Securities and Exchange Act of 1934 prohibit corporations from engaging in any act that is detrimental to its stockholders. Thus, a corporation must be very careful when trading in its stock.

Although treasury stock has a debit balance, it is reported under the stockholders' equity section of the balance sheet. (See Exhibit 13-2 on page 603 for an example of how treasury stock is reported.) The reason for this reporting is that, unlike acquiring shares of stock in another corporation, a corporation that acquires shares of its own stock does not have any of the basic stockholder rights. It does not have the right to vote for the board of directors, the right to receive a dividend when one is declared, or the right to participate in the distribution of assets at liquidation. Thus, a corporation does not acquire an asset when it acquires shares of its own stock, but instead it reduces its capitalization—and its legal capital.

The two generally accepted methods of accounting for treasury stock are the cost method and the par value method. The cost method is more widely used in practice and is discussed next, whereas the par value method is conceptually preferable, is supported by the Committee on Accounting Procedure,[15] and is covered in an appendix to this chapter.

Essentially, the cost method of accounting for treasury stock uses the same procedures as when long-lived assets are bought and sold, and it is for this reason that the method gets its name and is more widely used in practice than the par value method. When using the cost method, a corporation records the acquisition of its own stock by debiting a treasury stock account for the fair value of the consideration given. That price then becomes the "cost" of the treasury stock. The accounting procedures for subsequently reissuing the shares are as follows:

1. Debit Cash for the amount received.
2. Credit Treasury Stock for the "cost" of the shares of stock being reissued.

---

[14]During the 1980s, corporations paid disgruntled stockholders "green mail" for their shares, which is a substantial premium above the fair value of the stock. Such green mail should be expensed in the year incurred.

[15]See *ARB No. 43*, Chapter 1, par. 7.

3. The difference is accounted for as follows:
   a. When a credit is necessary to balance the entry, credit Paid-In Capital from Treasury Stock.
   b. When a debit is necessary to balance the entry, two options are permitted:
      (1) Debit Paid-In Capital from Treasury Stock up to the balance that is in that account and then debit Retained Earnings for the amount needed, or
      (2) Debit Retained Earnings for the entire amount.

Note that gains/losses on transactions with owners are not permitted[16] and that *Retained Earnings can be reduced because of treasury stock transactions, but it is never increased.* To illustrate the cost method of accounting for treasury stock, consider a corporation that conducts the following transactions:

Acquires 100 shares of its own $10 par value common stock at $15 per share:

Treasury Stock	1,500	
Cash		1,500

Explanation: The treasury stock account is debited for the fair value of the consideration given in the same manner as if it were an asset.

Reissues 20 shares at $15 per share:

Cash	300	
Treasury Stock		300

Explanation: The treasury stock account is credited for its "cost," and since its cost equals the cash received, no other account is affected.

Reissues 20 more shares at $20 per share:

Cash	400	
Treasury Stock		300
Paid-In Capital from Treasury Stock		100

Explanation: The "gain" is recorded in Paid-In Capital from Treasury Stock.

Reissues 20 more shares at $13 per share:

Cash	260	
Paid-In Capital from Treasury Stock[17]	40	
Treasury Stock		300

Explanation: The "loss" is recorded in Paid-In Capital from Treasury Stock because that account has a sufficient credit balance to absorb the loss.

Reissues the remaining 20 shares at $8 per share:

Cash	160	
Paid-In Capital from Treasury Stock	60	
Retained Earnings[18]	80	
Treasury Stock		300

Explanation: Only $60 of the "loss" can be recorded in Paid-In Capital from Treasury Stock, as that is the balance of that account; the rest of the loss is then debited to Retained Earnings.

---

[16]*APB Opinion No. 6*, "Status of Accounting Research Bulletins," par. 12-a(i).
[17]Alternatively, Retained Earnings could have been debited.
[18]As before, an acceptable alternative is to debit the entire $140 to Retained Earnings.

In summary, the cost method of accounting for treasury stock is very similar to accounting for the acquisition and disposal of long-lived assets. A "cost" is determined when the treasury stock is purchased, and that cost is equal to the fair value paid. Subsequently, when the treasury stock is reissued, the cost is removed from the books and a gain or loss is computed, which is credited or debited to Paid-In Capital from Treasury Stock or to Retained Earnings. Finally, corporations that use the cost method report treasury stock by subtracting the amount from the total of the contributed capital plus retained earnings, as Circus-Circus did in Exhibit 13-2 (p. 603).

Retiring Stock

When shares of stock (whether common or preferred) are acquired and then retired, all capital amounts that were received from the stockholders in relation to those shares are removed from the accounts. So both *the stock and the paid-in capital in excess accounts are debited for the amounts that the stockholders originally contributed.* The difference between the amount paid for the stock and the amount received when the stock was issued is accounted for as follows:

1. When the amount paid to acquire stock is less than the amounts contributed by the stockholders at the time the stock was issued originally (i.e., the debits exceed the credits in the journal entry to acquire the stock), *Paid-In Capital from Retirement is credited for the difference.*
2. When the amount paid exceeds the amounts contributed by the stockholders (i.e., the credits exceed the debits):
   a. *Paid-In Capital from Retirement may be debited up to the amount of any credit balance in that account, with any remaining difference debited to Retained Earnings.*
   b. Or, as an alternative, *Retained Earnings may be debited for the entire difference between the amount paid and the amounts contributed by the stockholders.*[19]

To illustrate, D'Souza issued 20,000 shares of $10 par common stock in 1999 at $18 per share. Then, on April 20, 2005, D'Souza reacquired 1,000 shares of stock at $14 per share and immediately retired them. The journal entry to retire these shares of stock is as follows:

Common Stock (1,000 shares at $10 par)	10,000	
Paid-In Capital in Excess of Par (1,000 shares at $8)	8,000	
Cash		14,000
Paid-In Capital from Retirement (difference)		4,000
To retire stock.		

The $8 per share debited to Paid-In Capital in Excess of Par is the amount in excess of par that was contributed when the stock was first issued. When several issuances of stock have occurred, such that it is impractical to identify the specific amounts that were contributed in excess of par for the specific shares of stock reacquired, an average paid-in capital amount can be used.

Illustration 13-5 shows the issuances of $5 par value stock that occurred over the time indicated. On June 30, 2006, the company bought back on the open market 20,000 shares of stock at $18 per share. Of course, the company could have kept track of the stock certificate numbers that were issued on each of the

---

[19]*APB Opinion No. 6*, "Status of Accounting Research Bulletins," par. 12-a(i).

ILLUSTRATION 13-5

Reacquiring Stocks Issued at Different Dates

Date	Stock Issued
January 1, 2001	100,000 shares at $10.25
February 25, 2002	50,000 shares at $12.50
August 12, 2002	20,000 shares at $14.00
March 3, 2004	50,000 shares at $15.40
November 30, 2005	40,000 shares at $15.70

above dates, but because the separating of legal capital from total capital is largely irrelevant information, a better way to record the entry to acquire and retire the shares of stock is to base the computations on the average paid-in capital amounts, as shown in Illustration 13-6.

ILLUSTRATION 13-6

Using an Average Paid-In Capital Amount for Retiring Stocks

Date	Stock Issued	Total Par	Total Paid-In Capital in Excess
January 1, 2001	100,000 shares at $10.25	$500,000	$ 525,000
February 25, 2002	50,000 shares at $12.50	250,000	375,000
August 12, 2002	20,000 shares at $14.00	100,000	180,000
March 3, 2004	50,000 shares at $15.40	250,000	520,000
November 30, 2005	40,000 shares at $15.70	200,000	428,000
	260,000 shares of stock		$2,028,000
	Average paid-in capital in excess per share of stock		$7.80

The required journal entry to retire the shares of stock, based upon these computations, is as follows:

Common Stock (20,000 shares × $5)	100,000	
Paid-In Capital in Excess of Par (20,000 shares × $7.80)	156,000	
Retained Earnings (difference)	104,000	
Cash (20,000 shares × $18)		360,000

To acquire shares of stock and retire them using an average paid-in capital amount.

Retiring stock causes both the number of shares outstanding and the number of shares issued to decrease but has no effect on the number of shares authorized.

Dividends

A **dividend** is a distribution of cash, other assets, or the corporation's own stock to owners. Ordinarily, dividends are distributed from current earnings or from retained earnings, and dividends represent a return to the owners on their investment. Dividends are never recognized as an expense under U.S. GAAP. As a result, dividends are not reported on the income statement but instead are reported on the statement of changes in stockholders' equity and, if the statement is prepared, on the statement of retained earnings.

Before a corporation distributes a dividend, it must ascertain whether the amount it desires to distribute is legally permissible and whether it has the economic ability to pay the desired amount. As with defining legal capital, the various states have adopted different laws defining what the maximum amount is that can be legally distributed as a dividend. Some of the more popular definitions of what can be legally distributed are: (1) current earnings or the balance in the retained earnings account and (2) the fair value of the corporation's net assets, which is defined as assets minus liabilities. Thus, determining whether a corporation is in compliance with applicable state laws is a legal question that should be answered by competent legal counsel.

In addition, the laws of some states reduce the maximum legal amount that can be distributed as a dividend by any balance in the treasury stock account because payments made by the corporation for treasury stock are considered to be distributions of assets to shareholders. If a corporation were permitted to acquire shares of treasury stock without limit and at any price, it could distribute all the assets to the stockholders and leave the creditors with no protection against future losses. Hence, when a corporation acquires treasury stock, the laws of some states require that the corporation disclose that its maximum legal ability to pay dividends is reduced by the balance in the treasury stock account.

Regardless of the amount that could legally be distributed, a corporation would rarely distribute all of its current earnings—let alone its accumulated earnings—as dividends. Hence, a more effective limitation on the amount that can be paid as a dividend is the corporation's economic ability to pay. Earnings are a principal source of funds that a corporation uses to replace existing assets and expand physical operations. So a corporation must consider its need for cash when deciding whether to pay a dividend and how much to pay. For this and other practical reasons, the amount distributed as dividends depends much more upon economic factors than upon some maximum legal restraint.

Many established corporations desire to create and continue a pattern of consistent dividend payments, and certainly financial markets react positively to such consistency. As a result, many corporations establish a dividend policy, and only in unusual circumstances will they deviate from this policy.

Important Dates Connected with Dividends

For accounting purposes, three dates regarding dividends are important:

- **Date of declaration:** This is the date that the board of directors announces—after having been approved by stockholders—that a dividend will be paid. In the Compaq example in Exhibit 13-6, the date of declaration is Decem-

EXHIBIT 13-6

Note Reporting of Dividends in Financial Reports

Note 9. Stockholders' Equity:

Dividends. On December 10, 1998, Compaq announced that the Board of Directors approved a cash dividend of $0.02 per share of common stock, or approximately $34 million, to shareholders of record as of December 31, 1998, to be paid in 1999.

ber 10. As part of the announcement, the board of directors stipulates: (a) the assets to be distributed, (b) the capital account to be charged (e.g., Retained Earnings), (c) the rate or amount of the dividend, and (d) the other dates of importance to the dividend. This information is not usually reported in the financial statements.

By announcing a dividend, the corporation is now committed to a formal liability that must be recorded. The general form of the journal entry to record this liability is as follows:

Retained Earnings[20]	Fair value of asset to be distributed.
Dividends Payable	Same as the debit entry.

- **Date of record:** Corporations do not keep a day-by-day record as to who owns their stock. Given the multitudes of daily trades on stock exchanges, it would be impossible to do so. So, in announcing a dividend, the board of directors also announces a day that all holders of stock, or their agents, must notify the corporation that they own stock. (In the Compaq example, the date of record is December 31, 1998.) It is to those individuals and institutional investors as of the date of record that dividends are paid. No journal entry is prepared on the date of record.
- **Date of payment:** This is the date that the liability, which was previously created by the board of directors, is satisfied by distributing the dividend. (In the Compaq example, the date of payment was specified to be some time in 1999.) The general form of the journal entry on the date of payment is as follows:

Dividends Payable	See declaration entry for amounts.
Cash, or Other Assets	See declaration entry for amounts.

Accounting for Cash Dividends

After five years of successful operations, Ponce de Leon's Fountain is ready to pay its first dividend. By that time, the corporation had issued 140,000 shares of common stock, of which 20,000 were in the treasury. The board of directors declares a $0.50 per share dividend to be paid in two months.

Date of declaration:

Retained Earnings (or Dividends)	60,000	
Dividends Payable		60,000

Note from this entry that dividends are not paid on treasury stock. From the previous discussion, remember that shares in the treasury do not have the *right* to receive dividends. However, there may be times when the board of directors may want to pay dividends, when payment is legal, on treasury shares.

Date of payment:

Dividends Payable	60,000	
Cash		60,000

[20]An acceptable alternative is to debit a dividends account. Also, if the board of directors had announced that a capital account other than Retained Earnings was to be charged (as in the case of a liquidating dividend), this journal entry would be modified accordingly.

Order of Dividend Payments

When a cash dividend is declared, the accountant must determine the amounts that are to be paid to each class of stockholder, given the nature of the preferences provided to the preferred stockholders. Regarding these dividend preferences, preferred stock may be:

- **Cumulative**: where the preferred stockholders do not lose the right to a dividend in those years that a dividend is not declared. Rather, the rights to those dividends accumulate and must be satisfied before dividends are paid in any year to the common stockholders. Cumulative dividends that have not been paid are called **dividends in arrears**, and such dividends should be disclosed in the notes to the financial statements.
- **Participating**: where the preferred stockholders receive an additional dividend above the stated yearly dividend. So holders of participating preferred stock, after receiving their regular preferred dividend, also participate with the common stockholders in receiving additional dividends up to a defined ceiling.[21]

Given these dividend preferences, dividends are distributed to common and preferred stockholders in the following order:

1. Dividends in arrears are paid to preferred stockholders (this is the cumulative preference).
2. Preferred stockholders are paid current-year dividends.
3. Common stockholders are paid the remainder of dividends to be distributed, unless the preferred stock is participating. In that case, the common stockholders are paid an equivalent percentage amount as was paid to the preferred stockholders for the current-year dividend.
4. Preferred and common stockholders share in dividends based upon the total par value of each class of stock up to any defined limit as to the amount of extra dividends to be received (this is the participating preference).
5. Common stockholders receive any remaining amounts.

To illustrate how these steps are applied, assume that in Year 11, Ponce de Leon's Fountain is very prosperous and the board of directors declares a dividend of $100,000 that will be distributed to all stockholders. At the time, there are outstanding 100,000 shares of $10 par common stock and 5,000 shares of 6%,[22] $50 par, cumulative (but not participating) preferred stock. Dividends on the preferred stock are one year in arrears. Based upon these facts, the $100,000 will be paid according to the calculations shown in Illustration 13-7.

Using the same information, except that the preferred stock is both cumulative and partially participating up to an additional 2%, the $100,000 is divided as shown in Illustration 13-8.

The participating feature does not "kick in" until an equivalent percentage amount is paid to the common stockholders as is paid to the preferred stockholders for the current year. That is, since the preferred stockholders are paid a 6% return for the current year, so too are the common stockholders paid a 6%

---

[21]Participating features are limited only by the imagination of those creating them, so the terms of participation must be read closely to be implemented correctly.

[22]Preferred stock dividend amounts may be given in dollar or percentage terms. For example, $4 preferred stock means the dividend amount is $4 per share, and 6% preferred stock with a $50 par value means that each share of stock will be paid a dividend amount of $3, which is computed as 6% times the par value of $50.

ILLUSTRATION 13-7

The Cumulative Feature on Distributing Dividends
(Stock Is Cumulative but Not Participating)

Order of Distribution	Paid to Preferred Stockholders	Paid to Common Stockholders	Amount Left to Be Distributed
			$100,000
Pay arrears.	$15,000*		85,000
Pay current-year 6% dividend to the preferred stockholders.	15,000		70,000
Pay the remaining amount to the common stockholders.		70,000	0

*Preferrred Stock Dividend = Total par value × 6% dividend rate
= (5,000 shares × $50/share) × 6%
= $15,000

ILLUSTRATION 13-8

The Participating Feature on Distributing Dividends
(Stock Is Cumulative and Partially Participating)

Order of Distribution	Paid to Preferred Stockholders	Paid to Common Stockholders	Amount Left to Be Distributed
			$100,000
Pay arrears.	$15,000		85,000
Pay current-year 6% dividend to the preferred stockholders.	15,000		70,000
Pay an equivalent 6% amount to the common stockholders		60,000*	10,000
Participating feature	2,000	8,000	0

*Amount is computed as follows:
Common stock dividend = Total par value × 6%
= (100,000 shares × $10 par/share) × 6%
= $60,000

return—before the preferred stockholders receive any amounts under the participating feature.

After paying $60,000 to the common stockholders, there is still $10,000 left to distribute. The simplest way to distribute this amount is to determine how much is needed—in total for both the preferred and common stockholders—to meet the participating feature, which in this example is $25,000.[23] When the amount still to be distributed is sufficient to pay the participating feature (i.e., $25,000), the preferred stockholders are paid the required amount under the participating provision, and the remainder is paid to the common stockholders.

---

[23]This $25,000 is computed as the total par value of $1,250,000 (i.e., $250,000 for common and $1,000,000 for preferred) multiplied by the 2% participating feature.

When the amount remaining to be distributed is not sufficient to pay the complete participating amount to both the preferred and common stockholders (which is the case in this example), the amount remaining to be distributed is divided between the preferred and common stockholders in relation to the total par value of each class of stock, as shown in Illustration 13-9.

ILLUSTRATION 13-9

Participating Feature When Remaining Cash Is Insufficient

Description of Stock	Total Par Value	Percent of Total Par Value	Amount of Dividends
Preferred stock	$ 250,000ª	20%	$ 2,000
Common stock	1,000,000ᵇ	80	8,000
	$1,250,000		$10,000

ª5,000 shares of preferred at $50 par value per share.
ᵇ100,000 shares of common at $10 par value per share.

Appropriated Retained Earnings

As the name indicates, retained earnings is the accumulated earnings of the company that the corporation has reinvested in assets rather than distributing the earnings to the owners. Retained earnings is measured as the net result of applying the revenue recognition and matching principles and is also affected by some transactions with owners. From the foregoing, it should be obvious that, contrary to what may be written about retained earnings in the popular press, it is not a sum of cash in a vault that the company can use to pay debts or settle lawsuits. From a business and accounting perspective, the essential characteristic of retained earnings is that it represents how much of the company's earnings has been kept and reinvested in assets as compared to financing the acquisition of those assets through borrowing money or having the owners contribute more capital.

Normally, retained earnings is increased only by net income and occasionally by prior-period adjustments. Retained earnings is decreased by:

1. Net losses;
2. Prior-period adjustments, which are covered in the next chapter;
3. Treasury stock transactions; and
4. Declarations of dividends.

Retained earnings may be divided and reported as an appropriated amount and an unappropriated amount. *The purpose of appropriating retained earnings is to disclose existing management policy of curtailing or restricting normal dividends for a period of time.* Appropriating retained earnings has no effect on cash or on any other asset; nor does appropriating retained earnings actually restrict or set aside an asset. An example of a legal restriction on dividends is that, as mentioned earlier, in some states a corporation's legal capital is reduced when it acquires treasury stock, and as a result, the corporation is required to disclose that the maximum legal amount that can be paid as dividends has been reduced. Such disclosure can be done in the notes to the financial statements or by appropriating retained earnings. An example of a contractual restriction on dividends is borrowing money where the lender requires the corporation to restrict dividends for the time that the money is owed, which increases the likelihood that the creditor will be paid. Again, the corporation can disclose such a restriction on paying dividends either in the notes or by appropriating retained earnings. An example of a corporation voluntarily restricting dividends for a period of time is the need to retain cash for internal purposes, such as for a major construction project or to expand operations. This corporate policy too can be disclosed by appropriating retained earnings.

The required journal entry for appropriating retained earnings is as follows:

Retained Earnings	Some amount	
Appropriated Retained Earnings		Some amount

Since the purpose of the entry is only to disclose managerial policy, the amount of the journal entry is not really important; but if desired, the amount can be an estimate of the amount of cash or other assets that is expected to be used for the purpose of the appropriation. When the corporation has no further reason for restricting dividends, it reverses the above entry.

Preparing the Stockholders' Equity Section of the Balance Sheet

The stockholders' equity section of a balance sheet is reported in various ways. [For examples, see Exhibits 13-2 (p. 603), 13-4 (p. 606), and 13-5 (p. 611).] Given this, the following seems only to be some of the more generally used guidelines. The stockholders' equity section is divided into three main sections: (1) Contributed capital, (2) Retained earnings, and (3) Other comprehensive income, which is covered in the next chapter. The contributed capital section contains the amounts contributed by the owners, with the legal capital amounts captured in the stock accounts. These amounts are described regarding the number of shares authorized, issued, and outstanding, and for preferred stock, the dividend rate and various preferences. Regarding the paid-in capital accounts, as mentioned in the chapter, corporations report either a paid-in capital for common stock and a separate amount for preferred, or—more typically—just one paid-in capital account. The typical order in which the various accounts are listed under contributed capital is to list the stock accounts first, beginning with preferred stock, then followed by the paid-in capital accounts. As with any balance sheet section, there should be a subtotal of the total contributed capital.

Usually, the Retained earnings section includes only the one account, Retained Earnings. When such is the case, neither a heading nor a subtotal is necessary; all that needs to be reported is the line "Retained earnings." When retained earnings is appropriated, the appropriated retained earnings account is listed first, labeled "Appropriated retained earnings," and is followed by retained earnings, which then is labeled "Unappropriated retained earnings." These two amounts are added together, and the total is reported as total retained earnings. When accumulated losses exceed accumulated income, the amount is not labeled "Retained earnings," but instead is labeled "Deficit" or "Accumulated deficit" (see Exhibit 13-4, p. 606). Treasury stock accounted for under the cost method is reported after total contributed capital and retained earnings (see Exhibit 13-2, p. 603). Exhibit 13-7 is an example of a stockholders' equity section that includes all items mentioned in this chapter.

EXHIBIT 13-7

Stockholders' Equity Section

Contributed Capital:	
6% Preferred stock $50 par value, 10,000 shares issued and outstanding	$ 500,000
Common stock, $1 par value, 500,000 issued, 480,000 outstanding	500,000
Common stock subscribed	20,000
Additional paid-in capital—common	680,000
Additional paid-in capital—preferred	40,000
Total contributed capital	$1,740,000
Retained Earnings:	
Appropriated retained earnings	$ 50,000
Unappropriated retained earnings	897,000
Total retained earnings	$ 947,000
Total contributed capital and retained earnings	$2,687,000
Less: Subscriptions receivable	(80,500)
Treasury stock	(165,000)
Total stockholders' equity	$2,441,500

International Practices for Stockholders' Equity Transactions

INTERNATIONAL

Most of the material covered in this chapter is followed in most non-U.S. countries as generally accepted accounting practices. However, some significant differences arise in classifying treasury stock on the balance sheet, accounting for cash dividends, and the definition of legal capital.

Classification of Treasury Stock

Consistent with the view that gains/losses are not recognized on transactions with owners, the generally accepted accounting principles of most other countries also do not allow gains and losses to be recognized when shares of stock are bought and sold. Also, treasury stock is typically reported as a contra stockholders' equity account. However, in some countries, such as Germany and Italy, companies are allowed to report treasury shares as an asset, usually in the "Other investments" category. The treasury shares are recorded at cost, and when the shares are resold, a gain or loss is recognized.

Recognizing Dividends as a Liability

Unlike U.S. GAAP, some countries require that dividends be deducted from retained earnings and recorded as a liability when proposed by the board of directors, that is, before being approved by the stockholders. Included in this group of countries is the United Kingdom. Similar to U.S. GAAP, international GAAP require dividends to be recorded as a liability only after stockholders approve the dividend. If a dividend proposal is made and the stockholders' approval is given subsequent to year-end, but before the issuance of the financial statements, revised *IAS No. 10* does not allow the accrual of the dividends in the year of proposal. This represents a major change from the old standard, which provided companies with a choice of accruing the dividends either in the year of proposal or the year of stockholder approval.

Legal Reserves (Compare to Par Value Concept)

In many countries where debt is the primary source of capital (e.g., Japan, Germany, Switzerland, and Mexico), laws have been established that are intended to protect debtors from the company distributing capital to equity holders in the form of dividends. In Japan, companies are required to appropriate retained earnings to a legal reserve account that is equal to 10% of the amount of dividends and bonuses paid to stockholders and managers until the total appropriated is equal to 25% of the capital stock accounts. This legal reserve account is not available for dividend distribution.

Exhibit 13-8, with emphasis added, presents the stockholders' equity section and the corresponding note related to the legal reserve as extracted from the 1999 financial statements of Canon Inc., a large company domiciled in Japan that is famous for cameras.

EXHIBIT 13-8

CANON Stockholders' Equity Section of Balance Sheet

Millions of Yen

	1999	1998
Stockholders' Equity:		
Common stock of 50 yen par value		
Authorized 2,000,000,000 shares;		
issued and outstanding 871,555,698 shares in 1999		
and 870,305,870 shares in 1998	163,969	163,033
Additional paid-in capital	376,848	375,913
Legal reserve	*33,518*	*31,396*
Retained earnings	735,975	682,663
Accumulated other comprehensive income	(108,307)	(97,485)
Total stockholders' equity	1,202,003	1,155,520

NOTE 13—Legal Reserve and Cash Dividend

The Japanese Commercial Code provides that an amount equal to at least 10% of appropriations paid in cash be appropriated as a legal reserve until such reserve equals 25% of stated capital. This reserve is not available for dividends but may be used to reduce a deficit or may be transferred to stated capital.

International Accounting Standards

IAS No. 1 (which was revised by the IASC to be effective for years beginning on or after July 1, 1998) provides guidance on the presentation and disclosure of financial statements, including the stockholders' equity section of the balance sheet. However, guidance for the actual accounting for many stockholders' equity transactions is noticeably lacking under international GAAP. For example, international GAAP does not mention how to account for treasury stock transactions. Only recently, the IASC took the position that treasury stock should be presented

This Is the Real World

Bass PLC is a large multinational company domiciled in the United Kingdom. The company owns, manages, and franchises several leading brands, including hotels and resorts (e.g., Crowne Plaza and Holiday Inn), bars and restaurants (e.g., All Bar One and Goose), and beers and softdrinks (Carling and Hooch). The company is listed on the New York Stock Exchange and thus must comply with all U.S. GAAP requirements. However, rather than issue financial statements based on U.S. GAAP, the company retains UK accounting principles and reconciles differences in its notes.

The following is the company's stockholders' equity section extracted from its 1999 annual report. Notice the different terminology used by UK companies. Specifically, "non-equity share capital" is equivalent to preferred stock, and "capital redemption reserve" is a reserve set up by the company for purposes of purchasing its own shares. Similar to appropriated retained earnings in the United States, this amount is not distributable as dividends. What other differences in terminology can you identify?

Bass PLC's preferred stock is redeemable; thus, where would these shares be disclosed under U.S. GAAP?

Bass PLC
Stockholders' Equity Section of Balance Sheet

| | Group | | Company | |
	1999 £m	1998 £m	1999 £m	1998 £m
Capital and reserves				
Equity share capital	223	223	223	223
Nonequity share capital	18	48	18	48
Called up share capital	241	271	241	271
Equity reserves				
Share premium account	53	40	53	40
Revaluation reserve	1,354	680	1	—
Capital redemption reserve	831	801	831	801
Profit and loss account	834	785	484	768
Shareholders' funds	3,313	2,577	1,610	1,880

in the stockholders' equity section (as opposed to allowing it to be reported in the investments section of the balance sheet). The IASC ruled that detailed guidance is not needed for these issues as long as the company provides full disclosure for investors to analyze.

Summary

In the United States, legal capital is the basis for accounting for transactions involving stockholders' equity accounts. Legal capital is defined by the various state laws, but essentially it is total par value, total stated value, or the total amount paid when stock is issued. When accounting for stock transactions, the legal capital amount is identified and accounted in the stock account, with additional contributed amounts being reported in descriptive paid-in capital in excess accounts. Accounting for stock transactions also requires that the source of funds be identified (i.e., whether the funds came from preferred stockholders or common stockholders).

The typical way a corporation accounts for acquiring shares of its stock is the cost method, where the cost of the treasury stock is equal to the fair value of the consideration paid. Subsequently, when those shares are sold, the corporation credits the treasury stock account for the "cost" of the shares reissued, debits Cash for the amount received, and then accounts for the difference either by (1) crediting a descriptive paid-in capital account or (2) debiting a descriptive paid-in capital account up to the amount of any available balance and then debiting the rest to Retained Earnings, or debiting Retained Earnings for the total amount.

Dividends are distributions of the corporation's assets to its owners. Usually, dividends reduce retained earnings. The amount of dividends paid to the preferred and common stockholders depends upon the preferences given the preferred stock, with the order of payments being:

1. Any preferred stock dividends in arrears,
2. Current-year preferred stock dividend,
3. Current-year common stock dividend that is equal to the preferred stock dividend percentage,
4. If the preferred stock is participating, the preferred and common stockholders participate in additional dividends up to some defined amount; otherwise,
5. Residual is paid to the common stockholders.

Retained earnings is the result of applying the revenue recognition and matching principles and also is affected by some transactions with owners. Retained earnings is not cash or any other asset. The account balance is increased by net income and decreased by net losses, dividends, and some treasury stock transactions. Retained earnings also may be increased or decreased by prior-period adjustments. Appropriating retained earnings is done to disclose management's intent to restrict or curtail dividends. Assets are not affected by such appropriation, nor are they restricted or set aside.

APPENDIX: Treasury Stock Transactions—Par Value Method

The par value method of accounting for treasury stock transactions is theoretically preferred to the cost method because it accounts for treasury stock as if the stock were reacquired, retired, and then reissued, rather than treating the stock as if it were a long-term asset that is being acquired and later sold.

Unlike the cost method that has one standard entry when treasury stock is acquired and a variation of entries when the treasury stock is reissued, the par value method has a variety of entries when the treasury stock is acquired and only one standard entry when it is reissued. Under the par value method, the following procedures are followed when a corporation acquires treasury stock:

- Debit Treasury Stock for the par value of the shares.
- Debit Paid-In Capital in Excess of Par for the amount that was received when the stock was initially issued (or, as illustrated in the chapter, for an average amount that was paid-in in excess of par).
- Credit Cash for the amount paid to acquire the shares.
- Debit/credit Paid-In Capital from Treasury Stock for the difference. Or, if necessary or desired, debit Retained Earnings for the difference.[24]

When the treasury shares are subsequently reissued, they are accounted for in the same way as stock that is being issued for the first time, which is:

[24]APB Opinion No. 6, "Status of Accounting Research Bulletins," par. 12-a(i).

Cash	XXX	
Treasury Stock		Par value
Paid-In Capital in Excess of Par		Difference

To illustrate the par value method of accounting for treasury stock, consider a corporation that conducted the following treasury stock transactions:

1. Acquired 20 shares of its own $10 par value common stock at $15 per share that had originally been issued for $15 per share.

Treasury Stock (at par)	200	
Paid-In Capital in Excess of Par (The $5 excess when the shares were issued originally)	100	
Cash		300

   Explanation: The entire amount originally received (i.e., $15 per share) is removed from the accounts.

2. Acquired another 20 shares of its own $10 par value common stock at $10 per share that had originally been issued for $15 per share.

Treasury Stock	200	
Paid-In Capital in Excess of Par	100	
Cash		200
Paid-In Capital from Treasury Stock		100 (plug figure)

   Explanation: The entire amount originally received is removed from the accounts, and since there is a "gain," a paid-in capital from treasury stock account is created.

3. Acquired another 20 shares of its own $10 par value common stock at $18 per share that had originally been issued for $15 per share.

Treasury Stock	200	
Paid-In Capital in Excess of Par	100	
Paid-In Capital from Treasury Stock[25]	60	
Cash		360

   Explanation: The "loss" is debited to the paid-in capital from treasury stock account because it had a balance of $100 and is able to absorb the loss.

4. Acquired another 20 shares of its own $10 par value common stock at $21 per share that had originally been issued for $15 per share.

Treasury Stock	200	
Paid-In Capital in Excess of Par	100	
Paid-In Capital from Treasury Stock	40	
Retained Earnings	80	
Cash		420

   Explanation: The paid-in capital from treasury stock account is able to absorb only $40 of the "loss," and the rest of the loss is debited to Retained Earnings.

In summary, the par value method accounts for acquiring treasury stock as if the stock had been retired. That is, all the capital initially contributed by stockholders is removed from the books, and a "gain" or "loss" is computed that is credited or debited to a paid-in capital from treasury stock account or, if necessary, debited to Retained Earnings. Later, when the treasury shares are reissued, the journal entry is the same as when shares are initially issued.

---

[25]Alternatively, the $60 amount could have been debited to Retained Earnings.

Companies that use the par value method of accounting for treasury stock transactions *report the account as a reduction in the related stock account*. This reporting is illustrated in Exhibit 13-1(A), which uses the Circus-Circus example with the numbers adjusted to conform to the par value method. Note that the total stockholders' equity for Circus-Circus in Exhibits 13-2 (p. 603) and 13-1(A) under the cost method and the par value method, respectively, are identical, but the balances of the additional paid-in capital and retained earnings are considerably different between the two methods.

EXHIBIT 13-1(A)

Reporting Treasury Stock under the Par Value Method

Circus-Circus

	(in thousands)	
	1998	1997
Preferred stock $0.01 par value		
Authorized—75,000,000 shares	—	—
Common stock $0.01 2/3 par value		
Authorized—450,000,000 shares		
Issued—113,609,008 and 112,808,337 shares	$ 1,893	$ 1,880
Treasury stock (18,496,125 and 18,749,209 shares),		
at par value	(309)	(313)
Additional paid-in capital	467,501	415,803
Retained earnings	654,664	554,421
Total stockholders' equity	$1,123,749	$971,791

Questions

1. What is the definition of *legal capital*? What factors contributed to the emergence of legal capital? Is legal capital effective in accomplishing its primary objective of protecting creditors?

2. Describe the primary difference between common and preferred stock. Which class of stock represents the basic ownership interests of the company?

3. Identify where each of the following items is classified on a balance sheet.
   a. Unappropriated retained earnings
   b. Common stock
   c. Subscribed common stock
   d. Paid-in capital in excess of par
   e. Cumulative preferred stock
   f. Dividends payable
   g. Appropriated retained earnings
   h. Redeemable preferred stock
   i. Bond securities
   j. Treasury stock
   k. Stock that has been repurchased and retired
   l. Reserves for contingent liabilities

4. Briefly describe the general sequence of events to incorporate a business.

5. List the three general rules in accounting for transactions involving stockholders' equity accounts.

6. BioLife Sciences, Inc., received an asset from Chemical Solutions, Inc., in exchange for 20,000 shares of BioLife's $1 par value common stock. The asset had a book value on Chemical Solutions' balance sheet of $170,000 with $90,000 accumulated depreciation. The fair value of the asset at the time it was acquired by BioLife was $120,000. At what amount should the acquired asset be recorded on BioLife's balance sheet?

7. Bryant Corporation issued 10,000 shares of common stock for $300,000. Provide the necessary journal entry in each of the following situations:
   a. The stock has a $10 par value.
   b. The stock has a $10 stated value.
   c. The stock does not have a par value.
   d. The stock has a $40 par value.

8. Explain how costs associated with issuing stock, e.g., legal, accounting, and underwriter's fees, are accounted for.

9. John and Sally subscribed to a total of 10,000 shares of stock of Piston Mechanics, Inc., at the specified price of $5. They have six months to pay for the stock, at which time the $1 par value common stock will be issued. John and Sally paid 20% of the subscription price today. Prepare the journal entries to record the subscribing to the stock and the subsequent paying and issuing of the common stock by Piston Mechanics. Indicate where all accounts, except Cash, are presented on the balance sheet.

10. Spencer's Electronics issued the following securities, as a package, in exchange for $100,000:
   a. 3,000 shares of Class A $1 par value common stock
   b. 2,000 shares of Class B $0.01 par value common stock
   c. 1,000 shares of no-par preferred stock

   The market values of one share of each type of security are: $20 for Class A common, $15 for Class B common, and $12 for preferred stock. Using the proportional method, prepare the journal entry to record issuing these securities.

11. What is treasury stock? Describe (i.e., do more than list) the two acceptable methods of accounting for treasury stock. Which method did the Committee on Accounting Procedures prefer? Which method is more widely used in practice?

12. Gray Furniture purchased 100 shares of its own $1 par value common stock on the open market for $300, which was equal to the amount that was received when the stock was originally issued. Subsequently, the company reissued the shares. Using the cost method and then the par value method, provide the journal entries to record reissuing the treasury stock, assuming that the proceeds received were as follows:
   a. $500
   b. $300
   c. $100

13. Describe how total stockholders' equity and the balances in Additional Paid-In Capital in Excess of Par, Additional Paid-In Capital, Treasury Stock, and Retained Earnings will differ between the cost method and the par value method of accounting for treasury stock.

14. When does a cash dividend become a liability that is recorded on the general ledger of the corporation?

15. Explain the significance of the date of record with respect to a dividend.

16. Define *dividends in arrears*. To what kind of security are dividends in arrears related?

17. What is participating preferred stock? Would this type of security have a greater or smaller market value compared to ordinary preferred stock of the same company? Why?

18. Rockport Appliances, Inc., has the following different types of securities outstanding: 8% long-term bonds, common stock, 8% ordinary preferred stock, and 8% fully participating preferred stock. Rank these securities based on their level of risk to an investor, from lowest risk to highest, and give the reason for ranking the securities that way.

Exercises

Exercise 13-1: Multiple-Choice Questions.

1. Which of the following statements is *true*?
   a. Distinguishing between debt and equity securities is not always easy.
   b. A company must record a liability on the balance sheet for unpaid dividends on cumulative preferred stock, even when the dividends are not declared.
   c. The number of shares issued by the company is always equal to the number of shares outstanding.
   d. Stockholders' equity is defined as the residual interest in the company's assets after deducting its liabilities and retained earnings.

2. Which of the following statements is *not* true with respect to U.S. GAAP and international GAAP? Under both sets of standards:
   a. Dividends are recorded as a liability when proposed by the company's board of directors and approved by stockholders.
   b. Liquidating dividends are taxable transactions, since they result in a cash flow to stockholders.
   c. Treasury stock is reported as a deduction from stockholders' equity.
   d. Treasury stock does not reduce the number of shares issued but does reduce the number of shares outstanding.

3. Which of the following statements is *true* under U.S. GAAP?
   a. Paid-in capital in excess of par represents the capital contributed by the owners to a corporation at the time stock is issued, other than that defined as legal capital.
   b. Transactions in a corporation's own stock can result in a corporation recognizing losses on the income statement but not gains.
   c. Treasury stock should be recorded as an asset and reported under the investments classification of the balance sheet.
   d. All of the above are true statements.

4. When a corporation issues stock without a par or stated value, the appropriate journal entry to record this transaction is:
   a. Cash   XXX
          Retained Earnings   XXX

b. Cash   XXX
    Common Stock   XXX
c. Cash   XXX
    Paid-In Capital in Excess of Par   XXX
d. Cash   XXX
    Common Stock (arbitrary amount)   XXX
    Paid-In Capital in Excess of Par   XXX

5. When stock is issued as compensation for services rendered:
   a. The transaction should be recorded at the par value of the stock, because in these types of transactions fair value cannot be objectively determined.
   b. The transaction should be recorded at the fair value of the stock issued.
   c. The transaction should be recorded at the fair value of the services rendered.
   d. The transaction is sometimes recorded at the fair value of the stock issued and sometimes at the fair value of services rendered, whichever is more clearly measured.

Exercise 13-2: Exchanging Stock for Goods and Services. During its first month of operations, McFadd Corporation entered into the following transactions:

1. On January 1, 2004, McFadd Corporation issued 2,000 shares of its $2 par value common stock to the company's founder Charles McFadd in exchange for his registered patent. Charles had worked on the patent on a part-time basis over many years and had kept meticulous notes as to the costs he had incurred to obtain the patent, which were as follows:

Cost of materials	$ 4,000
Cost to register the patent with the government	100
Attorney's fees	2,500
Time spent (valued at what he was paid on his full-time job while developing the patent at home in the garage)	45,000

Several companies, upon hearing about the patent, had expressed interest in obtaining it, with the best offer received being $250,000. However, McFadd believes the offer was too low and so decided to form this corporation.
2. Also, on January 1, 2004, McFadd Corporation issued 1,000 shares of common stock to James Lyson in exchange for a building where the company can house its operations. The building had cost Lyson $120,000, and at the time of selling it to McFadd, it had accumulated depreciation of $40,000. Competent real estate appraisal indicates that its fair value is approximately $180,000.
3. On March 1, 2004, McFadd issued 3,000 shares of common stock for $550,000 cash.
4. On April 1, 2004, McFadd issued 2,000 shares of $100 par value, 8% preferred stock for $230,000.
5. Legal, accounting, and underwriting fees for issuing the common stock were $50,000, and for the preferred stock the fees were $25,000, which were paid in cash.

Using the information from any transaction to assist in measuring any other transaction, prepare the journal entries necessary to record the issuing of the common and preferred shares.

Exercise 13-3: Issuing Stock. Transcend Media, Inc., was incorporated in 2004, and during that year it had the following transactions related to its stock.

Jan. 20   Registered 500,000 shares of $5 par common stock and 40,000 shares of $100 par preferred stock for future issuance.

Feb. 1   Issued 100,000 shares of common stock at $8 per share.

Mar. 15   Issued 50,000 shares of common stock at $10 per share.

Apr. 7   Paid underwriter's fees of $38,000 relating to registering and issuing the common stock.

June 10   Issued 5,000 shares of cumulative, 6%, preferred stock for $110 per share.

June 10   1,000 shares of common stock were issued to the lawyers and accountants as payment for their professional services in registering the common and preferred shares. The market price of the common shares on this date was $12 per share. (Round amounts to the nearest hundred dollars.)

Aug. 20   Exchanged 20,000 shares of common stock for a building with an asking price of $240,000. The market price of the securities on this date was $11 per share.

1. Prepare journal entries to record each transaction.
2. Show how the entries would change, assuming that the common stock did not have a par value.

Exercise 13-4: Subscribing to Stock. Knight Imaging Services has been in business as a private organization for several years, but in 2004, the company decided to incorporate. Preparatory to its initial public offering (IPO), the company initiated contact with an investment banker and then went on the road advertising the company. At various cities, the company's founders gave a presentation to potential investors and afterwards accepted subscriptions to the company's stock. The stock was to have a par value of $0.10 and be sold in the IPO at $10 per share. The investors were required to pay 25% at the time they subscribed, and the remaining funds were due at the time of the IPO. Prepare the following journal entries:

1. At a particular presentation, subscriptions were received for 20,000 shares and the appropriate amount collected in cash.
2. Subsequently, subscribers to 16,000 shares paid in full and the shares of stock were issued.
3. Subscribers to the other 4,000 shares defaulted on their shares, and in accordance with state law, the shares that had been paid for were issued and the balance in the subscriptions receivable account was written off.

Exercise 13-5: Issuing Multiple Types of Securities. Disk Zipper, Inc., was in need of additional capital in order to take advantage of some investment opportunities, so the company decided to issue a package of securities to an institutional investor for a lump sum of $450,000. The package of securities included 10,000 shares of common stock, 1,000 shares of preferred stock, and 50 bonds. The following table presents the details of each security.

Security	Par/Face Value	Interest or Dividend Rate	Expiration Date	Market Value
Common stock	$ 1.00	N/A	N/A	$ 31.00
Preferred stock	100.00	9%	N/A	109.25
Bond	1,000.00	6	Dec. 31, 2014	990.00

1. Using the proportional method, prepare the journal entry to record issuing the security package.

(continued)

2. Assume that the market value of the preferred stock was not known. Prepare the new journal entry.

Exercise 13-6: Issuing Multiple Types of Securities. Seinfeld Company issued 3,000 shares of its no-par common stock and also 15 bonds (with a face amount of $1,000) on July 1, 2004, in exchange for administrative services and equipment. The retail values of the services and equipment were $20,000 and $25,000, respectively. On that date, the market value of Seinfeld's common stock was $10. The bonds had a stated interest rate of 6%, and the market rate of interest for similar bonds was 8%. The bonds pay interest annually and mature in 10 years.

1. Using the fair value of the securities to measure the transaction and the values of the services and equipment as allocation bases, prepare the appropriate journal entry for this transaction. (Round amounts to the nearest hundred dollars.)
2. Using the proportional method and the fair value of the services and assets received, prepare the appropriate journal entry for this transaction. (Round amounts to the nearest hundred dollars.)
3. Assuming that the market value of the common stock could not be ascertained, prepare the appropriate journal entry, using the values of the services and equipment to measure the transaction. (Round amounts to the nearest hundred dollars.)

Exercise 13-7: Retiring Stock (Appendix). Harris Inc. reacquired 500 shares of its own $5 par common stock on January 15, 2004, at $45 per share. The shares had been issued originally at $25 per share. Two months after reacquiring these shares, Harris retired them. (Assume that there is no balance in any appropriate paid-in capital account that Harris can debit.)

1. Using the cost method, prepare the journal entry that would have been made to reacquire the shares of stock and then to retire them.
2. **(Appendix)** Prepare the journal entries that would have been made to reacquire the shares of stock and then to retire them, using the par value method.

Exercise 13-8: Treasury Stock (Appendix). Roger Moore Inc. purchased 700 shares of its own stock for $31 per share. The par value of the stock is $10 per share and had been originally issued at $22 per share. Two years later, Roger Moore reissued 400 shares of the treasury stock for services valued at $14,000. Later, a total of 200 of the remaining shares of treasury stock were reissued for $28 per share, and the other 100 shares were retired.

1. Using the cost method, prepare the journal entries for Roger Moore Inc. to record (a) the acquisition of the treasury shares, (b) the subsequent reissuing of the 400 and the 200 shares, and (c) the retiring of the 100 shares.
2. **(Appendix)** Repeat Part (1), using the par value method.

Exercise 13-9: Treasury Stock (Appendix). Longfellow Corporation reacquired 100 shares of its own stock by paying cash of $2,000. The par value of the stock is $2 per share, and the stock was originally issued for a total of $1,500. Longfellow made the following entry to record the transaction:

Treasury Stock	200	
Paid-In Capital in Excess of Par	1,300	
Retained Earnings	500	
Cash		2,000

1. What method is Longfellow using to account for the treasury stock?
2. Prepare the journal entry that Longfellow would have made if the other method of accounting for the treasury stock had been used.
3. Assume that Longfellow purchased the shares of stock for $1,300. Provide the appropriate journal entries to record the purchase, using (a) the cost method and (b) the par value method.

Exercise 13-10: Redeemable Preferred Stock. On January 15, 2001, Reynolds Corporation issued 2,000 shares of $100 par value redeemable preferred stock. The net cash proceeds from the sale of the securities was $220,000. Five years later, with the agreement of those holding the preferred stock, Reynolds redeemed 500 shares by exchanging 2,000 shares of common stock. Each share of common had a $2 par value and a $25 market value.

1. Prepare the journal entry to record the issuance of the preferred stock on January 15, 2001.
2. Prepare the journal entry to record the redemption of the 500 shares of preferred stock.
3. Identify the characteristics of the preferred stock that are similar to debt and the characteristics that are similar to equity. Should redeemable preferred stock always be classified as debt or equity? Would your answer change if the redemption feature was at the option of the holder? What if the redemption feature was mandatory after a certain time period?

Exercise 13-11: Cash Dividends. Lortek, Inc., had the following equity securities outstanding as of December 31, 2003:

- Class A, $1 par value common shares: 1,000,000 shares registered, 500,000 issued and 450,000 shares outstanding.
- Class B, $10 par value common shares: 100,000 shares registered and 80,000 shares issued and outstanding.
- $100 par value, 8%, cumulative preferred shares: 50,000 shares registered, issued, and outstanding.

Dividends on preferred stock were one year in arrears. On December 31, 2003, the board of directors declared a cash dividend of $2 per share on common stock. The date of record is January 10, 2004, and the payment date is February 15, 2004. Concurrently, the board approved payment of all necessary dividends on preferred shares.

1. On what date do the cash dividends on common stock become a liability?
2. Given the declaration of cash dividends on common stock, what amount of dividends is the company required to pay on preferred stock?
3. Does the company have any treasury stock? How can you tell?
4. Record all necessary journal entries to record the dividends on common and preferred stock for: (a) December 31, 2003, (b) January 10, 2004, and (c) February 15, 2004.

Exercise 13-12: Dividend Distributions. Winner Corp. has the following stock outstanding:

Common, $50 par value, 6,000 shares outstanding
Preferred, 6%, $100 par value, 1,000 shares outstanding

Compute the amount of dividends to be paid in total and per share to the common and preferred stockholders, respectively, for each of the following separate cases:

Case A: Preferred is noncumulative and nonparticipating; $21,000 of dividends to be paid.

Case B: Preferred is cumulative and nonparticipating; preferred dividends are two years in arrears; $40,500 of dividends to be paid.

Case C: Preferred is noncumulative and fully participating; $32,000 of dividends to be paid.

Case D: Preferred is cumulative and fully participating; preferred dividends are two years in arrears; $52,000 dividends to be paid.

Case E: Preferred is cumulative and partially participating up to an additional 2%; preferred dividends are two years in arrears; $60,000 dividends to be paid.

Case F: Preferred is cumulative and partially participating up to an additional 2%; preferred dividends are two years in arrears; $42,000 dividends to be paid.

Exercise 13-13: Dividend Distributions. Price Corporation declared dividends during four successive years as follows: $10,000, $12,000, $20,000, and $48,000. The capital stock consists of 50,000 shares of $10 par common stock and 3,000 shares of $100, 5% preferred stock.

Determine the amount to be paid in total on each class of stock for each of the four years, assuming:

Case A: Preferred is noncumulative and nonparticipating.

Case B: Preferred is cumulative and nonparticipating.

Case C: Preferred is noncumulative and fully participating.

Exercise 13-14: Preparing the Stockholders' Equity Section. As of December 31, 2003, Josiah's Widgets Company had the following balances in its stockholders' equity accounts:

Common stock, $1 par	$200,000
Paid-in-capital in excess of par	75,000
Retained earnings	175,000

During 2004, the company incurred the following stockholders' equity transactions:

a. Registered an additional 100,000 shares of $1 par value common stock.
b. Issued 25,000 shares of common stock for $20 per share, on average.
c. Registered and issued at par 2,000 shares of $100 par value, 8%, mandatorily redeemable, cumulative preferred stock. The shares will be redeemed in 10 years.
d. Purchased 5,000 shares of treasury stock at $16 per share.
e. Reissued 2,000 shares of the treasury stock at $21 per share.
f. Retired 2,000 shares of treasury stock; the original proceeds from these shares averaged $8 per share.
g. Appropriated retained earnings in the amount of $50,000 for the purchase of land.
h. Reported a net loss of $54,000.
i. Declared dividends on the preferred stock, which will be paid in 2005.

1. Prepare the journal entries to record these transactions, assuming that the cost method is used to account for treasury stock transactions.

2. Prepare the stockholders' equity section of the balance sheet for Josiah's Widgets Company, assuming that the paid-in capital accounts are combined for financial reporting purposes into one line item.

Exercise 13-15: Stockholders' Equity; Comprehensive. The following stockholders' equity information was obtained from the balance sheet of Thomas Company as of December 31, 2004:

Common stock ($10 par value)	$500,000
Additional paid-in capital	300,000
Retained earnings	100,000
Treasury stock (4,000 shares)	(48,000)

Thomas uses the cost method to account for treasury stock transactions. Answer the following *independent* questions:

1. How many shares of stock have been issued? How many shares of stock are outstanding?
2. What was the average price at which a share of stock was issued?
3. Assuming that Thomas Co. declared a dividend of $1 per share, how much cash normally would be paid to stockholders?
4. Prepare the journal entry that Thomas would make to record cash dividends of (a) $1 per share and (b) $5 per share.
5. Using the average price at which the stock was issued, as computed in Part (2), prepare the journal entry to retire the treasury shares.
6. Prepare the journal entry that Thomas would make if the treasury shares were resold for (a) $18 per share and (b) $10 per share.

Problems

Problem 13-1: Common versus Preferred Stock. With the proliferation of several different types of securities having innovative features, it is not always easy to identify a corporation's common stock. For example, consider the following statement that was extracted from a recent 10-K of the Pepsi Bottling Group Inc.

> The 154,917,354 common shares and 88,350 Class B common shares are substantially identical, except for voting rights. Holders of our common stock are entitled to one vote per share and holders of our Class B common stock are entitled to 250 votes per share. Each share of Class B common stock held by PepsiCo is, at PepsiCo's option, convertible into one share of common stock. Holders of our common stock and holders of our Class B common stock share equally on a per-share basis in any dividend distributions.

Required:
Evaluate the features of the different classes of stock and determine whether both classes of stock should be referred to as common stock or whether one class is, in substance, preferred stock.

1. Does it appear that one class of stock has a preference? If so, what are the specific features that result in this preference?
2. Is it possible for a company to have more than one class of common stock?

Problem 13-2: Issuing Multiple Types of Securities. An institutional investor has agreed to invest in Leading Edge but desires to diversify the investment into various types of securities. Leading Edge has decided to provide the following package to the investor in exchange for $4,200,000:

> 50,000 shares of $10 par value common stock
> 1,000 shares of $50 par value preferred stock
> 2,000 bonds with a face value of $1,000

Further details related to each security are as follows:
- *Common stock:* The common stock of Leading Edge is actively traded on an organized exchange, and the closing price as of the date of the agreement was $44.20 per share.
- *Preferred stock:* The preferred stock is cumulative with an 8% dividend rate. In 10 years, each share of preferred must be redeemed for two shares of common stock. The market value of these securities was $85 per share on the date of the agreement.
- *Bonds:* The bonds have a 10-year life and pay semiannual interest, with the first payment due six months from the date of the agreement. The stated interest rate on the bonds is $9\frac{2}{3}\%$, and the market rate of interest for similar bonds is 10%, so the bonds sold at $97\frac{3}{4}$.

Required:
1. Provide the necessary journal entry to record the issuing of these securities, using the proportional method.
2. Assume that the market value of the preferred shares could not be determined. Using the incremental method, prepare the journal entry for issuing these securities.

Problem 13-3: Treasury Stock Transactions. Accutron Inc. has been in business for several years. During 2004, the company's stock price was depressed due to the company announcing that product demand in some foreign markets was less than expected. As a result, the company is planning to support the stock price by purchasing some of its shares on the open market. Details relating to the company's stockholders' equity at the beginning of the year are as follows.

Common stock (2,000,000 shares registered, 1,200,000 shares issued and outstanding)	$2,400,000
Paid-in capital in excess of par	7,200,000
Retained earnings	1,800,000

On May 19, 2004, Accutron purchased 150,000 shares of its common stock at a price of $6 per share. Six months later, the company resold 100,000 shares of the stock for $775,000. The remaining 50,000 shares were retired. Assume that the original proceeds received from the retired shares was equal to the average proceeds received from all shares outstanding.

Required:
1. What is the par value of Accutron's stock?
2. Using the cost method, prepare the journal entry to record the purchase of Accutron's stock.
3. Prepare the journal entry to sell the 100,000 shares of treasury stock.

4. How would the entry in Requirement 3 differ if the proceeds were $550,000?
5. Prepare the journal entry to retire the 50,000 treasury shares.
6. **(Appendix)** Redo Requirements 2 through 5 using the par value method.
7. Would purchasing treasury stock affect EPS? Would purchasing treasury stock affect the company's stock price? Why? How would the stock price be affected when the treasury shares are resold?
8. Considering your answers to Requirement 7 and all other possible factors, what are some reasons a company might repurchase its own shares?

Problem 13-4: Preparing the Stockholders' Equity Section. Baker's Bread, Inc., was organized several years ago and has operated at a profit. The balances of the stockholders' equity accounts as of January 1, 2004, are as follows:

Common stock ($1 par value)	$ 50,000
Paid-in capital in excess of par	250,000
Retained earnings	184,000

During 2004, the company had the following transactions:

Feb. 15	Declared cash dividends of $1 per share.
Mar. 1	Extraordinary loss was recorded in the amount of $15,000.
May 5	Appropriated retained earnings for $100,000 for future plant expansion.
June 10	Paid the dividends that were declared in February.
July 1	Issued 5,000 shares of $100 par value, 8%, preferred stock at $104.
Aug. 15	Purchased 2,000 shares of common stock at $7. The company uses the cost method.
Nov. 1	Accepted subscriptions to 5,000 shares of common stock at $15 per share. Collected 30% and the rest is due by February 1.
Dec. 31	In addition to the extraordinary loss on March 1, income from operations was $72,000.
Dec. 31	Declared dividends on preferred stock.

Required:
Prepare the company's stockholders' equity section in good form for the year ending December 31, 2004. Use separate paid-in capital accounts for the common and preferred stock.

Problem 13-5: Stockholders' Equity Transactions (Comprehensive). The charter of KeKee authorized issuing 20,000 shares of $100 par, 6% preferred stock, and 200,000 shares of no par, common stock. The following transactions occurred during the first year of operations:

a. The promoters sold 10,000 shares of preferred stock at $110 per share.
b. Subscriptions were received for an additional 1,000 shares of preferred stock at $112 per share, 25% of the subscription amount was collected, and the balance is to be paid in three months.
c. Each of the four promoters was issued 2,000 shares of common stock at $25 per share. Each promoter paid 25% of the price, and the remaining amount was considered to be payment for promotional activities. The shares were issued.
d. Purchased 400 shares of the company's own preferred stock at $98 a share. KeKee uses the cost method to account for treasury stock transactions.
e. An institutional investor was sold 100 shares of preferred stock and 500 shares of common stock for $22,000. The stock was issued. At the time, the preferred

stock was selling for $110 per share, but the common stock was not being publicly traded.

f. Collected the complete amount owed from the subscribers of 900 shares of stock (see Transaction No. 2) and issued the shares of stock. The subscribers to the other 100 shares defaulted on their shares, and according to state law, the amounts previously collected are refunded and the subscription contract canceled.

g. Reissued 250 shares of the previously acquired preferred stock. The stock was issued at $105 a share.

h. Retired 100 shares of the preferred stock that was being carried in the treasury. The shares are not identified with any particular issuance.

i. Issued 5,000 shares of common stock for a used plant. The plant had been independently appraised at $100,000 and was carried on the seller's books at $40,000.

j. The company reported a net income of $20,000 for the year.

k. $10,000 of dividends were declared and distributed.

Required:

1. Prepare journal entries for these transactions.
2. Prepare the stockholders' equity section for KeKee, using just one paid-in capital account.

Problem 13-6: Stockholders' Equity (Comprehensive). The following transactions were incurred by the XYZ Corporation during its first year of operations:

May 15   Received authorization to issue 1 million shares of $5 par value common stock and 100,000 shares of $50 par, 5%, preferred stock.

June 1   Issued 85,000 shares of common stock for $595,000.

June 1   Issued 32,000 shares of common stock for a tract of land with building. No available fair value could be obtained on the land and building, so the fair value of the stock was used to measure the transaction. Thirty percent of the total value was assigned as the cost of the land, and the rest was assigned as the cost of the building.

July 1   Accepted subscriptions to 30,000 shares of common stock at $8 per share and collected 30% of the subscription price. The remaining amount is to be paid equally by September 1.

July 1   Issued 10,000 shares of common and 2,000 shares of preferred stock for some equipment that was valued at $220,000.

Sept. 1   Subscribers to 90% of the subscribed stock finished paying for their stock, and the appropriate number of shares were issued. Subscribers to the other 10% were considered to be in default, and according to state statute, the amounts they had paid previously were refunded to them.

Nov. 1   Purchased on the open market 10,000 shares of common stock at $10 per share and held them in the treasury. XYZ uses the cost method of accounting for treasury stock transactions.

Nov. 15   Purchased on the open market 10,000 shares of common stock at $11 per share and retired them. (Base computations to the paid-in capital in excess of par account on the average paid-in amounts.)

Dec. 1   Reissued 3,000 shares of the common stock that were being held in the treasury at $14 per share. (As necessary, use the paid-in capital, treasury stock account.)

Dec. 29   Reissued 3,000 shares of the common stock that were being held in the treasury at $8 per share. (As necessary, use the paid-in capital, treasury stock account.)

Required:

1. Prepare journal entries for these transactions.
2. Assuming that net income for the year was $40,000, prepare the stockholders' equity section of the balance sheet as of December 31. Use only one paid-in capital account.

Problem 13-7: Stockholders' Equity Transactions (Comprehensive). Cher Inc. is a public company whose shares are traded in the over-the-counter market. At December 31, 2003, Cher had 6,000,000 authorized shares of $5 par value common stock, of which 2,000,000 shares were issued and outstanding. The stockholders' equity accounts at December 31, 2003, had the following balances:

Common stock, $5 par	$10,000,000
Additional paid-in capital	7,500,000
Retained earnings	3,250,000

Transactions during 2004 and other information relating to the stockholders' equity accounts were as follows:

a. On January 5, 2004, Cher issued at $54 per share 100,000 shares of $50 par value, 9%, cumulative, preferred stock. Cher had 250,000 authorized shares of preferred stock. The preferred stock has a liquidation value of $55 per share.

b. On February 1, 2004, Cher reacquired 20,000 shares of its common stock for $16 per share. Cher uses the cost method to account for treasury stock.

c. On April 30, 2004, Cher completed an additional public offering of 50,000 shares of its $5 par value common stock. The stock was sold to the public at $12 per share, not including costs of $10,000.

d. On June 17, 2004, Cher declared a cash dividend of $1 per share of common stock, payable on July 10, 2004, to stockholders of record on July 1, 2004.

e. On November 6, 2004, Cher sold 10,000 shares of treasury stock for $21 per share.

f. On December 7, 2004, Cher declared the yearly cash dividend on preferred stock, payable on January 7, 2005, to stockholders of record on December 31, 2004.

g. On December 24, 2004, Cher accepted subscriptions to 20,000 shares of common stock at $20 per share. Cash was collected for $150,000. The remaining amount is due by March 1, 2005.

h. On December 31, 2004, Cher appropriated retained earnings for $100,000 for future plant expansion.

i. On January 17, 2005, before the books were closed for 2004, Cher became aware that the ending inventories at December 31, 2003, were overstated by $200,000. The after-tax effect on 2003 net income was $140,000. Cher uses a perpetual inventory system.

j. After correction of the beginning inventories, net income for 2004 was $2,250,000.

Required:

1. Prepare journal entries (where required) for each of these transactions.
2. Prepare the stockholders' equity section of Cher's balance sheet at December 31, 2004, keeping the paid-in capital on preferred stock separate from the paid-in capital on common stock.

Problem 13-8: Stockholders' Equity Section.

Required:

Use the following information and construct in columnar format the stockholders' equity for Magleby & Sons for 2005, with the 2004 data presented for comparison.

Data	2005	2004
Number of shares of common stock issued at January 1	To be computed	993,350
Par value of the common stock	$10	$10
Shares of common stock issued during the year	11,200 at $50 per share	4,500 at $40 per share
Number of shares in the treasury at January 1; Magleby uses the cost method to account for treasury stock	To be computed	3,000 that had been reacquired at an average cost of $38 per share
Shares of treasury stock acquired during the year	37,500 at $48 per share	2,600 at $45 per share
Shares of treasury stock issued under option plans during the year	2,800 at option price of $35 per share	2,600 at option price of $35 per share
Net income/(loss) for the year	$120,000	$(178,000)
Balance of paid-in capital at January 1 (all sources)	To be computed	$920,000
Balance of retained earnings at January 1	To be computed	$890,000

No attempt was made to identify the particular shares of treasury stock that were issued under the stock option plans. There is no paid-in capital from treasury stock transactions.

Problem 13-9: Stockholders' Equity Section.

Required:

From the following information, prepare in columnar format the stockholders' equity section of the balance sheet for Appalachian Mountains Computer Manufacturers.

Data	2005	2004
Beginning balances, January 1		
Number of common shares issued, $5 par	To be computed	146,000
Number of shares in the treasury at a total cost of $596,800	To be computed	23,000
Total amount received from issuing common stock	To be computed	$1,168,000
Retained earnings	To be computed	$1,777,000
Accumulated other comprehensive income	To be computed	$154,000 credit
Common stock issued during the year	None	50,000 shares at $69 per share
Common stock repurchased; Appalachian uses the cost method to account for treasury stock	5,000 shares at $64	11,500 shares at $64 per share
Treasury shares used in acquiring another company that became a subsidiary of Appalachian; shares were from those acquired in 2004	None	9,800

Data	2005	2004
Treasury stock retired that was repurchased prior to 2004	None	10,000
Translation adjustments: gain/(loss)	$4,000	$(5,600)
Unrealized holding gain/(loss) on available-for-sale securities	$15,000	$12,300
Net income	$750,000	$1,050,000
Dividends declared	$400,000	$400,000
Dividends paid	$200,000	$400,000

The treasury shares at December 31, 2004, had been reacquired at an average price of $40. The treasury shares that were retired had been purchased before 2004.

Cases

Case 13-1: Safeway Incorporated. Look up Safeway Incorporated's Form 10-K for the fiscal year 2001, registered with the SEC. Refer to the company's financial statements and accompanying notes to answer the following questions:

1. What types of shareholders' equity accounts does the company have?
2. Identify the dividends paid by the company. Using the stock price at the close of the fiscal year, what is the dividend yield (Dividends/Stock price)?
3. What is the company's return on equity? Does the company have treasury stock? If so, what would have been the company's return on equity if the Italian way of classifying treasury stock as an asset had been followed?
4. What is the company's earnings per share? Book value per share? Market value per share? What does a comparison of the company's book value per share and market value per share reveal about the company?

Research Activities

Activity 13-1: Dividends, Treasury Stock, and Stock Prices. An article by Christopher Farrel appeared in the May 11, 1998 issue of *Business Week*, entitled "Does the Dividend Yield Even Matter?" Read the article, and answer the following questions:

a. How is the dividend yield calculated? Explain the rule of thumb identified in the article related to a trading strategy that involves the dividend yield.
b. Is the author suggesting that the stock market was overvalued at the time of the article's writing? Why or why not?
c. The author suggests that stock repurchases are an alternative to dividends and help to boost the stock price. Explain the accounting for stock repurchases. Why is the stock price likely to increase after a repurchase?
d. Hindsight is 20/20. Provide a year-by-year analysis of the S&P 500 Index since the writing of the article in May 1998. Was the author correct in his assertion?

14

More Transactions
WITH AND
Reports TO Owners

At one time, it was relatively easy to differentiate between debt and equity securities, principally because there were very few varieties of either type and the characteristics of each were clearly different from the other. However, as the economy has become more complex, a greater variety of securities has been created, typically by intermixing the characteristics of debt and equity securities to form a hybrid security. Now, it is sometimes difficult to clearly distinguish between debt and equity securities, and with the increased variety of securities has come increased complexity of accounting and financial reporting. Consider, for example, the following scenario.

A company issues at par $1.25 billion of 4% notes payable that are convertible to shares of the company's common stock at the holders' option. In addition to a low interest rate, other features that make these notes unattractive as an investment is that they are unsecured and subordinated to all existing and future senior indebtedness. As discussed in Chapter 11, due to the lower-than-market interest rate (and other undesirable characteristics), these 4% notes should sell at a huge discount. However, the notes may sell at a premium. This can only be explained as the market perceiving that there is significant value to the opportunity to convert the notes into shares of common stock. Apparently, the market may place more value upon them as equity securities than as debt securities.

Questions

1. Regardless of the label, are these equity securities?

2. Due to having both debt and equity features, should the notes be viewed as two securities?

3. If it is logical to view the notes as two securities, how should the price be allocated between them—especially since exercising the conversion option means the security must be surrendered, and so there are not separate market quotations for the notes and the conversion feature?

4. Where on the balance sheet should this security be reported?

Another interesting accounting question concerns measuring compensation under stock option agreements. A large amount of publicity has surrounded large multinational companies regarding the compensation of their CEOs. As Exhibit 14-1 shows, most of this compensation is in the form of stock options. Also, many growth companies rely almost entirely on stock options to compensate executives because such companies do not have sufficient cash or other assets to pay for high-quality managerial talent.

When stock options are granted, the corporation issues executives the opportunity to acquire shares of stock at a price that may be at or below the market price when the options are granted. After the options are exercised, the executives may sell the stock on the open market and recognize a substantial profit. For the corporation, no cost is incurred, as no assets are distributed or liabilities incurred.

Questions

1. What amount should be reported as compensation expense?

2. If compensation expense is recorded, what is the offsetting account—is it a liability, a revenue, or a stockholders' equity account?

The accounting for dividends paid in cash was covered in Chapter 13. There remain unanswered issues about dividends.

Questions

1. How are dividend transactions recorded when assets other than cash are distributed?

2. How are dividend transactions recorded when the company's own stock is distributed as a dividend?

3. What is the appropriate accounting for stock splits?

EXHIBIT 14-1

Executive Compensation for Selected Companies for the 1998 Fiscal Year

Company Name	Executive Name	Salary	Bonus	Other Compensation	No. of Options Granted
Ebay Inc.	Margaret Whitman	$ 145,833	$ 100,000	$ 1,500	7,200,000
America Online Inc.	Stephen Case	500,000	1,000,000	0	900,000
Yahoo Inc.	Timothy Koogle	195,000	0	0	550,000
Lycos Inc.	Robert Davis	170,000	80,000	0	1,300,000
Time-Warner Inc.	Gerald Levine	1,000,000	7,800,000	186,861	1,400,000
Novell Inc.	Eric Schmidt	354,347	374,796	0	2,750,000

Learning Objectives

- Prepare the journal entries under the book value and the fair value methods for convertible debt at issuance and when converting the debt security to common stock.

- Prepare the journal entries for securities that have detachable warrants, where the security does not have to be surrendered to exercise the conversion feature, at issuance and when converting the security to common stock.

- Prepare the journal entries for stock warrants that are issued in connection with the preemptive right.

- Outline the political controversy that surrounded the formulating and issuing of *SFAS No. 123*.

- Explain how compensation expense is computed for stock options using the Black-Scholes option pricing model.

- Prepare the journal entries for executive (i.e., compensatory) stock options, using both the intrinsic and fair value methods.

- Explain the accounting for property, liquidating, script, and stock dividends.

- Compare the effects on total stockholders' equity and the various stockholders' equity accounts for (1) stock dividends, (2) stock splits, and (3) stock splits effected in the form of a dividend.

- Explain the financial reporting for prior-period adjustments and restate the statement of retained earnings or the statement of changes in stockholders' equity accordingly.

- Prepare the statement of changes in stockholders' equity.

Accounting for Securities with Some Equity Characteristics

Convertible Debt

Convertible debt is any debt security that may be converted, at the option of the holder, into shares of capital stock (usually common stock) of the issuing corporation. The contract between the corporation and the holder of the debt defines both the time when the conversion feature may be exercised and the number of shares to be received at conversion. The following features are typical of convertible debt.

- The contracted interest rate is below, sometimes considerably below, the interest rate that would have been required for nonconvertible bonds, thus indicating that part of the price at issuance is due to the opportunity to convert to equity securities.
- At the time the debt is issued, the value of the debt security is greater than the market value of the common stock into which it can be converted. For instance, a convertible bond is issued for $980, which can be converted into 50 shares of common stock; at the time the bond is issued, the common stock is selling for $9 per share. Hence, the initial value of the debt security (i.e., $980) is greater than the value of the common stock into which the bond can be converted (i.e., $450, which is computed as 50 shares multiplied by $9 per share). So the buyer of the convertible bond bears a risk that is reduced by the guaranteed interest received if conversion does not occur.
- The initial conversion rate does not decrease except for antidilution provisions, such as stock splits or stock dividends. Using the same example, the number of shares of common stock the bondholder would receive would not decrease below 50 per bond except for stock dividends, stock splits, etc., that are declared. If, for instance, a 2-for-1 reverse stock split is declared, then the bondholders would receive 25 shares for each bond converted.
- Usually, the convertible debt is callable at the option of the issuer. So the issuer can put some pressure on the bondholders to convert.

Convertible debt often has advantages for both the issuer and the holder. The issuer has the initial advantage of a lower interest rate. Also, if the market price of the underlying capital stock increases, the issuer of the debt can force conversion of the debt by exercising the call privilege, which effectively eliminates the debt. If the market price of the underlying capital stock does not increase, the issuer of the debt obtains the use of the cash at a relatively low interest cost. The advantages to the purchaser of the debt are the protection and security of a known, guaranteed interest rate coupled with the opportunity for price appreciation should the market price of the stock increase.

From the foregoing description of convertible debt, it can be seen that the price of the bond is partly due to its equity features (i.e., price appreciation of the bond because the stock of the company increases) and partly due to its debt features (i.e., guaranteed interest). Thus, convertible debt is a hybrid security. Because of its hybrid nature, two views of accounting are held for convertible debt. *One view is to account for the equity features separately from the debt features.* Proponents of this view propose that the amount to be assigned to the equity security (or to be accounted for as paid-in capital) can be computed as the difference between the amount received for the debt and the *expected amount* that would have been received if the debt had been issued without the conversion feature.

The other view of accounting for convertible debt is to account for the entire proceeds received as debt capital. Proponents of this view state that, although eq-

This Is the Real World

In mid-2002, Western investors were buying billions of dollars of convertible bonds on the Japanese stock market. Interestingly, the bonds offered little or no interest for years. Investors were buying them because (1) they were virtually guaranteed not to lose money, and (2) they were betting that the Japanese stock market would rebound. For example, in May 2002, Mitsubishi raised $1.2 billion from issuing zero-coupon bonds that matured in nine years. Before maturity, the bonds pay no interest, and at maturity the company will repay creditors in shares of the company's stock if the stock price is up more than 25% from the time of sale. If the shares do not rise that much, Mitsubishi will pay back only the principal of the debt.

uity features are present, the value of such are inseparable from the value of the debt. That is, the holder of the debt cannot sell one right (e.g., the debt portion) and retain the other (e.g., the equity portion); nor can the holder exercise the option to convert into stock and keep the right to receive interest. Even though an allocation of the issue price may be possible, proponents of this view state that accounting for the two features independently is practically impossible.

Conversion Feature Inseparable from the Debt

When considering the matter, the APB stated that *when the conversion feature is inseparable from the debt "no portion of the proceeds . . . should be accounted for as attributable to the conversion feature."*[1] The APB was swayed by the argument of the inseparability of the debt and equity features. It also ruled that it is not possible to give guidance on all types of debt with conversion features and that the accounting for all such should be done in accordance with the substance of the transaction.

To illustrate, assume that Smart Enterprises issued 1,000 convertible bonds on January 2, 2002, at 97¾, due in 10 years and paying 5% annual interest. Each bond is convertible into 40 shares of Smart's common stock any time after January 2, 2005. The journal entry to record the issuance of the convertible bonds is as follows:

Cash (1,000 bonds × $1,000/bond × 97¾)	977,500	
Discount on Bonds	22,500	
Bonds Payable		1,000,000

To record the issuance of convertible debt where the entire proceeds are assigned to debt.

The subsequent accounting for convertible debt entails accounting for interest and possible early retirements, as illustrated in Chapter 11, and expedited by preparing a bond amortization table. As always, the effective-interest method should be used to amortize any bond discount or premium, unless the results obtained from the straight-line method are not materially different.

Converting Debt to Equity—Book Value Method

The **book value method** seems to be the most popular method of accounting for bonds or any other debt instrument that is converted into equity securities or for preferred stock that is converted into common stock. It is the method most in accord with GAAP. Under this method:

- The bonds (or other debt securities) are amortized up to the date that they are converted. (This procedure was illustrated in Chapter 11.)

---

[1] *APB Opinion No. 14,* "Accounting for Convertible Debt and Debt Issued with Stock Purchase Warrants," par. 12, emphasis added.

- The carrying amount of the bonds (or other debt) being converted is removed from the books, along with its associated bond premium/discount. The common stock account is credited for the par value of the number of shares issued.
- Any unamortized bond issue costs associated with the bonds being converted is removed from the accounts.
- The difference is accounted for as additional paid-in capital; no gain or loss is recognized. (This accords with the notion that gains/losses are not recognized on transactions with owners in their role as owners.)

Thus, the entire transaction is accounted for at the book value of the bonds being retired. Continuing with the previous example, suppose that on January 2, 2006, 40% of the holders of Smart Enterprises' bonds exercised their option and converted their bonds into 16,000[2] shares of Smart's $10 par common stock that was selling at $26 per share.[3] Smart elects to use the straight-line method of amortization, since the results were not materially different from what would have resulted under the effective-interest method. At the date of conversion, the balance in Discount on Bonds was $13,500. The entry to record this conversion, using the book value method, is as follows:

Bonds Payable (400 bonds × $1,000 face amount)	400,000	
Discount on Bonds (40% × $13,500)		5,400
Common Stock (16,000 shares × $10)		160,000
Paid-In Capital, Bond Conversion (difference)		234,600

To record the conversion of bonds into shares of common stock using the book value method.

Converting Debt to Equity—Fair Value Method

Some accountants prefer that the converting of securities into common stock be measured at the fair value of the common stock being issued rather than the book value of the securities being surrendered. This method is called the **fair value** or **market method**. When using the fair value method, the securities being surrendered are removed from the books in the same way as described under the book value method, but the paid-in capital account that relates to the common stock being issued is credited for the difference between the fair value and the par value of the common stock. As a result, a gain or loss is recorded for the difference between the fair value of the stock issued and the carrying value of the bonds retired, including any amount for bond issue costs.

Suppose, in the previous example, that Smart Enterprises uses the market value method to account for converting bonds. Then, converting 40% of the bonds on January 2, 2006, when Smart's common stock is selling for $26 per share is recorded as follows:

Bonds Payable (400 bonds × $1,000 face amount)	400,000	
Loss on Conversion (difference)	21,400	
Discount on Bonds (40% × $13,500)		5,400
Common Stock (16,000 shares × $10)		160,000
Paid-In Capital, Bond Conversion [16,000 × ($26 − $10)]		256,000

To record the conversion of bonds into shares of common stock using the fair value method.

---

[2]The 16,000 shares is computed as 400 bonds (which is 40% of the 1,000 bonds issued) multiplied by 40 shares per bond.
[3]Note that with the stock selling at $26 per share, the bondholders have an economic incentive to convert their bonds into shares of stock.

Note that the only differences between the two methods of accounting for converting bonds into stock are (1) the amount credited to Paid-In Capital and (2) the presence of a gain/loss under the fair value method.

Book Value versus Fair Value

Those accountants who express a preference for the book value method base their position upon the idea that the selling and subsequent converting of bonds into stock is a single transaction. That is, the converting of bonds into stock is the culmination of the transaction that began when the bonds were issued. So any difference between the carrying amount of the bonds and the par value of the stock is accounted for as paid-in capital. Accountants who favor the fair value method defend their position using the idea that the selling and subsequent converting of bonds into stock are two transactions. Hence, the issuing of the bonds is accounted for at the fair value of that transaction, and the converting of bonds into stock, being a separate transaction, is also accounted for at fair value. Currently, GAAP indicates a preference for the book value method in that *APB Opinion No. 14* explains the book value method when bonds are converted and does not mention the fair value method.

Induced Conversions

Occasionally, the issuer of convertible debt desires that the debt holders convert their debt securities into stock. Typically, the issuer's incentive is to avoid paying interest. To encourage conversion, the issuer adds an inducement, called a **sweetener**, to the conversion privilege. Examples of such inducements include more favorable conversion ratios, cash payments, and opportunities to acquire additional stock at a later date. The accounting for all such sweeteners is to expense the fair value of them in the period that conversion occurs.[4]

Suppose, for example, that the holders of the remaining Smart Enterprises bonds (i.e., 60% of them) were encouraged to convert their bonds into stock by Smart adding a sweetener. The sweetener allows the debt holders for a limited time to convert their bonds into 45 shares of stock per bond, which is 5 shares of stock more than previously. Assume further that at the time of conversion the market price of each share of stock was $23 per share and that the balance in Discount on Bonds was $8,100. Then, the entry to record the induced conversion under the book value method, including recognizing the value of the sweetener as an expense of the period, is as follows:

Bonds Payable	600,000	
Bond Conversion Expense		
(600 bonds × 5 shares/bond × $23 share)	69,000	
Discount on Bonds		8,100
Common Stock		
(600 bonds × 45 shares/bond × $10 par)		270,000
Paid-In Capital in Excess of Par (difference)		390,900

To record the fair value of the sweetener as an expense.

The book value method was used to prepare the preceding entry. When the fair value or market method is used to account for induced conversions, all amounts in this entry are computed in the same manner, except for the paid-in capital in excess of par. That amount is computed as the difference between the

---

[4]*Statement of Financial Accounting Standard No. 84*, "Induced Conversions of Convertible Debt," Stamford: Financial Accounting Standards Board, March 1985, par. 3.

current fair value of the stock and the par value, multiplied by the number of shares issued. Any difference between the debits and credits in the journal entry is accounted for as a gain or loss, whichever is appropriate.

Debt Issued with Detachable Stock Warrants (i.e., Rights)

When the conversion feature can be separated from the debt,[5] as when debt is issued with detachable stock warrants,[6] the APB stated that the *amount received is allocated between the debt and the warrants, based upon their relative values*, if known.[7] When the fair value of either security is not known, then the incremental method is used, where the cost of one security is determined based upon its fair value and the remaining amount is assigned as the cost of the other security.

Suppose that instead of issuing convertible bonds, Smart Enterprises issued 1,000 bonds on January 2, 2002, at $97\frac{3}{4}$, due in 10 years and paying 5% interest, with each bond having two detachable stock warrants that allow the holder to exchange each warrant for a share of stock at a specified price. After issuance, the bonds had a market price of $96\frac{1}{2}$, and the market price of a warrant was $4. Given these facts, the issue price of $977,500 (i.e., 1,000 bonds × $97\frac{3}{4}$ × $1,000 face amount) is allocated between the bonds and warrants, as follows:

Determining the relative fair values of the securities:

Fair value of the bonds:
  1,000 bonds × $1,000 face amount × $96\frac{1}{2}$% = $965,000
Fair value of the warrants:
  1,000 bonds × 2 warrants/bond × $4 each =   8,000
  Total fair value $973,000

Allocating issue price:

To the bonds: ($965,000/$973,000) × $977,500 = $969,463
To the warrants: ($8,000/$973,000) × $977,500 = $8,037

The journal entry to record issuing the debt with detachable stock warrants is as follows:

Cash (given)	977,500	
Discount on Bonds (difference between cost allocated to the bonds and the par value of the bonds)	30,537	
Bonds Payable (par value)		1,000,000
Paid-In Capital—Stock Warrants (allocated amount)		8,037

To record the issuing of bonds with detachable warrants.

[5]The wording used and the example given is in reference to a debt security, but the same concepts apply if warrants are attached to equity securities.
[6]A warrant is a certificate, either separate or attached to another security (such as a bond or preferred stock), that entitles the holder to purchase stock within a stated period at a stated price. The accounting procedures described here for warrants attached to debt are also used when detachable warrants are attached to stock.
[7]*APB Opinion No. 14*, "Accounting for Convertible Debt and Debt Issued with Stock Purchase Warrants," par. 12, emphasis added.

Exercising the warrants requires that they be surrendered and cash paid for the amount specified. Consistent with the notion that gains/losses are not recognized on transactions with owners, *exercising the conversion feature affects the paid-in capital accounts, and no gain/loss is recognized*, nor is Retained Earnings affected. So suppose that the holders of Smart Enterprises stock warrants exercised them and paid the required $20 per share at a time when the stock was selling for $25 each. The journal entry to record the exercising of the stock warrants is as follows:

Cash (2,000 warrants × $20 per share)	40,000	
Paid-In Capital—Stock Warrants (see previous entry)	8,037	
Common Stock (2,000 shares × $10 par)		20,000
Paid-In Capital in Excess of Par (difference)		28,037

To record the exercise of stock warrants.

If the holder of the warrants lets them lapse (perhaps because the market price of the stock declined and made the warrants worthless), the issuing corporation does not recognize a loss but instead reclassifies the paid-in capital from stock warrants to another appropriately titled paid-in capital account, such as Paid-In Capital from Lapsing of Stock Warrants.

Stock Warrants

Other than issuing warrants with other securities to make the securities more attractive, a corporation may also issue warrants (1) in connection with the preemptive right, where a corporation (prior to issuing shares of stock to the public) sends warrants to present stockholders allowing them to buy shares of the company's stock, and (2) to executives and/or employees, granting them the opportunity to buy shares of the company's stock, which are called **stock options**. For both types of warrants, the certificate granting the right to acquire shares of the company's stock states:

- The stipulated price at which the stock can be purchased,
- The date that the warrant first can be exercised,
- The number of shares that can be purchased, and
- The expiration date.

Regardless of the way in which warrants are issued, generally one share of stock can be purchased for each warrant exercised. However, occasionally, several or even many warrants must be surrendered and the exercise price paid to acquire a share of stock.

Stock Warrants in Connection with the Preemptive Right

To encourage stockholders to exercise warrants, *the issuing corporation may state an exercise price that is less than the current market price of the stock, which then gives a value to the warrants*. The three important dates connected with stock warrants are:

- The date the corporation announces that the warrants will be offered,
- The date the warrants are issued, and
- The date the warrants expire.

Shares of the corporation's stock that are sold between the announcement date and the date the warrants are issued are sold **rights-on**, meaning that the buyer of the stock also buys the accompanying right to acquire stock at a reduced price. Shares of the corporation's stock that are sold after the date the warrants are issued and before the warrants expire are sold **ex-rights**, meaning that acquiring a share of stock does not carry with it the right to also buy the stock at a reduced price. From the time the stock warrants are issued to their expiration date, stock warrants are bought and sold just like any other security.

Issuing/Receipt of the Warrants

From the standpoint of the issuing corporation, issuing stock warrants does not result in assets of the corporation being distributed (or more assets being received), a liability or an expense being incurred, or revenue being earned. So when a corporation issues stock warrants in connection with the preemptive right, all the issuing corporation need do is make a memorandum entry stating the number of warrants that were issued, the number of shares that may be purchased, the exercise price, and the expiration date.

The percentage ownership in the corporation for investors who receive the stock warrants does not change nor does the value of their investment increase. However, investors have more pieces of paper over which the cost that they paid must be allocated. This allocating of the cost paid for the investment is done according to the relationship of the fair value of the stock purchased to the fair value of the warrants, when both fair values are known. When the fair values of both securities are not known, then the incremental method of allocating the cost is used.

To illustrate, assume that Jensen owns 500 shares of Shoot-the-Works Corporation's $5 par value common stock that Jensen purchased several years previously for $20 per share, for a total of $10,000. In the current year, Shoot-the-Works announced that warrants would be issued on April 1, permitting a share of stock to be obtained by surrendering four warrants and paying $24. On April 1, Jensen received 500 warrants when the stock price was $46 per share, and the warrants immediately began trading for $4 per share. Jensen accounts for the receipt of the stock warrants by allocating the $10,000 cost paid for the stock between the warrants and the stock, as follows:

Total fair value of the stock on April 1	
(500 shares × $46 per share)	$23,000
Total fair value of the warrants on April 1	
(500 warrants × $4/warrant)	2,000
Total fair value	$25,000

The amount of the $10,000 cost that is allocated to the warrants is then determined as follows: ($2,000/$25,000) × $10,000 = $800.

An important point in this allocation is that the cost of each share of stock to Jensen is no longer the $20 paid to acquire it, but is now $18.40, which is computed as the initial $10,000 paid to acquire the 500 shares less the $800 amount allocated to the stock warrants, divided by the 500 shares. In equation form, this amount is determined as follows:

$$\text{Cost per share of stock} = (\$10,000 - \$800)/500 \text{ shares}$$

$$= \$18.40 \text{ per share}$$

Also, the cost per stock warrant is the $800 amount divided by the 500 warrants owned, or $1.60 per right. Jensen's journal entry to record the allocation of the $10,000 between the stock and the stock warrants is as follows:

Investment in Stock Warrants	800	
Investment in Stock		800
To apportion the cost of the investment between the stock and the		
warrants.		

Subsequent Sale of Warrants and Stock

Following the receipt of warrants, the investor can (1) sell them, (2) exercise them and buy shares of stock, or (3) allow them to lapse. For any of these options, the accounting for the stock warrants is the same as with any other investment. So if Jensen subsequently sold 200 warrants at $4 each, Jensen's entry is as follows:

Cash (200 warrants × $4 per warrant)	800	
Investment in Stock Warrants (200 warrants × $1.60		
per warrant)		320
Gain on Sale of Stock Warrants		480
To record sale of warrants.		

If Jensen subsequently sold 200 shares of stock after having allocated the original cost between the shares and the warrants, the accounting is as follows:

Cash (200 shares × $46 per share)	9,200	
Investment in Stock (200 shares × $18.40 per share)		3,680
Gain on Sale of Stock		5,520
To record sale of shares of stock after allocating the original cost of the		
investment between the warrants and the stock.		

Exercising the Warrants

The investor exercises the warrants by surrendering them to the issuing corporation and paying the specified amount to acquire a share of stock. So if Jensen exercised 240 of the warrants and acquired 60 shares of stock at the specified exercise price of $24 per share, then Jensen's journal entry is as follows:

Investment in Stock	1,824	
Cash (60 shares × $24 per share)		1,440
Investment in Warrants (240 × $1.60)		384
To exercise warrants.		

The associated journal entry made by the issuing corporation is as follows:

Cash	1,440	
Common Stock		300
Paid-In Capital in Excess of Par		1,140
Issued common stock.		

Warrants Lapse

If Jensen allowed its remaining 60 warrants to lapse (perhaps because there was a sudden and marked decline in the stock price that made it unwise to buy additional shares of stock at $24 per share, and as a result, there also was no value to the warrants), then Jensen's journal entry is as follows:

Loss on Expiration of Warrants	96	
Investment in Warrants (60 warrants × $1.60		
per warrant)		96
To record expiration of warrants.		

The issuing corporation makes no journal entry when warrants lapse.

Stock Options

The granting of stock options to executives and other employees has become an extremely popular form of compensation for corporations. The notion behind employee stock options is that by employees becoming potential owners, they will be more likely to take actions that will be in harmony with the goals of other shareholders. Thus, stock options may motivate managers to work harder and build company loyalty. Furthermore, stock options can be a valuable source of executive compensation and thereby allow small, high-tech companies with smaller supplies of cash to nevertheless attract top managerial talent on the potential that their stock price will increase significantly in the future.

Not all stock option plans are meant to compensate executives for services rendered or to be rendered. At times, the corporation's intent is to raise additional funds through the issuing of stock. For these noncompensatory plans, the corporation does not recognize any expense. The essential nature of **noncompensatory stock option plans** is that:

- Substantially all full-time employees may participate;
- Stock is offered equally to all eligible employees, even though the plan may limit the number of shares that can be purchased;
- The time period to exercise the options is limited to a reasonable time; and
- The grant or option price is essentially equivalent to the market price when the stock options are granted.

© PRNEWSFOTO/CHICAGO STOCK EXCHANGE

All stock option plans that do not have these characteristics are **compensatory stock option plans** and are accounted for either according to *APB Opinion No. 25*, "Accounting for Stock Issued to Employees," or *SFAS No. 123*, "Accounting for Stock-Based Compensation."

The long and tedious process of issuing *SFAS No. 123* is an excellent example of the political nature of accounting standard setting and how ultimate standards often are the best compromise acceptable to all parties. In an exposure draft, the FASB proposed that the fair value of all stock options granted to employees be expensed on the income statement as compensation expense. Political pressure from various constituents resulted in the final standard allowing companies to either record the fair value as an expense or disclose pro forma earnings-per-share numbers in the notes as if the fair value had been expensed. Virtually all companies have chosen the latter option of disclosing in the notes to the financial statements instead of expensing the amount in the income statement. Although issuing stock options to employees is not accompanied by the transfer of any asset, current stockholders should be concerned about the potential dilution of their ownership and the dilutive effect that stock options will have on their share of earnings if the options are exercised.[8]

APB Opinion No. 25: The Intrinsic Value Method

For many years, *APB Opinion No. 25*, which was issued in 1972, was the only standard for accounting for stock options. In 1972, models for measuring the fair value of stock options had not been developed, and so *Opinion No. 25* adopted an

---

[8]The whole controversy of including the fair value of stock options on the income statement resurfaced following the Enron scandal. Several bills were debated in Congress, and a bill introduced by Carl Levin would deny lucrative tax benefits to any corporation that did not report the cost of options on the income statement in the same way that other forms of employee compensation are reported.

approach that required companies to expense the **intrinsic value** of the stock options. An intrinsic value is the amount that is considered to be the "true" or "real" worth of an item, given the available facts. *The intrinsic value of a stock option is the difference between the exercise price of the option and the market price of the stock at the **measurement date**, which is the earliest date that both the option price and the number of options are known.* Under the intrinsic method, stock options have no value where the option price and the market price of the stock are the same, or where the option price is less than the market price. When the option price is less than the market price of the stock, the option has value, which is accounted for as compensation expense and is allocated among the years that must be worked to receive the right to the options (i.e., **vesting** or **holding period**).

Fixed Compensatory Plans: Measurement Date Is the Same as the Option Date. Suppose that on December 31, 2003, Dell Computer grants 100,000 stock options to its CEO, Michael Dell. The options expire in five years, but Michael can exercise the options at any time.[9] At the time the options are granted, the market price of Dell Computer stock is $32 per share, and the options have an exercise price of $30 per share. Based upon this information, the measurement date is December 31, 2003, because that is the earliest date that both the number of options (i.e., 100,000) and the option price (i.e., $30) are known, so this is the date that compensation is measured. These options are considered to be "in-the-money," since at grant date the holder of the option can purchase the stock for an amount (i.e., $30) that is lower than the market price of the stock (i.e., $32). Given this information, the compensation expense is $200,000, which is computed by multiplying the $2 difference between the option price and the stock price by the number of options granted. Finally, since the options are immediately exercisable, it appears that they are granted for services already rendered, and therefore the entire compensation amount is recognized immediately. So at the time the options are granted, Dell Computer prepares the following entry. Note that the credit is to a paid-in capital account.

Compensation Expense		
(100,000 options × $2/option)	200,000	
Paid-In Capital—Stock Options		200,000

To record compensation expense for stock options under the intrinsic method as prescribed in APB Opinion No. 25.

To illustrate the accounting for the exercise of stock options, assume that Michael Dell exercised 50,000 options, or one-half of the total options, two years later when the market price of the stock is $40. Also, assume that the par value of the stock is $1. The following journal entry would be made to record the transaction:

Paid-In Capital—Stock Options		
(1/2 of the amount in prior entry)	100,000	
Cash (50,000 options × $30/option)	1,500,000	
Common Stock (50,000 shares × $1 par value)		50,000
Paid-In Capital in Excess of Par (difference)		1,550,000

To record the exercise of stock options.

If the holder of the options fails to exercise some of them, then at the time the options expire, any paid-in capital associated with the options is reclassified from "paid-in capital—stock options" to "paid-in capital—expiration of stock options."

---

[9]The long expiration date is typical of employee stock options, whereas most standardized option contracts that are traded on option exchanges have an expiration date within one year.

To further illustrate the accounting for fixed stock option plans, suppose that Michael Dell was granted 100,000 stock options on December 31, 2003, at an option price of $30 each, but he cannot exercise the options until December 1, 2006. In this situation, it appears that the granting of stock options is not for past services but is intended to compensate Mr. Dell for services that he will render during the next three years. However, the measurement date is still December 31, 2003, because that is the earliest date that both the option price and the number of options are known, and total compensation is still $200,000. However, this compensation amount is recognized over the next three years, and in each year, the following journal entry is prepared:

Compensation Expense	66,666	
Paid-In Capital—Stock Options		66,666

To recognize compensation expense under a stock option plan where the executive must work for three years before exercising the options.

EXTENDING THE CONCEPT

Suppose that on January 1, 2004, a company granted 50,000 stock options to its CEO at an option price of $30 when the stock was selling for $30. The options are exercisable any time from January 1, 2007, through December 31, 2008. Subsequently, on December 31, the stock price was $35 per share. How much compensation expense should the company record for the fiscal year ending December 31, 2004? Why?

Answer: No compensation expense should be recognized because there is no difference between the option price and the stock price on the measurement date.

The entries for exercising stock options under this type of arrangement are the same as previously illustrated.

Variable Compensatory Plans: Measurement Date Is Not the Same as the Option Date. In some stock compensation plans, the number of options, the option price, or both are not known at the date of grant. An example of such a stock compensation plan is **stock appreciation rights**, which differ from traditional stock option plans in that the executive does not have to buy stock and then sell it to obtain the benefit of the plan. Instead he receives a gift of cash (or receives shares of stock or a combination of both) for the difference between the market price and some predetermined price for a specified number of shares of stock. For such plans, the measurement date is subsequent to the grant date and may not occur until several years after the grant date. Hence, estimates of the unknown factors must be used to measure compensation expense. As with traditional stock option plans, *once the estimated compensation expense has been calculated, it is allocated to the years that the executive must work before exercising the rights.*

To illustrate, On January 1, 2005, Olin Computers grants stock appreciation rights to its chief executive. The options are exercisable on January 1, 2008, and the CEO will be paid the increase in the share price from January 1, 2005, to December 31, 2007, multiplied by 50,000 rights. The CEO may choose to be paid in cash or shares of stock of equivalent value. The market price on January 1, 2005, is $40 per share, and on December 31, 2005, it is $43 per share. At December 31, 2005, Olin computes the total compensation expense as the difference between the current market price of $43 and the market price of $40 at January 1, 2005, and then allocates this amount over the 3-year vesting period. Then, the following journal entry is prepared:

Compensation Expense		
[50,000 × ($43 − $40)/3 years]	50,000	
Compensation Liability		50,000

To record estimated compensation expense for a variable stock option plan.

A liability is recognized in this case because, according to the agreement, the CEO can choose to be paid in cash. If the agreement had required shares of stock to be distributed, the credit would be to a paid-in capital account.

Continuing the example, if at December 31, 2006, the market price of the stock is $46 per share, then total compensation expense and the compensation expense to recognize for 2006 are computed as follows:

Market price, December 31, 2006	$ 46 per share
Market price, January 1, 2005 (grant date)	− 40 per share
Stock appreciation	$ 6 per share
Number of stock appreciation rights	× 50,000
Total compensation expense	$300,000
Percent of vesting time elapsed	× 2/3
Total amount of compensation expense to recognize for 2005 and 2006	$200,000
Amount recognized in 2005	50,000
Amount to recognize in 2006	$150,000

Once this amount has been computed, the same journal entry as was done in 2005 is made.

Finishing the example, suppose that at December 31, 2007, the stock price is $45 per share. Then, the amount to recognize as compensation expense for 2007 is computed as follows:

Market price, December 31, 2007	$ 45 per share
Market price, January 1, 2005	− 40 per share
Stock appreciation	$ 5 per share
Number of stock appreciation rights	× 50,000
Total compensation expense	$250,000
Percent of vesting time elapsed	× 100%
Total amount of compensation expense to recognize for 2005, 2006, and 2007	$250,000
Amount recognized in 2005 and 2006	200,000
Amount to recognize in 2007	$ 50,000

So the journal entry at December 31, 2007, is to debit Compensation Expense and credit Compensation Liability for $50,000.

On January 1, 2008, the CEO decided to be paid cash. The entry is to debit Compensation Liability and credit Cash. However, if the CEO opted to receive stock for the total appreciation of $250,000, the following computations, with accompanying journal entry, would be made:

Total compensation expense	$250,000
Stock price at December 31, 2007	÷ $45 per share
Number of shares the CEO is entitled to receive	5,556 (rounded)
Par value of the stock	$10 per share

Compensation Liability	250,000	
Common Stock		55,560
Paid-In Capital in Excess of Par		194,440

To settle with the CEO according to the terms of a variable stock option plan where shares of stock are issued.

If it had happened that a fraction of a share was owed, then (1) the executive may be paid the value of that fractional share, (2) the executive may be required to pay enough so as to receive one more share of stock, or (3) since a fractional share is immaterial, the executive may be given the additional fractional amount of a share to make one share (the alternative used in this example).

In the preceding example, the only unknown component of the stock option plan on the grant date of January 1, 2005, was the price that the stock would be on January 1, 2008. For stock option plans that have more than one unknown component, (e.g., both the market price and the number of options are not known), the same estimation procedures are used. The concept is to estimate the total compensation expense at the end of a year and allocate that amount over the vesting period. The compensation expense for a year is determined by subtracting the amount already recognized from the estimated total compensation expense that should be recognized as of the end of that year. (This is another example of accounting for a change in an accounting estimate.) *It is possible that for a particular year compensation expense is credited, and this is acceptable as long as the total compensation expense in the stock compensation plan for the current and all previous years is not less than zero.*

To illustrate, on December 31, 2005, Dynamics Inc. granted stock options to its president at a time when the stock of the company was $45 per share. The options can be exercised beginning on December 31, 2008, and they expire December 31, 2009. Both the number of options and the option price will be determined when the options first become exercisable, but it is anticipated that there will be 100,000 options granted and that the option price will be 85% of whatever the stock price is on December 31, 2008. The stock prices at the end of each of the years 2006–2008 were as follows:

Year	Stock Price	Estimated Option Price	Compensation
Dec. 31, 2006	$50	$42.50	$7.50
Dec. 31, 2007	54	45.90	8.10
Dec. 31, 2008	48		

Since neither the number of options nor the option price is known when the options were first granted, compensation expense for each year must be estimated, which is done based upon the best estimate of the number of options to be granted and the stock price at the end of the year. So compensation expense for 2006 and 2007 is computed as follows:

2006:　Total estimated compensation expense:
　　　　$7.50 \times 100,000$ options = $750,000
　　　　Compensation expense for 2006:
　　　　$750,000 \times 1/3 = \$250,000$

2007:　Total estimated compensation expense:
　　　　$8.10 \times 100,000$ options = $810,000
　　　　Compensation expense for 2007:
　　　　$(\$810,000 \times 2/3) - \$250,000 = \$290,000$

On December 31, 2008, the board of directors established that 80,000 options would be granted, and the option price would be $45. Based upon this data, the compensation expense for 2008—which *may be negative for one year but cannot be less than zero when totaled for all years*—is computed as follows:

Total compensation expense at 2008:
　　$(\$48 - \$45) \times 80,000$ options = $240,000
Compensation expense for 2008:
　　$\$240,000 - \$250,000 - \$290,000 = \$(300,000)$

The journal entry is to debit Paid-In Capital (or if there was an opportunity to be paid an equivalent amount of cash, the debit is to a liability account) and to credit Compensation Expense.

Criticism of the Intrinsic Method. The conceptual problem with the intrinsic method of accounting for stock options is that most options are granted with an exercise price equal to the current market price at the time of grant. When that happens, no compensation expense is recorded. Many accountants perceive this nonrecognition as not being reflective of economic reality (i.e., there is value in the stock option), and not recognizing the event is inconsistent with other types of equity transactions. For example, when stock is issued for equipment, the fair market value of the stock is ultimately expensed as depreciation. In 1996, Disney's Michael Eisner signed a contract that gave him eight million options exercisable over 15 years. Since the exercise price of each option was equal to or greater than the market price on the grant date, Disney did not report compensation expense for this transaction. However, the value of the options is obviously greater than zero. Eisner has become a very rich man through the exercise of stock options.

The Fair Value Method

Fischer Black and Myron Scholes published an academic paper in 1973 that presented a model to value stock options that is now referred to as the Black-Scholes option pricing model. The development of this model (and others), combined with growing dissatisfaction over the intrinsic value method of accounting for stock options, prompted the FASB to place stock-based compensation on its agenda in March 1984.

Initially, the FASB proposed that the fair value of options granted must be recognized as an expense on the income statement, but this proposal was met with great opposition. Company managers claimed that recognizing the fair value of executive stock options as an expense would adversely affect their stock price, which would result in many companies having to cut stock option plans, which then would negatively affect their ability to attract managerial talent. The ultimate result, according to company managers, would be serious harm to the U.S. economy due to (1) the stifling of new business, (2) lost jobs from companies going out of business, and (3) a competitive disadvantage compared to foreign companies that do not follow a fair value method.

Another argument made against the FASB's exposure draft concerned the reliability of the Black-Scholes model in measuring the fair value of executive stock options. That is, the trading restrictions contained in most executive stock options and the longer exercise dates give rise to the possibility of risk-averse executives exercising options early. Together with the long vesting requirements, these restrictions could result in the option pricing models overstating the cost of executive stock options to companies.

Problems with the Black-Scholes option pricing model, its possible negative impact on the economy, and the fact that using it will always result in compensation expense being measured led to a long and controversial FASB due process procedure, which eventually introduced *SFAS No. 123*. (See Appendix A at the end of the chapter for a review of the significant events during the due process procedure for stock-based compensation.)

In the midst of the due process procedure, the chairman of the SEC was quoted as saying that he had never seen the amount of corporate anxiety that this issue had raised.

Eventually, the FASB gave in to political pressure and allowed companies to choose either (1) to recognize compensation expense on the income statement according to the fair value method or (2) to recognize compensation expense on the income statement according to the intrinsic method and then disclose in the notes to the financial statements pro forma EPS as if the fair value method had been adopted. This required note disclosure is shown in Exhibit 14-2, which was extracted from the published financial report of Cisco Systems.

EXHIBIT 14-2

Extracted Note from 1998 Annual Report for Cisco Systems, Inc.

SFAS No. 123, "Accounting for Stock-Based Compensation," ("SFAS 123") requires the Company to disclose pro forma information regarding option grants made to its employees. SFAS No. 123 specifies certain valuation techniques that produce estimated compensation charges that are included in the pro forma results below. These amounts have not been reflected in the Company's Statements of Operations, because APB 25, "Accounting for Stock Issued to Employees," specifies that no compensation charge arises when the price of the employees' stock options equal the market value of the underlying stock at the grant date, as in the case of options granted to the Company's employees.

SFAS No. 123 pro forma numbers are as follows (in thousands, except per-share amounts and percentages):

	1998	1997	1996
Net income as reported under APB 25	$1,350,072	$1,048,679	$913,324
Net income pro forma under SFAS 123	$1,108,809	$897,939	$872,263
Basic net income per common share—as reported under APB 25	$0.88	$0.71	$0.64
Diluted net income per common share—as reported under APB 25	$0.84	$0.68	$0.61
Basic net income per common share—pro forma under SFAS 123	$0.72	$0.60	$0.61
Diluted net income per common share—pro forma under SFAS 123	$0.70	$0.59	$0.59

Under SFAS No. 123, the fair value of each option grant is estimated on the date of grant using the Black-Scholes option pricing model with the following weighted average assumptions:

	Employee Stock Options			Employee Stock Purchase Plan		
	1998	1997	1996	1998	1997	1996
Expected dividend yield	0.0%	0.0%	0.0%	0.0%	0.0%	0.0%
Risk-free interest rate	5.7%	6.4%	5.9%	5.4%	5.3%	5.4%
Expected volatility	35.6%	32.8%	32.9%	44.8%	44.4%	44.9%
Expected life (in years)	3.1	3.1	3.1	0.5	0.5	0.5

The Black-Scholes option valuation model was developed for use in estimating the fair value of traded options that have no vesting restrictions and are fully transferable. In addition, option valuation models require the input of highly subjective assumptions including the expected stock price volatility. Because the Company's employee stock options have characteristics significantly different from those of traded options and because changes in the subjective input assumptions can materially affect the fair value estimate, in management's opinion the existing models do not necessarily provide a reliable single measure of the fair value of the Company's options. The weighted average estimated fair values of employee stock options granted during fiscal 1998, 1997, and 1996 were $14.27, $6.93, and $5.93 per share, respectively.

On February 8, 2000, PBS broadcast a documentary highlighting the Black-Scholes option pricing model. The companion Web site for the PBS special (**http:// www.pbs.org/wgbh/nova/ stockmarket/**) provides an interesting perspective on the model's contribution to finance and business.

Employing the Black-Scholes Model to Determine Fair Value of Options

Although *SFAS No. 123* does not require recognizing the fair value of granted options as compensation expense on the income statement, familiarization with fair value models is important to accounting students in order to construct and interpret the disclosures in notes. This section introduces the use of the Black-Scholes model to compute the fair value expense.

The Black-Scholes model, adjusted for dividend paying stocks, is expressed as:

$$F = e^{-dL}S\phi(Z) - e^{-rL}X\phi(Z - \sigma\sqrt{L}),$$

where

F = the fair value of the option,
d = the stock's expected dividend yield,
L = the expected life of the option,
S = the current stock price,
ϕ = the cumulative standard normal distribution function,
r = the risk-free interest rate,
X = the option's exercise price,
σ = the volatility of the stock's instantaneous return, and

$$Z = \frac{\ln\left(\dfrac{S}{X}\right) + \left(r - d + \dfrac{\sigma^2}{2}\right)L}{\sigma\sqrt{L}}.$$

This formula can be very intimidating. Fortunately, the formula can be broken down into manageable segments. Appendix B to this chapter contains some Excel spreadsheet formulas that calculate the value of the options, given the input variables.[10]

SFAS No. 123 does not restrict the measurement of stock-based compensation to just using the Black-Scholes option pricing model but allows the use of any option pricing model so long as the model employs the following factors in determining fair value:

(1) The option's exercise price,
(2) The market price of the underlying stock,
(3) The risk-free interest rate,
(4) The expected life of the option,
(5) The volatility of the stock price, and
(6) The stock's dividend yield.

The following paragraphs explain the relationship of each factor with the fair value of the option.

Exercise Price of Option. The relationship between an option's exercise price and its fair value is negative. That is, as the exercise price of the option decreases, the value of the option increases.

Market Price of the Underlying Stock. The relationship between an option's fair value and this factor is positive. Given an exercise price, the value of the option will increase as the value of the stock increases.

---

[10]D. Crawford, D. R. Franz, and G. R. Smith, Jr., "Michael Eisner's Compensation Agreement with Disney," *Issues in Accounting Education*, November 1998, pp. 957–974. The student is referred to this article for an excellent explanation of the spreadsheet formulas.

Risk-Free Interest Rate. The relationship between an option's exercise price and the risk-free interest rate is positive. This relationship is probably the least intuitive. The authors of the Black-Scholes model have demonstrated that it is possible to form a risk-free portfolio by taking a short position in a call option (i.e., writing a call option) and a long position in the stock. Given the risk-free nature of this portfolio, its expected return should be equal to the risk-free rate of return that exists in the market. As the expected return of any asset increases, its fair value also increases. Thus, the value of the option will increase with the risk-free rate.

Expected Life of the Option. The longer the time to maturity, the more valuable is the option. The reason is that as the time to maturity increases, the probability increases that the stock price will increase above the exercise price.

Volatility of the Stock Price. The relationship between an option's value and the volatility of the stock price is positive. The value of any asset is a weighted average of all possible outcomes. Since the holder of an option has no obligation to purchase stock when the market price declines below the exercise price, options have no downside risk. Therefore, their values are based on the weighted average of all possible positive outcomes. More volatile stocks experience large price swings. The likelihood of experiencing large positive returns increases the value of the option.

© GETTY IMAGES, INC./EYEWIRE

Dividend Yield. This factor is negatively related to the price of the underlying stock. Dividends are a return on an investment, which results in reducing the stock price. A reduction in stock price reduces the value of the options.

Stock Options vs. Restricted Stock

Many corporate compensation committees are creative when determining the best methods of attracting and retaining executive talent. Besides stock options, another popular form of compensation is granting restricted stock. Stock options provide the executive with a right to purchase stock at some price (i.e., the option or strike price), and if the stock price increases, the executive can buy at the strike price and realize an immediate gain. However, if the stock price declines in value, the options are worthless and the executive has received nothing. Alternatively, **restricted stock** is a gift of actual shares of stock. This stock is restricted in the sense that, like options granted to executives, a vesting period must pass before the executive receives the shares of stock, and some restricted stock is tied to performance requirements. However, the main advantage of restricted stock over options is that it virtually *guarantees* the executive *some* compensation.

The principal advantage to a corporation of issuing options over restricted stock is that options are usually granted to executives with a strike price that equals the current market price at the grant date so that no compensation expense need be recognized. This "free" compensation has no adverse effect on corporate earnings. Also, executives usually prefer receiving options in contrast to restricted stock because, since there is no cost to the company to issue them, a company typically is willing to grant more options than shares of restricted stock. Hence, a greater upside potential exists.

To illustrate the comparative advantages of options and restricted stock, consider the compensation package awarded to Hugh L. McColl, former CEO for Bank of America Corp. Mr. McColl's annual salary and bonus for a particular year was $3.75 million. In addition, he was granted 600,000 shares of restricted stock and 1.4 million options[11] with a strike price of $74.50, which was also equal to the stock's market price at the date of grant. Supposedly, both the options and the restricted stock awards provide incentives to Mr. McColl to make decisions that will maximize shareholder wealth, since any increase in stock price will increase the value to the stockholders and also to his compensation package. Since the options' strike price was equal to the market value of the stock on the date of the grant, Bank of America did not recognize any compensation expense for the options. However, Bank of America did recognize $44.7 million of compensation expense due to issuing restricted stock. This expense is computed as the market price of the stock on the date the shares were issued multiplied by the number of shares issued.[12]

Of interest is that by the end of the award year, the market value of Bank of America's stock had declined from $74.50 to about $50 per share. Assuming that is when Mr. McColl can exercise the options and restricted stock, the value of the restricted stock would still be the substantial amount of $30 million ($50 × 600,000 shares). However, the 1.4 million options would be worthless, since the strike price of $74.50 is much greater than the stock's market value. So an interesting question is that, given these facts about the future, what is the "correct" amount of compensation expense that the Bank of America should have recorded for the award year?

From the graph in Exhibit 14-3, it can be seen that Mr. McColl's total compensation increases as the value of Bank of America's stock appreciates. The graph

EXHIBIT 14-3

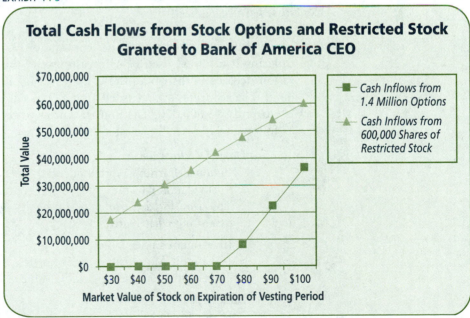

Total Cash Flows from Stock Options and Restricted Stock Granted to Bank of America CEO

- Cash Inflows from 1.4 Million Options
- Cash Inflows from 600,000 Shares of Restricted Stock

Total Value

Market Value of Stock on Expiration of Vesting Period

---

[11]Note the significantly greater number of options granted as compared to shares of restricted stock, which illustrates the comparative advantage to executives of receiving options versus restricted stock.

[12]Recognizing no expense for the options versus $44.7 million of expense for the restricted stock illustrates the comparative advantage to the company of issuing options versus shares of restricted stock.

illustrates the distribution of total cash inflows to Mr. McColl from the options and restricted stock, given a range of prices for Bank of America's stock. As can be seen, most of Mr. McColl's compensation came from restricted stock and is particularly significant compared to his base salary and bonus of $3.75 million. Although restricted stock is more expensive to companies in that it requires the recognition of compensation expense, it is becoming more popular recently, given the very competitive job market for top management talent.

More on Dividends and Stock Splits

Dividends are usually paid in cash, as discussed in Chapter 13. However, dividends also may be paid (1) in assets other than cash, (2) in shares of the corporation's stock, or (3) by incurring a liability. Regardless of the nature of the dividend, the accounting is still tied to three important dates:

- Date of declaration—the date the corporation declares that a dividend will be paid/distributed.
- Date of record—the date on which ownership of shares of stock is determined and it is known who will receive the dividend.
- Date of distribution—date that cash, other assets, or stock of the company is paid/distributed.

Property Dividends

Dividends where assets other than cash are distributed are called **property dividends**. Common examples of property dividends include the distribution of securities of other corporations and merchandise. One of the more exotic property dividends has been ounces of gold. Property dividends are accounted at the fair value (at the date of declaration) of the assets to be distributed, and gains or losses are recognized.[13]

Suppose that a corporation is found to be in violation of antitrust laws because of its investment in another corporation. To comply with the court decree ordering it to divest itself of its investment in the other corporation, the corporation decides to distribute those shares to its stockholders in a property dividend. The securities are recorded on the books at $4,000,000, but their fair value is currently $6,000,000. The journal entries to record the property dividend are as follows:

Date of declaration:
Retained Earnings (or Dividends)   6,000,000
  Dividends Payable   6,000,000
To record the declaration of a property dividend at the fair value of the assets to be distributed.

Investment in Securities   2,000,000
  Gain on Appreciation of Securities   2,000,000
To recognize the increase in the value of the securities to be distributed.

Date of payment:
Dividends Payable   6,000,000
  Investment in Securities   6,000,000
To distribute the securities as a property dividend.

---

[13]*APB Opinion No. 29*, "Accounting for Nonmonetary Transactions," pars. 20 and 23.

Liquidating Dividends

A dividend that is distributed from a capital account other than Retained Earnings or from current earnings is a liquidating dividend and is a return to the owners of their investment. For a liquidating dividend to occur, the board of directors must specifically indicate that the distribution is being made from some capital account other than Retained Earnings. The journal entry at the date of declaration is of the following form:

Paid-In Capital in Excess of Par	XXX	
Dividends Payable		XXX

The journal entry when the dividend is paid is the same journal entry for paying a cash dividend, as illustrated in Chapter 13.

Scrip Dividends

As mentioned in Chapter 13, corporations generally like to establish a history of paying dividends. Normally, dividends are paid within a few weeks after they are declared; but when a corporation is temporarily short of cash, it may distribute **promissory notes** (called **scrip**) that bear interest and include the corporation's promise to pay a dividend at a time that is longer than usual. The two changes in the accounting for scrip dividends from the cash dividend entries are that at the date of declaration an account such as Scrip Dividends Payable or Notes Payable to Stockholders is used, and interest expense is recognized on the date of payment. Illustrative entries are as follows:

Date of declaration:

Retained Earnings (or Dividends)	XXX	
Scrip Dividends Payable		XXX

Date of payment:

Scrip Dividends Payable	XXX	
Interest Expense	XXX	
Cash		XXX

Stock Dividends

A **stock dividend** occurs when a corporation distributes shares of its own stock to existing stockholders, with the desire to give the stockholders evidence of their interest in the accumulated earnings of the corporation. To be considered a stock dividend for accounting purposes, the number of shares distributed must be 20%–25%, or less, of the number of shares outstanding. Distributing amounts of stock greater than that are theoretically not stock dividends but are called stock splits effected in the form of a dividend, or simply large stock dividends. *Stock dividends do not result in distributing corporate assets, or the incurring of a liability.* Neither do stock dividends increase the percentage of any shareholder's interest in the net assets of the corporation. Instead, each shareholder has more pieces of paper representing the same percentage ownership. However, the number of shares outstanding does increase, and therefore legal capital also increases. So *an entry must be prepared to reclassify an amount from Retained Earnings to other capital accounts, so that the legal capital amount can be identified in the appropriate stockholders' equity accounts.* This process of moving capital among the stockholders' equity accounts is called **capitalizing retained earnings**. The CAP decided that stock dividends should be accounted for at the *fair value of the stock at the date of declaration*, as illustrated in the following journal entry:[14]

Date of declaration:

Retained Earnings	Fair value of the stock
Common Stock Dividends Distributable	Par value of the stock
Paid-In Capital from Stock Dividends	Difference

Common Stock Dividends Distributable is not a liability account. Rather, it is a stockholders' equity account, and in this example, since the stock dividend is declared on common stock, the dividends distributable account is reported next to it. The prior journal entry does not affect total stockholders' equity. Instead, Retained Earnings is decreased, and two other stockholders' equity accounts are increased. Later, when the shares of common stock are distributed, the journal entry is as follows:

Date of distribution:

Common Stock Dividends Distributable	Par value of the stock
Common Stock	Par value of the stock

Fractional share rights are issued when a stock dividend will result in a stockholder needing to receive a fraction of a share. For example, suppose that a stockholder has 75 shares in a corporation that has just declared a 15% stock dividend. So the stockholder should receive 11.25 shares of stock, but fractional shares are never issued. In this case, the stockholder will receive 11 shares and a fractional share right for one-fourth share. These fractional share rights are traded on exchanges shortly after the distribution of the stock dividend, and this stockholder can either sell his one-fourth fractional share right or acquire fractional share rights for three-fourths of a share, which then can be surrendered to the corporation for one additional share.

Stock Split Effected in the Form of a Dividend (Large Stock Dividend)

Stock distributions of more than 20%–25% of the stock outstanding are referred to as stock splits effected in the form of a dividend or, more simply, large stock dividends. Like stock dividends (i.e., those where less than 20%–25% of the outstanding stock is distributed), large stock dividends do not have any impact on total stockholders' equity and retained earnings. Also, like stock dividends, the number of shares outstanding is increased; hence, it is necessary to capitalize retained earnings so as to correctly state legal capital. However, according to GAAP, *the amount capitalized is par value* instead of fair value. So at the date of declaration, the journal entry to record a stock split that is effected in the form of a dividend is as follows:

Date of declaration:

Retained Earnings	Par value
Common Stock Dividends Distributable	Par value
To record a stock split effected in the form of a dividend.	

When the common stock is distributed, the journal entry is to debit Common Stock Dividends Distributable and credit Common Stock in the same way as was done for a stock dividend.

---

[14]As with cash dividends, stock dividends are not usually paid on treasury stock. Some states specifically prohibit the paying of stock dividends on treasury stock.

Capitalizing par value for large stock dividends and fair value for stock dividends causes the interesting situation where, on occasion, retained earnings can be capitalized for a greater amount when a 20% stock dividend is declared than when a much larger stock split effected in the form of a dividend is declared. Suppose that Bailey Company has the following stockholders' equity account balances as of September 1, 2004:

Common stock, $2 par value, 30,000 shares authorized and 20,000 shares issued and outstanding	$ 40,000
Additional paid-in capital	16,000
Retained earnings	60,000
Total stockholders' equity	$116,000

If Bailey declares a 10% stock dividend and the fair value of a share of stock is $15, the following journal entry is prepared:

Retained Earnings (20,000 shares × 10% × $15)	30,000	
Common Stock Dividends Distributable		4,000
Additional Paid-In Capital, Stock Dividends		26,000

If Bailey declares a 40% stock split effected in the form of a dividend, the following journal entry is prepared:

Retained Earnings (20,000 shares × 40% × $2)	16,000	
Common Stock Dividends Distributable		16,000

Stock Splits

A **stock split**, as contrasted to a stock dividend, occurs when a corporation distributes shares of its own stock to existing stockholders, with the principal desire of increasing the number of shares outstanding and thereby reducing the share price. A stock split increases, rather dramatically, the number of shares outstanding, but it reduces the par value proportionally. That is, a 2-for-1 stock split (i.e., giving two new shares of stock for each old share surrendered) doubles the number of shares outstanding, but the par value of each share is reduced by one-half. Thus, *legal capital is not changed*, and *no journal entry is required* to capitalize retained earnings or to move amounts among any capital accounts. If the accountant desires, a memo entry can be made as follows:

> January 15. The corporation declared a 2-for-1 stock split today that increased the number of shares outstanding from 10,000,000 to 20,000,000 but reduced the par value from $10 per share to $5 per share. Total par value remains unchanged.

Just as there are stock splits that dramatically increase the number of shares outstanding, so too there are **reverse stock splits** that dramatically decrease the number of shares outstanding and increase the par value per share. So, a 1-for-3 reverse stock split (i.e., giving one new share of stock for each three shares surrendered) will result in only one-third the number of shares outstanding as previously and will triple the par value per share. But again, the total par value—and the legal capital—do not change, and no journal entry, other than a memo entry, is necessary to record the transaction. Reverse stock splits may be done (1) to "penny stocks" to increase the stock price and, thus, to bring greater prestige to the stock, (2) to "buy out" vocal minority shareholders, or (3) to concentrate greater control of the corporation to fewer stockholders.

This Is the Real World

Why Do Companies Split Their Stock?

On March 29, 1999, Microsoft executed a 2-for-1 stock split. As a result, the number of shares outstanding doubled, and the share price was cut approximately in half (from a close of $178 prior to the split to an opening price on March 29 of $90). In substance, the intrinsic value of the company had not changed: the company still held the same amount of cash and operating assets, the executives were still the same people, and total revenues and net income were not affected. However, companies incur legal and investment banking fees to execute a stock split, so they must see some value in them.

A recent study has found that companies earn, on average, a 3.5% return on the day that a stock split is announced. In addition, the stock of companies that execute splits tend to outperform the stock of nonsplit companies by about eight percent over the next year. One explanation presented for this phenomenon is that a stock split sends a positive signal to investors about the likelihood of future capital gains. So,

presumably, managers with less optimistic expectations about future performance will not opt to split shares, since the perceived benefits will not exceed the costs of executing the split. Another explanation for why stock prices increase is that individual investors are resistant to buying stock at higher prices, and research has shown the tendency for individual investors to curtail purchases of stock when the price exceeds approximately $45 per share.

© PRNEWSFOTO/WAGGENER EDSTROM

SOURCE: *Ikenberry, David L.; Rankine, Graeme; Stine, Earl K., "What Do Stock Splits Really Signal?"* Journal of Financial and Quantitative Analysis, *September 1996, pp. 357–375.*

Summary of Stock Dividends and Stock Splits

Exhibit 14-4 compares and contrasts the effects of stock dividends, stock splits, and stock dividends effected in the form of a split upon stockholders' equity and the various components of stockholders' equity. A significant difference between stock dividends and stock splits pertains to their effects on the par value of the stock, on legal capital, and on retained earnings. *Stock dividends do not change the*

EXHIBIT 14-4

Comparison of Stock Dividends, Stock Splits, and Stock Dividends Effected in the Form of a Stock Split

Effect on	Stock Dividend	Stock Split	Stock Dividend Effected in the Form of a Stock Split (i.e., Large Stock Dividends)
Total number of shares outstanding	Increase	Increase	Increase
Par value per share	No effect	Decrease	No effect
Legal capital	Increase	No effect	Increase
Retained earnings	Decrease	No effect	Decrease
Total contributed capital	Increase	No effect	Increase
Total stockholders' equity	No effect	No effect	No effect

par value per share, whereas stock splits do. Also, stock dividends increase legal capital and decrease retained earnings, whereas stock splits have no effect on either total.

In all cases, the number of shares of stock outstanding increases. But for stock splits, because par value decreases proportionately, there is no effect on any stockholders' equity account or on total stockholders' equity. However, for all stock dividends, because the number of shares increases but there is no resulting decrease in par value per share, legal capital increases, which causes an amount to be reclassified from retained earnings to the contributed capital accounts. However, there still is no effect on total stockholders' equity.

Statement of Changes in Stockholders' Equity

Transactions between a company and its shareholders or owners have long been considered important information to the readers of financial statements. To that end, *APB Opinion No. 12* requires that a statement of changes in stockholders' equity be included as part of the financial report whenever financial statements are issued that purport to present the financial position and operating results of a company.[15] This is also the statement where comprehensive income is most commonly reported.

The statement of changes in stockholders' equity is a columnar statement, with each of the columns reporting a component of stockholders' equity. The statement begins with the balance as of the beginning of the reporting period, shows in summary form the transactions that changed the account balance during the year, and ends with the balances as of the end of the reporting period. In addition to reporting on the transactions of the reporting period, most companies report on several prior years as well. Exhibit 14-5, extracted from a recently published financial report of E.I. du Pont de Nemours and Company, illustrates a typical statement of changes in stockholders' equity.

In addition to providing a statement of stockholders' equity, companies also must provide the following information (usually in the notes to the financial statements) about each class of outstanding stock:

- Dividend and liquidation preferences,
- Participating rights,
- Call prices and dates,
- Conversion or exercise prices and dates,
- Sinking fund requirements,
- Unusual voting rights, and
- Significant contractual terms to issue additional shares.[16]

Reporting to Owners

In *Concept Statement No. 5*, the FASB stated that a full set of financial statements for a period should show:

- Financial position at the end of the period,
- Net income for the period,
- Cash flows for the period,
- Comprehensive income for the period, and
- Investments and distributions to owners during the period.

---

[15]*APB Opinion No. 12*, "Omnibus Opinion—1967," par. 10.
[16]*FAS No. 129*, "Disclosure of Information about Capital Structure," Norwalk, CT: Financial Accounting Standards Board, 1997.

EXHIBIT 14-5

E.I. du Pont de Nemours and Company Consolidated Statement of Changes in Stockholders' Equity

(Dollars in millions, except per share)

	Preferred Stock	Common Stock	Additional Paid-In Capital	Reinvested Earnings	Accumulated Other Comprehensive Income	Flexitrust	Treasury Stock	Total Stockholders' Equity	Total Comprehensive Income
Balance January 1, 1999	$237	$342	$7,854	$ 6,705	$(432)	$(752)	$ —	$13,954	
1999									
Net income				7,690					$7,690
Cumulative translation adjustment					172				172
Minimum pension liability					76				76
Net unrealized gain on securities					51				51
Total comprehensive income									$7,989
Common dividends ($1.40 per share)				(1,501)					
Preferred dividends				(10)					
Treasury stock									
Acquisition							(12,095)		
Businesses acquired			(5)	(1,147)			5,324		
Retirement			(6)	(38)			44		
Common stock issued			(220)						
Flexitrust			159			427			
Compensation plans									

(continued)

EXHIBIT 14-5 CONTINUED

	Preferred Stock	Common Stock	Additional Paid-In Capital	Reinvested Earnings	Accumulated Other Comprehensive Income	Flexitrust	Treasury Stock	Total Stockholders' Equity	Total Comprehensive Income
Adjustments to market value			159			(159)			
Balance December 31, 1999	$237	$342	$7,941	$11,699	$(133)	$(484)	$(6,727)	$12,875	
2000									
Net income				$2,314					$2,314
Cumulative translation adjustment					(38)				(38)
Minimum pension liability					4				4
Net unrealized (loss) on securities					(21)				(21)
Total comprehensive income									$2,259
Common dividends ($1.40 per share)				(1,455)					
Preferred dividends				(10)					
Treasury stock Acquisition							(462)		
Retirement		(3)	(64)	(395)			462		
Common stock issued			(96)						
Flexitrust			(16)			204			
Compensation plans						106			
Adjustments to market value			(106)						
Balance December 31, 2000	$237	$339	$7,659	$12,153	$(188)	$(174)	$(6,727)	$13,299	

The measuring and reporting of financial position and net income have been the focus of much of the book to this point. The statement of cash flows is the subject of Chapter 16, and the reporting of comprehensive income will be covered in Chapter 15. The remainder of this chapter covers the format of the statement of changes in stockholders' equity and the reporting for prior-period adjustments.

Prior-Period Adjustments

Two events trigger the recognizing of a prior-period adjustment. One is to correct an error of a prior period. An **error** may arise from a mathematical mistake, a mistake in the application of an accounting principle (e.g., recognizing revenue before it is earned and is realized or realizable), or an oversight or misuse of facts that existed at the time the financial statements were prepared. Also, changing from an accounting principle that is not generally accepted to one that is corrects an error and gives rise to reporting a prior-period adjustment. Errors that occur and are corrected in the same year do not require the reporting of a prior-period adjustment.

The second event that triggers the reporting of a prior-period adjustment is the changing of certain accounting principles mandated by the FASB or its predecessors. As discussed in Chapter 9, the reporting for a change in an accounting principle generally is done by reporting a cumulative effect on the income statement and also reporting pro forma data showing what net income would be if the new principle had always been used. However, there are several exceptions to this general case when—instead of reporting a cumulative effect and pro forma data—a prior-period adjustment is reported. The primary exceptions are as follows:

1. A change from the LIFO cost-flow assumption to another cost-flow assumption.
2. A change in the method of accounting for long-term construction contracts.
3. A change either to or from the "full cost" method in the extractive industries.
4. When a newly issued financial standard requires retroactive restatement for companies that must change their accounting principles to comply with the new standard.

Whether the reporting of a prior-period adjustment occurs because of an error or is due to one of the preceding listed accounting changes, the reporting is the same. This reporting entails (1) restating the financial statements of prior periods that are presented in the current year for comparative purposes and (2) reporting a prior-period adjustment. *The prior-period adjustment amount is computed in the same way as the cumulative effect of a change in an accounting principle*, which is that it is the difference between what the beginning balance of retained earnings is as compared to what it would be if the error had not been made or if the new accounting principle had been used.

To illustrate, suppose that in 2006 D&L Company decides to switch its inventory cost-flow assumption from LIFO to FIFO. This is an example of an accounting change that requires the prior-year financial statements that are included in the current year's financial report to be restated and a prior-period adjustment to be reported. D&L Company had begun operations in 2003 and had reported the net income amounts as shown in Exhibit 14-6.

As shown in the exhibit, the net income to be reported for 2006 is $32,000, which is the amount computed under the newly adopted accounting principle.

EXHIBIT 14-6

Computing the Prior-Period Adjustment Amount

Year	Net Income, LIFO	Net Income, FIFO	Changing to FIFO Cumulative Difference
2003	$18,000	$21,000	$ 3,000
2004	22,000	24,000	5,000
2005	25,000	29,000	9,000
2006	30,000	32,000	11,000

EXTENDING THE CONCEPT

The reporting of a prior period adjustment when an error occurs is as illustrated earlier. That is, the impact on the beginning balance of retained earnings is computed, which is the difference between the beginning balance of retained earnings as reported and what the balance of retained earnings would be if the error had not occurred.

Suppose that an asset is acquired on January 1, 2004, for $40,000 but is mistakenly expensed. The asset has a useful life of five years, and the company uses the straight-line method of depreciation. The error is discovered in 2007 before depreciation for the year is computed. Verify that the prior-period adjustment amounts that should be reported are $0 for 2004, $32,000 for 2005, and $24,000 for 2006. Also, note that the prior-period adjustment amounts will increase retained earnings.

Further, assume that the income tax rate is 30%; then verify that the prior-period adjustment amounts are $0 for 2004, $22,400 for 2005, and $16,800 for 2006.

The net income to be reported for 2005, which is presented in the 2006 financial statements for comparative purposes, is $29,000, which is also the amount as computed under the newly adopted accounting principle. Thus, *the prior year's income statement is restated.* If more than one prior years' financial statements are presented for comparative purposes, those amounts are also computed using the newly adopted accounting principle. Since these reported income amounts are comparable, there is no need to report pro forma numbers, as is done under the general method of accounting for a change in an accounting principle.

In addition to retroactively restating the prior-year financial statements, a prior-period adjustment is reported. Exhibit 14-7A shows how the statement of retained earnings is presented under the LIFO cost-flow assumption (i.e., as originally stated), and Exhibit 14-7B shows how the statement of retained earnings would be presented when reporting a prior-period adjustment, assuming that all prior years are presented for comparative purposes.

EXHIBIT 14-7A

D&L Company Statement of Retained Earnings—*As Originally Issued* For the Year Ended December 31, 2005

	2005	2004	2003	
Retained earnings, January 1	$28,000	$13,000	$ 0	As computed under LIFO (See Exhibit 14-5)
Net income	25,000	22,000	18,000	
	$53,000	$35,000	$18,000	
Dividends	10,000	7,000	5,000	Author constructed
Retained earnings, December 31	$43,000	$28,000	$13,000	

EXHIBIT 14-7B

D&L Company Statement of Retained Earnings—*As Restated*
For the Year Ended December 31, 2006

	2006	2005	2004	2003	
Retained earnings, January 1— as reported	$43,000	$28,000	$13,000	$ 0	These are the same amounts as originally reported
Prior-period adjustment	9,000	5,000	3,000	0	Cumulative differences (See Exhibit 14-5)
Retained earnings, January 1— as adjusted	$52,000	$33,000	$16,000	$ 0	
Net income	32,000	29,000	24,000	21,000	All amounts are computed using the newly adopted principle
	$84,000	$62,000	$40,000	$21,000	
Dividends	12,000	10,000	7,000	5,000	
Retained earnings, December 31	$72,000	$52,000	$33,000	$16,000	

In computing and reporting the prior-period adjustment amounts, particularly note the following points:

- The "Retained earnings, January 1—as reported" are the same numbers as previously reported when the LIFO cost-flow assumption was used. Verify these amounts.
- The prior-period adjustment amounts are the cumulative differences between the old LIFO method of inventory pricing and the new FIFO method of inventory pricing. These numbers can be traced to the computations in Exhibit 14-5. This is the same calculation used under the general case for computing the cumulative effect of a change in an accounting principle; only the location where it is reported in the financial report is different.
- The prior-period amounts are reported as an adjustment to the beginning balance of Retained Earnings—as originally reported. This permits the financial statement users (if they desire) to relate previously issued financial reports to the current report that is being restated.
- The "Retained Earnings, January 1—as adjusted" agrees with the prior year's "Retained Earnings, December 31" balance, thus showing the tie from year to year.

APPENDIX A: Significant Events Leading to *SFAS No. 123*

Date	Event
March 1984	FASB places issue of stock-based compensation on agenda; nothing more than deliberations occurs for next eight years.
January 1992	President Bush visits Japan while accompanied by 12 American executives; Japan insinuates that the wide compensation disparity between American and Japanese executives contributes to expensive American products and the trade deficit between the two countries.
April 1992	Senator Levin (D-Michigan) introduces legislation that would require companies to deduct from earnings the fair value of options granted.
1993	President Clinton changes tax code to make CEO compensation in excess of $1 million nondeductible as a corporate business expense if the compensation is not tied to performance. This tax law change further encourages companies to use stock options as a form of compensation.
June 1993	FASB issues an exposure draft that proposes companies must recognize fair value of options granted as compensation expense. Over 1,700 letters of comment, almost all of which are in opposition, are received by the FASB.
1993	Coopers and Lybrand release a study suggesting that financial statement users may want to remove the impact of the stock-based compensation expense as required by the exposure draft from the financial statements when analyzing the company.
	Senator Joseph Lieberman (D-Conneticut) introduced the Equity Expansion Act of 1993, which, if enacted, would have overruled any decision by the FASB that required expensing the fair value of granted options.
	Treasury Secretary Lloyd Bentsen encourages the FASB to carefully consider retaining the current accounting treatment for options.
	President Clinton warns of the possibility that the FASB's proposal would undermine the competitiveness of America's high-tech firms.
	The Coalition for American Equity Expansion is formed to fight the exposure draft.
1994	The Accounting Standards Executive Committee votes 9 to 6 in disagreement with the FASB's exposure draft proposal based on their belief that the measurement methods are not sufficiently reliable to be helpful.
	California state officials and federal legislatures address a rally held in San Jose, California, while the FASB is there holding public hearings on the exposure draft.
	One of the SEC commissioners expresses his strong opinion that the adoption of the exposure draft would be an economic casualty.
October 1995	FASB votes 5 to 2 in favor of allowing companies the option of disclosing in notes pro forma EPS as if the fair value of stock-based compensation was recognized.

APPENDIX B: Excel Spreadsheet Formulas for the Black-Scholes Option Pricing Model

	A	B	C
1	Current stock price (in dollars)		Input
2	Exercise price (in dollars)		Input
3	Risk-free interest rate (as percent)		Input
4	Expected life of option (in years)		Input
5	Volatility (as decimal value)		Input
6	Dividend yield (as percent)		Input
7	Value per option		Formula
8	Number of options granted		Input
9	Total value of options		Formula
10			
11	Intermediate computations	Formula	
12		Formula	
13		Formula	Formula
14		Formula	Formula
15		Formula	Formula
16		Formula	Formula
17		Formula	Formula

Formula Notes

Cell Address	Cell Formula
C7	+C1*B17/EXP(C4*C6)-C2*C17/EXP(C3*C4)
C9	+C7*C8
B11	+C5^2*C4
B12	(LN($C1/$C2)+$C3*$C4-$C6*$C4+$B11/2)/SQRT($B11)
B13	ABS(B12)
B14	EXP(B13^2/-2)/2.506628
B15	1/(1+B13*0.2316419)
B16	0.31938153*B15-0.356563782*B15^2+1.781477937*B15^3-1.821255978*B15^4+1.330274429*B15^5
B17	IF(B12>0,1-B14*B16,B14*B16)
C12	(LN($C1/$C2)+$C3*$C4-$C6*$C4-$B11/2)/SQRT($B11)
C13	ABS(C12)
C14	EXP(C13^2/-2)/2.506628
C15	1/(1+C13*0.2316419)
C16	0.31938153*C15-0.356563782*C15^2+1.781477937*C15^3-1.821255978*C15^4+1.330274429*C15^5
C17	IF(C12>0,1-C14*C16,C14*C16)

Questions

1. Explain the accounting at issuance and when the conversion feature is exercised for convertible debt where, in order to exercise the conversion feature, the debt must be surrendered. Use the book value method and the fair value method.

2. Explain the accounting for any "sweetener" that is added to encourage holders of convertible debt to convert to stock.

3. Explain the accounting from the viewpoint of the issuing corporation for a security that is issued with a detachable warrant(s) when (a) the security and warrant are issued, (b) the warrant is exercised, and (c) the warrant is allowed to lapse.

4. Define a *stock warrant* or *right*.

5. A company issued stock warrants to its existing shareholders to purchase additional shares of its $10 par common stock at a price of $25 per share. When should additional paid-in capital be recorded? When should the investor compute a new cost per share of stock, and how is this new cost per share computed?

6. Contrast the difference between how compensation is measured for stock options under *APB Opinion No. 25* (i.e., the intrinsic method) and *SFAS No. 123* (i.e., the fair value method).

7. Under *APB Opinion No. 25* (i.e., the intrinsic method), how is yearly compensation expense computed for stock options?

8. List the factors that affect the value of stock options, and indicate whether each factor is positively or negatively associated with the stock option value.

9. What are stock options, stock appreciation rights, and restricted stock? If given the choice between receiving one of them, which would you select? Why?

10. Define the following and explain why it is used:
    a. Scrip dividend
    b. Property dividend
    c. Stock dividend
    d. Stock split
    e. Stock split effected in the form of a dividend

11. Bouncing Boxers Inc. declared a 20% stock dividend on its $2 par value common stock when there were 50,000 shares outstanding and the market value of each share was $5. Prepare the journal entries to record the declaration and payment of the stock dividend.

12. Assume the same facts as in Question #11, except that the dividend was a 50% stock dividend (i.e., it was a stock split effected in the form of a dividend). Prepare the journal entries.

13. How do stock dividends and stock splits affect a company's legal capital, par value per share, and total stockholders' equity?

14. EBS Equity Systems has 10,000 shares of $0.10 par value common stock outstanding, and the market value of each share of stock is $22. Which of the following will result in capitalizing more of retained earnings: a 100% stock dividend, or a 10% stock dividend? Why?

15. What specific events or accounting changes are accounted for as prior-period adjustments? Explain the accounting for a prior-period adjustment.

Exercises

Exercise 14-1: Convertible Debt. Scholzen has $10 million of 8%, convertible debt outstanding. Interest payment dates are June 30 and December 31. The terms of conversion are that, at the bond holder's option, each $1,000 bond can be converted into 24 shares of the company's $5 par common stock. The bond indenture also allows the company to call the bonds at 106 any time after December 31, 2007. On June 30, 2006, holders of $9,000,000 exercised the conversion privilege when the market price of the stock was $50 per share and the market price of the bonds was $1,030. The total unamortized bond premium and bond issue costs were $300,000 and $80,000, respectively.

1. Prepare the appropriate journal entry for the conversion of the bonds, using the book value method.
2. Prepare the appropriate journal entry for the conversion of the bonds, using the fair value method.
3. Assume that on July 4, 2006, Scholzen (in an effort to induce conversion of the remaining bonds) offered to exchange 27 shares of stock for each bond. Prepare the journal entries under both the book value method and fair value methods, assuming that the rest of the bonds were converted and that the market price of the stock was still $50 per share.

Exercise 14-2: Convertible Debt. Reynolds Metals had $5,000,000 of 10%, convertible debt outstanding, with each $1,000 bond convertible into 50 shares of Reynolds $2 par value common stock. On December 31, 2006, when the balance in the bond premium account was $90,000 and the balance in the bond issue costs account was $20,000, bond holders of 1,000 of the bonds converted their bonds into shares of common stock. At the time, the market value of the bonds was 101¾, and the market value of the stock was $21 per share.

On January 3, 2007, as an inducement for others to exchange their bonds for common stock, Reynolds offered to exchange 54 shares of stock for each $1,000 bond. The holders of the other 4,000 bonds promptly converted them into shares of common stock. The market price of the common stock at the time was $22 per share.

1. Prepare the appropriate journal entries for all of these transactions, assuming the use of the book value method.
2. Prepare the same entries, assuming the use of the fair value method.

Exercise 14-3: Issuing Stock with Detachable Stock Warrants. On August 1, 2008, Round Company issued 5,000 shares of $10 par common stock for $80,000. Each share has a detachable warrant that allows the holder the right to acquire an additional share of common stock for $15 and that expires six months after issuance. At the time of selling these securities, Round's common stock was selling for $14 per share. On December 1, 2008, when Round's common stock was selling for $19 per share, 4,000 of the rights were exercised.

1. For Round Company,
   a. Prepare the journal entry to record the issuance of the stock with detachable warrants.
   b. Prepare the journal entry to record the exercise of the 4,000 warrants.

2. Prepare the journal entries for an investor who purchased 1,000 of these shares of common stock with detachable warrants.
3. Prepare the subsequent journal entries for the stock warrants, presuming the investor:
   a. Exercised the warrants.
   b. Allowed the warrants to lapse.

Exercise 14-4: Receipt of Stock Warrants after Purchasing Stock. Sunset Storage owns 50 shares of Cove Creek's $5 par common stock that were purchased in 1999 for $40 per share. On May 1, 2004, Cove Creek issued to Sunset 50 stock warrants that entitle Sunset to purchase one new share of common stock for $90 cash and two stock warrants. On May 1, each share of stock had a market value of $132 without warrants.

1. What is the implicit fair value of each stock warrant?
2. What cost should Sunset assign to Investment in Stock Warrants?
3. Assuming that Sunset exercised the 50 stock warrants, prepare the appropriate journal entry.
4. Assuming that Sunset exercised 40 stock warrants and allowed the others to lapse, prepare the appropriate journal entry for the lapsing of the stock warrants.

Exercise 14-5: Stock Dividends. The following information was extracted from the stockholders' equity section of Splashes Inc.'s 2003 balance sheet:

Common stock ($5 par value; 200,000 shares issued and outstanding)	$1,000,000
Paid-in capital in excess of par	2,500,000
Retained earnings	800,000

During 2004, the company declared a 10% stock dividend when the market price of its stock was $12 per share.

1. Prepare the necessary journal entries to record the declaration and distribution of the 10% stock dividend.
2. Assuming that the company announced an additional 50% stock dividend subsequent to the 10% dividend, when the market price of the stock was $14 per share, prepare the necessary journal entry to record the 50% dividend.
3. Assuming that Splashes earned a net income of $100,000 during 2004, what is the balance in the retained earnings account at December 31, 2004?

Exercise 14-6: Stock Dividends and Splits. By December 31, 2003, Alice, Inc., had issued 100,000 shares of $10 par value common stock, of which 8,000 were held in treasury. On December 31, 2003, the company declared a 100% stock dividend.

1. Prepare the journal entry to record the stock dividend.
2. Suppose that instead of declaring a 100% stock dividend, the company declared a 2-for-1 stock split. Prepare the journal entry to record the stock split.
3. Explain the effects of a 100% stock dividend versus a 2-for-1 stock split on retained earnings, contributed capital, and total stockholders' equity.
4. What are the likely effects on the stock's market value from a 100% stock dividend versus a 2-for-1 stock split?
5. Does a stock split or stock dividend provide any real value to the recipients?

Exercise 14-7: Dividends. Scrapp Company had the following balances in its stockholders' equity accounts as of June 1, 2004:

Common stock, $5 par value	$325,000
Paid-in capital in excess of par (common)	225,000
Cumulative preferred stock, 8%, $50 par value	150,000
Discount on preferred stock	(14,000)
Treasury stock (7,000 shares)	(56,000)
Retained earnings	268,000

Dividends on the preferred stock are in arrears for 2003. In June 2004, the company declared and distributed a 50% common stock dividend and then paid a $1 dividend on all common stock. The preferred stockholders received a dividend in the form of merchandise that had a book value of $15,000 and a market value of $26,000. By agreement, this dividend fulfills all obligations to preferred stockholders, including dividends in arrears.

1. Prepare the journal entries to record declaring and paying the dividends.
2. Prepare the stockholders' equity section of Scrapp's balance sheet after the payment of dividends.
3. Considering the stock dividend and the property dividend and the balance in retained earnings, show how the accounting in Part (1) would change if the cash dividend on common stock was $3 per share.

Exercise 14-8: Effect of Transactions on Financial Statements. Companies have a wide array of options when choosing to distribute assets to their stockholders, including either paying a dividend or buying treasury stock. Listed below are various dividend and other stockholders' equity transactions. In the table provided, indicate how each transaction will affect the financial statement item or ratio. Assume that there is an adequate credit balance in the paid-in capital from treasury stock account.

Transaction:

1. Declared a cash dividend.
2. Paid a cash dividend.
3. Declared a property dividend when the market value of the distributed item is greater than its book value.
4. Declared and distributed a small stock dividend when the market value of stock is greater than its par value.
5. Declared and distributed a large stock dividend when the market value of stock is greater than the par value.
6. Purchased treasury shares, using the cost method.
7. Sold treasury shares that were purchased using the cost method, and the selling price is greater than the price at which they were purchased.
8. Purchased treasury shares, using the par value method, and the purchase price is greater than the price at which the shares were originally issued.
9. Appropriated retained earnings.
10. Declared a liquidating dividend.
11. Declared a scrip dividend.

Transaction	Assets	Stockholders' Equity	Debt/Equity Ratio*	Net Income	Return on Assets**	Total Contributed Capital	Retained Earnings
1.							
2.							
3.							
4.							
5.							
6.							
7.							
8.							
9.							
10.							
11.							

+ = Improved   − = Not improved   NE = No effect   ? = Cannot be determined

*Assume that there is more equity than debt before the indicated transaction is journalized. Also, if the amount of equity increases as compared to debt, then the ratio has improved (i.e., +).
**Assume that this ratio is positive initially. Also, a larger positive number means that the ratio has improved (i.e., +).

Exercise 14-9: Stock Splits and Dividends. Korrel Inc. was organized in 1995 and has been profitable since 1998. Cash dividends were declared for the first time in 2002, and the dividend amount was maintained in 2003. The company's stock price has appreciated from around $2–$5 per share in 1995 to $120–$145 in 2004. Stockholders' equity accounts as of December 31, 2003, are as follows:

Common stock ($0.01 par)	$ 8,000
Paid-in capital in excess of par	4,000,000
Retained earnings	837,668
Treasury stock (25,000 shares; cost method)	(62,500)

The company has decided to maintain the annual cash dividend for the year 2004 at $0.50 per share before any adjustments for splits and/or dividends. (That is, if there is a 2-for-1 stock split, then the dividend is not $0.50 per share, but $0.25 per share, etc.). In addition, the company desires to provide additional shares of stock to its current investors. Accordingly, the company is investigating the possibility of providing a stock split or a stock dividend.

1. Prepare the journal entries to record the declaration and payment of the cash dividend.
2. Prepare the journal entry, assuming that when the market price of Korrel's stock was $140, the company declared and distributed:
   a. A 2-for-1 stock split.
   b. A 100% stock dividend.
   c. A 10% stock dividend.
3. Which method would you recommend to Korrel to accomplish its desire to increase the number of shares outstanding? Why?
4. Why would a company desire to provide shareholders with a stock dividend and/or split?
5. What effect would a 2-for-1 stock split as compared to a cash dividend have on the following:

a. Earnings per share?
b. Stock price?
c. P/E ratio (price/EPS)? Include a brief discussion of the significance of the P/E ratio.

Exercise 14-10: Stock Options (Intrinsic Method). On December 31, 2004, Southern Rentals granted its key employees 10,000 stock options as additional compensation. The options permit the employees to purchase shares of Southern Rentals' $10 par common stock at $40 per share. On the date of grant, Southern Rental's common stock is selling for $50 per share. The options are exercisable on December 31, 2006, after the key employees have worked for two years. All 10,000 options were exercised on December 31, 2006, when the market price was $74 per share.

1. Compute the total compensation expense related to these options.
2. How much compensation expense should Southern Rentals recognize on its financial statements for 2004, 2005, and 2006?
3. Prepare any necessary journal entries on December 31, 2004, through December 31, 2006, to recognize compensation expense and to record the exercise of the stock options.

Exercise 14-11: Stock Options (Intrinsic Method). On January 1, 2005, Karma Korporation hired a new CEO and, as part of the compensation package, granted her stock options to acquire 20,000 shares of its $10 par common stock. The market price on that date was $40 per share. The options become exercisable after the CEO has worked for Karma for three years. The subsequent market price of Karma's stock was as follows:

January 1, 2006	$50 per share
January 1, 2007	64 per share
December 31, 2007	70 per share

1. Assume that on January 1, 2005, it is determined that the exercise price will be $40 per share, how much should Karma record as total compensation expense over the three years?
2. Assume that on January 1, 2005, it is determined that the exercise price will be $30 per share, how much should Karma record as total compensation expense over the three years?
3. Assume that on January 1, 2005, it is determined that the exercise price will be 90% of the market price on December 31, 2007. Compute the amount of compensation expense Karma should recognize for the 12-month period ending (a) December 31, 2005, (b) December 31, 2006, and (c) December 31, 2007.

Exercise 14-12: Stock Options (Fair Value Method). In addition to the facts provided in Exercise 14-11, assume that on January 1, 2005, the interest yield on government-issued short-term treasury bills was 5%. Also, assume the following information related to the stock of Karma Korporation:

Expected stock volatility	22.5%
Dividend yield	4.0

Determine the amount of pro forma compensation expense that Karma Korporation should recognize in its notes, assuming that the exercise price for each share of stock is determined to be (1) $40 and (2) $30.

Exercise 14-13: Variable Stock Option Plan. On December 31, 2006, as incentive compensation for services to be rendered during the next three years, Red Mountain Corporation offered Lynn, its CEO, stock appreciation rights with the following terms:

Market price, Dec. 31, 2006	$60 per share
Number of SARs	10,000
Earliest date SARs can be exercised	January 1, 2008
Expiration date	December 31, 2010

The appreciation in stock value will be paid in shares (computed at the market price as of December 31, 2006) of Red Mountain's no-par common stock, with any fractional shares paid in cash. For example, if the shares are exercised when the market price of the stock is $70 per share, then Lynn's total compensation is $100,000, which is computed as the increase of $10 per share in excess of the current market price multiplied by the 10,000 rights. This $100,000 is equivalent to 1,666 shares of Red Mountain stock at its current market price of $60, with the difference of $40 paid in cash to Lynn.

Lynn exercised the rights on December 31, 2009. Between December 31, 2006, and December 31, 2009, the market value of Red Mountain's stock was as follows:

December 31, 2007	$57 per share
December 31, 2008	61 per share
December 31, 2009	65 per share

Provide the journal entries to accrue compensation expense for 2007 through 2009, and also record the payment of the stock and cash on December 31, 2009.

Exercise 14-14: Prior-Period Adjustment. O'Bannon Construction Company began business in 2000 and used the completed-contract method to recognize revenue. On December 1, 2005, the decision was made to switch to the percentage-of-completion method to recognize revenue. Prior to making the change, the following data were accumulated:

Income Reported for	Completed-Contract Method	Percentage-of-Completion Method
2000	$ 0	$ 500,000
2001	1,000,000	1,000,000
2002	0	1,200,000
2003	2,000,000	1,750,000
2004	0	2,000,000
2005	5,000,000	2,400,000

Prepare a statement of retained earnings for December 31, 2005, with the data for 2004 and 2003 also being reported for comparative purposes.

Exercise 14-15: Statement of Changes in Stockholders' Equity. The following information was extracted from the balance sheet of Bannigan Inc. as of December 31, 2003:

Common stock (50,000 shares authorized, $10 par)	$100,000
Additional paid-in capital in excess of par	75,000
Retained earnings	50,000
Accumulated other comprehensive income	(20,000)

During 2004, the company reported net income of $45,000 and declared and paid a cash dividend of $15,000. In addition, the company issued 10,000 shares of common stock for cash of $220,000. Bannigan also had a foreign currency translation credit adjustment of $8,000 and an unrealized loss on available-for-sale securities of $5,000.

Prepare a statement of changes in stockholders' equity for Bannigan Inc. for the 2004 fiscal year.

Problems

Problem 14-1: Stock Options (Intrinsic Method). On January 2, 2003, the stockholders of American Dixie Company authorized a stock option plan for key employees to purchase 50,000 shares of the company's $1 par value common stock at $20 per share. These shares are not exercisable until December 31, 2005, and they expire on December 31, 2006. The following day, the stockholders approved another stock option plan to grant an additional 4,000 shares to the president at 90% of the market price on the date the shares become exercisable. One thousand of these shares are exercisable at the end of each year for the next four years and expire six months later.

The president exercised his 1,000 options on December 31, 2003 and December 31, 2004, but did not exercise the options for 2005 and 2006. Various key employees exercised 15,000 options on December 31, 2005, but the rest of the 50,000 options expired.

The market price of the options at various dates were as follows:

January 2, 2003	$22 per share
December 31, 2003	25 per share
December 31, 2004	28 per share
December 31, 2005	20 per share
December 31, 2006	21 per share

Required:

1. Prepare all necessary journal entries to account for these two stock options (i.e., recognizing compensation expense and exercising the options) for the years 2003 through 2006.
2. Comment on the general advantages of a variable stock option plan (as structured in this problem) versus a fixed stock option plan and the amount of compensation expense recognized by American Dixie versus the benefit received by employees from the stock option plan.

Problem 14-2: Stock Options (Intrinsic Method). Ollie Corporation has 100,000 shares of $20 par common stock authorized, of which 40,000 shares are outstanding. Also, the company has a stock option plan for certain key executives that has the following provisions:

- Each executive will receive on January 1, 2005, a computed number of shares of common stock at a computed option exercise price per share. The computation of the number of options and the option exercise price shall be made on December 31, 2007, and will be related to the increase in net income over the 3-year period.
- The plan provides compensation in addition to salary for services to be performed approximately equally during the years 2005–2008.

- The options are nontransferable and must be exercised not earlier than three years and not later than five years from the date of grant. Employment with the company is required through the exercise date.

On January 1, 2005, one key executive to receive stock options was Kim, the chief financial officer. At that date, the common stock was trading for $50 per share. On January 1, 2005, the following information was also available:

	Estimates made on January 1, 2005, as to what the amounts would be on December 31, 2007	Actual amounts on December 31, 2007
Number of options for each executive	500	510
Option exercise price	$60	$63
Market price	$70	$75

Kim exercised the options on December 31, 2008, when the stock was selling for $80 per share.

Required:
1. When is the measurement date? Explain your answer.
2. Over what period should total compensation expense for Kim be assigned? Explain your answer.
3. Give appropriate entries for the stock options given to Kim at:
    a. January 1, 2005.
    b. December 31, 2005.
    c. December 31, 2007.
    d. December 31, 2008.
4. How much actual incentive compensation did Kim "earn?"
5. How much additional compensation did Ollie Corporation report?

Problem 14-3: Stock Options (Fair Value Method). Zippity Inc. is a small company with high growth potential but limited liquid resources. To attract a top executive, Tom Landers, the company offered Mr. Landers a compensation package that included a large number of stock options in lieu of a reduced cash salary. On January 1, 2003, Zippity Inc. granted 300,000 stock options to Mr. Landers. Each option provides for the purchase of one share of no-par common stock for $5. The shares vest evenly over three years (i.e., 100,000 shares vest each December 31 over the next three years), and upon vesting, Mr. Landers has one year to exercise the options.

Additional relevant information is as follows:

Risk-free interest rate	4.5%
Volatility of stock	45.0%
Dividend yield	0.0%

Assume that on December 31, 2005, the market price of Zippity Inc. stock is $7.50, and Mr. Landers decided to exercise 200,000 of the options. On December 31, 2006, the market price of Zippity Inc. stock deteriorated such that the remaining options were "out-of-the-money," and accordingly, Mr. Landers allowed the options to expire unexercised.

Required:

1. Assume that Zippity Inc. chooses to follow the fair value method according to the requirements of *SFAS No. 123*. Assuming that the market value of the stock on the grant date was (a) $3, (b) $5, and (c) $7, provide all necessary journal entries to account for the stock options on:
   a. January 1, 2003.
   b. December 31, 2003.
   c. December 31, 2004.
   d. December 31, 2005.
   e. December 31, 2006.

2. Compare the compensation expense amounts in Part (1) with the actual benefit that Tom Landers realized from holding the options.

Problem 14-4: Dividends. For the past five years, Dappall Co. has striven to provide some type of dividend to its stockholders. However, in each case, the type of dividend was different and depended on the company's circumstances. A brief description of the dividend for each year is provided below.

Year	Description of Dividend
2004	The company declared a dividend of $2 per share on all outstanding shares of common stock.
2005	The company paid a dividend in the form of merchandise to all holders of the company's stock. The book value of the merchandise was $80,000, and the market value was $100,000.
2006	The company announced a dividend of $2 per share to all holders of its common stock but issued 2-year promissory notes to the shareholders in lieu of cash.
2007	The company declared a dividend of $2 per share on all outstanding shares of common stock.
2008	The company announced a dividend in the form of additional shares. Each shareholder would receive an increase of 20% of the shares held.

The following table provides additional information pertaining to the equity of Dappall Co. for the period analyzed:

The Year Ended December 31,	Shares Outstanding Prior to Dividend Paid in Given Year	Market Value Prior to Dividend Paid in Given Year	Retained Earnings Prior to Payment of Dividend in Given Year
2004	60,000	$15	$180,000
2005	55,000	10	130,000
2006	50,000	8	125,000
2007	50,000	6	50,000
2008	60,000	12	165,000

Required:

1. Prepare the necessary journal entry to record the dividend declaration for each year.
2. Determine the ending balance of retained earnings for each year subsequent to the dividend declaration.

3. Prepare the journal entry to record a 2-for-1 stock split.
4. Prepare the journal entry to record a 100% stock dividend.

Problem 14-5: Dividends. Whitney, Inc., began business on January 2, 2004, and had the following reported net income or loss for their first five years:

2004	$ 150,000 loss
2005	240,000 loss
2006	120,000 loss
2007	250,000 income
2008	1,000,000 income

On December 31, 2008, Whitney's capital accounts were as follows:

Common stock, par value $10 per share: authorized, 100,000 shares; issued and outstanding, 50,000 shares	$ 500,000
4% cumulative preferred stock, participating up to an additional 2%, par value $100 per share: authorized, issued, and outstanding, 1,000 shares	100,000
7% fully participating, cumulative preferred stock, par value $100 per share: authorized, issued, and outstanding, 10,000 shares	1,000,000

Whitney has never paid a cash dividend or a stock dividend. The capital accounts have not changed since Whitney began operations. The appropriate state law permits dividends only from retained earnings.

Required:
1. Prepare a schedule showing the maximum amount available for cash dividends on December 31, 2008.
2. Prepare another schedule showing how that maximum amount should be distributable to the holders of the common shares and each class of preferred shares on December 31, 2008.

Problem 14-6: Errors and Preparing the Statement of Retained Earnings. In 1999, Dewey Cheatum, out of concern that the end of the world was fast approaching, began storing nitrogen-packed food, camping supplies, and other such materials. The "Big One" never occurred in 2000 as he had anticipated, but he found that money could be made in selling such supplies. So he and Ed Howe, a neighbor who had similar thoughts and ideas, formed a corporation that was called Dewey Cheatum and Howe. Business was immediately successful, and from 2000 through 2003, the corporation reported net income of $50,000, $67,000, $78,000, and $92,000, respectively. Also, Dewey and Ed paid dividends of $40,000, $60,000, $60,000, and $80,000 for those same four years, respectively.

In 2004, after issuing the 2003 financial statements, it was discovered that in addition to making an error as to when the end of the world would occur, Dewey and Ed had also made an error in 2000 in expensing equipment costing $20,000 that should have been capitalized. The equipment has an 8-year life, after which time it will not be worth anything. Dewey Cheatum and Howe uses the straight-line method of depreciation.0

Required:
Prepare the statement of retained earnings, as restated, in comparative form for each of the years 2000 through 2003. Assume a tax rate of 20%.

Problem 14-7: Accounting Changes, Correction of Errors, and Statement of Retained Earnings. ACAFS Corporation is negotiating a loan and, as part of the application process, ACAFS must submit audited financial statements, which it has never before done. During the audit of the 2004 financial statements, the auditor made the following work paper comments concerning errors that needed to be corrected:

- The count of merchandise inventory at December 31, 2004, was understated by $100,000. Also, an extension error was found in computing the merchandise inventory at December 31, 2003, such that inventory was overstated by $40,000, which had flowed through the cost of goods sold for 2004. ACAFS uses a perpetual inventory system.
- Equipment costing $240,000 that was purchased on July 1, 2002, was inappropriately expensed. The life of the equipment is six years, at which time it is anticipated that the equipment will be worthless.
- A 3-year insurance policy premium of $18,000 that was paid on August 1, 2003, was charged to expense.

ACAFS has an income tax rate of 30%.

Required:
1. Prepare the necessary journal entries to correct these errors, assuming that the books for 2004 have not been closed.
2. Assuming that the balance of retained earnings at January 1, 2004, was $1,000,000 and that income as reported and dividends for 2004 were $240,000 and $80,000, respectively, prepare the statement of retained earnings.

Problem 14-8: Stockholders' Equity (Comprehensive). Davin Corporation is a publicly owned corporation whose shares are traded on a national stock exchange. At December 31, 2004, Davin had 25,000,000 shares of $10 par value common stock authorized, of which 15,000,000 shares were issued and 14,000,000 shares were outstanding. Other stockholder equity accounts were as follows:

Paid-In Capital in Excess of Par	$120,000,000
Paid-In Capital, Stock Options	1,200,000
Paid-In Capital, Treasury Stock	24,000,000
Retained Earnings	90,000,000
Treasury Stock	(16,000,000)

The paid-in capital from stock options relates to 150,000 stock options that have been given to various key employees.

During 2005, Davin had the following transactions that affected stockholders' equity:

a. On February 1, a secondary distribution of 2,000,000 shares of the $10 par value common stock was issued at $19 per share.
b. On March 12, Davin issued at $110 per share, 100,000 shares of $100 par value, 8%, cumulative preferred stock with 100,000 detachable warrants. Each warrant with $20 could be exchanged for one share of $10 par value common stock. On March 12, the market price for one stock warrant was $1. Use the incremental method to account for the transaction.
c. On April 13, Davin reacquired 40,000 shares of its common stock for $17 per share. Davin uses the cost method to account for treasury stock.
d. On May 31, Davin declared a semiannual cash dividend on common stock of $0.15 per share, payable on June 10, 2005.

e. On July 1, when the market price of the stock warrants was $2 each and the market price of the common stock was $23 per share, 80,000 stock warrants were exercised. Davin issued new shares of stock to honor the warrants.

f. On August 15, executives exercised 100,000 options that were granted in 2000. When the options were granted, each option entitled the executive to purchase one share of common stock for $18 per share. On August 15, the market price of the common stock was $25 per share. Davin used treasury stock that had been purchased in a previous year to honor the stock options.

g. On September 1, when the market price of the common stock was $26 per share, Davin declared a 5% stock dividend that is distributable on October 1. State law prohibits stock dividends on treasury stock.

h. On November 15, Davin reissued 20,000 shares of treasury stock at $22 per share that had been acquired on April 13.

i. On November 30, Davin declared a semiannual cash dividend on common stock of $0.15 per share and the yearly dividend on preferred stock that is to be paid on December 20.

j. On December 30, the remaining stock warrants expired.

k. Net income for 2005 was $5,000,000.

Required:

1. Prepare journal entries for the preceding transactions.
2. Using one column for all paid-in capital amounts, prepare a statement of changes in stockholders' equity for 2005, rounding all amounts to the nearest thousand. Combine transactions as necessary.

Problem 14-9: Stockholders' Equity (Comprehensive and Cumulative). At the beginning of the current year, Erica Corporation had the following stockholders' equity balances in its general ledger:

Common Stock, $10 par value	$2,500,000
Paid-In Capital in Excess of Par	1,500,000
Paid-In Capital, Treasury Stock	450,000
Paid-In Capital, Stock Options	200,000
Retained Earnings	5,000,000
Treasury Stock (15,000 shares)	(300,000)

The paid-in capital from stock options relates to 50,000 options that were granted to the CEO as incentive compensation. The exercise price is $18 per share.

During the current year, Erica engaged in the following transactions, which are listed in chronological order:

a. On January 2, Erica purchased 5,000 shares of its common stock for $16 per share. Erica uses the cost method of accounting for treasury stock transactions.

b. On April 1, Erica issued 20,000 shares of $50 par, noncumulative, convertible preferred stock for $60 per share, where one share of preferred stock is convertible into three shares of common stock.

c. Declared and paid a cash dividend of $2 per share on the outstanding common stock.

d. On July 1, Erica reissued 2,000 shares of treasury stock that had been purchased in a prior year for $21 per share.

e. Also on July 1, holders of 10,000 shares of preferred stock converted their shares into common stock when the market value of the common stock was $22 per share. Erica uses the book value method of accounting for conversions.

f. On October 1, Erica declared and distributed a 1% stock dividend on common stock when the market price of the stock was $24 per share.

g. Corrected an error that was made several years ago, when land that had been purchased for $100,000 was inadvertently expensed.

h. Recorded net income of $1,000,000.

The combined income tax rate of all taxing districts is 30%, the average market price of the common stock during the year was $20, and no dividends were declared on the preferred stock.

Required:
1. Prepare journal entries for each of these transactions.
2. Using one column for all paid-in capital amounts, prepare a statement of changes in stockholders' equity for the current year. Round amounts to the nearest thousand.
3. Compute the basic and diluted earnings per share for the current year.

Cases

Case 14-1: Dell Computer Corporation. Dell Computer Corporation was founded by Michael Dell in 1984 and incorporated in 1987. As of 1999, the company was the largest direct computer systems company in the world, with $18.2 billion in annual revenues. The company provides a wide array of computer products and prides itself on high-quality customer service through on-line technical support and next-day, on-site product service. The company's common stock trades on the NASDAQ exchange under the ticker symbol "DELL."

As founder and CEO of the company, Michael Dell has benefited from the success of the company through a generous compensation package. For the annual period ending January 29, 1999, Michael Dell's compensation consisted of a salary of $844,231, a bonus of $2.6 million, and 12,800,000 stock options (along with other miscellaneous compensation that is not material—at least not material to Michael Dell).

The following selected information was obtained from the company's 10-K report filed with the SEC for the fiscal period ending January 29, 1999:

	For the Fiscal Year Ended January 29, 1999 (in millions, except per-share data)
Net income	$1,460
Weighted-average shares outstanding:	
Basic	2,531
Employee stock options and other	241
Diluted	$2,772
Earnings per share:	
Basic	$ 0.58
Diluted	$ 0.53

Dividends

The Company has never paid cash dividends on its common stock. The Company intends to retain its earnings for use in its business and, therefore, does not anticipate paying any cash dividends on the common stock for at least the next 12 months.

Note 1—Accounting Principles

Stock-Based Compensation—The Company applies the intrinsic value method in accounting for its stock option and employee stock purchase plans. Accordingly, no compensation expense has been recognized for options granted with an exercise price equal to market value at the date of grant or in connection with the employee stock purchase plan.

Note 7—Benefit Plans

Incentive and Employee Stock Purchase Plans—The Dell Computer Corporation Incentive Plan (the "Incentive Plan"), which is administered by the Compensation Committee of the Board of Directors, provides for the granting of incentive awards in the form of stock options, stock appreciation rights ("SARs"), restricted stock, stock and cash to directors, executive officers and key employees of the Company and its subsidiaries, and certain other persons who provide consulting or advisory services to the Company.

The right to purchase shares under the existing stock option agreements typically vests pro rata at each option anniversary date over a five-year period. Stock options must be exercised within 10 years from date of grant. Stock options are generally issued at fair market value. Under the Incentive Plan, each nonemployee director of the Company automatically receives nonqualified stock options annually.

The weighted-average fair value of options and purchase rights under the employee stock purchase plan was determined based on the Black-Scholes model, utilizing the following assumptions:

	Fiscal Year Ended January 29, 1999
Expected term	5 years
Risk-free interest rate	5.42%
Volatility	52.12%
Dividends	0%

In addition to the above 10-K information, the following disclosure was provided in Dell Computer's proxy statement filed with the SEC:

POLICY WITH RESPECT TO THE $1 MILLION DEDUCTION LIMIT

Section 162(m) of the Internal Revenue Code generally limits the U.S. corporate income tax deduction for compensation paid to executive officers named in the summary compensation table in the proxy statement of a public company to $1 million, unless the compensation is "performance-based compensation" or qualifies under certain other exceptions. When structuring awards to the executive officers, the Committee considers the potential loss of deduction under Section 162(m), as well as the financial statement effect of a particular award.

Additional information in Dell Computer's proxy statements filed with the SEC indicates that Dell Computer sets the exercise price of the stock options equal to the fair market value of the stock on the date of the grant. In addition, disclosures reveal that the weighted-average exercise price of all options granted to Michael Dell during the fiscal year is $21.25.

Using the preceding information, answer the following questions:

1. Based on the Black-Scholes option pricing model, what is the estimated value of the stock options provided to Michael Dell for the January 29, 1999 fiscal year? What percentage of Michael Dell's total compensation is represented by stock options?

2. How would earnings be affected if Dell Computer Corporation had recorded compensation expense based on the fair value of the options granted to Michael Dell? To answer this question, assume that the 12,800,000 options granted to Michael Dell for the period ending January 29, 1999, were all granted at the beginning of the reporting period, and the options vest evenly throughout the 5-year vesting period. In your opinion, is the compensation provided to Michael Dell a form of compensation expense that should be recognized in the financial statements?

3. How would the value of the stock options granted to Michael Dell change under the Black-Scholes model under each of the following independent assumptions?

   a. The exercise price was $2 below the market price at the date of issue. What would the compensation expense be using the intrinsic value method under this assumption?

   b. The risk-free interest rate increased by one percentage point.

   c. The volatility of the stock price increased by 10 percentage points.

   d. Dividend yield increased to 5%.

   e. Expected life of the option was 10 years.

4. Indicate whether the relationship is positive or negative between the value of stock options granted and the independent variables in Question (3). Provide some intuition for each relationship.

5. Why do you think Michael Dell's salary represents such a minor portion of his total compensation?

Research Activities

Activity 14-1: Stock Splits. In the April 12, 1999 edition of *Business Week Online*, an article by Anne Tergesen entitled "Stock Splits: Your Road to Riches?" discusses stock splits. Read the article and answer the following questions:

1. Why might a company want to split its stock?

2. Explain why a stock split might give the company's stock price a boost.

3. What kind of trading strategy is suggested in the article to earn excess stock returns? How might an investor identify companies that are susceptible to splitting their stock?

Activity 14-2: Stock Options—Fair Value Method. In most compensation packages that provide for the award of employee stock options, the number of shares that can be purchased and the exercise price for those shares are determined at the time the options are granted (referred to as "fixed" plans). However, in some more unusual cases, firms will tie the compensation to some type of performance measure, in which case the number of shares that can be purchased and/or the exercise price is not known on the date of grant (referred to as "variable" or "performance" plans). Accounting for the variable plans using the intrinsic value method was discussed in the text. To see how variable plans are accounted for using the fair value method, consider the following example.

Sam Stone is an executive for Rock Products, Inc., and on January 1, 2003, he accepted a compensation package that included the grant of stock options. The total number of options to be received depends on the earnings performance of the company over the next three years, as follows:

Cumulative Earnings Increase over the Next Three Years	Options to Be Granted
<5%	1,000
5–20%	2,000
>20%	3,000

As of January 1, 2003, the company expects that the cumulative increase in earnings over the next three years will be 8%. However, on December 31, 2003, the expectations of the company have changed, such that it now believes that cumulative earnings growth will be 23%. All options granted are expected to be exercised.

Other relevant information is as follows:

	January 1, 2003	December 31, 2003
Market price of stock	$8	$12
Exercise price of options	$8	$8
Risk-free interest rate	5%	5%
Volatility of stock	25%	23%
Dividend yield	0%	0%
Expected exercise date of options	January 1, 2006	January 1, 2006

Research *SFAS No. 123* to determine the amount of compensation expense that would be recognized under the fair value method of accounting for the options in the 2003 fiscal year. (*Hint:* You must consider how many options should be used to calculate the compensation expense recognized in 2003 and, given the change in estimate, whether the new or original market price and volatility values should be used in the calculation.)

15

Financial Reporting FOR Marketable Securities AND Comprehensive Income

Investments—Cost or Market?

One result of having a free market economy is that companies can invest in (or acquire) the debt and equity securities of other companies. Sometimes, this investment is made with the intent of earning a return on an investment. Other times, the intent is to acquire control over the operating and financing activities of another entity, as in the situation of a company wanting to ensure a continuing supply of some needed material or an outlet for a company's products. An investment may even be made when the intent is to buy out the competition. Whatever the reason, all investments in the debt and equity securities of other companies are accounted for at acquisition in accordance with the historical cost principle as discussed in Chapter 5. This historical cost amount is defined to be the sum of the expenditures incurred to acquire the investment, including such expenditures as broker's fees.

Prior to the issuance of *SFAS No. 115*, "Accounting for Certain Investments in Debt and Equity Securities," there was considerable controversy as to how investments in the securities of other companies should be reported on the balance sheet

following their acquisition. Since markets usually exist for most investments in securities, critics of reporting securities at historical cost referred to such accounting as "fairy tale" accounting. Further, critics pointed to the savings and loan fiasco of the 1980s as evidence of the detrimental effects that can occur when investments in securities are reported at historical cost. On the other side of the argument were many notable bankers and the chairman of the Federal Reserve, Allen Greenspan, who argued that reporting investments in securities at current value would cause valuations (and the resulting balance sheets of investors) to gyrate up and down as interest rates and other credit factors changed, which certainly does not communicate very relevant information.

Given these passionate and well-presented arguments, *SFAS No. 115* is a compromise where the accounting for investments in the securities of other companies depends upon management's intent for acquiring the investment. So, when reviewing how a particular company accounts for its investments in debt and equity securities, the readers of financial statements are granted a window into management's expectations.

Learning Objectives

- Explain how it is determined whether marketable securities are reported in the trading, available-for-sale, or held-to-maturity portfolios.
- Compute the unrealized holding gains/losses on marketable securities at year-end on the securities in the trading and the available-for-sale portfolios, and describe where these holding gains/losses are reported.
- Describe the year-end reporting on the balance sheet (i.e., valuation and classification) for securities in all portfolios.
- Describe the accounting procedures, and prepare the journal entries for transferring securities between portfolios.
- Define comprehensive income, and identify its two major components.
- Identify the items that comprise other comprehensive income.
- Prepare the statement of comprehensive income, using the three recommended formats.
- Compute and properly report the reclassification adjustment that results when a security is sold on which a holding gain/loss was previously recognized.
- Explain when and why the equity method of accounting is used for investments in equity securities.
- Prepare journal entries under the equity method to recognize the proportionate share of the investee's income, dividends declared, and amortization of any excess paid over the book value of the investee's net assets.

Marketable Securities—Significant Influence Not Achieved

At year-end, all investments in debt or equity securities (except equity securities accounted for under the equity method) are classified into one of three portfolios according to management's intention for acquiring and holding them. These three portfolios and the reasons that identify a security as belonging to each one are as follows:

1. **Trading securities portfolio:** Securities belonging to this portfolio were purchased and are being held primarily for the purpose of selling them in the near future. As a result, they are bought and sold frequently for the purpose of generating gains due to short-term differences in price.
2. **Held-to-maturity securities portfolio:** Securities belonging to this portfolio are *debt securities* where the company has both the intent—and the ability—to hold them to maturity. Equity securities can never be included in the held-to-maturity portfolio because equity securities have no maturity date.
3. **Available-for-sale securities portfolio:** All other securities belong to this portfolio.

Equity securities are ownership shares (e.g., preferred and common stock) or the right to acquire[1] or dispose[2] of ownership shares. Distinguishing charac-

---

[1]The right to acquire ownership shares occurs, for example, through stock warrants, rights, and call options.
[2]The right to dispose of ownership shares is done, for example, through put options.

teristics of equity securities are that they do not have a maturity date, but they do have the right to share in dividends and—for the common stockholders—the right to vote for management. Regardless of the portfolio into which they are classified, all investments in marketable[3] equity securities where the investor does not have the ability to *significantly influence* the operating and financing activities of the investee are reported on the balance sheet at fair value, as determined from current market quotations.

For securities to be considered marketable, there must be a current market quotation (i.e., bid-and-ask prices) available on a securities exchange registered with the SEC or on an over-the-counter market. Securities whose trading is restricted either by governmental or contractual requirement are not marketable. Securities trading on a foreign market are marketable when the breadth and scope of the foreign market are comparable to a U.S. market. Shares of a mutual fund are marketable when the per-share fair value is published and is the basis for current exchanges. Securities that are not marketable are reported at cost.

A corporation is assumed to have significant influence when it owns 20% or more of the outstanding voting common stock of a corporation. Investments where significant influence has been achieved are accounted for using the equity method rather than being reported at fair value.

Debt securities are differentiated from equity securities in that debt securities have (1) a maturity value, (2) an interest rate, and (3) a maturity date. Also, holders of debt securities receive interest (rather than dividends) and do not have the right to vote for management. Debt securities classified in the held-to-maturity portfolio are reported at amortized cost, using the effective-interest method.[4] Such securities are valued at amortized cost rather than fair value because—since they will be held to maturity—information about their current fair value is not considered too relevant. Intending to hold debt securities for an indefinite period of time does not justify reporting the securities at amortized cost. Investments in debt securities in the trading and the available-for-sale portfolios are reported at current market quotations.

These concepts of classifying debt and equity securities into portfolios and the accounting for the various portfolios are summarized in Exhibit 15-1.

The following discussion of the accounting and financial reporting for investments focuses on the year-end reporting issues. Accordingly, the issues of recognizing revenue during the year or amortizing premiums/discounts on investments in debt securities are covered only as considered necessary.[5]

Trading Securities Portfolio

Securities classified in the trading portfolio are reported on the balance sheet at fair value, and the resulting holding gains/losses are reported on the income statement. Assuming an increase in market value, the journal entry to record the adjustment to market and to recognize the resulting holding gain is as follows:

Adjustment to Market—Trading Portfolio   XXX
    Unrealized Holding Gain on Trading Securities   XXX
To write up marketable securities to fair value and recognize a resulting holding gain.

---

[3]This appears to be the FASB's term for saying that the market quotation is sufficiently reliable.
[4]The straight-line method may also be used when the results obtained are not materially different from those obtained when using the effective-interest method.
[5]If a review of these topics is needed, see Chapters 8 and 11.

EXHIBIT 15-1

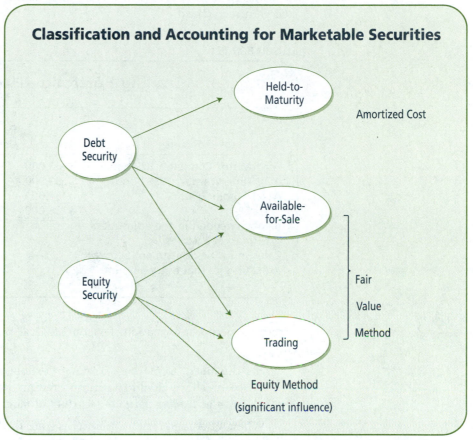

Classification and Accounting for Marketable Securities

The gain is labeled *unrealized* because it is the result of holding securities and having their price increase. Gains that result from selling securities are *realized* gains. When the fair value of the securities in the trading portfolio falls, the adjusting journal entry is to debit an unrealized holding loss account and to credit the adjustment to market account. Because trading securities are held for short periods of time, any premiums and discounts associated with debt securities are not amortized.

To illustrate, assume that during its first year of existence, Beacon Medical acquired the securities shown in Illustration 15-1, which it purchased and is holding with the intent of actively trading them. Accordingly, the company classifies the securities in the trading portfolio. At year-end, information is compiled about the cost and fair value of the securities, which are evaluated in total rather than security by security. For this particular example, the total fair value is $5,000 higher than the total cost of the securities, and so the

securities need to be written up by $5,000, with a corresponding $5,000 unrealized gain recognized.

ILLUSTRATION 15-1

Trading Portfolio—First Year

Security	Cost	Fair Value at December 31	Increase (Dr.) or Decrease (Cr.) in Fair Value
Ford Motor Company, 8% bonds	$ 43,000	$ 47,000	
AOL Time Warner, 10% bonds	89,000	87,000	
AT&T common stock	34,000	37,000	
Totals	$166,000	$171,000	
Balance needed in the adjustment to market account			$5,000 Dr.
Balance in the adjustment account[6]			0
Adjusting journal entry amount			$5,000 Dr.

Based upon this information, Beacon Medical prepares the following journal entry:

Adjustment to Market—Trading Portfolio	5,000	
Unrealized Holding Gain on Trading Securities		5,000
To value trading portfolio securities at market.		

When a trading portfolio security is sold, *the historical cost amount—not the fair value amount reported on the last balance sheet—is removed from the general ledger, and a gain or loss on the sale is recognized and reported as a component of operating income.* So suppose that in 2006, Beacon Medical sells its investment in AOL Time Warner for $81,000. The entry to record the sale is:

Cash	81,000	
Loss on Sale of Marketable Securities	8,000	
Marketable Securities—Trading Portfolio		89,000
To record the sale of a trading security and the resulting loss.		

The $8,000 loss is the difference between the historical cost amount and the selling price, or it can be viewed as being composed of the $2,000 holding loss that occurred in 2005 and a further price decrease of $6,000 in 2006. From this observation, it may appear that the $2,000 holding loss was counted twice—once as a holding loss in 2005 and again as a loss on sale in 2006. However, no double counting occurs. The double counting is avoided in the way the year-end adjustment-to-market entry is prepared. To illustrate this point, suppose that at December 31, 2006, Beacon Medical's trading portfolio is as shown in Illustration 15-2. For clarity of the example, it is assumed that the fair values of the securities still held by Beacon Medical did not change during the year. (Compare Illustration 15-2 with Illustration 15-1.) From this illustration, it can be seen that at December 31, 2006, a $7,000 debit balance is needed in the adjustment to market account. However, this $7,000 is not the amount of the adjusting entry. In determining that amount, consideration must be given to the existing balance in

---

[6]The beginning balance in the adjustment account is zero because this is the first year of the company's existence. In all other years, the balance probably will not be zero.

ILLUSTRATION 15-2

Trading Portfolio—Second Year

Security	Cost	Fair Value at December 31 (These did not change.)	Adjustment to Market Account
Ford Motor Company, 8% bonds	$43,000	$47,000	
AOL Time Warner, 10% bonds	0	0	
AT&T common stock	34,000	37,000	
Totals	$77,000	$84,000	
Balance needed in the adjustment account			$ 7,000 Dr.
Previous balance in the adjustment to market account			(5,000) Dr.
Amount of the year-end adjusting journal entry			$ 2,000 Dr.

the account. In this example, since the adjustment to market account already has a debit balance of $5,000, the adjusting entry at the end of 2006 is as follows:

Adjustment to Market—Trading Portfolio	2,000	
Unrealized Holding Gain on Trading Securities		2,000
To value trading portfolio securities at market.		

The effect of this entry is to reverse the previous year's holding gain on the securities that were sold. In summary, as a result of the preceding two journal entries, Beacon Medical recognized an $8,000 loss on sale of the securities and a $2,000 holding gain on the other two securities, meaning that the net amount Beacon Medical reports on the income statement is a $6,000 loss. Not coincidently, this $6,000 loss is the amount by which the price of the AOL Time Warner securities decreased during the year. *The point is, regardless of what gain/loss a company has on selling its securities, the amount that is reported on the income statement is the amount by which the price of the securities changes during the year.*

The important points of accounting for securities in the trading portfolio are:

1. Securities are reported on the year-end balance sheet at fair value.
2. Unrealized holding gains/losses are reported on the income statement.
3. When securities are sold, the gain/loss on the sale is computed as the difference between the cost of the securities and the selling price.
4. When preparing the year-end adjusting entry to value the securities at market, consideration must be given to the existing balance in the account.

Held-to-Maturity Securities

Securities in the held-to-maturity portfolio are reported on the balance sheet at amortized cost, and holding gains and losses are not recognized. In determining the amortized cost amounts, amortization tables like those for amortizing long-term liabilities, as illustrated in Chapter 11, are prepared. Such amortization tables assist in determining the amount of interest revenue to recognize for the year and the amount of debt premium/discount to amortize.

To illustrate the accounting and financial reporting for debt securities in the held-to-maturity portfolio, assume that on January 1, 2004, J&J Enterprises paid $48,360 for 50 bonds that were issued by Jackman and Person Corporation. Each bond has a face amount of $1,000, will mature in 10 years, and pays interest each December 31 at a coupon rate of 8%. At acquisition, the market interest rate on bonds of similar risk was $8\frac{1}{2}$%. At acquisition and in accordance with the historical cost principle, the entire cost is debited to the investment account. No separate premium/discount account is kept. Because the coupon rate of interest on the Jackman and Person bonds is less than the market rate of interest, the bonds sell at a discount and the amortization table as shown in Illustration 15-3 is prepared, using the effective-interest method.

ILLUSTRATION 15-3

Bond Amortization Table				
Period	Cash	Interest	Discount/ Premium	Carrying Amount
Amount paid at acquisition:				$48,360[7]
2004	$4,000	$4,111	$111	48,470
2005	4,000	4,120	120	48,590
2006	4,000	4,130	130	48,720
2007	4,000	4,141	141	48,862
2008	4,000	4,153	153	49,015
2009	4,000	4,166	166	49,181
2010	4,000	4,180	180	49,361
2011	4,000	4,196	196	49,557
2012	4,000	4,212	212	49,770
2013	4,000	4,230	230	50,000

The amount reported on the year-end balance sheet for any given year is shown in the column headed "Carrying Amount." From this amortization table, it can be seen that the bonds will be reported at December 31, 2004, at $48,470, the bonds will be reported at December 31, 2005, at $48,590, and so forth.

When the amortization of the premium/discount is recorded, the amount is recorded directly to the investment account, as follows (see Illustration 15-3):

Cash	4,000	
Investment in Bonds	111	
Interest Revenue		4,111

When discussing the trading portfolio, an example was given of selling equity securities. Those same general procedures are used when selling bonds in the held-to-maturity portfolio. That is, the unamortized cost of the securities is written off, and a gain/loss is recognized for the difference between fair value and unamortized cost. To illustrate and using the amortization table in Illustration 15-3, assume that one-fourth of the bonds are sold at December 31, 2006, for $14,000. The journal entry to record the sale is as follows:

Cash	14,000	
Investment in Bonds (1/4 × $48,720)		12,180
Gain on Sale of Bonds		1,820
To sell bonds on an interest payment date.		

---

[7]Rounding errors of $1 occur periodically throughout the table.

Recording the sale of bonds between interest payment dates requires that those bonds being sold be amortized since the last interest payment date. To review those procedures and again using the bond amortization table in Illustration 15-3 (but ignoring the prior entry for selling the bonds at 2006), assume instead that on May 31, 2007, one-third of the bonds are sold for $17,000. Then, the accounting for the sale is done in two steps: (1) amortizing the premium/discount since December 31, 2006, and (2) writing off the unamortized cost and recognizing any gain/loss. The computations for doing this are as follows:

Total amount of the discount that will be amortized in 2007 (see table in Illustration 15-3)	$141
Percentage of the year for which the bonds must be amortized	×5/12
Amortization of the bonds since the last interest payment date	$ 59
Percentage of the bonds that are being sold	× 1/3
Amount of the discount that must be amortized	$ 20

Investment in Bonds	20	
Interest Revenue		20

To amortize bond premium/discount since the last interest payment date.

Then, the entry to record the sale of the bonds is as follows, which is similar in all respects to the entry when the bonds were sold on an interest payment date.

Cash	17,000	
Investment in Bonds		16,260
Gain on Sale of Bonds		740

The amount in Investment in Bonds is determined as follows:

One-third of amount at December 31, 2006 (1/3 × $48,720)	$16,240
Amortization amount since December 31, 2006 (see prior entry)	20
Total	$16,260

The important points of the discussion of the accounting and financial reporting of securities in the held-to-maturity portfolio are summarized as follows:

1. Securities are reported in the year-end balance sheet at amortized cost.
2. No holding gains/losses are recognized or reported.
3. When sold, gains/losses are computed as the difference between fair value and amortized cost (with the premium/discount being amortized since the last interest payment date).

Available-for-Sale Securities

The accounting and financial reporting for available-for-sale securities is a mixture of the accounting and financial reporting procedures for trading and held-to-maturity securities, but it also has some unique characteristics. The key points of the accounting and reporting for these securities—in comparison to the accounting for securities in the other two portfolios—are as follows:

1. Like the trading portfolio, all securities (both debt and equity) in the available-for-sale portfolio *are reported on the balance sheet at fair value*, which gives rise to unrealized holding gains/losses. These unrealized holding gains/losses are computed in *exactly* the same fashion as was illustrated for securities in the trading portfolio.

2. However, *the unrealized holding gains/losses are part of other comprehensive income*[8] (rather than part of net income) and are reported in stockholders' equity in Accumulated Other Comprehensive Income, rather than being closed to Retained Earnings.[9]

3. Like securities in the held-to-maturity portfolio, *premiums and discounts on investments in debt securities are amortized*. Thus, for debt securities, an amortization table is prepared. But, unlike securities in the held-to-maturity portfolio, all securities in the available-for-sale portfolio are reported at fair value and not at amortized cost.

4. Finally, like securities in the trading portfolio, any balance in the adjustment to market account is ignored when a security is sold, and it is the historical cost amount (as adjusted for amortization) that is removed from the general ledger.

To illustrate the principles of accounting for debt and equity securities in the available-for-sale portfolio, suppose that on January 1, 2006, Victorian Charm Corporation had investments in securities as shown in Illustration 15-4. Also, assume that on January 1, 2006, the adjustment to market account had a debit balance of $4,000.

ILLUSTRATION 15-4

Securities in the Available-for-Sale Securities Portfolio
(beginning of the year)

Investments	Cost or Amortized Cost	Fair Value
Amazon.com stock	$ 76,000	$ 73,300
Jackman & Person, bonds	48,590	49,090
AT&T common stock	34,000	40,200
Totals	$158,590	$162,590
Balance in the adjustment to market account	$ 4,000	

During 2006, the following transactions occurred:

1. **Sale of securities.** Sold ½ of the Amazon.com stock for $34,000.

Cash	34,000	
Loss on Sale of Marketable Securities	4,000	
Marketable Securities—AFS Portfolio		38,000

To sell securities and recognize a gain/loss.

Supporting computations:

Total cost of the securities	$76,000
Percent being sold	50%
Cost of the securities being sold	$38,000

---

[8]The FASB's rationale for excluding the unrealized holding gain or loss from the determination of net income is that valuing assets at fair value without also valuing corresponding liabilities at fair value may lead to undue volatility of reported earnings.

[9]In Chapter 2, other comprehensive income was defined as gains and losses that affect owners' equity but are not the result of an exchange transaction. Holding gains/losses on marketable securities in the available-for-sale portfolio is the first example of an item included in other comprehensive income.

The important point in the previous entry is that the amount credited to the marketable securities account is one-half of the "cost." As with selling securities in the other portfolios, the market value is ignored, and it is the historical cost, or amortized cost for debt securities, that is removed from the general ledger.

2. **Amortization of bond premium/discount.** At year-end, the receipt (or accrual) of the interest and the amortization of the discount on the Jackman & Person bonds are recorded. (See Period 2006 from the amortization table in Illustration 15-3, p. 700.)

Cash	4,000	
Available-for-Sale Security Portfolio	130	
Interest Revenue		4,130

To recognize interest revenue, cash received, and amortize discount on an interest payment date.

This entry is the same as for recording the interest and amortizing the premium/discount for debt securities in the held-to-maturity portfolio, which is reinforced by using the same amortization table.

3. **Year-end mark to market.** At December 31, 2006, the fair values of the securities being held are determined as shown in Illustration 15-5.

ILLUSTRATION 15-5

Securities in the Available-for-Sale Securities Portfolio
(end of the year)

Investments	Cost/ Amortized Cost	Fair Value December 31	Adjustment to Market Account
Amazon.com stock	$ 38,000	$ 36,000	
Jackman & Person bonds	48,720[10]	49,000	
AT&T common stock	34,000	32,000	
Totals, including amount needed in the adjustment to market account	$120,720	$117,000	$3,720 Cr.
Amount presently in the adjustment to market account			4,000 Dr.
Adjusting journal entry amount			$7,720 Cr.

Based upon these data, the following adjusting journal entry is prepared on December 31, 2006:

Unrealized Holding Loss—AFS Portfolio	7,720	
Adjustment to Market		7,720

To mark securities to market when market is below cost.

Note that the unrealized gain/loss amount is computed in exactly the same way as is done for securities in the trading portfolio and that debt securities are reported at fair value rather than amortized cost. The only difference is where the gain/loss is reported. For the trading portfolio, the unrealized gain/loss is reported on the income statement; but for the available-for-sale portfolio, the unrealized gain/loss is included as a component of other comprehensive income.

---

[10]See Period 2006 in the amortization table of Illustration 15-3, p. 700.

Finally, at year-end and during the closing of the books, the unrealized holding loss is closed to accumulated other comprehensive income in the same way that revenues, gains, expenses, and losses are closed to Retained Earnings, except that an intermediate account like Income Summary is not used.

Permanent Decline in Value

For securities classified in the available-for-sale or the held-to-maturity portfolios, a determination is made at year-end as to whether any declines in the market price of the securities are permanent; that is, it is not expected that the price will return to historical cost in the foreseeable future. When a price decline is determined to be permanent, *the cost of the security is written down to fair value, and the loss is reported on the income statement*. This fair value amount then becomes the security's new cost basis, and that cost basis is not changed for any subsequent price recoveries. The most important ramification of this requirement is when security's are sold. Any gain/loss is determined by comparing the amount received to this new cost basis.

If this rule of recognizing permanent declines in market on the income statement did not exist, it would be possible for companies to postpone recognizing losses on securities in these two portfolios indefinitely. That is, by not selling securities on which the market price had declined substantially or not including them in the trading portfolio, actual losses due to permanent market price declines would never be recognized. The reason why it is not necessary to make the determination of permanent price declines on securities in the trading portfolio is that all holding losses already are reported on the income statement.

EXTENDING THE CONCEPT

Since securities cannot be written up above their new historical cost amount once they have written down, it is a matter of some concern as to whether a market decline at the end of the year is permanent, temporary, or partially permanent and partially temporary. For example, in the 1980s, junk bonds, which received their name because they are not backed by any asset, received a lot of attention because of the high returns that they promised. However, due to the high risk of these junk bonds, some of them subsequently became worthless, and the prices of others decreased substantially but later recovered. Thus, at the end of any particular year, companies who had invested in these bonds had to decide whether any price decrease was permanent or temporary. And there is the possibility that income could be manipulated by deciding that just a part of the price decrease—that part which benefits the company—is permanent.

Financial Reporting

For accounting purposes securities are classified into three portfolios, but for financial reporting purposes these three portfolios are reported as either current assets or long-term assets, depending upon when it is anticipated that they will be sold. *Trading securities are classified as current assets; held-to-maturity securities are classified as investments and funds, unless such securities will mature during the coming year; and available-for-sale securities are classified according to their maturity date or according to management's intent in selling or holding them for the coming year.*

The information in Exhibit 15-2 was extracted from the financial statements of Pfizer Inc. and illustrates how that company reported its investments in marketable securities on its year-end balance sheet.

Summary of Key Points

The following is a review of the more important points in accounting for marketable securities:

- Marketable securities are categorized into three portfolios: (1) trading, (2) available-for-sale, and (3) held-to-maturity.
- Primarily, it is company management's intent for acquiring and holding the securities that determines in which portfolio the securities are classified.

EXHIBIT 15-2

Illustration of the Financial Reporting for Marketable Securities by Pfizer Inc.

(millions, except per-share data)	Year 3	Year 2	Year 1
Assets:			
Current assets			
Cash and cash equivalents	$ 739	$1,552	$ 877
Short-term investments	3,703	2,377	712
Long-term loans and investments	1,721	1,756	1,330

Those securities where it is management's intent to trade them to generate gains on short-term price differences are included in the trading portfolio. Those debt securities where it is management's intent to hold them to maturity—and there is also the ability to hold them to maturity—are included in the held-to-maturity portfolio. All other securities are included in the available-for-sale portfolio. Because equity securities do not have a maturity date, they are never included in the held-to-maturity portfolio.

• At year-end, securities are reported as indicated in the table in Illustration 15-6.

ILLUSTRATION 15-6

Reporting Marketable Securities

	Trading	Available-for-Sale	Held-to-Maturity
Reported on balance sheet at:	Fair value	Fair value	Amortized cost
Unrealized holding gains/losses reported as:	Part of net income	Part of other comprehensive income	Not applicable

• At year-end, a determination is made as to whether any price declines on securities in the available-for-sale or held-to-maturity portfolios are permanent. When such is the case, the securities are written down and the loss is included in net income.

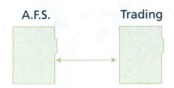

A.F.S.   Trading

Transferring Marketable Securities between Portfolios

When management's intent for holding a security changes, the accounting for the transfer of a security between portfolios is done as follows:

1. Compute the holding gains/losses at the time of transfer, and account for such according to the rules of the portfolio in which the securities are presently classified.
2. Reclassify the security along with any *accumulated unrecognized* gain/loss. Unrecognized gains/losses are those that have not been reported on the income statement. This reclassification is done by:
   a. Writing off the account balances of the security in its present portfolio,
   b. Establishing the account balances of the security in the new portfolio at fair value, and

3. Finally, account for the accumulated unrecognized gain/loss according to the rules of the portfolio into which the security is being transferred.

Exhibit 15-3 summarizes the accounting procedures for the unrecognized gains/losses when transferring securities between classifications.

EXHIBIT 15-3

Accounting for Gains/Losses on Transferring Securities

Transferred to

Transferred from	Trading	Available-for-Sale	Held-to-Maturity
Trading		Holding gains/losses have been reported in the income statement, so there are no *unrecognized* gains/losses to reclassify.	Holding gains/losses have been reported in the income statement, so there are no *unrecognized* gains/losses to reclassify.
Available-for-Sale	The accumulated holding gain/loss in accumulated other comprehensive income is reported on the income statement.		The accumulated gain/loss in accumulated other comprehensive income is amortized over the remaining life of the debt security.
Held-to-Maturity	The difference between fair value and amortized cost is reported on the income statement.	The difference between fair value and amortized cost is recorded in accumulated other comprehensive income and is not amortized.	

The FASB noted that because securities in the held-to-maturity portfolio were acquired with the intent of holding them to maturity, *transfers from that portfolio should be rare*. Also, because securities in the trading portfolio are acquired with the intent of generating gains through frequent buying and selling, *transfers to or from that portfolio should be rare*.

To illustrate the application of the above accounting procedures for transferring securities among portfolios, the information in Illustration 15-7 is used.

ILLUSTRATION 15-7

Securities Data

| | Cost/Amortized Cost | Fair Value | |
		Last Year	Currently
MNO security	$24,000	$25,000	$28,000

Transferring Securities from the Available-for-Sale Portfolio to the Trading Portfolio

Note that the cumulative gain on the MNO securities is $4,000. Also, remember that because the securities are in the available-for-sale portfolio, this gain is being reported in accumulated other comprehensive income. Then, the journal entry to transfer these securities to the trading portfolio is done as follows:

Investment in MNO—Trading Portfolio	28,000 (2. fair value)	
Unrealized Holding Gain—Other Comprehensive Income	4,000 (1. write off old balance)	
Investment in MNO—Available-for-Sale Portfolio		24,000 (1. write off old balance)
Adjustment to Market—Available-for-Sale Portfolio		4,000 (1. write off old balance)
Unrealized Holding Gain/Loss—Income Statement		4,000 (3. recognize this income)

Note the following points, which are associated with the references to the accounts in the preceding journal entry.

1. The cost of the old security, including the balances in the associated adjustment to market account and the unrealized holding gain account, are removed;
2. The securities are reported in the trading portfolio (its new classification) at fair value; and
3. The accumulated unrecognized holding gain is reported in net income because the security is being transferred into the trading portfolio, and that is the rule for accounting for unrealized gains in that portfolio.

Transferring Securities from the Trading Portfolio to the Available-for-Sale Portfolio or to the Held-to-Maturity Portfolio

Having demonstrated the procedures as they apply to transferring securities from the available-for-sale portfolio to the trading portfolio, the following journal entries illustrate the application of the accounting procedures for transferring securities between any other portfolios. The same data used in the previous illustration is used for all transfers; the only difference is the assumption as to what portfolios are affected.

Investment in MNO—AFS/HTM Portfolio	28,000 (2. fair value)	
Investment in MNO—Trading Portfolio		24,000 (1. write off old balance)
Adjustment to Market—Trading Portfolio		4,000 (1. write off old balance)

For securities in the trading portfolio, unrealized gains are reported in the income statement; thus, there are no cumulative unrecognized gains to reclassify. Hence, the only accounting procedures are (1) to write off the old balances (the balances in the investment and the adjustment accounts) and (2) to report the security in its new portfolio at fair value.

Transferring Securities from the Available-for-Sale Portfolio to the Held-to-Maturity Portfolio

Investment in MNO—Held-to-Maturity Portfolio	28,000 (2. fair value)	
Unrealized Holding Gain/Loss—Other Comprehensive Income	4,000 (1. write off old balance)	
Investment in MNO—Available-for-Sale Portfolio		24,000 (1. write off old balance)
Adjustment to Market—Available-for-Sale Portfolio		4,000 (1. write off old balance)
Unrealized Holding Gain/Loss—Other Comprehensive Income		4,000 (3. recognize this income)

Note that the unrealized holding gain/loss is really not affected by the previous entry. The only reason the account was both debited and credited was for completeness of the example. In subsequent years, because held-to-maturity securities are amortized, the holding gain in comprehensive income is also amortized over the remaining life of the debt security. This is done by debiting the holding gain/loss account and crediting the investment account, so that when the debt security matures, the balance in the investment account is equal to the maturity value of the debt.

Transferring Securities from the Held-to-Maturity Portfolio to the Trading Portfolio

Investment in MNO—Trading Portfolio	28,000 (2. fair value)	
Investment in MNO—Held-to-Maturity Portfolio		24,000 (1. write off old balance)
Unrealized Holding Gain—Income Statement		4,000 (3. recognize this income)

Note that there is no holding gain/loss account or adjustment to market account to reclassify or reverse because securities in the held-to-maturity portfolio are reported at amortized cost.

Transferring Securities from the Held-to-Maturity Portfolio to the Available-for-Sale Portfolio

Investment in MNO—Available-for-Sale Portfolio	28,000 (2. fair value)	
Investment in MNO—Held-to-Maturity Portfolio		24,000 (1. write off old balance)
Unrealized Holding Gain—Other Comprehensive Income		4,000 (3. recognize this income)

The only change in this journal entry, as compared to the previous one, is puting the unrealized holding gain/loss in other comprehensive income rather than on the income statement.

Other Comprehensive Income and Comprehensive Income

Comprehensive income includes net income and also the effects of other events that change owners' equity but are not included on the income statement. Thus, comprehensive income is divided into two major sections: (1) net income and (2) all other changes in owners' equity. The other changes in owners' equity that occur during the year are titled "Other Comprehensive Income," and the cumulative amount (similar to retained earnings) is titled "Accumulated Other Comprehensive Income."

Currently, the concept of comprehensive income is not fully implemented; but in addition to net income the FASB has identified the following three items of other comprehensive income that must be reported:

- Changes in the market value of investments that are reported in the available-for-sale securities portfolio and the cumulative unrealized holding gains/losses that result when securities are transferred into the available-for-sale securities portfolio.
- In pension accounting, the equity adjustment that sometimes results from computing the minimum liability. (This is covered in Chapter 18.)
- Certain adjustments that result from translating the financial statements of a foreign subsidiary prior to consolidation, including the adjustments required from a derivative that is designated as a hedge of the net investment. (This is covered in Chapter 21.)

Although reporting amounts other than net income as a separate component of stockholders' equity has been a practice since 1975, it was not until the issuance of *SFAS No. 130*, "Reporting Comprehensive Income," that guidance was pro-

INTERNATIONAL

EXTENDING
the Concept

The notion of comprehensive income is unique to U.S. GAAP.

vided as to how such amounts should be reported. Of importance, *SFAS No. 130* does not discuss how the elements of comprehensive income are measured—those issues are covered in other standards. Rather, *SFAS No. 130* provides acceptable alternative formats for reporting comprehensive income, including the items that comprise other comprehensive income.

Alternative Reporting Formats

The first acceptable format for reporting comprehensive income is in a statement titled, "Statement of Comprehensive Income." (See Illustration 15-8.) This approach is sometimes referred to as the "two-statement" approach because two operating statements are prepared: the income statement and the statement of comprehensive income. The statement of comprehensive income is prepared after the income statement and begins with net income, includes the other comprehensive income elements, and ends with comprehensive income.

ILLUSTRATION 15-8

Barbara's Warm Fuzzys
Statement of Comprehensive Income
For the Year Ended December 31, 2005

Net income		$100,000
Other comprehensive income:		
Foreign currency translation adjustment		$ (8,000)
Unrealized gains/losses on available-for-sale securities:		
Unrealized gains arising during the period	$ 9,000	
Reclassification adjustment	(3,000)	6,000
Minimum pension liability adjustment		4,000
Total other comprehensive income		$ 2,000
Comprehensive income		$102,000

The second acceptable approach to reporting comprehensive income is to report the other comprehensive income items on the income statement, which is titled "Statement of Earnings and Comprehensive Income." The first part of this statement is a traditional income statement, and after net income is determined, the various elements of other comprehensive income are reported. This approach is also called the "single-statement" approach and is shown as Illustration 15-9.

The third acceptable approach to reporting comprehensive income is within the statement of changes in stockholders' equity. Although the FASB expressly stated a preference for either of the first two approaches, it is this third approach that is used most frequently to report other comprehensive income. This reporting format was illustrated in Exhibit 14-7 in Chapter 14.

Whichever format is chosen, the yearly amount of other comprehensive income is transferred to a separate component of stockholders' equity called accumulated other comprehensive income. Using the information shown in the illustrations above for other comprehensive income, the typical year-end journal entry to close these amounts to accumulated other comprehensive income is as follows:

ILLUSTRATION 15-9

Barbara's Warm Fuzzys
Statement of Earnings and Comprehensive Income
For the Year Ended December 31, 2005

Revenues		$ XXX
Expenses		(XXX)
Net income		$100,000
Other comprehensive income:		
Foreign currency translation adjustment		$ (8,000)
Unrealized gains/losses on available-for-sale securities:		
Unrealized gain arising during the period	$ 9,000	
Reclassification adjustment	(3,000)	6,000
Minimum pension liability adjustment		4,000
Total other comprehensive income		$ 2,000
Comprehensive income		$102,000

Unrealized Gains/Losses on AFS Securities	6,000	
Minimum Pension Liability Adjustment	4,000	
Accumulated Other Comprehensive Income		2,000
Foreign Currency Translation Adjustment		8,000

To close the various other comprehensive income accounts to accumulated other comprehensive income.

On a balance sheet, the accumulated other comprehensive income account is reported just after Retained Earnings, as illustrated in Illustration 15-10.

ILLUSTRATION 15-10

Barbara's Warm Fuzzys
Stockholders' Equity
As of December 31

(all amounts in thousands)	2005	2004
Stockholders' equity:		
Common stock $0.01 par value, authorized 500,000,000 shares, issued 164,215,383 shares in 2004 and 164,215,383 shares in 2003	$ 2	$ 2
Additional paid-in capital	613	613
Retained earnings	722	622
Accumulated other comprehensive income (loss)	(78)	(80)
Less treasury stock, at cost (5,167,801 shares in 2004 and 3,945,843 shares in 2003)	(21)	(17)
Total shareholders' equity	$1,238	$1,140

Reclassification Adjustments

The basic characteristic of items included in other comprehensive income is that they are reported in the financial statements before they meet the criteria to be recognized as revenues, expenses, gains, or losses. Later, when these items meet the criteria to be reported on the income statement, they must be reversed out of accumulated other comprehensive income or they would be reported twice in comprehensive income, once as part of other comprehensive income and again as part of net income.

To illustrate how this reclassification or reversal is done, assume that Caleb Corporation at the end of its first year of operations had investments in marketable securities that were classified in the available-for-sale portfolio, as shown in Illustration 15-11A.

ILLUSTRATION 15-11A

Available-for-Sale Securities at the End of 2004
Cost and Market Value

Investments	Cost	Market	Adjustment to Market Account
Virgin Valley, 8% bonds	$ 48,360	$ 49,010	
Mountain America, 10% bonds	89,000	90,350	
Blue Heron, common stock	34,000	37,000	
Totals, including balance needed in the adjustment to market account	$171,360	$176,360	$5,000 Dr.

Based upon the analysis in Illustration 15-11A, the adjusting journal entry to report the securities at market and recognize the resulting holding gain is as follows:

Adjustment to Market—AFS Securities	5,000	
Holding Gain on AFS Securities		5,000

Accordingly, Caleb's statement of comprehensive income (using reporting alternative 1) for 2004 is as shown in Exhibit 15-4.

EXHIBIT 15-4

Caleb Corporation
Statement of Comprehensive Income
For the Year Ended December 31, 2004

Net income		$52,000
Other comprehensive income:		
Unrealized gain on AFS securities	$5,000	
Total other comprehensive income		5,000
Comprehensive income		$57,000

Then, through the closing process at the end of the year, the $52,000 net income is transferred to retained earnings, and the $5,000 other comprehensive income is transferred to accumulated other comprehensive income.

Continuing with the example—and this is the important part of illustrating the reclassification of amounts from other comprehensive income—during 2005, Caleb sold the investment in Blue Heron stock for $49,000, realizing a gain of $15,000. At the end of 2005, the cost and market values of Caleb's investments are as shown in Illustration 15-11B.

ILLUSTRATION 15-11B

Available-for-Sale Securities at the End of 2005
Cost and Market Value

Investments	Cost	Market	Adjustment to Market Account
Virgin Valley, 8% bonds	$ 48,360	$ 50,140	
Mountain America, 10% bonds	89,000	94,550	
Totals, including balance needed in the adjustment to market account	$137,360	$144,690	$7,330 Dr.
Balance already in the adjustment to market account			5,000 Dr.
Adjusting journal entry amount			$2,330 Dr.

Thus, the year-end adjusting entry to update the adjustment to market account to the needed balance of $7,330 is as follows:

Adjustment to Market—AFS Portfolio	2,330	
Holding Gain		2,330

From this analysis, it can be seen that the ending balance in both the adjustment to market account and the accumulated other comprehensive income account is $7,330. Importantly, this $7,330 no longer includes the $3,000 holding gain related to Blue Heron from 2004. This is so because the above journal entry for $2,330 accomplishes two things. First, it recognizes the holding gains/losses for the current year. Second, it reverses the $3,000 holding gain on the Blue Heron stock.

To verify that this adjusting entry accomplishes these two results, note that current year holding gains/losses are computed as the change in the stock price of the securities during the year. These gains/losses are computed by comparing the end-of-year market values to the end-of-the-prior-year market values as shown in Illustration 15-11C.

ILLUSTRATION 15-11C

Computing Holding Gains and Losses for 2005

Col. A	Col. B	Col. C	Col. D
Investments	Market Price, 2005 (See Illustration 15-11B)	Market Price, 2004 (See Illustration 15-11A)	Current Year's Gain/Loss (Col. B − Col. C)
Virgin Valley, 8% bonds	$ 50,140	$ 49,010	$1,130
Mountain America, 10% bonds	94,550	90,350	4,200
Totals	$144,690	$139,360	$5,330

Having computed the current year holding gains/losses, it can be verified that the prior journal entry does accomplish the two objectives of (1) recognizing the current year holding gains/losses, and (2) reversing the prior year holding gains/losses that are now realized. This is done as follows:

Current year holding gains	$ 5,330
Reversal of the holding gain on Blue Heron	(3,000)
Adjusting journal entry amount	$ 2,330

The way the holding gains for the current year and the reversal of the holding gains for the prior year are reported is shown in Exhibit 15-5.

EXHIBIT 15-5

Caleb Corporation
Statement of Earnings and Comprehensive Income
For the Year Ended December 31, 2005

Revenues		$ XXX
Expenses		(XXX)
Gain on sale of securities—classified as AFS		*15,000*
Net income		$100,000
Other comprehensive income, net of income taxes:		
Unrealized gains on securities:		
Unrealized gain arising during the period	*$ 5,330*	
Reclassification adjustment	*(3,000)*	
Total other comprehensive income		*2,330*
Comprehensive income		$102,330

This reclassification of the prior year's holding gains/losses is also necessary when securities are reclassified from the available-for-sale portfolio to the trading portfolio. Then, all previous holding gains/losses that were part of other comprehensive income are reported on the income statement.

In summary, the adjusting journal entry amount to report the available-for-sale securities at market is determined by comparing the amount needed in the adjustment to market account to what is currently in the account. The amount obtained consists of (1) the holding gains for the current year and (2) the reversal of any holding gains of the prior year that are now reported on the income statement. Such reversal is necessary to avoid double counting those gains/losses in comprehensive income: once as a holding gain/loss and then again as a gain/loss on sale. For reporting purposes, the holding gains for the current year are reported separately from the reversal of the holding gains for prior years, with the net amount being equal to the adjusting journal entry amount.

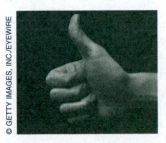

Equity Method of Accounting— Significant Influence Achieved

The equity method of accounting is used to account for all investments in common stock where the investor has the ability to exercise significant influence over the operating and financing activities of the investee. As a rule of thumb, it is presumed that an investor who owns 20% or more of the outstanding voting common stock of the investee has significant influence. However, there are exceptions to this 20% guideline. Some examples of these exceptions are as follows:

- A company owning even 100% of the outstanding voting common stock of an investee does not have significant influence if the investee is in bankruptcy, because then the courts have control.
- A company owning less than 20% of the outstanding voting common stock of an investee has significant influence if a majority of the board of directors of the investee are officers of the investor corporation.
- A company owning more than 20% of the outstanding common stock of an investee may not have significant influence if the investee is domiciled in a foreign country and the foreign government has imposed restrictions that deny the investor the ability to significantly influence the financing and operating policies of the investee.

Also, significant influence can be obtained through a large investment in bonds or preferred stock of the investee corporation. So many and varied are the relationships that can exist among corporations that it is impractical to list all situations in which significant influence could be achieved. Thus, regardless of the actual percentage of the voting common stock owned, all facts and circumstances must be evaluated to determine whether an investor actually has significant influence over the financing and operating policies of the investee.

The Theory of the Equity Method

The notion that a business entity is separate from other businesses or from its owners is a basic assumption of accounting. Because of this separate entity assumption, a business does not record the transactions of other companies or of the owners of the business. However, it is also obvious that an exception to the separate entity assumption occurs when one company owns 100% of the outstanding voting common stock of another company. Then, the two companies are in essence one company, and as a result, the operating results of the investee/subsidiary are reported on the books and financial statements of the investor/parent.

If an investor is separate from an investee at one level of ownership (e.g., 1%), but the two companies are actually the same company when the investor owns 100% of the outstanding voting common stock of the investee, then it follows that there is a point where the two companies begin to blend together. This relationship between the investor and investee with its range of possibilities is illustrated in Exhibit 15-6.

According to Exhibit 15-6, there exists a range of possibilities of the relationship between two companies, which for the sake of convenience is divided into three ranges or stages, as follows:

- In Range I, the investor and investee are totally separate from each other, and the transactions and events that occur to the investee are not recorded on the investor's accounting records or reflected on the investor's financial statements.
- Range II begins where the investor has *significant influence* over the operating and financing policies of the investee and ends when the investor has control.
- In Range III, the investor and investee are actually one entity. Range III begins when the investor has *control* over the operating and financing policies of the investee, which generally is defined to occur when the investor owns 50% or more of the outstanding voting common stock of the investee. In this stage, consolidated statements are issued.

EXHIBIT 15-6

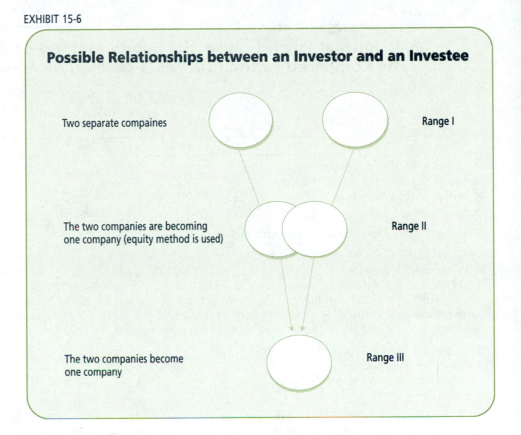

Accounting for Basic Transactions under the Equity Method

On January 3, 2004, Dudley Corporation, realizing the potential for profit in genetic research, acquired 20% of the outstanding common stock of Dallas Labs Corporation by paying $2,000,000. At the time of acquisition, the book value of Dallas Labs' net assets (i.e., assets minus liabilities) was $10,000,000. During the year, Dallas Labs reported an income of $1,000,000 and declared dividends of $400,000. At year-end, the market value of Dudley's 20% investment was $2,100,000, an increase of $100,000 above the amount paid.

In Illustration 15-12, journal entries are prepared under the equity method and under the fair value method, as discussed in the first part of the chapter. This is done to facilitate comparison of the accounting for investments where the investor has significant influence and where the investor does not have significant influence (i.e., the fair value method).

Intricacies to the Equity Method

For ease of illustrating the basic entries of the equity method, the prior example assumed that the shares of common stock of the investee were purchased for their underlying book value. Another simplifying assumption was that the acquisition occurred on January 1. Now, assume that on March 31, 2004, Dudley purchased 25,000 (i.e., 25%) shares of common stock in Dallas Labs for $2,210,000, which gave Dudley the ability to exercise significant influence over the operating and

ILLUSTRATION 15-12

Basic Journal Entries under the Equity Method of Accounting As Compared to the Fair Value Method of Accounting

Transaction	Journal Entries When Significant Influence Is Present		Journal Entries When Significant Influence Is Not Present	
	Debit	Credit	Debit	Credit
Acquire 20% of the outstanding common stock of the investee for $2 million:				
Investment in Investee	2,000,000		2,000,000	
Cash		2,000,000		2,000,000

Comment: No difference in the accounting.

Investee earned income of $1,000,000:				
Investment in Investee	200,000		No entry	
Equity in Net Income of Investee		200,000		No entry

Comment: To reflect the influential relationship the investor has on the investee, a journal entry is required under the equity method. Since the investor owns 20% of the outstanding common stock of the investee, the investor recognizes 20% of the income that the investee earned.

Investee declared a $400,000 dividend:				
Dividends Receivable	80,000		80,000	
Investment in Investee		80,000		—
Dividend Revenue[11]			—	80,000

Comment: Under the fair value method, where the investor does not have significant influence, dividends are recognized as revenue. Under the equity method, where the investor has significant influence, dividends are accounted for as a reduction of the investor's investment because the subsidiary now has fewer assets than previously.

Year-end adjustment to market:				
Adjustment to Market	No entry		100,000	
Unrealized Holding Gain		No entry		100,000

Comment: Under the equity method, securities are not valued at fair value at the end of the year.

[11]An exception to recognizing a dividend as revenue occurs when the dividend is a liquidating dividend, i.e., when the amount of dividends exceeds the investor's share of the investee's earnings subsequent to the date of investment. Then, the investor credits the investment account.

financing policies of Dallas Labs. At the time of acquisition, the underlying book value of Dallas Labs was $8,000,000. During 2004, Dallas Labs reported a net loss of $576,000, which was earned uniformly throughout the year, and did not pay any dividends.

The accounting for the investment in Dallas Labs begins with recording the acquisition of the 25,000 shares, as follows:

Investment in Dallas Labs	2,210,000	
Cash		2,210,000

To record the acquisition of common stock under the equity method.

Accounting for the investment in Dallas Labs continues by determining the excess above book value that Dudley paid. These calculations are made in the following way:

Book value of Dallas Labs	$8,000,000
Multiplied by the percentage acquired	× 25%
Book value of the net assets acquired	$2,000,000
Amount paid by Dudley	2,210,000
Excess amount paid	$ 210,000

There are two possible reasons why Dudley was willing to pay more than book value. First, the assets on the books of Dallas Labs were worth more than the amounts at which they were recorded; and second, Dallas Labs had valuable unrecorded assets (i.e., goodwill). To continue with the example, suppose that the land and building of Dallas Labs were worth $160,000 and $280,000 more, respectively, than the amounts recorded on the general ledger and that any remaining difference is attributable to unidentifiable intangible assets that are labeled "goodwill." Also, the useful lives of the land and goodwill are indefinite, and the life of the building is 20 years.

Having determined that Dudley paid $210,000 more than the underlying book value of the net assets of Dallas Labs, the next step is to determine how much of this excess is attributable to land, building, and goodwill, which is done as follows:

Excess amount paid (see calculation)	$210,000
Amounts attributable to identifiable assets:	
Land (25% × $160,000)	(40,000)
Building (25% × $280,000)	(70,000)
Amount attributable to goodwill (difference)	$100,000

Note that goodwill is determined in a "residual" fashion; that is, the amount paid for the shares of Dallas stock in excess of book value that cannot be attributed to any identifiable asset is labeled as goodwill. Also, note that no journal entry is recorded to write up the land or building or to record the goodwill,[12] but determining the amounts applicable to them greatly expedites the subsequent accounting for every year in which the investment in Dallas Labs is held.

Since no dividends were declared or paid during the year, the only journal entry to record for the year is to recognize Dudley's percentage share of Dallas Labs' reported net loss of $576,000. Computing that amount is done as follows:

Reported loss	$576,000
Multiplied by Dudley's percentage ownership	× 25%
Dudley's loss, assuming investment was held for the entire year	$144,000
Percent of the year in which Dudley owned its investment (9 mos./12mos.)	× 75%
Amount Dudley should recognize for 2004	$108,000

The journal entry to record Dudley's share of the net loss is as follows:

Equity in Net Loss of Dallas Labs	108,000	
Investment in Dallas Labs		108,000
To record investor's share of investee's net loss.		

---

[12]Actually, by recording the investment at the amount paid rather than at book value, the land and building are recorded on the investor's balance sheet at their fair value amounts, and goodwill is also included on the investor's balance sheet, although they are "buried" in the investment account.

Note that just as the investor's share of the investee's net income increases the net assets of the investor, so too does the investor's share of the investee's net loss decrease the net assets of the investor. Also, note that *the investor recognizes just the proportionate share of the investee's net loss.* So, since Dudley held its investment for 9 months, Dudley recognized only that portion of the investee's reported yearly net loss. (This assumes that the loss was incurred uniformly during the year, which was the stated condition in the problem.)

Classifying the Investee's Income

The investor accounts for its share of the reported income in a manner that retains the underlying nature of the income. So if the investee reported an extraordinary item, then the investor also accounts for its share of that gain/loss as an extraordinary item, and the journal entry is prepared accordingly. To illustrate this, assume that of the $576,000 loss reported by the investee, $48,000 was an extraordinary loss that was incurred on September 1. Then, Dudley would record the following journal entry, with supporting computations, to recognize its proportionate share of the reported net loss:

Equity in Net Loss of Dallas Labs, Ordinary	99,000	
Equity in Net Loss of Dallas Labs, Extraordinary	12,000	
Investment in Dallas Labs		111,000
To record and classify investee's income/loss.		

Supporting computations:

		Percent Owned by Dudley	Proportion of Year	To Be Reported
Reported net loss	$576,000			
Extraordinary loss	48,000	25%	100%	$12,000
Ordinary loss	$528,000	25	75	99,000

Dudley takes a full 25% of the extraordinary item (rather than 9/12) because the extraordinary loss is not incurred throughout the year but is incurred at a specific point in time. So if *the extraordinary event occurs after Dudley acquired its investment, then Dudley recognizes its full share of the extraordinary item, and if the extraordinary item occurs before Dudley acquired its investment, then Dudley does not recognize any portion of the extraordinary item.*

This same rule applies to dividends. Either Dudley recognizes a full 25% or it does not recognize any amount, depending upon when the dividends were declared in relation to when Dudley acquired the investment. Thus, using the same assumption that Dudley acquired its investment in Dallas Labs on March 31, 2004, it would not record any journal entry for dividends that were declared before March 31, and it would record 25% for any dividends that were declared after March 31.

Amortizing the Amount Paid in Excess of Book Value

Other than recognizing its proportionate share of the investee's income, another entry that Dudley records at December 31 is amortizing the excess amounts paid for the building and, if applicable, any other under/overvalued assets. The reason for this amortization is that when Dudley paid more than book value for its investment in Dallas Labs it, in effect, recorded the land, building, and goodwill on its general ledger at their fair values—but these amounts were not changed or recorded on Dallas Labs' general ledger. Thus, *Dallas Labs continues to depre-*

ciate these assets at their book values, but Dudley needs to record depreciation based on their fair values.

Using the amounts previously computed for the adjustments to land and building and the calculation of goodwill, these adjustments are computed as shown in Illustration 15-13.

ILLUSTRATION 15-13

Depreciation and Amortization Adjustments

Account	Amount (see prior computation)	Life	Portion of a Year	Amortization Amount
Land	$ 40,000	Indefinite	9/12	$ 0
Building	70,000	20 years	9/12	2,625
Goodwill	100,000	Indefinite	9/12	0
	Total depreciation and amortization			$2,625

The entry to record the additional depreciation and amortization is as follows:

Equity in Net Loss of Dallas Labs	2,625	
Investment in Dallas Labs		2,625

To adjust the depreciation expense from March 31 to December 31 for the difference between fair value and book value of under- or overvalued assets.

This adjustment is made for all undervalued or overvalued assets, including inventory and accounts receivable. For these assets, the amortization period is very short, which is just the normal period of time to collect the receivables or turn over the inventory. Hence, usually all differences between cost to the investee and fair value to the investor are completely amortized within a few months.

Summary of the Investment Account

Because additional expenses are being recorded in the previous amortization entry the equity in net income account is debited. Thus, from Dudley's view, a loss of $113,625 was incurred from its investment in Dallas Labs (which is the sum of its share of Dallas's net loss of $111,000 and the additional depreciation of $2,625). At December 31, the balance in Dudley's investment in Dallas Labs account is $2,096,375, which is computed as shown in this T-account.

Investment in Dallas Labs

Initial investment	2,210,000	
Recognize 25% of loss		111,000
Amortization		2,625
Balance at December 31, 2004	2,096,375	

Recognized Losses Exceed the Amount Invested

In the Dudley/Dallas Labs example, the investee incurred a loss for the year, causing the investor's investment account balance to decrease. It is possible for losses over a period of years to actually exceed the investor's investment, meaning that the balance in the investment account is reduced to zero, or even that it could have a credit balance. When such occurs, *the investor stops using the equity method when the investment account reaches zero*, unless the investee's return to profitability is imminent and assured. In the case where the investor stops using the equity method, the investor resumes using the equity method only after its share of the investee's net income equals the share of the net losses not recognized when the use of the equity method was suspended.

Selling Shares of Stock

Computing the gain/loss when shares of stock are sold is done in the same way as selling shares of stock under the fair value method. That is, the gain/loss is computed as the difference between the carrying value of the shares being sold and the amount received. Supposing that Dudley sold 5,000 shares (or 20% of its shares) in Dallas Labs common stock on January 2, 2005, for $90 per share, the journal entry is as follows:

© GETTY IMAGES, INC./EYEWIRE

Cash (5,000 shares × $90/share)	450,000	
Investment in Dallas Labs		419,275
Gain on Sale		30,725

To record the sale of stock in an investee.

Supporting computations:

Carrying amount of Dudley's investment in Dallas Labs	$2,096,375
Percentage sold	× 20%
Carrying amount of the investment that was sold	$ 419,275

Summary of the Equity Method

An investor uses the equity method when it has the ability to significantly influence the operating and financing policies of the investee. The basics of the accounting under the equity method are as follows:

- When the investee reports income, the investor increases its investment account, reflecting that its net assets have increased, and also records revenue in an account called "Equity in Net Income of Subsidiary." The opposite entry is made when the investee reports a loss.
- The investor records only its percentage share of the investee's income, which is also weighted by the fraction of the year that the investment in the investee was held.
- When reporting its share of the investee's net income, the investor records the underlying nature of the income. For example, extraordinary items for the investee are recorded as extraordinary items for the investor.
- When the investee pays a dividend, the investor prepares a journal entry decreasing the investment account.
- At year-end, no entry is made to adjust the investment account to market.
- When the investor pays an amount greater than the underlying book value of the net assets, the excess is allocated first to identifiable assets, with any residual being goodwill. Any excess amounts allocated to identifiable assets are then amortized over the life of the respective assets.

Questions

1. Name the three securities portfolios in which marketable securities are classified, and explain how the intent of management impacts the classification of these securities.

2. Discuss how temporary holding gains/losses on securities are accounted for under each of the three portfolios in which marketable securities are classified.

3. At what value are securities in the trading, available-for-sale, and held-to-maturity portfolios reported on the balance sheet?

4. Explain the accounting for a permanent decline in the market value of a marketable security and for which portfolio(s) it is not necessary to account for a permanent decline.

5. When is it appropriate to use the equity method of accounting?

6. Is it possible to own more than the presumed minimum percentage of the outstanding voting common stock of an investee and not have significant influence? Describe some situations where this would be the case. Also, is it possible to have less than this presumed minimum percentage and still have significant influence? Describe some situations where this could happen.

7. Under the equity method of accounting for investments, what entry (if any) does the investor prepare when the investee reports earnings? What entry does the investor prepare when the investee declares dividends?

8. Describe the accounting when an investor acquires an investment in the common stock of another corporation that results in having significant influence and the investor pays more for the investment than the underlying book value. Be specific, including the writing up of identifiable assets and the determination of goodwill and subsequent amortization of those amounts.

9. a. On January 1, an investor acquired 25% of the outstanding common stock of a corporation, which gave the investor the ability to exercise significant influence over the operating and financing decisions of the investee. During the year, the investee reported net income of $40,000, which included an extraordinary gain of $10,000. Prepare the journal entry the investor corporation would prepare for these facts.

   b. Prepare the journal entry for (a), assuming that the investor acquired the ability to exercise significant influence on April 1, the investee company's year-end is December 31, and the extraordinary gain was incurred on September 1.

   c. Prepare the journal entry for (a), assuming that the investor acquired the ability to exercise significant influence on April 1, the investee's year-end is December 31, and the extraordinary gain was incurred on February 1.

10. ABC purchased 100 shares of XYZ common stock at book value. During the year, XYZ earned $1.50 per share and paid dividends of $2.00 per share. Thus, a portion of the dividend is a liquidating dividend. Prepare the journal entry for the dividend, assuming that (a) ABC does not have the ability to exercise significant influence and (b) ABC does have the ability to exercise significant influence.

11. Identify the major components of (a) comprehensive income and (b) other comprehensive income.

12. Explain and give examples of the three approaches to reporting comprehensive income.

13. Where is accumulated other comprehensive income reported in the financial statements?

Exercises

Exercise 15-1: Classification of Marketable Securities (CPA Adapted). Camp purchased various securities:

a. Debt securities purchased with the intent of selling them in the near term.
b. U.S. Treasury bonds, where Camp has both the positive intent and the ability to hold them to maturity.
c. Debt securities purchased and being held with the intent of selling them in three years and using the proceeds to pay Camp's $2 million long-term note payable when it matures.
d. Convertible preferred stock that Camp intends to hold indefinitely.

1. For each type of security, determine whether it should be classified in the held-to-maturity, trading, or available-for-sale portfolio.
2. Explain why you classified the securities as you did.

Exercise 15-2: Holding Gains/Losses on Marketable Securities. In October 2004, Johnson Company purchased two marketable equity securities, the details of which are as follows:

Security A was purchased for $60,000. Its fair value on December 31, 2004 (the fiscal year-end), was $70,000, and it was sold on March 28, 2005, for $80,000.

Security B was purchased for $100,000. Its fair value on December 31, 2004, was $80,000, and it was sold on April 2, 2005, for $125,000.

1. Assuming that the securities are classified in the trading portfolio, determine the amount of gains/losses, including holding gains and losses for the years ended December 31, 2004 and 2005, and indicate how each should be reported on the year-end financial statements.
2. Assuming that the securities are classified in the available-for-sale portfolio, indicate where each of the gains and losses should be reported.

Exercise 15-3: Securities in the Various Portfolios. International Copper had the following securities by portfolio at December 31, 2004:

Security	Portfolio	Cost	Market, at December 31, 2004
A	Trading	$20,000	$15,000
B	Trading	30,000	33,000
C	Available-for-sale	10,000	12,000
D	Available-for-sale	70,000	72,000
E	Held-to-maturity	50,000	55,000
F	Held-to-maturity	40,000	42,000

1. What entry (or entries) would International Copper prepare at year-end, assuming that the balances in all adjustment-to-market accounts are zero at January 1, 2004?
2. If net income, before considering the adjustments in Part (1), is $100,000, what would net income be after the adjustments?
3. Ignoring your answers to Parts (1) and (2), what entry (or entries) would International Copper prepare at year-end assuming that the balances in the adjustment-to-market accounts, before preparing the year-end adjusting entries, are a $10,000 credit balance and a $9,000 debit balance in the trading and the available-for-sale portfolio, respectively?

Exercise 15-4: Available-for-Sale Securities. On January 1, 2004, Alliance Systems, Inc., purchased debt securities for $320,000 and classified them in the available-for-sale portfolio. The purchase price was $40,000 less than the maturity value of the securities. The securities coupon rate is 12%, interest is paid on June 30 and December 31, and the bonds mature 10 years from the date of purchase. Alliance uses the straight-line method of amortization. At December 31, 2004, the market value of the securities was $330,000. On April 2, 2005, Alliance sold one-fourth of its investment and received cash of $85,000, which includes the accrued interest. As of December 31, 2005, the market value of the securities still being held is $245,000.

1. Prepare the journal entries to record the transactions in the available-for-sale portfolio during 2004 and 2005. (*Hint:* When preparing the entry to record the sale of the bonds, be sure to record amortization from December 31, 2004, to April 2, 2005.)
2. Using parenthetical notations where appropriate, show how the investment in these bonds would be reported on the balance sheets as of December 31, 2004 and 2005.
3. How would the accounting and financial reporting change if these securities had been classified in the held-to-maturity portfolio?

Exercise 15-5: Held-to-Maturity Portfolio. On February 1, 2005, Moon and Sun purchased 10% bonds that have a maturity value of $1,000,000 for $958,933, which includes the accrued interest, and classified them in the held-to-maturity portfolio. The bonds mature on March 31, 2010, and pay interest semiannually on March 31 and September 30. Moon and Sun uses the straight-line method of amortization, and its fiscal year-end is December 31. At December 31, 2005, the bonds have a fair value of $945,000.

1. Prepare the journal entries to record the purchase of the bonds on February 1, the receipt of interest on March 31 and September 30, and the accrual of interest on December 31.
2. Prepare the adjusting entry, if necessary, to value these securities at market.
3. Show how all items related to the investment would be reported on the 2005 year-end balance sheet and income statement.

Exercise 15-6: Changes in Market-Adjustment Accounts. Precision Inc. reported the following balances in its adjustment-to-market accounts for the years 2004–2007:

	2004	2005	2006	2007
Adjustment to market: trading	$0	$4,000 cr.	$1,000 dr.	$7,000 dr.
Adjustment to market: available-for-sale	0	3,000 dr.	2,000 dr.	4,000 cr.

Using these data, reconstruct the journal entries that Precision Inc. prepared at the end of each year to value the securities at market.

Exercise 15-7: Temporary and Permanent Changes. Tulume Corp. reported the following investments in equity securities:

Securities	Initial Cost	Market Value December 31, 2004	Market Value December 31, 2005
MNO Co.	$40,000	$30,000	$25,000
PQR Co.	70,000	50,000	40,000

At December 31, 2005, Tulume decided that the decline in the market value of the PQR securities was permanent.

1. Assuming that the securities are reported in the trading portfolio, what would the effect be on net income for December 31, 2004, and December 31, 2005, as a result of these declines in value?
2. Assuming that the securities are reported in the available-for-sale portfolio, what would the effect be on net income for December 31, 2004, and December 31, 2005, as a result of these declines in value?

Exercise 15-8: Reclassifications. At December 31, 2004, the following information was available for an investment in debt securities:

	Cost	Market Value December 31, 2004
	$20,000	$24,000

The appropriate entry was prepared on December 31, 2004, to recognize the holding gain before the security was reclassified.

1. Assuming that the securities are in the trading portfolio, prepare the entry necessary to transfer them to the available-for-sale portfolio.
2. Assuming that the securities are in the available-for-sale portfolio, prepare the entry necessary to transfer them to the trading portfolio.
3. Assuming that the securities are in the available-for-sale portfolio, prepare the entry necessary to transfer them to the held-to-maturity portfolio.
4. Assuming that the securities are in the held-to-maturity portfolio, prepare the necessary journal entry to transfer them to the trading portfolio.

Exercise 15-9: Reclassifications. The following information is available for various securities in regard to their reclassifications to be done on December 31, 2005:

Security	Old Classification	New Classification	Cost	Market, December 31, 2005	Balance Related to This Security in the Adjustment-to-Market Account, January 1, 2005
A	Trading	Available-for-sale	$10,000	$12,000	$4,000 dr.
B	Available-for-sale	Trading	26,000	21,000	3,000 cr.
C	Available-for-sale	Held-to-maturity	15,000	13,000	1,000 dr.
D	Held-to-maturity	Available-for-sale	14,000	11,000	6,000 cr.

1. Prepare the necessary entries to reclassify the above securities at December 31, 2005, assuming that the appropriate journal entry has been prepared to recognize any holding gain/loss for the year.
2. Assuming that net income before the reclassifications was $50,000, what will be the net income after the adjustments to market and the reclassifications?

Exercise 15-10: Comparing the Accounting and Financial Reporting between Portfolios. On January 1, 2005, Martin-Kronzek purchased $500,000 par value, 12% bonds when the market was demanding 10% on similar bonds. The bonds pay interest annually and mature on December 31, 2010. Martin-Kronzek uses the effective-interest method of amortization. At December 31, 2005, the market value of these bonds was $540,000.

1. Using the time value of money concept, compute the amount at which the bonds will sell, and then prepare the journal entry to record the acquisition of the bonds, regardless of the portfolio in which they are to be classified.
2. Prepare all necessary journal entries for 2005 after acquiring the bonds, assuming that the bonds were classified in the trading portfolio.
3. Prepare all necessary journal entries for 2005 after acquiring the bonds, assuming that the bonds were classified in the available-for-sale portfolio.
4. Prepare all necessary journal entries for 2005 after acquiring the bonds, assuming that the bonds were classified in the held-to-maturity portfolio.
5. What is the net amount reported on the income statement for 2005 for each of the three portfolios?

Exercise 15-11: Comprehensive Income. In 2004, Cedar Branches Inc. reported the following information in its fiscal year-end income statement:

Revenues	$2,000,000
Cost of goods sold	1,200,000
Gross profit	$ 800,000
Selling and administrative expenses	500,000
Operating income	$ 300,000
Income tax expense	120,000
Net income	$ 180,000

In addition, the company had an unrealized holding gain on securities in its available-for-sale portfolio in the amount of $25,000, and dividends of $30,000 were declared and paid.

Show how comprehensive income would be reported, using the single-statement approach and the two-statement approach.

Exercise 15-12: Comprehensive Income. At December 31, 2004, Northern Lights Financial had the following securities in its available-for-sale portfolio:

Security	No. of Shares	Cost	Fair Value
ABC stock	1,000 shares	$13 per share	$15 per share
JKL stock	2,000 shares	20 per share	26 per share
XYZ stock	1,500 shares	31 per share	28 per share

During 2005, Northern Lights sold 40% of the shares in JKL for $28 per share and used the proceeds to buy 1,000 shares of QRS stock at $24 per share. At December 31, 2005, the following information was available regarding the various securities:

Security	No. of Shares	Cost	Fair Value
ABC stock	1,000 shares	$13 per share	$17 per share
JKL stock	1,200 shares	20 per share	29 per share
XYZ stock	1,500 shares	31 per share	25 per share
QRS stock	1,000 shares	24 per share	23 per share

1. Prepare the journal entry at December 31, 2004, to mark the securities to market.
2. For December 31, 2004, prepare a statement of comprehensive income, assuming that net income was $120,000 and that in addition to the holding gains/losses on the available-for-sale securities, there was a gain of $5,000 on a foreign currency translation adjustment.
3. Prepare the journal entry to sell the shares of JKL.
4. Prepare the journal entry at December 31, 2005, to mark the securities to market.
5. For December 31, 2005, prepare a statement of comprehensive income, assuming that net income was $140,000, and that in addition to the holding gains/losses on the available-for-sale securities, there was a foreign currency translation gain of $6,000.

Exercise 15-13: Reclassification of Accumulated Other Comprehensive Income.
On January 1, 2002, Laundry, Inc., purchased marketable securities at a cost of $18,000. These securities were placed in the available-for-sale portfolio. At the end of the year, the securities had a market value of $23,000. On March 13, 2003, management reclassified the securities as trading when their market value was $22,000. On April 20, 2003, the securities were sold for $24,000.

1. Provide the journal entry as of December 31, 2002, to record the change in market value of the securities.
2. Record the appropriate journal entries on March 13 and April 20 to record the reclassification and subsequent sale of the securities.
3. Assuming a net income for 2003 of $50,000, including the effects of the above entries, prepare the statement of comprehensive income.

Exercise 15-14: Other Comprehensive Income. During 2003, Momma-Loves-Pizza Company purchased various marketable securities and placed them in the available-for-sale portfolio. As of December 31, 2004, the cost basis and market values of these investments are as listed as follows:

Security	Cost Basis	Market Value December 31, 2003	December 31, 2004
Paper Products, Inc., common stock	$35,000	$41,000	$22,000*
Northern Lights Co., common stock	22,000	20,000	18,000
Kornigan Corp., 8% preferred stock	10,000	9,000	8,000
Totals	$67,000	$70,000	$48,000

*This is the market value for only the one-half of the securities that Momma still has.

During 2004, Momma sold half of the shares held in Paper Products, Inc., for $25,000. In addition, the company realized net income during 2003 and 2004 of $22,000 and $41,000, respectively. The only other comprehensive income item besides the unrealized gains/losses from the available-for-sale securities was a foreign currency translation adjustment, which was a credit adjustment of $6,000 in 2003 and a debit adjustment of $11,000 in 2004. The balance in the company's accumulated other comprehensive income account as of January 1, 2003, was a credit of $18,000.

1. Other than the entry to acquire the securities, prepare the necessary journal entries for 2003 and 2004.
2. Using the two-statement approach, prepare a comprehensive income statement for the years 2003 and 2004 for Momma-Loves-Pizza Company.
3. Determine the balance in the accumulated other comprehensive income account as of December 31, 2004. Where is the account reported on the financial statements?

Exercise 15-15: Proper Use of the Equity Method. Determine for each of the following situations whether the investment should be accounted for by using the equity method in the consolidated financial statements of the GSL Corporation, and give a reason for your decisions:

1. Owning 2,000 of the 50,000 issued and outstanding common shares of Superior Company, a domestic corporation.
2. Owning 3,000 of the 10,000 issued and outstanding preferred shares of Michigan Corporation.
3. Owning 15,000 of the 60,000 issued and outstanding common shares of Ontario Corporation, which is domiciled in a foreign country where the national government has imposed strict limitations on the amount of money that can be withdrawn and on other aspects of the operations of Ontario Corporation.
4. Owning 20,000 of the 25,000 issued and outstanding common shares of Erie Corporation, which is in federal bankruptcy.
5. Owning 18,000 of the 100,000 issued shares of Huron Corporation, where there are 20,000 shares in the treasury.
6. Owning 18,000 of the 100,000 issued and outstanding shares of the Great Lakes Corporation. Also, five members of the Great Lakes Corporation's board of directors are executives of GSL Corporation.

Exercise 15-16: Comparing the Fair Value and Equity Methods. Celebrations acquired 30% of the outstanding common stock of Park Place for $300,000, which gave Celebrations the ability to exercise significant influence over the operating and financing policies of Park Place. During the year, Park Place earned income of $50,000 and declared dividends of $20,000. Also, at year-end, the fair value of its investment exceeded the cost to Celebrations by $5,000. To record these events, Celebrations prepared the following journal entries:

Cash	6,000	
Investment Revenue		6,000
Fair Value Adjustment Accounts	5,000	
Unrealized Holding Gain		5,000
(reported in stockholders' equity)		

1. Determine (a) the correct amount that Celebrations should report for Investment Income (or Equity in Net Income of Investee) and (b) the correct balance in the investment account.
2. Determine the effects of these errors on (a) the investment account, (b) net income, and (c) total stockholders' equity.

Exercise 15-17: The Equity Method of Accounting. On January 3, Yokohama acquired a 30% interest in Quality Tires and appropriately used the equity method of accounting. At the time, the underlying book value of Quality Tires was $620,000, and Yokohama assigned a life of 20 years to any excess cost. Quality's net income for the year was $180,000, and dividends of $20,000 were paid during the year.

What is the ending balance of Yokohama's investment account at December 31, assuming that Yokohama paid (a) $186,000 for its investment, and (b) $258,000 for its investment?

Exercise 15-18: The Equity Method of Accounting. On December 1, 2005, Ryan Corporation purchased 20,000 shares, representing 20% of the outstanding common stock, of Artistic Skin Tattooing for $400,000 and appropriately used the equity method of accounting. For the year, Artistic Skin reports income of $30,000, of which $2,000 was earned in December. Artistic declared dividends of $5,000 on December 20 and paid those dividends on January 20, 2006. The appropriate amount of amortization to be recorded by Ryan is $1,500. As a result of these transactions, what is the amount Ryan should report as Equity in Net Income of Subsidiary and as the ending balance of its investment in the Artistic Skin account?

Exercise 15-19: The Equity Method of Accounting, Two Years. Investor acquired a 30% interest in Investee Corporation on January 1, 2004, for $240,000 when the book value of Investee's net assets was $700,000. The fair value of the assets approximated their carrying value, except for some land, whose fair value was $100,000 more than its carrying value. Investee reported earnings during 2004 and 2005 of $30,000 and $20,000, respectively. Also, Investee declared dividends of $10,000 in each year.

1. How much goodwill was in the acquisition because of Investor paying more than the book value of the net assets?
2. What is the balance in Investor's investment in Investee account at December 31, 2005?

Problems

Problem 15-1: Accounting for Debt Securities. On January 1, 2004, Basic Networks Inc. purchased $1,000,000 bonds issued on that date by Yankee Company. The bonds expire on December 31, 2013, and pay interest annually on December 31 at a rate of 6%. The bonds were issued to yield an effective interest rate of 8%. Basic Networks uses the effective-interest method of amortization.

Required:
1. Using time value of money concepts and a period of 9.75 years, how much did Basic Networks pay for the bonds (including accrued interest) on March 31, 2004? Prepare the journal entry. (The time value of money tables can be used after making appropriate interpolation adjustments, but it is better to use a financial calculator or an electronic spreadsheet.)
2. Construct an amortization table for the life of the investment.
3. Prepare the journal entries to recognize interest revenue on the bonds at December 31, 2004, and December 31, 2005.
4. Suppose that on December 31, 2005, the market rate of interest for bonds of this type is 10%. Calculate the market value of the bonds.

5. Assuming that Basic Networks has classified the bonds in the available-for-sale portfolio, how should Basic Networks recognize the change in the market value?

Problem 15-2: Journal Entries for Marketable Securities. Memory Lane, Inc., is a scrapbooking company that invests excess cash in marketable securities. During the 2004 fiscal year, the following transactions occurred:

Mar.	3	Purchased 500 shares of Company A common stock for $15,500.
June	10	Purchased 700 shares of Company B common stock for $49,000.
Sept.	1	Purchased 100, 8% bonds of Company C at 98, not including accrued interest. Each bond has a face value of $1,000 and will mature on June 30, 2009. Interest is paid annually. Memory Lane uses the straight-line method of amortization.
Oct.	1	Received a dividend on the Company B shares of $1,000.
Dec.	1	Company A announced a 2-for-1 stock split.
	10	Sold 400 shares of Company A common stock for $8,000.
	31	Accrued interest, recorded amortization on Company C bonds, and marked to market those securities that are reported at fair value.

The quoted market prices of each investment as of December 31, 2004, are as follows:

Company A stock	$ 18
Company B stock	$ 83
Company C bonds	101

Management of Memory Lane classifies Company B common stock as trading and the other securities as available-for-sale.

Required:
1. Prepare all necessary journal entries to record these transactions.
2. Prepare the journal entry to sell 500 shares of stock in Company B for $80 per share on February 1, 2005.
3. At December 31, 2005, the market price of each investment is as follows:

Company A stock	$20
Company B stock	$78
Company C bonds	99

Prepare the entries at year-end to report the securities at market.
4. Prepare a statement of comprehensive income for 2005, assuming that net income is $60,000.

Problem 15-3: Multiple-Year, Marketable Securities. On January 1, 2005, Ikon Office Supply purchased $300,000 par value of 12% bonds that pay interest annually on December 31. On that same day, Ikon prepared the following amortization table:

Period	Cash	Interest	Carrying Value
			$322,745
December 31, 2005	$36,000	$32,274	319,019
December 31, 2006	36,000	31,902	314,921
December 31, 2007	36,000	31,492	310,413
December 31, 2008	36,000	31,041	305,455
December 31, 2009	36,000	30,545	300,000

The fair values of the bonds for the first three years were as follows:

Period	Fair Value
December 31, 2005	$314,111
December 31, 2006	313,000
December 31, 2007	305,138

There is no balance in any adjustment-to-market account before acquiring this investment in bonds.

Required:
1. Assuming that Ikon classified the bonds in the held-to-maturity portfolio, prepare all required journal entries from acquisition through December 31, 2007, including entries (if necessary) to recognize holding gains/losses.
2. Assuming that Ikon classified the bonds in the available-for-sale portfolio, prepare all required journal entries from acquisition through December 31, 2007, including entries (if necessary) to recognize holding gains/losses.

Problem 15-4: Marketable Securities, Comprehensive, Multiple-Year. The following information is available for securities classified in the available-for-sale portfolio for Alma Corporation at December 31, 2004:

Security	Cost, at Acquisition	Fair Value December 31, 2004
7,000 shares of stock in Abysmal Corp.	$ 70,000	$ 63,000
10,000 shares of stock in Hi-Flyer Corp.	45,000	47,000
100, 8% bonds of Cross-Ways Corp.	102,000	101,500

There is no balance in the adjustment-to-market account related to the available-for-sale portfolio securities at December 31, 2004, nor does Alma have securities in either the trading or the held-to-maturity portfolios. Alma uses the straight-line method of amortization for bond premiums or discounts, with $50 being amortized each month on the Cross-Ways bonds, which were acquired on April 30. The bonds pay interest annually on December 31. When the bonds were acquired, an interest revenue account was debited for the accrued interest.

The following transactions occurred during 2005:

- Purchased 5,000 shares of Slider Corp. stock for $12,500.
- Received a dividend of $0.10 per share on Hi-Flyer Corp. stock.
- Sold 4,000 shares of the Abysmal Corp. stock at $8.00 per share.

At December 31, 2005, the market values of the various securities were as follows:

Security	Fair Value per Share
Stock of Abysmal Corp.	$5.50
Stock of Hi-Flyer Corp.	$4.00
Bonds of Cross-Ways Corp.	101%
Stock of Slider Corp.	$2.25

The following transactions occurred during 2006:

- Reclassified the stock of Hi-Flyer to the trading portfolio when the price per share was $3.50.
- Reclassified the bonds to the held-to-maturity portfolio on June 30 when the fair value of the bonds was 100. (Amortize the bond premium from January 1 through June 30.)
- Sold 2,000 shares of the stock of Abysmal Corp. at $5.00.

At December 31, 2006, the market values of the various securities were as follows:

Security	Fair Value per Share
Stock of Abysmal Corp.	$4.50
Stock of Hi-Flyer Corp.	$3.00
Bonds of Cross-Ways Corp.	99½%
Stock of Slider Corp.	$1.25

The price decline on the Abysmal stock was considered to be permanent.

Required:
1. Prepare the necessary entries at December 31, 2004, to recognize the receipt of interest and to mark to market.
2. Prepare the appropriate entries for 2005, and then prepare a statement of comprehensive income, assuming that the income before considering any effects of the journal entries you have prepared was $50,000.
3. Prepare the appropriate entries for 2006 for all securities in all portfolios, and then prepare a statement of comprehensive income, assuming that the income before any effects of the journal entries you have prepared was $30,000.

Problem 15-5: Equity Method of Accounting. On March 31, 2006, Hicaliber acquired a 30% interest in Camelot Corporation by paying $1,311,000 when the book value of Camelot's net assets was $4,000,000. Except for the following accounts, the book values of Camelot's assets and liabilities were equal to their fair values.

Account	Book Value	Fair Value	Remaining Life
Inventory	$200,000	$220,000	4 months
Equipment	350,000	400,000	5 years
Land	100,000	200,000	Indefinite

Any other excess amount paid is assigned to goodwill.

Camelot reported income from operations of $960,000 for the year, all of which was earned uniformly. Camelot also reported an extraordinary loss of $40,000 that was incurred on August 1. Dividends of $300,000 were declared on December 15, 2006, and were paid on February 1, 2007.

Required:
1. Compute the amount of goodwill in the purchase.
2. Compute the amount Hicaliber will report as "Equity in Net Income of Subsidiary," both from operations and from the extraordinary loss for the year.

(continued)

3. Compute the balance at December 31, 2006, in the investment in Camelot account.
4. On January 2, 2007, Hicaliber sold one-third of its investment in Camelot for $500,000. Compute the gain/loss on the sale.

Problem 15-6: Equity Method—Multiple Years. On July 1, 2006, seeing possible synergies in their respective businesses, We-Plant-Em (a company that runs funeral homes and cemeteries) acquired a 25% interest in You-Plug-Em (a retail outlet that sells handguns) by paying $13,000,000 when the book value of You-Plug-Em's net assets was $40,000,000. Except for the following accounts, the book values of You-Plug-Em's assets and liabilities were equal to their fair values.

Account	Book Value	Fair Value	Remaining Life
Accounts Receivable	$ 3,000,000	$ 2,400,000	2 months
Inventory	6,400,000	7,200,000	3 months
Buildings	20,000,000	24,000,000	20 years
Land	1,000,000	4,000,000	Indefinite

Any excess amount paid is assigned to goodwill.

You-Plug-Em reported a loss from operations of $2,400,000 for 2006, all of which was earned uniformly during the year. The company also reported an extraordinary loss of $5,000,000 that occurred on December 24, 2006. Dividends of $1,000,000 were declared on December 31, 2006, and were paid on February 28, 2007.

During 2007, You-Plug-Em reported a net loss of $3,600,000. Due to cash flow problems, You-Plug-Em did not pay a dividend for 2007.

On January 3, 2008, seeing that its investment was unprofitable and hoping to avoid any further losses, We-Plant-Em sold its shares in You-Plug-Em for $11,000,000.

Required:
1. Compute the amount of goodwill implied in the purchase.
2. Determine the effect on We-Plant-Em's 2006 and 2007 income statement as a result of its investment in You-Plug-Em.
3. Determine the balance in the investment in the You-Plug-Em account at December 31, 2006, and December 31, 2007.
4. Compute the amount of the gain on January 3, 2008, from selling the shares in You-Plug-Em.

Problem 15-7: Equity Method and Fair Value Method. Wishing to assure itself of a continuing supply of material, Manufacturer purchased 40% of the outstanding voting common stock of Supplier Corporation on April 1, 2004, which gave Manufacturer significant influence over the operating and investing policies of Supplier. Manufacturer paid $5,000,000 for its investment when the book value of Supplier's net assets was $10,000,000. Any excess paid is allocated to equipment, which has a life of five years.

During 2004, Supplier reported an income of $500,000, all of which was earned uniformly throughout the year. Supplier also paid dividends of $100,000. During 2005, Supplier reported an income of $600,000 and paid dividends of $150,000. The market value of Manufacturer's investment in Supplier's stock was $5,200,000 at the end of 2004, and $5,350,000 at the end of 2005.

On January 2, 2006, wanting to free up cash and realizing that its supply of material was not threatened, Manufacturer disposed of 60% of its investment (leaving it with 16% of the outstanding voting common stock of Supplier) for $3,200,000. As a result of the sale, Manufacturer no longer has significant influence over Supplier, and accordingly, the securities were classified in the available-for-sale portfolio. During 2006, Supplier reported an income of $650,000 and paid dividends of $100,000. The market value of Manufacturer's investment in Supplier's stock at the end of the year was $2,200,000.

On January 2, 2007, Manufacturer sold one-half of its remaining stock in Supplier for $1,200,000. During 2007, Supplier reported an income of $400,000 but did not pay a dividend. The market value of Manufacturer's investment in Supplier's stock at the end of the year was $850,000.

Required:
1. Prepare the necessary journal entries from acquisition to December 31, 2007.
2. Prepare a statement of comprehensive income at December 31, 2007, assuming that net income for the year was $100,000.

Research Activities

Activity 15-1: Fair Value Method vs. Equity Method. Explain when it is known that an investor is receiving a liquidating dividend. Explain the difference in the accounting for the receipt of a dividend that is a return *on* the investment and one that is a return *of* the investment if (a) the fair value method of accounting is used and (b) the equity method is used.

16

*S*tatement

OF

Cash Flows

Regina Company

During the mid-1980s, Regina Company became a household name in the vacuum cleaner industry. Through an aggressive advertising campaign, Regina attempted to take a significant market share of vacuum sales away from Hoover Company, the leading company in the industry. Figure 16-1 illustrates the growth in reported net income for Regina from the time the company went public in 1985 through the 1988 fiscal year-end (June 30).

Late in 1988, because of the impressive earnings pattern, several analysts gave glowing reports of the company's future. However, on April 26, 1989, the company filed for Chapter 11 bankruptcy, and in June of that year, Regina agreed to be acquired by Electrolux Corporation.

An obvious question is, why were the analysts so wrong in their predictions of Regina's future? The answer is that they were projecting from incomplete data. Regina Company was experiencing severe cash flow problems; but at the time, companies were not required to provide a statement of cash flows as prescribed by *SFAS No. 95*. Had the company provided relevant cash flow information, financial analysts and the public would have easily recognized the serious operating problems within the company, as illustrated

in Figure 16-2, which presents Regina's cash flows from operations during the same time period.

Today, financial analysts not only examine reported net income but also rely heavily on cash flow information. For example, Lockheed Martin Corp. reported on September 21, 2000, that it probably would meet analysts' earnings forecasts, but its cash flows would be higher than expected. The news of meeting analysts' forecasts for earnings was neutral information, which probably would not have impacted the stock price. However, the cash flow information caused the company's stock price to increase almost 2% in one day. Other examples can be found where cash flow information augments or even supersedes information on earnings.

Questions

1. How can a company report positive net income while simultaneously realizing significant net cash outflows from operations? (*Hint:* Fraudulent activity is not necessary for this phenomenon to occur.)

2. How can a cash flow statement be prepared using only an income statement and a balance sheet?

FIGURE 16-1

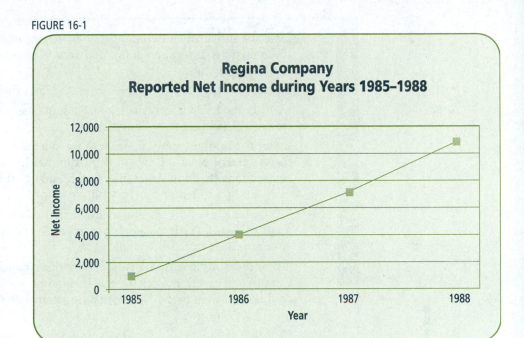

Regina Company
Reported Net Income during Years 1985–1988

FIGURE 16-2

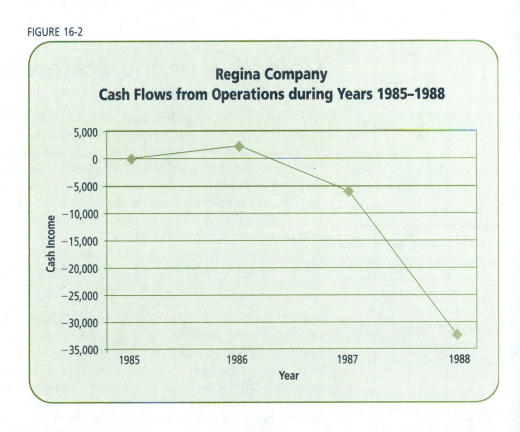

Regina Company
Cash Flows from Operations during Years 1985–1988

Objective of the Statement of Cash Flows

INTERNET

An interesting Web site that provides fundamental information on accounting, finance, and economics topics is **http://www.moneychimp.com/**. The Web site provides valuable insights for the average investor, including guides to economic indicators, monte carlo calculators, capital gains calculators, and information on how to interpret financial statements. The link **http://www.moneychimp.com/articles/financials/cashflow.htm** provides information on how to analyze the cash flow statement.

Chapter 4 introduced the fundamental ideas of the FASB's conceptual framework, including the notion that an objective of financial reporting is to communicate information that helps decision makers forecast the amount, timing, and uncertainty of future cash flows. Also, in Chapter 4 it was pointed out that accrual data are better for forecasting *long-run* future cash flows because accrual accounting (unlike cash accounting) records the financial effects of transactions in the periods in which they occur, rather than focusing only on the beginning and ending of transactions. Further, in Chapter 3, it was shown that information about an entity's liquidity, solvency, and management's ability to manage assets is best derived from accrual-based numbers. Because of this superiority of accrual-based numbers, the majority of this text focuses on accrual accounting.

But, as useful as accrual-based numbers are, cash-based numbers are also needed. Decision makers need information about the short run, particularly about cash flows in the short run. After all, both current-year dividends and interest are paid from short-run cash flows. And if a company fails to manage its cash in the short run, there may not be a long run. Thus, accrual-based numbers need to be supplemented with cash-based numbers. But rather than keeping a second set of records to obtain cash-based numbers, the accountant obtains the cash-based numbers by modifying the accrual-based numbers. The purpose of this chapter is to show how those adjustments are derived to prepare the statement of cash flows.

The primary objective of the statement of cash flows is to provide "relevant information about the cash receipts and cash disbursements of an enterprise during a period." Reporting cash flow information aids the readers of financial statements to assess:

1. The enterprise's ability to generate future cash flows;

2. The enterprise's ability to meet its current obligations, including paying dividends; and

3. The effect of an enterprise's cash and noncash activities on its financial position.

A statement of cash flows is required whenever a business enterprise provides a set of financial statements, and it must present one for each period in which an income statement is presented. That is, when a company prepares a comparative income statement, it must also prepare a comparative statement of cash flows. And, if a company prepares an income statement that reports on the results of operations for three years, it must also prepare a statement of cash flows that reports on cash flows for three years.

Focus on Cash and Cash Equivalents

Although the statement is called a cash flow statement, the FASB mandates that the statement concentrate on the changes in cash and cash equivalents. As defined in Chapter 10, **cash equivalents** are short-term, highly liquid securities that are readily convertible to known amounts of cash and are so near their maturity when purchased that there is no significant risk of a change in value due to a change in interest rates. Typically, securities with a maturity date of three months or less from the time that the securities were acquired are considered cash equivalents. Examples of securities that could be considered as cash equivalents include Treasury bills, commercial paper, money market funds, and federal funds. However, each company should establish its own policy as to what constitutes cash equivalents and then classify its securities accordingly.

Reconciliation

A completed statement of cash flows must explain the reasons for the change in cash and cash equivalents during the period. Most companies do this by showing, at the bottom of the statement, the adding (or subtracting) of the total cash flows during the year to (or from) the beginning balance of cash and cash equivalents, which results in the ending balance of cash and cash equivalents. This reconciliation is shown in Exhibit 16-1, which was extracted from an annual financial report of Compaq Computer Corporation.

EXHIBIT 16-1

Reconciliation of the Statement of Cash Flows

	1998	1997
Net (decrease) increase in cash and cash equivalents	$(2,327)	$3,410
Cash and cash equivalents at the beginning of the year	6,418	3,008
Cash and cash equivalents at the end of the year	$ 4,091	$6,418

Categories on the Statement

Exhibit 16-2 illustrates a typical statement of cash flows. The cash receipts and cash disbursements that give rise to the "Net (decrease) increase in cash and cash equivalents" are classified into three categories, which are called activities, and are named operating, investing, and financing activities. Also, note the reconcil-

EXHIBIT 16-2

Statement of Cash Flows
Compaq Computer Corporation
For the Year Ended December 31, 1998

YEAR ENDED DECEMBER 31 (IN MILLIONS)	1998	1997	
Cash flows from operating activities:			
Net income (loss)	$ (2,743)	$1,855	
Adjustments to reconcile net income (loss) to net cash provided by operating activities:			Note the three
Depreciation and amortization	893	545	classifications:
Provision for bad debts	61	19	operating,
Purchased in-process technology	3,196	208	investing, and
Deferred income taxes	(130)	202	financing.
Restructuring and asset impairment charges	393	—	
Changes in operating assets and liabilities, net of effects of purchased businesses:			
Accounts receivable	(1,736)	614	
Inventories	857	(335)	
Other current assets	114	63	
Accounts payable	589	756	
Income taxes payable	(265)	(319)	
Accrued restructuring costs	(575)	—	
Other current liabilities	(10)	80	
Net cash provided from operating activities	$ 644	$3,688	
Cash flows from investing activities:			
Purchases of property, plant, and equipment, net	$ (600)	$ (729)	
Purchases of short-term investments	(77)	(2,405)	These activities
Proceeds from sale of short-term investments	421	3,134	deal with long-term
Acquisition of businesses, net of cash acquired	(1,413)	(268)	asset transactions.
Acquisition of lease portfolio	(361)	—	
Other, net	(437)	(31)	
Net cash used in investing activities	$ (2,467)	$ (299)	
Cash flows from financing activities:			
Repayment of long-term debt	$ (788)	$ (293)	
Purchase of treasury shares	(384)	—	These activities
Issuance of common stock pursuant to stock option plans	407	188	deal with long-term
Tax benefit associated with stock options	234	156	liability and
Dividends paid	(95)	—	stockholders'
Other, net	(18)	(37)	equity transactions.
Net cash provided by (used in) financing activities	(644)	$ 14	
Effect of exchange rate changes on cash and cash equivalents	$ 140	$ 7	
Net (decrease) increase in cash and cash equivalents	$ (2,327)	$3,410	Here's the
Cash and cash equivalents at the beginning of the year	6,418	3,008	reconciliation.
Cash and cash equivalents at the end of the year	$ 4,091	$6,418	
Supplemental Cash Flow Information			
Acquisitions (Note 2)			
Fair value of:			
Assets acquired	$16,124	$ 362	And here is the
Liabilities assumed	(7,109)	(74)	significant noncash
Stock issued	(4,284)	0	information.
Options issued	(249)	(10)	
Cash paid	4,482	278	
Less cash acquired	(3,069)	(10)	
Net cash paid for acquisitions	$ 1,413	$ 268	

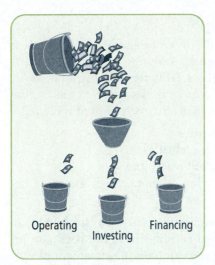

iation of cash and cash equivalents near the bottom of the statement. Finally, at the bottom of the statement, note the schedule labeled "Supplemental Cash Flow Information" and the types of transactions that are reported there.

Investing activities consist of (a) those transactions involving the long-term assets of the corporation and (b) those transactions in securities classified as current assets. Examples of investing activities include:

- Cash disbursements for making loans,
- Cash receipts from collecting loans,
- Cash disbursements for purchasing long-lived assets categorized as property, plant, and equipment or intangible assets,
- Cash receipts from disposing of long-lived assets,
- Cash disbursements for buying investments in debt and equity securities, whether those investments are classified as investments and funds or as current assets, and
- Cash receipts from selling investments.

Financing activities consist of (a) those transactions involving long-term liabilities, (b) those transactions of borrowing and repaying amounts borrowed that are classified as current liabilities, and (c) those transactions affecting stockholders' equity accounts. Examples of financing activities include:

- Cash receipts obtained from owners;
- Cash disbursements to owners, whether they are a return on the investment (i.e., dividends) or a return of the investment;
- Cash receipts obtained from creditors (e.g., notes payable); and
- Cash disbursements to creditors for the principal portion on amounts borrowed.

All other cash receipt and disbursement transactions are operating activities, and most of these transactions are associated with the current asset and current liability accounts of the corporation. The major exception to operating activities being connected only with current accounts is all deferred tax accounts. These are always operating activities, regardless of where they are reported on the balance sheet. The most typical examples of operating activities consist of the following:

- Cash receipts from sales of goods or services;
- Cash receipts from interest and dividends;
- Cash disbursements to acquire materials to resell or to manufacture;
- Cash disbursements to other suppliers and employees for goods and services;
- Cash disbursements to governmental entities for taxes, fines, etc.; and
- Cash disbursements for interest (but not dividends).

This Is the Real World

Although information about cash flows may point out problems with reported net income, cash flows are not immune to management manipulation. Following the collapse of Enron, the market immediately punished other companies that it considered to be involved in fraudulent accounting practices, with the stock of Tyco (for example) dropping 61% in less than nine weeks. During the past decade, Tyco has ac- quired hundreds of small businesses, with an astounding 700 acquired from 1999 to 2002. In conducting these acquisitions, Tyco was accused of (1) accelerating the paying of expenses immediately before the acquisition date and (2) postponing the recognizing of receipts until after the acquisition date. The effect was to make the cash flow look significantly better after acquisition than it looked previously.

Significant Noncash Transactions

In addition to reporting cash transactions in the three categories or activities as described, *the FASB mandates that all major noncash investing and financing activities must be reported on the statement of cash flows*. This reporting is done at the bottom of the statement, either in narrative form or in a schedule (see Exhibit 16-2). Examples of such noncash transactions that must be reported include:

- Converting debt securities to equity securities,
- Acquiring assets by issuing debt or equity securities,
- Obtaining an asset by entering into a capital lease, and
- Exchanging noncash assets or liabilities for other noncash assets or liabilities.

Traditionally, dividends paid in the corporation's own stock, stock splits of the company's stock, and appropriating retained earnings have not been considered to be significant transactions that require reporting on the statement of cash flows.

For transactions that are partly cash and partly noncash, such as when a $1 million asset is acquired by paying a cash down payment of $200,000 and financing the remainder with a mortgage, only the $200,000 cash portion is reflected on the statement. For the present example, the $200,000 would be shown as a cash outflow, and since the transaction relates to acquiring a long-term asset, it would be reported in the investing activities section. The financing of the purchase by obtaining a mortgage is then reported in the supplemental information at the bottom of the statement.

Steps in Preparing the Statement of Cash Flows

Unlike the income statement and the balance sheet, the statement of cash flows is not prepared from the adjusted trial balance. Rather, the major sources for the statement are (1) the income statement for the current year and (2) balance sheets for the current and prior year. From these three major sources and other information provided, the statement of cash flows is prepared in the following three major steps:

1. *From the comparative balance sheet, the change in cash for the year is computed.* The change in cash provides a check figure as to what the sum of the cash provided from or used in operating, investing, and financing activities should total.
2. *Prepare the operating activities section.* The operating activities section is prepared by using either the indirect method or the direct method, with the indirect method being used almost exclusively in practice. The difference between the indirect and direct methods is one of detail. For the indirect method, the operating activities section begins with the reported net income, and then adjustments are made to that number for the noncash transactions. (See Exhibit 16-2 for an example.) In contrast, for the direct method the individual income statement accounts (as compared to net income) are adjusted for the noncash transactions. (See Illustration 16-1A, p. 772, in the appendix to this chapter.)[1] The same adjustments are used, regardless of the method used.
3. *Prepare the investing and financing sections.* This step is covered later in the text.

---

[1]Illustration 16-2A (p. 772) and Illustration 16-16 (p. 760) are statements of cash flows using the same data. Note the differences in the operating activities sections, with all other items being identical.

Preparing the Operating Activities Section—The Indirect Method

Since the indirect method is used predominantly in practice, the procedures comprising it are addressed first. Later, the procedures comprising the direct method are covered. Note in Exhibit 16-2 that the operating activities section begins with net income and is followed by two categories of adjustments. The first category of adjustments (e.g., depreciation and amortization) is for amounts on the income statement that never affect cash. The second category of adjustments (e.g., change in the accounts receivable balance) is for transactions that do affect cash but in a different period from when they are recognized under accrual accounting. By adjusting net income for these two types of adjustments, net income is converted to a "net cash provided from operating activities" amount. (See the description of the last line of the operating activities section of Exhibit 16-2).

Adjustments for Noncash Transactions on the Income Statement

Typical adjustments for amounts reported on the income statement that do not affect cash are depreciation and amortization expense. That these adjustments do not affect cash is evident both from the journal entries to record such, noting that no entry is made to cash, and from knowing that depreciation and amortization are merely allocations of cost. *Since these and other like expenses never affect cash, they are treated in opposite ways on the statement of cash flows from how they were handled on the income statement so as to reverse (or negate) their effect on net income.* So any noncash items that were deducted from sales on the income statement (e.g., depreciation expense) are added back to net income on the statement of cash flows. And any noncash amounts that were added to sales on the income statement (e.g., gains) are deducted from net income on the statement of cash flows.

Other than depreciation and amortization, another common example of an adjustment that is made to net income because it was included on the income statement but did not affect cash is gains and losses. Regarding why gains and losses are adjusted, assume that the following journal entry was prepared for disposing of a long-lived depreciable asset:

Cash	1,000	
Loss on Disposing of Equipment	5,000	
Accumulated Depreciation	39,000	
Equipment		45,000

From this entry, it is seen that the amount of cash received is $1,000, and this is the amount that should be reported on the statement of cash flows. However, when the income statement was prepared, the $5,000 loss was included in determining net income. So on the statement of cash flows, if this loss is not added back to net income, the amount of cash provided from operating activities would be understated. Because the disposing of the long-lived asset is an investing activity, the $1,000 cash amount is reported in the investing activities section (not the operating activities section).

In summary, the first category of adjustments in the operating activities section of the statement of cash flows is for all the items on the income statement that do not affect cash. Primary examples of these adjustments are depreciation, amortization, and all gains and losses, of which the gain/loss on disposing of a long-lived asset is an example. In the operating activities section of the statement of cash flows, all of these items are treated just the opposite of how they were treated on the income statement, so as to negate their effect.

Adjustments that Affect Cash in a Different Period

In identifying the adjustments needed to convert net income to cash, the accountant compares the effects of transactions as recorded under accrual accounting to how and when they affect cash. For instance, under accrual accounting, both cash and credit sales are revenue. In contrast, under cash accounting, only cash sales affect cash; credit sales do not. So one difference between accrual accounting and cash collected is credit sales. But cash is also affected by collecting accounts receivable, which does not affect revenue under accrual accounting. Thus, this is another difference between the amount of revenue earned and the amount of cash collected. Both of these differences between revenue under accrual accounting and cash collected are reflected in the balance of accounts receivable. Thus, *to convert from revenue to cash collected requires adjusting revenue for the change in accounts receivable during the year.*

Converting Revenue to Cash Collected

To illustrate using numbers, assume that the following transactions occurred during the first year of a company's existence:

 a. Cash sales of $10,000,
 b. Credit sales of $50,000,
 c. Collections on account of $35,000.

From the transactions, it can be seen in Illustration 16-1 that under accrual accounting the total revenue is $60,000, which is the sum of the cash and credit sales. It also can be seen that the total cash collected is $45,000, which is the sum of the cash sales and collections of accounts receivable. So the difference between revenue and cash collected is $15,000. After posting the transactions to the T-accounts, note that this $15,000 difference equals the change in the account receivable balance.

ILLUSTRATION 16-1

Comparing Cash Collected to Revenue Earned

| Cash Accounting | Accrual Accounting |

Cash Accounting

Cash
(a)	10,000	
(c)	35,000	
	45,000	

Revenue
		10,000	(a)
		35,000	(c)
		45,000	

Accrual Accounting

Cash
(a)	10,000	
(c)	35,000	
	45,000	

Receivables
| (b) | 50,000 | 35,000 | (c) |
| | 15,000 | | |

Revenue
		10,000	(a)
		50,000	(b)
		60,000	

In sum, the amount of revenue earned can be converted to the amount of cash collected by adjusting revenue for the change in accounts receivable. Also, just as importantly, the amount of cash collected can be converted to the amount of revenue earned by adjusting the amount of cash collected by the change in accounts receivable. This reverse procedure is important, as many businesses (e.g., physicians, plumbers, and other professionals) keep their books on a cash basis during the year and then convert them to accrual accounting at the end of the year. These procedures of converting from revenue to cash or vice-versa apply whether the beginning balance in accounts receivable is zero (as in the given example) or some other amount. What is significant when making the change from accrual to cash or vice-versa is the change in the accounts receivable balance, not the magnitude of the beginning and ending balances.

When the accounts receivable balance remains unchanged, the amount of cash collected equals revenues. When the accounts receivable balance increases (as it did in the prior illustration), the amount of cash collected is less than revenue by the change in the accounts receivable balance. And when the accounts receivable balance decreases, the amount of cash collected is greater than revenue by the change in the accounts receivable balance. (See Exhibit 16-3 for a summary of this concept.) *Thus, when the statement of cash flows is prepared under the indirect method, the change in the accounts receivable balance is added to or subtracted from net income.* (See the second category of operating activities adjustments in Exhibit 16-2, p. 738, for how this change in accounts receivable is included in the statement of cash flows.)

EXHIBIT 16-3

Difference between Revenue and Cash Collected

Included in Accrual Basis	Reconciling Amount	Included in Cash
Cash Sales	No Difference	Cash Sales
+		+
Sales on Account	Change in Accounts Receivable	Collection of Accounts Receivable
=		=
Total Sales		Total Cash Collected

Converting Cost of Goods Sold to Cash Disbursements for Inventory

Just as the amount of cash collected can be derived from revenue, so too can cash disbursed for purchases of inventory be derived from the cost of goods sold. To illustrate, and again using numbers, assume that the beginning balances of the inventory and accounts payable accounts are $40,000 and $35,000, respectively, as shown in the following T-accounts. Also, assume that purchases on account during the year totaled $350,000, the cost of goods sold is $320,000, and the ending balance of accounts payable is $28,000. The question is: How much cash was disbursed for purchases of inventory?

Inventory				Accounts Payable		
Beginning bal.	40,000				35,000	Beginning bal.
Purchases	350,000				350,000	Purchases
Cost of goods		320,000				Cash disbursed
				?		for purchases
Ending bal.	70,000				28,000	Ending balance

From analyzing the inventory account, it is determined that purchases of inventory were $358,000. Then, after posting this amount to the accounts payable account, it can be determined that $357,000 was spent for purchases of inventory. However, this amount can also be determined by adding (or subtracting) the changes in the inventory and accounts payable accounts to (from) the cost of goods sold number, as follows:

Cost of goods sold	$320,000
Change in inventory account	30,000
Change in accounts payable account	7,000
Cash paid for purchases of inventory	$357,000

This procedure of adjusting the cost of goods sold by the changes in the account balances of inventory and accounts payable has the advantage over the previous T-account approach in that the amount of purchases need not be known, as it does when using the T-account approach. In regard to whether the changes in the account balances should be added to or subtracted from the cost of goods sold, the following rationale is used:

- For inventory, because the account balance increased, more inventory was acquired than was sold. Thus, to convert from the amount sold to the amount purchased requires that the change in the account balance be added to the cost of goods sold.
- For accounts payable, because the account balance decreased, more cash was paid than the amount that was purchased on account. So to convert from the amount purchased on account to the cash paid requires again that the change in the account balance be added to the cost of goods sold.

This relationship between the cost of goods sold and the cash disbursed for purchases is graphically illustrated in Exhibit 16-4. (See the operating activities section of Exhibit 16-2, p. 739, for an example of how the changes in inventory and accounts payable are included in the statement of cash flows.)

EXHIBIT 16-4

Difference between Cost of Goods Sold and Cash Disbursements for Purchases

Accrual Basis	Reconciling Amount	Cash Basis
Purchases for Cash	No Difference	Purchases for Cash
+		+
Purchases on Account	Change in Accounts Payable	Payments on Account
+		+
Change in Inventory	Change in Inventory	Not Applicable
=		=
Cost of Goods Sold		Cash Disbursements for Purchases

General Rule for Changing Balance Sheet Operating Accounts to Cash

Just as sales and the cost of goods sold were changed to cash numbers, so can all other revenue and expense amounts on the income statement be changed to cash numbers by adding to them or subtracting from them the change in the balance of the balance sheet accounts to which they relate. (This is exactly what is done under the direct method of preparing the operating activities section of the statement of cash flows.) However, under the indirect method, rather than adjusting the individual revenue and expense accounts to cash numbers, it is net income that is adjusted.

Under the indirect method, one way of determining whether the changes in the balance sheet accounts are added to or deducted from net income is by using the same rationale as shown in the previous example for changing cost of goods sold to cash disbursed for purchases of inventory. However, another method of determining whether the change in the balance sheet account should be added to or deducted from net income is by referring to the basic accounting equation. That equation is as follows:

$$Assets = Liabilities + Owners' \ Equity$$

Defining Assets as Cash and Other Assets results in the following equation:

$$Cash + Other \ Assets = Liabilities + Owners' \ Equity$$

Finally, that equation is algebraically manipulated to solve for cash and results in the following:

$$Cash = Liabilities + Owners' \ Equity - Other \ Assets$$

This form of the basic accounting equation states that *changes in cash move in the same direction as changes in liabilities, and that changes in cash move in the opposite direction as changes in assets.*

In summary, the second category of adjustments consists of the changes in the balance sheet accounts that are connected with operating activities. Generally, these balance sheet accounts are the current asset and current liability accounts. However, some current accounts are not operating activity accounts but are connected with investing activities (e.g., marketable securities) or financing activities (e.g., notes payable), and occasionally operating activities are found in long-term accounts. Whether the changes in the balance sheet operating accounts are added to or deducted from net income is determined either (1) by reasoning as to their effect on the accrual accounts as compared to their effect on cash or (2) by referring to the basic accounting equation. Both techniques were demonstrated.

Illustration

Beginning with Illustration 16-2, which presents the relevant portions of the comparative balance sheets and the current-year income statement for Mountain West Health Care, we demonstrate (1) the computing of the change in cash to obtain the check figure for the statement and (2) preparing the operating activities section of the statement of cash flows, using the indirect method.

Step 1: The change in cash as determined from the comparative balance sheets is an increase of $51,000.

Step 2: Prepare the operating activities section of the statement of cash flows.

The operating activities section begins with net income of $32,000, which is reported in the statement of cash flows as shown in Illustration 16-3.

After the net income figure is entered on the statement of cash flows, the changes in all the balance sheet operating accounts are entered. To review, when the operating account is an asset and its balance increases (or decreases), the effect is to decrease (or increase) cash. Hence, the change in the account balance is deducted from (or added to) net income to determine the amount of cash generated.

ILLUSTRATION 16-2

Mountain West Health Care Comparative Partial Balance Sheets

	At December 31, 2006	At December 31, 2005
Current assets:		
Cash and cash equivalents	$ 56,000	$ 5,000
Accounts receivable, net	77,000	52,000
Inventory	50,000	55,000
Prepaids	21,000	6,000
Total current assets	$204,000	$118,000
Current liabilities:		
Accounts payable	$ 55,000	$ 60,000
Accrued liabilities	48,000	41,000
Taxes payable	18,000	22,000
Total current liabilities	$121,000	$123,000

Mountain West Health Care
Income Statement
For the Year Ended December 31, 2006

Sales, net	$795,000
Cost of goods sold	515,000
Gross profit	$280,000
Operating expenses:	
Selling expenses	$120,000
Administrative expenses	70,000
Depreciation expense	50,000
Total expenses	$240,000
Operating income	$ 40,000
Gains and losses:	
Gain on sale of equipment	4,000
Income before taxes	$ 44,000
Income taxes	12,000
Net income	$ 32,000

Additional information:
During the year, equipment costing $26,000 and on which accumulated depreciation was $20,000 was sold for $10,000.

ILLUSTRATION 16-3

Mountain West Health Care
Statement of Cash Flows
For the Year Ended December 31, 2006

Operating activities:	
Net income	$32,000
Adjustments to reconcile net income to net cash:	

And when the operating account is a liability and its balance increases (or decreases), the effect is to increase (or decrease) cash, and the amount is added to (or deducted from) net income. Implementing these procedures results in Illustration 16-4.

ILLUSTRATION 16-4

Mountain West Health Care
Statement of Cash Flows
For the Year Ended December 31, 2006

Operating activities:		
Net income		$32,000
Adjustments to reconcile net income to net cash:		
Changes in operating assets and liabilities:		
Increase in accounts receivable	$(25,000)	
Decrease in inventory	5,000	
Increase in prepaids	(15,000)	
Decrease in accounts payable	(5,000)	
Increase in accrued liabilities	7,000	
Decrease in taxes payable	(4,000)	

The final category of adjustments is the items on the income statement that do not affect cash. In this example, there are two such items: depreciation expense and the gain on disposing of the equipment. They are reported on the statement of cash flows in the opposite way in which they were treated on the income statement, so as to cancel their effect on net income. Since depreciation was deducted on the income statement, on the statement of cash flows it is added back to net income. Since the gain increased net income, it is deducted from net income on the statement of cash flows to determine the amount of cash generated from operating activities.

After these adjustments are entered in the operating activities section, the section is complete and looks as shown in Illustration 16-5.

ILLUSTRATION 16-5

Mountain West Health Care
Statement of Cash Flows
For the Year Ended December 31, 2006

Operating activities:		
Net income		$32,000
Adjustments to reconcile net income to net cash:		
Depreciation expense	$ 50,000	
Gain on disposing of equipment	(4,000)	
Changes in operating assets and liabilities:		
Increase in accounts receivable	(25,000)	
Decrease in inventory	5,000	
Increase in prepaids	(15,000)	
Decrease in accounts payable	(5,000)	
Increase in accrued liabilities	7,000	
Decrease in taxes payable	(4,000)	9,000
Net cash provided from operating activities		$41,000

In Step 1, the total change in cash was computed to be $51,000; but as shown here, operating activities accounted for cash of only $41,000. The remaining $10,000 was generated from selling the equipment, which is an investing activity. After including this amount, the completed statement of cash flows, with reconciliation at the bottom of the statement, is shown in Illustration 16-6.

ILLUSTRATION 16-6

Mountain West Health Care
Statement of Cash Flows
For the Year Ended December 31, 2006

Operating activities:		
Net income		$32,000
Adjustments to reconcile net income to net cash:		
Depreciation expense	$ 50,000	
Gain on disposing of equipment	(4,000)	
Changes in operating assets and liabilities:		
Increase in accounts receivable	(25,000)	
Decrease in inventory	5,000	
Increase in prepaids	(15,000)	
Decrease in accounts payable	(5,000)	
Increase in accrued liabilities	7,000	
Decrease in taxes payable	(4,000)	9,000
Net cash provided from operating activities		$41,000
Investing activities:		
Disposal of equipment		10,000
Net increase in cash and cash equivalents		$51,000
Cash and cash equivalents at the beginning of the year		5,000
Cash and cash equivalents at the end of the year		$56,000

The Direct Method

Having illustrated the indirect method of preparing the operating activities section of the statement of cash flows, attention is now turned to the direct method. Earlier in the chapter, two important statements were made concerning the direct method. The first statement was that the difference between the indirect and direct methods is one of detail, where the indirect method adjusts net income and the direct method adjusts the individual items on the income statement. The second statement was that the adjustments made under the direct method are the same adjustments that are made under the indirect method.

Based upon the statement that the individual items of the income statement are adjusted rather than adjusting net income, a worksheet as shown in Illustration 16-7 is prepared. This worksheet is the same as the company's income statement, except that (1) "Operating expenses" is substituted for the various individual operating expenses and (2) all headings and subtotals are deleted from the worksheet. Parentheses around amounts indicate that the amount is a debit balance. The preparation of the worksheet in Illustration 16-7 should be verified by comparing it with the income statement found as part of Illustration 16-2 (p. 746).

The next step in completing the worksheet is to enter the adjustments as determined previously under the indirect method and as shown in Illustration 16-6. *When entering the adjustments on the worksheet, each amount is entered next*

ILLUSTRATION 16-7

Mountain West Health Care
Worksheet—Direct Method

	Income Statement (see Illustration 16-2)	Adjustments Dr.	Cr.	Cash Flows
Sales, net	$ 795,000			
Cost of goods sold	(515,000)			
Operating expenses	(190,000)			
Depreciation expense	(50,000)			
Gain on sale of equipment	4,000			
Income taxes	(12,000)			
Net income	$ 32,000			

to the income statement account to which it relates. That is, the adjustment for the change in the accounts receivable balance in Illustration 16-6 is entered on the "Sales, net" line because, as explained previously, sales is changed to a cash receipt number by adjusting it for the change in accounts receivable. Likewise, as explained previously, the changes in inventory and accounts payable are entered on the "Cost of goods sold" line so as to change that expense to a cash disbursement for purchases of inventory amount. So, too, the depreciation and gain adjustments are reported with "Depreciation expense" and "Gain on sale of equipment," respectively, on the worksheet. And the change in the taxes payable in Illustration 16-6 is reported with "Income taxes" on the preceding worksheet. Finally, the changes in the balances of the prepaids and accrued liabilities in Illustration 16-6 relate to the operating expenses and are reported accordingly.

Regarding in which column to put the adjustments, those amounts in Illustration 16-6 that are deducted from net income (i.e., have a debit balance) are entered in the debit column on the worksheet, and those amounts in Illustration 16-6 that are added to net income (i.e., have a credit balance) are entered in the credit column. After entering the adjustments in this manner and completing the worksheet by adding across each line, the result is as shown in Illustration 16-8.

ILLUSTRATION 16-8

Mountain West Health Care
Worksheet—Direct Method

	Income Statement	Adjustments Dr.	Cr.	Cash Flows
Sales, net	$ 795,000	$25,000		$ 770,000
Cost of goods sold	(515,000)	5,000ᵃ	$ 5,000ᵇ	(515,000)
Operating expenses	(190,000)	15,000	7,000	(198,000)
Depreciation expense	(50,000)		50,000	0
Gain on sale of equipment	4,000	4,000		0
Income taxes	(12,000)	4,000		(16,000)
Net income	$ 32,000			$ 41,000

ᵃThis adjustment relates to the decrease in Accounts Payable.
ᵇThis adjustment relates to the decrease in Inventory.

Having completed the worksheet to convert the individual income statement items to cash amounts, the operating activities section of the cash flow statement is completed by changing the names of the income statement accounts to descriptions of cash flow activities, as shown in Illustration 16-9. Note that the amount of cash provided from operating activities as reported under the direct method is the same as that reported under the indirect method in Illustration 16-6 (p. 748).

ILLUSTRATION 16-9

Mountain West Health Care
Statement of Cash Flows
For the Year Ended December 31, 2006

Operating activities:	
Cash received from customers	$770,000
Cash paid for purchases of inventory	(515,000)
Cash paid for operating expenses	(198,000)
Cash paid for income taxes	(16,000)
Net cash provided from operating activities	$ 41,000

The advantage of the direct method in preparing the operating activities section is that it is more consistent with the objective of the cash flow statement of showing the cash receipts and disbursements of the business enterprise. Those who support using the direct method argue that knowledge of the specific sources of cash receipts and reasons for cash disbursements in prior years is more relevant in forecasting future cash flows and that information about major sources and uses of cash is more relevant than one total.

However, if the direct method is used, *a supplemental schedule must be attached that reconciles net income to net cash provided from operating activities*, which is what the indirect method does. Although the FASB expressed a preference for the direct method, when that method is used, the results of applying the indirect method must be reported as a separate supplemental schedule; but if the indirect method is used, there is no such requirement for preparing a supplemental schedule showing the results of the direct method. Perhaps this is why the indirect method is used predominantly in practice.

Preparing the Investing and Financing Activities Sections

Just as the operating activities section was prepared by analyzing balance sheet accounts connected with operating activities, so too are the investing and financing activities sections prepared by analyzing the respective balance sheet accounts connected with those activities. As mentioned at the beginning of this chapter, transactions reported under investing activities are those associated with the long-term asset accounts and those current asset accounts having to do with investments. And transactions reported under financing activities are those associated with long-term liabilities, stockholders' equity accounts, and current liability accounts dealing with financing transactions.

A key to understanding how the investing and financing activities sections are prepared is to note that when the operating activities section was prepared, all changes in the balance sheet accounts connected with operating activities are included on the statement of cash flows. In a similar way, the changes in the balance sheet accounts connected with investing and financing activities are determined. The one difference is that the changes in the balance sheet accounts connected with investing and financing activities cannot be handled by reporting the net change, as was done with accounts receivable, inventory, etc. Rather, *all reasons that caused an account balance to change must be identified, and then those transactions that affect cash are reported on the statement of cash flows.*

Illustration 16-10 shows Red Rock Candy Mountain Company's income statement and comparative balance sheets, along with various information to

ILLUSTRATION 16-10

Red Rock Candy Mountain Company
Balance Sheets

For the Year Ending December 31	2005	2004	Increase (Decrease)	Type of Account
Assets				
Current assets:				
Cash and cash equivalents	$ 2,183	$ 4,420	$(2,237)	
Short-term investments	279	729	(450)	Investing
Accounts receivable, net	6,801	6,392	409	Operating
Deferred income taxes	1,495	1,765	(270)	Operating
Inventories	8,349	8,967	(618)	Operating
Total current assets	$19,107	$22,273		
Fixed assets:				
Investments (less allowance to value to market)	$ 4,930	$ 4,339	591	Investing
Property, plant, and equipment	25,577	20,112	5,465	Investing
Less accumulated depreciation	(11,650)	(10,900)	(750)	Investing
Intangible assets	2,290	2,395	(105)	Investing
Deferred income taxes	411	15	396	Operating
Total fixed assets	$21,558	$15,961		
Total assets	$40,665	$38,234		
Current liabilities:				
Accounts payable	$10,733	$11,548	(815)	Operating
Accrued liabilities	1,251	1,575	(324)	Operating
Income taxes payable	569	298	271	Operating
Currently maturing debt	869	731	138	Financing
Total current liabilities	$13,422	$14,152		
Long-term liabilities:				
Accrued retiree health care	4,831	4,796	35	Operating[2]
Long-term debt	6,103	6,123	(20)	Financing
Total liabilities	$24,356	$25,071		
Stockholders' equity:				
Common stock	$ 5,459	$ 5,000	459	Financing
Paid-in capital in excess of par	2,667	1,090	1,577	Financing
Retained earnings	8,206	7,073	1,133	Financing
Accumulated other comprehensive income	(23)	0	(23)	Investing or Financing
Total stockholders' equity	$16,309	$13,163		
Total liabilities and stockholders' equity	$40,665	$38,234		

(continued)

[2]This is an operating activities item because the expense associated with it is reported on the income statement.

ILLUSTRATION 16-10 CONTINUED

Red Rock Candy Mountain Company
Income Statement
For the Year Ending December 31, 2005

	2005
Sales	$56,154
Cost of goods sold	39,309
Gross profit	$16,845
Operating expenses:	
Selling expenses	9,599
General and administrative expenses	3,888
Depreciation and amortization expense	1,491
Operating income	$ 1,867
Other revenue and expenses:	
Gain on sale of equipment	75
Gain on sale of securities	208
Interest expense	(453)
Income before taxes	$ 1,697
Income taxes	277
Net income	$ 1,420

Additional information:

- Some securities classified as short-term investments were sold during the year.
- The only transactions affecting the accumulated depreciation account are the recording of depreciation expense and the sale of some equipment for $1,339.
- No new short-term debt was incurred during the year.
- The "Accrued retiree health care liability" consists of the estimated costs of health care benefits that current employees will receive upon retirement. The offsetting expense is included in the "General and administrative expenses." No part of this expense involved a cash payment.
- Common stock was issued during the year.
- Accumulated other comprehensive income consists of the holding gain/loss on securities categorized as available-for-sale, which is included under fixed assets. All securities purchased during the year were classified as available-for-sale securities.

assist in preparing the statement of cash flows. For convenience in preparing the statement, two additional columns have been added to the balance sheet. The first column shows the net change in the various account balances from the beginning of the year to the end of the year, and the second column shows to which section of the statement of cash flows the account relates.

Step 1: Computing the change in cash and cash equivalents. The change in cash and cash equivalents is identified on the comparative balance sheets as a decrease of $2,237.

Step 2: Preparing the operating activities section—indirect method. The adjustments to net income are identified in the following ways:

- **Category One adjustments**—those items on the income statement that never affect cash. From reviewing the income statement, these adjustments consist of the items shown in Illustration 16-11.

ILLUSTRATION 16-11

Items that Do Not Affect Cash

Depreciation and amortization expense	$1,491
Gain on sale of equipment	(75)
Gain on sale of securities	(208)

In addition to the preceding items that were separately reported on the income statement, an item in the additional information alerts us that there is a noncash expense connected with the "Accrued retiree health care liability." Reviewing that balance sheet account, it is determined that the account balance increased by $35, and so this noncash expense is also added back to net income on the statement of cash flows. (This item was included in this illustration to emphasize that all balance sheet accounts must be reviewed to make certain that all noncash items have been identified.)

- **Category Two adjustments**—items that affect cash in a different time period from when they are recognized under accrual accounting. These items are the changes in the balance sheet accounts connected with operating activities, stated as follows in Illustration 16-12.

ILLUSTRATION 16-12

Items that Affect Cash in a Different Time Period

Increase in accounts receivable	(409)
Decrease in deferred income taxes, current	270
Decrease in inventories	618
Increase in deferred income taxes, noncurrent	(396)
Decrease in accounts payable	(815)
Decrease in accrued liabilities	(324)
Increase in income taxes payable	271

Amounts in parentheses are deducted from net income on the statement of cash flows. Whether an amount is added or deducted is determined by whether the balance sheet account increased or decreased and then by what effect such a change in that account balance has on cash.

Having identified these adjustments, the operating activities section is now prepared and looks as shown in Illustration 16-13.

Step 3: Preparing the investing and financing activities sections. A good starting point in preparing the financing and investing activities sections is to identify the balance sheet accounts that relate to each activity, as follows:

ILLUSTRATION 16-13

Red Rock Candy Mountain
Statement of Cash Flows
For the Year Ending December 31, 2005

Operating activities:		
Net income		$1,420
Adjustments to reconcile net income to net cash:		
Depreciation and amortization expense	$1,491	
Gain on sale of equipment	(75)	
Gain on sale of securities	(208)	
Retiree health care expense	35	
Changes in operating assets and liabilities:		
Increase in accounts receivable	(409)	
Increase in deferred income taxes	(126)[a]	
Decrease in inventories	618	
Decrease in accounts payable	(815)	
Decrease in accrued liabilities	(324)	
Increase in income taxes payable	271	458
Net cash provided from operating activities		$1,878

[a]The two deferred tax accounts were netted.

Investing accounts:

a. Short-Term Investments
b. Investments
c. Property, Plant, and Equipment
d. Accumulated Depreciation
e. Intangible Assets

Financing accounts:

a. Currently Maturing Debt
b. Long-Term Debt
c. Common Stock and Paid-In Capital in Excess of Par, which are always analyzed together
d. Retained Earnings
e. Accumulated Other Comprehensive Income

Once these accounts have been identified, journal entries that caused the changes in the account balances are reconstructed. Sources of information for preparing the entries are (1) the "Additional information provided," (2) the insights into transactions, gained while the operating activities section was being prepared, and (3) a knowledge of basic transactions. Starting with the investing balance sheet accounts and then continuing with the financing balance sheet accounts, these steps are illustrated below.

Intangible Assets

Since Red Rock has intangible assets, amortization expense is expected. However, in reviewing the income statement it is seen that amortization expense was not separately reported but is included in "Depreciation and amortization." There is no information indicating that additional intangible assets were acquired or disposed of during the year, so it is concluded that the only transaction that affects the balance in the intangible assets account is the amortization expense of $105, shown in the following T-account.

Intangible Assets

Beginning balance	2,395		
Amortization amount		105 #9[3]	
Ending balance	2,290		

Having identified all the transactions that changed the intangible assets account balance and finding none that affected cash, no amount is entered on the statement of cash flows in connection with intangible assets.

Property, Plant, and Equipment, Including Accumulated Depreciation

Following the analysis of intangible assets, it is now possible to determine the amount of depreciation expense that was incurred during the year, as follows:

Depreciation and amortization expense (from the income statement)	$1,491
Less amortization expense (see prior analysis of intangible assets)	105
Depreciation expense	$1,386

Posting this depreciation expense amount to the accumulated depreciation account does not completely reconcile the account. (See the following T-account.) Rather, some other transaction is missing.

Accumulated Depreciation

	10,900	Beginning balance
	1,386	Depreciation expense #9
	11,650	Ending balance

From the additional information, it is learned that this other transaction is in connection with some equipment that was sold for $1,339. In preparing the entry to dispose of the long-lived asset, remember that both the cost of the asset and its accumulated depreciation are written off, and a gain or loss, as appropriate, is recognized. Further, from the income statement it is learned that there was a $75 gain from disposing of this equipment. Putting this information together, the following journal entry is prepared:

Cash (given in the problem)	1,339	
Accumulated Depreciation (balance needed to reconcile the accumulated depreciation account)	636	
Property, Plant, and Equipment (amount needed to balance this entry)		1,900
Gain on Sale of Equipment (from the income statement)		75

Trace these amounts to entry #10 on the worksheet, Illustration 16-17 (pp. 765–766).

---

[3]On page 765 is a worksheet used to prepare a statement of cash flows. Such a worksheet is normally used when there are a large number of adjustments in preparing the statement. These reference numbers refer to the adjustments on that worksheet.

Since this transaction of disposing of the equipment affects cash, the amount of $1,339 is reported on the statement of cash flows under the investing activities section. Posting the prior journal entry to the appropriate balance sheet accounts (see the following T-accounts) results in the accumulated depreciation account being reconciled but not the property, plant, and equipment account. It is missing a debit amount of $7,365.

Property, Plant, and Equipment				Accumulated Depreciation			
Beginning bal.	20,112					10,900	Beginning bal.
Disposing of equip.		*1,900*				1,386	Depreciation exp.
Unknown trans.	7,365				636		*Disposing of equip.*
Ending bal.	25,577					11,650	Ending bal.

No other information is available to help ascertain the nature of the missing transaction in the property, plant, and equipment account; but from an understanding of accounting, it is known that the only transaction that increases this account is the acquiring of assets. So the following entry is prepared:

Property, Plant, and Equipment	7,365	
Cash		7,365

Trace these amounts to entry #11 on the worksheet, Illustration 16-17.

Since this transaction affects cash, the amount of $7,365 is reported in the investing section of the statement of cash flows as a use of cash. Also, after posting this transaction, the property, plant, and equipment account reconciles.

To review, the analyses of the accumulated depreciation and the property, plant, and equipment accounts have demonstrated several useful analysis techniques to determine the transactions that affect an account balance. One technique is to use the additional information. This is always a useful first place to begin. Another analysis technique is to use the insight gained from analyzing another account, as was done in determining the amount of depreciation expense following the analysis of intangible assets. The third analysis technique is to apply what has been learned previously in the study of accounting. These three analysis techniques will be used repeatedly to reconcile the various investing and financing accounts in the Red Rock example.

Investments

The final balance sheet investing accounts to reconcile are those connected with investments. Again, using the additional information, it is learned that a holding loss was recognized on the investment classified under fixed assets; and from the accumulated other comprehensive income account, it is seen that the amount is a holding loss of $23. Posting this amount results in reconciling the accumulated other comprehensive income account, but not the investments account, as shown in the following T-accounts.

Investments				Accumulated Other Comprehensive Income			
Beginning bal.	4,339			Beginning bal.	0		
Holding loss		*23*[4]		*Holding loss*	23		
Ending balance	4,930			Ending balance	23		

[4]Trace these amounts to entry #12 on the worksheet.

Continuing, the additional information also alerts us that securities were purchased during the year, and that these securities were classified in the available-for-sale portfolio, which is classified under fixed assets. Since the investment account balance needs a debit of $614 to be reconciled, it is presumed that this is the cost of the securities that were purchased, and the following journal entry is prepared:

Investments	614	
Cash		614

Trace these amounts to entry #13 on the worksheet, Illustration 16-17.

From this entry, $614 is reported as a use of cash in the investing activities section of the statement of cash flows. This entry also reconciles the investments account.

Regarding the short-term investments, the additional information informs us that (1) some securities in this account were sold and (2) that all securities purchased during the year were classified as fixed assets (i.e., no purchase of securities affected the short-term investment account). Thus, the only entry in short-term investments is for the sale of securities, and the resulting journal entry (with the gain obtained from reviewing the income statement) is reconstructed as follows:

Cash	658	
Short-Term Investment		450
Gain on Sale of Securities		208

Trace these amounts to entry #14 on the worksheet, Illustration 16-17.

The cash of $658 is included in the investing activities section of the statement of cash flows.

Having analyzed all the account balances of the balance sheet accounts connected with investing activities, the investing activities section of the statement of cash flows is prepared from the cash amounts from the above entries, as shown in Illustration 16-14.

ILLUSTRATION 16-14

Investing Activities Section

Cash from investing activities:	
Cash from sale of equipment	$ 1,339
Cash used to purchase equipment	(7,365)
Cash used to purchase securities	(614)
Cash from sale of short-term investments	658
Net cash used in investing activities	$(5,982)

Stockholders' Equity

Having analyzed the balance sheet accounts connected with investing activities, the accounts connected with financing activities are now analyzed. The retained earnings account is considered first. After posting the net income to Retained Earnings, the account needs a debit of $287 to be reconciled. The most obvious transaction causing a debit to Retained Earnings is for dividends, so the reconstructed journal entry is as follows:

Retained earnings	287	
Cash		287 (financing)

Trace these amounts to entry #15 on the worksheet, Illustration 16-17.

Retained Earnings

			7,073	
Dividends	287	1,420	Net income
		8,206	Ending bal.

The cash of $287 is reported in the financing section of the statement of cash flows as a use of cash, and the retained earnings account is reconciled.

The common stock and paid-in capital in excess of par accounts are *always analyzed together* because almost always these accounts are affected by the same transactions. From the additional information, it is learned that common stock was issued during the year, and from reviewing these two accounts, it can be seen that the common stock and paid-in capital accounts need credits of $459 and $1,577, respectively, to be reconciled. The reason for such increases is explained by the issuing of additional shares of stock, and the reconstructed journal entry to issue the stock is as follows:

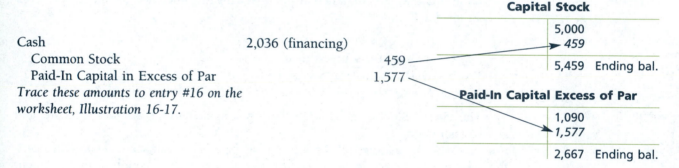

Cash	2,036 (financing)	
Common Stock		459
Paid-In Capital in Excess of Par		1,577

Trace these amounts to entry #16 on the worksheet, Illustration 16-17.

Capital Stock

	5,000
	459
	5,459 Ending bal.

Paid-In Capital Excess of Par

	1,090
	1,577
	2,667 Ending bal.

The cash amount of $2,036 is reported in the financing section of the statement of cash flows as a source of cash.

Liabilities

Finally, the debt accounts (i.e., Currently Maturing Debt and Long-Term Debt) are analyzed. These require careful analysis. First, it is known that amounts reported in the prior year's financial statements as currently maturing debt (i.e., $731) will have been liquidated by using cash. So the first journal entry affecting the debt accounts is as follows:

Currently Maturing Debt	731	
Cash		731

Trace these amounts to entry #17 on the worksheet, Illustration 16-17.

From this journal entry, cash of $731 is reported as a use of cash in the financing activities section of the statement of cash flows.

Continuing with the analysis of the current liability account, since the company did not incur any new short-term debt during the year, as explained in the additional information, the only explanation for the $869 balance in Currently Maturing Debt is that debt was reclassified from the long-term liability section. So the next reconstructed journal entry is as follows:

Long-Term Debt	869	
Currently Maturing Debt		869

Trace these amounts to entry #19 on the worksheet, Illustration 16-17.

After posting these two journal entries, the T-accounts of these liabilities appear as follows:

Currently Maturing Debt				Long-Term Debt		
Beginning bal.		731			6,123	
Payment	731					
Reclassification		*869*		*869*		*Reclassification*
					849	Unknown trans.
		869			6,103	Ending bal.

So the currently maturing debt account is reconciled, but the long-term debt account is not. It needs a credit amount of $849, which must represent new borrowings. Hence, that reconstructed journal entry is as follows:

Cash   849

    Long-Term Debt   849

Trace these amounts to entry #19 on the worksheet, Illustration 16-17.

As before, the cash amount of $849 is reported in the financing activities section of the statement of cash flows. Having reconciled all balance sheet accounts connected with financing activities, the financing activities section of the statement of cash flows is prepared from the cash amounts in the above entries, as shown in Illustration 16-15.

ILLUSTRATION 16-15

Financing Activities Section

Cash from financing activities:		
Cash used to pay dividends	$ (287)	
Cash from issuing stock	2,036	
Cash used to pay currently maturing portion of		
long-term debt	(731)	
Cash from new borrowings	849	
Net cash provided from financing activities		$1,867

Preparing and Interpreting the Statement of Cash Flows

All that remains now is putting the statement of cash flows together, including the reconciling of the beginning cash balance to the ending cash balance. Illustration 16-16 is the completed statement for Red Rock Candy Mountain.

Of importance is that the statement showing the "Net change in cash" of $2,237 agrees with the amount determined in Step 1. In the Red Rock illustration, there were no significant noncash transactions that need to be reported in a separate supplemental schedule. Finally, if the statement of cash flows was prepared using the direct method, the format of the operating activities section would change (as shown in the appendix to this chapter) and the investing and financing activities sections would remain unchanged.

ILLUSTRATION 16-16

Red Rock Candy Mountain
Statement of Cash Flows (Indirect Method)
For the Year Ending December 31, 2005

Cash from operating activities:

Net income		$ 1,420
Noncash items reported on the income statement:		
Depreciation and amortization	$ 1,491	
Accrued retiree health care	35	
Gain on sale of securities	(208)	
Gain on sale of equipment	(75)	
Changes in assets and liabilities:		
Increase in accounts receivable	(409)	
Increase in deferred income taxes	(126)	
Decrease in inventories	618	
Decrease in accounts payable	(815)	
Decrease in accrued liabilities	(324)	
Increase in income taxes payable	271	458
Net cash generated from operating activities		**$ 1,878**
Cash from investing activities:		
Cash from sale of equipment	$ 1,339	
Cash used to purchase equipment	(7,365)	
Cash used to purchase securities	(614)	
Cash from sale of short-term investments	658	
Net cash used in investing activities		**$(5,982)**
Cash from financing activities:		
Cash used to pay dividends	$ (287)	
Cash from issuing stock	2,036	
Cash used to pay currently maturing portion of long-term debt	(731)	
Cash from new borrowings	849	
Net cash provided from financing activities		**$ 1,867**
Net change in cash		**$(2,237)**
Beginning balance of cash and cash equivalents		**4,420**
Ending balance of cash and cash equivalents		**$ 2,183**

An objective of financial reporting is to provide useful information, which is defined as information about the amount, timing, and uncertainty of future cash flows. A company's ability to generate future cash flows is important because cash is the means by which eventually all business transactions are settled. For instance, cash is the means of repaying maturing debts and of paying returns to investors. Thus, creditors, in deciding to loan money to a business enterprise, and investors, in deciding in which company to invest, are interested in being able to forecast that entity's ability to generate future cash flows from which the debt will be repaid or dividends will be received. A company's ability to generate cash flows also affects the market price of the company's stock. Cash is also the means of conducting business. Cash is used to pay employee salaries, expand operations, and take advantage of business opportunities. It also increases a company's ability to endure economic recessions.

One way that a statement of cash flows increases the ability to forecast the amount, timing, and uncertainty of future cash flows is by comparing the amount of cash provided from operating activities to sales, net income, or some other financial number. Another way the statement provides useful information is that cash is not subject to estimation in the same way that determining net income is. Measuring net income is the result of various assumptions and measurement principles, which some critics of financial reporting contend make the resulting net income number highly suspect. However, measuring cash is not subject either to measurement principles or assumptions and is, therefore, a much more reliable number. It is generally conceded that net income is still a better estimator of the long-run future success of a business, but cash is a short-term measure of the success of a business. And without regard to the short-term, there is no long-term.

For the investing and financing activities sections, all reported items have significance and can be used to indicate from what activities and transactions a business entity generated its cash and where that cash was spent. Using these, the reader can estimate to what degree future cash flows will persist and to what extent they should be viewed as one-time events. For example, business expansion activities usually require commitments for several years. Having this information, the financial statement reader can forecast that, since the business will have need for cash, there is an increased possibility that little cash will be available to pay dividends. However, because of the expansion, the reader can also forecast possible stock price appreciation, and the possibility increases for greater future dividends after the expansion is completed. So it is with other items in the investing and financing activities sections—they, too, can be used to forecast future cash flows.

When the direct method is used to prepare the operating activities section of the statement of cash flows, each line is significant and can be read as a source of or use of cash and has meaning in the same way as indicated in the prior paragraph for investing and financing activities. So the reader can, with some degree of confidence, determine to what extent operating activities are generating cash and to what extent those cash flows can be expected to persist. But when the indirect method is used to prepare the operating activities section, only the "net cash" line has significance. For example, in Illustration 16-16, depreciation and amortization is the largest number in the operating activities section and is one of the biggest numbers on the entire statement; yet depreciation and amortization do not provide any cash. Both are only the allocations of historical cost amounts. Remember that the indirect method does not directly compute the amount of cash generated or used from operating activities. Instead, the approach begins with an accrual number—net income—and then adjustments are made to that number for the noncash transactions to derive a cash number.

The adjustments to net income in the operating activities section still contain useful information. For example, a significant increase in accounts receivable might be a signal about the deteriorating ability of the company to collect outstanding accounts. Also, a large increase in inventory could alert the analyst that the company is having difficulty moving obsolete merchandise.

At the beginning of this chapter, it was pointed out how accrual numbers by themselves may not reveal the complete picture for a business. In the Regina Company example, the accrual numbers portrayed a glowing picture, while the cash flow numbers told a completely different situation. This same conflict of information exists for other companies. However, sometimes the conflicting information has the income statement (under accrual accounting) reporting bleak numbers and the cash statement reporting better numbers. For example, Priceline.com was criticized in the late 1990s because of its continuing large losses; but during the period from 1997 through 1999, Priceline.com reported positive cash flows. This dichotomy is particularly startling because in 1999 Priceline.com reported a loss of over $1 billion but reported positive cash flows of $133 million. The reason the company reported positive cash flows from 1997 through

1999 was through issuing stock. The important point of this example is that cash flow information can tell a completely different story from that which accrual accounting tells. Hence, it is important that both sets of data be provided and reviewed by the reader of financial statements.

Other Issues in Preparing the Statement of Cash Flows

Not all the potential difficulties in preparing a statement of cash flows were covered in the Red Rock Candy Mountain example. Some other frequently incurred difficulties include:

- Presenting the statement of cash flows when extraordinary items, discontinued operations, and gains/losses from changing an accounting principle are present,
- Reporting transactions connected with uncollectible accounts, and
- Reporting the amortizing of premiums/discounts connected with long-term debt.

Accounting for these difficulties when preparing the cash flow statement is discussed next.

Reporting Extraordinary Items, Etc.

Under the indirect method, gains/losses from extraordinary items, from discontinued operations, and from changing an accounting principle are *added back to or deducted from net income* in the same way as is done for other gains/losses. Any cash received/paid on extraordinary items or discontinued operations is reported on the statement, most likely in the investing activities section. No cash is ever affected from a change in an accounting principle. Du Pont's statement of cash flows shown in Exhibit 16-5 is an example of reporting of a discontinued oper-

EXHIBIT 16-5

Reporting Extraordinary Items E.I. du Pont de Nemours and Company and Consolidated Subsidiaries Consolidated Statement of Cash Flows (dollars in millions)			
Cash and Cash Equivalents at Beginning of Year	$ 1,004	$1,066	$1,408
Cash Provided by Continuing Operations			
Net Income	4,480	2,405	3,636
Adjustments to Reconcile Net Income to Cash Provided by Continuing Operations:			
Net Income from Discontinued Operations	(3,033)	(973)	(705)
Extraordinary Charge from Early Retirement of Debt (Note 8)	275	0	0
Investment Activities of Continuing Operations (Note 23)			
Net Proceeds from Sale of Interest in Petroleum Operations (Note 2)	4,206	0	0

ation and of an extraordinary item on a statement of cash flows. There, it can be seen that the gains and losses are added back to net income, and any cash received is reported in investing activities.

Under the direct method, gains/losses from changing an accounting principle, extraordinary items, and discontinued operations are ignored in preparing the operating activities section in the same way that other gains/losses are ignored. Remember that gains/losses are always the difference between the carrying value of an asset(s) and the amount of cash received. Hence, all gains/losses—not being the amount of cash paid or received—are never included as a source or use of cash under the direct method. If any cash is received/paid on extraordinary items or discontinued operations, such cash is always reported on the statement of cash flows, usually in the investing activities section of the statement.

Bad Debts Expense and the Allowance for Doubtful Accounts

Bad debts expense does not affect the preparation of the operating activities section of the statement of cash flows under the indirect method. The reason is because the operating activities section contains only the net changes in the balance sheet accounts. Thus, it is not relevant whether the change in the accounts receivable balance is due to collecting an amount owed or to writing off an uncollectible account. It is the net change in the account balance that is important. So *when the indirect method is used, the easiest way to analyze accounts receivable and the allowance for doubtful accounts is to view them as one net amount and to adjust net income for the net change*, as was done in the examples and illustrations in the chapter.

However, when the direct method is used to prepare the operating activities section, it is important to distinguish between the change in accounts receivable that is due to sales—because that affects the amount of cash receipts—and the change in accounts receivable that is due to uncollectible accounts transactions—as these affect the amount of cash disbursements for expenses. So *under the direct method, the adjustment to convert sales to cash received is the change in the net accounts receivable reduced by the amount of uncollectible accounts expense.*

To illustrate, assume the following data:

Sales	$56,154
Accounts written off as uncollectible	355
Accounts receivable:	
Beginning balance	1,575
Ending balance	1,451
Allowance for doubtful accounts:	
Beginning balance	320
Ending balance	280
Uncollectible accounts expense	315
Operating expenses	11,200

Also, uncollectible accounts expense is included in the operating expenses of $11,200. Given these assumptions, the net change in accounts receivable is determined as follows in Exhibit 16-6.

EXHIBIT 16-6

Net Changes in Accounts Receivable

	Beginning of Year	End of Year
Accounts receivable balance	$1,575	$1,451
Less allowance for doubtful accounts	320	280
Net accounts receivable balance	$1,255	$1,171
Decrease in net accounts receivable		$ 84

Under the direct method, it would be incorrect to adjust sales by $84 because the change is due to items that affect both cash receipts and cash disbursements, not just cash receipts. If only the sales account were adjusted for the $84, the result would be that both cash receipts from customers and cash disbursements for operating expenses would be misstated. So under the direct method of preparing the operating activities section, the effects due to collecting accounts receivable must be separated from the effects of writing off bad debts.

Using the same data as given earlier, assume that uncollectible accounts expense was $315. (This is not the same as the amount of uncollectible accounts written off; rather, it is the amount of the year-end adjusting entry.) Then, the adjustment for the change in net accounts receivable is as shown in Exhibit 16-7.

EXHIBIT 16-7

Adjustments to Accounts Receivable

	Income Statement	Adjustments Dr.	Cr.	Cash Flows
Sales, net	$ 56,154	$315	$ 84	$55,923
Operating expenses	(11,200)		315	(10,885)

Bond Premiums and Discounts

Earlier in the text, it was demonstrated how bonds and other long-term debt are issued at premiums or discounts, depending upon the relationship between the coupon interest rate and the market rate. It also was shown that such premiums or discounts are amortized to interest expense (or revenue when the bonds are purchased as an investment) over the life of the debt. The effect of this is that the amount recognized as interest expense (or revenue) on the income statement is different from the amount of cash paid (or received). Thus, the problem is that under accrual accounting the interest expense (or revenue) as reported on the income statement is not equal to the amount of cash paid (or received).

Since the earning and paying of interest are operating activities, so too are the amortizing of premiums and discounts. Under the indirect method, the adjustment to net income for premium/discount amortization is handled—as always—by adjusting net income for the change in the premium/discount account. *For bonds payable, amortization amounts related to bond discounts are added back to net income, and amortization amounts related to bond premiums are deducted from net income.* And, of course, the accounting is the opposite for discounts/premiums relating to bond investments. Under the direct method, rather than adjusting net income for the amortization amount, *interest expense is adjusted.*

Preparing a Worksheet

When many adjustments must be made to net income to convert it to a cash number, or when there are many accounts to analyze to prepare the statement of cash flows, preparing a worksheet to assemble and classify the data is often used. Illustration 16-17 is an example of such a worksheet and was prepared using the Red Rock Candy Mountain data. In preparing such a worksheet, the following guidelines are helpful:

- Instead of preparing the worksheet in the typical balance sheet format (i.e., assets, liabilities, and equity), it is prepared in a debit and credit format. So such accounts as Allowance for Doubtful Accounts and Accumulated Depreciation are listed with the other accounts having credit balances. This listing of the balance sheet accounts comprises the top portion of the worksheet.
- For computational ease, the comparative balance sheets are presented with the most recent year in the right column and the prior year in the left column. These two balance sheet columns are separated by two other columns in which the debit and credit adjustments, respectively, are entered.
- The bottom portion of the worksheet is apportioned into the three major sections of the statement of cash flows: operating, investing, and financing activities. In these sections are gathered the adjusting amounts and transaction amounts that are reported on the statement.

ILLUSTRATION 16-17

Red Rock Candy Mountain
Worksheet, Statement of Cash Flows
(For Indirect Method)

	Balance, Beginning Year	Reconciling Items Debits	Reconciling Items Credits	Balance, Year-End
Debit accounts:				
Cash and cash equivalents	$ 4,420		(1) $ 2,237	$ 2,183
Short-term investments	729		(14) 450	279
Accounts receivable, net	6,392	(3) $ 409		6,801
Deferred income taxes	1,780	(4) 126		1,906
Inventories	8,967		(5) 618	8,349
Investments (less allowance)	4,339	(13) 614	(12) 23	4,930
Property, plant, and equipment	20,112	(11) 7,365	(10) 1,900	25,577
Intangible assets	2,395		(9) 105	2,290
Other comprehensive income		(12) 23		23
Total debits	$49,134	$ 8,537	$ 5,333	$52,338

(continued)

ILLUSTRATION 16-17 CONTINUED

	Balance, Beginning Year	Reconciling Items Debits	Reconciling Items Credits	Balance, Year-End
Credit accounts:				
Accumulated depreciation	$10,900	(10) $ 636	(9) $ 1,386	$11,650
Accounts payable	11,548	(6) 815		10,733
Accrued liabilities	1,575	(7) 324		1,251
Income taxes payable	298		(8) 271	569
Currently maturing debt	731	(17) 731	(18) 869	869
Accrued retiree health care	4,796		(4) 35	4,831
Long-term debt	6,123	(18) 869	(19) 849	6,103
Common stock	5,000		(16) 459	5,459
Paid-in capital in excess of par	1,090		(16) 1,577	2,667
Retained earnings	7,073	(15) 287	(2) 1,420	8,206
Total credits	$49,134	$ 3,662	$ 6,866	$52,338
Statement of cash flows:				
Operating activities:				
Net income		(2) $ 1,420		
Depreciation and amortization		(9) 1,491		
Accrued retiree health care		(4) 35		
Gain on sale of securities			(14) $ 208	
Gain on sale of equipment			(10) 75	
Accounts receivable			(3) 409	
Deferred income taxes			(4) 126	
Inventories		(5) 618		
Accounts payable			(6) 815	
Accrued liabilities			(7) 324	
Income taxes payable		(8) 271		
Investing activities:				
Cash from sale of equipment		(10) 1,339		
Cash used to purchase equipment			(11) 7,365	
Cash used to purchase securities			(13) 614	
Cash from sale of short-term investments		(14) 658		
Financing activities:				
Cash used to pay dividends			(15) 287	
Cash from issuing stock		(16) 2,036		
Cash used to pay currently maturing debt			(17) 731	
Cash from new borrowings		(19) 849		
Totals		$20,916	$23,153	
Net change in cash		(1) 2,237		
Worksheet totals		$23,153	$23,153	

Explanation of entries:
(1) Change in cash.
(2) Net income.
(3)–(8) Change in the operating accounts on the comparative balance sheets.
(9)–(19) Ties to the entries prepared earlier in the text that relate to the Red Rock Candy Mountain example.

After setting up the worksheet in the manner described, it is completed by using the same steps or procedures as were described earlier, which are:

- Step 1: Compute the change in cash and enter it as a debit and a credit in the worksheet. (See item #1 in Illustration 16-17.)
- Step 2: Complete the operating activities section. The net income (or loss) is entered with an adjustment to the retained earnings account and as the

first item in the operating activities section. (See item #2 in Illustration 16-17.) Following this, the other adjustments necessary to convert net income to a cash number are entered, with corresponding entries made to appropriate balance sheet accounts.

- Step 3: Complete the investing and financing activities sections by entering the adjustments in the appropriate sections of the statement of cash flows with an offsetting amount in the appropriate balance sheet account.

The worksheet is complete when (1) all balance sheet accounts have been reconciled, which is verified by adding across the worksheet, and (2) the worksheet reconciles to the change in cash number as computed in Step 1. Once the worksheet is complete, the statement of cash flows is prepared. The worksheet does not take the place of preparing the statement.

International Comparative Practices

In the international arena, a statement that provides information about the flow of funds within a company is increasingly becoming an integral part of financial reports. Many countries, including France, Brazil, Australia, and New Zealand, require a funds statement to be included in the annual report as a primary statement. However, there are some differences across countries in the definition of funds. As discussed in this chapter, U.S. GAAP bases the funds statement on changes in *cash and cash equivalents*, the position adopted in 1987. (Prior to that date, U.S. companies provided information on either the change in cash or working capital.) The U.S. adoption of a cash and cash equivalent emphasis has had a significant influence on standard-setting bodies in other countries. For example, in 1991 the United Kingdom adopted a new

standard that requires the focus of the funds statement to be on changes in cash and cash equivalents. In spite of the UK statement emphasizing cash and cash equivalents, significant format differences exist between U.S. and UK cash flow statements.

Exhibit 16-8 presents a cash flow statement for Vodafone Air Touch Plc, a British multinational company. The first line item is net cash flow from operating activities, which an examination of the corresponding note (not presented in the text) indicates is operating profit adjusted for noncash expenses (i.e., depreciation and amortization) and changes in inventory, accounts payable, and accounts receivable.

The next line items provide summary cash flow information for the following major categories:

- Dividends received
- Net interest payments
- Taxation
- Capital expenditures and investments
- Mergers, acquisitions, and disposals
- Dividend payments

EXHIBIT 16-8

Vodafone Air Touch Plc
Consolidated Cash Flow
For the Year Ending 31 March 2000

	Note	2000 £m	1999 £m
Net cash inflow from operating activities	25	2,510	1,045
Dividends received from joint ventures and associated undertakings		236	3
Net cash outflow for returns on investments and servicing of finance	25	(406)	(90)
Taxation		(325)	(195)
Net cash outflow for capital expenditure and financial investment	25	(756)	(688)
Net cash outflow for acquisitions and disposals	25	(4,756)	(317)
Equity dividends paid		(221)	(118)
Cash outflow before management of liquid resources and financing		(3,718)	(360)
Management of liquid resources			
Short-term deposits		(33)	—
Net cash inflow from financing			
Issue of ordinary share capital		362	11
Issue of shares to minorities		37	—
Purchase of shares from minorities		—	(18)
Debt due within one year:			
Increase/(decrease) in short-term debt		598	(130)
Repayment of debt acquired		(449)	—
Debt due after one year:			
(Decrease)/increase in bank loans		(550)	490
Repayment of debt acquired		(377)	—
Issue of new bonds		4,246	—
Net cash inflow from financing		3,867	353
Increase/(decrease) in cash in the year		116	(7)
Reconciliation of net cash flow to movement in net debt			
Increase/(decrease) in cash in the year		116	(7)
Cash inflow from increase in debt		(3,468)	(360)
Cash outflow from increase in liquid resources		33	—
Increase in net debt resulting from cash flows		(3,319)	(367)
Debt acquired on acquisition of subsidiary undertakings		(2,133)	—
Translation difference		316	(19)
Other movements		1	(5)
Increase in net debt in the year		(5,135)	(391)
Opening net debt		(1,508)	(1,117)
Closing net debt		(6,643)	(1,508)

The sum of all these categories is labeled "Cash flows before management of liquid resources and financing." This subtotal is meant to communicate the amount of cash used by the company for its primary operations and expenditures necessary to continue operating (i.e., investments). If compared to the U.S. cash flow statement, this subtotal would be similar to cash flows from operating and investing activities. Note that the "management of liquid resources" refers to cash equivalents. Thus, the final amount in the cash flow statement is based solely on cash.

Cash flows from financing activities are presented last on the statement. It is also interesting to note that the financing section is the only section that provides detailed information on the face of the cash flow statement. Other major categories refer the analyst to the notes to find the details of the corresponding subtotal.

Finally, after the total cash flows are derived for the period, UK GAAP require that this cash flow amount be the starting point at the bottom of the statement to reconcile the beginning and ending balances of net debt.

All of the cash flows statements in the United Kingdom follow this same format. This illustration demonstrates that even when a country has the same focus on cash flows as U.S. GAAP, the final product that provides this information can do so in a very different manner. To effectively compare cash flow results between two companies, where one follows U.S. GAAP and the other follows UK GAAP, the analyst must be familiar with the different formats used in the two countries.

International Accounting Standards

The International Accounting Standards Committee was also greatly influenced by U.S. GAAP when it issued *IAS No. 7*, "Cash Flow Statements." All of the major requirements of *IAS No. 7* are essentially equivalent to the U.S. GAAP standards and are summarized as follows:

- The statement's focus is on changes in cash and cash equivalents.
- Changes in cash are classified into operating, investing, and financing activities.
- Either the direct or indirect method can be used for the operating section.
- Major noncash transactions are excluded from the cash flow statement but disclosed in a separate schedule.

The similarities between U.S. GAAP and *IAS No. 7* are so great that the U.S. Securities and Exchange Commission stated as early as 1998 that non-U.S. companies following *IAS No. 7* to prepare their cash flow statements do not need to reconcile the differences to U.S. GAAP.

Despite these prevailing similarities, however, there are some differences between *IAS No. 7* and U.S. GAAP that should be noted. These differences are summarized in the following paragraphs.

Classification of Interest and Dividends

Under U.S. GAAP,

- Both interest received and interest paid are classified as operating activities.
- Dividends received are classified as an operating activity, but dividends paid are classified as a financing activity.

To some people, the rationale for these classification requirements is peculiar. The reason for the inconsistent treatment of dividends paid is that the FASB determined that any transaction related to a company's own stock should be classified as a financing activity, and so paying dividends is viewed as a necessary cost of obtaining equity financing. However, using this same rationale, one could argue that paying interest is a necessary cost of obtaining debt financing, and thus, interest paid should be a financing activity. In addition, one could also argue that interest and dividends received are returns from an investment and, thus, should be classified as an investing activity.

IAS No. 7 allows several options for classifying dividends and interest. One option is to classify them as operating activities. A second option is to classify interest and dividend payments as financing activities, and interest and dividend receipts as investing activities. A third option is to allow any combination of these. For example, the statement states that financial institutions should probably classify interest and dividend receipts and interest payments as operating activities and dividend payments as financing activities. This added flexibility potentially allows managers to provide more relevant information.

Definition of "Cash and Cash Equivalents"

U.S. GAAP requires disclosure in the notes to the financial statements of how companies define cash equivalents. In close contrast, instead of disclosing the definition of cash equivalents, *IAS No. 7* requires disclosure of what is included in cash equivalents. Also, U.S. GAAP requires the "cash and cash equivalents" line item on the balance sheet to correspond with what is being reported in the cash flow statement. *IAS No. 7 requires that a company reconcile its balance sheet cash and cash equivalent line item to what is shown on the cash flow statement, implying that the two amounts do not need to be equal.*

Cash Flow per Share

Both the FASB in Statement No. 95 and the SEC in Accounting Series Release No. 142 explicitly state that *cash flows per share must not be disclosed*. To do so, they argue, might lead financial statement readers to put undue emphasis on that number to the exclusion of other, more important measures (such as earnings per share) of performance. *IAS No. 7* makes no such statement, so companies following IAS can voluntarily provide a cash flow per share amount.

Comparison of Funds Flow Requirements

Exhibit 16-9 presents a comparative analysis of requirements across countries related to a funds flow statement. It should be noted, however, that the global market demand for a funds flow statement has resulted (in countries where an explicit requirement for such a statement is lacking) in many companies voluntarily providing a funds flow statement.

EXHIBIT 16-9

National Comparative Practices of Funds Flow Statement Requirements

Countries that Require a Cash Flow Statement	Countries that Require a Funds Flow Statement Without an Explicit Focus on Cash	Countries Without a Funds Flow Requirement
United States	Sweden	Italy
United Kingdom	South Korea	Switzerland
Australia		
Japan		
Germany		
France		
IASB		

Summary

In summary, the purpose of the statement of cash flows is to provide information about a business enterprise's cash receipts and cash disbursements, which then can be used to assess its ability to generate cash flows, meet its obligations, etc. These cash receipts and cash disbursements are categorized into three activities: operating, investing, and financing. Basically, investing activities are those that involve the long-term assets of the enterprise and also investments in securities categorized as current assets; financing activities are those that involve long-term liabilities, short-term borrowings, and stockholders' equity accounts. All other activities are operating activities. The statement includes a reconciliation of the beginning and ending balances of cash and cash equivalents, and finally a supplemental schedule or narrative description is included of significant noncash transactions. This is what the FASB requires when preparing a statement of cash flows.

The operating activities section may be prepared using either the indirect or the direct method. Under the indirect method, net income is converted to a cash number by (a) reversing on the statement of cash flows the effect of non-cash items that were reported on the income statement and (b) adjusting net income for the net change in those balance sheet accounts that are connected with operating activities. Under the direct method, each account on the income statement is converted to a cash number by analyzing the changes in those balance sheet accounts that are connected with it.

Regardless of which method is used to prepare the operating activities section, the investing and financing sections are prepared exactly the same way. The items reported in these sections are identified by analyzing the balance sheet accounts connected with them, determining the individual transactions that caused the account balance to change, and reporting the effect on cash on the statement. A good approach to preparing these sections is to establish T-accounts for each balance sheet account that is connected to either investing or financing activities, enter the beginning and ending balances, and then reconstruct the original journal entries by reviewing the available information until the accounts are reconciled. When there are many adjustments to be made or there are many accounts to analyze, preparing a worksheet expedites the process.

Although all accounting systems in the world require a statement of cash flows to be reported, there are differences in how the statement is prepared. Primary among these differences are (1) the focus on or way in which cash and cash equivalents are defined and (2) the place where interest and dividends are reported.

APPENDIX: Direct Method—Red Rock Candy Mountain Company

On the following worksheet, the numbers reported under the Income Statement column come from Illustration 16-10 on pages 751–752. They are the same numbers as reported on the income statement, except that several expenses have been combined into operating expenses, and all headings and subtotals on the income statement have been deleted from this worksheet.

The amounts reported in the Adjustments column are the same adjustments found in Illustration 16-13 on page 754. Each adjustment is reported next to the income statement account to which it relates. Also, each adjustment that is added to net income in Illustration 16-13 is included in the credit column here, and each adjustment that is deducted from net income in Illustration 16-13 is included in the debit column.

Of importance is that regardless of whether the indirect method (as shown in Illustration 16-13) or the direct method (Illustration 16-1A) is used, the amount of cash from operating activities remains the same.

ILLUSTRATION 16-1A

Red Rock Candy Mountain Company
Worksheet for Direct Method

	Income Statement	Adjustments Dr.	Adjustments Cr.	Cash Flow
Sales	$ 56,154	409		$ 55,745
Cost of goods sold	(39,309)	815	618	(39,506)
Operating expenses	(13,487)	324	35	(13,776)
Depreciation and amortization expense	(1,491)		1,491	0
Gain on sale of equipment	75	75		0
Gain on sale of securities	208	208		0
Interest expense	(453)			(453)
Income taxes	(277)	396	271	(132)
			270	
Net income	$ 1,420			$ 1,878

The completed cash flow statement, using the direct method, is shown in Illustration 16-2A.

ILLUSTRATION 16-2A

Red Rock Candy Mountain Company
Statement of Cash Flows
For the Year Ending December 31, 2005

Cash from operating activities:		
Cash receipts from customers		$ 55,745
Cash payments for purchases of inventory		(39,506)
Cash payments for operating expenses		(13,776)
Cash payments for interest		(453)
Cash payments for income taxes		(132)
Net cash generated from operating activities		$ 1,878
Cash from investing activities:		
Cash from sale of equipment	$ 1,339	
Cash used to purchase equipment	(7,365)	
Cash used to purchase securities	(614)	
Cash from sale of short-term investments	658	
Net cash used in investing activities		$ (5,982)
Cash from financing activities:		
Cash used to pay dividends	$ (287)	
Cash from issuing stock	2,036	
Cash used to pay currently maturing portion of long-term debt	(731)	
Cash from new borrowings	849	
Net cash provided from financing activities		$ 1,867
Net change in cash		$ (2,237)
Beginning balance of cash and cash equivalents		4,420
Ending balance of cash and cash equivalents		$ 2,183

Questions

1. When constructing a statement of cash flows, how is the check figure for the statement obtained?

2. List the three sections of the statement of cash flows, and identify the types of transactions that are reported in each section.

3. Although there are some exceptions, typically in what section of the statement of cash flows do transactions affecting the following items appear: (a) current assets, (b) noncurrent assets, (c) current liabilities, (d) noncurrent liabilities, and (e) stockholders' equity?

4. Suppose that a company purchased a major piece of equipment by signing a 10-year note with no down payment. How is this transaction reported (if at all) on the statement of cash flows?

5. What are the two methods of preparing the operating activities section of the statement of cash flows? Which method begins with net income? Which method provides more detail with respect to the sources and uses of cash from operating activities? Is the preparation of the investing and financing sections affected by the choice of which method is used to prepare the operating activities section?

6. Refer to the Regina Company scenario at the beginning of the chapter (p. 734). Regina was able to report a steady increase in earnings, while simultaneously having significant negative cash flows from operating activities. Provide some examples of how this could occur.

7. PSINet Inc. (an Internet and e-commerce provider to businesses) recorded a loss in every quarter during 1998 and 1999 but had positive cash flows in all of those quarters. Explain how this can occur. (The company has declared bankruptcy.)

8. Gooseman Corp. reported net income for the current period of $75,000. The income statement showed depreciation expense of $38,000. Also, accounts receivable and inventory increased during the period by $10,000 and $19,000, respectively, and accounts payable decreased by $14,000. Calculate the cash flows from operating activities for the company.

9. Carlisle, Inc., reported a net loss of $44,000. Depreciation and amortization for the period was $38,000. In addition, there was a decrease in accounts receivable of $12,000, an increase in accounts payable of $7,000, and an increase in marketable securities of $15,000. (a) Calculate the cash flows from operating activities for Carlisle, Inc. (b) How would the answer change if, in addition to the information provided in Part (a), the allowance for bad debts decreased by $2,500 during the year (i.e., the net change in accounts receivable was $9,500)?

10. Magnum, Inc., reported cost of goods sold of $165,000 on the income statement. On the balance sheet, inventory increased by $10,000, and accounts payable increased by $12,000. Assuming that the accounts payable were related to purchases of inventory, calculate the amount of cash paid to purchase inventory.

11. RF Systems Inc. reported net income of $200,000. The company's effective tax rate was 40%. Income taxes payable during the period increased by $6,000, and there was an increase of $11,000 in the deferred tax liability. (A deferred tax liability account is related to income tax expense in the same way that income taxes payable is.) Determine the amount of cash paid for income taxes during the period.

12. Discuss how gains and losses on sales of property, plant, and equipment are accounted for in the operating activities section of the cash flows statement, using the indirect method. Explain the rationale for this procedure.

13. An analysis of the equipment and associated accumulated depreciation accounts for Jackson Corp. revealed the following beginning and ending balances for the period:

Equipment			Accumulated Depreciation		
1/1/04	123,000			48,000	1/1/04
12/31/04	128,000			37,000	12/31/04

(a) Depreciation expense for the period was $27,000. (b) One piece of equipment was sold for $50,000, and a gain of $10,000 was realized. (c) Finally, all purchases of equipment during the period were financed with cash. When using the indirect method of preparing the operating activities section, what information should be provided in the statement of cash flows with respect to equipment?

14. Accounting regulators claim that net income is a better predictor of future cash flows than are the current total cash flows or cash flows from operating activities. Explain why this is the case.

15. Explain some of the similarities and differences in the statement of cash flows prepared by using U.S. GAAP and UK GAAP.

16. In which section of the statement of cash flows are the following items classified according to U.S. GAAP?
    a. Interest received
    b. Interest paid
    c. Dividends received
    d. Dividends paid

    How are the above items classified under *IAS No. 7*?

17. Do U.S. GAAP allow companies to report a "cash flow per share"? Why or why not?

Exercises

Exercise 16-1: Transaction Classification. Indicate how each of the following accounting events is classified on a statement of cash flows under the indirect method and using the following coding scheme. (Note that more than one item can be used for each event.)

O = Operating section

I = Investing section

F = Financing section

NC = Noncash transaction that is shown in a separate schedule

NA = Not shown on the statement of cash flows using the indirect approach

a. Paying interest on bonds outstanding.
b. Increase in prepaid assets.

c. Exchanging shares of the company's stock for equipment.
d. Receiving a note as a result of selling land.
e. Issuing stock.
f. Depreciation expense.
g. Purchasing stock of another company.
h. Decrease in accounts payable.
i. Paying salaries and wages.
j. Increase in inventory.
k. Retiring bonds.
l. Receiving a loan from a bank.
m. Purchasing land.
n. Paying cash to have a building demolished and receiving cash for the scrap materials.
o. Receiving dividends.
p. Paying dividends.
q. Loss on selling marketable securities.

Exercise 16-2: Operating Section—Direct Method. Calvin Computers had total sales of $352,300 for the period. Of this amount, sixty percent were cash sales and the remaining amount were credit sales. The company's gross accounts receivable increased during the period by $3,500. In addition, the company recognized bad debt expense of $2,200, which was included in general operating expenses of $78,000. The company wrote off specific accounts of $1,600 as uncollectible. Balance sheet accounts associated with the general operating expenses are as follows:

	Beginning Balance	Ending Balance
Prepaid expenses	$3,100	$4,800
Accrued liabilities	2,700	1,400

1. Determine the amount of cash that Calvin Computers collected from customers during the period.
2. Assuming that prepaid expenses and accrued liabilities relate to general operating expenses, calculate the amount of cash Calvin Computers paid for general operating expenses during the period.

Exercise 16-3: Changing from Accrual to Cash. McFarlin Co. uses the accrual method of accounting for sales and purchases transactions. The following information was obtained from the accrual accounting records of the company:

Income statement accounts:	
Sales	$487,500
Cost of goods sold	265,000
Balance sheet accounts:	
Increase in accounts receivable	$ 12,000
Increase in inventory	23,000
Decrease in accounts payable	23,000
Increase in unearned revenues	19,000

1. Calculate the amount of cash collected from customers.
2. Calculate purchases for the period and the amount of cash paid for purchases.

Exercise 16-4: Changing from Cash to Accrual. Peabody Corp. keeps its books on the cash basis and then at year-end makes the necessary adjusting entries so as to publish accrual-based financial statements. The following information was available at December 31, 2003:

a. On January 2, 2003, Peabody Corp. paid $15,000 for a 3-year insurance policy and debited the entire amount to Insurance Expense.

b. An analysis of the accounts receivable subsidiary ledger revealed that the amounts owed at the end of the year totaled $45,000, as compared to the amount owed at the beginning of the year of $47,000.

c. Purchases of inventory during the year, which were debited to an expense account, were $400,000. A physical count of the inventory at December 31 showed that inventory on hand had increased to $36,000 from $27,000 at the beginning of the year. Also, an analysis of the accounts payable subsidiary ledger showed the amount owed to suppliers had increased by $4,000.

d. A review of the accrued liabilities account, which is connected with operating expenses, showed that the amounts owed had increased by $10,000 since the beginning of the year.

Prepare the necessary adjusting entry to switch to the accrual basis at December 31, 2003, for each of these cases.

Exercise 16-5: Changing the Bases of Accounting. Answer each of the following independent cases.

1. Kevin Chappell, D.D.S., keeps his books on the cash basis. During 2006, fees collected totaled $700,000, and a review of the accounts receivable ledger shows that the amount owed to Kevin had increased by $40,000. At December 31, 2006, Kevin also had unearned fees of $3,000, but did not have any at January 1, 2006. Compute how much Kevin earned on the accrual basis during 2006.

2. Burke, a management consultant, hires a professional accountant who keeps Burke's records on the accrual basis and at the end of each month provides him with an income statement and balance sheet. For the most recent month, the financial statements show revenues of $40,000, unearned fees (representing an advance to speak at a national convention) of $4,000, and an accounts receivable balance of $30,000. Last month these figures were $42,000 for revenues, no unearned fees, and accounts receivable of $23,000. How much cash did Burke collect during the month?

Exercise 16-6: Multiple-Choice Questions.
1. Of the following current asset and current liability accounts, which one is *not* included in determining cash flows from operating activities?
   a. Marketable securities
   b. Prepaid expenses
   c. Taxes payable
   d. Unearned revenue
2. When using the indirect method of computing cash flows from operating activities, which of the following items is subtracted from net income?
   a. An increase in accounts payable.
   b. A gain from the sale of investments.
   c. Depreciation expense.
   d. Interest received from investments.

3. Which of the following items is a cash inflow from financing activities, according to U.S. GAAP?
   a. Purchase of a new vehicle by signing a note payable.
   b. Reissue of shares of treasury stock.
   c. Interest received on an investment in bonds.
   d. An increase in accounts payable.
4. Which of the following is *not* a major category of the cash flow statement under U.S. GAAP?
   a. Operating
   b. Financing
   c. Acquisitions
   d. Investing
5. With respect to preparing a statement of cash flows, which of the following is treated differently under U.S. GAAP as compared to *IAS No. 7*?
   a. The classification of interest and dividend cash flows.
   b. The definition of cash.
   c. The primary classifications used in the statement (operating, investing, etc.).
   d. Both a and b.

Exercise 16-7: Short Problems from Past CPA Exams.

1. The following information is available from Sand Corp.'s accounting records for the year ended December 31, 2006:

Cash received from customers	$870,000
Rent received	10,000
Cash paid to suppliers and employees	510,000
Taxes paid	110,000
Cash dividends paid	30,000

   What was the net cash flow provided by operating activities in 2006?

2. Tara Company reported revenue of $1,980,000 in its income statement for the year ended December 31, 2006. Additional information was as follows:

	December 31, 2005	December 31, 2006
Accounts receivable	$415,000	$550,000
Allowance for doubtful accounts	25,000	40,000

   No uncollectible accounts were written off during 2006. How much cash did Tara receive from sales during 2006?

3. Brock Corp.'s transactions for the year ended December 31, 2007, included the following:
   - Acquired 50% of Hoag Corp.'s common stock for $225,000 cash that was borrowed from a bank.
   - Exchanged 5,000 shares of its preferred stock for land having a fair value of $400,000.
   - Issued 500 of its 11% debenture bonds, due 2012, for $490,000 cash.
   - Purchased a patent for $275,000 cash.
   - Paid $150,000 toward a bank loan.
   - Sold investment securities for $995,000.

   Determine Brock's net cash flows from (a) investing and (b) financing activities for 2007.

(continued)

4. Rory Co.'s prepaid insurance account balance was $50,000 at December 31, 2007, and $25,000 at December 31, 2006. Insurance expense was $20,000 for 2007 and $15,000 for 2006. What amount of cash disbursements for insurance would be reported in Rory's 2007 net cash flows from operating activities presented on a direct basis?

5. The following information was taken from the 2005 financial statements of Planet Corp.:

Accounts receivable, January 1, 2005	$ 21,600
Accounts receivable, December 31, 2005	30,400
Sales on account and cash sales	438,000

No accounts receivable were written off or recovered during the year. If the direct method is used for the 2005 statement of cash flows, how much cash was collected from customers?

6. During 2005, Teb Inc. had the following activities related to its financial operations:

Payment for the early retirement of long-term bonds payable (carrying value $740,000)	$750,000
Distribution in 2005 of cash dividends declared in 2004 to preferred shareholders	62,000
Carrying value of convertible preferred stock in Teb, converted into common shares	120,000
Proceeds from sale of treasury stock (carrying value at cost, $86,000)	95,000

In Teb's 2005 statement of cash flows, what should be the net cash used in financing activities?

Exercise 16-8: Transaction Classification. Lyle Corp. uses the indirect method to prepare the operating section of its statement of cash flows. Lyle Corp. completed several transactions during the year ending December 31, 2004.

a. A building and accompanying land were sold for $210,000 cash. These assets were acquired 15 years ago at a total cost of $200,000, 70% of which was allocated to the building account. At the time of sale, the building was 50% depreciated and had a fair market value of $85,000. The fair market value of the land was $115,000.

b. The company purchased land for $600,000 by paying 25% of the purchase price in cash and signing a 5-year mortgage for the remaining balance.

c. Treasury shares of the company were reissued for $165,000. The cost of the shares at the time they were purchased was $120,000. The company uses the cost method of accounting for treasury stock.

d. $1 million of bonds were converted to 50,000 shares of no-par common shares. There was no premium or discount on the bonds.

e. A patent was sold to another company for $45,000. The carrying value of the patent was $1,000.

For each transaction, prepare the appropriate journal entry and then explain how each transaction would affect the statement of cash flows by giving amounts and the section in which each amount is reported.

Exercise 16-9: Statement of Cash Flows. The following is a list of items from the accounts of Jefferson, Inc.:

a. Net income for the period—$480,000.
b. Proceeds from the sale of equipment—$25,000 (book value was $20,000).
c. Cash used to purchase land—$112,000.
d. Increase in net accounts receivable—$16,000.
e. Decrease in inventory—$8,000.
f. Decrease in accounts payable—$11,000.
g. Payment of current portion of long-term debt—$55,000.
h. Dividends declared and paid—$38,000.
i. Depreciation expense—$45,000.
j. Issuance of common stock for equipment—$7,000.
k. Unrealized gain on marketable securities classified as trading—$17,000.

Using the indirect method for preparing the operating activities section, prepare a statement of cash flows. Cash increased by $304,000 during the year.

Exercise 16-10: Operating Section. The condensed financial statements for Shane's Product, Inc. are as follows.

Income Statement
For the Year Ended December 31, 2004

Sales	$ 580,000
Cost of goods sold	(320,000)
Gross profit	$ 260,000
Less operating expenses	(125,000)
Depreciation and amortization	(80,000)
Operating income	$ 55,000
Loss on sale of securities	(7,000)
Income before taxes	$ 48,000
Tax expense (33% tax rate)	(16,000)
Net income	$ 32,000

Partial Balance Sheet
as of December 31,

	2004	2003
Available-for-sale marketable securities	$ 38,000	$55,000
Accounts receivable	37,000	25,000
Inventory	108,000	95,000
Prepaid assets	12,000	26,000
Accounts payable	$ 22,000	$13,000
Unearned revenues	41,000	33,000
Taxes payable	5,000	26,000

Prepare the operating section of the statement of cash flows, using (a) the indirect method and (b) the direct method.

Exercise 16-11: Operating Section. The following information was taken from the accounting records of Milken Enterprises, which consists of all the accounts used in preparing the company's income statement for the year ending December 31, 2004:

	Debit	Credit
Sales		$517,000
Interest revenue		38,000
Dividend revenue		19,000
Gain on sale of securities		22,000
Income tax benefit		21,000
Cost of goods sold	$175,000	
Operating expenses	290,000	
Depreciation expense	72,000	
Interest expense	45,000	
Extraordinary loss	82,000	

In addition, the following information with respect to changes in the balance sheet accounts was obtained.

Accounts receivable	$16,000 debit
Inventory	8,000 credit
Accounts payable	10,000 credit
Wages payable	5,000 debit
Income taxes payable	24,000 debit

1. Using the direct method, prepare the operating section of the statement of cash flows for Milken Enterprises for the year ending December 31, 2004.
2. Repeat Part (1), using the indirect method.

Exercise 16-12: Cash Flows from Operations. R&R Resources, Inc., has gathered the following selected data from its accounts for the year ended December 31, 2004:

Sales	$434,000
Gross profit percentage	50%
Profit margin	15%
Inventory turnover	7
Operating expenses (i.e., excluding depreciation expense)	$130,000
Change in net accounts receivable	$12,000 debit
Change in accounts payable	$8,000 credit
Beginning inventory	$30,000
Change in prepaid expenses	$3,000 credit

No gains or losses were recorded for the period.

1. From the information given, prepare in condensed format an income statement for the period.
2. Use the indirect method to prepare the operating activities section of the statement of cash flows.

Exercise 16-13: Investing and Financing Activities. To aid in preparing the statement of cash flows for the year ending December 31, 2004, GT Systems Inc. gathered the following information on some transactions that occurred during the year:

a. Equipment with a historical cost of $50,000 and accumulated depreciation of $30,000 was sold for $45,000.
b. Common stock of Intelligene Corp. was purchased for $220,000.
c. The company issued 1,000 shares of its common stock for $25,000.
d. Dividends were declared in the amount of $45,000.
e. The dividends were paid.
f. Long-term debt with a carrying amount of $48,000 was called and retired early by paying cash of $52,000.

Assuming that the direct method is being used to prepare the operating activities section, specify how each of these transactions should be reported on GT Systems' statement of cash flows for 2004.

Exercise 16-14: Analysis of Cash Flows. The following table provides cash flow information for three different companies:

	Company		
	A	B	C
Net cash flows from:			
Operating activities	$(55,000)	$ 72,000	$ (35,000)
Investing activities	20,000	(22,000)	(75,000)
Financing activities	15,000	(30,000)	120,000
Net increase (decrease) in cash	$(20,000)	$ 20,000	$ 10,000

Additional information:

a. One company was just recently organized within a growing industry.
b. Another company is an old firm that is maintaining its size.
c. The other company is a firm with liquidity problems and on the verge of declaring bankruptcy.

From the cash flows, determine which company is the growth firm, which is the old firm, and which is the firm on the verge of bankruptcy.

Problems

Problem 16-1: Converting Accruals to Cash Flows. The following three scenarios are independent.

Scenario 1
Jackson's Hair Salon purchased supplies of $72,000 during the period, most of which were on account. A year-end physical count revealed that the cost of supplies on hand was $9,000. An inspection of the accounting records indicated that the beginning balance of supplies on hand was $6,000, and the payable account related to supplies payable increased by $5,000 during the period.

Required:
1. Calculate the amount of cash paid for supplies during the period by Jackson's Hair Salon.
2. Calculate the amount of supplies used during the period by Jackson's Hair Salon.

(continued)

Scenario 2

Thinking Products, Inc., is preparing its statement of cash flows and has gathered the following information related to income tax expense:

Income tax expense	$13,000
Current portion of deferred taxes, Jan. 1, 2004	3,000 debit
Current portion of deferred taxes, Dec. 31, 2004	1,000 credit
Noncurrent deferred taxes, Jan. 1, 2004	22,000 credit
Noncurrent deferred taxes, Dec. 31, 2004	17,000 credit
Taxes payable, Jan. 1, 2004	2,000
Taxes payable, Dec. 31, 2004	7,000

Required:

Calculate the amount of cash paid for income taxes.

Scenario 3

The current asset and liability sections of Simien's Corp.'s balance sheet showed the following beginning and ending balances:

	Ending Balance	Beginning Balance
Current assets:		
Cash	$ 5,000	$8,000
Accounts receivable	10,000	9,000
Prepaid expenses	7,000	2,000
Current liabilities:		
Accounts payable	1,000	4,000
Wages payable	2,000	2,000
Unearned revenues	5,000	2,000

The amount of cash collected from customers during the period was $112,000.

Required:

Calculate the amount of sales revenue that Simien's Corp. should recognize on its income statement.

Problem 16-2: Analysis of Balance Sheets. King's Cab's, Inc., completed operations for the year ending December 31, 2006, and prepared the following comparative balance sheet:

	As of December 31,	
	2006	2005
Assets:		
Cash	$ 160,000	$ 50,000
Short-term marketable securities	150,000	20,000
Accounts receivable, net	300,000	310,000
Inventory	430,000	300,000
Long-term investments	100,000	130,000
Property, plant, and equipment	750,000	550,000
Accumulated depreciation	(270,000)	(250,000)
Patent	80,000	120,000
Total assets	$1,700,000	$1,230,000

Liabilities and Stockholders' Equity:

Accounts payable	$ 150,000	$ 130,000
Unearned revenue	125,000	80,000
Short-term debt	75,000	60,000
Long-term debt	220,000	150,000
Common stock	300,000	250,000
Paid-in capital in excess of par	360,000	260,000
Accumulated other comprehensive income	(10,000)	20,000
Retained earnings	480,000	280,000
Total liabilities and stockholders' equity	$1,700,000	$1,230,000

The following additional information was obtained from the accounts of the company:

a. Net income for 2006 was $265,000.
b. Equipment costing $100,000 and having accumulated depreciation of $60,000 was sold during the year for $35,000.
c. A gain of $25,000 on some marketable securities in the available-for-sale portfolio was recognized. No securities were sold during the year.

Required:
Prepare a statement of cash flows for the year ended December 31, 2006, using the indirect method.

Problem 16-3: Statement of Cash Flows—Indirect Method. The balance sheet accounts of Micro-Age Inc. as of December 31, 2007 and 2006, are as follows.

	2007	2006
Assets:		
Cash	$ 69,000	$ 43,000
Marketable equity securities	115,000	55,000
Accounts receivable, net	110,000	102,000
Inventories	170,000	190,000
Property, plant, and equipment	580,000	530,000
Accumulated depreciation	(140,000)	(90,000)
Patent	225,000	250,000
Total assets	$1,129,000	$1,080,000
Liabilities and stockholders' equity:		
Accounts payable	$ 54,000	$ 60,000
Taxes payable	25,000	18,000
Wages payable	10,000	12,000
Long-term debt	360,000	390,000
Deferred taxes	91,000	85,000
Common stock, $1 par value	58,000	56,000
Paid in capital in excess of par	320,000	270,000
Retained earnings	211,000	189,000
Total liabilities and stockholders' equity	$1,129,000	$1,080,000

Additional information about the operations of the company during the year is as follows:

a. Net income for the year was $51,000.
b. Marketable securities in the amount of $30,000 were purchased during the year. No securities were sold. All securities are considered trading securities.

c. Equipment with a historical cost of $90,000 and a book value of $55,000 was sold for $35,000.

d. On December 31, dividends were paid in the amount of $0.50 per share.

Required:
Prepare a statement of cash flows for Micro-Age Inc. for the year ending December 31, 2007. Use the indirect method to prepare the operating section.

Problem 16-4: Statement of Cash Flows—Indirect and Direct Methods. The following is a trial balance that presents the beginning and ending balances (before closing) of Colonial World Co. for the year 2006:

Colonial World Co.
Adjusted Trial Balance
For the Year Ended December 31, 2006

	December 31, 2006 Dr. (Cr.)	January 1, 2006 Dr. (Cr.)
Cash	$ 21,700	$ 28,600
Accounts receivable	25,800	24,700
Inventory	75,000	81,200
Property, plant, and equipment	327,100	315,400
Accumulated depreciation	(185,700)	(167,300)
Intangible assets	95,800	105,400
Accounts payable	(17,700)	(21,000)
Income taxes payable	(12,600)	(5,500)
Current portion of long-term debt	(15,100)	(8,200)
Long-term debt	(117,100)	(193,700)
Deferred taxes	(16,500)	(14,400)
Common stock ($1 par)	(19,000)	(16,000)
Additional paid-in-capital	(137,400)	(122,500)
Retained earnings	31,300	(6,700)
Sales	(891,700)	
Cost of goods sold	531,600	
Selling and administrative expenses	188,700	
Depreciation and amortization expense	64,800	
Interest income	(15,000)	
Interest expense	22,000	
Dividends received	(5,000)	
Loss on sale of equipment	12,000	
Income tax expense	37,000	

Additional information about transactions incurred by the company are as follows:

a. Equipment costing $62,500 was purchased during the period to replace other equipment that was sold.

b. The only items affecting retained earnings during the period were dividends paid to common shareholders and net income.

c. Some long-term debt was extinguished. The amount of proceeds used to extinguish the debt was equal to the debt's carrying value. An amount was reclassified from long-term debt to the current portion of long-term debt, and the beginning balance in the current portion of long-term debt was paid.

Required:

1. Prepare the statement of cash flows for Colonial World Co. using the indirect method.
2. Redo the operating section of the statement of cash flows using the direct method.

Problem 16-5: Statement of Cash Flows (Indirect Method). The income statement and comparative balance sheets are provided below for Bradford, Inc.

Bradford, Inc.
Comparative Balance Sheet
As of December 31,

	2007	2006
Assets:		
Cash	$ 49,000	$ 17,000
Accounts receivable	57,000	68,000
Less allowance for bad debts	(3,000)	(4,000)
Inventory	468,000	435,000
Prepaid expenses	17,000	10,000
Long-term investments	70,000	75,000
Land	83,000	83,000
Building	128,000	128,000
Less accumulated depreciation	(24,000)	(16,000)
Furniture and fixtures	150,000	151,000
Less accumulated depreciation	(64,000)	(30,000)
Intangible asset	6,000	7,000
Total assets	$937,000	$924,000
Liabilities and stockholders' equity:		
Accounts payable	$129,000	$159,000
Salaries payable	6,000	5,000
Taxes payable	34,000	32,000
Long-term debt	103,000	92,000
Common stock	81,000	81,000
Additional paid-in-capital	181,000	180,000
Retained earnings	425,000	399,000
Less treasury stock	(22,000)	(24,000)
Total liabilities and stockholders' equity	$937,000	$924,000

Bradford, Inc.
Income Statement
For the Year Ended December 31, 2007

Sales		$1,900,000
Interest revenue		20,000
Total revenues		$1,920,000
Cost of goods sold	$1,070,000	
Depreciation and amortization expense	61,000	
Bad debt expense	32,000	
Salary expense	300,000	
Administrative expenses	276,000	
Interest expense	64,000	
Income tax expense	30,000	
Total expenses		1,833,000
Net income		$ 87,000

Additional information:

a. The only items that affected retained earnings are dividends and net income.
b. Treasury stock is recorded at cost.
c. Bradford did not acquire any securities during the year.
d. $20,000 of furniture and fixtures was purchased for cash during the year.
e. No gain or loss was incurred on sales of furniture and fixtures.
f. No long-term debt was liquidated during the year.
g. All changes in long-term debt and common stock accounts were the result of cash transactions.

Required:
Prepare a statement of cash flows for Bradford, Inc., for the year ending December 31, 2007. Use the indirect method to prepare the operating activities section.

Problem 16-6: Statement of Cash Flows (Direct Method). Refer to the information provided in Problem 16-5.

Required:
Prepare the operating activities section of the statement of cash flows for Bradford, Inc., using the direct method.

Problem 16-7: Statement of Cash Flows (Indirect Method). The following balance sheet is for 22nd Century Company for the year ending 2007.

	2007	2006
Accounts with debit balances:		
Cash		$ 30,000
Accounts receivable, net	$ 44,000	27,000
Inventory	46,000	40,000
Prepaids	3,000	5,000
Property, plant, and equipment	239,000	200,000
Intangibles	14,000	16,000
Cost of goods sold	81,000	
Operating expenses	72,000	
Depreciation and amortization expense	8,700	
Income tax expense	120	
Totals	$507,820	$318,000
Accounts with credit balances:		
Cash	$ 17,000	
Accumulated depreciation	70,700	$ 70,000
Accounts payable	22,000	25,000
Accrued liabilities	15,000	17,000
Taxes payable	120	5,000
Long-term notes payable	90,000	40,000
Common stock, $1 par	10,000	10,000
Paid-in capital	50,000	50,000
Retained earnings	71,000	101,000
Sales	160,000	
Gain on sale of equipment	2,000	
Totals	$507,820	$318,000

Additional information:

a. Equipment costing $9,000 was sold for cash.
b. New equipment was purchased for cash.
c. Dividends were declared and paid.

Required:
Prepare a statement of cash flows for 22nd Century Company, using the indirect method of preparing the operating section.

Problem 16-8: Statement of Cash Flows (Direct Method). Refer to the information given in Problem 16-7.

Required:
Prepare a statement of cash flows (including the investing and financing sections) using the direct method of preparing the operating activities section.

Problem 16-9: Statement of Cash Flows (Indirect Method)—Growth Company. Henderson Company was formed and incorporated in 2006, and despite a promising product and substantially increasing sales, the company has had severe cash flow problems. Until this year, the company has been able to survive by borrowing extensively and issuing shares of common stock, but both of those sources are "drying up." Company management is anxious to know where the cash is going, so steps can be taken to stop the outflow of cash. Previously, the company accountant had prepared balance sheets and income statements, shown as follows, but had never prepared a cash flow statement because "such was too hard." Facing severe cash flow problems (and the threat of losing his job), the company accountant decided to prepare a statement of cash flows this year and has come to you for help.

Henderson Company
Balance Sheet
At December 31,

	2008	2007
Assets		
Current assets:		
Cash	$ 31,000	$ 48,000
Accounts receivable, net	61,000	58,000
Inventory	78,000	66,000
Prepaids	6,000	8,000
Total current assets	$176,000	$180,000
Property, plant, and equipment:		
Land	$ 80,000	$ 45,000
Equipment	53,000	33,000
Building	240,000	240,000
Less accumulated depreciation	(58,900)	(48,000)
Intangibles	70,000	24,000
Total property, plant, and equipment	$384,100	$294,000
Total assets	$560,100	$474,000

(continued)

	2008	2007
Liabilities and Owners' Equity		
Current liabilities:		
Accounts payable	$ 51,000	$ 39,000
Accrued liabilities	20,000	18,000
Total current liabilities	$ 71,000	$ 57,000
Long-term liabilities:		
Note payable	$ 80,000	$ 75,000
Bonds payable	270,000	250,000
Total long-term liabilities	$350,000	$325,000
Stockholders' equity:		
Common stock	$200,000	$100,000
Retained earnings	(60,900)	(8,000)
Total stockholders' equity	$139,100	$ 92,000
Total liabilities and stockholders' equity	$560,100	$474,000

Henderson Company
Income Statement
For the Year Ended December 31, 2008

Sales, net	$205,000
Cost of goods sold	125,000
Gross profit	$ 80,000
Operating expenses:	
General and administrative expenses	(41,000)
Selling expenses	(41,000)
Depreciation expense	(14,400)
Amortization expense	(4,000)
Loss on sale of equipment	(2,500)
Interest expense	(30,000)
Net loss	$(52,900)

Additional information:

a. During the year, Henderson sold some used equipment for $2,000.
b. The balance due on January 1, 2008, on the note payable was paid when it came due.

Required:

1. Prepare a statement of cash flows using the indirect method to prepare the operating activities section.
2. From the information contained in the statement of cash flows, comment as to why many growth companies may experience cash flow problems.

Problem 16-10: Statement of Cash Flows (Direct Method). Refer to the information given in Problem 16-9.

Required:

Prepare a statement of cash flows (including the investing and financing sections) using the direct method of preparing the operating activities section.

Problem 16-11: Statement of Cash Flows (Indirect Method)—An Established Company. For several years, Simon's Sheetmetal Classics has been operating close to breakeven. However, Simon's has been generating large amounts of cash, and as a result has been paying large cash dividends. Although company management likes the present circumstances—low to no taxes and large cash dividends—company management is not certain how it is happening or how long it will last. Management is beginning to wonder if something other than paying dividends should be done with the excess cash. The company's trial balances and other information are shown as follows.

Simon's Sheetmetal Classics
Trial Balances

	2007	2006
Accounts with debit balances:		
Cash	$ 62,600	$ 50,000
Marketable securities, net of the adjustment account	42,000	40,000
Accounts receivable	72,000	65,000
Inventory	40,000	42,000
Prepaids	7,000	5,000
Land	60,000	60,000
Property, plant, and equipment	795,000	840,000
Intangibles	15,000	20,000
Cost of goods sold	602,000	
Operating expenses, including depreciation and amortization	370,500	
Loss on sale of marketable securities	16,000	
Loss on sale of equipment	4,000	
Interest expense	29,500	
Income tax expense	2,400	
Total	$2,118,000	$1,122,000
Accounts with credit balances:		
Allowance for doubtful accounts	$ 12,000	$ 4,000
Accumulated depreciation	167,500	140,000
Accounts payable	28,000	22,000
Accrued liabilities	38,000	28,000
Taxes payable	0	10,000
Bonds payable	250,000	250,000
Premium on bonds	3,500	4,000
Common stock, $1 par	15,000	15,000
Paid-in capital	80,000	80,000
Retained earnings	494,000	569,000
Sales	1,000,000	
Unrealized gains on trading securities	30,000	
Total	$2,118,000	$1,122,000

Additional information:

a. Marketable securities, which were classified as trading securities with a historical cost of $28,000, were sold for cash of $12,000. No marketable securities were purchased during the year. Simon appropriately reports all unrealized gains/losses on its trading portfolio securities.

b. Accounts receivable of $8,000 were written off as being uncollectible, and the allowance for uncollectible accounts was adjusted by $16,000 as the estimate of the bad debts incurred during the year.

c. Equipment costing $65,000, which had accumulated depreciation of $60,000, was sold.

d. No intangible assets were bought or sold during the year.

Required:

Prepare a statement of cash flows using the indirect method to prepare the operating section. Then answer the following questions:

1. What is the principal reconciling item between net income and the cash from operating activities (i.e., why is Simon having substantial cash flows from operating activities but reporting income close to breakeven)?

2. What are Simon's future prospects if it continues its current policy of paying large dividends? (Does the answer to this question give insight as to why the income statement is considered to be an indicator of a company's long-run ability to generate cash flows?)

3. Is this situation analogous to what happened to the railroads 100 years ago or to the steel industry 50 years ago?

Problem 16-12: Statement of Cash Flows (Direct Method). Use the information provided in Problem 16-11.

Required:

Prepare a statement of cash flows (including the investing and financing sections) using the direct method of preparing the operating activities section. Both depreciation and amortization expense relate to operating expenses.

Problem 16-13: Statement of Cash Flows (Indirect Method)—Comprehensive. The following information was prepared from the general ledger of Gently-Worn Clothing Co. for the current year:

Accounts with Debit Balances	End-of-the-Year	Beginning-of-the-Year
Cash	$ 123,000	$ 100,000
Marketable securities—trading portfolio, net	37,000	40,000
Accounts receivable	40,200	65,000
Inventory	92,000	80,000
Prepaids	4,000	24,000
Long-term investments—available-for-sale portfolio, nets	76,000	81,000
Land	112,000	72,000
Equipment	188,000	218,000
Buildings	560,000	400,000
Intangibles	52,500	60,000
Discount on bonds	5,000	8,000
Treasury stock	20,000	
Cost of goods sold	888,000	
Operating expenses (including depreciation and amortization)	324,200	
Loss on sale of marketable securities	4,000	
Interest expense	49,000	
Tax expense	17,100	
Dividends	20,000	
Totals	$2,612,000	$1,148,000

Accounts with Credit Balances	End-of-the-Year	Beginning-of-the-Year
Allowance for doubtful accounts	$ 8,200	$ 6,000
Accumulated depreciation—equipment	64,900	89,000
Accumulated depreciation—building	125,800	114,000
Accounts payable	60,000	55,000
Accrued liabilities	40,000	38,000
Taxes payable	13,100	17,000
Deferred taxes	14,000	10,000
Short-term notes payable	20,000	10,000
Long-term notes payable	245,000	100,000
Bonds payable	300,000	400,000
Common stock, $1 par	50,000	40,000
Paid-in capital	350,000	260,000
Retained earnings	5,000	5,000
Other comprehensive income	(1,000)	4,000
Sales	1,300,000	
Gain on sale of equipment	9,000	
Gain on retiring bonds payable	6,000	
Unrealized gain on securities	2,000	
Totals	$2,612,000	$1,148,000

Additional information:

a. Trading portfolio: Some securities in this portfolio were sold for $11,000 cash. Also, an unrealized gain of $2,000 was recognized. Additional securities were purchased for $10,000.

b. Accounts receivable: Accounts receivable of $9,800 were written off and no previously written-off accounts were collected. Uncollectible accounts expenses of $12,000 were recognized.

c. Available-for-sale portfolio: The company did not have any sales or purchases transactions in these securities during the year.

d. Land and building: A new building with land was acquired during the year by paying $50,000 cash and issuing a $150,000 note; $40,000 of the total purchase price was allocated as the cost of the land.

e. Equipment: Equipment with an original cost of $45,000 and a book value of $8,000 was sold. New equipment was acquired and financed with a note for $15,000.

f. Notes payable: At December 31, notes payable of $20,000 were classified as current, since they are due and payable in May. All necessary payments were paid during the year.

g. Bonds payable: One-fourth of the bonds were retired on December 30 by paying $92,000.

h. Common stock: Stock was issued during the year.

i. Treasury stock: Believing that its stock was undervalued and that the market would soon recognize that fact, the company purchased shares of its own stock, paying $40,000, and reissued one-half of them later in the year for $38,000.

j. Dividends of $20,000 were declared and paid.

Required:
Prepare a statement of cash flows for Gently-Worn Clothing Co. Use the indirect method to prepare the operating activities section.

Problem 16-14: Statement of Cash Flows (Direct Method). Use the information provided in Problem 16-13.

Required:
Prepare a statement of cash flows (including the investing and financing sections) using the direct method of preparing the operating section.

Problem 16-15: Statement of Cash Flows. B&B Bicycles, Inc., sells and repairs bikes. The company was founded in Witchita, Kansas, and has subsequently opened several other bike stores throughout Kansas and Missouri. The company's comparative balance sheets as of December 31, 2004 and 2003; and income statement for the year ended December 31, 2004 are as follows.

B&B Bicycles, Inc.
Balance Sheet
As of December 31

	2004	2003
Assets		
Current assets:		
Cash and cash equivalents	$ 37,000	$ 20,000
Short-term investments	77,000	53,000
Accounts receivable, net of allowance for doubtful accounts of $67 ($62 in 2003)	37,000	35,000
Inventories	15,000	16,000
Deferred tax assets	7,000	6,000
Total current assets	$173,000	$130,000
Property, plant, and equipment:		
Land and buildings	$ 72,000	$ 63,000
Machinery and equipment	149,000	131,000
	$221,000	$194,000
Less accumulated depreciation	118,000	95,000
Property, plant, and equipment, net	$103,000	$ 99,000
Patent and other amortizable intangibles	$ 49,000	$ 1,000
Total assets	$325,000	$230,000
Liabilities and Stockholders' Equity		
Current liabilities:		
Short-term debt	$ 2,000	$ 2,000
Accounts payable	10,000	12,000
Accrued compensation and benefits	15,000	13,000
Accrued advertising	6,000	5,000
Other accrued liabilities	12,000	11,000
Income taxes payable	17,000	10,000
Total current liabilities	$ 62,000	$ 53,000
Long-term debt	10,000	7,000
Deferred tax liabilities	31,000	14,000
Stockholders' equity:		
Common stock, $0.001 par value, 4,500 shares authorized, 3,334 issued and outstanding (3,315 in 2003); and capital in excess of par value	73,000	48,000
Retained earnings	114,000	80,000
Accumulated other comprehensive income	35,000	28,000
Total liabilities and stockholders' equity	$325,000	$230,000

B&B Bicycles, Inc.
Income Statement
For the Year Ended December 31, 2004

Net revenues	$294,000
Cost of sales	$118,000
Research and development	31,000
Marketing, general, and administrative	39,000
Amortization of goodwill and other acquisition-related intangibles	4,000
Purchased in-process research and development	4,000
Operating costs and expenses	$196,000
Operating income	$ 98,000
Interest expense	(1,000)
Interest income and other, net	15,000
Income before taxes	$112,000
Provision for taxes	(39,000)
Net income	$ 73,000

Additional information:

a. Marketable securities with a historical cost of $28,000 were sold during the period at a gain of $9,000.
b. Equipment was sold during the period at a loss of $2,000. The historical cost of the equipment was $30,000. It was being depreciated using the straight-line method over 10 years, with no salvage value. The company had had the equipment for eight years.
c. The company acquired a trademark from another company, which was the only intangible acquired during the period.

Required:
1. Use both the indirect and direct methods to prepare the operating activities section. Assume that the depreciation expense relates to the cost of goods sold.
2. Prepare the investing and financing sections of the statement of cash flows.

Problem 16-16: Financial Statement Analysis. A balance sheet and income statement as presented in the 2004 annual report of Advanced Fiber Electronics, Inc., follows.

Advanced Fiber Electronics, Inc.
Consolidated Balance Sheet

December 31 (in thousands)	2004	2003
Assets:		
Cash	$ 126	$ 79
Accounts receivable, net	2,622	2,671
Finance receivables, net	5,115	5,220
Inventories	2,961	3,269
Deferred taxes and other current assets	1,161	1,236
Total current assets	$11,985	$12,475
Finance receivables due after one year, net	$ 8,203	$ 9,093
Land, buildings and equipment, net	2,456	2,366
Investments in affiliates, at equity	1,615	1,456
Other intangibles	4,555	4,634
Total assets	$28,814	$30,024

(continued)

December 31 (in thousands)	2004	2003
Liabilities and equity:		
Short-term debt and current portion of long-term debt	$ 3,957	$ 4,104
Accounts payable	1,016	948
Accrued compensation and benefits costs	630	722
Unearned income	186	210
Other current liabilities	2,161	2,523
Total current liabilities	$ 7,950	$ 8,507
Long-term debt	10,994	10,867
Postretirement medical benefits	1,133	1,092
Deferred taxes and other liabilities	2,519	3,376
Preferred stock	1,307	1,325
Common stock	1,711	2,257
Retained earnings	3,200	2,600
Total liabilities and equity	$28,814	$30,024

Advanced Fiber Electronics, Inc.
Consolidated Income Statement

Year ended December 31 (in thousands, except per-share data)	2004	2003	2002
Revenues:			
Sales	$10,346	$10,696	$ 9,881
Service and rentals	7,856	7,678	7,257
Finance income	1,026	1,073	1,006
Total revenues	$19,228	$19,447	$18,144
Costs and expenses:			
Cost of sales	$ 5,744	$ 5,662	$ 5,330
Cost of service and rentals	4,481	4,318	3,778
Research and development expenses	1,526	1,610	1,585
Selling, administrative and general expenses	4,209	5,321	4,473
Depreciation and amortization	935	821	739
Writedown of equipment	0	710	0
Interest	297	242	98
Total costs and expenses	$17,192	$18,684	$16,003
Income before income taxes and equity income	$ 2,036	$ 763	$ 2,141
Income taxes	(631)	(207)	(728)
Equity in net income of unconsolidated affiliates	117	119	215
Net income	$ 1,522	$ 675	$ 1,628
Basic earnings per share	$ 2.09	$ 0.53	$ 2.16

Additional information:

a. Proceeds from the sale of land, buildings, and equipment during 2004 were $99,000. The company realized a net gain on these transactions in the amount of $15,000, which was included in finance income.
b. Shares of preferred and common stock were purchased during the year and retired, but no shares were issued. Losses on retiring stock were charged to the retained earnings account.
c. Dividends for the year were $200,000.

    d. The change in intangible assets is due to amortization.

    e. No dividends were received during the year from the company's investments in affiliates, but additional shares of stock of the affiliates were acquired.

Required:

1. Prepare a statement of cash flows for the year ended December 31, 2004. Use the direct method to prepare the operating activities section.
2. Provide a schedule that reconciles net income to cash flows from operating activities.
3. Based on an analysis of the statement of cash flows, provide a statement about the cash position of the company. Your statement might include an assessment of the following:
   a. Does the company appear to be in a growth stage?
   b. Is the company experiencing liquidity problems?
   c. Are the cash flows from operating activities sufficient to fund the company's business?

Cases

Case 16-1: XYZ, Inc. From the following information:

1. Fill in the missing numbers for the most recent balance sheet.
2. Compare the operating performance of the company as indicated by the income statement and cash flow statement. How would you judge the performance of the company?

XYZ, Inc.
Consolidated Balance Sheet
(dollars in millions)

	September 30, 2003	September 30, 2002
Assets		
Cash and cash equivalents	$	$ 1,154
Receivables less allowances of $362 in 2003 and $416 in 2002		7,405
Inventories		4,538
Deferred income taxes—net		1,775
Other current assets		912
Total current assets	$21,931	$15,784
Property, plant, and equipment—net		5,693
Prepaid pension costs		3,754
Deferred income taxes—net		761
Capitalized software development costs		298
Investments		3,073
Total assets	$38,775	$29,363

(continued)

	September 30, 2003	September 30, 2002
Liabilities		
Accounts payable	$	$ 2,157
Payroll and benefit-related liabilities		2,592
Postretirement and postemployment benefit liabilities	137	187
Debt maturing within one year		2,231
Other current liabilities		3,718
Total current liabilities	$11,777	$10,885
Postretirement and postemployment benefit liabilities		6,380
Long-term debt		4,389
Total liabilities	$25,190	$21,654
Shareowners' Equity		
Common stock, par value $0.01 per share Authorized shares: 6,000,000,000 Issued and outstanding shares: 3,071,750,726 at September 30, 2003; 3,022,369,264 at September 30, 2002	$	$ 30
Additional paid-in capital		6,589
Guaranteed ESOP obligation		(49)
Retained earnings		1,422
Accumulated other comprehensive income (loss)		(283)
Total shareowners' equity	$13,584	$ 7,709
Total liabilities and shareowners' equity	$38,775	$29,363

XYZ, Inc.
Consolidated Statements of Income
(dollars in millions)
For the Year Ended September 30, 2003

Revenues	$38,303
Costs	19,688
Gross margin	$18,615
Operating expenses:	
Selling, general, and administrative	$ 8,417
Research and development	4,510
Purchased in-process research and development	282
Total operating expenses	$13,209
Operating income	$ 5,406
Other income—net	443
Interest expense	(406)
Income before income taxes	$ 5,443
Provision for income taxes	(1,985)
Income before cumulative effect of accounting change	$ 3,458
Cumulative effect of accounting change (net of income taxes of $842)	1,308
Net income	$ 4,766

XYZ, Inc.
Consolidated Statements of Cash Flows
(dollars in millions)
For the Year Ended September 30, 2003

Operating activities:

Net income	$ 4,766
Adjustments to reconcile net income to net cash (used in) provided by operating activities, net of effects from acquisitions of businesses:	
Cumulative effect of accounting change	(1,308)
Business restructuring reversal	(141)
Asset impairment and other charges	236
Depreciation and amortization	1,806
Deferred income taxes and income taxes payable	1,026
Increase in receivables—net	(3,183)
Increase in inventories	(1,612)
Increase (decrease) in accounts payable	668
Changes in other current assets and other current liabilities	(2,534)
Net cash (used in) provided by operating activities	$ (276)
Investing activities:	
Capital expenditures	$(2,215)
Proceeds from the sale or disposal of property, plant and equipment	97
Purchases of equity investments	(307)
Sales of equity investments	156
Purchases of investment securities	(450)
Sales or maturity of investment securities	1,132
Dispositions of businesses	72
Acquisitions of businesses—net of cash acquired	(272)
Net cash used in investing activities	$(1,787)
Financing activities:	
Repayments of long-term debt	$(2,244)
Issuance of long-term debt	4,406
Proceeds from issuance of common stock	696
Dividends paid	(222)
S-Corp distribution to stockholder	(40)
Increase in short-term borrowings—net	89
Net cash provided by financing activities	$ 2,685
Effect of exchange rate changes on cash and cash equivalents	$ 40
Net increase (decrease) in cash and cash equivalents	$ 662
Cash and cash equivalents at beginning of period	1,154
Cash and cash equivalents at end of period	$ 1,816

Additional information:

a. There are no long-term deferred income taxes at the end of 2003, and the current deferred income taxes decreased by $192.

b. The accounting change related to a change in the method of depreciating long-term fixed assets.

c. The Business restructuring reversal, Asset impairment and other charges, and all items connected with disposing and acquiring businesses in the investing activities section relate to property, plant, and equipment.

d. Amortization expense was $130, and related to capitalized software development costs. Of the capital expenditures incurred, $300 related to capitalized software development costs.

e. Other income consisted of (1) gains of $45 from disposing of property, plant, equipment, and "businesses" and (2) gains from transactions in selling investment securities.

f. The items on the cash flow statement Repayments of long-term debt, Issuance of long-term debt, and Increase in short-term borrowing—net all relate to the balance sheet items Long-term debt and Debt maturing in one year.

g. The ESOP obligation had a debit balance of $33 million at the end of the year.

Research Activities

Activity 16-1: International Reporting of Cash Flows. Look up the most recent annual report of any company domiciled in the following countries that is *not* listed on a U.S. exchange:

a. Brazil
b. France
c. Switzerland

Determine what set of GAAP the company follows (i.e., country-specific GAAP or international GAAP). Identify as many differences as you can in these companies' statements of cash flows with what would be required under U.S. GAAP.

3

$\mathcal{S}$pecial Reporting Issues

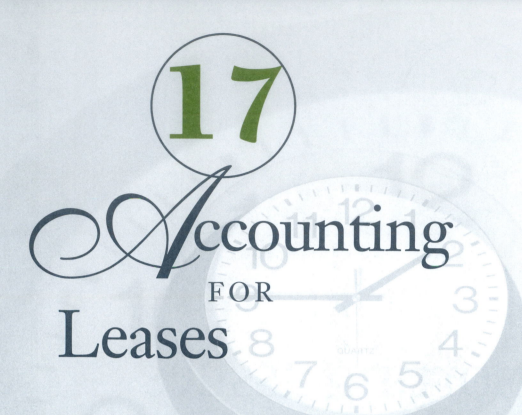

17

Accounting FOR Leases

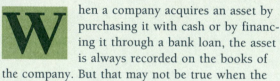

When a company acquires an asset by purchasing it with cash or by financing it through a bank loan, the asset is always recorded on the books of the company. But that may not be true when the company finances an asset through a lease.

To an increasing extent, airlines are leasing aircraft rather than buying them. For example, in a recent year, United Airlines reported that of its 577 aircraft, 309 were being leased. Other airlines show similar patterns. The typical length of these leases is from 10–30 years, during which time the airline must make periodic payments of predetermined amounts as if the airplanes had been financed through a bank. Obviously, the finance company sets the lease payments at an amount high enough to recover the cost of the aircraft and also earn a reasonable profit.

Questions

1. Since these leases are seemingly a means of financing the acquisition of airplanes, should the airplanes and the related lease obligations be reported on the airline's balance sheet?

2. Does it surprise you to learn that, of the 309 airplanes being leased by United Airlines, an asset and a long-term liability had been recorded for only 68 of them? Why can United keep the other airplanes and the related lease obligations off the balance sheet?

Other companies also use leases and do not report any related liability. For example, one company (as a lessee) entered into a $300 million lease to finance the construction of new stores. Later, the company increased its available funding under the lease agreement to $600 million. Later still, through a second lease agreement, the available funding was increased to a total of $882 million. Under the lease agreements, the lessor/lendor purchases the properties, pays the construction costs, and subsequently leases the facilities to the company. Given this information, it seems that the leases are financing arrangements, and, as a result, both the assets and related lease liabilities should be recorded on the company's books. However, the company has recorded none of the $882 million as an asset or a liability.

Questions

1. If financial statement readers disagree with this accounting treatment, what can they do to adjust the published financial statements so that the adjusted statements reflect the recording of assets and liabilities?

2. Is it "good accounting" (i.e., does accounting reflect economic reality) when the recording of an asset depends upon how it is financed?

- Paraphrase the criteria for determining when a lease liability (and the related asset) is reported on the balance sheet.
- Prepare the journal entries for an operating lease.
- Prepare the journal entries for a capital lease for both the lessee and the lessor.
- Explain the difference between a direct financing lease and a sales-type lease from the lessor's view.
- Account for a capital lease that has guaranteed or unguaranteed residual values.
- Account for a capital lease that has a bargain purchase option.
- Account for the initial direct costs incurred by the lessor.
- Using the information contained in the notes to the financial statements for operating leases, adjust a company's published financial statements by treating the operating leases as capital leases.

History and Theory of Leasing

Leasing is a popular method—and the fastest growing method—for businesses to acquire fixed assets. The reason for its growth is the perceived advantages of off-balance-sheet financing[1] that it provides. A **lease** is a contractual agreement that gives specific rights to the lessee to use stipulated property for a defined period of time in return for specified cash payments. For the lessor, the typical advantages to leasing are the opportunity to earn interest by carrying the leasing contract and/or to generate increased sales. For the lessee, the common advantages of leasing include:

©PRNEWSFOTO/CONTINENTAL AIRLINES

1. Enhanced cash flow, in that the lessor often will provide much, if not all, of the financing.
2. Protection against obsolescence, particularly in rapidly evolving technological areas.
3. Flexibility, in that the lease can be tailored specifically to the lessee's needs and the timing of cash inflows.
4. Tax advantages, because lease payments are not preference items subject to the alternative minimum tax computations.
5. Off-balance-sheet financing, in that the liability is frequently excluded from the balance sheet, which enhances financial ratios.

The early history of setting accounting standards for leases illustrates the popularity of off-balance-sheet financing—and also the apparent futility of setting standards for all accounting and financial reporting issues. Since the late

---

[1]Off-balance-sheet financing refers to a method of financing the acquisition of fixed assets such that both the asset and—more importantly—the liability are not recorded on the lessee's general ledger.

This Is the Real World

Following the collapse of Enron, the U.S. Congress demanded that J. P. Morgan Chase & Co. turn over documents related to transactions that allowed Enron to borrow money without the debt appearing on its balance sheet as a loan. The transaction, known as the Sequoia transaction, involved a string of special-purpose entities and was the means by which J. P. Morgan channeled $500 million to Enron. The loan was structured so that on the last day of each month—the date on which financial statements are prepared—the loan could be reported as paid in full, even though the repayment never actually occurred.

SOURCE: *The Wall Street Journal*, April 16, 2002, p. C1.

INTERNET

www

Leasing an automobile is probably the most common leasing arrangement for consumers. One of the better Internet sites that explains the terms and definitions of a lease, describes the advantages and disadvantages of a lease, and assists in computing a lease payment is **www .autoleasingsoftware.com/ LeaseTips/LeaseTips.htm**.

1960s, it has been fashionable to exclude as much debt as possible (and the related assets) from the balance sheet. The idea is that leaving debt off the balance sheet causes the financial statements to look better, and the market responds favorably to such "window-dressing." For this reason, beginning in the 1960s, businessmen structured lease agreements so that leased assets and the corresponding liabilities were not recorded on the lessee's general ledger. However, accounting standard-setting bodies viewed many lease agreements with skepticism, thinking that they were only methods of financing the acquisition of assets, and so businesses should be recording both the assets and the associated long-term liabilities.

With businessmen wanting to keep lease liabilities off the balance sheet and standard-setting bodies trying to formulate fair rules, but rules that would result in liabilities being recorded for most leases, the world of business was ripe for an interesting conflict of wills. The eventual outcome was that each time an accounting standard was issued requiring lease obligations to be recorded for new leases (accounting standards are never retroactive), businessmen wrote the terms of new leases so that the liabilities and corresponding assets could be excluded from the balance sheet. Illustrating this conflict of wills is that 10% of the APB's opinions deal with leases, and seven of the FASB's standards numbered between 13 and 28 deal with leases. Evidently, at that point, the FASB saw the futility of trying to define all the rules for when lease liabilities and corresponding assets must be recorded and so stopped issuing standards on leases.

Criteria and Terminology

For accounting purposes, leases are classified as either operating leases or capital leases. A **capital lease** is one that substantially transfers the rights and risks of ownership to the lessee. Capital leases result in assets and liabilities being recorded. Any other lease is an **operating lease**.[2]

Rather than leaving the determination to the parties of the lease as to whether a lease is a capital lease or an operating lease, the FASB has stipulated that, from the standpoint of the lessee, if the terms of a lease meet *any* of four criteria, the lease is a capital lease. Leases that do not meet any of these four criteria are, by default, operating leases. From the standpoint of the lessor, the lease must meet one of the four criteria *and* two other criteria as well to be classified as a capital lease.

---

[2]Assets may also be acquired through sale-leaseback transactions, which are discussed in Appendix B at the end of the chapter.

The four criteria for determining whether a lease is a capital lease are as follows:

1. *The lease transfers ownership of the property* to the lessee.
2. *The lease contains a **bargain purchase option***, which is that the option price (determined when the lease is signed) is anticipated to be significantly lower than the anticipated fair value of the property when the lease expires, such that exercise of the purchase option is reasonably assured.
3. *The lease term is equal to 75% or more of the estimated economic life of the leased property.* This criterion is not used when the beginning of the lease term falls within the last 25% of the economic life of the leased property. Generally, the **lease term** is the fixed, noncancelable term of the lease. However, the lease term is extended by the time included under a **bargain renewal option**, which exists when the rental payments for renewing a lease are sufficiently lower than the expected fair rental, such that renewal of the lease is reasonably assured.
4. *The present value of the minimum lease payments (excluding executory costs) is 90% or more of the fair value of the leased property.* Again, this criterion is not used when the beginning of the lease term falls within the last 25% of the economic life of the leased property. For most leases, the **minimum lease payments (MLP)** comprise (a) the minimum rental payments specified in the lease[3] and (b) any bargain purchase option. When a lease does not contain a bargain purchase option, then the MLP consists of (a) the rental payments, (b) plus any residual value of the leased property that the lessee guarantees, and (c) any payment the lessee will be required to make for failing to renew or extend the lease at the end of the lease term. **Executory costs** are payments made for maintenance, insurance, and property taxes and are not part of the minimum lease payments.[4]

The essence of these four criteria is that when the lessee is obtaining the right to buy the asset (see criteria 1 and 2), is substantially obtaining the exclusive use to the leased asset (see criteria 3), or is paying a price that is equivalent to the fair value of the asset (see criteria 4), the lessee should record an asset and liability on its general ledger.

To reiterate, the terms of a lease must meet only one of the above criteria for the lessee to consider the lease as a capital lease. For the lessor, the lease must meet one of the above criteria and both of the following criteria:

1. The collectibility of the minimum lease payments must be reasonably assured. All receivables have a degree of uncertainty of collectibility, and a lessor is not prohibited from recording a capital lease just because there is some degree of uncollectibility.
2. There are no important uncertainties regarding the amount of unreimbursable costs still to be incurred. Such uncertainties might include commitments by the lessor (a) to guarantee performance of the leased property beyond the typical product warranty or (b) to protect the lessee from obsolescence.

Key:

Lessee: Any 1 = capital lease

Lessor: Any 1 + both = capital lease

---

[3]It is important to distinguish between a minimum lease payment and a rental payment, which is a component of a minimum lease payment. In addition to rental payments, minimum lease payments include any guaranteed residual value and any penalties for failure to renew or extend a lease. When these other two components are not present, the minimum lease payments are equal to (or synonymous with) the rental payments.

[4]*Statement of Financial Accounting Standards No. 13*, "Accounting for Leases," Stamford: Financial Accounting Standards Board, November 1976.

From the preceding explanation as to what constitutes a capital lease for the lessee and the lessor, is it possible that

a. The lessee could account for a lease as a capital lease, and the lessor could account for it as an operating lease?

b. The lessee could account for a lease as an operating lease, and the lessor could account for it as a capital lease?

(*Hint:* One answer is "Yes," and the other answer is "No.")

Answer: Situation (a) is possible; situation (b) is not.

When a lease qualifies as a capital lease, the leased asset and associated liability are recorded at the present value of the minimum lease payments. (Review the definitions given earlier and note that the minimum lease payments consist of several items.) The discount rate with which to discount the minimum lease payments is determined as follows:

1. The lessor uses his **implicit rate**, which is the rate he used to determine the minimum lease payments, based upon the asset's fair value.
2. The lessee uses his incremental borrowing rate unless it is practicable to learn the lessor's implicit interest rate, and that rate is *lower* than the lessee's incremental borrowing rate. The **lessee's incremental borrowing rate** is the interest rate at which the lessee could have borrowed money to purchase the asset. (Using a lower discount rate results in the asset and the liability being recorded at higher amounts.)

Operating Leases

In the preceding paragraphs, much new terminology has been introduced; a key to learning the accounting and financial reporting for leases is to quickly become familiar with the new terminology. Before covering the accounting for a capital lease, the requirements for operating leases (those that do not meet one of the aforementioned four criteria) are covered.

The theory of an operating lease is that the lessee is paying a rent for the use of the asset, but that ownership remains with the lessor. For operating leases, the lessee does not record either an asset or a liability, and therefore, present value concepts are not used. Rather, the lessee and lessor recognize rent expense or rent revenue, respectively, in an amount typically equal to the cash payments to be made or received. For the lessee, the journal entry for an operating lease consists of the following:

Lease (or Rent) Expense	XXX	
Cash		XXX

The journal entry for the lessor is the mirror image of the preceding entry, as follows:

Cash	XXX	
Lease (or Rent) Revenue		XXX

The only exception to this scheme of entries is when the cash payments fluctuate as, for example, when a nonrefundable deposit is required. Then, expenses and revenues are recognized *as if* the cash is received in equal yearly amounts. Thus, it is assumed that equal benefits are received from using the asset for each period of time, regardless of the actual cash flows.

For example, Oak Company leases office space from Forester for a 5-year term beginning January 1, 2004. The terms of the lease do not meet any of the FASB's four criteria for identifying a capital lease, and so both the lessee and lessor classify the lease as an operating lease. The terms of the lease specify yearly payments of $12,000 for the first three years and payments of $15,000 for Years 4 and 5. Thus, the total cash to be received is $66,000, which is recognized as revenue/expense equally for each of the five years. This average yearly amount is $13,200, and the journal entries for the lessee and lessor are as shown in Illustration 17-1.

ILLUSTRATION 17-1

Operating Lease Journal Entries for Years 1–3

Lessee Accounting			Lessor Accounting		
Lease Expense	13,200		Cash	12,000	
Cash		12,000	Deferred Lease Receivable	1,200	
Deferred Lease Obligation		1,200	Lease Revenue		13,200
To record lease expense and cash payment for any of the first three years of an operating lease.			*To record lease expense and cash received for any of the first three years of an operating lease.*		

Journal Entries for Years 4–5

Lessee Accounting			Lessor Accounting		
Lease Expense	13,200		Cash	15,000	
Deferred Lease Obligation	1,800		Deferred Lease Receivable		1,800
Cash		15,000	Lease Revenue		13,200
To record lease expense and cash payment for either Year 4 or 5 of an operating lease.			*To record lease expense and cash received for either Year 4 or 5 of an operating lease.*		

Note that for the first three years of the lease, the balances in Deferred Lease Obligation and Deferred Lease Receivable increase, but those balances decrease in the fourth and fifth years and finally have a zero balance.

For the first three years, the deferred lease obligation and the deferred lease receivable are classified as a long-term liability and receivable, respectively. In the fourth and fifth years, that portion of the obligation that will be liquidated and that portion of the receivable that will be collected within the next operating cycle are classified as current. The equipment being leased remains the property of the lessor, is reported on his balance sheet, and is depreciated over the life of the asset in a manner consistent with depreciating other similar assets (e.g., depreciated in accordance with the company's policy for all such assets).

This completes the discussion of accounting for operating leases. The rest of this chapter covers the accounting for capital leases, beginning with a summary of the accounting and financial reporting requirements.

© GETTY IMAGES, INC./PHOTODISC

Capital Leases for the Lessee

The theory underlying the accounting for capital leases is that the lessee has acquired an asset and that the lease is the financing mechanism. Therefore, both the acquired asset and the associated liability should be recorded on the general ledger of the lessee. At the inception of the lease, the lessee measures the leasing transaction, using discounted cash flow concepts, and records an asset and a liability at the present value of the future cash flows. Subsequently, the accounting for the leased asset is independent of the accounting for the lease liability.

The accounting for the liability is based on an amortization table that is prepared at the inception of the lease, using the effective-interest method. The amortization table begins with the present value of the minimum lease payments, and, like the amortization tables used to account for other long-term liabilities as discussed in Chapter 11, it is used (1) to separate cash payments into the principal and interest components and (2) at year-end to separate the liability into its current and long-term portions for reporting on the balance sheet.

The cost of the asset is depreciated either over the life of the asset or the length of the lease, depending upon which of the FASB's criteria the lease agreement meets. When the terms of the lease transfer ownership at the end of the lease term or there is a bargain purchase option, the cost of the asset is depreciated over the life of the asset. Otherwise, the cost of the asset is depreciated over the lease term. (This process of allocating the asset's cost is referred to as either amortization or depreciation, with the terms used interchangeably for leases.)

Depreciation Rule

If:	Depreciate over:
Ownership transfers	Economic life
Ownership does not transfer	Lease term

Applying the Capital Lease Criteria

To illustrate, assume that on January 1, 2004, Pine Company leased equipment from Forest for 10 years with an annual rental payment (which does not include executory costs) of $25,152 that is due each January 1. Pine paid the first payment on the day the lease contract was signed. The fair value of the equipment is $170,000, and its useful life is 10 years. The lessee's incremental borrowing rate is 10%, and the lessor's implicit interest rate is not known, nor can the lessee reasonably determine it.

To determine whether this lease is a capital lease, the terms of the lease must be compared to each of the four criteria. That comparison yields the following results:

1. Transfers ownership: The given terms do not state that this occurs. Hence, this criterion is not met.
2. Bargain purchase option: There is no indication of a bargain purchase option so this criterion is not met either.
3. Lease term is 75% or more of the economic life: The economic life of the equipment is 10 years, and the lease term is also 10 years, so this criterion is met. The lease is a capital lease. Since one of the criteria has been met, there is no need to apply the last criterion. However, such is done to illustrate how the fourth criterion is applied.
4. Present value of the minimum lease payments (MLP) is 90% or more of the asset's fair value: The fair value of the equipment is $170,000, and the present value of the MLP is also $170,000, which is computed as follows:

Present Value Factor of an Annuity Due at 10%, 10 years (since the first payment is paid immediately)	Payment	Present Value Amount
6.75902	$25,152	$170,000

So, this criterion is also met.

Suppose that the fair value of the asset does not change, and the lease contract requires Pine Company to make the first lease payment one year after signing the lease contract. How would this affect the payment amount and the amount recorded for the equipment and the lease obligation? Would the amounts be greater, smaller, or the same?

Answer: The amount of the payments would increase, but the total present value would be unaffected so the amounts recorded for the asset and obligation would be unchanged.

Initial Recording of a Capital Lease

Since the lease is a capital lease, Pine prepares a journal entry to record both the lease liability and the associated asset at *the present value of the minimum lease payments*, which is the amount computed in applying the fourth criterion. The following entry is then prepared:

Equipment under Capital Lease	170,000	
Capital Lease Obligation		170,000

To record a capital lease.

Because the first payment is due at the inception of the lease, the following entry is also made at the signing of the lease:

Capital Lease Obligation	25,152	
Cash		25,152

To record first lease payment.

Subsequent Accounting for the Asset

Since the terms of the lease do not transfer ownership and there also was not a bargain purchase option, the cost of the asset is depreciated over the lease term of 10 years. So assuming the use of the straight-line method of depreciation, at December 31, 2004 (one year after signing the lease), the following journal entry is prepared:

Depreciation Expense	17,000	
Accumulated Depreciation		17,000

To record depreciation expense for an asset acquired under a capital lease.

Subsequent Accounting for the Liability

The subsequent accounting for the lease liability requires preparing an amortization table using the effective-interest method, which is shown in Table 17-1. The amortization table begins with the present value amount. From it, journal entries are prepared at each December 31 to recognize interest expense for the year. The journal entry at December 31, 2004, for example, is as follows:

Interest Expense	14,485	
Capital Lease Obligation[5]		14,485

To record interest expense for the year.

The journal entries to record the payment at January 1, 2005, and to record the interest expense at December 31, 2005, are as follows, respectively:

Capital Lease Obligation	25,152	
Cash		25,152

To record the lease payment on January 1, 2005.

Interest Expense	13,418	
Lease Obligation		13,418

To recognize interest expense for 2005.

---

[5]An interest payable account could have been used just as easily. If so, the next payment entry is modified accordingly.

808

TABLE 17-1

Lease Amortization Table (annuity due)				
Period	Lease Payment	Interest*	Reduction of Principal	Capital Lease Obligation
				$170,000
Jan. 1, 2004	$25,152	$ 0	$ 25,152	144,848
Jan. 1, 2005	25,152	14,485	10,667	134,181
Jan. 1, 2006	25,152	13,418	11,734	122,447
Jan. 1, 2007	25,152	12,244	12,908	109,539
Jan. 1, 2008	25,152	10,954	14,198	95,341
Jan. 1, 2009	25,152	9,534	15,618	79,723
Jan. 1, 2010	25,152	7,972	17,180	62,543
Jan. 1, 2011	25,152	6,254	18,898	43,645
Jan. 1, 2012	25,152	4,364	20,788	22,857
Jan. 1, 2013	25,152	2,295	22,857	0
Totals		$81,520	$170,000	

*Interest amounts are determined by multiplying the prior year capital lease obligation amount by the effective interest amount. Thus, $144,848 \times 10\% = $14,485.

This pattern of using the amortization table and preparing the journal entries is followed for all subsequent years.

Financial Reporting of a Capital Lease

Typically (but not always), leased assets are reported separately from other assets on the balance sheet. When the leased assets are not separately reported, then that detail is found in the notes to the financial statements.

Similarly, lease obligations are usually reported separately from other liabilities. Also, like other liabilities that are due in installments, the lease obligation is separated into its current and long-term components on the balance sheet. These amounts are derived from the amortization table. It can be seen from the amortization table that the total amount owing at December 31, 2004, is the principal amount of $144,848 plus the accrued interest of $14,485, for a total amount of $159,333. It can also be seen that the amount that will be owing (excluding interest, which has not yet been earned) one year in the future is $134,181. It is this $134,181 that is reported as a long-term liability, as that is the amount that will not be liquidated during the upcoming year by using a current asset. The difference between the total amount owing of $159,333 and the long-term portion of $134,181 is the current liability portion. This amount—not coincidentally—is the amount of the next lease payment of $25,152.

In general and regardless of when in the year a lease is signed, the amounts to report as current or long-term (for either the lessee or the lessor) are determined as follows:

1. The total amount owing is the amount in the Capital Lease Obligation column for the current year plus any accrued interest since the last payment date,
2. The long-term portion is the amount in the Capital Lease Obligation column for the next year, and
3. The current portion is the change in the amounts in the Capital Lease Obligation column for the current year as compared to the next year, plus any accrued interest (i.e., the difference between the amount in Step 1 and the amount in Step 2).

The date on which a lease is signed affects the amount that is reported as the current liability. The above lease was entered into on January 1, and, therefore, the accrued interest for the year of $14,485 is included in the current liability. In contrast, if the lease had been signed on December 31, 2003, the $14,485 would have been paid on December 31, 2004, and that amount would not need to be reported on the balance sheet. So, the current liability portion would be just the $10,667, which can be obtained from the amortization table and is the amount by which the obligation will be reduced during the coming year. For leases signed at the first day of the fiscal year, the current liability includes a full year of accrued interest, whereas for leases signed on the last day of the fiscal year, no accrued interest is included.

Exhibit 17-1 was taken from a recent financial report of United Airlines and illustrates these concepts of separately reporting the assets and liabilities under capital leases and separating the lease liabilities into their current and long-term components.

EXHIBIT 17-1

Financial Reporting of a Capital Lease—Lessee
(emphasis added)

Assets

Operating property and equipment			
Owned:			
Flight equipment	$12,006	$10,382	
Advances on flight equipment	985	972	
Other property and equipment	3,134	2,842	
	$16,125	$14,196	
Accumulated depreciation and amortization	(5,174)	(5,116)	
	$10,951	$ 9,080	
Capital leases:			
Flight equipment	$ 2,605	$ 2,221	Note the separate
Other property and equipment	97	98	reporting of assets
	$ 2,702	$ 2,319	acquired by financing
Accumulated amortization	(599)	(625)	through a capital
	$ 2,103	$ 1,694	lease.
Current liabilities:			
Notes payable	$ 184	$ —	
Long-term debt maturing within one year	98	235	Note the current and
Current obligation under capital leases, etc.	176	171	long-term portions of
Long-term debt	5,668	5,248	the capital lease
Long-term obligations under capital leases	2,858	2,092	obligation.

Example Problem: Capital Lease—Lessee

On the first day of a fiscal year, a capital lease was signed that requires 10 yearly payments of $8,408. The lessee's incremental borrowing rate is 14%. The first payment is due and payable upon signing of the lease contract. Complete the following requirements and then see Appendix A at the end of the chapter (p. 829) for the solutions.

1. Compute the present value of the minimum lease payments.
2. Prepare the amortization table.
3. From the amortization table, prepare the journal entry to recognize interest expense at the end of the first year of the lease.
4. From the amortization table, determine the total liability and separate it into its current and long-term portions at the end of the first year of the lease.
5. Prepare the journal entry to record the second lease payment.

Capital Leases for the Lessor— Direct Financing

Unlike the lessee, who has only one type of capital lease, the lessor must determine whether a capital lease is a direct financing lease or a sales-type lease. The difference between them is that a sales-type lease has **dealer's** or **manufacturer's profit**, which is the difference between the cost of the asset to the lessor and the fair value of the leased property. **Sales-type leases** arise because the manufacturer or dealer uses leases as a way of financing a sale. So, for example, the cost of an automobile to a car dealer is less than the selling price (i.e., fair value), and in order to sell the car, the dealer uses a capital lease. **Direct financing leases** do not have this profit element and are the type of lease used by leasing or financing companies that buy an asset at its fair market value and then lease it, with their profit coming from interest. The accounting for direct financing leases is demonstrated first, and the accounting for sales-type leases is covered later.

Initial Recording of a Direct Financing Capital Lease

Recall the previous example of Forest leasing equipment to Pine Company and assume that the lessor's implicit interest rate is the same as the lessee's incremental borrowing rate. Forest, the lessor, debits a lease receivable account for the *gross amount* to be received, credits the asset for the present value of the minimum lease payment (which usually is also the asset's fair value), and credits the difference to an unearned interest income account, as follows:

Lease Receivable (10 payments at $25,152 each)	251,520	
Equipment (previously computed in the lessee example)		170,000
Unearned Interest Income		81,520

To record a direct financing capital lease.

Then, the entry to record the first lease payment, which is paid at the signing of the lease, is:

Cash	25,152	
Lease Receivable		25,152

To record receipt of the first payment.

Although the entries for the lessor look different from those prepared by the lessee, upon closer examination it can be seen that they are mirror images of one another. The only difference is that the lessor separates the interest component from the receivable, rather than reporting them as one number like the lessee does with its obligation. As a result of this mirror-image accounting, the lessor's amortization table looks like the amortization table that the lessee prepares. The only difference is that the most right-hand column, rather than being labeled "Capital Lease Obligation," is labeled "Net Investment in Lease" to reflect the fact that the amortization table is being used to account for a lease receivable rather than a lease obligation.

Subsequent Accounting for a Direct Financing Capital Lease

Using the previously prepared amortization table (see Table 17-1 on page 808), the following journal entry is made for the accrual of interest at December 31, 2004:

Unearned Interest Income	14,485	
Interest Income		14,485

To recognize interest income for the year ended December 31, 2004.

The entries to record the lease payment at January 1, 2005, and to recognize interest income on December 31, 2005, are as follows, respectively:

Cash	25,152	
Lease Receivable		25,152

To record receipt of the lease payment on January 1, 2005.

Unearned Interest Income	13,418	
Interest Income		13,418

To recognize interest income for the year ended December 31, 2005.

Both interest income amounts in these entries are derived from the amortization table and are the same amounts as recognized by the lessee for those years as interest expense.

Financial Reporting for a Direct Financing Capital Lease

Regarding the lessor's financial reporting, the lease receivable and the unearned interest income are netted and labeled "Net investment in capital leases." This net investment amount is then separated between its current and noncurrent portions, using the amortization table in the same manner as illustrated previously for the lessee. From the amortization table it can be seen that the total amount to be received at the end of 2004 is $159,333, which consists of the principal of $144,848 and the accrued interest of $14,485. Of this amount, $134,181 is classified as a long-term asset, and the remaining amount of $25,152 is reported as a current asset.

Capital Leases for the Lessor— Sales-Type

With one modification, the Pine Company/Forest example can be used to illustrate the lessor's accounting for a sales-type lease. The modification is that the cost to Forest of the equipment being leased is $125,000, rather than the $170,000 that was used earlier. All other facts remain the same. Thus, because the fair value of the leased equipment of $170,000 is now greater than the cost of the equipment of $125,000, the lease is a sales-type capital lease. (Note that it is irrelevant to the lessee whether the lessor has a direct financing lease or a sales-type lease; the lessee's accounting is the same.)

Initial Recording for a Sales-Type Capital Lease

Illustration 17-2 shows the accounting for a sales-type lease in comparison to a direct financing lease for the lessor. The important differences in the journal entries are shown in italics. Note that the entry for the sales-type lease results in profit of $45,000 being recognized immediately, which is the difference between the sales amount of $170,000 and the cost of goods sold of $125,000. However, the amount of interest that will be earned on a sales-type lease is the same amount as will be recognized under a direct financing lease.

Subsequent Accounting for a Sales-Type Capital Lease

Because the present value of the minimum lease payments for a sales-type lease is the same as the present value for a direct financing lease, the amortization table prepared for a sales-type lease is exactly the same as the amortization table prepared previously for a direct financing lease. Also, the amortization table for a sales-type lease is used in exactly the same way (1) to recognize yearly interest and (2) to separate the net investment in the lease into its current and long-term portions at year-end for financial reporting purposes.

Thus, the entries to recognize the receipt of payment and the earning of interest for the next two years are as shown.

	2004		2005	
Unearned Interest Income	14,485		13,418	
Interest Income		14,485		13,418

To recognize interest income for the year.

Cash	25,152		25,152	
Lease Receivable		25,152		25,152

To recognize the receipt of the yearly lease payment and the resulting decrease of the receivable account. Note that these entries are the same as were prepared for a direct financing lease.

EXTENDING THE CONCEPT

Referring back to Table 17-1 on page 808, what amounts will be reported as a noncurrent receivable and as a current receivable at the end of 2008?

Answer: From the amortization table, the total amount owing at December 31, 2008, is $95,341 plus accrued interest of $9,534. Of this amount, $79,723 is a noncurrent asset, and the difference of $25,152 is a current asset.

Financial Reporting for a Sales-Type Capital Lease

As with direct financing leases, the amortization table is used to separate the net investment in a sales-type lease into its current and noncurrent portions at year-end for financial reporting purposes. This separating of the current and noncurrent portions is done the same as previously. So, after accruing interest for 2004, the total amount to be received per the amortization table is $159,333. Of this total, the long-term amount is $134,181, and the current portion is $25,152.

ILLUSTRATION 17-2

Comparison of Sales-Type Leases to Direct Financing Leases

Sales-Type Leases			Direct Financing Leases		
Lease Receivable	251,520		Lease Receivable	251,520	
Cost of Goods Sold	*125,000*		Equipment		170,000
Inventory		125,000	Unearned Interest		81,520
Sales		170,000	Revenue		
Unearned Interest		81,520			
Revenue					

Explanation of the above entry:

Lease receivable: The amount that is reported in this account is no different between a direct financing lease and a sales-type lease. The account *is still debited for the gross amount to be received.* The account is subsequently reduced by the amount of each payment in the same way as was done for a direct financing lease. This lease receivable amount is also referred to as the **gross investment in the lease**.

Inventory and cost of goods sold: A manufacturer or dealer carries the leased asset in finished goods inventory—at cost—until it is sold, when it is removed from that account and recorded in the cost of goods sold account. In contrast, for a direct financing lease, the lessor (e.g., Forest) buys the equipment, records the asset in an equipment account at its fair market value, and leases it to the lessee for the same amount. (Often, the buying and leasing of the asset are simultaneous transactions.) This difference in the nature of the asset to the two entities (i.e., inventory versus equipment) is the reason why Inventory is credited for a sales-type lease and Equipment is credited for a direct financing lease. The reason for recording different amounts for a sales-type lease versus a direct financing lease is due to the difference in cost to a manufacturer or dealer versus fair value to a financing agent.

Sales: The amount recorded as sales is the present value of the minimum lease payments. This present value amount is often equivalent to the fair value of the asset. The sales account is used because the manufacturer (or dealer) is using the lease as a mechanism to sell the product. This sales amount is usually also the **net investment in the lease**, which is defined to be the gross investment in the lease (i.e., the lease receivable amount) less the unearned interest income. The only time when the sales amount at the inception of the lease is not also the net investment in the lease is when the amounts recorded in the inventory and the cost of goods sold accounts are not the same. This occurs when there is an unguaranteed residual value.

Unearned interest income: As with the lease receivable account, what is recorded in this account between a sales-type lease and a direct financing lease is the same; it is the difference between the gross investment in the lease and the net investment in the lease. This amount can also be determined by adding the interest column on the amortization table. Subsequently, this amount is recognized as interest, using the effective-interest method, over the life of the lease.

Capital Leases with Guaranteed Residual Values

Seemingly, the particular contractual terms of a lease are limited only by the imagination of those entering into them. A typical lease provision included in many leases is a **residual value** for the leased asset, which is the estimated residual value (at the signing of the lease) that the leased asset will have at the end of the lease term. This residual value may be guaranteed or unguaranteed. A lease with a **guaranteed residual value** is one where the lessee (or some third party) agrees to make up any deficiency if the fair value of the leased asset when the lease expires is below a stated amount. Guaranteed residual values are included in lease contracts to protect the lessor from any loss; thus, the lessor is guaranteed that the desired rate of return will be earned. To the lessee, the advantage of including a residual value in a lease (whether guaranteed or not) is that the annual lease payments are reduced. In accounting for leases, a guaranteed residual value—by definition—is included in the minimum lease payments and, therefore, is included in the present value calculations for recording the asset and the liability for the lessee and the net investment in the lease for the lessor.

To illustrate the impact of a guaranteed residual value, again return to the Forest and Pine Company illustration, where the lease was a sales-type lease. Previously, the minimum lease payments were computed to be $25,152; but now suppose that Pine (the lessee) guarantees that the leased asset, which will return to the possession of Forest, will have a residual value of $10,000 at the termination of the lease. With this guaranteed residual value, the yearly payments are determined as shown in Illustration 17-3.

ILLUSTRATION 17-3

Computing the Yearly Payments for a Lease with a Guaranteed Residual Value

Fair value, which is the amount the lessor desires to recoup	$170,000
Present value of guaranteed residual value, discounted using the present value factor of a single sum at 10% for 10 years (i.e., 0.38554 × $10,000)	3,855
Net amount to recoup through the minimum rental payments	$166,145

Then, the yearly rental payments are computed by dividing the $166,145 by the present value of an annuity due (because the first payment is made immediately) at 10% for 10 years. This annual payment amount is computed as follows:

Minimum Rental Payment = $166,145/Present value of annuity due, 10%, 10 years
= $166,145/6.75902
= $24,581

As noted earlier, the presence of a guaranteed residual value makes the recapture of the fair value of the asset more likely by the lessor and reduces the rental payments.

Initial Recording of a Capital Lease with a Guaranteed Residual Value

At the inception of the lease, the journal entries for a lease with a guaranteed residual value for both the lessee and the lessor are as shown in Illustration 17-4. The important differences between a sales-type lease with a guaranteed residual value and a sales-type lease without residual value are italicized.

ILLUSTRATION 17-4

Journal Entries to Record a Sales-Type Lease with Guaranteed Residual Value
(at inception of the lease)

Accounting for the Lessor			Accounting for the Lessee		
Lease Receivable	*255,810*		Leased Property	170,000	
Cost of Goods Sold	125,000		Capital Lease		170,000
Inventory		125,000	Obligation		
Sales		170,000			
Unearned Interest		*85,810*			
Income					

Explanation of the above entry for the lessor:
Lease receivable: As before, the amount in Lease Receivable is the gross amount of the lease (i.e., undiscounted cash flow amount), which now includes the guaranteed residual value. Thus, the $255,810 amount in Lease Receivable is the sum of the 10 payments of $24,581 each and the $10,000 residual amount.

Sales: As before, this amount is the present value of the minimum lease payments, which (by definition) includes the present value of the guaranteed residual amount. Thus, the present value of the 10 payments of $24,581 (which is $166,145) and the present value of the guaranteed residual value of $10,000 (which is $3,855) give the total present value of $170,000.

Unearned interest income: This amount is still the difference between the gross investment in the lease (i.e., the lease receivable) and the net investment in the lease (i.e., sales).

Although the amounts have changed from a lease that does not have a residual value, the concepts behind how the amounts were obtained have not changed; they are exactly the same.

Explanation of the above entry for the lessee:
There is no difference in the initial journal entry above for the lessee when there is a guaranteed residual value and in the prior illustration when the lease did not have a residual value. The leased asset and related obligation are still recorded at the present value of the minimum lease payments. For the prior illustration, the minimum lease payments consisted only of the rental payments; but in the illustration above, the minimum lease payments consist of the minimum rental payments and the guaranteed residual value.

Subsequent Accounting for a Capital Lease with Guaranteed Residual Value

Regarding the subsequent accounting of the asset for the lessee, since the lease does not transfer ownership and there is no bargain purchase option, the lessee depreciates the cost less the guaranteed residual value over the life of the lease term. The guaranteed residual value is treated as if it were a salvage value.[6] Assuming the use of the straight-line depreciation method, the lessee's annual depreciation amount is $16,000, which is computed as follows:

$$\text{Depreciation Expense} = \frac{\text{Cost of Asset} - \text{Guaranteed Residual Value}}{\text{Life (in years)}}$$

$$\text{Depreciation Expense} = (\$170,000 - \$10,000)/10 = \$16,000$$

Regarding the subsequent accounting for the lessee's lease liability, the lessor's receivable, and both the lessee's and lessor's recognizing interest, an amortization table is prepared as shown in Table 17-2. Again, the amortization table begins with the present value amount.

TABLE 17-2

Lease Amortization Table— Guaranteed Residual Value
(for lessee and lessor)

Period	Cash	Interest Expense	Lease Obligation/ Net Investment in Lease
			$170,000
Jan. 1, 2004	$24,581	—	145,419
Jan. 1, 2005	24,581	$14,542	135,380
Jan. 1, 2006	24,581	13,538	124,337
Jan. 1, 2007	24,581	12,434	112,190
Jan. 1, 2008	24,581	11,219	98,828
Jan. 1, 2009	24,581	9,882	84,129
Jan. 1, 2010	24,581	8,413	67,961
Jan. 1, 2011	24,581	6,796	50,176
Jan. 1, 2012	24,581	5,018	30,613
Jan. 1, 2013	24,581	3,061	9,093
Jan. 1, 2014[7]		907	10,000
Total Interest		$85,810	

[6]Note that assets are depreciated over their useful life when title to the asset passes to the lessee or there is a bargain purchase option. Neither of these events occurs when there is a guaranteed residual value. That is, the lessor includes a guaranteed residual value to protect his investment in the asset when the asset reverts to him at the end of the lease term. If title to the asset is to pass to the lessee or there is a bargain purchase option, then the lessor has no need to protect his investment.

[7]Table 17-2 has this extra period because the lease will not be settled until the end of 2013. There is no additional payment, but interest continues to accrue until the lease is settled.

The major difference between this amortization table and the one prepared when the lease did not contain a guaranteed residual value is that *the amortization table ends at the residual value amount of $10,000*. However, the amortization table is used in the same way as before to prepare the journal entries to recognize interest income or expense amounts, as shown in Illustration 17-5, and for separating the obligation/receivable between the current and noncurrent portions.

ILLUSTRATION 17-5

Journal Entries to Recognize Interest for a Lease with Guaranteed Residual Value

Accounting for the Lessor			Accounting for the Lessee		
Dec. 31, 2004 Unearned Interest Income	14,542		Interest Expense	14,542	
Interest Income		14,542	Capital Lease Obligation		14,542
Jan 1, 2005 Cash	24,581		Capital Lease Obligation	24,581	
Lease Receivable		24,581	Cash		24,581

Using the amortization table for financial reporting purposes, at the end of 2004, both the lessor and lessee report a noncurrent amount (receivable and liability, respectively) of $135,380 and a current amount of $24,581.

Settling a Capital Lease with a Guaranteed Residual Value

At the termination of the lease, either (1) the asset's fair value is at least equal to the guaranteed residual value or (2) the asset's fair value is less than the guaranteed residual value. In accounting for the situation where the asset's fair value is at least equal to the guaranteed residual value, the lessee removes the asset and liability from the accounts and does not recognize either a gain or a loss because any excess of fair value above the guaranteed residual value belongs to the lessor. The lessor records the asset at its fair value, removes the remaining receivable from the books, and recognizes a gain for the difference. These entries for the lessor and lessee are demonstrated in Illustration 17-6 for the Forest/Pine Company example, where it is assumed that the asset's fair value at the termination of the lease is $12,000, or $2,000 more than the guaranteed residual amount.

ILLUSTRATION 17-6

Settlement of a Lease Fair Value Equals or Exceeds the Guaranteed Residual Value

Lessor's Accounting			Lessee's Accounting		
Asset	12,000		Lease Obligation	10,000	
Lease Receivable		10,000	Accumulated Depreciation	160,000	
Gain on Settling Lease		2,000	Asset		170,000

The accounting for terminating a lease where the fair value of the asset is less than the guaranteed residual value requires that the lessee (or some third party) pay such a difference. As a result, *the lessee recognizes a loss, but the lessor recognizes neither a gain nor a loss.* Avoiding a loss is the purpose of including a guaranteed residual value in the terms of the lease. Other than the lessee recognizing a loss, the accounting is the same as before, which is that the lessee removes the asset and liability from the books, and the lessor accounts for the asset at its fair value and removes the remaining receivable. Illustration 17-7 illustrates these journal entries, assuming the fair value of the leased asset is $7,000.

ILLUSTRATION 17-7

Settlement of a Lease
Fair Value Is Less Than the
Guaranteed Residual Value

Lessor's Accounting			Lessee's Accounting		
Cash	3,000		Loss on Settling Lease	3,000	
Asset	7,000		Lease Obligation	10,000	
Lease Receivable		10,000	Accumulated Deprec.	160,000	
			Asset		170,000
			Cash		3,000

Leases with Unguaranteed Residual Values

A residual value does not have to be guaranteed. The lessor may plan on a residual amount, but the lessee does not necessarily have to guarantee it. When a lease contract contains an unguaranteed residual value, the lessor computes the yearly rental payments in the same manner as if the residual value were guaranteed (see Illustration 17-4 on page 815). Treating the residual value as if it were guaranteed means that the yearly rental payments are not impacted; they do not change in amount. However, the lessor does have the following changes in the initial entry to record the inception of a lease:

• The cost of goods sold is reduced by the present value of the unguaranteed residual value.
• Sales does not include the present value of the unguaranteed residual value because unguaranteed residual is not part of the minimum lease payments.

These changes are made because, essentially, the lessor did not sell that portion of the asset represented by the unguaranteed residual value.

Once the lessee has been notified of the annual lease payments, the lessee computes the present value of those payments and records an asset and a liability for that amount, the same as done previously. By recording the present value of only the payments—and not including also the present value of the unguaranteed residual value—the *lessee does not account for the unguaranteed residual value.* Because the lessor accounts for the residual value and the lessee does not, the mirror-image accounting that has been demonstrated to this point for leases does not exist for leases with unguaranteed residual values.

To illustrate the accounting for a lease where the residual value is not guaranteed, the same Forest and Pine Company example will be used, but now the

$10,000 residual value is not guaranteed. Because the lessor's accounting is not affected by whether the residual value is guaranteed, the determination of the yearly payments is unchanged. So the annual payments are still $24,581.

Initial Recording of a Capital Lease with an Unguaranteed Residual Value

The journal entries to record a lease with an unguaranteed residual value by both the lessee and the lessor are as shown in Illustration 17-8. The differences in accounting for a sales-type lease with unguaranteed residual value versus when the residual is guaranteed are italicized.

ILLUSTRATION 17-8

Journal Entries to Record a Sales-Type Lease with Unguaranteed Residual Value
(at inception of the lease)

Accounting for the Lessor			Accounting for the Lessee		
Lease Receivable	255,810		*Leased Property*	*166,145*	
Cost of Goods Sold	*121,145*		*Capital Lease Obligation*		*166,145*
Inventory		125,000			
Sales		*166,145*			
Unearned Interest Income		85,810			

Explanation of the above entry for the lessor:
Lease receivable: As before, the amount in the lease receivable is the gross amount that will be received. This amount includes the unguaranteed residual value and the yearly payments. The $255,810 amount in the lease receivable account is the sum of the 10 payments of $24,581 each and the $10,000 residual amount.

Cost of goods sold: This amount is the cost of the inventory minus the present value of the unguaranteed residual value.

Sales: As before, this amount is the present value of the minimum lease payments, and since the definition of the minimum lease payments does not include an unguaranteed residual value, the present value of that amount is excluded. Thus, this amount is only the present value of the yearly payments.

Unearned interest income: For a lease with an unguaranteed residual value, this amount is computed by determining the amount required to make the journal entry balance or by adding the interest column in the amortization table.

Explanation of the above entry for the lessee:
When the lessee learns that the annual rental payments are $24,581, the present value of the rental payments is computed using the appropriate discount rate. This amount is $166,145. The reason the asset and liability are not recorded at the $170,000 amount, as was done when the residual value was guaranteed, is that the unguaranteed residual value is not included in the definition of what constitutes the minimum lease payments.

Subsequent Accounting for a Capital Lease with Unguaranteed Residual Value

To aid in the subsequent accounting for interest, the lessor prepares the same amortization table as when the residual value is guaranteed, which is replicated in the left-hand side of Table 17-3. But, because the lessee records the liability at $166,145, his amortization table is based upon that amount, as shown in the right-hand side of Table 17-3. Observe that the total interest the lessee incurs is not equal to the total interest the lessor earns.

Although the lessor and lessee use different amortization tables, the amortization tables are used exactly as before (1) to determine the amount of interest income/expense to recognize for a particular year and (2) to separate the amounts to be received or owing between the current and noncurrent portions for financial reporting purposes.

TABLE 17-3

Lease with Unguaranteed Residual Value

	Lessor			Lessee		
Period	Cash	Interest	Carrying Amount	Cash	Interest	Carrying Amount
			$170,000			$166,145
Jan. 1, 2004	$24,581	$ —	145,419	$24,581	$ —	141,564
Jan. 1, 2005	24,581	14,542	135,380	24,581	14,156	131,139
Jan. 1, 2006	24,581	13,538	124,337	24,581	13,114	119,672
Jan. 1, 2007	24,581	12,434	112,190	24,581	11,967	107,058
Jan. 1, 2008	24,581	11,219	98,828	24,581	10,706	93,183
Jan. 1, 2009	24,581	9,882	84,129	24,581	9,318	77,920
Jan. 1, 2010	24,581	8,413	67,961	24,581	7,792	61,131
Jan. 1, 2011	24,581	6,796	50,176	24,581	6,113	42,663
Jan. 1, 2012	24,581	5,018	30,613	24,581	4,266	22,348
Jan. 1, 2013	24,581	3,061	9,093	24,581	2,233	0
		907	10,000			
Totals		$85,810			$79,665	

The lessor must review periodically the unguaranteed residual value. When estimates are that the residual value has declined, the accounting for the lease must be revised accordingly, with a loss recognized in the year. For example, if for the above lease it was determined in 2007 that the residual value will only be $7,000 rather than $10,000, the amortization table is adjusted so that the ending amount is $7,000. The amount by which the amortization table needs to be adjusted in 2007 is the amount of the loss. In the above example, the carrying value needs to be changed from $98,828 to $97,133, for a loss of $1,695. Unearned Interest is debited for $1,305, and Lease Receivable is credited for $3,000. Upward adjustments to residual value are not recognized.

Leases with a Bargain Purchase Option

A bargain purchase option allows the lessee, at his option, to purchase the leased property at a price that is expected to be sufficiently below the expected fair value of the property at the date the option becomes exercisable, such that exercise of the purchase option is reasonably assured. For both the lessor and the lessee, *there is no difference in the accounting for a lease containing a bargain purchase option from a lease having a guaranteed residual value.*

For the lessor:

- The yearly payments are computed by assuming that the option will be exercised.
- The lease receivable is the sum of the amounts to be received, including the bargain purchase option.
- Sales is the present value of the minimum lease payments, which includes the bargain purchase option.
- Unearned interest income is computed as the difference between the lease receivable and sales.
- The amount in the amortization table at the termination of the lease is the bargain purchase amount.
- At the end of the lease term, if the bargain purchase option is exercised, the lessor debits Cash and credits Lease Receivable. If the lessee does not exercise the bargain purchase option, the lessor records the asset at its fair value, credits Lease Receivable, and recognizes the difference as a gain or loss (see Illustrations 17-6 and 17-7 on pages 817 and 818, respectively).

For the lessee:

- The amount recorded as the cost of the leased asset and the amount of the lease obligation are computed by discounting the minimum lease payments, which include the bargain purchase option amount.
- The leased asset is depreciated over its economic life (rather than over the lease term) using whatever salvage value is appropriate.
- The amount in the amortization table at the termination of the lease is the bargain purchase amount.
- At the end of the lease term, if the bargain purchase option is exercised, the lessee debits the liability account and credits Cash. If the lessee does not exercise the bargain purchase option, the liability amount and the cost of the asset with its accumulated depreciation are removed from the books, and if necessary, a gain or loss is recognized.

The amortization table in Illustration 17-9 was constructed for a 5-year direct financing lease that was entered into on January 1 and contains a $1,000 bargain purchase option. The interest rate is 14%, the first payment is due at the signing of the lease contract, and the economic life of the asset is eight years. Entries for selected events in the accounting for the lease for both the lessor and the lessee are also shown in the illustration.

ILLUSTRATION 17-9

Lease with Bargain Purchase Option
(lessor and lessee)

Period	Cash	Interest	Net Investment in Lease/ Lease Obligation
			$20,000
1	$4,978	$ —	15,022
2	4,978	2,104	12,148
3	4,978	1,701	8,871
4	4,978	1,243	5,136
5	4,978	719	877
6		123	1,000
		$5,890	

ILLUSTRATION 17-9 (CONTINUED)

a. Initial Entries for a Lease with a Bargain Purchase Option

Lessor			Lessee		
Lease Receivable	25,890		Leased Asset	20,000	
Sales		20,000	Lease Obligation		20,000
Unearned Interest Income		5,890			
Cash	4,978		Lease Obligation	4,978	
Lease Receivable		4,978	Cash		4,978

Explanation of the above entry for the lessor:
Lease receivable:

Five payments of $4,978	$24,890
Bargain purchase option	1,000
Total	$25,890

Sales:

Present value of an annuity due of five payments of $4,978 at 14%	$19,481
Present value of a single sum of $1,000, five periods, 14%	519
Total	$20,000

The unearned interest income is the difference between the gross receivable and the net investment or sales amount.

Explanation of the above entry for the lessee:
The leased asset and the lease obligation are recorded at the present value of the future cash flows, discounted at 14%.

b. Year-End Entries for Interest and Depreciation

Unearned Interest Income	2,104		Interest Expense	2,104	
Interest Income		2,104	Lease Obligation		2,104
			Depreciation Expense	2,500	
			Accumulated Depreciation		2,500

Explanation of entry:
The interest amounts come from the amortization table. Since the lease contains a bargain purchase option, the lessee depreciates the fair value of the asset over its economic life of eight years. In this illustration, the straight-line method of depreciation is used.

c. Termination of the Lease, Assuming the Bargain Purchase Option Is Exercised

Cash	1,000		Lease Obligation	1,000	
Lease Receivable		1,000	Cash		1,000

Explanation of entry:
The lessor records the receipt of cash and removes the remaining receivable amount from the books. No other accounts on the lessor's books are affected by the lease. The lessee pays the cash required to exercise the bargain purchase option and, as a result, removes the remaining obligation from the books. The asset has already been recorded.

ILLUSTRATION 17-9 (CONTINUED)

d. Termination of the Lease, Assuming the Bargain Purchase Option Is Not Exercised

Asset	6,000		Lease Obligation	1,000	
Lease Receivable		1,000	Accumulated Depreciation	12,500	
Gain on Settling Lease		5,000	Loss on Settling Lease	6,500	
			Asset		20,000

Explanation of entry:
The lessor records the asset at fair value, which is assumed to be $6,000, removes the lease receivable from the books, and recognizes a gain for the difference. The lessee removes the asset and its accumulated depreciation from the books. The lessee also removes the remaining lease obligation. In this case, because the asset had not been depreciated to the bargain purchase option amount, the lessee recognizes a loss. The accumulated depreciation amount is computed by multiplying the yearly depreciation expense of $2,500 [see entry in b] by the five years of the lease term.

Initial Direct Costs

Initial direct costs (IDCs) are those costs that (1) the lessor incurs to originate a lease and (2) directly relate to activities performed by the lessor for the lease.[8] IDCs include such costs as:

- A finder's fee;
- Fees for evaluating the prospective lessee's financial condition;
- Fees for evaluating and recording guarantees, collateral, and other security arrangements; and
- Fees for negotiating lease terms, preparing and processing lease documents, and closing the transaction.

IDCs do not include any internal indirect costs related to advertising, servicing existing leases, or credit activities.

The accounting for IDCs depends upon the type of lease entered into and is accounted for as shown in Table 17-4. The rationale for treating IDCs as de-

TABLE 17-4

Accounting for Initial Direct Costs

Type of Lease	Accounting Treatment
Operating	Deferred and then allocated equally over the lease term.
Direct Financing	Deducted from the unearned interest income. Consequently, a new interest rate is computed that recognizes the unearned interest income over the life of the lease. This new interest rate will be lower than the initial rate of return.
Sales-Type	Expensed in the year incurred.

[8]*Statement of Financial Accounting Standards No. 91*, "Accounting for Nonrefundable Fees and Costs Associated with Originating or Acquiring Loans and Initial Direct Costs of Leases," Stanford: Financial Accounting Standards Board, Dec. 1986.

pending upon the nature of the lease is to obtain an appropriate matching of revenues and expenses. For operating and direct financing leases, since no profit is recognized immediately, the IDCs are spread over the lease term in a manner that is consistent with the way in which revenue is recognized. But sales-type leases have the manufacturer's (or dealer's) profit that is recognized immediately, so IDCs for sales-type leases are recognized immediately.

Since the accounting for IDCs for operating and sales-type leases is straightforward, only the accounting for IDCs for a direct financing lease is illustrated. Suppose that a 5-year lease is entered into at a 10% effective interest rate. The fair value of the asset is $100,000, and the first payment is made immediately. As a result, the yearly payments are determined by referring to an annuity due table at 10% and five years. These payments are computed to be $23,982. The IDCs are $1,000. Given these facts, the lessor's entries at the inception of the lease are as follows:

Lease Receivable (5 payments of $23,982)	119,910	
Sales (present value of $119,910)		100,000
Unearned Interest Income		19,910
Unearned Interest Income (the IDC)	1,000	
Cash		1,000

Because of incurring the IDCs, the return to the lessor will be $1,000 less than what it otherwise would have been. The amortization table to subsequently account for interest is shown in Illustration 17-10.

ILLUSTRATION 17-10

Amortization Table When There Are IDCs

Period	Cash	Unearned Interest Income	Net Investment in the Lease
			$101,000
1	$23,982	$ 0	77,018
2	23,982	7,240	60,276
3	23,982	5,666	41,960
4	23,982	3,944	21,922
5	23,982	2,060	0
		$18,910	

Unearned interest income is computed by multiplying the 9.4% effective interest rate by the remaining principal. The 9.4% effective interest rate was computed as the rate that would (1) bring the net investment to zero at the end of the lease term and (2) result in recognizing interest income of $18,910 over the life of the lease. The new effective interest rate can be computed from an electronic calculator, electronic spreadsheet, or by trial and error.

Using the amortization table in Illustration 17-10, the journal entry to record the payment at the beginning of the second year and the interest income is as follows:

Cash	23,982	
Unearned Interest Income	7,240	
Lease Receivable		23,982
Interest Income		7,240

The entries for all other years follow the same pattern.

Treating an Operating Lease as a Capital Lease

Leasing assets under an operating lease is an example of off-balance-sheet financing, meaning that neither the assets nor—primarily—the liabilities are shown on the balance sheet. A review of financial statements indicates that today most leases are not being accounted for as capital leases. Some may suppose that, as a result, the financial statements of companies that are heavily involved in leasing activities do not correctly reflect the companies' financial position. If this is a concern, there is sufficient information in the notes to the financial statements to adjust a company's financial statements to reflect what the financial statements would be had the operating leases been treated as capital leases.

Companies with operating leases must disclose in the notes to the financial statements their future minimum rental payments as of the balance sheet date in the aggregate and for each of the next five fiscal years. Having access to this information allows the financial statement reader to adjust the financial statements as if those operating leases had been treated as capital leases.

To illustrate how this can be done, some information was extracted from a recently published financial report of American Airlines. The financial report stated that American flies a total of 697 airplanes, of which 205 (approximately 29%) are being financed through operating leases. In the notes to the financial statements, American disclosed the following information about its future minimum lease payments under operating leases:

Year Ending December 31,	Rental Payments for Operating Leases (in millions)
2000	$ 965
2001	972
2002	929
2003	944
2004	934
2005 and subsequent	12,096
Total	$16,840

Having the pattern of cash payments allows the analyst to determine a present value for them and then to adjust the financial statements, assuming that the operating leases were treated as capital leases. To do this, the analyst (a) assumes some pattern of payment for the $12,096 that will be paid subsequent to 2005 and (b) selects an acceptable discount rate. For this example, it is assumed that the $12,096 will be paid evenly over the next 10 years, and a 9% discount rate is used.[9] Based upon the above payments and assumptions, the present value of the minimum lease payments is $9,530, which is computed as shown in Table 17-5.

TABLE 17-5

Using Cash Flow Information in Financial Statements to Treat Operating Leases as Capital Leases

Period	Cash Flow Amount	Present Value Factor (present value of a single sum, 9%)	Present Value Amount
1	$ 965	1	$ 965
2	972	0.91743	892
3	929	0.84168	782
4	944	0.77218	729
5	934	0.70843	662
6	1,210	0.64993	786
7	1,210	0.59627	721
8	1,210	0.54703	662
9	1,210	0.50187	607
10	1,210	0.46043	557
11	1,210	0.42241	511
12	1,210	0.38753	469
13	1,210	0.35554	430
14	1,210	0.32618	395
15	1,210	0.29925	362
	Total present value		$9,530

Having determined the approximate present value of the future minimum lease payments, the financial statements can be adjusted to treat these operating leases as capital leases. This is done by adjusting the financial statements as if a journal entry had been prepared, debiting a long-term asset account for $9,530 and crediting a liability account for $9,530. Also, from Table 17-5 it can be seen that the amount of the obligation that will be paid in the first year is $965, which is the current liability portion, with the rest of the $9,530 being the noncurrent portion. Following these adjustments, some significant balance sheet subtotals and ratios as reported by American Airlines and as adjusted by treating the operating leases as capital leases are as shown in Table 17-6.

---

[9]The farther into the future that amounts are paid, the less impact they have on determining a present value amount. So, although it is unlikely that the actual cash payments subsequent to 2005 will be as assumed, it is also unlikely that any differences will have a significant impact on the present value of the rental payments.

TABLE 17-6

Significant Balance Sheet Subtotals, as Reported and as Adjusted

	Description	As Reported	Adjustment	As Adjusted
a.	Current assets	$ 4,881		$ 4,881
b.	Long-term assets (net)	16,838	$9,530	26,368
c.	Total assets	21,719	9,530	31,249
d.	Current liabilities	5,307	965	6,272
e.	All other liabilities	9,262	8,565	17,827
f.	Stockholders' equity	7,150		7,150
g.	Net income	627		627

Significant Ratios

Current ratio	0.920		0.778
Return on assets	2.89%		2.01%
Debt-to-equity	1.30:1		2.49:1

These adjustments reflect only those for the assets and liabilities. If desired, more precision could be made by adjusting or reversing out the operating lease payments for the year and substituting for them (1) depreciation on the newly capitalized lease assets and (2) interest expense on the lease obligation. Information is available in the financial report upon which to make these adjustments or to make reasonable assumptions.

The purpose of this discussion and example is to demonstrate that the information provided in the notes is useful and can be used to gain an understanding of a company. Other information is available in the notes to the financial statements to adjust the financial statements in a multitude of ways.

International Accounting Standards

INTERNATIONAL

Most countries and the International Accounting Standards Board require companies to capitalize leases that transfer substantially all the risks and rewards of ownership to the lessee.[10] However, Italy is an exception. There, accounting principles are prescribed and regulated by the government, making Italy a code-law country. Italy's civil code does not provide for capital leases, and, therefore, the form of the transaction, not the substance, determines the accounting for leases.

Even in countries that allow leases to be capitalized, significant differences from U.S. GAAP arise. For example, in South Korea, there is no criterion for determining a capital lease based on the length of the lease period relative to the asset's useful life. Thus, leases that must be capitalized in the United States could presumably be classified as operating leases under Korean GAAP. This accounting difference could have a material impact on total liabilities and total assets reported by the company and the resulting expenses for the lease period.

---

[10]Instead of being referred to as a capital lease, the term most often used is a *finance lease*.

1. In your opinion, is it better to provide managers with flexibility to exercise their discretion or to establish rigid criteria to guide accounting decisions?

2. Why do you suppose *IAS No. 17*, which became effective on January 1, 1999, leaves the classification of leases to the judgment of managers? Do you believe the experience of the FASB with respect to lease accounting had an impact on this decision?

In *IAS No. 17*, the International Accounting Standards Committee adopted the concept of requiring the capitalization of leases when "substantially all the risks and rewards incident to ownership" are transferred to the lessee. However, unlike U.S. GAAP, specific criteria were not established to determine whether a lease should be classified as a capital lease (or *finance lease* per IAS terminology). Instead, companies must exercise their own judgment based on the details of individual lease contracts. Thus, lease accounting under international GAAP is another area where managers can exercise significant influence over the content of financial statements. Skeptics of *IAS No. 17* suggest that this is just another area provided to managers that will allow them to "cook the books." On the other hand, given that managers have the best knowledge about the financial condition of the company, providing managers with discretion allows them to signal their superior information to investors.

Comprehensive Example Problem

Thurston Enterprises is a dealer of certain farm equipment that, to provide a full range of equipment, also arranges various direct financing leases that Thurston does not carry. During the month of January 2005, Thurston entered into two capital leases, each with slightly different leasing terms, as follows:

Lease 1: Thurston leased to D&M Ranches some equipment on its lot that had cost Thurston $40,000 but that had a fair value of $65,000. The terms of the lease call for five annual payments of $13,890 each, with the first payment due immediately, and the equipment will revert to Thurston at the end of the lease term. Thurston thinks the equipment will have a residual value of $7,500 at the end of the lease, but D&M does not guarantee this amount. Thurston's implicit interest rate on these types of leases is 8%, and this amount is known to D&M Ranches and is less than its incremental borrowing rate. Thurston incurred initial direct costs of $2,500 in consummating this lease.

Lease 2: Thurston arranged a second lease between a manufacturer of farm equipment and D&M for some equipment that Thurston did not normally carry. The cost to Thurston for the equipment was $30,000, which is the same amount at which Thurston sold it to D&M. The terms of the lease require annual payments of $10,888 for three years, at the end of which time D&M will be allowed to buy the equipment for $1,000—a price considerably less than what it is anticipated the equipment will be worth. The economic life of the equipment is five years. Thurston uses a 12% interest rate for this type of lease, which is known to D&M. Thurston incurred initial direct costs of $1,000 in consummating this lease. Complete the following requirements and then see Appendix A at the end of the chapter for the solutions.

1. Determine whether the above leases are capital leases.
2. Prepare the journal entries for the lessor and the lessee at the inception of the leases, including the initial direct costs.
3. Prepare the respective amortization tables for the lessor and lessee for both leases.
4. Prepare the journal entries for the lessor and the lessee at the end of the lease term, assuming for Lease 1 that the actual value of the equipment was $12,000, and for Lease 2 that the bargain purchase option was exercised.

APPENDIX A: Solutions to Example Problems

Example Problem: Capital Lease—Lessee (p. 810)

1. The present value of the minimum lease payments (MLP) is $50,000. This amount is computed by multiplying the MLP of $8,408 by the present value of an annuity due for 10 years at 14%, a factor that is approximately 5.94637.
2. The amortization table is as shown in Illustration 17A-1:

ILLUSTRATION 17A-1

Amortization Table for a Capital Lease

Period	Cash	Interest	Carrying Amount
			$50,000
1	$8,408	—	41,592
2	8,408	$5,823	39,007
3	8,408	5,461	36,060
4	8,408	5,048	32,700
5	8,408	4,576	28,868
6	8,408	4,040	24,500
7	8,408	3,429	19,521
8	8,408	2,733	13,846
9	8,408	1,938	7,376
10	8,408	1,032	0

3. The journal entry to recognize interest at the end of the first year after signing the lease is as follows:

| Interest Expense | 5,823 | |
| Capital Lease Obligation | | 5,823 |

4. The total amount due one year after signing the lease is $41,592 plus the accrued interest of $5,823, which is a total of $47,415. Of this amount, the long-term portion is $39,007, and the current portion is the difference of $8,408.
5. The journal entry to record the second lease payment is as follows:

| Capital Lease Obligation | 8,408 | |
| Cash | | 8,408 |

Comprehensive Example Problem (p. 828)

1. These two leases are capital leases if any of the four criteria are met. Not enough information is available to apply any of the capital-lease criteria, except for the present value of the minimum lease payments criterion. For Lease 1, the minimum lease payments consist of the minimum yearly payments of $13,890, but not the unguaranteed residual value. Discounting these cash flows at 8% results in the following:

Present value of yearly payments: $13,890 \times 4.3121[11] = $59,895$

[11]This is the present value factor of an annuity due for five periods at 8%.

Since this present value amount of the minimum lease payments is more than 90% of the fair value of the asset of $65,000, Lease 1 is a capital lease.

For Lease 2, the minimum lease payments consist of the minimum yearly payments of $10,888 and the bargain purchase option of $1,000. Discounting these cash flows at 12% results in the following calculation:

$$
\begin{array}{llr}
\text{Present value of yearly payments: } \$10,888 \times 2.69005^{12} & = \$29,288 \\
\text{Present value of bargain purchase option: } \$1,000 \times 0.71178^{13} = & \underline{712} \\
\text{Total present value (rounded)} & \$30,000 \\
\end{array}
$$

Since the present value of the minimum lease payments of $30,000 is 90% or more of the fair value of the asset, Lease 2 is also a capital lease.

2. The entries at the inception of these two leases, for the lessor and the lessee, are shown in Illustration 17A-2.

ILLUSTRATION 17A-2

Journal Entries at Inception
(unguaranteed residual value)

Entries for the Lessor (Thurston)			Entries for the Lessee (D&M)		
Lease 1: Sales-Type Lease			**Lease 1: Sales-Type Lease**		
Lease Receivable	76,950		Leased Property	59,895	
Cost of Goods Sold	34,895		Capital Lease Obligation		59,895
Inventory		40,000			
Sales		59,895			
Unearned Interest					
Income		11,950			

To record a sales-type lease with unguaranteed residual value.

To record a capital lease with unguaranteed residual value.

Leasing Expense	2,500				
Cash		2,500			

To expense the initial direct costs incurred.

Journal Entries at Inception
(bargain purchase option)

Lease 2: Direct Financing Lease			Lease 2: Direct Financing Lease		
Lease Receivable	33,664		Leased Property	30,000	
Sales		30,000	Capital Lease Obligation		30,000
Unearned Interest					
Income		3,664			

To record a direct financing lease having a bargain purchase option.

To record a capital lease having a bargain purchase option.

Unearned Interest Income	1,000				
Cash		1,000			

To include the initial direct costs as part of the net investment in the lease.

[12]This is the present value factor of an annuity due for three periods at 12%.
[13]This is the present value factor of a single sum for three periods at 12%.

In these journal entries, note the different treatment of the initial direct costs, which are expensed for the sales-type lease, as there is a profit against which to match it, but are not expensed for the direct financing lease because there is no initial profit against which it can be matched. Instead, the initial direct costs are deferred and recognized in relationship to the amount of interest recognized. Also, the amount for cost of goods sold for Lease 1 is computed as follows:

Cost of inventory	$40,000
Less present value of the unguaranteed residual value ($7,500 × 0.68058, rounded)	(5,105)
Cost of goods sold	$34,895

3. Continuing with the above illustration, the lessor and lessee prepare their respective amortization tables for Lease 1—a sales-type lease with an unguaranteed residual value—as shown in Illustration 17A-3. Because of the unguaranteed residual value, these amortization tables are not identical, and so the amounts recognized as interest expense by the lessee and as interest income by the lessor are not identical. The lessor's amortization table begins with the fair value of the asset, and the lessee's amortization table begins with the present value of the minimum lease payments.

ILLUSTRATION 17A-3

Amortization Table—Lease 1 with Unguaranteed Residual Value

	For the Lessor: Lease 1			For the Lessee: Lease 1		
Period	Cash	Interest	Net Investment in the Lease	Cash	Interest	Carrying Amount of Obligation
			$65,000			$59,895
1	$13,890	$ 0	51,110	$13,890	$ 0	46,005
2	13,890	4,089	41,308	13,890	3,680	35,795
3	13,890	3,305	30,723	13,890	2,864	24,769
4	13,890	2,458	19,291	13,890	1,982	12,861
5	13,890	1,543	6,944	13,890	1,029	0
6	0	556	7,500			
Total interest		$11,951			$9,555	

During the life of the lease, since the equipment will revert to Thurston, D&M depreciates the $59,895 over the life of the lease term.

The amortization tables for Lease 2—a direct financing lease with a bargain purchase option—are shown in Illustration 17A-4. Because of the IDCs and the fact that this is a direct financing lease, again the amortization tables do not begin with the same carrying amounts. The lessor's amortization table begins with the present value of the minimum lease payments plus the IDCs. By including the IDCs in the net investment in the lease and computing a new effective interest rate, the interest income of $2,664 (i.e., $3,664 − $1,000) is recognized over the life of the lease. The new effective interest rate of 8.341% is computed.

ILLUSTRATION 17A-4

Amortization Table—Lease 2 with a Bargain Purchase Option

	For the Lessor: Lease 2				For the Lessee: Lease 2		
Period	Cash	Interest	Net Investment in the Lease	Period	Cash	Interest	Carrying Amount of Obligation
			$31,000				$30,000
1	$10,888	$ —	20,112	1	$10,888	$ —	19,112
2	10,888	1,678	10,902	2	10,888	2,293	10,517
3	10,888	909	923	3	10,888	1,263	892
4		77	1,000	4		108	1,000
Totals interest		$2,664				$3,664	

EXTENDING the Concept

What entries would be made by the lessee and the lessor if the fair value of the equipment at the end of the Lease 1 term was $7,000?

Answer:

Lessor

Loss	500	
Equipment	7,000	
Lease Receivable		7,500

Lessee

Accumulated		
Depreciation	59,895	
Leased Property		59,895

4. At the conclusion of the lease term for Lease 1 and using the amortization table in Illustration 17A-3, the following entry is made by the lessor, assuming that the equipment actually has a fair value of $12,000:

Equipment	12,000	
Lease Receivable		7,500
Gain on Settling the Lease		4,500

To finalize a sales-type lease where the equipment reverts to the lessor and the fair value is greater than the estimated residual value.

The lessee writes off the asset with its accumulated depreciation. Since the asset was amortized over the lease term and the lessee did not guarantee the residual value, the asset will be completely amortized. So there will not be any gain or loss to recognize.

The journal entries to record the exercise of the bargain purchase option for Lease 2 at the end of the lease term for both the lessor and the lessee are as follows:

Entries to Exercise the Bargain Purchase Option

Entries for the Lessor

Cash	1,000	
Lease Receivable		1,000

To record the exercise of a bargain purchase option.

Entries for the Lessee

Lease Obligation	1,000	
Cash		1,000

To record the exercise of a bargain purchase option.

What entries would the lessee and the lessor prepare if the bargain purchase option was not exercised, and the fair value of the equipment was $5,000?

Answer:

Lessor

Equipment	5,000	
Lease Receivable		1,000
Gain on Settling Lease		4,000

Lessee

Lease Obligation	1,000	
Accumulated Depreciation	18,000	
Loss on Settling Lease	11,000	
Equipment		30,000

APPENDIX B: Sale-Leasebacks[14]

A **sale-leaseback** is a transaction where the owner of property sells it and simultaneously leases it back without actually transferring the asset. (The initial owner is the seller-lessee, and the other party is the purchasor-lessor.) Sale-leaseback transactions cause difficulties because the leasing back of the asset may not be an independent (i.e., arms-length) transaction. As a result, the question arises as to how to account for a sale-leaseback. Some suggest that a sale-leaseback should be viewed as two separate transactions: a sale and then a leasing back. If this viewpoint is accepted, then a gain/loss should be recognized on the sale, and the lease should be accounted for according to whether it meets the criteria for a capital lease or an operating lease. Others suggest that rather than being two transactions, a sale-leaseback is a single transaction. If a sale and resulting leaseback is viewed as two aspects of a single transaction, then no gain/loss would be recognized on the sale portion of the transaction. Thus, the accounting question is whether a gain/loss should be recognized for the sale portion of the transaction. The accounting and financial reporting for the leasing of the asset is the same as for any other lease (i.e., determine whether it is an operating or capital lease and treat accordingly).

Accounting for Losses on the Sale

For sale-leaseback transactions, *losses incurred on selling the asset—unless they are artificial losses—are recognized*, because to not recognize them would result in reporting assets above their fair value. Artificial losses occur when the sales price of an asset is less than the book value of the asset, but the book value is less than the asset's fair value. An artificial loss is graphically illustrated in Figure 17B-1. Artificial losses are deferred and amortized, according to the following rules:

- For capital leases—in proportion to depreciation expense, and
- For operating leases—an equal amount per year.

---

[14]*Statement of Financial Accounting Standards No. 28,* "Accounting for Sales with Leasebacks," August 1, 1979.

FIGURE 17B-1

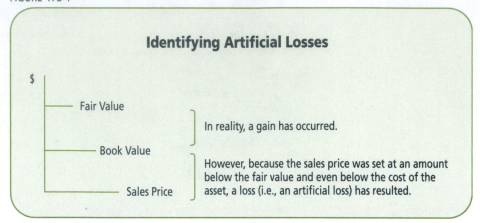

To illustrate the accounting for an artificial loss, Blue Water Marine Company sold equipment for $120,000 that had a carrying value of $150,000 and simultaneously leased it back. The equipment has an economic life of eight years, and the lease term is six years. The equipment's fair value is $170,000, which is also the present value of the yearly rental payments. Because the sales price of $120,000 is less than the carrying value of the equipment of $150,000, a loss on the sale is indicated. However, the loss is an artificial loss because the equipment's fair value is more than the equipment's carrying value. So no loss is recognized on the sale, and the journal entry for the sale part of the sale-leaseback transaction is as follows:

Cash	120,000	
Deferred Loss on Sale	30,000	
Equipment (net)		150,000

To record the sale of equipment in a sale-leaseback transaction.

The entry to record the capital lease is to debit Equipment and credit Lease Obligation for the present value of the minimum lease payments, which, from the information given, is $170,000.

Because this lease qualifies as a capital lease (e.g., the lease term is 75% or more of the economic life), the deferred loss is recognized in proportion to the depreciation expense. Assuming that Blue Water Marine uses the straight-line method of depreciation, the following yearly journal entry is necessary to amortize the deferred loss:

Depreciation Expense	33,333	
Deferred Loss on Sale		5,000
Accumulated Depreciation		28,333

To record depreciation expense for the year and amortize a portion of the deferred loss in the same pattern in which depreciation is recognized.

The computations for the amounts in this journal entry are as follows:

Accumulated depreciation: $170,000/6 yrs. = $28,333
Deferred loss to reverse: $30,000/6 yrs. = $5,000

Accounting for Gains on the Sale

Although losses are recognized (except artificial losses) on sale-leaseback transactions, whether gains are recognized depends upon the amount of rights that are subsequently leased back. The FASB set forth the following criteria for recognizing gains on the sale portion of a sale-leaseback transaction:

- When the seller-lessee leases back only *minor* rights to use the asset, then the sale-leaseback transaction is accounted for as two transactions, and the *gain on the sale of the asset is recognized.*
- When the seller-lessee leases back *substantially all* the rights to use the asset, then the sale-leaseback transaction is viewed as the lessee's method of financing the asset, rather than a sale, and *no gain on the sale of the asset is recognized.*
- When the seller-lessee leases back *more than minor rights to use the asset but less than substantially all the rights*, then *some of the gain on the sale of the asset is recognized.*

Thus, in sale-leaseback transactions, the meaning of the terms *minor* and *substantially all* are important to properly account for the sale portion. Their definitions are as follows:

- The seller-lessee retains substantially all the rights to use the asset when *any of the criteria for treating the lease as a capital lease are met.* As a result, the asset and related liability are recorded on the lessee's books at the present value of the minimum lease payments.
- The seller-lessee retains only minor rights to use the asset when the *present value of the rental payments is no more than 10% of the asset's fair value.*

A Sale-Leaseback Where Only Minor Rights Are Leased

Assume that Blue Water Marine Company sells equipment for $170,000, which approximates the equipment's fair value, and simultaneously leases it back for a 1-year term by paying $15,000 immediately. The carrying value of the equipment is $150,000, and the equipment has an economic life of 12 years. The accounting for this sale-leaseback begins with recognizing that there is a gain of $20,000, which is the difference between the selling price of $170,000 and the carrying value of the equipment of $150,000. The next step is to determine what percentage of the rights is leased back by Blue Water. In this example, Blue Water leases back less than 10% of the rights because the present value of the rental payment is less than 10% of the fair value of the asset. Since Blue Water retains only minor rights to the asset, the sale-leaseback is treated as two transactions, and the entire gain on the sale portion of the transaction is recognized, as follows:

Cash	170,000	
Equipment (net)		150,000
Gain on Sale		20,000

To record the sale portion of a sale-leaseback transaction in which a gain is indicated and only minor rights are leased back.

The only exception to this accounting for the sale in a sale-leaseback transaction when the seller-lessee retains only minor rights to the use of the equipment is when the yearly rentals are clearly unreasonable. Then, the amount of gain to be recognized is adjusted to an amount that results in reasonable rentals. Using the same example as in the preceding paragraph and supposing that a reasonable rental is $24,500, as compared to the $15,000 that Blue Water is required to pay, then the journal entry to record the sale of the asset and recognize the appropriate amount of the gain is as follows:

Cash	170,000	
Deferred Rent Expense	9,500	
Equipment (net)		150,000
Gain on Sale		29,500

To record the sale portion of a sale-leaseback transaction in which a gain is indicated, only minor rights are leased back, and the rental payments are clearly unreasonable.

Subsequently, the seller-lessee prepares the following journal entry to record the rental payment for the lease:

Rent Expense	24,500	
Deferred Rent Expense		9,500
Cash		15,000

To record the rental payments for the lease portion of a sale-leaseback transaction where only minor rights are retained.

Preparing the journal entries this way when the rental payment(s) are clearly unreasonable allows the appropriate gain to be recognized and an appropriate rental expense to be recorded as indicated by the substance of the transaction rather than by its form.

A Sale-Leaseback Where Substantially All Rights Are Leased

These sale-leaseback transactions are deemed to be financing transactions. For this reason, any indicated gain on the sale portion of the transaction is deferred.

Now assume that Blue Water Marine Company sells some equipment for $170,000, which is also the equipment's fair value, simultaneously leases it back under a 12-year lease at a yearly rental of $24,500 per year, and pays the first payment immediately. The carrying value of the equipment is $150,000, and the equipment has an economic life of 12 years. As with the previous example, the first step in accounting for this sale-leaseback is recognizing that there is a gain of $20,000. Then, it is established that the lease meets at least one of the criteria for being treated as a capital lease, and, therefore, Blue Water has leased back substantially all the rights to use the asset. Thus, the gain on the sale portion of the transaction is deferred, and since the lease is a capital lease, *the deferred gain is recognized in relation to the depreciation charge*. The journal entries for Blue Water to (1) record the sale and defer the gain, (2) record the lease as a capital lease, (3) pay the first lease payment, and (4) recognize the portion of the gain for the first year are shown in Illustration 17B-1.

In regard to entry (4), as with the amortization of the artificial loss, it seems more appropriate to reduce the amount of depreciation expense rather than recognize a gain.

A Sale-Leaseback Where More than Minor but Less than Substantially All Rights Are Leased

For sale-leasebacks in which the lessee leases back more than a minor portion of the rights to the asset but less than substantially all, the FASB decided to limit the recognition of profit to an amount that could not represent borrowings to be repaid, which it defined to be the lesser of the present value of the lease payments or the fair value of the asset. Determining this amount is done using the following steps.

- Step 1: Determine the fair value of the asset.
- Step 2: Compute the present value of the minimum lease payments.

ILLUSTRATION 17B-1

Journal Entries When Substantially All Rights Are Leased Back

(1) Cash   170,000
       Equipment (net)   150,000
       Deferred Gain on Sale   20,000

To record the sale portion of a sale-leaseback transaction in which a gain is indicated and substantially all the rights are leased back.

(2) Asset under Capital Lease   170,000
       Obligation under Capital Lease   170,000

To record the asset and related liability at the present value of the minimum lease payments at 12% for 12 years.

(3) Obligation under Capital Lease   24,500
       Cash   24,500

To record the first lease payment, which was made at time of signing of the sale-leaseback.

(4) Deferred Gain on Sale   1,667
       Depreciation Expense   1,667

To amortize the deferred gain in a straight-line manner, which is consistent with the company's use of the straight-line method of depreciating assets under capital leases.

Computations:
   Deferred gain: $20,000
   Amortization period: 12 years
   Amortization amount/Year: $1,667

- Step 3: Select the smaller of the fair value of the asset (amount in Step 1) and the present value of the minimum lease payments (amount in Step 2).
- Step 4: Compute the gain on the sale of the asset.
- Step 5: Compare the amount of the gain in Step 4 with the amount determined in Step 3. *The amount of the gain recognized is the portion of the gain that exceeds the amount in Step 3.* The rest of the gain is deferred and amortized over the life of the lease in proportion to the amount of depreciation expense on the leased asset.

Consider the following scenarios where Blue Water Marine Company sells equipment that has a carrying value of $150,000 for $210,000, which approximates the fair value of the asset, and then simultaneously leases it back for a yearly rental payment of $30,550.[15] The equipment has an economic life of eight years. In the first scenario, Blue Marine leases the equipment back for two years, and in the second scenario, Blue Marine leases the equipment back for five years. For both scenarios, the indicated gain is $60,000, which is the difference between the fair value of the asset of $210,000 and its carrying value of $150,000. The appropriate journal entries are shown in Illustration 17B-2.

---

[15]The rental payment was computed using annuity due tables and a 12% return.

Chapter 17

ILLUSTRATION 17B-2

Journal Entries When More than Minor but Less than Substantially All Rights Are Leased Back
(sale portion of the transaction)

	2-Year Leaseback	5-Year Leaseback
Step 1: Fair value of the asset	$210,000	$210,000
Step 2: Present value of the rental payments	57,827	123,341
Step 3: Select the smaller of the amounts in Steps 1 and in 2	57,827	123,241
Step 4: Gain on the sale of the asset	60,000	60,000
Step 5: Gain in excess of amount in Step 3 (i.e., the amount to be recognized)	2,173	0

	2-Year Leaseback		5-Year Leaseback	
Cash	210,000		210,000	
Equipment		150,000		150,000
Deferred Gain		57,827		60,000
Gain on Sale		2,173		0

As before, it seems more appropriate to reduce depreciation expense as the deferred gain is amortized, rather than to recognize a gain. So assuming that the straight-line method of depreciation is used to allocate the cost of the asset, the journal entries to amortize the deferred gain in a consistent manner are as follows:

	2-Year Leaseback		5-Year Leaseback	
Deferred Gain	28,914		12,000	
Depreciation Expense		28,914		12,000

To recognize the portion of the deferred gain in relation to the yearly amount of depreciation expense, assuming the use of the straight-line method of depreciation.

Computations:
2-year leaseback:
  Deferred gain: $57,827
  Amount of gain to recognize each year: $57,827/2 years = $28,914

5-year leaseback:
  Deferred gain: $60,000
  Amount of gain to recognize each year: $60,000/5 years = $12,000

Questions

1. Identify the potential advantages to the lessee and the lessor of leasing assets instead of purchasing them.

2. From an accounting perspective, what are the two types of leases? What is the theoretical basis for classifying leases into these major categories? (Don't list the criteria for determining whether a lease is a capital lease. Instead, mention the economic difference between the two leases.)

3. Briefly define the following terms:
   a. Lease term.
   b. Bargain purchase option.
   c. Minimum lease payments.
   d. Minimum rental payments.
   e. Implicit interest rate.
   f. Incremental interest rate.

4. What are the four specific criteria that must be considered by both the lessee and the lessor when classifying a lease contract? Identify the additional two criteria that a lessor must meet before classifying a lease as a capital lease.

5. Why is the amount of the receivable for the lessor of a capital lease different from the amount shown as the payable for the lessee of the same capital lease?

6. ABC Corporation (the lessee) leases an asset from XYZ Inc. (the lessor), making the first payment when the lease is signed. Without determining the amounts to be recorded, explain how the initial journal entries for both the lessee and the lessor are prepared, assuming the lease is (a) an operating lease and (b) a direct financing capital lease.

7. Under what circumstances does the lessee in a capital lease agreement use the lessor's implicit interest rate to determine the present value of the minimum lease payments and to construct an amortization table from which interest expense is recognized?

8. From the standpoint of the lessor, what is the difference between a direct financing lease and a sales-type lease?

9. Identify the specific revenues and expenses of an operating lease and of a capital lease (both direct financing and sales-type) for both the lessor and the lessee.

10. From the standpoint of the lessor, what impact does a guaranteed or an unguaranteed residual value have over the term of the lease? Does either a guaranteed or an unguaranteed residual value impact the accounting for the lessee? How?

11. What are initial direct costs? Which party incurs initial direct costs?

12. (Appendix) Describe a sale-leaseback transaction. Why do such transactions cause accounting difficulties?

13. (Appendix) Define an *artificial loss* in a sale-leaseback transaction.

14. Indicate whether the following statements are *true* or *false*.
   a. For a capital lease, initial direct costs incurred by the lessee should be expensed as incurred.
   b. For a sales-type lease, the lessor should use the lessee's incremental borrowing rate when it is known and it is lower than the lessor's implicit interest rate.
   c. Minimum lease payments include any guaranteed residual value.
   d. Under direct financing leases, initial direct costs are recognized in relationship to the amount of interest earned each period.
   e. (Appendix) Profit or loss on the sale portion of a sale-leaseback transaction is always deferred and recognized in relation to depreciation expense.
   f. In a capital lease for a lessee, each yearly rental payment is allocated between a reduction of the obligation and interest expense, so as to produce a constant rate of return.
   g. Under an operating lease, the lessee assigns lease expense to the period in equal amounts over the life of the lease but never records the obligation to make future lease payments.

Exercises

Exercise 17-1: Computing Lease Payments. Hornacek, Inc. (a lessor) entered into a 10-year noncancelable lease agreement that is considered a capital lease. The terms of the lease require payments at the beginning of the year. The fair value of the asset is $40,000, and Hornacek's cost of capital is 10%.

1. Determine the minimum yearly rental payments.
2. Determine the minimum yearly rental payments, assuming that the payments are due at the end of each lease period.

Exercise 17-2: Computing Yearly Payment Amounts. Compute the minimum lease payments for each of the following situations. (Round amounts to the nearest dollar.)

1. On January 2, 2005, a 5-year lease requiring annual payments with the first payment due immediately was signed. The fair value of the asset is $100,000. The lessor's implicit interest rate is 14%, and the lessee's incremental borrowing rate is 10%.
2. On February 1, 2005, the lessor signed a 17-year lease for some equipment with a fair value of $160,800. The lessor's implicit interest rate is 12%. The lessee guaranteed a residual value of $9,000. The first payment is due immediately.
3. Same as Part (2), except that the residual value is not guaranteed.
4. Same as Part (2), except that the $9,000 is the amount at which the lessee can acquire the leased asset at the end of the lease term, and this amount is anticipated to be considerably less than the fair value of the asset.

Exercise 17-3: Classifying a Lease, with Entries. On January 1, H&K Truck Company leased $60,000 of equipment for three years at an annual payment of $15,000 and also paid a nonrefundable deposit of $12,000. The rental payments are due at the beginning of each lease period, and the equipment is expected to have a 10-year life, at the end of which time it will have no residual value. H&K depreciates similar equipment, using the straight-line method over its useful life. The current rate of interest on similar leases is 12%.

1. How should this lease be classified? Why?
2. Prepare the journal entries for H&K Truck Company for the three years of the lease term.

Exercise 17-4: Computing Lease Revenues. On October 1, 2002, to induce a lessee to enter a lease for office space, Valley Title Company granted the lessee the right to use the office space for the rest of the year without paying rent. Thereafter, the lessee is to pay a monthly rental fee of $1,000 a month. The lease term ends on December 31, 2005.

1. Assuming that this lease is an operating lease, what amount should be reported as lease revenue for 2002? For 2005?
2. What account(s) and associated amount(s), other than lease revenue, would be disclosed on Valley's 2002 financial statements?

Exercise 17-5: Lease Classification, Amortization Table, and Entries. On January 1 of the current year, Jacob, Inc. entered into a lease agreement with Jeremy Enterprises that requires Jacob to make annual payments of $22,000 over eight years, with the first payment due at the signing of the lease. Jacob's incremental borrowing rate is 9%, which is also Jeremy's implicit interest rate. The leased equipment has a fair value of $137,000 at the inception of the lease, which is also the cost to Jeremy. The useful life of the equipment is 10 years. At the end of the lease agreement, Jeremy retains owner-ship of the equipment, and the lease does not contain a bargain purchase option.

1. Is this an operating lease or a capital lease? Why?
2. Prepare the journal entries for Jacob (the lessee) at the lease's inception.
3. Prepare an amortization table for the eight years.
4. Assuming that Jacob's fiscal year-end is December 31, and using the amortiza-tion table from Part (3), prepare the journal entries required on December 31 of the year in which the lease was signed and on January 1 of the next year.

Exercise 17-6: Accounting for Leases. On January 1, 2004, Boone, Inc. entered into a capital lease agreement for some specialized equipment worth $107,000. Boone is required to make five equal annual payments, with the first payment due immedi-ately. The useful life of the equipment is also five years, after which time it is ex-pected the equipment will not have any residual value. Boone's incremental interest rate is 8%, which is also the lessor's implicit interest rate. Boone uses the straight-line method of depreciation.

1. Compute the amount of the minimum payments. Prepare an amortization schedule for the lease obligation for the 5-year period.
2. Prepare all journal entries related to the leased equipment for Boone, Inc. through December 31, 2005.

Exercise 17-7: Classification of Lease and Entries—Lessee. On January 1, 2004, John Long, Inc. leased a vehicle for a 2-year period. The fair value of the vehicle is $25,000, and it has an expected useful life of seven years. The lease agreement calls for $2,840 down and end-of-month payments of $450. At the end of the lease term, John Long has the option to purchase the vehicle for $16,600, which is expected will approximate the vehicle's fair value. John Long, Inc. depreciates all assets using the straight-line method, and its incremental borrowing rate is 12%.

1. How should this lease be classified? Why?
2. Prepare the journal entries for John Long, Inc. at the inception of the lease and at the next three lease payments.

Exercise 17-8: Direct Financing Lease Entries for the Lessee and Lessor. On Jan-uary 1, McCormick leased a machine from Garrett, Inc. under a direct financing lease. At the lease's inception, the machine had a fair market value of $161,500, an ex-pected useful life of 10 years, and no salvage value. The lease term is five years, and annual payments of $40,000 are required at the beginning of each year. McCormick's cost of capital is 12%, which is also Garrett's implicit interest rate in the lease. At the end of the lease term, Garrett will retain ownership of the machine, and there is no bargain purchase option.

Prepare the journal entries related to the leased machine for both McCormick and Garrett for the first two years of the lease, assuming that both McCormick and Garrett have a fiscal year ending on December 31.

Exercise 17-9: Ownership with Subsequent Leasing of an Asset. Nelson Corpora-tion purchased equipment on January 2, 2001, at a cost of $74,000. Nelson depreci-ates such equipment using the straight-line method over its useful life of eight years.

On January 1, 2004, Nelson leased the equipment to Morrell, Inc. for four years at an annual lease payment of $12,000 (first payment due at inception of lease). Nelson will retain ownership of the equipment at the end of the lease term. Morrell's depreciation policy is the same as Nelson's. Assume that at the inception of the lease, the interest rate on similar leases is 10%, and the fair value of the equipment was approximately $43,000, with no change in its estimated useful life.

1. Is this an operating lease or a capital lease? Why?
2. Prepare the journal entries at the inception of the lease for both Morrell and Nelson.
3. Prepare the necessary journal entries for both companies at the end of the current fiscal year.
4. Redo Parts (1) through (3), assuming that the lease term is for only three years instead of four.

Exercise 17-10: Accounting for a Sales-Type Lease (Residual Value). At the beginning of a year, the lessor enters into an agreement that qualifies as a sales-type lease. The following facts are available:

Fair value of the asset	$90,000
Residual value	$6,500
Cost of asset leased	$75,000
Lease term	6 years
Interest rate	14%

The first payment is due immediately.

1. Compute the minimum rental payments.
2. Prepare the journal entry for the lessor at the inception of the lease, assuming that the residual value is guaranteed.
3. How much income should the lessor recognize at the inception of the lease?
4. How much interest income should the lessor recognize for Year 1?
5. Repeat Parts (2) through (4), assuming that the residual value is unguaranteed.

Exercise 17-11: Accounting and Reporting for a Sales-Type Lease. The following information relates to a sales-type capital lease that was entered into on the first day of the company's fiscal year:

Annual payment beginning at the time of signing the lease	$20,000
Nonguaranteed residual value	$10,000
Costs of manufacturing the leased equipment	$100,000
Fair value of the asset	$144,126
Lease term	10 years
Implicit and incremental interest rates	9%

1. Record the journal entries at the inception of the lease for the lessee and lessor.
2. Prepare amortization tables for the lessor and the lessee for all periods.
3. From the amortization table, prepare the journal entries to accrue the interest at the end of the first year.
4. Show how the lessor and the lessee would report the lease accounts on the balance sheet at the end of the first year, being sure to report amounts as either current or long term. The lessee uses the straight-line method of depreciation.

Exercise 17-12: Differentiating between the Effects of Sales-Type Leases and Operating Leases. On the first day of its fiscal year, Lessor leased a machine for 13 years at an annual rental of $10,000 and received the initial payment immediately. The leased property had cost Lessor $70,000, but is usually sold for $85,000. The machine has an estimated useful life of 15 years, and Lessor's implicit interest rate is 8%. Lessor should have accounted for this lease as a sale, but mistakenly treated the lease as an operating lease.

1. What was the effect on Lessor's net earnings and total assets during the first year as a result of this error?
2. What was the effect on Lessor's net earnings and total assets during the second year as a result of this error?
3. At the end of the lease term (i.e., 13 years), will there be any difference in stockholders' equity from treating this lease as an operating lease rather than a sales-type lease? That is, will the error reverse itself over the lease term? Prove your answer mathematically.

Exercise 17-13: Capital Lease—Lessee. On January 1, 2006, Marshall Company entered into a 10-year lease in which title to the equipment will pass to Marshall at the end of the lease term. Payments of $14,295 are made each January, and the first payment was made immediately. The fair value of the leased asset is $100,000, and its economic life is 12 years. Marshall uses the straight-line method of depreciation and assumes a salvage value of zero.

1. Prepare a lease amortization table.
2. Prepare the journal entries for Marshall that are required at January 1, 2006.
3. Show how the amounts related to the leased asset and related obligation will be reported on Marshall's balance sheet and income statement at December 31, 2008.

Exercise 17-14: Capital Lease—Lessee. On September 1, 2005, Russell Company entered into a 5-year lease for a luxury automobile. Title to the automobile does not pass to Russell at the end of the lease, but Russell may purchase the automobile at the end of the lease term for $20,000, which is thought will be its fair value at that time. Russell does not intend to exercise the purchase option. Russell paid $15,000 down and will make monthly payments of $1,188, beginning on October 1, 2005. The annual interest rate on such leases is 9%. The economic life of the asset is six years.

1. Without computing the present value of the minimum lease payments, is this lease a capital lease? Why?
2. Prepare a lease amortization table for Russell.
3. Prepare the journal entry required at September 1, 2005.
4. Show how the amounts related to the leased asset and related obligation will be reported on Russell's balance sheet and income statement at December 31, 2007.

Exercise 17-15: Knowing Some Intricacies of Capital Leases. Answer the questions for each of the following independent situations.

1. A machine with an expected useful life of 15 years is leased under a capital lease agreement for a term of 12 years. The terms of the lease stipulate that title to the leased asset will pass to the lessee at the end of the lease term. Over what period of time should the lessee depreciate the asset?

(continued)

2. A lessee signs a lease to finance the acquisition of some equipment, which allows the purchase of the equipment at the end of five years for an amount that is considered to be a bargain. The lessee could have borrowed the money from the bank at 12%, and he also knows that the lessor normally earns a 15% return on leases of this type. What interest rate should the lessee use in computing the present value of the minimum lease payments?

3. A lessee signs a 10-year lease for a corporate jet. At the time it was built, the jet had an estimated life of 40 years, and it was manufactured 30 years ago. The jet has had excellent maintenance, and the company considers the terms of the lease, including the monthly payment amount, to be the "best deal around." Title to the jet will not pass to the lessee at the end of the lease term, at which time the lessor will most likely scrap or sell it and then finance the acquisition of another jet. Is this a capital lease?

4. **(Research Question)** A lease is entered into that requires monthly lease payments of $5,000 for five years. Title to the asset does not pass to the lessee, and the lessee guarantees that the minimum fair value of the leased asset at the time the lease expires will be $40,000. The lessor wants the lease to continue for the full life of the equipment (which is 15 years) and accordingly included a provision that the lessee would pay a penalty of $25,000 (which is considered a substantial penalty) if the lessee fails to renew the lease at the end of the initial 5-year term. Identify the items that comprise the minimum lease payments, and state what the length of the lease term is.

Exercise 17-16: (Appendix) Sale-Leaseback (AICPA Adapted). On December 31, 2005, Pell, Inc., sold a machine to Flax and simultaneously leased it back for one year. Pertinent information at this date is as follows:

Sales price	$360,000
Carrying amount	$315,000
Estimated remaining useful life	12 years
Present value of lease payments	$34,100
($3,000 for 12 months @ 12%)	

At December 31, 2005, how much should Pell report as deferred revenue from the sale of the machine?

Exercise 17-17: (Appendix) Sale-Leaseback (AICPA Adapted). On January 1, 2004, Marsh Company sold an airplane with an estimated useful life of 10 years. At the same time, Marsh leased back the airplane for three years under a lease classified as an operating lease. Pertinent data are:

Sales price	$500,000
Book value of airplane	100,000
Monthly rental under leaseback	5,100
Present value of lease rentals	153,000

1. How much profit should Marsh report from the sale of the airplane?
2. Using the straight-line method of depreciation, what is Marsh's net depreciation expense for the airplane for the year ended December 31, 2004?

Exercise 17-18: (Appendix) Sale-Leaseback (AICPA Adapted). The following information pertains to equipment sold by Bard Co. to Kerr on December 31, 2004:

Sales price	$300,000
Book value	$100,000
Estimated remaining economic life	20 years

Simultaneously with the sale, Bard leased back the equipment for a period of 16 years.

1. How much profit should Bard report from the sale of the airplane?
2. Using the straight-line method of depreciation, what is Bard's net depreciation expense for the airplane for the year ended December 31, 2005?

Problems

Problem 17-1: Classifying and Accounting for Operating and Capital Leases. On January 1, 2003, Hopwood, Inc. leased a piece of machinery from Distill Corporation. The market value of the machinery at the beginning of the lease was $200,000, which is also its cost to Distill. Its estimated useful life is 10 years, and the lease term is six years. Quarterly payments are $9,500, and the first payment is payable at the inception of the lease. Hopwood uses the straight-line method of depreciation, but Distill Corporation uses the sum-of-the-years'-digits method of depreciation. The cost of capital for both Hopwood and Distill is 12%. For Hopwood, there are no important uncertainties regarding unreimbursable future costs, and the collectibility of the minimum lease payments is reasonably assured.

Required:
1. With regard to the lessor and the lessee, is this lease an operating lease or a capital lease? Explain your answer.
2. Prepare the necessary journal entries related to the leased machinery for the first year of the lease for both the lessee and the lessor.
3. Redo Requirements 1 and 2, assuming all the same facts except that the lease period is for eight years.

Problem 17-2: Classification and Effects of Misclassification. On January 1, 2003, Myron Company leased equipment to Heidi's Jeans & Apparel. The lease is noncancelable and requires semiannual lease payments of $21,000 for five years, with the first payment due at the lease inception. The equipment has a cost to Myron of $225,000, which is also its fair value. The expected useful life of the equipment is nine years. At the lease's expiration, Myron will retain ownership of the equipment, and there is no bargain purchase option. Both Myron and Heidi's depreciate all equipment using the straight-line method over its useful life. The current cost of capital is 6% for both Myron and Heidi's. For Myron, there are no important uncertainties regarding unreimbursable future costs, and the collectibility of the minimum lease payments is reasonably assured.

Required:
1. Should the lease be classified as an operating lease or a capital lease? Why?
2. Suppose that Myron and Heidi's both misclassified the lease and that December 31 is the fiscal year-end for both Myron and Heidi's. Determine the effect of this error on their 2003 and 2004 income statements. (Show your work.)

Problem 17-3: Accounting for Leases. On January 1, 2003 (the first day of its fiscal year), Royce Industries entered into a 12-year noncancelable lease that requires annual payments of $70,000, with the first payment due immediately. Royce's incremental borrowing rate is 10%, and the lessor's implicit interest rate, which is known to Royce, is 12%. Ownership of the asset remains with the lessor at the expiration of the lease, and there is no bargain purchase option. The leased property has an economic life of 15 years. Royce depreciates all assets by using the straight-line method.

Required:
1. Explain why the lease qualifies as a capital lease for Royce.
2. Prepare the journal entry necessary by Royce at the inception of the lease.
3. Prepare a lease amortization table for the 12-year period.
4. Prepare the journal entries for 2005 and 2008 (a) to accrue interest at year-end, (b) to record the lease payments, and (c) to record depreciation.

Problem 17-4: Accounting and Reporting for a Sales-Type Lease. Melville leased equipment from Ahab Corporation on July 1, 2003, for an 8-year period. Payments of $60,000 are due each year, beginning on the date the lease was signed. Ahab's implicit interest rate was 10%. Melville was aware of Ahab's implicit interest rate, and his incremental borrowing rate was 12%. The cost of the equipment to Ahab was $280,000. Ownership of the property does not pass to the lessor at the end of the lease, and neither was there a bargain purchase option. Both the lessor and the lessee have a June 30 fiscal year-end.

Required:
For the lessor:

1. Record the journal entry at the inception of the lease.
2. Prepare an amortization table for all periods.
3. From the amortization table, prepare the journal entry to accrue the interest at the end of the first year.
4. Show how the lease—all accounts affected—would be reported on the June 30, 2004 balance sheet, being sure to separate the net investment between the current and long-term portions.

For the lessee:

1. Record the journal entry at the inception of the lease.
2. Prepare an amortization table for all periods.
3. From the amortization table, prepare the journal entry to accrue the interest at the end of the first year.
4. Show how the lease—all accounts affected—would be reported on the balance sheet at the end of the first year, being sure to separate (if necessary) the lease obligation between current and long term.

Problem 17-5: Accounting and Reporting for Sales-Type Leases. On January 1, 2005, Tarzan Company entered into a noncancelable lease agreement with Burroughs Company to lease a machine that was carried in the accounting records of Tarzan at $16,000. Total payments under the lease agreement, which expires on December 31, 2014, aggregate $29,590. Payments of $2,959 are due each January 1, and the first payment was made on January 1, 2005. The lessor's implicit interest rate is 10%. The lessee does not know the lessor's implicit interest rate, nor is it practical for him to learn it; his incremental borrowing rate is 14%. Burroughs expects to be able to collect all amounts owed, and there are no important uncertainties regarding any unre-imbursable costs.

Required:
For the lessor:

1. Record the journal entry at the inception of the lease for this sales-type lease.
2. Prepare an amortization table for all periods.
3. From the amortization table, prepare the journal entry to accrue the interest at the end of the first year.
4. Show how the lease—all accounts affected—would be reported on the balance sheet at December 31, 2005, being sure to separate the lease receivable between current and long term.

For the lessee:

1. Record the journal entry at the inception of the lease for this sales-type lease.
2. Prepare an amortization table for all periods.
3. From the amortization table, prepare the journal entry to accrue the interest at the end of the first year.
4. Show how the lease—all accounts affected—would be reported on the balance sheet at December 31, 2005, being sure to separate the lease obligation between current and long term.

Problem 17-6: Guaranteed Residual Value. Speedy Leasing entered into a 5-year lease with Acme Corporation on January 1, 2005, for a machine that has a fair value of $63,914. The cost to Speedy is $40,000. The terms of the lease require Acme to pay equal annual amounts at the beginning of each year. Further, Acme guarantees that the asset will have a fair value of $20,000 at the end of the lease term. Speedy will retain ownership of the leased asset at the end of the lease term, and there is no bargain purchase option. The economic life of the asset is eight years. Speedy's implicit interest rate, of which Acme is aware, is 15%. Both companies have a December 31 fiscal year-end.

Required:
1. Compute the annual rental payments.
2. Prepare amortization tables for both the lessee and the lessor.
3. Record the following journal entries for both the lessee and the lessor:
   a. The inception of the lease.
   b. Adjusting entry(ies) at December 31, 2005.
4. For both the lessee and the lessor, show how the amounts related to this lease would be reported on their year-end balance sheets.
5. Prepare the necessary journal entries at the end of the lease term for both the lessee and the lessor, assuming that the actual residual value is:
   a. $24,000.
   b. $15,000.

Problem 17-7: Unguaranteed Residual Value.

Required:
Using the information in Problem 17-6, redo the requirements, assuming that the residual value is not guaranteed.

Problem 17-8: Guaranteed and Unguaranteed Residual Values. The following data apply to a capital lease entered into on January 3, 2004:

a. Leased asset—construction crane.
b. Cost to lessor, $450,000.
c. Estimated useful life, 20 years.
d. Lessor's normal selling price, $600,000.
e. Lease provisions:
   (1) The asset will remain with the lessor at the end of the lease.
   (2) Lease term, 15 years.
   (3) Estimated residual value at the end of the lease term, $100,000 (80% of which is guaranteed).
   (4) Payments due each January 3, beginning at the signing of the lease.
f. Lessor's implicit interest rate, which is known by the lessee, is 12%.

Required:
1. Without computing the present value of the minimum lease payments, why is it known that this is a capital lease?
2. Compute the annual rental payments.
3. Prepare amortization tables for both the lessee and the lessor.
4. Record the following journal entries for both the lessee and the lessor:
   a. The inception of the lease.
   b. Adjusting entry(ies) at December 31, 2005 (i.e., the end of the second year).
5. Show for both the lessee and the lessor the amounts that would be reported on their year-end financial statements for 2005 (i.e., the end of the second year).
6. Prepare the necessary journal entries at the end of the lease term for both the lessee and the lessor, assuming that the actual residual value is:
   a. $120,000.
   b. $70,000.

Problem 17-9: Bargain Purchase Option. A lease was entered into with the following terms:

a. Lessor's cost of the asset being leased is $150,000, and the fair value of the asset at the time the lease was entered into is $225,000.
b. Lease term is for four years, starting July 1, 2006.
c. Payments are due every July 1, with the first payment due immediately.
d. The lessor's implicit interest rate is 12%, and the lessee is aware of this.
e. The terms of the lease do not transfer ownership, but there is a provision allowing the lessee to acquire the asset for $17,000 at the end of the lease term, which is thought will be significantly below its fair value on that date.

Required:
1. Compute the annual rental payments.
2. Prepare amortization tables for both the lessee and the lessor.
3. Prepare the necessary journal entries at the end of the lease term for both the lessee and the lessor, assuming that the:
   a. Bargain purchase option is exercised.
   b. Bargain purchase option is not exercised, and the fair value of the asset at the time was $50,000. Also, assume that the lessee had been depreciating the asset over its economic life of six years, with the assumption that it would have no salvage value.

Problem 17-10: Bargain Purchase Option. Lessor and Lessee contract for the lease of an automobile for 12 rentals of $1,780 each, with the first rental due immediately and the other payments to be paid at the beginning of each of the next 11 quarters. They agree that, at the end of the lease term, Lessee can acquire the automobile for $2,500, which they believe will be a bargain. The interest rate is 3% per quarter. The cost of the automobile to Lessor is $14,000. The automobile has a useful life of six years.

Required:

1. Prepare the journal entries at the inception of the lease for both Lessee and Lessor.
2. Prepare an amortization table that can be used by either Lessee or Lessor.
3. Prepare the journal entries required at the end of the lease term by Lessee and Lessor, assuming that Lessee exercises the purchase option and the fair value of the automobile is $5,000.
4. Prepare the journal entries required at the end of the lease term by Lessee and Lessor, assuming that Lessee does not exercise the purchase option, and the fair value of the automobile is $5,000.

Problem 17-11: High-Risk Lease. Silver Reef Leasing is considering leasing some equipment to a high-risk lessee, meaning that there is a higher-than-normal probability that the lessee is not a going concern. The factors significant to the lease are as follows:

a. The cost and fair value of the equipment is $30,000.
b. The term of the lease will be six years, which is also the economic life of the equipment. The estimated residual value at the end of the six years is zero.
c. Silver Reef's implicit interest rate is 12%.
d. The lessee is wanting to lease the equipment because it is considered a high risk, and the best interest rate it can obtain from a bank to borrow the money and buy the equipment is 18%.
e. Title to the leased asset will stay with Silver Reef at the end of the lease.
f. Both Silver Reef and the lessee use the straight-line method to depreciate similar assets, and both have a fiscal year-end of December 31.

Required:

1. How should Silver Reef classify this asset? Discuss the various elements of the lease that cause uncertainty regarding the lease's classification.
2. Assuming that Silver Reef decides to classify the lease as a capital lease, which interest rate (i.e., 12% or 18%) should Silver Reef use to determine the annual lease payments? Why?
3. Based upon your answer to Requirement 2, determine the yearly payments, assuming that the first payment is to be paid at the signing of the lease, and prepare the journal entry for Silver Reef at the inception of the lease.

Problem 17-12: Korean GAAP vs. U.S. GAAP. Samwoo Co. is considering the possibility of listing its equity shares on the New York Stock Exchange and understands that in order to do this it must reconcile its accounting practices to U.S. GAAP. A significant difference between its accounting practices and U.S. GAAP is the way that certain leases are accounted for. To determine the effect of this accounting difference on its financial statements, the company has gathered the following details related to a typical lease contract:

Useful life of the leased asset	10 years
Lease period	8 years
Annual lease payment (due at end of year)	$30,000
Expected residual value at the end of lease period	$25,000

Ownership of the leased asset is retained by the lessor at the expiration of the lease, and a bargain purchase option does not exist. However, the residual value is guaranteed by a third party. Samwoo accounts for this type of lease as an operating lease. Samwoo depreciates all equipment by using the straight-line method, and the company's cost of capital is 8%.

Required:

Analyze the balance sheet and income statement effects of conforming to U.S. GAAP for the above lease over the lease period, instead of the typical method followed by Samwoo.

Problem 17-13: Alternatives for Financing the Acquisition of Assets. Montgomery Services is in need of an item of equipment that has an expected life of five years. After exploring various alternatives, the method of financing the purchase has been narrowed to the following three options:

Option 1: A bank will finance the acquisition. Montgomery then will make monthly payments of $2,450 to the bank, with the first payment due one month from delivery of the equipment. Montgomery also will pay $1,800 to have the equipment delivered. Maintenance costs are expected to be approximately $2,000 for the first three years, $4,500 for the fourth year, and $6,000 for the fifth year. Presume that payments are made at the end of each year.

Option 2: Leasing Co. has offered to lease the equipment to Montgomery for five years at a monthly payment of $3,000, with the first payment due immediately. Leasing Co. will incur all shipping costs and any necessary maintenance costs on the equipment over the life of the lease.

Option 3: XYZ Co. will sell the equipment to Montgomery at a discounted price of $98,000. Shipping and handling costs of $2,500 will be charged to Montgomery. Payment is due on delivery. In addition, XYZ offers an optional maintenance contract for an additional $15,000, whereupon XYZ will perform all maintenance services over the life of the equipment at no cost to Montgomery.

Required:

Determine from a discounted cash-flow perspective which of the three options is preferable. Montgomery's cost of capital is 12%.

Cases

Case 17-1: Delta Air Lines, Incorporated. Delta Air Lines is one of the largest airline companies in the world. Based on 1998 data, Delta had the most departures and carried more passengers than any other airline in the United States. Like most airlines, it leases many of its assets, including aircraft, airport terminal and maintenance facilities, ticket offices, and other property and equipment. As of the end of the 1999 fiscal year, the company operated a total of 584 aircraft. Of these, 256 were leased. Most of these lease arrangements are structured so as to avoid meeting any of the FASB's criteria for a capital lease; hence, both the asset and related liability are excluded from the balance sheet.

The following balance sheet is for the fiscal year ending June 30, 1999. In addition, the note that explains Delta's leasing obligations is presented. Delta's net income for 1999 was $1.1 billion. Use this information to answer the questions that follow it.

Delta Air Lines
Balance Sheet
For the Period Ending June 30, 1999 and 1998
(in millions)

Assets	1999	1998
CURRENT ASSETS:		
Cash and cash equivalents	$ 1,124	$ 1,077
Short-term investments	19	557
Accounts receivable, net of allowance for uncollectible accounts of $30 at June 30, 1999 and $36 at June 30, 1998	602	938
Deferred income taxes	403	464
Prepaid expenses and other	524	326
Total current assets	$ 2,672	$ 3,362
PROPERTY AND EQUIPMENT:		
Flight equipment	$13,389	$11,180
Less accumulated depreciation	4,405	3,895
	$ 8,984	$ 7,285
Flight equipment under capital leases	$ 515	$ 515
Less accumulated amortization	264	216
	$ 251	$ 299
Ground property and equipment	$ 3,862	$ 3,285
Less accumulated depreciation	2,123	1,854
	$ 1,739	$ 1,431
Advance payments for equipment	493	306
Total property and equipment	$11,467	$ 9,321
OTHER ASSETS:		
Marketable equity securities	$ 523	$ 424
Investments in associated companies	300	326
Cost in excess of net assets acquired, net of accumulated amortization of $121 at June 30, 1999, and $112 at June 30, 1998	782	265
Leasehold and operating rights, net of accumulated amortization of $220 at June 30, 1999, and $209 at June 30, 1998	113	124
Other noncurrent assets	687	781
Total other assets	$ 2,405	$ 1,920
Total assets	$16,544	$14,603

Liabilities and Shareowners' Equity	1999	1998
CURRENT LIABILITIES:		
Current maturities of long-term debt	$ 660	$ 67
Current obligations under capital leases	39	63
Accounts payable and misc. accrued liabilities	2,144	2,025
Air traffic liability	1,819	1,667
Accrued rent	195	202
Accrued salaries and vacation pay	470	553
Total current liabilities	$ 5,327	$ 4,577
NONCURRENT LIABILITIES:		
Long-term debt	$ 1,756	$ 1,533
Postretirement benefits	1,894	1,873
Accrued rent	720	651
Capital leases	196	249
Deferred income taxes	820	262
Other	470	511
Total noncurrent liabilities	$ 5,856	$ 5,079
DEFERRED CREDITS:		
Deferred gain on sale and leaseback transactions	$ 642	$ 694
Manufacturers' and other credits	76	55
Total deferred credits	$ 718	$ 749
Total Employee Stock Ownership Plan Preferred Stock	$ 195	$ 175
SHAREOWNERS' EQUITY:		
Common stock, $1.50 par value; authorized 450,000,000 shares; issued 179,763,547 shares at June 30, 1999 and 176,566,178 shares at June 30, 1998	$ 270	$ 265
Additional paid-in capital	3,208	3,034
Retained earnings	2,756	1,687
Accumulated other comprehensive income	149	89
Treasury stock at cost, 41,209,828 shares at June 30, 1999 and 26,115,784 shares at June 30, 1998	(1,935)	(1,052)
Total shareowners' equity	$ 4,448	$ 4,023
Total liabilities and shareowners' equity	$16,544	$14,603

NOTE 6. LEASE OBLIGATIONS

Our Company leases aircraft, airport terminal and maintenance facilities, ticket offices and other property and equipment. We record rent expense on a straight-line basis over the life of the lease. Rental expense for operating leases totaled $1.1 billion in fiscal 1999, $0.9 billion in fiscal 1998 and $0.9 billion in fiscal 1997. Amounts due under capital leases are recorded as liabilities, and our interest in assets acquired under capital leases are shown as assets on our Consolidated Balance Sheets.

The following table summarizes our minimum rental commitments under capital leases and operating leases with initial or remaining terms of more than one year as of June 30, 1999:

Year Ending June 30 (In millions)	Capital Leases	Operating Leases
2000	$ 63	$ 1,020
2001	57	1,030
2002	57	1,040
2003	48	1,020
2004	32	980
After 2004	40	9,440
Total minimum lease payments	$297	$14,530
Less amounts of lease payments which represent interest	62	
Present value of future minimum capital lease payments	$235	
Less current obligations under capital leases	39	
Long-term capital lease obligations	$196	

As of June 30, 1999, we operated 208 aircraft under operating leases and 48 aircraft under capital leases. These leases have remaining terms ranging from 6 months to 18 years. Several municipalities and airport authorities have issued special facility revenue bonds to build or improve airport terminal and maintenance facilities that we lease. Under these operating lease agreements, we are required to make rental payments that are sufficient to pay principal and interest on these bonds.

1. How many of the leased aircraft are capital leases, and how many are operating leases? What are the potential advantages to Delta of leasing?
2. Explain the theory behind the classification of leases as capital leases and operating leases. Given that Delta's lease payments on most of its capital leases are noncancelable, in your opinion, should Delta be required to show a liability for these payments on its balance sheet?
3. Using the balance sheet for 1999, calculate Delta's debt/equity ratio.
4. Estimate the average interest rate for the capital leases. (*Hint:* Either the internal rate of return—IRR—function of a calculator or a spreadsheet can be used.) Using this average interest rate, compute the present value of the minimum lease payments for the operating leases above. If Delta had classified all of its noncancelable leases as capital leases, what would be the effect on its:
   a. debt/equity?
   b. return on assets?
   c. return on equity?
   (Assume the net earnings effect from depreciating leased assets versus recognizing lease expense.)

18

*A*ccounting FOR Pensions

A company sponsors a pension plan in which, for every year an employee works, the employee receives a benefit upon retirement of 3% of his highest year's salary multiplied by the number of years he has worked. If an employee works 20 years for the company and his highest salary was $50,000, upon retirement he will receive an annual payment of $30,000 (3% × 20 years × $50,000). So if during the current year the company employs 20 people whose average age is 35, average salary is $30,000, and average retirement age is 62, how much is the liability (and the associated expense) that the company should record for the current year, assuming that a person lives for 18 years after retiring?

Even though this scenario is for a relatively small company, the important questions surrounding the measuring of the pension liability and associated expense are illustrated. The starting point in measuring the pension liability and expense is to measure the pension benefits as defined by the pension benefit formula, which means that the following questions have to be answered:

- How many of the 20 people employed will work to retirement so as to be able to receive a retirement benefit?
- At retirement, how many years will they have worked so that their retirement benefits can be computed?
- What will be their highest salary during employment?

Once these questions are answered, the yearly retirement benefits can be computed. Then, to measure the company's pension liability, the following additional set of questions needs to be answered:

- How many years after retiring will a worker receive pension benefits?
- Since all liabilities are recorded at their present value, what discount rate should be used?

These are not all the questions that must be answered when measuring pension liabilities and expenses, but they are sufficient to illustrate the difficulty of these measuring pension liabilities and the associated expenses.

Learning Objectives

- Explain the difference between a defined contribution pension plan and a defined benefit pension plan.
- Prepare the journal entries for a defined contribution pension plan.
- Define the elements that comprise pension expense under a defined benefit pension plan.
- Compute pension expense for a defined benefit plan.
- Illustrate how the balance of the prepaid asset/accrued liability account is determined.
- Explain when a minimum pension liability is reported, how it is recorded, and when it is necessary to report part of it as a component of other comprehensive income.

Theory and Definitions

In Chapter 12, the three basic accounting and reporting problems for any liability were introduced as: existence, valuation (or measurement), and classification.

Accounting for leases is an example of where the primary question is whether a liability exists. Once it has been determined that a liability exists (i.e., a capital lease has been entered into), the accounting problems of measurement and classification can be handled. In a similar way, the major problem in accounting for pensions is measuring the amount (i.e., the valuation) of the pension liability and the related expense.[1] Once this question has been answered, the basic journal entries are easily prepared.

© GETTY IMAGES, INC./PHOTODISC

A **pension plan** is an arrangement between a company and its employees where the company promises to pay the employees an annuity when they retire or are disabled in return for their working for the company before they retire. A pension plan in which the employer satisfies his pension obligation *by paying into the pension plan a specified amount each year* is called a **defined contribution pension plan**. This amount is usually some percentage of the employee's salary that is invested by a third party. For these plans, the benefits the retiree ultimately receives depend upon how well the funds are invested and the strength or performance of the national and global economy. So the employee/retiree bears the investment risk and receives the associated rewards of that risk. Once the employer has made the guaranteed payments to the pension plan, he is absolved of any further responsibility. An example of this type of pension plan is TIAA/CREF, which is likely the pension plan arrangement your professors have with your educational institution.

---

[1]Liabilities for postretirement benefits and postemployement benefits are discussed in Appendix B at the end of this chapter.

A pension plan where the *employer guarantees the annuity amount to be received at retirement or disability* is called a **defined benefit pension plan**. This guaranteed amount is defined in the plan and is based on such factors as age at retirement, years of service, and salary. The opening scenario is an example of a defined benefit plan. The employer has the responsibility to fund such a pension plan at a sufficient level so that an adequate amount of money will be available to pay retirement benefits when the employees retire. Determining the required periodic amounts to pay a third party so that a sufficient amount is accumulated is the task of an actuary and is based upon such estimates as mortality tables, expected ages at retirement, and expected future rates of return.[2]

Thus, the difference between defined contribution plans and defined benefit plans is that a defined contribution plan defines the amount to be contributed and leaves undefined the amount the retiree will receive at retirement. A defined benefit plan defines the amount the retiree will receive at retirement and leaves undefined the amount the employer is to contribute each year to the plan.

Interestingly, when corporations first began implementing pension plans, defined benefit plans predominated, and the typical (and inappropriate) accounting was to recognize as yearly expense only the cash paid to retirees during the year. With the implementation of pension accounting rules requiring accrual accounting—and the resulting recognition of rather large estimated liabilities—corporations began moving away from defined benefit plans to defined contribution plans that had smaller liabilities of a known amount. This is an example of the impact that appropriate financial accounting and reporting standards have had on business and the economy. By measuring the economic cost of implementing pension plans, more informed decisions were made that changed business practice and affected the economy.

An understanding of some additional terms is necessary to comprehending pensions and pension accounting. A **contributory pension plan** is a defined contribution plan or defined benefit plan that requires the employee to contribute some amount to the fund from which the future retirement payments will be paid. In contrast, under a **noncontributory pension plan**, the employer contributes all amounts to the retirement fund. When the benefits that an employee will receive upon retirement are no longer contingent upon his continuing employment, the pension benefits are said to be **vested benefits**. For most plans, a certain minimum number of years must be worked before the retirement benefits become partially or fully vested.

Under current GAAP, the *theory and objective of accounting for all pension plans, whether they are defined contribution plans or defined benefit plans, is to recognize the pension costs in the period that they are incurred and not when the cash is paid.*

Accounting and Reporting for Defined Contribution Plans

For defined contribution plans, the employer recognizes an expense for the year in the amount that *should be contributed* to the pension plan. The employer reports a liability on the balance sheet only when the accumulated payments to the

---

[2]A pay-as-you-go retirement plan is one where pension plan administrators intend that the amounts collected during the year will be sufficient to pay retirement benefits to retirees that year. The only retirement plan where such a funding pattern is still legal is the federal social security system.

pension plan are less than the total required payments, and the employer recognizes an asset when the accumulated payments to the plan are greater than the total required payments. Assuming that a company with a defined contribution plan has a pension expense of $200,000 for the year but is able to fund only $150,000 of that amount, the journal entry to record the pension expense, the related liability/asset, and the funding is as follows:

Pension Expense	200,000	
Pension Liability		50,000
Cash		150,000

To record pension expense, funding, and the related liability for a defined contribution pension plan.

In the same way, a pension asset is recognized when the accumulated amount paid to the pension plan exceeds the total pension expense.

In the notes to the financial statements, the employer is required to disclose a description of the pension plan (including the employee groups covered), how the required contributions are determined, and the nature and effect of significant matters that affect comparability between periods.[3] This is the extent of what needs to be known regarding the accounting and financial reporting for a defined contribution plan.

Accounting and Reporting for Defined Benefit Plans

Balance Sheet Reporting:

Funding > Expense = Report Asset

Expense > Funding = Report Liability

The accounting for defined benefit plans is much the same as the accounting for defined contribution plans in that a liability is recognized when the accumulated amount a company has paid is less than the accumulated amount that should have been paid, and a pension asset arises when the accumulated amount paid exceeds the accumulated amount that should have been contributed. However, the computing of the yearly pension expense, in contrast to defined contribution plans, is based upon many estimates, including actuarial calculations.

For defined benefit pension plans, pension expense is comprised of the following components:

1. Service cost.
2. Interest on the projected benefit obligation.
3. Expected return on plan assets.
4. Amortization of prior service cost.
5. Amortization of net gains and losses.

To illustrate how each of these elements is included in determining pension expense for a year, an extended (and simplified) example will be used. Suppose that Jared is 40 years old and has worked five years for Castro & Co., which on January 1, 2005, adopts a defined benefit pension plan. The plan defines the retirement benefit according to the following **pension benefit formula**:

$$\text{Retirement Annuity} = 3\% \times \begin{array}{c}\text{Number of Years}\\\text{of Service}\end{array} \times \begin{array}{c}\text{Average Salary}\\\text{for Last 3 Years}\end{array}$$

Note that no credit is given for the five years Jared worked prior to January 1, 2005.

[3]*FASB Statement No. 87*, "Employers' Accounting for Pension Plans," par. 63–66.

To illustrate how this benefit formula is used to compute the retirement benefits and the resulting pension expense and pension liability amounts, assume that Jared plans to retire from Castro & Co. at age 65 and it is anticipated that his average salary for the last three years of employment will be $50,000. In this case, Jared can anticipate receiving a yearly retirement annuity of $37,500, which is computed as:

$37,500 = (3% per year) × (25 years he will work) × ($50,000 average salary)

Component 1 of Pension Expense: Service Cost

Importantly, Castro & Co. decides to fund its pension plan by placing an amount *at the end of each year* in a trust (under the control of a third party), so that when Jared retires, the amount accumulated will be sufficient to pay Jared $37,500 at the *end of each year* of retirement. (The reason for italicizing "end of each year" is that the computations will now involve ordinary annuity, instead of annuity due, calculations.) For purposes of making some necessary calculations in this illustration, it is presumed that:

• Jared will work until age 65, or for 25 years after inception of the pension plan,
• Jared will live for 20 years after retiring (or to age 85), and
• An appropriate interest rate is 8%.

Figure 18-1 illustrates the growth of the monies invested by Castro & Co. for Jared's retirement and the subsequent withdrawal of retirement funds.

FIGURE 18-1

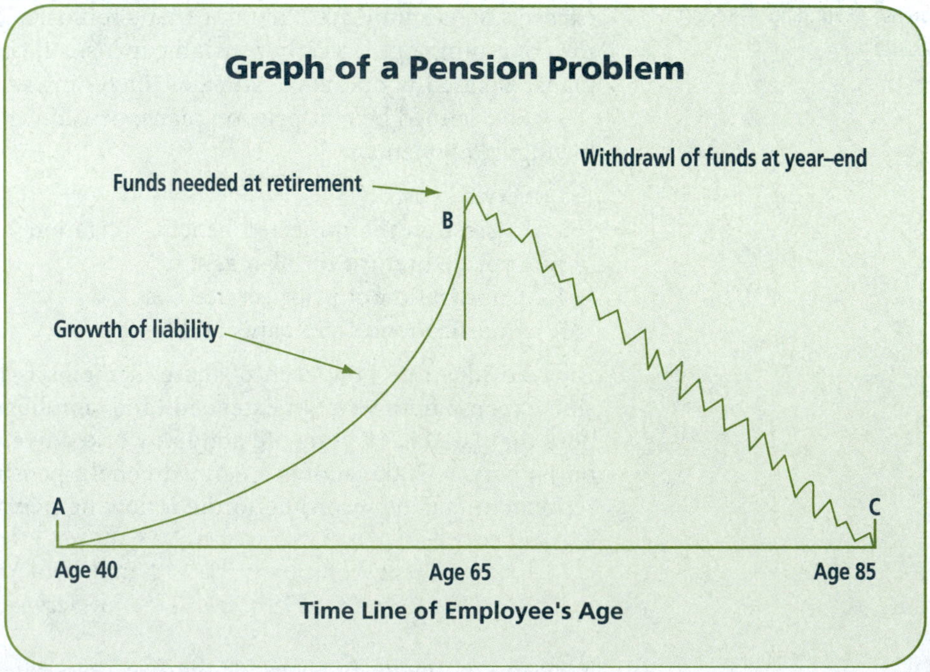

Graph of a Pension Problem

Funds needed at retirement
Withdrawl of funds at year–end
B
Growth of liability
A
C
Age 40
Age 65
Age 85
Time Line of Employee's Age

The first part of the graph in Figure 18-1 (with the upward sloping curve) represents the growth of Castro's pension liability. At first, the liability is very small because Jared has worked only a few years. The longer Jared works, the greater becomes Castro's liability, primarily because of the compounding nature of interest.

The second part of the graph in Figure 18-1 (with the downward stair-stepping curve) represents the decrease in the pension liability because of payments made to Jared after his retirement. If one year after retiring (remember the ordinary annuity assumption), Jared is paid $37,500, the pension liability is reduced by that much. But during the next year, the liability grows due to the earning of interest. Then, two years after retiring, Jared is paid another $37,500, which again reduces the pension liability. During the third year, the liability grows again because of interest earned. And so it continues for 20 years, at which time the liability is zero.

Point B on Figure 18-1 represents the pension liability at the time Jared retires. This liability is the present value of the yearly retirement payments of $37,500 until Jared is 85, or for 20 years. Using the present value of an ordinary annuity table, the pension liability when Jared retires is $368,181, which is computed as the present value of an annuity for 20 years at 8% (i.e., 9.81815) multiplied by the $37,500 yearly retirement benefit. [See Table 18-1A in Appendix A at the end of the chapter (p. 875) for mathematical verification of the $368,181.]

This $368,181 is neither Castro's expense for the year nor its liability at the end of 2005. To determine those amounts, a second calculation is required, which is the yearly amount that will accumulate to the $368,181. This yearly amount is Castro's expense. It is computed by dividing the $368,181 by the future amount of an ordinary annuity for 25 years[4] at 8% (the factor is 73.10594), which is $5,036. [See Table 18-2A in Appendix A (p. 876) for mathematical verification of this amount.] This $5,036 is called **service cost**, which is defined as the actuarial present value of benefits attributed by the pension benefit formula to services rendered by employees during that period.

Note the following important aspects of what was covered earlier.

1. By working during 2005, Jared has earned retirement benefits for only one year, but the calculations assume that he will work at Castro until he retires.
2. Once various assumptions have been made, Castro's yearly service cost and liability can be computed for any year until Jared retires. (See Table 18-2A in Appendix A.)
3. Jared's current salary was not used in the previous computations; rather, his projected salary was used in computing the retirement benefits. By using Jared's projected salary, the $368,181—and the liability balance for any particular year—is called the **projected benefit obligation (PBO)**. The PBO is defined as the actuarial present value as of a date of all benefits attributed by the pension benefit formula to employee service rendered, using assumptions as to future compensation levels.

Hopefully, the elements of the technical definition can be seen in the prior example, and, as a result, the essence of the definition can be restated in your words. The PBO is used extensively in accounting for defined benefit plans, and therefore an understanding of its essential nature is critical.

[4]The 25 years is the length of time from the current year-end to the time that Jared will receive his first retirement payment, which, because of using ordinary annuities, will be one year after he retires. So being 40 when the plan was adopted and having worked one year, that means there will be 25 years for the fund to grow to $368,181 before Jared receives his first payment.

This Is the Real World

Considering that companies hire many employees at different ages—and therefore with different expectations regarding the number of years that will be worked before retirement—along with estimates of turnover, mortality rates, etc., it is easy to understand why computing service cost is difficult. Those estimations are the actuary's job. This example is given primarily to help in understanding what the various pension terms mean. The authors consider it more valuable for the student to be able to define those terms in their own words rather than memorizing definitions.

EXTENDING
the Concept

Using Table 18-2A in Appendix A, what is the service cost for 2010 and the liability at December 31, 2010?

Answers: The expense is $5,036, and the PBO is $36,944.

In the given example, if Jared's present salary had been used in the calculations, rather than an estimate of his future salary, Castro's liability at any year-end or when Jared retires (i.e., Point B in Figure 18-1, p. 858) is called the **accumulated benefit obligation (ABO)**. In computing the ABO, it is still assumed that Jared will work 25 years and then retire and receive benefits for 20 years after retiring. So the only difference between the PBO and the ABO is which salary to use—the projected salary or the actual salary.

For the first year of Castro & Co.'s pension plan (i.e., 2005), service cost is the only element of pension expense. The journal entry for the first year, assuming that Castro & Co. fully funds the pension plan, is as follows:

Journal Entry #1—Pension expense with only service cost

Pension Expense	5,036	
Cash		5,036

To recognize pension expense and the pension funding for 2005.

As with defined contribution plans, a liability is recognized if Castro & Co. underfunds the pension plan, or an asset is recognized if Castro overfunds the pension plan.

Components 2 and 3 of Pension Expense: Interest Cost and Return on Plan Assets

Continuing with the Castro & Co. example, pension expense for the second year (i.e., 2006) consists of several components. The first component is the same service cost amount of $5,036. Unless the pension benefit formula or one of the actuarial assumptions change (e.g., the interest rate, how long Jared will live after retiring, etc.), this $5,036 is the service cost for every year until Jared retires.

The second component of pension expense in 2006 is an **interest cost**, which is defined as the expected increase in the PBO due to the passage of time. (See the first part of the graph in Figure 18-1, p. 858.) So an interest cost of $403[5] is added to the current year's service cost in determining the pension expense for 2006. (See Table 18-2A, p. 876, for the computations of interest cost for the 25 years that Jared works.) The interest rate used to compute the interest component of pension expense is referred to as the **discount rate**. This rate should re-

---

[5]This amount is computed by multiplying the prior year PBO balance of $5,036 by the 8% discount rate.

flect the rates at which pension benefits could be settled, such as the implicit rates in current annuity contracts, and not the assumed rate at which the pension assets will increase.

Two points to stress are that (1) the interest component is computed *on the beginning of the current year PBO balance (or the end of the prior year)* and (2) it is the *expected increase* that is included in computing pension expense and not the actual increase in the PBO. Any difference between the actual increase in the PBO and the expected increase is a gain or loss, and the accounting for such is discussed later in this chapter.

Just as interest on the PBO increases the pension expense for the year, so too does the *expected increase in the fair value of the pension assets decrease pension expense* for the year. The expected return is computed by multiplying the actuary's long-run rate of return on plan assets by the **market-related asset value** of the plan assets.[6] Again, the difference between the **expected return on plan assets** and the actual return[7] is a gain or loss, which is also discussed later in the chapter.

For the Castro example, a calculated asset value is used because of the ease in following the calculations, and it is assumed that the plan assets will grow by 9%. Because different factors affect the PBO versus the return on assets, it is not to be expected that the PBO and assets will grow at the same rates. For instance, the assets will grow according to the assumptions made about the growth of the economy and the assumed rate of growth of the type of assets in which the funds are invested. Conversely, the rate at which the PBO will grow depends upon assumptions about mortality, average salary, etc. Based upon the assumed return of 9%, the expected return on plan assets for 2006 is $453, which is computed as 9% of the beginning of the year market-related asset value. (See Table 18-3A, p. 877, for computations of the expected return on plan assets for all years in the Castro & Co. example.)

Combining the three elements of service cost, interest cost on the PBO, and the expected return on plan assets, the pension expense for 2006 is computed as follows:

Service cost	$5,036
Interest on PBO	403
Expected return on plan assets	(453)
Pension expense	$4,986

[6]The market-related asset value is defined to be either the fair value of the plan assets or a calculated value that recognizes changes in fair value in a systematic manner over not more than five years, which is done to dampen the effects of price changes.

[7]The **actual return on plan assets** is computed as the difference between the beginning and ending balances of the plan assets as adjusted for benefits paid and contributions. In other words, the actual return is equal to the ending balance of plan assets, minus contributions to the plan, plus benefits paid, and minus the beginning balance of plan assets.

EXTENDING
the Concept

Using Tables 18-2A and 18-3A in Appendix A (pp. 876 and 877) for computations of interest on the PBO and expected return on the plan assets, compute the pension expenses for 2007 and 2008 for Castro & Co.

Answer: The pension expenses are $4,927 and $4,858, respectively.

Presuming that Castro again fully funds the pension expense, the journal entry to recognize pension expense and the payment to the pension plan for 2006 is as follows:

Journal Entry #2: Service cost, interest on PBO, and expected return on plan assets

Pension Expense	4,986	
Cash		4,986

To recognize pension expense and the pension funding for 2006.

Component 4 of Pension Expense: Amortization of Prior Service Costs

The costs incurred by the company due to a change in the pension plan benefit formula—*when the changes are retroactive*—are called **prior service costs (PSC)**. The amortization of prior service costs is the fourth component of pension expense. For example, assume that *on January 3, 2014*, an amendment to the pension benefit formula is implemented, whereby employees will receive $3\frac{1}{2}$% credit (instead of 3%) for each year of work, and *this change is retroactive to 2005*, the year in which the pension plan was adopted. The effect of such an amendment to the pension plan is that there is a "jump" in the PBO, as illustrated in Figure 18-2.

FIGURE 18-2

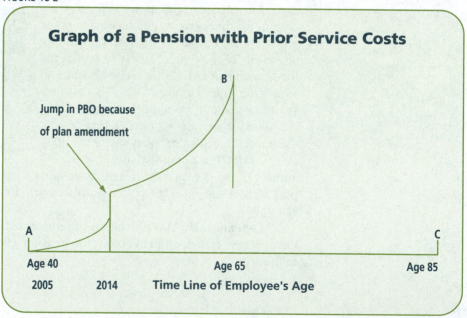

That is, Jared will now receive a larger yearly amount on retirement, which in turn requires that Castro & Co. have a larger amount accumulated when Jared retires than previously estimated. Since the **plan amendment** is retroactive, a greater amount should have been accumulated by 2014, in comparison to the previous benefit plan formula. The amount of the increase or jump in the PBO is the prior service cost. If the plan had been amended but not made retroactive, there would not have been a jump in the PBO. Instead, the graph of the PBO would have become steeper at the date the plan was amended.

Prior service costs also can arise when a pension plan is adopted and retroactive benefits are granted to employees. Such a situation can be illustrated by referring to Figure 18-2 and imagining that Point A, rather than touching the x-axis, is somewhat above the x-axis. This sudden appearance of the PBO is prior service cost. So prior service costs are the costs of retroactive benefits granted because of a pension plan being amended or implemented, with credit being given to employees for services they rendered previously.

To illustrate how prior service costs are computed, the Castro & Co. example will be used again. On January 3, 2014, the pension plan is amended, giving Jared 3.5% credit for each year worked. As a result, the prior service costs are computed as follows (using the same steps as previously demonstrated in the chapter):

1. The newly computed yearly retirement benefit is:

$$\text{Retirement Annuity} = 3.5\% \times \begin{array}{c}\text{Number of Years}\\\text{of Service}\end{array} \times \begin{array}{c}\text{Average Salary}\\\text{for Last 3 Years}\end{array}$$

$$= 3.5\% \times 25 \text{ years} \times \$50,000$$

$$= \$43,750, \text{ which compares to the previous } \$37,500$$

2. The new amount needing to be accumulated when Jared retires is:

   This amount needing to be accumulated is computed by finding the present value of an ordinary annuity of $43,750 for 20 years at 8%, which is $429,544 and compares with the $368,181, as previously computed.

3. The new service cost amount is:

   This new service cost amount is computed by dividing the $429,544 by the future amount of an annuity for 25 years at 8%, which is $5,875 and compares to the previously computed service cost amount of $5,036.

4. Then, the new PBO as of January 3, 2014 (or December 31, 2013), is:

   This new PBO amount at January 3, 2014, is $73,364, which compares with the previous PBO amount at December 31, 2013, of $62,887. [See Table 18-2A (p. 876) in Appendix A.]

5. Finally, the prior service cost is the difference between the new PBO amount at December 31, 2013, and what it previously was at that date. For this example, the prior service costs are $10,477, which is the difference between $73,364 and $62,887. [See Table 18-3A (p. 877) in Appendix A for all computations for the amended pension plan, using Excel spreadsheets.]

Regarding the accounting for prior service costs, the FASB mandates that they be accounted for as a change in an accounting estimate, meaning that no retroactive adjustment is made. Rather, *the increase (i.e., the "jump") in the PBO is amortized in the current and future years.* Their rationale for this position is that a company would not grant benefits to its employees for services prior to a plan being adopted or amended unless the company expected to receive some *future* benefits from them. Thus, companies granting such retroactive benefits apparently think that their employees will have greater loyalty and the company will then experience less employee turnover; or companies think that happier employees are more productive employees, etc. As a result of the FASB's position, the prior service costs are amortized over the remaining years to be worked by all employees, using either (1) the years-of-service amortization method or (2) the average-remaining-years-of-service amortization method.

To illustrate these two amortization methods, suppose that Castro & Co. actually covered 15 employees with its pension plan, and prior service costs for all 15 employees totaled $270,000 (as compared to the $10,477 that was computed previously for Jared). The first step in using either amortization method is to compute the number of years that each employee will work before retiring, which is presented in Table 18-1.

TABLE 18-1

Computing the Remaining Years of Service
(as of January 3, 2014)

Employee Number	Years of Service Remaining
1	15
2	20
3	13
4	5
5	7
6	2
7	12
8	14
9	6
10	19
11	1
12	4
13	8
14	16
15	2
Total years of service to be worked by employees	144

Years-of-Service Amortization Method

Having computed the remaining years that each employee is expected to work and summing the results, the years-of-service amortization method consists of dividing the total prior service costs (i.e., $270,000) by the 144 to obtain a cost per service-year. Then, this cost-per-service-year amount is multiplied by the number of service-years provided for any given year. It is this amount that is included as the fourth component of pension expense. Of the two amortization techniques mentioned earlier, this years-of-service amortization method is the preferred procedure.

To illustrate, dividing the total prior service costs of $270,000 by 144 results in a cost-per-service amount of $1,875 per service-year. So for 2014, the amortization amount that is included in determining pension expense is computed by multiplying $1,875 by 15 service-years that were worked that year (all employees worked, none retired). The amortization amount to include in determining pension expense for 2014 is $28,125.

From Table 18-1, it can be seen that Employee 11 retires at the end of 2014, and so there will be only 14 employees working during 2015. Thus, the amount of prior service costs that will be included in computing pension expense for

EXTENDING
the Concept

Compute the amount of prior service costs that will be included in determining pension expense for 2017 and 2018.

Answer: The amount of prior service costs will be $22,500 and $20,625, respectively.

2015 is computed by multiplying the $1,875 cost per service-year by 14 service-years, which results in an amortization amount of $26,250.

Each time an employee retires, the number of service-years that were worked that year declines by one. From Table 18-1, it can be seen that Employees 6 and 15 will retire at the end of 2015, so the amortization amount for 2016 will be $22,500, which is the $1,875 multiplied by 12 service-years. Thus, like the units-of-production depreciation method, the amortization amount to include as a component of pension expense is determined by multiplying the cost per service-year of $1,875 by the number of service-years for any given year.

Average-Remaining-Years-of-Service Amortization Method

In pension calculations, the FASB allows the use of estimates, averages, and computational shortcuts as long as it is reasonably expected that the results will not be materially different from the results of a detailed application. Thus, another acceptable approach to amortizing prior service costs is to use the straight-line method over the **average remaining years of service**. Using the data in Table 18-1, the average remaining years of service for Castro & Co. is computed by dividing the total remaining years of service of 144 by the number of employees (i.e., 15), which is 9.6. Using this method of amortization, the total prior service costs of $270,000 is amortized over 9.6 years, which gives an amortization amount of $28,125 per year. This is the amount of prior service cost that is included each year—for 9.6 years—in determining pension expense.

Funding Requirements and Journal Entries

To this point, it has been assumed that Castro & Co. always fully funded pension expense, meaning that the amount of cash it invested for future retirement benefits was always equal to the pension expense amount. This may not always happen. Minimum funding requirements are established by the Employee Retirement Income Security Act (ERISA), which was passed by Congress in 1974. ERISA is a lengthy and complex set of requirements that management, in connection with legal counsel, needs to consider when determining funding levels for any particular year.

The Castro & Co. example is used to illustrate how a journal entry is prepared when a plan is underfunded and also how pension expense is computed using four of the five components of pension expense. Previously, it was determined that the amortization amount of the prior service cost for Jared was $10,477. Also, since the plan amendment was made on January 3, 2014, Jared will work 16 more years before retiring. So the amount of prior service cost that will be included in determining pension expense for 2014 and subsequent years is $655, which is computed by dividing the prior service cost of $10,477 by 16 years. And, pension expense for 2014 is computed as follows:

Service cost	$5,875	(This amount changed due to the plan amendment)
Interest on PBO	5,869	(See Table 18-3A, p. 877)[8]
Expected return on plan assets	(5,902)	(given)
Amortization of prior service costs	655	(Computed as $10,477/16 years)
Pension expense	$6,497	

[8]Because of the plan amendment, the interest included in pension expense will not be found in Table 18-2A. Rather, Table 18-3A will have to be used, based upon the new assumptions regarding the PBO.

Assuming that Castro & Co. can fund only $5,000 during 2014, the appropriate journal entry is as follows:

Journal Entry 3: Service cost, interest on PBO, expected return on plan assets, and amortization of prior service costs

Pension Expense	6,497	
Prepaid/Accrued Pension Cost		1,497
Cash		5,000

To record pension expense and funding for 2014.

Prepaid/Accrued Pension Cost	
Debit balance	Credit balance
Asset reported	Liability reported

As illustrated in this entry and as mentioned previously, a liability is recognized only when the cumulative amount funded is less than the cumulative pension expense. The projected benefit obligation is not reported as a liability on a company's balance sheet. Neither are the prior service costs that result when a pension plan is implemented or amended reported as a liability. When a liability is reported, it represents the amount by which the fund is underfunded in relation to pension expense. Likewise, when a pension plan is funded at an amount in excess of pension expense, the difference is reported as an asset on the balance sheet and represents the amount by which the fund is overfunded in relation to pension expense. Instead of using two accounts (an asset account and a liability account) to report the funding status of a pension plan, a combined prepaid/accrued pension cost account is used. When this account has a debit balance, the amount is reported as a noncurrent asset, and when the account has a credit balance, it is reported as a noncurrent liability.

Component 5 of Pension Expense: Amortization of Unrecognized Gains and Losses

The accounting for gains and losses is the final component of pension expense. A **gain** or **loss** arises because actual experience is different from what was expected. So gains/losses result because:

1. The actual projected benefit obligation is different from what was expected, which is the likely result of a change in an actuarial assumption (such gains/losses are called liability gains/losses or actuarial gains/losses); and
2. The actual fair value of the plan assets is different from what was expected, which is likely due to the market either under- or overperforming from what was expected (such gains/losses are called asset gains/losses).

When the FASB was considering what ultimately became the current rules for pension accounting and reporting, companies were very concerned about possible wide fluctuations in pension expense from year to year due to fluctuations in the market value of the pension assets or in the actuarial assumptions regarding the PBO. Initially, the FASB thought that if volatility was a characteristic of the market, financial measures should reflect that volatility.[9] But eventually the FASB decided (strictly from a practical view) that reducing the volatility in the markets was desirable, and as a result, the FASB implemented several smoothing techniques to including gains/losses in pension expense.

One smoothing technique is that the liability gains/losses are netted with the asset gains/losses, thus resulting in the possibility that the two amounts—

---

[9]*SFAS No. 87*, par. 174. The FASB argued that financial measures are not representationally faithful (one of the characteristics of information being relevant) if they do not show volatility when such is present.

especially over time—will offset each other. A second smoothing technique is to permit only the unrecognized gains/losses, at the beginning of the year, that exceed a "corridor" to be considered for inclusion in calculating pension expense. The **corridor** is defined as 10% of the greater of the beginning of the year PBO or the beginning of the year market-related asset value. Once this excess amount is determined, a third smoothing technique is to amortize the amount over a period not to exceed the average remaining years of service of those employees expecting to receive benefits from the plan.[10]

Table 18-2 illustrates the calculation of the corridor for Castro & Co. from 2006–2010. The amounts in the projected benefit obligation column (Column B) come from Appendix A, Table 18-2A (p. 876). The other columns are prepared according to the FASB's guidelines for determining the corridor, as summarized in the previous paragraph.

TABLE 18-2

Determining the Corridor

(A) Year	(B) Projected Benefit Obligation (See Table 18-2A)	(C) Market-Related Asset Value (given)	(D) Higher of Col. B or Col. C	(E) Corridor (10% of Col. D)
2005	$ 0	$ 0	$ 0	$ 0
2006	5,036	5,036	5,036	504
2007	10,475	10,415	10,475	1,048
2008	16,349	15,685	16,349	1,635
2009	22,693	23,020	23,020	2,302
2010	29,544	29,752	29,752	2,975

Having determined the corridor for each of the periods presented, it is now possible to determine the amount by which any unrecognized gains/losses exceed the corridor, which is then amortized and included in pension expense. These procedures are illustrated in Table 18-3.

Note the effectiveness of the smoothing techniques of using a corridor and then amortizing the excess. Of the $3,500 losses, only a net of $2 has been included in pension expense.

Finishing the Castro & Co. example, pension expense for 2014—considering all the components that comprise it—is computed as follows:

Service cost	$ 5,875	(This amount changed due to the plan amendment.)
Interest on PBO	5,869	(See Table 18-3A, p. 877)[11]
Expected return on plan assets	(5,902)	(given)
Amortization of prior service costs	655	
(Gains)/losses	70	(Assumed)
Pension expense	$ 6,567	

[10]A shorter time period to amortize the amount in excess of the corridor is permitted as long as (1) the method is applied consistently (2) the method is applied to both gains and losses, and (3) the amortization method is disclosed.

TABLE 18-3

Determining the Amount in Excess of the Corridor, and the Amount of the Gain/Loss to Include in Pension Expense

Col. A Year	Col. B Current Yr's. Net Gain/(Loss) (given)	Col. C Amount Amortized from Prior Year	Col. D Unrecognized Gain/(Loss)	Col. E Corridor (See Table 18-2)	Col. F Amount in Excess of Corridor	Col. G Amorti- zation
2005	$ 0		$ 0	NA	$ 0	$ 0
2006	400	$ 0	400	$ 504	0	0
2007	1,250	0	1,650	1,048	602	63
2008	(2,000)	63	(413)	1,635	0	0
2009	(1,800)	0	(2,213)	2,302	0	0
2010	(1,350)	0	(3,563)	2,975	(588)	(61)
Totals	$(3,500)					$ 2

Explanations:

The amounts in Column B are assumed.
The amounts in Column C come from the prior-year row of Column G.
The amounts in Column D are computed as the prior-year amount in Column D plus/minus the amounts in Columns B and C.
The amounts in Column F are the amounts by which Column D exceeds Column E.
The amounts in Column G are the amounts that are included in pension expense for the year and are computed by dividing the amounts in Column F by 9.6 years, which is the average remaining years of service in the Castro & Co. example.

The journal entry to record the pension expense for 2014, assuming that Castro & Co. funds $6,000 of it, is as follows:

Journal Entry 4: Service cost, interest on PBO, expected return on plan assets, amortization of prior service costs, and amortization of gains/losses

Pension Expense	6,567	
Prepaid/Accrued Pension Cost		567
Cash		6,000

An exception to using the corridor/amortization technique for including gains/losses in pension expense is gains/losses arising from a single occurrence not directly related to the employer's business, such as closing a plant. Such gains/losses immediately become part of pension expense.

[11]Because of the plan amendment, the interest included in pension expense will not be found in Table 18-2A. Rather, Table 18-3A will have to be used, based upon the new assumptions regarding the PBO.

Reinforcing Illustration

Stoker Inc. has the following information related to its defined benefit pension plan as of December 31, 2005:

Projected benefit obligation, January 1, 2005	$960,000
Accumulated benefit obligation, January 1, 2005	$740,000
Discount rate	10%
Service costs	$50,000
Plan assets, January 1, 2005	$800,000
Actual return on plan assets	$80,000
Expected return on plan assets	9%
Prior service costs	$240,000
Average remaining years of service	20 years
Unrecognized actuarial gains	$116,000

Using this information, pension expense is computed as follows:

Service cost	$ 50,000
Interest on projected benefit obligation ($960,000 × 0.10)	96,000
Expected return on plan assets ($800,000 × 0.09)	(72,000)
Amortization of prior service costs ($240,000/20 yrs.)	12,000
Gains/losses (see the following computations)	(1,000)
Total pension expense for the year	$ 85,000

Corridor: 10% of higher of PBO or assets.
 Corridor is $96,000.
 Amount by which unrecognized gains exceed the corridor: $20,000.
 Amortization of unrealized gains: $1,000.

Analysis of the Prepaid/Accrued Cost Account with Pension Worksheet

Previously, it was indicated that a balance in the prepaid/accrued cost account arises when the total amount funded to a pension plan is either greater than or less than the total amount of pension expense. This statement is correct, but it is a simplistic description of the balance in the account. In a more precise sense, the balance in the prepaid/accrued cost account represents in a net amount the projected benefit obligation, the fair value of the plan assets, unamortized prior service costs, unrecognized actuarial and asset gains and losses, and any other amounts related to the pension plan that are not reported on the balance sheet.

Exhibit 18-1 is a worksheet for a fictitious defined benefit pension plan that shows the effects of the various elements of pension expense on the financial numbers of the plan, both those that are reported on the financial statements and those off-balance-sheet amounts. For example, the service costs are recognized as part of pension expense and are reported on the financial statements. They also impact the PBO, which is not reported on the financial statements. Likewise, the interest on the PBO impacts pension expense and is reported on the financial statements, and it also impacts the PBO, which is not recorded on the financial statements. So it is with each item; the worksheet indicates those accounts, both reported on the financial statements and not reported on the financial statements, which are impacted by pension events and transactions. Trace each item on the worksheet carefully to identify its impact on the accounts.

EXHIBIT 18-1

Worksheet for Pension Expense

	Financial Statement Accounts			Memorandum Accounts			
	Pension Expense	Cash	Prepaid/ (Accrued)	PBO	Value Assets	Prior Service	(Gains)/ Losses
January 1			$(31)	$(8,342)	$9,121	$390	$(1,200)
Service cost	$ 240			(240)			
Interest cost	585			(585)			
Return on assets	(310)				310		
Actuarial loss				(158)			158
Asset gain					466		(466)
Plan amend.				(30)		30	
Amortize PSC	21					(21)	
Amortize gains/losses	(30)						30
Benefits paid				456	(456)		
Funding		$(450)			450		
Subtotals	$ 506	$(450)	$(31)	$(8,899)	$9,891	$399	$(1,478)
Journal entry	$ 506	$(450)	(56)				
December 31 balance			$(87)				

Note that the totals of the memorandum accounts at January 1 and December 31 equal the balance in the prepaid/accrued account, thus illustrating that the balance in the prepaid/accrued account represents, in a net fashion, the PBO, the fair value of plan assets, unamortized prior service costs, and any unrecognized gains/losses. This worksheet (which is similar to worksheets customarily prepared by accountants and reported in the notes to published financial statements) helps explain the nature of the prepaid/accrued account.

Also, from the worksheet in Exhibit 18-1, the journal entry can be prepared to recognize pension expense for the year as follows:

Pension Expense	506	
Prepaid/Accrued Pension Cost		56
Cash		450

Minimum Liability

The FASB chose to report the various assets and liabilities of a defined benefit pension plan in a net fashion in the prepaid/accrued cost account for several reasons. Two of those reasons were (1) expediency (to get some standard adopted that would improve financial reporting, even though everything desired could not be implemented at the time) and (2) recognizing a liability for some items was too significant a departure from current practice to be implemented. Another reason was that there was theoretical justification for not recognizing these pension liabilities immediately but instead recognizing them over time. (For example, the justification for recognizing prior service costs in the future is that future benefits will be derived from amending the pension plan.)

However, the FASB does require that a **minimum liability** be reported on the balance sheet when, and by the amount that, the accumulated benefit obligation (ABO)[12] exceeds the fair value of the plan assets *at year-end*. Note that the actual fair value of the plan assets is used and not some computed value. When preparing the journal entry to recognize this minimum liability, the balance in the prepaid/accrued pension cost account must be considered. Suppose, for example, that the ABO exceeds the fair value of the plan assets by $75,000 (and so a minimum liability of $75,000 must be recognized) and there is already an $18,000 *credit balance* in the prepaid/accrued pension cost account. Then, an additional liability of $57,000 must be recognized, which is computed as follows:

Minimum liability to be recognized	$75,000 credit
Balance in the prepaid/accrued pension cost account	18,000 credit
Additional liability to be recognized	$57,000 credit

The adjusting journal entry to recognize the additional liability is:

Deferred Pension Cost[13]	57,000	
Prepaid/Accrued Pension Cost		57,000

To record the minimum pension liability that is required when, at year-end, the ABO exceeds the fair value of the plan assets.

The deferred pension cost account is classified with the intangible assets. The amount is not amortized but is adjusted at each year-end when the ABO is again compared with the fair value of the plan assets.

The recording of a liability and offsetting it with an intangible asset in the same journal entry may not be logical. However, the rationale for doing so is that companies institute pension plans (or make amendments thereto) and incur pension obligations with the expectation of receiving future benefits, and so this journal entry essentially recognizes both the future liability and the future benefits.

As mentioned, the balance in the prepaid/accrued pension cost account has to be considered when determining the journal entry to record the additional liability. So when the prepaid/accrued pension cost account has a debit balance, the additional liability must be increased accordingly. Assume again that the ABO exceeds the fair value of the plan assets by $75,000 but that the prepaid/accrued pension cost account has an $18,000 *debit balance*. Then, the journal entry to record the additional liability is as follows:

Deferred Pension Cost	93,000	
Prepaid/Accrued Pension Cost		93,000

To record the minimum pension liability that is required when, at year-end, the ABO exceeds the fair value of the plan assets.

In both examples, the minimum liability reported on the balance sheet is $75,000. In the first example, the $18,000 credit balance in the prepaid/accrued pension cost account plus the $57,000 additional liability amount results in a total liability of $75,000. In the second example, the initial $18,000 debit balance in the prepaid/accrued pension cost account and the $93,000 additional liability amount again results in a total liability of $75,000.

---

[12]Remember that the accumulated benefit obligation is computed the same way that the PBO is, except that the accumulated benefit obligation is based on current salaries rather than on projected salaries.

[13]Another acceptable title for this account is "Intangible Pension Asset."

One complication that may arise in recording the additional liability is that the *amount in the deferred pension cost account cannot exceed the* unrecognized *prior service costs as of the beginning of the year.* (Remember, prior service costs arise when a plan is implemented or amended and credit is given to employees for services rendered prior to the plan being implemented or amended.) *When the* minimum liability *is greater than the* unrecognized *prior service costs, then the excess amount is reported as a reduction of other comprehensive income.*

To illustrate, assume that the ABO exceeds the fair value of the plan assets by $75,000, the credit balance in the prepaid/accrued pension cost account is $18,000, and unrecognized prior service costs are $40,000. Also, assume that there is no balance in the deferred pension cost account. Given these facts, the minimum liability that must be reported is $75,000, and an additional liability must be recorded for $57,000 (all as previously computed). But since the un-recognized prior service costs are $40,000, the maximum amount that can be reported in the deferred pension cost account is $40,000, and the rest of the $57,000 is reported in an account called Minimum Pension Liability Adjustment, as follows:

Minimum Pension Liability Adjustment		
(part of other comprehensive income)	17,000	
Deferred Pension Cost (intangible asset)	40,000	
Prepaid/Accrued Pension Cost		57,000

To record the minimum liability when the amount in Deferred Pension Cost cannot exceed the prior service costs.

In subsequent years when recording the minimum liability, adjustments are made as needed to both the deferred pension cost account and the minimum pension liability adjustment account. So suppose that in the subsequent year, a minimum liability of $80,000 needs to be reported, after funding the pension plan there is a credit balance of $71,000 in the prepaid/accrued pension cost account, and the unrecognized prior service costs after amortizing $5,000 to pension expense is $35,000. Then the appropriate journal entry to recognize the additional liability is as follows:

Minimum Pension Liability Adjustment	14,000[3]	
Deferred Pension Cost Account		5,000[2]
Prepaid/Accrued Pension Cost		9,000[1]

[1]The difference between the minimum liability amount of $80,000 and the balance in the prepaid/accrued pension cost account.
[2]Before this journal entry, the balance in the deferred pension cost account was $40,000 (see prior entry), but the balance cannot exceed the amount of unrecognized prior service cost, which now is $35,000. So the account must be reduced by $5,000.
[3]Balancing amount.

The rationale for reporting an adjustment to other comprehensive income is that a minimum liability always represents a level of significant underfunding. When that underfunding is due to a plan amendment, then it seems appropriate to offset the liability with an intangible asset. However, when the underfunding results from unrecognized net losses, then it seems more appropriate to show that amount in other comprehensive income.

International Accounting Standards

Due to the complexity of accounting for pensions, even when an accounting system requires accrual accounting, significant differences in accounting for pensions among countries can arise. Similar to U.S. GAAP, *IAS No. 19* requires

This Is the Real World

The extended bull market during the late 1990s significantly increased the market values of many companies' funded pension plans. This is a good thing for current and retired employees because the risk of future pension payouts is reduced. Companies also benefit because future payments to the funds are reduced, being offset by expectations of higher returns. However, this phenomenon has created a new challenge of interpreting the effect of pension costs on operating earnings.

As an example, Northrop Grumman reported in its 1999 annual report the following components of net pension cost for its defined benefit plans:

	1999	1998
($ in millions)		
Service cost	$ 200	$ 187
Interest cost	659	642
Expected return on plan assets	(1,136)	(1,008)
Amortization of:		
Prior service costs	35	35
Transition assets, net	(42)	(42)
Net gain from previous years	(69)	(80)
Net periodic benefit cost (income)	$ (353)	$ (266)

Northrop Grumman's total net income for 1999 was $467 million, which includes the net pension income of $353 million. Therefore, the net pension income increased net income by over 300%. Also, net income reported in 1998 was $194 million, so if it wasn't for the net pension income of $266 million, the company would have reported a net loss for the period.

So what's the problem? Several factors complicate the appropriate interpretation of the net pension cost as it relates to firm value. First, although the net pension cost was obviously a very important contributor to Northrop Grumman's overall net income in 1999 and 1998, the company did not report the item separately on its income statement. The only way an investor could determine the effect of the pension cost on earnings was to search the notes. The fact that the company's primary operations are not related to pension assets emphasizes the concern that this component of earnings should be clearly disclosed to investors and creditors.

Second, the accounting rules for pensions, as discussed in this chapter, allow companies to defer any unexpected gain/loss on pension assets and amortize this amount only when the accumulated gains/losses exceed the corridor amount. Northrop Grumman's expected rate of return on plan assets in 1999 was 9.5% or $1,136 million; by comparison, its actual return was $2,284, or over 18%. The significant gains realized by companies during the bull market have resulted in a large pool of reserves available to management. Northrop Grumman's accumulated unrecognized gain is over $3.6 *billion*. This amount could find its way to earnings very quickly if Northrop Grumman was to revise its expected rate of return on plan assets. As an extreme example, consider what the net pension cost would have been if Northrop Grumman changed its expected rate of return from 9.5% to 19% for 1999. The pension cost component, expected return on plan assets, would have doubled to $2,272 million, which would have had a very significant effect on net income.

Finally, a related concern that accompanied the bull market of the late 1990s was the percentage of a pension plan's assets invested in equity securities. In 1995, pension funds allocated about 59.8% of their assets to equity securities. Five years later, this percentage had increased to 67.5%. This allocation is a good move for companies during a bull market, but it represents increased risk that the beneficiaries might not appreciate. Keep in mind that for defined benefit plans, the beneficiaries' cash receipts are not improved by unexpected gains but might be affected adversely if the plan realizes significant losses and goes bankrupt.

companies to accrue pension benefits that arise due to employees performing services in the current period. The same pension cost components specified in *SFAS No. 87* are also identified in *IAS No. 19*. In addition, the pension obligation is based on expected future salaries, and the "corridor" approach is used to amortize actuarial gains and losses. However, the following rules under *IAS No. 19* can result in significant differences in pension accounting under IAS versus U.S. GAAP:

- Accounting for prior service costs.
- Recognition of a minimum liability.

Under U.S. GAAP, when a company adopts or amends a pension plan and grants the new benefits to employees for prior service, the cost of this amendment related to active nonvested employees is to amortize the costs over the remaining service period of the active employees.[14] However, in contrast to the FASB's requirement, *IAS No. 19* requires that all prior service costs related to retirees and vested active employees be expensed immediately. Finally, *IAS No. 19* does not have a minimum liability requirement.

Summary

Pensions come in two basic versions: defined contribution plans and defined benefit plans. Defined contribution plans define the amount to be contributed each year to the plan and leave undefined the amount to be received in retirement. Defined benefit plans define the amount to be received in retirement and leave undefined the amount to be contributed each year to the plan. To account for defined contribution plans, Pension Expense is debited for the amount that should be contributed each year to the plan, with the cumulative difference between that amount and the actual funding being reported on the balance sheet as either a long-term asset or long-term liability.

For defined benefit plans, pension expense is comprised of the following items:

1. Service cost,
2. Interest on the projected benefit obligation,
3. Expected return on plan assets,
4. Amortization of prior service cost, and
5. Amortization of net gains and losses.

Service cost is the actuarial present value of benefits attributed by the pension benefit formula to services rendered by employees during that period. Interest on the projected benefit obligation is the increase in the projected benefit obligation due to the passage of time. The expected return on plan assets is a calculated amount based on the long-term rate of return on plan assets. Prior service costs are the cost of retroactive benefits granted in a plan amendment or at the inception of a pension plan and are amortized using the remaining years of service or the average remaining years of service methods. The net gains/losses that exceed the corridor (which is 10% of the greater of the projected benefit obligation or the fair value of the plan assets) are amortized using the remaining years of service method.

As with defined contribution plans, the amount reported on the balance sheet (called Prepaid/Accrued Pension Cost and reported as either a long-term asset or long-term liability) is the cumulative difference between pension expense and the amount of cash contributed to the fund. In addition, a minimum liability is reported on the balance sheet when the accumulated benefit obligation exceeds the fair value of the plan assets. In reporting this amount, the present

---

[14]Alternatively, the prior service cost can be amortized over the remaining life expectancy of retired employees if the costs associated with the plan amendment relate primarily to retired employees.

balance in the prepaid/accrued account is considered, with an additional liability recorded such that the balance in the prepaid/accrued account plus the additional liability equals the minimum liability amount. When recording this additional liability, the debit is usually recorded to a deferred pension cost account. The exception is that the amount so recorded cannot exceed the amount of unrecognized prior service costs. When another account needs to be debited to balance the journal entry, the account used is Minimum Pension Liability Adjustment, which is reported as a component of other comprehensive income.

APPENDIX A: Pension Expense for Jared and Castro & Co. Example

This appendix illustrates the principles of computing service cost, interest on service cost, and the calculation of the projected benefit obligation for the Jared example used throughout the chapter. All journal entries to record pension expense for Jared and Castro & Co. in the chapter can be traced to this appendix and the detail reviewed as to how the amounts were computed.

Table 18-1A illustrates that if Castro & Co. has $368,181 at the time Jared retires, that amount will be sufficient to pay Jared $37,500 per year for 20 years. The ending balance of $2 is due to cumulative small rounding errors.

TABLE 18-1A

Verification of Amount Castro & Co. Needs When Jared Retires

Year	Retirement Payment	Interest	Assets Remaining
			$368,181
2030	$37,500	$29,454	360,135
2031	37,500	28,811	351,446
2032	37,500	28,116	342,062
2033	37,500	27,365	331,927
2034	37,500	26,554	320,981
2035	37,500	25,678	309,160
2036	37,500	24,733	296,392
2037	37,500	23,711	282,604
2038	37,500	22,608	267,712
2039	37,500	21,417	251,629
2040	37,500	20,130	234,259
2041	37,500	18,741	215,500
2042	37,500	17,240	195,240
2043	37,500	15,619	173,359
2044	37,500	13,869	149,728
2045	37,500	11,978	124,206
2046	37,500	9,937	96,643
2047	37,500	7,731	66,874
2048	37,500	5,350	34,724
2049	37,500	2,778	2

Table 18-2A verifies that if Castro & Co. deposits $5,036 in the bank for 25 years, at the end of that time (i.e., when Jared retires) the fund will have accumulated to $368,181, assuming an interest rate of 8%. The $19 difference is due to small rounding errors.

TABLE 18-2A

Verification of Yearly Expense by Castro & Co.

Year	Service Cost	Interest	Liability (i.e., PBO)
2005	$5,036	—	$ 5,036
2006	5,036	$ 403	10,475
2007	5,036	838	16,349
2008	5,036	1,308	22,693
2009	5,036	1,815	29,544
2010	5,036	2,364	36,944
2011	5,036	2,955	44,935
2012	5,036	3,595	53,566
2013	5,036	4,285	62,887
2014	5,036	5,031	72,954
2015	5,036	5,836	83,827
2016	5,036	6,706	95,569
2017	5,036	7,646	108,250
2018	5,036	8,660	121,946
2019	5,036	9,756	136,738
2020	5,036	10,939	152,713
2021	5,036	12,217	169,966
2022	5,036	13,597	188,599
2023	5,036	15,088	208,723
2024	5,036	16,698	230,457
2025	5,036	18,437	253,930
2026	5,036	20,314	279,280
2027	5,036	22,342	306,659
2028	5,036	24,533	336,227
2029	5,036	26,898	368,162

Table 18-3A replicates Tables 18-1A and 18-2A for verifying the PBO and the annual deposit amount, given the change in the plan amendment as specified in the Castro & Co. example.

TABLE 18-3A

Verifications of PBO and Annual Deposits, Given the Amendment in the Pension Plan

	Verifying the Asset Accumulation (Similar to Table 18-1A)				Verifying the Annual Expense and Liability (Similar to Table 18-2A)		
Year	Retirement Payment	Interest	Assets Remaining	Year	Service Cost	Interest	Liability (i.e., PBO)
			$429,544				
2030	$43,750	$34,364	420,158	2005	$5,875	—	$ 5,875
2031	43,750	33,613	410,020	2006	5,875	$ 470	12,220
2032	43,750	32,802	399,072	2007	5,875	978	19,073
2033	43,750	31,926	387,247	2008	5,875	1,526	26,473
2034	43,750	30,980	374,477	2009	5,875	2,118	34,466
2035	43,750	29,958	360,685	2010	5,875	2,757	43,099
2036	43,750	28,855	345,790	2011	5,875	3,448	52,421
2037	43,750	27,663	329,704	2012	5,875	4,194	62,490
2038	43,750	26,376	312,330	2013	5,875	4,999	73,364
2039	43,750	24,986	293,566	2014	5,875	5,869	85,109
2040	43,750	23,485	273,301	2015	5,875	6,809	97,792
2041	43,750	21,864	251,416	2016	5,875	7,823	111,491
2042	43,750	20,113	227,779	2017	5,875	8,919	126,285
2043	43,750	18,222	202,251	2018	5,875	10,103	142,263
2044	43,750	16,180	174,681	2019	5,875	11,381	159,519
2045	43,750	13,974	144,906	2020	5,875	12,761	178,155
2046	43,750	11,592	112,748	2021	5,875	14,252	198,283
2047	43,750	9,020	78,018	2022	5,875	15,863	220,020
2048	43,750	6,241	40,509	2023	5,875	17,602	243,497
2049	43,750	3,241	0	2024	5,875	19,480	268,852
				2025	5,875	21,508	296,235
				2026	5,875	23,699	325,808
				2027	5,875	26,065	357,748
				2028	5,875	28,620	392,243
				2029	5,875	31,379	429,497

APPENDIX B: Liabilities for Postretirement Benefits[15]

Employees in recent years have been very successful in getting their employers to fund various benefits after retirement, including health care, life insurance, legal and tax services, and tuition assistance. Previously, employers accounted for the cost of such benefits on a pay-as-you-go (cash) basis. But with the increasing popularity of such benefits and with the magnitude of such liabilities increasing, the *FASB now requires an accrual measurement focus for all postretirement benefits*. Hence, the cost of providing such benefits must now be recognized during the periods in which the employees render the service that qualifies them to receive the postretirement benefits.

To the extent that other postretirement benefits (OPEB) are similar to pensions, the accounting and financial reporting for OPEBs uses the same fundamental framework as pensions. However, some fundamental differences exist between pensions and OPEBs, and where there are compelling reasons, the accounting and financial reporting differs. Table 18-1B summarizes some of the major differences between pensions and OPEBs.

TABLE 18-1B

Comparison of Pensions to OPEBs

Item	Pensions	OPEBs
Funding	Generally well funded	Generally *not* funded
Benefit	Well defined and equal dollar amount each year	Generally no upper limit and great variability each year
Beneficiary	Retiree (and occasionally the surviving spouse)	Retiree, spouse, and dependents
Benefit payable	Monthly	As needed
Predictability	Reasonably predictable	Difficult to predict, as cost varies geographically and over time

As with pensions, an important definition is the expected postretirement benefit obligation (EPBO), which is similar to the PBO for pensions. The EPBO is the present value, at a particular date, of the *total postretirement benefits expected to be paid* to the retiree, spouse, or other dependents as a result of services performed in the current year. As with pensions, this amount is not recorded in a company's balance sheet but is used to compute OPEB expense for a period. There is also an accumulated postretirement benefit obligation (APBO), which is the present value, at a particular date, of the *postretirement benefits that are attributed to employees' services to date*. The APBO is computed from the EPBO using the following formula:

APBO = EPBO × (Years of Service/Total Years to Be Fully Eligible)

---

[15]*FASB Statement No. 106*, "Employers' Accounting for Postretirement Benefits Other than Pensions."

As with accounting for pensions, the OPEB expense consists of the following components:

1. *Service cost*. The portion of the expected postretirement benefit obligation attributed to employee service during the period. (This is the same as for pensions.)
2. *Interest cost*. The increase in the accumulated postretirement benefit obligation due to the passage of time. (This is computed differently than for pensions.)
3. *Actual return on plan assets*. The increase in the fair value of plan assets adjusted for contributions and benefits paid. Again, this amount is really the expected return on plan assets because of the same adjustment for current-period gains/losses that is included in component #5. (This is the same as for pensions.)
4. *Amortization of prior service costs*. The amortization of retroactive benefits due to the implementation of or an amendment to an OPEB plan. The amortization period is the remaining service period. (This is the same as for pensions.)
5. *Gains and losses*. Changes in the APBO resulting from changed actuarial assumptions or experience being different from expectations. For funded OPEB plans, gains/losses also arise from actual returns on plan assets being different from expected returns. As with pensions, the current year's gain/loss is included in the determination of OPEB expense, and the cumulative prior year's gains/losses are amortized over the remaining service lives, using the corridor approach. (For funded OPEB plans, this is the same as for pensions.)
6. *Amortization of the transition obligation*. Because OPEB benefits are largely unfunded, an immediate obligation arises, which may either be recognized immediately or be amortized by using the straight-line method over a period of time not to exceed 20 years. (This is different than for pensions.)

As with pensions, the sum of these components is the expense amount, and the credit to Cash is determined by the company's funding policy. Any difference between the amount expensed and the amount funded is recorded in an accrued postretirement benefit cost account. The FASB does not require the reporting of a minimum liability for an OPEB.

Liabilities for Postemployment Benefits

Benefits provided to former/inactive employees after their employment but before they retire are called postemployment benefits. The nature of such benefits parallel those provided under postretirement benefits and includes such benefits as health care, life insurance, severance pay, and disability benefits. The accounting for all such postemployment is done in accordance with *SFAS No. 112*, "Employers' Accounting for Postemployment Benefits," except for those postemployment benefits that are specifically covered under another accounting standard. For example, special or contractual termination benefits are addressed in *SFAS Nos. 88* and *106*, deferred compensation plans for individual employees are covered under *APB No. 12*, etc. For those postemployment benefits not covered by other specific standards, the accrual of the cost of such benefits is the same as for compensated absences, which is as follows:

- The employer's obligation to compensate employees arises from services already performed,

- The obligation vests or accumulates,
- Payment is probable, and
- The amount of the payment can be reasonably estimated.

Questions

1. Distinguish between a defined contribution pension plan and a defined benefit pension plan. Briefly describe how pension expense is determined for each type of pension plan. During a period of significant growth in stock prices, which plan would a rational employee probably prefer?

2. Distinguish between a contributory and a noncontributory pension plan.

3. What does it mean for pension benefits to be vested?

4. Vickers Corporation has a pension plan in which it matches contributions made by its employees. At retirement, each employee receives an annuity based upon the rate of return earned by the fund. Identify whether this pension plan is (a) a contributory or noncontributory pension plan and (b) a defined contribution or a defined benefit pension plan.

5. Define each of the following components of pension expense:
   a. Service cost
   b. Interest cost
   c. Expected return on plan assets
   d. Prior service costs
   e. Actuarial gains and losses

6. What is the difference between the "projected benefit obligation" and the "accumulated benefit obligation"? What significance does the projected benefit obligation have in pension accounting? What significance does the accumulated benefit obligation have in pension accounting?

7. Which is more reliable—calculating the projected benefit obligation or calculating the accumulated benefit obligation? Which number is more relevant? Why?

8. What circumstances or events would cause a company to report a "prepaid pension cost"? An "accrued pension cost"?

9. Explain the "deferred pension cost" (or the intangible pension asset) account. Under what circumstances is it shown on the financial statements?

10. When a pension plan amendment occurs and causes a change (either an increase or a decrease) in the projected benefit obligation, how does this change affect (i.e., be included in) yearly pension expense?

11. How are asset gains/losses and actuarial gains/losses included in pension expense? (Describe all of the smoothing techniques.) Why did the FASB adopt this approach rather than have the gains/losses recognized immediately in pension expense?

12. Describe when it is necessary to recognize a minimum pension liability. Generally, what is the offsetting credit to recognizing the minimum pension liability? Under what circumstances does recognizing an additional pension liability affect other comprehensive income?

13. What are the main differences in pension accounting between U.S. GAAP and *IAS No. 19*?

Exercises

Exercise 18-1: Basic Journal Entries. Candice Corp. has correctly determined that the pension expense for the year is $420,000. Prepare the journal entry and describe how the difference between pension expense and the amount funded is reported (a) if Candice funds an amount equal to the pension expense, (b) if Candice funds $400,000, and (c) if Candice funds $450,000.

Exercise 18-2: Reporting Accrued/Prepaid Pension Costs. Heit Incorporated has pension expense of $160,000 in 2004 and $190,000 in 2005. Prepare the appropriate journal entries, assuming that the company funds $170,000 in both 2004 and 2005. Identify the accounts that will be reported on the balance sheet for both years and where they will be reported.

Exercise 18-3: Computing Service Cost. Mandy is the only employee of Broadway Guitar. She is 35 years old and plans to retire when she is 62 years old. On December 31, 2005, Broadway instituted a defined benefit plan in which Mandy will receive a retirement benefit equal to $2\frac{1}{2}\%$ of her highest salary for each year she works, commencing from December 31, 2005. The actuary has made the following assumptions:

> Mandy will live 18 years after retiring.
>
> The discount rate is 8%.
>
> Mandy's current salary is $24,000.
>
> Annual salary increases will be 2%.
>
> Retirement payments will be made yearly and will begin one year after retirement.
>
> Payments to fund the benefits will be made at the end of each year during the 27 years that Mandy works.

1. Compute the anticipated retirement benefits.
2. Compute the amount needed in the fund when Mandy retires (i.e., PBO).
3. Compute the service cost amount.

Round all answers to the nearest dollar.

Exercise 18-4: Computing Service Cost. Using an electronic spreadsheet, redo Exercise 18-3, assuming:

1. A benefit formula of 3% of the highest salary and a discount rate of 12%.
2. A benefit formula of 3.5% of the highest salary and a discount rate of 10%.

Exercise 18-5: Computing Balance in Prepaid/Accrued Pension. Goodwin Inc. has the following information related to pensions for the year beginning January 1, 2004:

Market-related value of plan assets	$400,000
Projected benefit obligation	375,000
Prepaid pension cost	20,000

The actuary has determined that an appropriate discount rate is 10% and that the long-run return on plan assets is expected to be 9%. Assume that Goodwin's service cost and funding amounts are $150,000 and $160,000, respectively, for every year.

Determine the balance in the prepaid/accrued pension account at (a) December 31, 2004, and (b) December 31, 2012.

Exercise 18-6: Computing Pension Expense. The following information pertains to 2004 for Do-Right Corp.'s defined benefit pension plan:

Service cost	$280,000
Expected return on plan assets	60,000
Interest cost on projected benefit obligation	144,000
Amortization of actuarial loss	20,000
Amortization of unrecognized prior service costs	50,000

What is Do-Right's pension cost for 2004?

Exercise 18-7: Computing Pension Expense. Skeeter Corp. provides a defined benefit pension plan for all its employees. At the end of the 2004 fiscal year, the company's actuary provided the following information related to the pension expense for the year:

Service cost	$75,000
Interest cost	32,000
Expected return on pension plan assets	35,000
Amortization of actuarial loss	3,000
Amortization of unrecognized prior service cost	5,000

Determine the amount of pension expense that Skeeter Corp. should recognize for the 2004 fiscal year.

Exercise 18-8: Pension Expense—Multi-Year. On December 31, 2003, Jacob's Ladder Company established a noncontributory defined benefit pension plan covering all the employees of the company and immediately contributed $400,000 to a pension trust fund. No credit was given to employees for services previously rendered. The following selected information about the plan is presented for the years ending December 31, 2004 and 2005:

	2004	2005
Service cost	$380,000	$380,000
Amount funded at beginning of year	$400,000	$420,000
Expected rate of return on plan assets	9%	9%
Discount rate	8%	8%

Jacob's also funded the 2005 amount on January 1, 2005. There were no other components of pension expense for the company during the year.

1. Compute the pension expense for Jacob's Ladder Company for the 2004 fiscal year.
2. Compute the pension expense for Jacob's Ladder Company for the 2005 fiscal year.

Exercise 18-9: Computing Pension Expense with Prior Service Costs. Christy Anderson Co. adopted a defined benefit pension plan on December 31, 2003, and incurred prior service costs of $334,000 by giving employees credit for service rendered prior to the adoption of the pension plan. Christy assumes that the projected benefit obligation will grow at 9% and amortizes the prior service cost over 16 years but funds it by making equal payments to the fund trustee at the end of each of the next 10 years. It is presumed that the fund assets will grow at an average rate of 8½%. Service cost is determined to be $85,000 and is fully funded at the end of each year.

1. Determine the pension expense for 2004 and 2005.
2. What is the balance in the prepaid/accrued account at the end of 2005?

Exercise 18-10: Pension Expense, Multi-Year with Prior Service Costs. Topsy-Turvey Corp. adopted a defined benefit pension plan on January 1, 2005, and gave present employees some credit for services already rendered. The cost of these benefits was $800,000, which is being amortized to pension expense over 15 years but is being funded over 20 years. Payments, including service cost, are made to a trustee on December 31 of each year. The following information is available for 2005 and 2006:

	2005	2006
Service cost	$240,000	$245,000
Discount rate		6%
Expected return on plan assets		5%

1. What is the amount of Topsy's prepaid/accrued pension cost account at December 31, 2006?
2. What is Topsy's projected benefit obligation at December 31, 2006?

Exercise 18-11: Pension Expense, Multi-Year with Prior Service Costs and Journal Entries. Joni Anderson Inc. adopted a noncontributory defined benefit pension plan on January 1, 2005, and gave employees credit for services already rendered. As a result, the prior service costs at January 1, 2005, were $170,000, which Joni decides to amortize over 17 years. All contributions to the fund will be made at the end of each year. The following information relating to Joni's pension plan is available for 2005 and 2006:

	2005	2006
Projected benefit obligation, January 1	$170,000	?
Discount rate	8%	8%
Fair value of plan assets, January 1	0	?
Expected rate of return on assets	9%	9%
Service costs	$50,000	$50,000
Amount funded	$60,000	$70,000

1. Compute the pension expense for 2005.
2. Prepare the appropriate journal entry to recognize pension expense and the amount funded for 2005.
3. Compute the pension expense for 2006.
4. Prepare the appropriate journal entry to recognize pension expense and the amount funded for 2006.
5. What is the balance in the prepaid/accrued pension cost account at the end of 2006?

Exercise 18-12: Amortizing Prior Service Cost. On January 1, 2004, Judkins amended its defined benefit pension plan, which resulted in prior service costs of $114,000. Judkins has 12 employees who are expected to retire as follows:

Two employees will retire at the end of 2005.

Four employees will retire at the end of 2008.

Three employees will retire at the end of 2014.

Two employees will retire at the end of 2016.

One employee will retire at the end of 2020.

1. Assuming that the prior service costs will be amortized over the future years of service of the employees, compute the amount of prior service costs that will be included in pension cost for the years 2004–2020.
2. Redo Part (1), using the average remaining years of service of the employees.

Exercise 18-13: Recognizing Gains/Losses. Determine the amount of gain/loss to recognize as a component of pension expense in each of the following independent situations:

Situation	Projected Benefit Obligation	Fair Value of Plan Assets	Remaining Service Period of Employees	Cumulative Unrecognized Gain/(Loss)
1	$1,000,000	$ 800,000	10	$ 120,000
2	1,200,000	1,400,000	6	(120,000)
3	1,400,000	1,100,000	4	(150,000)
4	1,500,000	1,600,000	6	150,000
5	2,000,000	2,100,000	12	200,000

Exercise 18-14: Minimum Pension Liability (CPA Adapted). On June 1, 2003, Paula Alger Corp. established a defined benefit pension plan for its employees. The following information was available one year later at May 31, 2004:

Projected benefit obligation	$14,500,000
Accumulated benefit obligation	12,000,000
Prepaid/accrued pension cost	200,000 cr.
Plan assets at fair market value	7,000,000
Unrecognized prior service cost	2,550,000

1. What is the amount of the additional liability that Paula should record to properly report its pension liability in its May 31, 2004 balance sheet?
2. How would your answer change if the unfunded prepaid/accrued pension cost account had a debit balance of $400,000? Prepare the appropriate journal entry.

Exercise 18-15: Minimum Pension Liability Entries. Scholz has a defined benefit pension plan for which it has always funded an amount equal to pension expense. Also, until December 31, 2004, the accumulated benefit obligation had always been less than the fair value of the plan assets. At December 31, 2005, these factors changed. First, Scholz had pension expense of $280,000 but only funded $250,000 of that amount. Also, because of a plan amendment, the unrecognized prior service costs were $40,000 at December 31, 2005, and with a downturn in the market the accumulated benefit obligation exceeded the fair value of the plan assets by $50,000.

1. Prepare the appropriate journal entry to recognize the additional liability.
2. Redo Part (1), assuming that the accumulated benefit obligation exceeded the fair value of the plan assets by $90,000.

Exercise 18-16: Minimum Pension Liability. The following information was extracted from the records of Laurie Harris Company as of December 31, 2004:

Accumulated benefit obligation at December 31, 2003	$314,000
Projected benefit obligation at December 31, 2003	355,000
Fair value of pension plan assets at December 31, 2003	289,000
Unrecognized prior service costs	30,000
Accrued pension cost (credit)	12,000

1. Determine whether Laurie should report a minimum liability for the pension obligation and, if necessary, prepare the journal entry to do so.
2. Assuming that the unrecognized prior service costs were $10,000, determine whether Laurie should report an additional liability for the pension obligation and, if necessary, prepare the appropriate journal entry.

Exercise 18-17: Comprehensive—Multi-Year. Alicia, Inc., has a defined benefit pension plan that covers all salaried employees. At the beginning of 2004, the prepaid/accrued pension cost account had a credit balance of $20,000. The following information was obtained at December 31, 2004 and 2005:

	2004	2005
Pension expense for the year	$ 250,000	$ 300,000
Amount funded at year-end	260,000	280,000
Accumulated benefit obligation at the end of the year	1,250,000	1,500,000
Fair value of plan assets at the end of the year	1,200,000	1,425,000
Unrecognized prior service costs at the end of the year	24,000	22,000

1. Record the pension expense and funding for each year.
2. Record any necessary entries for the additional pension liability, so as to recognize the appropriate pension minimum liability.
3. In comparative columns for 2004 and 2005, indicate the amounts that will be reported on the income statement and on the balance sheet related to this pension plan.

Problems

Problem 18-1: Pension Expense. Calvin Inc. provides a defined benefit pension plan for all its employees. As of January 1, 2004, the projected benefit obligation was $720,000, the fair value of plan assets was $600,000, there was a credit balance in the prepaid/accrued pension cost account of $65,000, and the unrecognized actuarial losses were $103,000. Other information related to the pension plan for 2004 is as follows:

Service cost	$79,000
Amortization of unrecognized prior service costs	$28,000
Expected return on plan assets	10%
Assumed discount rate on PBO	8%

Calvin contributed $100,000 to the pension fund just prior to year-end and paid pension benefits of $80,000 from pension plan assets. The average remaining service lives of the employees is 10 years.

Required:
1. What is the balance of the projected benefit obligation, and what is the market-related asset value at the end of the year?
2. Prepare the necessary journal entries to record the pension expense and the contribution to the pension fund. (*Hint:* Be sure to consider all the items that comprise pension expense.)
3. As of December 31, 2004, what is the balance in the prepaid/accrued pension cost account?

Problem 18-2: Amortizing Unrecognized Gains/Losses. On January 1, 2005, LaTesha Incorporated adopted a defined benefit pension plan for all full-time employees. The following information was obtained about the pension plan between 2005–2009:

| Year Ended December 31 | Estimated Change in: | | Actual Change in: | |
	PBO	Market-Related Value of Plan Assets	PBO	Market-Related Value of Plan Assets
2005	$220,000	$180,000	$222,000	$200,000
2006	242,000	196,000	258,000	220,000
2007	266,000	214,000	240,000	330,000
2008	293,000	233,000	290,000	510,000
2009	322,000	254,000	330,000	255,000

LaTesha amortizes any gains/losses in excess of the corridor over the average remaining years of service of its employees of 17 years. Each year's estimates are based on the prior year's actual amounts, so each year's gains/losses are new gains/losses and not cumulative.

Required:
Compute the amount of gains/losses that should be included in determining pension expense for the years 2005 through 2009.

Problem 18-3: Pension Expense. Bert & Ernie, Inc., provide a defined benefit pension plan to all its employees, and the following information was extracted from the company records as of January 1, 2004:

Accumulated benefit obligation	$660,000
Projected benefit obligation	750,000
Prepaid/accrued pension cost (debit)	20,000
Unrecognized prior service cost	220,000
Unrecognized net actuarial (gain) or loss	160,000

The assumptions used in the pension plan include a discount rate of 8%, an expected rate of return on plan assets of 10%, and an average employee service life of 15 years. Information related to the pension plan during 2004 is as follows:

Contributions to the pension trust, at year-end	$ 95,000
Service cost	154,000
Benefits to retirees	79,000

Required:

1. Assuming that the market-related asset value at January 1, 2004, is $815,000, determine the amount of pension expense to record for 2004.
2. Redo Requirement 1, assuming that the market-related asset value at January 1, 2004, is $500,000.
3. Ignoring any minimum liability, comment on the impact that the market-related asset/fair value of plan assets has on any liability that is reported on the balance sheet.

Problem 18-4: Minimum Liability. Thomas Company adopted a defined benefit pension plan for all its employees. The following information relates to the plan as of December 31, 2004:

	2004	2005
Accumulated benefit obligation, December 31	$425,000	$460,000
Fair value of plan assets, December 31	375,000	420,000
Pension expense	95,000	97,000
Unrecognized prior service cost	10,000	8,000
Prepaid/accrued pension cost January 1 (debit balance)	(12,000)	?

During 2004, Thomas contributed $90,000 to the pension fund for both years. The year 2004 was the first year that the accumulated benefit obligation had exceeded the fair value of the plan assets.

Required:

1. Determine the amount of the prepaid/accrued pension cost at December 31, 2004, before any adjustment for the minimum liability.
2. Determine whether Thomas Company should record a minimum liability at December 31, 2004, and if necessary, prepare the journal entry to do so.
3. Repeat Requirements 1 and 2 for 2005.

Problem 18-5: Minimum Liability with Entries. The following information as of the end of a fiscal year has been provided regarding various pension plans:

	Plan 1	Plan 2	Plan 3	Plan 4
Projected benefit obligation	$288,210	$326,795	$370,010	$420,150
Accumulated benefit obligation	216,150	250,100	297,500	340,000
Fair value of the plan assets	222,100	242,000	264,610	285,000
Unrecognized prior service costs	24,000	20,000	16,000	12,000

Required:

1. For each pension plan, determine the amount of any additional liability that is reported as part of other comprehensive income, assuming that the amount in the prepaid/accrued pension cost account before any adjustment to recognize the minimum liability is as follows:

	Plan 1	Plan 2	Plan 3	Plan 4
Prepaid/accrued pension costs at year-end, before adjustment to recognize the minimum liability	$3,000 dr.	$5,000 dr.	$9,100 cr.	$14,000 cr.

2. Assume that instead of being individual plans, these data are for successive years of the same plan. Determine the amount of any additional liability that is reported as part of other comprehensive income, assuming that the amount in the prepaid/accrued pension cost account before any adjustment to recognize the minimum liability at the *end of the first year* is a $3,000 debit balance. Also, assume that pension expense was $100,000, and the amount funded was $90,000 for the second and all succeeding years.

Problem 18-6: Conceptual Pension Problem (CPA Adapted). Carson Company sponsors a defined benefit pension plan that provides for pension benefits based on age, years of service, and compensation. Among the components that should be included in the net pension cost recognized for a period are service cost, interest cost, and return on plan assets.

Required:

1. What two accounting problems result from the nature of the defined benefit pension plan? Why do these problems arise?
2. How is the service cost component of the net pension expense determined?
3. How is the interest cost component of the net pension expense determined?
4. How is the estimated return on plan assets determined?
5. How is the actual return on plan assets determined?

Problem 18-7: Pension Expense, Journal Entries, Minimum Liability. Josie Stilson Company adopted an amendment to its defined benefit pension plan on January 1, 2005, which resulted in $525,000 of prior service costs. Stilson elected to amortize the costs over the average remaining years of service of the covered employees of 12.5 years. At December 31, 2005, the actuary determined the following:

	Jan. 1, 2005	Dec. 31, 2005	Dec. 31, 2006
Market-related value of plan assets	$2,490,000	$2,800,000	$3,400,000
Projected benefit obligation	3,825,000	4,164,000	4,439,000
Accumulated benefit obligation	3,250,000	3,500,000	3,850,000

The actuary also determined that the present value of the future benefits to be received by employees because of service rendered in any given year was $122,000. When making her calculations, the actuary assumed a discount rate of 8% and a return on assets of 10%. Total unrecognized losses at December 31, 2005, were $420,000.

At December 31, 2005, and before preparing the entry to recognize pension expense for the year, Stilson had a credit balance in the prepaid/accrued pension cost account of $30,000 and no balance in the deferred pension cost account. Stilson contributed $250,000 to the pension fund on December 30, 2005, and $300,000 on December 30, 2006. The market-related asset value and the fair value of the plan assets are the same amounts.

Required:

1. Compute pension expense for 2005, and prepare the necessary journal entry to record pension expense and the funding for the year.
2. Determine if a minimum liability must be reported, and if necessary, prepare the journal entry to record the additional liability.
3. Repeat Requirements (1) and (2) for 2006, assuming that the net asset/actuarial gains for the year were $20,000.

Problem 18-8: Pension Worksheet. Prepare a pension worksheet like that in Exhibit 18-1 (p. 870) for the years 2004 and 2005, using the following information. Then prepare the appropriate journal entries to recognize pension expense, the funding, and if necessary, the minimum liability.

	2004	2005
Projected benefit obligation, January 1	$9,000,000	?
Fair value of plan assets, January 31	8,100,000	?
Unamortized prior service costs, January 1	800,000	?
Prepaid/(accrued) pension costs, January 1	(290,000)	?
Unrecognized gains/(losses), January 1	(190,000)	?
Accumulated benefit obligation, December 1	7,900,000	$8,080,000
Service cost	300,000	300,000
Interest cost	630,000	650,000
Estimated return on plan assets	770,000	777,000
Actuarial gain (loss)	(124,000)	(92,000)
Asset gain (loss)	40,000	55,000
Pension benefits paid	800,000	825,000
Amortization of prior service costs	50,000	50,000
Funding	140,000	150,000

The average remaining service-years of the employees over which net unrecognized gains/losses are being amortized is 25 years. Note that the fair value of the plan assets at December 31, 2005, will have to be computed.

Problem 18-9: Pension Worksheet. Prepare a pension worksheet like that in Exhibit 18-1 (p. 870) for the years 2004 and 2005, using the following information. Then prepare the appropriate journal entries to recognize pension expense, the funding, and if necessary, the minimum liability.

	2004	2005
Projected benefit obligation, January 1	$6,550,000	?
Fair value of plan assets, January 31	5,270,000	?
Unamortized prior service costs, January 1	425,000	?
Prepaid/(accrued) pension costs, January 1	(355,000)	?
Unrecognized gains/(losses), January 1	(500,000)	?
Accumulated benefit obligation, December 1	5,400,000	$6,480,000
Service cost	185,000	185,000
Interest cost	393,000	426,420
Return on plan assets	168,500	147,920
Actuarial gain (loss)	(79,000)	28,300
Asset gain (loss)	(96,000)	(135,000)
Pension benefits paid	100,000	115,000
Amortization of prior service costs	40,000	40,000
Funding	320,000	600,000
Amortization of gains/losses	?	?

The average remaining service-years of the employees over which net unrecognized gains/losses are being amortized is 20 years. Note that the fair value of the plan assets at December 31, 2005, will have to be computed.

Problem 18-10: Comprehensive Pension Problem. McAffey Inc. has five full-time employees. On January 1, 2005, the company adopted a defined benefit pension plan covering all its full-time employees. The plan provides that, upon retirement, an annual payment will be made to each employee for the rest of his/her life, based on the following formula:

Number of Years Worked for Company × 5% × Highest Expected Salary

Credit for prior service is not granted. The following chart indicates the expected remaining service life of each employee and the expected highest salary they will earn with the company:

Employee	Remaining Service Life	Expected Highest Salary
B. Johnson	10 years	$70,000
J. Bradford	12 years	45,000
A. Smith	5 years	90,000
K. Larson	20 years	70,000
S. Whitmore	8 years	60,000

The average number of years that each employee is expected to live after retirement is 15 years, with the first retirement payment being paid one year after retiring. The company intends to contribute funds to a trust at the end of each year that equals the annual pension expense. These funds are expected to earn an annual return of 8%. A 6% discount rate is used to calculate the pension obligation.

Required:
1. Calculate the projected benefit obligation for McAffey Inc. as of December 31, 2005 and 2006.
2. Using just the information given (i.e., no plan amendments and no actuarial gains/losses), calculate the annual pension expense for 2005 and 2006.
3. Assume that at the end of 2007, the company amended the pension plan granting employees benefits for work provided up to five years prior to the adoption of the plan. All employees except K. Larson had been with the company during 2000–2004, and K. Larson had joined the company at the beginning of 2004. Compute the prior service cost, and calculate the amount of amortization that should be included in pension expense for 2008, amortizing the prior service costs by using the remaining-years-of-service method.
4. Calculate the accumulated benefit obligation for 2007 after the plan has been amended. Assume that current salaries for each employee are 80% of the expected highest salary. Also, assume that the company funded $125,000 to the pension plan at the end of 2007. Should the company record a minimum pension liability, and if so, how much is the minimum liability?

Problem 18-11: Comprehensive Pension Problem. For the past several years, JLR Music, Inc., has provided a defined benefit pension plan for all of its employees. For years prior to 2006, the company has funded the pension plan in an amount equal to pension expense.

On January 1, 2006, the company amended the plan to provide annual retirement payments for a greater percentage of salary. The amendment became effective immediately and caused an immediate increase in the projected benefit obligation. To fund the amendment, management decided to increase the contributions to the pension plan over an extended period of time. The amount of the prior service costs because of this amendment is reported below.

The following information relates to the pension plan for the year 2006 and was provided by the company's actuary.

Projected benefit obligation—January 1, 2006 (before the plan amendment)	$575,000
Accumulated benefit obligation—December 31, 2006	$440,000
Fair value of plan assets—January 1, 2006	$500,000
Fair value of plan assets—December 31, 2006	$640,000
Expected rate of return on plan assets	10%
Actual return on plan assets	$45,000
Unrecognized actuarial losses, January 1, 2006	$88,700
Unrecognized prior service costs because of January's amendment	$72,000
Service cost for the year 2006	$160,000
Discount rate	9%
Prepaid pension cost, January 1, 2006	$13,700

The company has decided to amortize the unrecognized prior service costs on a straight-line basis over the average remaining years of service of the employees, which is 12 years. Actual payments to retirees during the year were $95,000. The fair value of the plan assets at January 1, 2006, is equivalent to the market-related asset value on that date.

Required:
1. Prepare a schedule computing pension expense for 2006.
2. Before considering any minimum liability, determine the balance in the prepaid/accrued pension cost account as of December 31, 2006. (*Hint:* The amount funded will have to be determined by analyzing the plan asset balances at the beginning and end of the year.)
3. Using a pension worksheet as illustrated in Exhibit 18-1 (p. 870), reconcile this amount to the projected benefit obligation.
4. Determine whether a minimum liability should be recorded by the company.
5. Prepare all necessary journal entries related to the pension plan for the year 2006.

19
Accounting
FOR
Income Taxes

Two Sets of Books

Numerous novels have been written and movies produced in which the villain is a dishonest businessman because he keeps two sets of books—one set that he uses to report desired numbers and the other set that shows the real numbers. As a result of this characterization, you may be puzzled to learn that all companies—reputable companies—*must keep two sets of books*. The reason is that financial accounting rules as established by the SEC, the FASB, and its predecessors do not always agree with the tax rules and regulations passed by Congress and interpreted by the IRS and the tax courts. Thus, a company must keep two sets of books in order to comply with the conflicting requirements of two authoritative bodies. Further, some companies find it necessary to keep additional sets of books. For example, companies having governmental contracts are required to determine the cost of projects in conformity with the cost accounting rules established by the Cost Accounting Standards Board, which are different from those established by the FASB or the taxing

authorities. Thus, those companies keep a third set of books.

Having two sets of books does not mean that a company has two general journals or two general ledgers or prepares two sets of journal entries for every transaction. Rather, what occurs is that in addition to the general ledger, the company also keeps a *record of the differences* in the way that it accounts for various revenues, expenses, assets, liabilities, etc., for financial reporting purposes versus how it accounts for them for tax reporting. Thus, the company's accounting system is not changed in any way from how it has been explained in this text. Exhibit 19-1, which was taken from a recently published financial report of AT&T Corporation, is an example of such a worksheet, where the differences are identified between income taxes payable per the tax return and income tax expense per the income statement.

This chapter covers the accounting for the difference in income taxes as computed in accordance with tax rules and regulations and as computed for financial accounting purposes.

EXHIBIT 19-1

Worksheet Reconciling Taxes under GAAP vs. Income Tax Regulations (AT&T Corporation)

The following table shows the principal reasons for the difference between the effective income tax rate and the U.S. federal statutory income tax rate:

For the Years Ended December 31,	Year 3	Year 2	Year 1
U.S. federal statutory income tax rate	35%	35%	35%
Federal income tax at statutory rate (This is income tax payable, emphasis added.)	$2,908	$2,440	$3,044
Amortization of investment tax credits	(13)	(14)	(21)
State and local income taxes, net of federal income tax effect	201	183	273
Amortization of intangibles	28	23	14
Foreign rate differential	63	117	131
Taxes on repatriated and accumulated foreign income, net of tax credits	(36)	(32)	19
Legal entity restructuring	(84)	—	(195)
Research credits	(74)	(63)	(13)
Other differences—net	79	69	(13)
Provision for income taxes (This is income tax expense, emphasis added.)	$3,072	$2,723	$3,239
Effective income tax rate	37.0%	39.0%	37.2%

Learning Objectives

- Reconcile pretax income as reported on the income statement to taxable income as reported on the tax return.
- Classify the differences that result in pretax accounting income being different from taxable income as either temporary differences or permanent differences.
- Classify temporary differences as those that result in future taxable amounts and those that result in future deductible amounts.
- Explain the purpose of deferred tax accounts.
- Prepare the journal entry that records income taxes payable, the changes in the deferred tax accounts, and income tax expense.
- Account for the impact of changes in tax rates on the deferred tax accounts.
- Correctly report the deferred tax accounts on the balance sheet.
- Determine the effects of operating loss carrybacks and carryforwards in computing income taxes payable.

Theory—Reconciling Net Income with Taxable Income

The first part of accounting for income taxes is to compute income taxes payable (or refundable) for the current year, according to the rules of the Internal Revenue Code, rulings of tax courts, etc. Tax rules are not covered in this chapter, since they are covered in other accounting courses, and you can compute basic income taxes payable in accordance with tax rules. Computing such for all end-of-chapter materials is a relatively simple matter.

The second part of accounting for income taxes is to account for the differences between taxes per the income statement versus the tax return. These differences are called deferred taxes. Essentially, deferred taxes are the future tax consequences of events that are reported on the tax return in a different period from when they are reported on the income statement.

The final part of accounting for income taxes is to compute income tax expense for the year. This amount is the sum of the income taxes payable (as computed in Part #1) and deferred taxes (as computed in Part #2). Thus, the journal entry to record income tax expense, changes in deferred tax amounts, and income taxes payable is as follows:

Income Tax Expense	XXX		Balancing figure
Deferred Tax Accounts		XXX	Computed second
Income Tax Payable		XXX	Computed first

These three parts of accounting for income taxes comprise what is called the **asset-liability method**, which is the method required by U.S. GAAP. Since computing income taxes payable is ignored in this text and income tax expense is computed as the amount needed to balance the prior journal entry, the principal step in applying the asset-liability method (or in accounting for income taxes) is to account for deferred taxes. This is the topic of this chapter.

Defining Permanent and Temporary Differences

Assuming that income taxes payable have been computed (Part #1), the first step in accounting for deferred taxes (Part #2) is to identify all the reasons that accounting income before taxes on the income statement is different from taxable income on the tax return, as illustrated in Exhibit 19-1. Once these differences are identified, the second step is to categorize them as either permanent or temporary differences. **Permanent differences** are those that arise because various tax laws have been implemented that prevent certain revenues and expenses from ever being included on the tax return. For example, interest income from state and municipal bonds is never included on the tax return because Congress wants to encourage investment in such securities. However, interest income from such securities is reported on the income statement. Thus, interest from state and municipal securities is a permanent difference. *The key to identifying permanent differences is to know enough about the tax code to recognize those items of revenue or expense that are never included on the tax return.* Examples of permanent differences include:

- Interest income from state and municipal bonds.
- Life insurance premium expense on key officers and employees when the corporation is the beneficiary.
- Proceeds from life insurance on the death of key officers and employees.
- Payment of certain penalties or fines.

In contrast to permanent differences, **temporary differences** have the same total impact on the income statement as they do on the tax return; however, the effect in a particular year is different. An example of a temporary difference is the depreciating of an asset. The total depreciation of an asset over its life is exactly the same, regardless of the depreciation method used. However, the amount of depreciation in any year may be different. So if an accelerated method of depreciation is used to compute taxable income and the straight-line method is used to compute accounting income, the income in any particular year—and the taxes for any year—may be different. But over the life of the asset, the total income and the total taxes will be the same. Thus, temporary differences are the result of timing; the amount of revenue/expense on the income statement may be different for a given year from what is reported on the tax return.

In describing a temporary difference, the wording used in *SFAS No. 109*, "Accounting for Income Taxes," is that temporary differences arise when the *tax basis of an asset (or liability) differs from the amount that is reported on the financial statements*. Referring to the depreciation example, note that when the asset was first acquired, the tax basis of the asset was also the historical cost of the asset. But because the company uses a different depreciation method to compute taxable income than what is used to compute pretax accounting income, the tax basis in the years subsequent to purchase will be different from the undepreciated historical cost of the asset for financial reporting. So in the words of *SFAS No. 109*, the tax basis of the asset is different from the amount reported on the financial statements.

From the definitions of permanent and temporary differences, it can be seen that temporary differences give rise to deferred taxes and permanent differences do not. This is the reason why all the differences between taxable income and pretax accounting income are classified as being either permanent or temporary differences. Besides the depreciation example given earlier, other examples of temporary differences are as follows:

- Pension funding exceeds pension expense, where the tax return is prepared using the cash basis and the income statement is prepared on the accrual basis.
- Prepaid expenses are deducted for tax purposes when paid, but are deducted on the income statement when used.
- Sales or other revenue is recognized on the income statement on the accrual basis and on the cash basis for tax purposes.
- Involuntary conversion of assets, where the gain is deferred for tax purposes.
- Estimated warranty liabilities and expenses are recognized on the income statement when accrued but are deducted on the tax return when paid.
- Contingent losses are expensed on the income statement when accrued but are deducted on the tax return when paid.
- Bad debts are recognized on the income statement when accrued but are deducted on the tax return when the receivable is written off.
- Revenue received in advance (rent, subscriptions, etc.) is reported for tax purposes on the cash basis but is recognized on the income statement when earned.

To illustrate how temporary differences affect deferred tax amounts, assume that a company uses an accelerated method to compute taxable income on the tax return and the straight-line method to compute pretax accounting income on the income statement. Refer to Exhibit 19-2 and note that in the earlier years of the life of the asset, the accelerated depreciation method results in greater depreciation deductions on the tax return than will be reported as an expense on the income statement under the straight-line method. The result is that the company initially records a deferred tax liability, indicating that the company is postponing paying taxes. But sometime in the future these taxes will be paid; they are only being deferred. This deferred tax liability increases as long as the depreciation amounts under the accelerated method are greater than under the straight-line method. Then, in the later years of the asset's life, when the amount of depreciation under the accelerated method is less than under the straight-line method, the deferred tax liability begins to decrease and the company begins paying the deferred taxes. When the asset is completely depreciated, the balance in the deferred tax liability account is zero.

EXHIBIT 19-2

Illustrating a Temporary Difference and Deferred Taxes

	Col. 2	Col. 3		Col. 4	Col. 5

Cost of an asset: $10,000
Life of the asset: 5 years
Tax rate: 30%

Yr.	Accelerated Depreciation	Straight-Line Depreciation	Difference	Increase/(Decrease) in Deferred Tax for the Year (30% times amount in Col. 3)	Balance in Deferred Tax Account (Previous amount plus amount in Col. 4)
1	$ 4,000	$ 2,000	$2,000	$ 600	$600
2	2,400	2,000	400	120	720
3	1,440	2,000	(560)	(168)	552
4	1,080	2,000	(920)	(276)	276
5	1,080	2,000	(920)	(276)	0
	$10,000	$10,000	$ 0	$ 0	

In Exhibit 19-2, the temporary differences that cause the deferred tax account to increase are referred to as **originating differences**, and the differences that later cause the same deferred tax account to decrease are referred to as **reversing differences**. This is true of all temporary differences and not just those relating to depreciation.

Deferred Tax Assets and Deferred Tax Liabilities

As mentioned previously, temporary differences result in deferred taxes; permanent differences do not. Further, temporary differences result in either future taxable amounts (i.e., **deferred tax liabilities**) or future deductible amounts (i.e., **deferred tax assets**). Whether a temporary difference results in a future taxable or a future deductible amount is determined by when, or how much, is recognized on the income statement versus when, or how much, is reported on the tax return. In the accelerated depreciation example given, more depreciation was deducted on the tax return in the earlier years of the asset's life than was reported on the income statement, which gave rise to a deferred tax liability. So a deferred tax liability arises when tax deductions are initially greater than accounting expenses. A deferred tax liability also arises when revenue is recognized earlier on the income statement than when it is reported on the tax return. In both cases, a deferred tax liability *indicates that at some time in the future the taxes to be paid* *will be more than they would have been if the same accounting principles had been used on the tax return as are being used on the income statement.*

A deferred tax asset arises when expenses are recognized earlier or revenues are recognized later on the income statement as compared to when they are reported on the tax return. A deferred tax asset indicates that future taxes to be paid will be less than what they would have been if the same accounting principles had been used on the tax return as are being used on the income statement. Note that the timing patterns for deferred tax assets are just the opposite of those for deferred tax liabilities. Exhibit 19-3 summarizes the timing pattern of temporary differences that give rise to deferred tax liabilities and assets.

EXHIBIT 19-3

Identifying Deferred Taxes as Assets or Liabilities

Deferred tax liabilities arise when:

Expenses are reported on the tax return earlier than on the income statement.

Revenues are reported on the income statement earlier than on the tax return.

Deferred tax assets arise when:

Expenses are reported on the income statement earlier than on the tax return.

Revenues are reported on the tax return earlier than on the income statement.

When identifying whether a temporary difference gives rise to a deferred tax asset or a deferred tax liability, the guidance in Exhibit 19-3 is applied only to originating, not reversing, differences. Once it has been decided whether an originating difference gives rise to a deferred tax asset or liability, the reversing difference is classified the same way.

Having defined some fundamental concepts, the steps in applying the asset-liability method are shown in Exhibit 19-4. These steps represent suggestions for a logical way to proceed in accounting for income taxes.

EXHIBIT 19-4

Steps in Applying the Asset-Liability Method

1. Reconcile pretax accounting income on the income statement to taxable income on the tax return, and identify the differences as either permanent or temporary.

2. Compute income taxes payable.

3. Determine whether the temporary differences affect deferred tax assets or deferred tax liabilities.

4. Compute deferred tax amounts.

5. Classify the deferred taxes as either current or noncurrent, and prepare the appropriate journal entry, including income tax expense.

Following are three examples to illustrate and reinforce these steps in accounting for income taxes. Follow each example carefully, making sure that all the steps illustrated are clearly understood.

Example #1—Basic Procedures

The following information pertains to Aladdin Air Company for the year ended December 31, 2004:

- Income before taxes on the income statement is $213,000.
- The tax rate of all taxing entities (i.e., federal, state, local, etc.) is 40%, and Aladdin Air thinks this tax rate will be in effect for all future years.
- During the year, a fine of $9,000 was paid that is not deductible on the tax return.
- At the beginning of 2003, Aladdin Air had purchased equipment with a life of 6 years for $60,000. The equipment is being depreciated using the straight-line method for book purposes, and the straight-line election under MACRS using a 3-year life is employed for tax purposes. The resulting depreciation schedules are as follows:

	Year	Book Depr.	Tax Depr.	Difference
	2003	$10,000	$10,000	$ —
Current year	2004	10,000	20,000	(10,000)
	2005	10,000	20,000	(10,000)
	2006	10,000	10,000	—
	2007	10,000	—	10,000
	2008	10,000	—	10,000
		$60,000	$60,000	$ 0

- On June 30, 2004, Aladdin Air prepaid $24,000 of insurance premiums that cover it against damage to property for the next two years. For tax purposes, the entire amount was deducted in 2004.
- During 2004, a lawsuit was filed against Aladdin Air, and the company determined that it was probable it would realize a loss. Accordingly, a liability of $50,000 was accrued. Aladdin Air expects to settle the lawsuit in 2005.
- At the beginning of 2004, there was no balance in any deferred tax account.

Steps #1 and #2: Reconcile Pretax Accounting Income to Taxable Income, Identify the Differences as Permanent or Temporary, and Compute Income Taxes Payable.

A convenient way of reconciling accounting income before taxes to taxable income is to construct a schedule, as shown in Illustration 19-1, Table 1. Such a schedule identifies all differences between pretax accounting income and taxable income, with the differences then labeled as either temporary or permanent, based upon a knowledge of the tax regulations and financial accounting standards.

ILLUSTRATION 19-1, TABLE 1

Reconciling Pretax Accounting Income to Taxable Income

Pretax accounting income	$213,000	
Fines paid	9,000	Permanent difference
Depreciation	(10,000)	Temporary difference
Insurance premiums	(18,000)	Temporary difference
Lawsuit	50,000	Temporary difference
Taxable income	$244,000	

Explanation:

Fines paid: The problem identifies this difference as not being deductible for tax purposes. So it is a permanent difference and must be added back to accounting income to determine taxable income.

Depreciation: This is a temporary difference. The $10,000 difference is identified in the depreciation table, and since more depreciation is deducted on the tax return than on the income statement, this additional $10,000 is deducted from accounting income.

Insurance premiums: The insurance was purchased at mid-year and covers a two-year period. The entire amount is deducted on the tax return (as specified in the problem), but for financial reporting purposes only one-fourth is expensed and the rest is a prepaid asset. Therefore, the difference of $18,000 ($24,000 − $6,000) is deducted from pretax accounting income to determine taxable income.

Lawsuit: The probable loss is recognized on the income statement, but it is not deductible on the tax return until the amount is paid, which is anticipated to be in 2005. So this amount is added back to pretax accounting income.

Having determined taxable income, it is possible to determine taxes payable, which is done by multiplying taxable income by the tax rate of 40%, as follows:

Taxable income	$244,000
Tax rate	40%
Income taxes payable	$ 97,600

Step #3: Determine whether Temporary Differences Affect Deferred Tax Assets or Deferred Tax Liabilities.

Using the concepts of timing in Exhibit 19-3, the temporary differences are analyzed as follows:

1. For the temporary differences for depreciation and insurance:
   a. More deductions are being taken on the tax return in the current year than are being expensed on the income statement.
   b. There will be fewer taxes paid in the current year than the amount that would have been paid.
   c. These taxes eventually will be paid in the future.
   d. The company has a deferred tax liability.
2. For the temporary difference for the lawsuit:
   a. More expenses are being reported on the income statement than are being deducted on the tax return.

b. In the current year, there are more taxes being paid as compared to income tax expense on the income statement.

c. It is probable that this lawsuit will be settled and the company will pay cash, which then will be deducted on the tax return.

d. The company has an amount that can be deducted sometime in the future, which is a benefit to the company; so the company has a deferred tax asset.

The results of the previous thinking process are summarized in Illustration 19-1, Table 2.

ILLUSTRATION 19-1, TABLE 2

Determining Deferred Tax Asset or Deferred Tax Liability

Depreciation	$(10,000)	Temporary difference	Deferred tax liability (i.e., future taxable amount)
Insurance premiums	(18,000)	Temporary difference	Deferred tax liability (i.e., future taxable amount)
Lawsuit	50,000	Temporary difference	Deferred tax asset (i.e., future deductible amount)

These steps are critical components of accounting for deferred taxes. The conclusions reached will be used later to prepare the appropriate journal entry.

Step #4: Compute Deferred Tax Amounts.

The deferred tax amounts are computed using **enacted tax rates**, which are the tax rates expected to apply when the deferred tax liabilities/assets are settled. These enacted tax rates are the sum of the tax rates of the national, state, local, and foreign governments. Enacted tax rates are the current legislated rates. Tax rates merely proposed (or anticipated) but not yet enacted should not be used.

In computing deferred taxes, a schedule like that in Illustration 19-1, Table 3 is very useful. It is particularly helpful to schedule the temporary differences in this way when enacted tax rates change in future years.

ILLUSTRATION 19-1, TABLE 3

Scheduling Temporary Differences as to the Year They Will Reverse

Temporary Difference	Differences at End of 2004	Future Years and Differences				Net Difference
		2005	2006	2007	2008	
Depreciation	$(10,000)	$(10,000)	$ 0	$10,000	$10,000	$0
Insurance premiums	(18,000)	12,000	6,000			0
Lawsuit	50,000	(50,000)				0

The amounts in the column labeled "Differences at End of 2004" are the same reconciling items as found in Table 2. The amounts in the other columns represent when the differences at the end of 2004 (and 2005, in the case of depreciation) will reverse. The "Net Difference" column is included only to illustrate that the total amounts reported on the income statement eventually will be equal to the total amounts reported on the tax return. Having demonstrated this, this column will not be used in any future illustration.

Once the differences have been scheduled by year (as shown in Table 3), the deferred tax amounts are computed by multiplying the amounts in Table 3 by the enacted tax rates. This procedure is shown in Illustration 19-1, Table 4, the first part of which is a duplication of Table 3.

ILLUSTRATION 19-1, TABLE 4

Computing Deferred Taxes

Temporary Difference	Differences at End of 2004	Future Years and Differences				Net Difference
		2005	2006	2007	2008	
Depreciation	$(10,000)	$(10,000)	$ 0	$10,000	$10,000	$ 0
Insurance premiums	$(18,000)	$ 12,000	$6,000			0
Lawsuit	$ 50,000	$(50,000)				0
Enacted tax rate		40%	40%	40%	40%	
Tax effect of depreciation difference		$ (4,000)	$ 0	$ 4,000	$ 4,000	$ 4,000
Tax effect of insurance difference		$ 4,800	$2,400			7,200
Tax effect of lawsuit difference		$(20,000)				(20,000)
				Deferred taxes for 2004		$ (8,800)

The total deferred taxes that are reported on the 2004 balance sheet are $8,800. Illustration 19-1, Table 5 summarizes the results of the analysis to this point.

ILLUSTRATION 19-1, TABLE 5

Combining the Results of Table 2 and Table 4

Temporary Difference	Tax Amount (Table 4)	Liability or Asset (Table 2)
Depreciation	$ 4,000	Deferred tax liability
Insurance premiums	7,200	Deferred tax liability
Lawsuit	(20,000)	Deferred tax asset
Total deferred taxes	$ (8,800)	

Step #5: Classify the Deferred Taxes as Current/Noncurrent and Prepare the Journal Entry.

The last step is to determine whether the deferred tax amounts are current or noncurrent and to prepare the appropriate journal entry. In determining how the deferred taxes are to be classified, the FASB has two rules. The first rule is that the *deferred tax amounts are classified in a consistent manner with the assets or liabilities that gave rise to them.* For example, since a depreciable asset is classified as a noncurrent asset on the balance sheet, the deferred taxes that result from using different depreciation methods are also classified in a noncurrent category.

EXHIBIT 19-5

Classification of Deferred Taxes:

1. Consistent with asset or liability that gave rise to them, or

2. According to the date that the deferred taxes reverse.

If Rule #1 does not apply because the deferred tax amounts do not relate to specific assets or liabilities, the second rule is that the *deferred tax amounts are classified according to when they will reverse.* Those amounts that will reverse in the next fiscal year or operating cycle are classified as current, and all other deferred tax amounts are classified as noncurrent. Applying these rules to Aladdin Air results in Illustration 19-1, Table 6, which is a continuation of Table 5.

ILLUSTRATION 19-1, TABLE 6

Determining Balance Sheet Classification of Deferred Taxes

Temporary Difference	Tax Amount (Table 4)	Liability or Asset (Table 2)	Current Portion	Noncurrent Portion
Depreciation	$ 4,000	Deferred tax liability	$ 0	$4,000
Insurance premiums	7,200	Deferred tax liability	7,200	0
Lawsuit	(20,000)	Deferred tax asset	(20,000)	0
Total deferred taxes	$ (8,800)		$(12,800)	$4,000

Explanation:
All the deferred tax amounts were classified using the FASB's first rule of classification: classifying the deferred tax amounts in a manner consistent with the balance sheet items to which they relate. So because depreciation relates to a noncurrent asset, the deferred taxes related to depreciation are also noncurrent. Insurance premiums relate to a current asset (Prepaid Insurance), so the tax effects are also current. Finally, the lawsuit relates to an accrued liability, which, because the lawsuit is expected to be settled next year, is classified as a current liability; so the tax effects are also current.

The accounting for deferred taxes is now complete and the journal entry can be prepared. Income taxes payable of $97,600 as computed in Step 2 is entered first. Next, the deferred taxes as summarized in Table 6 are journalized. This is done by netting the current amounts together and the noncurrent amounts together. Finally, income tax expense is computed as the amount needed to balance the entry.

Income Tax Expense (balancing amount)	88,800	
Deferred Tax Asset, current (see Table 6)	12,800	
Deferred Tax Liability, noncurrent (see Table 6)		4,000
Income Taxes Payable (see analysis p. 899)		97,600

To record income tax expense, the change in the deferred tax accounts, and income taxes payable when there are no prior balances in the deferred tax accounts.

Because the income tax expense consists of the sum of the deferred taxes and the income taxes currently payable, income taxes payable is also termed "the *current* provision for income tax expense."

Example #2—Beginning Balance in Deferred Tax Accounts and Changes in Tax Rates

In the previous example, because there were no temporary differences prior to 2004, the beginning balances in the deferred tax accounts were zero. As a result, the end-of-the-year balances for the deferred tax accounts as computed in Illustration 19-1, Table 4 (p. 901), are also the year-end journal entry amounts. The purposes of this next example are to introduce (1) the preparing of the journal entry when the deferred tax accounts do not have a zero balance, and (2) the computing of the deferred tax amounts when income tax rates change. Important changes in this illustration as compared to the prior illustration are noted in italics.

Continuing with the Aladdin Air example, assume the additional following data for the year ended December 31, 2005:

- Financial statement accounting income before taxes is $230,000.
- *Recently enacted tax legislation changes the effective tax rate to 35% for all years, beginning after 2006 (i.e., the first year the tax rate becomes effective is 2007).*
- The depreciation schedule for Aladdin Air Company is replicated below.

	Year	Book Depr.	Tax Depr.	Difference
	2003	$10,000	$10,000	$ —
	2004	10,000	20,000	(10,000)
Current year	2005	10,000	20,000	(10,000)
	2006	10,000	10,000	—
	2007	10,000	—	10,000
	2008	10,000	—	10,000
		$60,000	$60,000	$ 0

- Because Aladdin Air had paid insurance premiums of $24,000 on June 1, 2004, for two years, no further insurance premiums are paid during 2005.
- The lawsuit that had been filed against Aladdin Air in 2004 was settled out-of-court for $60,000.
- Due to a recently inaugurated advertising and marketing campaign, Aladdin Air had presold some airline tickets in 2005 that will be redeemed and used in 2006. The total amount of such tickets is $20,000, which is included on the tax return but will not be considered revenue on the income statement until 2006.

© GETTY IMAGES, INC./PHOTODISC

Steps #1 and #2: Reconcile Pretax Accounting Income to Taxable Income, Identify the Differences as Permanent or Temporary, and Compute Income Taxes Payable.

Illustration 19-2, Table 1 is the reconciliation between pretax accounting income and taxable income and is similar in all respects to that previously illustrated. The important point is that all differences between pretax accounting income and taxable income are identified.

ILLUSTRATION 19-2, TABLE 1

Reconciling Pretax Accounting Income to Taxable Income

	2005	
Financial statement pretax income (given)	$230,000	
Depreciation: amount greater on the tax return	(10,000)	Temporary
Insurance: more expense on income statement than deducted on tax return	12,000	Temporary
Lawsuit: $60,000 deducted on tax return, $10,000 expensed on the income statement	(50,000)	Temporary
Presold tickets; taxed but not earned	20,000	Temporary
Taxable income	$202,000	

Explanation:

Depreciation: This difference is identified in the depreciation table.

Insurance premiums: The entire amount was deducted on the tax return in 2004, and so nothing is deducted this year. For financial reporting purposes, one-half of the $24,000 paid is expensed in 2005. Therefore, the difference in what was reported on the tax return for 2005 and the amount reported on the income statement for 2005 is $12,000. This amount is added back to accounting income to determine taxable income.

Lawsuit: The probable loss of $50,000 was recognized on the income statement last year, and an additional $10,000 is recognized this year. The entire $60,000 is deducted on the tax return this year, meaning that the difference between the amount deducted on the tax return and the amount expensed on the income statement is $50,000. This is deducted from the pretax accounting income to determine taxable income.

Presold tickets: This amount will not be included on the income statement until the services are rendered; however, the amount is included on the tax return for 2005, which is when the cash was received. So this amount is added to accounting income to determine taxable income.

Having computed taxable income, income taxes payable are now computed as follows:

Taxable income	$202,000
Income tax rate	40%
Income taxes payable	$ 80,800

Step #3: Determine whether Temporary Differences Affect Deferred Tax Assets or Deferred Tax Liabilities.

Regarding whether the above temporary differences affect deferred tax assets or deferred tax liabilities, note the following, using the guidance in Exhibit 19-3:

- The *depreciation difference affects a deferred tax liability* because the amount deducted on the tax return is greater than the amount deducted on the income statement.
- The $12,000 is a reversal of the prior year's difference. Last year, the difference was identified as a deferred tax liability, and so this year this difference will reduce that deferred tax liability.

- The lawsuit is another adjustment of a prior-year difference. Last year, the difference was identified as a deferred tax asset, and so this year this difference affects that deferred tax asset.
- The presold tickets are a new temporary difference, and since the amount of revenue reported on the tax return is greater than what is reported on the income statement, the difference is a future deductible amount. Therefore, according to the guidance in Exhibit 19-3, p. 897, this difference gives rise to a deferred tax asset.

These results are summarized in Illustration 19-2, Table 2.

ILLUSTRATION 19-2, TABLE 2

Deferred Tax Asset or Deferred Tax Liability

Depreciation	$(10,000)	Temporary difference	Deferred tax liability
Insurance premiums	12,000	Temporary difference	Deferred tax liability
Lawsuit	(50,000)	Temporary difference	Deferred tax asset
Presold tickets	20,000	Temporary difference	Deferred tax asset

Step #4: Compute Deferred Tax Amounts.

Having identified the temporary differences and whether they affect deferred tax assets or liabilities, the next step is to compute the deferred taxes. In Illustration 19-1, those computations were done in two tables to make the process as clear as possible; but having introduced that process, this step is simplified in this illustration by using one table. As before, the steps in preparing the table are:

- Schedule the differences by year. For most of the differences, this is done already in Illustration 19-1, Table 3 (p. 900). All that need be done is to copy the numbers into Illustration 19-2, Table 3. It is only for the new temporary difference that the schedule will have to be modified.
- Having scheduled the differences, those differences are then multiplied by the enacted tax rates for those years. The change in tax rates does not cause any difficulties; the schedule is completed the same as before. Changes in tax rates are just another change in an accounting estimate, and like all other changes in estimates, they are handled in the current and future periods.

Step #5: Classify the Deferred Taxes as Current/Noncurrent and Prepare the Journal Entry.

As before, Illustration 19-2, Table 4 summarizes the results of the preceding analysis. In addition, Table 4 also identifies whether the ending balances are classified as current or noncurrent. To review how this determination was made, because depreciation relates to assets that are categorized in a noncurrent balance sheet category, the deferred taxes related to depreciation are also classified in a noncurrent category. Because insurance premiums relate to an asset that is classified

ILLUSTRATION 19-2, TABLE 3

Determining Deferred Taxes

Temporary Difference	Differences for 2005	Years and Amounts in which the Difference Will Reverse				
		2006	2007	2008	2009	Totals
Depreciation	$(10,000)	$ 0	$10,000	$10,000		
Insurance premiums	12,000	6,000				
Lawsuit	(50,000)					
Presold tickets	20,000	$(20,000)				
Enacted tax rate		*40%*	*35%*	*35%*	*35%*	
Tax effect of depreciation difference		$ 0	$ 3,500	$ 3,500	$0	$ 7,000
Tax effect of insurance difference		2,400				2,400
Tax effect of lawsuit difference						0
Tax effect of presold tickets		(8,000)				(8,000)
Total deferred taxes		$ (5,600)	$ 3,500	$ 3,500	$0	$ 1,400

Explanation:
All amounts in the "Totals" column are the balances needed in the deferred tax accounts at the end of the fiscal year; they are not the adjusting journal entry amounts. For example, the balance of deferred taxes related to the lawsuit is now zero because there is no difference in the total amounts that have been reported on the income statement versus what has been reported on the tax return.

as a current asset, the related tax effects are also classified in a current category. And, because the presold tickets relate to a current liability (Unearned Revenue), the related tax effects are also classified in a current category.

ILLUSTRATION 19-2, TABLE 4

Summary of Steps #1 through #5 and Classification

Temporary Difference	Desired Ending Balances (Table 4)	Liability or Asset (Table 2)	Current Portion	Noncurrent Portion
Depreciation	$ 7,000	Deferred tax liability		$7,000
Insurance premiums	2,400	Deferred tax liability	$ 2,400	
Lawsuit	0	Deferred tax asset		
Presold tickets	(8,000)	Deferred tax asset	(8,000)	
Total deferred taxes	$ 1,400		$(5,600)	$7,000

The final step—and new procedure in this illustration—is to compare the balances needed in the various deferred accounts (as shown in Illustration 19-2, Table 4) to what the present balances are in the deferred accounts. The present balances were computed in Illustration 19-1, Table 6 (p. 902), and are shown in Illustration 19-2, Table 5. The adjusting journal entry amounts are the differences as shown in Table 4. When preparing the journal entry, as before, income tax expense is computed as a balancing amount.

ILLUSTRATION 19-2, TABLE 5

Determining Amounts for the Journal Entry

	Beginning-of-Year Balances (Illustration 19-1, Table 6)	Adjustments Necessary	End-of-Year Balances (Illustration 19-2, Table 4)
Current assets	$12,800 dr.	$ 7,200 cr.	$5,600 dr.
Noncurrent assets	0	0	0
Noncurrent liability	4,000 cr.	3,000 cr.	7,000 cr.
Total adjustment	$ 8,800 dr.	$10,200 cr.	$1,400 cr.

Income Tax Expense	91,000	
Deferred Tax Asset, current		7,200
Deferred Tax Liability, noncurrent		3,000
Income Taxes Payable		80,800

To record income tax expense, the change in the deferred tax accounts, and income taxes payable when balances exist in the deferred tax accounts.

Regarding the amounts to report on the year-end balance sheet, $5,600 is reported under current assets due to the netting of the two current accounts, and $7,000 is reported under long-term liabilities.

Example #3—Comprehensive Practice Problem

This example continues the previous examples for Aladdin Air, except for the year 2006, and allows all the necessary numbers to be computed and the final journal entry to be prepared. Check figures are provided throughout the problem, and the computations are provided in Appendix A at the end of this chapter (p. 917).

- Financial statement pretax accounting income is $180,000. The decline in income was caused by the economy entering a slight recession during the latter part of the year.
- Because of the recession, Congress decided to postpone for one year the reduction in tax rates, and as a result, the effective tax rate remained at 40% for 2007. However, the enacted tax rate for 2008 and all future years is still 35%.
- The depreciation schedule for the equipment that Aladdin Air acquired in 2003 is replicated below.

	Year	Book Depr.	Tax Depr.	Difference
	2003	$10,000	$10,000	$ —
	2004	10,000	20,000	(10,000)
	2005	10,000	20,000	(10,000)
Current year	2006	10,000	10,000	—
	2007	10,000	—	10,000
	2008	10,000	—	10,000
		$60,000	$60,000	$ 0

- At mid-year, Aladdin's insurance carrier billed Aladdin $30,000 for coverage for the next two years. Aladdin paid the amount and, as before, deducted the entire $30,000 on the tax return for 2006, but it pro-rated the amount for financial reporting purposes.

- Aladdin earned $10,000 from an investment in municipal bonds during the year.
- Individuals who had purchased airline tickets in 2005 due to Aladdin's advertising campaign did use their tickets during 2006. In addition, Aladdin continued the campaign, and at the end of 2006, it had another $30,000 of presold tickets that will be used in 2007.

Steps #1 and #2: Reconcile Pretax Accounting Income to Taxable Income, Identify the Differences as Permanent or Temporary, and Compute Income Taxes Payable.

Answer: Taxable income is $163,500. Income taxes payable is $65,400.

Step #3: Determine whether Temporary Differences Affect Deferred Tax Assets or Liabilities.

Answer: The tax effects of depreciation and insurance are deferred tax liabilities, and the tax effect of the presold tickets is a deferred tax asset.

Step #4: Compute Deferred Tax Amounts.

Answer: Total deferred taxes are $4,125. This is comprised of a deferred tax asset of $12,000 and a deferred tax liability of $16,125.

Step #5: Classify the Deferred Taxes as Current/Noncurrent and Prepare the Journal Entry.

Partial answer: Credit to Deferred Tax Asset, current, for $2,225, and credit to Deferred Tax Liability, noncurrent, for $500.

Valuation Allowance

SFAS No. 109 requires that deferred tax asset accounts be evaluated each year and that they be reduced by a **valuation allowance** when it is more likely than not (i.e., the probability is greater than 50%) that not all of the deferred tax asset amounts will be realized. Deferred tax asset amounts will not be realized when it is anticipated that future income will be insufficient for the company to fully take advantage of the tax savings from them. When making the determination of whether the deferred tax asset accounts should be reduced by a valuation allowance, all available evidence—both positive and negative—is considered. Some examples of information that might be pertinent to assessing whether a valuation allowance is needed are given here.

Negative evidence:

- Cumulative losses in recent years.
- A history of operating losses or tax credit carryforwards that the company did not use.
- Losses are expected in early future years (by a presently profitable entity).
- Unsettled circumstances that, if unfavorably resolved, would adversely affect future operations and profit levels on a continuing basis in future years.
- A carryback/carryforward period so brief that it would limit realization of tax benefits if:

    (1) Significant deductible temporary differences are expected to reverse in a single year, or

    (2) The enterprise operates in a traditionally cyclical business.

Positive evidence:

- Existing contracts or sales backlog that will provide future taxable income.
- An excess of appreciated asset value over the tax basis of the entity's net assets.
- A strong history of income, despite the loss resulting in the carryforward. The loss should show evidence that it was unusual, infrequent, or extra-ordinary.

When a valuation account should be established, the offsetting account is to the income tax expense account. To illustrate how this is done, assume that in 2005 Aladdin Air decides to reduce its deferred tax asset account by $1,000. Illustration 19-3 shows the journal entry as it had been prepared previously and how it changes because of establishing an allowance account.

ILLUSTRATION 19-3

Journal Entry with Valuation Account

	As Prepared Previously		With Valuation Account	
Income Tax Expense	91,000		*92,000*	
Deferred Tax Asset, current		7,200		7,200
Deferred Tax Liability, noncurrent		3,000		3,000
Valuation Allowance				*1,000*
Income Taxes Payable		80,800		80,800

Thus, income tax expense is increased if it is thought to be more likely than not that all the income tax benefits from deferred tax asset accounts will not be realized.

After a valuation allowance account is established, it should be evaluated at the end of each fiscal year and a determination made as to the adequacy of the amount. Any subsequent adjustments, either to further increase the allowance account or to reduce the amount, are adjusted to the income tax expense account.

Financial Reporting

Regarding the reporting of deferred taxes on the income statement, the income tax expense amount may be presented either as a single sum or separated into its current and deferred tax amounts.[1] Either way is acceptable, and both are used frequently. Exhibit 19-6 illustrates how the income tax expense is reported under either alternative for Aladdin Air for 2005. When the income tax expense amount is reported as a single sum on the income statement, the separation between the current and deferred portions is done in the notes to the financial statements.

---

[1]U.S. GAAP also requires that income from continuing operations and every line thereafter be shown net of tax. How these amounts are computed is discussed in Appendix B at the end of the chapter.

EXHIBIT 19-6

Presentation of Income Tax Expense on the Income Statement

OPTION #1: Presenting the income tax expense as one amount:

Income from continuing operations before income taxes	$230,000
Provision for income taxes	(91,000)
Income from continuing operations	$139,000

OPTION #2: Breaking the income tax expense amount into its components:

Income from continuing operations before income taxes		$230,000
Provision for income taxes:		
Current	$80,800	
Deferred	10,200	(91,000)
Income from continuing operations		$139,000

The reporting of deferred taxes on the balance sheet corresponds to the way in which the adjusting journal entry is prepared. That is, on the balance sheet the current deferred tax asset and liability amounts are netted and reported as either a current asset or a current liability. Also, the noncurrent deferred tax accounts are netted and reported as either a noncurrent asset or noncurrent liability. This is illustrated in Exhibit 19-7, which was taken from a recently published statement of AT&T.

EXHIBIT 19-7

Presentation of Income Tax Expense on the Balance Sheet

(dollars in millions)	Year 2	Year 1
Assets:		
Cash and cash equivalents	$ 3,160	$ 318
Marketable securities	—	307
Receivables, less allowances of $1,060 and $988		
Accounts receivable	8,652	8,675
Other receivables	403	5,684
Deferred income taxes (emphasis added)	*1,310*	*1,252*
Other current assets	593	541
Total current assets	$14,118	$16,777
Liabilities:		
Long-term debt	$ 5,556	$ 7,857
Long-term benefit-related liabilities	4,255	3,142
Deferred income taxes (emphasis added)	*5,453*	*5,711*
Other long-term liabilities and deferred credits	3,322	3,390

In the notes to the financial statements, companies usually disclose information about the total taxes owing and how much is owed to foreign governments and also reconcile the income tax payable amount to the income tax expense amount. Exhibit 19-8 illustrates some typical note disclosures regarding deferred taxes that were taken from a recently published report of AT&T.

EXHIBIT 19-8

Typical Note Disclosures

The U.S. and foreign components of income from continuing operations before income taxes and the provision for income taxes are presented in this table.

For the Year Ended December 31,		Comments
Income from continuing operations before income taxes		
United States	$8,318	
Foreign	(11)	
Total	$8,307	Reported as income from continuing operations on the income statement.
Provision for income taxes		
Current:		
Federal	$2,908	
State and local	251	
Foreign	41	
Total	$3,200	This is the income taxes payable amount as computed from the tax return.
Deferred:		
Federal	$ (172)	
State and local	58	
Foreign	(5)	
	$ (119)	This is the total change in the deferred tax accounts.
Deferred investment tax credits	$ (14)	
Provision for income taxes	$3,067	This is the income tax expense amount, which is the sum of the income taxes payable and the deferred tax adjustment amounts.

Net Operating Loss Carrybacks/Carryforwards

When tax deductions exceed tax revenues, the result is a **net operating loss (NOL)**. Currently, federal tax law permits a NOL to be offset against profits in other years, either by *carrying back the loss two years or carrying forward the loss up to 20 years.* Doing so results either in receiving a refund of taxes paid in previous years when the NOL is carried back, or a deferred tax asset when the NOL is carried forward. To receive the tax advantage of a NOL requires that a company earn income and pay taxes in any of the two previous years or earn an income and pay taxes in a future year.

When a NOL can be carried back, it is usually preferable to do so rather than carrying the NOL forward. This is because the tax advantage of carrying back the NOL is assured (i.e., taxes have been paid in a prior year), whereas the tax advantage of carrying forward a NOL is not assured but is dependent upon the company earning a profit and paying taxes in the future. A second reason for preferring to carry back a NOL when possible is the time value of money. Carrying back a NOL results in an immediate refund of taxes that were paid in prior years, whereas any refund that will be received in the future is not immediate.[2]

---

[2]There are various exceptions to this general rule of first carrying back a loss, one of which is that, because of changing tax rates, a larger refund will be obtained by carrying forward the NOL.

When a company elects and is able to carry back a NOL, it should first apply the NOL to the earliest year possible (i.e., two years prior to the current year), then to the prior year. If any loss remains, that amount is then carried forward. Carrying back a NOL to the earliest year possible ensures that the company can take the best advantage of the NOL. For example, assume that the Gold & Diamond Ranch incurred the net incomes and net losses shown in Illustration 19-4:

ILLUSTRATION 19-4

Net Incomes and Net Losses

Year	Taxable Income	Comments
2006	$ 62,000	Best to offset to earliest
2007	44,000	year possible.
2008	(80,000)	
2009	(40,000)	
2010	30,000	

In 2008, carrying back $62,000 of the NOL to 2006 and then carrying back the rest of the $80,000 loss (i.e., $18,000) to 2007 results in taking advantage of the entire $80,000 and permits part of the loss of $40,000 in 2009 to be carried back to 2007. However, if the $80,000 loss is first offset against the 2007 income of $44,000 and then the rest of the loss is carried back to 2006, the Gold & Diamond Ranch will not receive the maximum possible tax advantage of the 2009 loss of $40,000 because that loss cannot be carried back to 2006.

Illustration 19-5 shows the accounting for carrying back and carrying forward a NOL. The Gold & Diamond Ranch data are used, along with tax rates and the amount of taxes that were paid in prior years. In 2008, the Ranch first carries back $62,000 of the NOL to 2006, which results in a refund of $21,700. Then, the Ranch carries back the rest of the $80,000 NOL (or $18,000) to 2007, which results in a further refund of $6,300 ($18,000 × 35%). So the total refund the Ranch will receive in 2008 for the NOL is $28,000. Note that, in carrying back the NOL, the Ranch uses the tax rates in effect in the years in which net income was earned, not the tax rates in effect when the NOL was incurred. In other words, the Ranch cannot claim a refund of taxes for an amount more than what was paid. To claim the refund for taxes previously paid, the Ranch will have to file amended tax returns for 2006 and 2007.

ILLUSTRATION 19-5

Carrying Back the NOL

Year	Taxable Income	Tax Rates	Taxes Paid
2006	$ 62,000	35%	$21,700
2007	44,000	35%	15,400
2008	(80,000)	40%	
2009	(40,000)	40%	
2010	30,000	40%	

The journal entry in 2008 to record the tax benefit from the NOL is as follows:

Tax Refund Receivable	28,000	
Tax Benefit Due to NOL		28,000

To record the tax benefit of carrying back a NOL.

The tax benefit due to NOL is reported on the income statement in the same way that income tax expense is reported.

In 2009, the Ranch first carries back $26,000 to 2007,[3] which results in another tax refund and tax benefit of $9,100. Since the NOL in 2009 is not fully absorbed, the rest of the NOL ($14,000) is carried forward to a future year. Carrying forward this NOL results in a deferred tax asset of $5,600, which is computed as $14,000 × 40%. Assuming that it is more likely than not that the tax benefits of the deferred tax asset will be assured, the following journal entry records the tax effects of the $40,000 NOL for 2009:

Tax Refund Receivable ($26,000 × 35%)	9,100	
Deferred Tax Asset ($14,000 × 40%)	5,600	
Tax Benefit Due to NOL		14,700

To record in 2009 the tax benefits resulting from a NOL.

Like other deferred tax assets, the loss carryforward amount should be evaluated as to whether a valuation allowance account is necessary, considering that realization of the tax benefit is dependent upon future earnings. When appropriate, a valuation allowance account is established and the tax benefit due to NOL account is reduced accordingly.

International Financial Reporting Practices

INTERNATIONAL

Companies that follow U.S. GAAP must use a **comprehensive allocation method** of accounting for deferred taxes, which is the recognition of all temporary differences between tax and financial reporting rules. This method has been criticized on the basis that many companies report a deferred tax liability in their financial statements that is not representative of their true future tax obligation. That is, many temporary differences between tax and financial reporting rules are recurring in nature, and therefore, as one temporary difference begins to reverse, a new temporary difference occurs that offsets the reversing effect of the old difference.

As an example, a common temporary difference that occurs in companies' books is related to depreciation. Typically, for tax purposes, an accelerated method is employed, whereas, for financial reporting purposes, the straight-line method is used. This creates a deferred tax liability in the early years of the asset's life that begins to reverse in the later years. However, a company (particularly a growth company) is likely to purchase new depreciable assets that will offset the reversing effect of old assets. As a result, many companies report deferred tax liabilities that are virtually certain not to reverse in the future.

Exhibit 19-9 presents deferred tax liabilities reported by various companies in their 1999 annual reports and how the liabilities compare to reported total debt and total liabilities. Each company reports a deferred tax liability that represents a significant portion of its total liabilities. Intel Corp. reported a deferred tax liability of $3,130 million, which is the largest liability presented on its balance sheet. A convincing argument could be presented that Intel's deferred taxes

---

[3]Since $18,000 of the NOL in 2008 has already been offset against the $44,000 in 2007, the maximum amount of the NOL in 2009 that can be carried back to 2007 is $26,000.

do not meet the definition of a liability. That is, it is unlikely that the liability actually represents an obligation of $3,130 of future taxes due to the probability that recurring temporary differences will offset the reversals of current temporary differences.

EXHIBIT 19-9

Deferred Tax Liabilities Reported by Companies

Company	Deferred Tax Liability ($m)	Percentage of Total Debt	Percentage of Total Liabilities
McDonalds	$1,174	16.1%	10.3%
Honeywell International	864	17.1	5.8
PepsiCo	1,209	39.7	11.3
MCI Worldcom Inc.	4,877	26.9	12.2
GTE Corp.	3,406	24.4	14.5
Intel Corp.	3,130	74.3	27.7

As an alternative to comprehensive allocation, UK GAAP requires that a deferred tax liability not be recognized if, in the opinion of the directors, the temporary differences between tax and financial reporting that give rise to the liability are not expected to reverse in the foreseeable future. UK GAAP defines "foreseeable future" in this case as three years. This method is referred to as the **partial allocation method**. Obviously, partial allocation gives more discretion to managers, which has the potential disadvantage of increased earnings manipulation by managers. However, the method has a potential advantage of providing more relevant information about the actual liability that is associated with future taxes payable. Mexico is another country that follows the partial allocation method.

Compared to the comprehensive allocation method, partial allocation will result in higher profitability ratios due to recognizing lower income tax expense. This effect will also increase stockholders' equity through retained earnings. In addition, companies will report lower total liabilities under the partial allocation method, and thus some risk measures (e.g., debt/equity ratios) will be affected.

The International Accounting Standards Committee in *IAS No. 12* requires the comprehensive allocation method. As a result, except for some differences in disclosure requirements, U.S. GAAP and *IAS No. 12* provide similar results when accounting for income taxes.

Tax Effects of Changes in Accounting Principles

In Chapter 9, the financial reporting for a change in an accounting principle was illustrated but without the complicating factor of the associated tax effect. As mentioned in the early part of this chapter, deferred taxes become an issue when there is a timing difference between when the effects of a transaction are reported on the income statement and when they are included in taxable income. Thus, when a change in an accounting principle occurs, there are several possible impacts on deferred taxes. For example, assuming that a change is made in a depreciation method for income statement purposes, the following possibilities exist:

1. Initially, there was no difference in the depreciation methods for computing pretax accounting income and taxable income. Thus, with the change to a new depreciation method for financial reporting, there is now a difference in the accumulated depreciation amounts, and a deferred tax account must be established, assuming that the new depreciation method had been used since the asset was acquired.

2. Initially, there was a difference in the depreciation methods for computing pretax accounting income and taxable income, and so a deferred tax account was established. But with the change to a new depreciation method, there is no difference in the accumulated depreciation amounts, and the amount in the deferred tax account has to be reversed. This is done as an adjustment to the current year's income tax expense.

3. Initially, there was a difference in the depreciation methods for computing pretax accounting income and taxable income, and so a deferred tax account was established. The new depreciation method is still not the same method as is used for tax purposes, so a deferred tax account is still necessary, but the amount has to be adjusted.

To illustrate the first possibility, suppose that in December 2006, the L&B Company, which has been using an accelerated depreciation method for financial reporting purposes, switched to the straight-line method. For tax purposes, L&B was using and will continue to use the accelerated depreciation method. Thus, prior to the change in an accounting principle, L&B did not need a deferred tax account, but now it must establish one. The depreciation amounts shown in Table 19-1 were computed for all assets for all prior periods and summarized by year. The enacted tax rate for all taxing districts for all years is 40%.

TABLE 19-1

Computing the Cumulative Effect of an Accounting Principle Change

switching to

	Accelerated Method	Straight-Line	Difference
Years prior to the change:			
Prior to 2005	$1,980,000	$1,740,000	$240,000
2005	220,000	188,000	32,000
		Total difference	$272,000
The year of change:			
2006	$ 208,000	$ 190,000	$ 18,000

As shown in the table, the accumulated depreciation account must be decreased by $272,000 as a result of the accounting principle change. But the net-of-tax amount of the cumulative effect is $163,200. (The tax effect is computed as $272,000 × 40%. So the net-of-tax effect is computed as $272,000 × 60%.) Thus, the journal entry—considering deferred tax consequences—for this accounting principle change is as follows:

Accumulated Depreciation	272,000	
Deferred Tax Liability		108,800
Cumulative Effect of an Accounting		
Principle Change		163,200

To record an accounting principle change, which causes a deferred tax account to be created.

The second possibility mentioned is that because of the change in the depreciation method, there is now no need for a deferred tax account. This would be the case when L&B had used an accelerated method of depreciation on the tax return and the straight-line method on the income statement and then changed to an accelerated method on the income statement. So the amount in the deferred tax liability account of $108,800 has to be reversed. In that case, the resulting journal entry is as follows:

Accumulated Depreciation	272,000	
Deferred Tax Liability	108,800	
Cumulative Effect of an Accounting		
Principle Change		380,800

To record an accounting principle change and also reverse the deferred tax account, which is no longer necessary.

The third possibility, where a deferred tax account is still necessary but the amount has to be changed, follows this same pattern and, therefore, is not illustrated. This same concept of accounting for deferred taxes is applied when a change in an accounting principle has to be reported as a prior-period adjustment.

Summary

The result of financial accounting rules not being consistent with tax rules is that every company that issues a public financial report and pays taxes must keep two sets of books. The differences between pretax accounting income and taxable income are caused by both permanent and temporary differences. Temporary differences result in deferred tax accounts being created; permanent differences do not.

Accounting for income taxes consists of (1) computing the amount of taxes payable or refundable for the current year according to the rules of the Internal Revenue Code, (2) computing deferred tax assets and liabilities, and (3) computing income tax expense. The procedures illustrated in this chapter to account for deferred taxes are as follows:

1. Reconcile pretax accounting income on the income statement to taxable income on the tax return, and identify the differences as either permanent or temporary.
2. Compute income taxes payable.
3. Determine whether the temporary differences give rise to deferred tax assets or deferred tax liabilities.
4. Compute deferred tax amounts.
5. Classify the deferred taxes as either current or noncurrent, and prepare the appropriate journal entry, including income tax expense.

In preparing that journal entry, income tax expense is computed as the amount needed to balance the journal entry.

For financial reporting purposes, the income tax expense amount is reported on the income statement, either as a single amount or separated into its current and deferred components. On the balance sheet, the deferred tax amount is reported as a net current amount and a net noncurrent amount. The deferred tax amounts are classified in the same way as the underlying asset or liability that gave rise to them. For example, since long-lived assets are classified as noncurrent, the deferred taxes that result from using a different depreciation method for accounting purposes as compared to what is used for tax purposes are also classified as noncurrent. When the deferred taxes do not associate with some asset or liability, the deferred taxes are classified according to when they will reverse. The deferred taxes that will reverse within the next year are classified as current, and all other deferred taxes are classified as noncurrent.

At the end of each reporting period, any deferred tax asset is reduced by a valuation allowance when it is more likely than not that the entire amount of the deferred tax asset will not be realized. In making this determination, both positive and negative evidence is considered. The effect of establishing a valuation allowance is to increase income tax expense for the period.

A deferred tax asset also may be established for a NOL. According to current tax rules, a NOL may be carried back, and income taxes recouped, for two years or forward up to 20 years. A carryback results in an income tax benefit (as contrasted to income tax expense) and is reported on the income statement in the same way as income tax expense. A carryforward may result in a deferred tax asset, which results in an income tax benefit.

APPENDIX A: Solution to Comprehensive Practice Problem

Steps #1 and #2: Reconcile Pretax Accounting Income to Taxable Income, Identify the Differences as Permanent or Temporary, and Compute Income Taxes Payable.

Financial statement pretax income	$180,000	
Interest income from municipals	(10,000)	Permanent
Depreciation difference	0	
Insurance premiums	(16,500)	Temporary
Presold tickets	10,000	Temporary
Taxable income	$163,500	
Income tax rate	× 0.40	
Income taxes payable	$ 65,400	

Supporting computations:

Insurance:	
Amount per the income statement, to June 30	$ 6,000
Amount per the income statement, from June 30 to December 31	7,500
Total per the income statement	$13,500
Amount per the tax return (i.e., amount paid)	30,000
Difference	$16,500
Presold tickets:	
Amount collected this year—on the tax return	$30,000
Amount earned, sold last year—on income statement	20,000
Difference	$10,000

Step #3: Determine whether Temporary Differences Affect Deferred Tax Asset or Liability Accounts.

Deferred Tax Asset or Deferred Tax Liability

Internet income	10,000	Permanent	NA
Depreciation	0	Temporary difference	Deferred tax liability
Insurance premiums	16,500	Temporary difference	Deferred tax liability
Presold tickets	10,000	Temporary difference	Deferred tax asset

Step #4: Compute the Deferred Tax Amounts.

Description	Differences for 2006	2007	2008	Totals
Depreciation	$ 0	$ 10,000	$10,000	
Insurance premiums	(16,500)	15,000	7,500	
Presold tickets	10,000	(30,000)	0	
Tax rates		40%	35%	
Depreciation		$ 4,000	$ 3,500	$ 7,500
Insurance premiums		6,000	2,625	8,625
Presold tickets		(12,000)		(12,000)
Total deferred taxes		$ (2,000)	$ 6,125	$ 4,125

Step #5: Classify the Deferred Taxes as Current/Noncurrent and Prepare the Journal Entry.

Summary of Steps #1 through #5 and Classification

Temporary Difference	Desired Ending Balances (See Step #4)	Liability or Asset (See Step #3)	Current Portion	Noncurrent Portion
Depreciation	$ 7,500	Deferred tax liability		$7,500 cr.
Insurance premiums	8,625	Deferred tax liability	$ 8,625 cr.	
Presold tickets	(12,000)	Deferred tax asset	(12,000) dr.	
Total deferred taxes	$ 4,125		$ (3,375) dr.	$7,500 cr.
January 1, 2006 balances (See Illustration 19-2, Table 5, p. 907)			(5,600) dr.	7,000 cr.
Adjusting journal entry			$ 2,225 cr.	$ 500 cr.

Income Tax Expense	68,125	
Deferred Tax Asset, current		2,225
Deferred Tax Liability, noncurrent		500
Income Taxes Payable		65,400

To record income tax expense, the change in the deferred tax accounts, and income taxes payable.

APPENDIX B: Intraperiod Tax Allocation[4]

U.S. GAAP requires that, beginning with income from continuing operations, every line on the income statement be shown net of tax. This is called **intraperiod tax allocation**, or allocating the tax expense to the various categories on the income statement. The purpose of intraperiod tax allocation is to show each component of net income net of its associated tax effect. Intraperiod tax allocation procedures have been used throughout the text, but a simplifying assumption was made that there was only one tax rate for all levels and types of income (i.e., capital gains/losses, ordinary income, etc.). Using this simplifying assumption made it possible to view the reporting requirements without worrying about how the tax amounts were actually computed. However, it is now appropriate to demonstrate how the income tax expense is allocated to the various components of net income when there are multiple tax rates. In illustrating intraperiod tax allocation procedures, it is first assumed that there are no temporary or permanent differences between taxable income and pretax accounting income, and as a result, the income tax expense amount is the same as the income tax payable amount.

Intraperiod tax allocation is required for all items on the income statement after income from continuing operations and also for prior-period adjustments. Intraperiod tax allocation requires that the income tax expense amount (as determined by the asset-liability method discussed in the chapter) be allocated to the components of income that caused the tax expense/benefit. Allocating the computed income tax expense amount is done in four steps, as follows:

1. Determine income tax expense for income from continuing operations, using enacted tax rates. (This was demonstrated in the chapter.)
2. For capital gains, income tax expense is computed at the capital gains tax rate.
3. Determine the effect on total income tax expense (or benefit) of all loss items that are reported on the income statement after income from continuing operations. Then, apportion the computed tax benefit ratably to the loss items.
4. Determine the amount of income tax expense that remains and apportion it to the remaining gain items.

ScareWest Air is a small regional air service that flies twice daily to the major cities to the north and south of its hub. During 2004, ScareWest had several unusual transactions and events that caused its income statement to have many categories of income (as shown in Exhibit 19-1B), and its accountant was having difficulty determining how the income tax expense should be reported.

---

[4]Directions for intraperiod tax procedures are found in *FASB No. 109*, "Accounting for Income Taxes," par. 38.

EXHIBIT 19-1B

> ### ScareWest Air
> ### Categories of Income
> ### For the Year Ended December 31, 2004
>
> | | |
> |---|---:|
> | Income from continuing operations before taxes | $100,000 |
> | Discontinued operations: | |
> | Income from discontinued operations | 40,000 |
> | Extraordinary item #1 | 60,000 |
> | Extraordinary item #2 | (25,000) |
> | Extraordinary item #3 | (12,000) |
> | Accounting principle change | (24,000) |
> | Pretax income | $139,000 |

The extraordinary gain qualifies for capital gains treatment. All other items are taxed as ordinary income.

Enacted tax rates are as follows:

Ordinary income:	
First $50,000	25%
Next $50,000	30%
Above $100,000	35%
Capital gains	15%

To intertwine the intraperiod tax allocation procedures with the earlier material in this chapter, all the steps of accounting for taxes will be reiterated, even though they are not relevant (because there are no temporary or permanent differences), so that the total picture of accounting for income taxes is presented.

Steps #1 and #2: Reconcile Pretax Accounting Income to Taxable Income, Identify the Differences as Permanent or Temporary, and Compute Income Taxes Payable.

It is not necessary to reconcile account pretax income to taxable income, since there are no temporary or permanent differences, so they are the same amount, $139,000. Computing income taxes payable is done as follows:

Categories of Income	Amount	Tax Rate	Taxes
Ordinary:			
First $50,000	$ 50,000	25%	$12,500
Next $50,000	29,000	30%	8,700
Remainder	0	35%	0
Capital gains	60,000	15%	9,000
Total	$139,000		$30,200

Step #3: Determine whether Temporary Differences Affect Deferred Tax Assets or Liabilities.

There are no temporary differences, so this step is not necessary.

Step #4: Compute the Deferred Tax Amounts.

Not necessary.

Step #5: Classify the Deferred Taxes as Current/Noncurrent and Prepare the Journal Entry.

Income Tax Expense	30,200	
Income Tax Payable		30,200

This is where intraperiod tax allocation procedures begin.

Step #6: Compute the Income Tax Expense (or Benefit) on Income from Continuing Operations.

All of the income from continuing operations is ordinary income, so applying the graduated tax rates to the $100,000 of income results in taxes of $27,500, which is computed as follows:

Income from Continuing Operations	Amount	Tax Rate	Taxes
First $50,000	$ 50,000	25%	$12,500
Next $50,000	50,000	30%	15,000
Remainder	0	35%	0
Totals	$100,000		$27,500

Step #7: For Capital Gains, Income Tax Expense Is Computed at the Capital Gain Tax Rates.

The extraordinary gain is a capital gain and is taxed at 15%, so the income tax expense associated with the extraordinary gain is $9,000.

Step #8: Determine the Effect on Income Tax Expense of All Loss Items, and Apportion the Computed Tax Benefit Ratably to the Loss Items.

Income, assuming no loss items (see Exhibit 19-1B)		$200,000
Extraordinary item, to be taxed at 15%		(60,000)
Ordinary income, assuming no loss items		$140,000
Tax on first $50,000 is	$12,500	
Tax on next $50,000 is	15,000	
Tax on remaining $40,000 is	14,000	
Tax on capital gains is	9,000	
Total taxes, assuming no loss items		$ 50,500
Total tax expense with loss items (see Steps 2 and 5)		(30,200)
Tax benefit because of incurring losses during the year		$ 20,300

Apportioning the $20,300 benefit to the loss items:

	Amount of Item	Percent of Total	Tax Effect
Extraordinary item #2	$25,000	41.0%	$ 8,320
Extraordinary item #3	12,000	19.7	3,993
Accounting principle change	24,000	39.3	7,987
Totals	$61,000	100.0%	$20,300

Step #9. Determine the Amount of Income Tax Expense that Remains and Apportion It to the Gain Items.

Total tax expense (Steps 2 and 5)		$30,200
Less: Taxes on continuing operations (Step 6)	$ 27,500	
Capital gains tax (Step 7)	9,000	
Tax effect of loss items (Step 8)	(20,300)	16,200
Income taxes remaining to be allocated		$14,000

Since there is only one gain item (i.e., the income from discontinued operations), the $14,000 is the tax effect of that item. If there had been two or more items with a gain, the $14,000 would have been allocated between them, based upon the relative amounts, the same as was done for the loss items in Step #8.

This completes the example of applying intraperiod tax allocation procedures. The corrected income statement for ScareWest Air is shown in Exhibit 19-2B.

EXHIBIT 19-2B

ScareWest Air
Condensed Income Statement
For the Year Ended December 31, 2004

Income from continuing operations (net of taxes of $27,500⁵)	$ 72,500
Discontinued operations:	
Income from discontinued operations (net of taxes of $14,000)	26,000
Income before extraordinary items	$ 98,500
Extraordinary item #1 (net of taxes of 9,000)	51,000
Extraordinary item #2 (net of taxes of 8,320)	(16,680)
Extraordinary item #3 (net of tax effect of $3,993)	(8,007)
Accounting principle change (net of tax effect of $7,987)	(16,013)
Net income	$108,800

Questions

1. Your friend, who is not an accountant, does not understand why companies whose stock is publicly traded must keep "two sets of books." Write a brief memo to him, explaining why two sets of books are necessary.

2. Taxable income on the tax return can be different from accounting income before taxes on the income statement, because of either permanent differences or temporary differences. Define permanent and temporary differences, and give some examples of each type.

---

⁵On the actual income statement, this income tax expense amount could have been divided between the current and deferred portion, as discussed earlier in the chapter.

3. What type of difference (i.e., permanent or temporary) gives rise to deferred tax assets and liabilities? Explain what a deferred tax asset is and what a deferred tax liability is.

4. A company depreciates equipment for financial reporting purposes using the straight-line method, but it uses the accelerated depreciation method for tax purposes. When in the asset's life do originating differences occur, and when do reversing differences occur? Explain your answer.

5. Suppose that Garden Park Nursery's current combined tax rate is 35% and that Congress is debating a tax bill that would reduce that combined tax rate to 33%, if it is eventually passed. When preparing its 2005 fiscal year-end financial statements, and before the tax bill is passed, what rate should Garden Park use for computing its deferred taxes?

6. Refer to Question 5, and suppose that at the beginning of the next fiscal year the tax bill is passed, effective as of January 1, 2006, and Garden Park's combined effective tax rate is reduced to the anticipated 33%. Explain what effect, if any, this tax rate change would have on Garden Park's accounting for its 2006 deferred tax amounts.

7. Suppose that H.J. Grant begins a new business that requires a heavy investment in fixed assets that Grant will depreciate over five years. Also, suppose that inflation is typically 5%, meaning that the cost of acquiring new assets is steadily increasing. Finally, assume that Grant is successful in this business venture, so that the total fixed assets are growing, both in number and as to the cost per item. Speculate as to what will happen to the deferred tax liability account related to Grant's fixed assets over time. Will it increase, stay about the same, grow to a certain amount and then remain the same, etc.? Explain your thinking.

8. Describe how deferred tax assets and deferred tax liabilities are reported on a classified balance sheet.

9. a. Describe how it is determined whether the tax effect of a temporary difference is classified as current or noncurrent. (Give the two rules and rank them as to which should be applied first.)
   b. Based upon your rules in 9(a), determine whether the following temporary differences should be classified as current or noncurrent.

      i. Difference in rental income related to an unearned revenue account that is classified as a current liability.

      ii. Difference in rental income related to an account receivable that is classified as a current asset.

      iii. Difference in depreciation on an asset that was acquired ten years ago and that will be fully depreciated during the forthcoming year and is classified as property, plant, and equipment.

      iv. Difference in depreciation on an asset that was acquired during the current year and is classified as property, plant, and equipment.

      v. Difference in pension expense, where the amount reported on the tax return as an expense is the amount paid, but the amount recognized on the income statement is based upon the FASB's rules.

      vi. A gain on the sale of an item of equipment that is reported on the income statement in the current fiscal year, but the cash will not be received until the next fiscal year.

      vii. Holding gain on marketable securities in the trading portfolio.

10. (**Research Question.**) As explained in Chapter 11, conceptually long-term liabilities are reported at their present value. Are time value of money concepts applied to valuing long-term deferred tax liabilities? Why?

11. Explain why a valuation allowance account may be needed for deferred tax assets but is not necessary for deferred tax liabilities. What part of the FASB's conceptual framework, if any, justifies this difference in accounting treatment?

12. Describe the two alternatives that are available for obtaining the tax benefit of an operating loss. Which alternative should the company select first if it is available? Why?

13. (**Appendix**) Explain the concept of intra-period tax allocation. What items on the income statement must be reported net of tax?

14. (**Appendix**) Beginning with income tax expense for continuing operations, describe the sequence in determining the tax effect of the other income statement items that must be reported net of tax.

Exercises

Exercise 19-1: Reconciling Financial Reporting Income to Taxable Income (AICPA Adapted). L. Snow Corporation's books showed pretax accounting income of $1,000,000 for the year ended December 31, 2006. In computing its federal income taxes, the following data are to be considered:

Gain on an involuntary conversion	$200,000
(L. Snow has elected to replace the property within the statutory period.)	
Depreciation deductible for tax purposes in excess of depreciation deducted for book purposes	150,000
Federal estimated tax payments, 2006	140,000
Enacted federal tax rates, 2006	35%

What amount should L. Snow report as its current federal income tax liability on its December 31, 2006 balance sheet?

Exercise 19-2: Reconciling Accounting Income and Taxable Income. During the current year of operations, S. Kimball Company reported taxable income of $100,000 for the year ending December 31, 2004. Using that taxable income amount and the following information, determine what amount Kimball should report as pretax accounting income on its income statement.

• Interest earned on municipal bonds was $10,000, but only $8,000 was received by year-end.
• Rental income of $4,000 was earned, of which $3,000 was received by year-end.
• Accelerated depreciation, the method used for computing taxable income, exceeded straight-line depreciation, which is the method used for financial reporting, by $7,000.
• Life insurance premiums paid on a corporate executive, where the company is the beneficiary, were $2,400.

- Amortization of goodwill for tax purposes was $5,000.
- Bad debts expense under an allowance method was $3,500, but $4,000 was actually written off during the year.
- Sales of $1,200 were made during the year. One-third was collected during the current year, and the remaining amount will be collected over the next two years. Only the amount collected is taxable.

Exercise 19-3: Computing Taxes Payable and Deferred Taxes. Using the information in Exercise 19-2:

1. Compute Kimball's income taxes payable, assuming an effective tax rate of 30% for all taxing districts.
2. Assuming that the enacted tax rate for all future years is 30%, compute the required total balance in Kimball's deferred income tax accounts.
3. Assuming that Kimball had a credit balance in its deferred income tax account of $5,000 prior to the calculations in Part (2), compute Kimball's income tax expense.

Exercise 19-4: Recognizing Temporary Differences and Knowing Their Effect. For each item listed below, indicate whether it is a temporary difference or a permanent difference. Then, for each temporary difference, explain whether it will affect a deferred tax asset or a deferred tax liability. Your solution should look somewhat like this, with the answer to the first item as an illustration:

Item	Type of Difference	Deferred Asset/Liability
a.	Temporary	Liability

a. In the earlier years of an asset's life, depreciation on the income tax return is larger than depreciation on the income statement.
b. In the later years of an asset's life, depreciation on the income tax return is smaller than depreciation on the income statement.
c. Just prior to year-end, rent revenue is collected in advance that will not be earned until the next fiscal year.
d. Interest earned, but not yet received, on an investment in municipal bonds.
e. Organization costs were amortized over 60 months for tax purposes but expensed as incurred for financial reporting.
f. An advance payment on an operating lease obligation was received.
g. Warranty expenses on the income statement are estimated based upon a percentage of sales, whereas warranty expenses on the tax return are the actual cost incurred by the company in warranty work performed during the year. Sales have been steadily increasing for several years.
h. Life insurance premiums paid on an officer of the corporation.
i. Goodwill was amortized over 15 years for tax purposes.
j. Gross profit is recognized using the percentage-of-completion method for financial reporting purposes, but the completed-contract method is used for tax purposes.

Exercise 19-5: Income Taxes Payable, Expense, and Deferred Taxes. Young, Inc., prepared the following table reconciling the company's pretax accounting income to taxable income for the year ending December 31, 2004, which is its first year of operations:

Pretax financial income	$59,000
Holding gain on trading securities	(3,000)
Accrual of contingent loss, not deductible until paid	25,000
Interest on municipal bonds	(5,000)
Depreciation for tax purposes in excess of depreciation for financial reporting	(9,000)
Taxable income	$67,000

Young, Inc., has an effective tax rate of 40%.

1. What amount should Young report as income taxes payable at December 31, 2004?
2. What amount should Young report as deferred taxes on its 2004 balance sheet?
3. What amount should Young report as income tax expense for the year ending December 31, 2004?

Exercise 19-6: Current and Deferred Income Taxes and Balance Sheet Disclosures (AICPA adapted). McKay Corporation began business in 2006 and reported a pretax accounting income of $400,000 for its fiscal year ending December 31, 2006. Included in that figure were the following items, which were handled differently on the tax return than they were for financial reporting:

	Tax Return	Accounting Records
Warranty expense	$190,000	$205,000
Depreciation expense	150,000	100,000
Premiums on officers' life insurance	none	24,000

The enacted tax rate for all taxing authorities in which McKay does business for 2006 and all future years is 40%. Assume that all temporary differences will reverse equally over 2 years, and that McKay reports both a current and a noncurrent liability for its estimated liability for warranties.

On McKay's balance sheet, the liability for warranties is classified as a current liability.

1. What is the current portion of McKay's income tax expense for 2006?
2. What is the deferred portion of McKay's income tax expense for 2006?
3. What is McKay's total income tax expense for 2006?
4. Illustrate, or explain, how the deferred taxes would be reported on McKay's 2006 balance sheet.

Exercise 19-7: Worksheet for Deferred Taxes, Multiple Tax Rates. Using the information in Exercise 19-6 and assuming that the enacted tax rates are 40% for 2006 and 2007 but 42% thereafter, *prepare a worksheet*, compute the current and deferred portions of McKay's total income tax expense for 2006, and prepare the appropriate journal entry.

Exercise 19-8: Worksheet for Computing Deferred Taxes. Monson Corporation began business in 2004 and reported the following financial accounting and taxable incomes for the years 2004 through 2006:

	2004	2005	2006
Financial accounting income	$180,000	$220,000	$235,000
Taxable income	160,000	210,000	265,000

The tax rate for each of the three years is 30%. All differences between accounting income and taxable income are temporary differences, and they will completely reverse by the end of 2006.

For each year, prepare a worksheet that computes (a) the current taxes payable, (b) the ending balance of the deferred tax account and indicate whether it is an asset or a liability, (c) the adjustment required to the deferred tax account, and (d) income tax expense. Then prepare the required journal entry.

Exercise 19-9: Computing Deferred Taxes, Various Tax Rates, and Balance Sheet Reporting. During 2004, its first year of operations, Clark Corporation reported on its income statement depreciation expense of $300,000 and accrued warranty expenses of $40,000. On its tax return, Clark reported depreciation of $480,000 and no warranty expense. Clark's enacted tax rates for all taxing districts are 30% for 2004 and 2005, and 25% for 2006 and 2007. The depreciation difference and warranty expense will reverse over the next three years, as follows:

	Depreciation Difference	Warranty Expense
2005	$ 60,000	$10,000
2006	(60,000)	12,000
2007	(180,000)	18,000
	$(180,000)	$40,000

On Clark's balance sheet, the liability for warranties is separated between a current and a noncurrent portion.

1. Compute the total amount of deferred income taxes that Clark should report on its balance sheet for 2004.
2. Of the deferred taxes computed in Part (1), how much is current and how much is noncurrent? Explain.
3. Should the current and noncurrent deferred taxes be reported as assets or liabilities? Explain.

Exercise 19-10: Valuation Allowance Account. On January 1, 2005, the balance in H.J. Company's deferred tax asset account was $24,000, and there were no indications of the need for a valuation allowance account. At year-end, H.J. Company preliminarily had determined that the following journal entry was necessary—before considering the necessity of an allowance account:

Income Tax Expense	35,000	
Deferred Tax Asset		10,000
Income Tax Payable		25,000

However, after reviewing the available evidence, H.J. Company decided that it is more likely than not that $5,000 of the remaining deferred tax asset may not be realized.

Correct the journal entry to include a valuation account.

Exercise 19-11: Valuation Allowance Account. H.B. Lee Company has been successful for many years, but in recent years the changing global business environment has reduced H.B. Lee's sales. In the current year, 2006, H.B. Lee incurred its first net operating loss (NOL) of $110,000. Even after carrying back the NOL to previous periods, H.B. Lee has a NOL carryforward of $20,000. H.B. Lee's effective tax rate for all periods is 30%.

1. Discuss the evidence that H.B. Lee should consider in deciding whether the tax benefits associated with this operating loss carryforward can be recognized. Be specific.
2. Assuming that H.B. Lee decided it is more likely than not that all of the tax benefits of the operating loss carryforward will be realized, prepare H.B. Lee's journal entry to recognize the income tax benefit for 2006.
3. Assuming that H.B. Lee decided it will not realize all the tax benefits of the operating loss carryforward, prepare H.B. Lee's journal entry to recognize the income tax benefit for 2006.

Exercise 19-12: Net Operating Losses. The following information, along with income tax rates, was reported by Hinckley Company for the years 2003 through 2008:

Year	Financial Income (Loss)	Tax Rate	Taxes Paid
2003	$ 5,000	35%	$1,750
2004	15,000	40%	6,000
2005	(25,000)	40%	
2006	(40,000)		
2007	10,000		
2008	15,000		

1. Prepare the journal entry for the tax benefit of the 2005 NOL, assuming that Hinckley uses the carryback provision and that it is more likely than not that the tax benefits of any NOL carryforward will be realized, and at the end of 2005 the enacted tax rate for all future years is 40%.
2. Prepare the journal entry for the tax benefit of the 2006 NOL, assuming that it is more likely than not that the tax benefits of any NOL carryforward will be realized, taking into account the tax benefit of the NOL of 2005, and that at the end of 2005 the enacted tax rate for all years subsequent to 2005 is changed from the previous 40% to 30%.

Exercise 19-13: Net Operating Losses. On its income statement, E.T. Benson reported the following income (losses) before taxes for its first four years of operations:

2004	2005	2006	2007
$40,000	$(50,000)	$(10,000)	$25,000

For each year the effective tax rate was 40%. E.T. Benson elected to first carry back any NOLs, and for any year in which it is applicable, a valuation account is not considered necessary. Also, there are no permanent or temporary differences.

For each year, determine:

1. Income taxes payable, refundable (i.e., receivable).
2. Change in the deferred tax asset account for the year.
3. Income tax expense or benefit, and the journal entry.
4. Net income or loss.

Exercise 19-14: Multiple-Choice Questions.
1. Under the asset-liability method of accounting for income taxes, when a change in tax rates occurs, the effect of this change on deferred tax assets and liabilities is:
   a. Not reported.

      b. Reported in the current year's income tax expense related to continuing operations.

      c. Reported as a prior-period adjustment.

      d. None of the above.

2. Which of the following is considered a temporary difference?

      a. Revenue recognized on the accrual basis for financial reporting purposes and the cash basis for tax purposes.

      b. Recognition of interest income on municipal bonds.

      c. Payment of penalties or fines for polluting the environment.

      d. Life insurance proceeds on key employees.

3. What taxing authorities must a company consider in determining its income taxes payable and its deferred tax amounts?

      I.   Federal government.

      II. State and local taxing authorities.

      III. Foreign governments in which the company conducts operations

      a. Only I.

      b. I and II.

      c. I and III.

      d. I, II, and III.

4. When a company revises its expectations concerning the realizability of a deferred tax asset from unlikely to probable:

      a. The amount of the change in the deferred tax asset is amortized to earnings.

      b. The company recognizes a prior-period adjustment for the amount of the change in the deferred tax asset.

      c. The amount of the change in the deferred tax asset is recognized in the current year as an extraordinary item.

      d. The amount of the change in the deferred tax asset is recognized in the current year's continuing operations.

5. When is the tax benefit from a net operating loss carryforward recorded as a deferred tax asset?

      a. Always.

      b. When it is more likely than not that it will be realized.

      c. When it is probable it will be realized.

      d. When it is virtually certain it will be realized.

6. For accounting purposes, companies may keep four deferred tax accounts, consisting of a current asset, noncurrent asset, current liability, and a noncurrent liability account. However, for financial reporting, the company:

      a. Reports two items, a net asset amount and a net liability amount.

      b. Reports two items, a net current amount and a net noncurrent amount.

      c. Reports all four accounts in their respective classifications.

      d. Reports just one net amount and classifies it appropriately.

7. (AICPA adapted) Temporary differences arise when expenses are included on the tax return:

	After they are included on the income statement	*Before they are included on the income statement*
a.	No	No
b.	No	Yes
c.	Yes	Yes
d.	Yes	No

8. (AICPA adapted) On January 1, 2006, Lu-lu, Inc., purchased a machine for $90,000 that will be depreciated $9,000 per year for financial reporting. For income tax reporting, Lu-lu elects to expense immediately $10,000 and to use straight-line depreciation that will allow a cost recovery deduction of $8,000 for

2006. Assume that the present and future enacted income tax rate is 30%. What amount should be added to Lu-lu's deferred income tax liability for this temporary difference at December 31, 2006?

a. $5,400
b. $3,000
c. $2,700
d. $2,400

9. (AICPA adapted) Town, a calendar-year corporation incorporated in January 2003, experienced a $600,000 net operating loss (NOL) in 2005. For the years 2003 and 2004, Town reported a taxable income in each year and a total of $450,000 for the two years. Assume that: (1) there is no difference between pretax accounting income and taxable income for all years, (2) the income tax rate is 40% for all years, (3) the NOL will be carried back to the profit years 2003–2004 to the extent of $450,000, and (4) $150,000 will be carried forward to future periods, where it is more likely than not that the tax benefits of the carryforward will be realized. In its 2006 income statement, what amount should Town report as the income tax benefit due to the NOL carryback and carryforward?

a. $60,000
b. $180,000
c. $240,000
d. $360,000

10. (AICPA adapted) Tell Corp.'s 2004 income statement had pretax financial income of $38,000 in its first year of operations. Tell uses an accelerated cost recovery method on its tax return and straight-line depreciation for financial reporting. The difference between the book and tax deductions for depreciation over the five-year life of the assets acquired in 2004 and the enacted tax rates for 2004 to 2008 are as follows:

	Book Deductions Over (Under) Tax	Tax Rates
2004	$ (8,000)	35%
2005	(13,000)	30%
2006	(3,000)	30%
2007	10,000	25%
2008	14,000	25%

There are no other temporary differences. In Tell's December 31, 2004 balance sheet, the gross noncurrent deferred income tax liability and the income taxes currently payable are:

	Gross Noncurrent Deferred Income Tax Liability	Income Taxes Currently Payable
a.	$1,200	$ 7,500
b.	$1,200	$10,500
c.	$4,800	$ 7,500
d.	$4,800	$10,500

Exercise 19-15 (Appendix B): Intraperiod Tax Allocation. The accountant for G.A. Smith & Company has prepared the following preliminary income statement for the year ending December 31, 2007. Generally, the company had a successful year but had incurred several unusual losses. The accountant has chosen to use the single-step format.

G.A. Smith & Company
Income Statement
For the Year Ended December 31, 2007

Revenues:	
Sales	$140,000
Interest income	4,000
Total revenue	$144,000
Expenses:	
Cost of goods sold	$ 52,000
Operating expenses	28,000
Loss on expropriation of assets in foreign country	14,000
Litigation loss	30,000
Loss from earthquake	15,000
Income tax expense	1,000
Total expenses	$140,000
Net income	$ 4,000

Assuming that the expropriation loss and the earthquake loss are considered extraordinary items and keeping the single-step format, correctly prepare the income statement, using intraperiod tax allocation. The income tax rate is 20% on the first $20,000 and 25% on all additional income. Round tax amounts to the nearest tens of dollars.

Exercise 19-16 (Appendix B): Intraperiod Tax Allocation. Hunter Corporation has the following items before considering the tax effect that it needs to appropriately classify its income statement. The income tax rate is 30% up to $20,000 and 35% on all additional amounts.

Cumulative effect of an accounting principle change	$ 7,000
Loss on restructuring	30,000
Income from discontinued operations that was incurred before the measurement date	15,000
Estraordinary loss	20,000
Extraordinary gain	4,000
Sales	160,000
Cost of goods sold	60,000
Operating expenses	18,000
Settlement of legal issue wherein Hunter paid the plaintiff	40,000
Interest income	12,000
Loss incurred when plans to acquire another company were discontinued. This amount is the cost Hunter had incurred and deferred in connection with the proposed acquisition.	30,000
Increase in property owned by Hunter when a valuable mineral was discovered	100,000
Holding gain on sale of securities classified in the trading portfolio	17,000

Additional information:

1. The accounting principle change resulted from changing the cost-flow assumption from average cost to FIFO. Prices have been rising for all years since Hunter was in business.
2. There were 50,000 shares of common stock outstanding for the entire year, and there were no potentially dilutive securities. A preferred dividend was paid of $2,000.

Prepare a multiple-step income statement in proper form (i.e., proper heading, using columns to expedite ease of reading, intraperiod tax allocation, correct EPS presentation, etc.). Round tax amounts to the nearest tens of dollars.

Problems

Problem 19-1: Extracting Information from Financial Reports. The following information was extracted from the notes to the 1998 annual report of Microsoft regarding income taxes.

> Income tax expense includes U.S. and international income taxes, plus an accrual for U.S. taxes on undistributed earnings of international subsidiaries. Certain items of income and expense are not reported in tax returns and financial statements in the same year. The tax effect of this difference is reported as deferred income taxes. Tax credits are accounted for as a reduction of tax expense in the year in which the credits reduce taxes payable.
>
> The provision for income taxes consisted of:

Year Ended June 30	1996	1997	1998
Current taxes:			
U.S. and state	$1,139	$1,710	$2,518
International	285	412	526
Current taxes	$1,424	$2,122	$3,044
Deferred taxes	(240)	(262)	(417)
Provision for income taxes	$1,184	$1,860	$2,627

> The effective income tax rate was 35.0% in 1996 and 1997. The effective tax rate increased to 36.9% in 1998 due to the nondeductible write-off of WebTV in-process technologies.
>
> Income taxes payable were $466 million for 1997 and $915 million for 1998.

Required:

1. From the information given, what were the income tax expense amounts for 1997 and 1998?
2. Prepare the journal entries for 1997 and 1998 to record income tax expense.

Problem 19-2: Understanding Notes to the Financial Statements. That portion of Note #1 that relates to income taxes and most of Note #6 of the 1999 financial report of Nike, Inc., are given below:

> **NOTE 1—Summary of Significant Accounting Policies:**
> **Income taxes:** Income taxes are provided currently on financial statement earnings of non-U.S. subsidiaries expected to be repatriated. The Company intends to determine annually the amount of undistributed non-U.S. earnings to invest indefinitely in its non-U.S. operations.
>
> The Company accounts for income taxes using the asset and liability method. This approach requires the recognition of deferred tax assets and liabilities for the expected future tax consequences of temporary differences between the carrying amounts and the tax bases of other assets and liabilities. See Note 6 for further discussion.

NOTE 6—INCOME TAXES:

Income before income taxes and the provision for income taxes are as follows:

(in millions)

YEAR ENDED MAY 31,	1999	1998	1997
Income before income taxes:			
United States	$598.7	$ 648.2	$1,008.0
Foreign	147.4	4.8	287.2
	$746.1	$ 653.0	$1,295.2
Provision for income taxes:			
Current:			
United States			
Federal	$210.2	$ 258.4	$ 359.4
State	34.3	43.1	74.7
Foreign	50.1	69.4	112.7
	$294.6	$ 370.9	$ 546.8
Deferred:			
United States			
Federal	$ (7.6)	$ (40.2)	$ (21.1)
State	4.0	(8.8)	(5.1)
Foreign	3.7	(68.5)	(21.2)
	0.1	(117.5)	(47.4)
	$294.7	$ 253.4	$ 499.4

A reconciliation from the U.S. statutory federal income tax rate to the effective income tax rate follows:

YEAR ENDED MAY 31,	1999	1998
U.S. Federal statutory rate	35.0%	35.0%
State income taxes, net of federal benefit	3.3	3.4
Other, net	1.2	0.4
Effective income tax rate	39.5%	38.8%

Required:

1. Is Nike accounting for income taxes in accordance with what is prescribed by U.S. GAAP? Explain.
2. From the information given, what were the income tax expense amounts for 1998 and 1999?
3. Prepare the journal entries for 1998 and 1999 to record income tax expense.
4. Nike reported income taxes payable amounts of $0 for 1999 and $28.9 million for 1998. How much cash did Nike pay in income taxes during 1999?
5. At the end of 1999, the deferred tax assets were partially comprised of the following (in millions):

Allowance for doubtful accounts	$16.2
Inventory reserves	17.8
Accrued liabilities	59.0
Depreciation	33.7

How much of the deferred taxes should be classified as current, and how much should be classified as noncurrent?

Problem 19-3: Multiple Differences, Two Years. Heidi Swenson, the owner of the Extremely Successful Company, has compiled information prior to reporting income tax data on the 2005 financial reports, which is the company's first year of operations.

For tax purposes, Extremely Successful elected to use accelerated depreciation, recognize revenue under the installment sales method, and deduct warranty expenses when paid. However, for financial reporting purposes, Extremely Successful uses the straight-line method of depreciation, recognizes revenue when the sale is made, and warranty expenses in the same year that the sale is made. The only other difference between net income as reported on the income statement and taxable income on the tax return is $10,000 of interest on municipal bonds. The table below summarizes the dollar amount of these differences. The parentheses represent reversing differences.

Differences	2005	2006	2007	Subsequent Years
Interest on municipal bonds being held to maturity	$10,000			
Accelerated depreciation in excess of straight-line	37,500	$ 9,375	$(11,700)	$(35,175)
Revenue in excess of that recognized under the installment sales method	15,000	(10,000)	(5,000)	
Difference in warranty expense and warranty deductions	10,000	(10,000)		

Required:

1. Determine whether the differences will give rise to future deductible amounts or future taxable amounts.
2. Assuming that the accounting income before taxes on the income statement is $100,000 and that the tax rate for all years is 40%, compute taxable income per the tax return.
3. Assuming that installment accounts receivable are classified on the balance sheet under Other Assets, and that the liability for warranties is reported as a current liability, compute the deferred income tax amounts and determine the amount that should be reported as a current asset/liability and the amount that should be reported as a noncurrent asset/liability.
4. Prepare the appropriate journal entry to record income tax expense, appropriately classifying the deferred taxes as current and noncurrent.
5. Assuming that the accounting income in 2006 is $140,000 and there are no new temporary differences, repeat Requirements (2)–(4).

Problem 19-4: Computing Deferred Taxes. J. Faust Corporation began business in 2005, and for tax purposes chose those policies that would minimize taxes payable in the earlier years of the business. However, for financial reporting purposes, other policies were adopted. During 2005 through 2008, Faust Corporation reported the following:

	2005	2006	2007	2008	2009
Accounting income	$35,000	$45,000	$60,000	$50,000	$70,000
Taxable income	10,000	35,000	65,000	70,000	80,000

At 2005, the enacted tax rate for all years was 30%. However, at the beginning of 2007, legislation was passed that changed the enacted tax rates for that and all subsequent years to 35%. All differences are temporary differences, and at 2005 the differences will reverse as follows:

2006	$(10,000)
2007	5,000
2008	20,000
2009	10,000

Required:
For each year, prepare a worksheet and determine (a) the current taxes payable, (b) the ending balance of the deferred tax account, (c) the adjustment required to the deferred tax account, and (d) income tax expense. Then prepare the required journal entry.

Problem 19-5: Current and Deferred Taxes, Several Years. On January 1, 2004, J.F. Smith Company acquired a fixed asset for $15,000 for use in its business. For financial reporting purposes, Smith chose to depreciate the asset using the straight-line method over a five-year life, with no salvage value. For tax return purposes, Smith used the MACRS convention, and from 2004 through 2008, Smith deducted $3,000, $4,800, $2,880, $1,728, and $1,728, respectively. The remaining $864 will be deducted in 2009. From 2004 through 2008, J.F. Smith reported taxable income (i.e., on the tax return) before depreciation and taxes of $4,000, $6,000, $7,500, $12,000, and $13,000, respectively. The enacted income tax rate was 30% for all years.

Required:
1. Prepare the journal entries to record income taxes payable, deferred taxes, and income tax expense for the years 2004 through 2007. (Round amounts to the nearest dollar.)
2. What is the balance in the deferred tax account at December 31, 2008? Is it a deferred tax asset or liability? Why?

Problem 19-6: Current and Deferred Taxes, Several Years, Multiple Tax Rates. Using the information in Problem 19-5, redo Requirement (1), but assume in 2006 that the enacted tax rate is changed to 35% for 2007 and all subsequent years.

Problem 19-7: Three Differences, Multiple Rates. The accountant for Derek Co. compiled the following information for computing the deferred tax amounts to report on the company's financial report for 2003, its first year of operations:

Taxable/(deductible) amounts	Future (Deductible) and Taxable Amounts by Year			
	2004	2005	2006	2007
Rent received and taxable but not earned	$10,000	$10,000		
Warranties incurred but not taxable until paid	3,000	5,000		
Excess depreciation per the tax return	10,000	0	$(10,000)	$(20,000)

The company's accounting income before taxes was $150,000. Currently, the enacted tax rates are 35% for 2003–2005 and 30% for all years after 2005. For financial reporting purposes, Derek reports as current liabilities those portions of unearned rent and estimated warranty liabilities that will be settled next year.

Required:

1. Compute taxable income for 2003.
2. Compute income taxes payable for 2003.
3. Compute the deferred taxes for 2003.
4. Prepare the journal entry to recognize income tax expense for 2003, appropriately classifying the deferred taxes as current and noncurrent.
5. Beginning with "Income before taxes," illustrate the proper reporting of income tax expense on the income statement, separating the income tax expense between its current and deferred portions.

Problem 19-8: Multiple Differences, Changing Tax Rates, Beginning Balance in Deferred Tax Accounts. Shoddy Co. began operations on January 2, 2001. Certain of its accounting policies were different from the IRS rules, which gave rise to deferred taxes. As of January 1, 2009, Shoddy had a debit balance of $2,000 in its current deferred tax account and a credit balance of $8,500 in its noncurrent deferred tax account. At December 31, 2009, Shoddy prepared the following reconciliation between pretax accounting income and taxable income:

Pretax accounting income	$410,000
Excess depreciation taken on tax return	(26,000)
Warranty expenses on the income statement in excess of amounts paid	10,000
Accrued revenue on the income statement in excess of the amount received	(5,000)
Interest from municipal bonds	(15,000)
Taxable income	$374,000

Shoddy also prepared the following schedule as to future expected differences between accounting and tax income:

Description	2010	2011	2012	Future Years
Depreciation	$(15,000)	$ (5,000)	$ 5,000	$ 60,000
Warranty expense	(12,000)	(2,000)		
Revenue	5,000	0	0	0
Interest on municipal bonds	(15,000)	(15,000)	(15,000)	(15,000)

In all prior years Shoddy's effective income tax rate had been 30%, but recently enacted legislation had raised that rate to 35%, effective for years beginning in 2011, and Shoddy expects that rate to persist into the foreseeable future. Warranty liabilities are classified as current on the balance sheet.

Required:

1. Prepare the journal entry to recognize income tax expense, deferred taxes, and taxes payable for 2009. Show all computations.
2. Beginning with income before taxes, show how income tax expense would be reported on the income statement.

Problem 19-9: Change in an Accounting Principle and Deferred Taxes. M. Ekker Co. started business on January 2, 1999, with an initial public offering of stock that netted (after all fees) $5 million. Ekker immediately acquired fixed assets totaling $1 million, and for financial reporting purposes began using the straight-line method of depreciation, with a salvage value of 5% and a life of 10 years. However, for tax purposes Ekker used double-declining balance, with a half-year convention and no salvage value. The income tax rate is 30% for all years.

Required:

1. Compute the balance in the deferred tax account as of December 31, 2004.
2. Assume that as of January 1, 2005, Ekker decided to change the method of depreciation being used for financial reporting purposes from the straight-line method to the sum-of-the-years'-digits method. Prepare the appropriate journal entry to adjust the accumulated depreciation account and the deferred tax account.

Problem 19-10: Short Problems Adapted from CPA Exams.

1. On its December 31, 2004 balance sheet, Shin Co. had income taxes payable of $13,000 and a current deferred tax asset of $20,000 before determining the need for a valuation account. Shin had reported a current deferred tax asset of $15,000 at December 31, 2003. No estimated tax payments were made during 2004. At December 31, 2004, Shin determined that it was more likely than not that 10% of the deferred tax asset would not be realized. In its 2004 income statement, what amount should Shin report as total income tax expense?

2. As a result of differences between depreciation for financial reporting purposes and tax purposes, the financial reporting basis of Noor Co.'s sole depreciable asset, acquired in 2004, exceeded its tax basis by $250,000 at December 31, 2004. This difference will reverse in future years. The enacted tax rate is 30% for 2004 and 40% for future years. Noor has no other temporary differences. In its December 31, 2004 balance sheet, how much should Noor report as the deferred tax effect of this difference?

3. At December 31, 2004, Bren Co. had the following deferred income tax items:
   - A deferred income tax liability of $15,000 related to a noncurrent asset
   - A deferred income tax asset of $3,000 related to a noncurrent liability
   - A deferred income tax asset of $8,000 related to a current liability

   How should Bren report the above items in its December 31, 2004 balance sheet?

4. Quinn Co. reported a net deferred tax asset of $9,000 in its December 31, 2003 balance sheet. For 2004, Quinn reported pretax financial statement income of $300,000. Temporary differences of $100,000 resulted in taxable income of $200,000 for 2004. At December 31, 2004, Quinn had cumulative taxable differences of $70,000. Quinn's effective income tax rate is 30%. In its December 31, 2004 income statement, what should Quinn report as deferred income tax expense?

5. For the year ended December 31, 2003, Grim Co.'s pretax financial statement income was $200,000, and its taxable income was $150,000. The difference is due to the following:

Interest on municipal bonds	$ 70,000
Premium expense on keyman life insurance	(20,000)

Grim's enacted income tax rate is 30%. In its 2003 income statement, what amount should Grim report as the current provision for income tax expense?

6. At the end of 2003, the tax effects of temporary differences were as follows:

	Deferred Tax Assets (Liabilities)	Classification
Accelerated tax depreciation	$(75,000)	Noncurrent
Additional costs in inventory for tax purposes	$25,000	Current

A valuation allowance was not considered necessary. Thorn anticipates that $10,000 of the deferred tax liability will reverse in 2004. On Thorn's December 31, 2003 balance sheet, what amount should Thorn report as noncurrent deferred tax liability?

Problem 19-11 (Appendix B): Intraperiod Tax Allocation with Graduated Tax Rates. Current U.S. GAAP requires that tax expense or benefit be allocated to continuing operations, discontinued operations, extraordinary items, cumulative effect of accounting changes, and prior-period adjustments. Using the following information, compute the tax effect of the various items where intraperiod tax allocation is required.

Income from continuing operations	$ 740,000
Income on discontinuance of W Division	98,000
Extraordinary item #1	(310,000)
Extraordinary item #2	(405,000)
Accounting principle change	42,000

The applicable income tax rates are as follows:

First $100,000	20%
Next $100,000	33%
Over $200,000	45%

Problem 19-12 (Appendix B): Deferred Taxes and Intraperiod Tax Allocation. Using the following information, prepare in good form a multiple-step income statement and also prepare those portions of the balance sheet connected with deferred income taxes.

The Just-Right Company
Income Statement
For the Year Ended December 31, 2004

Sales	$ 7,000,000
Cost of goods sold	(2,950,000)
Gross profit	$ 4,050,000
Selling expenses	(1,350,000)
General and administrative expenses	(950,000)
Income from operations	$ 1,750,000
Other revenue	250,000
Other expenses	(475,000)
Income before discontinued operations and extraordinary items	$ 1,525,000
Loss from operations of discontinued segment	(40,000)
Extraordinary loss #1	(100,000)
Extraordinary loss #2	(35,000)
Extraordinary gain	50,000
Income before taxes	$ 1,400,000

Additional information:

a. The differences between income as reported on the income statement and income per the tax return are as follows:

	Tax Return	Accounting Records
Interest on municipal bonds	$ 0	$200,000
Depreciation expense	120,000	80,000
Warranty expense	70,000	100,000

The estimated liability for warranties is classified as a current liability on Just-Right's balance sheet.

b. 2004 was the first year that taxable income on the tax return differed from net income as reported on the income statement.

c. There were 100,000 shares of common stock outstanding for the entire year, and there were no potentially dilutive securities. Preferred dividends were $250,000.

d. The income tax rates are 25% on the first one million dollars and 30% on all amounts above that.

20
Foreign Currency Transactions

Derek Newmann is the Chief Executive Officer of Software Innovations, Inc., a small company that sells software products that assist businesses in organizing clientele records and tracking investment performance. During the past few years, the company has experienced significant growth, and this year (2004), for the first time, the company sold inventory to foreign customers where the sale was denominated in foreign currency. Specifically, in December, the company sold software valued at $100,000 to a British customer. The exchange rate for British pounds on the date of the sale was $1.60 = £1. Accordingly, Software Innovations billed the British customer for £62,500 ($100,000/$1.60), which is payable in January 2005.

On December 31, 2004 (the company's fiscal year-end), the exchange rate for British pounds had changed to $1.50 = £1. Therefore, the £62,500 to be received in January can be exchanged for only $93,750, instead of $100,000. Heidi Jenson, the company's chief financial officer, comes into Derek's office and explains that the company's EPS will be lower than expected because of the $6,250 loss that they had not anticipated. The following discussion ensues.

Derek: Heidi, I don't believe recognizing a loss on this year's income statement is appropriate. Exchange rates are extremely volatile, and there is a good chance that any gain or loss realized today will be offset by an equal gain or loss tomorrow. Recognizing unrealized gains/losses due to fluctuations in exchange rates will introduce volatility into our earnings, which communicates to our investors that we are a risky firm.

Heidi: I agree with you that exchange rates are volatile, but if we are dealing with foreign currencies, shouldn't this additional risk be reflected in our financial statements?

Derek: Heidi, if these were actual gains or losses, I would agree that they should be reflected in earnings, but they're not—they are *unrealized*. We won't actually know whether we have a gain or loss until our customer pays us in January. By that time, the exchange rate might be fully recovered, and who knows, we might actually realize a gain from this transaction.

Heidi: Yes, but it's just as likely that we'll realize a bigger loss. If we don't recognize our unrealized loss this year, next year our earnings might take a bigger hit.

Derek: OK, what about a compromise? Let's defer recognition of this unrealized loss in earnings until we know what the actual gain or loss will be, which is when payment is made in January. I propose we adjust the amount of the receivable to reflect the new exchange rate and take the unrealized loss to comprehensive income, which will show up in stockholders' equity.

Heidi: That sounds like a possibility, but I'm still not sure what justifies not recognizing this loss in earnings in the same way we do for unrealized gains and losses on trading securities.

Derek: Heidi, as manager of this company, my performance should be evaluated based on things that I can control, which are sales to customers and expenditures incurred. I have absolutely no control over exchange rate fluctuations. Therefore, recognizing their effects in earnings prior to realization just doesn't seem appropriate to me.

Questions

1. Has Software Innovations incurred additional risk by allowing customers to pay their obligations in a foreign currency?

2. How should Software Innovations recognize the unrealized loss from holding a receivable denominated in a foreign currency?

3. Should Derek's performance be evaluated based on earnings that include unrealized gains/losses from foreign currency fluctuations? Does Derek have control over these gains/losses?

Learning Objectives

- Describe the role that international trade plays within a company's operating environment and national economy.
- Explain the general concept of foreign exchange and the factors that determine the relationship between two countries' currencies.
- Explain the general concept of foreign currency risk.
- Describe the most basic types of methods employed by companies to reduce foreign currency risk.
- Describe U.S. GAAP requirements to account for transactions denominated in a foreign currency.

Introduction

This chapter provides an overview of accounting for transactions that are denominated in a currency other than the entity's primary economic operating environment. These types of transactions usually take the form of importing or exporting goods, services, and capital. The economy we live in is becoming increasingly global, as indicated by the fact that international trade, as measured by total imports and exports, has increased from a very hefty $500 billion in 1970 to nearly $7 trillion in 1999. Many large multinational enterprises obtain a majority of their sales from foreign sources (Exhibit 20-1). Similarly, cross-border investments have increased nearly four times over the last two decades.

Foreign trade is not restricted to only large companies. A 1992 survey conducted by Deloitte Touche Tohmatsu International revealed that 86 percent of managers from companies ranked as "medium-sized" in developed countries engage in importing and/or exporting transactions. Thus, foreign currency transactions are an increasingly important aspect of most businesses.

Foreign trade has many potential advantages to both seller and buyer. The seller has the potential of expanding sales volume and taking better advantage of economies of scale. The buyer has an opportunity to receive goods and/or services at perhaps a more favorable price. Moreover, without foreign trade, some goods/services might not even be available in the buyer's domestic market. In addition, both buyer and seller can develop relationships that perhaps will allow them access to other benefits, such as increased technology and/or superior knowledge.

EXHIBIT 20-1

Contribution of Foreign Operations to Company Profits

Company Name	Total Sales ($m) (2001)	Foreign Sales ($m) (2001)	Foreign Sales as a Percentage of Total Sales	Net Income ($m) (2001)	Foreign Net Income ($m) (2001)	Foreign Income as a Percentage of Total Income
Gillette Co.	$ 8,961	$ 5,204	58.1%	$ 910	$ 199	21.9%
PepsiCo	26,935	8,720	32.4	2,662	889	33.3
Procter & Gamble	39,244	18,910	48.2	2,992	799	26.7
Microsoft Corp.	25,296	7,500	29.6	7,785	961	12.3
Wal-Mart Stores Inc.	217,799	35,501	16.3	6,671	1,458	21.9
Phillip Morris	89,924	33,944	37.7	8,877	3,548	40.0
Nike	9,489	4,670	49.2	590	376	63.7
Oracle	10,860	5,318	49.0	2,561	822	32.1

However, these advantages are also accompanied by increased risk. This condition was magnified during the late 1990s, when several non-U.S. markets experienced problems with the value of their currencies. Consistent with the global nature of the economy, the consequences of currency devaluations in Korea, Thailand, Brazil, and other countries were felt by many U.S. companies. Exhibit 20-2 summarizes the advantages and risks that are associated with foreign trade.

EXHIBIT 20-2

Advantages and Risks of Foreign Trade

Advantages to Seller	Risks to Seller
1. Expansion of operations through increased sales. 2. Increased efficiency (economies of scale). 3. Broaden customer base. 4. Establish relationships with foreign customers that may provide future benefit.	1. Increased credit risk due to difficulty in collecting overdue debts from foreign customers. 2. Foreign currency exchange risk when sale is denominated in foreign currency.

Advantages to Buyer	Risks to Buyer
1. Additional suppliers of needed goods. 2. Increased competition, which could favorably affect price of goods. 3. Establish relationships with foreign suppliers that may provide future benefit.	1. Increased probability that purchased goods will not be delivered on a timely basis. 2. Increased risk related to quality of products. 3. Foreign currency exchange risk when purchase is denominated in foreign currency.

This chapter focuses on accounting for foreign transactions that are denominated in a foreign currency and the associated foreign currency exchange rate risk that accompanies such transactions. Of course, when companies measure transactions and issue financial statements, they must do so using a common currency. Matching the cost of goods sold measured in U.S. dollars with revenues measured in Japanese yen would produce nonsensical results. Thus, a U.S. company must measure all transactions in U.S. dollars, including transactions denominated in a different currency. If the foreign currency transaction is on a cash basis, accounting for the transaction is straightforward, since the foreign currency paid or received can be immediately converted into U.S. dollars and the journal entry is based on the U.S. dollar amount. However, when credit terms are provided, exchange rate fluctuations from the date of sale to the date of cash settlement can lead to the recognition of foreign currency gains/losses on the income statement, as illustrated in the opening scenario (pp. 940–941).

The U.S. GAAP authoritative literature on accounting for foreign currency transactions is *SFAS No. 52*, "Foreign Currency Translation." In addition, a relatively new standard provides guidance on accounting for derivative instruments that hedge against foreign currency transaction gains and losses—*SFAS No. 133*, "Accounting for Derivative Instruments and Hedging Activities." The international standard for foreign currency transactions is *IAS No. 21*, "The Effects of Changes in Foreign Exchange Rates." The IASC approved a final standard in 1999 on derivative instruments as the final step in developing a core set of standards to be reviewed by the U.S. Securities and Exchange Commission: *IAS No. 39*, "Financial Instruments: Recognition and Measurement." This chapter discusses the most basic type of foreign currency transactions under *SFAS No. 52* and accounting for simple derivative instruments per *SFAS No. 133*. The next chapter reviews more complex hedge accounting requirements per *SFAS No. 133* and *IAS No. 39*.

Foreign Exchange

Before we discuss measurement and financial reporting issues related to foreign currency transactions, we provide a brief overview of the foreign exchange market. An **exchange rate** represents the relative unit value of one currency compared to another, or in other words, *the price stated in one currency to purchase a unit of another currency.* An exchange rate can be quoted either directly or indirectly. A **direct quote** represents the amount of local currency needed to purchase one unit of foreign currency. An example of a direct quote that expresses the relationship between U.S. dollars and British pounds is:

© GETTY IMAGES, INC./PHOTODISC

$$\$1.50 = £1.$$

Alternatively, an **indirect quote** represents the amount of foreign currency needed to purchase one unit of local currency. If we were to express the above rate indirectly, an equivalent quote would be:

$$\$1 = £0.666.$$

Exhibit 20-3 contains the U.S. dollar exchange rates for various other currencies, as listed in the May 2, 2002 edition of *The Wall Street Journal*. For each

EXHIBIT 20-3

Exchange Rates

The New York foreign exchange mid-range rates below apply to trading among banks in amounts of $1 million and more, as quoted at 4 p.m. Eastern time by Reuters and other sources. Retail transactions provide fewer units of foreign currency per dollar.

Country	U.S. $ EQUIVALENT Wed.	U.S. $ EQUIVALENT Tue.	CURRENCY PER U.S. $ Wed.	CURRENCY PER U.S. $ Tue.
Argentina (Peso)-y	.3356	.3356	2.9800	2.9800
Australia (Dollar)	.5394	.5384	1.8539	1.8572
Brazil (Real)	.4235	.4235	2.3610	2.3610
Britain (Pound)	1.4631	1.4574	.6835	.6862
1-month forward	1.4604	1.4546	.6847	.6875
3-months forward	1.4551	1.4495	.6872	.6899
6-months forward	1.4477	1.4418	.6908	.6936
Canada (Dollar)	.6407	.6376	1.5607	1.5683
1-month forward	.6405	.6373	1.5613	1.5690
3-months forward	.6397	.6366	1.5633	1.5708
6-months forward	.6384	.6353	1.5663	1.5741

EXHIBIT 20-3 CONTINUED

Country	U.S. $ EQUIVALENT Wed.	Tue.	CURRENCY PER U.S. $ Wed.	Tue.
Chile (Peso)	.001546	.001546	646.85	646.85
China (Renminbi)	.1208	.1208	8.2773	8.2773
Columbia (Peso)	.0004389	.0004389	2278.50	2279.55
Czech. Rep. (Koruna)				
Commerical rate	.02952	.02948	33.875	33.925
Denmark (Krone)	.1220	.1211	8.1950	8.2557
Ecuador (U.S. Dollar)	1.0000	1.0000	1.0000	1.0000
Hong Kong (Dollar)	.1282	.1282	7.7991	7.7991
Hungary (Forint)	.003727	.003703	268.30	270.05
India (Rupee)	.02044	.02044	48.930	48.930
Indonesia (Rupiah)	.0001072	.0001072	9328	9330
Israel (Shekel)	.2048	.2043	4.8830	4.8950
Japan (Yen)	.007845	.007777	127.47	128.59
1-month forward	.007857	.007789	127.27	128.38
3-months forward	.007882	.007814	126.87	127.98
6-months forward	.007927	.007859	125.14	127.24
Jordan (Dinar)	1.4104	1.4104	.7090	.7090
Kuwait (Dinar)	3.2723	3.2690	.3056	.3059
Lebanon (Pound)	.0006605	.0006605	1514.00	1514.00
Malaysia (Ringgit)-b	.2632	.2632	3.8001	3.8001
Malta (Lira)	2.2482	2.2396	.4448	.4465
Mexico (Peso)				
Floating rate	.1062	.1064	9.4205	9.3985
New Zealand (Dollar)	.4490	.4480	2.2272	2.2321
Norway (Krone)	.1197	.1188	8.3543	8.4174
Pakistan (Rupee)	.01667	.01667	59.975	59.975
Peru (new Sol)	.2918	.2913	3.4275	3.4325
Philippines (Peso)	.01977	.01975	50.575	50.625
Poland (Zloty)	.2512	.2506	3.9810	3.9903
Russia (Ruble)-a	.03201	.03201	31.240	31.240
Saudi Arabia (Riyal)	.2666	.2666	3.7504	3.7504
Singapore (Dolar)	.5538	.5507	1.8058	1.8158
Slovak Rep. (Koruna)	.02148	.02136	46.562	46.824
South Africa (Rand)	.0946	.0938	10.566	10.665
South Korea (Won)	.0007758	.0007758	1289.00	1289.00
Sweden (Krona)	.0978	.0976	10.2263	10.2509
Switzerland (Franc)	.6236	.6182	1.6037	1.6175
1-month forward	.6238	.6184	1.6031	1.6170
3-months forward	.6243	.6188	1.6018	1.6160
6-months forward	.6253	.6197	1.5992	1.6136
Taiwan (Dollar)	.02884	.02884	34.670	34.670
Thailand (Baht)	.02314	.02312	43.220	43.245
Turkey (Lira)	.00000073	.00000075	1367500	1341000
United Arab (Dirham)	.2722	.2723	3.6731	3.6730
Uruguay (Peso)				
Financial	.06024	.06116	16.600	16.350
Venezuela (Bolivar)	.001169	.001169	855.50	855.50
SDR	1.2677	1.2677	.7888	.7888
Euro	.9054	.9004	1.1045	1.1106

Special Drawing Rights (SDR) are based on exchange rates for the U.S., British, and Japanese currencies. *Source:* International Monetary Fund.

a-Russian Central Bank rate. b-Government rate. y-Floating rate.

Source: The Wall Street Journal, May 2, 2002, p. C11.

listed currency, four columns are presented. The first two columns represent direct quotes for Wednesday, May 1 and Tuesday, April 30. The last two columns represent the same exchange rate for the same days, using indirect quotes. Focusing on the Australian dollar (A$), we see from Exhibit 20-3 that on Wednesday, May 1, 2002, $0.5394 = A$1, or equivalently using an indirect quote, $1 = A$1.8539.

The exchange rate quote provided in Exhibit 20-3 for the Australian dollar is called the **spot rate**, which represents the price of the currency if conversion were to take place immediately. Oftentimes, currency traders are interested in exchange rates that will be effective at some specified point in the future, which are referred to as **forward rates**.

Exhibit 20-3 also contains forward rates for most major currencies for specified time periods. For example, the spot rate for the British pound on Wednesday, May 1 (using the direct quote) is $1.4631. In addition, there are also quotes for traders desiring to enter into 1-month, 3-month, and 6-month forward contracts. The rate for the 1-month forward contract is $1.4604. Thus, if a trader entered into a 1-month forward contract to purchase £1,000, the trader would be required to deliver on May 31, 2002, $1,460.40 in exchange for the pounds. As will be discussed later in this chapter, forward contracts can be very useful to managers who desire to minimize earnings variability associated with foreign currency exchange rate fluctuations. In addition, traders might use forward contracts as a means of speculating in a foreign currency.

Exchange Rate Arrangements

Prior to 1973, exchange rates among the world's currencies were fixed by the International Monetary Fund (IMF). The IMF was established in 1944 for the purpose of promoting economic stability. A fixed exchange rate means that the price of a currency relative to another currency remains constant. However, the fixed rate system established by the IMF proved difficult to maintain, especially for underdeveloped countries that experienced chronic currency devaluations.

Finally, in 1973 the IMF allowed countries the option of breaking away from the fixed rate system. Several countries, including all the major developed countries of the world, allowed their currency to float, which means that exchange rates can fluctuate on a daily basis and are determined by market forces. Many other countries desired the stability that accompanies having a fixed exchange rate. Several of these countries, such as Thailand, Argentina, and the Bahamas, peg their currency to another stable currency. The most common currency used as a peg is the U.S. dollar.

As an example, prior to reverting to Chinese administration on July 1, 1997, Hong Kong pegged its currency to the U.S. dollar at a fixed rate of HK$7.8 = US$1. No matter how the value of the U.S. dollar changed relative to other currencies in the world, the exchange rate between U.S. and Hong Kong dollars would remain constant (unless, by decree, the governments establish a new fixed rate). By pegging its currency to the U.S. dollar, Hong Kong realized several advantages. The relatively low inflation and interest rates in the United States facilitated keeping inflation and interest rates under control in Hong Kong. Also, the fixed exchange rate significantly reduced the level of foreign currency risk associated with transactions with the United States since the amount of cash flows is known. This lessening of currency risk enhances trade and investment levels in Hong Kong. This is a particularly attractive benefit for developing countries, such as Argentina, because of its dependence on international trade for economic growth.

Other countries have chosen to use a basket of currencies as their peg. For example, in Exhibit 20-3, an exchange rate for SDR (Special Drawing Rights) is listed with a direct quote of $1.2677. The SDR was established by the IMF and is based on bundled exchange rates from the United States, Great Britain, and Japan. The reason for a country's decision to use the SDR (or any other basket of currencies) as a peg for its own currency as opposed to just one currency is that, supposedly, a basket of currencies will have less variability.

However, as with anything else in a world economy, the benefits derived from a pegged currency do not come without a price. If the U.S. dollar appreciates significantly, then other currencies that are pegged to the U.S. dollar will also appreciate, which has the result of hindering exports from that country since its goods will become relatively more expensive after the currency appreciation. Since one of the primary reasons for pegging a currency to another is to facilitate international trade, this problem is potentially serious.

Another problem with fixed exchange rate arrangements is that foreign currency traders must believe that the peg is credible; otherwise, the traders will speculate in the currency to such a degree that the local government will not be able to continue to support the peg. For example, assume that foreign currency traders did not believe that the Hong Kong peg of HK$7.8 = US$1 was credible, and instead believed the real value to be somewhere around HK$9 = US$1. In this case, traders believe that the Hong Kong dollars are actually weaker than the peg indicates. Such a belief would encourage traders to sell Hong Kong dollars in exchange for U.S. dollars. In the short term, the Hong Kong government

 This Is the Real World

During October 1997, South Korea was experiencing a currency crisis (along with several other Asian countries) where the value of the Korean won was declining at a rapid rate. Investor confidence in the South Korean economy was very low, and the government was unable to support the extreme amounts of Korean currency that investors were trying to sell. As a desperate attempt to stop the devaluation in its currency, the government established a daily limit of 2.25%, for which it would allow the won to devalue. Once the limit was reached, all trading in the currency would be suspended.

The first day this rule was in effect, trading in won during the first few minutes was furious, and the limit was reached within 10 minutes. As promised, trading in the currency was suspended. This process continued for several days until the Korean

government increased the limit to a 10 percent decline. The first day after the limit was extended, trading was suspended after only 30 minutes. Finally, after several weeks of this trading activity, in December 1997 the Korean won began to settle at about 1,900 won per dollar, which was about 50% below its value in October 1997.

Questions:
1. The Korean government established the trading rule to stop the decline in its currency's value. Was the rule effective?
2. Suppose that the Korean government decided to peg its currency to the U.S. dollar, i.e., decree an exchange rate instead of allowing the value of its currency to be determined by the market. Would this action solve the currency devaluation problems? How would this action likely affect the Korean economy?

might be able to support the peg by continuing to purchase Hong Kong dollars from the speculators. However, after a time, the continued sell pressure would ultimately result in the Hong Kong government devaluing its currency (or some other negative repercussion, such as higher interest rates, increasing unemployment, rising bankruptcies, and collapsing securities markets).

Determinants of Exchange Rates

Recall that we expressed exchange rates as a price relationship between two currencies. Like any other price, exchange rates are established by supply and demand market forces. A high demand for a currency will cause it to strengthen against (i.e., enable it to purchase more of) other currencies; in contrast, an oversupply of a currency will cause it to weaken against other currencies.

During the early 1980s, the United States was experiencing a very strong dollar relative to other developed nations. In late 1984, one U.S. dollar (US$1) could purchase approximately 250 Japanese yen (¥250). Referring to Exhibit 20-3 (pp. 944–945), we see that the direct spot rate for the Japanese yen on May 1, 2002, was around 127. What factors would cause such a substantial weakening in the U.S. dollar relative to the Japanese yen? The following paragraphs briefly discuss some of the factors that affect the price of currency.

Trade Balances

A country's trade balance has a positive relationship with the value of that country's currency. Every time a U.S. company exports goods or services to a foreign nation, the demand for U.S. dollars increases because the foreign buyer must sell its local currency in order to purchase U.S. dollars to pay for the goods and services. Imports have the opposite effect. The U.S. has experienced a prolonged trade deficit with Japan, which has certainly affected the weakening of the U.S. dollar relative to the Japanese yen.

What is the effect of exports and imports when the seller of goods/services (for example, Coca-Cola Company) does not require payment in its local currency (i.e., the U.S. dollar)? This might occur for two reasons. First, by allowing the foreign importer to pay for the goods/services in its domestic currency, Coca-Cola has shifted all risk associated with changes in exchange rates from the foreign customer to itself, and by so doing, could increase sales to foreign customers. Second, Coca-Cola might desire to reinvest the proceeds in the foreign country, and thus, payment in the foreign currency would facilitate this process. In both of these cases, however, the act of exporting goods/services has still created an increased demand for the U.S. dollar. In the first case, instead of the foreign buyer selling the foreign currency to purchase U.S. dollars, Coca-Cola does so, and therefore, the demand for U.S. dollars has still increased. The second case can be thought of as two separate transactions resulting in a net zero trade balance: the purchase of the U.S. goods requiring U.S. dollars increases the demand for U.S. dollars, while the reinvestment in the foreign country requires the foreign currency and increases the demand for the foreign currency.

Interest Rates

Holding all other things equal, if you had a choice of investing in a riskless investment in the United States and earning a return of 5% or investing in a similar riskless investment in the United Kingdom and earning a return of 6%, which investment would you choose? The answer is obvious—anyone would prefer the higher return investment. As a result, the demand for British pounds would increase, and it would strengthen against the U.S. dollar. Exchange rates and, in particular, forward rates would adjust to an equilibrium that would eliminate any arbitrage opportunities.

Inflation Rates

Inflation rates are closely linked to interest rates since inflation is a key component of an interest rate. However, it should be noted that the effect on a currency's strength is opposite for inflation rates compared to interest rates. As a country's interest rates increase, their currency strengthens; however, as the country's inflation rate increases, their currency weakens. A high inflation rate results in the value of a currency depreciating quickly, which lowers the demand for that currency.

Capital Market Stability

This factor has been very important to the United States in maintaining a strong currency. The stability of capital markets in the United States is very attractive to foreign investors, which results in a high inflow of foreign direct investment and increases the demand for the U.S. dollar.

Other Factors

Several other factors can affect exchange rates, as indicated in Exhibit 20-4, including attitude of governments about foreign investment, confidence in the economic system, national growth, and foreign exchange reserves. Exhibit 20-4 shows the relationship between a change in one factor with exchange rates, *holding all other factors constant*. However, the assumption that all other factors remain constant while one factor changes is not very realistic. All of these factors are interrelated, and it is extremely difficult to predict the long-term (or even the short-term) effects on exchange rates of a change in one of these factors in isolation.

EXHIBIT 20-4

Some Determinants of Exchange Rates

Factor	Relationship with Exchange Rates*
1. Trade balance	Positive
2. Interest rates	Positive
3. Inflation rates	Negative
4. Capital market stability	Positive
5. National growth	Positive
6. Attitude of local government to foreign trade	Positive
7. Foreign exchange reserves	Positive

*A positive (negative) relationship indicates that an increase in the specific factor causes the local currency to strengthen (weaken).

For example, an increase in interest rates by the Federal Reserve will by itself attract more foreign investors to U.S. markets, which will strengthen the U.S. dollar. However, an increase in interest rates can also have a negative effect on the overall economy. The cost of borrowing will increase, which will cause people to spend less for houses, cars, and other items. The cost of capital to businesses will increase, causing them to reduce their investments in new projects

This Is the Real World

The following excerpt from the business press illustrates the interrelationship of several economic variables and the difficulty in evaluating the financial repercussions of changes in foreign currency exchange rates.

Asian Currency Chaos Roils U.S. Tech Firms, But It Isn't All Bad

In October, the world's biggest drive maker, Seagate Technology Inc., took a $63 million charge because of a badly timed hedging bet on the plunging currencies of Thailand and Malaysia, where Seagate has many of its plants. While the charge was a shock for shareholders, there was also an upside: The currency declines that triggered it also meant lower manufacturing costs for Seagate, the biggest private employer in those two countries.

That bit of good news, though, was quickly offset by bad news in South Korea, where a weakening won gave Seagate's competitors like Samsung Group the chance to cut their prices. Because of the same South Korean crisis, the likes of Samsung are facing a credit crunch that appears likely to curb their ability to expand operations. That's potentially a big plus for Seagate, because the company is struggling with an industrywide glut of disk drives. But a scarcity of credit is also bad news, of course, since consumers and corporations in South Korea and the rest of Asia will be buying fewer personal computers, in which most of Seagate's drives are used.

SOURCE: Lee Gomes, Dean Takahashi, and Kuala Lumpur, *The Wall Street Journal, December 12, 1997,* Page A1.

and research and development. The net effect of all these factors could be that corporate profits will be seriously damaged, and the growth of the economy will slow down, which will have a weakening influence on the U.S. dollar.

European Monetary Union (EMU)

On January 1, 1999, eleven of the European Union's 15 member nations officially adopted the euro as a common currency among the nations. Greece subsequently joined the EMU to bring the number of euro-adopting countries to twelve.[1] The adoption of the euro is the culminating effort in the EU's attempt to cultivate a common market among the European nations. The currencies of the euro-adopting countries were phased out over a 3-year transition period until on December 31, 2001, they officially disappeared in place of the euro. The main advantage of a common currency is that it will facilitate investment and trade among the participating nations, since cost comparisons are made easier and the costs of exchanging currencies are eliminated.[2]

Although many EU officials are optimistic about the monetary union, history indicates that its success is certainly not guaranteed. In the past 130 years, there have been three other monetary unions that ultimately failed: the Scandinavian Monetary Union, the Latin Monetary Union, and the East African Community.

The Scandinavian Monetary Union began in 1873 and was comprised of Denmark, Norway, and Sweden. The problem in this union began when Sweden's economy grew at a rate significantly less than that of Norway's and Denmark's economies. The result was that Sweden experienced lower inflation rates, and the fixed exchange rate among the nations lost credibility among foreign currency

---

[1]The 12 adopting countries are Austria, Belgium, Finland, France, Germany, Greece, Ireland, Italy, Luxembourg, the Netherlands, Portugal, and Spain. Denmark, Sweden, and the United Kingdom are part of the European Union but have not joined the EMU.

[2]Similar to trading in stocks, exchange rates are quoted at a bid-and-ask rate, the difference being the broker's compensation for executing the exchange.

traders. Sweden's coins were perceived to be more valuable, even though the fixed exchange rate among all three nations was set at one-for-one. The demand for Sweden's coins became so great that the Swedish government could no longer support the currency link. The union was formally disbanded in 1924.

The Latin Monetary Union was formed in 1865 and was comprised of France, Belgium, Italy, Switzerland, and Greece. Italy continually ran up trade deficits, which weakened its currency relative to the other currencies. The union lingered until World War I, when several of the nations issued large amounts of paper money to finance the war effort. These paper currencies were not accepted as legal tender among the other union nations.

Kenya, Tanzania, and Uganda formed the East African Community in 1967. As part of the community, they issued a common shilling. However, cooperation among the nations did not last, and the union was disbanded only ten years later in 1977.

Critics of the European Monetary Union (EMU) point to the above failed endeavors to establish a monetary union and argue that the euro will not last. However, there is a key difference between the past monetary unions and the EMU. In June 1998, the EU formed a central bank, the European Central Bank, which will have powers similar to the Federal Reserve Bank in the United States. To qualify for entrance into the union, nations must exercise strict discipline over their monetary policies. The European Central Bank will monitor all member nations to ensure that they comply with certain rules and regulations. Proponents of the EMU suggest that this model will ensure the union's success.

In fact, some proponents suggest that it is this model that allowed the United States to adopt a common currency. In the nineteenth century, U.S. banks issued their own notes. The actual amount given in exchange for these notes was almost never equal to their face value. For example, $1 notes issued from Planters Bank in Nashville, TN, and State Bank of Illinois would return 80 and 50 cents, respectively, in Philadelphia. The value of the note depended on the reputation of and the distance from the issuing bank. It wasn't until the Civil War when the Union needed large amounts of funds to finance the war that a common paper currency was issued in the United States.

Many people are watching very closely to see whether the European Monetary Union will be successful. Currently, because of its liquidity, the U.S. dollar is the most traded currency in the world. Even when an Australian company, for example, pays for Swedish goods, it is not uncommon for the company to trade Australian dollars for U.S. dollars and then immediately convert the U.S. dollars into Swedish krona. The high liquidity of the U.S. dollar often results in lower trading costs from executing two currency trades in U.S. dollars, compared to only one trade between Australian dollars and Swedish krona. With the emergence of the euro, it is possible that the U.S. dollar will take a back seat to this newly formed currency as the most widely traded in the world. However, the U.S. economy is also expected to benefit since the liquidity of the euro will be greater than any single European currency by itself, which means that exchange costs will be less for U.S. companies conducting business in the European nations that use the euro.

Accounting for Foreign Exchange Transactions

Now that we have briefly discussed the foreign exchange market, you are more prepared to study and understand the economic and accounting effects of foreign currency transactions. The first example provides a simple scenario of a U.S. importing company conducting a business transaction with a Canadian exporting company. We will build upon this example by introducing a situation where credit terms are granted to the importer. As will be seen, exchange rate fluctuations from the date of sale to the date of cash settlement might result in a **foreign currency transaction gain or loss**. Finally, this section concludes by illustrating the accounting for some procedures that can be pursued by company management to minimize the risk associated with exchange rate fluctuations.

Foreign Exchange Transaction— Cash Basis

To illustrate the straightforward procedures of accounting for foreign currency transactions where no credit is granted to the purchaser, assume the following conditions.

> Total Distributors, Inc. (TDI) is a retail company based in Albany, New York, that purchases and distributes various products to retail stores. Recently, TDI discovered that it could purchase clothing products from Luis Co. at a favorable price. Luis is based in Ottawa, Canada, and requires that all transactions be paid in Canadian dollars (C$), and payment is required upon delivery of the goods.
>
> TDI decides to purchase 10,000 units of clothing inventory from Luis, the average cost of which is C$10. Delivery of the goods occurred on May 1, 2002. Referring to Exhibit 20-3 (pp. 944–945), the exchange rate for Canadian dollars on May 1, 2002, is:
>
> $$C\$1 = US\$0.6407.$$

Given this information, the following journal entries would be made by TDI and Luis to record the transaction on May 1.

Journal entry made by TDI:

Inventory	$64,070	
Cash		$64,070

[(10,000 × C$10) × $0.6407]
To record purchase of inventory.

Journal entry made by Luis:

Cash	C$100,000	
Sales		C$100,000

(10,000 × C$10)
To record sale of inventory.

As can be seen, no special problems are presented when credit is not extended to the purchasing party. Both parties record the transaction using the historical cost amounts based on their local currencies.

Foreign Exchange Transaction—Credit Sale

This section expands the previous example to a situation where credit terms are granted. It is this type of situation where decisions need to be made concerning how to account for changes in exchange rates.

CONCEPTUAL
Question

Conceptual Question: Has the Canadian dollar strengthened or weakened relative to the U.S. dollar from May 1 to June 30? From June 30 to July 31?

Assume the same facts as detailed in the cash transaction, except that on the date of delivery, Luis allows TDI to delay payment for 90 days, and TDI's fiscal year ends on June 30. Assume that on July 30, 2002, TDI remits full payment of C$100,000 when the exchange rate is $0.66. In addition, assume that on June 30, 2002 (TDI's fiscal year-end), the exchange rate for one Canadian dollar is $0.65.

To summarize the exchange rates on the relevant dates:

May 1, 2002—C$1 = US$0.6407
June 30, 2002—C$1 = US$0.65
July 30, 2002—C$1 = US$0.66

The journal entry for TDI to record the purchase on May 1 is the same as what was recorded earlier for the cash purchase, except that Cash is replaced by Accounts Payable for TDI and Accounts Receivable for Luis. The accounting problem comes into play later when the spot rate changes.

From May 1 to June 30, the U.S. dollar weakened relative to the Canadian dollar. As a result, if payment was made on June 30, TDI would have been required to pay $65,000. This amount is $930 more than what was paid under the cash transaction scenario and represents a foreign currency transaction loss to TDI. In this case, the measurement of the $930 loss is straightforward (the difference in the amounts payable in U.S. dollars on May 1 and June 30). However, two conceptual financial reporting issues must be addressed. First, how should the loss be reported: as an adjustment to the acquisition cost of the asset, or as an operating loss on the income statement? Second, should the loss be deferred until the cash settlement date or recognized immediately?

The first financial reporting issue has been relatively free of controversy. A foreign currency transaction gain or loss is generally regarded as a cost of conducting business in a foreign currency, *not* a cost of acquiring an asset. Therefore, the gain or loss should be reported in the operating section of the income statement, and the historical cost of the asset is *not* adjusted.

With respect to the second financial reporting issue, the FASB initially proposed that this type of transaction gain or loss should be reported as a component of operating earnings. However, during deliberations, several FASB constituents suggested that the gain or loss should be deferred until the settlement date. They argued that recognition in the income statement would cause undue variability in earnings, since the exchange rate might easily reverse prior to cash settlement. The FASB rejected this argument and concluded that immediate recognition of foreign currency gains and losses reflects the cash flow impacts of exchange rate fluctuations. In addition, deferring the transaction gain or loss until the settlement date violates the matching principle, since this method would result in gains or losses being recognized in periods that are unrelated to exchange rate changes.

Given this guidance, TDI should make the following journal entries to record the transaction:

Journal entries made by TDI:

May 1	Inventory	$64,070	
	Accounts Payable to Luis in C$		$64,070

[(10,000 × C$10) × $0.6407]
To record purchase of inventory.

June 30	Foreign Currency Transaction Loss	$930	
	Accounts Payable to Luis in C$		$930

[(C$100,000 × $0.6407) − (C$100,000 × $0.65)]
To update value of payable.

July 30	Accounts Payable to Luis in C$	$65,000	
	Foreign Currency Transaction Loss	$1,000	

[(C$100,000 × $0.65) − (C$100,000 × $0.66)]

	Cash		$66,000

(C$100,000 × $0.66)
To record cash payment for inventory.

Note that the total loss to TDI due to exchange rate fluctuations is $1,930, of which $930 was recognized from May 1 through June 30, and $1,000 was recognized in July (the subsequent fiscal year).

With respect to Luis Co., the accounting for this transaction is straightforward.

Journal entries made by Luis:

May 1	Accounts Receivable	$100,000	
	Sales		$100,000

(10,000 × C$10)
To record sale of inventory.

July 30	Cash	$100,000	
	Accounts Receivable		$100,000

To record cash received.

It should be noted that from Luis Co.'s perspective, this transaction is *not* a foreign currency transaction. By requiring that payment be made in Canadian dollars, Luis is able to avoid the risk associated with exchange rate fluctuations.

Using Forward Contracts to Eliminate Foreign Currency Risk

Many managers are evaluated and sometimes even compensated based on accounting earnings. Since currency fluctuations, which cause foreign currency transaction gains and losses, are beyond the control of company management, managers might choose to engage in **hedging activities** that protect against an unfavorable movement in exchange rates. A popular method of hedging against foreign currency risk is to invest in forward contracts.

A forward contract is a type of **derivative instrument**. *SFAS No. 133* defines a derivative instrument as a security consisting of three main characteristics:

1. It has one or more **underlyings** and one or more **notional amounts** or payment provisions, or both.

EXTENDING THE CONCEPT

Using the information provided in the example of TDI and Luis Co., return to the opening scenario (pp. 940–941) and determine how Software Innovations should account for its unrealized foreign currency exchange loss.

Both TDI and Software Innovations must recognize a foreign currency loss on their respective income statements. In TDI's case, this loss was a result of holding a monetary liability in a foreign currency during a period when the U.S. dollar weakened with respect to the foreign currency. What was the cause of Software Innovations' loss?

What if . . .

- TDI held a *monetary asset* denominated in a foreign currency during a time when the U.S. dollar was *strengthening* against the foreign currency?

- TDI held a *monetary liability* denominated in a foreign currency during a time when the U.S. dollar was *strengthening* against the foreign currency?

- TDI held a *monetary asset* denominated in a foreign currency during a time when the U.S. dollar was *weakening* against the foreign currency?

2. It requires no initial net investment or an initial net investment that is smaller than would be required for other types of contracts that would be expected to have a similar response to changes in market factors.

3. Its terms require or permit net settlement, it can readily be settled net by a means outside the contract, or it provides for delivery of an asset that puts the recipient in a position not substantially different from net settlement.

With respect to foreign currency forward contracts, the underlying is an exchange rate, and the notional amount is the amount of foreign currency units to be bought or sold. The interaction between the exchange rate and the foreign currency units determines the amount of cash required to settle the forward contract. Consistent with the second characteristic, typical forward contracts do not require a net investment. The third characteristic generally refers to an ability to settle a contract through one transaction rather than two or more transactions, which would be required if the contract were interpreted literally.

The use of and accounting for forward contracts to hedge foreign currency transaction gains/losses will be illustrated by extending the example used earlier involving TDI and Luis Co.

Assume the same facts as were used in the credit sale example. That is, TDI purchases C\$100,000 worth of inventory from Luis on May 1, 2002, when the spot rate for Canadian dollars was \$0.6407. Also, Luis grants credit terms for 90 days, and the spot rate between the purchase date and the payment date fluctuates as before.

May 1, 2002—C\$1 = US\$0.6407
June 30, 2002—C\$1 = US\$0.650
July 30, 2002—C\$1 = US\$0.660

Now, however, the example changes in that TDI enters into a 90-day forward contract on May 1, 2002, with a foreign currency broker to purchase C\$100,000. Referring to Exhibit 20-3 (pp. 944–945), we see that the 90-day forward rate for Canadian dollars is \$0.6397.

EXTENDING THE CONCEPT

The discussion in this section focuses on using forward contracts to reduce (or eliminate) risk associated with foreign currency exchange rates. However, companies can be exposed to other types of risk that could significantly affect the overall operating performance of the business, such as changes in interest rates and commodity prices. The concept of the forward contract is a popular tool to hedge against these types of risks, too.

Suppose that a company has debt outstanding that has a variable interest rate. Describe how a forward contract could be used to convert the variable interest payments to fixed interest payments. What is the underlying in this derivative instrument? What is the notional amount?

Could there be situations where a company would desire to convert fixed interest payments to variable interest payments?

The sequential flow of transactions and events within this example is illustrated in Figure 20-1. After purchasing inventory from Luis on credit, TDI agrees to pay a foreign currency broker (e.g., TDI's bank) \$63,970 (the notional amount of C\$100,000 multiplied by the forward rate or underlying of \$0.6397) in exchange for C\$100,000. TDI will then send the C\$100,000 received from the broker to Luis as payment for the inventory.

Through the purchase of the forward contract, TDI can determine on May 1, rather than July 30, the amount of cash needed to pay for the inventory. No matter what happens to exchange rates between May 1 and July 30, TDI will be required to pay \$63,970. Thus, TDI has effectively hedged its foreign currency transaction risk.

The difference between the spot rate and the forward rate on the date the forward contract is entered into is referred to as a forward contract premium or

FIGURE 20-1

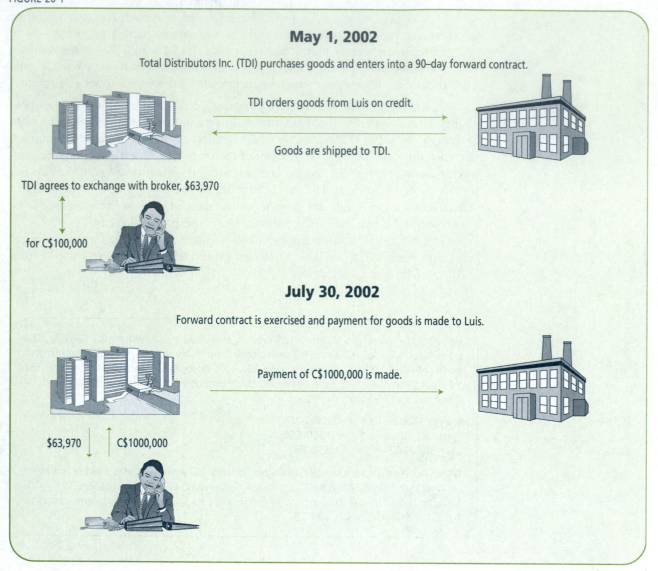

May 1, 2002

Total Distributors Inc. (TDI) purchases goods and enters into a 90–day forward contract.

TDI orders goods from Luis on credit.

Goods are shipped to TDI.

TDI agrees to exchange with broker, $63,970

for C$100,000

July 30, 2002

Forward contract is exercised and payment for goods is made to Luis.

Payment of C$1000,000 is made.

$63,970   C$1000,000

discount. In this case, since the forward rate is less than the spot rate, it is selling at a discount. As was mentioned in the previous section, the difference in interest rates between the Canadian and U.S. markets is a major determinant of the premium or discount. However, the premium or discount also represents compensation given to the foreign currency broker for providing liquidity in the foreign exchange market.

Accounting for the hedging transaction is stipulated by *SFAS No. 133*, which requires that *all derivative instruments be recognized at market values*. Prior to the issuance of *SFAS No. 133*, the rapid increase in the types and sophistication of derivative instruments and the lack of guidance from the FASB resulted in inconsistent accounting practices for hedging activities. The U.S. Securities and Exchange Commission pressured the FASB to provide a comprehensive framework for derivative instruments. Although *SFAS No. 133* was adopted in June 1998, due to its complexity and implementation difficulties, *SFAS No. 137* deferred its effective date to begin after June 15, 2000. (For example, for calendar-year entities, the standard became effective as of January 1, 2001.)

This Is the Real World

As is the case with many proposals issued by the Financial Accounting Standards Board, the proposal to value all derivatives at market value, which ultimately became *SFAS No. 133*, was met with controversy. Many critics, especially financial institutions, claimed that the standard would introduce added volatility to the income statement and sometimes result in misleading financial information. Even the Federal Reserve Chairman, Alan Greenspan, wrote a letter to the FASB, expressing concern over the proposal. According to Greenspan, the complexity and cost of the standard could discourage companies from participating in hedging activities. The Fed Chairman recommended that the FASB consider requiring supplemental disclosures about the market value of derivatives instead of recognizing the gains/losses on the financial statements.

Members of the United States Congress were also critical of the proposal. Senator Phil Gramm, a Texas Republican, expressed concern about the effects of the proposal. Implications were made that the accounting rule-making process, as conducted by the FASB, was failing in its attempt to provide cost-effective information that was useful to the public. The following comment was made by a staff member of the Senate Banking Committee: "Were FASB to disre-

gard [Greenspan's] letter, it would really throw into doubt their rulemaking process."*

When the FASB was met with a similar challenge in regards to accounting for stock-based employee compensation, the FASB backed down on its proposal to require companies to expense the market value of securities issued to employees as compensation expense. Instead, the FASB required pro forma EPS disclosures as if the fair-value method had been used.

To the FASB's credit in this case, the final standard issued on accounting for derivatives maintained the requirement that all derivative instruments must be reported at fair value. The FASB's position is that fair-value accounting will avoid the big surprises experienced in the past, when several companies reported liquidity problems due to sustained losses from trading in derivatives. Had banks and financial institutions been required to report their derivatives at market value in the 1980s, the public would have seen that many of them were insolvent, and perhaps the large expense related to the savings and loan crisis could have been avoided.

*"Greenspan Slams Stricter Derivatives Accounting," American Banker, *August 7, 1997*.

INTERNET

The following Web site can be used to look up current and historical exchange rates for all major currencies: **http://www.x-rates.com**. This Web site also provides fundamental information about exchange rates.

The passage of *SFAS No. 133* significantly altered the method of accounting for derivatives and was met with a great amount of resistance, particularly from financial institutions that had extensive operations in derivatives. Business executives feared that recognizing derivative instruments at market value would introduce increased variability in earnings, which would create an impression of a high level of risk.

Accounting for Forward Contracts

The journal entries made by TDI on the date of purchase, the fiscal year-end, and the settlement date to implement the requirements of *SFAS No. 133* are presented in this section, along with corresponding analyses.

May 1	Inventory	64,070
	Accounts Payable to Luis in C$	64,070
	[(10,000 × C$10) × $0.6407]	
	To record the purchase of inventory.	
	Memo Entry	
	To record the forward contract.	

The journal entry to record the purchase of inventory is exactly the same as what was recorded in the credit sale without the forward contract. Two items should be noted from the entry. First, the cost of the inventory is based on the spot rate that existed on the purchase date and not the forward rate. By taking advantage of the credit terms granted by Luis and purchasing the forward rate,

TDI paid $100 less in this transaction, compared to the cash price of $64,070. The $100 cash flow is related to the financing and locking in the price of the inventory by employing the forward contract (*not* part of the cost of inventory). As will be demonstrated later, the difference between forward and spot rates will be reflected in net income as a foreign currency transaction gain/loss.

The second item to note is that no entry is made for the forward contract, since no net investment is required to enter the contract. The main point to remember when accounting for derivative instruments is that *SFAS No. 133* requires them to be recorded at market value. At the date of initiation, market value is equal to historical cost (see Chapter 5), and since no cash was exchanged at the initiation of the forward contract, its market value on May 1, 2002, is $0.

Changes in the market value of a forward contract are a function of changes in *forward rates*. Therefore, in order to account for the forward contract on dates subsequent to its initiation, we need further information about the change in forward rates. Presented in Illustration 20-1 is a chart that outlines the assumptions we make with respect to forward and spot rates.

ILLUSTRATION 20-1

Assumed Spot and Forward Rates

Date	Spot Rates	Forward Rates for July 30, 2002
May 1, 2002	$0.6407	$0.6397
June 30, 2002	$0.6500	$0.6501
July 30, 2002	$0.6600	N/A

Given the assumed spot and forward rates, TDI would make the following journal entries on June 30, its fiscal year-end.

June 30	Foreign Currency Transaction Loss	930	
	Accounts Payable to Luis in C$		930

[(C$100,000 × $0.6407) − (C$100,000 × $0.65)]
To update the payable due to changes in the spot rate.

	Forward Contract	1,040	
	Foreign Currency Transaction Gain		1,040

[(C$100,000 × $0.6501) − (C$100,000 × $0.6397)]
To update the value of the forward contract due to changes in the forward rate.

The first entry made on June 30 is equivalent to what was made in the prior credit sale example without a forward contract. The foreign currency transaction loss is a function of the change in *spot rates*.

The second entry deserves special consideration. Consistent with the requirements of *SFAS No. 133*, the forward contract is recorded at its market value. The best determinant of market value will be a dealer's quote. In those cases where a dealer's quote is not available, *SFAS No. 133* indicates that the company should perform a discounted cash flow analysis. The cash flow analysis should be based on changes in *forward rates*. In our example, TDI holds a forward contract on June 30 that allows it to purchase C$100,000 at a price of $63,970 ($0.6397 × C$100,000). Similar forward contracts that exist on June 30 have a required payment of $65,010 ($0.6501 × C$100,000), which represents an increase in required cash outflows of $1,040.

Thus, the forward contract held by TDI has a positive value since it requires less cash to be paid in order to obtain the same amount of Canadian dollars. Another consideration to be made in order to determine the value of the forward contract is *when the net cash flows will be realized*. The $1,040 is a net cash inflow that will be received on July 30, 2002, and thus should be discounted to reflect its present value. However, the time to execution in our example is only 30 days and, given its immateriality, the discount is ignored for now. Thus, the forward contract is debited for the entire $1,040. The corresponding credit is a foreign currency transaction gain. The foreign currency transaction gain due to the increase in market value of the forward contract is almost identical (in absolute value) to the foreign currency transaction loss. Indeed, this is the objective of hedging activities. The $110 difference between the foreign currency gain and loss is a partial representation of the forward contract premium of $100.

Continuing with our example, the following entries are required on July 30, 2002, to record the payment for the purchased goods and the execution of the forward contract.

July 30	Accounts Payable to Luis in C$	65,000	
	Foreign Currency Transaction Loss	1,000	
	[(C$100,000 × $0.65) − (C$100,000 × $0.66)]		
	Cash		66,000
	(C$100,000 × $0.66)		

To record the payment of cash for the purchased inventory.

	Forward Contract	990	
	Foreign Currency Transaction Gain		990
	[(C$100,000 × $0.66) − (C$100,000 × $0.6501)]		

To update the value of the forward contract.

	Cash	2,030	
	Forward Contract		2,030

To record the net settlement of the forward contract.

EXTENDING THE CONCEPT

Derek Newmann in the opening scenario (pp. 940–941) argued that the foreign currency transaction loss should not be recognized in the income statement until actually realized because he had no control over exchange rate fluctuations, and he should not be evaluated on things that are out of his control. Having now studied forward contracts, evaluate Derek's argument.

TDI "bought forward" (i.e., agreed to purchase foreign currency in the future) C$100,000 to hedge against its exposure to exchange rate fluctuations as a result of holding a monetary liability denominated in a foreign currency. *What if...*

- TDI mistakenly agreed to "sell forward" C$100,000?

- Instead of the Canadian dollar strengthening against the U.S. dollar, the Canadian dollar weakened? What would happen to the value of the forward contract? What would be the net effect on the income statement?

What can Software Innovations (see the opening scenario) do to hedge against its risk associated with exchange rate fluctuations?

Once again, the first entry is the same as what was recorded in the example without the forward contract. The second and third entries could be easily combined; however, for instructive purposes, separation of the entries provides more intuition. The second entry represents the forward contract's increase in market value. On the date of settlement, the value of the forward contract should be equal to the amount of cash flows realized from executing the contract, which is the difference in the contracted forward rate ($0.6397) and the spot rate on the settlement date ($0.66—*the forward and spot rates on the expiration date of the forward contract are always the same*) multiplied by the notional amount. In this example, the cash flow realized from the forward contract is $2,030, which is reflected in the final entry.

As a result of entering into the forward contract, TDI's net cash outflow is $63,970 ($66,000 − $2,030). The difference in foreign currency transaction gains and losses of $100 recognized over the life of the contract represents the forward contract discount.

Speculation in Derivatives

Derivative instruments can also be used for speculative purposes. In this situation, traders use derivative instruments for the primary purpose of earning profits, instead of hedging against exposure to a certain type of risk. In the case of foreign currency derivatives, an investor might forecast that the British pound will weaken in the future, relative to the U.S. dollar. The investor could potentially profit from this forecast by purchasing a put option[3] to sell British pounds or by entering into a forward contract to sell British pounds at a specified rate in the future.

Referring once again to Exhibit 20-3 (pp. 944–945), the 6-month forward rate for British pounds on May 1, 2002, was $1.4477. If an investor entered into a forward contract to sell British pounds at this contracted rate and the British pound weakens so that the spot rate falls below the forward rate of $1.4477, the investor will realize a gain on the forward contract because he/she can purchase pounds at the cheaper spot rate and sell the pounds at the guaranteed forward rate.

Speculating with derivative instruments is very risky. Given the complexity of the global economy and the many interrelated factors that determine exchange rates, establishing a reliable forecast for future exchange rate fluctuations is extremely difficult. In fact, many academic studies indicate that the foreign exchange market that determines spot and forward rates is very efficient, and accordingly, whether one realizes a gain or a loss from speculating in the market is determined by a purely random process. This means that the chances of winning or losing

This Is the Real World

In February 1995, Barings PLC was the oldest merchant bank in Great Britain, with a reputation for conservative operations. The bank benefited from a high level of prestige and had clients such as the Queen of England and other members of the Royal Family. On February 26, 1995, the bank began proceedings that are similar to Chapter 11 bankruptcy proceedings in the United States. The sole cause of the bank's demise was derivative speculation by one man—Nicholas Leeson, general manager and head trader of Baring Futures (Singapore).

Mr. Leeson was heavily involved in arbitrage trading on futures contracts that were listed on both the Singapore International Monetary Exchange (SIMEX) and the Osaka Securities Exchange (OSE). Sometimes, securities listed on more than one exchange can be traded at different prices. Buying the security on the exchange where it is selling at a discount and immediately selling the same security on the other exchange results in arbitrage profits without carrying significant risk. However, what Barings PLC didn't know was that, beginning in 1992, Leeson began placing large bets on the direction that the Nikkei-225 (the Japanese version of the S&P 500 Index) would take. By the end

of 1992, Leeson had already realized losses of £2 million. These losses were hidden from the company by the creation of a new trading account that was not reported to company headquarters.

The speculation in derivatives became more intense as Leeson attempted to recover his previous losses. By the end of 1994, Leeson's cumulative losses in his fictitious account were £208 million. By comparison, Barings PLC reported £205 million profit for the year.

On January 17, 1995, a violent earthquake struck Kobe, Japan, which had a significant effect on the Japanese stock market. As the Nikkei-225 realized substantial losses, Leeson incurred magnified losses on his derivatives. In total, Leeson realized losses of £927 million (approximately US$1.4 billion). Barings total stockholders' equity was only £440 million.

Barings PLC was guilty of violating some significant internal control procedures which allowed a person inside the company to incur substantial losses. The case also illustrates the risk that is associated with trading in derivative instruments.

---

[3] A put option is a security that gives the holder the right, but not the obligation, to sell an asset (in this case, foreign currency) at a specified price.

are about fifty-fifty. One hedge fund that invests heavily in foreign currency derivatives realized a $1 billion gain from investing in the British pound in 1992. However, this same fund realized a $600 million loss on the Japanese yen in 1994.

Summary

The globalized economy requires that students become familiar with conducting international business, which includes accounting for transactions made in another currency. This chapter provides an introduction to foreign currency transactions and the risk that accompanies such transactions.

Engaging in credit transactions where the form of payment is denominated in a currency other than the operating currency introduces foreign currency risk, which arises when the relationship between two currencies fluctuates over time. Unrealized gains and losses that arise as a result of holding monetary assets and liabilities that are denominated in a foreign currency must be recognized immediately in the income statement. In addition, *SFAS No. 133* requires that all derivative instruments must be recorded at market value and that changes in market value must be recognized as gains or losses on the income statement. Thus, company managers can use derivative instruments as a means to hedge against foreign currency gains/losses from holding foreign currency monetary assets and liabilities.

Questions

1. What are some advantages to foreign trade that could be realized by an exporter? What are some advantages of foreign trade to an importer?

2. Identify specific risks that are associated with foreign trade.

3. The following is an exchange rate between U.S. dollars and British pounds expressed by a direct quote: $1.50 = £1. Provide an equivalent expression, using an indirect quote.

4. What is the difference between a spot rate and a forward rate?

5. Identify some factors that would affect demand for a particular currency. Indicate whether the factor identified would increase or decrease the demand and whether the factor would weaken or strengthen the value of the currency.

6. What is the European Monetary Union? Identify an arrangement within the United States that is similar to the European Monetary Union. Describe the role of the European Central Bank.

7. Describe the effect on a company's financial statements of holding monetary assets and liabilities denominated in a foreign currency during a time when the value of the foreign currency is decreasing.

8. Provide a theoretical argument for recognizing all foreign currency transaction gains and losses in the period when the exchange rate changed, instead of the period when cash is collected.

9. Describe at least two ways a domestic company that is involved in foreign currency transactions can avoid foreign currency risk.

10. Identify the three characteristics that describe a derivative. Relate these characteristics to a foreign currency forward contract.

11. Suppose that a company purchases inventory from a foreign supplier and is required to pay in the foreign currency 90 days from the date of purchase. To hedge against foreign currency risk, the company purchases a forward contract where the forward rate differs from the current spot rate. Should the cost of the inventory be recorded using the current spot rate or the forward rate? Why?

12. When a quoted market price is not available for a forward contract, should the market value of the contract be determined by referring to changes in the spot rate or changes in the forward rate? Why?

13. What is the market value of most forward contracts at the date of initiation?

14. What determines whether a purchased foreign currency forward contract is used for hedging purposes or whether it is used for speculative purposes? How is company risk affected under both scenarios?

15. Multiple-choice questions:

   (1) An exchange rate that represents a contract between a foreign currency broker and another party for delivery of goods in the future is referred to as:

      a. The spot rate.

      b. The current spot rate.

      c. The forward rate.

      d. The hedge rate.

   (2) Which of the following is the likely effect of the United States realizing a trade deficit with Japan for an extended period of time?

      a. The U.S. dollar is likely to weaken against the Japanese yen.

      b. The U.S. Federal Reserve is likely to decrease interest rates.

      c. The Japanese yen is likely to weaken against the U.S. dollar.

      d. Japanese goods are likely to become less expensive in the United States.

   (3) ABC Corp. has a receivable denominated in a foreign currency that is due after the end of the current fiscal year. At the end of the fiscal year, the foreign currency had strengthened relative to the U.S. dollar. Which of the following is true?

      a. ABC Corp. has realized a gain on the receivable that must be recognized immediately in the income statement.

      b. ABC Corp. has realized a loss on the receivable that must be recognized immediately in the balance sheet.

      c. ABC Corp. has realized a gain on the receivable that must be deferred and recognized when cash is collected.

      d. ABC Corp. has realized a loss on the receivable that must be deferred and recognized when cash is collected.

   (4) The appropriate accounting for realized gains and losses on derivatives that are held for speculative purposes is to:

      a. Defer all gains and losses until the settlement date.

      b. Recognize all gains and losses in the period realized.

      c. Recognize all losses in the period realized, but defer all gains until the settlement date.

      d. Report all gains and losses in comprehensive income.

Exercises

Exercise 20-1: Relative Strength of a Currency. Listed below are spot rates as of December 31, 2003, and December 31, 2004. The first set of rates is stated as the number of foreign currency units per one U.S. dollar, whereas, the second set of rates is stated as the number of U.S. dollars per one foreign currency unit.

No. of foreign currency units per one U.S. dollar as of:

December 31, 2003	December 31, 2004
1.61 Australian dollar	1.70 Australian dollar
116 Japanese yen	105 Japanese yen
8.5 Swedish krona	7.0 Swedish krona
1,350 Korean won	1,300 Korean won

No. of U.S. dollars per one foreign currency unit as of:

December 31, 2003	December 31, 2004
$0.10 per Mexican peso	$0.09 per Mexican peso
$0.025 per Indian rupee	$0.031 per Indian rupee
$0.55 per Brazilian real	$0.45 per Brazilian real
$0.65 per Singaporean dollar	$0.71 per Singaporean dollar

1. Determine which currencies have strengthened relative to the U.S. dollar and which have weakened.
2. From the information provided, determine which of the following currencies is more likely to have strengthened relative to the other.
   a. Australian dollar relative to the Japanese yen
   b. Swedish krona relative to the Mexican peso
   c. Mexican peso relative to the Indian repee
   d. Korean won relative to the Brazilian real
3. Suppose that a U.S. company has held receivables denominated in each of the listed foreign currencies during the 2004 calendar year, and the company did not hedge against any foreign currency risk. Has the U.S. company realized a gain or a loss from changes in the exchange rate? How would your answer change if the U.S. company had held debt that was denominated in the foreign currency?

Exercise 20-2: Transaction Gain or Loss. On September 22, 2004, Parker Corp. sold inventory to a Canadian company for C$10,000. The operating currency for Parker Corp. is the U.S. dollar, and the spot rate that existed on September 22, 2004, was $0.65 per Canadian dollar. Parker granted credit terms to the Canadian customer and received payment in full on March 20, 2005, when the spot rate was $0.72. The spot rate was $0.75 on December 31, 2004.

1. Determine whether Parker Corp. realized a foreign currency transaction gain or loss during the 2004 and 2005 fiscal years.
2. Provide all necessary journal entries that Parker Corp. must prepare related to the sale of the inventory. Assume that the cost of the inventory to Parker Corp. was $3,000, and the company maintains a perpetual inventory system.

Exercise 20-3: Transaction Gain or Loss. During the year 2003, Baskets, Inc., had the following foreign currency transactions:

- On January 20, 2003, the company sold inventory to a foreign customer for 25,000 units of the foreign currency (LCU). The invoice was paid in full on April 3, 2003.
- On July 1, 2003, the company borrowed 100,000 LCU and signed a note payable that required the total principal and accrued interest to be paid on July 1, 2004. The stated annual interest rate on the note was 10%.

The relevant spot rates are as follows:

January 20, 2003	$1 = 1.25 LCU
April 3, 2003	$1 = 1.35 LCU
July 1, 2003	$1 = 1.40 LCU
December 31, 2003	$1 = 1.45 LCU

1. Determine the amount of gain or loss that Baskets, Inc., should recognize on its 2003 income statement as a result of selling inventory to a foreign customer.
2. Determine the amount of gain or loss that Baskets, Inc., should recognize on its 2003 income statement as a result of holding the note payable.

Exercise 20-4: Recognition of Exchange Rate Gain or Loss. On November 1, 2003, Lockheart Co. purchased merchandise from a foreign supplier for 100,000 foreign currency units (FCU). On the date of the purchase, the spot rate was $1 = 0.29 FCU. Terms of the transaction required Lockheart to pay for the purchase on January 30, 2004. On December 31, 2003, which is the fiscal year-end for Lockheart Co., the spot rate was $1 = 0.22 FCU. However, on January 30, 2004, the date of payment, the foreign currency had recovered to $1 = 0.30. Lockheart Co. did not issue its annual financial statements until March 10, 2004.

1. Determine the amount of foreign currency gain or loss that Lockheart Co. should recognize on its income statements for the years ending December 31, 2003 and 2004.
2. Given that Lockheart has not filed its financial statements prior to the payment for the inventory, discuss the appropriateness of recognizing the entire gain/loss on the transaction in the year of purchase or the year of payment.

Exercise 20-5: Forward Contract for Speculative Purposes. On November 10, 2003, McFarlin Inc. purchased a forward contract that allowed it to sell 100,000 euro on February 9, 2004. McFarlin has a December 31 fiscal year-end. Relevant exchange rates for one euro are as follows:

	Spot Rate	Forward Rate (for Feb. 9, 2004)
November 10, 2003	$1.10	$1.08
December 31, 2003	$1.05	$1.06
February 9, 2004	$1.03	

Determine the amount of gain or loss related to this transaction that McFarlin should recognize in its income statements for the years ended December 31, 2003 and 2004.

Exercise 20-6: Leverage Using Derivatives. A hedge fund is a portfolio of investments, a large component of which is typically derivative instruments. Investing in these types of funds is highly risky. An example of a hedge fund is Tiger Management LLC, one of the biggest fund companies for rich investors. During one of its peak periods, the amount of capital invested in the fund was $20 billion. Shortly thereafter, however, the fund began to realize significant losses, which prompted management to liquidate part of its equity holdings. In a letter to shareholders, management disclosed that the fund had sold more than $37 billion of equity investments in less than one year.

1. Explain how Tiger Management LLC can liquidate more than $37 billion of equity investments while having only $20 billion invested in the fund.
2. Provide an example of a speculator investing in large amounts of foreign currency with very little money.

Problems

Problem 20-1: Relationship between Spot and Forward Rates. Answer each of the following independent situations:

1. Assume that the spot rate to exchange U.S. dollars for British pounds on December 31, 2004, is as follows: $1.50 = £1. Also, assume that on this date a 90-day U.S. Treasury bill yields an annual rate of return of 5.5% and that a similar type of riskless security in the UK yields a rate of 7.0%. *Using only the information about differences in interest rates and holding all other factors constant*, calculate a predicted 90-day forward rate between the British pound and U.S. dollar for December 31, 2004.
2. Assume the following exchange rates between the U.S. dollar and the Japanese yen as of December 31, 2004:

Spot rate	$1 = ¥130.0
180-day forward rate	$1 = ¥128.5

Also, assume that the interest rate on a 6-month U.S. Treasury bill yields an annual rate of return of 5.5%. *Using only the information about differences in spot and forward exchange rates and holding all other factors constant*, calculate a predicted rate of return on a 6-month riskless security issued by the Japanese government.

Problem 20-2: Forward Contracts for Hedging and Speculation. On November 1, 2003, OptiGon Co. purchased two 180-day forward contracts that allow it to purchase 100,000 foreign currency units (FCU) at a specified rate of $0.50 per unit. The first forward contract was purchased for the purpose of hedging a payable of 100,000 FCU that is due on May 1, 2004. The second forward contract was purchased for speculative purposes. Relevant exchange rates are as follows:

	Spot Rate	Forward Rate (for May 1, 2004)
November 1, 2003	$0.48	$0.50
December 31, 2003	0.51	0.52
May 1, 2004	0.54	?

Required:

1. On May 1, 2004, what is the forward rate for that date?
2. Provide all necessary journal entries to (a) purchase the forward contracts on November 1, (b) update the value of the forward contracts and the related payable on December 31, and (c) pay the payable and settle the forward contracts on May 1.
3. Why is the gain/loss on the payable not exactly offset by the gain/loss on the forward contract that is used to hedge the payable?

Problem 20-3: Importing Transactions. Champion, Inc., is a large company that engages in many foreign currency transactions. On March 2, 2004, the company received goods from a Mexican supplier for 1,000,000 Mexican pesos. Terms of the transaction were FOB destination, and Champion is required to pay for the goods in full within 90 days. Relevant exchange rates are as follows:

	Spot Rate	Forward Rate for May 31
March 2	$0.0984	$0.0990
March 31	0.0992	0.0994
May 31	0.1002	n/a

Champion made the required payment for the inventory on May 31. The first quarter ends on March 31, and the company is required to file quarterly financial statements with the Securities and Exchange Commission. Ignore present value calculations.

Required:

1. Provide the necessary journal entries on March 2, March 31, and May 31 to record the purchase of and payment for the goods, assuming that the Mexican supplier required Champion to pay for the goods in U.S. dollars, and no forward contract was entered into.
2. Repeat Requirement (1), assuming that payment is required in Mexican pesos, and no forward contract was employed.
3. Assume that on March 2, Champion entered into a forward contract to purchase 1,000,000 pesos on May 31 at the existing forward rate, and:
   a. The Mexican supplier requires payment in Mexican pesos.
   b. The Mexican supplier requires payment in U.S. dollars, based on the March 2 spot rate.
4. Which situation in Requirement (3) is descriptive of a hedging position, and which situation is descriptive of a speculative position?

Problem 20-4: Importing Transactions. Malcom Co. engages in importing inventory goods from a supplier in Great Britain. On December 11, 2004, Malcom acquired from the British supplier inventory with a cost of £100,000. Payment is due in pounds on Jan. 10, 2005, and Malcom made the payment on that date. The direct exchange rates for the applicable dates in December 2004 and January 2005 are as follows:

December 11, 2004	$1.50
December 31, 2004	1.55
January 10, 2005	1.57

Required:

1. Determine whether the U.S. dollar was weakening or strengthening relative to the British pound during the time period.

2. Assuming that no forward contract was entered into, provide all necessary journal entries for Malcom Co. to record the purchase of the inventory and payment.

3. To avoid the risk of an exchange rate change during the period from the transaction date to the settlement date, assume that Malcom entered into a 30-day forward exchange contract on December 11, 2004, whereby it agreed to purchase £100,000 on January 10, 2005, at the currently existing forward exchange rate. Prepare all journal entries required by Malcom related to the forward contract and the purchase of the inventory, assuming that all forward rates are equal to the spot rates.

4. Repeat Requirement (3), except assume that on December 11, 2004, when the spot rate for the British pound was $1.50, Malcom Co. bought £100,000 forward at the 30-day forward rate of $1.515.

5. Explain the effects on Malcom's income statement if the company mistakenly *sold* £100,000 forward at the 30-day forward rate of $1.515.

Problem 20-5: Importing Transactions. Willey's Widgets engages in several importing transactions during the year. On April 1, 2004, a British manufacturer sold equipment to Willey's Widgets and immediately shipped the equipment on the same day. The sale is denominated in pounds sterling £300,000. Terms of the purchase are FOB shipping point and are to be paid for on June 30. Assume the following exchange rates between the U.S. dollar and the British pound sterling:

	Spot Rate	3-Months Forward	2-Months Forward	1-Month Forward
April 1	$1.6290	$1.6095		
April 30	$1.6275		$1.6135	
May 31	$1.6005			$1.6000
June 30	$1.5950			

Required:

1. Assuming that no forward contract is entered into and the books are closed monthly, what would be the journal entries for Willey's Widgets on April 1, April 30, May 31, and June 30?

2. Assuming that a forward contract is entered into on April 1, what would be the journal entries for Willey's Widgets on April 1, April 30, May 31, and June 30?

3. If the sale were denominated in U.S. dollars at the April 1 exchange rate (i.e., £300,000 × 1.6290 = $488,700), what would be the journal entries for Requirements (1) and (2) in pounds sterling for the British exporter?

Problem 20-6: Exporting Transactions. On November 1, 2004, Casey Corp. sold inventory with a historical cost of $550,000 to a British customer for $970,000. Full payment is required no later than May 1, 2005. Relevant exchange rates between the U.S. dollar and British pound are as follows:

	Spot Rate	Forward Rate for May 31
November 1, 2004	$1.64	$1.63
December 31, 2004	1.55	1.58
May 1, 2005	1.60	n/a

Required:

1. Assume that Casey Corp. allows, but does not require, the foreign customer to pay 591,463 British pounds for the purchase ($970,000/$1.64). Provide all necessary journal entries for Casey Corp., assuming that no steps were taken to eliminate foreign currency exchange rate risk.
2. Provide all necessary journal entries, assuming that Casey Corp. entered into a foreign exchange contract to sell 591,463 British pounds on May 1, 2005.
3. Redo Requirement (2), assuming the following exchange rates (again, assume that Casey Corp. allows, but does not require, payment in pounds):

	Spot Rate	Forward Rate for May 1
November 1, 2004	$1.64	$1.63
December 31, 2004	1.75	1.73
May 1, 2005	1.70	n/a

   Has Casey Corp. effectively eliminated the foreign currency risk by using the forward contract?
4. Could Casey eliminate foreign currency risk by requiring the British customer to make payment in U.S. dollars?
5. Instead of using a forward contract and requiring payment in dollars, describe an alternative method that Casey could use to hedge the risk associated with the foreign currency.

Problem 20-7: Hedging a Fixed Payment Contract. Assume the same facts as those provided in Problem 20-6, except that the British customer signed a note payable that bears a 10% interest rate (similar to the market rate of interest for similar instruments) and requires six equal monthly installments in British pounds, due at the end of each month, with the first payment due on November 30, 2004.

Additional exchange rate information is as follows:

	Spot Rate	Forward Rates for					
		Nov. 30	Dec. 31	Jan. 31	Feb. 28	Mar. 31	Apr. 30
Nov. 1, 2004	$1.64	$1.64	$1.58	$1.57	$1.57	$1.57	$1.63
Nov. 30, 2004	1.60	—	1.60	1.59	1.60	1.60	1.61
Dec. 31, 2004	1.55	—	—	1.55	1.54	1.56	1.58
Jan. 31, 2005	1.51	—	—	—	1.51	1.52	1.52
Feb. 28, 2005	1.53	—	—	—	—	1.53	1.53
Mar. 31, 2005	1.57	—	—	—	—	—	1.57
Apr. 30, 2005	1.60	—	—	—	—	—	—

Required:

1. Calculate the monthly payment required for the British customer to service the note payable.
2. Assuming that no forward contract is entered into, prepare all necessary journal entries for Casey Corp. from the time of the sale through the date of the last payment received on April 30, 2005.
3. Describe the type of forward contract that Casey Corp. must purchase in order to perfectly hedge its foreign currency exposure related to the note receivable.
4. Calculate the gain or loss realized on the note receivable at the end of each month.

5. Calculate the gain or loss realized on the forward contract at the end of each month.

6. Prepare all necessary journal entries for Casey Corp., assuming that the forward contract was entered into.

Problem 20-8: Various. Solve each of the following independent problems.

1. On September 1, 2003, Bain Corp. received an order for equipment from a foreign customer for 300,000 local currency units (LCU), when the U.S. dollar equivalent was $96,000. Bain shipped the equipment on October 15, 2003, and billed the customer for 300,000 LCU when the U.S. equivalent was $100,000. Bain received the customer's remittance in full on November 16, 2003, and sold the 300,000 LCU for $105,000. In its income statement for the year ended December 31, 2003, for how much should Bain report a foreign exchange gain?

2. On April 8, 2003, Day Corp. purchased merchandise from an unaffiliated foreign company for 10,000 units of the foreign company's local currency. Day paid the bill in full on March 1, 2004, when the spot rate was $0.45. The spot rate was $0.60 on April 8, 2003, and $0.55 on December 31, 2003. Determine the amount of foreign currency transaction gain that Day Corp. should recognize for the year ended December 31, 2004.

3. Lindy, a U.S. corporation, bought inventory items from a supplier in West Germany on November 5, 2003, for 100,000 euro, when the spot rate was $0.9295. At Lindy's December 31, 2003 year-end, the spot rate was $0.9245. On January 15, 2004, Lindy bought 100,000 euro at the spot rate of $0.9345 and paid the invoice. How much should Lindy report in its income statements for 2003 and 2004 as a foreign exchange gain or (loss)?

4. On November 15, 2003, Celt, Inc., a U.S. company, ordered merchandise FOB shipping point from a German company for 200,000 euro. The merchandise was shipped and invoiced to Celt on December 10, 2003. Celt paid the invoice on January 10, 2004. The spot rates for euro on the respective dates are as follows:

November 15, 2003	$0.9955
December 10, 2003	$0.9875
December 31, 2003	$0.9675
January 10, 2004	$0.9475

Determine the amount of foreign exchange gain or (loss) that Celt should report on its December 31, 2003 income statement.

5. The following information pertains to Flint Co.'s sale of 10,000 foreign currency units under a forward contract dated November 1, 2004, for delivery on January 31, 2005:

	11/1/2004	12/31/2004
Spot rates	$0.80	$0.83
30-day forward rates	0.79	0.82
90-day forward rates	0.78	0.81

Flint entered into the forward contract in order to speculate in the foreign currency. In Flint's income statement for the year ended December 31, 2004, what amount of loss should be reported from this forward contract?

Research Activities

Activity 20-1: Effect of Foreign Sales and Foreign Net Income. Refer to the companies listed in Exhibit 20-1 (p. 942). For each company, look up the most recent financial statements and update the exhibit. Specifically, determine how foreign sales and foreign net income contribute to the corresponding total amounts.

Activity 20-2: Exchange Rates. Using editions of *The Wall Street Journal*, look up the most recent exchange rates for the following currencies relative to the U.S. dollar. Specify whether you are using the direct or indirect quote.
   a. Spot rate for Canadian dollars.
   b. Spot rate for Brazilian reals.
   c. Spot rate for South Korean won.
   d. Spot rate for Dutch guilders.
   e. Spot rate for euro.
   f. One-month forward rate for British pounds.
   g. Three-month forward rate for Japanese yen.
For these exchange rates, indicate whether the currencies have strengthened or weakened relative to the U.S. dollar during the past year.

Cases

Case 20-1: Speculation in Hedge Securities—Long-Term Capital Management LP. The types of securities that are traded in capital markets are many, and it seems that new kinds of sophisticated hybrid securities are invented every day. Investment banks and capital management groups often develop funds that invest in hedge securities, which are called hedge funds. Hedge funds are highly leveraged investment portfolios due to large amounts of borrowing and derivative investments. The speculation in derivatives can take many different forms, including speculation in the direction of interest rates, commodity prices, and foreign currency exchange rates. Even weather derivatives have been developed that essentially bet on future weather patterns. This type of derivative can be attractive to farmers, since unfavorable weather could be devastating to a farmer's crops.

Long-Term Capital Management LP was founded by John Meriwether in 1994, and Nobel economists Robert Merton and Myron Scholes later joined the group. Initially, the fund's performance was very impressive. Investors in Long-Term Capital realized a 43% return in 1995 and 41% in 1996. These types of returns, along with the impressive list of partners, facilitated the fund attracting over $6 billion, which the partners used to invest in derivatives with a notional amount of $1 trillion.

However, in 1997, the return on the hedge fund slipped to 17% while the S&P 500 index simultaneously realized a gain of 30%. In September of 1998, Meriweather announced that during the previous month, the fund had lost over 40% of its capital. Soon afterwards, the Federal Reserve Bank of New York, along with a consortium of banks, developed a rescue package for Long-Term Capital and took control of over 90% of the fund, with a $3.625 billion cash infusion.

The experience of Long-Term Capital illustrates the high risk that is associated with investing in derivatives for speculative purposes. Following its near collapse, regulators decided to evaluate whether additional oversight laws were needed for hedge funds and the derivatives market. The speculative bet played by Meriweather and his partners was not on whether particular securities would increase or decrease, but on how the relationship between different securities would change. An example of a hedge position taken by Long-Term Capital is described as follows.

In June of 1998, a 29-year Treasury bond had an effective yield that was 5-hundredths of a percent larger than the 30-year Treasury bond. For example, if the yield on the 30-year bond was 5%, then the yield on the 29-year bond was 5.05%. Long-Term Capital believed that such a relationship between the two types of bonds would not persist, that the yields on the two bonds would converge, and ultimately the rate on the 30-year bond would exceed the rate on the 29-year bond. Accordingly, Long-Term Capital decided to purchase 29-year bonds and sell short[3] 30-year bonds. Since funds received from the sale of 30-year bonds are used to purchase the 29-year bonds, this type of transaction is one that requires zero net investment, except for the small amount of margin that the brokers and bankers might require Long-Term Capital to have on hand.

By the end of September, instead of converging, the rates on the two Treasury investments drifted further apart, from 5-hundredths of a percentage point to 15-hundredths.

Required:
1. Suppose that Long-Term Capital Management invested in 29-year Treasury bonds with a face value of $10 million. The bonds were sold to yield an effective interest rate of 5.05%. The Treasury bonds are non-interest-bearing. Determine how much cash was required to purchase the bonds. How much 30-year Treasury bonds would Long-Term Capital need to sell short to have the necessary funds to purchase the 29-year bonds, if the 30-year bonds have an effective yield of 5%?
2. Assume that from June to September, the interest rates converged according to the expectations of Meriweather. That is, in September, both Treasury securities had an effective yield of 4.5%. Calculate the net gain or loss on the position. Also, assume that the bankers required a 1% margin, which means that 1% of the book value of the short position was required to be available and was the net cash required to make the hedge investment. Calculate the return on investment. How would the results change (if at all) if the interest rates had increased but still converged?
3. Now, calculate the actual net gain or loss on the position and the return on investment as a result of the interest rates drifting further apart. Assume that the interest rate in September on the 30-year bond was still 4.5%, but the interest rate on the 29-year bond was 4.65%.

Case 20-2: Metallgesellschaft AG. Founded in Germany in 1881, Metallgesellschaft AG initially concentrated on metal trading and soon expanded its operations to participate in mines, chemicals, and oil. After World War II, the company reconstructed its German production sites and began establishing numerous subsidiaries, while extending its research and development activities.

In 1993, the company was dangerously close to filing for bankruptcy. The company's supervisory board placed a large amount of the blame on the then cur-

---

[3]Selling short means to sell a security that is not actually in your possession. This type of transaction is similar to borrowing: you receive funds today and are required to "pay back" the funds later by purchasing the same security that you sold short. Purchasing the security is referred to as covering your short position.

rent managers, who invested heavily in derivatives. Subsequent to their being fired, the managers sued Metallgesellschaft, based on the argument that their actions related to derivatives were prudent and meant to hedge the risk associated with the company's operations. Some well-known academics supported the claims of these managers and argued that the company's board did not understand the purpose of the derivatives. However, others have claimed that the derivative investments were nothing more than speculation.

The company's troubles began in 1992, when a U.S. subsidiary followed an unconventional practice of agreeing to supply gasoline products at a fixed price for up to ten years in the future. This agreement placed Metallgesellschaft in a risky position. If oil prices were to increase significantly in the future, the company would be required to pay the higher costs but would not be free to charge a higher price to customers.

The company decided to hedge against this risk by investing in short-term oil futures that allowed them to purchase oil at a specified price. The execution prices on these future contracts fluctuated with near-term energy prices. At the end of each month, as the futures expired, they would "roll over" the futures into the next month, adding and removing some futures to correspond with the number of contracts to supply oil.

In December 1993, the spot price for oil crashed—decreasing by $4 a barrel—which significantly reduced the execution price on short-term future contracts. However, the long-term forward contract prices remained much more stable.

Required:

1. How does a drop in oil spot prices affect the value of the short-term future contracts?
2. How would the drop in the oil spot price affect the value of the near-term supply contracts? How do you suppose the value of the long-term supply contracts were affected? Do you suppose that, after the substantial drop in oil prices, the company faced additional risk associated with noncompliance with the supply contracts by the buyers?
3. Were the hedging practices implemented by the former managers effective in reducing the risk associated with the company's marketing campaign of providing fixed oil prices over an extended period of time? Can you think of a more effective way of eliminating this risk? Could the managers have hedged the risk associated with noncompliance?

Foreign Currency Hedge Accounting

Software Innovations, Part 2

Software Innovations (from the opening scenario in Chapter 20, p. 940) has continued to expand international operations throughout 2005. Foreign customers have been extremely pleased with the products offered by the company. One British customer, Royal Electronics, is engaged in internal expansion and has revealed to Derek Newmann (Software Innovations' CEO) its intent to purchase a substantial amount of software products from Software Innovations upon construction of a large plant to be completed in 2006, provided the price of the products in British pounds does not change significantly. Although no formal agreement was signed, Derek is confident that Royal Electronics will be true to its word. In addition, another British company, Thurston Corp., has signed a formal agreement with Software Innovations to purchase a predetermined level of software products at a specified price of £100,000 during 2006.

Derek is excited about the expanded operations overseas. Yet, he realizes from recent experience that dealing in foreign currencies introduces additional risks. If the U.S. dollar strengthens relative to the British pound, Software Innovations will realize a loss in U.S. dollars due to the change in the foreign currency exchange rate.

To eliminate the risk associated with these anticipated foreign transactions, Derek has approached the company's CFO, Heidi Jensen, to

discuss alternatives that could be pursued. Heidi suggests purchasing a derivative instrument that would allow Software Innovations to sell British pounds received from the British customers at a specified rate. Specifically, foreign currency forward contracts and options were discussed.

Derek also realizes that derivative instruments must be valued at market value on the balance sheet. This is of particular concern, since Software Innovations does not have an actual receivable from Royal Electronics or Thurston Corp. that could be used to offset any gain or loss realized on the derivative instruments. So, although Software Innovations will purchase the derivatives to reduce risk associated with foreign currency transactions, the gain/loss on the derivatives without an offsetting gain/loss on a monetary asset would introduce additional volatility in earnings, which would have the appearance of increased risk.

Questions

1. What are the advantages and disadvantages of forward contracts compared to options?

2. Thurston Corp. has signed a legally binding document to purchase the products of Software Innovations, i.e., a firm purchase commitment. If a gain/loss is recognized on the derivative instrument, should an offsetting gain/loss on the firm purchase commitment be recognized concurrently?

3. Royal Electronics is under no obligation to purchase products from Software Innovations; however, the likelihood of such a purchase is high if the price of the software products remains constant. Would it be wise for Derek Newmann to purchase a derivative for this forecasted transaction? By doing so, has risk associated with foreign currency fluctuations been eliminated or reduced? Should a gain or loss be recognized on derivatives associated with forecasted transactions?

Learning Objectives

- Describe the use of derivative instruments and natural hedges in reducing foreign currency risk.
- Explain the basics of option contracts and the advantages and disadvantages of forwards compared to options contracts.
- Describe the use of discounting to derive the market value of forward contracts.
- Describe the accounting rules for hedging risk associated with purchase commitments denominated in a foreign currency and how the rules differ for forecasted transactions.
- Describe the accounting rules for hedging risk associated with foreign currency denominated securities.

The Use of Forward Contracts as Foreign Currency Hedging Instruments

Developments in financial markets and the increased globalization of the economy have resulted in various types of risk that managers are exposed to daily. As a result, the number and type of derivatives have increased exponentially in the past decade. Some derivative instruments are very sophisticated and complex in nature; however, the basic types of derivatives are forwards and futures, swaps, and options contracts. Although this chapter focuses on accounting for only foreign currency derivative instruments, many of the concepts can be applied to other types of derivative instruments, such as interest-rate swaps, commodity futures contracts, and options to hedge against domestic purchases or sales.

The discussion on forward contracts in Chapter 20 focused on reducing (or eliminating) the risk associated with a current liability denominated in a foreign currency *for a transaction that already occurred.* There are many other circumstances that would expose companies to foreign currency risk. *SFAS No. 133* (paragraph 18d) indicates the different types of foreign currency hedges as follows: (1) an unrecognized firm commitment, (2) an available-for-sale security, (3) a forecasted transaction, or (4) a net investment in a foreign operation. This chapter presents an example of the first three types of hedges. The fourth type of hedge is related to translation of foreign currency financial statements into U.S. dollars and is covered in some advanced accounting textbooks.

Foreign currency hedges can be further classified as either fair-value hedges or cash-flow hedges. Changes in the market value of derivative instruments are accounted for differently, depending on the classification. Fair-value and cash-flow hedges are defined in *SFAS No. 133* as follows [paragraph 4(a)–(b)]:

> **Fair-value hedge**. A hedge of the exposure to changes in the fair value of a recognized asset or liability, or of an unrecognized firm commitment, that is attributable to a particular risk.

> **Cash-flow hedge**. A hedge of the exposure to variability in the cash flows of a recognized asset or liability, or of a forecasted transaction, that is attributable to a particular risk.

Changes in the market value of derivative instruments used as fair-value hedges are recognized on the income statement as an operating gain or loss. In contrast, derivative instruments that are effective in hedging foreign currency exposure related to forecasted transactions are classified as cash-flow hedges, and the market value changes in this type of derivative instrument are recognized in comprehensive income.

As will be discussed, special accounting rules are applied to fair-value and cash-flow hedges. These special rules are necessary in order for a gain or loss to be recognized that effectively offsets the gain or loss recognized on the derivative instrument. The term **hedge accounting** is typically used to refer to these special accounting rules.[1]

The illustrations presented in this chapter are not meant to be comprehensive of all possible methods in which companies can use forward contracts to hedge against foreign currency risk. *SFAS No. 133* provides more examples of hedging activities.

Foreign Currency Firm Commitments

A common practice among companies is to enter into a firm commitment with an unrelated entity to purchase or sell assets on a specified future date at a fixed price. Typically, the firm commitment is legally binding. The purchaser benefits from this type of arrangement by having a reliable source of supplies, and the seller benefits from the assured source of revenue. In addition, both sides are protected against future price changes, which reduces cash flow variability.

© GETTY IMAGES, INC./EYEWIRE

As a review of accounting for purchase commitments denominated in local currency, unrealized losses to the purchaser (where the market price of the item to be

---

[1]Interestingly, the use of forward contracts to hedge a single monetary asset and/or liability denominated in a foreign currency, as was discussed in Chapter 20, is not designated in *SFAS No. 133* as either a fair-value hedge or a cash-flow hedge. Initially, this omission might seem counterintuitive, since this is a common business practice and makes economic sense to do so. However, the lack of specific designation does not preclude the forward contract from accomplishing its objective. *SFAS No. 52* requires monetary foreign currency assets and liabilities to be translated by using the current spot rate, and *SFAS No. 133* requires all derivative instruments to be valued at market value. The resulting gains and losses are offsetting and required to be recognized in the income statement. Thus, no special accounting rules are necessary in order for the income statement to reflect the effectiveness of the derivative instrument in hedging the risk associated with a receivable or payable.

purchased is less than the agreed-upon purchase price) are recognized immediately in the financial statements, but unrealized gains are not recognized. An additional element of complexity is introduced when the purchase commitment is for goods denominated in a foreign currency. In this case, although the price is fixed in foreign currency units, future exchange rate fluctuations will result in cash flow uncertainty. Companies can reduce or even eliminate the cash flow uncertainty with respect to the firm commitment by entering into a forward contract. When this is done, special hedge accounting rules are followed in order for the income statement to properly reflect the substance of the transaction.

To illustrate the accounting for the various types of hedging activities discussed in this chapter, we will build upon the TDI and Luis example presented in Chapter 20, with minor changes.

On May 1, 2002, TDI committed with Luis to purchase 10,000 units of inventory at an agreed-upon price of C$10 per unit. In addition, to introduce the effects of discounting on the measurement principles (recall that all examples in Chapter 20 ignored the time value of money), assume that delivery of the goods is to take place three months in the future—on July 31, 2002. Luis continues to provide credit for three months, and TDI takes advantage of these credit terms by making payment on November 1, 2002.

Relevant exchange rates are as follows:

Date	Spot Rates	Forward Rates for November 1, 2002	
May 1, 2002	$0.6450	$0.6384	(purchase date)
June 30, 2002	$0.6500	$0.6507	(fiscal year-end)
July 31, 2002	$0.6600	$0.6601	(delivery date)
November 1, 2002	$0.6350	N/A	(payment date)

TDI's marginal annual borrowing rate is 12% (or 1% monthly rate).

On the date of the agreement, TDI realizes that it has an obligation to pay C$100,000 on November 1, 2002. Accordingly, it enters into a 6-month forward contract to purchase C$100,000 at the forward rate of $0.6384 (see Exhibit 20-3, pp. 944–945).

Given that Luis is not exposed to foreign currency fluctuations, we focus on the required entries only for TDI. Although two events occur on May 1—the purchase commitment and forward contract are initiated—neither event requires a net investment, and therefore both the purchase commitment and the forward contract have a market value of zero. No asset or liability is recorded.

On June 30, 2002, according to the requirements of *SFAS No. 133*, TDI must determine and record the market value of the forward contract. A dealer's quote for the forward contract is not available on June 30. One method for deriving the forward's market value is to perform a discounted cash flow analysis by analyzing the change in forward rates between May 1 and June 30, as follows:

$$(\$0.6507 \times C\$100,000) - (\$0.6384 \times C\$100,000) = \$1,230$$

Cash flows using June 30 − Cash flows using May 1 = Net cash
forward rate   forward rate   flows

The $1,230 represents the *undiscounted* net cash inflows that will be realized by TDI, assuming that the spot rate on May 1, 2002, is equal to the new forward rate on June 30, 2002. However, these expected cash flows are not realized until the execution of the contract in the future. As a result, the market value of the forward contract must be adjusted for the time value of money.

The present value of a single sum factor discounted at 1% for 4 periods is 0.96098.[2] Applying this factor to the net cash flows expected to be realized in four months results in a market value of $1,182 (0.96098 × $1,230) for the forward contract.

Although TDI does not have an actual payable to Luis, it still has an obligation to pay Canadian dollars in the future as a result of the purchase commitment. Therefore, the change in exchange rates has resulted in a loss on the purchase commitment identical to the situation where a payable existed. The amount of the loss to be recorded in this case is stipulated by the requirements in *SFAS No. 133*. (This is where hedge accounting special rules come into play.) The statement allows that, for designated hedges *that are fully effective*, the gain/loss on the hedging instrument (i.e., the forward contract) can be directly offset by a gain/loss on the hedged item (i.e., firm commitment). Since the amounts, dates, and currencies of the purchase commitment and forward contract are identical in this case, the hedging instrument is fully effective, and the loss to be recognized on the purchase commitment is identical to the gain on the forward contract. Accordingly, the journal entries by TDI on May 1 and June 30, 2002, are as follows.

Journal entries for TDI:
May 1   No entries required.

June 30 Forward Contract	1,182	
Gain on Forward Contract		1,182
To record the gain on forward contract.		
Loss on Firm Commitment to Luis in C$	1,182	
Firm Commitment to Luis in C$		1,182
To record the loss on firm commitment.		

In this example, TDI has realized a gain on the forward contract and recognized this gain in current period earnings. An exactly offsetting loss on the purchase commitment is recognized in current period earnings.[3] If the forward rates had moved in the opposite direction, TDI would have recognized a loss on the forward contract and a corresponding gain on the purchase commitment. Recognizing gains on foreign currency firm commitments is a classic example of hedge accounting, which refers to the application of special rules when company management is attempting to reduce risk. If a company uses a derivative instrument that is effective in hedging the risk associated with the firm commitment, then *SFAS No. 133* allows both gains and losses on the purchase commitment to offset the gains and losses on the derivative instrument.

Continuing with our example, the exchange rates have continued in their directional movement from June 30 to July 31. As a result, the forward contract has continued to increase in value. The market value of the contract on July 31 can be derived as before, as follows:

($0.6601 × C$100,000) − ($0.6384 × C$100,000) = $2,170   × 0.97059 = $2,106

Cash flows using July 31 − Cash flows using May 1 = Net cash × Present value
forward rate   forward rate   flows   factor

---

[2]$1/(1 + 0.01)^4 = 0.96098$

[3]Note that this loss on the purchase commitment is not related to price changes in the underlying asset but rather changes in exchange rates. If the market price of the inventory were to change in an unfavorable direction, an additional loss and liability would need to be recorded to recognize this additional loss.

The present value factor is based on a 1% monthly discount rate for three periods. The new value of the forward contract is a positive $2,106. Since the forward contract account already has a positive value of $1,182, the realized gain on the forward contract from June 30, 2002, to July 31, 2002, is $924, which is illustrated in the following T-account:

Forward contract T-account

Value as of June 30 $1,182	
Journal entry on July 31 924	
Value as of July 31 $2,106	

As before, the gain/loss on the forward contract is exactly offset by a gain/loss on the purchase commitment, according to the hedge accounting rules in *SFAS No. 133*. The journal entries related to the above transactions made by TDI on July 31 are as follows:

Journal entries for TDI:

July 31	Forward Contract	924	
	Gain on Forward Contract		924

To record the loss on forward contract.

Loss on Purchase Commitment to Luis in C$	924	
Purchase Commitment to Luis in C$		924

To record the gain on purchase commitment.

Inventory	63,894	
Purchase Commitment to Luis in C$	2,106	
Accounts Payable		66,000

To record the purchase of inventory.

The third entry made on July 31, 2002, recognizes the execution of the purchase commitment. Accordingly, the purchase commitment account is closed out. Two items are particularly noteworthy in this entry. First, the accounts payable is recorded at the *spot rate* on July 31. This is consistent with the requirements of *SFAS No. 52* that all foreign currency denominated monetary assets and liabilities be translated using the spot rate. Second, the inventory is merely a plug figure; i.e., it is not a function of the forward rate nor the spot rate. This result is due to inconsistent recognition rules for the purchase commitment and the accounts payable. The purchase commitment is recorded at a discounted cash flow amount, whereas the valuation of accounts payable gives no consideration to the time value of money.

All that is left to be recognized is the payment of cash to Luis and the settlement of the forward contract on November 1, 2002. The value of the forward contract at the settlement date is derived as before by analyzing the change in forward rates since the inception of the contract. The forward rate on the forward contract's expiration date is always equal to the spot rate on that date. Thus, the forward rate has reversed its directional movement from July 31 to November 1. In fact, the spot rate on November 1 is less than the contracted forward rate, which results in the forward contract having a negative market value on November 1 of $(340), which is computed as follows:

$$(\$0.635 \times C\$100{,}000) - (\$0.6384 \times C\$100{,}000) = \$(340) \times 1.000 = \$(340)$$

Cash flows using May 22 — Cash flows using Dec. 21 = Net cash × Present value
forward rate   forward rate   flows   factor

Prior to any adjustment, the forward contract carries a debit balance of $2,106, and accordingly, the change in its market value from July 31 to November 1, 2002, is a negative $(2,446).

As was discussed in Chapter 20, the gain/loss on the accounts payable is a function of the change in *spot rates* from July 31 to November 1 [($0.660 × C$100,000) − ($0.635 × C$100,000)]. Accordingly, TDI would make the following journal entries on November 1, 2002. The final journal entry represents the cash payment and the settlement of the forward contract.

Journal entries for TDI:

Nov. 1	Loss on Forward Contract	2,446	
	Forward Contract		2,446
	To record gain on forward contract.		
	Accounts Payable	2,500	
	Foreign Currency Transaction Gain		2,500
	To record loss on accounts payable.		
	Accounts Payable	63,500	
	Forward Contract	340	
	Cash		63,840
	To record the settlement of forward contract and account payable.		

EXTENDING THE CONCEPT

Refer to the opening scenario (pp. 973–974), where Software Innovations has two anticipated transactions: one with Royal Electronics and the other with Thurston Corp. Which of the two transactions is similar to the circumstances just described with TDI, i.e., a firm purchase commitment? Accordingly, assuming that Software Innovations purchases a derivative instrument to hedge the foreign currency risk associated with the purchase commitment, how should it account for the foreign currency gains/losses on the purchase commitment and the related derivative instrument?

The following is an excerpt from the 2000 annual report of Texaco Inc.:

Derivatives are contracts whose value is derived from changes in an underlying commodity price, interest rate or other item. We use derivatives to reduce our exposure to changes in foreign exchange rates, interest rates, and crude oil, petroleum products and natural gas prices. Our written policies restrict our use of derivatives to protecting existing positions and committed or anticipated transactions.

Does Texaco Inc. employ derivatives in a similar manner as what Software Innovations does? That is, does it appear as though Texaco Inc. uses derivatives to hedge against the risk associated with foreign currency purchase commitments?

Note that the loss on the forward contract is not exactly offset by the gain on the accounts payable, since the loss on the forward contract is derived using the change in the forward rates, and the gain on the payable is derived using the change in spot rates.

In summary, the use of a forward contract allows TDI to avoid the risk associated with foreign currency fluctuations on a firm commitment. Both the hedging instrument and the hedged item are recorded at market value and presented on the balance sheet as an asset if they carry a debit balance, and a liability if they carry a credit balance. The gain or loss associated with a change in the hedging instrument and the hedged item are recorded as an operating gain or loss on the income statement. However, the inconsistent valuation techniques for hedged items (market value) and short-term liabilities (undiscounted cash flows) result in gains and losses that are not completely offsetting.

Foreign Currency Forecasted Transactions

In the opening scenario of this chapter (pp. 973–974), Software Innovations expects to sell inventory to Royal Electronics in the future, provided that the price of the products in British pounds does not change significantly. Many managers in this situation would desire to lock in the price in British pounds to ensure that the sale will take place. Foreign currency forward contracts and/or options could be used to accomplish this objective. Software Innovations will know how much the customer is willing to pay in British pounds, and a forward contract would ensure that a desired level of dollars will be received, no matter how the exchange rate fluctuates.

However, accounting for these derivatives at market value introduces a special problem since the company does not have anything (e.g., a receivable or purchase commitment) that would offset any gain/loss associated with the derivative. For example, if Software Innovations purchases a forward contract and realizes a loss on the contract, recognizing a gain on the forecasted transaction would seem inappropriate, since no formal agreement or contract is held by the company. Recognizing gains/losses on forecasted events would appear to violate the principle of recognizing events and transactions only after they are realized. So, although the company is taking steps to reduce foreign currency risk, gains/losses in the income statement from holding derivatives without offsetting amounts would introduce additional volatility in earnings and have the appearance that the firm is holding derivatives for speculative purposes.

The FASB recognized this dilemma when drafting *SFAS No. 133* and allowed hedge accounting rules to be applied to these types of situations.[4] To illustrate the accounting for firms that hedge against foreign currency risk associated with forecasted transactions, the facts related to the TDI example are changed slightly.

Instead of entering into a firm commitment with Luis, assume that on May 1, 2002, TDI informs Luis of its decision to purchase inventory in July. However, the agreement to purchase from Luis is informal and specifies that TDI will be required to pay the prevailing market rate at the time of purchase.

Although no formal obligation to purchase inventory from Luis exists, TDI is still exposed to foreign currency fluctuations based on its *intent* to purchase in the future. To hedge against this exposure, TDI chooses to enter into a forward contract on May 1, 2002, similar to the previous example. All of the same spot rates, forward rates, and discount rates that were used in the preceding example are employed in this example and are reviewed here.

Date	Spot Rates	Forward Rates for November 1, 2002	
May 1, 2002	$0.6450	$0.6384	(purchase date)
June 30, 2002	$0.6500	$0.6507	(fiscal year-end)
July 31, 2002	$0.6600	$0.6601	(delivery date)
November 1, 2002	$0.6350	N/A	(payment date)

TDI's marginal annual borrowing rate is 12% (or 1% monthly rate).

This type of arrangement meets the following definition of a **forecasted transaction** provided in the glossary of *SFAS No. 133*:

A transaction that is expected to occur for which there is no firm commitment. Because no transaction or event has yet occurred and the fu-

---

[4]Recall that hedge accounting refers to special accounting rules that apply only to situations where the company is trying to reduce risk through hedging activities.

ture transaction or event will be at the prevailing market price, a forecasted transaction does not give an entity any present rights to future benefits or a present obligation for future sacrifices.

A derivative instrument that hedges foreign currency exposure associated with a forecasted transaction is classified in *SFAS No. 133* as a cash flow hedge. *The change in market value of a derivative instrument used as a cash-flow hedge is recorded in comprehensive income.* Accordingly, the journal entries to be made by TDI are as follows.

> *Journal entries for TDI:*
> May 1 No entries required.
>
> June 30 Forward Contract ... 1,182
>   Other Comprehensive Income ... 1,182
> *To record change in market value of forward contract.*
>
> July 31 Forward Contract ... 924
>   Other Comprehensive Income ... 924
> *To record change in market value of forward contract.*
>
> Inventory ... 66,000
>   Accounts Payable ... 66,000
> *To record purchase of inventory; payable recorded at spot rate.*
>
> Nov. 1 Loss on Forward Contract ... 2,446
>   Forward Contract ... 2,446
> *To record change in market value of forward contract.*
>
> Accounts Payable ... 2,500
>   Foreign Currency Transaction Gain ... 2,500
> *To record change in payable due to changes in exchange rates.*
>
> Accounts Payable ... 63,500
> Forward Contract ... 340
>   Cash ... 63,840
> *To record payment for payable and settlement of forward contract.*
>
> Cost of Goods Sold ... 63,894
> Accumulated Other Comprehensive Income ... 2,106
>   Inventory ... 66,000
> *To record sale of inventory.*

The derivation of the forward contract's fair value will not be repeated here since all of the specifics related to its valuation are provided in the previous example. The main item to note in the prior journal entries is that the change in market value of the forward contract is recognized in other comprehensive income (OCI) instead of in net income. Allowing the gain or loss on the forward contract to bypass the income statement makes sense, given that an offsetting gain or loss on a hedged item does not exist. Otherwise, increased variability would be introduced into earnings when, in fact, managers are taking steps to decrease variability in cash flows.

Note, however, that the change in the value of the forward contract from July 31 to November 1 is recorded as a loss and will be taken to net income instead of OCI. This is the case since, as of July 31, a hedged item exists (accounts payable) that has an offsetting gain. Also, note that the accounts payable on the date of the purchase is recorded at the spot rate on that date. Finally, the accumulated other comprehensive income associated with the transaction is closed out when the hedged item flows through the income statement.

Foreign-Currency-Denominated Securities

SFAS No. 115 stipulates that the measurement and financial reporting of marketable securities is determined by management's classification of the securities. Trading and available-for-sale securities are recorded at market value. The change in market value for trading securities is recorded as a gain or loss in the income statement, whereas the change in market value for available-for-sale securities is recorded in comprehensive income. Held-to-maturity debt securities are recorded at discounted present value, and the resulting discount or premium is amortized over the life of the debt.

When a security is denominated in a foreign currency, managers are motivated to hedge the risk of fair value changes in these securities associated with exchange rate fluctuations. The accounting requirements for derivative instruments that hedge this type of risk depend upon how the corresponding security is classified.

Trading Securities

In theory, hedging foreign currency risk associated with trading securities is difficult, if not impossible. The difficulty arises when determining the length to maturity of the derivative instrument. Trading securities are debt and equity instruments bought and sold for the purpose of realizing profit in the short term. Supposedly, trading in these securities could take place at any time and probably depends largely on the short-term price changes. Nevertheless, if a firm decides to purchase a derivative instrument to hedge trading securities, the accounting for such a transaction is relatively straightforward. Both the derivative instrument (per *SFAS No. 133*) and the corresponding security (per *SFAS No. 115*) are required to be valued at market value, and any changes in market value in both items are required to be recognized in net income. The gain or loss from holding the security will probably not be completely offset by the gain or loss on the derivative instrument since the market value of the security (which is the item being hedged) will depend not only on changes in exchange rates but also on the market value of the underlying foreign asset.

Available-for-Sale Securities

An example will be used here to illustrate the accounting for derivative instruments designed to hedge foreign-currency-denominated available-for-sale securities.

On November 1, 2002, XYZ purchases 500 shares of common stock of a foreign company, priced at FC100, and designates the stock as available-for-sale. The market values for these shares of stock at the relevant dates are also presented here, along with the corresponding spot and forward rates.

Date	Spot Rates	Forward Rates for June 30, 2003	Quoted Prices for Foreign Security
November 1, 2002	$0.5000	$0.5064	FC50,000
December 31, 2002	$0.5350	$0.5390	FC52,000
June 30, 2003	$0.5660	N/A	FC55,000

XYZ anticipates selling the investment on June 30, 2003, at which time XYZ will need cash for a planned expansion of its building. To hedge against changes in the value of the security due to foreign currency fluctuations, XYZ enters into a forward contract on November 1 to sell FC50,000 on June 30, 2003. XYZ's marginal annual borrowing rate is 12% (or 1% monthly rate). Finally, assume that the sale actually occurs on June 30, 2003.

A hedge of a foreign-currency-denominated available-for-sale security is classified in *SFAS No. 133* as a fair-value hedge, and the gain or loss from holding the forward contract must be recognized in earnings. Consistent with this requirement, the gain or loss on the available-for-sale security *that is attributable to hedged foreign currency exchange rate fluctuations* is also recognized in earnings.

Recall that market value changes in available-for-sale securities that are *not* denominated in a foreign currency are presented in comprehensive income. Therefore, companies must partition the total market value change of the foreign currency security into two components: (1) the change due to exchange rate fluctuations and (2) the change due to the underlying value of the foreign company. This is another example where special hedge accounting rules apply in an attempt to have the financial statements reflect the economic actions pursued by company management.

Before we proceed with the journal entries, an analysis of the change in the investment's market value is provided in Exhibit 21-1. As presented in the exhibit, the securities' change in market value in U.S. dollars from the date of purchase to the end of the reporting period (December 31) is $2,820 ($27,820 − $25,000). Part of this change in market value in U.S. dollars reflects a market value increase of the company, but part of it also reflects the fact that the foreign currency unit has strengthened relative to the U.S. dollar. The change in market value due to a change in exchange rates is calculated by comparing the market value of the securities in U.S. dollars *on the date of purchase (i.e., November 1, 2002)* using the old and new spot rates. After considering the effect on market value due to the change in exchange rates, the remaining market value change is due to the change in the underlying value of the company.

The market value of the forward contract is derived in Exhibit 21-2. The forward contract held by XYZ has a negative value on December 31 since it requires FC units to be sold at $0.5064 and current forward contracts allow the FC units to be sold at a more favorable higher price of $0.5390. The market value of the forward contract on the settlement date remains negative, given the unfavorable rate at which the contract requires the units to be sold compared to the spot rate.

EXHIBIT 21-1

Market Value Analysis of Available-for-Sale Equity Security

Date (A)	Market Value in FC (B)	Market Value in $[1] (C)	Change in Market Value from Date of Purchase in $ (D)	Change in Market Value Due to Change in Exchange Rates[2] (E)	Change in Market Value Due to Change in Underlying Value of Company[3] (F)
Nov. 1, 2002	FC50,000	$25,000	N/A	N/A	N/A
Dec. 31, 2002	FC52,000	$27,820	$2,820	$1,750	$1,070
June 30, 2003	FC55,000	$31,130	$6,130	$3,300	$2,830

[1] Calculated as the current spot rate multiplied by the market value of the security denominated in FC.
[2] Calculated as the difference in the market value of securities on the date of purchase converted to U.S. dollars, using the spot rate on the date of purchase and the spot rate on the reporting date.
[3] The difference between columns (D) and (E).

EXHIBIT 21-2

Derivation of Forward Contract's Market Values On Relevant Dates

Market value on November 1, 2002: $0

Market value on December 31, 2002: Difference in U.S. dollar equivalents, using changes in forward rates and discounted to present value.

$$[(FC50,000 \times \$0.5064) - (FC50,000 \times \$0.5390)] \times 0.9420 = (\$1,535)$$

Market value on June 30, 2003 (settlement date): Difference in U.S. dollar equivalents, using changes in forward rates (forward rate on settlement date of contract is equal to spot rate).

$$(\$0.5064 - \$0.5660) \times FC50,000 = (\$2,980)$$

The preceding analyses facilitate the accounting for the transactions. Using the values derived, the following journal entries would apply.

Nov. 1	Investment in Foreign Security	25,000	
	Cash		25,000

To record the purchase of securities: FC50,000 × $0.5000.

Dec. 31	Investment in Foreign Security	2,820	
	Gain on Foreign Security		1,750
	Other Comprehensive Income		1,070

To record the change in market value of foreign currency securities.

	Loss on Forward Contract	1,535	
	Forward Contract		1,535

To record the change in market value of forward contract.

June 30	Investment in Foreign Security	3,310	
	Gain on Foreign Security		1,550
	Other Comprehensive Income		1,760

To record the change in market value of foreign currency securities.

	Loss on Forward Contract	1,445	
	Forward Contract		1,445

To record the change in market value of forward contract.

	Cash	28,150	
	Acc. Other Comprehensive Income	2,830	
	Forward Contract	2,980	
	Investment in Foreign Security		31,130
	Realized Gain on Sale of Security		2,830

To record the sale of foreign security and settlement on forward contract.

The journal entries effectively record the forward contract and the equity security at market value. The portion of the gain on the equity security that is associated with the hedged foreign currency exposure is recognized in net income and offsets most of the loss associated with the forward contract. The loss on the forward contract that is not offset is attributable to the difference in the spot and forward rates on the date the contract was initiated. The remaining portion of the gain on the security is recognized in comprehensive income until actually realized, which is consistent with the requirements in *SFAS No. 115*.

© GETTY IMAGES, INC./PHOTODISC

It is important to note that the offsetting gain of $3,300 on the available-for-sale security can only be recognized in earnings when the hedging relationship qualifies as a fair-value hedge. *SFAS No. 133*, paragraphs 38(a)–(b), establishes the following criteria that must be met in order for an available-for-sale *equity* security to be part of a hedging relationship:

a. The security is not traded on an exchange (or other established marketplace) on which trades are denominated in the investor's functional currency.

b. Dividends or other cash flows to holders of the security are all denominated in the same foreign currency as the currency expected to be received upon sale of the security.

The functional currency in XYZ's case is the U.S. dollar. If the equity security does not meet these criteria, the entire gain or loss on the available-for-sale security must be recognized in comprehensive income. As a result, the gain or loss on the derivative instrument would introduce additional variability in earnings, which is looked upon unfavorably by company management.

Held-to-Maturity Securities

A derivative instrument employed to hedge foreign currency exposure on a held-to-maturity security follows the same general principle of being valued at market value. A new wrinkle is introduced, however, since these types of securities typically will make intermittent interest payments. To fully hedge this security, several different forward contracts must be initiated that correspond with every interest payment and the final principal payment, or one forward contract is made that integrates all these payments. The following example illustrates the accounting for a hedge of a held-to-maturity security.

Assume that on November 1, 2002, XYZ purchases a 1-year, FC10,000 bond that was issued on July 1, 2002, by a foreign company. The bond makes 6% semi-annual interest payments payable on December 31, 2002, and June 30, 2003. The bond's stated interest rate is equal to the market rate for similar securities on the date of purchase.

Also, on November 1, 2002, to fully hedge against foreign currency fluctuations, XYZ entered into two forward contracts. The first forward contract allowed XYZ to sell the interest receipt of FC600 on December 31 at the specified forward rate of $0.5020. The second forward contract hedged the interest and principal payment of FC10,600 to be made at the bond's expiration on June 30, 2003.

The same spot and forward rates from the previous example are used here.

Date	Spot Rates	Forward Rates for June 30, 2003
November 1, 2002	$0.5000	$0.5064
December 31, 2002	$0.5350	$0.5390
June 30, 2003	$0.5660	N/A

Using the facts given, XYZ paid $5,200 for the bond ($5,000 for the bond principal and $200 for accrued interest) and made the following journal entry:

Nov. 1	Investment in Foreign Bond	5,000	
	FC Interest Receivable	200	
	Cash		5,200

To record investment in foreign currency bond.

The company must keep track of the market value of two forward contracts and the corresponding gains/losses on the bond payments. The remaining journal entries to record all transactions associated with the bond and forward contracts are as follows.

Dec. 31	FC Interest Receivable	14	
	Gain on FC Interest Receivable		14

To update value of monetary interest receivable:
FC400 × $0.535 = $214.

	Cash	321	
	FC Interest Receivable		214
	Interest Revenue		107

To record the interest receipt of
FC10,000 × 0.06 × $0.5350 = $321.

Loss on Forward Contract No. 1	20	
Cash		20

To record settlement of first forward contract: ($0.5020 − $0.5350) × FC600.

Loss on Forward Contract No. 2	326	
Forward Contract No. 2		326

To record change in market value of second forward contract [(FC10,600 × $0.5064) − (FC10,600 × $0.5390)] × 0.942.

Investment in Foreign Bond	350	
Gain on Investment in Foreign Bond		350

To recognize the investment translated at the current spot rate (FC10,000 × $0.500) − (FC10,000 × $0.535).

June 30

Loss on Forward Contract No. 2	306	
Forward Contract No. 2		306

To update market value of second forward contract prior to settlement [(FC10,600 × $0.5064) − (FC10,600 × $0.566)] + 326.

Investment in Foreign Bond	310	
Gain on Investment in Foreign Bond		310

To update the value of the investment translated at current market rate (FC10,000 × $0.535) − (FC10,000 × $0.566).

Forward Contract No. 2	632	
Cash		632

To record settlement of second forward contract.

Cash	340	
Interest Revenue		340

To record the interest receipt of FC10,000 × 0.06 × $0.5660.

Cash	5,660	
Investment in Foreign Bond		5,660

To record redemption of bond.

The concept of accounting for the forward contracts is exactly the same as before. The only difference in this case is that there are more contracts to keep track of. In addition, the concept of updating the value of the bond and interest receivable according to changes in the exchange rates is exactly the same as what was done for other monetary assets and liabilities (e.g., accounts payable).

The pro forma financial statements to reflect the preceding entries are presented in Exhibit 21-3. In this case, the loss on the first forward contract offsets most of the interest revenue earned on the bond, instead of a "gain" on a hedged item. Once again, the net effect on earnings is not zero since the forward rate and the spot rate on the inception date are not equal.

EXHIBIT 21-3

Pro Forma Balance Sheet for XYZ

	Year	
	2002	2003
Current assets:		
Cash	$(4,899)	$ 469
Investment in foreign bond	5,350	0
Total assets	$ 451	$ 469
Current liabilities:		
Forward contract No. 2	$ 326	$ 0
Stockholders' equity:		
Retained earnings	125	469
Total liabilities and stockholders' equity	$ 451	$ 469

Pro Forma Income Statement for XYZ

	Year	
	2002	2003
Gain on interest receivable	$ 14	—
Interest revenue	107	$ 340
Loss on forward contract No. 1	(20)	—
Loss on forward contract No. 2	(326)	(306)
Gain on investment in foreign bond	350	310
Net income	$ 125	$ 344

The Use of Options to Hedge Foreign Currency Transactions

So far, we have focused exclusively on forward contracts as a means to hedge against exchange rate fluctuations. However, forward contracts are certainly not the only derivative instrument available to reduce foreign currency risk. Foreign currency options are also very popular in the business community. Similar to stock options, foreign currency options provide the investor with a right, but not the obligation, to trade foreign currency at a specified exchange rate. This arrangement protects against downside risk while allowing investors to reap the benefits of favorable changes in exchange rates. This asymmetrical distribution of rewards provided by options makes them more expensive than forward contracts, and they will require an investment of cash on the initiation date. Changes in market value will be based primarily on changes in exchange rates and the passage of time.

Similar to other derivative instruments, *SFAS No. 133* requires options to be valued on the balance sheet at market value. Dealer quotes are the most reliable source of market value data; however, if dealer quotes are not readily available, companies can use option pricing models, such as the Black-Scholes model, to value their options.

Exhibit 21-4 presents *The Wall Street Journal* listing of foreign currency options quoted on the Philadelphia Stock Exchange for December 21, 1998. For

EXHIBIT 21-4

OPTIONS
PHILADELPHIA EXCHANGE

	Calls		Puts			Calls		Puts			Calls		Puts	
	Vol.	Last	Vol.	Last		Vol.	Last	Vol.	Last		Vol.	Last	Vol.	Last
ADllr				61.88	**65 Mar.**	...	...	10	1.11	**Japanese Yen**				86.47
50,000 Australian Dollar EOM-European.					**66 Mar.**	...	...	24	1.79	**6,250,000 Yen-100ths of a cent per unit**				
62 Jan.	...	0.01	10	0.87						82 Mar.	...	...	510	1.12
					German Mark				59.80	86 Mar.	1	3.75	...	...
British Pound				168.24	**62,500 German Marks-European Style.**									
31,250 Brit. Pounds-European Style.					59 Feb.	...	0.01	80	0.48	**Swiss Franc**				74.30
167 Jan.	...	...	80	1.30						**62,500 Swiss Francs-European Style.**				
										73 Jan.	12	1.75	...	...
31,250 Brit. Pounds-cents per unit.					**62,500 German Marks-cents per unit.**					74 Jan.	12	1.13	...	...
170 Jan.	20	1.00	...	...	56 Mar.	...	0.01	2	0.11	**62,500 Swiss Francs-cents per unit**				
					60 Jan.	...	...	4	0.63	73 Mar.	10	2.26	...	...
British Pound-GMark				279.79	62 Mar.	...	...	2	2.48	76 Mar.	22	0.97	2	2.64
31,250 British Pound-German Mark cross.														
290 Mar.	19	1.34	...	0.01						**Call Vol.** 188		**Open Int.** 30,310		
										Put Vol. 759		**Open Int.** 33,227		
Canadian Dollar				64.76										
50,000 Canadian Dollars-cents per unit.														
64 1/2 Mar.	12	1.10	...	...										

Key Currency Cross Rates
Late New York Trading Dec. 21, 1998

	Dollar	ECU	Pound	SFranc	Guilder	Peso	Yen	Lira	D-Mark	FFranc	CdnDir
Canada	1.5505	1.8224	2.6115	1.1409	.82360	.15838	.01334	.00094	.92811	.27675	
France	5.6025	6.5850	9.4363	4.1225	2.9759	.57227	.04821	.00339	3.3536		3.6134
Germany	1.6706	1.9636	2.8138	1.2293	.88739	.17064	.01438	.00101		.29819	1.0775
Italy	1654.0	1944.1	2785.8	1217.1	878.57	168.95	14.234		990.06	295.23	1066.8
Japan	116.2	136.58	195.7	85.504	61.723	11.869		.07025	69.556	20.741	74.944
Mexico	9.7900	11.507	16.489	7.2038	5.2003		.08425	.00592	5.8602	1.7474	6.3141
Netherlands	1.8826	2.2127	3.1709	1.3853		.19230	.01620	.00114	1.1269	.33603	1.2142
Switzerland	1.3590	1.5973	2.2890		.72187	.13882	.01170	.00082	.81348	.24257	.87649
U.K.	.59372	.69784		.43688	.31537	.06065	.00511	.00036	.35539	.10597	.38292
ECU	.85080		1.4330	.62605	.45193	.08691	.00732	.00051	.50928	.15186	.54873
U.S.		1.1754	1.6843	.73584	.53118	.10215	.00861	.00060	.59859	.17949	.64495

SOURCE: The Wall Street Journal, *December 22, 1998, p. C18.*

each foreign currency option listed, information on "Calls" and "Puts" is provided. A call option gives the holder the right to *purchase* a specified amount of foreign currency, whereas a put option gives the holder the right to *sell* the foreign currency. Also, some currency options are designated as "European Style," which can only be exercised at the option's expiration date. In contrast, an American Style option can be exercised at any time up to the expiration date. All options are American Style unless otherwise designated.

The following example is used to illustrate the interpretation of the option information provided in Exhibit 21-4.

Assume that ABC has a receivable denominated in Japanese yen for ¥25,000,000 to be received on March 21, 1999. To hedge the foreign currency exposure associated with this position, on December 21, 1998, ABC decides to purchase options quoted on the Philadelphia Stock Exchange.

Referring to Exhibit 21-4, only two quoted options are available for Japanese yen. Both have a March 1999 expiration date. One of the options is a call option, and the other is a put option. Since ABC will be receiving yen, to hedge the foreign currency risk it should protect against the yen weakening by purchasing a put option, which allows it to sell the yen received at a specified rate.

The first row under the heading "Japanese Yen" in the exhibit indicates that each Japanese yen option allows the holder to trade ¥6,250,000. The first column under the listed option represents the contracted exchange rate or strike rate. As indicated in the exhibit, the numbers are quoted in 100ths of a cent per unit. Thus, the 82 strike rate can be written $0.0082, which is lower than the spot rate of $0.008647 and all forward rates on the same date. Of course, as the strike rate increases, put options become more expensive. The price of the contract is displayed under the column "Last," or 1.12 per unit. Thus, the price quote for one Japanese foreign currency put option is $0.000112 × ¥6,250,000 = $700. ABC must purchase four options to fully hedge the receivable position (¥25,000,000/¥6,250,000), and so if ABC decides to pursue this hedging alternative, it will require an initial investment of $2,800.

The decision of whether to exercise the option or not will depend on the spot rate that exists on the date that ABC receives the Japanese yen. If the spot rate is greater than $0.0082, the option is considered "out-of-the-money," since ABC will be better off selling the Japanese currency at the spot rate. Alternatively, if the spot rate declines to less than $0.0082, the option is considered to be "in-the-money," and ABC will receive more U.S. dollars from exercising the option. In either case, ABC has limited its loss on the Japanese receivable by guaranteeing a selling price of $0.0082 for the yen. In contrast, the amount of gain realized from holding the Japanese-yen-denominated receivable is unlimited and a function of the increase in the spot rate.

Assessment of Hedge Effectiveness

To qualify for hedge accounting under *SFAS No. 133*, changes in the market value of derivative instruments must be highly effective in offsetting the market value changes of the hedged item. Management is required to assess hedge effectiveness of all derivative instruments on a continual basis and at least every three months. Although the given Japanese put option was purchased by ABC to hedge against foreign currency risk, the option will not be fully effective since the strike rate is below the spot rate on the date of initiation. Assuming that the Japanese yen weakens to $0.0083 on March 21, 1999, ABC will realize a loss on the Japanese receivable, but the option will not provide any benefit since the strike rate is still below the spot rate. In fact, the option will not be effective in offsetting any loss on the receivable until the spot rate falls below the strike rate.

SFAS No. 133 requires that the ineffective portion of a derivative instrument be recognized currently in earnings. Furthermore, through the hedge effectiveness analysis, if it is concluded that the derivative instrument is not highly effective, the company is precluded from following hedge accounting. This means that (1) the derivative, as usual, is valued at market value, and the change in market value is recognized in earnings, and (2) accounting for the hedged item does not fall under *SFAS No. 133*. Therefore, gains on firm commitments, for example, cannot be used to offset losses on the derivative instrument, and gains/losses on an available-for-sale security cannot be used to offset gains/losses on a derivative instrument.

We did not refer to hedge effectiveness when discussing forward contracts. This was due to the critical terms of the forward contract being equivalent to those of the hedged item. In each example presented, the maturity of the forward contract was set equal to the settlement date of the hedged item, the notional amount was equal to the principal amount, and the forward rate was generally equal to the spot rate. As a result, it was not necessary to conduct an analysis in order to conclude that the hedging instrument was effective. The only ineffective portion of the forward contract was the discount/premium paid for the forward (the difference in the forward and spot rates on the date of initiation), which was included in earnings anyway.

Separating an Option's Market Value into Time Value and Intrinsic Value Components

The value of options can be separated into two components: (1) time value and (2) intrinsic value. Determining an option's time value is important, since *SFAS No. 133* permits the assessment of hedge effectiveness based solely on the option's intrinsic value. Paragraph 30(a) of *SFAS No. 133* indicates that when companies choose this method of assessing hedge effectiveness, changes in the option's time value must be included in earnings. We emphasize, however, that this method of assessing hedge effectiveness is merely an alternative, and companies are free to assess hedge effectiveness based on changes in the option's total market value.

On December 21, the Japanese yen put options given are considered to be "out-of-the-money," since the strike rate of $0.0082 is below the current spot rate of $0.008647. *Out-of-the-money options do not have any intrinsic value.* Therefore, the entire purchase price for the options is considered to be its time value or, in other words, the price paid for the *possibility* that the spot rate will drop below $0.0082 before the end of March 1999. If the strike rate on these options had been greater than $0.008647, the intrinsic value would be equal to the difference in the strike rate and the spot rate multiplied by the notional amount.

To illustrate the separation of an option's value into its time value and intrinsic value components, refer to the Japanese yen call option in Exhibit 21-4. The strike rate at which the option holder can purchase yen is $0.0086. Since this rate is less expensive than the current spot rate of $0.008647, the call option is considered to be "in-the-money." The total price of one option is $0.000375 × ¥6,250,000 = $2,344. The intrinsic amount is (¥6,250,000 × $0.008647) − (¥6,250,000 × $0.0086) = $293.75. The time value is the remaining amount of $2,050.25.

Accounting for Foreign Currency Options

Accounting for foreign currency options follows the same general rules as accounting for foreign currency forward contracts. Options must be reported on the balance sheet at market value, and the changes in market value are reported either in current earnings or comprehensive income, depending on whether the option is designated as a cash-flow or a fair-value hedge.

Although the general rules are the same, the differences between options and forward contracts result in some minor differences in accounting, which will be illustrated in two examples. The first example uses the scenario described at the beginning of this section, where ABC has a ¥25,000,000 receivable. The second example implements only one minor change, which is that, instead of holding a receivable, ABC forecasts sales in March of ¥25,000,000.

Example 1: Using an Option to Hedge a Foreign-Currency-Denominated Receivable

Assume that on December 21, 1998, ABC purchases four put options for $700 each to hedge against foreign currency risk associated with a ¥25,000,000 receivable, which is payable on March 21, 1999. The spot rates and market values for each option, which are determined by dealer quotes, are presented below.

Date	Spot Rates	Quoted Prices for Each Option	Time Value of Option	Intrinsic Value of Option
December 21, 1998	$0.008647 (from Exh. 21-4)	$700 (from Exh. 21-4)	$700 (calculated separately)	$0
December 31, 1998	$0.0084 (assumed)	$800 (assumed)	$800 (calculated separately)	$0
March 21, 1999	$0.0080 (assumed)	$1,250 (assumed)	$0 (calculated separately)	$1,250

Since the options are "out-of-the-money" on December 21 and December 31, all of their values are allocated to time value. This example also demonstrates that this partitioning is, to a large extent, quite artificial. In theory, the time value of an option should gradually decrease over the life of the option, since, as the expiration date of the option draws closer, the chances of the option becoming in-the-money decrease. On this basis, prior to *SFAS No. 133*, U.S. GAAP amortized the time value of options on a straight-line basis over the life of the option. However, in this example, the value of each option has increased by $100 from December 21 to December 31 due to the significant drop in spot rates over a relatively short amount of time. Nevertheless, since the intrinsic value of the option on December 31 is still zero, all of the option's value is allocated to time value.

Given the information on spot rates and the market values of the options at the relevant dates, journal entries are presented as follows.

Dec. 21   Accounts Receivable in ¥   216,175
        Sales   216,175
        To record sales in yen; ¥25,000,000 ×
        $0.008647.

        Foreign Currency Options   2,800
            Cash   2,800
        To record the purchase of foreign currency
        options.

Dec. 31	Loss on Foreign Currency Rec.	6,175	
	Accounts Receivable in ¥		6,175

To record the loss on receivable (¥25,000,000 × $0.0084) − (¥25,000,000 × $0.008647).

	Foreign Currency Options	400	
	Gain on Foreign Currency Options		400

To record gain on options.

Mar. 21	Loss on Foreign Currency Rec.	10,000	
	Accounts Receivable in ¥		10,000

To record the loss on receivable (¥25,000,000 × $0.0080) − (¥25,000,000 × $0.0084).

	Foreign Currency Options	1,800	
	Gain on Foreign Currency Options		1,800

To record gain on options.

	Cash	205,000	
	Foreign Currency Options		5,000
	Accounts Receivable in ¥		200,000

To record payment of receivable and exercise of options.

Analysis of these prior entries reveals that the purchase of the options establishes a lower limit for the cash inflows to be received from the receivable. This lower limit is equal to the strike rate of the options ($0.0082) multiplied by the receivable (¥25,000,000) less the amount paid for the options ($2,800). Thus, the net loss was limited to $13,975 (which is equal to the receivable's initial value less cash received).

If the Japanese yen had strengthened instead of weakened, ABC would have realized a gain on the receivable, but the loss on the options would have been limited to the amount paid to purchase the options. Also, it should be noted that the given entries are not affected by whether the company chooses to assess hedge effectiveness based on changes in the option's total value or intrinsic value. This is the case because the gains and losses on both the hedging instrument and the hedged item are required to be recognized in current earnings.

> **Example 2: Using an Option to Hedge a Foreign-Currency-Denominated Forecasted Transaction**
> All of the previous facts are used in this example, except that instead of holding a receivable in December 1998, ABC forecasts sales in Japanese yen in the amount of ¥25,000,000. Accordingly, ABC purchases four put options for $2,800 to hedge against foreign currency risk associated with the forecasted sales.

SFAS No. 133 designates a derivative instrument used to hedge foreign currency risk associated with a forecasted transaction as a foreign currency cash-flow hedge. Journal entries are provided in Exhibit 21-5 under both scenarios, where hedge effectiveness is based on the total change in the option's value and the change in the option's intrinsic value.

EXHIBIT 21-5

Journal Entries for Options Used to Hedge Foreign Currency Forecasted Transactions

		Hedge Effectiveness Based on:			
		Total Option Value		Intrinsic Value	
Dec. 21	Foreign Currency Options	2,800		2,800	
	Cash		2,800		2,800
	To purchase options.				
Dec. 31	Foreign Currency Options			400	
	Gain on Foreign Currency Options				400
	To record the change in the time value of options.				
	Foreign Currency Options	400			
	Other Comprehensive Income		400		
	To record the change in the total value of options.				
Mar. 21	Loss on Foreign Currency Options			3,200	
	Foreign Currency Options				3,200
	To record the change in the time value of options.				
	Foreign Currency Options	1,800		5,000	
	Other Comprehensive Income		1,800		5,000
	To record the change in the total value and intrinsic value of options.				
	Cash	200,000		200,000	
	Sales		200,000		200,000
	To record sales made on March 31, 1999, at spot rate.				
	Cash	5,000		5,000	
	Foreign Currency Options		5,000		5,000
	To record settlement of options.				
	Other Comprehensive Income	2,200		5,000	
	Sales		2,200		5,000
	To close out OCI account.				

The results from these entries are similar to the results from the first example. The net cash received as a result of purchasing the options is $202,200 (the same as what was received in the first example). However, the journal entries differ slightly, depending on how hedge effectiveness is assessed, because the time value component of the option is taken directly to earnings when it is not included as part of the assessment.

Note that when using intrinsic value to assess hedge effectiveness, gains and losses on the options are recorded in earnings without offsetting gains and losses on the hedged item, due to recognizing the option's time value changes in earnings.

Exhibit 21-6 presents the pro forma financial statements for the preceding example.

As a summary, Exhibit 21-7 presents the different accounting procedures for forward and option contracts, based on whether the derivative instrument is intended to be used as a hedge and the type of hedge.

EXHIBIT 21-6

Pro Forma Balance Sheet for ABC

	Hedge Effectiveness Based on			
	Total Option Value		Intrinsic Option Value	
	Year		Year	
	1998	1999	1998	1999
Current assets:				
Cash	$(2,800)	$202,200	$(2,800)	$202,200
Foreign currency options	3,200	0	3,200	0
Total assets	$ 400	$202,200	$ 400	$202,200
Stockholders' equity:				
Accumulated other comp. income	$ 400	$ 0	$ 0	$ 0
Retained earnings	0	202,200	400	202,200
Total liabilities and SE	$ 400	$202,200	$ 400	$202,200

Pro Forma Income Statement for ABC

	Hedge Effectiveness Based on			
	Total Option Value		Intrinsic Option Value	
	Year		Year	
	1998	1999	1998	1999
Sales	$ 0	$202,200	$ 0	$205,000
Gain on foreign currency options	0	0	400	0
Loss on foreign currency options	0	0	0	(3,200)
Net income	$ 0	$202,200	$ 400	$201,800

EXHIBIT 21-7

Summarization of Accounting for Foreign Currency Forward Contracts and Options

Derivative Instrument	Purpose of Derivative Instrument	Hedged Item	Qualifies as a Hedging Instrument under *SFAS No. 133*?	Accounting for Changes in Market Value of:	
				Derivative Instrument per *SFAS No. 133*	Hedged Item
Forward Contract and Option		Receivable, payable, long-term debt, etc.	No.*	Current operating earnings	Gain or loss due to translation at different spot rates is recognized in current operating earnings per *SFAS No. 52*.
	Hedge foreign currency exposure associated with holding a foreign-currency-denominated asset or liability.	Trading security	No.*	Current operating earnings	Both gain or loss due to translation at different spot rates and gain or loss due to market value of underlying asset are recognized in current operating earnings per *SFAS No. 115*.
		Available-for-sale security	Yes. Foreign currency fair-value hedge	Current operating earnings	Gain or loss due to translation at different spot rates is recognized in current operating earnings per *SFAS No. 133*. Gain or loss due to market value of underlying asset is recognized in other comprehensive income per *SFAS No. 115*.
		Held-to-maturity security	No.*	Current operating earnings	Gain or loss due to translation at different spot rates is recognized in current operating earnings due to *SFAS No. 52*.
	Hedge foreign currency exposure associated with a future transaction denominated in foreign currency.	Firm commitment	Yes. Foreign currency fair value hedge	Current operating earnings	Gain or loss of firm commitment is recognized in current operating earnings per *SFAS No. 133*.
		Forecasted sale or purchase	Yes. Foreign currency cash flow hedge	Other comprehensive income until transaction is realized	No recognition, since forecasted transactions are not recognized in financial statements.
	Speculation in foreign exchange rate movements	None	No hedging activity exists.	Current operating earnings	Hedged item does not exist.

*Designating a special hedge relationship for the hedged item is not necessary since gains and losses on the derivative instrument are naturally offset by the gains and losses on the hedged item without following special hedge accounting rules.

Natural Hedges

We have discussed the use of derivative instruments for reducing or eliminating the risk associated with foreign-currency-denominated transactions. However, companies can sometimes accomplish the same objective by using nonderivative instruments, which is sometimes referred to as a **natural hedge**. For example, if a company has a receivable denominated in a foreign currency, a natural hedge would be to create a liability in the same foreign currency, with equivalent principal amounts and maturity dates. With this arrangement, any gain or loss on the receivable as a result of exchange rate fluctuations will be offset by the gain or loss on the payable.

Natural hedges can also be set up for firm commitments or forecasted transactions. If a company forecasted sales of FC5,000,000 during the year 2003, a natural hedge could be established by borrowing debt in the amount of FC5,000,000 and repaying the debt using the revenue generated from the sales. The question that arises, however, is what are the effects of such an arrangement on the financial statements? Interestingly, when a nonderivative instrument is employed to hedge against foreign currency risk, *SFAS No. 133* allows hedge accounting to be followed when the hedged item is a firm commitment, but *not* when the hedged item is a forecasted transaction. Therefore, although a company that attempts to hedge a forecasted transaction with foreign currency debt is following sound risk management policies, the gain or loss on the debt will be recognized in current earnings, without an offsetting gain or loss on the hedged item.

International Accounting Standards

The international counterparts to *SFAS No. 52* and *SFAS No. 133* are *IAS No. 21, The Effects of Changes in Foreign Exchange Rates*, and *IAS No. 39, Financial Instruments: Recognition and Measurement*. *IAS No. 39* represented the last step in completing a core set of standards for evaluation by the U.S. SEC and IOSCO for cross-border capital raising and listings. However, it should be recognized that even the final standard is considered to be an interim solution for financial instruments. The IASB continues to work cooperatively with 13 other national standard-setting bodies throughout the world, including the FASB, on the task of creating a harmonized standard.

This section will highlight some of the main differences between the standards under U.S. GAAP and their international counterparts. Most of the differences relate to the translation of foreign financial statements, which is covered in most advanced accounting courses.

Foreign Currency Transactions

Similar to *SFAS No. 52, IAS No. 21* also requires that foreign currency transactions be recorded at the spot rate that exists at the time of the transaction. *IAS No. 21* also specifically mentions that an average rate for the period can be used if this method results in recorded transactions that are in close proximity to what would be recorded using the spot rate. This is accomplished when the entity experiences a constant pattern of transactions within the foreign currency, and the relevant exchange rate is stable over the period. However, this perceived difference is only on the surface, since, in practice, firms using U.S. GAAP that have large numbers of transactions in a foreign currency typically use an average rate to lower costs.

The benchmark method of accounting for exchange rate fluctuations related to a monetary asset or liability is to recognize the resulting gain or loss in current earnings in the period realized, which is the required method under U.S. GAAP. *IAS No. 21*, paragraph 21, indicates that under certain conditions, companies can adjust the carrying value of purchased assets denominated in a foreign currency instead of recording a gain or loss on the payable related to the purchase of the asset. This alternative treatment represents a significant departure from U.S. GAAP.

To qualify for the alternative treatment, all of the following conditions must be met:

- The foreign currency must have experienced a severe devaluation.
- At no time were there practical means available to hedge against the foreign currency risk.
- Acquisition of the asset must have been recent.
- The company must not be reporting in a hyperinflationary currency (*IAS No. 29*, paragraph 23).

All of these criteria probably deserve further elaboration. A "severe" devaluation implies that the currency depreciated suddenly as opposed to a steady deterioration. The second criterion indicates that no forward, future, or option contracts were available at any time, nor could the company establish a natural hedge. With regards to the third criterion, "recent" is not defined in the standard but is left open to judgment. The fourth criterion is necessary to include, since a severe devaluation of currency in a hyperinflationary economy would not be unusual, and thus, foreign currency gains and losses would be an important piece of information to provide to financial statement users.

Hedging Foreign Currency Transactions

IAS No. 39 provides guidance on accounting for all financial instruments. Those portions of the statement that discuss accounting for derivative instruments and hedge accounting closely parallel the requirements outlined in *SFAS No. 133*. *IAS No. 39* became effective for annual accounting periods beginning on or after January 1, 2001.

Similar to U.S. GAAP, all derivative instruments must be reported on the balance sheet at market value. Those derivatives that are used to hedge exposure to exchange rate fluctuations are to be designated as either a fair-value hedge or a cash-flow hedge. Also, *IAS No. 39* allows hedge accounting to be followed for forecasted transactions.

Changes in market values of derivatives are to be reported either directly in earnings or as a component of equity, depending on the type of hedging relationship that exists. However, determining market values for derivatives that are not readily traded and therefore have no market quotes is not addressed in *IAS No. 39*. U.S. GAAP stipulates that changes in forward rates are to be used to evaluate changes in market value, and presumably this method will be used extensively under IAS. However, it's possible that the forward rate will be compared to the existing spot rate at interim balance sheet dates. If so, although the cumulative gain or loss recognized on the hedging instrument over its life will be the same, the pattern of gains and losses will differ from U.S. GAAP.

Questions

1. In addition to hedging the risk associated with a receivable or payable denominated in a foreign currency, as discussed in Chapter 20, identify other circumstances where a company would be exposed to foreign currency risk and could use derivatives to hedge this risk.

2. What does the term "hedge accounting" mean? Provide an example where hedge accounting results in accounting for an item differently from what would be done had a company not employed hedge accounting.

3. Give an example discussed in the chapter of a fair-value hedge and a cash-flow hedge.

4. Explain the difference in accounting for gains and losses between fair-value and cash-flow hedges.

5. On November 1, 2003, GNG Inc. holds a forward contract that allows it to purchase £100,000 six months in the future. The current spot rate for British pounds is $1.70, and the 6-month forward rate is $1.68. On December 31, 2003, the forward rate for 4-month forward contracts is $1.65. Using a discounted cash flow analysis, derive the market value of the forward contract held by GNG Inc. on December 31, 2003.

6. Suppose that Mountain Hills Mines, Inc., has entered into a legally binding commitment with a foreign company to sell ore at a specified price in the future, denominated in the foreign currency. To hedge against the risk of exchange rate fluctuations, Mountain Hills Mines enters into a forward contract to sell the foreign currency at a specified rate. What type of hedge is this? How should Mountain Hills Mines account for the realized gains/losses on the forward contract and purchase commitment? Assuming that the forward contract is fully effective in hedging the risk associated with the purchase commitment, how is the gain/loss on the purchase commitment determined?

7. In Question 6, rather than entering into a purchase commitment with a foreign company, suppose that Mountain Hills Mines, Inc., forecasts that it will sell a certain amount of ore to foreign companies during the next year. The company desires to hedge against foreign currency risk associated with the forecasted sales and, accordingly, enters into a forward contract to sell foreign currency at a specified rate. What type of hedge is this? How should Mountain Hills Mines account for the realized gains/losses on the forward contract?

8. Discuss how a gain or loss on a derivative instrument used to hedge the risk associated with a foreign-currency-denominated security should be accounted for, assuming that the foreign security is classified as:
   a. A trading security
   b. An available-for-sale security
   c. A held-to-maturity debt security

9. Why is it difficult, if not impossible, to hedge the foreign currency risk associated with a security that is classified by management as a trading security?

10. Suppose that a foreign security has a market value as of June 30, 2003, of $10. Six months later, on December 31, the market value has changed to $12. Also, assume that on June 30, 2003, $1 could be exchanged for 2 foreign currency units (FCU), and this spot rate changes to $1 = 1.5 FCU as of December 31, 2003.

How much of the change in this security's market value was due to foreign currency fluctuations, and how much was due to a change in the value of the underlying net assets of the company? How should each of these components be reported on a U.S. investor's financial statements, supposing that the security was classified as available-for-sale?

11. Suppose that a U.S. company holds shares of Honda Motors Company, a Japanese company that has its shares listed on the New York Stock Exchange. Assuming that the U.S. company purchased derivatives to hedge foreign currency exposure associated with the investment in Honda, is it possible for the gain/loss on the Honda security to offset gain/loss on the derivative instrument? Why or why not?

12. What special characteristic must a derivative contain in order to effectively hedge against a bond security that pays intermittent interest payments?

13. What advantages and disadvantages does an option contract have over a forward contract when hedging foreign currency risk?

14. What is a call option, and how does it differ from a put option? If a company wanted to hedge a foreign currency asset position, which type of option should be purchased?

15. How should a gain or loss on a derivative instrument that is ineffective in hedging gains/losses on hedged items be recognized?

16. Suppose that Elliot Smith paid $300 for a British pounds call option with a strike price of $1.50 to hedge a payable of £10,000. The spot rate on the date that the option was purchased was $1.48. Is the option in-the-money or out-of-the-money on the date it was purchased? What is the maximum net loss that Elliot could realize on the payable and option? What is the maximum net gain that could be realized?

17. Assume the same facts provided in Question 16, except that the option purchased was a put option to hedge against a receivable. Calculate the option's intrinsic value and time value. In theory, as the option's expiration date draws closer, how will the option's time value change? Why?

18. Explain when a company might want to determine an option's time value and intrinsic value. Where in the financial statements are changes in an option's time value always presented?

19. Explain the concept of a natural hedge. What advantage does this type of hedge have over a derivative instrument?

20. Suppose that Yamashita Corp. expects to have total foreign sales during the next year in the amount of 50,000 foreign currency units (FCU). To protect itself against foreign currency fluctuations, the company issued debt denominated in 50,000 FCU. Has Yamashita effectively hedged against the forecasted foreign currency sales? How will the financial statements be affected by this hedging activity?

21. Assume the same facts provided in Question 20, except that instead of forecasting sales of 50,000 FCU, Yamashita has a legally binding agreement with several companies to sell products worth 50,000 FCU to the foreign customers. What are the financial statement effects of this agreement and the hedging activity of issuing debt in FCU?

22. In some cases, international GAAP allow companies to adjust the carrying value of purchased assets denominated in a foreign currency. Review the conditions that must be met before this accounting practice is allowed. In your opinion, what is the likelihood that all these criteria will be met?

23. Multiple-Choice Questions.
   (1) A security that gives the holder a right, but not the obligation, to purchase foreign currency is:
        a. A foreign currency forward contract
        b. A foreign currency call option contract
        c. A foreign currency put option contract
        d. A foreign currency swap contract
   (2) According to *SFAS No. 133*, a forward contract purchased to eliminate or reduce the risk associated with a forecasted transaction in a foreign currency is called a:
        a. Cash-flow hedge
        b. Speculative hedge
        c. Market-value hedge
        d. Premium hedge
   (3) Gary Grant Inc. entered into a call option contract with JP Morgan to purchase 50,000 Brazilian reals. The option's expiration date is March 31, 2004. The strike rate stipulated on the option is $0.20. The real spot rate that existed on March 31, 2004, is $0.21, and the 3-month forward rate is $0.19. Should Gary Grant exercise the option?
        a. Yes, since the spot rate on March 31, 2004, is greater than the strike rate.
        b. No, since the 3-month forward rate on March 31, 2004, is less than the strike rate.
        c. No, since the spot rate on March 31, 2004, is greater than the strike rate.
        d. Yes, since the 3-month forward rate on March 31, 2004, is less than the strike rate.
   (4) When a forward contract is used to hedge the risk associated with a firm purchase commitment denominated in a foreign currency:
        a. Any realized gains/losses on the forward contract are recognized in the current period as part of operating income.
        b. Any realized gains/losses on the forward contract are recognized in other comprehensive income until the forward contract is settled.
        c. Realized losses on the forward contract are recognized in the current period as part of operating income; however, realized gains are recognized in other comprehensive income until the forward contract is settled.
        d. There will not be any gains/losses to recognize, since the gains/losses on the forward contract will be exactly offset by the gains/losses on the purchase commitment.
   (5) A foreign currency call option contract that has a strike rate greater than the spot rate:
        a. Will always have a higher market value than a put option contract with the same strike rate and expiration date.
        b. Will never be fully effective in hedging exposure to foreign currency risk, since the strike rate is different from the spot rate.
        c. Will be less expensive than a forward contract, where the exercise rate is equal to the spot rate.
        d. Can be used as a market-value hedge but not as a cash-flow hedge.
   (6) Classy Clowns Co. has a note receivable from a major customer that is denominated in Korean won. Indicate which of the following would effectively hedge its exposure to foreign currency risk:
        a. Issue debt that is denominated in Korean won.
        b. Purchase a Korean won call option.
        c. Enter into a forward contract to purchase Korean won.
        d. All of the above are effective strategies in hedging the note receivable.

Exercises

Exercise 21-1: Hedging a Purchase Commitment. On November 1, 2003, Lenix Blinds Co. agreed with a foreign supplier to purchase inventory at a price of 60,000 foreign currency units (FC). The purchase is to take place on May 1, 2004. To hedge the foreign currency risk associated with this purchase commitment, Lenix Blinds entered into a forward contract on November 1, 2003, to purchase FC 60,000 at the existing forward rate. Relevant spot and forward rates are as follows:

	Spot Rate	Forward Rate (for May 1, 2004)
November 1, 2003	$1 = 0.70 FC	$1 = 0.68 FC
December 31, 2003	1 = 0.74 FC	1 = 0.72 FC
May 1, 2004	1 = 0.75 FC	n/a

Lenix Blinds Co. has an annual discount rate of 12%.

1. Determine the market value of the forward contract on November 1, December 31, and May 1.
2. Prepare all necessary journal entries related to the purchase commitment and forward contract for the years 2003 and 2004.

Exercise 21-2: Hedging a Purchase Commitment. On November 15, 2003, American Devices Inc. (ADI) has entered into a contract with a British customer where the British company is to purchase 10,000 units from American Devices for $10/unit on March 15, 2004. The exchange rates between U.S. dollars and British pounds are as follows:

	Spot Rate	Forward Rate (for March 15, 2004)
November 15, 2003	$1.74	$1.72
December 31, 2003	1.76	1.76
March 15, 2004	1.75	n/a

1. Prepare all journal entries for ADI related to the purchase commitment, assuming that ADI requires all payments be made in U.S. dollars.
2. Repeat Part (1), assuming that no forward contract was entered into and ADI allows the foreign customer to pay in British pounds.
3. Repeat Part (2), assuming that ADI enters into a forward contract on November 15, 2003, to fully hedge against the foreign currency risk associated with the purchase commitment. Ignore time value of money calculations.

Exercise 21-3: Forecasted Transaction. Terra Gardens, Inc., expects to sell inventory during 2004 to a Mexican customer that makes payment in Mexican pesos. Terra Gardens is concerned with the inflationary economy in Mexico and the resulting effect it would have on the exchange rate between U.S. dollars and Mexican pesos. Accordingly, the company determines to enter into a 6-month forward contract on December 15, 2003, to sell 500,000 Mexican pesos. The relevant exchange rates are as follows:

	Spot Rate	Forward Rate (for June 15, 2004)
December 15, 2003	$0.095	$0.091
December 31, 2003	0.100	0.094
June 15, 2004	0.085	n/a

Ignore time value of money calculations.

1. Suppose that the Mexican peso has a severe devaluation during 2004. What is the likely effect of this on the U.S. dollar/Mexican peso exchange rate and the market value of the forward contract entered into in 2003?
2. Suppose that Terra Gardens actually sold inventory worth 500,000 Mexican pesos on June 15, 2004. Prepare all necessary journal entries for 2003 and 2004 related to this transaction and the corresponding hedging activity.
3. Repeat Part (2), except assume that the actual sales made on June 15, 2004, were for 420,000 Mexican pesos.

Exercise 21-4: Forecasted Transaction. Kyle Turf, Inc., has agreed in principle to purchase some office equipment from a German company. The planned purchase is to take place during the first quarter of 2004, and euro will be used for payment. No documents were signed, and Kyle is under no obligation to execute the transaction; however, Kyle fully intends to honor the agreement and expects the German company to do so. To hedge the risk associated with the transaction, Kyle enters into a 4-month forward contract on December 1, 2003, to purchase 200,000 euro (the cost of the office equipment).

The relevant exchange rates are as follows:

	Spot Rate	Forward Rate (for March 31, 2004)
December 1, 2003	$0.555	$0.554
December 31, 2003	0.552	0.551
March 31, 2004	0.557	n/a

Kyle will depreciate the office equipment over 5 years, using the straight-line method.

1. Assuming that the purchase was made on March 31, 2004, prepare all necessary journal entries related to the transaction, including depreciation expense for the year ending December 31, 2004.
2. Repeat Part (1), except that instead of entering into a forward contract, Kyle purchased an option to purchase 200,000 euro with a strike rate of $0.556. The cost of the option was $7,000, and the option's market value on December 31, 2003, was $2,500.

Exercise 21-5: Hedging Foreign Securities. On June 30, 2003, Magnum Inc. purchased equity stock in Higgins, Inc., which is a small British company not listed on a U.S. exchange, and pays all dividends in British pounds. The cost of the investment was £45,000, and the spot rate on this date was £1 = $1.44. Concurrent with purchasing the security, Magnum also entered into a forward contract to sell £45,000 at a contracted rate of $1.42. The forward contract has an expiration date of one year.

As of December 31, 2003, the market value of the investment in Higgins, Inc., is £49,000. The new spot and forward rates on that date are $1.48 and $1.49, respectively.

1. Determine the market value of the investment in Higgins, Inc., in U.S. dollars on June 30, 2003, and December 31, 2003.
2. How much of the change in market value in U.S. dollars from June 30 to December 31 is due to a change in exchange rates? How should this gain/loss be reported on Magnum's financial statements, assuming that the investment is classified as:
   a. Trading securities.
   b. Available-for-sale securities.
3. How much of the change in market value in U.S. dollars from June 30 to December 31 is due to a change in the underlying assets of Higgins, Inc.? How should this gain/loss be reported on Magnum's financial statements, assuming that the investment is classified as:
   a. Trading securities.
   b. Available-for-sale securities.
4. Calculate the gain or loss on the forward contract (ignore time value of money). How should this gain/loss be reported on Magnum's financial statements, assuming that the investment in Higgins, Inc., is classified as:
   a. Trading securities.
   b. Available-for-sale securities.
5. Prepare all journal entries related to the security and the corresponding forward contract, assuming that the investment is classified as:
   a. Trading.
   b. Available-for-sale.

Exercise 21-6: Option's Time Value and Intrinsic Value. A foreign currency option is listed on an exchange with a quoted price of $1,850. The option allows the holder to purchase 50,000 Australian dollars at a rate of $0.75 when the spot rate is $0.73.

1. Calculate the option's intrinsic and time value.
2. Calculate the option's intrinsic and time value, assuming that the spot rate was $0.76.

Exercise 21-7: Reading an Options Table. Presented below is a foreign currency options table that was presented in the October 31, 2000 edition of *The Wall Street Journal*. (The rates are closing quotes as of October 30, 2000.)

PHILADELPHIA EXCHANGE OPTIONS

	CALLS		PUT			CALLS		PUT			CALLS		PUT	
	Vol.	Last	Vol.	Last		Vol.	Last	Vol.	Last		Vol.	Last	Vol.	Last
Euro				88.15	British Pounds				147.69	Euro				88.15
62,500 Euro—cents per unit					31,250 Brit. Pounds—European style					62,500 Euro—European style				
86 Nov.	50	0.80	—	—	148 Dec.	16	1.67	—	—	84 Nov.	—	—	5	1.02
86 Mar.	30	2.56	—	0.00	Canadian Dollar				66.48	90 Dec.	—	—	6	5.92
88 Nov.	50	0.28	—	—	50,000 Canadian Dollars—cents per unit									
90 Dec.	10	0.38	—	—	68 Dec.	12	0.05	—	—					

1. How many euro options are available?
2. The euro spot rate on October 30, 2000, was $1 = 1.1912 euros. Which of the euro options are "in-the-money"?
3. What is the exercise price for the Canadian dollar call option?
4. Suppose that a company has an exposed euro asset position of 125,000 euros. How many options should be bought to fully hedge against this exposure? Should a put or call option be bought? How much money will the company need to spend to fully hedge its position? What is the expiration date of these options?

Exercise 21-8: Comparison of U.S. GAAP and International GAAP. Axmate Inc. entered into a 90-day forward contract on November 20, 2003, to hedge against the risk associated with a receivable denominated in a foreign currency (FC). The relevant spot and forward rates are summarized as follows:

	Spot Rate	Forward Rate (for Feb. 18, 2004)
November 20, 2003	$1 = 2.20 FC	$1 = 2.25 FC
December 31, 2003	1 = 2.26 FC	1 = 2.27 FC
February 18, 2004	1 = 2.15 FC	n/a

The amount of the receivable was FC90,000, and the forward contract was fully effective. The company's annual discount rate is 12% (1% monthly rate).

1. Determine the amount of gain or loss that the company would record on the forward contract in 2003 and 2004, following U.S. GAAP.
2. Suppose that the company chose to calculate the market value of the forward contract using the change in spot rates as allowed under international GAAP. Determine the amount of the gain or loss to be reported on the company's 2003 and 2004 financial statements, and compare these amounts to what was reported under U.S. GAAP. Did the total gain/loss over the life of the contract differ between the two methods?

Problems

Problem 21-1: Hedging a Purchase Commitment and Forecasted Transaction. Harland Industries, Inc., is a company domiciled in Hong Kong. During the year 2003, the company determined that a new piece of machinery would be necessary in order to effectively keep up with its competition. The company located the desired machine from a dealer in France. The French supplier requires Harland to purchase the equipment, using euros, and the purchase price of the machine is 95,000 euros. The machine has an estimated useful life of 10 years, with no salvage value. Harland depreciates all equipment using the straight-line method.

Required:
1. Suppose that Harland Industries purchased the machine on October 1, 2003, by making a down payment of 15,000 euros and signing a note payable for the remaining amount due in six months. The relevant exchange rates are as follows:

	Spot Rate	Forward Rate (for April 1, 2004)
October 1, 2003	HK$1 = €0.20	HK$1 = €0.18
December 31, 2003	HK$1 = €0.23	HK$1 = €0.21
April 1, 2004	HK$1 = €0.25	n/a

Calculate the gain or loss on the note payable for the years 2003 and 2004.

(continued)

2. Suppose that Harland Industries entered into a forward contract to hedge the risk associated with the note payable. What is the gain or loss on the forward contract for the years 2003 and 2004 (ignore present value calculations)? Where is this gain or loss reported on the financial statements? Make all appropriate journal entries related to this transaction for the years 2003 and 2004, including depreciation.

3. Suppose that Harland did not actually purchase the machine on October 1, 2003, but instead forecasted that the transaction would take place on April 1, 2004. Accordingly, the company purchased a forward contract to hedge the foreign currency risk associated with this transaction on October 1, 2003. Make all appropriate journal entries related to this transaction for the years 2003 and 2004, including depreciation.

4. Assume the same facts as in Requirement 1, but instead of entering into a forward contract to exchange Hong Kong dollars for euros, the company entered into a U.S. dollar/euro forward contract. Hong Kong dollars have a fixed exchange rate with U.S. dollars of $1 = HK$7.45. The relevant forward rates between U.S. dollars and euros are as follows:

	Forward Rate (for April 1, 2004)
October 1, 2003	$1 = €0.90
December 31, 2003	1 = €0.88
April 1, 2004	1 = €0.87

Make all necessary journal entries for 2003 and 2004, including depreciation.

Problem 21-2: Forecasted Transactions. Ingrid Company has been experiencing substantial growth over the past few years and expects foreign sales to increase dramatically next year due to a large advertising campaign in selected foreign markets. The company is concerned about the foreign currency risk that accompanies transactions in a foreign currency. Management is particularly concerned with the Japanese market, since a large portion of its foreign sales is denominated in Japanese yen, and the U.S. dollar/Japanese yen exchange rate has experienced large fluctuations during the past couple of years.

Management has approached you to discuss alternative methods that could be pursued to hedge risk associated with the exposure in Japanese yen.

Required:
1. Explain how Ingrid Company could hedge its foreign currency exposure in Japanese yen by using forward contracts, option contracts, and natural hedges. Discuss the advantages and disadvantages of each method.
2. Suppose that management enters into a forward contract on December 31, 2003, to exchange ¥20 million. The contract exchange rate on the forward contract is $1 = ¥123 and can be exercised anytime during the next year. The spot rate on December 31, 2003, was $1 = ¥120. On June 30, 2004, the company has realized cash sales in Japanese yen of ¥12 million and exchanges the cash into U.S. dollars. (For simplicity purposes, assume that all sales are made on June 30.) The spot and forward rates on this date are ¥118 and ¥119, respectively. On December 31, 2004, additional sales of ¥13 million are exchanged into U.S. dollars. The exchange rate on this date is ¥131. Prepare all necessary journal entries for these transactions.

3. Assume the same facts as provided in Requirement (2), except that instead of entering into a forward contract, Ingrid Company purchases a Japanese yen put option to sell ¥20 million. The strike rate on the option is $1 = ¥123 and can be exercised anytime during the next year. The cost of the option is $10,000, and its market value on June 30, 2004, is $3,000. Prepare all necessary journal entries for these transactions, assuming that hedge effectiveness is based on the option's full value.

Problem 21-3: Hedging Foreign Securities. Tyler Corp. has invested in a foreign security that is not listed on a U.S. exchange and pays dividends in the foreign currency. The investment was made on September 1, 2003, at a cost of 75,000 foreign currency units (FC) when the spot rate was $1 = FC1. The foreign security was sold one year later for FC90,000. Additional exchange rate and market price information is as follows:

Date	Spot Rates	Forward Rates for Sept. 1, 2003	Quoted Prices for Foreign Security
Sept. 1, 2003	$1.00	$1.02	FC75,000
Dec. 31, 2004	$1.05	$1.08	FC82,000
Sept. 1, 2004	$1.16	n/a	FC90,000

Assume that Tyler Corp enters into a forward contract on September 1, 2003, to sell FC75,000 to hedge against the foreign currency risk associated with the foreign security. The company's discount rate is 8%.

Required:

1. Prepare all journal entries related to the security, assuming that it was classified by management as a trading security. What are the inherent difficulties in hedging against trading foreign securities?
2. Repeat Requirement (1), assuming that the security was classified by management as available-for-sale.

Problem 21-4: Held-to-Maturity Foreign Securities. Family Toys Company wanted to take advantage of a favorable interest rate on some bonds offered by a foreign company, Norwitz, Inc. Family Toys purchased 20 bonds on March 1, 2003. The bonds have a stated annual interest rate of 10%, and annual interest payments are made on December 31 of each year. The bonds expire on December 31 of 2005. Each bond has a face value of 10,000 foreign currency units (FC). To protect against foreign currency risk associated with holding the bonds, Family Toys entered into a forward contract that allowed the company to sell FC20,000 each December 31, and also FC200,000 on December 31, 2005. Relevant foreign currency exchange rates are as follows:

	Spot Rate	Forward Rate (Dec. 31, 2003)	Forward Rate (Dec. 31, 2004)	Forward Rate (Dec. 31, 2005)
March 1, 2003	$1.17	$1.18	$1.18	$1.16
Dec. 31, 2003	1.25	—	1.26	1.26
Dec. 31, 2004	1.50	—	—	1.48
Dec. 31, 2005	1.21	—	—	—

The company's cost of capital is 8%.

Required:

1. Prepare the journal entry on March 1, 2003, to record the purchase of the foreign bonds.
2. Prepare the journal entry on December 31, 2003, to record the interest payment and the change in market value of the forward contract. If you prefer, you may treat the forward contract as four separate contracts—one for each interest payment and one for the principal payment.
3. Prepare a pro forma comparative balance sheet and income statement for Family Toys Company for the period ending December 31, 2003.

Problem 21-5: Continuation of Problem 21-4. Refer to the facts provided in Problem 21-4.

Required:

Calculate the market value of the forward contract as of December 31, 2004. Prepare a pro forma comparative balance sheet and income statement for Family Toys Company for the period ending December 31, 2004.

Problem 21-6: Accounting for Foreign Currency Options. Tally's Manufacturing, Inc., has a major inventory supplier domiciled in Canada. During the previous year, the U.S./Canadian exchange rate changed dramatically, which caused Tally's to incur a significant foreign exchange loss. To avoid a similar occurrence in the current year, Tally's has decided to purchase Canadian dollar options to hedge its exposure to the foreign currency risk.

Assume that on October 15, 2003, Tally's Manufacturing has a C$50,000 note payable denominated in Canadian dollars that is due on March 15, 2004. The company has decided to purchase a foreign currency option to fully hedge against the weakening of the U.S. dollar. The option's strike rate is $0.88, and it expires on March 15, 2004. Data related to the option and spot rates at various dates are provided in the following table:

	Spot Rates	Quoted Prices for Options
October 15, 2003	$0.86	$1,400
December 31, 2003	0.84	800
March 15, 2004	0.90	—

Required:

1. Determine the time value and intrinsic value of the options on October 15, December 31, and March 15.
2. Prepare all necessary journal entries related to the note payable and the options for the years 2003 and 2004.
3. Repeat Requirement (2), assuming that the options were purchased to hedge a forecasted transaction instead of a note payable, and Tally's Manufacturing assesses hedge effectiveness based on the total value of the options. Prepare pro forma balance sheets and income statements for the years 2003 and 2004.
4. Repeat Requirement (3), assuming that hedge effectiveness is assessed based on the options' intrinsic value.

SPREADSHEET

Problem 21-7: Foreign Currency Swap. Bubba Gump Shrimp Co. is a U.S. corporation that provides shrimp products to food companies and restaurants throughout the world. In January, 1995, the company was in need of additional capital. After investigating several options, the company decided to issue bonds. Given the capital structure of Bubba Gump Shrimp and its risk profile, the company's investment banker determines that U.S. bondholders would require an effective return of about 9% on Bubba Gump's bonds. However, investors in Norway would require only a 7% return. With this information, on January 1, 1995, the company sold bonds with a face value of 50 million Norwegian kroner (nok) to investors in Norway. The bonds carry an interest rate of 7% and require annual interest payments on December 31. The bonds expire on December 31, 2004.

To hedge against the foreign currency risk associated with the bonds, Bubba Gump Shrimp Co. entered into a swap agreement with First World Bank of Norway (FWBN). The terms of the agreement are as follows:

	Bubba Gump pays to FWBN:	FWBN pays to Bubba Gump:
Jan. 1, 1995	nok50 million	$8,333,333
Annual interest payments On Dec. 31	$666,666	nok3,500,000
Principal repayment Dec. 31, 2004	$8,333,333	nok50 million

The U.S. dollar/Norwegian kroner spot rates for relevant dates are as follows:*

January 1, 1995 $1 = nok5.3425
December 31, 1995 $1 = nok4.9075
December 31, 1996 $1 = nok5.2333
December 31, 1997 $1 = nok5.9997
December 31, 1998 $1 = nok5.6220
December 31, 1999 $1 = nok6.5329
December 31, 2000 $1 = nok7.6239
December 31, 2001 $1 = nok7.3321
December 31, 2002 $1 = nok7.9910
December 31, 2003 $1 = nok8.2391
December 31, 2004 $1 = nok8.3531
*Rates are assumed values.

Required:
1. What is the effective interest rate that Bubba Gump Shrimp will pay on its bonds as a result of entering into the swap agreement with FWBN?
2. Assuming that Bubba Gump Shrimp did not enter into the swap agreement, determine the cash flows in U.S. dollars to Bubba Gump Shrimp over the life of the bonds. Using a spreadsheet program, calculate the effective interest rate that would have been realized on the bonds. Comment on the effect that the change in spot rates over the life of the bonds has on the effective interest rate on the bonds.

Problem 21-8: Three Forward Contracts. On December 12, 2003, Imp Co. entered into three forward exchange contracts, each to purchase 100,000 euro in 90 days. The relevant exchange rates are as follows:

	Spot Rate	Forward Rate (for March 12, 2004)
December 12, 2003	$0.88	$0.90
December 31, 2003	$0.98	$0.93

Imp entered into the first forward contract to hedge a purchase of inventory in November 2003, payable in March 2004. Imp entered into the second forward contract to hedge a March 2004 commitment to purchase equipment being manufactured to Imp's specifications. The third forward contract was for purposes of hedging a forecasted transaction that was to take place in March 2004.

Required:
What amount of foreign currency transaction gain should Imp include in its 2003 income from these forward contracts (ignore present value calculations)?

Research Activities

Activity 21-1: Cash Flow Statement. The standard promulgated by the FASB that requires companies to prepare a statement of cash flows is *SFAS No. 95*, "Statement of Cash Flows." Soon after its release, two other statements were issued that modify how cash flows from hedging activities are reported on the statement: *SFAS No. 102*, "Statement of Cash Flows—Exemption of Certain Enterprises and Classification of Cash Flows from Certain Securities Acquired for Resale," and *SFAS No. 104*, "Statement of Cash Flows—Net Reporting of Certain Cash Receipts and Cash Payments and Financial Instruments with Concentrations of Credit Risk."

1. Determine how *SFAS No. 95* requires the reporting of cash flows from debt or equity instruments of other entities (i.e., operating, investing, or financing activities). Cite the appropriate paragraph(s) that provides this information.
2. How does *SFAS No. 102* modify this requirement? Cite the appropriate paragraph(s) that provides this information.
3. How does *SFAS No. 104* modify this requirement with respect to derivative securities? Cite the appropriate paragraph(s) that provides this information.
4. Suppose that a company purchases a forward contract to hedge the risk associated with inventory price changes. How should a company classify the cash flows associated with the forward contract on the statement of cash flows?

Cases

Case 21-1: Barings PLC. Barings PLC was founded in 1762 by the sons of German immigrants. Prior to its demise in February 1995, it was the oldest merchant bank in Great Britain. It enjoyed a distinguished history as the institution that arranged the financing for the Louisiana Purchase by the United States of America. The bank's reputation was permanently marred in February 1995, when it was discovered that one of its head traders, Nicholas Leeson, had incurred huge losses from derivative trading. The bank had not adopted adequate internal controls to prevent such actions and was declared insolvent.

Beginning in 1992, Leeson had speculated on the movements of the Nikkei-225 by purchasing forward contracts. As time passed and his losses increased, his speculation bets became more sophisticated. Some time in 1994, he began selling large numbers of option straddles. Option straddles involve the simultaneous sale of both call and put options.

In January 1995, a violent earthquake in Kobe, Japan, caused a large drop in the Japanese stock market. As a result, Leeson sustained losses of £68 million on the option straddles.

1. The purchaser of a call (put) option has the right to buy (sell) an underlying (stock, foreign currency, commodity, etc.) at a specified price. Thus, if the price of the underlying remains unchanged, the purchaser will not gain from the option. However, if the price increases significantly, the purchaser of the call (put) option will realize a gain (loss). Explain the payout profile for the seller of a call option and the seller of a put option.

2. Were the sustained losses by Nicholas Leeson the result of selling call options or put options?

3. Nicholas Leeson sustained an extensive loss due to the Nikkei-225 decreasing significantly in January 1995. What would have been the result if the Nikkei-225 increased significantly? Explain the payout profile of an option straddle. When selling the option straddles, what was Nicholas Leeson betting on?

4. The following is an excerpt from *The Wall Street Journal* article, "Salomon Puts Loss in October at Less than $60 Million," November 26, 1997:

   "Salomon lost as much as $50 million in stock derivatives trading during the week of October 27. . . . The losses stem from a bearish bet Salomon had made on what's known in the derivatives business as volatility. Salomon had in effect bet that the markets wouldn't be very volatile. But when global stock markets started plummeting that week, Salomon racked up sizable losses . . ."

   Given this statement, what type of derivatives was Salomon probably trading? Nicholas Leeson was sentenced to $6\frac{1}{2}$ years of prison for his part in the Barings case. What is the difference in the trading activity conducted by Salomon and Nicholas Leeson?

A

Account A record that gathers information about a particular type of transaction.

Accounting cycle The sequence of procedures to process the year's transactions, prepare the financial statements, and get ready to process the next year's transactions.

Accounting equation The expression in mathematical form that the total of the dollar amount of a business entity's assets always equals the sum of the dollar amounts of its liabilities and owners' equity.

Accounting information system The set of procedures used to record, classify, and summarize accounting data, along with the necessary controls to prevent mistakes and guard against dishonesty.

Accounting Principles Board (APB) During its existence, the APB was the senior technical committee of the AICPA, whose mission was to issue timely guidance on accounting and financial reporting matters and to develop a conceptual framework of accounting. The APB was organized in 1959 to replace the Committee on Accounting Procedure. During the APB's tenure, it issued 31 authoritative pronouncements, called *Opinions*. Despite several attempts, the APB was not successful in developing a conceptual framework. During its tenure, it was embroiled frequently in conflicts and controversy, and eventually its critics outnumbered its supporters in influence. It was replaced by the FASB in 1973.

Accounting Principles Board's Opinions (APBO) The authoritative pronouncements of the APB. Those Opinions that have not been superceded are still in force, and all financial statements of corporations whose securities are publicly traded should conform to those pronouncements. Issuing financial statements to the public that do not conform to the policies set forth in these Opinions constitutes a violation of Rule 203 of the CPA's code of professional conduct.

Accounting Research Bulletins (ARB) The authoritative pronouncements of the CAP. Those Bulletins that have not been superceded are still in force, and all financial statements of corporations whose securities are publicly traded should conform to those pronouncements. Issuing financial statements to the public that do not conform to the policies set forth in these Bulletins constitutes a violation of Rule 203 of the CPA's code of professional conduct.

Accounting Series Releases (ASR) The official pronouncements of the Securities and Exchange Commission (SEC). They deal with accounting, financial reporting, and auditing matters, as well as the actions taken by the SEC on the rights of certain CPA firms and individuals to practice before it.

Accretion method A revenue recognition method that recognizes the increase in value of assets due to natural growth. Currently, this method is not acceptable under U.S. GAAP.

Accrual In reference to adjusting entries, it is to recognize transactions or events that have occurred.

Accrual accounting The method of accounting where revenues and expenses are identified with specific periods and are recognized as incurred and not when the cash is paid or received.

Accumulated benefit obligation The actuarial present value of benefits attributed by the pension benefit formula to employee service rendered and based on employee service and compensation prior to that date. The accumulated benefit obligation differs from the projected benefit obligation in that it includes no assumption about future compensation levels.

Accumulated other comprehensive income The gains and losses that affects owners' equity but are not the result of exchange transactions.

Activity methods of depreciation Methods of allocating the cost of long-lived assets based upon the assumption that use is the most important factor of an asset's decline in usefulness. For any such method, the denominator is a measure of the asset's output and can be measured, for example, in units or hours. The numerator is the number of units or hours (for example) that the long-lived asset produced that year.

Actual return on plan assets The difference between fair value of pension plan assets at the end of the period and the fair value at the beginning of the period, adjusted for contributions and payments of benefits during the period.

Additions Capital expenditures that increase the productive capacity of an asset.

Adjusted trial balance The trial balance taken from the general ledger after the adjusting journal entries have been posted.

Adjusting journal entries The record prepared, usually prior to preparing the financial statements, to update account balances for continuous transactions or for errors.

All-inclusive concept An approach to preparing an income statement in which all revenue, expenses, gains, and losses should be included in computing net income. Current GAAP largely supports this concept, except that items defined to be prior-period adjustments are not included on the income statement. (*See* **Current operating concept**.)

American Accounting Association (AAA) A voluntary organization of persons, primarily academics, interested in accounting education and research.

American Institute of Accountants (AIA) The predecessor of the AICPA. Its name was changed in 1953.

American Institute of Certified Public Accountants (AICPA) A leading professional accounting body that, through various committees, provides advice to its members, government agencies, et al., and issues technical bulletins in accounting matters. These bulletins do not have the same authority as those issued by the FASB or by the predecessors of the FASB, but they should be looked to as authoritative guidance on accounting and financial reporting matters that are not addressed in pronouncements of the FASB and its predecessors.

Amortization In a narrow sense, it is the allocating of the cost of a long-lived intangible asset over the periods in which the asset is used and reporting the amount on the income statement. In a general sense, it refers to the allocating of the cost of any long-lived asset.

Annuity A series of equal payments at fixed intervals of time. Also, it is the right to receive such payments.

Annuity due An annuity in which the first payment is paid (or due) immediately. (*See* **Ordinary annuity**.)

Anticipated useful life The length of time the business entity estimates it will use an asset as determined at the time the asset is acquired or modified thereafter.

Anti-dilution A term used when computing diluted earnings per share that indicates that the assumption of the conversion of convertible securities into shares of common stock would increase earnings per share.

Appropriated retained earnings An amount of retained earnings that has been segregated into a separate account and is reported separately on the balance sheet. Its purpose is to indicate that for a temporary period normal dividends will be curtailed. When the legal, contractual, or other reason for the restriction has been met or has occurred, the amount is returned undiminished to the retained earnings account.

As-if converted method The approach used in computing diluted earnings per share in which it is assumed that convertible securities are converted into shares of common stock on the later of (1) the beginning of the current year or (2) when the shares were issued.

Asset management Measurements of how successfully a company is utilizing its resources.

Asset-liability method The method of accounting for deferred income taxes that places emphasis on measuring balance sheet amounts.

Available-for-sale portfolio all other securities that are not reported in the trading or the held-to-maturity portfolios belong to this portfolio. (*See* **Trading portfolio** and **Held-to-maturity portfolio**.)

Average Cost An inventory cost-flow assumption where inventory and cost of goods sold are determined by averaging inventory costs. (*See* **Weighted-average** and **Moving average**.)

Avoidable interest An amount of interest that theoretically could have been avoided if a company had chosen not to construct an asset.

B

Bank Overdrafts A negative balance in a bank account due to writing checks for more than the amount of cash deposited in the account.

Bargain purchase option A provision in a lease agreement that allows the lessee the option to purchase the leased asset at a price that is expected to be significantly lower than the anticipated fair value of the property when the lease expires, such that exercise of the purchase option is reasonably assured.

Bargain renewal option A provision in a lease agreement that allows the lessee the right to renew a lease at a rental that is expected to be significantly less than the anticipated fair rental when exercise of the renewal option is reasonably assured.

Bearer bonds Bonds that do not have the name of the owner printed on the bond certificate and are sold to another owner by delivering the bond certificate. (*See* **Registered bonds**.)

Betterments Capital expenditures that replace a worn-out component of an asset with a higher-quality component or add something to an asset that improves the quality of the asset.

Bond discount The amount by which the par value of a bond exceeds its selling price. A discount indicates that at the time a bond is sold, the coupon interest rate is less than the rate demanded by the market, given the relative risk of the bond.

Bond indenture The written agreement between the bondholders and the issuer of the bonds of the rights and duties of each party.

Bond issue costs The legal, accounting, underwriting, and other direct costs of issuing bonds. These amounts are accumulated in a deferred charge account (which is included with the assets on the balance sheet) and then amortized over the life of the bonds using the straight-line method.

Bond premium The amount by which the sale price of a bond exceeds its par value. A premium indicates that at the time a bond is sold, the coupon interest rate exceeds the rate demanded by the market, given the relative risk of the bond.

Bond Debt where the amount to be borrowed is too large for a single entity to supply, and so the amount is borrowed from the public. Bonds may be issued in the form of bearer bonds or registered in the name of the owner. They may be classified by the (a) type of issuing body (e.g., state, municipal, corporate, etc.), (b) nature of the project being financed, (c) special privileges (e.g., callable, convertible, etc.), (d) type of lien (e.g., first- or second-mortgage, etc.), or (e) maturity (e.g., term, serial, etc.). (*See* **Bond indenture**.)

Boot Something in addition. In regards to exchanging assets, that something is usually cash.

C

Callable bonds Bonds that may be called prior to maturity and retired at the option of the issuer. Typically, there is a specified call premium.

Callable preferred stock A feature that allows the corporation to acquire the preferred stock at its option, usually at specified prices and times. The call price typically is higher than the original issuing price, thus giving the holder some incentive to buy the stock and some reward for having held it, should the corporation exercise the call option.

Capital expenditure An expenditure incurred that will provide benefits for more than one reporting period. These expenditures are not recorded as expenses in the period incurred. (*See* **Additions**, **Replacements**, **Betterments**, **Rearrangements** and **reinstallations**, and **Extraordinary repairs**.)

Capital lease A lease that substantially transfers the rights and risks of ownership to the lessee. Both the asset and related liability are reported on the balance sheet of the lessee. (*See* **Operating lease**.)

Capitalize Refers to recording an expenditure as an asset, rather than expensing the amount.

Carrying amount of the bonds The par value of the bonds plus any unamortized premium or minus any unamortized discount.

Cash discount A discount given because of prompt settlement of a debt arising from a sale.

Cash equivalent A highly liquid security that can be converted into cash with no risk of loss.

Cash Equivalents Low-risk securities with a short maturity date (typically, 90 days or less) that can be readily converted into cash.

Cash Money, that which is used as a medium of exchange.

Cash-flow hedge A hedge of the exposure to variability in the cash flows of a recognized asset or liability, or of a forecasted transaction, that is attributable to a particular risk.

Cause-and-effect *See* **Matching principle**.

Certified Public Accountant (CPA) The title conferred by a particular state agency upon individuals, allowing them to render an opinion on the publicly issued financial statements of corporations as to whether those statements conform in all material aspects to generally accepted accounting principles. Generally, a person qualifies to become a CPA by completing a course of education, passing a uniform national examination, and completing a minimum number of hours working under the direction of another CPA. However, since the license to practice as a CPA is state administered, there are many variations of these requirements.

Chain discount More than one trade discount. Chain discounts are applied in steps, with each discount applied to the previously discounted price.

Change in accounting estimate A change in a previous estimate that results because of better information being available.

Chart of accounts A list of the account names and numbers, if any, which is used by a specific business.

Code-law countries Countries where a branch of the federal government sets the rules governing a profession (i.e., establishes financial reporting rules).

Committee on Accounting Procedure (CAP) Organized by the AIA, the CAP was the first committee with the charge to develop authoritative accounting and financial reporting standards. Their authoritative pronouncements are called Accounting Research Bulletins, and except where they have been superceded, they are still in force today. The CAP was replaced by the APB in 1959.

Commodity-backed bonds Bonds that are redeemable in units of a commodity, such as barrels of oil, ounces of gold, etc.

Common-size financial statement A financial statement that displays all amounts as a percentage of some base, rather than dollars. The base is usually net sales or total revenue on a common-size income statement and total assets on a common-size balance sheet.

Common-law countries Countries where the federal government allows a private-sector organization to establish the rules governing a profession.

Comparability That quality of information that enables readers of financial statements to identify similarities in and differences between sets of data of two or more enterprises.

Comparative statements Any financial statement that reports the numbers for the current period and the comparable numbers for one or more prior periods.

Compensating balance The amount a lender requires to be retained in a demand deposit to support an existing loan arrangement.

Compensatory (noncompensatory) stock options plans/Stock distribution plans administered by companies with (without) the purpose of providing compensation for services rendered. To be classified as noncompensatory, the plan must meet the following criteria: (1) substantially all full-time employees may participate, (2) stock is offered equally to all eligible employees, even though the plan may limit the number of shares that can be purchased, (3) the time period to exercise the options is limited to a reasonable time, and (4) the grant or option price is essentially equivalent to the market price when the stock options are granted.

Completed-contract method A revenue recognition method that recognizes all revenues when production is complete. This method is used for short-term contracts and long-term contracts only when reliable cost estimates cannot be made.

Complex capital structure Used to denote that a corporation has securities outstanding that could become common stock and that, if converted, would dilute earnings per share. Corporations having a complex capital structure must present both basic earnings per share and diluted earnings per share. (*See* **Diluted earnings per share** and **Dual presentation**.)

Composite depreciation method A depreciation method that applies a single rate to a large group of assets that are not of the same general type. Essentially, it is a special application of the straight-line depreciation method. (*See* **Group depreciation**.)

Comprehensive allocation The method of accounting for deferred taxes that recognizes the tax effects of all temporary differences between accounting income before taxes and taxable income.

Conservatism The concept that when two or more equally good alternatives exist, the accountant should select the one that is least likely to overstate net income and/or total assets.

Consignment transaction A transaction where the potential seller (consignor) delivers merchandise to an agent (the consignee) to sell.

Consistency That quality of information that enables readers of financial statements to identify similarities in and differences between sets of data of the same enterprise over two or more years.

Contingency Existing condition or situation that has given rise to an uncertain gain or loss, which will be resolved when a future event occurs or fails to occur.

Contra-asset account An account that partially or wholly offsets the balance of another account. In reference to the depreciation of long-lived assets, it is intended to show how much of the cost of the asset has been allocated and reported as an expense.

Contributed capital That section of stockholders' equity that reports the contributions made by stockholders.

Contributory plan A pension plan under which employees contribute part of the cost.

Convenience translation Financial statements of a company based in a foreign country that are prepared in the English language and sometimes translated into U.S. dollars.

Conventional retail One form of the retail method, which includes markups and markup cancellations in calculating the cost-to-retail percentage.

Convertible bonds Bonds that are convertible into other types of securities, usually common stock, for a specified time period at the option of the holder.

Convertible debt Any debt security that may be converted, at the option of the holder, into shares of capital stock (usually common stock) of the issuing corporation.

Convertible preferred stock A feature that allows the holder of the preferred stock at his option to exchange his stock for shares of the corporation's common stock at specified times, rates of exchange, and perhaps subject to other conditions as well. This gives the holder the opportunity to participate in the greater rewards that accrue to the common stockholders, should the corporation become very profitable, but also the security of a set return if such does not occur.

Cost-benefit constraint The control placed in financial reporting that requires that the benefits received from information exceed the cost of providing it.

Cost-flow assumption An assumption of how inventory costs flow from purchase (or manufacture) to sale, which determines how much of the inventory cost becomes an expense and how much remains as an asset.

Cost-recovery method A revenue recognition method that is employed when the probability is high that future cash flows will not be realized. This method results in the recognition of profit from sales only when cash receipts exceed the total cost of the goods sold.

Counter-balancing error An error that affects net income and total assets in one direction during the current year and in the opposite direction by the same magnitude during the subsequent year. Therefore, the combined effect on total assets and retained earnings is zero.

Coupon interest rate The annual interest rate used to determine the periodic interest payments. It is also known as the nominal or stated interest rate as compared to the yield rate of interest.

Credit The recording of an amount on the right side of an account.

Cross-sectional analysis Compares the performance of two or more companies on the same dimension at a point in time.

Cumulative dividend Dividends that do not lapse if not paid in the current year, but must be paid in a future year before dividends are paid to the common stockholders.

Cumulative preferred stock The feature where the right to dividends is not lost in those years in which a dividend is not declared, but the right to those dividends accumulates and must be satisfied before dividends are paid to the common stockholders in any later year.

Current assets A balance sheet classification consisting of cash or other assets that will be converted into cash within the year or operating cycle, whichever is longer. By tradition, prepayments are also included in this category.

Current liabilities A balance sheet classification reporting any liability that will be liquidated (1) within the year or operating cycle, (2) by using a current asset or incurring another current liability.

Current operating concept An approach to preparing an income statement in which only the revenues and expenses connected with operations are included in computing net income. (*See* **All-inclusive concept**.)

D

Date of declaration The date that the board of directors announces—after having been approved by stockholders—that a dividend will be paid.

Date of payment The date that the liability for dividends previously created by the board of directors is satisfied by distributing the dividend.

Date of record The day by which all holders of stock, or their agents, must notify the corporation that they own stock in order to receive a dividend.

Debit The recording of an amount on the left side of an account.

Deep discount bonds Bonds that do not pay interest periodically. Rather, the total payout (principal and interest) is paid/received when the bond matures. Since bonds are measured at the present value of their cash flows and because the cash flows are being delayed, the result is that the bonds are sold at a price considerably below the face amount of the bonds.

Deferral To postpone recognizing the expending of cash as an expense.

Deferred charge An expenditure that is not expensed in the period in which it was incurred. Most deferred charges are assets because future economic benefits will be derived from the expenditure. Other deferred charges are not technically assets but are reported with the assets on the balance sheet because a standard-setting body has decided it is inappropriate to expense the amount in the period in which it was incurred.

Deferred tax asset A difference in accounting income before taxes and taxable income that causes current taxable income to be greater than accounting income but will result in future taxable income being less than accounting income.

Deferred tax liability A difference in accounting income before taxes and taxable income that causes current taxable income to be less than accounting income but will result in future taxable income being greater than accounting income.

Deficit The label substituted for retained earnings when the accumulated losses and dividends exceeds accumulated profits.

Defined benefit pension plan A pension plan that defines an amount of pension benefit to be provided. Usually, this benefit is based on one or more factors such as age, years of service, or compensation.

Defined contribution pension plan A pension plan that provides pension benefits in return for services rendered and specifies how contributions are to be determined instead of specifying the amount of benefits the individual is to receive.

Depletion The allocating of the cost of natural resources to time periods.

Deposit method This method of revenue recognition is employed when revenue is realized or realizable but the revenue has not been earned. Under this method, revenue is recognized gradually as the seller performs his/her obligation.

Depreciation The allocating of the cost of a long-lived tangible asset over the periods in which the asset is used (i.e., the time periods benefited) and reporting the amount on the income statement.

Derivative instrument A security consisting of three main characteristics: (1) it has one or more underlyings and one or more notional amounts or payment provisions or both, (2) it requires no initial net investment or a smaller initial net investment than would be required for other types of contracts that would be expected to have a similar response to changes in market factors, and 3) its terms require or permit net settlement, it can readily be settled net by a means outside the contract, or it provides for delivery of an asset that puts the recipient in a position not substantially different from net settlement.

Development stage corporation A corporation that is devoting substantially all its efforts to establishing a new business, and either planned principal operations have not commenced or they have commenced but there have been no significant revenues therefrom.

Diluted earnings per share An earnings per share figure that is computed for corporations having a complex capital structure and that indicates the maximum potential dilution of earnings per share, assuming conversion of dilutive securities. Corporations having a complex capital structure must use a dual presentation in which diluted earnings per share is reported with equal prominence with basic earnings per share.

Direct exchange rate quote An expression of the amount of local currency needed to purchase one unit of foreign currency.

Direct financing lease A lease that does not include the manufacturer's or dealer's profit for the lessor.

Discount interest rate The interest rate used to discount the future cash flows of a liability to determine its present value. The discount rate is the rate demanded by the market, given the risk involved.

Discount rate The interest rate used to adjust for the time value of money.

Discovery method A revenue recognition method that recognizes the sudden discovery of an asset's increased value. Currently, this method is not acceptable under U.S. GAAP.

Dividend A distribution of cash, or other assets, or the corporation's own stock to owners.

Dividends in arrears The amount of undeclared dividends that has accumulated and is to be paid on cumulative preferred stock.

Dollar-value LIFO retail One form of the retail method of estimating inventory where the dollar-value LIFO procedures are used.

Dollar-value LIFO An inventory cost-flow procedure that is applied to pools of inventory instead of individual units, using price indices rather than unit prices.

Double-declining-balance depreciation method The allocating of the cost of a long-lived asset such that a greater portion of the cost is expensed in the earlier years of the asset's useful life. The depreciation amount is computed by multiplying a constant percentage (2 divided by the asset's useful life) by the book value of the asset. This method is based on the assumption that time is the most significant reason for a decline in a long-lived asset's usefulness, but that the impact of time is greater in the earlier years.

Double-entry The method of capturing data in an accounting information system such that information is classified into at least two accounts.

Dual presentation For corporations with a complex capital structure, this consists of the reporting, with equal prominence, basic and diluted earnings per share.

E

Earned The business has substantially done what it must to be entitled to the benefits represented by the revenues.

Earnings process A series of transactions whereby cash is converted into goods (or services), which then are sold to customers, and cash is collected.

Effective interest method of amortization The method of amortizing any debt premium/discount in which interest expense is computed by multiplying the carrying amount of the debt at the beginning of the period by the effective interest rate. This method results in a constant rate of interest over the life of the debt.

Effective interest rate *See* **Yield rate of interest**.

Emerging Issues Task Force (EITF) The EITF assists the FASB in identifying emerging issues and in providing timely guidance on those issues. It is a part-time body consisting of the senior technical partners of the major CPA firms and representatives from the major associations of financial statement preparers.

Enacted tax rates The tax rates expected to apply when a deferred tax asset or liability is settled. Enacted tax rates are not proposed or anticipated tax rates, but are the rates in effect due to current legislation.

Equity method of accounting The method of accounting for an investment when significant influence over the operating and financing activities of the investee has been obtained. Under the equity method, the investor (1) records income as the investee earns that income, (2) records the declaration of a dividend as a decrease in its investment account, (3) does not value the investment at market at the end of the year, and (4) amortizes any cost paid over the book value of the underlying assets.

European Monetary Union (EMU) A cooperative arrangement among twelve European nations to adopt the euro as the official national currency.

Exchange rate The relative unit value of one currency compared to another.

Executory contract A contract where one or more parties have yet to completely fulfill their promise.

Executory costs Payments made for maintenance, insurance, and property taxes.

Expected return on plan assets A calculated amount based on the long-term rate of return on plan assets.

Extraordinary repairs Capital expenditures that were not anticipated when the asset was acquired but are necessary for the company to continue deriving benefits from the asset.

F

Factoring receivables Transferring receivables to another party (i.e., the factor). Factoring can be done with or without recourse. Factoring with (without) recourse means the transferor (factor) must bear the cost of uncollectible receivables.

Fair-value hedge A hedge of the exposure to changes in the fair value of a recognized asset or liability, or of an unrecognized firm commitment, that is attributable to a particular risk.

Feedback value The quality of information that enables decision makers to confirm or correct prior expectations.

Financial Accounting Standards Board (FASB) This is the designated organization in the private sector to issue accounting and financial accounting pronouncements, and to establish a conceptual framework of accounting. It was established in 1973, and unlike its predecessors (the APB and the CAP), it is not a committee of the AICPA. The pronouncements establishing accounting and financial reporting policies are called *Statements of Financial Accounting Standards* and *Interpretations*. The pronouncements constructing the conceptual framework are called *Statements of Financial Accounting Concepts*.

Financial flexibility Refers to a company's ability to effectively respond to unexpected cash demands and to take advantage of new opportunities.

Financial leverage The tendency for net income to vary disproportionately in relation to sales because a company has chosen to raise capital through debt financing rather than through equity financing.

Financial statement analysis To synthesize information in such a manner that insight into the operating performance and financial health of the company is provided.

First-In, First-Out (FIFO) An inventory cost-flow assumption where the first inventory items purchased are assumed to be the first inventory items sold. Thus, the older inventory cost is assigned to the cost of goods sold and the newer costs are assigned as the value of the inventory on the balance sheet.

Forecasted transaction A transaction that is expected to occur for which there is no firm commitment. Because no transaction or event has yet occurred and the transaction or event when it occurs will be at the prevailing market price, a forecasted transaction does not give an entity any present rights to future benefits or a present obligation for future sacrifices.

Foreign currency transaction gain/loss A gain/loss realized and reported on the income statement from holding monetary assets/liabilities denominated in a foreign currency.

Forward rate An exchange rate that will be effective at a specified point in the future.

G

General journal The record in which seldom-encountered transactions and the end-of-period adjustments are initially recorded.

General ledger A ledger containing all the company's accounts showing their respective balances and the transaction amounts giving rise to those balances.

Generally Accepted Accounting Principles (GAAP) The official written pronouncements and the traditions that accountants follow when accounting for transactions and issuing financial statements to the public. The written pronouncements have various levels of authority, with the most authoritative pronouncements being the Rule 203 documents.

General-purpose financial statements Financial statement(s) issued with the intent of meeting the common informational needs of all parties external to a business entity.

Going concern assumption The notion that the existence of a business will continue at least into the foreseeable future so as to be able to complete its contemplated operations, contracts, and commitments.

Goods-in-transit Goods that have been shipped by the seller to the buyer but have not arrived at their destination.

Goodwill (1) The intangible asset(s) that represents a company's ability to generate more than normal profits. (2) The price paid in excess of the fair values of the individual assets less the fair values of the individual liabilities.

Gross investment in a lease To the lessor, it is the sum of the minimum lease payment plus any unguaranteed residual value.

Gross method Recording purchases of inventory at the sales price without regard to any cash discounts received or that could have been received. Cost of goods sold is this gross price less any cash discounts received.

Gross profit percentage method A method for estimating the value of inventory on hand without physically counting it. The method estimates cost of goods sold by multiplying sales by a gross profit percentage; then ending inventory is computed as the difference between the cost of goods available for sale and the cost of goods sold.

Group depreciation method A depreciation method that applies a single rate to a large group of assets of the same general type. Essentially, it is a special application of the straight-line depreciation method. (*See* **Composite depreciation**.)

Guaranteed residual value The amount at the signing of a lease that the lessee or some third party guarantees the leased asset will be worth at the end of the lease.

H

Hedge accounting Special accounting rules that reflect the reduction of risk from implementing hedging activities.

Hedging activities Actions taken by management to reduce specific risk associated with company operations.

Held-to-maturity portfolio Securities belonging to this portfolio are *debt securities* where the company has both the intent—and the ability—to hold them to maturity. Equity securities can never be included in the held-to-maturity portfolio because equity securities have no maturity date.

Historical cost The principle of measuring assets at acquisition at the sum of the cash, or its equivalent, that was paid to acquire the asset. In this regard, it is only the necessary and reasonable costs incurred to acquire the asset and get it ready for its intended use that becomes the historical cost of the asset.

Horizontal analysis Focuses on changes—both in magnitude and percentage change—in the account balances of a company over time.

I

Immediate recognition *See* **Matching principle**.

Implicit rate on a lease The interest rate the lessor uses to determine the minimum lease payments based upon the asset's fair value.

Inadequacy The decline in usefulness of a long-lived asset because it is not capable of meeting the demands placed on it.

Income smoothing The process of selecting measurement principles that decrease income in very successful years and boost income in unsuccessful years.

Incremental borrowing rate on a lease The interest rate at which the lessee could have borrowed money to purchase the leased asset.

Indirect exchange rate quote An expression of the amount of foreign currency needed to purchase one unit of local currency.

Initial direct costs on a lease The costs the lessor incurs (1) to originate a lease and (2) that directly relate to activities performed by the lessor for the lease.

Installment-sales method A revenue recognition method that is employed when a more-than-normal uncertainty surrounds the collection of future cash flows. This method results in only a portion of total gross profit being recognized at each cash installment.

Intangible assets The balance sheet classification reporting those long-lived assets that are not tangible and are used in operations.

International Accounting Standards (IAS) The official pronouncements of the IASB. In the United States, CPAs do not need to make sure that financial statements issued to the public conform to these standards; they are not Rule 203 documents.

International Accounting Standards Board (IASB) Formed in 2001 from a major restructuring of the IASC, the IASB is the foremost group that is seeking to establish uniform accounting and financial reporting standards throughout the world.

International Accounting Standards Committee (IASC) The predecessor of the IASB, it was organized in 1973 with the objective of developing a harmonized set of accounting principles that could be used internationally.

International Organization of Securities Commissions (IOSCO) The IOSCO consists of representatives from securities regulation agencies from more than 100 countries, including the SEC. Its purpose is to improve the efficiency of securities markets on both the domestic and international level.

Intraperiod tax allocation Distribution of the tax expense among the various categories of the income statement, thus showing the events in a net-of-tax manner.

Inventory Goods held for sale in the ordinary course of business. Also, for manufacturing entities, raw materials that will become part of the finished product and work-in-process that is becoming a finished product.

Investments and funds A balance sheet classification consisting of assets where the company's intent is to hold them for future use of long-term price appreciation.

J

Journal In a manual accounting information system, it is the record in which transactions are initially recorded. It may be the general journal or special journals.

L

Last-In, First-Out (LIFO) An inventory cost-flow assumption where the last inventory items purchased are assumed to be the first inventory items sold. Thus, the newer inventory cost is assigned to the cost of goods sold, and the older costs are assigned as the value of the inventory on the balance sheet.

Lease A contractual agreement that gives specific rights to the lessee to use stipulated property for a defined period of time in return for specified cash payments. (*See* **Capital lease** and **Operating lease**.)

Leasehold improvements Improvements made to a leased property to the condition where it can be used or to improve its usefulness.

Legal capital An arbitrary amount defined in state statute, which because stockholders are not personally liable for the corporation's debts, must be retained in a corporation to protect its creditors.

Liability Probable future sacrifice of economic benefits that arises from a present obligation to transfer assets or provide services to other entities as a result of a past transaction or event.

LIFO conformity rule A law within the United States that stipulates that if LIFO is used to determine taxable income, it must also be used to determine income for financial reporting purposes.

LIFO reserve The difference in inventory cost between using FIFO in the general ledger and LIFO on the financial statements.

Liquidating dividends Dividends distributed from a capital account other than retained earnings and is a return to owners of their investment.

Liquidity A measure of an entity's ability to pay its short-term liabilities as they mature.

Long-term liability A balance sheet classification that reports those liabilities that will not be liquidated within the year or operating cycle by using a current asset.

M

Manufacturer's or dealer's profit on a lease This occurs when the cost of the leased asset to the lessor is less than the asset's fair value.

Market interest rate See **Yield rate of interest**.

Marketable securities Equity and debt securities for which sales prices or bid and ask prices are available in a securities exchange registered with the SEC or in the over-the-counter market. Stock whose trading is restricted either by governmental or contractual requirement is not marketable. Equity securities trading on a foreign market are marketable when the breadth and scope of the foreign market are comparable to a U.S. market. Shares of a mutual fund are marketable when the per-share fair value is published and is the basis for current exchanges.

Market-related value of pension plan assets A balance used to calculate the expected return on pension plan assets. It can be either fair market value or a calculated value that recognizes changes in fair value in a systematic and rational manner over not more than five years.

Matching principle The principle that determines when costs become expenses. The three aspects of the matching principle are: (1) immediate recognition, which expenses an expenditure when it does not result in probable future benefits; (2) cause-and-effect, which expenses those costs connected to a product when the product is sold; and (3) systematic and rational allocation, which expenses the cost of long-lived assets.

Materiality The provision in financial reporting that permits an exception to the rule because the information provided from the exception is not considerably different from the information that would have been provided by adhering to the rule.

Minimum lease payment (MLP) The payments the lessee is obligated to make in connection with leased property. When a lease has a bargain purchase option, the MLP comprises (a) the minimum rental payments specified in the lease and (b) any bargain purchase option. When a lease does not contain a bargain purchase option, then the MLP consists of (a) the rental payments, (b) plus any residual value of the leased property that the lessee guarantees, and (c) any payment the lessee will be required to make for failing to renew or extend the lease at the end of the lease term.

Minimum liability A liability that must be recognized when the accumulated benefit obligation at the end of the year exceeds the fair value of the pension plan assets at the end of the year.

Modified perpetual inventory control system An inventory system where changes in quantity are recorded as they occur but not in the general ledger.

Monetary account Any balance sheet account that is fixed as to dollar amount, regardless of price changes.

Moving-average An inventory cost-flow assumption used with the perpetual inventory control system where the inventory unit cost is computed after every purchase by averaging the cost of the inventory and the most recent purchase.

Multiple-step income statement A form of the income statement where revenues are reported separately from gains, and expenses are reported separately from losses.

N

Net assets The value of assets minus the value of liabilities, where value is defined either as book value or fair value.

Net investment in the lease The gross investment in a lease less the amount of unearned interest. At the inception of the lease, this amount is usually equal to the fair value or sales price of the leased asset.

Net method Recording purchases of inventory at the sales price less all cash discounts that could be received, without regard to whether they actually were received.

Net operating loss The result when tax deductions exceed tax revenues.

Net realizable value Net benefits received minus any expected costs that will be incurred. For receivables, net realizable value refers to the gross amount of the receivables minus an allowance for uncollectible accounts. For inventory or other assets to be sold, net realizable value refers to the selling price less any costs to dispose.

Neutrality Information that is reasonably free from error and bias.

Nominal dollars Measuring and reporting amounts on the financial statements in terms of dollars, assuming that the dollar does not change in purchasing power over time.

Nominal interest rate *See* **Coupon interest rate**.

Nonmonetary accounts Accounts on the balance sheet that are not monetary.

Normal balance The expected balance of an account. A debit balance is the normal balance of asset, expense and the owners' drawing accounts. A credit balance is the normal balance of liability, owners' contribution, and revenue accounts.

O

Obsolescence A catch-all phrase used to indicate the decline in usefulness of a long-lived asset that is not due to inadequacy or supersession.

Off-balance-sheet financing The practice of using loopholes in accounting pronouncements to avoid reporting liabilities on the balance sheet.

Operating lease A lease that does not transfer the rights and risks of ownership to the lessee. The lessor reports the asset on its balance sheet. (*See* **Capital lease**.)

Operating leverage The tendency for net income to vary disproportionately in relation to sales because a company is utilizing fixed costs rather than variable costs.

Ordinary annuity An annuity in which the first payment is paid (or due) one time period in the future. (*See* **Annuity due**.)

Organization costs The costs incurred in starting up a business or when a business opens a new facility, introduces a new product or service, or conducts business in a new territory or with a new customer.

Other assets A balance sheet classification that, when used, reports those assets that do not nicely fit in any other classification.

Owners' equity A balance sheet classification reporting the residual claims on assets.

P

Partial allocation The method of accounting for deferred taxes that recognizes the tax effects of only those temporary differences that will reverse in the foreseeable future.

Participating preferred stock Allows preferred stockholders to receive an additional dividend, above the regular preferred dividend, usually after certain conditions are met.

Pension benefit formula The basis for determining payments to which participants may be entitled under a pension plan.

Pension interest cost The increase in the projected benefit obligation due to the passage of time.

Pension plan amendment A change in the terms of an existing pension plan or the initiation of a new pension plan.

Pension plan gain or loss A change in the value of either the projected benefit obligation or the plan assets resulting from experience differing from that assumed or from a change in an actuarial assumption.

Pension service cost The actuarial present value of benefits attributed by the pension benefit formula to services rendered by employees during that period.

Percentage-of-completion method A revenue recognition method typically employed for long-term construction contracts that recognizes revenue during the production process.

Period costs Expenditures that are recorded as expenses based upon the time that they are incurred rather than when the goods are sold. Period costs are reported in the Operating Expense section of the income statement.

Periodic inventory control system An accounting system where the quantity of inventory and its cost as reported in the general ledger are the amounts as of the last inventory count.

Periodic inventory system The method of accounting for inventory that depends upon a physical count of the inventory to determine the value of the inventory on hand.

Periodicity assumption The notion that it is possible to measure the performance of a business for a time interval that is shorter than its existence.

Permanent decline in value In regards to securities in either the available-for-sale or the held-to-maturity portfolios, a permanent decline in value occurs when it is not expected that the price of a security will return to its historical cost in the foreseeable future.

Permanent difference A difference between accounting income before taxes and taxable income arising from a transaction that, according to income tax laws and regulations, will not be offset in future periods.

Perpetual inventory control system An accounting system where both the quantity and cost of inventory are shown in the general ledger at any point in time.

Perpetual inventory system The method of accounting for inventory where the amount of inventory shown in the account agrees with the amount of inventory on hand.

Pledging As used with receivables, pledging refers to the use of receivables as collateral on a loan.

Posting The process of transferring data from the journals to the ledgers, particularly in a manual accounting system.

Predictive value The quality of information that increases the likelihood of correctly predicting future events.

Preemptive right The privilege given common stockholders to acquire shares of newly offered stock, so as to preserve their ownership percentage in a corporation. In recent years, this right has been eliminated by many corporations.

Prepayments To pay for goods or services in a period where the benefits from that payment extend over several months and in some cases for several years.

Present value of a liability The hypothetical amount that would be required at the balance sheet date to liquidate the liability.

Present value principle The concept that liabilities are reported at the theoretical amount that would be required to liquidate them at the balance sheet date, given the time value of money.

Prior service cost The cost of retroactive benefits granted in a pension plan amendment or at the inception of a pension plan.

Product costs The cost of material, labor, and overhead that constitutes the cost of the product. Product costs are reported as expenses in the period in which the goods are sold and are reported in the Cost of Goods Sold section of the income statement.

Product financing arrangement An arrangement where one party (the borrower) receives financing to complete a project, and the lender has an interest in seeing the project completed.

Productive output depreciation method See **Activity methods of depreciation**.

Profit margin A measure of how much profit a company earns from each dollar of sales.

Profitability A measure of the increase in net assets a company is generating from operations.

Pro forma financial statements "As if" financial statements. In regards to financial analysis, pro forma financial statements are future statements given the assumptions of the analyst.

Projected benefit obligation The actuarial present value as of a date of all benefits attributed by the pension benefit formula to employee service rendered prior to that date. The projected benefit obligation is measured using assumptions as to future compensation levels if the pension benefit formula is based on those compensation levels.

Property dividends Dividends where other assets other than cash are distributed to stockholders.

Property, plant and equipment A balance sheet classification reporting those assets that are (1) tangible, (2) long-lived, and (3) used in operations.

Prudence An accounting convention that discourages early recognition of assets and/or income.

Q

Quality of earnings The phrase used to indicate that current earnings are an indication of future earnings. Companies whose earnings are a good indication of future earnings (or that current earnings will persist) are said to have high-quality earnings.

R

Rational In regards to the allocating of costs to periods, it means that the allocation method is defensible in associating cost with the time period.

Real rate of interest See **Yield rate of interest**.

Realizable Goods or services have been exchanged for assets that are readily convertible into known amounts of cash or a claim to cash.

Realized Goods or services have been exchanged for cash or a claim to cash.

Rearrangements and reinstallations Capital expenditures that enhance the effectiveness and productivity of current and future operations.

Receivable Amounts expected to be collected from customers, officers, employees, and affiliates.

Recoverability (i.e., Impairment) Test A test to determine whether the carrying value of a long-term asset or group of assets should be written down. The test consists of comparing the undiscounted estimated future cash flows that will be realized from holding the asset (group of assets) to its (their) carrying value(s).

Redeemable preferred stock Preferred stock that has a fixed or determinable redemption date, or is redeemable at the option of the holder, or has conditions regarding redemption that are not totally within the control of the issuer. Such stock cannot be reported under the stockholders' equity caption.

Refunding bonds Bonds where the proceeds are used to retire other (usually higher interest rate) bonds.

Registered bonds Bonds with the name of the owner printed on the bonds. Selling the bonds requires the surrender of the bond certificate and the issuance of a new bond certificate. (See **Bearer bonds**.)

Relevance or relevant The quality of information that makes a difference in a decision.

Reliable The measure of confidence that can be placed in information.

Replacements Capital expenditures to replace a worn-out component of an asset with the same quality component.

Representational faithfulness The concept indicating a close relationship between financial numbers and the economic substance of reality.

Reserve accounting A practice of recognizing reserves on the balance sheet for future contingencies, losses, and cash payments. Reserve accounting has the effect of creating pools of earnings that managers can use in periods of poor performance in order to smooth earnings.

Residual value At the signing of the lease, the estimated value that the leased asset will have at the end of the lease.

Restricted stock Company stock, usually granted to company employees, that is restricted from being traded for a certain time period.

Retail method A method of estimating the cost of inventory on hand without actually counting it by employing a cost-to-retail percentage. (*See* **Conventional retail** and **Dollar-value LIFO retail**.)

Retained earnings Accumulated net income that has not been distributed to stockholders.

Revaluation reserve A stockholders' equity account that is increased when fixed assets are written up to their current values. This account is employed in accounting regimes that adopt a current-value accounting system.

Revenue expenditure An expenditure incurred to maintain assets in normal operating condition and incurred routinely as part of the ongoing operations of the company. These expenditures are recorded as expenses in the period incurred.

Revenue recognition principle A fundamental principle of accounting that dictates when companies should recognize revenue on their income statement. The principle requires that, prior to recognition, revenue must be (1) earned and (2) realized or realizable. Revenue is earned when the company has substantially accomplished what it must do to receive the benefits represented by the revenues. Revenue is realized when goods or services are exchanged for cash or claims to cash. Revenue is realizable when goods or services are exchanged for an asset that is readily convertible to cash or a claim to cash.

Rule 203 That part of the AICPA's Code of Professional Conduct that requires the CPA to only issue financial statements to the pubic for corporations whose statements conform with *Accounting Research Bulletins* of the CAP, *Opinions* of the APB, and the *Statements of Financial Accounting Standards* and *Interpretations* of the FASB. For this reason, these four documents are called Rule 203 documents. Issuing financial statements that contain material departures from these four documents is a violation of Rule 203 and could lead to punitive action by the AICPA and by state licensing boards, which could include the loss of the license to practice as a CPA.

S

Sale with a buy-back agreement A transaction where a company transfers inventory to another company and agrees to buy back the inventory at a specified price over an agreed period of time.

Sale-leaseback A transaction where the owner of property sells it and simultaneously leases it back without actually transferring the asset.

Sales-type lease Leases that include the manufacturer's or dealer's profit for the lessor.

Salvage value The expected amount to be realized through sale or trade-in that will be received at the end of the asset's useful life as determined when the asset was acquired or modified thereafter.

Scrip dividends Distributions to owners where the time between the declaration and payment dates is longer than usual. Scrip dividends typically are in the form of a promissory note and bear interest.

Secured bonds Bonds backed by collateral. Mortgage bonds that are secured by a claim on real estate are an example of secured bonds.

Securities and Exchange Commission (SEC) The federal regulatory agency created to administer the federal securities acts. The SEC has the statutory authority to prescribe the accounting and financial reporting standards that must be adhered to when issuing financial statements of corporations whose securities (either debt or equity) are publicly traded. Historically, the SEC has looked to the private sector to determine what constitutes generally accepted accounting principles, while reserving the right to approve or direct the development of GAAP. However, the SEC also issues *Accounting Series Releases*, in which it too prescribes acceptable accounting and financial reporting procedures, and its staff issues additional guidance through its *Staff Accounting Bulletins*.

Separate-entity assumption The notion that the business is a separate economic unit from its owners and from other business enterprises.

Serial bonds Bonds that mature in installments. State and local governments and governmental entities where the principal is paid through specially levied taxes use this type of bond most frequently.

Service hours depreciation method *See* **Activity methods of depreciation**.

Service life *See* **Anticipated useful life**.

Significant influence Indicates the investor has the ability to exercise significant influence over the operating and financing activities of the investee. As a rule-of-thumb, it is presumed that an investor who owns 20 percent, or more, of the outstanding voting common stock of the investee has significant influence. The investor uses the equity method of accounting to account for its investment when it has achieved significant influence.

Single-step income statement A form of the income statement were revenues and gains are reported in the same section and expenses and losses are reported in another section.

Solvency A measure of a company's ability to pay its long-term obligations.

Special journals The record in which frequently used transactions are initially recorded. There is a different special journal for each type of frequently encountered transaction. So, there is a special journal for cash disbursements, another for cash receipts, etc.

Specific identification An inventory cost-flow method where the inventory cost is matched with the physical units.

Spot rate An exchange rate quote that represents the price of a currency if conversion were to take place immediately.

Start-up costs The initial costs of establishing a business, division, or new facility and incurred before principle operations have commenced and significant revenues are earned.

Stated interest rate *See* **Coupon interest rate**.

Statements of Financial Accounting Concepts (SFAC) Those pronouncements of the FASB that constitute their conceptual framework of accounting. These pronouncements are not Rule 203 documents; thus, the accountant does not have to adhere to them when publishing the financial statements of corporations whose securities are publicly traded. Rather, they are for providing guidance, particularly to the FASB, in developing future Statements of Financial Accounting Standards.

Statements of Financial Accounting Concepts The set of guidelines issued by the FASB that forms its conceptual framework of accounting.

Statements of Financial Accounting Standards (SFAS) The authoritative pronouncements of the FASB, setting forth policies on accounting and financial accounting standards. All Standards that have not been superceded are still in force and all financial statements of corporations whose securities are publicly traded should conform to those pronouncements. Issuing financial statements to the public that do not conform to these Standards constitutes a violation of Rule 203 of the CPA's code of professional conduct.

Stock appreciation rights Rights granted to employees that provide compensation based on the price appreciation of company stock.

Stock dividends Distribution of additional shares of company stock to owners. Stock dividends can either be in the form of a large stock dividend or a small stock dividend.

Stock splits Distribution to owners of additional shares without affecting the overall legal and contributed capital. Reverse stock splits can also occur, which reduces the number of outstanding shares but again, does not affect legal and contributed capital.

Stock subscription A contract or agreement between a corporation and prospective stockholders to purchase shares of stock.

Stockholders' equity *See* **Owners' equity**.

Straight-line depreciation method The allocating of the cost of a long-lived asset in such a manner that equal amounts are allocated to equal periods of time. The method is based on the assumption that time is the most significant reason for a decline in a long-lived asset's usefulness.

Straight-line method of discount/premium amortization The method of amortizing any debt premium/discount so that equal amounts of interest expense are recognized in each period. This is done by dividing any premium/discount by the number of interest periods, and this amount is then added to cash paid for interest (when a discount is present) or subtracted from the cash paid for interest (when a premium is present).

Subsidiary ledgers A supporting ledger containing the details of specific accounts the total of which agrees with the balance of an account in the general ledger.

Sum-of-the-years'-digits depreciation method The allocating of the cost of a long-lived asset in such a manner that larger amounts are expensed in the earlier years of the asset's useful life. The denominator of the percentage applied to the cost of the asset is the sum of the years of the asset's life, and the numerator is the number of years remaining in the life of the asset. This method is based on the assumption that time is the most significant reason for a decline in a long-lived asset's usefulness, but that the impact of time is greater in the earlier years.

Supersession The decline in usefulness of an asset because another is more efficient or economical.

Systematic and rational allocation *See* **Matching principle**.

Systematic In regards to the allocating of costs to periods, it means that clear, unambiguous guidance is provided in advance as to the amount of the cost that is expensed in any particular time period.

T

T-accounts A representation of an account used to demonstrate the effect of a transaction or transactions, or for solving accounting problems.

Take-or-pay contract A type of product financing arrangement where the purchaser of goods promises to make specified payments to the seller, even if no goods are shipped, which enables the seller to make payments on any loan obtained to finance a project of mutual benefit to both buyer and seller.

Temporary difference A difference between accounting income before taxes and taxable income arising because the year in which a transaction enters into accounting income before taxes is different than the year in which it enters into taxable income. However, the total impact, over all years, is the same on accounting income before taxes as it is on taxable income.

Term bonds Bonds that mature on a single date.

Through-put contract Similar to a take-or-pay contract, except that the agreement is for a service rather than for a product.

Time deposits Funds deposited in a bank where prior notification is legally required before the amounts can be withdrawn without incurring a penalty.

Timeliness An attribute of information that has the capacity to affect a decision.

Trade discount A discount given to a class of customers on a sale before considering credit terms.

Trading on the equity Synonymous with financial leverage.

Trading portfolio Securities belonging to this portfolio are those that were purchased and are being held primarily for the purpose of selling them in the near future. As a result, they are bought and sold frequently for the purpose of generating gains due to short term differences in price.

Transaction An external event that changes a business entity's assets, liabilities, owners' equity, or its revenues (and gains) and expenses (and losses).

Transaction processing system An information system that captures data only when a transaction occurs.

Transactions approach The approach used in accounting to measure net income where revenue, expense, etc. are measured for each transaction in which a business engages.

Treasury bonds Bonds that a corporation has issued, then reacquired, but that have not been retired. Instead, the bonds are held with the expectation that they will be reissued at some future time.

Treasury stock method The approach used to compute the effect on diluted earnings per share for stock options, rights, and warrants. The approach assumes that all outstanding options, rights, and warrants are converted into shares of common stock at the average stock price for the year, and then the corporation uses the money received to buy shares of its own stock (which is called treasury stock) at the end-of-year prices.

Trend analysis Refers to the performance of one company or one aspect of a company (e.g., sales) over an extended period of time.

Trial balance A list of the accounts in the general ledger and their respective balances, which is prepared to verify that the total debits in the general ledger equals the total credits. The books are said to be in balance when the total debits equals the total credits.

Troubled debt restructuring An arrangement where the creditor grants a concession that he ordinarily would not, which is done with the objective of recovering as much money as possible.

U

Unappropriated retained earnings That portion of retained earnings that has not been appropriated.

Unasserted claims Lawsuits that have not yet been filed but are expected to be filed sometime in the future.

Unrecognized net gain or loss The cumulative net gain or loss that has not been recognized as a part of net periodic pension cost.

Unrecognized prior service cost That portion of prior service cost that has not been recognized as a part of net periodic pension cost.

Unsecured bonds Bonds that are not backed by collateral. Debentures are unsecured bonds. Junk bonds are unsecured bonds that are very risky. Risky means that there is a higher probability of default that is offset by a higher rate of interest.

V

Valuation allowance The amount by which a deferred tax asset is reduced when it is more likely than not that the entire amount of the deferred tax asset will not be realized.

Verifiable An attribution of information indicating a consensus among measurers.

Vertical analysis Using common-size financial statements.

Vested benefits Benefits for which the employee's right to receive a present or future pension benefit is no longer contingent on remaining in the service of the employer.

Vesting period the time that must pass in order to claim certain rights.

W

Weighted-average An inventory cost-flow assumption used with the periodic inventory control system where the inventory unit cost is the average of all purchases during the year and the beginning of the period inventory cost.

Y

Yield rate of interest The economic or effective rate of return on a bond. It is also known as the effective, market, or real interest rate.

Z

Zero interest bonds *See* **Deep discount bonds**.

Company Index

Subject Index